Bill James presents. . .

STATS™
Major League Handbook
1996

STATS, Inc. • Bill James

Published by STATS Publishing
A Division of Sports Team Analysis & Tracking Systems, Inc.
Dr. Richard Cramer, Chairman • John Dewan, President

**To my dad, Neil, for warm summer evenings at Percy
Ruhe Park, and to my mom, Sylvia, for making sure
the Easter Bunny always brought baseball cards.
— Steve Moyer**

Cover by John Grimwade and Excel Marketing

Photo by Otto Greule/Allsport Photography

Second Edition: January, 1996

Printed in the United States of America

ISBN 1-884064-17-5

Acknowledgments

The *STATS Major League Handbook* is our most popular book, one which helped STATS become the unquestioned leader in sports-data collection and analysis. Producing it involves most of the people who work for us, and we'd like to thank them.

John Dewan, STATS President and CEO, and Dick Cramer, STATS Chairman and founder, continue to spearhead our company's remarkable growth. It's hard to believe how far we've come in such a short time, and Dick and John are the guys who got us here. (And they're not gonna stop *here*, either.)

This is a book full of fascinating numbers, and the Systems Department, headed by Sue Dewan with the assistance of Mike Canter, is responsible for producing them. Stefan Kretschmann was the "book man" who handled many of the details involved in getting the numbers on the page. Dave Mundo helped with both programming and with our publications software, and David Pinto produced the manager tendencies section. Jeff Schinski and Madison Smith also contributed to the programming effort, and as always, Art Ashley made certain our hardware was running properly.

The Operations Department, headed by Steve Moyer, collects the data through our reporter network, then makes sure that it's accurate. Steve's staff consists of Ethan Cooperson, Mike Hammer, Kenn Ruby, Allan Spear and Peter Woelflein.

My guys in the Publications Department are responsible for the prose parts of the book and for making sure the manuscript meets "STATS standards" before it goes out the door. Rob Neyer and Scott McDevitt are my ace helpers in the office; while we're tending to the baseball books, Jim Henzler works with the ESPN sports staff.

The Marketing Department, headed by Ross Schaufelberger, sells STATS products and services. Ross' staff, which includes Kristen Beauregard, Drew Faust, Ron Freer, Chuck Miller and Jim Musso, also produces the cover, the park diagrams, and other graphical elements of this book. Jim Capuano, who serves as STATS' Director of National Sales, plays a key role in marketing our products.

The Department of Finances and Human Resources, headed by Bob Meyerhoff, processes the orders, handles the paperwork and makes sure our books get to you. Bob's staff consists of Brian Ersnberger, Ginny Hamill, Tim Harbert, Marge Morra, Betty Moy, Brynne Orlando, Jim Osborne, Pat Quinn and Leena Sheth. Stephanie Seburn is our Assistant Director of Marketing Support and Administration, and Buffy Cramer-Hammann serves as John Dewan's assistant.

Last of all, thanks to Bill James for presenting this book, and for continuing to be the best friend STATS has ever had.

— Don Zminda, STATS Director of Publications

Table of Contents

Introduction

The 1995 season forced all of us here at STATS to recalibrate our sights toward analyzing baseball once again. Three divisions in each league, a 144-game schedule, a playoff format we're *still* trying to understand, a bionic man in Atlanta, a Japanese tornado in Los Angeles, a launching pad in Colorado, postseason play in Cleveland, an assistant manager in Cincinnati—whew! It was a hectic 1995 season to say the least. But at least there *was* a 1995 season, and we here at STATS are greatly thankful for that fact.

With that in mind, we're very pleased to present the *STATS 1996 Major League Handbook*—one of three publications (along with the *STATS Minor League Handbook* and *STATS Player Profiles*) that serves as one leg of the triathalon our dedicated employees complete each October. It's a lot of work to put together three books in such a short amount of time, but darn it, you fans keep on buying them—and that's incentive enough for us to keep churning them out.

If you're already a fan of the *Handbook*, you'll know you can find a little bit of everything in here. In addition to the career register section, you'll find fielding stats (including special stats like "catcher ERA"), ballpark data (yes, Coors Field made *quite* a difference), lefty/righty splits, Leader Boards, 1996 player projections, manager tendencies, and a whole lot more. You'll be hard pressed to find a wider array of major league stats anywhere—and certainly not in a book available just days after the World Series.

As always, we'd be happy to hear any suggestions you have toward making this book better. You've chosen to buy it—and that makes *you* the ultimate judge.

—Scott McDevitt

What's Official and What's Not

The stats in this book are technically unofficial. The official Major League Baseball stats are not released until December, but we can't wait that long. If you compare these stats to the official ones, you'll find no major differences. We take extraordinary efforts to ensure accuracy.

Career Stats

The career data section of this book includes the records of all players who saw major league action in 1995.

You probably know what most of the abbreviations stand for, but just in case:

Age is seasonal age based on July 1, 1996.

For Batters, **G** = Games; **AB** = At Bats; **H** = Hits; **2B** = Doubles; **3B** = Triples; **HR** = Home Runs; **Hm** = Home Runs at Home; **Rd** = Home Runs on the Road; **TB** = Total Bases; **R** = Runs; **RBI** = Runs Batted In; **TBB** = Total Bases on Balls; **IBB** = Intentional Bases on Balls; **SO** = Strikeouts; **HBP** = Times Hit by Pitches; **SH** = Sacrifice Hits; **SF** = Sacrifice Flies; **SB** = Stolen Bases; **CS** = Times Caught Stealing; **SB%** = Stolen Base Percentage; **GDP** = Times Grounded into Double Plays; **Avg** = Batting Average; **OBP** = On-Base Percentage; **SLG** = Slugging Percentage.

For Pitchers, **G** = Games Pitched; **GS** = Games Started; **CG** = Complete Games; **GF** = Games Finished; **IP** = Innings Pitched; **BFP** = Batters Facing Pitcher; **H** = Hits Allowed; **R** = Runs Allowed; **ER** = Earned Runs Allowed; **HR** = Home Runs Allowed; **SH** = Sacrifice Hits Allowed; **SF** = Sacrifice Flies Allowed; **HB** = Hit Batsmen; **TBB** = Total Bases on Balls; **IBB** = Intentional Bases on Balls; **SO** = Strikeouts; **WP** = Wild Pitches; **Bk** = Balks; **W** = Wins; **L** = Losses; **Pct.** = Winning Percentage; **ShO** = Shutouts; **Sv** = Saves; **ERA** = Earned Run Average.

An asterisk (*) by a player's minor league stats indicates that these are his 1995 minor league numbers only; previous minor league experience is not included. Figures in **boldface** indicate that the player led the league in that category.

For pitchers, thirds of an inning were not kept officially until 1982. Therefore, there are no thirds of innings for 1981 and before.

For players who played for more than one major league team in a season, stats for each team are shown just above the bottom-line career totals.

Jim Abbott

Pitches: Left **Bats:** Left **Pos:** SP   **Ht:** 6' 3" **Wt:** 210 **Born:** 9/19/67 **Age:** 28

			HOW MUCH HE PITCHED						WHAT HE GAVE UP									THE RESULTS				
Year Team	Lg	G	GS	CG	GF	IP	BFP	H	R	ER	HR	SH	SF	HB	TBB	IBB	SO	WP	Bk	W	L	Pct.	ShO	Sv	ERA
1989 California	AL	29	29	4	0	181.1	788	190	95	79	13	11	5	4	74	3	115	8	2	12	12	.500	2	0	3.92
1990 California	AL	33	33	4	0	211.2	925	246	116	106	16	9	6	5	72	6	105	4	3	10	14	.417	1	0	4.51
1991 California	AL	34	34	5	0	243	1002	222	85	78	14	7	7	5	73	6	158	1	4	18	11	.621	1	0	2.89
1992 California	AL	29	29	7	0	211	874	208	73	65	12	8	4	4	68	3	130	2	0	7	15	.318	0	0	2.77
1993 New York	AL	32	32	4	0	214	906	221	115	104	22	12	4	3	73	4	95	9	0	11	14	.440	1	0	4.37
1994 New York	AL	24	24	2	0	160.1	692	167	88	81	24	9	5	2	64	1	90	8	1	9	8	.529	0	0	4.55
1995 ChA-Cal	AL	30	30	4	0	197	842	209	93	81	14	8	4	2	64	1	86	1	0	11	8	.579	1	0	3.70
1995 Chicago	AL	17	17	3	0	112.1	474	116	50	42	10	5	1	1	35	1	45	0	0	6	4	.600	0	0	3.36
California	AL	13	13	1	0	84.2	368	93	43	39	4	3	3	1	29	0	41	1	0	5	4	.556	1	0	4.15
7 ML YEARS		211	211	30	0	1418.1	6029	1463	665	594	115	64	35	25	488	24	779	33	10	78	82	.488	6	0	3.77

Kurt Abbott

Bats: Right **Throws:** Right **Pos:** SS   **Ht:** 6' 0" **Wt:** 185 **Born:** 6/2/69 **Age:** 27

							BATTING												BASERUNNING				PERCENTAGES		
Year Team	Lg	G	AB	H	2B	3B	HR	(Hm	Rd)	TB	R	RBI	TBB	IBB	SO	HBP	SH	SF	SB	CS	SB%	GDP	Avg	OBP	SLG
1995 Charlotte *	AAA	5	18	5	0	0	1			8	3	3	1	0	3	0	0	0	1	0	1.00	0	.278	.316	.444
1993 Oakland	AL	20	61	15	1	0	3	(0	3)	25	11	9	3	0	20	0	3	0	2	0	1.00	3	.246	.281	.410
1994 Florida	NL	101	345	86	17	3	9	(4	5)	136	41	33	16	1	98	5	3	2	3	0	1.00	5	.249	.291	.394
1995 Florida	NL	120	420	107	18	7	17	(12	5)	190	60	60	36	4	110	5	2	5	4	3	.57	6	.255	.318	.452
3 ML YEARS		241	826	208	36	10	29	(16	13)	351	112	102	55	5	228	10	8	7	9	3	.75	14	.252	.304	.425

Kyle Abbott

Pitches: Left **Bats:** Left **Pos:** RP   **Ht:** 6' 4" **Wt:** 215 **Born:** 2/18/68 **Age:** 28

				HOW MUCH HE PITCHED						WHAT HE GAVE UP									THE RESULTS				
Year Team	Lg	G	GS	CG	GF	IP	BFP	H	R	ER	HR	SH	SF	HB	TBB	IBB	SO	WP	Bk	W	L	Pct.	ShO	Sv	ERA
1991 California	AL	5	5	0	0	19.2	90	22	11	10	2	3	0	1	13	0	12	1	1	1	2	.333	0	0	4.58
1992 Philadelphia	NL	31	19	0	0	133.1	577	147	80	76	20	6	5	1	45	0	88	9	1	1	14	.067	0	0	5.13
1995 Philadelphia	NL	18	0	0	3	28.1	122	28	12	12	3	0	1	0	16	0	21	2	1	2	0	1.000	0	0	3.81
3 ML YEARS		54	22	0	3	181.1	789	197	103	98	25	9	6	2	74	0	121	12	3	4	16	.200	0	0	4.86

Juan Acevedo

Pitches: Right **Bats:** Right **Pos:** SP/RP   **Ht:** 6' 2" **Wt:** 195 **Born:** 5/5/70 **Age:** 26

				HOW MUCH HE PITCHED						WHAT HE GAVE UP									THE RESULTS				
Year Team	Lg	G	GS	CG	GF	IP	BFP	H	R	ER	HR	SH	SF	HB	TBB	IBB	SO	WP	Bk	W	L	Pct.	ShO	Sv	ERA
1992 Bend	A	1	0	0	0	2	13	4	3	3	0	1	0	1	1	0	3	0	0	0	0	.000	0	0	13.50
Visalia	A	12	12	1	0	64.2	289	75	46	39	2	2	2	3	33	0	37	1	2	3	4	.429	0	0	5.43
1993 Central Val	A	27	20	1	3	118.2	529	119	68	58	8	5	4	9	58	0	107	12	4	9	8	.529	0	0	4.40
1994 New Haven	AA	26	26	5	0	174.2	697	142	56	46	16	4	3	5	38	0	161	4	5	17	6	.739	2	0	2.37
1995 Colo. Sprng	AAA	3	3	0	0	14.2	68	18	11	10	0	1	1	2	7	0	7	2	1	1	1	.500	0	0	6.14
Norfolk	AAA	2	2	0	0	3	9	0	0	0	0	0	0	0	1	0	2	0	0	0	0	.000	0	0	0.00
1995 Colorado	NL	17	11	0	0	65.2	291	82	53	47	15	4	2	6	20	2	40	2	1	4	6	.400	0	0	6.44

Mark Acre

Pitches: Right **Bats:** Right **Pos:** RP   **Ht:** 6' 8" **Wt:** 240 **Born:** 9/16/68 **Age:** 27

				HOW MUCH HE PITCHED						WHAT HE GAVE UP									THE RESULTS				
Year Team	Lg	G	GS	CG	GF	IP	BFP	H	R	ER	HR	SH	SF	HB	TBB	IBB	SO	WP	Bk	W	L	Pct.	ShO	Sv	ERA
1991 Athletics	R	6	0	0	2	10	44	10	3	3	0	0	0	0	6	0	6	0	1	2	0	1.000	0	0	2.70
1992 Reno	A	35	8	0	11	77	347	67	56	39	5	5	1	1	50	1	65	13	4	4	4	.500	0	2	4.56
1993 Madison	A	28	0	0	27	31.1	115	9	1	1	1	1	0	0	13	0	41	4	0	0	0	.000	0	20	0.29
Huntsville	AA	19	0	0	19	22.1	89	22	10	6	2	1	1	0	3	1	21	2	0	1	1	.500	0	10	2.42
1994 Tacoma	AAA	20	0	0	16	28.2	120	24	7	6	1	2	0	1	11	1	31	1	0	1	1	.500	0	6	1.88
1994 Oakland	AL	34	0	0	6	34.1	147	24	13	13	4	3	1	1	23	3	21	1	0	5	1	.833	0	0	3.41
1995 Oakland	AL	43	0	0	10	52	236	52	35	33	7	1	2	2	28	2	47	2	1	1	2	.333	0	0	5.71
2 ML YEARS		77	0	0	16	86.1	383	76	48	46	11	4	3	3	51	5	68	3	1	6	3	.667	0	0	4.80

Terry Adams

Pitches: Right **Bats:** Right **Pos:** RP   **Ht:** 6' 3" **Wt:** 205 **Born:** 3/6/73 **Age:** 23

				HOW MUCH HE PITCHED						WHAT HE GAVE UP									THE RESULTS				
Year Team	Lg	G	GS	CG	GF	IP	BFP	H	R	ER	HR	SH	SF	HB	TBB	IBB	SO	WP	Bk	W	L	Pct.	ShO	Sv	ERA
1991 Huntington	R	14	13	0	0	57.2	300	67	56	37	1	1	2	6	62	0	52	4	4	0	9	.000	0	0	5.77
1992 Peoria	A	25	25	3	0	157	682	144	95	77	7	8	6	9	86	0	96	13	1	7	12	.368	1	0	4.41
1993 Daytona	A	13	13	0	0	70.2	320	78	47	39	2	2	3	1	43	0	35	9	2	3	5	.375	0	0	4.97
1994 Daytona	A	39	7	0	21	84.1	383	87	47	41	5	4	2	4	46	3	64	8	1	9	10	.474	0	7	4.38

3

Year	Team	Lg	G	GS	CG	GF	IP	BFP	H	R	ER	HR	SH	SF	HB	TBB	IBB	SO	WP	Bk	W	L	Pct.	ShO	Sv	ERA
1995	Orlando	AA	37	0	0	30	37.2	149	23	9	6	2	0	1	2	16	1	26	4	1	2	3	.400	0	19	1.43
	Iowa	AAA	7	0	0	6	6.1	25	3	0	0	0	0	0	0	2	0	10	1	0	0	0	.000	0	5	0.00
1995	Chicago	NL	18	0	0	7	18	86	22	15	13	0	0	0	0	10	1	15	1	0	1	1	.500	0	1	6.50

Rick Aguilera

Pitches: Right **Bats:** Right **Pos:** RP **Ht:** 6' 5" **Wt:** 203 **Born:** 12/31/61 **Age:** 34

			HOW MUCH HE PITCHED						WHAT HE GAVE UP												THE RESULTS					
Year	Team	Lg	G	GS	CG	GF	IP	BFP	H	R	ER	HR	SH	SF	HB	TBB	IBB	SO	WP	Bk	W	L	Pct.	ShO	Sv	ERA
1985	New York	NL	21	19	2	1	122.1	507	118	49	44	8	7	4	2	37	2	74	5	2	10	7	.588	0	0	3.24
1986	New York	NL	28	20	2	2	141.2	605	145	70	61	15	6	5	7	36	1	104	5	3	10	7	.588	0	0	3.88
1987	New York	NL	18	17	1	0	115	494	124	53	46	12	7	2	3	33	2	77	9	0	11	3	.786	0	0	3.60
1988	New York	NL	11	3	0	2	24.2	111	29	20	19	2	2	0	1	10	2	16	1	1	0	4	.000	0	0	6.93
1989	Min-NYN		47	11	3	19	145	594	130	51	45	8	7	1	3	38	4	137	4	3	9	11	.450	0	7	2.79
1990	Minnesota	AL	56	0	0	54	65.1	268	55	27	20	5	0	0	4	19	6	61	3	0	5	3	.625	0	32	2.76
1991	Minnesota	AL	63	0	0	60	69	275	44	20	18	3	1	3	1	30	6	61	3	0	4	5	.444	0	42	2.35
1992	Minnesota	AL	64	0	0	61	66.2	273	60	28	21	7	1	2	1	17	4	52	5	0	2	6	.250	0	41	2.84
1993	Minnesota	AL	65	0	0	61	72.1	287	60	25	25	9	2	1	1	14	3	59	1	0	4	3	.571	0	34	3.11
1994	Minnesota	AL	44	0	0	40	44.2	201	57	23	18	7	4	1	0	10	3	46	2	0	1	4	.200	0	23	3.63
1995	Min-Bos	AL	52	0	0	51	55.1	223	46	16	16	6	1	4	1	13	1	52	0	0	3	3	.500	0	32	2.60
1989	Minnesota	AL	11	11	3	0	75.2	310	71	32	27	5	2	0	1	17	1	57	1	0	3	5	.375	0	0	3.21
	New York	NL	36	0	0	19	69.1	284	59	19	18	3	5	1	2	21	3	80	3	3	6	6	.500	0	7	2.34
1995	Minnesota	AL	22	0	0	21	25	99	20	7	7	2	0	2	1	6	1	29	0	0	1	1	.500	0	12	2.52
	Boston		30	0	0	30	30.1	124	26	9	9	4	1	2	0	7	0	23	0	0	2	2	.500	0	20	2.67
	11 ML YEARS		469	70	8	351	922	3838	868	382	333	82	38	23	24	257	34	739	38	9	59	56	.513	0	211	3.25

Pat Ahearne

Pitches: Right **Bats:** Right **Pos:** SP **Ht:** 6' 3" **Wt:** 195 **Born:** 12/10/69 **Age:** 26

			HOW MUCH HE PITCHED						WHAT HE GAVE UP												THE RESULTS					
Year	Team	Lg	G	GS	CG	GF	IP	BFP	H	R	ER	HR	SH	SF	HB	TBB	IBB	SO	WP	Bk	W	L	Pct.	ShO	Sv	ERA
1992	Lakeland	A	1	1	0	0	4.2	17	4	2	1	0	0	0	0	0	0	4	0	0	0	0	.000	0	0	1.93
1993	Lakeland	A	25	24	2	0	147.1	650	160	87	73	8	7	4	6	48	0	51	3	1	6	15	.286	0	0	4.46
1994	Trenton	AA	30	13	2	3	108.2	467	126	55	48	8	1	6	5	25	1	57	5	0	7	5	.583	0	0	3.98
1995	Toledo	AAA	25	23	1	0	139.2	599	165	83	73	11	2	5	5	37	3	54	2	0	7	9	.438	0	0	4.70
1995	Detroit	AL	4	3	0	0	10	55	20	13	13	2	0	0	0	5	1	4	1	0	0	2	.000	0	0	11.70

Jose Alberro

Pitches: Right **Bats:** Right **Pos:** RP **Ht:** 6' 2" **Wt:** 190 **Born:** 6/29/69 **Age:** 27

			HOW MUCH HE PITCHED						WHAT HE GAVE UP												THE RESULTS					
Year	Team	Lg	G	GS	CG	GF	IP	BFP	H	R	ER	HR	SH	SF	HB	TBB	IBB	SO	WP	Bk	W	L	Pct.	ShO	Sv	ERA
1991	Rangers	R	19	0	0	16	30.1	121	17	6	5	1	1	0	4	9	0	40	1	2	2	0	1.000	0	6	1.48
	Charlotte	A	5	0	0	0	5.2	33	8	9	6	0	1	0	1	7	2	3	3	0	0	1	.000	0	0	9.53
1992	Gastonia	A	17	0	0	6	20.2	84	18	8	8	2	0	1	1	4	0	26	1	0	1	0	1.000	0	1	3.48
	Charlotte	A	28	0	0	20	45	175	37	10	6	0	2	0	3	9	0	29	1	1	1	1	.500	0	15	1.20
1993	Tulsa	AA	17	0	0	16	19	78	11	2	2	2	1	0	0	8	1	24	2	1	0	0	.000	0	5	0.95
	Okla. City	AAA	12	0	0	7	17	85	25	15	13	2	1	2	0	11	0	14	4	0	0	0	.000	0	0	6.88
1994	Okla. City	AAA	52	0	0	35	69.2	314	79	40	35	6	4	6	5	36	8	50	3	0	4	3	.571	0	11	4.52
1995	Okla. City	AAA	20	10	0	7	77.2	331	73	34	29	4	2	3	4	27	2	55	6	0	4	2	.667	0	0	3.36
1995	Texas	AL	12	0	0	7	20.2	101	26	18	17	2	0	1	1	12	1	10	2	0	0	0	.000	0	0	7.40

Mike Aldrete

Bats: Left **Throws:** Left **Pos:** 1B/LF **Ht:** 5'11" **Wt:** 185 **Born:** 1/29/61 **Age:** 35

			BATTING																	BASERUNNING				PERCENTAGES		
Year	Team	Lg	G	AB	H	2B	3B	HR	(Hm	Rd)	TB	R	RBI	TBB	IBB	SO	HBP	SH	SF	SB	CS	SB%	GDP	Avg	OBP	SLG
1986	San Francisco	NL	84	216	54	18	3	2	(1	1)	84	27	25	33	4	34	2	4	1	1	3	.25	3	.250	.353	.389
1987	San Francisco	NL	126	357	116	18	2	9	(7	2)	165	50	51	43	5	50	0	4	2	6	0	1.00	6	.325	.396	.462
1988	San Francisco	NL	139	389	104	15	0	3	(3	0)	128	44	50	56	13	65	0	1	3	6	5	.55	10	.267	.357	.329
1989	Montreal	NL	76	136	30	8	1	1	(0	1)	43	12	12	19	0	30	1	1	2	1	3	.25	4	.221	.316	.316
1990	Montreal	NL	96	161	39	7	1	1	(0	1)	51	22	18	37	2	31	1	1	0	1	2	.33	2	.242	.385	.317
1991	Cle-SD		97	198	48	6	1	1	(0	1)	59	24	20	39	1	41	0	1	2	1	3	.25	1	.242	.364	.298
1993	Oakland	AL	95	255	68	13	1	10	(5	5)	113	40	33	34	2	45	0	3	0	1	1	.50	7	.267	.353	.443
1994	Oakland	AL	76	178	43	5	0	4	(2	2)	60	23	18	20	1	35	0	0	3	2	0	1.00	2	.242	.337	.337
1995	Oak-Cal	AL	78	149	40	8	0	4	(2	2)	60	19	24	19	1	31	1	0	3	0	0	.00	4	.268	.349	.403
1991	Cleveland	AL	85	183	48	6	1	1	(0	1)	59	22	19	36	1	37	0	1	2	1	2	.33	0	.262	.380	.322
	San Diego	NL	12	15	0	0	0	0	(0	0)	0	2	1	3	0	4	0	0	0	0	1	.00	1	.000	.167	.000
1995	Oakland	AL	60	125	34	8	0	4	(2	2)	54	18	21	19	1	23	1	0	2	0	0	.00	3	.272	.367	.432
	California	AL	18	24	6	0	0	0	(0	0)	6	1	3	0	0	8	0	0	1	0	0	.00	1	.250	.240	.250
	9 ML YEARS		867	2039	542	98	9	35	(20	15)	763	261	251	300	29	362	5	14	17	19	17	.53	39	.266	.359	.374

Manny Alexander

Bats: Right   **Throws:** Right   **Pos:** 2B   **Ht:** 5'10"   **Wt:** 150   **Born:** 3/20/71   **Age:** 25

Year	Team	Lg	G	AB	H	2B	3B	HR	(Hm	Rd)	TB	R	RBI	TBB	IBB	SO	HBP	SH	SF	SB	CS	SB%	GDP	Avg	OBP	SLG
1989	Bluefield	R	65	274	85	13	2	2	--	--	108	49	34	20	1	49	3	0	2	19	8	.70	2	.310	.361	.394
1990	Wausau	A	44	152	27	3	1	0	--	--	32	16	11	12	1	41	1	1	3	8	3	.73	2	.178	.238	.211
1991	Frederick	A	134	548	143	17	3	3	--	--	175	81	42	44	0	68	2	3	1	47	14	.77	4	.261	.318	.319
	Hagerstown	AA	3	9	3	1	0	0	--	--	4	3	2	1	0	3	1	0	1	0	0	.00	0	.333	.417	.444
1992	Hagerstown	AA	127	499	129	23	8	2	--	--	174	69	41	25	0	62	6	4	4	43	12	.78	10	.259	.300	.349
	Rochester	AAA	6	24	7	1	0	0	--	--	8	3	3	1	0	3	0	1	0	2	2	.50	0	.292	.320	.333
1993	Rochester	AAA	120	471	115	23	8	6	--	--	172	55	51	22	0	60	4	2	1	19	7	.73	11	.244	.283	.365
1994	Rochester	AAA	111	426	106	23	6	6	--	--	77	63	39	16	0	67	3	4	5	30	8	.79	7	.249	.278	.373
1992	Baltimore	AL	4	5	1	0	0	0	(0	0)	1	1	0	0	0	3	0	0	0	0	0	.00	0	.200	.200	.200
1993	Baltimore	AL	3	0	0	0	0	0	(0	0)	0	1	0	0	0	0	0	0	0	0	0	.00	0	.000	.000	.000
1995	Baltimore	AL	94	242	57	9	1	3	(2	1)	77	35	23	20	0	30	2	4	0	11	4	.73	2	.236	.299	.318
	3 ML YEARS		101	247	58	9	1	3	(2	1)	78	37	23	20	0	33	2	4	0	11	4	.73	2	.235	.297	.316

Edgardo Alfonzo

Bats: Right   **Throws:** Right   **Pos:** 3B/2B   **Ht:** 5'11"   **Wt:** 187   **Born:** 8/11/73   **Age:** 22

Year	Team	Lg	G	AB	H	2B	3B	HR	(Hm	Rd)	TB	R	RBI	TBB	IBB	SO	HBP	SH	SF	SB	CS	SB%	GDP	Avg	OBP	SLG
1991	Mets	R	54	175	58	8	4	0	--	--	74	29	27	34	0	12	2	3	7	6	4	.60	1	.331	.431	.423
1992	St. Lucie	A	4	5	0	0	0	0	--	--	0	0	0	0	0	0	0	0	0	0	0	.00	0	.000	.000	.000
	Pittsfield	A	74	298	106	13	5	1	--	--	132	41	44	18	1	31	0	2	4	7	5	.58	6	.356	.388	.443
1993	St. Lucie	A	128	494	145	18	3	11	--	--	202	75	86	57	3	51	5	4	9	26	16	.62	13	.294	.366	.409
1994	Binghamton	AA	127	498	146	34	2	15	--	--	229	89	75	64	6	55	0	5	7	14	11	.56	9	.293	.369	.460
1995	New York	NL	101	335	93	13	5	4	(0	4)	128	26	41	12	1	37	1	4	4	1	1	.50	7	.278	.301	.382

Luis Alicea

Bats: Both   **Throws:** Right   **Pos:** 2B   **Ht:** 5' 9"   **Wt:** 177   **Born:** 7/29/65   **Age:** 30

Year	Team	Lg	G	AB	H	2B	3B	HR	(Hm	Rd)	TB	R	RBI	TBB	IBB	SO	HBP	SH	SF	SB	CS	SB%	GDP	Avg	OBP	SLG
1988	St. Louis	NL	93	297	63	10	4	1	(1	0)	84	20	24	25	4	32	2	4	2	1	1	.50	12	.212	.276	.283
1991	St. Louis	NL	56	68	13	3	0	0	(0	0)	16	5	0	8	0	19	0	0	0	1	0	1.00	0	.191	.276	.235
1992	St. Louis	NL	85	265	65	9	11	2	(2	0)	102	26	32	27	1	40	4	2	4	2	5	.29	5	.245	.320	.385
1993	St. Louis	NL	115	362	101	19	3	3	(2	1)	135	50	46	47	2	54	4	1	7	11	1	.92	9	.279	.362	.373
1994	St. Louis	NL	88	205	57	12	5	5	(3	2)	94	32	29	30	4	38	3	1	3	4	5	.44	1	.278	.373	.459
1995	Boston	AL	132	419	113	20	3	6	(0	6)	157	64	44	63	0	61	7	13	9	13	10	.57	10	.270	.367	.375
	6 ML YEARS		569	1616	412	73	26	17	(8	9)	588	197	175	200	11	244	20	21	25	31	23	.57	37	.255	.340	.364

Andy Allanson

Bats: Right   **Throws:** Right   **Pos:** C   **Ht:** 6' 5"   **Wt:** 225   **Born:** 12/22/61   **Age:** 34

Year	Team	Lg	G	AB	H	2B	3B	HR	(Hm	Rd)	TB	R	RBI	TBB	IBB	SO	HBP	SH	SF	SB	CS	SB%	GDP	Avg	OBP	SLG
1995	Lk Elsinore *	A	22	82	26	9	0	4	--	--	47	22	22	16	0	8	1	0	1	2	2	.50	4	.317	.430	.573
1986	Cleveland	AL	101	293	66	7	3	1	(0	1)	82	30	29	14	0	36	1	11	4	10	1	.91	7	.225	.260	.280
1987	Cleveland	AL	50	154	41	6	0	3	(2	1)	56	17	16	9	0	30	0	4	5	1	1	.50	2	.266	.298	.364
1988	Cleveland	AL	133	434	114	11	0	5	(4	1)	140	44	50	25	2	63	3	8	4	5	9	.36	6	.263	.305	.323
1989	Cleveland	AL	111	323	75	9	1	3	(1	2)	95	30	17	23	2	47	4	6	3	4	4	.50	7	.232	.289	.294
1991	Detroit	AL	60	151	35	10	0	1	(0	1)	48	10	16	7	0	31	0	2	0	0	1	.00	3	.232	.266	.318
1992	Milwaukee	AL	9	25	8	1	0	0	(0	0)	9	6	0	1	0	2	0	2	0	3	1	.75	1	.320	.346	.360
1993	San Francisco	NL	13	24	4	1	0	0	(0	0)	5	3	2	1	0	2	0	1	0	0	0	.00	1	.167	.200	.208
1995	California	AL	35	82	14	3	0	3	(1	2)	26	5	10	7	0	12	1	1	0	0	1	.00	0	.171	.244	.317
	8 ML YEARS		512	1486	357	48	4	16	(8	8)	461	145	140	87	4	223	9	35	16	23	18	.56	27	.240	.283	.310

Roberto Alomar

Bats: Both   **Throws:** Right   **Pos:** 2B   **Ht:** 6' 0"   **Wt:** 185   **Born:** 2/5/68   **Age:** 28

Year	Team	Lg	G	AB	H	2B	3B	HR	(Hm	Rd)	TB	R	RBI	TBB	IBB	SO	HBP	SH	SF	SB	CS	SB%	GDP	Avg	OBP	SLG
1988	San Diego	NL	143	545	145	24	6	9	(5	4)	208	84	41	47	5	83	3	16	0	24	6	.80	15	.266	.328	.382
1989	San Diego	NL	158	623	184	27	1	7	(3	4)	234	82	56	53	4	76	1	17	8	42	17	.71	10	.295	.347	.376
1990	San Diego	NL	147	586	168	27	5	6	(4	2)	223	80	60	48	1	72	2	5	5	24	7	.77	16	.287	.340	.381
1991	Toronto	AL	161	637	188	41	11	9	(6	3)	278	88	69	57	3	86	4	16	5	53	11	.83	5	.295	.354	.436
1992	Toronto	AL	152	571	177	27	8	8	(5	3)	244	105	76	87	5	52	5	6	2	49	9	.84	8	.310	.405	.427
1993	Toronto	AL	153	589	192	35	6	17	(8	9)	290	109	93	80	5	67	5	4	5	55	15	.79	13	.326	.408	.492
1994	Toronto	AL	107	392	120	25	4	8	(4	4)	177	78	38	51	2	41	2	7	3	19	8	.70	14	.306	.386	.452

5

Year Team	Lg	G	AB	H	2B	3B	HR	(Hm	Rd)	TB	R	RBI	TBB	IBB	SO	HBP	SH	SF	SB	CS	SB%	GDP	Avg	OBP	SLG
1995 Toronto	AL	130	517	155	24	7	13	(7	6)	232	71	66	47	3	45	0	6	7	30	3	.91	16	.300	.354	.449
8 ML YEARS		1151	4460	1329	230	48	77	(42	35)	1886	697	499	470	28	522	22	77	35	296	76	.80	97	.298	.365	.423

Sandy Alomar

Bats: Right **Throws:** Right **Pos:** C **Ht:** 6' 5" **Wt:** 215 **Born:** 6/18/66 **Age:** 30

							BATTING												BASERUNNING				PERCENTAGES		
Year Team	Lg	G	AB	H	2B	3B	HR	(Hm Rd)	TB	R	RBI	TBB	IBB	SO	HBP	SH	SF	SB	CS	SB%	GDP	Avg	OBP	SLG
1995 Canton-Akrn *	AA	6	15	6	1	0	0	(-- --)	7	3	1	1	0	1	0	0	0	0	0	.00	1	.400	.438	.467
1988 San Diego	NL	1	1	0	0	0	0	(0 0)	0	0	0	0	0	0	1	0	0	0	0	.00	0	.000	.000	.000
1989 San Diego	NL	7	19	4	1	0	1	(1 0)	8	1	6	3	1	3	0	0	0	0	0	.00	0	.211	.318	.421
1990 Cleveland	AL	132	445	129	26	2	9	(5 4)	186	60	66	25	2	46	2	5	6	4	1	.80	10	.290	.326	.418
1991 Cleveland	AL	51	184	40	9	0	0	(0 0)	49	10	7	8	1	24	4	2	1	0	4	.00	4	.217	.246	.266
1992 Cleveland	AL	89	299	75	16	0	2	(1 1)	97	22	26	13	3	32	5	3	0	3	3	.50	7	.251	.293	.324
1993 Cleveland	AL	64	215	58	7	1	6	(3 3)	85	24	32	11	0	28	6	1	4	3	1	.75	3	.270	.318	.395
1994 Cleveland	AL	80	292	84	15	1	14	(4 10)	143	44	43	25	2	31	2	0	1	8	4	.67	7	.288	.347	.490
1995 Cleveland	AL	66	203	61	6	0	10	(4 6)	97	32	35	7	0	26	3	4	1	3	1	.75	8	.300	.332	.478
8 ML YEARS		490	1658	451	80	4	42	(18 24)	665	193	215	92	9	191	22	15	13	21	14	.60	40	.272	.317	.401

Moises Alou

Bats: Right **Throws:** Right **Pos:** LF/RF **Ht:** 6' 3" **Wt:** 195 **Born:** 7/3/66 **Age:** 29

							BATTING												BASERUNNING				PERCENTAGES		
Year Team	Lg	G	AB	H	2B	3B	HR	(Hm Rd)	TB	R	RBI	TBB	IBB	SO	HBP	SH	SF	SB	CS	SB%	GDP	Avg	OBP	SLG
1990 Mon-Pit	NL	16	20	4	0	1	0	(0 0)	6	4	0	0	0	3	0	1	0	0	0	.00	1	.200	.200	.300
1992 Montreal	NL	115	341	96	28	2	9	(6 3)	155	53	56	25	0	46	1	5	5	16	2	.89	5	.282	.328	.455
1993 Montreal	NL	136	482	138	29	6	18	(10 8)	233	70	85	38	9	53	5	3	7	17	6	.74	9	.286	.340	.483
1994 Montreal	NL	107	422	143	31	5	22	(9 13)	250	81	78	42	10	63	2	0	5	7	6	.54	7	.339	.397	.592
1995 Montreal	NL	93	344	94	22	0	14	(4 10)	158	48	58	29	6	56	9	0	4	4	3	.57	9	.273	.342	.459
1990 Montreal	NL	14	15	3	0	1	0	(0 0)	5	4	0	0	0	3	0	1	0	0	0	.00	0	.200	.200	.333
Pittsburgh	NL	2	5	1	0	0	0	(0 0)	1	0	0	0	0	0	0	0	0	0	0	.00	0	.200	.200	.200
5 ML YEARS		467	1609	475	110	14	63	(29 34)	802	256	277	134	25	221	17	9	21	44	17	.72	31	.295	.351	.498

Tavo Alvarez

Pitches: Right **Bats:** Right **Pos:** SP **Ht:** 6' 3" **Wt:** 245 **Born:** 11/25/71 **Age:** 24

				HOW MUCH HE PITCHED				WHAT HE GAVE UP											THE RESULTS					
Year Team	Lg	G	GS	CG	GF	IP	BFP	H	R	ER	HR	SH	SF	HB	TBB	IBB	SO	WP	Bk	W	L	Pct.	ShO	Sv	ERA
1990 Expos	R	11	10	0	0	52	214	42	17	15	0	1	3	1	16	0	47	1	0	5	2	.714	0	0	2.60
1991 Sumter	A	25	25	3	0	152.2	663	152	68	55	6	4	3	11	58	0	158	3	6	12	10	.545	1	0	3.24
1992 W. Palm Bch	A	19	19	7	0	139	542	124	30	23	0	2	1	3	24	0	83	2	0	13	4	.765	4	0	1.49
Harrisburg	AA	7	7	2	0	47.1	191	48	15	15	3	1	1	2	9	0	42	0	0	4	1	.800	1	0	2.85
1993 Ottawa	AAA	25	25	1	0	140.2	636	163	80	66	10	5	7	4	55	2	77	6	0	7	10	.412	0	0	4.22
1995 Harrisburg	AA	3	3	0	0	16	70	17	8	4	0	0	0	0	5	0	14	0	0	2	1	.667	0	0	2.25
Ottawa	AAA	3	3	0	0	21.2	83	17	6	6	1	0	0	1	5	0	11	1	0	2	1	.667	0	0	2.49
1995 Montreal	NL	8	8	0	0	37.1	173	46	30	28	2	1	0	3	14	0	17	1	0	1	5	.167	0	0	6.75

Wilson Alvarez

Pitches: Left **Bats:** Left **Pos:** SP **Ht:** 6' 1" **Wt:** 235 **Born:** 3/24/70 **Age:** 26

				HOW MUCH HE PITCHED				WHAT HE GAVE UP											THE RESULTS					
Year Team	Lg	G	GS	CG	GF	IP	BFP	H	R	ER	HR	SH	SF	HB	TBB	IBB	SO	WP	Bk	W	L	Pct.	ShO	Sv	ERA
1989 Texas	AL	1	1	0	0	0	5	3	3	3	2	0	0	0	2	0	0	0	0	0	0	.000	0	0	----
1991 Chicago	AL	10	9	2	0	56.1	237	47	26	22	9	3	1	0	29	0	32	2	0	3	2	.600	1	0	3.51
1992 Chicago	AL	34	9	0	4	100.1	455	103	64	58	12	3	4	4	65	2	66	2	0	5	3	.625	0	1	5.20
1993 Chicago	AL	31	31	1	0	207.2	877	168	78	68	14	13	6	7	122	8	155	2	1	15	8	.652	1	0	2.95
1994 Chicago	AL	24	24	2	0	161.2	682	147	72	62	16	6	3	0	62	1	108	3	0	12	8	.600	1	0	3.45
1995 Chicago	AL	29	29	3	0	175	769	171	96	84	21	6	5	2	93	4	118	1	2	8	11	.421	0	0	4.32
6 ML YEARS		129	103	8	4	701	3025	639	339	297	74	31	19	13	373	15	479	10	3	43	33	.566	3	1	3.81

Rich Amaral

Bats: Right **Throws:** Right **Pos:** LF/CF **Ht:** 6' 0" **Wt:** 175 **Born:** 4/1/62 **Age:** 34

							BATTING												BASERUNNING				PERCENTAGES		
Year Team	Lg	G	AB	H	2B	3B	HR	(Hm Rd)	TB	R	RBI	TBB	IBB	SO	HBP	SH	SF	SB	CS	SB%	GDP	Avg	OBP	SLG
1991 Seattle	AL	14	16	1	0	0	0	(0 0)	1	2	0	1	0	5	1	0	0	0	0	.00	1	.063	.167	.063
1992 Seattle	AL	35	100	24	3	0	1	(0 1)	30	9	7	5	0	16	0	4	0	4	2	.67	4	.240	.276	.300
1993 Seattle	AL	110	373	108	24	1	1	(0 1)	137	53	44	33	0	54	3	7	5	19	11	.63	5	.290	.348	.367
1994 Seattle	AL	77	228	60	10	2	4	(2 2)	86	37	18	24	1	28	1	7	2	5	1	.83	3	.263	.333	.377
1995 Seattle	AL	90	238	67	14	2	2	(1 1)	91	45	19	21	0	33	1	0	0	21	2	.91	3	.282	.342	.382
5 ML YEARS		326	955	260	51	5	8	(3 5)	345	146	88	84	1	136	6	19	7	49	16	.75	16	.272	.333	.361

Ruben Amaro

Bats: Both **Throws:** Right **Pos:** CF   **Ht:** 5'10" **Wt:** 175 **Born:** 2/12/65 **Age:** 31

												BATTING								BASERUNNING				PERCENTAGES		
Year Team	Lg	G	AB	H	2B	3B	HR	(Hm	Rd)	TB	R	RBI	TBB	IBB	SO	HBP	SH	SF	SB	CS	SB%	GDP	Avg	OBP	SLG
1995 Buffalo *	AAA	54	213	65	15	4	6	--	--	104	42	22	18	1	29	7	3	1	6	1	.86	5	.305	.377	.488
1991 California	AL	10	23	5	1	0	0	(0	0)	6	0	2	3	1	3	0	0	0	0	0	.00	1	.217	.308	.261
1992 Philadelphia	NL	126	374	82	15	6	7	(5	2)	130	43	34	37	1	54	9	4	2	11	5	.69	11	.219	.303	.348
1993 Philadelphia	NL	25	48	16	2	2	1	(0	1)	25	7	6	6	0	5	0	3	1	0	0	.00	1	.333	.400	.521
1994 Cleveland	AL	26	23	5	1	0	2	(0	2)	12	5	5	2	0	3	0	0	0	2	1	.67	0	.217	.280	.522
1995 Cleveland	AL	28	60	12	3	0	1	(1	0)	18	5	7	4	0	6	2	2	0	1	3	.25	1	.200	.273	.300
5 ML YEARS		215	528	120	22	8	11	(6	5)	191	60	54	52	2	71	11	9	3	14	9	.61	14	.227	.308	.362

Brady Anderson

Bats: Left **Throws:** Left **Pos:** LF/CF   **Ht:** 6'1" **Wt:** 195 **Born:** 1/18/64 **Age:** 32

												BATTING								BASERUNNING				PERCENTAGES		
Year Team	Lg	G	AB	H	2B	3B	HR	(Hm	Rd)	TB	R	RBI	TBB	IBB	SO	HBP	SH	SF	SB	CS	SB%	GDP	Avg	OBP	SLG
1988 Bal-Bos	AL	94	325	69	13	4	1	(1	0)	93	31	21	23	0	75	4	11	1	10	6	.63	3	.212	.272	.286
1989 Baltimore	AL	94	266	55	12	2	4	(2	2)	83	44	16	43	6	45	3	5	0	16	4	.80	4	.207	.324	.312
1990 Baltimore	AL	89	234	54	5	2	3	(1	2)	72	24	24	31	2	46	5	4	5	15	2	.88	4	.231	.327	.308
1991 Baltimore	AL	113	256	59	12	3	2	(1	1)	83	40	27	38	0	44	5	11	3	12	5	.71	1	.230	.338	.324
1992 Baltimore	AL	159	623	169	28	10	21	(15	6)	280	100	80	98	14	98	9	10	9	53	16	.77	2	.271	.373	.449
1993 Baltimore	AL	142	560	147	36	8	13	(2	11)	238	87	66	82	4	99	10	6	6	24	12	.67	4	.263	.363	.425
1994 Baltimore	AL	111	453	119	25	5	12	(7	5)	190	78	48	57	3	75	10	3	2	31	1	.97	7	.263	.356	.419
1995 Baltimore	AL	143	554	145	33	10	16	(10	6)	246	108	64	87	4	111	10	4	2	26	7	.79	3	.262	.371	.444
1988 Baltimore	AL	53	177	35	8	1	1	(1	0)	48	17	9	8	0	40	0	7	0	6	4	.60	1	.198	.232	.271
Boston	AL	41	148	34	5	3	0	(0	0)	45	14	12	15	0	35	4	4	1	4	2	.67	2	.230	.315	.304
8 ML YEARS		945	3271	817	164	44	72	(39	33)	1285	512	346	459	33	593	56	54	28	187	53	.78	28	.250	.349	.393

Brian Anderson

Pitches: Left **Bats:** Both **Pos:** SP   **Ht:** 6'1" **Wt:** 190 **Born:** 4/26/72 **Age:** 24

			HOW MUCH HE PITCHED					WHAT HE GAVE UP										THE RESULTS				
Year Team	Lg	G	GS	CG	GF	IP	BFP	H	R	ER	HR	SH	SF	HB	TBB	IBB	SO	WP	Bk	W	L	Pct.	ShO	Sv	ERA
1995 Lk Elsinore *	A	3	3	0	0	14	51	10	3	3	0	0	1	0	1	0	13	1	0	1	1	.500	0	0	1.93
1993 California	AL	4	1	0	3	11.1	45	11	5	5	1	0	0	0	2	0	4	0	0	0	0	.000	0	0	3.97
1994 California	AL	18	18	0	0	101.2	441	120	63	59	13	3	6	5	27	0	47	5	5	7	5	.583	0	0	5.22
1995 California	AL	18	17	1	0	99.2	433	110	66	65	24	5	5	3	30	2	45	1	3	6	8	.429	0	0	5.87
3 ML YEARS		40	36	1	3	212.2	919	241	134	129	38	8	11	8	59	2	96	6	8	13	13	.500	0	0	5.46

Garret Anderson

Bats: Left **Throws:** Left **Pos:** LF   **Ht:** 6'3" **Wt:** 190 **Born:** 6/30/72 **Age:** 24

												BATTING								BASERUNNING				PERCENTAGES		
Year Team	Lg	G	AB	H	2B	3B	HR	(Hm	Rd)	TB	R	RBI	TBB	IBB	SO	HBP	SH	SF	SB	CS	SB%	GDP	Avg	OBP	SLG
1990 Angels	R	32	127	27	2	0	0	--	--	29	5	14	2	0	24	2	0	3	3	0	1.00	3	.213	.231	.228
Boise	A	25	83	21	3	1	1	--	--	29	11	8	4	0	17	0	0	1	0	1	.00	3	.253	.284	.349
1991 Quad City	A	105	392	102	22	2	2	--	--	134	40	42	20	0	89	0	0	2	5	6	.45	16	.260	.295	.342
1992 Palm Spring	A	81	322	104	15	2	1	--	--	126	46	62	21	3	61	1	0	0	1	1	.50	9	.323	.366	.391
Midland	AA	39	146	40	5	0	2	--	--	51	16	19	9	2	30	0	0	0	2	1	.67	8	.274	.316	.349
1993 Vancouver	AAA	124	467	137	34	4	4	--	--	191	57	71	31	8	95	0	1	5	3	4	.43	15	.293	.334	.409
1994 Vancouver	AAA	123	505	162	42	6	12	--	--	252	75	102	28	2	93	1	0	3	3	3	.50	7	.321	.356	.499
1995 Vancouver	AAA	14	61	19	7	0	0	--	--	26	9	12	5	0	14	0	0	0	0	0	.00	3	.311	.364	.426
1994 California	AL	5	13	5	0	0	0	(0	0)	5	0	1	0	0	2	0	0	0	0	0	.00	0	.385	.385	.385
1995 California	AL	106	374	120	19	1	16	(7	9)	189	50	69	19	4	65	1	2	4	6	2	.75	8	.321	.352	.505
2 ML YEARS		111	387	125	19	1	16	(7	9)	194	50	70	19	4	67	1	2	4	6	2	.75	8	.323	.353	.501

Scott Anderson

Pitches: Right **Bats:** Right **Pos:** SP   **Ht:** 6'5" **Wt:** 200 **Born:** 8/1/62 **Age:** 33

			HOW MUCH HE PITCHED					WHAT HE GAVE UP										THE RESULTS				
Year Team	Lg	G	GS	CG	GF	IP	BFP	H	R	ER	HR	SH	SF	HB	TBB	IBB	SO	WP	Bk	W	L	Pct.	ShO	Sv	ERA
1984 Burlington	A	14	13	2	0	86.1	366	79	33	24	8	3	4	4	28	0	81	2	1	3	6	.333	0	0	2.50
1985 Tulsa	AA	28	27	2	0	174.1	735	177	87	71	15	1	0	4	51	1	123	3	1	9	6	.600	1	0	3.67
1986 Tulsa	AA	10	0	0	7	18.2	76	11	4	3	0	0	2	0	8	0	13	0	0	0	0	.000	0	5	1.45
Okla. City	AAA	48	0	0	39	82	355	82	36	27	6	5	7	1	28	3	51	1	0	5	7	.417	0	15	2.96
1987 Okla. City	AAA	49	0	0	36	64	294	79	44	40	4	1	1	2	35	7	39	2	0	5	3	.625	0	8	5.63
1988 Okla. City	AAA	38	10	0	10	97	421	101	51	49	6	5	4	3	49	3	44	2	3	4	6	.400	0	2	4.55
1989 Indianapols	AAA	29	19	1	3	127.2	560	139	62	45	7	12	6	4	44	1	88	5	2	7	8	.467	2	0	3.17
1990 Indianapols	AAA	27	25	6	2	182	750	166	74	67	16	8	5	0	61	2	116	6	1	12	10	.545	2	0	3.31
1993 Edmonton	AAA	44	1	0	14	66.1	285	74	30	26	6	2	0	2	15	2	52	1	0	5	4	.556	0	4	3.53
1994 New Orleans	AAA	8	3	0	1	24.1	111	34	20	19	4	0	1	1	6	0	17	0	0	0	2	.000	0	0	7.03

								IP	BFP	H	R	ER	HR	SH	SF	HB	TBB	IBB	SO	WP	Bk	W	L	Pct.	ShO	Sv	ERA
1995 Omaha	AAA	15	11	1	0	73.1	294	63	37	34	9	0	1	2	16	0	47	0	0	5	3	.625	0	0	4.17
1987 Texas	AL	8	0	0	2	11.1	59	17	12	12	1	0	1	1	8	2	6	2	0	0	1	.000	0	0	9.53
1990 Montreal	NL	4	3	0	1	18	71	12	6	6	1	1	1	0	5	0	16	0	0	0	1	.000	0	0	3.00
1995 Kansas City	AL	6	4	0	0	25.1	109	29	15	15	3	0	0	1	8	0	6	0	0	1	0	1.000	0	0	5.33
3 ML YEARS		18	7	0	3	54.2	239	58	33	33	4	2	1	2	21	2	28	2	0	1	2	.333	0	0	5.43

Shane Andrews

Bats: Right **Throws:** Right **Pos:** 3B/1B **Ht:** 6' 1" **Wt:** 215 **Born:** 8/28/71 **Age:** 24

					BATTING												BASERUNNING				PERCENTAGES		
Year Team	Lg	G	AB	H	2B	3B	HR	(Hm | Rd)	TB	R	RBI	TBB	IBB	SO	HBP	SH	SF	SB	CS	SB%	GDP	Avg	OBP	SLG
1990 Expos	R	56	190	45	7	1	3	--	--	63	31	24	29	0	46	3	1	1	10	4	.71	7	.237	.345	.332
1991 Sumter	A	105	356	74	16	7	11	--	--	137	46	49	65	2	132	3	0	0	5	4	.56	8	.208	.335	.385
1992 Albany	A	136	453	104	18	1	25	--	--	199	76	87	107	4	174	7	0	3	8	3	.73	4	.230	.382	.439
1993 Harrisburg	AA	124	442	115	29	1	18	--	--	200	77	70	64	2	118	1	1	4	10	6	.63	8	.260	.352	.452
1994 Ottawa	AAA	137	460	117	25	2	16	--	--	194	79	85	80	5	126	5	0	5	6	5	.55	11	.254	.367	.422
1995 Montreal	NL	84	220	47	10	1	8	(2 | 6)	83	27	31	17	2	68	1	1	2	1	1	.50	4	.214	.271	.377

Luis Andujar

Pitches: Right **Bats:** Right **Pos:** SP **Ht:** 6' 2" **Wt:** 175 **Born:** 11/22/72 **Age:** 23

		HOW MUCH HE PITCHED						WHAT HE GAVE UP										THE RESULTS				
Year Team	Lg	G	GS	CG	GF	IP	BFP	H	R	ER	HR	SH	SF	HB	TBB	IBB	SO	WP	Bk	W	L	Pct.	ShO	Sv	ERA
1991 White Sox	R	10	10	1	0	62.1	255	60	27	17	0	1	2	4	10	0	52	3	1	4	4	.500	1	0	2.45
1992 South Bend	A	32	15	1	11	120.1	516	109	49	39	5	2	0	6	47	0	91	5	1	6	5	.545	1	3	2.92
1993 Sarasota	A	18	11	2	4	86	345	67	26	19	2	7	0	3	28	0	72	1	0	6	6	.500	0	1	1.99
Birmingham	AA	6	6	0	0	39.2	169	31	9	8	3	3	1	5	18	0	48	1	0	5	0	1.000	0	0	1.82
1994 White Sox	R	2	0	0	0	6	22	3	1	0	0	0	0	1	1	0	6	0	0	1	0	1.000	0	0	0.00
Birmingham	AA	15	15	0	0	76.2	344	90	50	43	5	1	2	8	25	0	64	5	0	3	7	.300	0	0	5.05
1995 Birmingham	AA	27	27	2	0	167.1	689	147	64	53	10	1	5	7	44	0	146	3	1	14	8	.636	1	0	2.85
1995 Chicago	AL	5	5	0	0	30.1	128	26	12	11	4	0	0	1	14	2	9	0	0	2	1	.667	0	0	3.26

Eric Anthony

Bats: Left **Throws:** Left **Pos:** RF/1B **Ht:** 6' 2" **Wt:** 195 **Born:** 11/8/67 **Age:** 28

					BATTING												BASERUNNING				PERCENTAGES		
Year Team	Lg	G	AB	H	2B	3B	HR	(Hm | Rd)	TB	R	RBI	TBB	IBB	SO	HBP	SH	SF	SB	CS	SB%	GDP	Avg	OBP	SLG
1995 Indianapolis *	AAA	7	24	7	0	0	4	--	--	19	7	8	6	3	4	0	0	0	2	0	1.00	2	.292	.433	.792
1989 Houston	NL	25	61	11	2	0	4	(2 | 2)	25	7	7	9	2	16	0	0	0	0	0	.00	1	.180	.286	.410
1990 Houston	NL	84	239	46	8	0	10	(5 | 5)	84	26	29	29	3	78	2	1	6	5	0	1.00	4	.192	.279	.351
1991 Houston	NL	39	118	18	6	0	1	(0 | 1)	27	11	7	12	1	41	0	0	2	1	0	1.00	2	.153	.227	.229
1992 Houston	NL	137	440	105	15	1	19	(9 | 10)	179	45	80	38	5	98	1	0	4	5	4	.56	7	.239	.298	.407
1993 Houston	NL	145	486	121	19	4	15	(5 | 10)	193	70	66	49	2	88	2	0	2	3	5	.38	9	.249	.319	.397
1994 Seattle	AL	79	262	62	14	1	10	(3 | 7)	108	31	30	23	4	66	0	2	1	6	2	.75	7	.237	.297	.412
1995 Cincinnati	NL	47	134	36	6	0	5	(3 | 2)	57	19	23	13	2	30	0	0	3	2	1	.67	1	.269	.327	.425
7 ML YEARS		556	1740	399	70	6	64	(27 | 37)	673	209	242	173	19	417	5	3	18	22	12	.65	31	.229	.298	.387

Kevin Appier

Pitches: Right **Bats:** Right **Pos:** SP **Ht:** 6' 2" **Wt:** 195 **Born:** 12/6/67 **Age:** 28

		HOW MUCH HE PITCHED						WHAT HE GAVE UP										THE RESULTS				
Year Team	Lg	G	GS	CG	GF	IP	BFP	H	R	ER	HR	SH	SF	HB	TBB	IBB	SO	WP	Bk	W	L	Pct.	ShO	Sv	ERA
1989 Kansas City	AL	6	5	0	0	21.2	106	34	22	22	3	0	3	0	12	1	10	0	0	1	4	.200	0	0	9.14
1990 Kansas City	AL	32	24	3	1	185.2	784	179	67	57	13	5	9	6	54	2	127	6	1	12	8	.600	3	0	2.76
1991 Kansas City	AL	34	31	6	1	207.2	881	205	97	79	13	6	2	6	61	3	158	7	1	13	10	.565	3	0	3.42
1992 Kansas City	AL	30	30	3	0	208.1	852	167	59	57	10	8	3	2	68	5	150	4	0	15	8	.652	0	0	2.46
1993 Kansas City	AL	34	34	5	0	238.2	953	183	74	68	8	3	5	1	81	3	186	5	0	18	8	.692	1	0	2.56
1994 Kansas City	AL	23	23	1	0	155	653	137	68	66	11	9	7	4	63	7	145	11	1	7	6	.538	0	0	3.83
1995 Kansas City	AL	31	31	4	0	201.1	832	163	90	87	14	3	3	8	80	1	185	6	0	15	10	.600	1	0	3.89
7 ML YEARS		190	178	22	2	1218.1	5061	1068	477	436	72	36	36	23	419	22	961	38	3	81	54	.600	8	0	3.22

Luis Aquino

Pitches: Right **Bats:** Right **Pos:** RP **Ht:** 6' 1" **Wt:** 190 **Born:** 5/19/65 **Age:** 31

		HOW MUCH HE PITCHED						WHAT HE GAVE UP										THE RESULTS				
Year Team	Lg	G	GS	CG	GF	IP	BFP	H	R	ER	HR	SH	SF	HB	TBB	IBB	SO	WP	Bk	W	L	Pct.	ShO	Sv	ERA
1995 San Jose *	A	4	4	0	0	10.1	38	9	1	0	0	0	0	1	1	0	13	1	0	0	0	.000	0	0	0.00
1986 Toronto	AL	7	0	0	3	11.1	50	14	8	8	2	0	1	0	3	1	5	1	0	1	1	.500	0	0	6.35
1988 Kansas City	AL	7	5	1	0	29	136	33	15	9	1	0	1	1	17	0	11	1	1	1	0	1.000	0	0	2.79
1989 Kansas City	AL	34	16	2	7	141.1	591	148	62	55	6	2	4	4	35	4	68	4	0	6	8	.429	1	0	3.50
1990 Kansas City	AL	20	3	1	3	68.1	287	59	25	24	6	5	2	4	27	6	28	3	1	4	1	.800	0	0	3.16

Year Team	Lg	G	GS	CG	GF	IP	BFP	H	R	ER	HR	SH	SF	HB	TBB	IBB	SO	WP	Bk	W	L	Pct.	ShO	Sv	ERA
1991 Kansas City	AL	38	18	1	9	157	661	152	67	60	10	2	7	4	47	5	80	1	0	8	4	.667	1	3	3.44
1992 Kansas City	AL	15	13	0	1	67.2	293	81	35	34	5	2	3	1	20	1	11	1	1	3	6	.333	0	0	4.52
1993 Florida	NL	38	13	0	5	110.2	471	115	43	42	6	7	2	5	40	1	67	4	0	6	8	.429	0	0	3.42
1994 Florida	NL	29	1	0	3	50.2	214	39	22	21	3	1	2	3	22	4	22	2	0	2	1	.667	0	0	3.73
1995 Mon-SF	NL	34	0	0	9	42.1	199	57	34	24	6	1	1	3	13	2	26	3	0	0	3	.000	0	2	5.10
1995 Montreal	NL	29	0	0	8	37.1	171	47	24	16	4	0	1	3	11	1	22	3	0	0	2	.000	0	2	3.86
San Francisco	NL	5	0	0	1	5	28	10	10	8	2	1	0	0	2	1	4	0	0	0	1	.000	0	0	14.40
9 ML YEARS		222	69	5	40	678.1	2902	698	311	277	45	20	23	25	224	24	318	20	3	31	32	.492	3	5	3.68

Alex Arias

Bats: Right **Throws:** Right **Pos:** SS/3B   **Ht:** 6' 3" **Wt:** 185 **Born:** 11/20/67 **Age:** 28

							BATTING											BASERUNNING				PERCENTAGES		
Year Team	Lg	G	AB	H	2B	3B	HR	(Hm	Rd)	TB	R	RBI	TBB	IBB	SO	HBP	SH	SF	SB	CS	SB%	GDP	Avg	OBP	SLG
1992 Chicago	NL	32	99	29	6	0	0	(0	0)	35	14	7	11	0	13	2	1	0	0	0	.00	4	.293	.375	.354
1993 Florida	NL	96	249	67	5	1	2	(1	1)	80	27	20	27	0	18	3	1	3	1	1	.50	5	.269	.344	.321
1994 Florida	NL	59	113	27	5	0	0	(0	0)	32	4	15	9	0	19	1	1	1	0	1	.00	5	.239	.298	.283
1995 Florida	NL	94	216	58	9	2	3	(2	1)	80	22	26	22	1	20	2	3	3	1	0	1.00	8	.269	.337	.370
4 ML YEARS		281	677	181	25	3	5	(3	2)	227	67	68	69	1	70	8	6	7	2	2	.50	22	.267	.339	.335

Jack Armstrong

Pitches: Right **Bats:** Right **Pos:** SP   **Ht:** 6' 5" **Wt:** 220 **Born:** 3/7/65 **Age:** 31

		HOW MUCH HE PITCHED						WHAT HE GAVE UP											THE RESULTS					
Year Team	Lg	G	GS	CG	GF	IP	BFP	H	R	ER	HR	SH	SF	HB	TBB	IBB	SO	WP	Bk	W	L	Pct.	ShO	Sv	ERA
1988 Cincinnati	NL	14	13	0	0	65.1	293	63	44	42	8	4	5	0	38	2	45	3	2	4	7	.364	0	0	5.79
1989 Cincinnati	NL	9	8	0	1	42.2	187	40	24	22	5	2	1	0	21	4	23	0	0	2	3	.400	0	0	4.64
1990 Cincinnati	NL	29	27	2	1	166	704	151	72	63	9	8	5	6	59	7	110	7	5	12	9	.571	1	0	3.42
1991 Cincinnati	NL	27	24	1	1	139.2	611	158	90	85	25	6	9	2	54	2	93	2	1	7	13	.350	0	0	5.48
1992 Cleveland	AL	35	23	1	5	166.2	735	176	100	86	23	6	5	3	67	0	114	6	3	6	15	.286	0	0	4.64
1993 Florida	NL	36	33	0	2	196.1	879	210	105	98	29	8	10	7	78	6	118	7	2	9	17	.346	0	0	4.49
1994 Texas	AL	2	2	0	0	10	41	9	4	4	3	0	0	0	2	0	7	1	0	0	1	.000	0	0	3.60
7 ML YEARS		152	130	4	10	786.2	3450	807	439	400	102	34	35	18	319	21	510	26	13	40	65	.381	1	0	4.58

Rene Arocha

Pitches: Right **Bats:** Right **Pos:** RP   **Ht:** 6' 0" **Wt:** 180 **Born:** 2/24/66 **Age:** 30

		HOW MUCH HE PITCHED						WHAT HE GAVE UP											THE RESULTS					
Year Team	Lg	G	GS	CG	GF	IP	BFP	H	R	ER	HR	SH	SF	HB	TBB	IBB	SO	WP	Bk	W	L	Pct.	ShO	Sv	ERA
1993 St. Louis	NL	32	29	1	0	188	774	197	92	79	20	8	5	3	31	2	96	3	1	11	8	.579	0	0	3.78
1994 St. Louis	NL	45	7	1	25	83	360	94	42	37	9	5	1	4	21	4	62	2	0	4	4	.500	1	11	4.01
1995 St. Louis	NL	41	0	0	13	49.2	216	55	24	22	6	8	2	3	18	4	25	2	0	3	5	.375	0	0	3.99
3 ML YEARS		118	36	2	38	320.2	1350	346	155	138	35	21	8	10	70	10	183	7	1	18	17	.514	1	11	3.87

Andy Ashby

Pitches: Right **Bats:** Right **Pos:** SP   **Ht:** 6' 5" **Wt:** 190 **Born:** 7/11/67 **Age:** 28

		HOW MUCH HE PITCHED						WHAT HE GAVE UP											THE RESULTS					
Year Team	Lg	G	GS	CG	GF	IP	BFP	H	R	ER	HR	SH	SF	HB	TBB	IBB	SO	WP	Bk	W	L	Pct.	ShO	Sv	ERA
1991 Philadelphia	NL	8	8	0	0	42	186	41	28	28	5	1	3	3	19	0	26	6	0	1	5	.167	0	0	6.00
1992 Philadelphia	NL	10	8	0	0	37	171	42	31	31	6	2	2	1	21	0	24	2	0	1	3	.250	0	0	7.54
1993 SD-Col	NL	32	21	0	3	123	577	168	100	93	19	6	7	4	56	5	77	6	3	3	10	.231	0	1	6.80
1994 San Diego	NL	24	24	4	0	164.1	682	145	75	62	16	11	3	6	43	12	121	5	0	6	11	.353	0	0	3.40
1995 San Diego	NL	31	31	2	0	192.2	800	180	79	63	17	10	4	11	62	3	150	7	0	12	10	.545	2	0	2.94
1993 San Diego	NL	12	12	0	0	69	300	79	46	42	14	3	4	1	24	1	44	4	0	3	6	.333	0	0	5.48
Colorado	NL	20	9	0	3	54	277	89	54	51	5	3	3	3	32	4	33	2	3	0	4	.000	0	1	8.50
5 ML YEARS		105	92	6	3	559	2416	576	313	277	63	30	19	22	201	20	398	26	3	23	39	.371	2	1	4.46

Billy Ashley

Bats: Right **Throws:** Right **Pos:** LF   **Ht:** 6' 7" **Wt:** 235 **Born:** 7/11/70 **Age:** 25

							BATTING											BASERUNNING				PERCENTAGES		
Year Team	Lg	G	AB	H	2B	3B	HR	(Hm	Rd)	TB	R	RBI	TBB	IBB	SO	HBP	SH	SF	SB	CS	SB%	GDP	Avg	OBP	SLG
1992 Los Angeles	NL	29	95	21	5	0	2	(2	0)	32	6	6	5	0	34	0	0	0	0	0	.00	2	.221	.260	.337
1993 Los Angeles	NL	14	37	9	0	0	0	(0	0)	9	0	0	2	0	11	0	0	0	0	0	.00	0	.243	.282	.243
1994 Los Angeles	NL	2	6	2	1	0	0	(0	0)	3	0	0	0	0	2	0	0	0	0	0	.00	0	.333	.333	.500
1995 Los Angeles	NL	81	215	51	5	0	8	(6	2)	80	17	27	25	4	88	2	0	2	0	0	.00	8	.237	.320	.372
4 ML YEARS		126	353	83	11	0	10	(8	2)	124	23	33	32	4	135	2	0	2	0	0	.00	10	.235	.301	.351

9

Paul Assenmacher

Pitches: Left **Bats:** Left **Pos:** RP **Ht:** 6' 3" **Wt:** 210 **Born:** 12/10/60 **Age:** 35

		HOW MUCH HE PITCHED						WHAT HE GAVE UP										THE RESULTS					
Year Team	Lg	G	GS	CG	GF	IP	BFP	H	R	ER	HR	SH	SF	HB	TBB	IBB	SO	WP	Bk	W	L	Pct.	ShO	Sv	ERA
1986 Atlanta	NL	61	0	0	27	68.1	287	61	23	19	5	7	1	0	26	4	56	2	3	7	3	.700	0	7	2.50
1987 Atlanta	NL	52	0	0	10	54.2	251	58	41	31	8	2	1	1	24	4	39	0	0	1	1	.500	0	2	5.10
1988 Atlanta	NL	64	0	0	32	79.1	329	72	28	27	4	8	1	1	32	11	71	7	0	8	7	.533	0	5	3.06
1989 Atl-ChN	NL	63	0	0	17	76.2	331	74	37	34	3	9	3	1	28	8	79	3	1	3	4	.429	0	0	3.99
1990 Chicago	NL	74	1	0	21	103	426	90	33	32	10	10	3	1	36	8	95	2	0	7	2	.778	0	10	2.80
1991 Chicago	NL	75	0	0	31	102.2	427	85	41	37	10	8	4	3	31	6	117	4	0	7	8	.467	0	15	3.24
1992 Chicago	NL	70	0	0	23	68	298	72	32	31	6	1	2	3	26	5	67	4	0	4	4	.500	0	8	4.10
1993 NYA-ChN		72	0	0	21	56	237	54	21	21	5	4	0	1	22	6	45	0	0	4	3	.571	0	0	3.38
1994 Chicago	AL	44	0	0	11	33	134	26	13	13	2	1	3	1	13	2	29	1	0	1	2	.333	0	1	3.55
1995 Cleveland	AL	47	0	0	12	38.1	160	32	13	12	3	1	2	3	12	3	40	1	0	6	2	.750	0	0	2.82
1989 Atlanta	NL	49	0	0	14	57.2	247	55	26	23	2	7	2	1	16	7	64	3	1	1	3	.250	0	0	3.59
Chicago	NL	14	0	0	3	19	84	19	11	11	1	2	1	0	12	1	15	0	0	2	1	.667	0	0	5.21
1993 New York	AL	26	0	0	6	17.1	71	10	6	6	0	4	0	1	9	3	11	0	0	2	2	.500	0	0	3.12
Chicago	NL	46	0	0	15	38.2	166	44	15	15	5	0	0	0	13	3	34	0	0	2	1	.667	0	0	3.49
10 ML YEARS		622	1	0	205	680	2880	624	282	257	56	51	20	15	250	57	638	24	4	48	36	.571	0	48	3.40

Pedro Astacio

Pitches: Right **Bats:** Right **Pos:** RP/SP **Ht:** 6' 2" **Wt:** 195 **Born:** 11/28/69 **Age:** 26

		HOW MUCH HE PITCHED						WHAT HE GAVE UP										THE RESULTS					
Year Team	Lg	G	GS	CG	GF	IP	BFP	H	R	ER	HR	SH	SF	HB	TBB	IBB	SO	WP	Bk	W	L	Pct.	ShO	Sv	ERA
1992 Los Angeles	NL	11	11	4	0	82	341	80	23	18	1	3	2	2	20	4	43	1	0	5	5	.500	4	0	1.98
1993 Los Angeles	NL	31	31	3	0	186.1	777	165	80	74	14	7	8	5	68	5	122	8	9	14	9	.609	2	0	3.57
1994 Los Angeles	NL	23	23	3	0	149	625	142	77	71	18	6	5	4	47	4	108	4	0	6	8	.429	1	0	4.29
1995 Los Angeles	NL	48	11	1	7	104	436	103	53	49	12	5	3	4	29	5	80	5	0	7	8	.467	1	0	4.24
4 ML YEARS		113	76	11	7	521.1	2179	490	233	212	45	21	18	15	164	18	353	18	9	32	30	.516	8	0	3.66

Rich Aude

Bats: Right **Throws:** Right **Pos:** 1B **Ht:** 6' 5" **Wt:** 209 **Born:** 7/13/71 **Age:** 24

		BATTING																BASERUNNING				PERCENTAGES		
Year Team	Lg	G	AB	H	2B	3B	HR	(Hm | Rd)	TB	R	RBI	TBB	IBB	SO	HBP	SH	SF	SB	CS	SB%	GDP	Avg	OBP	SLG
1989 Pirates	R	24	88	19	3	0	0	--	--	22	13	7	5	0	17	3	0	1	2	0	1.00	1	.216	.278	.250
1990 Augusta	A	128	475	111	23	1	6	--	--	154	48	61	41	1	133	7	0	4	3	1	.75	11	.234	.302	.324
1991 Salem	A	103	366	97	12	2	3	--	--	122	45	43	27	5	72	9	0	0	3	0	1.00	7	.265	.331	.333
1992 Salem	A	122	447	128	26	4	9	--	--	189	63	60	50	2	79	8	0	1	11	2	.85	10	.286	.368	.423
Carolina	AA	6	20	4	1	0	2	--	--	11	4	3	1	0	3	0	0	0	0	0	.00	0	.200	.238	.550
1993 Buffalo	AAA	21	64	24	9	0	4	--	--	45	17	16	10	0	15	1	0	1	0	0	.00	1	.375	.461	.703
Carolina	AA	120	422	122	25	3	18	--	--	207	66	73	50	7	79	12	1	6	8	4	.67	6	.289	.376	.491
1994 Buffalo	AAA	138	520	146	38	4	15	--	--	237	66	79	41	3	83	11	0	2	9	5	.64	14	.281	.345	.456
1995 Calgary	AAA	50	195	65	14	2	9	--	--	110	34	42	12	1	30	4	0	5	3	2	.60	11	.333	.375	.564
1993 Pittsburgh	NL	13	26	3	1	0	0	(0 | 0)	4	1	4	1	0	7	0	0	0	0	0	.00	0	.115	.148	.154
1995 Pittsburgh	NL	42	109	27	8	0	2	(1 | 1)	41	10	19	6	0	20	0	0	0	1	2	.33	4	.248	.287	.376
2 ML YEARS		55	135	30	9	0	2	(1 | 1)	45	11	23	7	0	27	0	0	0	1	2	.33	4	.222	.261	.333

Rich Aurilia

Bats: Right **Throws:** Right **Pos:** SS **Ht:** 6' 1" **Wt:** 170 **Born:** 9/2/71 **Age:** 24

		BATTING																BASERUNNING				PERCENTAGES		
Year Team	Lg	G	AB	H	2B	3B	HR	(Hm | Rd)	TB	R	RBI	TBB	IBB	SO	HBP	SH	SF	SB	CS	SB%	GDP	Avg	OBP	SLG
1992 Butte	R	59	202	68	11	3	3	--	--	94	37	30	42	0	18	0	5	2	13	9	.59	2	.337	.447	.465
1993 Charlotte	A	122	440	136	16	5	5	--	--	177	80	56	75	4	57	3	9	7	15	18	.45	9	.309	.408	.402
1994 Tulsa	AA	129	458	107	18	6	12	--	--	173	67	57	53	0	74	4	8	5	10	13	.43	8	.234	.315	.378
1995 Shreveport	AA	64	226	74	17	1	4	--	--	105	29	42	27	3	26	1	5	2	10	3	.77	8	.327	.398	.465
Phoenix	AAA	71	258	72	12	0	5	--	--	99	42	34	35	2	29	0	0	3	2	2	.50	4	.279	.361	.384
1995 San Francisco	NL	9	19	9	3	0	2	(0 | 2)	18	4	4	1	0	2	0	1	1	1	0	1.00	1	.474	.476	.947

Joe Ausanio

Pitches: Right **Bats:** Right **Pos:** RP **Ht:** 6' 1" **Wt:** 205 **Born:** 12/9/65 **Age:** 30

		HOW MUCH HE PITCHED						WHAT HE GAVE UP										THE RESULTS					
Year Team	Lg	G	GS	CG	GF	IP	BFP	H	R	ER	HR	SH	SF	HB	TBB	IBB	SO	WP	Bk	W	L	Pct.	ShO	Sv	ERA
1988 Watertown	A	28	0	0	23	47.2	200	29	10	7	1	6	1	3	27	5	56	3	0	2	4	.333	0	13	1.32
1989 Salem	A	54	0	0	51	89	368	51	29	21	9	7	2	3	44	6	97	5	0	5	4	.556	0	20	2.12
1990 Harrisburg	AA	43	0	0	38	54	211	36	15	11	2	6	1	2	16	4	49	4	0	3	2	.600	0	15	1.83
1991 Carolina	AA	3	0	0	3	3	9	0	0	0	0	0	0	0	0	0	2	0	0	0	0	.000	0	2	0.00
Buffalo	AAA	22	0	0	14	30.1	144	33	17	13	5	1	3	0	19	3	26	2	1	2	2	.500	0	3	3.86
1992 Buffalo	AAA	53	0	0	39	83.2	352	64	35	27	5	6	2	1	40	6	66	4	0	6	4	.600	0	15	2.90

Year Team	Lg	G	GS	CG	GF	IP	BFP	H	R	ER	HR	SH	SF	HB	TBB	IBB	SO	WP	Bk	W	L	Pct.	ShO	Sv	ERA
1993 Expos	R	5	0	0	0	5	18	3	1	0	0	1	0	0	1	0	6	0	0	0	0	.000	0	0	0.00
Harrisburg	AA	19	0	0	15	22.1	86	16	3	3	1	0	0	0	4	1	30	0	0	2	1	1.000	0	6	1.21
1994 Columbus	AAA	44	0	0	29	60.1	243	45	21	16	5	2	6	1	16	1	69	3	0	3	3	.500	0	13	2.39
1995 Columbus	AAA	11	0	0	9	12	53	12	10	10	1	1	2	1	5	0	20	1	0	1		1.000	0	3	7.50
1994 New York	AL	13	0	0	5	15.2	69	16	9	9	3	0	0	0	6	0	15	0	0	2	1	.667	0	0	5.17
1995 New York	AL	28	0	0	10	37.2	173	42	24	24	9	1	2	0	23	0	36	3	0	2		1.000	0	1	5.73
2 ML YEARS		41	0	0	15	53.1	242	58	33	33	12	1	2	0	29	0	51	3	0	4	1	.800	0	1	5.57

Brad Ausmus

Bats: Right **Throws:** Right **Pos:** C

Ht: 5'11" **Wt:** 190 **Born:** 4/14/69 **Age:** 27

					BATTING												BASERUNNING				PERCENTAGES		
Year Team	Lg	G	AB	H	2B	3B	HR	(Hm | Rd)	TB	R	RBI	TBB	IBB	SO	HBP	SH	SF	SB	CS	SB%	GDP	Avg	OBP	SLG
1993 San Diego	NL	49	160	41	8	1	5	(4 | 1)	66	18	12	6	0	28	0	0	0	2	0	1.00	2	.256	.283	.413
1994 San Diego	NL	101	327	82	12	1	7	(6 | 1)	117	45	24	30	12	63	1	6	2	5	1	.83	8	.251	.314	.358
1995 San Diego	NL	103	328	96	16	4	5	(2 | 3)	135	44	34	31	3	56	2	4	4	16	5	.76	6	.293	.353	.412
3 ML YEARS		253	815	219	36	6	17	(12 | 5)	318	107	70	67	15	147	3	10	6	23	6	.79	16	.269	.324	.390

Steve Avery

Pitches: Left **Bats:** Left **Pos:** SP

Ht: 6'4" **Wt:** 205 **Born:** 4/14/70 **Age:** 26

		HOW MUCH HE PITCHED						WHAT HE GAVE UP											THE RESULTS					
Year Team	Lg	G	GS	CG	GF	IP	BFP	H	R	ER	HR	SH	SF	HB	TBB	IBB	SO	WP	Bk	W	L	Pct.	ShO	Sv	ERA
1990 Atlanta	NL	21	20	1	1	99	466	121	79	62	7	14	4	2	45	2	75	5	1	3	11	.214	1	0	5.64
1991 Atlanta	NL	35	35	3	0	210.1	868	189	89	79	21	8	4	3	65	0	137	4	1	18	8	.692	1	0	3.38
1992 Atlanta	NL	35	35	2	0	233.2	969	216	95	83	14	12	8	0	71	3	129	7	3	11	11	.500	2	0	3.20
1993 Atlanta	NL	35	35	3	0	223.1	891	216	81	73	14	12	8	0	43	5	125	3	1	18	6	.750	1	0	2.94
1994 Atlanta	NL	24	24	1	0	151.2	628	127	71	68	15	4	6	4	55	4	122	5	2	8	3	.727	0	0	4.04
1995 Atlanta	NL	29	29	3	0	173.1	724	165	92	90	22	6	4	6	52	4	141	3	0	7	13	.350	1	0	4.67
6 ML YEARS		179	178	13	1	1091.1	4546	1034	507	455	93	56	34	15	331	18	729	27	8	65	52	.556	6	0	3.75

Bobby Ayala

Pitches: Right **Bats:** Right **Pos:** RP

Ht: 6'3" **Wt:** 200 **Born:** 7/8/69 **Age:** 26

		HOW MUCH HE PITCHED						WHAT HE GAVE UP											THE RESULTS					
Year Team	Lg	G	GS	CG	GF	IP	BFP	H	R	ER	HR	SH	SF	HB	TBB	IBB	SO	WP	Bk	W	L	Pct.	ShO	Sv	ERA
1992 Cincinnati	NL	5	5	0	0	29	127	33	15	14	1	2	0	1	13	2	23	0	0	2	1	.667	0	0	4.34
1993 Cincinnati	NL	43	9	0	8	98	450	106	72	61	16	9	2	7	45	4	65	5	0	7	10	.412	0	3	5.60
1994 Seattle	AL	46	0	0	40	56.2	236	42	25	18	2	1	2	0	26	0	76	2	0	4	3	.571	0	18	2.86
1995 Seattle	AL	63	0	0	50	71	320	73	42	35	9	2	3	6	30	4	77	3	0	6	5	.545	0	19	4.44
4 ML YEARS		157	14	0	98	254.2	1133	254	154	128	28	14	7	14	114	10	241	10	0	19	19	.500	0	40	4.52

Carlos Baerga

Bats: Both **Throws:** Right **Pos:** 2B

Ht: 5'11" **Wt:** 200 **Born:** 11/4/68 **Age:** 27

					BATTING												BASERUNNING				PERCENTAGES		
Year Team	Lg	G	AB	H	2B	3B	HR	(Hm | Rd)	TB	R	RBI	TBB	IBB	SO	HBP	SH	SF	SB	CS	SB%	GDP	Avg	OBP	SLG
1990 Cleveland	AL	108	312	81	17	2	7	(3 | 4)	123	46	47	16	2	57	4	1	5	0	2	.00	4	.260	.300	.394
1991 Cleveland	AL	158	593	171	28	2	11	(9 | 2)	236	80	69	48	5	74	6	4	3	3	2	.60	12	.288	.346	.398
1992 Cleveland	AL	161	657	205	32	1	20	(9 | 11)	299	92	105	35	10	76	13	2	9	10	2	.83	15	.312	.354	.455
1993 Cleveland	AL	154	624	200	28	6	21	(8 | 13)	303	105	114	34	7	68	6	3	13	15	4	.79	17	.321	.355	.486
1994 Cleveland	AL	103	442	139	32	2	19	(8 | 11)	232	81	80	10	1	45	6	3	8	8	2	.80	10	.314	.333	.525
1995 Cleveland	AL	135	557	175	28	2	15	(7 | 8)	252	87	90	35	6	31	3	0	5	11	2	.85	15	.314	.355	.452
6 ML YEARS		819	3185	971	165	15	93	(37 | 56)	1445	491	505	178	31	351	38	13	43	47	14	.77	73	.305	.345	.454

Jeff Bagwell

Bats: Right **Throws:** Right **Pos:** 1B

Ht: 6'0" **Wt:** 195 **Born:** 5/27/68 **Age:** 28

					BATTING												BASERUNNING				PERCENTAGES		
Year Team	Lg	G	AB	H	2B	3B	HR	(Hm | Rd)	TB	R	RBI	TBB	IBB	SO	HBP	SH	SF	SB	CS	SB%	GDP	Avg	OBP	SLG
1995 Jackson *	AA	4	12	2	0	0	0	--	--	2	0	0	3	1	2	1	0	0	0	0	.00	0	.167	.375	.167
1991 Houston	NL	156	554	163	26	4	15	(6 | 9)	242	79	82	75	5	116	13	1	7	7	4	.64	12	.294	.387	.437
1992 Houston	NL	162	586	160	34	6	18	(8 | 10)	260	87	96	84	13	97	12	2	13	10	6	.63	17	.273	.368	.444
1993 Houston	NL	142	535	171	37	4	20	(9 | 11)	276	76	88	62	6	73	3	0	9	13	4	.76	20	.320	.388	.516
1994 Houston	NL	110	400	147	32	2	39	(23 | 16)	300	104	116	65	14	65	4	0	10	15	4	.79	12	.368	.451	.750
1995 Houston	NL	114	448	130	29	0	21	(10 | 11)	222	88	87	79	12	102	6	0	6	12	5	.71	9	.290	.399	.496
5 ML YEARS		684	2523	771	158	16	113	(56 | 57)	1300	434	469	365	50	453	38	3	45	57	23	.71	70	.306	.395	.515

Cory Bailey

Pitches: Right **Bats:** Right **Pos:** RP

Ht: 6' 1" **Wt:** 210 **Born:** 1/24/71 **Age:** 25

		HOW MUCH HE PITCHED						WHAT HE GAVE UP											THE RESULTS					
Year Team	Lg	G	GS	CG	GF	IP	BFP	H	R	ER	HR	SH	SF	HB	TBB	IBB	SO	WP	Bk	W	L	Pct.	ShO	Sv	ERA
1991 Red Sox	R	1	0	0	1	2	9	2	1	0	0	0	0	0	1	0	1	0	0	0	0	.000	0	1	0.00
Elmira	A	28	0	0	25	39	151	19	10	8	2	1	0	3	12	0	54	2	0	2	4	.333	0	15	1.85
1992 Lynchburg	A	49	0	0	43	66.1	272	43	20	18	3	6	2	2	30	2	87	5	0	5	7	.417	0	23	2.44
1993 Pawtucket	AAA	52	0	0	40	65.2	264	48	21	21	1	2	2	1	31	3	59	5	1	4	5	.444	0	20	2.88
1994 Pawtucket	AAA	53	0	0	43	61.1	264	44	25	22	4	4	0	1	38	2	52	7	0	4	3	.571	0	19	3.23
1995 Louisville	AAA	55	0	0	40	59.1	258	51	30	30	6	6	2	0	30	4	49	7	0	5	3	.625	0	25	4.55
1993 Boston	AL	11	0	0	5	15.2	66	12	7	6	0	1	1	0	12	3	11	2	1	0	1	.000	0	0	3.45
1994 Boston	AL	5	0	0	2	4.1	24	10	6	6	2	0	0	0	3	1	4	0	0	0	1	.000	0	0	12.46
1995 St. Louis	NL	3	0	0	0	3.2	15	2	3	3	0	0	0	0	2	1	5	1	0	0	0	.000	0	0	7.36
3 ML YEARS		19	0	0	7	23.2	105	24	16	15	2	1	1	0	17	5	20	3	1	0	2	.000	0	0	5.70

Roger Bailey

Pitches: Right **Bats:** Right **Pos:** RP/SP

Ht: 6' 1" **Wt:** 180 **Born:** 10/3/70 **Age:** 25

		HOW MUCH HE PITCHED						WHAT HE GAVE UP											THE RESULTS					
Year Team	Lg	G	GS	CG	GF	IP	BFP	H	R	ER	HR	SH	SF	HB	TBB	IBB	SO	WP	Bk	W	L	Pct.	ShO	Sv	ERA
1992 Bend	A	11	11	1	0	65.1	271	48	19	16	4	2	1	4	30	0	81	2	1	5	2	.714	0	0	2.20
1993 Central Val	A	22	22	1	0	111.2	515	139	78	60	9	1	3	6	56	1	84	7	1	4	7	.364	1	0	4.84
1994 New Haven	AA	25	24	1	1	159	675	157	70	57	8	5	7	5	56	1	112	6	0	9	9	.500	1	0	3.23
1995 Colo. Sprng	AAA	3	3	0	0	16.2	71	15	9	5	0	0	0	0	8	0	7	0	0	0	0	.000	0	0	2.70
1995 Colorado	NL	39	6	0	9	81.1	360	88	49	45	9	7	2	1	39	3	33	7	1	7	6	.538	0	0	4.98

Harold Baines

Bats: Left **Throws:** Left **Pos:** DH

Ht: 6' 2" **Wt:** 195 **Born:** 3/15/59 **Age:** 37

		BATTING																	BASERUNNING				PERCENTAGES		
Year Team	Lg	G	AB	H	2B	3B	HR	(Hm	Rd)	TB	R	RBI	TBB	IBB	SO	HBP	SH	SF	SB	CS	SB%	GDP	Avg	OBP	SLG
1980 Chicago	AL	141	491	125	23	6	13	(3	10)	199	55	49	19	7	65	1	2	5	2	4	.33	15	.255	.281	.405
1981 Chicago	AL	82	280	80	11	7	10	(3	7)	135	42	41	12	4	41	2	0	2	6	2	.75	6	.286	.318	.482
1982 Chicago	AL	161	608	165	29	8	25	(11	14)	271	89	105	49	10	95	0	2	9	10	3	.77	12	.271	.321	.469
1983 Chicago	AL	156	596	167	33	2	20	(12	8)	264	76	99	49	13	85	1	3	6	7	5	.58	15	.280	.333	.443
1984 Chicago	AL	147	569	173	28	10	29	(16	13)	308	72	94	54	9	75	0	1	5	1	2	.33	12	.304	.361	**.541**
1985 Chicago	AL	160	640	198	29	3	22	(13	9)	299	86	113	42	8	89	1	0	10	1	1	.50	23	.309	.348	.467
1986 Chicago	AL	145	570	169	29	2	21	(8	13)	265	72	88	38	9	89	2	0	8	2	1	.67	14	.296	.338	.465
1987 Chicago	AL	132	505	148	26	4	20	(12	8)	242	59	93	46	2	82	1	0	2	0	0	.00	12	.293	.352	.479
1988 Chicago	AL	158	599	166	39	1	13	(5	8)	246	55	81	67	14	109	1	0	7	0	0	.00	21	.277	.347	.411
1989 ChA-Tex	AL	146	505	156	29	1	16	(5	11)	235	73	72	73	13	79	1	3	4	0	3	.00	15	.309	.395	.465
1990 Oak-Tex	AL	135	415	118	15	1	16	(9	7)	183	52	65	67	10	80	0	3	7	0	3	.00	17	.284	.378	.441
1991 Oakland	AL	141	488	144	25	1	20	(11	9)	231	76	90	72	22	67	1	0	5	0	1	.00	12	.295	.383	.473
1992 Oakland	AL	140	478	121	18	0	16	(12	8)	187	58	76	59	6	61	0	0	6	1	3	.25	14	.253	.331	.391
1993 Baltimore	AL	118	416	130	22	0	20	(12	8)	212	64	78	57	9	52	0	1	6	0	0	.00	14	.313	.390	.510
1994 Baltimore	AL	94	326	96	12	1	16	(11	5)	158	44	54	30	6	49	1	0	0	0	0	.00	9	.294	.356	.485
1995 Baltimore	AL	127	385	115	19	1	24	(7	17)	208	60	63	70	13	45	0	0	4	0	2	.00	17	.299	.403	.540
1989 Chicago	AL	96	333	107	20	1	13	(4	9)	168	55	56	60	13	52	1	0	3	0	1	.00	11	.321	.423	.505
Texas	AL	50	172	49	9	0	3	(1	2)	67	18	16	13	0	27	0	0	1	0	2	.00	4	.285	.333	.390
1990 Oakland	AL	32	94	25	5	0	3	(3	0)	39	11	21	20	1	17	0	0	0	0	0	.00	4	.266	.381	.415
Texas	AL	103	321	93	10	1	13	(6	7)	144	41	44	47	9	63	0	0	3	0	1	.00	13	.290	.377	.449
16 ML YEARS		2183	7871	2271	387	48	301	(148	153)	3657	1033	1261	804	155	1163	12	9	86	30	30	.50	225	.289	.352	.465

Scott Baker

Pitches: Left **Bats:** Left **Pos:** RP

Ht: 6' 2" **Wt:** 175 **Born:** 5/18/70 **Age:** 26

		HOW MUCH HE PITCHED						WHAT HE GAVE UP											THE RESULTS					
Year Team	Lg	G	GS	CG	GF	IP	BFP	H	R	ER	HR	SH	SF	HB	TBB	IBB	SO	WP	Bk	W	L	Pct.	ShO	Sv	ERA
1990 Johnson Cty	R	32	0	0	7	51.1	223	44	21	12	2	1	3	0	29	2	62	6	3	4	2	.667	0	0	2.10
1991 Savannah	A	8	8	0	0	46.2	200	42	27	15	1	1	3	1	25	0	41	2	0	2	3	.400	0	0	2.89
St. Pete	A	19	16	1	2	93.2	401	98	47	45	2	4	6	3	42	0	50	5	0	3	9	.250	0	0	4.32
1992 St. Pete	A	24	24	0	0	151.2	610	123	48	33	3	9	4	5	54	0	125	11	8	10	9	.526	0	1	1.96
1993 Huntsville	AA	25	25	1	0	130.1	589	141	73	60	7	3	1	4	84	0	97	8	4	10	4	.714	1	0	4.14
1994 Huntsville	AA	30	14	3	5	111	453	86	28	22	4	7	2	0	46	2	67	4	2	10	4	.714	2	2	1.78
1995 Edmonton	AAA	22	20	1	0	107.1	474	123	69	63	9	2	2	3	46	4	56	4	0	4	7	.364	0	0	5.28
1995 Oakland	AL	1	0	0	0	3.2	22	5	4	4	1	1	1	1	5	0	3	0	0	0	0	.000	0	0	9.82

James Baldwin

Pitches: Right **Bats:** Right **Pos:** SP   **Ht:** 6' 3" **Wt:** 210 **Born:** 7/15/71 **Age:** 24

Year Team	Lg	HOW MUCH HE PITCHED						WHAT HE GAVE UP												THE RESULTS					
		G	GS	CG	GF	IP	BFP	H	R	ER	HR	SH	SF	HB	TBB	IBB	SO	WP	Bk	W	L	Pct.	ShO	Sv	ERA
1990 White Sox	R	9	7	0	1	37.1	164	32	29	17	1	1	2	0	18	0	32	6	3	1	6	.143	0	0	4.10
1991 White Sox	R	6	6	0	0	34	132	16	8	8	0	0	1	1	16	0	48	3	1	3	1	.750	0	0	2.12
Utica	A	7	7	1	0	37.1	180	40	26	22	0	0	1	2	27	0	23	4	2	1	4	.200	0	0	5.30
1992 South Bend	A	21	21	1	0	137.2	570	118	53	37	6	2	2	3	45	0	137	8	2	9	5	.643	1	0	2.42
Sarasota	A	6	6	1	0	37.2	149	31	13	12	2	3	0	1	7	0	39	1	0	1	2	.333	0	0	2.87
1993 Birmingham	AA	17	17	4	0	120	491	94	48	30	6	9	3	6	43	0	107	7	2	8	5	.615	0	0	2.25
Nashville	AAA	10	10	1	0	69	279	43	21	20	5	2	2	0	36	0	61	3	1	5	4	.556	0	0	2.61
1994 Nashville	AAA	26	26	2	0	162	696	144	75	67	14	2	2	1	83	1	156	9	4	12	6	.667	0	0	3.72
1995 Nashville	AAA	18	18	0	0	95.1	448	120	76	62	27	1	3	2	44	1	89	10	3	5	9	.357	0	0	5.85
1995 Chicago	AL	6	4	0	0	14.2	81	32	22	21	6	0	0	0	9	1	10	1	0	0	1	.000	0	0	12.89

Scott Bankhead

Pitches: Right **Bats:** Right **Pos:** RP   **Ht:** 5'10" **Wt:** 185 **Born:** 7/31/63 **Age:** 32

Year Team	Lg	HOW MUCH HE PITCHED						WHAT HE GAVE UP												THE RESULTS					
		G	GS	CG	GF	IP	BFP	H	R	ER	HR	SH	SF	HB	TBB	IBB	SO	WP	Bk	W	L	Pct.	ShO	Sv	ERA
1995 Edmonton *	AAA	12	0	0	5	18.1	90	28	18	16	2	3	1	1	7	2	15	0	0	1	3	.250	0	1	7.85
1986 Kansas City	AL	24	17	0	2	121	517	121	66	62	14	5	5	3	37	7	94	1	0	8	9	.471	0	0	4.61
1987 Seattle	AL	27	25	2	1	149.1	642	168	96	90	35	3	6	3	37	0	95	2	2	9	8	.529	0	0	5.42
1988 Seattle	AL	21	21	2	0	135	557	115	53	46	8	3	1	1	38	5	102	3	1	7	9	.438	1	0	3.07
1989 Seattle	AL	33	33	3	0	210.1	862	187	84	78	19	4	8	3	63	1	140	2	0	14	6	.700	2	0	3.34
1990 Seattle	AL	4	4	0	0	13	63	18	16	16	2	0	2	0	7	0	10	1	0	0	2	.000	0	0	11.08
1991 Seattle	AL	17	9	0	2	60.2	271	73	35	33	8	0	2	2	21	2	28	0	0	3	6	.333	0	0	4.90
1992 Cincinnati	NL	54	0	0	10	70.2	299	57	26	23	4	3	3	3	29	5	53	6	0	10	4	.714	0	1	2.93
1993 Boston	AL	40	0	0	4	64.1	272	59	28	25	7	3	4	0	29	3	47	1	0	2	1	.667	0	0	3.50
1994 Boston	AL	27	0	0	3	37.2	156	34	21	19	5	0	2	0	12	3	25	7	0	3	2	.600	0	0	4.54
1995 New York	AL	20	1	0	8	39	175	44	26	26	9	0	1	0	16	0	20	1	0	1	1	.500	0	0	6.00
10 ML YEARS		267	110	7	30	901	3814	876	451	418	111	21	34	15	289	26	614	24	3	57	48	.543	3	1	4.18

Willie Banks

Pitches: Right **Bats:** Right **Pos:** SP/RP   **Ht:** 6' 1" **Wt:** 200 **Born:** 2/27/69 **Age:** 27

Year Team	Lg	HOW MUCH HE PITCHED						WHAT HE GAVE UP												THE RESULTS					
		G	GS	CG	GF	IP	BFP	H	R	ER	HR	SH	SF	HB	TBB	IBB	SO	WP	Bk	W	L	Pct.	ShO	Sv	ERA
1991 Minnesota	AL	5	3	0	2	17.1	85	21	15	11	1	0	0	0	12	0	16	3	0	1	1	.500	0	0	5.71
1992 Minnesota	AL	16	12	0	2	71	324	80	46	45	6	2	5	2	37	0	37	5	1	4	4	.500	0	0	5.70
1993 Minnesota	AL	31	30	0	1	171.1	754	186	91	77	17	4	4	3	78	2	138	9	5	11	12	.478	0	0	4.04
1994 Chicago	NL	23	23	1	0	138.1	598	139	88	83	16	5	2	2	56	3	91	8	1	8	12	.400	1	0	5.40
1995 ChN-LA-Fla	NL	25	15	0	2	90.2	430	106	71	57	14	6	3	2	58	7	62	9	1	2	6	.250	0	0	5.66
1995 Chicago	NL	10	0	0	0	11.2	73	27	23	20	5	1	1	0	12	4	9	3	0	0	1	.000	0	0	15.43
Los Angeles	NL	6	6	0	0	29	138	36	21	13	2	1	1	1	16	2	23	4	1	0	2	.000	0	0	4.03
Florida	NL	9	9	0	0	50	219	43	27	24	7	4	1	1	30	1	30	2	0	2	3	.400	0	0	4.32
5 ML YEARS		100	83	1	7	488.2	2191	532	311	273	54	17	14	9	241	12	344	34	8	26	35	.426	1	0	5.03

Brian Barber

Pitches: Right **Bats:** Right **Pos:** RP/SP   **Ht:** 6' 1" **Wt:** 175 **Born:** 3/4/73 **Age:** 23

Year Team	Lg	HOW MUCH HE PITCHED						WHAT HE GAVE UP												THE RESULTS					
		G	GS	CG	GF	IP	BFP	H	R	ER	HR	SH	SF	HB	TBB	IBB	SO	WP	Bk	W	L	Pct.	ShO	Sv	ERA
1991 Johnson Cty	R	14	13	0	0	73.1	325	62	48	44	5	1	1	5	38	0	84	4	6	4	6	.400	0	0	5.40
1992 Springfield	A	8	8	0	0	50.2	215	39	21	21	7	2	0	1	24	0	56	2	1	3	4	.429	0	0	3.73
St. Pete	A	19	19	1	0	113.1	473	99	51	41	7	1	2	5	46	0	102	4	0	5	5	.500	0	0	3.26
1993 Arkansas	AA	24	24	1	0	143.1	625	154	70	64	19	7	4	4	56	2	126	10	2	9	8	.529	0	0	4.02
Louisville	AAA	1	1	0	0	5.2	25	4	3	3	0	1	0	0	4	0	5	0	1	0	1	.000	0	0	4.76
1994 Arkansas	AA	6	6	0	0	36	152	31	15	13	4	1	0	0	16	2	54	2	0	1	3	.250	0	0	3.25
Louisville	AAA	19	18	0	1	85.1	376	79	58	51	7	4	3	5	46	1	95	7	0	4	7	.364	0	1	5.38
1995 Louisville	AAA	20	19	0	0	107.1	465	105	67	56	14	2	6	4	40	1	94	1	0	6	5	.545	0	0	4.70
1995 St. Louis	NL	9	4	0	2	29.1	130	31	17	17	4	0	3	0	16	0	27	3	0	2	1	.667	0	0	5.22

Bret Barberie

Bats: Both **Throws:** Right **Pos:** 2B   **Ht:** 5'11" **Wt:** 180 **Born:** 8/16/67 **Age:** 28

Year Team	Lg	BATTING																		BASERUNNING				PERCENTAGES		
		G	AB	H	2B	3B	HR	(Hm	Rd)	TB	R	RBI	TBB	IBB	SO	HBP	SH	SF	SB	CS	SB%	GDP	Avg	OBP	SLG
1991 Montreal	NL	57	136	48	12	2	2	(2	0)	70	16	18	20	2	22	2	1	3	0	0	.00	4	.353	.435	.515
1992 Montreal	NL	111	285	66	11	0	1	(0	1)	80	26	24	47	3	62	8	1	2	9	5	.64	4	.232	.354	.281
1993 Florida	NL	99	375	104	16	2	5	(2	3)	139	45	33	33	2	58	7	5	3	2	4	.33	7	.277	.344	.371
1994 Florida	NL	107	372	112	20	2	5	(2	3)	151	40	31	23	3	65	9	2	0	2	0	1.00	4	.301	.356	.406

Year Team	Lg	G	GS	CG	GF	IP	BFP	( )	H	R	ER	HR	SH	SF	HB	TBB	IBB	SO	WP	Bk	W	L	Pct.	Sv	Avg	OBP	SLG
1995 Baltimore	AL	90	237	57	14	0	2	(1 1)	77	32	25	36	0	50	6	6	3	3	3	.50	6	.241	.351	.325			
5 ML YEARS		464	1405	387	73	6	15	(7 8)	517	159	131	159	10	257	32	15	11	16	12	.57	25	.275	.360	.368			

Brian Bark

Pitches: Left   **Bats:** Left   **Pos:** RP   **Ht:** 5' 9"   **Wt:** 170   **Born:** 8/26/68   **Age:** 27

		HOW MUCH HE PITCHED						WHAT HE GAVE UP												THE RESULTS					
Year Team	Lg	G	GS	CG	GF	IP	BFP	H	R	ER	HR	SH	SF	HB	TBB	IBB	SO	WP	Bk	W	L	Pct.	ShO	Sv	ERA
1990 Pulaski	R	5	5	0	0	23.2	100	17	19	7	3	1	0	1	13	0	33	2	0	2	2	.500	0	0	2.66
1991 Durham	A	13	13	0	0	82.1	330	66	23	23	0	3	2	6	24	0	76	4	3	4	3	.571	0	0	2.51
Greenville	AA	9	3	1	2	17.2	79	19	10	7	0	0	0	2	8	1	15	3	1	2	1	.667	0	1	3.57
1992 Greenville	AA	11	11	2	0	55	215	36	11	7	1	0	1	3	13	0	49	3	0	5	0	1.000	1	0	1.15
Richmond	AAA	22	4	0	4	42	197	63	32	28	3	1	2	1	15	1	50	1	1	1	2	.333	0	2	6.00
1993 Richmond	AAA	29	28	1	0	162	705	153	81	66	13	6	7	9	72	4	110	9	0	12	9	.571	1	0	3.67
1994 Richmond	AAA	37	16	0	8	126.2	543	128	76	67	15	8	4	3	51	5	87	8	0	4	9	.308	0	0	4.76
1995 Richmond	AAA	13	5	0	0	40.2	168	42	16	16	2	1	1	0	17	0	22	1	0	2	2	.500	0	0	3.54
Pawtucket	AAA	30	0	0	15	31.2	123	21	8	8	1	1	1	1	14	0	21	3	0	3	1	.750	0	7	2.27
1995 Boston	AL	3	0	0	2	2.1	8	2	0	0	0	0	0	0	1	0	1	0	0	0	0	.000	0	0	0.00

Jeff Barry

Bats: Both   **Throws:** Right   **Pos:** LF   **Ht:** 6' 0"   **Wt:** 200   **Born:** 9/22/68   **Age:** 27

		BATTING															BASERUNNING				PERCENTAGES		
Year Team	Lg	G	AB	H	2B	3B	HR	(Hm | Rd)	TB	R	RBI	TBB	IBB	SO	HBP	SH	SF	SB	CS	SB%	GDP	Avg	OBP	SLG
1990 Jamestown	A	51	197	62	6	1	4	--	--	82	30	23	17	2	25	0	2	0	25	5	.83	1	.315	.369	.416
1991 W. Palm Bch	A	116	437	92	16	3	4	--	--	126	47	31	34	4	67	4	2	2	20	14	.59	7	.211	.273	.288
1992 St. Lucie	A	3	9	3	2	0	0	--	--	5	0	1	0	0	0	0	0	0	0	0	.00	0	.333	.333	.556
Mets	R	8	23	4	1	0	0	--	--	5	5	2	6	1	2	0	0	0	2	0	1.00	1	.174	.345	.217
1993 St. Lucie	A	114	420	108	17	5	4	--	--	147	68	50	49	4	37	5	2	6	17	14	.55	7	.257	.338	.350
1994 Binghamton	AA	110	388	118	24	3	9	--	--	175	48	69	35	4	62	6	1	8	10	11	.48	10	.304	.364	.451
1995 Norfolk	AAA	12	41	9	2	0	0	--	--	11	3	6	3	0	6	1	0	2	0	0	.00	2	.220	.277	.268
Binghamton	AA	80	290	78	17	6	11	--	--	140	49	53	31	6	61	9	0	9	4	1	.80	4	.269	.348	.483
1995 New York	NL	15	15	2	1	0	0	(0 0)	3	2	0	1	0	8	0	0	0	0	0	.00	0	.133	.188	.200	

Shawn Barton

Pitches: Left   **Bats:** Right   **Pos:** RP   **Ht:** 6' 1"   **Wt:** 195   **Born:** 5/14/63   **Age:** 33

		HOW MUCH HE PITCHED						WHAT HE GAVE UP												THE RESULTS					
Year Team	Lg	G	GS	CG	GF	IP	BFP	H	R	ER	HR	SH	SF	HB	TBB	IBB	SO	WP	Bk	W	L	Pct.	ShO	Sv	ERA
1984 Bend	A	13	8	1	1	58.1	0	46	28	14	3	0	0	4	24	0	47	2	1	4	5	.444	0	0	2.16
1985 Peninsula	A	22	22	7	0	140.2	555	108	45	36	5	5	4	1	43	1	82	4	2	12	4	.750	5	0	2.30
1986 Reading	AA	17	17	3	0	92.2	404	92	53	39	10	5	2	2	41	2	62	2	1	8	7	.533	1	0	3.79
1987 Maine	AAA	7	4	0	3	26.2	119	25	14	13	2	2	1	0	15	1	19	3	2	1	1	.500	0	1	4.39
Reading	AA	32	12	3	9	82.1	367	108	50	45	8	1	2	1	31	2	53	5	1	6	5	.545	0	3	4.92
1988 Jackson	AA	22	8	0	8	71.2	305	74	33	26	5	2	1	1	26	3	58	3	3	2	4	.333	0	1	3.27
Tidewater	AAA	19	2	0	5	32.1	140	34	13	11	1	1	1	0	11	0	27	2	2	2	2	.500	0	0	3.06
1989 Tidewater	AAA	38	0	0	20	33.2	152	41	22	16	3	4	1	3	9	2	27	1	1	0	3	.000	0	5	4.28
1990 Tidewater	AAA	16	0	0	4	21.2	103	27	17	14	1	0	1	1	10	0	23	1	0	0	0	.000	0	0	5.82
Greenville	AA	15	0	0	11	16.2	79	24	15	15	2	1	0	1	9	1	8	0	0	0	1	.000	0	1	8.10
1991 Jacksonville	AA	14	4	1	3	34.2	143	36	16	12	0	2	0	1	8	0	24	0	1	3	3	.500	1	0	3.12
Calgary	AAA	17	0	0	6	31	127	25	11	9	3	1	0	0	8	0	22	1	0	2	0	1.000	0	1	2.61
1992 Calgary	AAA	30	0	0	17	53	231	57	31	25	4	3	1	2	24	4	31	1	1	3	5	.375	0	4	4.25
1993 Calgary	AAA	51	0	0	18	60.2	266	64	29	24	5	1	2	2	27	6	29	3	0	3	1	.750	0	4	3.56
1994 Phoenix	AAA	38	0	0	17	54.2	230	51	16	12	2	5	3	2	22	4	39	3	0	1	2	.333	0	4	1.98
1995 Phoenix	AAA	15	0	0	2	25	95	20	5	5	0	2	0	0	5	0	25	0	0	2	0	1.000	0	0	1.80
1992 Seattle	AL	14	0	0	2	12.1	50	10	5	4	1	1	0	0	7	2	4	2	0	0	1	.000	0	0	2.92
1995 San Francisco	NL	52	0	0	11	44.1	181	37	22	21	3	1	3	2	19	1	22	0	1	4	1	.800	0	0	4.26
2 ML YEARS		66	0	0	13	56.2	231	47	27	25	4	2	3	2	26	3	26	2	1	4	2	.667	0	0	3.97

Kevin Bass

Bats: Both   **Throws:** Right   **Pos:** RF/LF/DH   **Ht:** 6' 0"   **Wt:** 190   **Born:** 5/12/59   **Age:** 37

		BATTING															BASERUNNING				PERCENTAGES		
Year Team	Lg	G	AB	H	2B	3B	HR	(Hm | Rd)	TB	R	RBI	TBB	IBB	SO	HBP	SH	SF	SB	CS	SB%	GDP	Avg	OBP	SLG
1982 Mil-Hou		30	33	1	0	0	0	(0 0)	1	6	1	1	0	9	0	1	0	0	0	.00	1	.030	.059	.030	
1983 Houston	NL	88	195	46	7	3	2	(2 0)	65	25	18	6	1	27	0	4	1	2	2	.50	2	.236	.257	.333
1984 Houston	NL	121	331	86	17	5	2	(1 1)	119	33	29	6	1	57	3	2	0	5	5	.50	2	.260	.279	.360
1985 Houston	NL	150	539	145	27	5	16	(9 7)	230	72	68	31	1	63	6	4	2	19	8	.70	10	.269	.315	.427
1986 Houston	NL	157	591	184	33	5	20	(5 15)	287	83	79	38	11	72	6	1	4	22	13	.63	15	.311	.357	.486
1987 Houston	NL	157	592	168	31	5	19	(10 9)	266	83	85	53	13	77	4	0	5	21	8	.72	15	.284	.344	.449

14

Year	Team	Lg	G	AB	H	2B	3B	HR	(Hm	Rd)	TB	R	RBI	TBB	IBB	SO	HBP	SH	SF	SB	CS	SB%	GDP	Avg	OBP	SLG
1988	Houston	NL	157	541	138	27	2	14	(5	9)	211	57	72	42	10	65	6	3	3	31	6	.84	16	.255	.314	.390
1989	Houston	NL	87	313	94	19	4	5	(2	3)	136	42	44	29	3	44	1	1	4	11	4	.73	2	.300	.357	.435
1990	San Francisco	NL	61	214	54	9	1	7	(3	4)	86	25	32	14	3	26	2	2	1	2	2	.50	5	.252	.303	.402
1991	San Francisco	NL	124	361	84	10	4	10	(5	5)	132	43	40	36	8	56	4	2	3	7	4	.64	12	.233	.307	.366
1992	NYN-SF	NL	135	402	108	23	5	9	(7	2)	168	40	39	23	3	70	1	1	3	14	9	.61	8	.269	.308	.418
1993	Houston	NL	111	229	65	18	0	3	(2	1)	92	31	37	26	3	31	1	2	0	7	1	.88	4	.284	.359	.402
1994	Houston	NL	82	203	63	15	1	6	(3	3)	98	37	35	28	6	24	1	1	2	2	3	.40	5	.310	.393	.483
1995	Baltimore	AL	111	295	72	12	0	5	(2	3)	99	32	32	24	0	47	2	4	2	8	8	.50	15	.244	.303	.336
1982	Milwaukee	AL	18	9	0	0	0	0	(0	0)	0	4	0	1	0	1	0	1	0	0	0	.00	0	.000	.100	.000
	Houston	NL	12	24	1	0	0	0	(0	0)	1	2	1	0	0	8	0	0	0	0	0	.00	1	.042	.042	.042
1992	New York	NL	46	137	37	12	2	2	(2	0)	59	11	9	7	2	17	0	0	1	7	2	.78	2	.270	.303	.431
	San Francisco	NL	89	265	71	11	3	7	(5	2)	109	25	30	16	1	53	1	1	2	7	7	.50	6	.268	.310	.411
14 ML YEARS			1571	4839	1308	248	40	118	(56	62)	1990	609	611	357	63	668	37	28	30	151	73	.67	112	.270	.323	.411

Jason Bates

Bats: Both **Throws:** Right **Pos:** 2B/3B/SS   **Ht:** 5'11" **Wt:** 170 **Born:** 1/5/71 **Age:** 25

			BATTING																BASERUNNING				PERCENTAGES		
Year	Team	Lg	G	AB	H	2B	3B	HR	(Hm	Rd)	TB	R	RBI	TBB	IBB	SO	HBP	SH	SF	SB	CS	SB%	GDP	Avg	OBP	SLG
1992	Bend	A	70	255	73	10	3	6	--	--	107	57	31	56	1	55	5	2	4	18	4	.82	5	.286	.419	.420
1993	Colo. Sprng	AAA	122	449	120	21	2	13	--	--	184	76	62	45	4	99	10	3	3	9	8	.53	8	.267	.345	.410
1994	Colo. Sprng	AAA	125	458	131	19	5	10	--	--	190	68	76	60	4	57	4	2	5	4	6	.40	11	.286	.370	.415
1995	Colorado	NL	116	322	86	17	4	8	(4	4)	135	42	46	42	3	70	2	2	0	3	6	.33	4	.267	.355	.419

Allen Battle

Bats: Right **Throws:** Right **Pos:** LF/RF   **Ht:** 6' 0" **Wt:** 170 **Born:** 11/29/68 **Age:** 27

			BATTING																BASERUNNING				PERCENTAGES		
Year	Team	Lg	G	AB	H	2B	3B	HR	(Hm	Rd)	TB	R	RBI	TBB	IBB	SO	HBP	SH	SF	SB	CS	SB%	GDP	Avg	OBP	SLG
1991	Johnson Cty	R	17	62	24	6	1	0	--	--	32	26	7	14	0	6	1	1	0	7	1	.88	2	.387	.506	.516
	Savannah	A	48	169	42	7	1	0	--	--	51	27	20	27	0	34	1	0	2	12	3	.80	1	.249	.352	.302
1992	Springfield	A	67	235	71	10	4	4	--	--	101	49	24	41	0	34	10	1	2	22	12	.65	1	.302	.424	.430
	St. Pete	A	60	222	71	9	2	1	--	--	87	34	15	35	2	38	4	4	2	21	11	.66	2	.320	.418	.392
1993	Arkansas	AA	108	390	107	24	12	3	--	--	164	71	40	45	0	75	6	2	3	20	12	.63	4	.274	.356	.421
1994	Louisville	AAA	132	520	163	44	7	6	--	--	239	104	69	59	2	82	6	1	7	23	8	.74	14	.313	.385	.460
1995	Louisville	AAA	47	164	46	12	1	3	--	--	69	28	18	28	0	32	1	5	0	7	1	.88	3	.280	.389	.421
1995	St. Louis	NL	61	118	32	5	0	0	(0	0)	37	13	2	15	0	26	1	3	0	3	3	.50	0	.271	.358	.314

Howard Battle

Bats: Right **Throws:** Right **Pos:** 3B   **Ht:** 6' 0" **Wt:** 197 **Born:** 3/25/72 **Age:** 24

			BATTING																BASERUNNING				PERCENTAGES		
Year	Team	Lg	G	AB	H	2B	3B	HR	(Hm	Rd)	TB	R	RBI	TBB	IBB	SO	HBP	SH	SF	SB	CS	SB%	GDP	Avg	OBP	SLG
1990	Medicne Hat	R	61	233	62	17	1	5	--	--	96	25	32	15	2	38	2	0	0	5	2	.71	2	.266	.316	.412
1991	Myrtle Bch	A	138	520	147	33	4	20	--	--	248	82	86	49	2	88	3	0	4	15	7	.68	1	.283	.345	.477
1992	Dunedin	A	136	520	132	27	3	17	--	--	216	76	85	49	3	89	5	1	5	6	8	.43	5	.254	.321	.415
1993	Knoxville	AA	141	521	145	21	5	7	--	--	197	66	70	45	3	94	7	1	3	12	9	.57	8	.278	.342	.378
1994	Syracuse	AAA	139	517	143	26	8	14	--	--	227	72	75	40	4	82	3	1	7	26	2	.93	15	.277	.324	.439
1995	Syracuse	AAA	118	443	111	17	4	8	--	--	160	43	48	39	2	73	3	1	2	10	11	.48	7	.251	.314	.361
1995	Toronto	AL	9	15	3	0	0	0	(0	0)	3	3	0	4	0	8	0	0	0	1	0	1.00	0	.200	.368	.200

Danny Bautista

Bats: Right **Throws:** Right **Pos:** RF   **Ht:** 5'11" **Wt:** 170 **Born:** 5/24/72 **Age:** 24

			BATTING																BASERUNNING				PERCENTAGES		
Year	Team	Lg	G	AB	H	2B	3B	HR	(Hm	Rd)	TB	R	RBI	TBB	IBB	SO	HBP	SH	SF	SB	CS	SB%	GDP	Avg	OBP	SLG
1995	Toledo *	AAA	18	58	14	3	0	0	--	--	17	6	4	1	0	10	3	1	0	2	1	.33	1	.241	.290	.293
1993	Detroit	AL	17	61	19	3	0	1	(0	1)	25	6	9	1	0	10	0	0	1	3	1	.75	1	.311	.317	.410
1994	Detroit	AL	31	99	23	4	1	4	(1	3)	41	12	15	3	0	18	0	0	0	1	2	.33	2	.232	.255	.414
1995	Detroit	AL	89	271	55	9	0	7	(3	4)	85	28	27	12	0	68	0	6	0	4	1	.80	6	.203	.237	.314
3 ML YEARS			137	431	97	16	1	12	(4	8)	151	46	51	16	0	96	0	6	1	8	4	.67	10	.225	.252	.350

Jose Bautista

Pitches: Right **Bats:** Right **Pos:** RP/SP   **Ht:** 6' 2" **Wt:** 205 **Born:** 7/26/64 **Age:** 31

			HOW MUCH HE PITCHED						WHAT HE GAVE UP											THE RESULTS					
Year	Team	Lg	G	GS	CG	GF	IP	BFP	H	R	ER	HR	SH	SF	HB	TBB	IBB	SO	WP	Bk	W	L	Pct.	ShO	Sv	ERA
1988	Baltimore	AL	33	25	3	5	171.2	721	171	86	82	21	2	3	7	45	3	76	4	5	6	15	.286	0	0	4.30
1989	Baltimore	AL	15	10	0	4	78	325	84	46	46	17	1	1	1	15	0	30	0	0	3	4	.429	0	0	5.31
1990	Baltimore	AL	22	0	0	9	26.2	112	28	15	12	4	1	1	0	7	3	15	2	0	1	0	1.000	0	0	4.05
1991	Baltimore	AL	5	0	0	3	5.1	34	13	10	10	1	0	0	1	5	0	3	1	0	0	1	.000	0	0	16.88
1993	Chicago	NL	58	7	1	14	111.2	459	105	38	35	11	4	3	5	27	3	63	4	1	10	3	.769	0	2	2.82

Year Team	Lg	G	GS	CG	GF	IP	BFP	H	R	ER	HR	SH	SF	HB	TBB	IBB	SO	WP	Bk	W	L	Pct.	ShO	Sv	ERA
1994 Chicago	NL	58	0	0	24	69.1	293	75	30	30	10	5	4	3	17	7	45	2	1	4	5	.444	0	1	3.89
1995 San Francisco	NL	52	6	0	19	100.2	451	120	77	72	24	8	5	5	26	3	45	1	2	3	8	.273	0	0	6.44
7 ML YEARS		243	48	4	78	563.1	2395	596	302	287	88	21	17	22	142	19	277	14	9	27	36	.429	0	3	4.59

Billy Bean

Bats: Left **Throws:** Left **Pos:** LF **Ht:** 6' 0" **Wt:** 190 **Born:** 5/11/64 **Age:** 32

					BATTING														BASERUNNING				PERCENTAGES		
Year Team	Lg	G	AB	H	2B	3B	HR	(Hm Rd)	TB	R	RBI	TBB	IBB	SO	HBP	SH	SF	SB	CS	SB%	GDP	Avg	OBP	SLG
1995 Las Vegas *	AAA	119	445	129	34	2	15	-- --	212	67	77	46	9	55	9	0	9	2	2	.50	9	.290	.361	.476
1987 Detroit	AL	26	66	17	2	0	0	(0 0)	19	6	4	5	0	11	0	0	0	1	1	.50	1	.258	.310	.288
1988 Detroit	AL	10	11	2	0	1	0	(0 0)	4	2	0	0	0	2	0	1	0	0	0	.00	0	.182	.182	.364
1989 Det-LA		60	82	14	4	0	0	(0 0)	18	7	3	6	0	13	2	0	0	0	2	.00	0	.171	.244	.220
1993 San Diego	NL	88	177	46	9	0	5	(4 1)	70	19	32	6	1	29	2	2	5	2	4	.33	4	.260	.284	.395
1994 San Diego	NL	84	135	29	5	1	0	(0 0)	36	7	14	7	1	25	0	1	3	0	1	.00	4	.215	.248	.267
1995 San Diego	NL	4	7	0	0	0	0	(0 0)	0	1	0	1	0	4	0	0	0	0	0	.00	0	.000	.125	.000
1989 Detroit	AL	9	11	0	0	0	0	(0 0)	0	0	0	2	0	3	1	0	0	0	0	.00	0	.000	.214	.000
Los Angeles	NL	51	71	14	4	0	0	(0 0)	18	7	3	4	0	10	1	0	0	0	2	.00	0	.197	.250	.254
6 ML YEARS		272	478	108	20	2	5	(4 1)	147	42	53	25	2	84	4	4	8	3	8	.27	9	.226	.266	.308

Rod Beck

Pitches: Right **Bats:** Right **Pos:** RP **Ht:** 6' 1" **Wt:** 236 **Born:** 8/3/68 **Age:** 27

		HOW MUCH HE PITCHED						WHAT HE GAVE UP												THE RESULTS					
Year Team	Lg	G	GS	CG	GF	IP	BFP	H	R	ER	HR	SH	SF	HB	TBB	IBB	SO	WP	Bk	W	L	Pct.	ShO	Sv	ERA
1991 San Francisco	NL	31	0	0	10	52.1	214	53	22	22	4	4	2	1	13	2	38	0	0	1	1	.500	0	1	3.78
1992 San Francisco	NL	65	0	0	42	92	352	62	20	18	4	6	2	2	15	2	87	5	2	3	3	.500	0	17	1.76
1993 San Francisco	NL	76	0	0	71	79.1	309	57	20	19	11	6	3	3	13	4	86	4	0	3	1	.750	0	48	2.16
1994 San Francisco	NL	48	0	0	47	48.2	207	49	17	15	10	3	3	0	13	2	39	0	0	2	4	.333	0	28	2.77
1995 San Francisco	NL	60	0	0	52	58.2	255	60	31	29	7	4	3	2	21	3	42	2	0	5	6	.455	0	33	4.45
5 ML YEARS		280	0	0	222	331	1337	281	110	103	36	23	13	8	75	13	292	11	2	14	15	.483	0	127	2.80

Rich Becker

Bats: Left **Throws:** Left **Pos:** CF **Ht:** 5'10" **Wt:** 199 **Born:** 2/1/72 **Age:** 24

					BATTING														BASERUNNING				PERCENTAGES		
Year Team	Lg	G	AB	H	2B	3B	HR	(Hm Rd)	TB	R	RBI	TBB	IBB	SO	HBP	SH	SF	SB	CS	SB%	GDP	Avg	OBP	SLG
1990 Elizabethtn	R	56	194	56	5	1	6	-- --	81	54	24	53	0	54	3	5	0	16	2	.89	3	.289	.448	.418
1991 Kenosha	A	130	494	132	38	3	13	-- --	215	100	53	72	3	108	2	1	4	19	4	.83	7	.267	.360	.435
1992 Visalia	A	136	506	160	37	2	15	-- --	246	118	82	114	2	122	4	1	6	29	15	.66	5	.316	.441	.486
1993 Nashville	AA	138	516	148	25	7	15	-- --	232	93	66	94	5	117	3	2	3	29	7	.81	10	.287	.398	.450
1994 Salt Lake	AAA	71	282	89	21	3	2	-- --	122	64	38	40	0	56	0	2	0	7	1	.88	9	.316	.401	.433
1995 Salt Lake	AAA	36	123	38	7	0	6	-- --	63	26	28	26	0	24	1	0	2	6	1	.86	1	.309	.428	.512
1993 Minnesota	AL	3	7	2	2	0	0	(0 0)	4	3	0	5	0	4	0	0	0	1	1	.50	0	.286	.583	.571
1994 Minnesota	AL	28	98	26	3	0	1	(1 0)	32	12	8	13	0	25	0	1	0	6	1	.86	2	.265	.351	.327
1995 Minnesota	AL	106	392	93	15	1	2	(1 1)	116	45	33	34	0	95	4	6	2	8	9	.47	9	.237	.303	.296
3 ML YEARS		137	497	121	20	1	3	(2 1)	152	60	41	52	0	124	4	7	2	15	11	.58	11	.243	.319	.306

Steve Bedrosian

Pitches: Right **Bats:** Right **Pos:** RP **Ht:** 6' 3" **Wt:** 205 **Born:** 12/6/57 **Age:** 38

		HOW MUCH HE PITCHED						WHAT HE GAVE UP												THE RESULTS					
Year Team	Lg	G	GS	CG	GF	IP	BFP	H	R	ER	HR	SH	SF	HB	TBB	IBB	SO	WP	Bk	W	L	Pct.	ShO	Sv	ERA
1981 Atlanta	NL	15	1	0	5	24	106	15	14	12	2	0	1	1	15	2	9	0	0	1	2	.333	0	0	4.50
1982 Atlanta	NL	64	3	0	30	137.2	567	102	39	37	7	9	2	4	57	5	123	0	0	8	6	.571	0	11	2.42
1983 Atlanta	NL	70	1	0	52	120	504	100	50	48	11	8	4	4	51	8	114	2	0	9	10	.474	0	19	3.60
1984 Atlanta	NL	40	4	0	28	83.2	345	65	23	22	5	1	1	1	33	5	81	4	0	9	6	.600	0	11	2.37
1985 Atlanta	NL	37	37	0	0	206.2	907	198	101	88	17	6	7	5	111	6	134	6	0	7	15	.318	0	0	3.83
1986 Philadelphia	NL	68	0	0	56	90.1	381	79	39	34	12	3	3	0	34	10	82	5	2	8	6	.571	0	29	3.39
1987 Philadelphia	NL	65	0	0	56	89	366	79	31	28	11	2	1	1	28	5	74	3	1	5	3	.625	0	40	2.83
1988 Philadelphia	NL	57	0	0	49	74.1	322	75	34	31	6	0	3	0	27	5	61	0	0	6	6	.500	0	28	3.75
1989 Phi-SF	NL	68	0	0	60	84.2	342	56	31	27	12	1	4	1	39	5	58	2	0	3	7	.300	0	23	2.87
1990 San Francisco	NL	68	0	0	53	79.1	349	72	40	37	6	3	1	2	44	9	43	3	0	9	9	.500	0	17	4.20
1991 Minnesota	AL	56	0	0	22	77.1	332	70	42	38	11	2	4	3	35	6	44	2	0	5	3	.625	0	6	4.42
1993 Atlanta	NL	49	0	0	12	49.2	198	34	11	9	4	3	4	2	14	2	33	5	1	5	2	.714	0	0	1.63
1994 Atlanta	NL	46	0	0	9	46	196	41	20	17	4	5	2	2	18	5	43	1	0	0	2	.000	0	0	3.33
1995 Atlanta	NL	29	0	0	7	28	129	40	21	19	6	1	2	1	12	2	22	0	0	2	3	.333	0	0	6.11
1989 Philadelphia	NL	28	0	0	27	33.2	135	21	13	12	7	0	2	1	17	1	24	0	0	2	3	.400	0	6	3.21
San Francisco	NL	40	0	0	33	51	207	35	18	15	5	1	2	0	22	4	34	2	0	1	4	.200	0	17	2.65
14 ML YEARS		732	46	0	439	1190.2	5044	1026	496	412	114	44	39	27	518	75	921	33	4	76	79	.490	0	184	3.38

Tim Belcher

Pitches: Right **Bats:** Right **Pos:** SP   **Ht:** 6' 3" **Wt:** 220 **Born:** 10/19/61 **Age:** 34

			HOW MUCH HE PITCHED					WHAT HE GAVE UP									THE RESULTS					
Year Team	Lg	G	GS	CG	GF	IP	BFP	H	R	ER	HR	SH	SF	HB	TBB	IBB	SO	WP	Bk	W	L	Pct.	ShO	Sv	ERA
1995 Indianapols *	AAA	2	2	0	0	10	36	6	2	2	2	0	0	1	1	0	8	0	0	0	0	.000	0	0	1.80
1987 Los Angeles	NL	6	5	0	1	34	135	30	11	9	2	2	1	0	7	0	23	0	1	4	2	.667	0	0	2.38
1988 Los Angeles	NL	36	27	4	5	179.2	719	143	65	58	8	6	1	2	51	7	152	4	0	12	6	.667	1	4	2.91
1989 Los Angeles	NL	39	30	10	6	230	937	182	81	72	20	6	6	7	80	5	200	7	2	15	12	.556	8	1	2.82
1990 Los Angeles	NL	24	24	5	0	153	627	136	76	68	17	5	6	2	48	0	102	6	1	9	9	.500	2	0	4.00
1991 Los Angeles	NL	33	33	2	0	209.1	880	189	76	61	10	11	3	2	75	3	156	7	0	10	9	.526	1	0	2.62
1992 Cincinnati	NL	35	34	2	1	227.2	949	201	104	99	17	12	11	3	80	2	149	3	1	15	14	.517	1	0	3.91
1993 ChA-Cin		34	33	5	0	208.2	886	198	108	103	19	8	4	8	74	4	135	6	0	12	11	.522	3	0	4.44
1994 Detroit	AL	25	25	3	0	162	750	192	124	106	21	3	3	4	78	10	76	6	1	7	15	.318	0	0	5.89
1995 Seattle	AL	28	28	1	0	179.1	802	188	101	90	19	4	5	5	88	5	96	6	0	10	12	.455	0	0	4.52
1993 Chicago	AL	12	11	1	0	71.2	296	64	36	35	8	2	1	1	27	0	34	0	0	3	5	.375	1	0	4.40
Cincinnati	NL	22	22	4	0	137	590	134	72	68	11	6	3	7	47	4	101	6	0	9	6	.600	2	0	4.47
9 ML YEARS		260	239	32	13	1583.2	6685	1459	746	666	133	57	40	33	581	36	1089	45	6	94	90	.511	16	5	3.78

Stan Belinda

Pitches: Right **Bats:** Right **Pos:** RP   **Ht:** 6' 3" **Wt:** 215 **Born:** 8/6/66 **Age:** 29

			HOW MUCH HE PITCHED					WHAT HE GAVE UP									THE RESULTS					
Year Team	Lg	G	GS	CG	GF	IP	BFP	H	R	ER	HR	SH	SF	HB	TBB	IBB	SO	WP	Bk	W	L	Pct.	ShO	Sv	ERA
1995 Sarasota *	A	1	1	0	0	2	7	2	1	1	1	0	0	0	0	0	2	0	0	0	0	.000	0	0	4.50
1989 Pittsburgh	NL	8	0	0	2	10.1	46	13	8	7	0	0	0	0	2	0	10	1	0	0	1	.000	0	0	6.10
1990 Pittsburgh	NL	55	0	0	17	58.1	245	48	23	23	4	2	2	1	29	3	55	1	0	3	4	.429	0	8	3.55
1991 Pittsburgh	NL	60	0	0	37	78.1	318	50	30	30	10	4	3	4	35	4	71	2	0	7	5	.583	0	16	3.45
1992 Pittsburgh	NL	59	0	0	42	71.1	299	58	26	25	8	4	6	0	29	5	57	1	0	6	4	.600	0	18	3.15
1993 KC-Pit		63	0	0	44	69.2	287	65	31	30	6	3	2	2	17	4	55	2	0	4	2	.667	0	19	3.88
1994 Kansas City	AL	37	0	0	10	49	220	47	36	28	6	0	3	5	24	3	37	1	0	2	2	.500	0	1	5.14
1995 Boston	AL	63	0	0	30	69.2	285	51	25	24	5	0	4	4	28	3	57	2	0	8	1	.889	0	10	3.10
1993 Kansas City	AL	23	0	0	7	27.1	116	30	13	13	2	2	0	1	6	0	25	2	0	1	1	.500	0	0	4.28
Pittsburgh	NL	40	0	0	37	42.1	171	35	18	17	4	1	2	1	11	4	30	0	0	3	1	.750	0	19	3.61
7 ML YEARS		345	0	0	182	406.2	1700	332	179	167	39	13	20	16	164	22	342	10	0	30	19	.612	0	72	3.70

David Bell

Bats: Right **Throws:** Right **Pos:** 2B   **Ht:** 5'10" **Wt:** 175 **Born:** 9/14/72 **Age:** 23

					BATTING															BASERUNNING				PERCENTAGES		
Year Team	Lg	G	AB	H	2B	3B	HR	(Hm	Rd)	TB	R	RBI	TBB	IBB	SO	HBP	SH	SF	SB	CS	SB%	GDP	Avg	OBP	SLG
1990 Indians	R	30	111	29	5	1	0	--	--	36	18	13	10	1	8	4	0	1	1	1	.50	5	.261	.341	.324
Burlington	R	12	42	7	1	1	0	--	--	10	4	2	2	0	5	1	0	1	2	1	.67	1	.167	.217	.238
1991 Columbus	A	136	491	113	23	1	5	--	--	153	47	63	37	2	49	5	3	7	3	2	.60	22	.230	.287	.312
1992 Kinston	A	123	464	117	17	2	6	--	--	156	52	47	54	1	66	1	2	7	2	4	.33	13	.252	.327	.336
1993 Canton-Akrn	AA	129	483	141	20	2	9	--	--	192	69	60	43	0	54	3	2	6	3	4	.43	12	.292	.350	.398
1994 Charlotte	AAA	134	481	141	17	4	18	--	--	220	66	88	41	5	54	9	1	7	2	5	.29	9	.293	.355	.457
1995 Buffalo	AAA	70	254	69	11	1	8	--	--	106	34	34	22	0	37	4	1	3	0	3	.00	4	.272	.336	.417
Louisville	AAA	18	76	21	3	1	1	--	--	29	9	9	2	1	10	3	1	0	4	0	1.00	2	.276	.321	.382
1995 Cle-StL		41	146	36	7	2	2	(1	1)	53	13	19	4	0	25	2	0	1	1	2	.33	0	.247	.275	.363
1995 Cleveland	AL	2	2	0	0	0	0	(0	0)	0	0	0	0	0	0	0	0	0	0	0	.00	0	.000	.000	.000
St. Louis	NL	39	144	36	7	2	2	(1	1)	53	13	19	4	0	25	2	0	1	1	2	.33	0	.250	.278	.368

Derek Bell

Bats: Right **Throws:** Right **Pos:** RF/CF   **Ht:** 6' 2" **Wt:** 215 **Born:** 12/11/68 **Age:** 27

					BATTING															BASERUNNING				PERCENTAGES		
Year Team	Lg	G	AB	H	2B	3B	HR	(Hm	Rd)	TB	R	RBI	TBB	IBB	SO	HBP	SH	SF	SB	CS	SB%	GDP	Avg	OBP	SLG
1991 Toronto	AL	18	28	4	0	0	0	(0	0)	4	5	1	6	0	5	1	0	0	3	2	.60	0	.143	.314	.143
1992 Toronto	AL	61	161	39	6	3	2	(2	0)	57	23	15	15	1	34	5	2	1	7	2	.78	6	.242	.324	.354
1993 San Diego	NL	150	542	142	19	1	21	(12	9)	226	73	72	23	5	122	12	0	8	26	5	.84	7	.262	.303	.417
1994 San Diego	NL	108	434	135	20	0	14	(8	6)	197	54	54	29	5	88	1	0	2	24	8	.75	14	.311	.354	.454
1995 Houston	NL	112	452	151	21	2	8	(3	5)	200	63	86	33	2	71	8	0	6	27	9	.75	10	.334	.385	.442
5 ML YEARS		449	1617	471	66	6	45	(25	20)	684	218	228	106	13	320	27	2	17	87	26	.77	37	.291	.342	.423

Jay Bell

Bats: Right **Throws:** Right **Pos:** SS   **Ht:** 6' 0" **Wt:** 185 **Born:** 12/11/65 **Age:** 30

					BATTING															BASERUNNING				PERCENTAGES		
Year Team	Lg	G	AB	H	2B	3B	HR	(Hm	Rd)	TB	R	RBI	TBB	IBB	SO	HBP	SH	SF	SB	CS	SB%	GDP	Avg	OBP	SLG
1986 Cleveland	AL	5	14	5	2	0	1	(0	1)	10	3	4	2	0	3	0	0	0	0	0	.00	0	.357	.438	.714
1987 Cleveland	AL	38	125	27	9	1	2	(1	1)	44	14	13	8	0	31	1	3	0	2	0	1.00	0	.216	.269	.352
1988 Cleveland	AL	73	211	46	5	1	2	(2	0)	59	23	21	21	0	53	1	1	2	4	2	.67	3	.218	.289	.280

Year Team	Lg	G	AB	H	2B	3B	HR	(Hm	Rd)	TB	R	RBI	TBB	IBB	SO	HBP	SH	SF	SB	CS	SB%	GDP	Avg	OBP	SLG
1989 Pittsburgh	NL	78	271	70	13	3	2	(1	1)	95	33	27	19	0	47	1	10	2	5	3	.63	9	.258	.307	.351
1990 Pittsburgh	NL	159	583	148	28	7	7	(1	6)	211	93	52	65	0	109	3	39	6	10	6	.63	14	.254	.329	.362
1991 Pittsburgh	NL	157	608	164	32	8	16	(7	9)	260	96	67	52	1	99	4	30	3	10	6	.63	15	.270	.330	.428
1992 Pittsburgh	NL	159	632	167	36	6	9	(5	4)	242	87	55	55	0	103	4	19	2	7	5	.58	12	.264	.326	.383
1993 Pittsburgh	NL	154	604	187	32	9	9	(3	6)	264	102	51	77	6	122	6	13	1	16	10	.62	16	.310	.392	.437
1994 Pittsburgh	NL	110	424	117	35	4	9	(3	6)	187	68	45	49	1	82	3	8	3	2	0	1.00	15	.276	.353	.441
1995 Pittsburgh	NL	138	530	139	28	4	13	(8	5)	214	79	55	55	1	110	4	3	1	2	5	.29	13	.262	.336	.404
10 ML YEARS		1071	4002	1070	220	43	70	(31	39)	1586	598	390	403	9	759	27	126	20	58	37	.61	97	.267	.337	.396

Juan Bell

Bats: Both **Throws:** Right **Pos:** SS **Ht:** 5'11" **Wt:** 170 **Born:** 3/29/68 **Age:** 28

Year Team	Lg	G	AB	H	2B	3B	HR	(Hm	Rd)	TB	R	RBI	TBB	IBB	SO	HBP	SH	SF	SB	CS	SB%	GDP	Avg	OBP	SLG
1995 Pawtucket *	AAA	68	262	69	18	1	6	--	--	107	42	23	21	0	46	0	1	0	4	5	.44	7	.263	.318	.408
1989 Baltimore	AL	8	4	0	0	0	0	(0	0)	0	2	0	0	0	1	0	0	0	1	0	1.00	0	.000	.000	.000
1990 Baltimore	AL	5	2	0	0	0	0	(0	0)	0	1	0	0	0	1	0	0	0	0	0	.00	0	.000	.000	.000
1991 Baltimore	AL	100	209	36	9	2	1	(0	1)	52	26	15	8	0	51	0	4	2	0	0	.00	1	.172	.201	.249
1992 Philadelphia	NL	46	147	30	3	1	1	(1	0)	38	12	8	18	5	29	1	0	2	5	0	1.00	1	.204	.292	.259
1993 Mil-Phi		115	351	80	12	3	5	(2	3)	113	47	36	41	0	76	2	5	1	6	7	.46	4	.228	.311	.322
1994 Montreal	NL	38	97	27	4	0	2	(0	2)	37	12	10	15	0	21	0	1	0	4	0	1.00	1	.278	.372	.381
1995 Boston	AL	17	26	4	2	0	1	(0	1)	9	7	2	2	0	10	0	1	0	0	0	.00	0	.154	.207	.346
1993 Milwaukee	AL	91	286	67	6	2	5	(2	3)	92	42	29	36	0	64	1	3	1	6	6	.50	4	.234	.321	.322
Philadelphia	NL	24	65	13	6	1	0	(0	0)	21	5	7	5	0	12	1	2	0	0	1	.00	0	.200	.268	.323
7 ML YEARS		329	836	177	30	6	10	(3	7)	249	107	71	84	5	189	3	10	7	16	7	.70	7	.212	.284	.298

Albert Belle

Bats: Right **Throws:** Right **Pos:** LF **Ht:** 6' 2" **Wt:** 210 **Born:** 8/25/66 **Age:** 29

Year Team	Lg	G	AB	H	2B	3B	HR	(Hm	Rd)	TB	R	RBI	TBB	IBB	SO	HBP	SH	SF	SB	CS	SB%	GDP	Avg	OBP	SLG
1989 Cleveland	AL	62	218	49	8	4	7	(3	4)	86	22	37	12	0	55	2	0	2	2	2	.50	4	.225	.269	.394
1990 Cleveland	AL	9	23	4	0	0	1	(1	0)	7	1	3	1	0	6	0	1	0	0	0	.00	1	.174	.208	.304
1991 Cleveland	AL	123	461	130	31	2	28	(8	20)	249	60	95	25	2	99	5	0	5	3	1	.75	24	.282	.323	.540
1992 Cleveland	AL	153	585	152	23	1	34	(15	19)	279	81	112	52	5	128	4	1	8	8	2	.80	18	.260	.320	.477
1993 Cleveland	AL	159	594	172	36	3	38	(20	18)	328	93	129	76	13	96	8	1	14	23	12	.66	18	.290	.370	.552
1994 Cleveland	AL	106	412	147	35	2	36	(21	15)	294	90	101	58	9	71	5	1	4	9	6	.60	5	.357	.438	.714
1995 Cleveland	AL	143	546	173	52	1	50	(25	25)	377	121	126	73	5	80	6	0	4	5	2	.71	24	.317	.401	.690
7 ML YEARS		755	2839	827	185	13	194	(93	101)	1620	468	603	297	34	535	30	4	37	50	25	.67	94	.291	.360	.571

Rafael Belliard

Bats: Right **Throws:** Right **Pos:** SS/2B **Ht:** 5' 6" **Wt:** 160 **Born:** 10/24/61 **Age:** 34

Year Team	Lg	G	AB	H	2B	3B	HR	(Hm	Rd)	TB	R	RBI	TBB	IBB	SO	HBP	SH	SF	SB	CS	SB%	GDP	Avg	OBP	SLG
1982 Pittsburgh	NL	9	2	1	0	0	0	(0	0)	1	3	0	0	0	0	0	0	0	1	0	1.00	0	.500	.500	.500
1983 Pittsburgh	NL	4	1	0	0	0	0	(0	0)	0	1	0	0	0	1	0	0	0	0	0	.00	0	.000	.000	.000
1984 Pittsburgh	NL	20	22	5	0	0	0	(0	0)	5	3	0	0	0	1	0	0	0	4	1	.80	0	.227	.227	.227
1985 Pittsburgh	NL	17	20	4	0	0	0	(0	0)	4	1	1	0	0	5	0	0	0	0	0	.00	0	.200	.200	.200
1986 Pittsburgh	NL	117	309	72	5	2	0	(0	0)	81	33	31	26	6	54	3	11	1	12	2	.86	8	.233	.298	.262
1987 Pittsburgh	NL	81	203	42	4	3	1	(0	1)	55	26	15	20	6	25	3	2	1	5	1	.83	4	.207	.286	.271
1988 Pittsburgh	NL	122	286	61	0	4	0	(0	0)	69	28	11	26	3	47	4	5	0	7	1	.88	10	.213	.288	.241
1989 Pittsburgh	NL	67	154	33	4	0	0	(0	0)	37	10	8	8	2	22	0	3	0	5	2	.71	1	.214	.253	.240
1990 Pittsburgh	NL	47	54	11	3	0	0	(0	0)	14	10	6	5	0	13	1	1	0	1	2	.33	2	.204	.283	.259
1991 Atlanta	NL	149	353	88	9	2	0	(0	0)	101	36	27	22	2	63	2	7	1	3	1	.75	4	.249	.296	.286
1992 Atlanta	NL	144	285	60	6	1	0	(0	0)	68	20	14	14	4	43	3	13	0	0	1	.00	6	.211	.255	.239
1993 Atlanta	NL	91	79	18	5	0	0	(0	0)	23	6	6	4	0	13	3	3	0	0	0	.00	1	.228	.291	.291
1994 Atlanta	NL	46	120	29	7	1	0	(0	0)	38	9	9	2	1	29	2	2	1	0	2	.00	2	.242	.264	.317
1995 Atlanta	NL	75	180	40	2	1	0	(0	0)	44	12	7	6	2	28	2	4	0	2	2	.50	3	.222	.255	.244
14 ML YEARS		989	2068	464	45	14	1	(0	1)	540	198	135	133	26	344	23	51	4	40	15	.73	44	.224	.278	.261

Esteban Beltre

Bats: Right **Throws:** Right **Pos:** SS/2B **Ht:** 5'10" **Wt:** 155 **Born:** 12/26/67 **Age:** 28

Year Team	Lg	G	AB	H	2B	3B	HR	(Hm	Rd)	TB	R	RBI	TBB	IBB	SO	HBP	SH	SF	SB	CS	SB%	GDP	Avg	OBP	SLG
1991 Chicago	AL	8	6	1	0	0	0	(0	0)	1	0	0	1	0	1	0	0	0	1	0	1.00	0	.167	.286	.167
1992 Chicago	AL	49	110	21	2	0	1	(1	0)	26	21	10	3	0	18	0	2	1	1	0	1.00	3	.191	.211	.236
1994 Texas	AL	48	131	37	5	0	0	(0	0)	42	12	12	16	0	25	0	5	1	2	5	.29	3	.282	.358	.321
1995 Texas	AL	54	92	20	8	0	0	(0	0)	28	7	7	4	0	15	0	3	0	0	0	.00	1	.217	.250	.304
4 ML YEARS		159	339	79	15	0	1	(1	0)	97	40	29	24	0	59	0	10	2	4	5	.44	7	.233	.282	.286

Marvin Benard

Bats: Left **Throws:** Left **Pos:** CF **Ht:** 5' 9" **Wt:** 180 **Born:** 1/20/70 **Age:** 26

		BATTING																	BASERUNNING				PERCENTAGES		
Year Team	Lg	G	AB	H	2B	3B	HR	(Hm	Rd)	TB	R	RBI	TBB	IBB	SO	HBP	SH	SF	SB	CS	SB%	GDP	Avg	OBP	SLG
1992 Everett	A	64	161	38	10	2	1	--	--	55	31	17	24	0	39	6	1	0	17	3	.85	1	.236	.356	.342
1993 Clinton	A	112	349	105	14	2	5	--	--	138	84	50	56	1	66	4	2	0	42	10	.81	1	.301	.403	.395
1994 Shreveport	AA	125	454	143	32	3	4	--	--	193	66	48	31	5	58	4	7	4	24	13	.65	14	.315	.361	.425
1995 Phoenix	AAA	111	378	115	14	6	6	--	--	159	70	32	50	3	66	5	5	3	10	13	.43	2	.304	.390	.421
1995 San Francisco	NL	13	34	13	2	0	1	(0	1)	18	5	4	1	0	7	0	0	0	1	0	1.00	1	.382	.400	.529

Alan Benes

Pitches: Right **Bats:** Right **Pos:** SP **Ht:** 6' 5" **Wt:** 215 **Born:** 1/21/72 **Age:** 24

		HOW MUCH HE PITCHED						WHAT HE GAVE UP												THE RESULTS					
Year Team	Lg	G	GS	CG	GF	IP	BFP	H	R	ER	HR	SH	SF	HB	TBB	IBB	SO	WP	Bk	W	L	Pct.	ShO	Sv	ERA
1993 Glens Falls	A	7	7	0	0	37	162	39	20	15	2	0	1	2	14	0	29	2	1	0	4	.000	0	0	3.65
1994 Savannah	A	4	4	0	0	24.1	95	21	5	4	1	0	0	1	7	0	24	1	0	2	0	1.000	0	0	1.48
St. Pete	A	11	11	0	0	78.1	299	55	18	14	0	3	0	2	15	0	69	4	1	7	0	.875	0	0	1.61
Arkansas	AA	13	13	1	0	87.2	341	58	38	29	8	1	2	4	26	0	75	3	1	7	2	.778	0	0	2.98
Louisville	AAA	2	2	1	0	15.1	61	10	5	5	1	0	0	0	4	0	16	3	0	1	0	1.000	0	0	2.93
1995 Louisville	AAA	11	11	2	0	56	215	37	16	15	5	0	0	1	14	1	54	2	0	4	2	.667	1	0	2.41
1995 St. Louis	NL	3	3	0	0	16	76	24	15	15	2	1	0	1	4	0	20	3	0	1	2	.333	0	0	8.44

Andy Benes

Pitches: Right **Bats:** Right **Pos:** SP **Ht:** 6' 6" **Wt:** 240 **Born:** 8/20/67 **Age:** 28

		HOW MUCH HE PITCHED						WHAT HE GAVE UP												THE RESULTS					
Year Team	Lg	G	GS	CG	GF	IP	BFP	H	R	ER	HR	SH	SF	HB	TBB	IBB	SO	WP	Bk	W	L	Pct.	ShO	Sv	ERA
1989 San Diego	NL	10	10	0	0	66.2	280	51	28	26	7	6	2	1	31	0	66	0	3	6	3	.667	0	0	3.51
1990 San Diego	NL	32	31	2	1	192.1	811	177	87	77	18	5	6	1	69	5	140	2	5	10	11	.476	0	0	3.60
1991 San Diego	NL	33	33	4	0	223	908	194	76	75	23	5	4	4	59	7	167	3	4	15	11	.577	1	0	3.03
1992 San Diego	NL	34	34	2	0	231.1	961	230	90	86	14	19	6	5	61	6	169	1	1	13	14	.481	2	0	3.35
1993 San Diego	NL	34	34	4	0	230.2	968	200	111	97	23	10	6	4	86	7	179	14	2	15	15	.500	2	0	3.78
1994 San Diego	NL	25	25	2	0	172.1	717	155	82	74	20	11	1	1	51	2	189	4	0	6	14	.300	2	0	3.86
1995 SD-Sea		31	31	1	0	181.2	809	193	107	96	18	4	8	6	78	5	171	5	0	11	9	.550	1	0	4.76
1995 San Diego	NL	19	19	1	0	118.2	518	121	65	55	10	3	4	4	45	3	126	3	0	4	7	.364	1	0	4.17
Seattle	AL	12	12	0	0	63	291	72	42	41	8	1	4	2	33	2	45	2	0	7	2	.778	0	0	5.86
7 ML YEARS		199	198	15	1	1298	5454	1200	581	531	123	60	33	22	435	32	1081	29	15	76	77	.497	8	0	3.68

Armando Benitez

Pitches: Right **Bats:** Right **Pos:** RP **Ht:** 6' 4" **Wt:** 220 **Born:** 11/3/72 **Age:** 23

		HOW MUCH HE PITCHED						WHAT HE GAVE UP												THE RESULTS					
Year Team	Lg	G	GS	CG	GF	IP	BFP	H	R	ER	HR	SH	SF	HB	TBB	IBB	SO	WP	Bk	W	L	Pct.	ShO	Sv	ERA
1991 Orioles	R	14	3	0	6	36.1	157	35	16	11	2	2	0	4	11	0	33	2	0	3	2	.600	0	0	2.72
1992 Bluefield	R	25	0	0	18	31.1	157	35	31	15	1	1	3	3	23	0	37	7	0	1	2	.333	0	5	4.31
1993 Albany	A	40	0	0	34	53.1	209	31	10	9	2	3	1	2	19	0	83	4	0	5	1	.833	0	14	1.52
Frederick	A	12	0	0	10	13.2	52	7	1	1	0	1	0	0	4	0	29	1	0	3	0	1.000	0	4	0.66
1994 Bowie	AA	53	0	0	36	71.2	298	41	29	25	6	0	1	2	39	0	106	3	0	8	4	.667	0	16	3.14
1995 Rochester	AAA	17	0	0	17	21.2	81	10	4	3	2	0	0	0	7	0	37	1	0	2	2	.500	0	8	1.25
1994 Baltimore	AL	3	0	0	1	10	42	8	1	1	0	0	0	1	4	0	14	0	0	0	0	.000	0	0	0.90
1995 Baltimore	AL	44	0	0	18	47.2	221	37	33	30	8	2	3	5	37	2	56	3	1	1	5	.167	0	2	5.66
2 ML YEARS		47	0	0	19	57.2	263	45	34	31	8	2	3	6	41	2	70	3	1	1	5	.167	0	2	4.84

Yamil Benitez

Bats: Right **Throws:** Right **Pos:** RF **Ht:** 6' 2" **Wt:** 190 **Born:** 5/10/72 **Age:** 24

		BATTING																	BASERUNNING				PERCENTAGES		
Year Team	Lg	G	AB	H	2B	3B	HR	(Hm	Rd)	TB	R	RBI	TBB	IBB	SO	HBP	SH	SF	SB	CS	SB%	GDP	Avg	OBP	SLG
1990 Expos	R	22	83	19	1	0	1	--	--	23	6	5	8	0	18	0	0	0	0	0	.00	1	.229	.297	.277
1991 Expos	R	54	197	47	9	5	5	--	--	81	20	38	12	1	55	1	1	5	10	5	.67	3	.239	.279	.411
1992 Albany	A	23	79	13	3	2	1	--	--	23	6	6	5	1	49	0	0	0	0	2	.00	1	.165	.214	.291
Jamestown	A	44	162	44	6	6	3	--	--	71	24	23	14	0	52	2	1	0	19	1	.95	5	.272	.337	.438
1993 Burlington	A	111	411	112	21	5	15	--	--	188	70	61	29	1	99	3	6	3	18	7	.72	8	.273	.323	.457
1994 Harrisburg	AA	126	475	123	18	4	17	--	--	200	58	91	36	2	134	2	1	4	18	15	.55	12	.259	.311	.421
1995 Ottawa	AAA	127	474	123	24	6	18	--	--	213	66	69	44	3	128	2	2	2	14	6	.70	10	.259	.324	.449
1995 Montreal	NL	14	39	15	2	1	2	(1	1)	25	8	7	1	0	7	0	0	0	0	2	.00	0	.385	.400	.641

Mike Benjamin

Bats: Right **Throws:** Right **Pos:** 3B/SS **Ht:** 6' 0" **Wt:** 169 **Born:** 11/22/65 **Age:** 30

Year Team	Lg	G	AB	H	2B	3B	HR	(Hm	Rd)	TB	R	RBI	TBB	IBB	SO	HBP	SH	SF	SB	CS	SB%	GDP	Avg	OBP	SLG
1989 San Francisco	NL	14	6	1	0	0	0	(0	0)	1	6	0	0	0	1	0	0	0	0	0	.00	0	.167	.167	.167
1990 San Francisco	NL	22	56	12	3	1	2	(2	0)	23	7	3	3	1	10	0	0	0	1	0	1.00	2	.214	.254	.411
1991 San Francisco	NL	54	106	13	3	0	2	(0	2)	22	12	8	7	2	26	2	3	2	3	0	1.00	1	.123	.188	.208
1992 San Francisco	NL	40	75	13	2	1	1	(0	1)	20	4	3	4	1	15	0	3	0	1	0	1.00	1	.173	.215	.267
1993 San Francisco	NL	63	146	29	7	0	4	(3	1)	48	22	16	9	2	23	4	6	0	0	0	.00	3	.199	.264	.329
1994 San Francisco	NL	38	62	16	5	1	1	(1	0)	26	9	9	5	1	16	3	5	0	5	0	1.00	1	.258	.343	.419
1995 San Francisco	NL	68	186	41	6	0	3	(1	2)	56	19	12	8	3	51	1	7	0	11	1	.92	3	.220	.256	.301
7 ML YEARS		299	637	125	26	3	13	(7	6)	196	79	51	36	10	142	10	24	2	21	1	.95	11	.196	.250	.308

Erik Bennett

Pitches: Right **Bats:** Right **Pos:** RP **Ht:** 6' 2" **Wt:** 205 **Born:** 9/13/68 **Age:** 27

Year Team	Lg	G	GS	CG	GF	IP	BFP	H	R	ER	HR	SH	SF	HB	TBB	IBB	SO	WP	Bk	W	L	Pct.	ShO	Sv	ERA
1989 Bend	A	15	15	2	0	96	422	96	58	37	4	3	2	3	36	0	96	8	6	6	8	.429	0	0	3.47
1990 Quad City	A	18	18	3	0	108.1	453	91	48	36	9	5	6	4	37	0	100	2	4	7	7	.500	1	0	2.99
1991 Palm Spring	A	8	8	1	0	43	192	41	15	12	2	3	0	3	27	0	31	0	0	2	3	.400	0	0	2.51
1992 Quad City	A	8	8	1	0	57.1	238	46	20	17	0	3	5	4	22	0	59	3	1	3	3	.500	1	0	2.67
Palm Spring	A	6	6	1	0	42	171	27	19	17	0	2	1	4	15	0	33	2	1	4	2	.667	0	0	3.64
Midland	AA	7	7	0	0	46	195	47	22	20	3	3	2	7	16	0	36	1	0	1	3	.250	0	0	3.91
1993 Midland	AA	11	11	0	0	69.1	308	87	57	50	12	2	6	6	17	1	33	1	0	5	4	.556	0	0	6.49
Vancouver	AAA	18	12	0	1	80.1	353	101	57	54	10	1	0	4	21	0	51	3	0	6	6	.500	0	1	6.05
1994 Vancouver	AAA	45	1	0	14	89.2	375	71	32	28	9	2	4	10	28	2	83	8	2	1	4	.200	0	3	2.81
1995 Vancouver	AAA	28	0	0	12	50.2	206	44	24	24	5	0	2	3	18	2	39	4	1	6	0	1.000	0	2	4.26
Tucson	AAA	14	1	0	4	22.2	110	27	17	12	1	0	3	2	14	2	24	0	0	3	1	.750	0	1	4.76
1995 California	AL	1	0	0	1	0.1	1	0	0	0	0	0	0	0	0	0	0	0	0	0	0	.000	0	0	0.00

Gary Bennett

Bats: Right **Throws:** Right **Pos:** PH **Ht:** 6' 0" **Wt:** 190 **Born:** 4/17/72 **Age:** 24

Year Team	Lg	G	AB	H	2B	3B	HR	(Hm	Rd)	TB	R	RBI	TBB	IBB	SO	HBP	SH	SF	SB	CS	SB%	GDP	Avg	OBP	SLG
1990 Martinsvlle	R	16	52	14	2	1	0	--	--	18	3	10	4	0	15	0	0	1	0	1	.00	0	.269	.316	.346
1991 Martinsvlle	R	41	136	32	7	0	1	--	--	42	15	16	17	0	26	5	1	1	0	1	.00	5	.235	.340	.309
1992 Batavia	A	47	146	30	2	0	0	--	--	32	22	12	15	0	27	2	3	0	2	1	.67	2	.205	.288	.219
1993 Spartanburg	A	42	126	32	4	1	0	--	--	38	18	15	12	0	22	1	2	1	0	2	.00	2	.254	.321	.302
Clearwater	A	17	55	18	0	0	1	--	--	21	5	6	3	0	10	1	2	0	0	1	.00	0	.327	.373	.382
1994 Clearwater	A	19	55	13	3	0	0	--	--	16	6	10	8	0	6	0	0	1	0	0	.00	1	.236	.328	.291
Reading	AA	63	208	48	9	0	3	--	--	66	13	22	14	0	26	0	3	3	0	1	.00	6	.231	.276	.317
1995 Reading	AA	86	271	64	11	0	4	--	--	87	27	40	22	1	36	3	3	2	0	0	.00	12	.236	.299	.321
Scranton-Wb	AAA	7	20	3	0	0	0	--	--	3	1	1	2	1	2	0	1	0	0	0	.00	0	.150	.227	.150
1995 Philadelphia	NL	1	1	0	0	0	0	(0	0)	0	0	0	0	0	0	1	0	0	0	0	.00	0	.000	.000	.000

Todd Benzinger

Bats: Both **Throws:** Right **Pos:** 1B **Ht:** 6' 1" **Wt:** 195 **Born:** 2/11/63 **Age:** 33

Year Team	Lg	G	AB	H	2B	3B	HR	(Hm	Rd)	TB	R	RBI	TBB	IBB	SO	HBP	SH	SF	SB	CS	SB%	GDP	Avg	OBP	SLG
1995 Columbus *	AAA	12	50	14	3	0	1	--	--	20	4	4	2	1	10	0	0	0	0	0	.00	2	.280	.308	.400
1987 Boston	AL	73	223	62	11	1	8	(5	3)	99	36	43	22	3	41	2	3	3	5	4	.56	5	.278	.344	.444
1988 Boston	AL	120	405	103	28	1	13	(6	7)	172	47	70	22	4	80	1	6	2	2	3	.40	8	.254	.293	.425
1989 Cincinnati	NL	161	628	154	28	3	17	(6	11)	239	79	76	44	13	120	2	4	8	3	7	.30	15	.245	.293	.381
1990 Cincinnati	NL	118	376	95	14	2	5	(4	1)	128	35	46	19	4	69	4	2	7	3	4	.43	3	.253	.291	.340
1991 KC-Cin		129	416	109	18	5	3	(2	1)	146	36	51	27	4	66	3	2	3	4	6	.40	7	.262	.310	.351
1992 Los Angeles	NL	121	293	70	16	2	4	(1	3)	102	24	31	15	1	54	0	0	5	2	4	.33	6	.239	.272	.348
1993 San Francisco	NL	86	177	51	7	2	6	(0	6)	80	25	26	13	1	35	0	1	3	0	0	.00	2	.288	.332	.452
1994 San Francisco	NL	107	328	87	13	2	9	(5	4)	131	32	31	17	4	84	2	3	2	2	1	.67	3	.265	.304	.399
1995 San Francisco	NL	9	10	2	0	0	1	(1	0)	5	2	2	2	1	3	0	0	0	0	0	.00	0	.200	.308	.500
1991 Kansas City	AL	78	293	86	15	3	2	(1	1)	113	29	40	17	2	46	3	1	1	2	6	.25	5	.294	.338	.386
Cincinnati	NL	51	123	23	3	2	1	(1	0)	33	7	11	10	2	20	0	1	2	2	0	1.00	2	.187	.244	.268
9 ML YEARS		924	2856	733	135	18	66	(30	36)	1102	316	376	181	35	552	14	21	34	21	29	.42	39	.257	.301	.386

Jason Bere

Pitches: Right **Bats:** Right **Pos:** SP **Ht:** 6' 3" **Wt:** 185 **Born:** 5/26/71 **Age:** 25

			HOW MUCH HE PITCHED				WHAT HE GAVE UP											THE RESULTS					
Year Team	Lg	G	GS	CG	GF	IP	BFP	H	R	ER	HR	SH	SF	HB	TBB	IBB	SO	WP	Bk	W	L	Pct.	ShO	Sv	ERA
1995 Nashville *	AAA	1	1	0	0	5.1	24	6	2	2	0	0	0	0	2	0	7	0	0	1	0	1.000	0	0	3.38
1993 Chicago	AL	24	24	1	0	142.2	610	109	60	55	12	4	2	5	81	0	129	8	0	12	5	.706	0	0	3.47
1994 Chicago	AL	24	24	0	0	141.2	608	119	65	60	17	4	4	1	80	0	127	2	0	12	2	**.857**	0	0	3.81
1995 Chicago	AL	27	27	1	0	137.2	668	151	120	110	21	4	7	6	106	6	110	8	0	8	**15**	.348	0	0	7.19
3 ML YEARS		75	75	2	0	422	1886	379	245	225	50	12	13	12	267	6	366	18	0	32	22	.593	0	0	4.80

Sean Bergman

Pitches: Right **Bats:** Right **Pos:** SP **Ht:** 6' 4" **Wt:** 230 **Born:** 4/11/70 **Age:** 26

			HOW MUCH HE PITCHED				WHAT HE GAVE UP											THE RESULTS					
Year Team	Lg	G	GS	CG	GF	IP	BFP	H	R	ER	HR	SH	SF	HB	TBB	IBB	SO	WP	Bk	W	L	Pct.	ShO	Sv	ERA
1995 Toledo *	AAA	1	1	0	0	3	13	4	2	2	1	0	0	1	0	0	4	0	0	0	1	.000	0	0	6.00
1993 Detroit	AL	9	6	1	1	39.2	189	47	29	25	6	3	2	1	23	3	19	3	1	1	4	.200	0	0	5.67
1994 Detroit	AL	3	3	0	0	17.2	82	22	11	11	2	0	1	1	7	0	12	1	0	2	1	.667	0	0	5.60
1995 Detroit	AL	28	28	1	0	135.1	630	169	95	77	19	5	3	4	67	8	86	13	0	7	10	.412	1	0	5.12
3 ML YEARS		40	37	2	1	192.2	901	238	135	113	27	8	6	6	97	11	117	17	1	10	15	.400	1	0	5.28

Geronimo Berroa

Bats: Right **Throws:** Right **Pos:** DH/LF/RF **Ht:** 6' 0" **Wt:** 195 **Born:** 3/18/65 **Age:** 31

				BATTING															BASERUNNING				PERCENTAGES		
Year Team	Lg	G	AB	H	2B	3B	HR	(Hm	Rd)	TB	R	RBI	TBB	IBB	SO	HBP	SH	SF	SB	CS	SB%	GDP	Avg	OBP	SLG
1989 Atlanta	NL	81	136	36	4	0	2	(1	1)	46	7	9	7	1	32	0	0	0	0	1	.00	2	.265	.301	.338
1990 Atlanta	NL	7	4	0	0	0	0	(0	0)	0	0	0	1	1	1	0	0	0	0	0	.00	0	.000	.200	.000
1992 Cincinnati	NL	13	15	4	1	0	0	(0	0)	5	2	0	2	0	1	1	0	0	0	1	.00	1	.267	.389	.333
1993 Florida	NL	14	34	4	1	0	0	(0	0)	5	3	0	2	0	7	0	0	0	0	0	.00	0	.118	.167	.147
1994 Oakland	AL	96	340	104	18	2	13	(4	9)	165	55	65	41	0	62	3	0	7	7	2	.78	5	.306	.379	.485
1995 Oakland	AL	141	546	152	22	3	22	(10	12)	246	87	88	63	2	98	1	0	6	7	4	.64	12	.278	.351	.451
6 ML YEARS		352	1075	300	46	5	37	(15	22)	467	154	162	116	4	201	5	0	13	14	8	.64	22	.279	.348	.434

Sean Berry

Bats: Right **Throws:** Right **Pos:** 3B **Ht:** 5'11" **Wt:** 200 **Born:** 3/22/66 **Age:** 30

				BATTING															BASERUNNING				PERCENTAGES		
Year Team	Lg	G	AB	H	2B	3B	HR	(Hm	Rd)	TB	R	RBI	TBB	IBB	SO	HBP	SH	SF	SB	CS	SB%	GDP	Avg	OBP	SLG
1990 Kansas City	AL	8	23	5	1	1	0	(0	0)	8	2	4	2	0	5	0	0	0	0	0	.00	0	.217	.280	.348
1991 Kansas City	AL	31	60	8	3	0	0	(0	0)	11	5	1	5	0	23	1	0	0	0	0	.00	1	.133	.212	.183
1992 Montreal	NL	24	57	19	1	0	1	(0	1)	23	5	4	1	0	11	0	0	0	2	1	.67	1	.333	.345	.404
1993 Montreal	NL	122	299	78	15	2	14	(5	9)	139	50	49	41	6	70	2	3	6	12	2	.86	4	.261	.348	.465
1994 Montreal	NL	103	320	89	19	2	11	(4	7)	145	43	41	32	7	50	3	2	2	14	0	**1.0**	7	.278	.347	.453
1995 Montreal	NL	103	314	100	22	1	14	(5	9)	166	38	55	25	1	53	2	2	5	3	8	.27	5	.318	.367	.529
6 ML YEARS		391	1073	299	61	6	40	(14	26)	492	143	154	106	14	212	8	7	13	31	11	.74	18	.279	.344	.459

Damon Berryhill

Bats: Both **Throws:** Right **Pos:** C **Ht:** 6' 0" **Wt:** 205 **Born:** 12/3/63 **Age:** 32

				BATTING															BASERUNNING				PERCENTAGES		
Year Team	Lg	G	AB	H	2B	3B	HR	(Hm	Rd)	TB	R	RBI	TBB	IBB	SO	HBP	SH	SF	SB	CS	SB%	GDP	Avg	OBP	SLG
1987 Chicago	NL	12	28	5	1	0	0	(0	0)	6	2	1	3	0	5	0	0	0	0	1	.00	1	.179	.258	.214
1988 Chicago	NL	95	309	80	19	1	7	(5	2)	122	19	38	17	5	56	0	3	3	1	0	1.00	11	.259	.295	.395
1989 Chicago	NL	91	334	86	13	0	5	(2	3)	114	37	41	16	4	54	2	4	5	1	0	1.00	13	.257	.291	.341
1990 Chicago	NL	17	53	10	4	0	1	(1	0)	17	6	9	5	1	14	0	0	1	0	0	.00	3	.189	.254	.321
1991 Atl-ChN	NL	63	160	30	7	0	5	(3	2)	52	13	14	11	1	42	1	0	1	1	2	.33	2	.188	.243	.325
1992 Atlanta	NL	101	307	70	16	1	10	(6	4)	118	21	43	17	4	67	1	0	3	0	2	.00	4	.228	.268	.384
1993 Atlanta	NL	115	335	82	18	2	8	(6	2)	128	24	43	21	1	64	2	2	3	0	0	.00	7	.245	.291	.382
1994 Boston	AL	82	255	67	17	2	6	(3	3)	106	30	34	19	0	59	0	0	2	0	1	.00	6	.263	.312	.416
1995 Cincinnati	NL	34	82	15	3	0	2	(2	0)	24	6	11	10	2	19	0	1	4	0	0	.00	3	.183	.260	.293
1991 Atlanta	NL	1	1	0	0	0	0	(0	0)	0	0	0	0	0	1	0	0	0	0	0	.00	0	.000	.000	.000
Chicago	NL	62	159	30	7	0	5	(3	2)	52	13	14	11	1	41	1	0	1	1	2	.33	2	.189	.244	.327
9 ML YEARS		610	1863	445	98	6	44	(28	16)	687	158	234	119	18	380	6	10	22	3	6	.33	50	.239	.284	.369

Mike Bertotti

Pitches: Left **Bats:** Left **Pos:** SP **Ht:** 6' 1" **Wt:** 185 **Born:** 1/18/70 **Age:** 26

Year	Team	Lg	G	GS	CG	GF	IP	BFP	H	R	ER	HR	SH	SF	HB	TBB	IBB	SO	WP	Bk	W	L	Pct.	ShO	Sv	ERA
1991	Utica	A	14	5	0	3	37.1	186	38	33	24	2	1	3	2	36	0	33	9	0	3	4	.429	0	0	5.79
1992	South Bend	A	11	0	0	5	19.1	86	12	8	8	1	1	1	1	22	0	17	1	1	0	3	.000	0	1	3.72
	Utica	A	17	1	0	5	33.1	164	36	28	23	2	0	1	2	31	0	23	7	1	2	2	.500	0	1	6.21
1993	Hickory	A	9	9	2	0	59.2	248	42	19	14	2	4	0	1	29	1	77	2	3	3	3	.500	0	0	2.11
	South Bend	A	17	16	2	0	111	466	93	51	43	5	6	6	6	44	2	108	7	1	5	7	.417	2	0	3.49
1994	Pr. William	A	16	15	2	0	104.2	435	90	48	41	13	2	1	3	43	0	103	8	1	7	6	.538	1	0	3.53
	Birmingham	AA	10	10	1	0	68.1	273	55	25	22	1	2	3	0	21	1	44	5	0	4	3	.571	1	0	2.90
1995	Birmingham	AA	12	12	1	0	63	279	60	38	35	4	0	4	2	36	0	53	8	0	2	7	.222	0	0	5.00
	Nashville	AAA	7	6	0	1	32	154	41	34	31	4	0	1	3	17	0	35	0	0	2	3	.400	0	0	8.72
1995	Chicago	AL	4	4	0	0	14.1	80	23	20	20	6	0	3	3	11	0	15	2	1	1	1	.500	0	0	12.56

Andres Berumen

Pitches: Right **Bats:** Right **Pos:** RP **Ht:** 6' 2" **Wt:** 205 **Born:** 4/5/71 **Age:** 25

Year	Team	Lg	G	GS	CG	GF	IP	BFP	H	R	ER	HR	SH	SF	HB	TBB	IBB	SO	WP	Bk	W	L	Pct.	ShO	Sv	ERA
1989	Royals	R	12	10	0	0	49	223	57	29	26	2	2	2	4	17	1	24	6	0	2	4	.333	0	0	4.78
1990	Royals	R	5	4	0	1	22.2	95	24	9	6	0	0	1	0	8	1	18	0	0	0	2	.000	0	1	2.38
	Baseball Cy	A	9	9	1	0	44	197	30	27	21	0	2	5	4	28	0	35	2	1	3	5	.375	1	0	4.30
1991	Baseball Cy	A	7	7	0	0	37	161	34	18	17	0	1	0	4	18	0	24	5	0	5	5	.000	0	0	4.14
	Appleton	A	13	13	0	0	56.1	254	55	33	22	0	3	4	3	26	0	49	2	1	2	6	.250	0	0	3.51
1992	Appleton	A	46	0	0	38	57.2	245	50	25	17	3	1	3	1	23	2	52	3	0	5	2	.714	0	13	2.65
1993	High Desert	A	14	13	1	0	92	396	85	45	37	8	0	4	7	36	1	74	6	1	9	2	.818	0	0	3.62
	Wichita	AA	7	7	0	0	26.2	120	35	17	17	2	1	1	1	11	2	17	3	0	3	1	.750	0	0	5.74
1994	Las Vegas	AAA	43	6	0	14	75.2	375	93	70	55	5	2	2	5	57	1	49	6	1	4	7	.364	0	1	6.54
1995	Las Vegas	AAA	3	0	0	0	3.1	16	4	2	2	0	0	0	1	2	0	3	0	0	0	0	.000	0	0	5.40
	Rancho Cuca	A	4	0	0	1	7.1	28	6	2	2	1	0	0	0	1	0	11	0	0	0	0	.000	0	1	2.45
1995	San Diego	NL	37	0	0	17	44.1	207	37	29	28	3	1	3	3	36	3	42	6	0	2	3	.400	0	1	5.68

Dante Bichette

Bats: Right **Throws:** Right **Pos:** LF/RF **Ht:** 6' 3" **Wt:** 235 **Born:** 11/18/63 **Age:** 32

Year	Team	Lg	G	AB	H	2B	3B	HR	(Hm	Rd)	TB	R	RBI	TBB	IBB	SO	HBP	SH	SF	SB	CS	SB%	GDP	Avg	OBP	SLG
1988	California	AL	21	46	12	2	0	0	(0	0)	14	1	8	0	0	7	0	0	4	0	0	.000	0	.261	.240	.304
1989	California	AL	48	138	29	7	0	3	(2	1)	45	13	15	6	0	24	0	0	2	3	0	1.00	0	.210	.240	.326
1990	California	AL	109	349	89	15	1	15	(8	7)	151	40	53	16	1	79	3	1	2	5	2	.71	9	.255	.292	.433
1991	Milwaukee	AL	134	445	106	18	3	15	(6	9)	175	53	59	22	4	107	1	1	6	14	8	.64	9	.238	.272	.393
1992	Milwaukee	AL	112	387	111	27	2	5	(3	2)	157	37	41	16	3	74	3	2	3	18	7	.72	13	.287	.318	.406
1993	Colorado	NL	141	538	167	43	5	21	(11	10)	283	93	89	28	2	99	7	0	8	14	8	.64	7	.310	.348	.526
1994	Colorado	NL	116	484	147	33	2	27	(15	12)	265	74	95	19	3	70	4	0	2	21	8	.72	17	.304	.334	.548
1995	Colorado	NL	139	579	197	38	2	40	(31	9)	359	102	128	22	5	96	4	0	7	13	9	.59	16	.340	.364	.620
	8 ML YEARS		820	2966	858	183	15	126	(76	50)	1449	413	488	129	18	556	22	4	34	88	42	.68	74	.289	.320	.489

Mike Bielecki

Pitches: Right **Bats:** Right **Pos:** SP/RP **Ht:** 6' 3" **Wt:** 195 **Born:** 7/31/59 **Age:** 36

Year	Team	Lg	G	GS	CG	GF	IP	BFP	H	R	ER	HR	SH	SF	HB	TBB	IBB	SO	WP	Bk	W	L	Pct.	ShO	Sv	ERA
1995	Lk Elsinore *	A	3	2	0	0	3.2	15	2	2	2	0	1	0	0	2	0	2	1	0	0	0	.000	0	0	4.91
	Vancouver *	AAA	3	1	0	0	5	21	2	3	0	0	0	0	0	2	0	4	0	0	1	0	1.000	0	0	0.00
1984	Pittsburgh	NL	4	0	0	1	4.1	17	4	0	0	0	1	0	0	0	1	0	1	0	0	0	.000	0	0	0.00
1985	Pittsburgh	NL	12	7	0	1	45.2	211	45	26	23	5	4	0	1	31	1	22	1	1	2	3	.400	0	0	4.53
1986	Pittsburgh	NL	31	27	0	0	148.2	667	149	87	77	10	7	6	2	83	3	83	7	5	6	11	.353	0	0	4.66
1987	Pittsburgh	NL	8	8	2	0	45.2	192	43	25	24	6	5	2	1	12	0	25	3	0	2	3	.400	0	0	4.73
1988	Chicago	NL	19	5	0	7	48.1	215	55	22	18	4	1	4	0	16	1	33	3	3	2	2	.500	0	0	3.35
1989	Chicago	NL	33	33	4	0	212.1	882	187	82	74	16	9	3	0	81	8	147	9	4	18	7	.720	3	0	3.14
1990	Chicago	NL	36	29	0	6	168	749	188	101	92	13	16	4	5	70	11	103	11	0	8	11	.421	0	1	4.93
1991	Atl-ChN	NL	41	25	0	9	173.2	727	171	91	86	18	10	6	2	56	6	75	6	0	13	11	.542	0	0	4.46
1992	Atlanta	NL	19	14	1	0	80.2	336	77	27	23	2	3	2	1	27	1	62	4	0	2	4	.333	1	0	2.57
1993	Cleveland	AL	13	13	0	0	68.2	317	90	47	45	8	0	2	2	23	3	38	1	0	4	5	.444	0	0	5.90
1994	Atlanta	NL	19	1	0	7	27	115	28	12	12	2	1	0	1	12	1	18	0	0	2	0	1.000	0	0	4.00
1995	California	AL	22	11	0	2	75.1	334	80	56	50	15	2	5	3	31	1	45	3	0	4	6	.400	0	0	5.97
1991	Atlanta	NL	2	0	0	1	1.2	9	2	0	0	0	0	0	0	2	0	3	0	0	0	0	.000	0	0	0.00

		G	GS	CG	GF	IP	BFP	H	R	ER	HR	SH	SF	HB	TBB	IBB	SO	WP	Bk	W	L	Pct.	ShO	Sv	ERA
Chicago	NL	39	25	0	8	172	718	169	91	86	18	10	6	2	54	6	72	6	0	13	11	.542	0	0	4.50
12 ML YEARS		257	173	7	33	1098.1	4762	1117	576	524	99	59	34	18	442	36	652	48	15	63	63	.500	4	1	4.29

Craig Biggio

Bats: Right **Throws:** Right **Pos:** 2B **Ht:** 5'11" **Wt:** 180 **Born:** 12/14/65 **Age:** 30

		BATTING																		BASERUNNING				PERCENTAGES		
Year Team	Lg	G	AB	H	2B	3B	HR	(Hm	Rd)	TB	R	RBI	TBB	IBB	SO	HBP	SH	SF	SB	CS	SB%	GDP	Avg	OBP	SLG
1988 Houston	NL	50	123	26	6	1	3	(1	2)	43	14	5	7	2	29	0	1	0	6	1	.86	1	.211	.254	.350
1989 Houston	NL	134	443	114	21	2	13	(6	7)	178	64	60	49	8	64	6	6	5	21	3	.88	7	.257	.336	.402
1990 Houston	NL	150	555	153	24	2	4	(2	2)	193	53	42	53	1	79	3	9	1	25	11	.69	11	.276	.342	.348
1991 Houston	NL	149	546	161	23	4	4	(0	4)	204	79	46	53	3	71	2	5	3	19	6	.76	2	.295	.358	.374
1992 Houston	NL	162	613	170	32	3	6	(3	3)	226	96	39	94	9	95	7	5	2	38	15	.72	5	.277	.378	.369
1993 Houston	NL	155	610	175	41	5	21	(8	13)	289	98	64	77	7	93	10	4	5	15	17	.47	10	.287	.373	.474
1994 Houston	NL	114	437	139	44	5	6	(4	2)	211	88	56	62	1	58	8	2	2	39	4	.91	5	.318	.411	.483
1995 Houston	NL	141	553	167	30	2	22	(6	16)	267	123	77	80	1	85	22	11	7	33	8	.80	6	.302	.406	.483
8 ML YEARS		1055	3880	1105	221	24	79	(30	49)	1611	615	389	475	32	574	58	43	25	196	65	.75	47	.285	.369	.415

Mike Birkbeck

Pitches: Right **Bats:** Right **Pos:** SP **Ht:** 6' 2" **Wt:** 185 **Born:** 3/10/61 **Age:** 35

		HOW MUCH HE PITCHED						WHAT HE GAVE UP												THE RESULTS					
Year Team	Lg	G	GS	CG	GF	IP	BFP	H	R	ER	HR	SH	SF	HB	TBB	IBB	SO	WP	Bk	W	L	Pct.	ShO	Sv	ERA
1995 Norfolk *	AAA	9	9	0	0	53.1	215	52	20	14	2	3	0	1	13	0	39	1	0	5	3	.625	0	0	2.36
1986 Milwaukee	AL	7	4	0	2	22	97	24	12	11	0	0	0	0	12	0	13	1	0	1	1	.500	0	0	4.50
1987 Milwaukee	AL	10	10	1	0	45	210	63	33	31	8	1	2	0	19	0	25	2	0	1	4	.200	0	0	6.20
1988 Milwaukee	AL	23	23	0	0	124	538	141	69	65	10	4	2	1	37	1	64	0	11	10	8	.556	0	0	4.72
1989 Milwaukee	AL	9	9	1	0	44.2	214	57	32	27	4	2	3	3	22	2	31	1	0	0	4	.000	0	0	5.44
1992 New York	NL	1	1	0	0	7	33	12	7	7	3	1	0	0	1	1	2	1	0	0	1	.000	0	0	9.00
1995 New York	NL	4	4	0	0	27.2	104	22	5	5	2	2	0	0	2	0	14	3	1	0	1	.000	0	0	1.63
6 ML YEARS		54	51	2	2	270.1	1196	319	158	146	27	10	7	4	93	4	149	8	12	12	19	.387	0	0	4.86

Bud Black

Pitches: Left **Bats:** Left **Pos:** SP **Ht:** 6' 2" **Wt:** 188 **Born:** 6/30/57 **Age:** 39

		HOW MUCH HE PITCHED						WHAT HE GAVE UP												THE RESULTS					
Year Team	Lg	G	GS	CG	GF	IP	BFP	H	R	ER	HR	SH	SF	HB	TBB	IBB	SO	WP	Bk	W	L	Pct.	ShO	Sv	ERA
1981 Seattle	AL	2	0	0	0	1	7	2	0	0	0	0	0	0	3	1	0	1	0	0	0	.000	0	0	0.00
1982 Kansas City	AL	22	14	0	2	88.1	386	92	48	45	10	4	3	3	34	6	40	4	7	4	6	.400	0	0	4.58
1983 Kansas City	AL	24	24	3	0	161.1	672	159	75	68	19	4	5	2	43	1	58	4	0	10	7	.588	0	0	3.79
1984 Kansas City	AL	35	35	8	0	257	1045	226	99	89	22	6	1	4	64	2	140	2	2	17	12	.586	1	0	3.12
1985 Kansas City	AL	33	33	5	0	205.2	885	216	111	99	17	8	4	8	59	4	122	9	1	10	15	.400	2	0	4.33
1986 Kansas City	AL	56	4	0	26	121	503	100	49	43	14	4	4	7	43	5	68	2	2	5	10	.333	0	9	3.20
1987 Kansas City	AL	29	18	0	4	122.1	520	126	63	49	16	1	3	5	35	2	61	6	0	8	6	.571	0	1	3.60
1988 Cle-KC	AL	33	7	0	9	81	358	82	47	45	8	6	3	4	34	3	63	5	6	4	4	.500	0	1	5.00
1989 Cleveland	AL	33	32	6	0	222.1	912	213	95	83	14	9	5	1	52	0	88	13	5	12	11	.522	3	0	3.36
1990 Cle-Tor	AL	32	31	5	1	206.2	857	181	86	82	19	6	7	5	61	1	106	6	1	13	11	.542	2	0	3.57
1991 San Francisco	NL	34	34	3	0	214.1	893	201	104	95	25	11	7	4	71	8	104	6	6	12	16	.429	3	0	3.99
1992 San Francisco	NL	28	28	2	0	177	749	178	88	78	23	8	4	1	59	11	82	3	7	10	12	.455	1	0	3.97
1993 San Francisco	NL	16	16	0	0	93.2	394	89	44	37	13	8	4	2	33	2	45	0	4	8	2	.800	0	0	3.56
1994 San Francisco	NL	10	10	0	0	54.1	227	50	31	27	9	2	2	3	16	1	28	3	1	4	2	.667	0	0	4.47
1995 Cleveland	AL	11	10	0	0	47.1	219	63	42	36	8	1	3	0	16	2	34	1	1	4	2	.667	0	0	6.85
1988 Cleveland	AL	16	7	0	4	59	260	59	35	33	6	5	3	4	23	1	44	5	4	2	3	.400	0	1	5.03
Kansas City	AL	17	0	0	5	22	98	23	12	12	2	1	0	0	11	2	19	0	2	2	1	.667	0	0	4.91
1990 Cleveland	AL	29	29	5	0	191	796	171	79	75	17	4	5	4	58	1	103	6	1	11	10	.524	2	0	3.53
Toronto	AL	3	2	0	1	15.2	61	10	7	7	2	2	2	1	3	0	3	0	0	2	1	.667	0	0	4.02
15 ML YEARS		398	296	32	42	2053.1	8627	1978	982	876	217	78	55	49	623	49	1039	65	43	121	116	.511	12	11	3.84

Willie Blair

Pitches: Right **Bats:** Right **Pos:** RP/SP **Ht:** 6' 1" **Wt:** 182 **Born:** 12/18/65 **Age:** 30

		HOW MUCH HE PITCHED						WHAT HE GAVE UP												THE RESULTS					
Year Team	Lg	G	GS	CG	GF	IP	BFP	H	R	ER	HR	SH	SF	HB	TBB	IBB	SO	WP	Bk	W	L	Pct.	ShO	Sv	ERA
1990 Toronto	AL	27	6	0	8	68.2	297	66	33	31	4	0	4	1	28	4	43	3	0	3	5	.375	0	0	4.06
1991 Cleveland	AL	11	5	0	1	36	168	58	27	27	7	1	2	1	10	0	13	1	0	2	3	.400	0	0	6.75
1992 Houston	NL	29	8	0	1	78.2	331	74	47	35	5	4	3	2	25	2	48	2	0	5	7	.417	0	0	4.00
1993 Colorado	NL	46	18	1	5	146	664	184	90	77	20	10	8	3	42	6	84	6	1	6	10	.375	0	0	4.75
1994 Colorado	NL	47	1	0	13	77.2	365	98	57	50	9	3	1	4	39	3	68	4	0	0	5	.000	0	3	5.79
1995 San Diego	NL	40	12	0	11	114	485	112	60	55	11	8	2	2	45	3	83	4	0	7	5	.583	0	0	4.34
6 ML YEARS		200	50	1	39	521	2310	592	314	275	56	26	20	13	189	16	339	20	1	23	35	.397	0	3	4.75

Jeff Blauser

Bats: Right **Throws:** Right **Pos:** SS **Ht:** 6' 1" **Wt:** 180 **Born:** 11/8/65 **Age:** 30

							BATTING													BASERUNNING				PERCENTAGES		
Year Team	Lg	G	AB	H	2B	3B	HR	(Hm	Rd)	TB	R	RBI	TBB	IBB	SO	HBP	SH	SF		SB	CS	SB%	GDP	Avg	OBP	SLG
1987 Atlanta	NL	51	165	40	6	3	2	(1	1)	58	11	15	18	1	34	3	1	0		7	3	.70	4	.242	.328	.352
1988 Atlanta	NL	18	67	16	3	1	2	(2	0)	27	7	7	2	0	11	1	3	1		0	1	.00	1	.239	.268	.403
1989 Atlanta	NL	142	456	123	24	2	12	(5	7)	187	63	46	38	2	101	1	8	4		5	2	.71	7	.270	.325	.410
1990 Atlanta	NL	115	386	104	24	3	8	(3	5)	158	46	39	35	1	70	5	3	0		3	5	.38	4	.269	.338	.409
1991 Atlanta	NL	129	352	91	14	3	11	(7	4)	144	49	54	54	4	59	2	4	3		5	6	.45	4	.259	.358	.409
1992 Atlanta	NL	123	343	90	19	3	14	(5	9)	157	61	46	46	2	82	4	7	3		5	5	.50	2	.262	.354	.458
1993 Atlanta	NL	161	597	182	29	2	15	(4	11)	260	110	73	85	0	109	16	5	7		16	6	.73	13	.305	.401	.436
1994 Atlanta	NL	96	380	98	21	4	6	(3	3)	145	56	45	38	0	64	5	5	6		1	3	.25	11	.258	.329	.382
1995 Atlanta	NL	115	431	91	16	2	12	(7	5)	147	60	31	57	2	107	12	2	2		8	5	.62	6	.211	.319	.341
9 ML YEARS		950	3177	835	156	23	82	(37	45)	1283	463	356	373	12	637	49	38	26		50	36	.58	52	.263	.347	.404

Ben Blomdahl

Pitches: Right **Bats:** Right **Pos:** RP **Ht:** 6' 2" **Wt:** 185 **Born:** 12/30/70 **Age:** 25

		HOW MUCH HE PITCHED						WHAT HE GAVE UP										THE RESULTS					
Year Team	Lg	G	GS	CG	GF	IP	BFP	H	R	ER	HR	SH	SF	HB	TBB	IBB	SO	WP	Bk	W	L	Pct.	ShO	Sv	ERA
1991 Niagara Fal	A	16	13	0	2	78.2	344	72	43	39	2	1	3	2	50	0	30	7	6	6	6	.500	0	0	4.46
1992 Fayetteville	A	17	17	2	0	103.1	423	94	46	31	5	2	0	4	26	0	65	6	3	10	4	.714	2	0	2.70
Lakeland	A	10	10	2	0	62	264	77	35	32	3	2	1	3	5	0	41	2	0	5	3	.625	0	0	4.65
1993 London	AA	17	17	3	0	119	498	108	58	49	7	4	6	7	42	1	72	4	3	6	6	.500	0	0	3.71
Toledo	AAA	11	10	0	0	62.2	264	67	34	34	8	1	4	2	19	0	27	4	0	3	4	.429	0	0	4.88
1994 Toledo	AAA	28	28	0	0	165.1	729	192	92	82	18	6	10	7	47	3	83	5	0	11	11	.500	0	0	4.46
1995 Toledo	AAA	41	0	0	23	56	232	55	24	22	6	1	1	2	13	4	39	3	0	5	4	.556	0	3	3.54
1995 Detroit	AL	14	0	0	5	24.1	115	36	21	21	5	1	0	0	13	0	15	2	0	0	0	.000	0	1	7.77

Mike Blowers

Bats: Right **Throws:** Right **Pos:** 3B **Ht:** 6' 2" **Wt:** 210 **Born:** 4/24/65 **Age:** 31

							BATTING													BASERUNNING				PERCENTAGES		
Year Team	Lg	G	AB	H	2B	3B	HR	(Hm	Rd)	TB	R	RBI	TBB	IBB	SO	HBP	SH	SF		SB	CS	SB%	GDP	Avg	OBP	SLG
1989 New York	AL	13	38	10	0	0	0	(0	0)	10	2	3	3	0	13	0	0	0		0	0	.00	1	.263	.317	.263
1990 New York	AL	48	144	27	4	0	5	(1	4)	46	16	21	12	1	50	1	0	0		1	0	1.00	3	.188	.255	.319
1991 New York	AL	15	35	7	0	0	1	(0	1)	10	3	1	4	0	3	0	1	0		0	0	.00	1	.200	.282	.286
1992 Seattle	AL	31	73	14	3	0	1	(0	1)	20	7	2	6	0	20	0	1	0		0	0	.00	0	.192	.253	.274
1993 Seattle	AL	127	379	106	23	3	15	(8	7)	180	55	57	44	3	98	2	3	1		1	5	.17	12	.280	.357	.475
1994 Seattle	AL	85	270	78	13	0	9	(3	6)	118	37	49	25	2	60	1	1	3		2	2	.50	12	.289	.348	.437
1995 Seattle	AL	134	439	113	24	1	23	(17	6)	208	59	96	53	0	128	0	3	3		2	1	.67	18	.257	.335	.474
7 ML YEARS		453	1378	355	67	4	54	(29	25)	592	179	229	147	6	372	4	9	7		6	8	.43	50	.258	.329	.430

Doug Bochtler

Pitches: Right **Bats:** Right **Pos:** RP **Ht:** 6' 3" **Wt:** 200 **Born:** 7/5/70 **Age:** 25

		HOW MUCH HE PITCHED						WHAT HE GAVE UP										THE RESULTS					
Year Team	Lg	G	GS	CG	GF	IP	BFP	H	R	ER	HR	SH	SF	HB	TBB	IBB	SO	WP	Bk	W	L	Pct.	ShO	Sv	ERA
1989 Expos	R	9	9	1	0	47.2	209	46	22	17	0	2	2	0	20	1	45	3	1	2	2	.500	0	0	3.21
1990 Rockford	A	25	25	1	0	139	602	142	82	54	3	6	4	8	54	2	109	6	5	9	12	.429	1	0	3.50
1991 W. Palm Bch	A	26	24	7	1	160.1	647	148	63	52	6	6	2	6	54	2	109	7	0	12	9	.571	2	0	2.92
1992 Harrisburg	AA	13	13	2	0	77.2	310	50	25	20	1	2	2	0	36	1	89	4	0	6	5	.545	1	0	2.32
1993 Central Val	A	8	8	0	0	47.2	205	40	23	18	2	1	0	1	28	0	43	2	0	3	1	.750	0	0	3.40
Colo. Sprng	AAA	12	11	0	0	50.2	239	71	41	39	3	2	2	1	26	1	38	2	0	1	4	.200	0	0	6.93
Las Vegas	AAA	7	7	1	0	39.2	177	52	26	23	2	1	1	0	11	1	30	1	0	0	5	.000	0	0	5.22
1994 Las Vegas	AAA	22	20	2	1	100.1	458	116	67	58	11	5	3	3	48	2	86	10	0	3	7	.300	1	0	5.20
1995 Las Vegas	AAA	18	2	0	7	36	161	31	18	17	1	5	1	2	26	6	32	2	0	2	3	.400	0	1	4.25
1995 San Diego	NL	34	0	0	11	45.1	181	38	18	18	5	2	1	0	19	0	45	1	0	4	4	.500	0	1	3.57

Brian Boehringer

Pitches: Right **Bats:** Both **Pos:** RP/SP **Ht:** 6' 2" **Wt:** 190 **Born:** 1/8/70 **Age:** 26

		HOW MUCH HE PITCHED						WHAT HE GAVE UP										THE RESULTS					
Year Team	Lg	G	GS	CG	GF	IP	BFP	H	R	ER	HR	SH	SF	HB	TBB	IBB	SO	WP	Bk	W	L	Pct.	ShO	Sv	ERA
1991 White Sox	R	5	1	0	2	12.1	54	14	9	9	1	0	1	0	5	0	10	3	1	1	1	.500	0	0	6.57
Utica	A	4	4	0	0	19	78	14	8	5	0	0	0	2	8	0	19	0	2	1	1	.500	0	0	2.37
1992 White Sox	R	2	2	0	0	12	47	9	3	2	0	1	0	1	2	0	8	0	0	1	1	.500	0	0	1.50
South Bend	A	15	15	2	0	86.1	381	87	52	42	5	3	3	6	40	0	59	6	4	6	7	.462	0	0	4.38
1993 Sarasota	A	18	17	3	0	119	495	103	47	37	2	3	6	1	51	2	92	2	2	10	4	.714	0	0	2.80
Birmingham	AA	7	7	1	0	40.2	173	41	20	16	3	1	1	2	14	0	29	1	1	2	1	.667	0	0	3.54

Year	Team	Lg	G	GS	CG	GF	IP	BFP	H	R	ER	HR	SH	SF	HB	TBB	IBB	SO	WP	Bk	W	L	Pct.	ShO	Sv	ERA
1994	Albany-Colo	AA	27	27	5	0	171.2	722	165	85	69	10	7	10	4	57	1	145	7	5	10	11	.476	1	0	3.62
1995	Columbus	AAA	17	17	3	0	104	439	101	39	32	6	3	3	4	31	1	58	9	0	8	6	.571	0	0	2.77
1995	New York	AL	7	3	0	0	17.2	99	24	27	27	5	0	1	1	22	1	10	3	0	0	3	.000	0	0	13.75

Joe Boever

Pitches: Right **Bats:** Right **Pos:** RP   **Ht:** 6' 1" **Wt:** 205 **Born:** 10/4/60 **Age:** 35

			HOW MUCH HE PITCHED						WHAT HE GAVE UP											THE RESULTS					
Year	Team	Lg	G	GS	CG	GF	IP	BFP	H	R	ER	HR	SH	SF	HB	TBB	IBB	SO	WP	Bk	W	L	Pct.	ShO	Sv	ERA
1985	St. Louis	NL	13	0	0	5	16.1	69	17	8	8	3	1	1	0	4	1	20	1	0	0	0	.000	0	0	4.41
1986	St. Louis	NL	11	0	0	4	21.2	93	19	5	4	2	0	0	0	11	0	8	1	0	0	1	.000	0	0	1.66
1987	Atlanta	NL	14	0	0	10	18.1	93	29	15	15	4	1	1	0	12	1	18	1	0	1	0	1.000	0	0	7.36
1988	Atlanta	NL	16	0	0	13	20.1	70	12	4	4	1	2	0	1	1	0	7	0	0	0	2	.000	0	1	1.77
1989	Atlanta	NL	66	0	0	53	82.1	349	78	37	36	6	5	0	1	34	5	68	5	0	4	11	.267	0	21	3.94
1990	Atl-Phi	NL	67	0	0	34	88.1	388	77	35	33	6	4	2	0	51	12	75	3	2	3	6	.333	0	14	3.36
1991	Philadelphia	NL	68	0	0	27	98.1	431	90	45	42	10	3	6	0	54	11	89	6	1	3	5	.375	0	0	3.84
1992	Houston	NL	81	0	0	26	111.1	479	103	38	31	3	10	4	4	45	9	67	4	0	3	6	.333	0	2	2.51
1993	Det-Oak	AL	61	0	0	22	102.1	449	101	50	41	9	5	7	4	44	7	63	1	0	6	3	.667	0	3	3.61
1994	Detroit	AL	46	0	0	27	81.1	349	80	40	36	12	4	2	2	37	12	49	4	0	9	2	.818	0	3	3.98
1995	Detroit	AL	60	0	0	27	98.2	463	128	74	70	17	7	8	3	44	12	71	1	1	5	7	.417	0	3	6.39
1990	Atlanta	NL	33	0	0	21	42.1	198	40	23	22	6	2	2	0	35	10	35	2	0	1	3	.250	0	8	4.68
	Philadelphia	NL	34	0	0	13	46	190	37	12	11	0	2	0	0	16	2	40	1	2	2	3	.400	0	6	2.15
1993	Detroit	AL	19	0	0	3	23	96	14	10	7	1	3	4	0	11	3	14	0	0	2	1	.667	0	3	2.74
	Oakland	AL	42	0	0	19	79.1	353	87	40	34	8	2	3	4	33	4	49	1	0	4	2	.667	0	0	3.86
11 ML YEARS			503	0	0	248	739.1	3233	734	351	320	73	42	31	15	337	70	535	27	4	34	43	.442	0	47	3.90

Tim Bogar

Bats: Right **Throws:** Right **Pos:** SS/3B   **Ht:** 6' 2" **Wt:** 198 **Born:** 10/28/66 **Age:** 29

			BATTING															BASERUNNING				PERCENTAGES		
Year	Team	Lg	G	AB	H	2B	3B	HR	(Hm | Rd)	TB	R	RBI	TBB	IBB	SO	HBP	SH	SF	SB	CS	SB%	GDP	Avg	OBP	SLG
1993	New York	NL	78	205	50	13	0	3	(1 | 2)	72	19	25	14	2	29	3	1	1	0	1	.00	2	.244	.300	.351
1994	New York	NL	50	52	8	0	0	0	(0 | 2)	14	5	5	4	1	11	0	2	1	1	0	1.00	1	.154	.211	.269
1995	New York	NL	78	145	42	7	0	1	(0 | 1)	52	17	21	9	0	25	0	2	1	1	0	1.00	1	.290	.329	.359
3 ML YEARS			206	402	100	20	0	6	(1 | 5)	138	41	51	27	3	65	3	5	3	2	1	.67	5	.249	.299	.343

Wade Boggs

Bats: Left **Throws:** Right **Pos:** 3B   **Ht:** 6' 2" **Wt:** 197 **Born:** 6/15/58 **Age:** 38

			BATTING															BASERUNNING				PERCENTAGES		
Year	Team	Lg	G	AB	H	2B	3B	HR	(Hm | Rd)	TB	R	RBI	TBB	IBB	SO	HBP	SH	SF	SB	CS	SB%	GDP	Avg	OBP	SLG
1982	Boston	AL	104	338	118	14	1	5	(4 | 1)	149	51	44	35	4	21	0	4	4	1	0	1.00	9	.349	.406	.441
1983	Boston	AL	153	582	210	44	7	5	(2 | 3)	283	100	74	92	2	36	1	3	7	3	5	.38	15	.361	.444	.486
1984	Boston	AL	158	625	203	31	4	6	(5 | 1)	260	109	55	89	6	44	0	8	4	3	2	.60	13	.325	.407	.416
1985	Boston	AL	161	653	240	42	3	8	(6 | 2)	312	107	78	96	5	61	4	3	2	2	1	.67	20	.368	.450	.478
1986	Boston	AL	149	580	207	47	2	8	(3 | 5)	282	107	71	105	14	44	0	4	4	0	4	.00	11	.357	.453	.486
1987	Boston	AL	147	551	200	40	6	24	(10 | 14)	324	108	89	105	19	48	2	1	8	1	3	.25	13	.363	.461	.588
1988	Boston	AL	155	584	214	45	6	5	(4 | 1)	286	128	58	125	18	34	3	0	7	2	3	.40	23	.366	.476	.490
1989	Boston	AL	156	621	205	51	7	3	(2 | 1)	279	113	54	107	19	51	7	0	7	2	6	.25	19	.330	.430	.449
1990	Boston	AL	155	619	187	44	5	6	(3 | 3)	259	89	63	87	19	68	1	0	6	0	0	.00	14	.302	.386	.418
1991	Boston	AL	144	546	181	42	2	8	(6 | 2)	251	93	51	89	25	32	0	1	6	1	2	.33	16	.332	.421	.460
1992	Boston	AL	143	514	133	22	4	7	(4 | 3)	184	62	50	74	19	31	4	0	6	1	3	.25	10	.259	.353	.358
1993	New York	AL	143	560	169	26	1	2	(1 | 1)	203	83	59	74	4	49	0	1	9	0	1	.00	10	.302	.378	.363
1994	New York	AL	97	366	125	19	1	11	(6 | 5)	179	61	55	61	3	29	1	2	4	2	1	.67	10	.342	.433	.489
1995	New York	AL	126	460	149	22	4	5	(4 | 1)	194	76	63	74	5	50	0	0	7	1	1	.50	13	.324	.412	.422
14 ML YEARS			1991	7599	2541	489	53	103	(60 | 43)	3445	1287	864	1213	162	598	23	26	81	19	30	.39	196	.334	.424	.453

Brian Bohanon

Pitches: Left **Bats:** Left **Pos:** RP/SP   **Ht:** 6' 3" **Wt:** 220 **Born:** 8/1/68 **Age:** 27

			HOW MUCH HE PITCHED						WHAT HE GAVE UP											THE RESULTS					
Year	Team	Lg	G	GS	CG	GF	IP	BFP	H	R	ER	HR	SH	SF	HB	TBB	IBB	SO	WP	Bk	W	L	Pct.	ShO	Sv	ERA
1990	Texas	AL	11	6	0	1	34	158	40	30	25	6	0	3	2	18	0	15	1	0	0	3	.000	0	0	6.62
1991	Texas	AL	11	11	1	0	61.1	273	66	35	33	4	2	5	2	23	0	34	3	1	4	3	.571	0	0	4.84
1992	Texas	AL	18	7	0	3	45.2	220	57	38	32	7	0	2	1	25	0	29	2	0	1	1	.500	0	0	6.31
1993	Texas	AL	36	8	0	4	92.2	418	107	54	49	8	2	5	4	46	3	45	10	0	4	4	.500	0	0	4.76
1994	Texas	AL	11	5	0	1	37.1	169	51	31	30	7	1	0	1	8	1	26	5	0	2	2	.500	0	0	7.23
1995	Detroit	AL	52	10	0	7	105.2	474	121	68	65	10	0	5	4	41	5	63	3	0	1	1	.500	0	1	5.54
6 ML YEARS			139	47	1	16	376.2	1712	442	256	234	42	5	20	14	161	9	212	24	1	12	14	.462	0	1	5.59

Rodney Bolton

Pitches: Right **Bats:** Right **Pos:** RP/SP | **Ht:** 6' 2" **Wt:** 190 **Born:** 9/23/68 **Age:** 27

			HOW MUCH HE PITCHED					WHAT HE GAVE UP											THE RESULTS				
Year	Team	Lg	G	GS	CG	GF	IP	BFP	H	R	ER	HR	SH	SF	HB	TBB	IBB	SO	WP	Bk	W	L	Pct.	ShO	Sv	ERA
1990	Utica	A	6	6	1	0	44	168	27	4	2	0	1	0	3	11	0	45	0	0	5	1	.833	1	0	0.41
	South Bend	A	7	7	3	0	51	196	34	14	11	0	1	1	1	12	1	50	1	1	5	1	.833	0	0	1.94
1991	Sarasota	A	15	15	5	0	103.2	412	81	29	22	2	5	1	2	23	0	77	3	1	7	6	.538	2	0	1.91
	Birmingham	AA	12	12	3	0	89	360	73	26	16	3	0	2	8	21	1	57	3	0	8	4	.667	2	0	1.62
1992	Vancouver	AAA	27	27	3	0	187.1	781	174	72	61	9	9	4	1	59	2	111	9	2	11	9	.550	2	0	2.93
1993	Nashville	AAA	18	16	1	1	115.2	486	108	40	37	10	2	3	3	37	2	75	11	0	10	1	.909	0	1	2.88
1994	Nashville	AAA	17	17	1	0	116	480	114	43	33	4	6	1	4	35	2	63	2	0	7	5	.583	0	0	2.56
1995	Nashville	AAA	20	20	3	0	131.1	534	127	44	42	13	2	2	7	23	1	76	2	0	14	3	.824	1	0	2.88
1993	Chicago	AL	9	8	0	0	42.1	197	55	40	35	4	1	4	1	16	0	17	4	0	2	6	.250	0	0	7.44
1995	Chicago	AL	8	3	0	2	22	109	33	23	20	4	0	1	0	14	1	10	1	0	0	2	.000	0	0	8.18
	2 ML YEARS		17	11	0	2	64.1	306	88	63	55	8	1	5	1	30	1	27	5	0	2	8	.200	0	0	7.69

Barry Bonds

Bats: Left **Throws:** Left **Pos:** LF | **Ht:** 6' 1" **Wt:** 190 **Born:** 7/24/64 **Age:** 31

			BATTING															BASERUNNING				PERCENTAGES		
Year	Team	Lg	G	AB	H	2B	3B	HR	(Hm | Rd)	TB	R	RBI	TBB	IBB	SO	HBP	SH	SF	SB	CS	SB%	GDP	Avg	OBP	SLG
1986	Pittsburgh	NL	113	413	92	26	3	16	(9 | 7)	172	72	48	65	2	102	2	2	2	36	7	.84	4	.223	.330	.416
1987	Pittsburgh	NL	150	551	144	34	9	25	(12 | 13)	271	99	59	54	3	88	3	0	3	32	10	.76	4	.261	.329	.492
1988	Pittsburgh	NL	144	538	152	30	5	24	(14 | 10)	264	97	58	72	14	82	2	0	2	17	11	.61	3	.283	.368	.491
1989	Pittsburgh	NL	159	580	144	34	6	19	(7 | 12)	247	96	58	93	22	93	1	1	4	32	10	.76	9	.248	.351	.426
1990	Pittsburgh	NL	151	519	156	32	3	33	(14 | 19)	293	104	114	93	15	83	3	0	6	52	13	.80	8	.301	.406	.565
1991	Pittsburgh	NL	153	510	149	28	5	25	(12 | 13)	262	95	116	107	25	73	4	0	13	43	13	.77	8	.292	.410	.514
1992	Pittsburgh	NL	140	473	147	36	5	34	(15 | 19)	295	109	103	127	32	69	5	0	7	39	8	.83	9	.311	.456	.624
1993	San Francisco	NL	159	539	181	38	4	46	(21 | 25)	365	129	123	126	43	79	2	0	7	29	12	.71	11	.336	.458	.677
1994	San Francisco	NL	112	391	122	18	1	37	(15 | 22)	253	89	81	74	18	43	6	0	3	29	9	.76	3	.312	.426	.647
1995	San Francisco	NL	144	506	149	30	7	33	(16 | 17)	292	109	104	120	22	83	5	0	4	31	10	.76	12	.294	.431	.577
	10 ML YEARS		1425	5020	1436	306	48	292	(135 | 157)	2714	999	864	931	196	795	33	3	51	340	103	.77	71	.286	.398	.541

Ricky Bones

Pitches: Right **Bats:** Right **Pos:** SP | **Ht:** 6' 0" **Wt:** 193 **Born:** 4/7/69 **Age:** 27

			HOW MUCH HE PITCHED					WHAT HE GAVE UP											THE RESULTS				
Year	Team	Lg	G	GS	CG	GF	IP	BFP	H	R	ER	HR	SH	SF	HB	TBB	IBB	SO	WP	Bk	W	L	Pct.	ShO	Sv	ERA
1991	San Diego	NL	11	11	0	0	54	234	57	33	29	3	0	4	0	18	0	31	4	0	4	6	.400	0	0	4.83
1992	Milwaukee	AL	31	28	0	0	163.1	705	169	90	83	27	2	5	9	48	0	65	3	2	9	10	.474	0	0	4.57
1993	Milwaukee	AL	32	31	3	1	203.2	883	222	122	110	28	5	7	8	63	3	63	6	1	11	11	.500	0	0	4.86
1994	Milwaukee	AL	24	24	4	0	170.2	708	166	76	65	17	4	5	3	45	1	57	8	0	10	9	.526	1	0	3.43
1995	Milwaukee	AL	32	31	3	0	200.1	877	218	108	103	26	3	11	4	83	2	77	5	2	10	12	.455	0	0	4.63
	5 ML YEARS		130	125	10	1	792	3407	832	429	390	101	14	32	24	257	6	293	26	5	44	48	.478	1	0	4.43

Bobby Bonilla

Bats: Both **Throws:** Right **Pos:** 3B/LF/RF | **Ht:** 6' 3" **Wt:** 240 **Born:** 2/23/63 **Age:** 33

			BATTING															BASERUNNING				PERCENTAGES		
Year	Team	Lg	G	AB	H	2B	3B	HR	(Hm | Rd)	TB	R	RBI	TBB	IBB	SO	HBP	SH	SF	SB	CS	SB%	GDP	Avg	OBP	SLG
1986	ChA-Pit		138	426	109	16	4	3	(2 | 1)	142	55	43	62	3	88	2	5	1	8	5	.62	9	.256	.352	.333
1987	Pittsburgh	NL	141	466	140	33	3	15	(7 | 8)	224	58	77	39	4	64	2	0	8	3	5	.38	8	.300	.351	.481
1988	Pittsburgh	NL	159	584	160	32	7	24	(9 | 15)	278	87	100	85	19	82	4	0	8	3	5	.38	4	.274	.366	.476
1989	Pittsburgh	NL	163	616	173	37	10	24	(13 | 11)	302	96	86	76	20	93	1	0	5	8	8	.50	10	.281	.358	.490
1990	Pittsburgh	NL	160	625	175	39	7	32	(13 | 19)	324	112	120	45	9	103	1	0	15	4	3	.57	11	.280	.322	.518
1991	Pittsburgh	NL	157	577	174	44	6	18	(9 | 9)	284	102	100	90	8	67	2	0	11	2	4	.33	14	.302	.391	.492
1992	New York	NL	128	438	109	23	0	19	(5 | 14)	189	62	70	66	10	73	1	0	1	4	3	.57	11	.249	.348	.432
1993	New York	NL	139	502	133	21	3	34	(18 | 16)	262	81	87	72	11	96	0	0	8	3	3	.50	12	.265	.352	.522
1994	New York	NL	108	403	117	24	1	20	(8 | 12)	203	60	67	55	9	101	0	0	2	1	3	.25	10	.290	.374	.504
1995	NYN-Bal		141	554	182	37	8	28	(14 | 14)	319	96	99	54	10	79	2	0	4	0	5	.00	22	.329	.388	.576
1986	Chicago	AL	75	234	63	10	2	2	(2 | 0)	83	27	26	33	2	49	1	2	1	4	1	.80	4	.269	.361	.355
	Pittsburgh	NL	63	192	46	6	2	1	(0 | 1)	59	28	17	29	1	39	1	3	0	4	4	.50	5	.240	.342	.307
1995	New York	NL	80	317	103	25	4	18	(7 | 11)	190	49	53	31	10	48	1	0	2	0	3	.00	11	.325	.385	.599
	Baltimore	AL	61	237	79	12	4	10	(7 | 3)	129	47	46	23	0	31	1	0	2	0	2	.00	11	.333	.392	.544
	10 ML YEARS		1434	5191	1472	306	49	217	(98 | 119)	2527	809	849	644	103	846	15	5	63	36	44	.45	111	.284	.360	.487

Bret Boone

Bats: Right **Throws:** Right **Pos:** 2B | **Ht:** 5'10" **Wt:** 180 **Born:** 4/6/69 **Age:** 27

			BATTING															BASERUNNING				PERCENTAGES		
Year	Team	Lg	G	AB	H	2B	3B	HR	(Hm | Rd)	TB	R	RBI	TBB	IBB	SO	HBP	SH	SF	SB	CS	SB%	GDP	Avg	OBP	SLG
1992	Seattle	AL	33	129	25	4	0	4	(2 | 2)	41	15	15	4	0	34	1	1	0	1	1	.50	4	.194	.224	.318

Year Team	Lg	G	AB	H	2B	3B	HR	(Hm	Rd)	TB	R	RBI	TBB	IBB	SO	HBP	SH	SF	SB	CS	SB%	GDP	Avg	OBP	SLG
1993 Seattle	AL	76	271	68	12	2	12	(7	5)	120	31	38	17	1	52	4	6	4	2	3	.40	6	.251	.301	.443
1994 Cincinnati	NL	108	381	122	25	2	12	(5	7)	187	59	68	24	1	74	8	5	6	3	4	.43	10	.320	.368	.491
1995 Cincinnati	NL	138	513	137	34	2	15	(6	9)	220	63	68	41	0	84	6	5	5	5	1	.83	14	.267	.326	.429
4 ML YEARS		355	1294	352	75	6	43	(20	23)	568	168	189	86	2	244	19	17	15	11	9	.55	34	.272	.323	.439

Pedro Borbon

Pitches: Left **Bats:** Left **Pos:** RP **Ht:** 6' 1" **Wt:** 205 **Born:** 11/15/67 **Age:** 28

		HOW MUCH HE PITCHED						WHAT HE GAVE UP												THE RESULTS					
Year Team	Lg	G	GS	CG	GF	IP	BFP	H	R	ER	HR	SH	SF	HB	TBB	IBB	SO	WP	Bk	W	L	Pct.	ShO	Sv	ERA
1988 White Sox	R	16	11	1	2	74.2	299	52	28	20	1	3	3	2	17	0	67	5	14	5	3	.625	1	1	2.41
1990 Burlington	A	14	14	6	0	97.2	381	73	25	16	3	0	0	3	23	0	76	4	1	11	3	.786	2	0	1.47
Durham	A	11	11	0	0	61.1	266	73	40	37	8	2	2	2	16	0	37	2	1	4	5	.444	0	0	5.43
1991 Durham	A	37	6	1	21	90.2	388	85	40	23	2	5	4	2	35	2	79	4	2	4	3	.571	0	5	2.28
Greenville	AA	4	4	0	0	29	120	23	12	9	1	1	0	3	10	0	22	2	0	0	1	.000	0	0	2.79
1992 Greenville	AA	39	10	0	14	94	384	73	36	32	6	1	3	3	42	1	79	2	0	8	2	.800	0	3	3.06
1993 Richmond	AAA	52	0	0	15	76.2	344	71	40	36	7	10	3	2	42	9	95	3	1	5	5	.500	0	1	4.23
1994 Richmond	AAA	59	0	0	20	80.2	337	66	29	25	3	2	3	1	41	5	82	1	0	3	4	.429	0	4	2.79
1992 Atlanta	NL	2	0	0	2	1.1	7	2	1	1	0	0	0	0	1	1	1	0	0	0	1	.000	0	0	6.75
1993 Atlanta	NL	3	0	0	0	1.2	11	3	4	4	0	1	0	0	3	0	2	0	0	0	0	.000	0	0	21.60
1995 Atlanta	NL	41	0	0	19	32	143	29	12	11	2	3	1	1	17	4	33	0	1	2	2	.500	0	2	3.09
3 ML YEARS		46	0	0	21	35	161	34	17	16	2	4	1	1	21	5	36	0	1	2	3	.400	0	2	4.11

Pat Borders

Bats: Right **Throws:** Right **Pos:** C **Ht:** 6' 2" **Wt:** 195 **Born:** 5/14/63 **Age:** 33

		BATTING																	BASERUNNING				PERCENTAGES		
Year Team	Lg	G	AB	H	2B	3B	HR	(Hm	Rd)	TB	R	RBI	TBB	IBB	SO	HBP	SH	SF	SB	CS	SB%	GDP	Avg	OBP	SLG
1988 Toronto	AL	56	154	42	6	3	5	(2	3)	69	15	21	3	0	24	0	2	1	0	0	.00	5	.273	.285	.448
1989 Toronto	AL	94	241	62	11	1	3	(1	2)	84	22	29	11	2	45	1	1	2	2	1	.67	7	.257	.290	.349
1990 Toronto	AL	125	346	99	24	2	15	(10	5)	172	36	49	18	2	57	0	1	3	0	1	.00	17	.286	.319	.497
1991 Toronto	AL	105	291	71	17	0	5	(2	3)	103	22	36	11	1	45	1	6	3	0	0	.00	8	.244	.271	.354
1992 Toronto	AL	138	480	116	26	2	13	(7	6)	185	47	53	33	3	75	2	1	5	1	1	.50	11	.242	.290	.385
1993 Toronto	AL	138	488	124	30	0	9	(6	3)	181	38	55	20	2	66	2	7	3	2	2	.50	18	.254	.285	.371
1994 Toronto	AL	85	295	73	13	1	3	(3	0)	97	24	26	15	0	50	0	1	0	1	1	.50	7	.247	.284	.329
1995 KC-Hou		63	178	37	8	1	4	(1	3)	59	15	13	9	2	29	0	0	0	0	0	.00	3	.208	.246	.331
1995 Kansas City	AL	52	143	33	8	1	4	(1	3)	55	14	13	7	1	22	0	0	0	0	0	.00	1	.231	.267	.385
Houston	NL	11	35	4	0	0	0	(0	0)	4	1	0	2	1	7	0	0	0	0	0	.00	2	.114	.162	.114
8 ML YEARS		804	2473	624	135	10	57	(32	25)	950	219	282	120	12	391	6	19	17	6	6	.50	76	.252	.287	.384

Mike Bordick

Bats: Right **Throws:** Right **Pos:** SS **Ht:** 5'11" **Wt:** 175 **Born:** 7/21/65 **Age:** 30

		BATTING																	BASERUNNING				PERCENTAGES		
Year Team	Lg	G	AB	H	2B	3B	HR	(Hm	Rd)	TB	R	RBI	TBB	IBB	SO	HBP	SH	SF	SB	CS	SB%	GDP	Avg	OBP	SLG
1995 Modesto *	A	1	2	0	0	0	0	(--	--)	0	0	0	0	0	0	1	0	0	0	1	.00	0	.000	.333	.000
1990 Oakland	AL	25	14	1	0	0	0	(0	0)	1	0	0	1	0	4	0	0	0	0	0	.00	0	.071	.133	.071
1991 Oakland	AL	90	235	56	5	1	0	(0	0)	63	21	21	14	0	37	3	12	1	3	4	.43	3	.238	.289	.268
1992 Oakland	AL	154	504	151	19	4	3	(3	0)	187	62	48	40	2	59	9	14	5	12	6	.67	10	.300	.358	.371
1993 Oakland	AL	159	546	136	21	2	3	(2	1)	170	60	48	60	2	58	11	10	6	10	10	.50	9	.249	.332	.311
1994 Oakland	AL	114	391	99	18	4	2	(1	1)	131	38	37	38	1	44	3	3	5	7	2	.78	9	.253	.320	.335
1995 Oakland	AL	126	428	113	13	0	8	(2	6)	150	46	44	35	2	48	5	7	8	11	3	.79	8	.264	.325	.350
6 ML YEARS		668	2118	556	76	11	16	(8	8)	702	227	198	188	7	250	31	46	20	43	25	.63	39	.263	.329	.331

Toby Borland

Pitches: Right **Bats:** Right **Pos:** RP **Ht:** 6' 6" **Wt:** 190 **Born:** 5/29/69 **Age:** 27

		HOW MUCH HE PITCHED						WHAT HE GAVE UP												THE RESULTS					
Year Team	Lg	G	GS	CG	GF	IP	BFP	H	R	ER	HR	SH	SF	HB	TBB	IBB	SO	WP	Bk	W	L	Pct.	ShO	Sv	ERA
1988 Martinsville	R	34	0	0	23	49	215	42	26	22	1	1	2	1	29	1	43	2	1	2	3	.400	0	12	4.04
1989 Spartanburg	A	47	0	0	46	66.2	296	62	29	22	3	2	2	7	35	1	48	15	1	4	5	.444	0	9	2.97
1990 Clearwater	A	44	0	0	23	59.2	257	44	21	15	1	7	1	3	35	4	44	6	1	1	2	.333	0	5	2.26
Reading	AA	14	0	0	5	25	100	16	6	4	1	0	2	1	11	1	26	2	0	4	1	.800	0	1	1.44
1991 Reading	AA	59	0	0	50	76.2	358	68	31	23	2	2	5	2	56	5	72	5	3	8	3	.727	0	24	2.70
1992 Scranton-Wb	AAA	27	0	0	6	27.1	131	25	23	22	2	3	1	2	26	3	25	4	0	0	1	.000	0	1	7.24
Reading	AA	32	0	0	18	42	196	39	23	16	2	2	1	1	32	3	45	3	0	2	4	.333	0	5	3.43
1993 Scranton-Wb	AAA	26	0	0	15	29.2	136	31	20	19	4	4	0	1	20	3	26	2	1	2	4	.333	0	5	5.76
Reading	AA	44	0	0	37	53.2	219	38	17	15	2	1	2	0	20	1	74	1	0	2	2	.500	0	13	2.52
1994 Scranton-Wb	AAA	27	1	0	15	53.2	214	36	12	10	2	1	3	1	21	7	61	2	0	4	1	.800	0	4	1.68
1995 Scranton-Wb	AAA	8	0	0	3	11.1	45	5	0	0	0	0	0	0	6	1	15	2	0	0	0	.000	0	1	0.00
1994 Philadelphia	NL	24	0	0	7	34.1	144	31	10	9	1	1	0	4	14	3	26	4	0	1	0	1.000	0	1	2.36

Year Team	Lg	G	GS	CG	GF	IP	BFP	H	R	ER	HR	SH	SF	HB	TBB	IBB	SO	WP	Bk	W	L	Pct.	ShO	Sv	ERA
1995 Philadelphia	NL	50	0	0	18	74	339	81	37	31	3	3	2	5	37	7	59	12	0	1	3	.250	0	6	3.77
2 ML YEARS		74	0	0	25	108.1	483	112	47	40	4	4	2	9	51	10	85	16	0	2	3	.400	0	7	3.32

Joe Borowski

Pitches: Right **Bats:** Right **Pos:** RP   **Ht:** 6' 2" **Wt:** 225 **Born:** 5/4/71   **Age:** 25

Year Team	Lg	G	GS	CG	GF	IP	BFP	H	R	ER	HR	SH	SF	HB	TBB	IBB	SO	WP	Bk	W	L	Pct.	ShO	Sv	ERA
1990 White Sox	R	12	11	0	0	61.1	286	74	47	38	3	1	2	2	25	0	67	2	2	2	8	.200	0	0	5.58
1991 Kane County	A	49	0	0	28	81	344	60	26	23	2	4	4	3	43	2	76	4	0	7	2	.778	0	13	2.56
1992 Frederick	A	48	0	0	36	80.1	362	71	40	33	3	5	6	3	50	3	85	2	0	5	6	.455	0	10	3.70
1993 Frederick	A	42	2	0	27	62.1	280	61	30	25	5	2	2	3	37	0	70	8	0	1	1	.500	0	11	3.61
Bowie	AA	9	0	0	5	17.2	75	11	0	0	0	3	0	0	11	3	17	0	1	3	0	1.000	0	0	0.00
1994 Bowie	AA	49	0	0	37	66	277	52	14	14	3	4	1	0	28	3	73	4	0	3	4	.429	0	14	1.91
1995 Bowie	AA	16	0	0	14	20.2	83	19	9	9	2	0	0	0	7	1	32	1	0	2	2	.500	0	7	3.92
Rochester	AAA	28	0	0	22	35.2	149	32	16	16	3	5	1	0	18	2	32	1	0	1	3	.250	0	6	4.04
1995 Baltimore	AL	6	0	0	3	7.1	30	5	1	1	0	0	0	0	4	0	3	0	0	0	0	.000	0	0	1.23

Chris Bosio

Pitches: Right **Bats:** Right **Pos:** SP   **Ht:** 6' 3" **Wt:** 225 **Born:** 4/3/63   **Age:** 33

Year Team	Lg	G	GS	CG	GF	IP	BFP	H	R	ER	HR	SH	SF	HB	TBB	IBB	SO	WP	Bk	W	L	Pct.	ShO	Sv	ERA
1986 Milwaukee	AL	10	4	0	3	34.2	154	41	27	27	9	1	0	0	13	0	29	2	1	0	4	.000	0	0	7.01
1987 Milwaukee	AL	46	19	2	8	170	734	187	102	99	18	3	3	1	50	3	150	14	2	11	8	.579	1	2	5.24
1988 Milwaukee	AL	38	22	9	15	182	766	190	80	68	13	7	9	2	38	6	84	1	2	7	15	.318	1	6	3.36
1989 Milwaukee	AL	33	33	8	0	234.2	969	225	90	77	16	5	5	6	48	1	173	4	2	15	10	.600	2	0	2.95
1990 Milwaukee	AL	20	20	4	0	132.2	557	131	67	59	15	4	4	3	38	1	76	7	0	4	9	.308	1	0	4.00
1991 Milwaukee	AL	32	32	5	0	204.2	840	187	80	74	15	2	6	8	58	0	117	5	0	14	10	.583	1	0	3.25
1992 Milwaukee	AL	33	33	4	0	231.1	937	223	100	93	21	6	5	4	44	1	120	8	2	16	6	.727	2	0	3.62
1993 Seattle	AL	29	24	3	2	164.1	678	138	75	63	14	7	4	6	59	3	119	5	0	9	9	.500	1	1	3.45
1994 Seattle	AL	19	19	4	0	125	546	137	72	60	15	3	6	2	40	3	67	4	0	4	10	.286	0	0	4.32
1995 Seattle	AL	31	31	0	0	170	766	211	98	93	18	5	11	5	69	3	85	10	0	10	8	.556	0	0	4.92
10 ML YEARS		291	237	39	28	1649.1	6947	1670	791	713	154	43	53	37	457	21	1020	60	9	90	89	.503	9	9	3.89

Shawn Boskie

Pitches: Right **Bats:** Right **Pos:** SP   **Ht:** 6' 3" **Wt:** 200 **Born:** 3/28/67   **Age:** 29

Year Team	Lg	G	GS	CG	GF	IP	BFP	H	R	ER	HR	SH	SF	HB	TBB	IBB	SO	WP	Bk	W	L	Pct.	ShO	Sv	ERA
1995 Lk Elsinore *	A	3	3	0	0	11	53	15	7	5	1	0	0	0	4	0	8	0	0	0	0	.000	0	0	4.09
Vancouver *	AAA	1	1	0	0	6	25	4	2	2	1	0	0	0	2	0	1	0	0	1	0	1.000	0	0	3.00
1990 Chicago	NL	15	15	1	0	97.2	415	99	42	40	8	8	2	1	31	3	49	3	2	5	6	.455	0	0	3.69
1991 Chicago	NL	28	20	0	2	129	582	150	78	75	14	8	6	5	52	4	62	1	1	4	9	.308	0	0	5.23
1992 Chicago	NL	23	18	0	2	91.2	393	96	55	51	14	9	6	4	36	3	39	5	1	5	11	.313	0	0	5.01
1993 Chicago	NL	39	2	0	10	65.2	277	63	30	25	7	4	1	7	21	2	39	5	0	5	3	.625	0	0	3.43
1994 Sea-ChN-Phi		22	15	1	1	90.2	394	92	58	51	15	2	3	3	30	3	61	7	0	4	7	.364	0	0	5.06
1995 California	AL	20	20	1	0	111.2	494	127	73	70	16	4	6	7	25	0	51	4	0	7	7	.500	0	0	5.64
1994 Seattle	AL	2	1	0	0	2.2	13	4	2	2	1	0	0	0	1	1	0	0	0	0	1	.000	0	0	6.75
Chicago	NL	2	0	0	0	3.2	14	3	0	0	0	0	0	0	0	0	2	1	0	0	0	.000	0	0	0.00
Philadelphia	NL	18	14	1	1	84.1	367	85	56	49	14	2	3	3	29	2	59	6	0	4	6	.400	0	0	5.23
6 ML YEARS		147	90	3	15	586.1	2555	627	336	312	74	35	24	27	195	15	301	25	4	30	43	.411	0	0	4.79

Ricky Bottalico

Pitches: Right **Bats:** Left **Pos:** RP   **Ht:** 6' 1" **Wt:** 209 **Born:** 8/26/69   **Age:** 26

Year Team	Lg	G	GS	CG	GF	IP	BFP	H	R	ER	HR	SH	SF	HB	TBB	IBB	SO	WP	Bk	W	L	Pct.	ShO	Sv	ERA
1991 Martinsvlle	R	7	6	2	0	33	144	32	20	15	2	0	1	1	13	0	38	2	1	3	2	.600	1	0	4.09
Spartanburg	A	2	2	0	0	15	52	4	0	0	0	0	0	1	2	0	11	1	0	2	0	1.000	0	0	0.00
1992 Spartanburg	A	42	11	1	24	119.2	501	94	41	32	6	6	0	3	56	0	118	5	0	5	10	.333	0	13	2.41
1993 Clearwater	A	13	0	0	9	19.2	79	19	6	6	0	0	0	0	5	0	19	0	0	1	0	1.000	0	4	2.75
Reading	AA	49	0	0	37	72	301	63	22	18	4	4	2	2	26	3	65	3	0	3	3	.500	0	20	2.25
1994 Scranton-Wb	AAA	19	0	0	14	22.1	123	32	27	22	4	2	1	0	22	2	22	1	0	3	1	.750	0	3	8.87
Reading	AA	38	0	0	33	42.2	165	29	13	12	6	1	1	0	10	0	51	4	0	2	2	.500	0	22	2.53
1994 Philadelphia	NL	3	0	0	3	3	13	3	0	0	0	0	0	0	1	0	3	0	0	0	0	.000	0	0	0.00
1995 Philadelphia	NL	62	0	0	20	87.2	350	50	25	24	7	3	1	4	42	3	87	1	0	5	3	.625	0	1	2.46
2 ML YEARS		65	0	0	23	90.2	363	53	25	24	7	3	1	4	43	3	90	1	0	5	3	.625	0	1	2.38

Ryan Bowen

Pitches: Right **Bats:** Right **Pos:** SP   **Ht:** 6' 0" **Wt:** 185 **Born:** 2/10/68 **Age:** 28

| | | | HOW MUCH HE PITCHED | | | | | WHAT HE GAVE UP | | | | | | | | | | | | THE RESULTS | | | | | |
Year Team	Lg	G	GS	CG	GF	IP	BFP	H	R	ER	HR	SH	SF	HB	TBB	IBB	SO	WP	Bk	W	L	Pct.	ShO	Sv	ERA
1995 Brevard Cty *	A	3	3	0	0	11	43	6	3	3	1	0	0	0	6	0	10	0	0	0	2	.000	0	0	2.45
Charlotte *	AAA	1	1	0	0	4.2	22	5	5	5	1	0	0	0	4	0	3	0	0	0	1	.000	0	0	9.64
1991 Houston	NL	14	13	0	0	71.2	319	73	43	41	4	2	6	3	36	1	49	8	1	6	4	.600	0	0	5.15
1992 Houston	NL	11	9	0	2	33.2	179	48	43	41	8	3	0	2	30	3	22	5	0	0	7	.000	0	0	10.96
1993 Florida	NL	27	27	2	0	156.2	693	156	83	77	11	5	4	3	87	7	98	10	4	8	12	.400	1	0	4.42
1994 Florida	NL	8	8	1	0	47.1	208	50	28	26	9	2	2	2	19	0	32	2	0	1	5	.167	0	0	4.94
1995 Florida	NL	4	3	0	0	16.2	85	23	11	7	3	1	2	0	12	2	15	0	0	2	0	1.000	0	0	3.78
5 ML YEARS		64	60	3	2	326	1484	350	208	192	35	13	14	10	184	13	216	25	5	17	28	.378	1	0	5.30

Terry Bradshaw

Bats: Left **Throws:** Right **Pos:** LF   **Ht:** 6' 0" **Wt:** 180 **Born:** 2/3/69 **Age:** 27

| | | | | | BATTING | | | | | | | | | | | | | | BASERUNNING | | | | PERCENTAGES | | |
Year Team	Lg	G	AB	H	2B	3B	HR	(Hm	Rd)	TB	R	RBI	TBB	IBB	SO	HBP	SH	SF	SB	CS	SB%	GDP	Avg	OBP	SLG
1990 Hamilton	A	68	236	55	5	1	3	--	--	71	37	13	24	1	60	1	2	1	15	3	.83	4	.233	.305	.301
1991 Savannah	A	132	443	105	17	1	7	--	--	145	90	42	99	1	117	10	4	5	64	15	.81	6	.237	.384	.327
1993 St. Pete	A	125	461	134	25	6	5	--	--	186	84	51	82	1	60	7	7	5	43	17	.72	8	.291	.402	.403
1994 Arkansas	AA	114	425	119	25	8	10	--	--	190	65	52	50	4	69	7	2	4	13	10	.57	5	.280	.362	.447
Louisville	AAA	22	80	20	4	0	4	--	--	36	16	8	6	0	10	2	1	0	5	1	.83	2	.250	.318	.450
1995 Louisville	AAA	111	389	110	24	8	8	--	--	174	65	42	53	0	60	3	7	1	20	7	.74	4	.283	.372	.447
1995 St. Louis	NL	19	44	10	1	1	0	(0	0)	13	6	2	2	0	10	0	0	0	1	2	.33	0	.227	.261	.295

Doug Brady

Bats: Both **Throws:** Right **Pos:** 2B   **Ht:** 5'11" **Wt:** 165 **Born:** 11/23/69 **Age:** 26

| | | | | | BATTING | | | | | | | | | | | | | | BASERUNNING | | | | PERCENTAGES | | |
Year Team	Lg	G	AB	H	2B	3B	HR	(Hm	Rd)	TB	R	RBI	TBB	IBB	SO	HBP	SH	SF	SB	CS	SB%	GDP	Avg	OBP	SLG
1991 Utica	A	65	226	53	6	3	2	--	--	71	37	31	31	0	31	1	3	4	21	6	.78	5	.235	.324	.314
1992 South Bend	A	24	92	27	5	1	0	--	--	34	12	7	17	1	13	0	2	1	16	3	.84	0	.293	.400	.370
White Sox	R	3	8	1	0	0	0	--	--	1	1	2	1	0	1	0	0	2	0	0	.00	0	.125	.182	.125
Sarasota	A	56	184	50	6	0	2	--	--	62	21	27	25	1	33	3	6	2	5	7	.42	4	.272	.364	.337
1993 Sarasota	A	115	449	113	16	6	5	--	--	156	75	44	55	2	54	6	4	5	26	9	.74	4	.252	.338	.347
Nashville	AAA	2	3	0	0	0	0	--	--	0	0	0	0	0	0	0	0	0	0	0	.00	0	.000	.000	.000
1994 Birmingham	AA	127	516	128	18	8	4	--	--	174	59	47	38	1	59	1	6	5	34	12	.74	0	.248	.298	.337
1995 Nashville	AAA	125	450	134	15	6	5	--	--	176	71	27	31	3	76	0	4	3	32	6	.84	0	.298	.341	.391
1995 Chicago	AL	12	21	4	1	0	0	(0	0)	5	4	3	0	0	4	0	0	0	0	1	.00	1	.190	.261	.238

Darren Bragg

Bats: Left **Throws:** Right **Pos:** LF/RF   **Ht:** 5' 9" **Wt:** 180 **Born:** 9/7/69 **Age:** 26

| | | | | | BATTING | | | | | | | | | | | | | | BASERUNNING | | | | PERCENTAGES | | |
Year Team	Lg	G	AB	H	2B	3B	HR	(Hm	Rd)	TB	R	RBI	TBB	IBB	SO	HBP	SH	SF	SB	CS	SB%	GDP	Avg	OBP	SLG
1991 Peninsula	A	69	237	53	14	0	3	--	--	76	42	29	66	0	72	2	1	1	21	9	.70	8	.224	.395	.321
1992 Peninsula	A	135	428	117	25	5	9	--	--	179	83	58	105	6	76	5	5	5	44	19	.70	8	.273	.418	.418
1993 Jacksonvlle	AA	131	451	119	26	3	11	--	--	184	74	46	81	3	82	7	4	3	19	11	.63	12	.264	.382	.408
1994 Calgary	AAA	126	500	175	33	6	17	--	--	271	112	85	68	3	72	6	3	9	28	12	.70	11	.350	.430	.542
1995 Tacoma	AAA	53	212	65	13	3	4	--	--	96	24	31	23	1	39	0	0	1	10	3	.77	3	.307	.373	.453
1994 Seattle	AL	8	19	3	1	0	0	(0	0)	4	4	2	2	1	5	0	0	0	0	0	.00	0	.158	.238	.211
1995 Seattle	AL	52	145	34	5	1	3	(1	2)	50	20	12	18	1	37	4	1	2	9	0	1.00	2	.234	.331	.345
2 ML YEARS		60	164	37	6	1	3	(1	2)	54	24	14	20	2	42	4	1	2	9	0	1.00	2	.226	.321	.329

Mark Brandenburg

Pitches: Right **Bats:** Right **Pos:** RP   **Ht:** 6' 0" **Wt:** 180 **Born:** 7/14/70 **Age:** 25

| | | | HOW MUCH HE PITCHED | | | | | WHAT HE GAVE UP | | | | | | | | | | | | THE RESULTS | | | | | |
Year Team	Lg	G	GS	CG	GF	IP	BFP	H	R	ER	HR	SH	SF	HB	TBB	IBB	SO	WP	Bk	W	L	Pct.	ShO	Sv	ERA
1992 Butte	R	24	1	0	16	62	268	70	32	28	3	1	1	5	14	1	78	1	0	7	1	.875	0	2	4.06
1993 Charlstn-Sc	A	44	0	0	18	80	320	62	23	13	2	4	2	3	22	6	67	0	0	6	3	.667	0	4	1.46
1994 Charlotte	A	25	0	0	15	41.1	159	23	5	4	1	2	1	2	15	4	44	0	0	2	0	.000	0	5	0.87
Tulsa	AA	37	0	0	26	62	248	50	17	12	2	2	1		12	6	63	0	0	5	4	.556	0	8	1.74
1995 Okla. City	AAA	35	0	0	15	58	235	52	16	13	2	3	1	2	15	5	51	0	2	0	5	.000	0	2	2.02
1995 Texas	AL	11	0	0	5	27.1	123	36	18	18	5	0	1	1	7	1	21	0	0	0	1	.000	0	0	5.93

Jeff Branson

Bats: Left **Throws:** Right **Pos:** 3B/SS   **Ht:** 6' 0" **Wt:** 180 **Born:** 1/26/67 **Age:** 29

								BATTING											BASERUNNING				PERCENTAGES		
Year Team	Lg	G	AB	H	2B	3B	HR	(Hm Rd)	TB	R	RBI	TBB	IBB	SO	HBP	SH	SF	SB	CS	SB%	GDP	Avg	OBP	SLG
1992 Cincinnati	NL	72	115	34	7	1	0	(0 0)	43	12	15	5	2	16	0	2	1	0	1	.00	4	.296	.322	.374
1993 Cincinnati	NL	125	381	92	15	1	3	(2 1)	118	40	22	19	2	73	0	8	4	4	1	.80	4	.241	.275	.310
1994 Cincinnati	NL	58	109	31	4	1	6	(1 5)	55	18	16	5	2	16	0	2	0	0	0	.00	4	.284	.316	.505
1995 Cincinnati	NL	122	331	86	18	2	12	(9 3)	144	43	45	44	14	69	2	1	6	2	1	.67	9	.260	.345	.435
4 ML YEARS		377	936	243	44	5	21	(12 9)	360	113	98	73	20	174	2	13	11	6	3	.67	21	.260	.311	.385

Jeff Brantley

Pitches: Right **Bats:** Right **Pos:** RP   **Ht:** 5'10" **Wt:** 190 **Born:** 9/5/63 **Age:** 32

			HOW MUCH HE PITCHED						WHAT HE GAVE UP										THE RESULTS					
Year Team	Lg	G	GS	CG	GF	IP	BFP	H	R	ER	HR	SH	SF	HB	TBB	IBB	SO	WP	Bk	W	L	Pct.	ShO	Sv	ERA
1988 San Francisco	NL	9	1	0	2	20.2	88	22	13	13	2	1	0	1	6	1	11	0	1	0	1	.000	0	1	5.66
1989 San Francisco	NL	59	1	0	15	97.1	422	101	50	44	10	7	3	2	37	8	69	3	2	7	1	.875	0	0	4.07
1990 San Francisco	NL	55	0	0	32	86.2	361	77	18	15	3	2	2	3	33	6	61	0	3	5	3	.625	0	19	1.56
1991 San Francisco	NL	67	0	0	39	95.1	411	78	27	26	8	4	4	5	52	10	81	6	0	5	2	.714	0	15	2.45
1992 San Francisco	NL	56	4	0	32	91.2	381	67	32	30	8	7	3	3	45	5	86	3	1	7	7	.500	0	7	2.95
1993 San Francisco	NL	53	12	0	9	113.2	496	112	60	54	19	5	5	7	46	2	76	3	4	5	6	.455	0	0	4.28
1994 Cincinnati	NL	50	0	0	35	65.1	262	66	20	18	6	5	1	0	28	5	63	1	0	6	6	.500	0	15	2.48
1995 Cincinnati	NL	56	0	0	49	70.1	283	53	22	22	11	2	3	1	20	3	62	2	2	3	2	.600	0	28	2.82
8 ML YEARS		405	18	0	213	641	2704	556	242	222	67	33	21	22	267	40	509	18	13	38	28	.576	0	85	3.12

Billy Brewer

Pitches: Left **Bats:** Left **Pos:** RP   **Ht:** 6' 1" **Wt:** 175 **Born:** 4/15/68 **Age:** 28

			HOW MUCH HE PITCHED						WHAT HE GAVE UP										THE RESULTS					
Year Team	Lg	G	GS	CG	GF	IP	BFP	H	R	ER	HR	SH	SF	HB	TBB	IBB	SO	WP	Bk	W	L	Pct.	ShO	Sv	ERA
1995 Springfield *	A	1	0	0	1	2	9	2	1	0	0	0	0	0	1	0	2	0	0	0	0	.000	0	1	0.00
Omaha *	AAA	6	0	0	1	7	25	1	0	0	0	0	0	0	7	0	5	2	1	0	0	.000	0	0	0.00
1993 Kansas City	AL	46	0	0	14	39	157	31	16	15	6	1	1	0	20	4	28	2	1	2	2	.500	0	1	3.46
1994 Kansas City	AL	50	0	0	17	38.2	157	28	11	11	4	2	2	2	16	1	25	3	0	4	1	.800	0	3	2.56
1995 Kansas City	AL	48	0	0	13	45.1	209	54	28	28	9	1	0	2	20	1	31	5	1	2	4	.333	0	0	5.56
3 ML YEARS		144	0	0	44	123	523	113	55	54	19	4	3	4	56	6	84	10	2	8	7	.533	0	3	3.95

Jamie Brewington

Pitches: Right **Bats:** Right **Pos:** SP   **Ht:** 6' 4" **Wt:** 190 **Born:** 9/28/71 **Age:** 24

			HOW MUCH HE PITCHED						WHAT HE GAVE UP										THE RESULTS					
Year Team	Lg	G	GS	CG	GF	IP	BFP	H	R	ER	HR	SH	SF	HB	TBB	IBB	SO	WP	Bk	W	L	Pct.	ShO	Sv	ERA
1992 Everett	A	15	11	1	1	68.2	317	65	40	33	2	0	3	5	47	2	63	9	1	5	2	.714	1	0	4.33
1993 Clinton	A	26	25	1	0	133.2	580	126	78	71	20	1	3	5	61	1	111	19	2	13	5	.722	0	0	4.78
1994 Clinton	A	10	10	0	0	53	226	46	29	29	5	1	3	2	24	0	62	7	1	2	4	.333	0	0	4.92
San Jose	A	13	13	0	0	76	310	61	38	27	3	2	2	2	25	0	65	7	1	7	3	.700	0	0	3.20
1995 Shreveport	AA	16	16	1	0	88.1	376	72	39	30	8	2	1	0	55	0	74	4	0	8	3	.727	1	0	3.06
1995 San Francisco	NL	13	13	0	0	75.1	334	68	38	38	8	4	4	4	45	6	45	3	0	6	4	.600	0	0	4.54

John Briscoe

Pitches: Right **Bats:** Right **Pos:** RP   **Ht:** 6' 3" **Wt:** 190 **Born:** 9/22/67 **Age:** 28

			HOW MUCH HE PITCHED						WHAT HE GAVE UP										THE RESULTS					
Year Team	Lg	G	GS	CG	GF	IP	BFP	H	R	ER	HR	SH	SF	HB	TBB	IBB	SO	WP	Bk	W	L	Pct.	ShO	Sv	ERA
1995 Modesto *	A	4	4	0	0	5.2	22	5	1	1	0	0	0	0	2	0	5	0	0	0	0	.000	0	0	1.59
Edmonton *	AAA	3	3	0	0	6	26	5	2	2	0	0	0	0	5	0	3	0	0	0	0	.000	0	0	3.00
1991 Oakland	AL	11	0	0	9	14	62	12	11	11	3	0	1	0	10	0	9	3	0	0	0	.000	0	0	7.07
1992 Oakland	AL	2	2	0	0	7	40	12	6	5	0	1	0	0	9	0	4	2	0	0	1	.000	0	0	6.43
1993 Oakland	AL	17	0	0	6	24.2	122	26	25	22	2	0	2	0	26	3	24	5	0	1	0	1.000	0	0	8.03
1994 Oakland	AL	37	0	0	8	49.1	210	31	24	22	7	1	1	1	39	2	45	8	1	4	2	.667	0	1	4.01
1995 Oakland	AL	16	0	0	7	18.1	99	25	17	17	4	2	2	2	21	1	19	1	0	0	0	.000	0	0	8.35
5 ML YEARS		83	2	0	30	113.1	533	106	83	77	16	4	6	3	105	6	101	19	1	5	4	.556	0	1	6.11

Bernardo Brito

Bats: Right **Throws:** Right **Pos:** DH   **Ht:** 6' 1" **Wt:** 210 **Born:** 12/4/63 **Age:** 32

								BATTING											BASERUNNING				PERCENTAGES		
Year Team	Lg	G	AB	H	2B	3B	HR	(Hm Rd)	TB	R	RBI	TBB	IBB	SO	HBP	SH	SF	SB	CS	SB%	GDP	Avg	OBP	SLG
1995 Salt Lake *	AAA	51	186	57	10	1	15	(-- --)	114	31	49	17	5	58	4	0	0	1	0	1.00	7	.306	.377	.613
1992 Minnesota	AL	8	14	2	1	0	0	(0 0)	3	1	2	0	0	4	0	0	1	0	0	.00	0	.143	.133	.214
1993 Minnesota	AL	27	54	13	2	0	4	(0 4)	27	8	9	1	0	20	0	0	0	0	0	.00	1	.241	.255	.500
1995 Minnesota	AL	5	5	1	0	0	1	(0 1)	4	1	1	0	0	3	1	0	0	0	0	.00	1	.200	.333	.800
3 ML YEARS		40	73	16	3	0	5	(0 5)	34	10	12	1	0	27	1	0	1	0	1	.00	2	.219	.237	.466

Jorge Brito

Bats: Right **Throws:** Right **Pos:** C   **Ht:** 6' 1" **Wt:** 190 **Born:** 6/22/66 **Age:** 30

								BATTING										BASERUNNING				PERCENTAGES		
Year Team	Lg	G	AB	H	2B	3B	HR	(Hm | Rd)	TB	R	RBI	TBB	IBB	SO	HBP	SH	SF	SB	CS	SB%	GDP	Avg	OBP	SLG
1986 Medford	A	21	59	9	2	0	0	--	--	11	4	5	4	0	17	2	0	1	0	2	.00	3	.153	.227	.186
1987 Medford	A	40	110	20	1	0	1	--	--	24	7	15	12	0	54	1	1	2	0	0	.00	3	.182	.264	.218
1988 Modesto	A	96	300	65	15	0	5	--	--	95	38	27	47	0	104	8	3	3	0	0	.00	6	.217	.335	.317
1989 Modesto	A	16	54	13	2	0	1	--	--	18	8	6	5	0	14	1	1	0	0	0	.00	2	.241	.317	.333
Tacoma	AAA	5	15	3	1	0	0	--	--	4	2	0	2	0	6	0	0	0	0	1	.00	2	.200	.294	.267
Huntsville	AA	24	73	16	2	2	0	--	--	22	13	8	20	0	23	0	2	0	1	1	.50	2	.219	.387	.301
Madison	A	43	143	30	4	1	3	--	--	45	20	14	22	1	46	2	1	0	1	0	1.00	9	.210	.323	.315
1990 Huntsville	AA	57	164	44	6	1	2	--	--	58	17	20	30	1	49	3	3	1	0	1	.00	6	.268	.389	.354
1991 Tacoma	AAA	22	73	17	2	0	1	--	--	22	6	3	4	0	20	0	0	0	0	0	.00	1	.233	.273	.301
Huntsville	AA	65	203	41	11	0	1	--	--	55	26	23	28	0	50	4	2	1	0	1	.00	6	.202	.309	.271
1992 Tacoma	AAA	18	35	5	2	0	0	--	--	7	4	1	2	0	17	0	0	0	0	0	.00	0	.143	.189	.200
Huntsville	AA	33	72	15	2	0	2	--	--	23	10	6	13	0	21	1	3	0	0	1	1.00	4	.208	.337	.319
1993 Huntsville	AA	18	36	10	3	0	4	--	--	25	6	11	10	1	10	2	0	1	0	0	.00	0	.278	.449	.694
1994 New Haven	AA	63	200	46	11	1	5	--	--	74	18	25	18	3	59	2	1	2	2	0	1.00	6	.230	.297	.370
Colo. Sprng	AAA	21	64	24	5	0	3	--	--	38	13	19	7	1	14	0	1	0	0	0	.00	3	.375	.437	.594
1995 Colo. Sprng	AAA	32	96	22	4	1	2	--	--	34	9	15	2	0	20	1	1	2	0	0	.00	3	.229	.248	.354
1995 Colorado	NL	18	51	11	3	0	0	(0 | 0)	14	5	7	2	0	17	1	1	0	1	0	1.00	1	.216	.259	.275

Doug Brocail

Pitches: Right **Bats:** Left **Pos:** RP/SP   **Ht:** 6' 5" **Wt:** 235 **Born:** 5/16/67 **Age:** 29

		HOW MUCH HE PITCHED						WHAT HE GAVE UP										THE RESULTS					
Year Team	Lg	G	GS	CG	GF	IP	BFP	H	R	ER	HR	SF	HB	TBB	IBB	SO	WP	Bk	W	L	Pct.	ShO	Sv	ERA
1995 Tucson *	AAA	3	3	0	0	16.1	74	18	9	7	1	0	1	4	0	16	0	0	1	0	1.000	0	0	3.86
1992 San Diego	NL	3	3	0	0	14	64	17	10	10	2	2	0	5	0	15	0	0	0	0	.000	0	0	6.43
1993 San Diego	NL	24	24	0	0	128.1	571	143	75	65	16	10	8	42	4	70	4	1	4	13	.235	0	0	4.56
1994 San Diego	NL	12	0	0	4	17	78	21	13	11	1	1	1	5	3	11	1	1	0	0	.000	0	0	5.82
1995 Houston	NL	36	7	0	12	77.1	339	87	40	36	10	1	1	22	2	39	1	1	6	4	.600	0	1	4.19
4 ML YEARS		75	34	0	16	236.2	1052	268	138	122	29	14	10	74	9	135	6	3	10	17	.370	0	1	4.64

Rico Brogna

Bats: Left **Throws:** Left **Pos:** 1B   **Ht:** 6' 2" **Wt:** 205 **Born:** 4/18/70 **Age:** 26

								BATTING										BASERUNNING				PERCENTAGES		
Year Team	Lg	G	AB	H	2B	3B	HR	(Hm	Rd)	TB	R	RBI	TBB	IBB	SO	HBP	SH	SF	SB	CS	SB%	GDP	Avg	OBP	SLG
1992 Detroit	AL	9	26	5	1	0	1	(1	0)	9	3	3	3	0	5	0	0	0	0	0	.00	0	.192	.276	.346
1994 New York	NL	39	131	46	11	2	7	(2	5)	82	16	20	6	0	29	0	1	0	1	0	1.00	2	.351	.380	.626
1995 New York	NL	134	495	143	27	2	22	(13	9)	240	72	76	39	7	111	2	2	2	0	0	.00	10	.289	.342	.485
3 ML YEARS		182	652	194	39	4	30	(16	14)	331	91	99	48	7	145	2	3	2	1	0	1.00	12	.298	.347	.508

Jeff Bronkey

Pitches: Right **Bats:** Right **Pos:** RP   **Ht:** 6' 3" **Wt:** 211 **Born:** 9/18/65 **Age:** 30

		HOW MUCH HE PITCHED						WHAT HE GAVE UP										THE RESULTS					
Year Team	Lg	G	GS	CG	GF	IP	BFP	H	R	ER	HR	SH	SF	HB	TBB	IBB	SO	WP	Bk	W	L	Pct.	ShO	Sv	ERA
1995 Beloit *	A	3	3	0	0	7.1	32	5	5	3	1	0	0	1	3	0	8	1	0	0	1	.000	0	0	3.68
New Orleans *	AAA	2	1	0	0	8	29	8	2	2	0	1	0	0	1	0	2	1	0	0	0	.000	0	0	2.25
1993 Texas	AL	21	0	0	6	36	152	39	20	16	4	1	2	1	11	4	18	2	0	1	1	.500	0	1	4.00
1994 Milwaukee	AL	16	0	0	9	20.2	93	20	10	10	3	0	0	0	12	4	13	1	0	1	1	.500	0	0	4.35
1995 Milwaukee	AL	8	0	0	4	12.1	56	15	6	5	0	2	0	0	6	0	5	1	0	0	0	.000	0	0	3.65
3 ML YEARS		45	0	0	19	69	301	74	36	31	7	3	2	1	29	8	36	4	0	2	2	.500	0	2	4.04

Scott Brosius

Bats: Right **Throws:** Right **Pos:** 3B/1B/CF/RF   **Ht:** 6' 1" **Wt:** 185 **Born:** 8/15/66 **Age:** 29

								BATTING										BASERUNNING				PERCENTAGES		
Year Team	Lg	G	AB	H	2B	3B	HR	(Hm	Rd)	TB	R	RBI	TBB	IBB	SO	HBP	SH	SF	SB	CS	SB%	GDP	Avg	OBP	SLG
1991 Oakland	AL	36	68	16	5	0	2	(1	1)	27	9	4	3	0	11	0	1	0	3	1	.75	2	.235	.268	.397
1992 Oakland	AL	38	87	19	2	0	4	(1	3)	33	13	13	3	1	13	2	0	1	3	0	1.00	0	.218	.258	.379
1993 Oakland	AL	70	213	53	10	1	6	(3	3)	83	26	25	14	0	37	1	3	2	6	0	1.00	6	.249	.296	.390
1994 Oakland	AL	96	324	77	14	1	14	(9	5)	135	31	49	24	0	57	2	4	6	2	6	.25	7	.238	.289	.417
1995 Oakland	AL	123	389	102	19	2	17	(12	5)	176	69	46	41	0	67	8	1	4	4	2	.67	5	.262	.342	.452
5 ML YEARS		363	1081	267	50	4	43	(26	17)	454	148	137	85	1	185	13	9	13	18	9	.67	20	.247	.306	.420

Jarvis Brown

Bats: Right **Throws:** Right **Pos:** CF **Ht:** 5' 7" **Wt:** 170 **Born:** 9/26/67 **Age:** 28

								BATTING												BASERUNNING				PERCENTAGES		
Year	Team	Lg	G	AB	H	2B	3B	HR	(Hm	Rd)	TB	R	RBI	TBB	IBB	SO	HBP	SH	SF	SB	CS	SB%	GDP	Avg	OBP	SLG
1995	Norfolk *	AAA	45	148	42	12	3	0	--	--	60	29	17	18	0	29	1	2	0	6	3	.67	3	.284	.365	.405
	Bowie *	AA	58	219	61	12	1	6	--	--	93	50	23	33	0	49	4	2	1	12	3	.80	5	.279	.381	.425
	Rochester *	AAA	17	70	22	4	2	0	--	--	30	12	4	10	0	20	0	2	0	1	1	.50	2	.314	.400	.429
1991	Minnesota	AL	38	37	8	0	0	0	(0	0)	8	10	0	2	0	8	0	1	0	7	1	.88	0	.216	.256	.216
1992	Minnesota	AL	35	15	1	0	0	0	(0	0)	1	8	0	2	0	4	1	0	0	2	2	.50	0	.067	.222	.067
1993	San Diego	NL	47	133	31	9	2	0	(0	0)	44	21	8	15	0	26	6	2	1	3	3	.50	4	.233	.335	.331
1994	Atlanta	NL	17	15	2	1	0	1	(0	1)	6	3	1	0	0	2	0	1	0	0	0	.00	1	.133	.133	.400
1995	Baltimore	AL	18	27	4	1	0	0	(0	0)	5	2	1	7	0	9	0	3	0	1	1	.50	0	.148	.324	.185
	5 ML YEARS		155	227	46	11	2	1	(0	1)	64	44	10	26	0	49	7	7	1	13	7	.65	5	.203	.303	.282

Kevin Brown

Pitches: Right **Bats:** Right **Pos:** SP **Ht:** 6' 4" **Wt:** 195 **Born:** 3/14/65 **Age:** 31

						HOW MUCH HE PITCHED					WHAT HE GAVE UP										THE RESULTS			
Year	Team	Lg	G	GS	CG	GF	IP	BFP	H	R	ER	HR	SH	SF	HB	TBB	IBB	SO	WP	Bk	W	L	Pct.	ShO	Sv	ERA
1986	Texas	AL	1	1	0	0	5	19	6	2	2	0	0	0	0	0	0	4	0	0	1	0	1.000	0	0	3.60
1988	Texas	AL	4	4	1	0	23.1	110	33	15	11	2	1	0	1	8	0	12	1	0	1	1	.500	0	0	4.24
1989	Texas	AL	28	28	7	0	191	798	167	81	71	10	3	6	4	70	2	104	7	2	12	9	.571	0	0	3.35
1990	Texas	AL	26	26	6	0	180	757	175	84	72	13	2	7	3	60	3	88	9	2	12	10	.545	2	0	3.60
1991	Texas	AL	33	33	0	0	210.2	934	233	116	103	17	6	4	13	90	5	96	12	3	9	12	.429	0	0	4.40
1992	Texas	AL	35	35	11	0	265.2	1108	262	117	98	11	7	8	10	76	2	173	8	2	21	11	.656	1	0	3.32
1993	Texas	AL	34	34	12	0	233	1001	228	105	93	14	5	3	15	74	5	142	8	1	15	12	.556	3	0	3.59
1994	Texas	AL	26	25	3	1	170	760	218	109	91	18	2	7	6	50	3	123	7	0	7	9	.438	0	0	4.82
1995	Baltimore	AL	26	26	3	0	172.1	706	155	73	69	10	5	2	9	48	1	117	3	0	10	9	.526	1	0	3.60
	9 ML YEARS		213	212	43	1	1451	6193	1477	702	610	95	31	37	61	476	21	859	55	10	88	73	.547	7	0	3.78

Jerry Browne

Bats: Both **Throws:** Right **Pos:** 2B/LF/CF/RF **Ht:** 5'10" **Wt:** 170 **Born:** 2/3/66 **Age:** 30

								BATTING												BASERUNNING				PERCENTAGES		
Year	Team	Lg	G	AB	H	2B	3B	HR	(Hm	Rd)	TB	R	RBI	TBB	IBB	SO	HBP	SH	SF	SB	CS	SB%	GDP	Avg	OBP	SLG
1995	Brevard Cty *	A	3	7	2	0	0	0	--	--	2	0	2	1	0	1	0	0	0	0	0	.00	0	.286	.333	.286
1986	Texas	AL	12	24	10	2	0	0	(0	0)	12	6	3	1	0	4	0	0	0	0	2	.00	0	.417	.440	.500
1987	Texas	AL	132	454	123	16	6	1	(1	0)	154	63	38	61	0	50	2	7	2	27	17	.61	6	.271	.358	.339
1988	Texas	AL	73	214	49	9	2	1	(1	0)	65	26	17	25	0	32	0	3	1	7	5	.58	5	.229	.308	.304
1989	Cleveland	AL	153	598	179	31	4	5	(1	4)	233	83	45	68	10	64	1	14	4	14	6	.70	9	.299	.370	.390
1990	Cleveland	AL	140	513	137	26	5	6	(2	4)	191	92	50	72	1	46	2	12	11	12	7	.63	12	.267	.353	.372
1991	Cleveland	AL	107	290	66	5	2	1	(1	0)	78	28	29	27	0	29	1	12	4	2	4	.33	5	.228	.292	.269
1992	Oakland	AL	111	324	93	12	2	3	(1	2)	118	43	40	40	0	40	4	16	6	3	3	.50	7	.287	.366	.364
1993	Oakland	AL	76	260	65	13	0	2	(1	1)	84	27	19	22	0	17	0	2	2	4	0	1.00	5	.250	.306	.323
1994	Florida	NL	101	329	97	17	4	3	(0	3)	131	42	30	52	3	23	2	3	2	3	0	1.00	5	.295	.392	.398
1995	Florida	NL	77	184	47	4	0	1	(0	1)	54	21	17	25	0	20	1	1	1	1	1	.50	7	.255	.346	.293
	10 ML YEARS		982	3190	866	135	25	23	(8	15)	1120	431	288	393	14	325	13	78	33	73	45	.62	65	.271	.351	.351

Tom Browning

Pitches: Left **Bats:** Left **Pos:** SP **Ht:** 6' 1" **Wt:** 190 **Born:** 4/28/60 **Age:** 36

						HOW MUCH HE PITCHED					WHAT HE GAVE UP										THE RESULTS			
Year	Team	Lg	G	GS	CG	GF	IP	BFP	H	R	ER	HR	SH	SF	HB	TBB	IBB	SO	WP	Bk	W	L	Pct.	ShO	Sv	ERA
1995	Wichita *	AA	1	1	0	0	6	28	10	5	5	0	0	2	0	1	0	5	0	0	1	0	1.000	0	0	7.50
	Omaha *	AAA	5	5	0	0	21	78	13	8	8	1	1	0	0	5	0	5	1	0	2	1	.667	0	0	3.43
1984	Cincinnati	NL	3	3	0	0	23.1	95	27	4	4	0	1	0	0	5	0	14	1	0	1	0	1.000	0	0	1.54
1985	Cincinnati	NL	38	38	6	0	261.1	1083	242	111	103	29	13	7	3	73	8	155	2	0	20	9	.690	4	0	3.55
1986	Cincinnati	NL	39	39	4	0	243.1	1016	225	123	103	26	14	12	1	70	6	147	3	0	14	13	.519	2	0	3.81
1987	Cincinnati	NL	32	31	2	1	183	791	201	107	102	27	10	7	5	61	7	117	2	0	10	13	.435	0	0	5.02
1988	Cincinnati	NL	36	36	5	0	250.2	1001	205	98	95	36	6	8	7	64	3	124	2	4	18	5	.783	2	0	3.41
1989	Cincinnati	NL	37	37	9	0	249.2	1031	241	109	94	31	12	6	3	64	10	118	2	1	15	12	.556	2	0	3.39
1990	Cincinnati	NL	35	35	2	0	227.2	957	235	98	96	24	13	5	5	52	13	99	5	1	15	9	.625	1	0	3.80
1991	Cincinnati	NL	36	36	1	0	230.1	983	241	124	107	32	8	9	4	56	4	115	3	1	14	14	.500	0	0	4.18
1992	Cincinnati	NL	16	16	0	0	87	386	108	49	49	6	5	4	2	28	7	33	2	1	6	5	.545	0	0	5.07
1993	Cincinnati	NL	21	20	0	0	114	505	159	61	60	15	4	2	1	20	2	53	1	1	7	7	.500	0	0	4.74
1994	Cincinnati	NL	7	7	2	0	40.2	169	34	20	19	8	0	2	1	13	1	22	1	0	3	1	.750	1	0	4.20
1995	Kansas City	AL	2	2	0	0	10	49	13	9	9	2	1	0	0	5	0	3	0	0	0	2	.000	0	0	8.10
	12 ML YEARS		302	300	31	2	1921	8066	1931	913	841	236	87	62	32	511	61	1000	25	13	123	90	.577	12	0	3.94

Jacob Brumfield

Bats: Right **Throws:** Right **Pos:** CF   **Ht:** 6' 0" **Wt:** 185 **Born:** 5/27/65 **Age:** 31

						BATTING													BASERUNNING				PERCENTAGES		
Year Team	Lg	G	AB	H	2B	3B	HR	(Hm	Rd)	TB	R	RBI	TBB	IBB	SO	HBP	SH	SF	SB	CS	SB%	GDP	Avg	OBP	SLG
1995 Carolina *	AA	3	12	5	0	0	2	--	--	11	2	2	1	0	2	0	0	0	0	2	.00	0	.417	.462	.917
1992 Cincinnati	NL	24	30	4	0	0	0	(0	0)	4	6	2	2	1	4	1	0	0	6	0	1.00	0	.133	.212	.133
1993 Cincinnati	NL	103	272	73	17	3	6	(1	5)	114	40	23	21	4	47	1	3	2	20	8	.71	1	.268	.321	.419
1994 Cincinnati	NL	68	122	38	10	2	4	(3	1)	64	36	11	15	0	18	0	2	2	6	3	.67	3	.311	.381	.525
1995 Pittsburgh	NL	116	402	109	23	2	4	(4	0)	148	64	26	37	0	71	5	0	1	22	12	.65	3	.271	.339	.368
4 ML YEARS		311	826	224	50	7	14	(8	6)	330	146	62	75	5	140	7	5	5	54	23	.70	7	.271	.335	.400

Mike Brumley

Bats: Both **Throws:** Right **Pos:** SS   **Ht:** 5'10" **Wt:** 175 **Born:** 4/9/63 **Age:** 33

						BATTING													BASERUNNING				PERCENTAGES		
Year Team	Lg	G	AB	H	2B	3B	HR	(Hm	Rd)	TB	R	RBI	TBB	IBB	SO	HBP	SH	SF	SB	CS	SB%	GDP	Avg	OBP	SLG
1995 Tucson *	AAA	94	330	86	20	10	4	--	--	138	56	33	41	5	67	3	1	3	17	6	.74	8	.261	.345	.418
1987 Chicago	NL	39	104	21	2	2	1	(0	1)	30	8	9	10	1	30	1	1	1	7	1	.88	2	.202	.276	.288
1989 Detroit	AL	92	212	42	5	2	1	(1	0)	54	33	11	14	0	45	1	3	0	8	4	.67	4	.198	.251	.255
1990 Seattle	AL	62	147	33	5	4	0	(0	0)	46	19	7	10	0	22	0	4	1	2	0	1.00	5	.224	.272	.313
1991 Boston	AL	63	118	25	5	0	0	(0	0)	30	16	5	10	0	22	0	4	0	2	0	1.00	0	.212	.273	.254
1992 Boston	AL	2	1	0	0	0	0	(0	0)	0	0	0	0	0	0	0	0	0	0	0	.00	0	.000	.000	.000
1993 Houston	NL	8	10	3	0	0	0	(0	0)	3	1	2	1	0	3	0	0	0	0	1	.00	0	.300	.364	.300
1994 Oakland	AL	11	25	6	0	0	0	(0	0)	6	0	2	1	0	8	0	0	0	0	0	.00	0	.240	.269	.240
1995 Houston	NL	18	18	1	0	0	1	(0	1)	4	1	2	0	0	6	0	0	0	1	0	1.00	0	.056	.056	.222
8 ML YEARS		295	635	131	17	8	3	(1	2)	173	78	38	46	1	136	2	12	2	20	6	.77	11	.206	.261	.272

Jim Bruske

Pitches: Right **Bats:** Right **Pos:** RP   **Ht:** 6' 1" **Wt:** 185 **Born:** 10/7/64 **Age:** 31

		HOW MUCH HE PITCHED						WHAT HE GAVE UP										THE RESULTS					
Year Team	Lg	G	GS	CG	GF	IP	BFP	H	R	ER	HR	SH	SF	HB	TBB	IBB	SO	WP	Bk	W	L	Pct.	ShO	Sv	ERA
1986 Batavia	A	1	0	0	1	1	7	1	2	2	0	0	0	0	3	0	3	2	0	0	0	.000	0	0	18.00
1989 Canton-Akrn	AA	2	0	0	2	2	11	3	3	3	0	0	0	0	2	0	1	1	0	0	0	.000	0	0	13.50
1990 Canton-Akrn	AA	32	13	3	6	118	511	118	53	43	6	2	3	4	42	2	62	5	0	9	3	.750	2	0	3.28
1991 Canton-Akrn	AA	17	11	0	3	80.1	337	73	36	31	3	0	1	2	27	3	35	2	0	5	2	.714	0	1	3.47
Colo. Sprng	AAA	7	1	0	3	25.2	100	19	9	7	3	0	1	0	8	0	13	1	1	4	0	1.000	0	2	2.45
1992 Colo. Sprng	AAA	7	0	0	1	17.2	83	24	11	9	2	0	0	2	6	1	8	2	0	2	0	1.000	0	0	4.58
Jackson	AA	13	9	1	1	61.2	258	54	23	18	2	2	2	4	14	1	48	1	1	4	3	.571	0	0	2.63
1993 Jackson	AA	15	15	1	0	97.1	391	86	34	25	6	1	1	2	22	1	83	2	0	9	5	.643	0	0	2.31
Tucson	AAA	12	9	0	1	66.2	290	77	36	28	4	2	1	0	18	2	42	3	0	4	2	.667	0	0	3.78
1994 Tucson	AAA	7	7	0	0	39	170	47	22	18	2	1	0	1	8	0	25	2	0	3	1	.750	0	0	4.15
1995 Albuquerque	AAA	43	6	0	13	114	492	128	54	52	6	4	4	3	41	2	99	3	0	7	5	.583	0	4	4.11
1995 Los Angeles	NL	9	0	0	3	10	45	12	7	5	0	0	0	1	4	0	5	1	0	0	0	.000	0	1	4.50

Steve Buechele

Bats: Right **Throws:** Right **Pos:** 3B   **Ht:** 6' 2" **Wt:** 200 **Born:** 9/26/61 **Age:** 34

						BATTING													BASERUNNING				PERCENTAGES		
Year Team	Lg	G	AB	H	2B	3B	HR	(Hm	Rd)	TB	R	RBI	TBB	IBB	SO	HBP	SH	SF	SB	CS	SB%	GDP	Avg	OBP	SLG
1995 Okla. City *	AAA	3	13	4	0	0	1	--	--	7	1	3	1	0	1	0	0	0	0	0	.00	0	.308	.357	.538
1985 Texas	AL	69	219	48	6	3	6	(5	1)	78	22	21	14	2	38	2	0	1	3	2	.60	11	.219	.271	.356
1986 Texas	AL	153	461	112	19	2	18	(6	12)	189	54	54	35	1	98	5	0	3	5	8	.38	10	.243	.302	.410
1987 Texas	AL	136	363	86	20	0	13	(6	7)	145	45	50	28	3	66	1	4	4	2	2	.50	7	.237	.290	.399
1988 Texas	AL	155	503	126	21	4	16	(8	8)	203	68	58	65	6	79	5	6	0	2	4	.33	8	.250	.342	.404
1989 Texas	AL	155	486	114	22	2	16	(7	9)	188	60	59	36	0	107	5	2	1	1	3	.25	21	.235	.294	.387
1990 Texas	AL	91	251	54	10	0	7	(5	2)	85	30	30	27	1	63	2	7	2	1	0	1.00	5	.215	.294	.339
1991 Tex-Pit		152	530	139	22	3	22	(9	13)	233	74	85	49	4	97	7	11	3	0	5	.00	14	.262	.331	.440
1992 ChN-Pit	NL	145	524	137	23	4	9	(4	5)	195	52	64	52	6	105	7	4	3	1	3	.25	10	.261	.334	.372
1993 Chicago	NL	133	460	125	27	2	15	(8	7)	201	53	65	48	5	87	5	4	3	1	1	.50	12	.272	.345	.437
1994 Chicago	NL	104	339	82	11	1	14	(7	7)	137	33	52	39	2	80	4	2	3	1	0	1.00	8	.242	.325	.404
1995 ChN-Tex		41	130	23	2	0	1	(0	1)	28	10	9	15	1	22	0	0	0	0	0	.00	1	.177	.262	.215
1991 Texas	AL	121	416	111	17	2	18	(7	11)	186	58	66	39	4	69	5	10	2	0	4	.00	11	.267	.335	.447
Pittsburgh	NL	31	114	28	5	1	4	(2	2)	47	16	19	10	0	28	2	1	1	0	1	.00	3	.246	.315	.412
1992 Chicago	NL	65	239	66	9	3	1	(0	1)	84	25	21	18	2	44	5	2	1	1	1	.50	5	.276	.338	.351
Pittsburgh	NL	80	285	71	14	1	8	(3	5)	111	27	43	34	4	61	2	2	2	0	2	.00	5	.249	.331	.389
1995 Chicago	NL	32	106	20	2	0	1	(0	1)	25	10	9	11	0	19	0	0	0	0	0	.00	1	.189	.265	.236
Texas	AL	9	24	3	0	0	0	(0	0)	3	0	0	4	1	3	0	0	0	0	0	.00	0	.125	.250	.125
11 ML YEARS		1334	4266	1046	183	21	137	(65	72)	1682	501	547	408	31	842	43	50	23	17	28	.38	107	.245	.316	.394

33

Damon Buford

Bats: Right **Throws:** Right **Pos:** CF/LF   **Ht:** 5'10" **Wt:** 170 **Born:** 6/12/70 **Age:** 26

Year Team	Lg	G	AB	H	2B	3B	HR	(Hm	Rd)	TB	R	RBI	TBB	IBB	SO	HBP	SH	SF	SB	CS	SB%	GDP	Avg	OBP	SLG
1995 Rochester *	AAA	46	188	58	12	3	4	--	--	88	40	18	17	0	26	1	1	1	17	4	.81	2	.309	.367	.468
1993 Baltimore	AL	53	79	18	5	0	2	(0	2)	29	18	9	9	0	19	1	1	0	2	2	.50	1	.228	.315	.367
1994 Baltimore	AL	4	2	1	0	0	0	(0	0)	1	2	0	0	0	1	0	0	0	0	0	.00	0	.500	.500	.500
1995 Bal-NYN		68	168	34	5	0	4	(2	2)	51	30	14	25	0	35	5	3	3	10	8	.56	3	.202	.318	.304
1995 Baltimore	AL	24	32	2	0	0	0	(0	0)	2	6	2	6	0	7	0	3	1	3	1	.75	0	.063	.205	.063
New York	NL	44	136	32	5	0	4	(2	2)	49	24	12	19	0	28	5	0	2	7	7	.50	3	.235	.346	.360
3 ML YEARS		125	249	53	10	0	6	(2	4)	81	50	23	34	0	55	6	4	3	12	10	.55	4	.213	.318	.325

Jay Buhner

Bats: Right **Throws:** Right **Pos:** RF   **Ht:** 6' 3" **Wt:** 210 **Born:** 8/13/64 **Age:** 31

Year Team	Lg	G	AB	H	2B	3B	HR	(Hm	Rd)	TB	R	RBI	TBB	IBB	SO	HBP	SH	SF	SB	CS	SB%	GDP	Avg	OBP	SLG
1987 New York	AL	7	22	5	2	0	0	(0	0)	7	0	1	1	0	6	0	0	0	0	0	.00	1	.227	.261	.318
1988 NYA-Sea	AL	85	261	56	13	1	13	(8	5)	110	36	38	28	1	93	6	1	3	1	1	.50	5	.215	.302	.421
1989 Seattle	AL	58	204	56	15	1	9	(7	2)	100	27	33	19	0	55	2	0	1	1	4	.20	0	.275	.341	.490
1990 Seattle	AL	51	163	45	12	0	7	(2	5)	78	16	33	17	1	50	4	0	1	2	2	.50	6	.276	.357	.479
1991 Seattle	AL	137	406	99	14	4	27	(14	13)	202	64	77	53	5	117	6	2	4	0	1	.00	10	.244	.337	.498
1992 Seattle	AL	152	543	132	16	3	25	(9	16)	229	69	79	71	2	146	6	1	8	0	6	.00	12	.243	.333	.422
1993 Seattle	AL	158	563	153	28	3	27	(13	14)	268	91	98	100	11	144	2	2	8	2	5	.29	12	.272	.379	.476
1994 Seattle	AL	101	358	100	23	4	21	(8	13)	194	74	68	66	3	63	5	2	5	0	1	.00	7	.279	.394	.542
1995 Seattle	AL	126	470	123	23	0	40	(21	19)	266	86	121	60	7	120	1	2	6	0	1	.00	15	.262	.343	.566
1988 New York	AL	25	69	13	0	0	3	(1	2)	22	8	13	3	0	25	3	0	1	0	0	.00	1	.188	.250	.319
Seattle		60	192	43	13	1	10	(7	3)	88	28	25	25	1	68	3	1	2	1	1	.50	4	.224	.320	.458
9 ML YEARS		875	2990	769	146	16	169	(82	87)	1454	463	548	415	30	794	32	10	36	6	21	.22	68	.257	.350	.486

Scott Bullett

Bats: Left **Throws:** Left **Pos:** LF/CF   **Ht:** 6' 2" **Wt:** 215 **Born:** 12/25/68 **Age:** 27

Year Team	Lg	G	AB	H	2B	3B	HR	(Hm	Rd)	TB	R	RBI	TBB	IBB	SO	HBP	SH	SF	SB	CS	SB%	GDP	Avg	OBP	SLG
1988 Pirates	R	21	61	11	1	0	0	--	--	12	6	8	7	1	9	0	1	1	2	5	.29	0	.180	.261	.197
1989 Pirates	R	46	165	42	7	3	1	--	--	58	24	16	12	2	31	5	1	0	15	5	.75	2	.255	.324	.352
1990 Welland	A	74	256	77	11	4	3	--	--	105	46	33	13	2	50	2	1	0	30	6	.83	7	.301	.339	.410
1991 Augusta	A	95	384	109	21	6	1	--	--	145	61	36	27	2	79	2	1	1	48	17	.74	1	.284	.333	.378
Salem	A	39	156	52	7	5	2	--	--	75	22	15	8	1	29	0	0	0	15	7	.68	0	.333	.366	.481
1992 Carolina	AA	132	518	140	20	5	8	--	--	194	59	45	28	5	98	10	2	7	29	21	.58	7	.270	.316	.375
Buffalo	AAA	3	10	4	0	2	0	--	--	8	1	0	0	0	2	0	0	0	0	0	.00	0	.400	.400	.800
1993 Buffalo	AAA	110	408	117	13	6	1	--	--	145	62	30	39	0	67	1	8	0	28	17	.62	5	.287	.350	.355
1994 Iowa	AAA	135	530	163	28	4	13	--	--	238	75	69	19	4	110	5	11	6	27	16	.63	5	.308	.334	.449
1991 Pittsburgh	NL	11	4	0	0	0	0	(0	0)	0	2	0	0	0	3	1	0	0	1	1	.50	0	.000	.200	.000
1993 Pittsburgh	NL	23	55	11	0	2	0	(0	0)	15	2	4	3	0	15	0	0	1	3	2	.60	1	.200	.237	.273
1995 Chicago	NL	104	150	41	5	7	3	(2	1)	69	19	22	12	2	30	1	1	0	8	3	.73	4	.273	.331	.460
3 ML YEARS		138	209	52	5	9	3	(2	1)	84	23	26	15	2	48	2	1	1	12	6	.67	5	.249	.304	.402

Jim Bullinger

Pitches: Right **Bats:** Right **Pos:** SP   **Ht:** 6' 2" **Wt:** 185 **Born:** 8/21/65 **Age:** 30

			HOW MUCH HE PITCHED					WHAT HE GAVE UP										THE RESULTS				
Year Team	Lg	G	GS	CG	GF	IP	BFP	H	R	ER	HR	SH	SF	HB	TBB	IBB	SO	WP	Bk	W	L	Pct.	ShO	Sv	ERA
1995 Orlando *	AA	1	1	0	0	4	16	3	0	0	0	0	0	0	1	0	2	0	0	0	0	.000	0	0	0.00
1992 Chicago	NL	39	9	1	15	85	380	72	49	44	9	9	4	4	54	6	36	4	0	2	8	.200	0	7	4.66
1993 Chicago	NL	15	0	0	6	16.2	75	18	9	8	1	0	1	0	9	0	10	0	0	1	0	1.000	0	1	4.32
1994 Chicago	NL	33	10	1	10	100	412	87	43	40	6	3	3	1	34	2	72	4	1	6	2	.750	0	2	3.60
1995 Chicago	NL	24	24	1	0	150	665	152	80	69	14	12	5	1	65	7	93	5	1	12	8	.600	1	0	4.14
4 ML YEARS		111	43	3	31	351.2	1532	329	181	161	30	24	13	14	162	15	211	13	2	21	18	.538	1	10	4.12

Mel Bunch

Pitches: Right **Bats:** Right **Pos:** RP/SP   **Ht:** 6' 1" **Wt:** 165 **Born:** 11/4/71 **Age:** 24

			HOW MUCH HE PITCHED					WHAT HE GAVE UP										THE RESULTS				
Year Team	Lg	G	GS	CG	GF	IP	BFP	H	R	ER	HR	SH	SF	HB	TBB	IBB	SO	WP	Bk	W	L	Pct.	ShO	Sv	ERA
1992 Royals	R	5	4	0	1	24	87	11	6	4	2	0	0	1	3	0	26	0	0	2	1	.667	0	0	1.50
Eugene	A	10	10	0	0	64.2	265	62	23	20	5	2	2	1	13	0	69	2	1	5	3	.625	0	0	2.78
1993 Rockford	A	19	11	1	8	85	337	79	24	20	4	7	3	2	18	0	71	6	1	6	4	.600	0	4	2.12
Wilmington	A	10	10	1	0	65.2	256	52	22	17	3	1	2	1	14	0	54	2	0	5	3	.625	0	0	2.33
1994 Wilmington	A	15	12	0	0	61	252	52	30	23	4	0	0	1	15	0	62	2	0	5	3	.625	0	0	3.39

Year Team	Lg	G	GS	CG	GF	IP	BFP	H	R	ER	HR	SH	SF	HB	TBB	IBB	SO	WP	Bk	W	L	Pct.	ShO	Sv	ERA
1995 Omaha	AAA	12	11	1	0	65	272	63	37	33	10	3	4	0	20	2	50	8	1	1	7	.125	0	0	4.57
1995 Kansas City	AL	13	5	0	3	40	175	42	25	25	11	0	0	0	14	1	19	6	0	1	3	.250	0	0	5.63

Dave Burba

Pitches: Right **Bats:** Right **Pos:** RP/SP **Ht:** 6' 4" **Wt:** 240 **Born:** 7/7/66 **Age:** 29

		HOW MUCH HE PITCHED						WHAT HE GAVE UP												THE RESULTS					
Year Team	Lg	G	GS	CG	GF	IP	BFP	H	R	ER	HR	SH	SF	HB	TBB	IBB	SO	WP	Bk	W	L	Pct.	ShO	Sv	ERA
1990 Seattle	AL	6	0	0	2	8	35	8	6	4	0	2	0	1	2	0	4	0	0	0	0	.000	0	0	4.50
1991 Seattle	AL	22	2	0	11	36.2	153	34	16	15	6	0	0	0	14	3	16	1	0	2	2	.500	0	1	3.68
1992 San Francisco	NL	23	11	0	4	70.2	318	80	43	39	4	2	4	2	31	2	47	1	1	2	7	.222	0	0	4.97
1993 San Francisco	NL	54	5	0	9	95.1	408	95	49	45	14	6	3	3	37	5	88	4	0	10	3	.769	0	0	4.25
1994 San Francisco	NL	57	0	0	13	74	322	59	39	36	5	3	1	6	45	3	84	3	0	3	6	.333	0	0	4.38
1995 SF-Cin	NL	52	9	1	7	106.2	451	90	50	47	9	4	1	0	51	3	96	5	0	10	4	.714	1	0	3.97
1995 San Francisco	NL	37	0	0	7	43.1	191	38	26	24	5	3	1	0	25	2	46	2	0	4	2	.667	0	0	4.98
Cincinnati	NL	15	9	1	0	63.1	260	52	24	23	4	1	0	0	26	1	50	3	0	6	2	.750	1	0	3.27
6 ML YEARS		214	27	1	46	391.1	1687	366	203	186	38	17	9	12	180	16	335	14	1	27	22	.551	1	1	4.28

Enrique Burgos

Pitches: Left **Bats:** Left **Pos:** RP **Ht:** 6' 4" **Wt:** 195 **Born:** 10/7/65 **Age:** 30

		HOW MUCH HE PITCHED						WHAT HE GAVE UP												THE RESULTS					
Year Team	Lg	G	GS	CG	GF	IP	BFP	H	R	ER	HR	SH	SF	HB	TBB	IBB	SO	WP	Bk	W	L	Pct.	ShO	Sv	ERA
1993 Omaha	AAA	48	0	0	26	62.2	263	36	26	22	4	2	3	1	37	0	91	9	0	2	4	.333	0	9	3.16
1994 Omaha	AAA	57	0	0	45	56.1	248	44	24	18	5	2	1	1	33	3	68	8	1	1	4	.200	0	19	2.88
1995 Phoenix	AAA	41	2	0	13	58.2	273	63	44	40	7	5	3	0	40	5	77	4	1	2	6	.250	0	2	6.14
1993 Kansas City	AL	5	0	0	3	5	28	5	5	5	0	0	0	1	6	1	6	3	0	0	1	.000	0	0	9.00
1995 San Francisco	NL	5	0	0	2	8.1	44	14	8	8	1	0	0	1	6	0	12	2	0	0	0	.000	0	0	8.64
2 ML YEARS		10	0	0	5	13.1	72	19	13	13	1	0	0	2	12	1	18	5	0	0	1	.000	0	0	8.78

John Burkett

Pitches: Right **Bats:** Right **Pos:** SP **Ht:** 6' 3" **Wt:** 211 **Born:** 11/28/64 **Age:** 31

		HOW MUCH HE PITCHED						WHAT HE GAVE UP												THE RESULTS					
Year Team	Lg	G	GS	CG	GF	IP	BFP	H	R	ER	HR	SH	SF	HB	TBB	IBB	SO	WP	Bk	W	L	Pct.	ShO	Sv	ERA
1987 San Francisco	NL	3	0	0	1	6	28	7	4	3	2	1	0	1	3	0	5	0	0	0	0	.000	0	0	4.50
1990 San Francisco	NL	33	32	2	1	204	857	201	92	86	18	6	5	4	61	7	118	3	3	14	7	.667	0	1	3.79
1991 San Francisco	NL	36	34	3	0	206.2	890	223	103	96	19	8	8	10	60	2	131	5	0	12	11	.522	1	0	4.18
1992 San Francisco	NL	32	32	3	0	189.2	799	194	96	81	13	11	4	4	45	6	107	0	0	13	9	.591	1	0	3.84
1993 San Francisco	NL	34	34	2	0	231.2	942	224	100	94	18	8	4	11	40	4	145	1	2	22	7	.759	1	0	3.65
1994 San Francisco	NL	25	25	0	0	159.1	676	176	72	64	14	12	5	7	36	7	85	2	0	6	8	.429	0	0	3.62
1995 Florida	NL	30	30	4	0	188.1	810	208	95	90	22	10	0	6	57	5	126	2	1	14	14	.500	0	0	4.30
7 ML YEARS		193	187	14	2	1185.2	5002	1233	562	514	106	56	26	43	302	31	717	13	6	81	56	.591	3	1	3.90

Ellis Burks

Bats: Right **Throws:** Right **Pos:** CF/LF **Ht:** 6' 2" **Wt:** 205 **Born:** 9/11/64 **Age:** 31

		BATTING															BASERUNNING				PERCENTAGES		
Year Team	Lg	G	AB	H	2B	3B	HR	(Hm | Rd)	TB	R	RBI	TBB	IBB	SO	HBP	SH	SF	SB	CS	SB%	GDP	Avg	OBP	SLG
1995 Colo. Sprng *	AAA	8	29	9	2	1	2	--	--	19	9	6	4	0	8	0	0	0	0	0	.00	1	.310	.394	.655
1987 Boston	AL	133	558	152	30	2	20	(11 | 9)	246	94	59	41	0	98	2	4	1	27	6	.82	1	.272	.324	.441
1988 Boston	AL	144	540	159	37	5	18	(8 | 10)	260	93	92	62	1	89	3	4	6	25	9	.74	8	.294	.367	.481
1989 Boston	AL	97	399	121	19	6	12	(6 | 6)	188	73	61	36	2	52	5	2	4	21	5	.81	8	.303	.365	.471
1990 Boston	AL	152	588	174	33	8	21	(10 | 11)	286	89	89	48	4	82	1	2	2	9	11	.45	18	.296	.349	.486
1991 Boston	AL	130	474	119	33	3	14	(8 | 6)	200	56	56	39	2	81	6	2	3	6	11	.35	7	.251	.314	.422
1992 Boston	AL	66	235	60	8	3	8	(4 | 4)	98	35	30	25	2	48	1	0	4	5	2	.71	5	.255	.327	.417
1993 Chicago	AL	146	499	137	24	4	17	(7 | 10)	220	75	74	60	2	97	4	3	8	6	9	.40	11	.275	.352	.441
1994 Colorado	NL	42	149	48	8	3	13	(7 | 6)	101	33	24	16	3	39	0	0	0	3	1	.75	3	.322	.388	.678
1995 Colorado	NL	103	278	74	10	6	14	(8 | 6)	138	41	49	39	0	72	2	1	1	7	3	.70	7	.266	.359	.496
9 ML YEARS		1013	3720	1044	202	40	137	(69 | 68)	1737	589	534	366	16	658	24	18	27	109	57	.66	68	.281	.347	.467

Jeromy Burnitz

Bats: Left **Throws:** Right **Pos:** LF **Ht:** 6' 0" **Wt:** 190 **Born:** 4/15/69 **Age:** 27

		BATTING															BASERUNNING				PERCENTAGES		
Year Team	Lg	G	AB	H	2B	3B	HR	(Hm	Rd)	TB	R	RBI	TBB	IBB	SO	HBP	SH	SF	SB	CS	SB%	GDP	Avg	OBP	SLG
1995 Buffalo *	AAA	128	443	126	26	7	19	--	--	223	72	85	50	8	83	3	1	3	13	5	.72	6	.284	.359	.503
1993 New York	NL	86	263	64	10	6	13	(6	7)	125	49	38	38	4	66	1	2	2	3	6	.33	2	.243	.339	.475
1994 New York	NL	45	143	34	4	0	3	(2	1)	47	26	15	23	0	45	1	1	0	1	1	.50	2	.238	.347	.329
1995 Cleveland	AL	9	7	4	1	0	0	(0	0)	5	4	0	0	0	0	0	0	0	0	0	.00	0	.571	.571	.714
3 ML YEARS		140	413	102	15	6	16	(8	8)	177	79	53	61	4	111	2	3	2	4	7	.36	4	.247	.345	.429

Terry Burrows

Pitches: Left **Bats:** Left **Pos:** RP/SP 　　　　**Ht:** 6' 0" **Wt:** 195 **Born:** 11/28/68 **Age:** 27

Year Team	Lg	G	GS	CG	GF	IP	BFP	H	R	ER	HR	SH	SF	HB	TBB	IBB	SO	WP	Bk	W	L	Pct.	ShO	Sv	ERA
1990 Butte	R	14	11	1	1	62.2	275	56	35	28	1	3	1	0	35	0	64	6	2	3	6	.333	0	0	4.02
1991 Gastonia	A	27	26	0	0	147.2	614	107	79	73	11	3	0	5	78	0	151	6	6	12	8	.600	0	0	4.45
1992 Charlotte	A	14	14	0	0	80	327	71	22	18	2	2	1	4	25	1	66	5	4	4	2	.667	0	0	2.03
Tulsa	AA	14	13	1	0	76	314	66	22	18	3	0	0	0	35	0	59	4	0	6	3	.667	0	0	2.13
Okla. City	AAA	1	1	0	0	8	30	3	1	1	1	0	0	0	5	0	2	0	0	1	0	1.000	0	0	1.13
1993 Okla. City	AAA	27	25	1	0	138	645	171	107	98	19	8	7	2	76	0	74	8	5	7	15	.318	0	0	6.39
1994 Okla. City	AAA	44	5	0	15	82.1	353	75	43	39	9	4	3	4	37	3	57	4	5	3	5	.375	0	1	4.26
1995 Okla. City	AAA	5	0	0	0	2.2	16	5	4	3	0	0	0	0	2	0	4	1	0	0	0	.000	0	0	10.13
1994 Texas	AL	1	0	0	0	1	5	1	1	1	1	0	0	0	1	0	0	0	0	0	0	.000	0	0	9.00
1995 Texas	AL	28	3	0	6	44.2	207	60	37	32	11	0	0	2	19	0	22	4	0	2	2	.500	0	1	6.45
2 ML YEARS		29	3	0	6	45.2	212	61	38	33	12	0	0	2	20	0	22	4	0	2	2	.500	0	1	6.50

Mike Busch

Bats: Right **Throws:** Right **Pos:** 3B 　　　　**Ht:** 6' 5" **Wt:** 225 **Born:** 7/7/68 **Age:** 27

Year Team	Lg	G	AB	H	2B	3B	HR	(Hm	Rd)	TB	R	RBI	TBB	IBB	SO	HBP	SH	SF	SB	CS	SB%	GDP	Avg	OBP	SLG
1990 Great Falls	R	61	220	72	18	2	13	--	--	133	48	47	39	2	50	3	0	3	3	2	.60	8	.327	.430	.605
1991 Bakersfield	A	21	72	20	3	1	4	--	--	37	13	16	12	0	21	0	0	1	0	1	.00	1	.278	.376	.514
1992 San Antonio	AA	115	416	99	14	2	18	--	--	171	58	51	36	2	111	4	0	3	3	2	.60	7	.238	.303	.411
1993 Albuquerque	AAA	122	431	122	32	4	22	--	--	228	87	70	53	4	89	8	0	5	1	2	.33	12	.283	.368	.529
1994 Albuquerque	AAA	126	460	121	23	3	27	--	--	231	73	83	50	0	101	4	0	1	2	3	.40	8	.263	.340	.502
1995 Albuquerque	AAA	121	443	119	32	1	18	--	--	207	68	62	42	3	103	7	0	0	2	2	.50	12	.269	.341	.467
1995 Los Angeles	NL	13	17	4	0	0	3	(0	3)	13	3	6	0	0	7	0	0	0	0	0	.00	0	.235	.235	.765

Mike Butcher

Pitches: Right **Bats:** Right **Pos:** RP 　　　　**Ht:** 6' 1" **Wt:** 200 **Born:** 5/10/66 **Age:** 30

Year Team	Lg	G	GS	CG	GF	IP	BFP	H	R	ER	HR	SH	SF	HB	TBB	IBB	SO	WP	Bk	W	L	Pct.	ShO	Sv	ERA
1992 California	AL	19	0	0	6	27.2	125	29	11	10	3	0	0	2	13	1	24	0	0	2	2	.500	0	0	3.25
1993 California	AL	23	0	0	11	28.1	124	21	12	9	2	1	3	2	15	1	24	0	0	1	0	1.000	0	8	2.86
1994 California	AL	33	0	0	12	29.2	140	31	24	22	2	2	0	2	23	5	19	2	0	2	1	.667	0	1	6.67
1995 California	AL	40	0	0	13	51.1	227	49	28	27	7	1	3	1	31	2	29	3	0	6	1	.857	0	0	4.73
4 ML YEARS		115	0	0	42	137	616	130	75	68	14	4	6	7	82	9	96	5	0	11	4	.733	0	9	4.47

Brett Butler

Bats: Left **Throws:** Left **Pos:** CF 　　　　**Ht:** 5'10" **Wt:** 161 **Born:** 6/15/57 **Age:** 39

Year Team	Lg	G	AB	H	2B	3B	HR	(Hm	Rd)	TB	R	RBI	TBB	IBB	SO	HBP	SH	SF	SB	CS	SB%	GDP	Avg	OBP	SLG
1981 Atlanta	NL	40	126	32	2	3	0	(0	0)	40	17	4	19	0	17	0	0	0	9	1	.90	0	.254	.352	.317
1982 Atlanta	NL	89	240	52	2	0	0	(0	0)	54	35	7	25	0	35	0	3	0	21	8	.72	1	.217	.291	.225
1983 Atlanta	NL	151	549	154	21	13	5	(1	4)	216	84	37	54	3	56	2	3	5	39	23	.63	5	.281	.344	.393
1984 Cleveland	AL	159	602	162	25	9	3	(1	2)	214	108	49	86	1	62	4	11	6	52	22	.70	6	.269	.361	.355
1985 Cleveland	AL	152	591	184	28	14	5	(1	4)	255	106	50	63	2	42	1	8	3	47	20	.70	8	.311	.377	.431
1986 Cleveland	AL	161	587	163	17	14	4	(0	4)	220	92	51	70	1	65	4	17	5	32	15	.68	8	.278	.356	.375
1987 Cleveland	AL	137	522	154	25	8	9	(4	5)	222	91	41	91	0	55	1	2	2	33	16	.67	3	.295	.399	.425
1988 San Francisco	NL	157	568	163	27	9	6	(1	5)	226	109	43	97	4	64	4	8	2	43	20	.68	2	.287	.393	.398
1989 San Francisco	NL	154	594	168	22	4	4	(2	2)	210	100	36	59	2	69	3	13	3	31	16	.66	4	.283	.349	.354
1990 San Francisco	NL	160	622	192	20	9	3	(3	0)	239	108	44	90	1	62	6	7	7	51	19	.73	3	.309	.397	.384
1991 Los Angeles	NL	161	615	182	13	5	2	(2	0)	211	112	38	108	4	79	1	4	2	38	28	.58	3	.296	.401	.343
1992 Los Angeles	NL	157	553	171	14	11	3	(1	2)	216	86	39	95	2	67	3	24	1	41	21	.66	4	.309	.413	.391
1993 Los Angeles	NL	156	607	181	21	10	1	(0	1)	225	80	42	86	1	69	5	14	4	39	19	.67	6	.298	.387	.371
1994 Los Angeles	NL	111	417	131	13	9	8	(2	6)	186	79	33	68	0	52	2	2	2	27	8	.77	2	.314	.411	.446
1995 NYN-LA	NL	129	513	154	18	9	1	(0	1)	193	78	38	67	2	51	0	10	6	32	8	.80	5	.300	.377	.376
1995 New York	NL	90	367	114	13	7	1	(0	1)	144	54	25	43	2	42	0	6	2	21	7	.75	4	.311	.381	.392
Los Angeles	NL	39	146	40	5	2	0	(0	0)	49	24	13	24	0	9	0	4	4	11	1	.92	1	.274	.368	.336
15 ML YEARS		2074	7706	2243	268	127	54	(21	33)	2927	1285	552	1078	23	845	36	131	48	535	244	.69	60	.291	.379	.380

Paul Byrd

Pitches: Right **Bats:** Right **Pos:** RP 　　　　**Ht:** 6' 1" **Wt:** 185 **Born:** 12/3/70 **Age:** 25

Year Team	Lg	G	GS	CG	GF	IP	BFP	H	R	ER	HR	SH	SF	HB	TBB	IBB	SO	WP	Bk	W	L	Pct.	ShO	Sv	ERA
1991 Kinston	A	14	11	0	0	62.2	263	40	27	22	7	3	3	0	36	0	62	6	7	4	3	.571	0	0	3.16

36

Year	Team	Lg	G	GS	CG	GF	IP	BFP	H	R	ER	HR	SH	SF	HB	TBB	IBB	SO	WP	Bk	W	L	Pct.	ShO	Sv	ERA
1992	Canton-Akrn	AA	24	24	4	0	152.1	654	122	68	51	4	5	4	4	75	2	118	10	0	14	6	.700	0	0	3.01
1993	Canton-Akrn	AA	2	1	0	1	10	41	7	4	4	1	0	1	0	3	0	8	1	0	0	0	.000	0	0	3.60
	Charlotte	AAA	14	14	1	0	81	351	80	43	35	9	1	3	6	30	0	54	4	1	7	4	.636	1	0	3.89
1994	Canton-Akrn	AA	21	20	4	0	139.1	594	135	70	59	10	5	5	2	52	3	106	1	2	5	9	.357	1	0	3.81
	Charlotte	AAA	9	4	0	2	36.2	149	33	19	16	5	3	3	0	11	1	15	3	0	2	2	.500	0	1	3.93
1995	Norfolk	AAA	22	10	1	10	87	341	71	29	27	6	0	1	5	21	0	61	1	0	3	5	.375	0	6	2.79
1995	New York	NL	17	0	0	6	22	91	18	6	5	1	0	2	1	7	1	26	1	2	2	0	1.000	0	0	2.05

Edgar Caceres

Bats: Both **Throws:** Right **Pos:** 2B **Ht:** 6' 1" **Wt:** 170 **Born:** 6/6/64 **Age:** 32

			BATTING																BASERUNNING				PERCENTAGES		
Year	Team	Lg	G	AB	H	2B	3B	HR	(Hm | Rd)	TB	R	RBI	TBB	IBB	SO	HBP	SH	SF	SB	CS	SB%	GDP	Avg	OBP	SLG
1984	Dodgers	R	20	77	23	3	1	0	--	--	28	11	11	10	0	6	0	1	0	5	2	.71	0	.299	.379	.364
1985	Dodgers	R	53	176	53	6	0	0	--	--	59	37	22	18	1	11	2	2	0	5	2	.71	4	.301	.372	.335
1986	W. Palm Bch	A	111	382	106	9	5	0	--	--	125	52	37	24	2	28	2	4	4	25	6	.81	4	.277	.320	.327
1987	Jacksonvlle	AA	18	62	8	0	1	0	--	--	10	7	3	3	0	7	0	0	0	2	0	1.00	2	.129	.169	.161
	W. Palm Bch	A	105	390	105	14	1	2	--	--	127	55	37	24	0	30	5	7	1	30	5	.86	4	.269	.324	.326
1988	Rockford	A	36	117	31	2	0	0	--	--	33	25	8	12	0	12	0	5	1	13	3	.81	2	.265	.331	.282
	Tampa	A	32	74	15	2	0	1	--	--	20	5	8	10	2	8	1	2	3	3	0	1.00	2	.203	.295	.270
1989	Sarasota	A	106	373	110	16	4	0	--	--	134	45	50	24	4	38	2	9	2	8	3	.73	12	.295	.339	.359
1990	Birmingham	AA	62	213	56	5	1	0	--	--	63	31	17	16	0	26	1	3	1	7	4	.64	7	.263	.296	.296
1992	El Paso	AA	114	378	118	14	6	2	--	--	150	50	52	23	4	41	2	5	1	9	2	.82	8	.312	.354	.397
1993	New Orleans	AAA	114	420	133	20	2	5	--	--	172	73	45	35	5	39	1	3	3	7	4	.64	14	.317	.368	.410
1994	Omaha	AAA	67	236	64	7	3	2	--	--	83	39	18	16	1	23	0	6	3	5	3	.63	7	.271	.314	.352
1995	Omaha	AAA	37	107	22	3	1	0	--	--	27	13	12	8	3	10	0	1	1	3	1	.75	2	.206	.259	.252
1995	Kansas City	AL	55	117	28	6	2	1	(0 | 1)	41	13	17	8	0	15	1	3	1	2	2	.50	3	.239	.291	.350

Mike Cameron

Bats: Right **Throws:** Right **Pos:** RF **Ht:** 6' 2" **Wt:** 190 **Born:** 1/8/73 **Age:** 23

			BATTING																BASERUNNING				PERCENTAGES		
Year	Team	Lg	G	AB	H	2B	3B	HR	(Hm | Rd)	TB	R	RBI	TBB	IBB	SO	HBP	SH	SF	SB	CS	SB%	GDP	Avg	OBP	SLG
1991	White Sox	R	44	136	30	3	0	0	--	--	33	21	11	17	0	29	4	1	0	13	2	.87	3	.221	.325	.243
1992	Utica	A	28	87	24	1	4	2	--	--	39	15	12	11	0	26	0	1	1	3	7	.30	0	.276	.354	.448
	South Bend	A	35	114	26	8	1	1	--	--	39	19	9	10	0	37	4	3	1	2	3	.40	0	.228	.310	.342
1993	South Bend	A	122	411	98	14	5	0	--	--	122	52	30	27	0	101	6	2	5	19	10	.66	8	.238	.292	.297
1994	Pr. William	A	131	468	116	15	17	6	--	--	183	86	48	60	2	101	8	2	0	22	10	.69	6	.248	.343	.391
1995	Birmingham	AA	107	350	87	20	5	11	--	--	150	64	60	54	0	104	6	5	4	21	12	.64	9	.249	.355	.429
1995	Chicago	AL	28	38	7	2	0	1	(0 | 1)	12	4	2	3	0	15	0	3	0	0	0	.00	0	.184	.244	.316

Ken Caminiti

Bats: Both **Throws:** Right **Pos:** 3B **Ht:** 6' 0" **Wt:** 200 **Born:** 4/21/63 **Age:** 33

			BATTING																BASERUNNING				PERCENTAGES		
Year	Team	Lg	G	AB	H	2B	3B	HR	(Hm | Rd)	TB	R	RBI	TBB	IBB	SO	HBP	SH	SF	SB	CS	SB%	GDP	Avg	OBP	SLG
1987	Houston	NL	63	203	50	7	1	3	(2 | 1)	68	10	23	12	1	44	0	2	1	0	0	.00	6	.246	.287	.335
1988	Houston	NL	30	83	15	2	0	1	(0 | 1)	20	5	7	5	0	18	0	0	1	0	0	.00	3	.181	.225	.241
1989	Houston	NL	161	585	149	31	3	10	(3 | 7)	216	71	72	51	9	93	3	3	4	4	1	.80	8	.255	.316	.369
1990	Houston	NL	153	541	131	20	2	4	(2 | 2)	167	52	51	48	7	97	0	3	4	9	4	.69	15	.242	.302	.309
1991	Houston	NL	152	574	145	30	3	13	(9 | 4)	220	65	80	46	7	85	5	3	4	4	5	.44	18	.253	.312	.383
1992	Houston	NL	135	506	149	31	2	13	(7 | 6)	223	68	62	44	13	68	1	2	4	10	4	.71	14	.294	.350	.441
1993	Houston	NL	143	543	142	31	0	13	(5 | 8)	212	75	75	49	10	88	0	1	3	8	5	.62	15	.262	.321	.390
1994	Houston	NL	111	406	115	28	2	18	(6 | 12)	201	63	75	43	13	71	2	0	3	4	3	.57	8	.283	.352	.495
1995	San Diego	NL	143	526	159	33	0	26	(16 | 10)	270	74	94	69	8	94	1	0	6	12	5	.71	11	.302	.380	.513
	9 ML YEARS		1091	3967	1055	213	13	101	(50 | 51)	1597	483	539	367	68	658	12	14	30	51	27	.65	98	.266	.328	.403

Kevin Campbell

Pitches: Right **Bats:** Right **Pos:** RP **Ht:** 6' 2" **Wt:** 231 **Born:** 12/6/64 **Age:** 31

			HOW MUCH HE PITCHED						WHAT HE GAVE UP											THE RESULTS					
Year	Team	Lg	G	GS	CG	GF	IP	BFP	H	R	ER	HR	SH	SF	HB	TBB	IBB	SO	WP	Bk	W	L	Pct.	ShO	Sv	ERA
1995	Tacoma *	AAA	31	0	0	8	49	211	50	28	20	6	0	2	5	14	3	34	3	1	3	2	.600	0	1	3.67
1991	Oakland	AL	14	0	0	2	23	94	13	7	7	4	1	0	1	14	0	16	0	0	1	0	1.000	0	0	2.74
1992	Oakland	AL	32	5	0	6	65	297	66	39	37	4	3	2	0	45	3	38	2	0	2	3	.400	0	1	5.12
1993	Oakland	AL	11	0	0	4	16	77	20	13	13	1	0	1	1	11	1	9	0	0	0	0		0	0	7.31
1994	Minnesota	AL	14	0	0	5	24.2	97	20	8	8	2	2	3	1	5	0	15	2	0	1	0	1.000	0	0	2.92
1995	Minnesota	AL	6	0	0	1	9.2	39	8	5	5	0	0	0	0	5	0	5	1	0	0	0	.000	0	0	4.66
	5 ML YEARS		77	5	0	18	138.1	604	127	72	70	11	6	6	3	80	4	83	5	0	4	3	.571	0	1	4.55

Tom Candiotti

Pitches: Right **Bats:** Right **Pos:** SP **Ht:** 6' 2" **Wt:** 221 **Born:** 8/31/57 **Age:** 38

Year Team	Lg	HOW MUCH HE PITCHED						WHAT HE GAVE UP										THE RESULTS					
		G	GS	CG	GF	IP	BFP	H	R	ER	HR	SH	SF	HB	TBB	IBB	SO	WP	Bk	W	L	Pct.	ShO	Sv	ERA
1983 Milwaukee	AL	10	8	2	1	55.2	233	62	21	20	4	0	2	2	16	0	21	0	0	4	4	.500	1	0	3.23
1984 Milwaukee	AL	8	6	0	0	32.1	147	38	21	19	5	0	0	0	10	0	23	1	0	2	2	.500	0	0	5.29
1986 Cleveland	AL	36	34	17	1	252.1	1078	234	112	100	18	3	9	8	106	0	167	12	4	16	12	.571	3	0	3.57
1987 Cleveland	AL	32	32	7	0	201.2	888	193	132	107	28	8	10	4	93	2	111	13	2	7	18	.280	2	0	4.78
1988 Cleveland	AL	31	31	11	0	216.2	903	225	86	79	15	12	5	6	53	3	137	5	7	14	8	.636	1	0	3.28
1989 Cleveland	AL	31	31	4	0	206	847	188	80	71	10	6	4	4	55	5	124	4	8	13	10	.565	0	0	3.10
1990 Cleveland	AL	31	29	3	1	202	856	207	92	82	23	4	3	6	55	1	128	9	3	15	11	.577	1	0	3.65
1991 Cle-Tor	AL	34	34	6	0	238	981	202	82	70	12	4	11	6	73	1	167	11	0	13	13	.500	0	0	2.65
1992 Los Angeles	NL	32	30	6	1	203.2	839	177	78	68	13	20	6	3	63	5	152	9	2	11	15	.423	2	0	3.00
1993 Los Angeles	NL	33	32	2	0	213.2	898	192	86	74	12	15	9	6	71	1	155	6	0	8	10	.444	0	0	3.12
1994 Los Angeles	NL	23	22	5	0	153	652	149	77	70	9	9	8	5	54	2	102	9	0	7	7	.500	0	0	4.12
1995 Los Angeles	NL	30	30	1	0	190.1	812	187	93	74	18	7	5	9	58	2	141	7	0	7	14	.333	1	0	3.50
1991 Cleveland	AL	15	15	3	0	108.1	442	88	35	27	6	1	7	2	28	0	86	6	0	7	6	.538	0	0	2.24
Toronto	AL	19	19	3	0	129.2	539	114	47	43	6	3	4	4	45	1	81	5	0	6	7	.462	0	0	2.98
12 ML YEARS		331	319	64	4	2165.1	9134	2054	960	834	167	88	72	59	707	22	1428	86	26	117	124	.485	11	0	3.47

John Cangelosi

Bats: Both **Throws:** Left **Pos:** CF/LF **Ht:** 5' 8" **Wt:** 160 **Born:** 3/10/63 **Age:** 33

Year Team	Lg	BATTING																		BASERUNNING				PERCENTAGES		
		G	AB	H	2B	3B	HR	(Hm	Rd)	TB	R	RBI	TBB	IBB	SO	HBP	SH	SF	SB	CS	SB%	GDP	Avg	OBP	SLG
1995 Tucson *	AAA	30	106	39	4	1	0	--	--	45	18	9	19	2	11	0	3	0	11	3	.79	1	.368	.464	.425
1985 Chicago	AL	5	2	0	0	0	0	(0	0)	0	2	0	0	0	1	1	1	0	0	0	.00	0	.000	.333	.000
1986 Chicago	AL	137	438	103	16	3	2	(1	1)	131	65	32	71	0	61	7	6	3	50	17	.75	5	.235	.349	.299
1987 Pittsburgh	NL	104	182	50	8	3	4	(2	2)	76	44	18	46	1	33	3	1	1	21	6	.78	3	.275	.427	.418
1988 Pittsburgh	NL	75	118	30	4	1	0	(0	0)	36	18	8	17	0	16	1	3	0	9	4	.69	0	.254	.353	.305
1989 Pittsburgh	NL	112	160	35	4	2	0	(0	0)	43	18	9	35	2	20	3	1	2	11	8	.58	1	.219	.365	.269
1990 Pittsburgh	NL	58	76	15	2	0	0	(0	0)	17	13	1	11	0	12	1	2	0	7	2	.78	3	.197	.307	.224
1992 Texas	AL	73	85	16	2	0	1	(0	1)	21	12	6	18	0	16	0	3	0	6	5	.55	0	.188	.330	.247
1994 New York	NL	62	111	28	4	0	0	(0	0)	32	14	4	19	1	20	2	3	0	5	1	.83	1	.252	.371	.288
1995 Houston	NL	90	201	64	5	2	2	(2	0)	79	46	18	48	2	42	4	2	1	21	5	.81	3	.318	.457	.393
9 ML YEARS		716	1373	341	45	11	9	(5	4)	435	232	96	265	6	221	22	22	7	130	48	.73	15	.248	.377	.317

Jose Canseco

Bats: Right **Throws:** Right **Pos:** DH **Ht:** 6' 4" **Wt:** 235 **Born:** 7/2/64 **Age:** 31

Year Team	Lg	BATTING																		BASERUNNING				PERCENTAGES		
		G	AB	H	2B	3B	HR	(Hm	Rd)	TB	R	RBI	TBB	IBB	SO	HBP	SH	SF	SB	CS	SB%	GDP	Avg	OBP	SLG
1995 Pawtucket *	AAA	2	6	1	0	0	0	--	--	1	1	1	1	0	5	0	0	1	0	0	.00	0	.167	.250	.167
1985 Oakland	AL	29	96	29	3	0	5	(4	1)	47	16	13	4	0	31	0	0	0	1	1	.50	1	.302	.330	.490
1986 Oakland	AL	157	600	144	29	1	33	(14	19)	274	85	117	65	1	175	8	0	9	15	7	.68	12	.240	.318	.457
1987 Oakland	AL	159	630	162	35	3	31	(16	15)	296	81	113	50	2	157	2	0	9	15	3	.83	16	.257	.310	.470
1988 Oakland	AL	158	610	187	34	0	42	(16	26)	347	120	124	78	10	128	10	1	6	40	16	.71	15	.307	.391	.569
1989 Oakland	AL	65	227	61	9	1	17	(8	9)	123	40	57	23	4	69	2	0	6	6	3	.67	4	.269	.333	.542
1990 Oakland	AL	131	481	132	14	2	37	(18	19)	261	83	101	72	8	158	5	0	5	19	10	.66	9	.274	.371	.543
1991 Oakland	AL	154	572	152	32	1	44	(16	28)	318	115	122	78	8	152	9	0	6	26	6	.81	16	.266	.359	.556
1992 Oak-Tex	AL	119	439	107	15	0	26	(15	11)	200	74	87	63	2	128	6	0	4	6	7	.46	16	.244	.344	.456
1993 Texas	AL	60	231	59	14	1	10	(6	4)	105	30	46	16	2	62	3	0	3	6	6	.50	6	.255	.308	.455
1994 Texas	AL	111	429	121	19	2	31	(17	14)	237	88	90	69	8	114	5	0	2	15	8	.65	20	.282	.386	.552
1995 Boston	AL	102	396	121	25	1	24	(10	14)	220	64	81	42	4	93	7	0	5	4	0	1.00	9	.306	.378	.556
1992 Oakland	AL	97	366	90	11	0	22	(12	10)	167	66	72	48	1	104	3	0	4	5	7	.42	15	.246	.335	.456
Texas	AL	22	73	17	4	0	4	(3	1)	33	8	15	15	1	24	3	0	0	1	0	1.00	1	.233	.385	.452
11 ML YEARS		1245	4711	1275	229	12	300	(140	160)	2428	796	951	560	49	1267	57	1	55	153	67	.70	124	.271	.351	.515

Ramon Caraballo

Bats: Both **Throws:** Right **Pos:** 2B **Ht:** 5' 7" **Wt:** 150 **Born:** 5/23/69 **Age:** 27

Year Team	Lg	BATTING																		BASERUNNING				PERCENTAGES		
		G	AB	H	2B	3B	HR	(Hm	Rd)	TB	R	RBI	TBB	IBB	SO	HBP	SH	SF	SB	CS	SB%	GDP	Avg	OBP	SLG
1989 Braves	R	20	77	19	3	1	1	--	--	27	9	10	10	0	14	0	1	1	5	4	.56	0	.247	.330	.351
Sumter	A	45	171	45	10	5	1	--	--	68	22	32	16	0	38	2	1	3	9	4	.69	5	.263	.328	.398
1990 Burlington	A	102	390	113	18	14	7	--	--	180	84	54	49	2	69	7	2	2	41	20	.67	9	.290	.377	.462
1991 Durham	A	120	444	111	13	8	6	--	--	158	73	52	38	1	91	3	3	2	53	23	.70	5	.250	.312	.356
1992 Greenville	AA	24	93	29	4	4	1	--	--	44	15	8	14	0	13	0	0	1	10	6	.63	1	.312	.398	.473
Richmond	AAA	101	405	114	20	3	2	--	--	146	42	40	22	1	60	3	7	1	19	16	.54	6	.281	.323	.360

Year Team	Lg	G	AB	H	2B	3B	HR	(Hm	Rd)	TB	R	RBI	TBB	IBB	SO	HBP	SH	SF	SB	CS	SB%	GDP	Avg	OBP	SLG
1993 Richmond	AAA	126	470	128	25	9	3	--	--	180	73	41	30	3	81	7	7	5	20	14	.59	3	.272	.322	.383
1994 Richmond	AAA	22	75	10	1	0	0	--	--	11	5	0	7	0	12	1	0	0	4	4	.50	1	.133	.217	.147
Greenville	AA	72	243	58	4	6	9	--	--	101	32	30	12	1	46	7	2	5	4	7	.36	3	.239	.288	.416
1995 Louisville	AAA	69	245	78	10	1	8	--	--	114	38	25	19	1	42	4	4	4	14	4	.78	5	.318	.371	.465
1993 Atlanta	NL	6	0	0	0	0	0	(0	0)	0	0	0	0	0	0	0	0	0	0	0	.00	0	.000	.000	.000
1995 St. Louis	NL	34	99	20	4	1	2	(0	2)	32	10	3	6	0	33	3	2	0	3	2	.60	1	.202	.269	.323
2 ML YEARS		40	99	20	4	1	2	(0	2)	32	10	3	6	0	33	3	2	0	3	2	.60	1	.202	.269	.323

Rafael Carmona

Pitches: Right **Bats:** Left **Pos:** RP/SP **Ht:** 6' 2" **Wt:** 185 **Born:** 10/2/72 **Age:** 23

	HOW MUCH HE PITCHED						WHAT HE GAVE UP											THE RESULTS					
Year Team	Lg	G	GS	CG	GF	IP	BFP	H	R	ER	HR	SH	SF	HB	TBB	IBB	SO	WP	Bk	W	L	Pct.	ShO	Sv	ERA
1993 Bellingham	A	23	0	0	9	35.2	159	33	19	15	1	5	1	1	14	1	30	4	0	2	3	.400	0	2	3.79
1994 Riverside	A	50	0	0	48	67.1	264	48	22	21	3	1	0	4	19	0	63	3	0	8	2	.800	0	21	2.81
1995 Port City	AA	15	0	0	15	15	59	11	5	3	0	1	1	1	3	0	17	2	0	0	1	.000	0	4	1.80
Tacoma	AAA	8	8	1	0	48	212	52	29	27	6	1	2	3	19	1	37	1	3	4	3	.571	1	0	5.06
1995 Seattle	AL	15	3	0	6	47.2	230	55	31	30	9	1	5	2	34	1	28	3	1	2	4	.333	0	1	5.66

Chuck Carr

Bats: Right **Throws:** Right **Pos:** CF **Ht:** 5'10" **Wt:** 165 **Born:** 8/10/68 **Age:** 27

	BATTING																	BASERUNNING				PERCENTAGES		
Year Team	Lg	G	AB	H	2B	3B	HR	(Hm	Rd)	TB	R	RBI	TBB	IBB	SO	HBP	SH	SF	SB	CS	SB%	GDP	Avg	OBP	SLG
1995 Charlotte	AAA	7	23	5	0	1	1	--	--	10	5	2	2	1	0	0	0	0	2	0	1.00	0	.217	.280	.435
1990 New York	NL	4	2	0	0	0	0	(0	0)	0	0	0	0	0	2	0	0	0	1	0	1.00	0	.000	.000	.000
1991 New York	NL	12	11	2	0	0	0	(0	0)	2	1	1	0	0	2	0	0	0	1	0	1.00	0	.182	.182	.182
1992 St. Louis	NL	22	64	14	3	0	0	(0	0)	17	8	3	9	0	6	0	3	0	10	2	.83	0	.219	.315	.266
1993 Florida	NL	142	551	147	19	2	4	(3	1)	182	75	41	49	0	74	2	7	4	58	22	.73	6	.267	.327	.330
1994 Florida	NL	106	433	114	19	2	2	(1	1)	143	61	30	22	1	71	5	6	2	32	8	.80	5	.263	.305	.330
1995 Florida	NL	105	308	70	20	0	2	(1	1)	96	54	20	46	1	49	2	7	2	25	11	.69	2	.227	.330	.312
6 ML YEARS		391	1369	347	61	4	8	(5	3)	440	199	95	126	2	204	9	23	8	127	43	.75	13	.253	.319	.321

Giovanni Carrara

Pitches: Right **Bats:** Right **Pos:** SP/RP **Ht:** 6' 2" **Wt:** 230 **Born:** 3/4/68 **Age:** 28

	HOW MUCH HE PITCHED						WHAT HE GAVE UP											THE RESULTS					
Year Team	Lg	G	GS	CG	GF	IP	BFP	H	R	ER	HR	SH	SF	HB	TBB	IBB	SO	WP	Bk	W	L	Pct.	ShO	Sv	ERA
1991 St. Cathrns	A	15	13	2	0	89.2	363	66	26	16	5	0	4	8	21	0	83	4	2	5	2	.714	2	0	1.61
1992 Dunedin	A	5	4	0	1	23.1	101	22	13	12	1	0	0	2	11	0	16	4	0	0	1	.000	0	0	4.63
Myrtle Bch	A	22	16	1	2	100.1	416	86	40	35	12	0	2	4	36	0	100	9	3	11	7	.611	1	0	3.14
1993 Dunedin	A	27	24	1	1	140.2	601	136	69	54	14	4	4	4	59	0	108	10	0	6	11	.353	0	0	3.45
1994 Knoxville	AA	26	26	1	0	164.1	705	158	85	71	16	2	7	7	59	0	96	9	0	13	7	.650	0	0	3.89
1995 Syracuse	AAA	21	21	0	0	131.2	565	116	72	58	11	3	2	4	56	2	81	3	0	7	7	.500	0	0	3.96
1995 Toronto	AL	12	7	1	2	48.2	229	64	46	39	10	1	2	1	25	1	27	1	0	2	4	.333	0	0	7.21

Hector Carrasco

Pitches: Right **Bats:** Right **Pos:** RP **Ht:** 6' 2" **Wt:** 180 **Born:** 10/22/69 **Age:** 26

	HOW MUCH HE PITCHED						WHAT HE GAVE UP											THE RESULTS					
Year Team	Lg	G	GS	CG	GF	IP	BFP	H	R	ER	HR	SH	SF	HB	TBB	IBB	SO	WP	Bk	W	L	Pct.	ShO	Sv	ERA
1988 Mets	R	14	2	0	3	36.2	166	37	29	17	0	1	2	1	13	0	21	5	0	0	2	.000	0	0	4.17
1989 Kingsport	R	12	10	0	1	53.1	258	69	49	34	6	2	1	1	34	1	55	4	5	1	6	.143	0	0	5.74
1990 Kingsport	R	3	1	0	0	6.2	27	8	3	3	1	0	0	0	1	0	5	2	0	0	0	.000	0	0	4.05
1991 Pittsfield	A	12	1	0	5	23.1	120	25	17	14	1	1	2	1	21	0	20	7	0	0	1	.000	0	1	5.40
1992 Asheville	A	49	0	0	30	78.1	338	66	30	26	5	6	3	3	47	6	67	11	3	5	5	.500	0	8	2.99
1993 Kane County	A	28	28	0	0	149	673	153	90	68	11	6	4	11	76	6	127	12	1	6	12	.333	0	0	4.11
1994 Cincinnati	NL	45	0	0	29	56.1	237	42	17	14	3	5	0	2	30	1	41	3	1	5	6	.455	0	6	2.24
1995 Cincinnati	NL	64	0	0	28	87.1	391	86	45	40	1	2	6	2	46	5	64	15	0	2	7	.222	0	5	4.12
2 ML YEARS		109	0	0	57	143.2	628	128	62	54	4	7	6	4	76	6	105	18	1	7	13	.350	0	11	3.38

Mark Carreon

Bats: Right **Throws:** Left **Pos:** 1B/RF **Ht:** 6' 0" **Wt:** 195 **Born:** 7/9/63 **Age:** 32

	BATTING																	BASERUNNING				PERCENTAGES		
Year Team	Lg	G	AB	H	2B	3B	HR	(Hm	Rd)	TB	R	RBI	TBB	IBB	SO	HBP	SH	SF	SB	CS	SB%	GDP	Avg	OBP	SLG
1987 New York	NL	9	12	3	0	0	0	(0	0)	3	0	1	1	0	1	0	0	0	0	1	.00	0	.250	.308	.250
1988 New York	NL	7	9	5	2	0	1	(0	1)	10	5	1	2	0	1	0	0	0	0	0	.00	0	.556	.636	1.111
1989 New York	NL	68	133	41	6	0	6	(4	2)	65	20	16	12	0	17	1	0	0	2	3	.40	1	.308	.370	.489
1990 New York	NL	82	188	47	12	0	10	(1	9)	89	30	26	15	0	29	2	0	0	1	0	1.00	1	.250	.312	.473
1991 New York	NL	106	254	66	6	0	4	(3	1)	84	18	21	12	2	26	2	1	1	2	1	.67	13	.260	.297	.331

39

Year	Team	Lg	G	AB	H	2B	3B	HR	(Hm	Rd)	TB	R	RBI	TBB	IBB	SO	HBP	SH	SF	SB	CS	SB%	GDP	Avg	OBP	SLG
1992	Detroit	AL	101	336	78	11	1	10	(5	5)	121	34	41	22	2	57	1	1	4	3	1	.75	12	.232	.278	.360
1993	San Francisco	NL	78	150	49	9	1	7	(2	5)	81	22	33	13	2	16	1	0	5	1	0	1.00	8	.327	.373	.540
1994	San Francisco	NL	51	100	27	4	0	3	(2	1)	40	8	20	7	0	20	2	0	2	0	0	.00	1	.270	.324	.400
1995	San Francisco	NL	117	396	119	24	0	17	(7	10)	194	53	65	23	1	37	4	0	3	1		.00	7	.301	.343	.490
9 ML YEARS			619	1578	435	74	2	58	(24	34)	687	190	224	107	7	204	13	2	15	9	7	.56	43	.276	.324	.435

Andy Carter

Pitches: Left **Bats:** Left **Pos:** RP **Ht:** 6' 5" **Wt:** 220 **Born:** 11/9/68 **Age:** 27

Year	Team	Lg	G	GS	CG	GF	IP	BFP	H	R	ER	HR	SH	SF	HB	TBB	IBB	SO	WP	Bk	W	L	Pct.	ShO	Sv	ERA
1987	Utica	A	12	1	0	1	28.2	140	27	25	18	1	1	2	4	19	0	19	2	1	0	1	.000	0	0	5.65
1988	Spartanburg	A	25	25	4	0	156.2	657	110	55	40	7	5	1	6	75	0	99	5	3	11	6	.647	1	0	2.30
1989	Clearwater	A	12	12	2	0	68.2	310	73	46	37	3	4	7	6	32	0	31	5	2	1	5	.167	1	0	4.85
	Spartanburg	A	15	15	1	0	90.2	393	73	38	33	5	2	2	3	51	0	72	7	1	6	5	.545	1	0	3.28
1990	Clearwater	A	26	26	2	0	131	582	121	82	71	8	3	7	9	69	2	90	10	1	4	14	.222	0	0	4.88
1991	Reading	AA	20	20	1	0	102.1	452	86	57	55	10	1	3	8	57	0	64	5	1	11	5	.688	0	0	4.84
1992	Reading	AA	7	6	0	0	25.1	127	37	28	26	3	2	0	1	15	0	17	3	0	0	4	.000	0	0	9.24
	Clearwater	A	16	13	1	1	87	340	60	30	18	2	3	2	4	13	1	68	9	0	3	4	.429	1	0	1.86
1993	Reading	AA	4	4	0	0	22.1	90	15	8	7	1	1	1	1	12	0	16	0	0	1	1	.500	0	0	2.82
	Scranton-Wb	AAA	30	13	0	6	109	462	104	59	55	7	2	4	8	35	0	68	10	1	7	7	.500	0	1	4.54
1994	Scranton-Wb	AAA	25	0	0	14	31	125	22	10	9	1	2	0	1	13	1	27	5	0	1	0	1.000	0	2	2.61
1995	Scranton-Wb	AAA	14	1	0	5	20.2	91	17	10	10	2	0	1	3	13	2	18	1	1	1	2	.333	0	0	4.35
1994	Philadelphia	NL	20	0	0	7	34.1	149	34	18	17	5	1	3	6	12	2	18	0	0	0	2	.000	0	0	4.46
1995	Philadelphia	NL	4	0	0	1	7.1	28	4	5	5	3	0	1	1	2	1	6	0	0	0	0	.000	0	0	6.14
2 ML YEARS			24	0	0	8	41.2	177	38	23	22	8	1	4	7	14	3	24	0	0	0	2	.000	0	0	4.75

Joe Carter

Bats: Right **Throws:** Right **Pos:** LF/CF **Ht:** 6' 3" **Wt:** 215 **Born:** 3/7/60 **Age:** 36

Year	Team	Lg	G	AB	H	2B	3B	HR	(Hm	Rd)	TB	R	RBI	TBB	IBB	SO	HBP	SH	SF	SB	CS	SB%	GDP	Avg	OBP	SLG
1983	Chicago	NL	23	51	9	1	1	0	(0	0)	12	6	1	0	0	21	0	1	0	0	1	1.00	1	.176	.176	.235
1984	Cleveland	AL	66	244	67	6	1	13	(9	4)	114	32	41	11	0	48	1	0	1	2	4	.33	2	.275	.307	.467
1985	Cleveland	AL	143	489	128	27	0	15	(5	10)	200	64	59	25	2	74	2	3	4	24	6	.80	9	.262	.298	.409
1986	Cleveland	AL	162	663	200	36	9	29	(14	15)	341	108	121	32	3	95	5	1	8	29	7	.81	8	.302	.335	.514
1987	Cleveland	AL	149	588	155	27	2	32	(9	23)	282	83	106	27	6	105	9	1	4	31	6	.84	8	.264	.304	.480
1988	Cleveland	AL	157	621	168	36	6	27	(16	11)	297	85	98	35	6	82	7	1	6	27	5	.84	6	.271	.314	.478
1989	Cleveland	AL	162	651	158	32	4	35	(16	19)	303	84	105	39	8	112	8	2	5	13	5	.72	6	.243	.292	.465
1990	San Diego	NL	162	634	147	27	1	24	(12	12)	248	79	115	48	18	93	7	0	8	22	6	.79	12	.232	.290	.391
1991	Toronto	AL	162	638	174	42	3	33	(23	10)	321	89	108	49	12	112	10	0	9	20	9	.69	6	.273	.330	.503
1992	Toronto	AL	158	622	164	30	7	34	(21	13)	310	97	119	36	4	109	11	1	13	12	5	.71	14	.264	.309	.498
1993	Toronto	AL	155	603	153	33	5	33	(21	12)	295	92	121	47	5	113	9	0	10	8	3	.73	10	.254	.312	.489
1994	Toronto	AL	111	435	118	25	2	27	(18	9)	228	70	103	33	6	64	2	0	13	11	0	1.00	6	.271	.317	.524
1995	Toronto	AL	139	558	141	23	0	25	(13	12)	239	70	76	37	5	87	3	0	5	12	1	.92	11	.253	.300	.428
13 ML YEARS			1749	6797	1782	345	41	327	(177	150)	3190	959	1173	419	75	1115	74	10	86	212	57	.79	99	.262	.308	.469

Larry Casian

Pitches: Left **Bats:** Right **Pos:** RP **Ht:** 6' 0" **Wt:** 173 **Born:** 10/28/65 **Age:** 30

Year	Team	Lg	G	GS	CG	GF	IP	BFP	H	R	ER	HR	SH	SF	HB	TBB	IBB	SO	WP	Bk	W	L	Pct.	ShO	Sv	ERA
1995	Iowa *	AAA	13	0	0	4	12.2	48	9	3	3	0	1	1	1	2	1	9	0	0	0	0	.000	0	1	2.13
1990	Minnesota	AL	5	3	0	1	22.1	90	26	9	8	2	0	1	0	4	0	11	0	0	2	1	.667	0	0	3.22
1991	Minnesota	AL	15	0	0	4	18.1	87	28	16	15	4	0	0	1	7	2	6	2	0	0	0	.000	0	0	7.36
1992	Minnesota	AL	6	0	0	1	6.2	28	7	2	2	0	0	0	0	1	0	2	0	0	1	0	1.000	0	0	2.70
1993	Minnesota	AL	54	0	0	4	56.2	241	59	23	19	1	3	3	1	14	2	31	2	0	5	3	.625	0	1	3.02
1994	Cle-Min	AL	40	0	0	10	49	231	73	43	40	12	7	2	2	16	3	20	1	0	1	5	.167	0	1	7.35
1995	Chicago	NL	42	0	0	5	23.1	107	23	6	5	1	1	0	0	15	6	11	0	0	1	0	1.000	0	0	1.93
1994	Cleveland	AL	7	0	0	2	8.1	43	16	9	8	1	1	0	0	4	1	2	1	0	0	2	.000	0	0	8.64
	Minnesota	AL	33	0	0	8	40.2	188	57	34	32	11	6	2	2	12	2	18	0	0	1	3	.250	0	0	7.08
6 ML YEARS			162	3	0	29	176.1	784	216	99	89	20	11	8	4	57	13	81	7	0	10	9	.526	0	2	4.54

Pedro Castellano

Bats: Right **Throws:** Right **Pos:** 3B **Ht:** 6' 1" **Wt:** 180 **Born:** 3/11/70 **Age:** 26

Year	Team	Lg	G	AB	H	2B	3B	HR	(Hm	Rd)	TB	R	RBI	TBB	IBB	SO	HBP	SH	SF	SB	CS	SB%	GDP	Avg	OBP	SLG
1989	Wytheville	R	66	244	76	17	4	9	--	--	128	55	42	46	2	44	3	1	3	5	2	.71	9	.311	.422	.525
1990	Peoria	A	117	417	115	27	4	2	--	--	156	61	44	63	2	72	3	3	4	7	1	.88	9	.276	.372	.374
	Winston-Sal	A	19	66	13	0	0	1	--	--	16	6	8	10	0	11	2	2	0	1	0	1.00	3	.197	.321	.242

	Lg	G	AB	H	2B	3B	HR	(Hm	Rd)	TB	R	RBI	TBB	IBB	SO	HBP	SH	SF	SB	CS	SB%	GDP	Avg	OBP	SLG
1991 Winston-Sal	A	129	459	139	25	3	10	--	--	200	59	88	72	4	97	3	2	5	11	10	.52	13	.303	.397	.436
Charlotte	AA	7	19	8	0	0	0	--	--	8	2	2	1	0	6	1	0	1	0	0	.00	1	.421	.455	.421
1992 Iowa	AAA	74	238	59	14	4	2	--	--	87	25	20	32	0	42	1	8	1	2	2	.50	6	.248	.338	.366
Charlotte	AA	45	147	33	3	0	1	--	--	39	16	15	19	0	21	4	3	2	1	0	1.00	2	.224	.326	.265
1993 Colo. Sprng	AAA	90	304	95	21	2	12	--	--	156	61	60	36	0	63	6	1	8	3	5	.38	8	.313	.387	.513
1994 Colo. Sprng	AAA	33	120	42	11	2	4	--	--	69	23	24	13	1	17	2	0	2	1	1	.50	3	.350	.416	.575
1995 Colo. Sprng	AAA	99	334	89	23	2	9	--	--	143	40	47	24	1	56	2	3	5	2	0	1.00	10	.266	.315	.428
1993 Colorado	NL	34	71	13	2	0	3	(1	2)	24	12	7	8	0	16	0	0	0	1	1	.50	1	.183	.266	.338
1995 Colorado	NL	4	5	0	0	0	0	(0	0)	0	0	0	2	0	3	0	0	0	0	0	.00	0	.000	.286	.000
2 ML YEARS		38	76	13	2	0	3	(1	2)	24	12	7	10	0	19	0	0	0	1	1	.50	1	.171	.267	.316

Vinny Castilla

Bats: Right **Throws:** Right **Pos:** 3B **Ht:** 6' 1" **Wt:** 180 **Born:** 7/4/67 **Age:** 28

			BATTING																BASERUNNING				PERCENTAGES		
Year Team	Lg	G	AB	H	2B	3B	HR	(Hm	Rd)	TB	R	RBI	TBB	IBB	SO	HBP	SH	SF	SB	CS	SB%	GDP	Avg	OBP	SLG
1991 Atlanta	NL	12	5	1	0	0	0	(0	0)	1	1	0	0	0	2	0	1	0	0	0	.00	0	.200	.200	.200
1992 Atlanta	NL	9	16	4	1	0	0	(0	0)	5	1	1	1	1	4	1	0	0	0	0	.00	0	.250	.333	.313
1993 Colorado	NL	105	337	86	9	7	9	(5	4)	136	36	30	13	4	45	2	0	5	2	5	.29	10	.255	.283	.404
1994 Colorado	NL	52	130	43	11	1	3	(1	2)	65	16	18	7	1	23	0	1	3	2	1	.67	3	.331	.357	.500
1995 Colorado	NL	139	527	163	34	2	32	(23	9)	297	82	90	30	2	87	4	4	6	2	8	.20	15	.309	.347	.564
5 ML YEARS		317	1015	297	55	10	44	(29	15)	504	136	139	51	8	161	7	6	14	6	14	.30	28	.293	.327	.497

Alberto Castillo

Bats: Right **Throws:** Right **Pos:** C **Ht:** 6' 0" **Wt:** 184 **Born:** 2/10/70 **Age:** 26

			BATTING																BASERUNNING				PERCENTAGES		
Year Team	Lg	G	AB	H	2B	3B	HR	(Hm	Rd)	TB	R	RBI	TBB	IBB	SO	HBP	SH	SF	SB	CS	SB%	GDP	Avg	OBP	SLG
1987 Kingsport	R	7	9	1	0	0	0	--	--	1	1	0	5	0	3	0	1	0	1	0	1.00	0	.111	.429	.111
1988 Mets	R	22	68	18	4	0	0	--	--	22	7	10	4	0	4	2	2	3	2	0	1.00	3	.265	.312	.324
Kingsport	R	24	75	22	3	0	1	--	--	28	7	14	15	1	14	0	1	1	0	1	.00	1	.293	.407	.373
1989 Kingsport	R	27	74	19	4	0	3	--	--	32	15	12	11	1	14	1	1	0	2	1	.67	2	.257	.360	.432
Pittsfield	A	34	123	29	8	0	1	--	--	40	13	13	7	0	26	1	2	2	2	0	1.00	3	.236	.278	.325
1990 Columbia	A	30	103	24	4	3	1	--	--	37	8	14	10	0	21	0	2	2	1	1	.50	2	.233	.296	.359
Pittsfield	A	58	185	41	8	1	4	--	--	63	19	24	28	2	35	5	1	2	3	3	.50	7	.222	.336	.341
St. Lucie	A	3	11	4	0	0	1	--	--	7	4	3	1	0	1	0	0	0	0	0	.00	2	.364	.417	.636
1991 Columbia	A	90	267	74	20	3	3	--	--	109	35	47	43	0	44	5	6	4	6	6	.50	6	.277	.382	.408
1992 St. Lucie	A	60	162	33	6	0	3	--	--	48	11	17	16	0	37	2	3	2	0	0	.00	4	.204	.280	.296
1993 St. Lucie	A	105	333	86	21	0	5	--	--	122	37	42	28	1	46	3	2	7	0	2	.00	5	.258	.315	.366
1994 Binghamton	AA	90	315	78	14	0	7	--	--	113	33	42	41	0	46	0	3	1	1	3	.25	11	.248	.333	.359
1995 Norfolk	AAA	69	217	58	13	1	4	--	--	85	23	31	26	0	32	1	3	2	2	3	.40	6	.267	.346	.392
1995 New York	NL	13	29	3	0	0	0	(0	0)	3	2	0	3	0	9	1	0	0	1	0	1.00	0	.103	.212	.103

Frank Castillo

Pitches: Right **Bats:** Right **Pos:** SP **Ht:** 6' 1" **Wt:** 190 **Born:** 4/1/69 **Age:** 27

		HOW MUCH HE PITCHED						WHAT HE GAVE UP									THE RESULTS					
Year Team	Lg	G	GS	CG	GF	IP	BFP	H	R	ER	HR	SH	SF	HB	TBB	IBB	SO	WP	Bk	W	L	Pct.	ShO	Sv	ERA
1991 Chicago	NL	18	18	4	0	111.2	467	107	56	54	13	3	3	2	33	2	73	5	1	6	7	.462	0	0	4.35
1992 Chicago	NL	33	33	0	0	205.1	856	179	91	79	19	11	5	6	63	6	135	11	0	10	11	.476	0	0	3.46
1993 Chicago	NL	29	25	2	0	141.1	614	162	83	76	20	10	3	9	39	4	84	5	3	5	8	.385	0	0	4.84
1994 Chicago	NL	4	4	1	0	23	96	25	13	11	3	1	0	0	5	0	19	0	0	2	1	.667	0	0	4.30
1995 Chicago	NL	29	29	2	0	188	795	179	75	67	22	11	3	6	52	4	135	3	1	11	10	.524	2	0	3.21
5 ML YEARS		113	109	9	0	669.1	2828	652	318	287	69	39	14	21	192	16	446	24	5	34	37	.479	2	0	3.86

Tony Castillo

Pitches: Left **Bats:** Left **Pos:** RP **Ht:** 5'10" **Wt:** 190 **Born:** 3/1/63 **Age:** 33

		HOW MUCH HE PITCHED						WHAT HE GAVE UP									THE RESULTS					
Year Team	Lg	G	GS	CG	GF	IP	BFP	H	R	ER	HR	SH	SF	HB	TBB	IBB	SO	WP	Bk	W	L	Pct.	ShO	Sv	ERA
1988 Toronto	AL	14	0	0	6	15	54	10	5	5	2	0	2	0	2	0	14	0	0	1	0	1.000	0	0	3.00
1989 Tor-Atl		29	0	0	9	27	127	31	19	17	0	3	4	1	14	6	15	3	0	1	2	.333	0	1	5.67
1990 Atlanta	NL	52	3	0	7	76.2	337	93	41	36	5	4	4	1	20	3	64	2	2	5	1	.833	0	1	4.23
1991 Atl-NYN	NL	17	3	0	6	32.1	148	40	16	12	4	2	1	0	11	1	18	0	0	2	1	.667	0	0	3.34
1993 Toronto	AL	51	0	0	10	50.2	211	44	19	19	4	5	2	0	22	5	28	1	0	3	2	.600	0	0	3.38
1994 Toronto	AL	41	0	0	8	68	291	66	22	19	7	3	3	3	28	1	43	0	0	5	2	.714	0	1	2.51
1995 Toronto	AL	55	0	0	31	72.2	298	64	27	26	7	3	5	3	24	1	38	0	0	1	5	.167	0	13	3.22
1989 Toronto	AL	17	0	0	8	17.2	86	23	14	12	0	2	4	1	10	5	10	3	0	1	1	.500	0	1	6.11
Atlanta	NL	12	0	0	1	9.1	41	8	5	5	0	1	0	0	4	1	5	0	0	0	1	.000	0	0	4.82
1991 Atlanta	NL	7	0	0	5	8.2	44	13	9	7	3	1	0	0	5	0	8	0	0	1	1	.500	0	0	7.27
New York	NL	10	3	0	1	23.2	104	27	7	5	1	1	1	0	6	1	10	0	0	1	0	1.000	0	0	1.90
7 ML YEARS		259	6	0	77	342.1	1466	348	149	134	29	20	21	8	121	17	220	6	2	18	13	.581	0	16	3.52

Juan Castro

Bats: Right **Throws:** Right **Pos:** 3B   **Ht:** 5'10" **Wt:** 163 **Born:** 6/20/72 **Age:** 24

								BATTING										BASERUNNING				PERCENTAGES		
Year	Team	Lg	G	AB	H	2B	3B	HR	(Hm	Rd)	TB	R	RBI	TBB	IBB	SO	HBP	SH	SF	SB	CS	SB%	GDP	Avg	OBP	SLG
1991	Great Falls	R	60	217	60	4	2	1	--	--	71	36	27	33	1	31	0	3	2	7	6	.54	2	.276	.369	.327
1992	Bakersfield	A	113	446	116	15	4	4	--	--	151	56	42	37	2	64	1	20	7	14	11	.56	7	.260	.314	.339
1993	San Antonio	AA	118	424	117	23	8	7	--	--	177	55	41	30	3	40	2	17	3	12	11	.52	14	.276	.325	.417
1994	San Antonio	AA	123	445	128	25	4	4	--	--	173	55	44	31	2	66	1	10	2	4	7	.36	9	.288	.334	.389
1995	Albuquerque	AAA	104	341	91	18	4	3	--	--	126	51	43	20	3	42	0	7	0	4	4	.50	11	.267	.307	.370
1995	Los Angeles	NL	11	4	1	0	0	0	(0	0)	1	0	0	1	0	1	0	0	0	0	0	.00	0	.250	.400	.250

Andujar Cedeno

Bats: Right **Throws:** Right **Pos:** SS   **Ht:** 6' 1" **Wt:** 170 **Born:** 8/21/69 **Age:** 26

								BATTING										BASERUNNING				PERCENTAGES		
Year	Team	Lg	G	AB	H	2B	3B	HR	(Hm | Rd)	TB	R	RBI	TBB	IBB	SO	HBP	SH	SF	SB	CS	SB%	GDP	Avg	OBP	SLG
1990	Houston	NL	7	8	0	0	0	0	(0 | 0)	0	0	0	0	0	5	0	0	0	0	0	.00	0	.000	.000	.000
1991	Houston	NL	67	251	61	13	2	9	(4 | 5)	105	27	36	9	1	74	1	1	2	4	3	.57	3	.243	.270	.418
1992	Houston	NL	71	220	38	13	2	2	(2 | 0)	61	15	13	14	2	71	3	0	0	2	0	1.00	1	.173	.232	.277
1993	Houston	NL	149	505	143	24	4	11	(6 | 5)	208	69	56	48	9	97	3	4	5	9	7	.56	17	.283	.346	.412
1994	Houston	NL	98	342	90	26	0	9	(5 | 4)	143	38	49	29	15	79	8	0	1	1	1	.50	5	.263	.334	.418
1995	San Diego	NL	120	390	82	16	2	6	(3 | 3)	120	42	31	28	7	92	5	0	1	5	3	.63	12	.210	.271	.308
	6 ML YEARS		512	1716	414	92	10	37	(20 | 17)	637	191	185	128	34	418	20	5	9	21	14	.60	38	.241	.300	.371

Domingo Cedeno

Bats: Both **Throws:** Right **Pos:** SS/2B   **Ht:** 6' 0" **Wt:** 170 **Born:** 11/4/68 **Age:** 27

								BATTING										BASERUNNING				PERCENTAGES		
Year	Team	Lg	G	AB	H	2B	3B	HR	(Hm | Rd)	TB	R	RBI	TBB	IBB	SO	HBP	SH	SF	SB	CS	SB%	GDP	Avg	OBP	SLG
1993	Toronto	AL	15	46	8	0	0	0	(0 | 0)	8	5	7	1	0	10	0	2	1	1	0	1.00	2	.174	.188	.174
1994	Toronto	AL	47	97	19	2	3	0	(0 | 0)	27	14	10	10	0	31	0	3	4	1	2	.33	1	.196	.261	.278
1995	Toronto	AL	51	161	38	6	1	4	(1 | 3)	58	18	14	10	2	35	2	1	0	0	1	.00	3	.236	.289	.360
	3 ML YEARS		113	304	65	8	4	4	(1 | 3)	93	37	31	21	2	76	2	6	5	2	3	.40	6	.214	.265	.306

Roger Cedeno

Bats: Both **Throws:** Right **Pos:** LF/CF   **Ht:** 6' 1" **Wt:** 165 **Born:** 8/16/74 **Age:** 21

								BATTING										BASERUNNING				PERCENTAGES		
Year	Team	Lg	G	AB	H	2B	3B	HR	(Hm	Rd)	TB	R	RBI	TBB	IBB	SO	HBP	SH	SF	SB	CS	SB%	GDP	Avg	OBP	SLG
1992	Great Falls	R	69	256	81	6	5	2	--	--	103	60	27	51	3	53	2	4	2	40	9	.82	4	.316	.431	.402
1993	San Antonio	AA	122	465	134	13	8	4	--	--	175	70	30	45	2	90	1	4	1	28	20	.58	5	.288	.352	.376
	Albuquerque	AAA	6	18	4	1	1	0	--	--	7	1	4	3	0	3	0	0	0	0	1	.00	0	.222	.333	.389
1994	Albuquerque	AAA	104	383	123	18	5	4	--	--	163	84	49	51	0	57	0	3	7	30	13	.70	4	.321	.395	.426
1995	Albuquerque	AAA	99	367	112	19	9	2	--	--	155	67	44	53	2	56	2	4	3	23	18	.56	5	.305	.393	.422
1995	Los Angeles	NL	40	42	10	2	0	0	(0	0)	12	4	3	3	0	10	0	0	1	0	1	1.00	0	.238	.283	.286

Wes Chamberlain

Bats: Right **Throws:** Right **Pos:** RF   **Ht:** 6' 2" **Wt:** 230 **Born:** 4/13/66 **Age:** 30

								BATTING										BASERUNNING				PERCENTAGES		
Year	Team	Lg	G	AB	H	2B	3B	HR	(Hm	Rd)	TB	R	RBI	TBB	IBB	SO	HBP	SH	SF	SB	CS	SB%	GDP	Avg	OBP	SLG
1995	Pawtucket *	AAA	48	183	64	17	1	12	--	--	119	28	40	3	0	45	3	0	1	5	3	.63	3	.350	.368	.650
	Omaha *	AAA	16	64	14	3	0	1	--	--	20	2	6	2	0	15	2	0	1	0	0	.00	4	.219	.261	.313
1990	Philadelphia	NL	18	46	13	3	0	2	(0	2)	22	9	4	1	0	9	0	0	0	4	0	1.00	1	.283	.298	.478
1991	Philadelphia	NL	101	383	92	16	3	13	(9	4)	153	51	50	31	0	73	2	1	0	9	4	.69	8	.240	.300	.399
1992	Philadelphia	NL	76	275	71	18	0	9	(3	6)	116	26	41	10	2	55	1	1	2	4	0	1.00	7	.258	.285	.422
1993	Philadelphia	NL	96	284	80	20	2	12	(5	7)	140	34	45	17	3	51	1	0	1	2	1	.67	8	.282	.320	.493
1994	Bos-Phi		75	233	61	14	1	6	(3	3)	95	20	26	15	2	50	0	0	0	0	2	.00	9	.262	.306	.408
1995	Boston	AL	19	42	5	1	0	1	(1	0)	9	4	1	3	0	11	0	0	0	1	0	1.00	2	.119	.178	.214
1994	Boston	AL	51	164	42	9	1	4	(3	1)	65	13	20	12	2	38	0	0	0	0	2	.00	6	.256	.307	.396
	Philadelphia	NL	24	69	19	5	0	2	(0	2)	30	7	6	3	0	12	0	0	0	0	0	.00	3	.275	.306	.435
	6 ML YEARS		385	1263	322	72	6	43	(21	22)	535	144	167	77	7	249	4	2	6	20	7	.74	34	.255	.299	.424

Norm Charlton

Pitches: Left **Bats:** Both **Pos:** RP   **Ht:** 6' 3" **Wt:** 205 **Born:** 1/6/63 **Age:** 33

							HOW MUCH HE PITCHED						WHAT HE GAVE UP								THE RESULTS				
Year	Team	Lg	G	GS	CG	GF	IP	BFP	H	R	ER	HR	SH	SF	HB	TBB	IBB	SO	WP	Bk	W	L	Pct.	ShO	Sv	ERA
1988	Cincinnati	NL	10	10	0	0	61.1	259	60	27	27	6	1	2	2	20	2	39	3	2	4	5	.444	0	0	3.96
1989	Cincinnati	NL	69	0	0	27	95.1	393	67	38	31	5	9	2	2	40	7	98	2	4	8	3	.727	0	0	2.93
1990	Cincinnati	NL	56	16	1	13	154.1	650	131	53	47	10	7	2	4	70	4	117	9	1	12	9	.571	1	2	2.74

Year Team	Lg	G	GS	CG	GF	IP	BFP	H	R	ER	HR	SH	SF	HB	TBB	IBB	SO	WP	Bk	W	L	Pct.	ShO	Sv	ERA
1991 Cincinnati	NL	39	11	0	10	108.1	438	92	37	35	6	7	1	6	34	4	77	11	0	3	5	.375	0	1	2.91
1992 Cincinnati	NL	64	0	0	46	81.1	341	79	39	27	7	7	3	3	26	4	90	8	0	4	2	.667	0	26	2.99
1993 Seattle	AL	34	0	0	29	34.2	141	22	12	9	4	0	1	0	17	0	48	6	0	1	3	.250	0	18	2.34
1995 Phi-Sea	AL	55	0	0	27	69.2	284	46	31	26	4	4	2	4	31	3	70	6	1	4	6	.400	0	14	3.36
1995 Philadelphia	NL	25	0	0	5	22	102	23	19	18	2	1	1	3	15	3	12	1	0	2	5	.286	0	0	7.36
Seattle	AL	30	0	0	22	47.2	182	23	12	8	2	3	1	1	16	0	58	5	1	2	1	.667	0	14	1.51
7 ML YEARS		327	37	1	152	605	2506	497	237	202	42	35	13	21	238	24	539	45	8	36	33	.522	0	61	3.00

Jason Christiansen

Pitches: Left   **Bats:** Right   **Pos:** RP   **Ht:** 6' 5"   **Wt:** 230   **Born:** 9/21/69   **Age:** 26

		HOW MUCH HE PITCHED						WHAT HE GAVE UP												THE RESULTS					
Year Team	Lg	G	GS	CG	GF	IP	BFP	H	R	ER	HR	SH	SF	HB	TBB	IBB	SO	WP	Bk	W	L	Pct.	ShO	Sv	ERA
1991 Pirates	R	6	0	0	4	8	29	4	0	0	0	0	0	0	1	0	8	0	0	1	0	1.000	0	0	0.00
Welland	A	8	1	0	1	21.1	85	15	9	6	1	0	0	1	12	1	17	5	0	0	1	.000	0	0	2.53
1992 Augusta	A	10	0	0	4	20	73	12	4	4	0	3	0	0	8	0	21	1	0	1	0	1.000	0	2	1.80
Salem	A	38	0	0	15	50	212	47	20	18	7	3	1	1	22	2	59	0	1	3	1	.750	0	2	3.24
1993 Salem	A	57	0	0	22	71.1	287	48	30	25	5	5	1	4	24	2	70	2	0	1	1	.500	0	4	3.15
Carolina	AA	2	0	0	1	2.2	12	3	0	0	0	0	0	0	1	0	2	0	0	0	0	.000	0	0	0.00
1994 Carolina	AA	28	0	0	9	38.2	158	30	10	9	2	3	1	1	14	1	43	2	0	2	1	.667	0	2	2.09
Buffalo	AAA	33	0	0	12	33.2	132	19	9	9	3	1	2	0	16	0	39	1	0	3	1	.750	0	0	2.41
1995 Pittsburgh	NL	63	0	0	13	56.1	255	49	28	26	5	6	3	3	34	9	53	4	1	1	3	.250	0	0	4.15

Mike Christopher

Pitches: Right   **Bats:** Right   **Pos:** RP   **Ht:** 6' 5"   **Wt:** 205   **Born:** 11/3/63   **Age:** 32

		HOW MUCH HE PITCHED						WHAT HE GAVE UP												THE RESULTS					
Year Team	Lg	G	GS	CG	GF	IP	BFP	H	R	ER	HR	SH	SF	HB	TBB	IBB	SO	WP	Bk	W	L	Pct.	ShO	Sv	ERA
1995 Toledo *	AAA	36	0	0	35	36.1	160	38	14	9	1	3	3	1	8	4	32	1	0	2	4	.333	0	21	2.23
1991 Los Angeles	NL	3	0	0	2	4	15	2	0	0	0	0	0	0	3	0	2	0	0	0	0	.000	0	0	0.00
1992 Cleveland	AL	10	0	0	4	18	79	17	8	6	2	1	1	0	10	1	13	2	0	0	0	.000	0	0	3.00
1993 Cleveland	AL	9	0	0	3	11.2	51	14	6	5	3	0	0	0	2	1	8	0	0	0	0	.000	0	0	3.86
1995 Detroit	AL	36	0	0	11	61.1	262	71	28	26	8	1	2	2	14	2	34	5	0	4	0	1.000	0	1	3.82
4 ML YEARS		58	0	0	20	95	407	104	42	37	13	2	3	2	29	4	57	7	0	4	0	1.000	0	1	3.51

Archi Cianfrocco

Bats: Right   **Throws:** Right   **Pos:** 1B/SS   **Ht:** 6' 5"   **Wt:** 215   **Born:** 10/6/66   **Age:** 29

		BATTING																BASERUNNING				PERCENTAGES		
Year Team	Lg	G	AB	H	2B	3B	HR	(Hm Rd)	TB	R	RBI	TBB	IBB	SO	HBP	SH	SF	SB	CS	SB%	GDP	Avg	OBP	SLG
1995 Las Vegas *	AAA	89	322	100	2	10	--	--	154	51	58	16	0	61	3	0	7	5	0	1.00	11	.311	.342	.478
1992 Montreal	NL	86	232	56	5	2	6	(3 3)	83	25	30	11	0	66	1	1	2	3	0	1.00	2	.241	.276	.358
1993 Mon-SD	NL	96	296	72	11	2	12	(6 6)	123	30	48	17	1	69	3	2	5	2	0	1.00	9	.243	.287	.416
1994 San Diego	NL	59	146	32	8	0	4	(1 3)	52	9	13	3	0	39	4	1	2	2	0	1.00	2	.219	.252	.356
1995 San Diego	NL	51	118	31	7	0	5	(1 4)	53	22	31	11	1	28	2	0	1	0	2	.00	3	.263	.333	.449
1993 Montreal	NL	12	17	4	1	0	1	(0 1)	8	3	1	2	0	5	0	0	0	0	0	.00	0	.235	.235	.471
San Diego	NL	84	279	68	10	2	11	(6 5)	115	27	47	17	1	64	3	2	5	2	0	1.00	9	.244	.289	.412
4 ML YEARS		292	792	191	31	4	27	(13 14)	311	86	122	42	2	202	10	4	10	7	2	.78	16	.241	.285	.393

Jeff Cirillo

Bats: Right   **Throws:** Right   **Pos:** 3B/2B   **Ht:** 6' 2"   **Wt:** 188   **Born:** 9/23/69   **Age:** 26

		BATTING																BASERUNNING				PERCENTAGES		
Year Team	Lg	G	AB	H	2B	3B	HR	(Hm Rd)	TB	R	RBI	TBB	IBB	SO	HBP	SH	SF	SB	CS	SB%	GDP	Avg	OBP	SLG
1991 Helena	R	70	286	100	16	2	10	-- --	150	60	51	31	3	29	4	2	2	3	1	.75	11	.350	.418	.524
1992 Stockton	A	7	27	6	1	0	0	-- --	7	2	5	2	0	2	0	0	0	0	0	.00	2	.222	.323	.259
Beloit	A	126	444	135	27	3	9	-- --	195	65	71	84	6	85	6	5	6	21	12	.64	7	.304	.417	.439
1993 El Paso	AA	67	249	85	16	2	9	-- --	132	53	41	26	1	37	5	0	3	2	3	.40	5	.341	.410	.530
New Orleans	AAA	58	215	63	13	2	3	-- --	89	31	32	29	0	33	3	4	0	2	1	.67	7	.293	.385	.414
1994 New Orleans	AAA	61	236	73	18	2	10	-- --	125	45	46	18	1	39	2	1	1	4	0	1.00	4	.309	.386	.530
1994 Milwaukee	AL	39	126	30	9	0	3	(1 2)	48	17	12	11	0	16	2	0	0	0	1	.00	4	.238	.309	.381
1995 Milwaukee	AL	125	328	91	19	4	9	(6 3)	145	57	39	47	0	42	4	1	4	7	2	.78	8	.277	.371	.442
2 ML YEARS		164	454	121	28	4	12	(7 5)	193	74	51	58	0	58	6	1	4	7	3	.70	12	.267	.354	.425

Dave Clark

Bats: Left   **Throws:** Right   **Pos:** LF/RF   **Ht:** 6' 2"   **Wt:** 209   **Born:** 9/3/62   **Age:** 33

		BATTING																BASERUNNING				PERCENTAGES		
Year Team	Lg	G	AB	H	2B	3B	HR	(Hm Rd)	TB	R	RBI	TBB	IBB	SO	HBP	SH	SF	SB	CS	SB%	GDP	Avg	OBP	SLG
1986 Cleveland	AL	18	58	16	1	0	3	(1 2)	26	10	9	7	0	11	0	2	1	1	0	1.00	1	.276	.348	.448
1987 Cleveland	AL	29	87	18	5	0	3	(1 2)	32	11	12	2	0	24	0	0	1	1	0	1.00	4	.207	.225	.368
1988 Cleveland	AL	63	156	41	4	1	3	(2 1)	56	11	18	17	2	28	0	0	1	0	2	.00	8	.263	.333	.359

Year Team	Lg	G	AB	H	2B	3B	HR	(Hm	Rd)	TB	R	RBI	TBB	IBB	SO	HBP	SH	SF	SB	CS	SB%	GDP	Avg	OBP	SLG
1989 Cleveland	AL	102	253	60	12	0	8	(4	4)	96	21	29	30	5	63	0	1	1	0	2	.00	7	.237	.317	.379
1990 Chicago	NL	84	171	47	4	2	5	(3	2)	70	22	20	8	1	40	0	0	2	7	1	.88	4	.275	.304	.409
1991 Kansas City	AL	11	10	2	0	0	0	(0	0)	2	1	1	1	0	1	0	0	0	0	0	.00	0	.200	.273	.200
1992 Pittsburgh	NL	23	33	7	0	0	2	(2	0)	13	3	7	6	0	8	0	0	1	0	0	.00	0	.212	.325	.394
1993 Pittsburgh	NL	110	277	75	11	2	11	(8	3)	123	43	46	38	5	58	1	0	2	1	0	1.00	10	.271	.358	.444
1994 Pittsburgh	NL	86	223	66	11	1	10	(7	3)	109	37	46	22	0	48	0	1	3	2	2	.50	5	.296	.355	.489
1995 Pittsburgh	NL	77	196	55	6	0	4	(2	2)	73	30	24	24	1	38	1	0	2	3	3	.50	9	.281	.359	.372
10 ML YEARS		603	1464	387	54	6	49	(30	19)	600	189	212	155	14	319	2	4	13	15	10	.60	48	.264	.333	.410

Jerald Clark

Bats: Right   **Throws:** Right   **Pos:** LF/1B   **Ht:** 6' 4"   **Wt:** 205   **Born:** 8/10/63   **Age:** 32

			BATTING																BASERUNNING				PERCENTAGES		
Year Team	Lg	G	AB	H	2B	3B	HR	(Hm	Rd)	TB	R	RBI	TBB	IBB	SO	HBP	SH	SF	SB	CS	SB%	GDP	Avg	OBP	SLG
1988 San Diego	NL	6	15	3	1	0	0	(0	0)	4	0	3	0	0	4	0	0	0	0	0	.00	0	.200	.200	.267
1989 San Diego	NL	17	41	8	2	0	1	(1	0)	13	5	7	3	0	9	0	0	0	0	1	.00	0	.195	.250	.317
1990 San Diego	NL	52	101	27	4	1	5	(2	3)	48	12	11	5	0	24	0	0	1	0	0	.00	0	.267	.299	.475
1991 San Diego	NL	118	369	84	16	0	10	(8	2)	130	26	47	31	2	90	6	1	4	2	1	.67	10	.228	.295	.352
1992 San Diego	NL	146	496	120	22	6	12	(9	3)	190	45	58	22	3	97	4	1	3	3	0	1.00	7	.242	.278	.383
1993 Colorado	NL	140	478	135	26	6	13	(8	5)	212	65	67	20	2	60	10	3	1	9	6	.60	12	.282	.324	.444
1995 Minnesota	AL	36	109	37	8	3	3	(1	2)	60	17	15	2	0	11	1	0	1	3	0	1.00	5	.339	.354	.550
7 ML YEARS		515	1609	414	79	16	44	(29	15)	657	170	208	83	7	295	21	5	10	17	8	.68	37	.257	.301	.408

Mark Clark

Pitches: Right   **Bats:** Right   **Pos:** SP   **Ht:** 6' 5"   **Wt:** 225   **Born:** 5/12/68   **Age:** 28

		HOW MUCH HE PITCHED						WHAT HE GAVE UP											THE RESULTS					
Year Team	Lg	G	GS	CG	GF	IP	BFP	H	R	ER	HR	SH	SF	HB	TBB	IBB	SO	WP	Bk	W	L	Pct.	ShO	Sv	ERA
1995 Buffalo *	AAA	5	5	0	0	35.1	151	39	14	14	0	1	2	2	10	0	17	0	0	4	0	1.000	0	0	3.57
1991 St. Louis	NL	7	2	0	1	22.1	93	17	10	10	3	0	3	0	11	0	13	2	0	1	1	.500	0	0	4.03
1992 St. Louis	NL	20	20	1	0	113.1	488	117	59	56	12	7	4	0	36	2	44	4	0	3	10	.231	1	0	4.45
1993 Cleveland	AL	26	15	1	1	109.1	454	119	55	52	18	1	1	1	25	1	57	1	0	7	5	.583	0	0	4.28
1994 Cleveland	AL	20	20	4	0	127.1	540	133	61	54	14	2	7	4	40	0	60	9	1	11	3	.786	1	0	3.82
1995 Cleveland	AL	22	21	2	0	124.2	552	143	77	73	13	3	6	4	42	0	68	8	0	9	7	.563	0	0	5.27
5 ML YEARS		95	78	8	2	497	2127	529	262	245	60	13	21	9	154	3	242	24	1	31	26	.544	2	0	4.44

Phil Clark

Bats: Right   **Throws:** Right   **Pos:** RF/LF   **Ht:** 6' 0"   **Wt:** 200   **Born:** 5/6/68   **Age:** 28

			BATTING																BASERUNNING				PERCENTAGES		
Year Team	Lg	G	AB	H	2B	3B	HR	(Hm	Rd)	TB	R	RBI	TBB	IBB	SO	HBP	SH	SF	SB	CS	SB%	GDP	Avg	OBP	SLG
1992 Detroit	AL	23	54	22	4	0	1	(0	1)	29	3	5	6	1	9	0	1	0	0	1	1.00	0	.407	.467	.537
1993 San Diego	NL	102	240	75	17	0	9	(6	3)	119	33	33	8	2	31	5	1	2	2	1	1.00	2	.313	.345	.496
1994 San Diego	NL	61	149	32	6	0	5	(4	1)	53	14	20	5	1	17	3	0	3	1	2	.33	1	.215	.250	.356
1995 San Diego	NL	75	97	21	3	0	2	(1	1)	30	12	7	8	1	18	1	0	2	0	2	.00	3	.216	.278	.309
4 ML YEARS		261	540	150	30	0	17	(11	6)	231	62	65	27	5	75	9	2	7	4	4	.50	8	.278	.319	.428

Terry Clark

Pitches: Right   **Bats:** Right   **Pos:** RP   **Ht:** 6' 2"   **Wt:** 196   **Born:** 10/10/60   **Age:** 35

		HOW MUCH HE PITCHED						WHAT HE GAVE UP											THE RESULTS					
Year Team	Lg	G	GS	CG	GF	IP	BFP	H	R	ER	HR	SH	SF	HB	TBB	IBB	SO	WP	Bk	W	L	Pct.	ShO	Sv	ERA
1995 Rochester *	AAA	9	0	0	7	10	37	5	3	3	2	0	1	0	2	1	10	0	1	1	2	.333	0	5	2.70
1988 California	AL	15	15	2	0	94	410	120	54	53	8	2	5	0	31	6	39	5	2	6	6	.500	1	0	5.07
1989 California	AL	4	2	0	2	11	48	13	8	6	0	2	1	0	3	0	7	2	1	0	0	.000	0	0	4.91
1990 Houston	NL	1	1	0	0	4	25	9	7	6	0	1	0	0	3	0	2	0	0	0	0	.000	0	0	13.50
1995 Atl-Bal		41	0	0	13	42.2	184	43	17	17	3	4	1	1	20	5	20	2	0	2	5	.286	0	1	3.59
1995 Atlanta	NL	3	0	0	1	3.2	18	3	2	2	0	0	0	0	5	0	2	1	0	0	0	.000	0	0	4.91
Baltimore	AL	38	0	0	12	39	166	40	15	15	3	4	1	1	15	5	18	1	0	2	5	.286	0	1	3.46
4 ML YEARS		61	18	2	15	151.2	667	185	86	82	11	9	7	1	57	11	68	9	3	8	13	.381	1	1	4.87

Tony Clark

Bats: Both   **Throws:** Right   **Pos:** 1B   **Ht:** 6' 7"   **Wt:** 240   **Born:** 6/15/72   **Age:** 24

			BATTING																BASERUNNING				PERCENTAGES		
Year Team	Lg	G	AB	H	2B	3B	HR	(Hm	Rd)	TB	R	RBI	TBB	IBB	SO	HBP	SH	SF	SB	CS	SB%	GDP	Avg	OBP	SLG
1990 Bristol	R	25	73	12	2	0	1	--	--	17	2	8	6	0	28	1	0	0	0	0	.00	0	.164	.238	.233
1992 Niagara Fal	A	27	85	26	9	0	5	--	--	50	12	17	9	0	34	1	0	0	1	0	1.00	0	.306	.372	.588
1993 Lakeland	A	36	117	31	4	1	1	--	--	40	14	22	18	2	32	0	2	2	0	1	.00	1	.265	.358	.342
1994 Trenton	AA	107	394	110	25	0	21	--	--	198	50	86	40	5	113	1	0	2	0	4	.00	9	.279	.346	.503
Toledo	AAA	25	92	24	4	0	2	--	--	34	10	13	12	1	25	0	0	2	2	0	1.00	1	.261	.340	.370

Year Team		Lg	G	AB	H	2B	3B	HR	(Hm	Rd)	TB	R	RBI	TBB	IBB	SO	HBP	SH	SF	SB	CS	SB%	GDP	Avg	OBP	SLG
1995 Toledo	AAA	110	405	98	17	2	14	--	--	161	50	63	52	1	129	3	0	3	0	2	.00	8	.242	.330	.398
1995 Detroit	AL	27	101	24	5	1	3	(0	3)	40	10	11	8	0	30	0	0	0	0	0	.00	2	.238	.294	.396

Will Clark

Bats: Left **Throws:** Left **Pos:** 1B **Ht:** 6' 1" **Wt:** 196 **Born:** 3/13/64 **Age:** 32

Year Team		Lg	G	AB	H	2B	3B	HR	(Hm	Rd)	TB	R	RBI	TBB	IBB	SO	HBP	SH	SF	SB	CS	SB%	GDP	Avg	OBP	SLG
1986 San Francisco		NL	111	408	117	27	2	11	(7	4)	181	66	41	34	10	76	3	9	4	4	7	.36	3	.287	.343	.444
1987 San Francisco		NL	150	529	163	29	5	35	(22	13)	307	89	91	49	11	98	5	3	2	5	17	.23	2	.308	.371	.580
1988 San Francisco		NL	162	575	162	31	6	29	(14	15)	292	102	109	100	27	129	4	0	10	9	1	.90	9	.282	.386	.508
1989 San Francisco		NL	159	588	196	38	9	23	(9	14)	321	104	111	74	14	103	5	0	8	8	3	.73	6	.333	.407	.546
1990 San Francisco		NL	154	600	177	25	5	19	(8	11)	269	91	95	62	9	97	3	0	13	8	2	.80	7	.295	.357	.448
1991 San Francisco		NL	148	565	170	32	7	29	(17	12)	303	84	116	51	12	91	2	0	4	4	2	.67	5	.301	.359	.536
1992 San Francisco		NL	144	513	154	40	1	16	(11	5)	244	69	73	73	23	82	4	0	11	12	7	.63	5	.300	.384	.476
1993 San Francisco		NL	132	491	139	27	2	14	(5	9)	212	82	73	63	6	68	6	1	6	2	2	.50	10	.283	.367	.432
1994 Texas		AL	110	389	128	24	2	13	(9	4)	195	73	80	71	11	59	3	0	6	5	1	.83	5	.329	.431	.501
1995 Texas		AL	123	454	137	27	3	16	(10	6)	218	85	92	68	6	50	4	0	11	0	1	.00	7	.302	.389	.480
10 ML YEARS			1393	5112	1543	300	42	205	(112	93)	2542	845	881	645	129	853	39	13	75	57	43	.57	59	.302	.379	.497

Royce Clayton

Bats: Right **Throws:** Right **Pos:** SS **Ht:** 6' 0" **Wt:** 183 **Born:** 1/2/70 **Age:** 26

Year Team		Lg	G	AB	H	2B	3B	HR	(Hm	Rd)	TB	R	RBI	TBB	IBB	SO	HBP	SH	SF	SB	CS	SB%	GDP	Avg	OBP	SLG
1991 San Francisco		NL	9	26	3	1	0	0	(0	0)	4	0	2	1	0	6	0	0	0	0	0	.00	1	.115	.148	.154
1992 San Francisco		NL	98	321	72	7	4	4	(3	1)	99	31	24	26	3	63	0	3	2	8	4	.67	11	.224	.281	.308
1993 San Francisco		NL	153	549	155	21	5	6	(5	1)	204	54	70	38	2	91	5	8	7	11	10	.52	16	.282	.331	.372
1994 San Francisco		NL	108	385	91	14	6	3	(1	2)	126	38	30	30	2	74	3	3	2	23	3	.88	7	.236	.295	.327
1995 San Francisco		NL	138	509	124	29	3	5	(2	3)	174	56	58	38	1	109	3	4	3	24	9	.73	7	.244	.298	.342
5 ML YEARS			506	1790	445	72	18	18	(11	7)	607	179	184	133	8	343	11	18	14	66	26	.72	42	.249	.302	.339

Roger Clemens

Pitches: Right **Bats:** Right **Pos:** SP **Ht:** 6' 4" **Wt:** 225 **Born:** 8/4/62 **Age:** 33

Year Team		Lg	G	GS	CG	GF	IP	BFP	H	R	ER	HR	SH	SF	HB	TBB	IBB	SO	WP	Bk	W	L	Pct.	ShO	Sv	ERA
1995 Sarasota *	A	1	1	0	0	4	14	0	0	0	0	0	0	0	2	0	7	0	0	0	0	.000	0	0	0.00
Pawtucket *	AAA	1	1	0	0	5	19	1	0	0	0	0	0	0	3	0	5	0	0	0	0	.000	0	0	0.00
1984 Boston	AL	21	20	5	0	133.1	575	146	67	64	13	2	3	2	29	3	126	4	0	9	4	.692	1	0	4.32
1985 Boston	AL	15	15	3	0	98.1	407	83	38	36	5	1	2	3	37	0	74	1	3	7	5	.583	1	0	3.29
1986 Boston	AL	33	33	10	0	254	997	179	77	70	21	4	6	4	67	0	238	11	3	24	4	.857	1	0	2.48
1987 Boston	AL	36	36	18	0	281.2	1157	248	100	93	19	6	4	9	83	4	256	4	3	20	9	.690	7	0	2.97
1988 Boston	AL	35	35	14	0	264	1063	217	93	86	17	6	3	6	62	4	291	4	7	18	12	.600	8	0	2.93
1989 Boston	AL	35	35	8	0	253.1	1044	215	101	88	20	9	5	8	93	5	230	7	0	17	11	.607	3	0	3.13
1990 Boston	AL	31	31	7	0	228.1	920	193	59	49	7	7	5	7	54	3	209	8	0	21	6	.778	4	0	1.93
1991 Boston	AL	35	35	13	0	271.1	1077	219	93	79	15	6	8	5	65	12	241	6	0	18	10	.643	4	0	2.62
1992 Boston	AL	32	32	11	0	246.2	989	203	80	66	11	5	5	9	62	5	208	3	0	18	11	.621	5	0	2.41
1993 Boston	AL	29	29	2	0	191.2	808	175	99	95	17	5	7	11	67	4	160	3	1	11	14	.440	1	0	4.46
1994 Boston	AL	24	24	3	0	170.2	692	124	62	54	15	2	5	4	71	1	168	4	0	9	7	.563	1	0	2.85
1995 Boston	AL	23	23	0	0	140	623	141	70	65	15	2	3	14	60	0	132	9	0	10	5	.667	0	0	4.18
12 ML YEARS		349	348	94	0	2533.1	10352	2143	939	845	175	55	56	82	750	41	2333	64	17	182	98	.650	36	0	3.00

Brad Clontz

Pitches: Right **Bats:** Right **Pos:** RP **Ht:** 6' 1" **Wt:** 180 **Born:** 4/25/71 **Age:** 25

Year Team		Lg	G	GS	CG	GF	IP	BFP	H	R	ER	HR	SH	SF	HB	TBB	IBB	SO	WP	Bk	W	L	Pct.	ShO	Sv	ERA
1992 Pulaski	R	4	0	0	3	5.2	23	3	1	1	0	0	0	2	2	0	7	1	0	0	0	.000	0	1	1.59
Macon	A	17	0	0	14	23	103	19	14	10	2	2	1	3	10	0	18	1	0	2	1	.667	0	2	3.91
1993 Durham	A	51	0	0	38	75.1	325	69	32	23	5	8	0	4	26	1	79	6	0	1	7	.125	0	10	2.75
1994 Greenville	AA	39	0	0	38	45	178	32	13	6	5	3	1	1	10	2	49	2	0	1	2	.333	0	27	1.20
Richmond	AAA	24	0	0	22	25.2	101	19	6	6	1	0	1	0	9	2	21	0	0	0	0	.000	0	11	2.10
1995 Atlanta	NL	59	0	0	14	69	295	71	29	28	5	3	2	4	22	4	55	0	0	8	1	.889	0	4	3.65

Greg Colbrunn

Bats: Right **Throws:** Right **Pos:** 1B **Ht:** 6' 0" **Wt:** 200 **Born:** 7/26/69 **Age:** 26

Year Team		Lg	G	AB	H	2B	3B	HR	(Hm	Rd)	TB	R	RBI	TBB	IBB	SO	HBP	SH	SF	SB	CS	SB%	GDP	Avg	OBP	SLG
1992 Montreal		NL	52	168	45	8	0	2	(1	1)	59	12	18	6	1	34	2	0	4	3	2	.60	1	.268	.294	.351

Year Team	Lg	G	AB	H	2B	3B	HR	(Hm	Rd)	TB	R	RBI	TBB	IBB	SO	HBP	SH	SF	SB	CS	SB%	GDP	Avg	OBP	SLG
1993 Montreal	NL	70	153	39	9	0	4	(2	2)	60	15	23	6	1	33	1	1	3	4	2	.67	1	.255	.282	.392
1994 Florida	NL	47	155	47	10	0	6	(3	3)	75	17	31	9	0	27	2	0	2	1	1	.50	3	.303	.345	.484
1995 Florida	NL	138	528	146	22	1	23	(12	11)	239	70	89	22	4	69	6	0	4	11	3	.79	15	.277	.311	.453
4 ML YEARS		307	1004	277	49	1	35	(18	17)	433	114	161	43	6	163	11	1	13	19	8	.70	20	.276	.309	.431

Alex Cole

Bats: Left   **Throws:** Left   **Pos:** CF   **Ht:** 6' 0"   **Wt:** 184   **Born:** 8/17/65   **Age:** 30

Year Team	Lg	G	AB	H	2B	3B	HR	(Hm	Rd)	TB	R	RBI	TBB	IBB	SO	HBP	SH	SF	SB	CS	SB%	GDP	Avg	OBP	SLG
1990 Cleveland	AL	63	227	68	5	4	0	(0	0)	81	43	13	28	0	38	1	0	0	40	9	.82	2	.300	.379	.357
1991 Cleveland	AL	122	387	114	17	3	0	(0	0)	137	58	21	58	2	47	1	4	2	27	17	.61	8	.295	.386	.354
1992 Cle-Pit		105	302	77	4	7	0	(0	0)	95	44	15	28	1	67	1	1	2	16	6	.73	4	.255	.318	.315
1993 Colorado	NL	126	348	89	9	4	0	(0	0)	106	50	24	43	3	58	2	4	2	30	13	.70	6	.256	.339	.305
1994 Minnesota	AL	105	345	102	15	5	4	(2	2)	139	68	23	44	2	60	1	6	2	29	8	.78	3	.296	.375	.403
1995 Minnesota	AL	28	79	27	3	2	1	(0	1)	37	10	14	8	0	15	1	2	0	1	3	.25	0	.342	.409	.468
1992 Cleveland	AL	41	97	20	1	0	0	(0	0)	21	11	5	10	0	21	1	0	1	9	2	.82	2	.206	.284	.216
Pittsburgh	NL	64	205	57	3	7	0	(0	0)	74	33	10	18	1	46	0	1	1	7	4	.64	2	.278	.335	.361
6 ML YEARS		549	1688	477	53	25	5	(2	3)	595	273	110	209	8	285	7	17	8	143	56	.72	23	.283	.362	.352

Vince Coleman

Bats: Both   **Throws:** Right   **Pos:** LF/RF   **Ht:** 6' 1"   **Wt:** 185   **Born:** 9/22/61   **Age:** 34

Year Team	Lg	G	AB	H	2B	3B	HR	(Hm	Rd)	TB	R	RBI	TBB	IBB	SO	HBP	SH	SF	SB	CS	SB%	GDP	Avg	OBP	SLG
1995 Omaha *	AAA	9	38	15	2	0	1	--	--	20	7	5	2	2	6	0	0	0	3	0	1.00	0	.395	.425	.526
1985 St. Louis	NL	151	636	170	20	10	1	(1	0)	213	107	40	50	1	115	0	5	3	110	25	.81	3	.267	.320	.335
1986 St. Louis	NL	154	600	139	13	8	0	(0	0)	168	94	29	60	0	98	2	3	5	107	14	.88	4	.232	.301	.280
1987 St. Louis	NL	151	623	180	14	10	3	(3	0)	223	121	43	70	0	126	3	5	1	109	22	.83	7	.289	.363	.358
1988 St. Louis	NL	153	616	160	20	10	3	(2	1)	209	77	38	49	4	111	1	8	5	81	27	.75	4	.260	.313	.339
1989 St. Louis	NL	145	563	143	21	9	2	(1	1)	188	94	28	50	0	90	2	7	2	65	10	.87	4	.254	.316	.334
1990 St. Louis	NL	124	497	145	18	9	6	(5	1)	199	73	39	35	1	88	2	4	1	77	17	.82	6	.292	.340	.400
1991 New York	NL	72	278	71	7	5	1	(0	1)	91	45	17	39	0	47	0	1	0	37	14	.73	3	.255	.347	.327
1992 New York	NL	71	229	63	11	1	2	(2	0)	82	37	21	27	3	41	2	2	1	24	9	.73	1	.275	.355	.358
1993 New York	NL	92	373	104	14	8	2	(2	0)	140	64	25	21	1	58	0	3	2	38	13	.75	2	.279	.316	.375
1994 Kansas City	AL	104	438	105	14	12	2	(1	1)	149	61	33	29	0	72	1	4	5	50	8	.86	2	.240	.285	.340
1995 KC-Sea	AL	115	455	131	23	6	5	(3	2)	181	66	29	37	2	80	2	5	1	42	16	.72	8	.288	.343	.398
1995 Kansas City	AL	75	293	84	13	4	4	(2	2)	117	39	20	27	1	48	1	2	1	26	9	.74	7	.287	.348	.399
Seattle	AL	40	162	47	10	2	1	(1	0)	64	27	9	10	1	32	1	3	0	16	7	.70	1	.290	.335	.395
11 ML YEARS		1332	5308	1411	175	88	27	(20	7)	1843	839	342	467	12	926	15	47	24	740	175	.81	44	.266	.326	.347

Darnell Coles

Bats: Right   **Throws:** Right   **Pos:** 3B/1B   **Ht:** 6' 1"   **Wt:** 180   **Born:** 6/2/62   **Age:** 34

Year Team	Lg	G	AB	H	2B	3B	HR	(Hm	Rd)	TB	R	RBI	TBB	IBB	SO	HBP	SH	SF	SB	CS	SB%	GDP	Avg	OBP	SLG
1983 Seattle	AL	27	92	26	7	0	1	(0	1)	36	9	6	7	0	12	0	1	0	0	3	.00	6	.283	.333	.391
1984 Seattle	AL	48	143	23	3	1	0	(0	0)	28	15	6	17	0	26	2	3	0	2	1	.67	5	.161	.259	.196
1985 Seattle	AL	27	59	14	4	0	1	(0	1)	21	8	5	9	0	17	1	0	2	0	1	.00	0	.237	.338	.356
1986 Detroit	AL	142	521	142	30	2	20	(12	8)	236	67	86	45	3	84	6	7	8	6	2	.75	8	.273	.333	.453
1987 Det-Pit		93	268	54	13	1	10	(8	2)	99	34	39	34	3	43	3	5	3	1	4	.20	4	.201	.295	.369
1988 Sea-Pit		123	406	106	23	2	15	(10	5)	178	52	70	37	1	67	7	2	10	4	3	.57	8	.261	.326	.438
1989 Seattle	AL	146	535	135	21	3	10	(4	6)	192	54	59	27	1	61	6	2	3	5	4	.56	13	.252	.294	.359
1990 Det-Sea	AL	89	215	45	7	1	3	(3	0)	63	22	20	16	2	38	1	1	2	0	4	.00	4	.209	.265	.293
1991 San Francisco	NL	11	14	3	0	0	0	(0	0)	3	1	0	0	0	2	0	0	0	0	0	.00	1	.214	.214	.214
1992 Cincinnati	NL	55	141	44	11	2	3	(1	2)	68	16	18	3	0	15	0	3	2	1	0	1.00	1	.312	.322	.482
1993 Toronto	AL	64	194	49	9	1	4	(3	1)	72	26	26	16	1	29	4	1	2	1	1	.50	3	.253	.319	.371
1994 Toronto	AL	48	143	30	6	1	4	(1	3)	50	15	15	10	0	25	1	0	2	0	0	.00	4	.210	.263	.350
1995 St. Louis	NL	63	138	31	7	0	3	(0	0)	47	13	16	16	1	20	3	0	1	0	0	.00	4	.225	.316	.341
1987 Detroit	AL	53	149	27	5	1	4	(3	1)	46	14	15	15	1	23	2	2	1	0	1	.00	1	.181	.263	.309
Pittsburgh	NL	40	119	27	8	0	6	(5	1)	53	20	24	19	2	20	1	3	2	1	3	.25	3	.227	.333	.445
1988 Seattle	AL	55	195	57	10	1	10	(9	1)	99	32	34	17	0	26	4	2	3	3	2	.60	5	.292	.356	.508
Pittsburgh	NL	68	211	49	13	1	5	(1	4)	79	20	36	20	1	41	3	0	7	1	1	.50	3	.232	.299	.374
1990 Detroit	AL	52	108	22	2	0	1	(1	0)	27	13	4	12	1	21	0	1	1	0	4	.00	3	.204	.281	.250
Seattle	AL	37	107	23	5	1	2	(2	0)	36	9	16	4	1	17	1	0	1	0	0	.00	1	.215	.248	.336
13 ML YEARS		936	2869	702	141	14	74	(45	29)	1093	332	366	237	12	439	34	25	35	20	23	.47	58	.245	.306	.381

David Cone

Pitches: Right **Bats:** Left **Pos:** SP　　　　**Ht:** 6' 1" **Wt:** 190 **Born:** 1/2/63 **Age:** 33

			HOW MUCH HE PITCHED						WHAT HE GAVE UP									THE RESULTS					
Year Team	Lg	G	GS	CG	GF	IP	BFP	H	R	ER	HR	SH	SF	HB	TBB	IBB	SO	WP	Bk	W	L	Pct.	ShO	Sv	ERA
1986 Kansas City	AL	11	0	0	5	22.2	108	29	14	14	2	0	0	1	13	1	21	3	0	0	0	.000	0	0	5.56
1987 New York	NL	21	13	1	3	99.1	420	87	46	41	11	4	3	5	44	1	68	2	4	5	6	.455	0	1	3.71
1988 New York	NL	35	28	8	0	231.1	936	178	67	57	10	11	5	4	80	7	213	10	10	20	3	.870	4	0	2.22
1989 New York	NL	34	33	7	0	219.2	910	183	92	86	20	6	4	4	74	6	190	14	4	14	8	.636	2	0	3.52
1990 New York	NL	31	30	6	1	211.2	860	177	84	76	21	4	6	1	65	1	233	10	4	14	10	.583	2	0	3.23
1991 New York	NL	34	34	5	0	232.2	966	204	95	85	13	13	7	5	73	2	241	17	1	14	14	.500	2	0	3.29
1992 Tor-NYN		35	34	7	0	249.2	1055	201	91	78	15	6	9	12	111	7	261	12	1	17	10	.630	5	0	2.81
1993 Kansas City	AL	34	34	6	0	254	1060	205	102	94	20	7	9	10	114	2	191	14	2	11	14	.440	1	0	3.33
1994 Kansas City	AL	23	23	4	0	171.2	690	130	60	56	15	1	5	7	54	0	132	5	1	16	5	.762	3	0	2.94
1995 Tor-NYA	AL	30	30	6	0	229.1	954	195	95	91	24	2	3	6	88	2	191	11	1	18	8	.692	2	0	3.57
1992 Toronto	AL	8	7	0	0	53	224	39	16	15	3	0	3	3	29	2	47	3	0	4	3	.571	0	0	2.55
New York	NL	27	27	7	0	196.2	831	162	75	63	12	6	6	9	82	5	214	9	1	13	7	.650	5	0	2.88
1995 Toronto	AL	17	17	5	0	130.1	537	113	53	49	12	2	2	5	41	2	102	6	1	9	6	.600	2	0	3.38
New York	AL	13	13	1	0	99	417	82	42	42	12	0	1	1	47	0	89	5	0	9	2	.818	0	0	3.82
10 ML YEARS		288	259	50	9	1922	7959	1589	746	678	151	54	51	55	716	29	1741	98	28	129	78	.623	21	1	3.17

Jeff Conine

Bats: Right **Throws:** Right **Pos:** LF/1B　　　　**Ht:** 6' 1" **Wt:** 220 **Born:** 6/27/66 **Age:** 30

					BATTING												BASERUNNING				PERCENTAGES		
Year Team	Lg	G	AB	H	2B	3B	HR	(Hm | Rd)	TB	R	RBI	TBB	IBB	SO	HBP	SH	SF	SB	CS	SB%	GDP	Avg	OBP	SLG
1990 Kansas City	AL	9	20	5	2	0	0	(0 | 0)	7	3	2	2	0	5	0	0	0	0	0	.00	1	.250	.318	.350
1992 Kansas City	AL	28	91	23	5	2	0	(0 | 0)	32	10	9	8	1	23	0	0	0	0	0	.00	1	.253	.313	.352
1993 Florida	NL	162	595	174	24	3	12	(5 | 7)	240	75	79	52	2	135	5	0	6	2	2	.50	14	.292	.351	.403
1994 Florida	NL	115	451	144	27	6	18	(8 | 10)	237	60	82	40	4	92	1	0	4	1	2	.33	8	.319	.373	.525
1995 Florida	NL	133	483	146	26	2	25	(13 | 12)	251	72	105	66	5	94	1	0	12	2	0	1.00	13	.302	.379	.520
5 ML YEARS		447	1640	492	84	13	55	(26 | 29)	767	220	277	168	12	349	7	0	22	5	4	.56	37	.300	.363	.468

Jim Converse

Pitches: Right **Bats:** Left **Pos:** RP　　　　**Ht:** 5' 9" **Wt:** 180 **Born:** 8/17/71 **Age:** 24

					HOW MUCH HE PITCHED						WHAT HE GAVE UP									THE RESULTS					
Year Team	Lg	G	GS	CG	GF	IP	BFP	H	R	ER	HR	SH	SF	HB	TBB	IBB	SO	WP	Bk	W	L	Pct.	ShO	Sv	ERA
1995 Tacoma *	AAA	17	12	0	3	73.2	337	96	57	49	5	4	5	1	36	1	43	4	4	4	7	.364	0	0	5.99
Omaha *	AAA	4	0	0	0	5	19	1	0	0	0	0	0	0	1	0	9	1	0	1	0	1.000	0	0	0.00
1993 Seattle	AL	4	4	0	0	20.1	93	23	12	12	0	0	1	0	14	2	10	0	0	1	3	.250	0	0	5.31
1994 Seattle	AL	13	8	0	1	48.2	253	73	49	47	5	2	3	1	40	4	39	3	0	0	5	.000	0	0	8.69
1995 Sea-KC	AL	15	1	0	4	23.1	109	28	17	17	2	2	0	0	16	2	14	2	0	1	3	.250	0	1	6.56
1995 Seattle	AL	6	1	0	3	11	55	16	9	9	2	1	0	0	8	0	9	0	0	0	3	.000	0	1	7.36
Kansas City	AL	9	0	0	1	12.1	54	12	8	8	0	1	0	0	8	2	5	2	0	1	0	1.000	0	0	5.84
3 ML YEARS		32	13	0	5	92.1	455	124	78	76	7	4	4	1	70	8	63	5	0	2	11	.154	0	1	7.41

Dennis Cook

Pitches: Left **Bats:** Left **Pos:** RP　　　　**Ht:** 6' 3" **Wt:** 190 **Born:** 10/4/62 **Age:** 33

					HOW MUCH HE PITCHED						WHAT HE GAVE UP									THE RESULTS					
Year Team	Lg	G	GS	CG	GF	IP	BFP	H	R	ER	HR	SH	SF	HB	TBB	IBB	SO	WP	Bk	W	L	Pct.	ShO	Sv	ERA
1988 San Francisco	NL	4	4	0	0	22	86	9	8	7	1	0	3	0	11	1	13	1	0	2	1	.667	0	0	2.86
1989 Phi-SF	NL	23	18	2	1	121	499	110	59	50	18	5	2	2	38	6	67	4	2	7	8	.467	1	0	3.72
1990 LA-Phi	NL	47	16	2	4	156	663	155	74	68	20	7	7	2	56	9	64	6	3	9	4	.692	1	1	3.92
1991 Los Angeles	NL	20	1	0	5	17.2	69	12	3	1	0	1	2	0	7	1	8	0	0	1	0	1.000	0	0	0.51
1992 Cleveland	AL	32	25	1	1	158	669	156	79	67	29	3	3	2	50	2	96	4	5	5	7	.417	0	0	3.82
1993 Cleveland	AL	25	6	0	2	54	233	62	36	34	9	3	2	2	16	1	34	0	1	5	5	.500	0	0	5.67
1994 Chicago	AL	38	0	0	8	33	143	29	17	13	4	3	0	0	14	3	26	0	1	3	1	.750	0	0	3.55
1995 Cle-Tex	AL	46	1	0	10	57.2	255	63	32	29	9	4	5	2	26	3	53	1	0	0	2	.000	0	2	4.53
1989 Philadelphia	NL	21	16	1	1	106	441	97	56	47	17	5	2	2	33	6	58	3	2	6	8	.429	1	0	3.99
San Francisco	NL	2	2	1	0	15	58	13	3	3	1	0	0	0	5	0	9	1	0	1	0	1.000	0	0	1.80
1990 Los Angeles	NL	5	3	0	0	14.1	69	23	13	12	7	2	2	0	2	0	6	0	0	1	1	.500	0	0	7.53
Philadelphia	NL	42	13	2	4	141.2	594	132	61	56	13	5	5	2	54	9	58	6	3	8	3	.727	1	1	3.56
1995 Cleveland	AL	11	0	0	1	12.2	62	16	9	9	3	1	0	1	10	2	13	0	0	0	0	.000	0	0	6.39
Texas	AL	35	1	0	9	45	193	47	23	20	6	3	5	1	16	1	40	1	0	0	2	.000	0	2	4.00
8 ML YEARS		235	71	6	31	619.1	2617	596	308	269	90	26	24	10	218	26	361	16	12	32	28	.533	3	3	3.91

Brent Cookson

Bats: Right **Throws:** Right **Pos:** LF　　　　**Ht:** 6' 0" **Wt:** 195 **Born:** 9/7/69 **Age:** 26

						BATTING												BASERUNNING				PERCENTAGES		
Year Team	Lg	G	AB	H	2B	3B	HR	(Hm	Rd)	TB	R	RBI	TBB	IBB	SO	HBP	SH	SF	SB	CS	SB%	GDP	Avg	OBP	SLG
1991 Sou. Oregon	A	6	9	0	0	0	0	--	--	0	0	0	0	0	7	0	0	0	0	0	.00	1	.000	.000	.000

Year	Team	Lg	G	AB	H	2B	3B	HR	(Hm	Rd)	TB	R	RBI	TBB	IBB	SO	HBP	SH	SF	SB	CS	SB%	GDP	Avg	OBP	SLG
	Athletics	R	1	1	0	0	0	0	--	--	0	0	0	0	0	1	0	0	0	0	0	.00	0	.000	.000	.000
1992	Clinton	A	46	145	31	5	1	8	--	--	62	30	20	22	0	48	3	1	1	9	3	.75	4	.214	.327	.428
	San Jose	A	68	255	74	8	4	12	--	--	126	44	49	25	0	69	3	0	2	9	5	.64	8	.290	.358	.494
1993	San Jose	A	67	234	60	10	1	17	--	--	123	43	50	43	1	73	3	2	5	14	6	.70	5	.256	.372	.526
1994	Shreveport	AA	62	207	67	21	3	11	--	--	127	32	41	18	2	57	1	2	2	4	1	.80	2	.324	.377	.614
	Phoenix	AAA	14	43	12	0	1	1	--	--	17	7	6	5	0	14	1	0	0	0	1	.00	1	.279	.367	.395
1995	Phoenix	AAA	68	210	63	9	3	15	--	--	123	38	46	25	2	36	1	1	2	3	3	.50	4	.300	.374	.586
	Omaha	AAA	40	137	55	13	0	4	--	--	80	28	20	17	0	24	4	0	2	0	0	.00	3	.401	.475	.584
1995	Kansas City	AL	22	35	5	1	0	0	(0	0)	6	2	5	2	0	7	0	1	0	1	0	1.00	0	.143	.189	.171

Ron Coomer

Bats: Right **Throws:** Right **Pos:** 1B/3B   **Ht:** 5'11" **Wt:** 205 **Born:** 11/18/66 **Age:** 29

						BATTING														BASERUNNING				PERCENTAGES		
Year	Team	Lg	G	AB	H	2B	3B	HR	(Hm	Rd)	TB	R	RBI	TBB	IBB	SO	HBP	SH	SF	SB	CS	SB%	GDP	Avg	OBP	SLG
1990	Huntsville	AA	66	194	43	7	0	3	--	--	59	22	27	21	1	40	1	4	3	3	1	.75	5	.222	.297	.304
1991	Birmingham	AA	137	505	129	27	5	13	--	--	205	81	76	59	1	78	1	6	8	0	3	.00	21	.255	.330	.406
1992	Vancouver	AAA	86	262	62	10	0	9	--	--	99	29	40	16	3	36	0	3	4	3	0	1.00	14	.237	.277	.378
1993	Birmingham	AA	69	262	85	18	0	13	--	--	142	44	50	15	3	43	0	0	2	1	1	.50	8	.324	.358	.542
	Nashville	AAA	59	211	66	19	0	13	--	--	124	34	51	10	1	29	1	0	3	1	2	.33	5	.313	.342	.588
1994	Albuquerque	AAA	127	535	181	34	6	22	--	--	293	89	123	26	4	62	2	0	7	4	3	.57	12	.338	.367	.548
1995	Albuquerque	AAA	85	323	104	23	2	16	--	--	179	54	76	18	1	28	2	0	4	5	2	.71	16	.322	.357	.554
1995	Minnesota	AL	37	101	26	3	1	5	(2	3)	46	15	19	9	0	11	1	0	0	0	1	.00	9	.257	.324	.455

Scott Cooper

Bats: Left **Throws:** Right **Pos:** 3B   **Ht:** 6'3" **Wt:** 205 **Born:** 10/13/67 **Age:** 28

						BATTING														BASERUNNING				PERCENTAGES		
Year	Team	Lg	G	AB	H	2B	3B	HR	(Hm	Rd)	TB	R	RBI	TBB	IBB	SO	HBP	SH	SF	SB	CS	SB%	GDP	Avg	OBP	SLG
1990	Boston	AL	2	1	0	0	0	0	(0	0)	0	0	0	0	0	1	0	0	0	0	0	.00	0	.000	.000	.000
1991	Boston	AL	14	35	16	4	2	0	(0	0)	24	6	7	2	0	2	0	0	0	0	0	.00	0	.457	.486	.686
1992	Boston	AL	123	337	93	21	0	5	(2	3)	129	34	33	37	0	33	0	2	2	1	1	.50	5	.276	.346	.383
1993	Boston	AL	156	526	147	29	3	9	(3	6)	209	67	63	58	15	81	5	4	3	5	2	.71	8	.279	.355	.397
1994	Boston	AL	104	369	104	16	4	13	(9	4)	167	49	53	30	2	65	1	1	5	0	3	.00	6	.282	.333	.453
1995	St. Louis	NL	118	374	86	18	2	3	(1	2)	117	29	40	49	3	85	3	0	4	0	3	.00	9	.230	.321	.313
6	ML YEARS		517	1642	446	88	11	30	(15	15)	646	185	196	176	20	267	9	7	14	6	9	.40	28	.272	.343	.393

Joey Cora

Bats: Both **Throws:** Right **Pos:** 2B   **Ht:** 5'8" **Wt:** 155 **Born:** 5/14/65 **Age:** 31

						BATTING														BASERUNNING				PERCENTAGES		
Year	Team	Lg	G	AB	H	2B	3B	HR	(Hm	Rd)	TB	R	RBI	TBB	IBB	SO	HBP	SH	SF	SB	CS	SB%	GDP	Avg	OBP	SLG
1987	San Diego	NL	77	241	57	7	2	0	(0	0)	68	23	13	28	1	26	1	5	1	15	11	.58	4	.237	.317	.282
1989	San Diego	NL	12	19	6	1	0	0	(0	0)	7	5	1	1	0	0	0	0	0	1	0	1.00	0	.316	.350	.368
1990	San Diego	NL	51	100	27	3	0	0	(0	0)	30	12	2	6	1	9	0	0	0	8	3	.73	1	.270	.311	.300
1991	Chicago	AL	100	228	55	2	3	0	(0	0)	63	37	18	20	0	21	5	8	3	11	6	.65	1	.241	.313	.276
1992	Chicago	AL	68	122	30	7	1	0	(0	0)	39	27	9	22	1	13	4	2	3	10	3	.77	2	.246	.371	.320
1993	Chicago	AL	153	579	155	15	13	2	(0	2)	202	95	51	67	0	63	9	**19**	4	20	8	.71	14	.268	.351	.349
1994	Chicago	AL	90	312	86	13	4	2	(0	2)	113	55	30	38	0	32	2	11	5	8	4	.67	8	.276	.353	.362
1995	Seattle	AL	120	427	127	19	2	3	(1	2)	159	64	39	37	0	31	6	13	4	18	7	.72	8	.297	.359	.372
8	ML YEARS		671	2028	543	67	25	7	(3	4)	681	318	163	219	3	195	27	58	20	91	42	.68	38	.268	.344	.336

Wil Cordero

Bats: Right **Throws:** Right **Pos:** SS/LF   **Ht:** 6'2" **Wt:** 195 **Born:** 10/3/71 **Age:** 24

						BATTING														BASERUNNING				PERCENTAGES		
Year	Team	Lg	G	AB	H	2B	3B	HR	(Hm	Rd)	TB	R	RBI	TBB	IBB	SO	HBP	SH	SF	SB	CS	SB%	GDP	Avg	OBP	SLG
1992	Montreal	NL	45	126	38	4	1	2	(1	1)	50	17	8	9	0	31	1	1	0	0	0	.00	3	.302	.353	.397
1993	Montreal	NL	138	475	118	32	2	10	(8	2)	184	56	58	34	8	60	7	4	1	12	3	.80	12	.248	.308	.387
1994	Montreal	NL	110	415	122	30	3	15	(5	10)	203	65	63	41	3	62	6	2	3	16	3	.84	8	.294	.363	.489
1995	Montreal	NL	131	514	147	35	2	10	(2	8)	216	64	49	36	4	88	9	1	4	9	5	.64	11	.286	.341	.420
4	ML YEARS		424	1530	425	101	8	37	(16	21)	653	202	178	120	15	241	23	8	8	37	11	.77	34	.278	.338	.427

Marty Cordova

Bats: Right **Throws:** Right **Pos:** LF/CF   **Ht:** 6'0" **Wt:** 193 **Born:** 7/10/69 **Age:** 26

						BATTING														BASERUNNING				PERCENTAGES		
Year	Team	Lg	G	AB	H	2B	3B	HR	(Hm	Rd)	TB	R	RBI	TBB	IBB	SO	HBP	SH	SF	SB	CS	SB%	GDP	Avg	OBP	SLG
1989	Elizabethtn	R	38	148	42	2	3	8	--	--	74	32	29	14	1	29	3	0	0	2	1	.67	7	.284	.358	.500
1990	Kenosha	A	81	269	58	7	5	7	--	--	96	35	25	28	0	73	5	0	1	6	3	.67	5	.216	.300	.357
1991	Visalia	A	71	189	40	6	1	7	--	--	69	31	19	17	0	46	2	2	0	2	3	.40	3	.212	.284	.365

Year	Team	Lg	G	AB	H	2B	3B	HR	(Hm	Rd)	TB	R	RBI	TBB	IBB	SO	HBP	SH	SF	SB	CS	SB%	GDP	Avg	OBP	SLG
1992	Visalia	A	134	513	175	31	6	28	--	--	302	103	131	76	5	99	9	3	5	13	5	.72	20	.341	.431	.589
1993	Nashville	AA	138	508	127	30	5	19	--	--	224	83	77	64	3	153	13	0	3	10	5	.67	10	.250	.347	.441
1994	Salt Lake	AAA	103	385	138	25	4	19	--	--	228	69	66	39	0	63	8	0	2	17	6	.74	9	.358	.426	.592
1995	Minnesota	AL	137	512	142	27	4	24	(16	8)	249	81	84	52	1	111	10	0	5	20	7	.74	10	.277	.352	.486

Rheal Cormier

Pitches: Left **Bats:** Left **Pos:** RP/SP **Ht:** 5'10" **Wt:** 185 **Born:** 4/23/67 **Age:** 29

			HOW MUCH HE PITCHED					WHAT HE GAVE UP								THE RESULTS						
Year	Team	Lg	G	GS	CG	GF	IP	BFP	H	R	ER	HR	SH	SF	HB	TBB	IBB	SO	WP	Bk	W	L	Pct.	ShO	Sv	ERA
1991	St. Louis	NL	11	10	2	1	67.2	281	74	35	31	5	1	3	2	8	1	38	2	1	4	5	.444	0	0	4.12
1992	St. Louis	NL	31	30	3	1	186	772	194	83	76	15	11	3	5	33	2	117	4	2	10	10	.500	0	0	3.68
1993	St. Louis	NL	38	21	1	4	145.1	619	163	80	70	18	10	4	4	27	3	75	6	0	7	6	.538	0	0	4.33
1994	St. Louis	NL	7	7	0	0	39.2	169	40	24	24	6	1	2	3	7	0	26	2	0	3	2	.600	0	0	5.45
1995	Boston	AL	48	12	0	3	115	488	131	60	52	12	6	2	3	31	1	69	4	0	7	5	.583	0	0	4.07
	5 ML YEARS		135	80	6	9	553.2	2329	602	282	253	56	29	14	17	106	8	325	18	3	31	28	.525	0	0	4.11

Reid Cornelius

Pitches: Right **Bats:** Right **Pos:** SP/RP **Ht:** 6'0" **Wt:** 200 **Born:** 6/2/70 **Age:** 26

			HOW MUCH HE PITCHED					WHAT HE GAVE UP								THE RESULTS						
Year	Team	Lg	G	GS	CG	GF	IP	BFP	H	R	ER	HR	SH	SF	HB	TBB	IBB	SO	WP	Bk	W	L	Pct.	ShO	Sv	ERA
1989	Rockford	A	17	17	0	0	84.1	391	71	58	40	6	3	3	11	63	0	66	13	3	5	6	.455	0	0	4.27
1990	W. Palm Bch	A	11	11	0	0	56	245	54	25	21	1	0	4	5	25	0	47	3	3	2	3	.400	0	0	3.38
1991	W. Palm Bch	A	17	17	0	0	109.1	449	79	31	29	3	9	4	7	43	1	81	3	6	8	3	.727	0	0	2.39
	Harrisburg	AA	3	3	1	0	18.2	76	15	6	6	3	0	0	2	7	0	12	0	0	2	1	.667	1	0	2.89
1992	Harrisburg	AA	4	4	0	0	23	92	11	8	8	0	2	0	6	8	0	17	1	0	1	0	1.000	0	0	3.13
1993	Harrisburg	AA	27	27	1	0	157.2	698	146	95	73	10	3	5	13	82	1	119	8	0	10	7	.588	0	0	4.17
1994	Ottawa	AAA	25	24	1	1	148	661	149	89	72	18	1	4	8	75	2	87	10	0	9	8	.529	0	0	4.38
1995	Ottawa	AAA	4	3	0	0	10.2	54	16	12	8	1	0	1	2	5	0	7	2	0	1	1	.500	0	0	6.75
	Norfolk	AAA	10	10	1	0	70.1	287	57	10	7	2	3	1	6	19	0	43	1	0	7	0	1.000	0	0	0.90
1995	Mon-NYN	NL	18	10	0	1	66.2	301	75	44	41	11	4	3	5	30	5	39	2	1	3	7	.300	0	0	5.54
1995	Montreal	NL	8	0	0	1	9	43	11	8	8	3	0	0	2	5	0	4	1	0	0	0	.000	0	0	8.00
	New York	NL	10	10	0	0	57.2	258	64	36	33	8	4	3	3	25	5	35	1	1	3	7	.300	0	0	5.15

Brad Cornett

Pitches: Right **Bats:** Right **Pos:** RP **Ht:** 6'3" **Wt:** 188 **Born:** 2/4/69 **Age:** 27

			HOW MUCH HE PITCHED					WHAT HE GAVE UP								THE RESULTS						
Year	Team	Lg	G	GS	CG	GF	IP	BFP	H	R	ER	HR	SH	SF	HB	TBB	IBB	SO	WP	Bk	W	L	Pct.	ShO	Sv	ERA
1992	St. Cathrns	A	25	0	0	13	60	241	54	30	24	6	1	0	3	10	0	64	5	0	4	1	.800	0	1	3.60
1993	Hagerstown	A	31	21	3	7	172.1	711	164	77	46	6	5	5	5	31	2	161	6	1	10	8	.556	1	3	2.40
1994	Knoxville	AA	7	7	1	0	37.1	151	34	18	10	2	1	0	1	6	0	26	3	0	2	3	.400	0	0	2.41
	Syracuse	AAA	3	3	0	0	19	85	18	8	3	0	0	1	0	9	1	12	0	0	1	2	.333	0	0	1.42
1995	Syracuse	AAA	3	3	0	0	11	49	13	6	6	1	0	1	0	4	0	3	0	0	0	1	.000	0	0	4.91
1994	Toronto	AL	9	4	0	0	31	141	40	25	23	1	4	2	3	11	2	22	2	0	1	3	.250	0	0	6.68
1995	Toronto	AL	5	0	0	2	5	25	9	6	5	1	0	1	1	3	0	4	1	0	0	0	.000	0	0	9.00
	2 ML YEARS		14	4	0	2	36	166	49	31	28	2	4	2	4	14	2	26	3	0	1	3	.250	0	0	7.00

Rod Correia

Bats: Right **Throws:** Right **Pos:** SS **Ht:** 5'11" **Wt:** 185 **Born:** 9/13/67 **Age:** 28

			BATTING																BASERUNNING				PERCENTAGES		
Year	Team	Lg	G	AB	H	2B	3B	HR	(Hm	Rd)	TB	R	RBI	TBB	IBB	SO	HBP	SH	SF	SB	CS	SB%	GDP	Avg	OBP	SLG
1995	Vancouver *	AAA	73	264	80	6	5	1	--	--	99	42	39	26	3	33	0	4	4	8	4	.67	7	.303	.361	.375
1993	California	AL	64	128	34	5	0	0	(0	0)	39	12	9	6	0	20	4	5	0	2	4	.33	1	.266	.319	.305
1994	California	AL	6	17	4	1	0	0	(0	0)	5	4	0	0	0	2	0	0	0	0	0	.00	0	.235	.316	.294
1995	California	AL	14	21	5	1	1	0	(0	0)	8	3	3	0	0	5	0	1	0	0	0	.00	0	.238	.238	.381
	3 ML YEARS		84	166	43	7	1	0	(0	0)	52	19	12	6	0	25	6	6	0	2	4	.33	2	.259	.309	.313

Jim Corsi

Pitches: Right **Bats:** Right **Pos:** RP **Ht:** 6'1" **Wt:** 220 **Born:** 9/9/61 **Age:** 34

			HOW MUCH HE PITCHED					WHAT HE GAVE UP								THE RESULTS						
Year	Team	Lg	G	GS	CG	GF	IP	BFP	H	R	ER	HR	SH	SF	HB	TBB	IBB	SO	WP	Bk	W	L	Pct.	ShO	Sv	ERA
1995	Edmonton *	AAA	3	0	0	3	3	10	0	0	0	0	0	0	0	1	0	3	0	0	0	0	.000	0	3	0.00
1988	Oakland	AL	11	0	0	7	21.1	89	20	10	9	1	3	3	0	6	1	10	1	1	0	0	.000	0	0	3.80
1989	Oakland	AL	22	0	0	14	38.1	149	26	8	8	2	2	2	1	10	0	21	0	0	1	2	.333	0	0	1.88
1991	Houston	NL	47	0	0	15	77.2	322	76	37	32	6	3	2	0	23	5	53	1	1	0	5	.000	0	3	3.71
1992	Oakland	AL	32	0	0	16	44	185	44	12	7	2	4	2	0	18	2	19	0	0	4	2	.667	0	0	1.43
1993	Florida	NL	15	0	0	6	20.1	97	28	15	15	1	3	1	0	10	3	7	0	0	0	2	.000	0	0	6.64

Year Team	Lg	G	GS	CG	GF	IP	BFP	H	R	ER	HR	SH	SF	HB	TBB	IBB	SO	WP	Bk	W	L	Pct.	ShO	Sv	ERA
1995 Oakland	AL	38	0	0	7	45	187	31	14	11	2	5	1	2	26	1	26	0	0	2	4	.333	0	2	2.20
6 ML YEARS		165	1	0	65	246.2	1029	225	96	82	14	20	11	3	93	12	136	2	2	7	16	.304	0	2	2.99

Craig Counsell

Bats: Left   **Throws:** Right   **Pos:** SS   **Ht:** 6' 0"   **Wt:** 177   **Born:** 8/21/70   **Age:** 25

							BATTING										BASERUNNING				PERCENTAGES		
Year Team	Lg	G	AB	H	2B	3B	HR	(Hm | Rd)	TB	R	RBI	TBB	IBB	SO	HBP	SH	SF	SB	CS	SB%	GDP	Avg	OBP	SLG
1992 Bend	A	18	61	15	6	1	0	--	--	23	11	8	9	1	10	1	1	0	1	2	.33	2	.246	.352	.377
1993 Central Val	A	131	471	132	26	3	5	--	--	179	79	59	95	1	68	3	5	4	14	8	.64	8	.280	.401	.380
1994 New Haven	AA	83	300	84	20	1	5	--	--	121	47	37	37	4	32	5	1	2	4	1	.80	6	.280	.366	.403
1995 Colo. Sprng	AAA	118	399	112	22	6	5	--	--	161	60	53	34	7	47	2	3	6	10	2	.83	11	.281	.336	.404
1995 Colorado	NL	3	1	0	0	0	0	(0 | 0)	0	0	0	1	0	0	0	0	0	0	0	.00	0	.000	.500	.000

John Courtright

Pitches: Left   **Bats:** Left   **Pos:** RP   **Ht:** 6' 2"   **Wt:** 185   **Born:** 5/30/70   **Age:** 26

		HOW MUCH HE PITCHED						WHAT HE GAVE UP												THE RESULTS					
Year Team	Lg	G	GS	CG	GF	IP	BFP	H	R	ER	HR	SH	SF	HB	TBB	IBB	SO	WP	Bk	W	L	Pct.	ShO	Sv	ERA
1991 Billings	R	1	1	0	0	6	21	2	0	0	0	0	0	0	1	0	4	0	1	1	0	1.000	0	0	0.00
1992 Charlstn-Wv	A	27	26	1	0	173	688	147	64	48	5	5	4	7	55	2	147	9	5	10	5	.667	1	0	2.50
1993 Chattanooga	AA	27	27	1	0	175	752	179	81	68	5	8	11	8	70	6	96	5	2	5	11	.313	0	0	3.50
1994 Chattanooga	AA	4	4	0	0	21.2	95	19	16	13	2	2	1	1	14	0	12	1	0	1	2	.333	0	0	5.40
Indianapols	AAA	24	23	2	0	142	595	144	61	56	9	8	1	4	46	3	73	2	1	9	10	.474	2	0	3.55
1995 Indianapols	AAA	13	2	0	1	33.2	147	29	18	16	2	2	1	2	15	1	13	4	1	2	1	.667	0	0	4.28
Salt Lake	AAA	18	17	1	0	84.2	384	108	70	64	6	5	7	0	36	7	42	4	2	3	7	.300	0	0	6.80
1995 Cincinnati	NL	1	0	0	0	1	5	2	1	1	0	1	0	0	0	0	0	0	0	0	0	.000	0	0	9.00

Danny Cox

Pitches: Right   **Bats:** Right   **Pos:** RP   **Ht:** 6' 4"   **Wt:** 250   **Born:** 9/21/59   **Age:** 36

		HOW MUCH HE PITCHED						WHAT HE GAVE UP												THE RESULTS					
Year Team	Lg	G	GS	CG	GF	IP	BFP	H	R	ER	HR	SH	SF	HB	TBB	IBB	SO	WP	Bk	W	L	Pct.	ShO	Sv	ERA
1995 Syracuse *	AAA	4	0	0	1	7	28	2	0	0	0	0	0	0	5	0	9	0	0	0	0	.000	0	0	0.00
1983 St. Louis	NL	12	12	0	0	83	352	92	38	30	6	6	1	0	23	2	36	2	0	3	6	.333	0	0	3.25
1984 St. Louis	NL	29	27	1	0	156.1	668	171	81	70	9	10	5	7	54	6	70	2	4	9	11	.450	1	0	4.03
1985 St. Louis	NL	35	35	10	0	241	989	226	91	77	19	12	9	3	64	5	131	3	1	18	9	.667	4	0	2.88
1986 St. Louis	NL	32	32	8	0	220	881	189	85	71	14	8	3	2	60	6	108	3	4	12	13	.480	0	0	2.90
1987 St. Louis	NL	31	31	2	0	199.1	864	224	99	86	17	14	4	3	71	6	101	5	1	11	9	.550	0	0	3.88
1988 St. Louis	NL	13	13	0	0	86	361	89	40	38	6	5	3	1	25	7	47	4	3	3	8	.273	0	0	3.98
1991 Philadelphia	NL	23	17	0	2	102.1	433	98	57	52	14	6	7	1	39	2	46	7	1	4	6	.400	0	0	4.57
1992 Phi-Pit	NL	25	7	0	8	62.2	278	66	37	32	5	5	3	0	27	2	48	1	0	5	3	.625	0	3	4.60
1993 Toronto	AL	44	0	0	13	83.2	348	73	31	29	8	0	1	0	29	5	84	5	0	7	6	.538	0	2	3.12
1994 Toronto	AL	10	0	0	5	18.2	72	7	3	3	0	1	1	1	7	1	14	1	0	1	1	.500	0	3	1.45
1995 Toronto	AL	24	0	0	7	45	218	57	40	37	4	1	3	1	33	4	38	7	0	1	3	.250	0	0	7.40
1992 Philadelphia	NL	9	7	0	0	38.1	178	46	28	23	3	3	2	0	19	1	30	0	0	2	2	.500	0	0	5.40
Pittsburgh	NL	16	0	0	8	24.1	100	20	9	9	2	2	1	0	8	1	18	1	0	3	1	.750	0	3	3.33
11 ML YEARS		278	174	21	35	1298	5464	1292	602	525	102	68	40	19	432	46	723	40	14	74	75	.497	5	8	3.64

Tim Crabtree

Pitches: Right   **Bats:** Right   **Pos:** RP   **Ht:** 6' 4"   **Wt:** 195   **Born:** 10/13/69   **Age:** 26

		HOW MUCH HE PITCHED						WHAT HE GAVE UP												THE RESULTS					
Year Team	Lg	G	GS	CG	GF	IP	BFP	H	R	ER	HR	SH	SF	HB	TBB	IBB	SO	WP	Bk	W	L	Pct.	ShO	Sv	ERA
1992 St. Cathrns	A	12	12	0	0	69	279	45	19	12	1	1	0	7	22	0	47	6	0	6	3	.667	0	0	1.57
Knoxville	AA	3	3	1	0	19	78	14	8	2	0	1	0	2	4	0	13	0	0	0	2	.000	0	0	0.95
1993 Knoxville	AA	27	27	2	0	158.2	707	178	93	72	11	10	7	10	59	0	67	7	3	9	14	.391	2	0	4.08
1994 Syracuse	AAA	51	9	0	15	108	474	125	56	50	5	4	2	2	49	6	58	4	0	2	6	.250	0	2	4.17
1995 Syracuse	AAA	26	0	0	16	31.2	148	38	25	19	1	1	1	1	12	2	22	5	1	0	2	.000	0	5	5.40
1995 Toronto	AL	31	0	0	19	32	141	30	16	11	1	0	1	2	13	0	21	2	0	0	2	.000	0	0	3.09

Doug Creek

Pitches: Left   **Bats:** Left   **Pos:** RP   **Ht:** 5'10"   **Wt:** 205   **Born:** 3/1/69   **Age:** 27

		HOW MUCH HE PITCHED						WHAT HE GAVE UP												THE RESULTS					
Year Team	Lg	G	GS	CG	GF	IP	BFP	H	R	ER	HR	SH	SF	HB	TBB	IBB	SO	WP	Bk	W	L	Pct.	ShO	Sv	ERA
1991 Hamilton	A	9	5	0	1	38.2	169	22	22	2	0	3	3	18	0	45	3	0	3	2	.600	0	1	5.12
Savannah	A	5	5	0	0	28.1	117	24	14	14	2	0	1	1	17	0	32	1	0	2	1	.667	0	0	4.45
1992 Springfield	A	6	6	0	0	38.1	155	32	11	11	4	1	0	0	13	1	43	0	1	4	1	.800	0	0	2.58
St. Pete	A	13	13	0	0	73.1	300	57	31	23	5	0	4	1	37	1	63	4	1	5	4	.556	0	0	2.82
1993 Arkansas	AA	25	25	1	0	147.2	620	142	75	66	15	5	5	3	48	1	128	10	1	11	10	.524	1	0	4.02

Year	Team	Lg	G	GS	CG	GF	IP	BFP	H	R	ER	HR	SH	SF	HB	TBB	IBB	SO	WP	Bk	W	L	Pct.	ShO	Sv	ERA
	Louisville	AAA	2	2	0	0	14	60	10	5	5	0	2	0	1	9	0	9	2	0	0	0	.000	0	0	3.21
1994	Louisville	AAA	7	7	0	0	26.1	132	37	26	25	2	0	2	1	23	0	16	2	1	1	4	.200	0	0	8.54
	Arkansas	AA	17	17	1	0	92	405	96	54	45	8	11	4	3	36	0	65	7	1	3	10	.231	0	0	4.40
1995	Arkansas	AA	26	0	0	11	34.1	143	24	12	11	4	3	0	3	16	2	50	1	0	4	2	.667	0	1	2.88
	Louisville	AAA	26	0	0	5	30.2	132	20	12	11	1	0	0	1	21	0	29	4	0	3	2	.600	0	0	3.23
1995	St. Louis	NL	6	0	0	1	6.2	24	2	0	0	0	0	0	0	3	0	10	0	0	0	0	.000	0	0	0.00

Tripp Cromer

Bats: Right **Throws:** Right **Pos:** SS/2B   **Ht:** 6' 2" **Wt:** 165 **Born:** 11/21/67 **Age:** 28

						BATTING															BASERUNNING				PERCENTAGES		
Year	Team	Lg	G	AB	H	2B	3B	HR	(Hm	Rd)	TB	R	RBI	TBB	IBB	SO	HBP	SH	SF	SB	CS	SB%	GDP	Avg	OBP	SLG
1989	Hamilton	A	35	137	36	6	3	0	--	--	48	18	6	17	0	30	1	2	1	4	4	.50	5	.263	.346	.350
1990	St. Pete	A	121	408	88	12	5	5	--	--	125	53	38	46	0	79	5	3	5	7	12	.37	11	.216	.300	.306
1991	St. Pete	A	43	137	28	3	1	0	--	--	33	11	10	9	0	17	1	3	1	0	0	.00	8	.204	.257	.241
	Arkansas	AA	73	227	52	12	1	1	--	--	69	28	18	15	1	37	3	2	3	0	1	.00	7	.229	.282	.304
1992	Arkansas	AA	110	339	81	16	6	7	--	--	130	30	29	22	1	82	4	4	2	4	6	.40	9	.239	.292	.383
	Louisville	AAA	6	25	5	1	1	1	--	--	11	5	7	1	0	6	0	0	1	0	0	.00	0	.200	.222	.440
1993	Louisville	AAA	86	309	85	8	4	11	--	--	134	39	33	15	3	60	2	2	0	1	3	.25	10	.275	.313	.434
1994	Louisville	AAA	124	419	115	23	9	9	--	--	183	53	50	33	1	85	3	6	2	5	6	.45	12	.274	.330	.437
1993	St. Louis	NL	10	23	2	0	0	0	(0	0)	2	1	0	1	0	6	0	0	0	0	0	.00	0	.087	.125	.087
1994	St. Louis	NL	2	0	0	0	0	0	(0	0)	0	0	1	0	0	0	0	0	0	0	0	.00	0	.000	.000	.000
1995	St. Louis	NL	105	345	78	19	0	5	(2	3)	112	36	18	14	2	66	4	1	5	0	0	.00	14	.226	.261	.325
	3 ML YEARS		117	368	80	19	0	5	(2	3)	114	38	18	15	2	72	4	1	5	0	0	.00	14	.217	.253	.310

Fausto Cruz

Bats: Right **Throws:** Right **Pos:** SS   **Ht:** 5'10" **Wt:** 165 **Born:** 5/1/72 **Age:** 24

						BATTING															BASERUNNING				PERCENTAGES		
Year	Team	Lg	G	AB	H	2B	3B	HR	(Hm	Rd)	TB	R	RBI	TBB	IBB	SO	HBP	SH	SF	SB	CS	SB%	GDP	Avg	OBP	SLG
1991	Modesto	A	18	58	12	1	0	0	--	--	13	9	0	8	0	13	1	0	0	1	2	.33	1	.207	.313	.224
	Athletics	R	52	180	49	-2	1	2	--	--	59	38	36	32	0	23	3	3	7	3	0	1.00	10	.272	.378	.328
1992	Reno	A	127	489	156	22	11	9	--	--	227	86	90	70	1	66	7	3	7	8	7	.53	17	.319	.407	.464
1993	Modesto	A	43	165	39	3	0	1	--	--	45	21	20	25	0	34	0	5	4	6	4	.60	2	.236	.330	.273
	Huntsville	AA	63	251	84	15	2	3	--	--	112	45	31	20	0	42	1	4	2	2	4	.33	8	.335	.383	.446
	Tacoma	AAA	21	74	18	2	1	0	--	--	22	13	6	5	0	16	0	2	0	3	3	.50	7	.243	.291	.297
1994	Tacoma	AAA	65	218	70	19	0	1	--	--	92	27	17	17	0	32	3	4	1	2	2	.50	7	.321	.377	.422
1995	Edmonton	AAA	114	448	126	23	2	11	--	--	186	72	67	34	2	67	5	4	7	7	5	.58	15	.281	.334	.415
1994	Oakland	AL	17	28	3	0	0	0	(0	0)	3	2	0	4	0	6	0	0	0	0	0	.00	0	.107	.219	.107
1995	Oakland	AL	8	23	5	0	0	0	(0	0)	5	0	5	3	0	5	0	2	2	1	1	.50	1	.217	.286	.217
	2 ML YEARS		25	51	8	0	0	0	(0	0)	8	2	5	7	0	11	0	2	2	1	1	.50	1	.157	.250	.157

John Cummings

Pitches: Left **Bats:** Left **Pos:** RP   **Ht:** 6' 3" **Wt:** 200 **Born:** 5/10/69 **Age:** 27

			HOW MUCH HE PITCHED						WHAT HE GAVE UP												THE RESULTS					
Year	Team	Lg	G	GS	CG	GF	IP	BFP	H	R	ER	HR	SH	SF	HB	TBB	IBB	SO	WP	Bk	W	L	Pct.	ShO	Sv	ERA
1995	Tacoma *	AAA	1	1	0	0	2.1	16	6	4	2	1	0	0	0	3	0	3	0	0	0	1	.000	0	0	7.71
	San Antonio *	AA	6	5	0	0	27.1	113	28	13	12	0	2	1	1	7	0	13	3	2	0	2	.000	0	0	3.95
1993	Seattle	AL	10	8	1	0	46.1	207	59	34	31	6	0	2	2	16	2	19	1	1	0	6	.000	0	0	6.02
1994	Seattle	AL	17	8	0	2	64	285	66	44	40	7	1	3	0	37	2	33	3	1	2	4	.333	0	0	5.63
1995	Sea-LA		39	0	0	11	44.1	195	46	24	20	3	3	3	0	17	6	25	5	1	3	1	.750	0	0	4.06
1995	Seattle	AL	4	0	0	0	5.1	30	8	8	7	0	1	2	0	7	2	4	4	1	0	0	.000	0	0	11.81
	Los Angeles	NL	35	0	0	11	39	165	38	16	13	3	2	1	0	10	4	21	1	0	3	1	.750	0	0	3.00
	3 ML YEARS		66	16	1	13	154.2	687	171	101	91	16	4	8	2	70	10	77	9	3	5	11	.313	0	0	5.30

Midre Cummings

Bats: Left **Throws:** Right **Pos:** CF/RF   **Ht:** 6' 0" **Wt:** 196 **Born:** 10/14/71 **Age:** 24

						BATTING															BASERUNNING				PERCENTAGES		
Year	Team	Lg	G	AB	H	2B	3B	HR	(Hm	Rd)	TB	R	RBI	TBB	IBB	SO	HBP	SH	SF	SB	CS	SB%	GDP	Avg	OBP	SLG
1990	Twins	R	47	177	56	3	4	5	--	--	82	28	28	13	1	32	2	0	4	13	9	.59	1	.316	.362	.463
1991	Kenosha	A	106	382	123	20	4	4	--	--	163	59	54	22	2	66	6	4	2	28	10	.74	7	.322	.367	.427
1992	Salem	A	113	420	128	20	5	14	--	--	200	55	75	35	2	67	4	0	3	23	9	.72	2	.305	.361	.476
1993	Carolina	AA	63	237	70	17	2	6	--	--	109	33	26	14	1	23	1	2	0	5	3	.63	5	.295	.337	.460
	Buffalo	AAA	60	232	64	12	1	9	--	--	105	36	21	22	4	45	0	0	2	5	1	.83	4	.276	.336	.453
1994	Buffalo	AAA	49	183	57	12	4	2	--	--	83	23	22	13	0	26	2	0	2	5	0	1.00	11	.311	.360	.454
1995	Calgary	AAA	45	159	44	9	1	1	--	--	58	19	16	6	4	27	2	0	5	1	1	.50	1	.277	.302	.365
1993	Pittsburgh	NL	13	36	4	1	0	0	(0	0)	5	5	3	4	0	9	0	0	1	0	0	.00	1	.111	.195	.139
1994	Pittsburgh	NL	24	86	21	4	0	1	(1	0)	28	11	12	4	0	18	1	0	1	0	0	.00	0	.244	.283	.326
1995	Pittsburgh	NL	59	152	37	7	1	2	(1	1)	52	13	15	13	3	30	0	0	0	1	0	1.00	1	.243	.303	.342
	3 ML YEARS		96	274	62	12	1	3	(2	1)	85	29	30	21	3	57	1	0	2	1	0	1.00	2	.226	.282	.310

Chad Curtis

Bats: Right **Throws:** Right **Pos:** CF **Ht:** 5'10" **Wt:** 175 **Born:** 11/6/68 **Age:** 27

Year	Team	Lg	G	AB	H	2B	3B	HR	(Hm	Rd)	TB	R	RBI	TBB	IBB	SO	HBP	SH	SF	SB	CS	SB%	GDP	Avg	OBP	SLG
1992	California	AL	139	441	114	16	2	10	(5	5)	164	59	46	51	2	71	6	5	4	43	18	.70	10	.259	.341	.372
1993	California	AL	152	583	166	25	3	6	(3	3)	215	94	59	70	2	89	4	7	7	48	24	.67	16	.285	.361	.369
1994	California	AL	114	453	116	23	4	11	(8	3)	180	67	50	37	0	69	5	7	4	25	11	.69	10	.256	.317	.397
1995	Detroit	AL	144	586	157	29	3	21	(11	10)	255	96	67	70	3	93	7	0	7	27	15	.64	12	.268	.349	.435
	4 ML YEARS		549	2063	553	93	12	48	(27	21)	814	316	222	228	7	322	22	19	22	143	68	.68	48	.268	.344	.395

Milt Cuyler

Bats: Both **Throws:** Right **Pos:** LF **Ht:** 5'10" **Wt:** 185 **Born:** 10/7/68 **Age:** 27

Year	Team	Lg	G	AB	H	2B	3B	HR	(Hm	Rd)	TB	R	RBI	TBB	IBB	SO	HBP	SH	SF	SB	CS	SB%	GDP	Avg	OBP	SLG
1995	Toledo *	AAA	54	203	62	10	4	6	--	--	98	33	28	20	0	40	5	0	4	6	7	.46	1	.305	.375	.483
1990	Detroit	AL	19	51	13	3	1	0	(0	0)	18	8	8	5	0	10	0	2	1	1	2	.33	1	.255	.316	.353
1991	Detroit	AL	154	475	122	15	7	3	(1	2)	160	77	33	52	0	92	5	12	2	41	10	.80	4	.257	.335	.337
1992	Detroit	AL	89	291	70	11	1	3	(1	2)	92	39	28	10	0	62	4	8	0	8	5	.62	4	.241	.275	.316
1993	Detroit	AL	82	249	53	11	7	0	(0	0)	78	46	19	19	0	53	3	4	1	13	2	.87	2	.213	.276	.313
1994	Detroit	AL	48	116	28	3	1	1	(1	0)	36	20	11	13	0	21	1	2	2	5	3	.63	3	.241	.318	.310
1995	Detroit	AL	41	88	18	1	4	0	(0	0)	27	15	5	8	0	16	0	2	0	2	1	.67	0	.205	.271	.307
	6 ML YEARS		433	1270	304	44	21	7	(3	4)	411	205	104	107	0	254	13	30	6	70	23	.75	14	.239	.304	.324

Omar Daal

Pitches: Left **Bats:** Left **Pos:** RP **Ht:** 6' 3" **Wt:** 185 **Born:** 3/1/72 **Age:** 24

Year	Team	Lg	G	GS	CG	GF	IP	BFP	H	R	ER	HR	SH	SF	HB	TBB	IBB	SO	WP	Bk	W	L	Pct.	ShO	Sv	ERA
1995	Albuquerque *	AAA	17	9	0	3	53.1	232	56	28	24	3	0	0	1	26	2	46	1	0	2	3	.400	0	1	4.05
1993	Los Angeles	NL	47	0	0	12	35.1	155	36	20	20	5	2	2	0	21	3	19	1	2	2	3	.400	0	0	5.09
1994	Los Angeles	NL	24	0	0	5	13.2	55	12	5	5	1	1	0	0	5	0	9	1	1	0	0	.000	0	0	3.29
1995	Los Angeles	NL	28	0	0	0	20	100	29	16	16	1	1	1	1	15	4	11	0	1	4	0	1.000	0	0	7.20
	3 ML YEARS		99	0	0	17	69	310	77	41	41	7	4	3	1	41	7	39	2	4	6	3	.667	0	0	5.35

Mark Dalesandro

Bats: Right **Throws:** Right **Pos:** C **Ht:** 6' 0" **Wt:** 185 **Born:** 5/14/68 **Age:** 28

Year	Team	Lg	G	AB	H	2B	3B	HR	(Hm	Rd)	TB	R	RBI	TBB	IBB	SO	HBP	SH	SF	SB	CS	SB%	GDP	Avg	OBP	SLG
1990	Boise	A	55	223	75	10	2	6	--	--	107	35	44	19	2	42	1	0	1	6	1	.86	6	.336	.389	.480
1991	Quad City	A	125	487	133	17	8	5	--	--	181	63	69	34	1	58	6	0	4	1	2	.33	10	.273	.326	.372
1992	Palm Spring	A	126	492	146	30	3	7	--	--	203	72	92	33	6	50	5	0	6	6	2	.75	20	.297	.343	.413
1993	Palm Spring	A	46	176	43	5	3	1	--	--	57	22	25	15	1	20	0	0	7	3	2	.60	9	.244	.293	.324
	Midland	AA	57	235	69	9	0	2	--	--	84	33	36	8	2	30	4	0	5	1	1	.50	9	.294	.321	.357
	Vancouver	AAA	26	107	32	8	1	2	--	--	48	16	15	6	1	13	1	0	1	1	0	1.00	4	.299	.339	.449
1994	Vancouver	AAA	51	199	63	9	1	1	--	--	77	29	31	7	0	19	1	0	2	1	0	1.00	6	.317	.340	.387
1995	Vancouver	AAA	34	123	41	13	1	1	--	--	59	16	18	6	0	12	1	1	0	2	0	1.00	2	.333	.366	.480
1994	California	AL	19	25	5	1	0	1	(1	0)	9	5	2	2	0	4	0	0	0	0	0	.00	2	.200	.259	.360
1995	California	AL	11	10	1	1	0	0	(0	0)	2	1	0	0	0	2	0	0	0	0	0	.00	0	.100	.100	.200
	2 ML YEARS		30	35	6	2	0	1	(1	0)	11	6	2	2	0	6	0	0	0	0	0	.00	2	.171	.216	.314

Johnny Damon

Bats: Left **Throws:** Left **Pos:** CF **Ht:** 6' 0" **Wt:** 175 **Born:** 11/5/73 **Age:** 22

Year	Team	Lg	G	AB	H	2B	3B	HR	(Hm	Rd)	TB	R	RBI	TBB	IBB	SO	HBP	SH	SF	SB	CS	SB%	GDP	Avg	OBP	SLG
1992	Royals	R	50	192	67	12	9	4	--	--	109	58	24	31	1	21	4	4	0	23	6	.79	1	.349	.449	.568
	Baseball Cy	A	1	1	0	0	0	0	--	--	0	0	0	0	0	0	0	0	0	0	0	.00	0	.000	.000	.000
1993	Rockford	A	127	511	148	25	13	5	--	--	214	82	50	51	1	83	6	3	3	59	18	.77	4	.290	.359	.419
1994	Wilmington	A	119	472	149	25	13	6	--	--	218	96	75	62	6	55	8	5	7	44	9	.83	4	.316	.399	.462
1995	Wichita	AA	111	423	145	15	9	16	--	--	226	83	54	67	13	35	2	10	1	26	15	.63	3	.343	.434	.534
1995	Kansas City	AL	47	188	53	11	5	3	(1	2)	83	32	23	12	0	22	1	2	3	7	0	1.00	2	.282	.324	.441

Ron Darling

Pitches: Right **Bats:** Right **Pos:** SP **Ht:** 6' 3" **Wt:** 195 **Born:** 8/19/60 **Age:** 35

Year	Team	Lg	G	GS	CG	GF	IP	BFP	H	R	ER	HR	SH	SF	HB	TBB	IBB	SO	WP	Bk	W	L	Pct.	ShO	Sv	ERA
1983	New York	NL	5	5	1	0	35.1	148	31	11	11	0	3	0	3	17	1	23	3	2	1	3	.250	0	0	2.80
1984	New York	NL	33	33	2	0	205.2	884	179	97	87	17	7	6	5	104	2	136	7	1	12	9	.571	2	0	3.81

Year Team		Lg	G	GS	CG	GF	IP	BFP	H	R	ER	HR	SH	SF	HB	TBB	IBB	SO	WP	Bk	W	L	Pct.	ShO	Sv	ERA
1985 New York		NL	36	35	4	1	248	1043	214	93	80	21	13	4	3	**114**	1	167	7	1	16	6	.727	2	0	2.90
1986 New York		NL	34	34	4	0	237	967	203	84	74	21	10	6	3	81	2	184	7	3	15	6	.714	2	0	2.81
1987 New York		NL	32	32	2	0	207.2	891	183	111	99	24	5	3	3	96	3	167	6	3	12	8	.600	0	0	4.29
1988 New York		NL	34	34	7	0	240.2	971	218	97	87	24	10	8	5	60	2	161	7	2	17	9	.654	4	0	3.25
1989 New York		NL	33	33	4	0	217.1	922	214	100	85	19	7	**13**	5	70	7	153	12	4	14	14	.500	0	0	3.52
1990 New York		NL	33	18	1	3	126	554	135	73	63	20	7	3	5	44	4	99	5	1	7	9	.438	0	0	4.50
1991 Oak-Mon-NYN			32	32	0	0	194.1	827	185	100	92	22	12	8	9	71	3	129	16	5	8	15	.348	0	0	4.26
1992 Oakland		AL	33	33	4	0	206.1	866	198	98	84	15	4	3	4	72	5	99	13	0	15	10	.600	3	0	3.66
1993 Oakland		AL	31	29	3	1	178	793	198	107	102	22	5	6	5	72	5	95	3	1	5	9	.357	0	0	5.16
1994 Oakland		AL	25	**25**	4	0	160	682	162	89	80	18	5	5	7	59	3	108	6	1	10	11	.476	0	0	4.50
1995 Oakland		AL	21	21	1	0	104	484	124	79	72	16	7	8	4	46	2	69	5	0	4	7	.364	0	0	6.23
1991 Oakland		AL	12	12	0	0	75	319	64	34	34	7	5	4	2	38	2	60	3	1	3	7	.300	0	0	4.08
Montreal		NL	3	3	0	0	17	81	25	16	14	6	0	0	1	5	0	11	4	0	0	2	.000	0	0	7.41
New York		NL	17	17	0	0	102.1	427	96	50	44	9	7	4	6	28	1	58	9	4	5	6	.455	0	0	3.87
13 ML YEARS			382	364	37	5	2360.1	10032	2244	1139	1016	239	95	73	59	906	40	1590	97	24	136	116	.540	13	0	3.87

Danny Darwin

Pitches: Right **Bats:** Right **Pos:** SP/RP   **Ht:** 6' 3" **Wt:** 202 **Born:** 10/25/55 **Age:** 40

			HOW MUCH HE PITCHED						WHAT HE GAVE UP												THE RESULTS					
Year Team		Lg	G	GS	CG	GF	IP	BFP	H	R	ER	HR	SH	SF	HB	TBB	IBB	SO	WP	Bk	W	L	Pct.	ShO	Sv	ERA
1995 Okla. City *		AAA	1	1	0	0	3	10	1	0	0	0	0	0	0	0	0	4	0	0	0	0	.000	0	0	0.00
1978 Texas		AL	3	1	0	2	9	36	11	4	4	0	0	1	0	1	0	8	0	0	1	0	1.000	0	0	4.00
1979 Texas		AL	20	6	1	4	78	313	50	36	35	5	3	6	5	30	2	58	0	1	4	4	.500	0	0	4.04
1980 Texas		AL	53	2	0	35	110	468	98	37	32	4	5	7	2	50	7	104	3	0	13	4	.765	0	8	2.62
1981 Texas		AL	22	22	6	0	146	601	115	67	59	12	8	3	6	57	5	98	1	0	9	9	.500	2	0	3.64
1982 Texas		AL	56	1	0	41	89	394	95	38	34	6	10	5	2	37	8	61	2	1	10	8	.556	0	7	3.44
1983 Texas		AL	28	26	9	0	183	780	175	86	71	9	7	7	3	62	3	92	2	0	8	13	.381	2	0	3.49
1984 Texas		AL	35	32	5	2	223.2	955	249	110	98	19	3	3	4	54	2	123	3	0	8	12	.400	1	0	3.94
1985 Milwaukee		AL	39	29	11	8	217.2	919	212	112	92	**34**	7	9	4	65	4	125	6	0	8	18	.308	1	2	3.80
1986 Mil-Hou			39	22	6	6	184.2	759	170	81	65	16	6	9	3	44	1	120	7	1	11	10	.524	1	0	3.17
1987 Houston		NL	33	30	3	0	195.2	833	184	87	78	17	8	3	5	69	12	134	3	1	9	10	.474	1	0	3.59
1988 Houston		NL	44	20	3	9	192	804	189	86	82	20	10	9	7	48	9	129	1	2	8	13	.381	0	3	3.84
1989 Houston		NL	68	0	0	26	122	482	92	34	32	8	8	5	2	33	9	104	2	3	11	4	.733	0	7	2.36
1990 Houston		NL	48	17	3	14	162.2	646	136	42	40	11	4	2	4	31	4	109	0	2	11	4	.733	0	2	**2.21**
1991 Boston		AL	12	12	0	0	68	292	71	39	39	15	1	2	4	15	1	42	2	0	3	6	.333	0	0	5.16
1992 Boston		AL	51	15	2	21	161.1	688	159	76	71	11	7	5	5	53	9	124	5	0	9	9	.500	0	3	3.96
1993 Boston		AL	34	34	2	0	229.1	919	196	93	83	31	6	9	3	49	8	130	5	1	15	11	.577	1	0	3.26
1994 Boston		AL	13	13	0	0	75.2	350	101	54	53	13	1	5	1	24	6	54	0	0	7	5	.583	0	0	6.30
1995 Tor-Tex		AL	20	15	1	0	99	448	131	87	82	25	3	5	4	31	3	58	2	0	3	10	.231	0	0	7.45
1986 Milwaukee		AL	27	14	5	4	130.1	537	120	62	51	13	5	6	3	35	1	80	5	0	8	6	.429	1	0	3.52
Houston		NL	12	8	1	2	54.1	222	50	19	14	3	1	3	0	9	0	40	2	1	5	2	.714	0	0	2.32
1995 Toronto		AL	13	11	1	0	65	303	91	60	55	13	3	5	3	24	2	36	1	0	1	8	.111	0	0	7.62
Texas		AL	7	4	0	0	34	145	40	27	27	12	0	0	1	7	1	22	1	0	2	2	.500	0	0	7.15
18 ML YEARS			618	297	52	168	2546.2	10687	2434	1169	1050	256	97	95	64	753	93	1673	44	12	148	150	.497	9	32	3.71

Darren Daulton

Bats: Left **Throws:** Right **Pos:** C   **Ht:** 6' 2" **Wt:** 200 **Born:** 1/3/62 **Age:** 34

			BATTING																BASERUNNING				PERCENTAGES		
Year Team		Lg	G	AB	H	2B	3B	HR	(Hm	Rd)	TB	R	RBI	TBB	IBB	SO	HBP	SH	SF	SB	CS	SB%	GDP	Avg	OBP	SLG
1983 Philadelphia		NL	2	3	1	0	0	0	(0	0)	1	1	0	1	0	1	0	0	0	0	0	.00	0	.333	.500	.333
1985 Philadelphia		NL	36	103	21	3	1	4	(0	4)	38	14	11	16	0	37	0	0	0	3	0	1.00	0	.204	.311	.369
1986 Philadelphia		NL	49	138	31	4	0	8	(4	4)	59	18	21	38	3	41	1	2	2	2	3	.40	1	.225	.391	.428
1987 Philadelphia		NL	53	129	25	6	0	3	(1	2)	40	10	13	16	1	37	0	4	1	0	0	.00	2	.194	.281	.310
1988 Philadelphia		NL	58	144	30	6	0	1	(0	1)	39	13	12	17	1	26	0	0	2	2	1	.67	2	.208	.288	.271
1989 Philadelphia		NL	131	368	74	12	2	8	(2	6)	114	29	44	52	8	58	2	1	1	2	1	.67	4	.201	.303	.310
1990 Philadelphia		NL	143	459	123	30	1	12	(5	7)	191	62	57	72	9	72	2	3	4	7	1	.88	6	.268	.367	.416
1991 Philadelphia		NL	89	285	56	12	0	12	(8	4)	104	36	42	41	4	66	2	2	5	5	0	1.00	5	.196	.297	.365
1992 Philadelphia		NL	145	485	131	32	5	27	(17	10)	254	80	**109**	88	11	103	6	0	6	11	2	.85	3	.270	.385	.524
1993 Philadelphia		NL	147	510	131	35	4	24	(10	14)	246	90	105	117	12	111	2	0	8	5	1	1.00	5	.257	.392	.482
1994 Philadelphia		NL	69	257	77	17	1	15	(7	8)	141	43	56	33	2	43	1	0	1	4	1	.80	3	.300	.367	.549
1995 Philadelphia		NL	98	342	85	19	3	9	(7	2)	137	44	55	55	2	52	5	0	2	3	1	1.00	4	.249	.359	.401
12 ML YEARS			1020	3223	785	176	17	123	(61	62)	1364	440	525	546	53	647	21	12	32	44	9	.83	30	.244	.354	.423

Chili Davis

Bats: Both **Throws:** Right **Pos:** DH **Ht:** 6' 3" **Wt:** 217 **Born:** 1/17/60 **Age:** 36

					BATTING													BASERUNNING				PERCENTAGES		
Year	Team	Lg	G	AB	H	2B	3B	HR	(Hm | Rd)	TB	R	RBI	TBB	IBB	SO	HBP	SH	SF	SB	CS	SB%	GDP	Avg	OBP	SLG
1981	San Francisco	NL	8	15	2	0	0	0	(0 | 0)	2	1	0	1	0	2	0	0	0	2	0	1.00	1	.133	.188	.133
1982	San Francisco	NL	154	641	167	27	6	19	(6 | 13)	263	86	76	45	2	115	2	7	6	24	13	.65	13	.261	.308	.410
1983	San Francisco	NL	137	486	113	21	2	11	(7 | 4)	171	54	59	55	6	108	0	3	9	10	12	.45	9	.233	.305	.352
1984	San Francisco	NL	137	499	157	21	6	21	(7 | 14)	253	87	81	42	6	74	1	2	2	12	8	.60	13	.315	.368	.507
1985	San Francisco	NL	136	481	130	25	2	13	(7 | 6)	198	53	56	62	12	74	0	1	7	15	7	.68	16	.270	.349	.412
1986	San Francisco	NL	153	526	146	28	3	13	(7 | 6)	219	71	70	84	23	96	1	2	5	16	13	.55	11	.278	.375	.416
1987	San Francisco	NL	149	500	125	22	1	24	(9 | 15)	221	80	76	72	15	109	2	0	4	16	9	.64	8	.250	.344	.442
1988	California	AL	158	600	161	29	3	21	(11 | 10)	259	81	93	56	14	118	0	1	10	9	10	.47	13	.268	.326	.432
1989	California	AL	154	560	152	24	1	22	(6 | 16)	244	81	90	61	12	109	0	3	6	3	0	1.00	21	.271	.340	.436
1990	California	AL	113	412	109	17	1	12	(10 | 2)	164	58	58	61	4	89	0	0	3	1	2	.33	14	.265	.357	.398
1991	Minnesota	AL	153	534	148	34	1	29	(14 | 15)	271	84	93	95	13	117	1	0	9	5	6	.45	9	.277	.385	.507
1992	Minnesota	AL	138	444	128	27	2	12	(6 | 6)	195	63	66	73	11	76	3	0	9	4	5	.44	11	.288	.386	.439
1993	California	AL	153	573	139	32	0	27	(13 | 14)	252	74	112	71	12	135	1	0	6	4	1	.80	18	.243	.327	.440
1994	California	AL	108	392	122	18	1	26	(14 | 12)	220	72	84	69	11	84	1	0	6	3	2	.60	12	.311	.410	.561
1995	California	AL	119	424	135	23	0	20	(11 | 9)	218	81	86	89	12	79	0	0	9	3	3	.50	12	.318	.429	.514
	15 ML YEARS		1970	7087	1934	348	29	270	(128 | 142)	3150	1026	1100	936	153	1385	12	19	80	127	91	.58	181	.273	.355	.444

Russ Davis

Bats: Right **Throws:** Right **Pos:** 3B **Ht:** 6' 0" **Wt:** 195 **Born:** 9/13/69 **Age:** 26

					BATTING													BASERUNNING				PERCENTAGES		
Year	Team	Lg	G	AB	H	2B	3B	HR	(Hm	Rd)	TB	R	RBI	TBB	IBB	SO	HBP	SH	SF	SB	CS	SB%	GDP	Avg	OBP	SLG
1988	Yankees	R	58	213	49	11	3	2	--	--	72	33	30	16	0	39	1	2	3	6	2	.75	2	.230	.283	.338
1989	Ft. Laud	A	48	147	27	5	1	2	--	--	40	8	22	11	0	38	0	4	0	3	1	.75	4	.184	.241	.272
	Oneonta	A	65	236	68	7	5	7	--	--	106	33	42	19	0	44	1	1	2	3	3	.50	3	.288	.341	.449
1990	Pr. William	A	137	510	127	37	3	16	--	--	218	55	71	37	1	136	5	0	6	3	1	.75	6	.249	.303	.427
1991	Albany-Colo	AA	135	473	103	23	3	8	--	--	156	57	58	50	1	102	5	1	6	3	0	1.00	8	.218	.296	.330
1992	Albany-Colo	AA	132	491	140	23	4	22	--	--	237	77	71	49	0	93	7	0	5	3	3	.50	11	.285	.355	.483
1993	Columbus	AAA	113	424	108	24	1	26	--	--	212	63	83	40	2	117	3	2	6	1	1	.50	7	.255	.319	.500
1994	Columbus	AAA	117	416	115	30	2	25	--	--	224	76	69	62	2	93	5	0	3	3	7	.30	5	.276	.374	.538
1995	Columbus	AAA	20	76	19	4	1	2	--	--	31	12	15	17	3	23	1	0	0	0	0	.00	0	.250	.389	.408
1994	New York	AL	4	14	2	0	0	0	(0	0)	2	0	1	0	0	4	0	0	0	0	0	.00	0	.143	.143	.143
1995	New York	AL	40	98	27	5	2	2	(2	0)	42	14	12	10	0	26	1	0	0	0	0	.00	1	.276	.349	.429
	2 ML YEARS		44	112	29	5	2	2	(2	0)	44	14	13	10	0	30	1	0	0	0	0	.00	1	.259	.325	.393

Tim Davis

Pitches: Left **Bats:** Left **Pos:** SP **Ht:** 5'11" **Wt:** 165 **Born:** 7/14/70 **Age:** 25

			HOW MUCH HE PITCHED					WHAT HE GAVE UP										THE RESULTS				
Year	Team	Lg	G	GS	CG	GF	IP	BFP	H	R	ER	HR	SH	SF	HB	TBB	IBB	SO	WP	Bk	W	L	Pct.	ShO	Sv	ERA
1993	Appleton	A	16	10	3	4	77.2	313	54	20	16	5	1	2	2	33	0	89	4	2	10	2	.833	2	2	1.85
	Riverside	A	18	0	0	17	30.2	117	14	6	6	1	0	1	1	9	0	56	1	0	3	0	1.000	0	7	1.76
1994	Calgary	AAA	6	6	1	0	39.2	161	35	13	8	1	1	1	0	8	0	43	0	0	3	1	.750	0	0	1.82
1995	Tacoma	AAA	2	2	0	0	13.1	57	15	8	8	2	0	0	0	4	0	13	0	0	0	0	.000	0	0	5.40
1994	Seattle	AL	42	1	0	12	49.1	225	57	25	22	4	3	3	1	25	5	28	6	0	2	2	.500	0	2	4.01
1995	Seattle	AL	5	5	0	0	24	117	30	21	17	2	0	1	0	18	2	19	0	0	2	1	.667	0	0	6.38
	2 ML YEARS		47	6	0	12	73.1	342	87	46	39	6	3	4	1	43	7	47	6	0	4	3	.571	0	2	4.79

Scott Davison

Pitches: Right **Bats:** Right **Pos:** RP **Ht:** 6' 0" **Wt:** 190 **Born:** 10/16/70 **Age:** 25

			HOW MUCH HE PITCHED					WHAT HE GAVE UP										THE RESULTS				
Year	Team	Lg	G	GS	CG	GF	IP	BFP	H	R	ER	HR	SH	SF	HB	TBB	IBB	SO	WP	Bk	W	L	Pct.	ShO	Sv	ERA
1994	Bellingham	A	13	0	0	11	15	66	11	5	3	0	1	0	1	6	1	21	3	2	0	1	.000	0	7	1.80
	Appleton	A	4	0	0	2	7.1	30	7	4	3	0	0	2	0	2	0	7	0	2	0	1	.000	0	0	3.68
	Calgary	AAA	11	0	0	3	14.2	67	20	10	10	1	0	0	1	6	0	17	2	1	0	1	.000	0	0	6.14
1995	Tacoma	AAA	8	3	0	2	22	91	21	14	13	1	1	1	0	4	0	12	1	1	1	1	.500	0	0	5.32
	Port City	AA	34	0	0	28	40.2	156	22	4	4	1	6	2	1	16	1	50	2	0	2	0	1.000	0	10	0.89
1995	Seattle	AL	3	0	0	3	4.1	21	7	3	3	0	0	0	0	1	0	3	0	0	0	0	.000	0	0	6.23

Andre Dawson

Bats: Right **Throws:** Right **Pos:** RF/LF **Ht:** 6' 3" **Wt:** 197 **Born:** 7/10/54 **Age:** 41

					BATTING													BASERUNNING				PERCENTAGES		
Year	Team	Lg	G	AB	H	2B	3B	HR	(Hm	Rd)	TB	R	RBI	TBB	IBB	SO	HBP	SH	SF	SB	CS	SB%	GDP	Avg	OBP	SLG
1995	Brevard Cty *	A	3	10	1	0	0	0	--	--	1	0	0	0	0	2	0	0	0	0	0	.00	1	.100	.100	.100
1976	Montreal	NL	24	85	20	4	1	0	(0	0)	26	9	7	5	1	13	0	2	0	1	2	.33	0	.235	.278	.306
1977	Montreal	NL	139	525	148	26	9	19	(7	12)	249	64	65	34	4	93	2	1	4	21	7	.75	6	.282	.326	.474

Year	Team	Lg	G	AB	H	2B	3B	HR	(Hm	Rd)	TB	R	RBI	TBB	IBB	SO	HBP	SH	SF	SB	CS	SB%	GDP	Avg	OBP	SLG
1978	Montreal	NL	157	609	154	24	8	25	(12	13)	269	84	72	30	3	128	12	4	5	28	11	.72	7	.253	.299	.442
1979	Montreal	NL	155	639	176	24	12	25	(13	12)	299	90	92	27	5	115	6	8	4	35	10	.78	10	.275	.309	.468
1980	Montreal	NL	151	577	178	41	7	17	(7	10)	284	96	87	44	7	69	6	1	10	34	9	.79	9	.308	.358	.492
1981	Montreal	NL	103	394	119	21	3	24	(9	15)	218	71	64	35	14	50	7	0	5	26	4	.87	6	.302	.365	.553
1982	Montreal	NL	148	608	183	37	7	23	(9	14)	303	107	83	34	4	96	8	4	6	39	10	.80	8	.301	.343	.498
1983	Montreal	NL	159	633	189	36	10	32	(10	22)	341	104	113	38	12	81	9	0	18	25	11	.69	14	.299	.338	.539
1984	Montreal	NL	138	533	132	23	6	17	(6	11)	218	73	86	41	2	80	2	1	6	13	5	.72	12	.248	.301	.409
1985	Montreal	NL	139	529	135	27	2	23	(11	12)	235	65	91	29	8	92	4	1	7	13	4	.76	12	.255	.295	.444
1986	Montreal	NL	130	496	141	32	2	20	(11	9)	237	65	78	37	11	79	6	1	6	18	12	.60	13	.284	.338	.478
1987	Chicago	NL	153	621	178	24	2	49	(27	22)	353	90	137	32	7	103	7	0	2	11	3	.79	15	.287	.328	.568
1988	Chicago	NL	157	591	179	31	8	24	(12	12)	298	78	79	37	12	73	4	1	7	12	4	.75	13	.303	.344	.504
1989	Chicago	NL	118	416	105	18	6	21	(6	15)	198	62	77	35	13	62	1	0	7	8	5	.62	16	.252	.307	.476
1990	Chicago	NL	147	529	164	28	5	27	(14	13)	283	72	100	42	21	65	2	0	8	16	2	.89	12	.310	.358	.535
1991	Chicago	NL	149	563	153	21	4	31	(22	9)	275	69	104	22	3	80	5	0	6	4	5	.44	13	.272	.302	.488
1992	Chicago	NL	143	542	150	27	2	22	(13	9)	247	60	90	30	8	70	4	0	6	6	2	.75	13	.277	.316	.456
1993	Boston	AL	121	461	126	29	1	13	(8	5)	196	44	67	17	4	49	13	0	7	2	1	.67	18	.273	.313	.425
1994	Boston	AL	75	292	70	18	0	16	(7	9)	136	34	48	9	3	53	4	0	1	2	2	.50	15	.240	.271	.466
1995	Florida	NL	79	226	58	10	3	8	(1	7)	98	30	37	9	1	45	8	0	3	0	0	.00	7	.257	.305	.434
20 ML YEARS			2585	9869	2758	501	98	436	(205	231)	4763	1367	1577	587	143	1496	110	24	118	314	109	.74	216	.279	.323	.483

Steve Decker

Bats: Right **Throws:** Right **Pos:** C **Ht:** 6' 3" **Wt:** 220 **Born:** 10/25/65 **Age:** 30

			BATTING																	BASERUNNING				PERCENTAGES		
Year	Team	Lg	G	AB	H	2B	3B	HR	(Hm	Rd)	TB	R	RBI	TBB	IBB	SO	HBP	SH	SF	SB	CS	SB%	GDP	Avg	OBP	SLG
1990	San Francisco	NL	15	54	16	2	0	3	(1	2)	27	5	8	1	0	10	0	1	0	0	0	.00	1	.296	.309	.500
1991	San Francisco	NL	79	233	48	7	1	5	(4	1)	72	11	24	16	1	44	3	2	4	0	1	.00	7	.206	.262	.309
1992	San Francisco	NL	15	43	7	1	0	0	(0	0)	8	3	1	6	0	7	1	0	0	0	0	.00	0	.163	.280	.186
1993	Florida	NL	8	15	0	0	0	0	(0	0)	0	0	1	3	0	3	0	0	1	0	0	.00	2	.000	.158	.000
1995	Florida	NL	51	133	30	2	1	3	(2	1)	43	12	13	19	1	22	0	0	2	1	0	1.00	1	.226	.318	.323
5 ML YEARS			168	478	101	12	2	11	(7	4)	150	31	47	45	2	86	4	3	7	1	1	.50	11	.211	.281	.314

Jim Dedrick

Pitches: Right **Bats:** Both **Pos:** RP **Ht:** 6' 0" **Wt:** 185 **Born:** 4/4/68 **Age:** 28

			HOW MUCH HE PITCHED						WHAT HE GAVE UP											THE RESULTS					
Year	Team	Lg	G	GS	CG	GF	IP	BFP	H	R	ER	HR	SH	SF	HB	TBB	IBB	SO	WP	Bk	W	L	Pct.	ShO	Sv	ERA
1990	Wausau	A	3	1	0	1	10	41	6	4	3	0	0	0	0	4	0	8	0	3	0	1	.000	0	0	2.70
1991	Kane County	A	16	15	0	0	88.1	380	84	38	29	2	1	2	5	38	1	71	5	2	4	5	.444	0	0	2.95
1992	Frederick	A	38	5	1	19	108.2	454	94	41	37	5	5	0	5	42	4	86	4	3	8	4	.667	0	3	3.06
1993	Bowie	AA	38	6	1	14	106.1	426	84	36	30	4	5	0	3	32	1	78	1	0	8	3	.727	1	3	2.54
	Rochester	AAA	1	1	1	0	7	27	6	2	2	2	0	0	0	0	0	3	0	0	1	0	1.000	0	0	2.57
1994	Rochester	AAA	44	1	0	18	99	421	98	56	42	7	3	1	3	35	7	70	4	1	3	6	.333	0	1	3.82
1995	Bowie	AA	10	10	0	0	60.1	267	59	24	20	7	2	2	5	25	2	48	5	1	4	2	.667	0	0	2.98
	Rochester	AAA	24	2	0	4	45.2	190	45	9	9	0	2	4	1	14	1	31	4	0	4	0	1.000	0	1	1.77
1995	Baltimore	AL	6	0	0	1	7.2	35	8	2	2	1	0	2	1	6	0	3	0	0	0	0	.000	0	0	2.35

Jose DeLeon

Pitches: Right **Bats:** Right **Pos:** RP **Ht:** 6' 3" **Wt:** 226 **Born:** 12/20/60 **Age:** 35

			HOW MUCH HE PITCHED						WHAT HE GAVE UP											THE RESULTS					
Year	Team	Lg	G	GS	CG	GF	IP	BFP	H	R	ER	HR	SH	SF	HB	TBB	IBB	SO	WP	Bk	W	L	Pct.	ShO	Sv	ERA
1983	Pittsburgh	NL	15	15	3	0	108	438	75	36	34	5	4	3	1	47	2	118	5	2	7	3	.700	2	0	2.83
1984	Pittsburgh	NL	30	28	5	0	192.1	795	147	86	80	10	7	7	3	92	5	153	6	2	7	13	.350	1	0	3.74
1985	Pittsburgh	NL	31	25	1	5	162.2	700	138	93	85	15	7	4	3	89	3	149	7	1	2	19	.095	0	3	4.70
1986	ChA-Pit		22	14	1	5	95.1	408	66	46	41	9	5	1	5	59	3	79	7	0	5	8	.385	0	1	3.87
1987	Chicago	AL	33	31	2	0	206	889	177	106	92	24	6	6	10	97	4	153	6	1	11	12	.478	0	0	4.02
1988	St. Louis	NL	34	34	3	0	225.1	940	198	95	92	13	10	7	2	86	7	208	10	0	13	10	.565	1	0	3.67
1989	St. Louis	NL	36	36	5	0	244.2	972	173	96	83	16	5	3	6	80	5	201	2	0	16	12	.571	3	0	3.05
1990	St. Louis	NL	32	32	0	0	182.2	793	168	96	90	15	11	8	5	86	9	164	5	0	7	19	.269	0	0	4.43
1991	St. Louis	NL	28	28	1	0	162.2	679	144	57	49	15	5	4	6	61	1	118	1	1	5	9	.357	0	0	2.71
1992	Phi-StL	NL	32	18	0	3	117.1	506	111	63	57	7	6	6	2	48	1	79	3	0	2	8	.200	0	0	4.37
1993	ChA-Phi		35	3	0	7	57.1	244	44	27	19	7	3	2	6	30	3	40	5	0	3	0	1.000	0	0	2.98
1994	Chicago	AL	42	0	0	11	67	288	48	28	25	5	6	5	6	31	5	67	1	0	3	2	.600	0	2	3.36
1995	ChA-Mon		45	0	0	5	76	333	67	48	46	12	2	7	7	35	2	65	2	1	5	4	.556	0	0	5.45
1986		AL	13	13	1	0	79	325	49	30	26	7	4	1	4	42	0	68	6	0	4	5	.444	0	0	2.96
	Pittsburgh	NL	9	1	0	5	16.1	83	17	16	15	2	1	0	1	17	3	11	1	0	1	3	.250	0	0	8.27
1992	Philadelphia	NL	3	3	0	0	15	63	16	7	5	0	1	0	0	5	0	7	0	0	0	1	.000	0	0	3.00
	St. Louis	NL	29	15	0	3	102.1	443	95	56	52	7	5	6	2	43	1	72	3	0	2	7	.222	0	0	4.57
1993	Chicago	AL	11	0	0	1	10.1	37	5	2	2	2	0	0	1	3	0	6	0	0	0	0	.000	0	0	1.74
	Philadelphia	NL	24	3	0	6	47	207	39	25	17	5	3	2	5	27	3	34	5	0	3	0	1.000	0	0	3.26

Year	Team	Lg	G	GS	CG	GF	IP	BFP	H	R	ER	HR	SH	SF	HB	TBB	IBB	SO	WP	Bk	W	L	Pct.	ShO	Sv	ERA
1995	Chicago	AL	38	0	0	4	67.2	293	60	41	39	10	2	5	6	28	2	53	2	1	5	3	.625	0	0	5.19
	Montreal	NL	7	0	0	1	8.1	40	7	7	7	2	0	2	1	7	0	12	0	0	0	1	.000	0	0	7.56
13 ML YEARS			415	264	21	36	1897.1	7985	1556	877	793	153	77	63	62	841	50	1594	60	8	86	119	.420	7	6	3.76

Carlos Delgado

Bats: Left **Throws:** Right **Pos:** LF **Ht:** 6' 3" **Wt:** 206 **Born:** 6/25/72 **Age:** 24

							BATTING											BASERUNNING				PERCENTAGES		
Year	Team	Lg	G	AB	H	2B	3B	HR	(Hm	Rd)	TB	R	RBI	TBB	IBB	SO	HBP	SH	SF	SB	CS	SB%	GDP	Avg	OBP	SLG
1995	Syracuse *	AAA	91	333	106	23	4	22	--	--	203	59	74	45	7	78	5	0	4	0	4	.00	8	.318	.403	.610
1993	Toronto	AL	2	1	0	0	0	0	(0	0)	0	0	0	1	0	0	0	0	0	0	0	.00	0	.000	.500	.000
1994	Toronto	AL	43	130	28	2	0	9	(5	4)	57	17	24	25	4	46	3	0	1	1	1	.50	5	.215	.352	.438
1995	Toronto	AL	37	91	15	3	0	3	(2	1)	27	7	11	6	0	26	0	0	2	0	0	.00	1	.165	.212	.297
3 ML YEARS			82	222	43	5	0	12	(7	5)	84	24	35	32	4	72	3	0	3	1	1	.50	6	.194	.300	.378

Rich DeLucia

Pitches: Right **Bats:** Right **Pos:** RP **Ht:** 6' 0" **Wt:** 185 **Born:** 10/7/64 **Age:** 31

			HOW MUCH HE PITCHED						WHAT HE GAVE UP										THE RESULTS					
Year	Team	Lg	G	GS	CG	GF	IP	BFP	H	R	ER	HR	SH	SF	HB	TBB	IBB	SO	WP	Bk	W	L	Pct.	ShO	Sv	ERA
1990	Seattle	AL	5	5	1	0	36	144	30	9	8	2	2	0	0	9	0	20	0	0	1	2	.333	0	0	2.00
1991	Seattle	AL	32	31	0	0	182	779	176	101	103	31	5	14	4	78	4	98	10	0	12	13	.480	0	0	5.09
1992	Seattle	AL	30	11	0	6	83.2	382	100	55	51	13	2	2	2	35	1	66	1	0	3	6	.333	0	1	5.49
1993	Seattle	AL	30	1	0	11	42.2	195	46	24	22	5	1	1	1	23	3	48	4	0	3	6	.333	0	0	4.64
1994	Cincinnati	NL	8	0	0	2	10.2	47	9	6	5	4	0	0	0	5	0	15	1	0	0	0	.000	0	0	4.22
1995	St. Louis	NL	56	1	0	8	82.1	342	63	38	31	9	5	2	3	36	2	76	5	0	8	7	.533	0	0	3.39
6 ML YEARS			161	49	1	27	437.1	1889	424	239	220	64	15	19	10	186	10	323	21	0	27	34	.443	0	1	4.53

Jim Deshaies

Pitches: Left **Bats:** Left **Pos:** SP **Ht:** 6' 5" **Wt:** 220 **Born:** 6/23/60 **Age:** 36

			HOW MUCH HE PITCHED						WHAT HE GAVE UP										THE RESULTS					
Year	Team	Lg	G	GS	CG	GF	IP	BFP	H	R	ER	HR	SH	SF	HB	TBB	IBB	SO	WP	Bk	W	L	Pct.	ShO	Sv	ERA
1995	Scrantn-WB *	AAA	19	19	2	0	117.1	476	105	51	45	8	2	3	5	26	0	79	2	1	7	8	.467	1	0	3.45
1984	New York	AL	2	2	0	0	7	40	14	9	9	1	0	1	0	7	0	5	0	0	0	1	.000	0	0	11.57
1985	Houston	NL	2	0	0	0	3	10	1	0	0	0	0	0	0	0	0	2	0	0	0	0	.000	0	0	0.00
1986	Houston	NL	26	26	1	0	144	599	124	58	52	16	4	3	2	59	2	128	0	7	12	5	.706	1	0	3.25
1987	Houston	NL	26	25	1	0	152	648	149	81	78	22	9	3	0	57	7	104	4	5	11	6	.647	0	0	4.62
1988	Houston	NL	31	31	3	0	207	847	164	77	69	20	8	13	2	72	5	127	1	6	11	14	.440	2	0	3.00
1989	Houston	NL	34	34	6	0	225.2	928	180	80	73	15	11	5	4	79	8	153	8	1	15	10	.600	3	0	2.91
1990	Houston	NL	34	34	2	0	209.1	881	186	93	88	21	17	12	8	84	9	119	3	3	7	12	.368	0	0	3.78
1991	Houston	NL	28	28	1	0	161	686	156	90	89	19	4	7	1	72	5	98	0	5	5	12	.294	0	0	4.98
1992	San Diego	NL	15	15	0	0	96	395	92	40	35	6	3	2	1	33	2	46	1	2	4	7	.364	0	0	3.28
1993	Min-SF	NL	32	31	1	1	184.1	770	183	94	90	26	5	7	7	57	1	85	1	4	13	15	.464	0	0	4.39
1994	Minnesota	AL	25	25	0	0	130.1	596	170	109	107	30	5	5	2	54	0	78	1	2	6	12	.333	0	0	7.39
1995	Philadelphia	NL	2	2	0	0	5.1	32	15	12	12	3	0	0	0	1	0	6	0	0	0	1	.000	0	0	20.25
1993	Minnesota	AL	27	27	1	0	167.1	693	159	85	82	24	4	7	6	51	1	80	0	4	11	13	.458	0	0	4.41
	San Francisco	NL	5	4	0	1	17	77	24	9	8	2	1	0	1	6	0	5	1	0	2	2	.500	0	0	4.24
12 ML YEARS			257	253	15	1	1525	6432	1434	743	702	179	66	58	27	575	39	951	19	35	84	95	.469	6	0	4.14

Delino DeShields

Bats: Left **Throws:** Right **Pos:** 2B **Ht:** 6' 1" **Wt:** 175 **Born:** 1/15/69 **Age:** 27

							BATTING											BASERUNNING				PERCENTAGES		
Year	Team	Lg	G	AB	H	2B	3B	HR	(Hm | Rd)	TB	R	RBI	TBB	IBB	SO	HBP	SH	SF	SB	CS	SB%	GDP	Avg	OBP	SLG
1990	Montreal	NL	129	499	144	28	6	4	(3 | 1)	196	69	45	66	3	96	4	1	2	42	22	.66	10	.289	.375	.393
1991	Montreal	NL	151	563	134	15	4	10	(3 | 7)	187	83	51	95	2	151	2	8	5	56	23	.71	6	.238	.347	.332
1992	Montreal	NL	135	530	155	19	8	7	(1 | 6)	211	82	56	54	4	108	3	9	3	46	15	.75	10	.292	.359	.398
1993	Montreal	NL	123	481	142	17	7	2	(2 | 0)	179	75	29	72	3	64	3	4	2	43	10	.81	6	.295	.389	.372
1994	Los Angeles	NL	89	320	80	11	3	2	(1 | 1)	103	51	33	54	0	53	0	1	1	27	7	.79	9	.250	.357	.322
1995	Los Angeles	NL	127	425	109	18	3	8	(2 | 6)	157	66	37	63	4	83	1	3	1	39	14	.74	6	.256	.353	.369
6 ML YEARS			754	2818	764	108	31	33	(12 | 21)	1033	426	251	404	16	555	13	26	14	253	91	.74	47	.271	.363	.367

John DeSilva

Pitches: Right **Bats:** Right **Pos:** SP **Ht:** 6' 0" **Wt:** 195 **Born:** 9/30/67 **Age:** 28

			HOW MUCH HE PITCHED						WHAT HE GAVE UP										THE RESULTS					
Year	Team	Lg	G	GS	CG	GF	IP	BFP	H	R	ER	HR	SH	SF	HB	TBB	IBB	SO	WP	Bk	W	L	Pct.	ShO	Sv	ERA
1989	Niagara Fal	A	4	4	0	0	24	95	15	5	5	0	1	0	2	8	0	24	3	1	3	0	1.000	0	0	1.88
	Fayettvlle	A	9	9	1	0	52.2	215	40	23	16	4	1	2	0	21	0	54	2	3	2	2	.500	0	0	2.73

Year	Team	Lg	G	GS	CG	GF	IP	BFP	H	R	ER	HR	SH	SF	HB	TBB	IBB	SO	WP	Bk	W	L	Pct.	ShO	Sv	ERA
1990	Lakeland	A	14	14	0	0	91	349	54	18	15	4	1	2	4	25	0	113	3	1	8	1	.889	0	0	1.48
	London	AA	14	14	1	0	89	372	87	47	37	4	1	4	2	27	0	76	3	0	5	6	.455	1	0	3.74
1991	London	AA	11	11	2	0	73.2	294	51	24	23	4	2	2	0	24	0	80	1	0	5	4	.556	1	0	2.81
	Toledo	AAA	11	11	1	0	58.2	254	62	33	30	10	0	1	1	21	0	56	1	0	5	4	.556	0	0	4.60
1992	Toledo	AAA	7	2	0	3	19	89	26	18	18	5	1	0	0	8	0	21	0	0	0	3	.000	0	0	8.53
	London	AA	9	9	1	0	52.1	216	51	24	24	4	1	2	1	13	0	53	2	1	2	4	.333	1	0	4.13
1993	Toledo	AAA	25	24	1	0	161	675	145	73	66	13	2	5	0	60	2	136	3	1	7	10	.412	0	0	3.69
1994	Albuquerque	AAA	25	6	0	4	66.2	317	90	62	58	7	1	3	4	27	0	39	3	0	3	5	.375	0	0	7.83
	San Antonio	AA	25	2	0	7	46	202	46	29	26	3	2	1	1	18	2	46	2	1	1	3	.250	0	2	5.09
1995	Rochester	AAA	26	25	2	1	150.2	644	156	78	70	19	3	3	6	51	0	82	2	1	11	9	.550	0	0	4.18
1993	Det-LA		4	0	0	3	6.1	27	8	5	5	0	0	1	0	1	0	6	0	0	0	0	.000	0	0	7.11
1995	Baltimore	AL	2	2	0	0	8.2	41	8	7	7	3	1	1	1	7	0	1	0	0	1	0	1.000	0	0	7.27
1993	Detroit	AL	1	0	0	1	1	4	2	1	1	0	0	0	0	1	0	0	0	0	0	0	.000	0	0	9.00
	Los Angeles	NL	3	0	0	2	5.1	23	6	4	4	0	0	0	0	1	0	6	0	0	0	0	.000	0	0	6.75
	2 ML YEARS		6	2	0	3	15	68	16	12	12	3	1	2	1	8	0	7	0	0	1	0	1.000	0	0	7.20

John Dettmer

Pitches: Right **Bats:** Right **Pos:** RP **Ht:** 6' 0" **Wt:** 185 **Born:** 3/4/70 **Age:** 26

			HOW MUCH HE PITCHED						WHAT HE GAVE UP											THE RESULTS					
Year	Team	Lg	G	GS	CG	GF	IP	BFP	H	R	ER	HR	SH	SF	HB	TBB	IBB	SO	WP	Bk	W	L	Pct.	ShO	Sv	ERA
1992	Gastonia	A	15	15	3	0	98	374	74	25	22	1	0	4	2	17	0	102	2	2	10	1	.909	1	0	2.02
1993	Charlotte	A	27	27	5	0	163	648	132	44	39	6	4	1	7	33	0	128	2	5	16	3	.842	2	0	2.15
1994	Tulsa	AA	10	10	2	0	74.2	288	57	23	20	3	1	2	1	12	1	65	1	0	6	1	.857	0	0	2.41
	Okla. City	AAA	8	8	1	0	46.1	209	59	33	29	7	1	4	2	11	0	26	1	0	3	2	.600	1	0	5.63
1995	Okla. City	AAA	5	0	0	3	8.2	37	10	3	2	1	1	0	0	4	0	10	1	1	0	0	.000	0	0	2.08
	Rochester	AAA	21	11	0	3	82.2	359	98	52	43	9	2	3	2	16	0	46	2	1	4	7	.364	1	1	4.68
1994	Texas	AL	11	9	0	0	54	250	63	42	26	10	2	5	3	20	3	27	1	0	0	6	.000	0	0	4.33
1995	Texas	AL	1	0	0	0	0.1	4	2	1	1	0	0	1	0	0	0	0	0	0	0	0	.000	0	0	27.00
	2 ML YEARS		12	9	0	0	54.1	254	65	43	27	10	2	6	3	20	3	27	1	0	0	6	.000	0	0	4.47

Cesar Devarez

Bats: Right **Throws:** Right **Pos:** C **Ht:** 5'10" **Wt:** 175 **Born:** 9/22/69 **Age:** 26

			BATTING																BASERUNNING				PERCENTAGES		
Year	Team	Lg	G	AB	H	2B	3B	HR	(Hm | Rd)	TB	R	RBI	TBB	IBB	SO	HBP	SH	SF	SB	CS	SB%	GDP	Avg	OBP	SLG
1989	Bluefield	R	12	42	9	4	0	0	--	--	13	3	7	1	0	5	0	0	0	0	0	.00	3	.214	.233	.310
1990	Wausau	A	56	171	34	4	1	3	--	--	49	7	19	7	0	28	0	2	0	2	3	.40	3	.199	.230	.287
1991	Frederick	A	74	235	59	13	2	3	--	--	85	25	29	14	0	28	4	2	1	2	2	.50	9	.251	.303	.362
1992	Hagerstown	AA	110	319	72	8	1	2	--	--	88	20	32	17	0	49	6	2	2	2	5	.29	3	.226	.276	.276
1993	Frederick	A	38	124	36	8	0	2	--	--	50	15	16	12	1	18	1	1	0	1	4	.20	2	.290	.358	.403
	Bowie	AA	57	174	39	7	1	0	--	--	48	14	15	5	0	21	2	2	2	5	1	.83	6	.224	.251	.276
1994	Bowie	AA	73	249	78	13	4	6	--	--	117	43	48	8	1	25	1	3	4	7	2	.78	10	.313	.332	.470
1995	Rochester	AAA	67	240	60	12	1	1	--	--	77	32	21	7	0	25	0	1	1	2	2	.50	8	.250	.270	.321
1995	Baltimore	AL	6	4	0	0	0	0	(0 | 0)	0	0	0	0	0	0	0	0	0	0	0	.00	0	.000	.000	.000

Mike Devereaux

Bats: Right **Throws:** Right **Pos:** RF/LF/CF **Ht:** 6' 0" **Wt:** 195 **Born:** 4/10/63 **Age:** 33

			BATTING																BASERUNNING				PERCENTAGES		
Year	Team	Lg	G	AB	H	2B	3B	HR	(Hm	Rd)	TB	R	RBI	TBB	IBB	SO	HBP	SH	SF	SB	CS	SB%	GDP	Avg	OBP	SLG
1987	Los Angeles	NL	19	54	12	3	0	0	(0	0)	15	7	4	3	0	10	0	1	0	3	1	.75	0	.222	.263	.278
1988	Los Angeles	NL	30	43	5	1	0	0	(0	0)	6	4	2	2	0	10	0	0	0	0	1	.00	0	.116	.156	.140
1989	Baltimore	AL	122	391	104	14	3	8	(4	4)	148	55	46	36	0	60	2	2	3	22	11	.67	7	.266	.329	.379
1990	Baltimore	AL	108	367	88	18	1	12	(6	6)	144	48	49	28	0	48	0	4	4	13	12	.52	10	.240	.291	.392
1991	Baltimore	AL	149	608	158	27	10	19	(10	9)	262	82	59	47	2	115	2	7	4	16	9	.64	13	.260	.313	.431
1992	Baltimore	AL	156	653	180	29	11	24	(14	10)	303	76	107	44	1	94	4	0	9	10	8	.56	14	.276	.321	.464
1993	Baltimore	AL	131	527	132	31	3	14	(8	6)	211	72	75	43	0	99	1	2	4	3	3	.50	13	.250	.306	.400
1994	Baltimore	AL	85	301	61	8	2	9	(5	4)	100	35	33	22	0	72	1	2	4	1	2	.33	6	.203	.256	.332
1995	ChA-Atl		121	388	116	24	1	11	(5	6)	175	55	63	27	3	62	0	0	3	8	6	.57	11	.299	.342	.451
1995	Chicago	AL	92	333	102	21	1	10	(4	6)	155	48	55	25	3	51	0	0	3	6	6	.50	10	.306	.352	.465
	Atlanta	NL	29	55	14	3	0	1	(1	0)	20	7	8	2	0	11	0	0	0	2	0	1.00	1	.255	.281	.364
	9 ML YEARS		921	3332	856	155	31	97	(52	45)	1364	434	438	252	6	570	10	18	31	76	53	.59	74	.257	.308	.409

Mark Dewey

Pitches: Right **Bats:** Right **Pos:** RP **Ht:** 6' 0" **Wt:** 216 **Born:** 1/3/65 **Age:** 31

			HOW MUCH HE PITCHED						WHAT HE GAVE UP											THE RESULTS					
Year	Team	Lg	G	GS	CG	GF	IP	BFP	H	R	ER	HR	SH	SF	HB	TBB	IBB	SO	WP	Bk	W	L	Pct.	ShO	Sv	ERA
1990	San Francisco	NL	14	0	0	5	22.2	92	22	7	7	1	2	0	0	5	1	11	0	1	1	1	.500	0	0	2.78
1992	New York	NL	20	0	0	6	33.1	143	37	16	16	2	1	0	0	10	2	24	0	1	1	0	1.000	0	0	4.32

Year Team	Lg	G	GS	CG	GF	IP	BFP	H	R	ER	HR	SH	SF	HB	TBB	IBB	SO	WP	Bk	W	L	Pct.	ShO	Sv	ERA
1993 Pittsburgh	NL	21	0	0	17	26.2	108	14	8	7	0	3	3	3	10	1	14	0	0	1	2	.333	0	7	2.36
1994 Pittsburgh	NL	45	0	0	18	51.1	226	61	22	21	4	2	1	3	19	3	30	0	0	2	1	.667	0	1	3.68
1995 San Francisco	NL	27	0	0	5	31.2	137	30	12	11	2	1	1	0	17	6	32	1	0	1	0	1.000	0	0	3.13
5 ML YEARS		127	0	0	51	165.2	706	164	65	62	9	9	5	6	61	13	111	1	2	6	4	.600	0	8	3.37

Alex Diaz

Bats: Both   **Throws:** Right   **Pos:** CF/LF   **Ht:** 5'11"   **Wt:** 180   **Born:** 10/5/68   **Age:** 27

										BATTING									BASERUNNING				PERCENTAGES		
Year Team	Lg	G	AB	H	2B	3B	HR	(Hm	Rd)	TB	R	RBI	TBB	IBB	SO	HBP	SH	SF	SB	CS	SB%	GDP	Avg	OBP	SLG
1995 Tacoma *	AAA	10	40	10	1	0	0	--	--	11	3	4	2	0	5	0	0	0	1	2	.33	0	.250	.286	.275
1992 Milwaukee	AL	22	9	1	0	0	0	(0	0)	1	5	1	0	0	0	0	0	0	3	2	.60	0	.111	.111	.111
1993 Milwaukee	AL	32	69	22	2	0	0	(0	0)	24	9	1	0	0	12	0	3	0	5	3	.63	3	.319	.319	.348
1994 Milwaukee	AL	79	187	47	5	7	1	(0	1)	69	17	17	10	1	19	0	3	3	5	5	.50	5	.251	.285	.369
1995 Seattle	AL	103	270	67	14	0	3	(3	0)	90	44	27	13	2	27	2	5	2	18	8	.69	3	.248	.286	.333
4 ML YEARS		236	535	137	21	7	4	(3	1)	184	75	46	23	3	58	2	11	5	31	18	.63	11	.256	.287	.344

Mario Diaz

Bats: Right   **Throws:** Right   **Pos:** 2B   **Ht:** 5'10"   **Wt:** 160   **Born:** 1/10/62   **Age:** 34

										BATTING									BASERUNNING				PERCENTAGES		
Year Team	Lg	G	AB	H	2B	3B	HR	(Hm	Rd)	TB	R	RBI	TBB	IBB	SO	HBP	SH	SF	SB	CS	SB%	GDP	Avg	OBP	SLG
1987 Seattle	AL	11	23	7	0	1	0	(0	0)	9	4	3	0	0	4	0	0	0	0	0	.00	0	.304	.304	.391
1988 Seattle	AL	28	72	22	5	0	0	(0	0)	27	6	9	3	0	5	0	0	1	0	0	.00	0	.306	.329	.375
1989 Seattle	AL	52	74	10	0	0	1	(0	1)	13	9	7	7	0	7	0	5	0	0	0	.00	2	.135	.210	.176
1990 New York	NL	16	22	3	1	0	0	(0	0)	4	0	1	0	0	3	0	0	1	0	0	.00	0	.136	.130	.182
1991 Texas	AL	96	182	48	7	0	1	(1	0)	58	24	22	15	0	18	0	4	1	0	1	.00	5	.264	.318	.319
1992 Texas	AL	19	31	7	1	0	0	(0	0)	8	2	1	1	1	2	0	1	0	0	1	.00	2	.226	.250	.258
1993 Texas	AL	71	205	56	10	1	2	(1	1)	74	24	24	8	0	13	1	7	5	1	0	1.00	6	.273	.297	.361
1994 Florida	NL	32	77	25	4	2	0	(0	0)	33	10	11	6	0	6	1	0	1	0	0	.00	1	.325	.376	.429
1995 Florida	NL	49	87	20	3	0	1	(0	1)	26	5	6	1	0	12	0	1	0	0	0	.00	2	.230	.239	.299
9 ML YEARS		374	773	198	31	4	5	(2	3)	252	84	84	41	1	70	2	18	9	1	2	.33	23	.256	.292	.326

Rob Dibble

Pitches: Right   **Bats:** Left   **Pos:** RP   **Ht:** 6'4"   **Wt:** 220   **Born:** 1/24/64   **Age:** 32

		HOW MUCH HE PITCHED						WHAT HE GAVE UP										THE RESULTS					
Year Team	Lg	G	GS	CG	GF	IP	BFP	H	R	ER	HR	SH	SF	HB	TBB	IBB	SO	WP	Bk	W	L	Pct.	ShO	Sv	ERA
1995 Birmingham *	AA	8	0	0	1	7.1	32	4	6	6	0	1	0	1	5	0	15	2	0	0	1	.000	0	1	7.36
New Orleans *	AAA	4	0	0	1	4	16	1	2	0	0	0	0	1	2	0	6	0	0	0	1	.000	0	0	0.00
1988 Cincinnati	NL	37	0	0	6	59.1	235	43	12	12	2	2	3	1	21	5	59	3	2	1	1	.500	0	0	1.82
1989 Cincinnati	NL	74	0	0	18	99	401	62	23	23	4	3	4	3	39	11	141	7	0	10	5	.667	0	2	2.09
1990 Cincinnati	NL	68	0	0	29	98	384	62	22	19	3	4	6	1	34	3	136	3	1	8	3	.727	0	11	1.74
1991 Cincinnati	NL	67	0	0	57	82.1	334	67	32	29	5	5	3	0	25	2	124	5	0	3	5	.375	0	31	3.17
1992 Cincinnati	NL	63	0	0	49	70.1	286	48	26	24	3	2	2	2	31	2	110	6	0	3	5	.375	0	25	3.07
1993 Cincinnati	NL	45	0	0	37	41.2	196	34	33	30	8	1	0	2	42	0	49	4	0	1	4	.200	0	19	6.48
1995 ChA-Mil	AL	31	0	0	8	26.1	143	16	21	21	2	3	6	3	46	2	26	8	0	1	2	.333	0	1	7.18
1995 Chicago	AL	16	0	0	4	14.1	78	7	10	10	1	1	2	3	27	2	16	5	0	0	1	.000	0	1	6.28
Milwaukee	AL	15	0	0	4	12	65	9	11	11	1	2	4	0	19	0	10	3	0	1	1	.500	0	0	8.25
7 ML YEARS		385	0	0	204	477	1979	332	169	158	27	20	24	12	238	25	645	36	3	27	25	.519	0	89	2.98

Jerry DiPoto

Pitches: Right   **Bats:** Right   **Pos:** RP   **Ht:** 6'2"   **Wt:** 200   **Born:** 5/24/68   **Age:** 28

		HOW MUCH HE PITCHED						WHAT HE GAVE UP										THE RESULTS					
Year Team	Lg	G	GS	CG	GF	IP	BFP	H	R	ER	HR	SH	SF	HB	TBB	IBB	SO	WP	Bk	W	L	Pct.	ShO	Sv	ERA
1993 Cleveland	AL	46	0	0	26	56.1	247	57	21	15	0	3	2	1	30	7	41	0	0	4	4	.500	0	11	2.40
1994 Cleveland	AL	7	0	0	1	15.2	79	26	14	14	1	0	4	1	10	0	9	0	0	0	0	.000	0	0	8.04
1995 New York	NL	58	0	0	26	78.2	330	77	41	33	2	6	3	4	29	8	49	3	1	4	6	.400	0	2	3.78
3 ML YEARS		111	0	0	53	150.2	656	160	76	62	3	9	9	6	69	15	99	3	1	8	10	.444	0	13	3.70

Gary DiSarcina

Bats: Right   **Throws:** Right   **Pos:** SS   **Ht:** 6'1"   **Wt:** 178   **Born:** 11/19/67   **Age:** 28

										BATTING									BASERUNNING				PERCENTAGES		
Year Team	Lg	G	AB	H	2B	3B	HR	(Hm	Rd)	TB	R	RBI	TBB	IBB	SO	HBP	SH	SF	SB	CS	SB%	GDP	Avg	OBP	SLG
1989 California	AL	2	0	0	0	0	0	(0	0)	0	0	0	0	0	0	0	0	0	0	0	.00	0	.000	.000	.000
1990 California	AL	18	57	8	1	1	0	(0	0)	11	8	0	3	0	10	0	1	0	1	0	1.00	3	.140	.183	.193
1991 California	AL	18	57	12	2	0	0	(0	0)	14	5	3	3	0	4	2	2	0	0	0	.00	0	.211	.274	.246
1992 California	AL	157	518	128	19	0	3	(2	1)	156	48	42	20	0	50	7	5	3	9	7	.56	15	.247	.283	.301
1993 California	AL	126	416	99	20	1	3	(2	1)	130	44	45	15	0	38	6	5	3	5	7	.42	13	.238	.273	.313
1994 California	AL	112	389	101	14	2	3	(2	1)	128	53	33	18	0	28	2	10	2	3	7	.30	10	.260	.294	.329

1995 California	AL	99	362	111	28	6	5	(1	4)	166	61	41	20	0	25	2	7	3	7	4	.64	10	.307	.344	.459
7 ML YEARS		532	1799	459	84	10	14	(7	7)	605	219	164	79	0	155	19	30	11	25	25	.50	51	.255	.292	.336

Glenn Dishman

Pitches: Left **Bats:** Right **Pos:** SP   **Ht:** 6' 1" **Wt:** 195 **Born:** 11/5/70 **Age:** 25

		HOW MUCH HE PITCHED						WHAT HE GAVE UP													THE RESULTS				
Year Team	Lg	G	GS	CG	GF	IP	BFP	H	R	ER	HR	SH	SF	HB	TBB	IBB	SO	WP	Bk	W	L	Pct.	ShO	Sv	ERA
1993 Spokane	A	12	12	2	0	77.2	307	59	25	19	3	2	1	1	13	0	79	3	1	6	3	.667	2	0	2.20
Rancho Cuca	A	2	2	0	0	11.1	52	14	9	9	0	0	0	1	5	0	6	1	1	0	0	.000	0	0	7.15
1994 Wichita	AA	27	27	1	0	169.1	693	156	73	53	6	8	3	3	42	2	165	4	1	11	8	.579	0	0	2.82
Las Vegas	AAA	2	2	0	0	13	55	15	7	5	1	0	2	0	1	0	12	0	0	1	1	.500	0	0	3.46
1995 Las Vegas	AAA	14	14	3	0	106	430	91	37	30	12	4	1	0	20	2	63	3	1	6	3	.667	1	0	2.55
1995 San Diego	NL	19	16	0	1	97	421	104	60	54	11	6	3	4	34	1	43	3	1	4	8	.333	0	0	5.01

John Doherty

Pitches: Right **Bats:** Right **Pos:** RP   **Ht:** 6' 4" **Wt:** 215 **Born:** 6/11/67 **Age:** 29

		HOW MUCH HE PITCHED						WHAT HE GAVE UP													THE RESULTS				
Year Team	Lg	G	GS	CG	GF	IP	BFP	H	R	ER	HR	SH	SF	HB	TBB	IBB	SO	WP	Bk	W	L	Pct.	ShO	Sv	ERA
1992 Detroit	AL	47	11	0	9	116	491	131	61	50	4	3	2	4	25	5	37	5	0	7	4	.636	0	3	3.88
1993 Detroit	AL	32	31	3	1	184.2	780	205	104	91	19	5	4	5	48	7	63	4	1	14	11	.560	2	0	4.44
1994 Detroit	AL	18	17	2	1	101.1	454	139	75	73	13	5	7	3	26	6	28	4	0	6	7	.462	0	0	6.48
1995 Detroit	AL	48	2	0	18	113	499	130	66	64	10	3	2	6	37	10	46	0	0	5	9	.357	0	6	5.10
4 ML YEARS		145	61	5	29	515	2224	605	306	278	46	16	15	18	136	28	174	13	1	32	31	.508	2	9	4.86

Chris Donnels

Bats: Left **Throws:** Right **Pos:** 3B   **Ht:** 6' 0" **Wt:** 185 **Born:** 4/21/66 **Age:** 30

		BATTING																	BASERUNNING				PERCENTAGES		
Year Team	Lg	G	AB	H	2B	3B	HR	(Hm	Rd)	TB	R	RBI	TBB	IBB	SO	HBP	SH	SF	SB	CS	SB%	GDP	Avg	OBP	SLG
1995 Jackson *	AA	4	12	2	1	0	0	--	--	3	1	1	4	0	4	0	0	0	0	0	.00	0	.167	.375	.250
Pawtucket *	AAA	4	15	6	0	0	0	--	--	9	1	4	1	0	3	0	0	0	0	0	.00	0	.400	.438	.600
1991 New York	NL	37	89	20	2	0	0	(0	0)	22	7	5	14	1	19	0	1	0	1	1	.50	0	.225	.330	.247
1992 New York	NL	45	121	21	4	0	0	(0	0)	25	8	6	17	0	25	0	1	0	1	0	1.00	1	.174	.275	.207
1993 Houston	NL	88	179	46	14	2	2	(0	2)	70	18	24	19	0	33	0	0	1	2	0	1.00	6	.257	.327	.391
1994 Houston	NL	54	86	23	5	0	3	(2	1)	37	12	5	13	0	18	0	0	0	1	0	1.00	1	.267	.364	.430
1995 Hou-Bos		59	121	32	2	2	2	(0	2)	44	17	13	12	2	24	0	0	1	0	0	.00	2	.264	.328	.364
1995 Houston	NL	19	30	9	0	0	0	(0	0)	9	4	2	3	2	6	0	0	0	0	0	.00	1	.300	.364	.300
Boston	AL	40	91	23	2	2	2	(0	2)	35	13	11	9	0	18	0	0	1	0	0	.00	1	.253	.317	.385
5 ML YEARS		283	596	142	27	4	7	(2	5)	198	62	53	75	3	119	0	2	2	5	1	.83	10	.238	.322	.332

Jim Dougherty

Pitches: Right **Bats:** Right **Pos:** RP   **Ht:** 6' 0" **Wt:** 210 **Born:** 3/8/68 **Age:** 28

		HOW MUCH HE PITCHED						WHAT HE GAVE UP													THE RESULTS				
Year Team	Lg	G	GS	CG	GF	IP	BFP	H	R	ER	HR	SH	SF	HB	TBB	IBB	SO	WP	Bk	W	L	Pct.	ShO	Sv	ERA
1991 Asheville	A	61	0	0	48	82	324	63	17	14	0	7	0	3	24	6	76	0	2	3	1	.750	0	27	1.54
1992 Osceola	A	57	0	0	52	81	325	66	21	14	1	4	2	2	22	4	77	0	1	5	2	.714	0	31	1.56
1993 Jackson	AA	52	0	0	50	53	207	39	15	11	3	0	0	1	21	0	55	0	0	2	2	.500	0	36	1.87
1994 Tucson	AAA	55	0	0	48	59	276	70	32	27	9	1	1	2	30	6	49	4	0	5	4	.556	0	21	4.12
1995 Tucson	AAA	8	0	0	3	11	46	11	4	4	1	0	0	0	5	0	12	0	1	1	0	1.000	0	1	3.27
1995 Houston	NL	56	0	0	11	67.2	294	76	37	37	7	3	3	3	25	1	49	1	0	8	4	.667	0	0	4.92

Doug Drabek

Pitches: Right **Bats:** Right **Pos:** SP   **Ht:** 6' 1" **Wt:** 185 **Born:** 7/25/62 **Age:** 33

		HOW MUCH HE PITCHED						WHAT HE GAVE UP													THE RESULTS				
Year Team	Lg	G	GS	CG	GF	IP	BFP	H	R	ER	HR	SH	SF	HB	TBB	IBB	SO	WP	Bk	W	L	Pct.	ShO	Sv	ERA
1986 New York	AL	27	21	0	2	131.2	561	126	64	60	13	5	2	3	50	1	76	2	0	7	8	.467	0	0	4.10
1987 Pittsburgh	NL	29	28	1	0	176.1	721	165	86	76	22	3	4	0	46	2	120	5	1	11	12	.478	1	0	3.88
1988 Pittsburgh	NL	33	32	3	0	219.1	880	194	83	75	21	7	5	6	50	4	127	4	1	15	7	.682	1	0	3.08
1989 Pittsburgh	NL	35	34	8	1	244.1	994	215	83	76	21	13	7	3	69	3	123	3	0	14	12	.538	5	0	2.80
1990 Pittsburgh	NL	33	33	9	0	231.1	918	190	78	71	15	10	3	3	56	2	131	6	0	22	6	.786	3	0	2.76
1991 Pittsburgh	NL	35	35	5	0	234.2	977	245	92	80	16	12	6	3	62	6	142	5	0	15	14	.517	2	0	3.07
1992 Pittsburgh	NL	34	34	10	0	256.2	1021	218	84	79	17	8	8	6	54	8	177	11	1	15	11	.577	4	0	2.77
1993 Houston	NL	34	34	7	0	237.2	991	242	108	100	18	14	8	3	60	12	157	12	0	9	18	.333	2	0	3.79
1994 Houston	NL	23	23	6	0	164.2	657	132	58	52	14	5	6	2	45	2	121	2	0	12	6	.667	2	0	2.84
1995 Houston	NL	31	31	2	0	185	797	205	104	98	18	4	3	8	54	4	143	8	1	10	9	.526	1	0	4.77
10 ML YEARS		314	305	51	3	2081.2	8517	1932	840	767	175	81	52	37	546	44	1317	58	4	130	103	.558	21	0	3.32

Matt Dunbar

Pitches: Left   **Bats:** Left   **Pos:** RP   **Ht:** 6' 0"   **Wt:** 160   **Born:** 10/15/68   **Age:** 27

					HOW MUCH HE PITCHED			WHAT HE GAVE UP											THE RESULTS					
Year	Team	Lg	G	GS	CG	GF	IP	BFP	H	R	ER	HR	SH	SF	HB	TBB	IBB	SO	WP	Bk	W	L	Pct.	ShO	Sv	ERA
1990	Yankees	R	3	0	0	2	6	24	4	2	2	0	1	0	2	3	0	7	0	1	0	0	.000	0	1	3.00
	Oneonta	A	19	2	0	8	30.1	145	32	23	14	1	2	2	1	24	2	24	5	1	1	4	.200	0	0	4.15
1991	Greensboro	A	24	2	1	14	44.2	184	36	14	11	1	0	1	3	15	0	40	2	0	2	2	.500	0	1	2.22
1992	Pr. William	A	44	0	0	21	81.2	350	68	37	26	5	7	4	6	33	2	68	7	1	5	4	.556	0	2	2.87
1993	Pr. William	A	49	0	0	20	73	292	50	21	14	0	6	0	3	30	1	66	6	0	6	2	.750	0	4	1.73
	Albany-Colo	AA	15	0	0	6	23.2	91	23	8	7	0	0	0	0	6	0	18	0	0	1	0	1.000	0	0	2.66
1994	Albany-Colo	AA	34	0	0	12	39.2	163	30	10	9	1	2	2	4	14	0	41	1	0	2	1	.667	0	4	2.04
	Columbus	AAA	19	0	0	6	26	104	20	5	5	1	0	1	1	10	1	21	2	1	0	1	.000	0	2	1.73
1995	Columbus	AAA	36	0	0	9	44.1	201	50	22	20	1	0	1	3	19	2	33	5	1	2	3	.400	0	0	4.06
1995	Florida	NL	8	0	0	1	7	45	12	9	9	0	2	0	1	11	3	5	1	0	0	1	.000	0	0	11.57

Mariano Duncan

Bats: Right   **Throws:** Right   **Pos:** 2B/1B/SS   **Ht:** 6' 0"   **Wt:** 185   **Born:** 3/13/63   **Age:** 33

									BATTING										BASERUNNING				PERCENTAGES		
Year	Team	Lg	G	AB	H	2B	3B	HR	(Hm	Rd)	TB	R	RBI	TBB	IBB	SO	HBP	SH	SF	SB	CS	SB%	GDP	Avg	OBP	SLG
1985	Los Angeles	NL	142	562	137	24	6	6	(1	5)	191	74	39	38	4	113	3	13	4	38	8	.83	9	.244	.293	.340
1986	Los Angeles	NL	109	407	93	7	0	8	(2	6)	124	47	30	30	1	78	2	5	1	48	13	.79	6	.229	.284	.305
1987	Los Angeles	NL	76	261	56	8	1	6	(3	3)	84	31	18	17	1	62	2	6	1	11	1	.92	4	.215	.267	.322
1989	Cin-LA	NL	94	258	64	15	2	3	(2	1)	92	32	21	8	0	51	5	2	0	9	5	.64	3	.248	.284	.357
1990	Cincinnati	NL	125	435	133	22	11	10	(5	5)	207	67	55	24	4	67	4	4	4	13	7	.65	10	.306	.345	.476
1991	Cincinnati	NL	100	333	86	7	4	12	(10	2)	137	46	40	12	0	57	3	5	3	5	4	.56	0	.258	.288	.411
1992	Philadelphia	NL	142	574	153	40	3	8	(3	5)	223	71	50	17	0	108	5	5	4	23	3	.88	15	.267	.292	.389
1993	Philadelphia	NL	124	496	140	26	4	11	(5	6)	207	68	73	12	0	88	4	4	2	6	5	.55	13	.282	.304	.417
1994	Philadelphia	NL	88	347	93	22	1	8	(6	2)	141	49	48	17	1	72	4	2	4	10	2	.83	10	.268	.306	.406
1995	Phi-Cin	NL	81	265	76	14	2	6	(3	3)	112	36	36	5	0	62	1	1	5	1	3	.25	7	.287	.297	.423
1989	Cincinnati	NL	45	174	43	10	1	3	(2	1)	64	23	13	8	0	36	3	1	0	6	2	.75	2	.247	.292	.368
	Los Angeles	NL	49	84	21	5	1	0	(0	0)	28	9	8	0	0	15	2	1	0	3	3	.50	1	.250	.267	.333
1995	Philadelphia	NL	52	196	56	12	1	3	(1	2)	79	20	23	0	0	43	1	1	3	1	2	.33	6	.286	.285	.403
	Cincinnati	NL	29	69	20	2	1	3	(2	1)	33	16	13	5	0	19	0	0	2	0	1	.00	1	.290	.329	.478
	10 ML YEARS		1081	3938	1031	185	34	78	(40	38)	1518	521	410	180	11	758	33	47	28	164	51	.76	77	.262	.298	.385

Steve Dunn

Bats: Left   **Throws:** Left   **Pos:** 1B   **Ht:** 6' 4"   **Wt:** 219   **Born:** 4/18/70   **Age:** 26

									BATTING										BASERUNNING				PERCENTAGES		
Year	Team	Lg	G	AB	H	2B	3B	HR	(Hm	Rd)	TB	R	RBI	TBB	IBB	SO	HBP	SH	SF	SB	CS	SB%	GDP	Avg	OBP	SLG
1988	Elizabethtn	R	26	95	27	4	0	2	--	--	37	9	14	8	0	22	0	0	0	0	0	.00	0	.284	.340	.389
1989	Kenosha	A	63	219	48	8	0	0	--	--	56	17	23	18	4	55	1	1	2	2	1	.67	2	.219	.279	.256
	Elizabethtn	R	57	210	64	12	3	6	--	--	100	34	42	22	2	41	0	1	4	0	2	.00	1	.305	.364	.476
1990	Kenosha	A	130	478	142	29	1	10	--	--	203	48	72	49	8	104	6	1	6	13	6	.68	4	.297	.365	.425
1991	Visalia	A	125	458	105	16	1	13	--	--	162	64	59	58	6	103	6	0	6	9	6	.60	12	.229	.320	.354
1992	Visalia	A	125	492	150	36	3	26	--	--	270	93	113	41	6	103	7	0	4	8	3	.73	13	.305	.364	.549
1993	Nashville	AA	97	366	96	20	2	14	--	--	162	48	60	35	3	88	1	0	4	1	2	.33	4	.262	.325	.443
1994	Salt Lake	AAA	90	330	102	21	2	15	--	--	172	61	73	24	6	75	2	0	8	0	0	.00	5	.309	.352	.521
1995	Salt Lake	AAA	109	402	127	31	1	12	--	--	196	57	83	30	4	63	1	0	6	3	2	.60	6	.316	.360	.488
1994	Minnesota	AL	14	35	8	5	0	0	(0	0)	13	2	4	1	0	12	0	0	0	0	0	.00	0	.229	.250	.371
1995	Minnesota	AL	5	6	0	0	0	0	(0	0)	0	0	0	1	0	3	0	0	0	0	0	.00	1	.000	.143	.000
	2 ML YEARS		19	41	8	5	0	0	(0	0)	13	2	4	2	0	15	0	0	0	0	0	.00	1	.195	.233	.317

Shawon Dunston

Bats: Right   **Throws:** Right   **Pos:** SS   **Ht:** 6' 1"   **Wt:** 180   **Born:** 3/21/63   **Age:** 33

									BATTING										BASERUNNING				PERCENTAGES		
Year	Team	Lg	G	AB	H	2B	3B	HR	(Hm	Rd)	TB	R	RBI	TBB	IBB	SO	HBP	SH	SF	SB	CS	SB%	GDP	Avg	OBP	SLG
1985	Chicago	NL	74	250	65	12	4	4	(3	1)	97	40	18	19	3	42	0	1	2	11	3	.79	3	.260	.310	.388
1986	Chicago	NL	150	581	145	37	3	17	(10	7)	239	66	68	21	5	114	3	4	2	13	11	.54	5	.250	.278	.411
1987	Chicago	NL	95	346	85	18	3	5	(3	2)	124	40	22	10	1	68	1	0	2	12	3	.80	6	.246	.267	.358
1988	Chicago	NL	155	575	143	23	6	9	(5	4)	205	69	56	16	8	108	2	4	4	30	9	.77	6	.249	.271	.357
1989	Chicago	NL	138	471	131	20	6	9	(3	6)	190	52	60	30	15	86	1	6	4	19	11	.63	7	.278	.320	.403
1990	Chicago	NL	146	545	143	22	8	17	(7	10)	232	73	66	15	1	87	3	4	6	25	5	.83	9	.262	.283	.426
1991	Chicago	NL	142	492	128	22	7	12	(7	5)	200	59	50	23	5	64	4	4	11	21	6	.78	9	.260	.292	.407
1992	Chicago	NL	18	73	23	3	1	0	(0	0)	28	8	2	3	0	13	0	0	0	2	3	.40	0	.315	.342	.384
1993	Chicago	NL	7	10	4	2	0	0	(0	0)	6	3	2	0	0	1	0	0	0	0	0	.00	0	.400	.400	.600
1994	Chicago	NL	88	331	92	19	0	11	(2	9)	144	38	35	16	3	48	2	5	2	3	8	.27	4	.278	.313	.435

Year Team	Lg	G	AB	H	2B	3B	HR	(Hm	Rd)	TB	R	RBI	TBB	IBB	SO	HBP	SH	SF	SB	CS	SB%	GDP	Avg	OBP	SLG
1995 Chicago	NL	127	477	141	30	6	14	(8	6)	225	58	69	10	3	75	6	7	3	10	5	.67	8	.296	.317	.472
11 ML YEARS		1140	4151	1100	208	44	98	(48	50)	1690	506	448	163	44	706	22	35	34	146	64	.70	57	.265	.294	.407

Ray Durham

Bats: Both **Throws:** Right **Pos:** 2B   **Ht:** 5' 8" **Wt:** 170 **Born:** 11/30/71 **Age:** 24

							BATTING													BASERUNNING				PERCENTAGES		
Year Team	Lg	G	AB	H	2B	3B	HR	(Hm	Rd)	TB	R	RBI	TBB	IBB	SO	HBP	SH	SF	SB	CS	SB%	GDP	Avg	OBP	SLG
1990 White Sox	R	35	116	31	3	3	0	--	--	40	18	13	15	0	35	4	0	1	22	9	.71	0	.267	.368	.345
1991 Utica	A	39	142	36	2	7	0	--	--	52	29	17	25	0	43	2	2	1	12	1	.92	0	.254	.371	.366
White Sox	R	6	23	7	1	0	0	--	--	8	3	4	3	0	5	0	0	0	5	1	.83	0	.304	.385	.348
1992 White Sox	R	5	13	7	2	0	0	--	--	9	3	2	3	0	1	0	0	0	1	0	1.00	0	.538	.625	.692
Sarasota	A	57	202	55	6	3	0	--	--	67	37	7	32	0	36	10	5	0	28	8	.78	2	.272	.398	.332
1993 Birmingham	AA	137	528	143	22	10	3	--	--	194	83	37	42	2	100	14	5	5	39	25	.61	5	.271	.338	.367
1994 Nashville	AAA	133	527	156	33	12	16	--	--	261	89	66	46	7	91	12	3	4	34	11	.76	5	.296	.363	.495
1995 Chicago	AL	125	471	121	27	6	7	(1	6)	181	68	51	31	2	83	6	5	4	18	5	.78	8	.257	.309	.384

Mike Dyer

Pitches: Right **Bats:** Right **Pos:** RP   **Ht:** 6' 3" **Wt:** 200 **Born:** 9/8/66 **Age:** 29

			HOW MUCH HE PITCHED						WHAT HE GAVE UP										THE RESULTS					
Year Team	Lg	G	GS	CG	GF	IP	BFP	H	R	ER	HR	SH	SF	HB	TBB	IBB	SO	WP	Bk	W	L	Pct.	ShO	Sv	ERA
1989 Minnesota	AL	16	12	1	0	71	317	74	43	38	2	5	2	2	37	0	37	1	1	4	7	.364	0	0	4.82
1994 Pittsburgh	NL	14	0	0	7	15.1	74	15	12	10	1	1	2	3	12	4	13	0	1	1	1	.500	0	4	5.87
1995 Pittsburgh	NL	55	0	0	15	74.2	327	81	40	36	9	3	1	5	30	3	53	4	1	4	5	.444	0	0	4.34
3 ML YEARS		85	12	1	22	161	718	170	95	84	12	9	5	10	79	7	103	5	3	9	13	.409	0	4	4.70

Lenny Dykstra

Bats: Left **Throws:** Left **Pos:** CF   **Ht:** 5'10" **Wt:** 190 **Born:** 2/10/63 **Age:** 33

							BATTING													BASERUNNING				PERCENTAGES		
Year Team	Lg	G	AB	H	2B	3B	HR	(Hm	Rd)	TB	R	RBI	TBB	IBB	SO	HBP	SH	SF	SB	CS	SB%	GDP	Avg	OBP	SLG
1985 New York	NL	83	236	60	9	3	1	(0	1)	78	40	19	30	0	24	1	4	2	15	2	.88	4	.254	.338	.331
1986 New York	NL	147	431	127	27	7	8	(4	4)	192	77	45	58	1	55	0	7	2	31	7	.82	4	.295	.377	.445
1987 New York	NL	132	431	123	37	3	10	(7	3)	196	86	43	40	3	67	4	4	0	27	7	.79	1	.285	.352	.455
1988 New York	NL	126	429	116	19	3	8	(3	5)	165	57	33	30	2	43	3	2	2	30	8	.79	3	.270	.321	.385
1989 NYN-Phi	NL	146	511	121	32	4	7	(5	2)	182	66	32	60	1	53	3	5	5	30	12	.71	7	.237	.318	.356
1990 Philadelphia	NL	149	590	192	35	3	9	(6	3)	260	106	60	89	14	48	7	2	3	33	5	.87	5	.325	.418	.441
1991 Philadelphia	NL	63	246	73	13	5	3	(3	0)	105	48	12	37	1	20	1	0	0	24	4	.86	1	.297	.391	.427
1992 Philadelphia	NL	85	345	104	18	0	6	(5	1)	140	53	39	40	4	32	3	0	4	30	5	.86	1	.301	.375	.406
1993 Philadelphia	NL	161	637	194	44	6	19	(12	7)	307	143	66	129	9	64	2	0	5	37	12	.76	8	.305	.420	.482
1994 Philadelphia	NL	84	315	86	26	5	5	(3	2)	137	68	24	68	11	44	2	0	1	15	4	.79	3	.273	.404	.435
1995 Philadelphia	NL	62	254	67	15	1	2	(2	0)	90	37	18	33	2	28	3	0	2	10	5	.67	1	.264	.353	.354
1989 New York	NL	56	159	43	12	1	3	(2	1)	66	27	13	23	0	15	2	4	4	13	1	.93	2	.270	.362	.415
Philadelphia	NL	90	352	78	20	3	4	(3	1)	116	39	19	37	1	38	1	1	1	17	11	.61	5	.222	.297	.330
11 ML YEARS		1238	4425	1263	275	40	78	(50	28)	1852	781	391	614	48	478	29	24	26	282	71	.80	38	.285	.374	.419

Damion Easley

Bats: Right **Throws:** Right **Pos:** 2B/SS   **Ht:** 5'11" **Wt:** 185 **Born:** 11/11/69 **Age:** 26

							BATTING													BASERUNNING				PERCENTAGES		
Year Team	Lg	G	AB	H	2B	3B	HR	(Hm	Rd)	TB	R	RBI	TBB	IBB	SO	HBP	SH	SF	SB	CS	SB%	GDP	Avg	OBP	SLG
1992 California	AL	47	151	39	5	0	1	(1	0)	47	14	12	8	0	26	3	2	1	9	5	.64	2	.258	.307	.311
1993 California	AL	73	230	72	13	2	2	(0	2)	95	33	22	28	2	35	3	1	2	6	6	.50	5	.313	.392	.413
1994 California	AL	88	316	68	16	1	6	(4	2)	104	41	30	29	0	48	4	4	2	4	5	.44	4	.215	.288	.329
1995 California	AL	114	357	77	14	2	4	(1	3)	107	35	35	32	1	47	6	6	4	5	2	.71	11	.216	.288	.300
4 ML YEARS		322	1054	256	48	5	13	(6	7)	353	123	99	97	3	156	16	13	9	24	18	.57	26	.243	.314	.335

Dennis Eckersley

Pitches: Right **Bats:** Right **Pos:** RP   **Ht:** 6' 2" **Wt:** 195 **Born:** 10/3/54 **Age:** 41

			HOW MUCH HE PITCHED						WHAT HE GAVE UP										THE RESULTS					
Year Team	Lg	G	GS	CG	GF	IP	BFP	H	R	ER	HR	SH	SF	HB	TBB	IBB	SO	WP	Bk	W	L	Pct.	ShO	Sv	ERA
1975 Cleveland	AL	34	24	6	5	187	794	147	61	54	16	6	7	7	90	8	152	4	2	13	7	.650	2	2	2.60
1976 Cleveland	AL	36	30	9	3	199	821	155	82	76	13	10	4	5	78	2	200	6	1	13	12	.520	3	1	3.44
1977 Cleveland	AL	33	33	12	0	247	1006	214	100	97	31	11	6	7	54	11	191	3	0	14	13	.519	3	0	3.53
1978 Boston	AL	35	35	16	0	268	1121	258	99	89	30	7	8	7	71	8	162	3	0	20	8	.714	3	0	2.99
1979 Boston	AL	33	33	17	0	247	1018	234	89	82	29	10	6	6	59	4	150	1	1	17	10	.630	2	0	2.99
1980 Boston	AL	30	30	8	0	198	818	188	101	94	25	7	8	2	44	7	121	0	0	12	14	.462	0	0	4.27
1981 Boston	AL	23	23	8	0	154	649	160	82	73	9	6	5	3	35	2	79	0	0	9	8	.529	2	0	4.27
1982 Boston	AL	33	33	11	0	224.1	926	228	101	93	31	4	4	2	43	3	127	1	0	13	13	.500	3	0	3.73

Year Team	Lg	G	GS	CG	GF	IP	BFP	H	R	ER	HR	SH	SF	HB	TBB	IBB	SO	WP	Bk	W	L	Pct.	ShO	Sv	ERA
1983 Boston	AL	28	28	2	0	176.1	787	223	119	110	27	1	5	6	39	4	77	1	0	9	13	.409	0	0	5.61
1984 Bos-ChN		33	33	4	0	225	932	223	97	90	21	11	9	5	49	9	114	3	2	14	12	.538	0	0	3.60
1985 Chicago	NL	25	25	6	0	169.1	664	145	61	58	15	6	2	3	19	4	117	0	3	11	7	.611	2	0	3.08
1986 Chicago	NL	33	32	1	0	201	862	226	109	102	21	13	10	3	43	3	137	2	5	6	11	.353	0	0	4.57
1987 Oakland	AL	54	2	0	33	115.2	460	99	41	39	11	3	3	3	17	3	113	1	0	6	8	.429	0	16	3.03
1988 Oakland	AL	60	0	0	53	72.2	279	52	20	19	5	1	3	1	11	2	70	0	2	4	2	.667	0	45	2.35
1989 Oakland	AL	51	0	0	46	57.2	206	32	10	10	5	0	4	1	3	0	55	0	0	4	0	1.000	0	33	1.56
1990 Oakland	AL	63	0	0	61	73.1	262	41	9	5	2	0	1	0	4	1	73	0	0	4	2	.667	0	48	0.61
1991 Oakland	AL	67	0	0	59	76	299	60	26	25	11	1	0	1	9	3	87	1	0	5	4	.556	0	43	2.96
1992 Oakland	AL	69	0	0	65	80	309	62	17	17	5	3	0	1	11	6	93	0	0	7	1	.875	0	51	1.91
1993 Oakland	AL	64	0	0	52	67	276	67	32	31	7	2	2	2	13	4	80	0	0	2	4	.333	0	36	4.16
1994 Oakland	AL	45	0	0	39	44.1	193	49	26	21	5	1	0	1	13	2	47	0	0	5	4	.556	0	19	4.26
1995 Oakland	AL	52	0	0	48	50.1	212	53	29	27	5	1	2	1	11	0	40	0	0	4	6	.400	0	29	4.83
1984 Boston	AL	9	9	2	0	64.2	270	71	38	36	10	3	3	1	13	2	33	2	0	4	4	.500	0	0	5.01
Chicago	NL	24	24	2	0	160.1	662	152	59	54	11	8	6	4	36	7	81	1	2	10	8	.556	0	0	3.03
21 ML YEARS		901	361	100	464	3133	12894	2916	1311	1212	324	104	89	67	716	86	2285	26	16	192	159	.547	20	323	3.48

Chris Eddy

Pitches: Left   **Bats:** Left   **Pos:** RP   **Ht:** 6' 3"   **Wt:** 200   **Born:** 11/27/69   **Age:** 26

| | | HOW MUCH HE PITCHED | | | | | | WHAT HE GAVE UP | | | | | | | | | | | | THE RESULTS | | | | | |
Year Team	Lg	G	GS	CG	GF	IP	BFP	H	R	ER	HR	SH	SF	HB	TBB	IBB	SO	WP	Bk	W	L	Pct.	ShO	Sv	ERA
1992 Eugene	A	23	0	0	11	45.1	191	25	13	8	1	2	2	6	23	1	63	3	3	4	2	.667	0	5	1.59
1993 Wilmington	A	55	0	0	38	54	237	39	23	18	4	4	6	3	37	1	67	8	1	2	2	.500	0	14	3.00
1994 Memphis	AA	43	0	0	19	78.1	336	74	37	34	3	4	2	1	32	3	86	5	0	9	2	.818	0	1	3.91
1995 Omaha	AAA	14	0	0	6	17.1	84	20	15	14	1	1	2	2	12	2	12	0	0	1	1	.500	0	0	7.27
Wichita	AA	9	0	0	5	9	38	8	4	4	1	0	0	1	3	0	10	0	0	1	0	1.000	0	1	4.00
1995 Oakland	AL	6	0	0	0	3.2	22	7	3	3	0	2	0	2	2	0	2	1	0	0	0	.000	0	0	7.36

Ken Edenfield

Pitches: Right   **Bats:** Right   **Pos:** RP   **Ht:** 6' 1"   **Wt:** 165   **Born:** 3/18/67   **Age:** 29

| | | HOW MUCH HE PITCHED | | | | | | WHAT HE GAVE UP | | | | | | | | | | | | THE RESULTS | | | | | |
Year Team	Lg	G	GS	CG	GF	IP	BFP	H	R	ER	HR	SH	SF	HB	TBB	IBB	SO	WP	Bk	W	L	Pct.	ShO	Sv	ERA
1990 Boise	A	31	0	0	24	54.1	225	38	15	10	1	5	1	4	20	3	57	2	0	8	4	.667	0	9	1.66
1991 Quad City	A	47	0	0	40	87	356	69	30	25	3	5	3	4	30	2	106	5	1	8	5	.615	0	15	2.59
1992 Palm Spring	A	13	0	0	13	18.1	70	12	1	1	0	0	0	0	7	0	20	0	0	0	0	.000	0	7	0.49
Midland	AA	31	0	0	17	49.2	225	60	35	33	5	3	2	4	24	3	43	4	0	1	5	.167	0	2	5.98
1993 Midland	AA	48	3	1	19	93.2	404	93	56	48	10	2	5	8	35	5	84	14	2	5	8	.385	0	4	4.61
Vancouver	AAA	2	0	0	2	3.2	13	1	0	0	0	0	0	1	1	0	5	0	0	0	0	.000	0	0	0.00
1994 Vancouver	AAA	51	0	0	28	87.2	368	69	38	33	7	3	4	9	36	3	84	12	0	9	4	.692	0	4	3.39
1995 Vancouver	AAA	33	0	0	4	60	259	56	24	23	2	3	3	5	25	2	44	5	0	7	2	.778	0	0	3.45
1995 California	AL	7	0	0	3	12.2	56	15	7	6	1	0	1	0	5	0	6	3	0	0	0	.000	0	0	4.26

Tom Edens

Pitches: Right   **Bats:** Left   **Pos:** RP   **Ht:** 6' 2"   **Wt:** 190   **Born:** 6/9/61   **Age:** 35

| | | HOW MUCH HE PITCHED | | | | | | WHAT HE GAVE UP | | | | | | | | | | | | THE RESULTS | | | | | |
Year Team	Lg	G	GS	CG	GF	IP	BFP	H	R	ER	HR	SH	SF	HB	TBB	IBB	SO	WP	Bk	W	L	Pct.	ShO	Sv	ERA
1995 Iowa *	AAA	20	3	0	5	41.2	175	36	17	16	3	1	0	3	17	1	28	2	0	2	0	1.000	0	0	3.46
1987 New York	NL	2	2	0	0	8	42	15	6	6	2	2	0	0	4	0	4	2	0	0	0	.000	0	0	6.75
1990 Milwaukee	AL	35	6	0	9	89	387	89	52	44	8	6	4	4	33	3	40	1	0	4	5	.444	0	2	4.45
1991 Minnesota	AL	8	6	0	0	33	143	34	15	15	2	0	0	0	10	1	19	1	0	2	2	.500	0	0	4.09
1992 Minnesota	AL	52	0	0	14	76.1	317	65	26	24	1	4	0	2	36	3	57	5	0	6	3	.667	0	3	2.83
1993 Houston	NL	38	0	0	20	49	203	47	17	17	4	4	1	0	19	7	21	3	0	1	1	.500	0	0	3.12
1994 Hou-Phi	NL	42	0	0	15	54	231	59	26	26	3	3	3	2	18	4	39	5	1	5	1	.833	0	1	4.33
1995 Chicago	NL	5	0	0	1	3	18	6	3	2	0	0	0	0	3	0	2	0	0	1	0	1.000	0	0	6.00
1994 Houston	NL	39	0	0	13	50	214	55	25	25	3	2	3	2	17	4	38	5	1	4	1	.800	0	1	4.50
Philadelphia	NL	3	0	0	2	4	17	4	1	1	0	1	0	0	1	0	1	0	0	1	0	1.000	0	0	2.25
7 ML YEARS		182	14	0	59	312.1	1341	315	145	134	20	19	8	8	123	18	182	17	1	19	12	.613	0	6	3.86

Jim Edmonds

Bats: Left   **Throws:** Left   **Pos:** CF   **Ht:** 6' 1"   **Wt:** 190   **Born:** 6/27/70   **Age:** 26

| | | BATTING | | | | | | | | | | | | | | | BASERUNNING | | | | PERCENTAGES | | |
Year Team	Lg	G	AB	H	2B	3B	HR	(Hm	Rd)	TB	R	RBI	TBB	IBB	SO	HBP	SH	SF	SB	CS	SB%	GDP	Avg	OBP	SLG
1993 California	AL	18	61	15	4	1	0	(0	0)	21	5	4	2	1	16	0	0	0	0	2	.00	1	.246	.270	.344
1994 California	AL	94	289	79	13	1	5	(3	2)	109	35	37	30	3	72	1	1	1	4	2	.67	3	.273	.343	.377
1995 California	AL	141	558	162	30	4	33	(16	17)	299	120	107	51	4	130	5	1	5	1	4	.20	10	.290	.352	.536
3 ML YEARS		253	908	256	47	6	38	(19	19)	429	160	148	83	8	218	6	2	6	5	8	.38	14	.282	.344	.472

Robert Eenhoorn

Bats: Right **Throws:** Right **Pos:** 2B   **Ht:** 6' 3" **Wt:** 185 **Born:** 2/9/68 **Age:** 28

			BATTING																	BASERUNNING				PERCENTAGES		
Year	Team	Lg	G	AB	H	2B	3B	HR	(Hm	Rd)	TB	R	RBI	TBB	IBB	SO	HBP	SH	SF	SB	CS	SB%	GDP	Avg	OBP	SLG
1990	Oneonta	A	57	220	59	9	3	2	--	--	80	30	18	18	0	29	1	2	2	9	4	.69	2	.268	.324	.364
1991	Yankees	R	13	39	14	4	1	1	--	--	23	6	7	4	0	8	0	0	0	1	0	1.00	1	.359	.419	.590
	Pr. William	A	29	108	26	6	1	1	--	--	37	15	12	14	0	21	0	0	1	0	0	.00	4	.241	.325	.343
1992	Ft. Laud	A	57	203	62	5	2	4	--	--	83	23	33	19	2	25	4	2	4	6	2	.75	3	.305	.370	.409
	Albany-Colo	AA	60	196	46	11	2	1	--	--	64	24	23	10	1	17	1	3	3	2	1	.67	7	.235	.271	.327
1993	Albany-Colo	AA	82	314	88	24	3	6	--	--	136	48	46	21	1	39	1	3	3	3	4	.43	11	.280	.324	.433
1994	Columbus	AAA	99	343	82	10	2	5	--	--	111	38	39	14	0	43	1	3	1	2	2	.50	7	.239	.270	.324
1995	Columbus	AAA	92	318	80	11	3	5	--	--	112	36	32	20	0	54	3	6	2	2	4	.33	5	.252	.300	.352
1994	New York	AL	3	4	2	1	0	0	(0	0)	3	0	0	0	0	0	0	0	0	0	0	.00	0	.500	.500	.750
1995	New York	AL	5	14	2	1	0	0	(0	0)	3	1	2	1	0	3	0	0	0	0	0	.00	1	.143	.200	.214
	2 ML YEARS		8	18	4	2	0	0	(0	0)	6	2	2	1	0	3	0	0	0	0	0	.00	1	.222	.263	.333

Mark Eichhorn

Pitches: Right **Bats:** Right **Pos:** RP   **Ht:** 6' 3" **Wt:** 210 **Born:** 11/21/60 **Age:** 35

			HOW MUCH HE PITCHED					WHAT HE GAVE UP											THE RESULTS					
Year	Team	Lg	G	GS	CG	GF	IP	BFP	H	R	ER	HR	SH	SF	HB	TBB	IBB	SO	WP	Bk	W	L	Pct.	ShO	Sv	ERA
1982	Toronto	AL	7	7	0	0	38	171	40	28	23	4	1	2	0	14	1	16	3	0	0	3	.000	0	0	5.45
1986	Toronto	AL	69	0	0	38	157	612	105	32	30	8	9	2	7	45	14	166	2	1	14	6	.700	0	10	1.72
1987	Toronto	AL	89	0	0	27	127.2	540	110	47	45	14	7	4	6	52	13	96	3	1	10	6	.625	0	4	3.17
1988	Toronto	AL	37	0	0	17	66.2	302	79	32	31	3	8	1	6	27	4	28	3	6	0	3	.000	0	1	4.19
1989	Atlanta	NL	45	0	0	13	68.1	286	70	36	33	6	7	4	1	19	8	49	0	1	5	5	.500	0	0	4.35
1990	California	AL	60	0	0	40	84.2	374	98	36	29	2	2	4	6	23	0	69	2	0	2	5	.286	0	13	3.08
1991	California	AL	70	0	0	23	81.2	311	63	21	18	2	5	3	2	13	1	49	0	0	3	3	.500	0	1	1.98
1992	Cal-Tor	AL	65	0	0	26	87.2	372	86	34	30	3	3	5	2	25	8	61	9	1	4	4	.500	0	2	3.08
1993	Toronto	AL	54	0	0	16	72.2	309	76	26	22	3	3	2	3	22	7	47	2	0	3	1	.750	0	0	2.72
1994	Baltimore	AL	43	0	0	20	71	290	62	19	17	1	4	4	5	19	4	35	1	0	6	5	.545	0	1	2.15
1992	California	AL	42	0	0	19	56.2	237	51	19	15	2	2	3	0	18	8	42	3	1	2	4	.333	0	2	2.38
	Toronto	AL	23	0	0	7	31	135	35	15	15	1	1	2	2	7	0	19	6	0	2	0	1.000	0	0	4.35
	10 ML YEARS		539	7	0	220	855.1	3567	789	311	278	46	49	31	38	259	60	616	25	10	47	41	.534	0	32	2.93

Dave Eiland

Pitches: Right **Bats:** Right **Pos:** RP   **Ht:** 6' 3" **Wt:** 210 **Born:** 7/5/66 **Age:** 29

			HOW MUCH HE PITCHED					WHAT HE GAVE UP											THE RESULTS					
Year	Team	Lg	G	GS	CG	GF	IP	BFP	H	R	ER	HR	SH	SF	HB	TBB	IBB	SO	WP	Bk	W	L	Pct.	ShO	Sv	ERA
1995	Columbus *	AAA	19	18	1	0	109	444	109	44	38	4	0	2	1	22	2	62	1	0	8	7	.533	0	3	3.14
1988	New York	AL	3	3	0	0	12.2	57	15	9	9	6	0	0	2	4	0	7	0	0	0	0	.000	0	0	6.39
1989	New York	AL	6	6	0	0	34.1	152	44	25	22	5	1	2	2	13	3	11	0	0	1	3	.250	0	0	5.77
1990	New York	AL	5	5	0	0	30.1	127	31	14	12	2	0	0	0	5	0	16	0	0	2	1	.667	0	0	3.56
1991	New York	AL	18	13	0	4	72.2	317	87	51	43	10	0	3	3	23	1	18	0	0	2	5	.286	0	0	5.33
1992	San Diego	NL	7	7	0	0	27	120	33	21	17	1	0	0	0	5	0	10	1	0	0	2	.000	0	0	5.67
1993	San Diego	NL	10	9	0	0	48.1	217	58	33	28	5	2	2	1	17	1	14	1	0	0	3	.000	0	0	5.21
1995	New York	AL	4	1	0	1	10	51	16	10	7	1	0	1	1	3	1	6	1	0	1	1	.500	0	0	6.30
	7 ML YEARS		53	44	0	5	235.1	1041	284	163	138	30	3	8	9	70	6	82	2	1	6	15	.286	0	0	5.28

Joey Eischen

Pitches: Left **Bats:** Left **Pos:** RP   **Ht:** 6' 1" **Wt:** 190 **Born:** 5/25/70 **Age:** 26

			HOW MUCH HE PITCHED					WHAT HE GAVE UP											THE RESULTS					
Year	Team	Lg	G	GS	CG	GF	IP	BFP	H	R	ER	HR	SH	SF	HB	TBB	IBB	SO	WP	Bk	W	L	Pct.	ShO	Sv	ERA
1989	Butte	R	12	12	0	0	52.2	248	50	45	31	4	1	0	6	38	0	57	13	11	3	7	.300	0	0	5.30
1990	Gastonia	A	17	14	0	0	73.1	311	51	36	22	0	3	4	3	40	0	69	8	9	3	7	.300	0	0	2.70
1991	Charlotte	A	18	18	1	0	108.1	467	99	59	40	5	6	3	4	55	1	80	8	1	4	10	.286	0	0	3.32
	W. Palm Bch	A	8	8	1	0	38.1	177	34	27	22	3	3	1	2	24	0	26	3	0	4	2	.667	1	0	5.17
1992	W. Palm Bch	A	27	26	3	0	169.2	705	128	68	58	5	4	3	8	83	2	167	6	0	9	8	.529	2	0	3.08
1993	Harrisburg	AA	20	20	0	0	119.1	533	122	62	48	11	3	6	4	60	0	110	9	1	14	4	.778	0	0	3.62
	Ottawa	AAA	6	6	0	0	40.2	166	34	18	16	3	1	2	0	15	0	29	1	0	2	2	.500	0	0	3.54
1994	Ottawa	AAA	48	2	0	20	62	274	54	38	34	7	3	4	0	40	4	57	10	0	2	6	.250	0	2	4.94
1995	Ottawa	AAA	11	0	0	3	15.2	61	9	4	3	0	1	0	0	8	1	13	0	0	2	1	.667	0	0	1.72
	Albuquerque	AAA	13	0	0	6	16.1	59	8	8	0	0	1	0	0	3	0	14	1	0	3	0	1.000	0	2	0.00
1994	Montreal	NL	1	0	0	0	0.2	7	4	4	4	0	0	0	1	0	0	1	0	0	0	0	.000	0	0	54.00
1995	Los Angeles	NL	17	0	0	8	20.1	95	19	9	7	1	0	0	2	11	1	15	1	0	0	0	.000	0	0	3.10
	2 ML YEARS		18	0	0	8	21	102	23	13	11	1	0	0	3	11	1	16	1	0	0	0	.000	0	0	4.71

Jim Eisenreich

Bats: Left **Throws:** Left **Pos:** RF/LF   **Ht:** 5'11" **Wt:** 195 **Born:** 4/18/59 **Age:** 37

Year	Team	Lg	G	AB	H	2B	3B	HR	(Hm	Rd)	TB	R	RBI	TBB	IBB	SO	HBP	SH	SF	SB	CS	SB%	GDP	Avg	OBP	SLG
1982	Minnesota	AL	34	99	30	6	0	2	(1	1)	42	10	9	11	0	13	1	0	0	0	0	.00	1	.303	.378	.424
1983	Minnesota	AL	2	7	2	1	0	0	(0	0)	3	1	0	1	0	1	0	0	0	0	0	.00	0	.286	.375	.429
1984	Minnesota	AL	12	32	7	1	0	0	(0	0)	8	1	3	2	1	4	0	0	2	2	0	1.00	0	.219	.250	.250
1987	Kansas City	AL	44	105	25	8	2	4	(3	1)	49	10	21	7	2	13	0	0	3	1	1	.50	2	.238	.278	.467
1988	Kansas City	AL	82	202	44	8	1	1	(0	1)	57	26	19	6	1	31	0	2	4	9	3	.75	2	.218	.236	.282
1989	Kansas City	AL	134	475	139	33	7	9	(4	5)	213	64	59	37	9	44	0	3	4	27	8	.77	8	.293	.341	.448
1990	Kansas City	AL	142	496	139	29	7	5	(2	3)	197	61	51	42	2	51	1	2	4	12	14	.46	7	.280	.335	.397
1991	Kansas City	AL	135	375	113	22	3	2	(2	0)	147	47	47	20	1	35	1	3	6	5	3	.63	10	.301	.333	.392
1992	Kansas City	AL	113	353	95	13	3	2	(1	1)	120	31	28	24	4	36	0	0	3	11	6	.65	6	.269	.313	.340
1993	Philadelphia	NL	153	362	115	17	4	7	(3	4)	161	51	54	26	5	36	1	3	2	5	0	1.00	6	.318	.363	.445
1994	Philadelphia	NL	104	290	87	15	4	4	(3	1)	122	42	43	33	3	31	1	3	2	6	2	.75	8	.300	.371	.421
1995	Philadelphia	NL	129	377	119	22	2	10	(5	5)	175	46	55	38	4	44	1	2	5	10	0	1.00	7	.316	.375	.464
	12 ML YEARS		1084	3173	915	175	33	46	(24	22)	1294	390	389	247	32	339	6	18	35	88	37	.70	58	.288	.337	.408

Cal Eldred

Pitches: Right **Bats:** Right **Pos:** SP   **Ht:** 6' 4" **Wt:** 236 **Born:** 11/24/67 **Age:** 28

Year	Team	Lg	G	GS	CG	GF	IP	BFP	H	R	ER	HR	SH	SF	HB	TBB	IBB	SO	WP	Bk	W	L	Pct.	ShO	Sv	ERA
1991	Milwaukee	AL	3	3	0	0	16	73	20	9	8	2	0	0	0	6	0	10	0	0	2	0	1.000	0	0	4.50
1992	Milwaukee	AL	14	14	2	0	100.1	394	76	21	20	4	1	0	2	23	0	62	3	0	11	2	.846	1	0	1.79
1993	Milwaukee	AL	36	36	8	0	258	1087	232	120	115	32	5	12	10	91	5	180	2	0	16	16	.500	1	0	4.01
1994	Milwaukee	AL	25	25	6	0	179	769	158	96	93	23	5	7	4	84	0	98	2	0	11	11	.500	0	0	4.68
1995	Milwaukee	AL	4	4	0	0	23.2	104	24	10	9	4	1	0	1	10	0	18	1	1	1	1	.500	0	0	3.42
	5 ML YEARS		82	82	16	0	577	2427	510	256	245	65	12	19	17	214	5	368	8	1	41	30	.577	2	0	3.82

Donnie Elliott

Pitches: Right **Bats:** Right **Pos:** RP   **Ht:** 6' 5" **Wt:** 225 **Born:** 9/20/68 **Age:** 27

Year	Team	Lg	G	GS	CG	GF	IP	BFP	H	R	ER	HR	SH	SF	HB	TBB	IBB	SO	WP	Bk	W	L	Pct.	ShO	Sv	ERA
1988	Martinsvlle	R	15	10	0	2	59	257	47	37	24	4	0	0	3	31	0	77	4	9	4	2	.667	0	1	3.66
1989	Batavia	A	8	8	0	0	57	231	45	21	9	2	1	0	0	14	1	48	4	0	4	1	.800	0	0	1.42
	Spartanburg	A	7	7	1	0	43.2	183	46	19	12	1	1	1	0	14	0	36	4	0	2	3	.400	1	0	2.47
1990	Spartanburg	A	20	20	0	0	105.1	450	101	52	41	6	3	5	2	46	0	109	7	1	4	8	.333	0	0	3.50
1991	Spartanburg	A	10	10	0	0	51	235	42	37	24	1	1	0	3	36	0	81	8	0	3	4	.429	0	0	4.24
	Clearwater	A	18	18	1	0	107	435	78	34	33	1	4	4	1	51	0	103	10	1	8	5	.615	1	0	2.78
1992	Clearwater	A	3	3	0	0	18	71	12	6	6	1	0	0	0	8	0	12	2	0	1	1	.500	0	0	3.00
	Reading	AA	6	6	0	0	35.2	153	37	10	10	2	2	1	0	11	1	23	0	0	3	3	.500	0	0	2.52
	Greenville	AA	19	17	0	0	103.2	416	76	28	24	8	1	3	5	35	1	100	4	0	7	2	.778	0	0	2.08
1993	Richmond	AAA	18	18	1	0	103	449	108	65	54	16	3	2	0	39	0	99	5	0	8	5	.615	0	0	4.72
	Las Vegas	AAA	8	7	0	0	41	198	48	32	29	6	1	2	1	24	0	44	3	0	2	5	.286	0	0	6.37
1994	Las Vegas	AAA	6	0	0	1	13.1	65	13	11	8	3	0	1	0	11	2	12	5	0	2	0	1.000	0	0	5.40
1995	Las Vegas	AAA	7	0	0	3	8	35	8	4	4	1	1	1	0	4	1	2	0	0	1	0	1.000	0	0	4.50
1994	San Diego	NL	30	1	0	10	33	148	31	12	12	3	2	0	1	21	2	24	2	0	0	1	.000	0	0	3.27
1995	San Diego	NL	1	0	0	1	2	9	2	0	0	0	0	0	0	1	0	3	0	0	0	0	.000	0	0	0.00
	2 ML YEARS		31	1	0	11	35	157	33	12	12	3	2	0	1	22	2	27	2	0	0	1	.000	0	0	3.09

Kevin Elster

Bats: Right **Throws:** Right **Pos:** SS   **Ht:** 6' 2" **Wt:** 200 **Born:** 8/3/64 **Age:** 31

Year	Team	Lg	G	AB	H	2B	3B	HR	(Hm	Rd)	TB	R	RBI	TBB	IBB	SO	HBP	SH	SF	SB	CS	SB%	GDP	Avg	OBP	SLG
1995	Omaha *	AAA	11	42	10	4	0	0	--	--	14	5	6	5	0	8	0	0	1	0	0	.00	0	.238	.313	.333
	Scrantn-WB *	AAA	5	17	5	3	0	0	--	--	8	2	2	2	0	3	0	0	1	0	0	.00	1	.294	.368	.471
1986	New York	NL	19	30	5	1	0	0	(0	0)	6	3	0	3	1	8	0	0	0	0	0	.00	0	.167	.242	.200
1987	New York	NL	5	10	4	2	0	0	(0	0)	6	1	1	0	0	1	0	0	0	0	0	.00	1	.400	.400	.600
1988	New York	NL	149	406	87	11	1	9	(6	3)	127	41	37	35	12	47	3	6	0	2	1	.67	10	.214	.282	.313
1989	New York	NL	151	458	106	25	2	10	(5	5)	165	52	55	34	11	77	2	6	8	4	3	.57	13	.231	.283	.360
1990	New York	NL	92	314	65	20	1	9	(2	7)	114	36	45	30	2	54	1	1	6	2	0	1.00	4	.207	.274	.363
1991	New York	NL	115	348	84	16	2	6	(3	3)	122	33	36	40	6	53	1	1	4	2	3	.40	4	.241	.318	.351
1992	New York	NL	6	18	4	0	0	0	(0	0)	4	0	0	2	0	0	0	1	0	0	0	.00	1	.222	.222	.222
1994	New York	AL	7	20	0	0	0	0	(0	0)	0	0	0	1	0	6	0	1	0	0	0	.00	0	.000	.048	.000
1995	NYA-Phi		36	70	13	5	1	1	(1	0)	23	11	9	8	1	19	1	2	2	0	0	.00	1	.186	.272	.329
1995	New York	AL	10	17	2	1	0	0	(0	0)	3	1	0	1	0	5	0	0	0	0	0	.00	0	.118	.167	.176

	Lg	G	AB	H	2B	3B	HR	(Hm	Rd)	TB	R	RBI	TBB	IBB	SO	HBP	SH	SF	SB	CS	SB%	GDP	Avg	OBP	SLG
Philadelphia	NL	26	53	11	4	1	1	(1	0)	20	10	9	7	1	14	1	2	2	0	0	.00	1	.208	.302	.377
9 ML YEARS		580	1674	368	80	7	35	(17	18)	567	177	183	151	33	267	8	17	20	10	6	.63	29	.220	.284	.339

Alan Embree

Pitches: Left **Bats:** Left **Pos:** RP **Ht:** 6' 2" **Wt:** 190 **Born:** 1/23/70 **Age:** 26

		HOW MUCH HE PITCHED						WHAT HE GAVE UP										THE RESULTS					
Year Team	Lg	G	GS	CG	GF	IP	BFP	H	R	ER	HR	SH	SF	HB	TBB	IBB	SO	WP	Bk	W	L	Pct.	ShO	Sv	ERA
1990 Burlington	R	15	15	0	0	81.2	351	87	36	24	3	1	3	0	30	0	58	5	4	4	4	.500	0	0	2.64
1991 Columbus	A	27	26	3	0	155.1	651	125	80	62	4	5	3	4	77	1	137	7	0	10	8	.556	1	0	3.59
1992 Kinston	A	15	15	1	0	101	418	89	48	37	10	3	1	2	32	0	115	6	3	10	5	.667	0	0	3.30
Canton-Akrn	AA	12	12	0	0	79	316	61	24	20	2	3	1	2	28	1	56	2	1	7	2	.778	0	0	2.28
1993 Canton-Akrn	AA	1	1	0	0	5.1	20	3	2	2	0	0	0	0	3	0	4	0	0	0	0	.000	0	0	3.38
1994 Canton-Akrn	AA	30	27	2	1	157	698	183	106	96	15	2	6	4	64	3	81	8	1	9	16	.360	1	0	5.50
1995 Buffalo	AAA	30	0	0	19	40.2	170	31	10	4	0	1	2	1	19	2	56	0	0	3	4	.429	0	5	0.89
1992 Cleveland	AL	4	4	0	0	18	81	19	14	14	3	0	2	1	8	0	12	1	1	0	2	.000	0	0	7.00
1995 Cleveland	AL	23	0	0	8	24.2	111	23	16	14	2	2	2	0	16	0	23	1	0	3	2	.600	0	1	5.11
2 ML YEARS		27	4	0	8	42.2	192	42	30	28	5	2	4	1	24	0	35	2	1	3	4	.429	0	1	5.91

Angelo Encarnacion

Bats: Right **Throws:** Right **Pos:** C **Ht:** 5' 8" **Wt:** 180 **Born:** 4/18/73 **Age:** 23

		BATTING																	BASERUNNING				PERCENTAGES		
Year Team	Lg	G	AB	H	2B	3B	HR	(Hm	Rd)	TB	R	RBI	TBB	IBB	SO	HBP	SH	SF	SB	CS	SB%	GDP	Avg	OBP	SLG
1991 Welland	A	50	181	46	3	2	0	--	--	53	21	15	5	0	27	1	0	0	4	3	.57	5	.254	.278	.293
1992 Augusta	A	94	314	80	14	3	1	--	--	103	39	29	25	1	37	1	4	2	2	4	.33	5	.255	.310	.328
1993 Salem	A	70	238	61	12	1	3	--	--	84	20	24	13	1	27	0	0	1	1	4	.20	5	.256	.294	.353
Buffalo	AAA	3	9	3	0	0	0	--	--	3	1	2	0	0	0	0	0	0	0	0	.00	0	.333	.333	.333
1994 Carolina	AA	67	227	66	17	0	3	--	--	92	26	32	11	1	28	2	0	4	2	2	.50	4	.291	.324	.405
1995 Calgary	AAA	21	80	20	3	0	1	--	--	26	8	6	1	1	12	0	0	0	1	0	1.00	2	.250	.259	.325
1995 Pittsburgh	NL	58	159	36	7	2	2	(2	0)	53	18	10	13	5	28	0	3	0	1	1	.50	3	.226	.285	.333

John Ericks

Pitches: Right **Bats:** Right **Pos:** SP **Ht:** 6' 7" **Wt:** 225 **Born:** 9/16/67 **Age:** 28

		HOW MUCH HE PITCHED						WHAT HE GAVE UP										THE RESULTS					
Year Team	Lg	G	GS	CG	GF	IP	BFP	H	R	ER	HR	SH	SF	HB	TBB	IBB	SO	WP	Bk	W	L	Pct.	ShO	Sv	ERA
1988 Johnson Cty	R	9	9	1	0	41	174	27	20	17	1	1	2	0	27	0	41	5	4	3	2	.600	0	0	3.73
1989 Savannah	A	28	28	1	0	167.1	695	90	59	38	4	4	5	9	101	0	211	11	2	11	10	.524	1	0	2.04
1990 St. Pete	A	4	4	0	0	23	88	16	5	4	0	0	1	0	6	0	25	1	1	2	1	.667	0	0	1.57
Arkansas	AA	4	4	1	0	15.1	83	17	19	16	2	0	2	1	19	0	19	3	1	1	2	.333	1	0	9.39
1991 Arkansas	AA	25	25	1	0	139.2	630	138	94	74	6	5	4	7	84	3	103	15	3	5	14	.263	0	0	4.77
1992 Arkansas	AA	13	13	1	0	75	316	69	36	34	4	4	3	3	29	1	71	6	0	2	6	.250	0	0	4.08
1994 Salem	A	17	5	0	3	52.1	219	42	22	18	4	1	2	3	20	0	71	3	0	4	2	.667	0	1	3.10
Carolina	AA	11	11	0	0	57	234	42	22	17	2	2	1	3	19	0	64	5	0	2	4	.333	0	0	2.68
1995 Calgary	AAA	5	5	0	0	29	116	20	8	8	2	1	0	0	13	0	25	3	0	2	1	.667	0	0	2.48
1995 Pittsburgh	NL	19	18	1	0	106	472	108	59	54	7	5	5	2	50	0	80	11	1	3	9	.250	0	0	4.58

Scott Erickson

Pitches: Right **Bats:** Right **Pos:** SP **Ht:** 6' 4" **Wt:** 234 **Born:** 2/2/68 **Age:** 28

		HOW MUCH HE PITCHED						WHAT HE GAVE UP										THE RESULTS					
Year Team	Lg	G	GS	CG	GF	IP	BFP	H	R	ER	HR	SH	SF	HB	TBB	IBB	SO	WP	Bk	W	L	Pct.	ShO	Sv	ERA
1990 Minnesota	AL	19	17	1	0	113	485	108	49	36	9	5	2	1	51	4	53	3	0	8	4	.667	0	0	2.87
1991 Minnesota	AL	32	32	5	0	204	851	189	80	72	13	5	7	6	71	3	108	4	0	20	8	.714	3	0	3.18
1992 Minnesota	AL	32	32	5	0	212	888	197	86	80	18	9	7	8	83	3	101	6	1	13	12	.520	3	0	3.40
1993 Minnesota	AL	34	34	1	0	218.2	976	266	138	126	17	10	13	10	71	1	116	5	0	8	19	.296	0	0	5.19
1994 Minnesota	AL	23	23	2	0	144	654	173	95	87	15	3	4	9	59	0	104	10	0	8	11	.421	1	0	5.44
1995 Min-Bal	AL	32	31	7	1	196.1	836	213	108	105	18	3	3	5	67	0	106	3	2	13	10	.565	2	0	4.81
1995 Minnesota	AL	15	15	0	0	87.2	390	102	61	58	11	2	1	4	32	0	45	1	0	4	6	.400	0	0	5.95
Baltimore	AL	17	16	7	1	108.2	446	111	47	47	7	1	2	1	35	0	61	2	2	9	4	.692	2	0	3.89
6 ML YEARS		172	169	21	2	1088	4690	1146	556	506	90	35	36	43	402	11	588	31	3	70	64	.522	9	0	4.19

Vaughn Eshelman

Pitches: Left **Bats:** Left **Pos:** SP/RP **Ht:** 6' 3" **Wt:** 210 **Born:** 5/22/69 **Age:** 27

		HOW MUCH HE PITCHED						WHAT HE GAVE UP										THE RESULTS					
Year Team	Lg	G	GS	CG	GF	IP	BFP	H	R	ER	HR	SH	SF	HB	TBB	IBB	SO	WP	Bk	W	L	Pct.	ShO	Sv	ERA
1991 Bluefield	R	3	3	0	0	14	59	10	4	1	0	1	0	0	9	0	15	1	0	1	0	1.000	0	0	0.64
Kane County	A	11	11	2	0	77.2	319	57	23	20	3	3	1	3	35	0	90	2	2	5	3	.625	1	0	2.32
1993 Frederick	A	24	24	2	0	143.1	608	128	70	62	10	4	3	7	59	0	122	7	1	7	10	.412	1	0	3.89

65

Year	Team	Lg	G	GS	CG	GF	IP	BFP	H	R	ER	HR	SH	SF	HB	TBB	IBB	SO	WP	Bk	W	L	Pct.	ShO	Sv	ERA
1994	Bowie	AA	27	25	2	0	166.1	713	175	81	74	13	7	3	3	60	1	133	8	0	11	9	.550	2	0	4.00
1995	Trenton	AA	2	2	0	0	7	25	3	1	0	0	0	0	1	0	0	7	0	0	0	1	.000	0	0	0.00
1995	Boston	AL	23	14	0	4	81.2	356	86	47	44	3	0	3	1	36	0	41	4	0	6	3	.667	0	0	4.85

Alvaro Espinoza

Bats: Right **Throws:** Right **Pos:** 2B/3B/SS **Ht:** 6' 0" **Wt:** 190 **Born:** 2/19/62 **Age:** 34

			BATTING															BASERUNNING				PERCENTAGES		
Year	Team	Lg	G	AB	H	2B	3B	HR	(Hm | Rd)	TB	R	RBI	TBB	IBB	SO	HBP	SH	SF	SB	CS	SB%	GDP	Avg	OBP	SLG
1984	Minnesota	AL	1	0	0	0	0	0	(0 | 0)	0	0	0	0	0	0	0	0	0	0	0	.00	0	.000	.000	.000
1985	Minnesota	AL	32	57	15	2	0	0	(0 | 0)	17	5	9	1	0	9	1	3	0	0	1	.00	2	.263	.288	.298
1986	Minnesota	AL	37	42	9	1	0	0	(0 | 0)	10	4	1	1	0	10	0	2	0	0	1	.00	0	.214	.233	.238
1988	New York	AL	3	3	0	0	0	0	(0 | 0)	0	0	0	0	0	0	0	0	0	0	0	.00	0	.000	.000	.000
1989	New York	AL	146	503	142	23	1	0	(0 | 0)	167	51	41	14	1	60	1	23	3	3	3	.50	14	.282	.301	.332
1990	New York	AL	150	438	98	12	2	2	(0 | 2)	120	31	20	16	0	54	5	11	2	1	2	.33	13	.224	.258	.274
1991	New York	AL	148	480	123	23	2	5	(2 | 3)	165	51	33	16	0	57	2	9	2	4	1	.80	10	.256	.282	.344
1993	Cleveland	AL	129	263	73	15	0	4	(3 | 1)	100	34	27	8	0	36	1	8	3	2	2	.50	7	.278	.298	.380
1994	Cleveland	AL	90	231	55	13	0	1	(1 | 0)	71	27	19	6	0	33	1	4	2	1	3	.25	7	.238	.258	.307
1995	Cleveland	AL	66	143	36	4	0	2	(0 | 2)	46	15	17	2	0	16	1	2	2	0	2	.00	3	.252	.264	.322
	10 ML YEARS		802	2160	551	93	5	14	(6 | 8)	696	218	167	64	1	275	12	62	14	11	15	.42	56	.255	.279	.322

Shawn Estes

Pitches: Left **Bats:** Right **Pos:** SP **Ht:** 6' 2" **Wt:** 185 **Born:** 2/18/73 **Age:** 23

			HOW MUCH HE PITCHED						WHAT HE GAVE UP										THE RESULTS					
Year	Team	Lg	G	GS	CG	GF	IP	BFP	H	R	ER	HR	SH	SF	HB	TBB	IBB	SO	WP	Bk	W	L	Pct.	ShO	Sv	ERA
1991	Bellingham	A	9	9	0	0	34	185	27	33	26	2	2	3	1	55	0	35	6	10	1	3	.250	0	0	6.88
1992	Bellingham	A	15	15	0	0	77	354	84	55	37	6	2	2	3	45	0	77	10	3	3	3	.500	0	0	4.32
1993	Appleton	A	19	18	0	0	83.1	418	108	85	67	3	1	3	7	52	1	65	19	2	5	9	.357	0	0	7.24
1994	Mariners	R	5	5	0	0	20	86	16	9	7	0	1	0	1	6	0	31	7	0	3	0	.000	0	0	3.15
	Appleton	A	5	4	0	1	19.2	92	19	13	10	1	2	1	2	17	0	28	4	0	0	2	.000	0	0	4.58
1995	Wisconsin	A	2	2	0	0	10	38	5	1	1	0	0	1	0	5	0	11	2	1	0	0	.000	0	0	0.90
	Burlington	A	4	4	0	0	15.1	72	13	8	7	2	0	0	2	12	0	22	2	0	0	0	.000	0	0	4.11
	San Jose	A	9	8	0	0	49.2	191	32	13	12	1	0	3	1	17	0	61	7	0	5	2	.714	0	0	2.17
	Shreveport	AA	4	4	0	0	22.1	90	14	5	5	1	0	1	3	10	0	18	3	0	2	0	1.000	0	0	2.01
1995	San Francisco	NL	3	3	0	0	17.1	76	16	14	13	2	0	0	1	5	0	14	4	0	0	3	.000	0	0	6.75

Tony Eusebio

Bats: Right **Throws:** Right **Pos:** C **Ht:** 6' 2" **Wt:** 180 **Born:** 4/27/67 **Age:** 29

			BATTING															BASERUNNING				PERCENTAGES		
Year	Team	Lg	G	AB	H	2B	3B	HR	(Hm | Rd)	TB	R	RBI	TBB	IBB	SO	HBP	SH	SF	SB	CS	SB%	GDP	Avg	OBP	SLG
1991	Houston	NL	10	19	2	1	0	0	(0 | 0)	3	4	0	6	0	8	0	0	0	0	0	.00	1	.105	.320	.158
1994	Houston	NL	55	159	47	9	1	5	(1 | 4)	73	18	30	8	0	33	0	2	5	0	1	.00	4	.296	.320	.459
1995	Houston	NL	113	368	110	21	1	6	(5 | 1)	151	46	58	31	1	59	3	1	5	0	2	.00	12	.299	.354	.410
	3 ML YEARS		178	546	159	31	2	11	(6 | 5)	227	68	88	45	1	100	3	3	10	0	3	.00	17	.291	.343	.416

Carl Everett

Bats: Both **Throws:** Right **Pos:** RF **Ht:** 6' 0" **Wt:** 190 **Born:** 6/3/71 **Age:** 25

			BATTING															BASERUNNING				PERCENTAGES		
Year	Team	Lg	G	AB	H	2B	3B	HR	(Hm	Rd)	TB	R	RBI	TBB	IBB	SO	HBP	SH	SF	SB	CS	SB%	GDP	Avg	OBP	SLG
1995	Norfolk *	AAA	67	260	78	16	4	6	--	--	120	52	35	20	1	47	4	1	1	12	6	.67	2	.300	.358	.462
1993	Florida	NL	11	19	2	0	0	0	(0	0)	2	0	0	1	0	9	0	0	0	0	1	1.00	0	.105	.150	.105
1994	Florida	NL	16	51	11	1	0	2	(2	0)	18	7	6	3	0	15	0	0	0	4	1	1.00	0	.216	.259	.353
1995	New York	NL	79	289	75	13	1	12	(9	3)	126	48	54	39	2	67	2	1	0	2	5	.29	11	.260	.352	.436
	3 ML YEARS		106	359	88	14	1	14	(11	3)	146	55	60	43	2	91	2	1	0	7	5	.58	11	.245	.329	.407

Bryan Eversgerd

Pitches: Left **Bats:** Right **Pos:** RP **Ht:** 6' 1" **Wt:** 190 **Born:** 2/11/69 **Age:** 27

			HOW MUCH HE PITCHED						WHAT HE GAVE UP										THE RESULTS					
Year	Team	Lg	G	GS	CG	GF	IP	BFP	H	R	ER	HR	SH	SF	HB	TBB	IBB	SO	WP	Bk	W	L	Pct.	ShO	Sv	ERA
1989	Johnson Cty	R	16	1	0	5	29.2	127	30	16	12	1	2	6	0	12	1	19	2	0	2	3	.400	0	0	3.64
1990	Springfield	A	20	15	2	2	104.1	457	123	60	48	6	5	4	4	26	1	55	2	0	6	8	.429	0	0	4.14
1991	Savannah	A	72	0	0	22	93.1	390	71	43	36	7	2	0	3	34	4	98	11	0	1	5	.167	0	1	3.47
1992	St. Pete	A	57	1	0	13	74	305	65	25	22	0	9	4	2	25	4	57	1	1	3	2	.600	0	0	2.68
	Arkansas	AA	6	0	0	2	5.1	25	7	4	4	0	1	0	0	2	1	4	0	0	0	1	.000	0	0	6.75
1993	Arkansas	AA	62	0	0	32	66	269	60	24	16	3	2	1	0	19	4	68	7	1	4	4	.500	0	0	2.18
1994	Louisville	AAA	9	0	0	2	12	54	11	7	6	0	1	1	0	8	0	8	1	0	1	1	.500	0	0	4.50
1995	Ottawa	AAA	38	0	0	9	53	232	49	21	14	1	2	3	1	26	1	45	2	0	6	2	.750	0	2	2.38
1994	St. Louis	NL	40	1	0	8	67.2	283	75	36	34	8	5	2	2	20	1	47	3	1	2	3	.400	0	0	4.52

1995 Montreal	NL	25	0	0	5	21	95	22	13	12	2	2	1	9	2	8	1	0	0	0	.000	0	0	5.14
2 ML YEARS		65	1	0	13	88.2	378	97	49	46	10	6	4	3	29	3	55	4	1	2	3	.400	0	0	4.67

Jorge Fabregas

Bats: Left **Throws:** Right **Pos:** C **Ht:** 6' 3" **Wt:** 205 **Born:** 3/13/70 **Age:** 26

		BATTING																	BASERUNNING				PERCENTAGES		
Year Team	Lg	G	AB	H	2B	3B	HR	(Hm	Rd)	TB	R	RBI	TBB	IBB	SO	HBP	SH	SF	SB	CS	SB%	GDP	Avg	OBP	SLG
1992 Palm Spring	A	70	258	73	13	0	0	--	--	86	35	40	30	1	27	1	1	3	0	4	.00	13	.283	.356	.333
1993 Midland	AA	113	409	118	26	3	6	--	--	168	63	56	31	5	60	1	0	3	1	1	.50	15	.289	.338	.411
Vancouver	AAA	4	13	3	1	0	0	--	--	4	1	1	1	0	3	0	0	0	0	0	.00	1	.231	.286	.308
1994 Vancouver	AAA	66	211	47	6	1	1	--	--	58	17	24	12	0	25	1	2	3	1	1	.50	1	.223	.264	.275
1995 Vancouver	AAA	21	73	18	3	0	4	--	--	33	9	10	9	3	12	0	0	1	0	0	.00	1	.247	.325	.452
1994 California	AL	43	127	36	3	0	0	(0	0)	39	12	16	7	1	18	0	1	0	2	1	.67	5	.283	.321	.307
1995 California	AL	73	227	56	10	0	1	(1	0)	69	24	22	17	0	28	0	3	1	0	2	.00	9	.247	.298	.304
2 ML YEARS		116	354	92	13	0	1	(1	0)	108	36	38	24	1	46	0	4	1	2	3	.40	14	.260	.306	.305

Hector Fajardo

Pitches: Right **Bats:** Right **Pos:** RP **Ht:** 6' 4" **Wt:** 200 **Born:** 11/6/70 **Age:** 25

		HOW MUCH HE PITCHED						WHAT HE GAVE UP										THE RESULTS					
Year Team	Lg	G	GS	CG	GF	IP	BFP	H	R	ER	HR	SH	SF	HB	TBB	IBB	SO	WP	Bk	W	L	Pct.	ShO	Sv	ERA
1995 Ottawa *	AAA	11	0	0	5	15.1	69	18	7	7	2	1	0	2	6	0	9	1	0	0	0	.000	0	0	4.11
1991 Tex-Pit		6	5	0	1	25.1	119	35	20	19	2	0	3	1	11	0	23	3	0	0	2	.000	0	0	6.75
1993 Texas	AL	1	0	0	1	0.2	2	0	0	0	0	0	0	0	0	0	1	0	0	0	0	.000	0	0	0.00
1994 Texas	AL	18	12	0	0	83.1	370	95	67	64	15	4	4	2	26	0	45	4	0	5	7	.417	0	0	6.91
1995 Texas	AL	5	0	0	1	15	67	19	13	13	2	0	1	1	5	0	9	3	0	0	2	.000	0	0	7.80
1991 Texas	AL	4	3	0	1	19	84	25	13	12	2	0	3	1	4	0	15	0	0	0	2	.000	0	0	5.68
Pittsburgh	NL	2	2	0	0	6.1	35	10	7	7	0	0	0	0	7	0	8	3	0	0	0	.000	0	0	9.95
4 ML YEARS		30	17	0	3	124.1	558	149	100	96	19	4	7	4	42	0	78	10	0	5	9	.357	0	0	6.95

Rikkert Faneyte

Bats: Right **Throws:** Right **Pos:** CF/RF **Ht:** 6' 1" **Wt:** 170 **Born:** 5/31/69 **Age:** 27

		BATTING																	BASERUNNING				PERCENTAGES		
Year Team	Lg	G	AB	H	2B	3B	HR	(Hm	Rd)	TB	R	RBI	TBB	IBB	SO	HBP	SH	SF	SB	CS	SB%	GDP	Avg	OBP	SLG
1995 Phoenix *	AAA	38	135	37	8	1	1	--	--	50	22	17	15	1	22	0	2	1	2	5	.29	1	.274	.344	.370
1993 San Francisco	NL	7	15	2	0	0	0	(0	0)	2	2	0	2	0	4	0	0	0	0	0	.00	0	.133	.235	.133
1994 San Francisco	NL	19	26	3	3	0	0	(0	0)	6	1	4	3	0	11	0	0	0	0	0	.00	1	.115	.207	.231
1995 San Francisco	NL	46	86	17	4	1	0	(0	0)	23	7	4	11	0	27	0	1	0	1	0	1.00	2	.198	.289	.267
3 ML YEARS		72	127	22	7	1	0	(0	0)	31	10	8	16	0	42	0	1	0	1	0	1.00	3	.173	.266	.244

John Farrell

Pitches: Right **Bats:** Right **Pos:** RP **Ht:** 6' 4" **Wt:** 210 **Born:** 8/4/62 **Age:** 33

		HOW MUCH HE PITCHED						WHAT HE GAVE UP										THE RESULTS					
Year Team	Lg	G	GS	CG	GF	IP	BFP	H	R	ER	HR	SH	SF	HB	TBB	IBB	SO	WP	Bk	W	L	Pct.	ShO	Sv	ERA
1995 Buffalo *	AAA	29	28	2	1	184.1	792	198	97	93	17	2	9	16	61	1	92	11	1	11	9	.550	0	0	4.54
1987 Cleveland	AL	10	9	1	1	69	297	68	29	26	7	3	1	5	22	1	28	1	1	5	1	.833	0	0	3.39
1988 Cleveland	AL	31	30	4	1	210.1	895	216	106	99	15	9	6	9	67	3	92	2	3	14	10	.583	0	0	4.24
1989 Cleveland	AL	31	31	7	0	208	895	196	97	84	14	8	6	7	71	4	132	4	0	9	14	.391	2	0	3.63
1990 Cleveland	AL	17	17	1	0	96.2	418	108	49	46	10	5	2	1	33	1	44	1	0	4	5	.444	0	0	4.28
1993 California	AL	21	17	0	1	90.2	420	110	74	74	22	2	2	7	44	3	45	3	0	3	12	.200	0	0	7.35
1994 California	AL	3	3	0	0	13	61	16	14	13	2	0	0	1	8	0	10	0	0	1	2	.333	0	0	9.00
1995 Cleveland	AL	1	0	0	0	4.2	21	7	4	2	0	1	1	0	0	0	4	0	0	0	0	.000	0	0	3.86
7 ML YEARS		114	107	13	2	692.1	3007	721	373	344	70	28	18	30	245	12	355	11	4	36	44	.450	2	0	4.47

Jeff Fassero

Pitches: Left **Bats:** Left **Pos:** SP **Ht:** 6' 1" **Wt:** 195 **Born:** 1/5/63 **Age:** 33

		HOW MUCH HE PITCHED						WHAT HE GAVE UP										THE RESULTS					
Year Team	Lg	G	GS	CG	GF	IP	BFP	H	R	ER	HR	SH	SF	HB	TBB	IBB	SO	WP	Bk	W	L	Pct.	ShO	Sv	ERA
1991 Montreal	NL	51	0	0	30	55.1	223	39	17	15	1	6	0	1	17	1	42	4	0	2	5	.286	0	8	2.44
1992 Montreal	NL	70	0	0	22	85.2	368	81	35	27	1	5	2	2	34	6	63	7	1	8	7	.533	0	1	2.84
1993 Montreal	NL	56	15	1	10	149.2	616	119	50	38	7	7	4	0	54	0	140	6	1	12	5	.706	0	1	2.29
1994 Montreal	NL	21	21	1	0	138.2	569	119	54	46	13	7	2	1	40	4	119	6	0	8	6	.571	0	0	2.99
1995 Montreal	NL	30	30	1	0	189	833	207	102	91	15	19	7	2	74	3	164	7	1	13	14	.481	0	0	4.33
5 ML YEARS		228	66	3	62	618.1	2609	565	258	217	37	44	15	6	219	14	528	29	2	43	37	.538	0	10	3.16

Felix Fermin

Bats: Right **Throws:** Right **Pos:** SS/2B   **Ht:** 5'11" **Wt:** 170 **Born:** 10/9/63 **Age:** 32

					BATTING														BASERUNNING				PERCENTAGES		
Year Team	Lg	G	AB	H	2B	3B	HR	(Hm	Rd)	TB	R	RBI	TBB	IBB	SO	HBP	SH	SF	SB	CS	SB%	GDP	Avg	OBP	SLG
1995 Tacoma *	AAA	1	3	1	0	0	0	--	--	1	0	0	0	0	0	0	0	0	0	0	.00	0	.333	.333	.333
1987 Pittsburgh	NL	23	68	17	0	0	0	(0	0)	17	6	4	4	1	9	1	2	0	0	0	.00	3	.250	.301	.250
1988 Pittsburgh	NL	43	87	24	0	2	0	(0	0)	28	9	2	8	1	10	3	1	1	3	1	.75	3	.276	.354	.322
1989 Cleveland	AL	156	484	115	9	1	0	(0	0)	126	50	21	41	0	27	4	32	1	6	4	.60	15	.238	.302	.260
1990 Cleveland	AL	148	414	106	13	2	1	(1	0)	126	47	40	26	0	22	0	13	5	3	3	.50	13	.256	.297	.304
1991 Cleveland	AL	129	424	111	13	2	0	(0	0)	128	30	31	26	0	27	3	13	3	5	4	.56	17	.262	.307	.302
1992 Cleveland	AL	79	215	58	7	2	0	(0	0)	69	27	13	18	1	10	1	9	2	0	0	.00	7	.270	.326	.321
1993 Cleveland	AL	140	480	126	16	2	2	(0	2)	152	48	45	24	1	14	4	5	1	4	5	.44	12	.263	.303	.317
1994 Seattle	AL	101	379	101	21	0	1	(0	1)	144	52	35	11	0	22	4	12	5	4	4	.50	9	.317	.338	.380
1995 Seattle	AL	73	200	39	6	0	0	(0	0)	45	21	15	6	0	6	4	8	1	2	0	1.00	7	.195	.232	.225
9 ML YEARS		892	2751	716	85	11	4	(1	3)	835	290	206	164	4	147	24	95	19	27	21	.56	86	.260	.306	.304

Ramon Fermin

Pitches: Right **Bats:** Right **Pos:** RP   **Ht:** 6'3" **Wt:** 180 **Born:** 11/25/72 **Age:** 23

Year Team	Lg	HOW MUCH HE PITCHED						WHAT HE GAVE UP										THE RESULTS				
		G	GS	CG	GF	IP	BFP	H	R	ER	HR	SH	SF	HB	TBB	IBB	SO	WP	Bk	W	L	Pct.	ShO	Sv	ERA
1991 Athletics	R	7	3	1	1	25.1	102	20	6	6	2	1	0	4	4	0	11	0	1	3	0	1.000	0	0	2.13
Modesto	A	3	2	0	0	12.1	52	16	7	6	1	1	0	1	3	0	5	0	0	1	0	1.000	0	0	4.38
1992 Madison	A	14	14	1	0	77.2	330	66	33	21	2	2	4	1	35	0	37	6	2	5	5	.500	0	0	2.43
Modesto	A	14	5	0	4	42.2	196	50	31	27	5	1	0	2	19	1	18	3	1	2	3	.400	0	1	5.70
1993 Modesto	A	31	5	0	8	67.1	321	78	56	46	7	3	2	5	37	5	47	10	0	4	6	.400	0	1	6.15
1994 Modesto	A	29	18	0	8	133	565	129	71	53	12	3	3	9	42	1	120	16	1	9	6	.600	0	5	3.59
1995 Huntsville	AA	32	13	0	16	100.1	435	105	53	43	5	6	1	6	45	5	58	6	1	6	7	.462	0	7	3.86
1995 Oakland	AL	1	0	0	1	1.1	9	4	2	2	0	0	0	1	1	0	0	1	0	0	0	.000	0	0	13.50

Alex Fernandez

Pitches: Right **Bats:** Right **Pos:** SP   **Ht:** 6'1" **Wt:** 215 **Born:** 8/13/69 **Age:** 26

Year Team	Lg	HOW MUCH HE PITCHED						WHAT HE GAVE UP										THE RESULTS				
		G	GS	CG	GF	IP	BFP	H	R	ER	HR	SH	SF	HB	TBB	IBB	SO	WP	Bk	W	L	Pct.	ShO	Sv	ERA
1990 Chicago	AL	13	13	3	0	87.2	378	89	40	37	6	5	0	3	34	0	61	1	0	5	5	.500	0	0	3.80
1991 Chicago	AL	34	32	2	1	191.2	827	186	100	96	16	7	11	2	88	2	145	4	1	9	13	.409	0	0	4.51
1992 Chicago	AL	29	29	4	0	187.2	804	199	100	89	21	6	4	8	50	3	95	3	0	8	11	.421	2	0	4.27
1993 Chicago	AL	34	34	3	0	247.1	1004	221	95	86	27	9	3	6	67	5	169	8	0	18	9	.667	1	0	3.13
1994 Chicago	AL	24	24	4	0	170.1	712	163	83	73	25	4	6	1	50	4	122	3	1	11	7	.611	3	0	3.86
1995 Chicago	AL	30	30	5	0	203.2	858	200	98	86	19	4	6	4	65	7	159	3	0	12	8	.600	2	0	3.80
6 ML YEARS		164	162	21	1	1088.1	4583	1058	516	467	114	35	30	20	354	21	751	22	2	63	53	.543	8	0	3.86

Sid Fernandez

Pitches: Left **Bats:** Left **Pos:** SP   **Ht:** 6'1" **Wt:** 225 **Born:** 10/12/62 **Age:** 33

Year Team	Lg	HOW MUCH HE PITCHED						WHAT HE GAVE UP										THE RESULTS				
		G	GS	CG	GF	IP	BFP	H	R	ER	HR	SH	SF	HB	TBB	IBB	SO	WP	Bk	W	L	Pct.	ShO	Sv	ERA
1995 Bowie *	AA	2	2	1	0	12	41	4	2	1	0	0	0	0	3	0	10	1	0	1	0	1.000	1	0	0.75
1983 Los Angeles	NL	2	1	0	0	6	33	7	4	4	0	0	0	1	7	0	9	0	0	0	1	.000	0	0	6.00
1984 New York	NL	15	15	0	0	90	371	74	40	35	8	5	5	0	34	3	62	1	4	6	6	.500	0	0	3.50
1985 New York	NL	26	26	3	0	170.1	685	108	56	53	14	4	3	2	80	3	180	3	2	9	9	.500	0	0	2.80
1986 New York	NL	32	31	2	1	204.1	855	161	82	80	13	9	7	2	91	1	200	6	0	16	6	.727	1	1	3.52
1987 New York	NL	28	27	3	0	156	665	130	75	66	16	3	6	8	67	8	134	2	0	12	8	.600	1	0	3.81
1988 New York	NL	31	31	1	0	187	751	127	69	63	15	2	7	6	70	1	189	4	9	12	10	.545	1	0	3.03
1989 New York	NL	35	32	6	0	219.1	883	157	73	69	21	4	4	6	75	3	198	1	3	14	5	.737	2	0	2.83
1990 New York	NL	30	30	2	0	179.1	735	130	79	69	18	7	6	5	67	4	181	1	0	9	14	.391	1	0	3.46
1991 New York	NL	8	8	0	0	44	177	36	18	14	4	5	1	0	9	0	31	0	0	1	3	.250	0	0	2.86
1992 New York	NL	32	32	5	0	214.2	865	162	67	65	12	12	11	4	67	4	193	0	0	14	11	.560	2	0	2.73
1993 New York	NL	18	18	1	0	119.2	469	82	42	39	17	3	1	3	36	0	81	2	0	5	6	.455	1	0	2.93
1994 Baltimore	AL	19	19	2	0	115.1	494	109	66	66	27	4	3	2	46	2	95	1	0	6	6	.500	0	0	5.15
1995 Bal-Phi		19	18	0	1	92.2	400	84	51	47	20	2	1	1	38	2	110	0	1	6	5	.545	0	0	4.56
1995 Baltimore	AL	8	7	0	1	28	137	36	26	23	9	1	1	0	17	2	31	0	0	0	4	.000	0	0	7.39
Philadelphia	NL	11	11	0	0	64.2	263	48	25	24	11	1	0	1	21	0	79	0	1	6	1	.857	0	0	3.34
13 ML YEARS		295	288	25	2	1798.2	7383	1367	722	670	185	60	55	40	687	31	1663	21	19	110	90	.550	9	1	3.35

Tony Fernandez

Bats: Both **Throws:** Right **Pos:** SS **Ht:** 6' 2" **Wt:** 175 **Born:** 6/30/62 **Age:** 34

Year Team	Lg	G	AB	H	2B	3B	HR	(Hm	Rd)	TB	R	RBI	TBB	IBB	SO	HBP	SH	SF	SB	CS	SB%	GDP	Avg	OBP	SLG
1983 Toronto	AL	15	34	9	1	1	0	(0	0)	12	5	2	2	0	2	1	1	0	0	1	.00	1	.265	.324	.353
1984 Toronto	AL	88	233	63	5	3	3	(1	2)	83	29	19	17	0	15	0	2	2	5	7	.42	3	.270	.317	.356
1985 Toronto	AL	161	564	163	31	10	2	(1	1)	220	71	51	43	2	41	2	7	2	13	6	.68	12	.289	.340	.390
1986 Toronto	AL	163	687	213	33	9	10	(4	6)	294	91	65	27	0	52	4	5	4	25	12	.68	8	.310	.338	.428
1987 Toronto	AL	146	578	186	29	8	5	(1	4)	246	90	67	51	3	48	5	4	4	32	12	.73	14	.322	.379	.426
1988 Toronto	AL	154	648	186	41	4	5	(3	2)	250	76	70	45	3	65	4	3	4	15	5	.75	9	.287	.335	.386
1989 Toronto	AL	140	573	147	25	9	11	(2	9)	223	64	64	29	1	51	3	2	10	22	6	.79	9	.257	.291	.389
1990 Toronto	AL	161	635	175	27	17	4	(2	2)	248	84	66	71	4	70	7	2	6	26	13	.67	17	.276	.352	.391
1991 San Diego	NL	145	558	152	27	5	4	(1	3)	201	81	38	55	0	74	0	7	1	23	9	.72	12	.272	.337	.360
1992 San Diego	NL	155	622	171	32	4	4	(3	1)	223	84	37	56	4	62	4	9	3	20	20	.50	6	.275	.337	.359
1993 Tor-NYN		142	526	147	23	11	5	(1	4)	207	65	64	56	3	45	1	8	3	21	10	.68	16	.279	.348	.394
1994 Cincinnati	NL	104	366	102	18	6	8	(3	5)	156	50	50	44	8	40	5	4	3	12	7	.63	5	.279	.361	.426
1995 New York	AL	108	384	94	20	2	5	(3	2)	133	57	45	42	4	40	4	3	2	6	6	.50	14	.245	.322	.346
1993 Toronto	AL	94	353	108	18	9	4	(1	3)	156	45	50	31	3	26	0	5	1	15	8	.65	13	.306	.361	.442
New York	NL	48	173	39	5	2	1	(0	1)	51	20	14	25	0	19	1	3	2	6	2	.75	3	.225	.323	.295
13 ML YEARS		1682	6408	1808	312	89	66	(25	41)	2496	847	638	538	32	605	40	57	47	220	114	.66	126	.282	.339	.390

Mike Fetters

Pitches: Right **Bats:** Right **Pos:** RP **Ht:** 6' 4" **Wt:** 224 **Born:** 12/19/64 **Age:** 31

Year Team	Lg	G	GS	CG	GF	IP	BFP	H	R	ER	HR	SH	SF	HB	TBB	IBB	SO	WP	Bk	W	L	Pct.	ShO	Sv	ERA
1989 California	AL	1	0	0	0	3.1	16	5	4	3	1	0	0	0	1	0	4	2	0	0	0	.000	0	0	8.10
1990 California	AL	26	2	0	10	67.2	291	77	33	31	9	1	0	2	20	0	35	3	0	1	1	.500	0	1	4.12
1991 California	AL	19	4	0	8	44.2	206	53	29	24	4	1	0	3	28	2	24	4	0	2	5	.286	0	0	4.84
1992 Milwaukee	AL	50	0	0	11	62.2	243	38	15	13	3	5	2	7	24	2	43	4	1	5	1	.833	0	2	1.87
1993 Milwaukee	AL	45	0	0	14	59.1	246	59	29	22	4	5	5	2	22	4	23	0	0	3	3	.500	0	0	3.34
1994 Milwaukee	AL	42	0	0	31	46	202	41	16	13	0	2	3	1	27	5	31	3	1	1	4	.200	0	17	2.54
1995 Milwaukee	AL	40	0	0	34	34.2	163	40	16	13	3	2	1	0	20	4	33	5	0	0	3	.000	0	22	3.38
7 ML YEARS		223	6	0	108	318.1	1367	313	142	119	24	16	11	15	142	17	193	21	2	12	17	.414	0	42	3.36

Cecil Fielder

Bats: Right **Throws:** Right **Pos:** 1B/DH **Ht:** 6' 3" **Wt:** 250 **Born:** 9/21/63 **Age:** 32

Year Team	Lg	G	AB	H	2B	3B	HR	(Hm	Rd)	TB	R	RBI	TBB	IBB	SO	HBP	SH	SF	SB	CS	SB%	GDP	Avg	OBP	SLG
1985 Toronto	AL	30	74	23	4	0	4	(2	2)	39	6	16	6	0	16	0	0	1	0	0	.00	0	.311	.358	.527
1986 Toronto	AL	34	83	13	2	0	4	(0	4)	27	7	13	6	0	27	1	0	0	0	0	.00	3	.157	.222	.325
1987 Toronto	AL	82	175	47	7	1	14	(10	4)	98	30	32	20	2	48	1	0	1	0	1	.00	6	.269	.345	.560
1988 Toronto	AL	74	174	40	6	1	9	(6	3)	77	24	23	14	0	53	1	0	1	0	1	.00	6	.230	.289	.431
1990 Detroit	AL	159	573	159	25	1	51	(25	26)	339	104	132	90	11	182	5	0	5	0	1	.00	15	.277	.377	.592
1991 Detroit	AL	162	624	163	25	0	44	(27	17)	320	102	133	78	12	151	6	0	4	0	0	.00	17	.261	.347	.513
1992 Detroit	AL	155	594	145	22	0	35	(18	17)	272	80	124	73	8	151	2	0	7	0	0	.00	14	.244	.325	.458
1993 Detroit	AL	154	573	153	23	0	30	(20	10)	266	80	117	90	15	125	4	0	5	0	1	.00	22	.267	.368	.464
1994 Detroit	AL	109	425	110	16	2	28	(12	16)	214	67	90	50	4	110	2	0	4	0	0	.00	17	.259	.337	.504
1995 Detroit	AL	136	494	120	18	1	31	(16	15)	233	70	82	75	8	116	5	0	4	0	1	.00	17	.243	.346	.472
10 ML YEARS		1095	3789	973	148	6	250	(136	114)	1883	570	762	502	60	979	27	0	32	0	5	.00	119	.257	.345	.497

Chuck Finley

Pitches: Left **Bats:** Left **Pos:** SP **Ht:** 6' 6" **Wt:** 214 **Born:** 11/26/62 **Age:** 33

Year Team	Lg	G	GS	CG	GF	IP	BFP	H	R	ER	HR	SH	SF	HB	TBB	IBB	SO	WP	Bk	W	L	Pct.	ShO	Sv	ERA
1986 California	AL	25	0	0	7	46.1	198	40	17	17	2	4	0	1	23	1	37	2	0	3	1	.750	0	0	3.30
1987 California	AL	35	3	0	17	90.2	405	102	54	47	7	2	2	3	43	3	63	4	3	2	7	.222	0	0	4.67
1988 California	AL	31	31	2	0	194.1	831	191	95	90	15	7	10	6	82	7	111	5	8	9	15	.375	0	0	4.17
1989 California	AL	29	29	9	0	199.2	827	171	64	57	13	7	3	2	82	0	156	4	2	16	9	.640	1	0	2.57
1990 California	AL	32	32	7	0	236	962	210	77	63	17	12	3	2	81	3	177	9	0	18	9	.667	2	0	2.40
1991 California	AL	34	34	4	0	227.1	955	205	102	96	23	4	3	8	101	1	171	6	3	18	9	.667	2	0	3.80
1992 California	AL	31	31	4	0	204.1	885	212	99	90	24	10	10	3	98	2	124	6	0	7	12	.368	1	0	3.96
1993 California	AL	35	35	13	0	251.1	1065	243	108	88	22	11	7	6	82	1	187	8	1	16	14	.533	2	0	3.15
1994 California	AL	25	25	7	0	183.1	774	178	95	88	21	9	6	3	71	0	148	10	0	10	10	.500	0	0	4.32
1995 California	AL	32	32	2	0	203	880	192	106	95	20	4	5	7	93	1	195	13	1	15	12	.556	1	0	4.21
10 ML YEARS		309	252	48	24	1836.1	7782	1744	817	731	164	70	49	41	756	19	1369	67	18	114	98	.538	11	0	3.58

Steve Finley

Bats: Left **Throws:** Left **Pos:** CF **Ht:** 6' 2" **Wt:** 180 **Born:** 3/12/65 **Age:** 31

Year	Team	Lg	G	AB	H	2B	3B	HR	(Hm	Rd)	TB	R	RBI	TBB	IBB	SO	HBP	SH	SF	SB	CS	SB%	GDP	Avg	OBP	SLG
1989	Baltimore	AL	81	217	54	5	2	2	(0	2)	69	35	25	15	1	30	1	6	2	17	3	.85	3	.249	.298	.318
1990	Baltimore	AL	142	464	119	16	4	3	(1	2)	152	46	37	32	3	53	2	10	5	22	9	.71	8	.256	.304	.328
1991	Houston	NL	159	596	170	28	10	8	(0	8)	242	84	54	42	5	65	2	10	6	34	18	.65	8	.285	.331	.406
1992	Houston	NL	162	607	177	29	13	5	(5	0)	247	84	55	58	6	63	3	16	2	44	9	.83	10	.292	.355	.407
1993	Houston	NL	142	545	145	15	13	8	(1	7)	210	69	44	28	1	65	3	6	3	19	6	.76	8	.266	.304	.385
1994	Houston	NL	94	373	103	16	5	11	(4	7)	162	64	33	28	0	52	2	13	1	13	7	.65	3	.276	.329	.434
1995	San Diego	NL	139	562	167	23	8	10	(4	6)	236	104	44	59	5	62	3	4	2	36	12	.75	8	.297	.366	.420
	7 ML YEARS		919	3364	935	132	55	47	(15	32)	1318	486	292	262	21	390	16	65	21	185	64	.74	48	.278	.331	.392

John Flaherty

Bats: Right **Throws:** Right **Pos:** C **Ht:** 6' 1" **Wt:** 200 **Born:** 10/21/67 **Age:** 28

Year	Team	Lg	G	AB	H	2B	3B	HR	(Hm	Rd)	TB	R	RBI	TBB	IBB	SO	HBP	SH	SF	SB	CS	SB%	GDP	Avg	OBP	SLG
1992	Boston	AL	35	66	13	2	0	0	(0	0)	15	3	2	3	0	7	0	1	1	0	0	.00	0	.197	.229	.227
1993	Boston	AL	13	25	3	2	0	0	(0	0)	5	3	2	2	0	6	1	1	0	0	0	.00	0	.120	.214	.200
1994	Detroit	AL	34	40	6	1	0	0	(0	0)	7	2	4	1	0	11	0	2	1	0	0	.00	1	.150	.167	.175
1995	Detroit	AL	112	354	86	22	1	11	(6	5)	143	39	40	18	0	47	3	8	2	0	0	.00	8	.243	.284	.404
	4 ML YEARS		194	485	108	27	1	11	(6	5)	170	47	48	24	0	71	4	12	4	0	1	.00	9	.223	.263	.351

Dave Fleming

Pitches: Left **Bats:** Left **Pos:** RP/SP **Ht:** 6' 3" **Wt:** 200 **Born:** 11/7/69 **Age:** 26

Year	Team	Lg	G	GS	CG	GF	IP	BFP	H	R	ER	HR	SH	SF	HB	TBB	IBB	SO	WP	Bk	W	L	Pct.	ShO	Sv	ERA
1995	Royals *	R	1	1	0	0	3	11	2	1	0	0	0	0	0	0	0	1	0	0	0	0	.000	0	0	0.00
	Omaha *	AAA	3	3	0	0	16	72	17	6	6	1	1	0	2	7	0	8	0	0	1	0	1.000	0	0	3.38
1991	Seattle	AL	9	3	0	3	17.2	73	19	13	13	3	0	0	3	3	0	11	1	0	1	0	1.000	0	0	6.62
1992	Seattle	AL	33	33	7	0	228.1	946	225	95	86	13	3	2	4	60	3	112	8	1	17	10	.630	4	0	3.39
1993	Seattle	AL	26	26	1	0	167.1	737	189	84	81	15	4	8	6	67	6	75	2	0	12	5	.706	1	0	4.36
1994	Seattle	AL	23	23	0	0	117	561	152	93	84	17	4	3	1	65	4	65	4	0	7	11	.389	0	0	6.46
1995	Sea-KC	AL	25	12	1	3	80	374	84	61	53	19	3	4	2	53	4	40	5	0	1	6	.143	0	0	5.96
1995	Seattle	AL	16	7	1	2	48	233	57	44	40	15	2	3	0	34	3	26	4	0	1	5	.167	0	0	7.50
	Kansas City	AL	9	5	0	1	32	141	27	17	13	4	1	1	2	19	1	14	1	0	0	1	.000	0	0	3.66
	5 ML YEARS		116	97	9	6	610.1	2691	669	346	317	67	14	17	16	248	17	303	20	1	38	32	.543	5	0	4.67

Darrin Fletcher

Bats: Left **Throws:** Right **Pos:** C **Ht:** 6' 1" **Wt:** 205 **Born:** 10/3/66 **Age:** 29

Year	Team	Lg	G	AB	H	2B	3B	HR	(Hm	Rd)	TB	R	RBI	TBB	IBB	SO	HBP	SH	SF	SB	CS	SB%	GDP	Avg	OBP	SLG
1989	Los Angeles	NL	5	8	4	0	0	1	(1	0)	7	1	2	1	0	0	0	0	0	0	0	.00	0	.500	.556	.875
1990	LA-Phi	NL	11	23	3	1	0	0	(0	0)	4	3	1	1	0	6	0	0	0	0	0	.00	0	.130	.167	.174
1991	Philadelphia	NL	46	136	31	8	0	1	(1	0)	42	5	12	5	0	15	0	1	0	0	1	.00	2	.228	.255	.309
1992	Montreal	NL	83	222	54	10	2	2	(0	2)	74	13	26	14	3	28	2	2	4	0	2	.00	8	.243	.289	.333
1993	Montreal	NL	133	396	101	20	1	9	(5	4)	150	33	60	34	2	40	6	5	4	0	0	.00	7	.255	.320	.379
1994	Montreal	NL	94	285	74	18	1	10	(4	6)	124	28	57	25	4	23	3	0	12	0	0	.00	6	.260	.314	.435
1995	Montreal	NL	110	350	100	21	1	11	(3	8)	156	42	45	32	1	23	4	1	2	0	1	.00	15	.286	.351	.446
1990	Los Angeles	NL	2	1	0	0	0	0	(0	0)	0	0	0	0	0	1	0	0	0	0	0	.00	0	.000	.000	.000
	Philadelphia	NL	9	22	3	1	0	0	(0	0)	4	3	1	1	0	5	0	0	0	0	0	.00	0	.136	.174	.182
	7 ML YEARS		482	1420	367	78	5	34	(14	20)	557	125	203	112	10	135	15	9	22	0	4	.00	38	.258	.315	.392

Paul Fletcher

Pitches: Right **Bats:** Right **Pos:** RP **Ht:** 6' 1" **Wt:** 193 **Born:** 1/14/67 **Age:** 29

Year	Team	Lg	G	GS	CG	GF	IP	BFP	H	R	ER	HR	SH	SF	HB	TBB	IBB	SO	WP	Bk	W	L	Pct.	ShO	Sv	ERA
1988	Martinsvlle	R	15	14	1	1	69.1	320	81	44	36	4	1	3	4	33	0	61	3	1	1	3	.250	0	1	4.67
1989	Batavia	A	14	14	3	0	82.1	339	77	41	30	13	2	2	3	28	0	58	3	1	7	5	.583	0	0	3.28
1990	Spartanburg	A	9	9	1	0	49.1	207	46	24	18	3	1	1	2	18	0	53	7	1	2	4	.333	0	0	3.28
	Clearwater	A	20	18	2	1	117.1	498	104	56	44	3	6	6	13	49	0	106	7	2	5	8	.385	0	1	3.38
1991	Clearwater	A	14	4	0	5	29.1	119	22	6	4	1	1	2	0	8	1	27	2	0	0	1	.000	0	1	1.23
	Reading	AA	21	19	3	1	120.2	517	111	56	47	12	3	2	1	56	3	90	6	1	7	9	.438	1	0	3.51
1992	Reading	AA	22	20	2	0	127	521	103	45	40	10	1	1	5	47	2	103	7	0	9	4	.692	1	0	2.83
	Scranton-Wb	AAA	4	4	0	0	22.2	85	17	8	7	1	0	0	0	2	0	26	2	0	3	0	1.000	0	0	2.78
1993	Scranton-Wb	AAA	34	19	2	5	140	625	146	99	88	21	4	4	9	60	3	116	21	0	4	12	.250	1	0	5.66
1994	Scranton-Wb	AAA	42	13	3	8	138.1	604	144	78	72	12	4	1	6	54	0	92	6	0	4	9	.308	1	3	4.68

Year Team	Lg	G	GS	CG	GF	IP	BFP	H	R	ER	HR	SH	SF	HB	TBB	IBB	SO	WP	Bk	W	L	Pct.	ShO	Sv	ERA
1995 Scranton-Wb	AAA	52	0	0	7	61	257	45	33	21	7	7	3	1	28	4	48	8	0	4	1	.800	0	2	3.10
1993 Philadelphia	NL	1	0	0	0	0.1	1	0	0	0	0	0	0	0	0	0	0	1	0	0	0	.000	0	0	0.00
1995 Philadelphia	NL	10	0	0	1	13.1	64	15	8	8	2	1	1	1	9	2	10	2	0	1	0	1.000	0	0	5.40
2 ML YEARS		11	0	0	1	13.2	65	15	8	8	2	1	1	1	9	2	10	3	0	1	0	1.000	0	0	5.27

Scott Fletcher

Bats: Right **Throws:** Right **Pos:** 2B   **Ht:** 5'11" **Wt:** 172 **Born:** 7/30/58 **Age:** 37

												BASERUNNING				PERCENTAGES		
Year Team	Lg	G	AB	H	2B	3B	HR	(Hm | Rd)	TB	R	RBI	TBB	IBB	SO	HBP	SH	SF	SB	CS	SB%	GDP	Avg	OBP	SLG
1981 Chicago	NL	19	46	10	4	0	0	(0 | 0)	14	6	1	2	0	4	0	0	0	0	0	.00	0	.217	.250	.304
1982 Chicago	NL	11	24	4	0	0	0	(0 | 0)	4	4	1	4	0	5	0	0	0	1	0	1.00	0	.167	.286	.167
1983 Chicago	AL	114	262	62	16	5	3	(1 | 2)	97	42	31	29	0	22	2	7	2	5	1	.83	8	.237	.315	.370
1984 Chicago	AL	149	456	114	13	3	3	(2 | 1)	142	46	35	46	2	46	8	9	2	10	4	.71	5	.250	.328	.311
1985 Chicago	AL	119	301	77	8	1	2	(0 | 2)	93	38	31	35	0	47	0	11	1	5	5	.50	9	.256	.332	.309
1986 Texas	AL	147	530	159	34	5	3	(2 | 1)	212	82	50	47	0	59	4	10	3	12	11	.52	10	.300	.360	.400
1987 Texas	AL	156	588	169	28	4	5	(4 | 1)	220	82	63	61	3	66	5	12	2	13	12	.52	14	.287	.358	.374
1988 Texas	AL	140	515	142	19	4	0	(0 | 0)	169	59	47	62	1	34	12	15	5	8	5	.62	13	.276	.364	.328
1989 ChA-Tex	AL	142	546	138	25	2	1	(0 | 1)	170	77	43	64	1	60	3	11	5	2	1	.67	12	.253	.332	.311
1990 Texas	AL	151	509	123	18	3	4	(1 | 3)	159	54	56	45	3	63	3	11	5	1	3	.25	10	.242	.304	.312
1991 Chicago	AL	90	248	51	10	1	1	(0 | 1)	66	14	28	17	0	26	3	6	3	0	2	.00	3	.206	.262	.266
1992 Milwaukee	AL	123	386	106	18	3	3	(2 | 1)	139	53	51	30	1	33	7	6	4	17	10	.63	4	.275	.335	.360
1993 Boston	AL	121	480	137	31	5	5	(2 | 3)	193	81	45	37	1	35	5	6	3	16	3	.84	12	.285	.341	.402
1994 Boston	AL	63	185	42	9	1	3	(2 | 1)	62	31	11	16	1	14	2	3	0	8	1	.89	7	.227	.296	.335
1995 Detroit	AL	67	182	42	10	1	1	(1 | 0)	57	19	17	19	0	27	3	4	1	0	1	1.00	2	.231	.312	.313
1989 Chicago	AL	59	232	63	11	1	1	(0 | 1)	79	30	21	26	0	19	1	9	3	1	1	.50	4	.272	.344	.341
Texas	AL	83	314	75	14	1	0	(0 | 0)	91	47	22	38	1	41	2	2	2	1	0	1.00	8	.239	.323	.290
15 ML YEARS		1612	5258	1376	243	38	34	(17 | 17)	1797	688	510	514	13	541	57	111	36	99	58	.63	109	.262	.332	.342

Kevin Flora

Bats: Right **Throws:** Right **Pos:** CF   **Ht:** 6'0" **Wt:** 185 **Born:** 6/10/69 **Age:** 27

												BASERUNNING				PERCENTAGES		
Year Team	Lg	G	AB	H	2B	3B	HR	(Hm	Rd)	TB	R	RBI	TBB	IBB	SO	HBP	SH	SF	SB	CS	SB%	GDP	Avg	OBP	SLG
1987 Salem	A	35	88	24	5	1	0	--	--	31	17	12	21	0	14	0	3	0	8	4	.67	2	.273	.413	.352
1988 Quad City	A	48	152	33	3	4	0	--	--	44	19	15	18	4	33	0	1	0	5	3	.63	4	.217	.300	.289
1989 Quad City	A	120	372	81	8	4	1	--	--	100	46	21	57	2	107	6	5	3	30	10	.75	3	.218	.329	.269
1990 Midland	AA	71	232	53	16	5	5	--	--	94	35	32	23	0	53	0	3	1	11	5	.69	6	.228	.297	.405
1991 Midland	AA	124	484	138	14	15	12	--	--	218	97	67	37	0	92	3	3	3	40	8	.83	2	.285	.338	.450
1992 Edmonton	AAA	52	170	55	8	4	3	--	--	80	35	19	29	0	25	1	4	2	9	8	.53	6	.324	.421	.471
1993 Vancouver	AAA	30	94	31	2	0	1	--	--	36	17	12	10	0	20	1	2	1	6	2	.75	2	.330	.396	.383
1994 Vancouver	AAA	6	12	2	1	0	0	--	--	3	5	1	4	0	4	0	1	0	1	0	1.00	1	.167	.375	.250
Lk Elsinore	A	19	72	13	3	2	0	--	--	20	13	6	12	0	17	0	1	1	7	1	.88	2	.181	.294	.278
1995 Vancouver	AAA	38	124	37	7	0	3	--	--	53	22	14	16	0	33	0	1	0	7	4	.64	2	.298	.376	.427
1991 California	AL	3	8	1	0	0	0	(0	0)	1	1	0	1	0	5	0	1	0	1	0	1.00	1	.125	.222	.125
1995 Cal-Phi		26	76	16	3	0	2	(2	0)	25	13	7	4	0	23	0	2	0	1	0	1.00	5	.211	.250	.329
1995 California	AL	2	1	0	0	0	0	(0	0)	0	1	0	0	0	1	0	0	0	0	0	.00	0	.000	.000	.000
Philadelphia	NL	24	75	16	3	0	2	(2	0)	25	12	7	4	0	22	0	2	0	1	0	1.00	5	.213	.253	.333
2 ML YEARS		29	84	17	3	0	2	(2	0)	26	14	7	5	0	28	0	3	0	2	0	1.00	6	.202	.247	.310

Don Florence

Pitches: Left **Bats:** Right **Pos:** RP   **Ht:** 6'0" **Wt:** 195 **Born:** 3/16/67 **Age:** 29

		HOW MUCH HE PITCHED						WHAT HE GAVE UP												THE RESULTS					
Year Team	Lg	G	GS	CG	GF	IP	BFP	H	R	ER	HR	SH	SF	HB	TBB	IBB	SO	WP	Bk	W	L	Pct.	ShO	Sv	ERA
1988 Winter Havn	A	27	16	4	7	120.2	542	136	68	53	4	3	4	4	50	1	56	13	2	6	8	.429	0	0	3.95
1989 Winter Havn	A	51	2	0	31	93.2	395	81	46	30	1	7	2	2	34	3	71	7	1	2	7	.222	0	15	2.88
1990 New Britain	AA	34	4	0	12	79.2	341	85	37	31	3	2	3	1	26	3	39	4	0	6	4	.600	0	1	3.50
1991 New Britain	AA	55	2	0	28	84.1	382	85	59	52	7	6	5	7	43	4	73	4	1	3	8	.273	0	2	5.55
1992 New Britain	AA	58	0	0	30	74.2	311	65	23	20	0	8	0	3	27	3	51	4	0	3	1	.750	0	6	2.41
1993 Pawtucket	AAA	57	0	0	18	59	246	56	24	22	6	6	1	0	18	5	46	8	0	7	8	.467	0	2	3.36
1994 Pawtucket	AAA	61	0	0	24	59	259	66	24	24	2	3	1	1	24	4	43	1	0	1	4	.200	0	7	3.66
1995 Norfolk	AAA	41	0	0	16	47	191	37	6	5	0	5	1	1	17	3	29	2	0	0	1	.000	0	4	0.96
1995 New York	NL	14	0	0	3	12	57	17	3	2	0	1	0	0	6	0	5	0	0	3	0	1.000	0	0	1.50

Bryce Florie

Pitches: Right **Bats:** Right **Pos:** RP   **Ht:** 5'11" **Wt:** 190 **Born:** 5/21/70 **Age:** 26

		HOW MUCH HE PITCHED						WHAT HE GAVE UP												THE RESULTS					
Year Team	Lg	G	GS	CG	GF	IP	BFP	H	R	ER	HR	SH	SF	HB	TBB	IBB	SO	WP	Bk	W	L	Pct.	ShO	Sv	ERA
1988 Padres	R	11	6	0	2	38.1	190	52	44	34	1	2	1	2	22	0	29	5	0	4	5	.444	0	0	7.98
1989 Charlstn-Sc	A	12	12	0	0	44	234	54	47	34	2	4	2	1	42	0	22	10	2	1	7	.125	0	0	6.95

Team	Lg	G	GS	CG	SV	IP	BFP	H	R	ER	HR	SH	SF	HB	TBB	IBB	SO	WP	Bk		W	L	Pct.	ShO	Sv	ERA
Spokane	A	14	14	0	0	61	301	79	66	48	2	0	0	4	40	1	50	11	1		4	5	.444	0	0	7.08
1990 Waterloo	A	14	14	1	0	65.2	292	60	37	32	3	2	4	8	37	0	38	6	3		4	5	.444	0	0	4.39
1991 Waterloo	A	23	23	2	0	133	581	119	66	58	3	1	4	9	79	0	90	9	1		7	6	.538	0	0	3.92
1992 High Desert	A	26	24	0	0	137.2	612	99	79	63	8	1	6	12	114	2	106	10	2		9	7	.563	0	0	4.12
Charlstn-Sc	A	1	1	0	0	5	21	5	3	1	1	0	0	1	0	0	5	0	0		0	1	.000	0	0	1.80
1993 Wichita	AA	27	27	0	0	154.2	672	128	80	68	8	4	3	10	100	2	133	24	2		11	8	.579	0	0	3.96
1994 Las Vegas	AAA	50	0	0	15	71.2	336	76	47	41	3	3	3	8	47	2	67	9	2		2	5	.286	0	1	5.15
1994 San Diego	NL	9	0	0	4	9.1	37	8	1	1	0	0	1	0	3	0	8	1	0		0	0	.000	0	0	0.96
1995 San Diego	NL	47	0	0	10	68.2	290	49	30	23	8	5	1	4	38	3	68	7	2		2	2	.500	0	1	3.01
2 ML YEARS		56	0	0	14	78	327	57	31	24	8	5	2	4	41	3	76	8	2		2	2	.500	0	1	2.77

Cliff Floyd

Bats: Left **Throws:** Right **Pos:** 1B **Ht:** 6' 4" **Wt:** 230 **Born:** 12/5/72 **Age:** 23

				BATTING														BASERUNNING				PERCENTAGES		
Year Team	Lg	G	AB	H	2B	3B	HR	(Hm Rd)	TB	R	RBI	TBB	IBB	SO	HBP	SH	SF	SB	CS	SB%	GDP	Avg	OBP	SLG
1993 Montreal	NL	10	31	7	0	0	1	(0 1)	10	3	2	0	0	9	0	0	0	0	0	.00	0	.226	.226	.323
1994 Montreal	NL	100	334	94	19	4	4	(2 2)	133	43	41	24	0	63	3	2	3	10	3	.77	3	.281	.332	.398
1995 Montreal	NL	29	69	9	1	0	1	(1 0)	13	6	8	7	0	22	1	0	0	3	0	1.00	1	.130	.221	.188
3 ML YEARS		139	434	110	20	4	6	(3 3)	156	52	51	31	0	94	4	2	3	13	3	.81	4	.253	.307	.359

Tom Foley

Bats: Left **Throws:** Right **Pos:** 1B **Ht:** 6' 1" **Wt:** 185 **Born:** 9/9/59 **Age:** 36

				BATTING														BASERUNNING				PERCENTAGES		
Year Team	Lg	G	AB	H	2B	3B	HR	(Hm Rd)	TB	R	RBI	TBB	IBB	SO	HBP	SH	SF	SB	CS	SB%	GDP	Avg	OBP	SLG
1995 Ottawa *	AAA	23	62	19	5	0	0	-- --	24	13	7	8	0	7	0	2	0	1	0	1.00	4	.306	.386	.387
1983 Cincinnati	NL	68	98	20	4	1	0	(0 0)	26	7	9	13	2	17	0	2	0	1	0	1.00	1	.204	.297	.265
1984 Cincinnati	NL	106	277	70	8	3	5	(2 3)	99	26	27	24	7	36	0	1	2	3	2	.60	2	.253	.310	.357
1985 Cin-Phi	NL	89	250	60	13	1	3	(2 1)	84	24	23	19	8	34	0	0	0	2	3	.40	2	.240	.294	.336
1986 Mon-Phi	NL	103	263	70	15	3	1	(1 0)	94	26	23	30	6	37	0	2	4	10	3	.77	2	.266	.337	.357
1987 Montreal	NL	106	280	82	18	3	5	(3 2)	121	35	28	11	0	40	1	1	0	6	10	.38	6	.293	.322	.432
1988 Montreal	NL	127	377	100	21	3	5	(3 2)	142	33	43	30	10	49	1	0	3	2	7	.22	11	.265	.319	.377
1989 Montreal	NL	122	375	86	19	2	7	(4 3)	130	34	39	45	4	53	3	4	4	2	3	.40	2	.229	.314	.347
1990 Montreal	NL	73	164	35	2	1	0	(0 0)	39	11	12	12	2	22	0	1	1	0	1	.00	4	.213	.266	.238
1991 Montreal	NL	86	168	35	11	1	0	(0 0)	48	12	15	14	4	30	1	1	3	2	0	1.00	4	.208	.269	.286
1992 Montreal	NL	72	115	20	3	1	0	(0 0)	25	7	5	8	2	21	1	3	2	3	0	1.00	6	.174	.230	.217
1993 Pittsburgh	NL	86	194	49	11	1	3	(1 2)	71	18	22	11	1	26	0	2	4	0	0	.00	4	.253	.287	.366
1994 Pittsburgh	NL	59	123	29	7	0	3	(2 1)	45	13	15	13	2	18	0	0	1	0	0	.00	1	.236	.307	.366
1995 Montreal	NL	11	24	5	2	0	0	(0 0)	7	2	2	2	0	4	0	0	1	0	1	1.00	2	.208	.269	.292
1985 Cincinnati	NL	43	92	18	5	1	0	(0 0)	25	7	6	6	1	16	0	0	0	1	0	1.00	1	.196	.245	.272
Philadelphia	NL	46	158	42	8	0	3	(2 1)	59	17	17	13	7	18	0	0	0	1	3	.25	2	.266	.322	.373
1986 Montreal	NL	64	202	52	13	2	1	(1 0)	72	18	18	20	5	26	0	2	3	8	3	.73	2	.257	.320	.356
Philadelphia	NL	39	61	18	2	1	0	(0 0)	22	8	5	10	1	11	0	0	1	2	0	1.00	1	.295	.389	.361
13 ML YEARS		1108	2708	661	134	20	32	(18 14)	931	248	263	232	48	387	7	17	24	32	29	.52	49	.244	.303	.344

Chad Fonville

Bats: Both **Throws:** Right **Pos:** 2B/SS **Ht:** 5' 6" **Wt:** 155 **Born:** 3/5/71 **Age:** 25

				BATTING														BASERUNNING				PERCENTAGES		
Year Team	Lg	G	AB	H	2B	3B	HR	(Hm Rd)	TB	R	RBI	TBB	IBB	SO	HBP	SH	SF	SB	CS	SB%	GDP	Avg	OBP	SLG
1992 Everett	A	63	260	71	9	1	1	-- --	85	56	33	31	1	39	3	1	0	36	14	.72	2	.273	.357	.327
1993 Clinton	A	120	447	137	16	10	1	-- --	176	80	44	40	2	48	9	5	2	52	16	.76	0	.306	.373	.394
1994 San Jose	A	68	283	87	9	6	0	-- --	108	58	26	34	0	34	4	5	0	22	8	.73	5	.307	.389	.382
1995 Mon-LA	NL	102	320	89	6	1	0	(0 0)	97	43	16	23	1	42	1	6	0	20	7	.74	3	.278	.328	.303
1995 Montreal	NL	14	12	4	0	0	0	(0 0)	4	2	0	0	0	3	0	0	0	0	2	.00	0	.333	.333	.333
Los Angeles	NL	88	308	85	6	1	0	(0 0)	93	41	16	23	1	39	1	6	0	20	5	.80	3	.276	.328	.302

Brook Fordyce

Bats: Right **Throws:** Right **Pos:** PH **Ht:** 6' 1" **Wt:** 185 **Born:** 5/7/70 **Age:** 26

				BATTING														BASERUNNING				PERCENTAGES		
Year Team	Lg	G	AB	H	2B	3B	HR	(Hm Rd)	TB	R	RBI	TBB	IBB	SO	HBP	SH	SF	SB	CS	SB%	GDP	Avg	OBP	SLG
1989 Kingsport	R	69	226	74	15	0	9	-- --	116	45	38	30	1	26	1	3	2	10	6	.63	3	.327	.405	.513
1990 Columbia	A	104	372	117	29	1	10	-- --	178	45	54	39	0	42	0	1	2	4	1	.80	18	.315	.378	.478
1991 St. Lucie	A	115	406	97	19	3	7	-- --	143	42	55	37	2	51	4	0	6	4	5	.44	7	.239	.305	.352
1992 Binghamton	AA	118	425	118	30	0	11	-- --	181	59	61	37	1	78	4	3	6	1	2	.33	13	.278	.337	.426
1993 Norfolk	AAA	116	409	106	21	2	2	-- --	137	33	40	26	3	62	5	3	6	2	2	.50	10	.259	.307	.335
1994 Norfolk	AAA	66	229	60	13	3	3	-- --	88	26	32	19	1	26	1	2	1	1	0	1.00	9	.262	.320	.384
1995 Buffalo	AAA	58	176	44	13	0	0	-- --	57	18	9	14	0	20	2	3	0	1	0	1.00	2	.250	.313	.324
1995 New York	NL	4	2	1	1	0	0	(0 0)	2	1	0	1	0	0	0	0	0	0	0	.00	0	.500	.667	1.000

Tim Fortugno

Pitches: Left **Bats:** Left **Pos:** RP **Ht:** 6' 0" **Wt:** 185 **Born:** 4/11/62 **Age:** 34

Year Team	Lg	G	GS	CG	GF	IP	BFP	H	R	ER	HR	SH	SF	HB	TBB	IBB	SO	WP	Bk	W	L	Pct.	ShO	Sv	ERA
1995 Vancouver *	AAA	10	0	0	7	11.2	45	8	2	2	1	0	0	0	4	1	7	0	0	1	1	.500	0	1	1.54
1992 California	AL	14	5	1	5	41.2	177	37	24	24	5	0	1	0	19	0	31	2	1	1	1	.500	1	1	5.18
1994 Cincinnati	NL	25	0	0	9	30	132	32	14	14	2	3	1	3	14	0	29	4	2	1	0	1.000	0	0	4.20
1995 Chicago	AL	37	0	0	11	38.2	163	30	24	24	7	1	2	0	19	2	24	5	3	1	3	.250	0	0	5.59
3 ML YEARS		76	5	1	25	110.1	472	99	62	62	14	4	4	3	52	2	84	11	6	3	4	.429	1	1	5.06

Tony Fossas

Pitches: Left **Bats:** Left **Pos:** RP **Ht:** 6' 0" **Wt:** 187 **Born:** 9/23/57 **Age:** 38

Year Team	Lg	G	GS	CG	GF	IP	BFP	H	R	ER	HR	SH	SF	HB	TBB	IBB	SO	WP	Bk	W	L	Pct.	ShO	Sv	ERA
1988 Texas	AL	5	0	0	1	5.2	28	11	3	3	0	0	0	0	2	0	1	1	0	0	0	.000	0	0	4.76
1989 Milwaukee	AL	51	0	0	16	61	256	57	27	24	3	7	3	1	22	7	42	1	3	2	2	.500	0	1	3.54
1990 Milwaukee	AL	32	0	0	9	29.1	146	44	23	21	5	2	1	0	10	2	24	0	0	2	3	.400	0	0	6.44
1991 Boston	AL	64	0	0	18	57	244	49	27	22	3	5	0	3	28	9	29	2	0	3	2	.600	0	1	3.47
1992 Boston	AL	60	0	0	17	29.2	129	31	9	8	1	3	0	1	14	3	19	0	0	1	2	.333	0	2	2.43
1993 Boston	AL	71	0	0	19	40	175	38	28	23	4	0	1	2	15	4	39	1	1	1	1	.500	0	0	5.18
1994 Boston	AL	44	0	0	14	34	151	35	18	18	6	2	0	1	15	1	31	2	1	2	0	1.000	0	1	4.76
1995 St. Louis	NL	58	0	0	20	36.2	145	28	6	6	1	2	1	1	10	3	40	1	0	3	0	1.000	0	0	1.47
8 ML YEARS		385	0	0	114	293.1	1274	293	141	125	23	21	6	9	116	29	224	7	4	14	10	.583	0	5	3.84

Kevin Foster

Pitches: Right **Bats:** Right **Pos:** SP **Ht:** 6' 1" **Wt:** 170 **Born:** 1/13/69 **Age:** 27

Year Team	Lg	G	GS	CG	GF	IP	BFP	H	R	ER	HR	SH	SF	HB	TBB	IBB	SO	WP	Bk	W	L	Pct.	ShO	Sv	ERA
1993 Philadelphia	NL	2	1	0	0	6.2	40	13	11	11	3	0	0	0	7	0	6	2	0	0	1	.000	0	0	14.85
1994 Chicago	NL	13	13	0	0	81	337	70	31	26	7	1	1	1	35	1	75	1	1	3	4	.429	0	0	2.89
1995 Chicago	NL	30	28	0	1	167.2	703	149	90	84	32	4	6	6	65	4	146	2	2	12	11	.522	0	0	4.51
3 ML YEARS		45	42	0	1	255.1	1080	232	132	121	42	5	7	7	107	5	227	5	3	15	16	.484	0	0	4.27

Steve Foster

Pitches: Right **Bats:** Right **Pos:** RP **Ht:** 6' 0" **Wt:** 180 **Born:** 8/16/66 **Age:** 29

Year Team	Lg	G	GS	CG	GF	IP	BFP	H	R	ER	HR	SH	SF	HB	TBB	IBB	SO	WP	Bk	W	L	Pct.	ShO	Sv	ERA
1991 Cincinnati	NL	11	0	0	5	14	53	7	5	3	1	0	0	0	4	0	11	0	0	0	0	.000	0	0	1.93
1992 Cincinnati	NL	31	1	0	7	50	209	52	16	16	4	5	2	0	13	1	34	1	0	1	1	.500	0	2	2.88
1993 Cincinnati	NL	17	0	0	7	25.2	105	23	8	5	1	1	0	1	5	2	16	0	0	2	2	.500	0	0	1.75
3 ML YEARS		59	1	0	19	89.2	367	82	29	24	6	6	2	1	22	3	61	1	0	3	3	.500	0	2	2.41

Eric Fox

Bats: Both **Throws:** Left **Pos:** LF **Ht:** 5'10" **Wt:** 180 **Born:** 8/15/63 **Age:** 32

Year Team	Lg	G	AB	H	2B	3B	HR	(Hm	Rd)	TB	R	RBI	TBB	IBB	SO	HBP	SH	SF	SB	CS	SB%	GDP	Avg	OBP	SLG
1995 Okla. City *	AAA	92	349	97	22	5	6	--	--	147	52	50	30	7	68	2	4	3	5	5	.50	7	.278	.336	.421
1992 Oakland	AL	51	143	34	5	2	3	(0	3)	52	24	13	13	0	29	0	6	1	3	4	.43	1	.238	.299	.364
1993 Oakland	AL	29	56	8	1	0	1	(1	0)	12	5	5	2	0	7	0	3	0	0	2	.00	0	.143	.172	.214
1994 Oakland	AL	26	44	9	2	0	1	(0	1)	14	7	1	3	0	8	0	0	0	2	0	1.00	0	.205	.255	.318
1995 Texas	AL	10	15	0	0	0	0	(0	0)	0	2	0	3	0	4	0	1	0	0	0	.00	0	.000	.167	.000
4 ML YEARS		116	258	51	8	2	5	(1	4)	78	38	19	21	0	48	0	10	1	5	6	.45	1	.198	.257	.302

John Franco

Pitches: Left **Bats:** Left **Pos:** RP **Ht:** 5'10" **Wt:** 185 **Born:** 9/17/60 **Age:** 35

Year Team	Lg	G	GS	CG	GF	IP	BFP	H	R	ER	HR	SH	SF	HB	TBB	IBB	SO	WP	Bk	W	L	Pct.	ShO	Sv	ERA
1984 Cincinnati	NL	54	0	0	30	79.1	335	74	28	23	3	4	4	2	36	4	55	2	0	6	2	.750	0	4	2.61
1985 Cincinnati	NL	67	0	0	33	99	407	83	27	24	5	11	1	1	40	8	61	4	0	12	3	.800	0	12	2.18
1986 Cincinnati	NL	74	0	0	52	101	429	90	40	33	7	8	3	2	44	12	84	4	2	6	6	.500	0	29	2.94
1987 Cincinnati	NL	68	0	0	60	82	344	76	26	23	6	5	2	0	27	6	61	1	0	8	5	.615	0	32	2.52
1988 Cincinnati	NL	70	0	0	61	86	336	60	18	15	3	5	1	0	27	3	46	1	2	6	6	.500	0	39	1.57
1989 Cincinnati	NL	60	0	0	50	80.2	345	77	35	28	3	7	3	0	36	8	60	3	2	4	8	.333	0	32	3.12
1990 New York	NL	55	0	0	48	67.2	287	66	22	19	4	3	1	0	21	2	56	7	2	5	3	.625	0	33	2.53
1991 New York	NL	52	0	0	48	55.1	247	61	27	18	2	3	0	1	18	4	45	6	0	5	9	.357	0	30	2.93
1992 New York	NL	31	0	0	30	33	128	24	6	6	1	0	2	0	11	2	20	0	0	6	2	.750	0	15	1.64
1993 New York	NL	35	0	0	30	36.1	172	46	24	21	4	1	1	1	19	3	29	5	0	4	3	.571	0	10	5.20

Year	Team	Lg	G	GS	CG	GF	IP	BFP	H	R	ER	HR	SH	SF	HB	TBB	IBB	SO	WP	Bk	W	L	Pct.	ShO	Sv	ERA
1994	New York	NL	47	0	0	43	50	216	47	20	15	2	2	1	1	19	0	42	1	0	1	4	.200	0	30	2.70
1995	New York	NL	48	0	0	41	51.2	213	48	17	14	4	4	1	0	17	2	41	0	0	5	3	.625	0	29	2.44
12 ML YEARS			661	0	0	526	822	3459	752	290	239	46	56	20	8	315	54	600	34	8	68	54	.557	0	295	2.62

Julio Franco

Bats: Right   **Throws:** Right   **Pos:** DH/1B   **Ht:** 6' 1"   **Wt:** 190   **Born:** 8/23/61   **Age:** 34

					BATTING															BASERUNNING				PERCENTAGES		
Year	Team	Lg	G	AB	H	2B	3B	HR	(Hm	Rd)	TB	R	RBI	TBB	IBB	SO	HBP	SH	SF	SB	CS	SB%	GDP	Avg	OBP	SLG
1982	Philadelphia	NL	16	29	8	1	0	0	(0	0)	9	3	3	2	1	4	0	1	0	0	2	.00	1	.276	.323	.310
1983	Cleveland	AL	149	560	153	24	8	8	(6	2)	217	68	80	27	1	50	2	3	6	32	12	.73	21	.273	.306	.388
1984	Cleveland	AL	160	658	188	22	5	3	(1	2)	229	82	79	43	1	68	6	1	10	19	10	.66	23	.286	.331	.348
1985	Cleveland	AL	160	636	183	33	4	6	(3	3)	242	97	90	54	2	74	4	0	9	13	9	.59	26	.288	.343	.381
1986	Cleveland	AL	149	599	183	30	5	10	(4	6)	253	80	74	32	1	66	0	0	5	10	7	.59	28	.306	.338	.422
1987	Cleveland	AL	128	495	158	24	3	8	(5	3)	212	86	52	57	2	56	3	0	5	32	9	.78	23	.319	.389	.428
1988	Cleveland	AL	152	613	186	23	6	10	(3	7)	251	88	54	56	4	72	2	1	4	25	11	.69	17	.303	.361	.409
1989	Texas	AL	150	548	173	31	5	13	(9	4)	253	80	92	66	11	69	1	0	6	21	3	.88	27	.316	.386	.462
1990	Texas	AL	157	582	172	27	1	11	(4	7)	234	96	69	82	3	83	2	2	2	31	10	.76	12	.296	.383	.442
1991	Texas	AL	146	589	201	27	3	15	(7	8)	279	108	78	65	8	78	3	0	2	36	9	.80	13	.341	.408	.474
1992	Texas	AL	35	107	25	7	0	2	(2	0)	38	19	8	15	2	17	0	1	0	1	1	.50	3	.234	.328	.355
1993	Texas	AL	144	532	154	31	3	14	(6	8)	233	85	84	62	4	95	1	5	7	9	3	.75	16	.289	.360	.438
1994	Chicago	AL	112	433	138	19	2	20	(10	10)	221	72	98	62	4	75	5	0	5	8	1	.89	14	.319	.406	.510
13 ML YEARS			1658	6381	1922	299	45	120	(60	60)	2671	964	861	623	44	807	29	14	61	237	87	.73	224	.301	.363	.419

Matt Franco

Bats: Left   **Throws:** Right   **Pos:** 2B   **Ht:** 6' 2"   **Wt:** 200   **Born:** 8/19/69   **Age:** 26

					BATTING															BASERUNNING				PERCENTAGES		
Year	Team	Lg	G	AB	H	2B	3B	HR	(Hm	Rd)	TB	R	RBI	TBB	IBB	SO	HBP	SH	SF	SB	CS	SB%	GDP	Avg	OBP	SLG
1987	Wytheville	R	62	202	50	10	1	1	--	--	65	25	21	26	1	41	0	0	0	4	1	.80	3	.248	.333	.322
1988	Wytheville	R	20	79	31	9	1	0	--	--	42	14	16	7	0	5	0	0	0	1	0	1.00	2	.392	.442	.532
	Geneva	A	44	164	42	2	0	3	--	--	53	19	21	19	3	13	0	0	1	2	0	1.00	7	.256	.332	.323
1989	Charlstn-Wv	A	109	377	102	16	1	5	--	--	135	42	48	57	0	40	0	5	4	2	2	.50	10	.271	.363	.358
	Peoria	A	16	58	13	4	0	0	--	--	17	4	9	5	0	5	1	0	1	0	1	.00	1	.224	.292	.293
1990	Peoria	A	123	443	125	33	2	6	--	--	180	52	65	43	2	39	1	1	2	4	4	.50	19	.282	.346	.406
1991	Winston-Sal	A	104	307	66	12	1	4	--	--	92	47	40	46	2	41	2	2	6	4	1	.80	6	.215	.316	.300
1992	Charlotte	AA	108	343	97	18	3	2	--	--	127	35	31	26	1	46	1	0	3	3	3	.50	4	.283	.332	.370
1993	Orlando	AA	68	237	75	20	1	7	--	--	118	31	37	29	2	30	2	1	2	3	6	.33	2	.316	.393	.498
	Iowa	AAA	62	199	58	17	4	5	--	--	98	24	29	16	3	30	1	0	3	4	1	.80	6	.291	.342	.492
1994	Iowa	AAA	128	437	121	32	4	11	--	--	194	63	71	52	5	66	2	2	5	3	3	.50	7	.277	.353	.444
1995	Iowa	AAA	121	455	128	28	5	6	--	--	184	51	58	37	5	44	0	1	6	1	1	.50	11	.281	.331	.404
1995	Chicago	NL	16	17	5	1	0	0	(0	0)	6	3	1	0	0	4	0	0	0	0	0	.00	0	.294	.294	.353

John Frascatore

Pitches: Right   **Bats:** Right   **Pos:** RP/SP   **Ht:** 6' 1"   **Wt:** 200   **Born:** 2/4/70   **Age:** 26

				HOW MUCH HE PITCHED					WHAT HE GAVE UP										THE RESULTS					
Year	Team	Lg	G	GS	CG	GF	IP	BFP	H	R	ER	HR	SH	SF	HB	TBB	IBB	SO	WP	Bk	W	L	Pct.	ShO	Sv	ERA
1991	Hamilton	A	30	1	0	7	30.1	162	44	38	31	3	3	1	2	22	1	18	1	2	2	7	.222	0	1	9.20
1992	Savannah	A	50	0	0	44	58.2	266	49	32	25	4	8	1	3	29	2	56	4	5	5	7	.417	0	23	3.84
1993	Springfield	A	27	26	2	1	157.1	654	157	84	66	6	7	5	3	33	0	126	2	3	7	12	.368	1	0	3.78
1994	Arkansas	AA	12	12	4	0	78.1	324	76	37	27	3	1	2	3	15	0	63	3	0	7	3	.700	1	0	3.10
	Louisville	AAA	13	12	2	0	85	366	82	34	32	3	6	4	2	33	2	58	2	0	8	3	.727	1	0	3.39
1995	Louisville	AAA	28	10	1	15	82	370	89	54	36	5	5	2	3	34	3	55	5	0	2	8	.200	0	5	3.95
1994	St. Louis	NL	1	1	0	0	3.1	18	7	6	6	2	0	0	0	2	0	2	1	0	0	1	.000	0	0	16.20
1995	St. Louis	NL	14	4	0	3	32.2	151	39	19	16	3	1	1	2	16	1	21	0	0	1	1	.500	0	0	4.41
2 ML YEARS			15	5	0	3	36	169	46	25	22	5	1	1	2	18	1	23	1	0	1	2	.333	0	0	5.50

Willie Fraser

Pitches: Right   **Bats:** Right   **Pos:** RP   **Ht:** 6' 1"   **Wt:** 206   **Born:** 5/26/64   **Age:** 32

				HOW MUCH HE PITCHED					WHAT HE GAVE UP										THE RESULTS					
Year	Team	Lg	G	GS	CG	GF	IP	BFP	H	R	ER	HR	SH	SF	HB	TBB	IBB	SO	WP	Bk	W	L	Pct.	ShO	Sv	ERA
1995	Ottawa *	AAA	19	14	1	0	107.1	434	94	44	38	11	3	3	3	18	0	84	2	0	7	6	.538	1	0	3.19
1986	California	AL	1	1	0	0	4.1	20	6	4	4	0	1	1	0	1	0	2	0	0	0	0	.000	0	0	8.31
1987	California	AL	36	23	5	6	176.2	744	160	85	77	24	4	4	6	63	3	106	12	1	10	10	.500	1	1	3.92
1988	California	AL	34	32	2	0	194.2	861	203	129	117	33	2	9	9	80	2	86	12	6	12	13	.480	0	0	5.41
1989	California	AL	44	0	0	21	91.2	375	80	33	33	6	4	3	5	23	4	46	5	0	4	7	.364	0	2	3.24
1990	California	AL	45	0	0	20	76	315	69	29	26	4	2	3	0	24	3	32	1	0	5	4	.556	0	2	3.08

		G	AB	H	2B	3B	HR	IP	BFP	H	R	ER	HR	SH	SF	HB	TBB	IBB	SO	WP	Bk	W	L	Pct.	ShO	Sv	ERA
1991 Tor-StL		48	1	0	22	75.2	333	77	48	45	13	1	3	6	32	5	37	6	0	3	5	.375	0	0	5.35
1994 Florida	NL	9	0	0	4	12.1	63	20	9	8	1	2	1	0	6	3	7	2	0	2	0	1.000	0	0	5.84
1995 Montreal	NL	22	0	0	6	25.2	114	25	17	16	6	1	0	3	9	1	12	2	0			.667	0	2	5.61
1991 Toronto	AL	13	1	0	6	26.1	123	33	20	18	4	0	0	3	11	2	12	2	0	0	2	.000	0	0	6.15
St. Louis	NL	35	0	0	16	49.1	210	44	28	27	9	1	3	3	21	3	25	4	0	3	3	.500	0	0	4.93
8 ML YEARS		239	57	7	79	657	2825	640	354	326	89	18	24	29	238	26	328	40	7	38	40	.487	1	7	4.47

Lou Frazier

Bats: Both   **Throws:** Right   **Pos:** LF/CF   **Ht:** 6' 2"   **Wt:** 180   **Born:** 1/26/65   **Age:** 31

			BATTING															BASERUNNING				PERCENTAGES		
Year Team	Lg	G	AB	H	2B	3B	HR	(Hm | Rd)	TB	R	RBI	TBB	IBB	SO	HBP	SH	SF	SB	CS	SB%	GDP	Avg	OBP	SLG
1995 Ottawa *	AAA	31	110	24	3	0	1	--	--	30	11	10	13	0	20	1	1		10	1	.91	2	.218	.304	.273
1993 Montreal	NL	112	189	54	7	1	1	(1 | 0)	66	27	16	16	0	24	0	5	1	17	2	.89	3	.286	.340	.349
1994 Montreal	NL	76	140	38	3	1	0	(0 | 0)	43	25	14	18	0	23	1	1	0	20	4	.83	1	.271	.358	.307
1995 Mon-Tex		84	162	33	4	0	0	(0 | 0)	37	25	11	15	0	32	4	3	1	13	1	.93	3	.204	.286	.228
1995 Montreal	NL	35	63	12	2	0	0	(0 | 0)	14	6	3	8	0	12	2	0	1	4	0	1.00	1	.190	.297	.222
Texas	AL	49	99	21	2	0	0	(0 | 0)	23	19	8	7	0	20	2	3	0	9	1	.90	2	.212	.278	.232
3 ML YEARS		272	491	125	14	2	1	(1 | 0)	146	77	41	49	0	79	5	9	2	50	7	.88	7	.255	.327	.297

Marvin Freeman

Pitches: Right   **Bats:** Right   **Pos:** SP   **Ht:** 6' 7"   **Wt:** 222   **Born:** 4/10/63   **Age:** 33

		HOW MUCH HE PITCHED						WHAT HE GAVE UP												THE RESULTS					
Year Team	Lg	G	GS	CG	GF	IP	BFP	H	R	ER	HR	SH	SF	HB	TBB	IBB	SO	WP	Bk	W	L	Pct.	ShO	Sv	ERA
1986 Philadelphia	NL	3	3	0	0	16	61	6	4	4	0	0	1	0	10	0	8	1	0	2	0	1.000	0	0	2.25
1988 Philadelphia	NL	11	11	0	0	51.2	249	55	36	35	2	5	1	1	43	2	37	3	1	2	3	.400	0	0	6.10
1989 Philadelphia	NL	1	1	0	0	3	16	2	2	2	0	0	0	0	5	0	0	1	0	0	0	.000	0	0	6.00
1990 Atl-Phi	NL	25	3	0	5	48	207	41	24	23	5	2	0	5	17	2	38	4	0	1	2	.333	0	1	4.31
1991 Atlanta	NL	34	0	0	6	48	190	37	19	16	2	1	1	2	13	1	34	4	0	1	0	1.000	0	1	3.00
1992 Atlanta	NL	58	0	0	15	64.1	276	61	26	23	7	2	1	1	29	7	41	4	0	7	5	.583	0	3	3.22
1993 Atlanta	NL	21	0	0	5	23.2	103	24	16	16	1	0	0	1	10	2	25	3	0	2	0	1.000	0	0	6.08
1994 Colorado	NL	19	18	0	0	112.2	465	113	39	35	10	4	1	5	23	2	67	4	0	10	2	.833	0	0	2.80
1995 Colorado	NL	22	18	0	0	94.2	437	122	64	62	15	7	3	2	41	1	61	5	1	3	7	.300	0	0	5.89
1990 Atlanta	NL	9	0	0	1	15.2	60	7	3	3	0	1	0	2	3	0	12	0	0	1	0	1.000	0	1	1.72
Philadelphia	NL	16	3	0	4	32.1	147	34	21	20	5	1	0	3	14	2	26	4	0	0	2	.000	0	1	5.57
9 ML YEARS		194	54	0	31	462	2004	461	230	216	42	21	8	17	191	17	311	28	3	28	19	.596	0	5	4.21

Steve Frey

Pitches: Left   **Bats:** Left   **Pos:** RP   **Ht:** 5' 9"   **Wt:** 170   **Born:** 7/29/63   **Age:** 32

		HOW MUCH HE PITCHED						WHAT HE GAVE UP												THE RESULTS					
Year Team	Lg	G	GS	CG	GF	IP	BFP	H	R	ER	HR	SH	SF	HB	TBB	IBB	SO	WP	Bk	W	L	Pct.	ShO	Sv	ERA
1995 Scrantn-WB *	AAA	4	0	0	2	5	21	3	1	1	0	1	0	1	2	1	3	1	0	0	0	.000	0	0	1.80
1989 Montreal	NL	20	0	0	11	21.1	103	29	15	13	4	0	2	1	11	1	15	1	1	3	2	.600	0	0	5.48
1990 Montreal	NL	51	0	0	21	55.2	236	44	15	13	4	3	2	1	29	6	29	0	0	8	2	.800	0	9	2.10
1991 Montreal	NL	31	0	0	5	39.2	182	43	31	22	3	3	2	1	23	4	21	3	1	0	1	.000	0	4	4.99
1992 California	AL	51	0	0	20	45.1	193	39	18	18	6	2	3	2	22	3	24	1	0	4	2	.667	0	4	3.57
1993 California	AL	55	0	0	28	48.1	212	41	20	16	1	4	1	3	26	1	22	3	0	2	3	.400	0	13	2.98
1994 San Francisco	NL	44	0	0	12	31	137	37	17	17	6	1	4	2	15	3	20	1	0	1	0	1.000	0	0	4.94
1995 SF-Sea-Phi		31	0	0	7	28.1	121	26	14	10	2	5	2	1	10	2	14	0	0	0	4	.000	0	1	3.18
1995 San Francisco	NL	9	0	0	1	6.1	29	7	6	3	1	1	1	0	2	0	5	0	0	0	1	.000	0	0	4.26
Seattle	AL	13	0	0	3	11.1	56	16	7	.6	0	3	1	1	6	1	7	0	0	0	3	.000	0	0	4.76
Philadelphia	NL	9	0	0	3	10.2	36	3	1	1	1	1	0	0	2	1	2	0	0	0	0	.000	0	1	0.84
7 ML YEARS		283	0	0	104	269.2	1184	259	130	109	26	18	16	11	136	20	145	9	2	18	14	.563	0	28	3.64

Jeff Frye

Bats: Right   **Throws:** Right   **Pos:** 2B   **Ht:** 5' 9"   **Wt:** 165   **Born:** 8/31/66   **Age:** 29

			BATTING															BASERUNNING				PERCENTAGES		
Year Team	Lg	G	AB	H	2B	3B	HR	(Hm | Rd)	TB	R	RBI	TBB	IBB	SO	HBP	SH	SF	SB	CS	SB%	GDP	Avg	OBP	SLG
1992 Texas	AL	67	199	51	9	1	1	(0 | 1)	65	24	12	16	0	27	3	11	1	1	3	.25	2	.256	.320	.327
1994 Texas	AL	57	205	67	20	3	0	(0 | 0)	93	37	18	29	0	23	1	5	3	6	1	.86	1	.327	.408	.454
1995 Texas	AL	90	313	87	15	2	4	(2 | 2)	118	38	29	24	0	45	5	8	4	3	3	.50	7	.278	.335	.377
3 ML YEARS		214	717	205	44	6	5	(2 | 3)	276	99	59	69	0	95	9	24	8	10	7	.59	10	.286	.352	.385

Travis Fryman

Bats: Right   **Throws:** Right   **Pos:** 3B   **Ht:** 6' 1"   **Wt:** 195   **Born:** 3/25/69   **Age:** 27

			BATTING															BASERUNNING				PERCENTAGES		
Year Team	Lg	G	AB	H	2B	3B	HR	(Hm | Rd)	TB	R	RBI	TBB	IBB	SO	HBP	SH	SF	SB	CS	SB%	GDP	Avg	OBP	SLG
1990 Detroit	AL	66	232	69	11	1	9	(5 | 4)	109	32	27	17	0	51	1	1	0	3	3	.50	3	.297	.348	.470

Year Team	Lg	G	AB	H	2B	3B	HR	(Hm	Rd)	TB	R	RBI	TBB	IBB	SO	HBP	SH	SF	SB	CS	SB%	GDP	Avg	OBP	SLG
1991 Detroit	AL	149	557	144	36	3	21	(8	13)	249	65	91	40	0	149	3	6	6	12	5	.71	13	.259	.309	.447
1992 Detroit	AL	161	**659**	175	31	4	20	(9	11)	274	87	96	45	1	144	6	5	6	8	4	.67	13	.266	.316	.416
1993 Detroit	AL	151	607	182	37	5	22	(13	9)	295	98	97	77	1	128	4	1	6	9	4	.69	8	.300	.379	.486
1994 Detroit	AL	114	**464**	122	34	5	18	(10	8)	220	66	85	45	1	**128**	5	1	13	2	2	.50	6	.263	.326	.474
1995 Detroit	AL	144	567	156	21	5	15	(9	6)	232	79	81	63	4	100	3	0	7	4	2	.67	18	.275	.347	.409
6 ML YEARS		785	3086	848	170	23	105	(54	51)	1379	427	477	287	7	700	22	14	38	38	20	.66	61	.275	.337	.447

Gary Gaetti

Bats: Right **Throws:** Right **Pos:** 3B/1B **Ht:** 6' 0" **Wt:** 200 **Born:** 8/19/58 **Age:** 37

Year Team	Lg	G	AB	H	2B	3B	HR	(Hm	Rd)	TB	R	RBI	TBB	IBB	SO	HBP	SH	SF	SB	CS	SB%	GDP	Avg	OBP	SLG
1981 Minnesota	AL	9	26	5	0	0	2	(1	1)	11	4	3	0	0	6	0	0	0	0	0	.00	1	.192	.192	.423
1982 Minnesota	AL	145	508	117	25	4	25	(15	10)	225	59	84	37	2	107	3	4	13	0	4	.00	16	.230	.280	.443
1983 Minnesota	AL	157	584	143	30	3	21	(7	14)	242	81	78	54	2	121	4	0	8	7	1	.88	18	.245	.309	.414
1984 Minnesota	AL	**162**	588	154	29	4	5	(2	3)	206	55	65	44	1	81	4	3	5	11	5	.69	9	.262	.315	.350
1985 Minnesota	AL	160	560	138	31	0	20	(10	10)	229	71	63	37	3	89	7	3	1	13	5	.72	15	.246	.301	.409
1986 Minnesota	AL	157	596	171	34	1	34	(16	18)	309	91	108	52	4	108	6	1	6	14	15	.48	18	.287	.347	.518
1987 Minnesota	AL	154	584	150	36	2	31	(18	13)	283	95	109	37	7	92	3	1	3	10	7	.59	**25**	.257	.303	.485
1988 Minnesota	AL	133	468	141	29	2	28	(9	19)	258	66	88	36	5	85	5	1	6	7	4	.64	10	.301	.353	.551
1989 Minnesota	AL	130	498	125	11	4	19	(10	9)	201	63	75	25	5	87	3	1	9	6	2	.75	12	.251	.286	.404
1990 Minnesota	AL	154	577	132	27	5	16	(7	9)	217	61	85	36	1	101	3	1	8	6	1	.86	22	.229	.274	.376
1991 California	AL	152	586	144	22	1	18	(12	6)	222	58	66	33	3	104	8	2	5	5	5	.50	13	.246	.293	.379
1992 California	AL	130	456	103	13	2	12	(8	4)	156	41	48	21	4	79	6	0	3	3	1	.75	9	.226	.267	.342
1993 Cal-KC	AL	102	331	81	20	1	14	(6	8)	145	40	50	21	0	87	8	2	7	1	3	.25	7	.245	.300	.438
1994 Kansas City	AL	90	327	94	15	3	12	(5	7)	151	53	57	19	3	63	2	1	3	0	2	.00	9	.287	.328	.462
1995 Kansas City	AL	137	514	134	27	0	35	(16	19)	266	76	96	47	6	91	8	3	6	3	3	.50	7	.261	.329	.518
1993 California	AL	20	50	9	2	0	0	(0	0)	11	3	4	5	0	12	0	0	1	1	0	1.00	3	.180	.250	.220
Kansas City	AL	82	281	72	18	1	14	(6	8)	134	37	46	16	0	75	8	2	6	0	3	.00	2	.256	.309	.477
15 ML YEARS		1972	7203	1832	349	32	292	(142	150)	3121	914	1075	499	46	1301	70	23	83	86	58	.60	189	.254	.306	.433

Greg Gagne

Bats: Right **Throws:** Right **Pos:** SS **Ht:** 5'11" **Wt:** 180 **Born:** 11/12/61 **Age:** 34

Year Team	Lg	G	AB	H	2B	3B	HR	(Hm	Rd)	TB	R	RBI	TBB	IBB	SO	HBP	SH	SF	SB	CS	SB%	GDP	Avg	OBP	SLG
1983 Minnesota	AL	10	27	3	1	0	0	(0	0)	4	2	3	0	0	6	0	0	2	0	0	.00	0	.111	.103	.148
1984 Minnesota	AL	2	1	0	0	0	0	(0	0)	0	0	0	0	0	0	0	0	0	0	0	.00	0	.000	.000	.000
1985 Minnesota	AL	114	293	66	11	3	2	(0	2)	93	37	23	20	0	57	3	3	3	10	4	.71	5	.225	.279	.317
1986 Minnesota	AL	156	472	118	22	6	12	(10	2)	188	63	54	30	0	108	6	13	3	12	10	.55	4	.250	.301	.398
1987 Minnesota	AL	137	437	116	28	7	10	(7	3)	188	68	40	25	0	84	4	10	2	6	6	.50	3	.265	.310	.430
1988 Minnesota	AL	149	461	109	20	6	14	(5	9)	183	70	48	27	2	110	7	11	1	15	7	.68	13	.236	.288	.397
1989 Minnesota	AL	149	460	125	29	7	9	(5	4)	195	69	48	17	0	80	2	7	5	11	4	.73	10	.272	.298	.424
1990 Minnesota	AL	138	388	91	22	3	7	(3	4)	140	38	38	24	0	76	1	8	2	8	8	.50	5	.235	.280	.361
1991 Minnesota	AL	139	408	108	23	3	8	(3	5)	161	52	42	26	0	72	3	5	5	11	9	.55	15	.265	.310	.395
1992 Minnesota	AL	146	439	108	23	0	7	(1	6)	152	53	39	19	0	83	2	12	1	6	7	.46	11	.246	.280	.346
1993 Kansas City	AL	159	540	151	32	3	10	(3	7)	219	66	57	33	1	93	0	4	4	10	12	.45	7	.280	.319	.406
1994 Kansas City	AL	107	375	97	23	3	7	(2	5)	147	39	51	27	0	79	4	2	1	10	**17**	.37	8	.259	.314	.392
1995 Kansas City	AL	120	430	110	25	4	6	(2	4)	161	58	49	38	2	60	2	7	5	3	5	.38	11	.256	.316	.374
13 ML YEARS		1526	4731	1202	263	45	92	(41	51)	1831	615	492	286	5	908	34	82	34	102	89	.53	92	.254	.299	.387

Andres Galarraga

Bats: Right **Throws:** Right **Pos:** 1B **Ht:** 6' 3" **Wt:** 235 **Born:** 6/18/61 **Age:** 35

Year Team	Lg	G	AB	H	2B	3B	HR	(Hm	Rd)	TB	R	RBI	TBB	IBB	SO	HBP	SH	SF	SB	CS	SB%	GDP	Avg	OBP	SLG
1985 Montreal	NL	24	75	14	1	0	2	(0	2)	21	9	4	3	0	18	1	0	0	1	2	.33	0	.187	.228	.280
1986 Montreal	NL	105	321	87	13	0	10	(4	6)	130	39	42	30	5	79	3	1	1	6	5	.55	8	.271	.338	.405
1987 Montreal	NL	147	551	168	40	3	13	(7	6)	253	72	90	41	13	127	10	0	4	7	10	.41	11	.305	.361	.459
1988 Montreal	NL	157	609	**184**	**42**	8	29	(14	15)	**329**	99	92	39	9	**153**	10	0	3	13	4	.76	12	.302	.352	.540
1989 Montreal	NL	152	572	147	30	1	23	(13	10)	248	76	85	48	10	**158**	**13**	0	3	12	5	.71	12	.257	.327	.434
1990 Montreal	NL	155	579	148	29	0	20	(6	14)	237	65	87	40	8	**169**	4	0	5	10	1	.91	14	.256	.306	.409
1991 Montreal	NL	107	375	82	13	2	9	(3	6)	126	34	33	23	5	86	2	0	0	5	6	.45	6	.219	.268	.336
1992 St. Louis	NL	95	325	79	14	2	10	(4	6)	127	38	39	11	0	69	8	0	3	5	4	.56	8	.243	.282	.391
1993 Colorado	NL	120	470	174	35	4	22	(13	9)	283	71	98	24	12	73	6	0	6	2	4	.33	9	**.370**	.403	.602
1994 Colorado	NL	103	417	133	21	0	31	(16	15)	247	77	85	19	8	93	8	0	5	8	3	.73	10	.319	.356	.592
1995 Colorado	NL	143	554	155	29	3	31	(18	13)	283	89	106	32	6	**146**	13	0	5	12	2	.86	14	.280	.331	.511
11 ML YEARS		1308	4848	1371	267	23	200	(98	102)	2284	669	761	310	76	1171	78	1	35	81	46	.64	104	.283	.334	.471

Dave Gallagher

Bats: Right **Throws:** Right **Pos:** RF/CF **Ht:** 6' 0" **Wt:** 185 **Born:** 9/20/60 **Age:** 35

Year	Team	Lg	G	AB	H	2B	3B	HR	(Hm	Rd)	TB	R	RBI	TBB	IBB	SO	HBP	SH	SF	SB	CS	SB%	GDP	Avg	OBP	SLG
1987	Cleveland	AL	15	36	4	1	1	0	(0	0)	7	2	1	2	0	5	0	1	0	2	0	1.00	1	.111	.158	.194
1988	Chicago	AL	101	347	105	15	3	5	(1	4)	141	59	31	29	3	40	0	6	2	5	4	.56	8	.303	.354	.406
1989	Chicago	AL	161	601	160	22	2	1	(1	0)	189	74	46	46	1	79	2	16	2	5	6	.45	9	.266	.320	.314
1990	Bal-ChA	AL	68	126	32	4	1	0	(0	0)	38	12	7	7	0	12	1	7	1	1	2	.33	3	.254	.296	.302
1991	California	AL	90	270	79	17	0	1	(0	1)	99	32	30	24	0	43	2	10	0	2	4	.33	6	.293	.355	.367
1992	New York	NL	98	175	42	11	1	1	(1	0)	58	20	21	19	0	16	1	3	7	4	5	.44	7	.240	.307	.331
1993	New York	NL	99	201	55	12	2	6	(1	5)	89	34	28	20	1	18	0	7	1	1	1	.50	7	.274	.338	.443
1994	Atlanta	NL	89	152	34	5	0	2	(1	1)	45	27	14	22	2	17	1	2	0	0	2	.00	5	.224	.326	.296
1995	Phi-Cal		73	173	53	13	0	1	(1	0)	69	13	12	18	0	21	0	2	1	0	0	.00	1	.306	.370	.399
1990	Baltimore	AL	23	51	11	1	0	0	(0	0)	12	7	2	4	0	3	0	2	1	1	1	.50	0	.216	.268	.235
	Chicago		45	75	21	3	1	0	(0	0)	26	5	5	3	0	9	1	5	0	0	1	.00	3	.280	.316	.347
1995	Philadelphia	NL	62	157	50	12	0	1	(1	0)	65	12	12	16	0	20	0	2	1	0	0	.00	0	.318	.379	.414
	California	AL	11	16	3	1	0	0	(0	0)	4	1	0	2	0	1	0	0	0	0	0	.00	0	.188	.278	.250
9 ML YEARS			794	2081	564	100	10	17	(6	11)	735	273	190	187	7	251	7	54	14	20	24	.45	51	.271	.331	.353

Mike Gallego

Bats: Right **Throws:** Right **Pos:** 2B/3B/SS **Ht:** 5' 8" **Wt:** 175 **Born:** 10/31/60 **Age:** 35

Year	Team	Lg	G	AB	H	2B	3B	HR	(Hm	Rd)	TB	R	RBI	TBB	IBB	SO	HBP	SH	SF	SB	CS	SB%	GDP	Avg	OBP	SLG
1995	Edmonton *	AAA	6	18	5	1	0	0	--	--	6	1	1	0	0	4	2	0	0	0	0	.00	0	.278	.350	.333
1985	Oakland	AL	76	77	16	5	1	1	(0	1)	26	13	9	12	0	14	1	2	1	1	1	.50	2	.208	.319	.338
1986	Oakland	AL	20	37	10	2	0	0	(0	0)	12	2	4	1	0	6	0	2	0	0	2	.00	0	.270	.289	.324
1987	Oakland	AL	72	124	31	6	0	2	(0	2)	43	18	14	12	0	21	1	5	1	0	1	.00	5	.250	.319	.347
1988	Oakland	AL	129	277	58	8	0	2	(2	0)	72	38	20	34	0	53	1	8	0	2	3	.40	6	.209	.298	.260
1989	Oakland	AL	133	357	90	14	2	3	(2	1)	117	45	30	35	0	43	6	8	3	7	5	.58	10	.252	.327	.328
1990	Oakland	AL	140	389	80	13	2	3	(1	2)	106	36	34	35	0	50	4	17	2	5	5	.50	13	.206	.277	.272
1991	Oakland	AL	159	482	119	15	4	12	(6	6)	178	67	49	67	3	84	5	10	3	6	9	.40	8	.247	.343	.369
1992	New York	AL	53	173	44	7	1	3	(1	2)	62	24	14	20	0	22	4	3	1	0	1	.00	5	.254	.343	.358
1993	New York	AL	119	403	114	20	1	10	(5	5)	166	63	54	50	0	65	4	3	5	3	2	.60	16	.283	.364	.412
1994	New York	AL	89	306	73	17	1	6	(2	4)	110	39	41	38	1	46	4	5	4	0	1	.00	4	.239	.327	.359
1995	Oakland	AL	43	120	28	0	0	0	(0	0)	28	11	8	9	0	24	1	2	0	0	1	.00	3	.233	.292	.233
11 ML YEARS			1033	2745	663	107	12	42	(19	23)	920	356	277	313	4	428	31	65	20	24	31	.44	72	.242	.324	.335

Ron Gant

Bats: Right **Throws:** Right **Pos:** LF **Ht:** 6' 0" **Wt:** 200 **Born:** 3/2/65 **Age:** 31

Year	Team	Lg	G	AB	H	2B	3B	HR	(Hm	Rd)	TB	R	RBI	TBB	IBB	SO	HBP	SH	SF	SB	CS	SB%	GDP	Avg	OBP	SLG
1987	Atlanta	NL	21	83	22	4	0	2	(1	1)	32	9	9	1	0	11	0	1	1	4	2	.67	3	.265	.271	.386
1988	Atlanta	NL	146	563	146	28	8	19	(7	12)	247	85	60	46	4	118	3	2	4	19	10	.66	7	.259	.317	.439
1989	Atlanta	NL	75	260	46	8	3	9	(5	4)	87	26	25	20	0	63	1	2	2	9	6	.60	8	.177	.237	.335
1990	Atlanta	NL	152	575	174	34	3	32	(18	14)	310	107	84	50	0	86	1	1	4	33	16	.67	8	.303	.357	.539
1991	Atlanta	NL	154	561	141	35	3	32	(18	14)	278	101	105	71	8	104	5	0	5	34	15	.69	6	.251	.338	.496
1992	Atlanta	NL	153	544	141	22	6	17	(10	7)	226	74	80	45	5	101	7	0	6	32	10	.76	10	.259	.321	.415
1993	Atlanta	NL	157	606	166	27	4	36	(17	19)	309	113	117	67	2	117	2	0	7	26	9	.74	14	.274	.345	.510
1995	Cincinnati	NL	119	410	113	19	4	29	(12	17)	227	79	88	74	5	108	3	1	5	23	8	.74	11	.276	.386	.554
8 ML YEARS			977	3602	949	177	31	176	(88	88)	1716	594	568	374	24	708	22	7	34	180	76	.70	59	.263	.334	.476

Rich Garces

Pitches: Right **Bats:** Right **Pos:** RP **Ht:** 6' 0" **Wt:** 215 **Born:** 5/18/71 **Age:** 25

Year	Team	Lg	G	GS	CG	GF	IP	BFP	H	R	ER	HR	SH	SF	HB	TBB	IBB	SO	WP	Bk	W	L	Pct.	ShO	Sv	ERA
1988	Elizabethtn	R	17	3	1	10	59	254	51	22	15	1	2	1	1	27	2	69	7	0	5	4	.556	0	5	2.29
1989	Kenosha	A	24	24	4	0	142.2	596	117	70	54	5	5	5	5	62	1	84	5	6	9	10	.474	1	0	3.41
1990	Visalia	A	47	0	0	42	54.2	212	33	14	11	2	1	1	1	16	0	75	6	0	2	2	.500	0	28	1.81
	Orlando	AA	15	0	0	14	17.1	81	17	4	4	0	1	0	0	14	2	22	2	0	2	1	.667	0	8	2.08
1991	Portland	AAA	10	0	0	8	13	58	10	7	7	1	0	0	1	8	1	13	0	1	0	1	.000	0	3	4.85
	Orlando	AA	10	0	0	5	16.1	75	12	6	6	0	2	1	2	14	2	17	0	0	2	1	.667	0	0	3.31
1992	Orlando	AA	58	0	0	42	73.1	334	76	46	37	6	8	7	2	39	1	72	6	0	3	3	.500	0	13	4.54
1993	Portland	AAA	35	7	0	5	54	293	70	55	50	4	3	2	0	64	0	48	3	3	1	3	.250	0	0	8.33
1994	Nashville	AA	40	1	0	22	77.1	335	70	40	32	5	4	4	2	31	0	76	6	0	4	5	.444	0	3	3.72
1995	Iowa	AAA	23	0	0	15	28.1	116	25	10	9	3	0	0	1	8	1	36	0	1	0	2	.000	0	7	2.86
1990	Minnesota	AL	5	0	0	3	5.2	24	4	2	1	0	0	0	0	4	0	1	0	0	0	0	.000	0	2	1.59
1993	Minnesota	AL	3	0	0	1	4	18	4	2	0	0	0	0	0	2	0	3	0	0	0	0	.000	0	0	0.00

Year Team	Lg	G	GS	CG	GF	IP	BFP	H	R	ER	HR	SH	SF	HB	TBB	IBB	SO	WP	Bk	W	L	Pct.	ShO	Sv	ERA
1995 ChN-Fla	NL	18	0	0	7	24.1	108	25	15	12	1	1	0	0	11	2	22	0	0	0	2	.000	0	0	4.44
1995 Chicago	NL	7	0	0	4	11	46	11	6	4	0	0	0	0	3	0	6	0	0	0	0	.000	0	0	3.27
Florida	NL	11	0	0	3	13.1	62	14	9	8	1	1	0	0	8	2	16	0	0	0	2	.000	0	0	5.40
3 ML YEARS		26	0	0	11	34	150	33	19	13	1	1	0	0	17	2	26	0	0	0	2	.000	0	2	3.44

Carlos Garcia

Bats: Right **Throws:** Right **Pos:** 2B/SS   **Ht:** 6' 1" **Wt:** 193 **Born:** 10/15/67 **Age:** 28

									BATTING											BASERUNNING				PERCENTAGES		
Year Team	Lg	G	AB	H	2B	3B	HR	(Hm	Rd)	TB	R	RBI	TBB	IBB	SO	HBP	SH	SF	SB	CS	SB%	GDP	Avg	OBP	SLG
1990 Pittsburgh	NL	4	4	2	0	0	0	(0	0)	2	1	0	0	0	2	0	0	0	0	0	.00	0	.500	.500	.500
1991 Pittsburgh	NL	12	24	6	0	2	0	(0	0)	10	2	1	1	0	8	0	0	0	0	0	.00	1	.250	.280	.417
1992 Pittsburgh	NL	22	39	8	1	0	0	(0	0)	9	4	4	0	0	9	0	1	2	0	0	.00	1	.205	.195	.231
1993 Pittsburgh	NL	141	546	147	25	5	12	(7	5)	218	77	47	31	2	67	9	6	5	18	11	.62	9	.269	.316	.399
1994 Pittsburgh	NL	98	412	114	15	2	6	(4	2)	151	49	28	16	2	67	4	1	1	18	9	.67	6	.277	.309	.367
1995 Pittsburgh	NL	104	367	108	24	2	6	(4	2)	154	41	50	25	5	55	2	5	3	8	4	.67	4	.294	.340	.420
6 ML YEARS		381	1392	385	65	11	24	(15	9)	544	174	130	73	9	208	15	13	11	44	24	.65	21	.277	.317	.391

Freddy Garcia

Bats: Right **Throws:** Right **Pos:** LF   **Ht:** 6' 2" **Wt:** 190 **Born:** 8/1/72 **Age:** 23

									BATTING											BASERUNNING				PERCENTAGES		
Year Team	Lg	G	AB	H	2B	3B	HR	(Hm	Rd)	TB	R	RBI	TBB	IBB	SO	HBP	SH	SF	SB	CS	SB%	GDP	Avg	OBP	SLG
1993 Medicne Hat	R	72	264	63	8	2	11	--	--	108	47	42	31	1	71	2	1	4	5	4	.44	3	.239	.319	.409
1994 St. Cathrns	A	73	260	74	10	2	13	--	--	127	46	40	33	1	57	2	1	3	1	3	.25	6	.285	.366	.488
1995 Pittsburgh	NL	42	57	8	1	1	0	(0	0)	11	5	1	8	0	17	0	1	0	0	1	.00	0	.140	.246	.193

Karim Garcia

Bats: Left **Throws:** Left **Pos:** RF   **Ht:** 6' 0" **Wt:** 172 **Born:** 10/29/75 **Age:** 20

									BATTING											BASERUNNING				PERCENTAGES		
Year Team	Lg	G	AB	H	2B	3B	HR	(Hm	Rd)	TB	R	RBI	TBB	IBB	SO	HBP	SH	SF	SB	CS	SB%	GDP	Avg	OBP	SLG
1993 Bakersfield	A	123	460	111	20	9	19	--	--	206	61	54	37	4	109	2	0	2	5	3	.63	5	.241	.299	.448
1994 Vero Beach	A	121	452	120	28	10	21	--	--	231	72	84	37	8	112	1	0	6	8	3	.73	7	.265	.319	.511
1995 Albuquerque	AAA	124	474	151	26	10	20	--	--	257	88	91	38	5	102	2	3	3	12	6	.67	12	.319	.369	.542
1995 Los Angeles	NL	13	20	4	0	0	0	(0	0)	4	1	0	0	0	4	0	0	0	0	0	.00	0	.200	.200	.200

Mike Gardiner

Pitches: Right **Bats:** Both **Pos:** RP   **Ht:** 6' 0" **Wt:** 200 **Born:** 10/19/65 **Age:** 30

		HOW MUCH HE PITCHED						WHAT HE GAVE UP												THE RESULTS					
Year Team	Lg	G	GS	CG	GF	IP	BFP	H	R	ER	HR	SH	SF	HB	TBB	IBB	SO	WP	Bk	W	L	Pct.	ShO	Sv	ERA
1995 Toledo *	AAA	11	1	0	4	16.1	77	19	8	8	2	1	1	0	13	0	10	1	0	0	1	.000	0	0	4.41
1990 Seattle	AL	5	3	0	1	12.2	66	22	17	15	1	0	1	2	5	0	6	0	0	0	2	.000	0	0	10.66
1991 Boston	AL	22	22	0	0	130	562	140	79	70	18	1	3	0	47	2	91	1	0	9	10	.474	0	0	4.85
1992 Boston	AL	28	18	0	3	130.2	566	126	78	69	12	3	5	2	58	2	79	8	0	4	10	.286	0	0	4.75
1993 Det-Mon		34	2	0	4	49.1	224	52	33	27	3	2	3	1	26	3	25	2	0	2	3	.400	0	0	4.93
1994 Detroit	AL	38	1	0	14	58.2	254	53	35	27	10	2	2	0	23	5	31	1	0	2	2	.500	0	5	4.14
1995 Detroit	AL	9	0	0	1	12.1	66	27	20	20	5	3	2	0	2	1	7	1	0	0	0	.000	0	0	14.59
1993 Detroit	AL	10	0	0	1	11.1	51	12	5	5	0	1	0	0	7	1	4	2	0	0	0	.000	0	0	3.97
Montreal	NL	24	2	0	3	38	173	40	28	22	3	1	3	1	19	2	21	0	0	2	3	.400	0	0	5.21
6 ML YEARS		136	46	0	23	393.2	1738	420	262	228	49	11	16	5	161	13	239	13	0	17	27	.386	0	5	5.21

Mark Gardner

Pitches: Right **Bats:** Right **Pos:** RP/SP   **Ht:** 6' 1" **Wt:** 205 **Born:** 3/1/62 **Age:** 34

		HOW MUCH HE PITCHED						WHAT HE GAVE UP												THE RESULTS					
Year Team	Lg	G	GS	CG	GF	IP	BFP	H	R	ER	HR	SH	SF	HB	TBB	IBB	SO	WP	Bk	W	L	Pct.	ShO	Sv	ERA
1989 Montreal	NL	7	4	0	1	26.1	117	26	16	15	2	0	0	2	11	1	21	0	0	0	3	.000	0	0	5.13
1990 Montreal	NL	27	26	3	1	152.2	642	129	62	58	13	4	7	9	61	5	135	2	4	7	9	.438	3	0	3.42
1991 Montreal	NL	27	27	0	0	168.1	692	139	78	72	17	7	2	4	75	1	107	2	1	9	11	.450	0	0	3.85
1992 Montreal	NL	33	30	0	0	179.2	778	179	91	87	15	12	7	9	60	2	132	2	1	12	10	.545	0	0	4.36
1993 Kansas City	AL	17	16	0	0	91.2	387	92	65	63	17	1	7	4	36	0	54	2	0	4	6	.400	0	0	6.19
1994 Florida	NL	20	14	0	3	92.1	391	97	53	50	14	4	5	1	30	2	57	3	1	4	4	.500	0	0	4.87
1995 Florida	NL	39	11	1	7	102.1	456	109	60	51	14	7	0	5	43	5	87	3	1	5	5	.500	1	1	4.49
7 ML YEARS		170	128	4	13	813.1	3463	771	425	396	92	35	28	34	316	16	593	14	7	41	48	.461	4	1	4.38

Brent Gates

Bats: Both **Throws:** Right **Pos:** 2B **Ht:** 6' 1" **Wt:** 180 **Born:** 3/14/70 **Age:** 26

Year Team	Lg	G	AB	H	2B	3B	HR	(Hm	Rd)	TB	R	RBI	TBB	IBB	SO	HBP	SH	SF	SB	CS	SB%	GDP	Avg	OBP	SLG
1993 Oakland	AL	139	535	155	29	3	7	(4	3)	209	64	69	56	4	75	4	6	8	7	3	.70	17	.290	.357	.391
1994 Oakland	AL	64	233	66	11	1	2	(0	2)	85	29	24	21	1	32	1	3	6	3	0	1.00	8	.283	.337	.365
1995 Oakland	AL	136	524	133	24	4	5	(3	2)	180	60	56	46	2	84	0	4	11	3	3	.50	15	.254	.308	.344
3 ML YEARS		339	1292	354	64	7	14	(7	7)	474	153	149	123	7	191	5	13	25	13	6	.68	40	.274	.334	.367

Jason Giambi

Bats: Left **Throws:** Right **Pos:** 3B/1B **Ht:** 6' 2" **Wt:** 200 **Born:** 1/8/71 **Age:** 25

Year Team	Lg	G	AB	H	2B	3B	HR	(Hm	Rd)	TB	R	RBI	TBB	IBB	SO	HBP	SH	SF	SB	CS	SB%	GDP	Avg	OBP	SLG
1992 Sou. Oregon	A	13	41	13	3	0	3	--	--	25	9	13	9	1	6	0	0	0	1	1	.50	0	.317	.440	.610
1993 Modesto	A	89	313	91	16	2	12	--	--	147	72	60	73	7	47	10	1	3	2	3	.40	12	.291	.436	.470
1994 Huntsville	AA	56	193	43	9	0	6	--	--	70	31	30	27	2	31	2	3	4	0	0	.00	8	.223	.319	.363
Tacoma	AAA	52	176	56	20	0	4	--	--	88	28	38	25	2	32	0	0	8	1	0	1.00	1	.318	.388	.500
1995 Edmonton	AAA	55	190	65	26	1	3	--	--	102	34	41	34	4	26	2	0	3	0	0	.00	4	.342	.441	.537
1995 Oakland	AL	54	176	45	7	0	6	(3	3)	70	27	25	28	0	31	3	1	2	2	1	.67	4	.256	.364	.398

Ray Giannelli

Bats: Left **Throws:** Right **Pos:** 1B **Ht:** 6' 0" **Wt:** 195 **Born:** 2/5/66 **Age:** 30

Year Team	Lg	G	AB	H	2B	3B	HR	(Hm	Rd)	TB	R	RBI	TBB	IBB	SO	HBP	SH	SF	SB	CS	SB%	GDP	Avg	OBP	SLG
1988 Medcine Hat	R	47	123	30	8	3	4	--	--	56	17	28	19	2	22	0	1	3	0	0	.00	6	.244	.338	.455
1989 Myrtle Bch	A	127	458	138	17	1	18	--	--	211	76	84	78	4	53	5	1	8	2	6	.25	10	.301	.403	.461
1990 Dunedin	A	118	416	120	18	1	18	--	--	194	64	57	66	7	56	1	1	3	4	8	.33	12	.288	.385	.466
1991 Knoxville	AA	112	362	100	14	3	7	--	--	141	53	37	64	6	66	2	5	2	8	5	.62	6	.276	.386	.390
1992 Syracuse	AAA	84	249	57	9	2	5	--	--	85	23	22	48	2	44	0	0	2	2	2	.50	4	.229	.351	.341
1993 Syracuse	AAA	127	411	104	18	4	11	--	--	163	51	42	38	1	79	2	2	5	1	6	.14	8	.253	.316	.397
1994 Syracuse	AAA	114	327	94	19	1	10	--	--	145	43	51	48	2	77	2	0	3	0	1	.00	5	.287	.379	.443
1995 Louisville	AAA	119	390	115	19	1	16	--	--	184	56	70	44	5	85	3	0	4	3	7	.30	6	.295	.367	.472
1991 Toronto	AL	9	24	4	1	0	0	(0	0)	5	2	0	5	0	9	0	0	0	1	0	1.00	0	.167	.310	.208
1995 St. Louis	NL	9	11	1	0	0	0	(0	0)	1	0	0	3	0	4	0	0	0	0	0	.00	0	.091	.286	.091
2 ML YEARS		18	35	5	1	0	0	(0	0)	6	2	0	8	0	13	0	0	0	1	0	1.00	0	.143	.302	.171

Steve Gibralter

Bats: Right **Throws:** Right **Pos:** CF **Ht:** 6' 0" **Wt:** 190 **Born:** 10/9/72 **Age:** 23

Year Team	Lg	G	AB	H	2B	3B	HR	(Hm	Rd)	TB	R	RBI	TBB	IBB	SO	HBP	SH	SF	SB	CS	SB%	GDP	Avg	OBP	SLG
1990 Reds	R	52	174	45	11	3	4	--	--	74	26	27	23	3	31	3	3	1	8	2	.80	5	.259	.353	.425
1991 Charlstn-Wv	A	140	544	145	36	7	6	--	--	213	72	71	31	2	117	5	2	6	11	13	.46	14	.267	.309	.392
1992 Cedar Rapds	A	137	529	162	32	3	19	--	--	257	92	99	51	4	99	12	1	3	12	9	.57	8	.306	.378	.486
1993 Chattanooga	AA	132	477	113	25	3	11	--	--	177	65	47	20	2	108	7	3	4	7	12	.37	6	.237	.276	.371
1994 Chattanooga	AA	133	460	124	28	3	14	--	--	200	71	63	47	0	114	9	4	5	10	8	.56	5	.270	.345	.435
1995 Indianapols	AAA	79	263	83	19	3	18	--	--	162	49	63	25	3	70	4	1	2	0	2	.00	6	.316	.381	.616
1995 Cincinnati	NL	4	3	1	0	0	0	(0	0)	1	0	0	0	0	0	0	0	0	0	0	.00	0	.333	.333	.333

Kirk Gibson

Bats: Left **Throws:** Left **Pos:** DH **Ht:** 6' 3" **Wt:** 225 **Born:** 5/28/57 **Age:** 39

Year Team	Lg	G	AB	H	2B	3B	HR	(Hm	Rd)	TB	R	RBI	TBB	IBB	SO	HBP	SH	SF	SB	CS	SB%	GDP	Avg	OBP	SLG
1979 Detroit	AL	12	38	9	3	0	1	(0	1)	15	3	4	1	0	3	0	0	0	3	3	.50	0	.237	.256	.395
1980 Detroit	AL	51	175	46	2	1	9	(3	6)	77	23	16	10	0	45	1	1	2	4	7	.36	0	.263	.303	.440
1981 Detroit	AL	83	290	95	11	3	9	(4	5)	139	41	40	18	1	64	2	1	2	17	5	.77	9	.328	.369	.479
1982 Detroit	AL	69	266	74	16	2	8	(4	4)	118	34	35	25	2	41	1	1	1	9	7	.56	2	.278	.341	.444
1983 Detroit	AL	128	401	91	12	9	15	(5	10)	166	60	51	53	3	96	4	5	4	14	3	.82	2	.227	.320	.414
1984 Detroit	AL	149	531	150	23	10	27	(11	16)	274	92	91	63	6	103	8	3	6	29	9	.76	4	.282	.363	.516
1985 Detroit	AL	154	581	167	37	5	29	(18	11)	301	96	97	71	16	137	5	3	10	30	4	.88	5	.287	.364	.518
1986 Detroit	AL	119	441	118	11	2	28	(15	13)	217	84	86	68	4	107	7	1	4	34	6	.85	8	.268	.371	.492
1987 Detroit	AL	128	487	135	25	3	24	(14	10)	238	95	79	71	8	117	5	1	4	26	7	.79	5	.277	.372	.489
1988 Los Angeles	NL	150	542	157	28	1	25	(14	11)	262	106	76	73	14	120	7	3	7	31	4	.89	8	.290	.377	.483
1989 Los Angeles	NL	71	253	54	8	2	9	(4	5)	93	35	28	35	5	55	2	0	2	12	3	.80	5	.213	.312	.368
1990 Los Angeles	NL	89	315	82	20	0	8	(2	6)	126	59	38	39	0	65	3	0	2	26	2	.93	4	.260	.345	.400
1991 Kansas City	AL	132	462	109	17	6	16	(4	12)	186	81	55	69	3	103	6	1	2	18	4	.82	9	.236	.341	.403
1992 Pittsburgh	NL	16	56	11	0	0	2	(0	2)	17	6	5	3	0	12	0	1	0	3	1	.75	1	.196	.237	.304
1993 Detroit	AL	116	403	105	18	6	13	(5	8)	174	62	62	44	4	87	4	0	3	15	6	.71	2	.261	.337	.432

Year	Team	Lg	G	AB	H	2B	3B	HR	(Hm	Rd)	TB	R	RBI	TBB	IBB	SO	HBP	SH	SF	SB	CS	SB%	GDP	Avg	OBP	SLG
1994	Detroit	AL	98	330	91	17	2	23	(9	14)	181	71	72	42	3	69	3	2	5	4	5	.44	2	.276	.358	.548
1995	Detroit	AL	70	227	59	12	2	9	(7	2)	102	37	35	33	3	61	3	0	2	9	2	.82	6	.260	.358	.449
17	ML YEARS		1635	5798	1553	260	54	255	(119	136)	2686	985	870	718	72	1285	61	23	56	284	78	.78	72	.268	.352	.463

Benji Gil

Bats: Right **Throws:** Right **Pos:** SS **Ht:** 6' 2" **Wt:** 180 **Born:** 10/6/72 **Age:** 23

Year	Team	Lg	G	AB	H	2B	3B	HR	(Hm	Rd)	TB	R	RBI	TBB	IBB	SO	HBP	SH	SF	SB	CS	SB%	GDP	Avg	OBP	SLG
1991	Butte	R	32	129	37	4	3	2	--	--	53	25	15	14	1	36	0	0	1	9	3	.75	0	.287	.354	.411
1992	Gastonia	A	132	482	132	21	1	9	--	--	182	75	55	50	0	106	3	3	4	26	13	.67	16	.274	.343	.378
1993	Tulsa	AA	101	342	94	9	1	17	--	--	156	45	59	35	2	89	7	0	3	20	12	.63	9	.275	.351	.456
1994	Okla. City	AAA	139	487	121	20	6	10	--	--	183	62	55	33	2	120	4	7	6	14	8	.64	9	.248	.298	.376
1993	Texas	AL	22	57	7	0	0	0	(0	0)	7	3	2	5	0	22	0	4	0	1	2	.33	0	.123	.194	.123
1995	Texas	AL	130	415	91	20	3	9	(5	4)	144	36	46	26	0	147	1	10	2	2	4	.33	5	.219	.266	.347
2	ML YEARS		152	472	98	20	3	9	(5	4)	151	39	48	31	0	169	1	14	2	3	6	.33	5	.208	.257	.320

Brian Giles

Bats: Left **Throws:** Left **Pos:** RF **Ht:** 5'11" **Wt:** 195 **Born:** 1/21/71 **Age:** 25

Year	Team	Lg	G	AB	H	2B	3B	HR	(Hm	Rd)	TB	R	RBI	TBB	IBB	SO	HBP	SH	SF	SB	CS	SB%	GDP	Avg	OBP	SLG
1989	Burlington	R	36	129	40	7	0	0	--	--	47	18	20	11	2	19	1	0	1	6	3	.67	0	.310	.366	.364
1990	Watertown	A	70	246	71	15	2	1	--	--	93	44	23	48	1	23	0	0	1	10	8	.56	3	.289	.403	.378
1991	Kinston	A	125	394	122	14	0	4	--	--	148	70	47	68	2	70	2	3	3	19	7	.73	5	.310	.411	.376
1992	Canton-Akrn	AA	23	74	16	4	0	0	--	--	20	6	3	10	1	10	0	0	1	3	1	.75	4	.216	.310	.270
	Kinston	A	42	140	37	5	1	3	--	--	53	28	18	30	1	21	1	0	0	3	5	.38	5	.264	.398	.379
1993	Canton-Akrn	AA	123	425	139	16	6	8	--	--	191	64	64	57	4	43	4	7	3	18	12	.60	9	.327	.409	.449
1994	Charlotte	AAA	128	434	136	18	3	16	--	--	208	74	58	55	10	61	2	1	4	8	5	.62	5	.313	.390	.479
1995	Buffalo	AAA	123	413	128	18	8	15	--	--	207	67	67	54	4	40	8	5	6	7	3	.70	9	.310	.395	.501
1995	Cleveland	AL	6	9	5	0	0	1	(0	1)	8	6	3	0	0	1	0	0	0	0	0	.00	0	.556	.556	.889

Bernard Gilkey

Bats: Right **Throws:** Right **Pos:** LF **Ht:** 6' 0" **Wt:** 190 **Born:** 9/24/66 **Age:** 29

Year	Team	Lg	G	AB	H	2B	3B	HR	(Hm	Rd)	TB	R	RBI	TBB	IBB	SO	HBP	SH	SF	SB	CS	SB%	GDP	Avg	OBP	SLG
1995	Louisville *	AAA	2	6	2	1	0	1	--	--	6	3	1	1	0	0	0	0	0	0	0	.00	0	.333	.429	1.000
1990	St. Louis	NL	18	64	19	5	2	1	(0	1)	31	11	3	8	0	5	0	0	0	6	1	.86	1	.297	.375	.484
1991	St. Louis	NL	81	268	58	7	2	5	(2	3)	84	28	20	39	0	33	1	1	2	14	8	.64	14	.216	.316	.313
1992	St. Louis	NL	131	384	116	19	4	7	(3	4)	164	56	43	39	1	52	1	3	4	18	12	.60	5	.302	.364	.427
1993	St. Louis	NL	137	557	170	40	5	16	(7	9)	268	99	70	56	2	66	4	0	5	15	10	.60	16	.305	.370	.481
1994	St. Louis	NL	105	380	96	22	1	6	(0	6)	138	52	45	39	2	65	10	0	2	15	8	.65	6	.253	.336	.363
1995	St. Louis	NL	121	480	143	33	4	17	(5	12)	235	73	69	42	3	70	5	1	3	12	6	.67	17	.298	.358	.490
6	ML YEARS		593	2133	602	126	18	52	(17	35)	920	319	250	223	8	291	21	5	16	80	45	.64	59	.282	.354	.431

Ed Giovanola

Bats: Left **Throws:** Right **Pos:** 2B **Ht:** 5'10" **Wt:** 170 **Born:** 3/4/69 **Age:** 27

Year	Team	Lg	G	AB	H	2B	3B	HR	(Hm	Rd)	TB	R	RBI	TBB	IBB	SO	HBP	SH	SF	SB	CS	SB%	GDP	Avg	OBP	SLG
1990	Idaho Falls	R	25	98	38	6	0	0	--	--	44	25	13	17	0	9	0	2	1	6	2	.75	0	.388	.474	.449
	Sumter	A	35	119	29	4	0	0	--	--	33	20	8	34	1	17	0	3	0	8	6	.57	0	.244	.412	.277
1991	Durham	A	101	299	76	9	0	6	--	--	103	50	27	57	1	39	2	0	3	18	11	.62	6	.254	.374	.344
1992	Greenville	AA	75	270	72	5	0	5	--	--	92	39	30	29	2	40	0	1	2	4	1	.80	1	.267	.336	.341
1993	Greenville	AA	120	384	108	21	5	5	--	--	154	70	43	84	3	49	2	4	6	6	7	.46	11	.281	.408	.401
1994	Greenville	AA	25	84	20	6	1	4	--	--	40	13	16	10	1	12	0	1	0	2	0	1.00	0	.238	.319	.476
	Richmond	AAA	98	344	97	16	2	6	--	--	135	48	30	31	5	49	3	5	2	7	4	.64	5	.282	.345	.392
1995	Richmond	AAA	99	321	103	18	2	4	--	--	137	45	36	55	3	37	1	4	4	8	7	.53	10	.321	.417	.427
1995	Atlanta	NL	13	14	1	0	0	0	(0	0)	1	2	0	3	0	5	0	0	0	0	0	.00	1	.071	.235	.071

Joe Girardi

Bats: Right **Throws:** Right **Pos:** C **Ht:** 5'11" **Wt:** 195 **Born:** 10/14/64 **Age:** 31

Year	Team	Lg	G	AB	H	2B	3B	HR	(Hm	Rd)	TB	R	RBI	TBB	IBB	SO	HBP	SH	SF	SB	CS	SB%	GDP	Avg	OBP	SLG
1989	Chicago	NL	59	157	39	10	0	1	(0	1)	52	15	14	11	5	26	2	1	1	2	1	.67	4	.248	.304	.331
1990	Chicago	NL	133	419	113	24	2	1	(1	0)	144	36	38	17	11	50	3	4	4	8	3	.73	13	.270	.300	.344
1991	Chicago	NL	21	47	9	2	0	0	(0	0)	11	3	6	6	1	6	0	1	0	0	0	.00	0	.191	.283	.234
1992	Chicago	NL	91	270	73	3	1	1	(1	0)	81	19	12	19	3	38	1	0	1	0	2	.00	8	.270	.320	.300
1993	Colorado	NL	86	310	90	14	5	3	(2	1)	123	35	31	24	0	41	3	12	0	6	6	.50	6	.290	.346	.397

1994 Colorado	NL	93	330	91	9	4	4	(1	3)	120	47	34	21	1	48	2	6	2	3	3	.50	13	.276	.321	.364
1995 Colorado	NL	125	462	121	17	2	8	(6	2)	166	63	55	29	0	76	2	12	1	3	3	.50	15	.262	.308	.359
7 ML YEARS		608	1995	536	79	14	18	(11	7)	697	218	190	127	21	285	13	36	10	22	18	.55	59	.269	.315	.349

Brian Givens

Pitches: Left **Bats:** Right **Pos:** SP **Ht:** 6' 6" **Wt:** 220 **Born:** 11/6/65 **Age:** 30

		HOW MUCH HE PITCHED						WHAT HE GAVE UP									THE RESULTS					
Year Team	Lg	G	GS	CG	GF	IP	BFP	H	R	ER	HR	SH	SF	HB	TBB	IBB	SO	WP	Bk	W	L	Pct.	ShO	Sv	ERA
1984 Kingsport	R	14	10	0	2	44.1	227	41	36	32	2	0	1	3	52	0	51	20	1	4	1	.800	0	0	6.50
1985 Little Fall	A	11	11	3	0	73.2	315	54	28	24	1	4	2	2	43	0	81	2	0	3	4	.429	1	0	2.93
Columbia	A	3	3	1	0	21.1	88	15	7	7	2	0	0	0	13	0	25	6	0	1	2	.333	0	0	2.95
1986 Columbia	A	27	27	2	0	172	753	147	89	72	8	2	3	4	100	1	189	21	0	8	7	.533	1	0	3.77
1987 Tidewater	AAA	1	1	0	0	3.2	25	9	10	10	0	0	0	0	6	0	3	2	0	0	1	.000	0	0	24.55
Lynchburg	A	21	20	3	0	112.1	523	112	79	58	8	5	2	4	69	0	96	19	2	6	8	.429	0	0	4.65
1988 Jackson	AA	26	26	4	0	164.1	689	140	78	69	6	13	5	1	68	2	156	14	11	6	14	.300	3	0	3.78
1989 St. Lucie	A	1	1	0	0	5	25	7	6	0	1	0	0	0	1	0	8	0	0	0	1	.000	0	0	0.00
Jackson	AA	13	13	2	0	85	382	76	39	32	4	1	4	3	55	5	68	11	1	3	5	.375	0	0	3.39
1990 Tidewater	AAA	15	15	0	0	83	376	99	45	38	9	4	1	2	39	0	53	9	0	4	6	.400	0	0	4.12
Calgary	AAA	2	2	0	0	5.2	29	7	8	8	1	0	0	0	8	0	4	1	0	0	1	.000	0	0	12.71
1991 San Bernrdo	A	1	1	0	0	5	20	4	2	1	0	1	0	0	1	0	4	0	0	1	0	1.000	0	0	1.80
Calgary	AAA	3	3	0	0	14.2	65	16	8	8	1	1	0	1	6	0	8	4	1	1	0	1.000	0	0	4.91
1992 Memphis	AA	7	0	0	1	8.1	38	5	5	3	0	1	0	0	7	0	9	1	0	0	0	.000	0	0	3.24
1993 Royals	R	4	4	0	0	8	31	7	3	3	0	0	0	0	1	0	11	0	0	0	1	.000	0	0	3.38
Memphis	AA	14	4	0	7	35.1	154	37	22	18	4	2	3	1	11	0	29	3	0	1	3	.250	0	2	4.58
1994 Birmingham	AA	36	13	1	8	110	480	103	57	45	8	4	1	8	52	6	111	11	0	4	7	.364	1	1	3.68
1995 New Orleans	AAA	16	11	2	1	77.2	320	67	28	22	2	2	3	0	33	1	75	2	2	7	4	.636	1	0	2.55
1995 Milwaukee	AL	19	19	0	0	107.1	481	116	71	59	11	1	1	3	54	0	73	3	2	5	7	.417	0	0	4.95

Tom Glavine

Pitches: Left **Bats:** Left **Pos:** SP **Ht:** 6' 1" **Wt:** 185 **Born:** 3/25/66 **Age:** 30

		HOW MUCH HE PITCHED						WHAT HE GAVE UP									THE RESULTS					
Year Team	Lg	G	GS	CG	GF	IP	BFP	H	R	ER	HR	SH	SF	HB	TBB	IBB	SO	WP	Bk	W	L	Pct.	ShO	Sv	ERA
1987 Atlanta	NL	9	9	0	0	50.1	238	55	34	31	5	2	3	3	33	4	20	1	1	2	4	.333	0	0	5.54
1988 Atlanta	NL	34	34	1	0	195.1	844	201	111	99	12	17	11	8	63	7	84	2	2	7	17	.292	0	0	4.56
1989 Atlanta	NL	29	29	6	0	186	766	172	88	76	20	11	4	2	40	3	90	2	0	14	8	.636	4	0	3.68
1990 Atlanta	NL	33	33	1	0	214.1	929	232	111	102	18	21	2	1	78	10	129	8	1	10	12	.455	0	0	4.28
1991 Atlanta	NL	34	34	9	0	246.2	989	201	83	70	17	7	6	2	69	6	192	10	2	20	11	.645	1	0	2.55
1992 Atlanta	NL	33	33	7	0	225	919	197	81	69	6	2	6	2	70	7	129	5	0	20	8	.714	5	0	2.76
1993 Atlanta	NL	36	36	4	0	239.1	1014	236	91	85	16	10	2	2	90	7	120	4	0	22	6	.786	2	0	3.20
1994 Atlanta	NL	25	25	2	0	165.1	731	173	76	73	10	9	6	1	70	10	140	8	1	13	9	.591	0	0	3.97
1995 Atlanta	NL	29	29	3	0	198.2	822	182	76	68	9	7	5	5	66	0	127	3	0	16	7	.696	1	0	3.08
9 ML YEARS		262	262	33	0	1721	7252	1649	751	673	113	86	45	26	579	54	1031	43	7	124	82	.602	13	0	3.52

Jerry Goff

Bats: Left **Throws:** Right **Pos:** C **Ht:** 6' 3" **Wt:** 207 **Born:** 4/12/64 **Age:** 32

		BATTING																	BASERUNNING				PERCENTAGES		
Year Team	Lg	G	AB	H	2B	3B	HR	(Hm	Rd)	TB	R	RBI	TBB	IBB	SO	HBP	SH	SF	SB	CS	SB%	GDP	Avg	OBP	SLG
1995 Tucson *	AAA	68	207	46	11	1	6	--	--	77	23	34	29	3	56	0	0	2	0	0	.00	3	.222	.315	.372
1990 Montreal	NL	52	119	27	1	0	3	(0	3)	37	14	7	21	4	36	0	1	0	0	2	.00	0	.227	.343	.311
1992 Montreal	NL	3	3	0	0	0	0	(0	0)	0	0	0	0	0	3	0	0	0	0	0	.00	0	.000	.000	.000
1993 Pittsburgh	NL	14	37	11	2	0	2	(2	0)	19	5	6	8	1	9	0	1	0	0	0	.00	0	.297	.422	.514
1994 Pittsburgh	NL	8	25	2	0	0	0	(0	0)	2	0	1	0	0	11	0	1	0	0	0	.00	1	.080	.080	.080
1995 Houston	NL	12	26	4	2	0	1	(1	0)	9	2	3	4	0	13	0	0	0	0	0	.00	1	.154	.267	.346
5 ML YEARS		89	210	44	5	0	6	(3	3)	67	21	17	33	5	72	0	3	0	0	2	.00	2	.210	.317	.319

Greg Gohr

Pitches: Right **Bats:** Right **Pos:** RP **Ht:** 6' 3" **Wt:** 205 **Born:** 10/29/67 **Age:** 28

		HOW MUCH HE PITCHED						WHAT HE GAVE UP									THE RESULTS					
Year Team	Lg	G	GS	CG	GF	IP	BFP	H	R	ER	HR	SH	SF	HB	TBB	IBB	SO	WP	Bk	W	L	Pct.	ShO	Sv	ERA
1995 Toledo *	AAA	6	4	0	1	15.2	68	16	9	5	0	0	0	0	8	0	15	1	0	0	0	.000	0	0	2.87
1993 Detroit	AL	16	0	0	9	22.2	108	26	15	15	1	1	1	2	14	2	23	1	0	0	0	.000	0	0	5.96
1994 Detroit	AL	8	6	0	1	34	159	36	19	17	3	0	1	0	21	1	21	2	1	2	2	.500	0	0	4.50
1995 Detroit	AL	10	0	0	1	10.1	41	9	1	1	0	1	0	0	3	0	12	1	0	1	0	1.000	0	0	0.87
3 ML YEARS		34	6	0	11	67	308	71	35	33	4	2	2	2	38	3	56	4	1	3	2	.600	0	0	4.43

Chris Gomez

Bats: Right **Throws:** Right **Pos:** SS/2B   **Ht:** 6' 1" **Wt:** 188 **Born:** 6/16/71 **Age:** 25

Year	Team	Lg	BATTING																		BASERUNNING				PERCENTAGES		
			G	AB	H	2B	3B	HR	(Hm	Rd)	TB	R	RBI	TBB	IBB	SO	HBP	SH	SF	SB	CS	SB%	GDP	Avg	OBP	SLG
1993	Detroit	AL	46	128	32	7	1	0	(0	0)	41	11	11	9	0	17	1	3	0	2	2	.50	2	.250	.304	.320
1994	Detroit	AL	84	296	76	19	0	8	(5	3)	119	32	53	33	0	64	3	3	1	5	3	.63	8	.257	.336	.402
1995	Detroit	AL	123	431	96	20	2	11	(5	6)	153	49	50	41	0	96	3	3	4	4	1	.80	13	.223	.292	.355
	3 ML YEARS		253	855	204	46	3	19	(10	9)	313	92	114	83	0	177	7	9	5	11	6	.65	23	.239	.309	.366

Leo Gomez

Bats: Right **Throws:** Right **Pos:** 3B   **Ht:** 6' 0" **Wt:** 208 **Born:** 3/2/67 **Age:** 29

Year	Team	Lg	BATTING																		BASERUNNING				PERCENTAGES		
			G	AB	H	2B	3B	HR	(Hm	Rd)	TB	R	RBI	TBB	IBB	SO	HBP	SH	SF	SB	CS	SB%	GDP	Avg	OBP	SLG
1990	Baltimore	AL	12	39	9	0	0	0	(0	0)	9	3	1	8	0	7	0	1	0	0	0	.00	2	.231	.362	.231
1991	Baltimore	AL	118	391	91	17	2	16	(7	9)	160	40	45	40	0	82	2	5	7	1	1	.50	11	.233	.302	.409
1992	Baltimore	AL	137	468	124	24	0	17	(6	11)	199	62	64	63	4	78	8	5	8	2	3	.40	14	.265	.356	.425
1993	Baltimore	AL	71	244	48	7	0	10	(7	3)	85	30	25	32	1	60	3	3	2	0	1	.00	2	.197	.295	.348
1994	Baltimore	AL	84	285	78	20	0	15	(11	4)	143	46	56	41	0	55	3	0	4	0	0	.00	5	.274	.366	.502
1995	Baltimore	AL	53	127	30	5	0	4	(3	1)	47	16	12	18	1	23	2	0	2	0	1	.00	0	.236	.336	.370
	6 ML YEARS		475	1554	380	73	2	62	(34	28)	643	197	203	202	6	305	18	14	23	3	6	.33	34	.245	.334	.414

Pat Gomez

Pitches: Left **Bats:** Left **Pos:** RP   **Ht:** 5'11" **Wt:** 185 **Born:** 3/17/68 **Age:** 28

Year	Team	Lg	HOW MUCH HE PITCHED						WHAT HE GAVE UP												THE RESULTS					
			G	GS	CG	GF	IP	BFP	H	R	ER	HR	SH	SF	HB	TBB	IBB	SO	WP	Bk	W	L	Pct.	ShO	Sv	ERA
1995	Phoenix *	AAA	2	0	0	0	1.1	12	5	5	4	0	0	0	0	3	2	1	1	0	0	0	.000	0	0	27.00
	San Jose *	A	3	2	0	0	6.1	29	5	2	1	0	1	0	0	5	0	5	1	1	0	0	.000	0	0	1.42
1993	San Diego	NL	27	1	0	6	31.2	144	35	19	18	2	1	4	0	19	4	26	2	0	1	2	.333	0	0	5.12
1994	San Francisco	NL	26	0	0	11	33.1	133	23	14	14	2	2	2	0	20	1	14	5	0	0	1	.000	0	0	3.78
1995	San Francisco	NL	18	0	0	3	14	70	16	8	8	2	0	0	0	12	1	15	0	1	0	0	.000	0	0	5.14
	3 ML YEARS		71	1	0	20	79	347	74	41	40	6	3	6	0	51	6	55	7	1	1	3	.250	0	0	4.56

Rene Gonzales

Bats: Right **Throws:** Right **Pos:** 3B   **Ht:** 6' 3" **Wt:** 220 **Born:** 9/3/61 **Age:** 34

Year	Team	Lg	BATTING																		BASERUNNING				PERCENTAGES		
			G	AB	H	2B	3B	HR	(Hm	Rd)	TB	R	RBI	TBB	IBB	SO	HBP	SH	SF	SB	CS	SB%	GDP	Avg	OBP	SLG
1995	Midland *	AA	5	17	3	0	0	0	--	--	3	1	2	4	0	1	0	0	0	0	1	.00	0	.176	.333	.176
	Vancouver *	AAA	50	165	45	12	0	4	--	--	69	27	18	24	1	25	2	0	1	0	0	.00	7	.273	.370	.418
1984	Montreal	NL	29	30	7	1	0	0	(0	0)	8	5	2	2	0	5	1	0	0	0	0	.00	0	.233	.303	.267
1986	Montreal	NL	11	26	3	0	0	0	(0	0)	3	1	0	2	0	7	0	0	0	0	2	.00	0	.115	.179	.115
1987	Baltimore	AL	37	60	16	2	1	1	(1	0)	23	14	7	3	0	11	0	2	0	1	0	1.00	2	.267	.302	.383
1988	Baltimore	AL	92	237	51	6	0	2	(1	1)	63	13	15	13	0	32	3	5	2	2	0	1.00	5	.215	.263	.266
1989	Baltimore	AL	71	166	36	4	0	1	(0	1)	43	16	11	12	0	30	0	6	1	5	3	.63	5	.217	.268	.259
1990	Baltimore	AL	67	103	22	3	1	1	(1	0)	30	13	12	12	0	14	0	6	0	1	2	.33	3	.214	.296	.291
1991	Toronto	AL	71	118	23	3	0	1	(1	0)	29	16	6	12	0	22	4	6	1	0	0	.00	5	.195	.289	.246
1992	California	AL	104	329	91	17	1	7	(6	1)	131	47	38	41	1	46	4	5	1	7	4	.64	17	.277	.363	.398
1993	California	AL	118	335	84	17	0	2	(1	1)	107	34	31	49	2	45	1	2	2	5	5	.50	12	.251	.346	.319
1994	Cleveland	AL	22	23	8	1	1	1	(0	1)	14	6	5	5	0	3	0	1	1	2	0	1.00	0	.348	.448	.609
1995	California	AL	30	18	6	1	0	1	(0	1)	10	1	3	0	0	4	0	0	0	0	0	.00	1	.333	.333	.556
	11 ML YEARS		652	1445	347	55	4	17	(11	6)	461	166	130	151	3	219	13	33	8	23	16	.59	51	.240	.316	.319

Alex Gonzalez

Bats: Right **Throws:** Right **Pos:** SS   **Ht:** 6' 0" **Wt:** 182 **Born:** 4/8/73 **Age:** 23

Year	Team	Lg	BATTING																		BASERUNNING				PERCENTAGES		
			G	AB	H	2B	3B	HR	(Hm	Rd)	TB	R	RBI	TBB	IBB	SO	HBP	SH	SF	SB	CS	SB%	GDP	Avg	OBP	SLG
1991	Blue Jays	R	53	192	40	5	4	0	--	--	53	29	10	12	0	41	3	1	0	7	2	.78	1	.208	.266	.276
1992	Myrtle Bch	A	134	535	145	22	9	10	--	--	215	83	62	38	2	119	3	3	2	26	14	.65	9	.271	.322	.402
1993	Knoxville	AA	142	561	162	29	7	16	--	--	253	93	69	39	2	110	6	0	4	38	13	.75	9	.289	.339	.451
1994	Syracuse	AAA	110	437	124	22	4	12	--	--	190	69	57	53	1	92	1	4	2	23	6	.79	9	.284	.361	.435
1994	Toronto	AL	15	53	8	3	1	0	(0	0)	13	7	1	4	0	17	1	1	0	3	0	1.00	2	.151	.224	.245
1995	Toronto	AL	111	367	89	19	4	10	(8	2)	146	51	42	44	1	114	1	9	4	4	4	.50	7	.243	.322	.398
	2 ML YEARS		126	420	97	22	5	10	(8	2)	159	58	43	48	1	131	2	10	4	7	4	.64	9	.231	.310	.379

Juan Gonzalez

Bats: Right **Throws:** Right **Pos:** DH | **Ht:** 6' 3" **Wt:** 210 **Born:** 10/16/69 **Age:** 26

								BATTING											BASERUNNING				PERCENTAGES		
Year Team	Lg	G	AB	H	2B	3B	HR	(Hm	Rd)	TB	R	RBI	TBB	IBB	SO	HBP	SH	SF	SB	CS	SB%	GDP	Avg	OBP	SLG
1989 Texas	AL	24	60	9	3	0	1	(1	0)	15	6	7	6	0	17	0	2	0	0	0	.00	4	.150	.227	.250
1990 Texas	AL	25	90	26	7	1	4	(3	1)	47	11	12	2	0	18	2	0	1	0	1	.00	2	.289	.316	.522
1991 Texas	AL	142	545	144	34	1	27	(7	20)	261	78	102	42	7	118	5	0	3	4	4	.50	10	.264	.321	.479
1992 Texas	AL	155	584	152	24	2	43	(19	24)	309	77	109	35	1	143	5	0	8	0	1	.00	16	.260	.304	.529
1993 Texas	AL	140	536	166	33	1	46	(24	22)	339	105	118	37	7	99	13	0	1	4	1	.80	12	.310	.368	.632
1994 Texas	AL	107	422	116	18	4	19	(6	13)	199	57	85	30	10	66	7	0	4	6	4	.60	18	.275	.330	.472
1995 Texas	AL	90	352	104	20	2	27	(15	12)	209	57	82	17	3	66	0	0	5	0	0	.00	15	.295	.324	.594
7 ML YEARS		683	2589	717	139	11	167	(75	92)	1379	391	515	169	28	527	32	2	22	14	11	.56	77	.277	.326	.533

Luis Gonzalez

Bats: Left **Throws:** Right **Pos:** LF | **Ht:** 6' 2" **Wt:** 180 **Born:** 9/3/67 **Age:** 28

								BATTING											BASERUNNING				PERCENTAGES		
Year Team	Lg	G	AB	H	2B	3B	HR	(Hm	Rd)	TB	R	RBI	TBB	IBB	SO	HBP	SH	SF	SB	CS	SB%	GDP	Avg	OBP	SLG
1990 Houston	NL	12	21	4	2	0	0	(0	0)	6	1	0	2	1	5	0	0	0	0	0	.00	0	.190	.261	.286
1991 Houston	NL	137	473	120	28	9	13	(4	9)	205	51	69	40	4	101	8	1	4	10	7	.59	9	.254	.320	.433
1992 Houston	NL	122	387	94	19	3	10	(4	6)	149	40	55	24	3	52	2	1	2	7	7	.50	6	.243	.289	.385
1993 Houston	NL	154	540	162	34	3	15	(8	7)	247	82	72	47	7	83	10	3	10	20	9	.69	9	.300	.361	.457
1994 Houston	NL	112	392	107	29	4	8	(3	5)	168	57	67	49	6	57	3	0	6	15	13	.54	10	.273	.353	.429
1995 Hou-ChN	NL	133	471	130	29	8	13	(6	7)	214	69	69	57	8	63	6	1	6	8	8	.43	16	.276	.357	.454
1995 Houston	NL	56	209	54	10	4	6	(1	5)	90	35	35	18	3	30	3	1	3	1	3	.25	8	.258	.322	.431
Chicago	NL	77	262	76	19	4	7	(5	2)	124	34	34	39	5	33	3	0	3	5	5	.50	8	.290	.384	.473
6 ML YEARS		670	2284	617	141	27	59	(25	34)	989	300	332	219	29	361	29	6	28	58	44	.57	50	.270	.338	.433

Curtis Goodwin

Bats: Left **Throws:** Left **Pos:** CF | **Ht:** 5'11" **Wt:** 180 **Born:** 9/30/72 **Age:** 23

								BATTING											BASERUNNING				PERCENTAGES		
Year Team	Lg	G	AB	H	2B	3B	HR	(Hm	Rd)	TB	R	RBI	TBB	IBB	SO	HBP	SH	SF	SB	CS	SB%	GDP	Avg	OBP	SLG
1991 Orioles	R	48	151	39	5	0	0	--	--	44	32	9	38	0	25	1	5	0	26	5	.84	3	.258	.411	.291
1992 Kane County	A	134	542	153	7	5	1	--	--	173	85	42	38	0	106	2	14	0	52	18	.74	1	.282	.332	.319
1993 Frederick	A	138	555	156	15	10	2	--	--	197	98	42	52	0	90	1	7	1	61	15	.80	8	.281	.343	.355
1994 Bowie	AA	142	597	171	18	8	2	--	--	211	105	37	40	0	78	3	13	2	59	10	.86	7	.286	.333	.353
1995 Rochester	AAA	36	140	37	3	3	0	--	--	46	24	7	12	0	15	1	3	0	17	3	.85	4	.264	.327	.329
1995 Baltimore	AL	87	289	76	11	3	1	(0	1)	96	40	24	15	0	53	2	7	3	22	4	.85	5	.263	.301	.332

Tom Goodwin

Bats: Left **Throws:** Right **Pos:** CF/LF | **Ht:** 6' 1" **Wt:** 170 **Born:** 7/27/68 **Age:** 27

								BATTING											BASERUNNING				PERCENTAGES		
Year Team	Lg	G	AB	H	2B	3B	HR	(Hm	Rd)	TB	R	RBI	TBB	IBB	SO	HBP	SH	SF	SB	CS	SB%	GDP	Avg	OBP	SLG
1991 Los Angeles	NL	16	7	1	0	0	0	(0	0)	1	3	0	0	0	0	0	0	0	1	1	.50	0	.143	.143	.143
1992 Los Angeles	NL	57	73	17	1	1	0	(0	0)	20	15	3	6	0	10	0	0	0	7	3	.70	0	.233	.291	.274
1993 Los Angeles	NL	30	17	5	1	0	0	(0	0)	6	6	1	1	0	4	0	0	0	1	2	.33	1	.294	.333	.353
1994 Kansas City	AL	2	2	0	0	0	0	(0	0)	0	0	0	0	0	1	0	0	0	0	0	.00	0	.000	.000	.000
1995 Kansas City	AL	133	480	138	16	3	4	(2	2)	172	72	28	38	0	72	5	14	0	50	18	.74	7	.288	.346	.358
5 ML YEARS		238	579	161	18	4	4	(2	2)	199	96	32	45	0	87	5	14	0	59	24	.71	8	.278	.335	.344

Tom Gordon

Pitches: Right **Bats:** Right **Pos:** SP | **Ht:** 5' 9" **Wt:** 180 **Born:** 11/18/67 **Age:** 28

						HOW MUCH HE PITCHED					WHAT HE GAVE UP										THE RESULTS				
Year Team	Lg	G	GS	CG	GF	IP	BFP	H	R	ER	HR	SH	SF	HB	TBB	IBB	SO	WP	Bk	W	L	Pct.	ShO	Sv	ERA
1988 Kansas City	AL	5	2	0	0	15.2	67	16	9	9	1	0	0	0	7	0	18	0	0	0	2	.000	0	0	5.17
1989 Kansas City	AL	49	16	1	16	163	677	122	67	66	10	4	4	1	86	4	153	12	0	17	9	.654	1	1	3.64
1990 Kansas City	AL	32	32	6	0	195.1	858	192	99	81	17	8	2	3	99	1	175	11	0	12	11	.522	1	0	3.73
1991 Kansas City	AL	45	14	1	11	158	684	129	76	68	16	5	3	4	87	6	167	5	0	9	14	.391	0	1	3.87
1992 Kansas City	AL	40	11	0	13	117.2	516	116	67	60	9	2	6	4	55	4	98	5	2	6	10	.375	0	0	4.59
1993 Kansas City	AL	48	14	2	18	155.2	651	125	65	62	11	6	6	1	77	5	143	17	0	12	6	.667	0	1	3.58
1994 Kansas City	AL	24	24	0	0	155.1	675	136	79	75	15	3	8	3	87	3	126	12	1	11	7	.611	0	0	4.35
1995 Kansas City	AL	31	31	2	0	189	843	204	110	92	12	7	11	4	89	4	119	9	0	12	12	.500	0	0	4.43
8 ML YEARS		274	144	12	58	1149.2	4971	1040	572	514	91	35	40	20	587	27	999	71	3	79	71	.527	2	3	4.02

Jim Gott

Pitches: Right **Bats:** Right **Pos:** RP   **Ht:** 6' 4" **Wt:** 230 **Born:** 8/3/59 **Age:** 36

				HOW MUCH HE PITCHED			WHAT HE GAVE UP										THE RESULTS				
Year	Team	Lg	G	GS	CG	GF	IP	BFP	H	R	ER	HR	SH	SF	HB	TBB	IBB	SO	WP	Bk	W	L	Pct.	ShO	Sv	ERA
1982	Toronto	AL	30	23	1	4	136	600	134	76	67	15	3	2	3	66	0	82	8	0	5	10	.333	1	0	4.43
1983	Toronto	AL	34	30	6	2	176.2	776	195	103	93	15	4	3	5	68	5	121	2	0	9	14	.391	1	0	4.74
1984	Toronto	AL	35	12	1	11	109.2	464	93	54	49	7	7	6	3	49	3	73	1	0	7	6	.538	1	2	4.02
1985	San Francisco	NL	26	26	2	0	148.1	629	144	73	64	10	6	4	1	51	3	78	3	2	7	10	.412	0	0	3.88
1986	San Francisco	NL	9	0	0	3	13	66	16	12	11	0	1	1	0	13	2	9	1	1	0	0	.000	0	1	7.62
1987	Pit-SF	NL	55	3	0	30	87	382	81	43	33	4	2	1	2	40	7	90	5	0	1	2	.333	0	13	3.41
1988	Pittsburgh	NL	67	0	0	59	77.1	314	68	30	30	9	7	3	2	22	5	76	1	6	6	6	.500	0	34	3.49
1989	Pittsburgh	NL	1	0	0	0	0.2	4	1	0	0	0	0	0	0	1	0	1	0	0	0	0	.000	0	0	0.00
1990	Los Angeles	NL	50	0	0	24	62	270	59	27	20	5	2	4	0	34	7	44	4	0	3	5	.375	0	3	2.90
1991	Los Angeles	NL	55	0	0	26	76	322	63	28	25	5	6	1	1	32	7	73	6	3	4	3	.571	0	2	2.96
1992	Los Angeles	NL	68	0	0	28	88	369	72	27	24	4	6	1	1	41	13	75	9	3	3	3	.500	0	6	2.45
1993	Los Angeles	NL	62	0	0	45	77.2	313	71	23	20	6	7	2	1	17	5	67	5	0	4	8	.333	0	25	2.32
1994	Los Angeles	NL	37	0	0	17	36.1	172	46	24	24	3	5	1	3	20	4	29	4	0	5	3	.625	0	2	5.94
1995	Pittsburgh	NL	25	0	0	12	31.1	147	38	26	21	2	1	1	1	12	2	19	3	0	2	4	.333	0	3	6.03
1987	Pittsburgh	NL	25	0	0	22	31	129	28	11	5	0	1	0	0	8	2	27	2	0	0	2	.000	0	13	1.45
	San Francisco	NL	30	3	0	8	56	253	53	32	28	4	1	1	2	32	5	63	3	0	1	0	1.000	0	0	4.50
	14 ML YEARS		554	96	10	261	1120	4828	1081	546	481	85	57	30	23	466	63	837	52	15	56	74	.431	3	91	3.87

Mark Grace

Bats: Left **Throws:** Left **Pos:** 1B   **Ht:** 6' 2" **Wt:** 190 **Born:** 6/28/64 **Age:** 32

									BATTING											BASERUNNING				PERCENTAGES		
Year	Team	Lg	G	AB	H	2B	3B	HR	(Hm	Rd)	TB	R	RBI	TBB	IBB	SO	HBP	SH	SF	SB	CS	SB%	GDP	Avg	OBP	SLG
1988	Chicago	NL	134	486	144	23	4	7	(0	7)	196	65	57	60	5	43	0	0	4	3	3	.50	12	.296	.371	.403
1989	Chicago	NL	142	510	160	28	3	13	(8	5)	233	74	79	80	13	42	0	3	3	14	7	.67	13	.314	.405	.457
1990	Chicago	NL	157	589	182	32	1	9	(4	5)	243	72	82	59	5	54	5	1	8	15	6	.71	10	.309	.372	.413
1991	Chicago	NL	160	619	169	28	5	8	(5	3)	231	87	58	70	7	53	3	4	7	3	4	.43	6	.273	.346	.373
1992	Chicago	NL	158	603	185	37	5	9	(5	4)	259	72	79	72	8	36	4	2	8	6	1	.86	14	.307	.380	.430
1993	Chicago	NL	155	594	193	39	4	14	(5	9)	282	86	98	71	14	32	1	1	9	8	4	.67	25	.325	.393	.475
1994	Chicago	NL	106	403	120	23	3	6	(5	1)	167	55	44	48	5	41	0	0	3	0	1	.00	10	.298	.370	.414
1995	Chicago	NL	143	552	180	51	3	16	(4	12)	285	97	92	65	9	46	2	1	7	6	2	.75	10	.326	.395	.516
	8 ML YEARS		1155	4356	1333	261	28	82	(36	46)	1896	608	589	525	66	347	15	12	49	55	28	.66	100	.306	.379	.435

Mike Grace

Pitches: Right **Bats:** Right **Pos:** SP   **Ht:** 6' 4" **Wt:** 210 **Born:** 6/20/70 **Age:** 26

				HOW MUCH HE PITCHED			WHAT HE GAVE UP										THE RESULTS				
Year	Team	Lg	G	GS	CG	GF	IP	BFP	H	R	ER	HR	SH	SF	HB	TBB	IBB	SO	WP	Bk	W	L	Pct.	ShO	Sv	ERA
1991	Batavia	A	6	6	0	0	32.1	123	20	9	5	3	2	0	1	14	1	36	1	2	1	2	.333	0	0	1.39
	Spartanburg	A	6	6	0	0	33.1	127	24	7	7	1	2	1	0	9	0	23	1	0	3	1	.750	0	0	1.89
1992	Spartanburg	A	6	6	0	0	27.1	114	25	16	15	3	0	0	1	8	0	21	2	0	0	1	.000	0	0	4.94
1994	Spartanburg	A	15	15	0	0	80.1	345	84	50	43	6	4	1	8	20	1	45	2	0	5	5	.500	0	0	4.82
1995	Reading	AA	24	24	2	0	147.1	606	137	65	58	13	5	0	6	35	0	118	3	2	13	6	.684	0	0	3.54
	Scranton-Wb	AAA	2	2	1	0	17	68	17	3	3	0	0	0	0	2	0	13	2	0	2	0	1.000	0	0	1.59
1995	Philadelphia	NL	2	2	0	0	11.1	47	10	4	4	0	0	0	0	4	0	7	0	0	1	1	.500	0	0	3.18

Joe Grahe

Pitches: Right **Bats:** Right **Pos:** SP/RP   **Ht:** 6' 0" **Wt:** 200 **Born:** 8/14/67 **Age:** 28

				HOW MUCH HE PITCHED			WHAT HE GAVE UP										THE RESULTS				
Year	Team	Lg	G	GS	CG	GF	IP	BFP	H	R	ER	HR	SH	SF	HB	TBB	IBB	SO	WP	Bk	W	L	Pct.	ShO	Sv	ERA
1995	Colo. Sprng *	AAA	2	2	1	0	11	41	7	4	4	1	1	1	0	3	0	4	0	0	1	1	.500	0	0	3.27
1990	California	AL	8	8	0	0	43.1	200	51	30	24	3	0	0	3	23	1	25	1	0	3	4	.429	0	0	4.98
1991	California	AL	18	10	1	2	73	330	84	43	39	2	1	1	3	33	0	40	2	0	3	7	.300	0	0	4.81
1992	California	AL	46	7	0	31	94.2	399	85	37	37	5	4	4	6	39	2	39	3	0	5	6	.455	0	21	3.52
1993	California	AL	45	0	0	32	56.2	247	54	22	18	5	2	3	2	25	4	31	3	0	4	1	.800	0	11	2.86
1994	California	AL	40	0	0	32	43.1	218	68	33	32	5	3	3	6	18	4	26	4	1	2	5	.286	0	13	6.65
1995	Colorado	NL	17	9	0	0	56.2	265	69	42	32	6	3	3	3	27	2	27	3	2	4	3	.571	0	0	5.08
	6 ML YEARS		174	34	1	97	367.2	1659	411	207	182	26	13	14	23	165	13	188	16	3	21	26	.447	0	45	4.46

Craig Grebeck

Bats: Right **Throws:** Right **Pos:** SS/3B   **Ht:** 5' 7" **Wt:** 148 **Born:** 12/29/64 **Age:** 31

									BATTING											BASERUNNING				PERCENTAGES		
Year	Team	Lg	G	AB	H	2B	3B	HR	(Hm	Rd)	TB	R	RBI	TBB	IBB	SO	HBP	SH	SF	SB	CS	SB%	GDP	Avg	OBP	SLG
1990	Chicago	AL	59	119	20	3	1	1	(1	0)	28	7	9	8	0	24	2	3	3	0	0	.00	2	.168	.227	.235

Year	Team	Lg	G	AB	H	2B	3B	HR	(Hm	Rd)	TB	R	RBI	TBB	IBB	SO	HBP	SH	SF	SB	CS	SB%	GDP	Avg	OBP	SLG
1991	Chicago	AL	107	224	63	16	3	6	(3	3)	103	37	31	38	0	40	1	4	1	1	3	.25	3	.281	.386	.460
1992	Chicago	AL	88	287	77	21	2	3	(2	1)	111	24	35	30	0	34	3	10	3	0	3	.00	5	.268	.341	.387
1993	Chicago	AL	72	190	43	5	0	1	(0	1)	51	25	12	26	0	26	0	7	0	1	2	.33	9	.226	.319	.268
1994	Chicago	AL	35	97	30	5	0	0	(0	0)	35	17	5	12	0	5	1	3	0	0	0	.00		.309	.391	.361
1995	Chicago	AL	53	154	40	12	0	1	(0	1)	55	19	18	21	0	23	3	4	0	0	0	.00	4	.260	.360	.357
	6 ML YEARS		414	1071	273	62	6	12	(6	6)	383	129	110	135	0	152	10	31	7	2	8	.20	24	.255	.342	.358

Shawn Green

Bats: Left **Throws:** Left **Pos:** RF   **Ht:** 6' 4" **Wt:** 190 **Born:** 11/10/72 **Age:** 23

Year	Team	Lg	G	AB	H	2B	3B	HR	(Hm	Rd)	TB	R	RBI	TBB	IBB	SO	HBP	SH	SF	SB	CS	SB%	GDP	Avg	OBP	SLG
1992	Dunedin	A	114	417	114	21	3	1	--	--	144	44	49	28	0	66	4	5	8	22	9	.71	9	.273	.319	.345
1993	Knoxville	AA	99	360	102	14	2	4	--	--	132	40	34	26	2	72	5	6	1	4	9	.31	6	.283	.339	.367
1994	Syracuse	AAA	109	433	149	27	3	13	--	--	221	82	61	40	2	54	4	2	4	19	7	.73	5	.344	.401	.510
1993	Toronto	AL	3	6	0	0	0	0	(0	0)	0	0	0	0	0	1	0	0	0	0	0	.00	0	.000	.000	.000
1994	Toronto	AL	14	33	3	1	0	0	(0	0)	4	1	1	1	0	8	0	0	0	1	0	1.00	1	.091	.118	.121
1995	Toronto	AL	121	379	109	31	4	15	(5	10)	193	52	54	20	3	68	3	0	3	1	2	.33	4	.288	.326	.509
	3 ML YEARS		138	418	112	32	4	15	(5	10)	197	53	55	21	3	77	3	0	3	2	2	.50	5	.268	.306	.471

Tyler Green

Pitches: Right **Bats:** Right **Pos:** SP   **Ht:** 6' 5" **Wt:** 204 **Born:** 2/18/70 **Age:** 26

Year	Team	Lg	G	GS	CG	GF	IP	BFP	H	R	ER	HR	SH	SF	HB	TBB	IBB	SO	WP	Bk	W	L	Pct.	ShO	Sv	ERA
1991	Batavia	A	3	3	0	0	15	58	7	2	2	0	0	0	2	6	0	19	2	0	1	0	1.000	0	0	1.20
	Clearwater	A	2	2	0	0	13	50	3	2	2	0	0	0	0	8	0	20	2	0	2	0	1.000	0	0	1.38
1992	Reading	AA	12	12	0	0	62.1	249	46	16	13	2	4	1	1	20	0	67	5	0	6	3	.667	0	0	1.88
	Scranton-Wb	AAA	2	2	0	0	10.1	50	7	7	7	1	0	0	1	12	0	15	0	1	0	1	.000	0	0	6.10
1993	Scranton-Wb	AAA	28	14	4	6	118.1	496	102	62	52	8	3	4	5	43	2	87	8	2	6	10	.375	0	0	3.95
1994	Scranton-Wb	AAA	27	26	4	0	162	725	179	110	100	25	4	4	12	77	3	95	14	1	7	16	.304	0	0	5.56
1993	Philadelphia	NL	3	2	0	1	7.1	41	16	9	6	1	0	0	0	5	0	7	2	0	0	0	.000	0	0	7.36
1995	Philadelphia	NL	26	25	4	0	140.2	623	157	86	83	15	5	6	4	66	3	85	9	2	8	9	.471	2	0	5.31
	2 ML YEARS		29	27	4	1	148	664	173	95	89	16	5	6	4	71	3	92	11	2	8	9	.471	2	0	5.41

Tommy Greene

Pitches: Right **Bats:** Right **Pos:** SP/RP   **Ht:** 6' 5" **Wt:** 222 **Born:** 4/6/67 **Age:** 29

Year	Team	Lg	G	GS	CG	GF	IP	BFP	H	R	ER	HR	SH	SF	HB	TBB	IBB	SO	WP	Bk	W	L	Pct.	ShO	Sv	ERA
1995	Clearwater *	A	3	3	0	0	20	77	12	7	7	2	0	0	2	7	0	20	1	0	0	3	.000	0	0	3.15
	Scrantn-WB *	AAA	4	4	0	0	28.1	105	18	8	7	1	1	1	0	6	0	19	5	0	3	0	1.000	0	0	2.22
1989	Atlanta	NL	4	4	1	0	26.1	103	22	12	12	5	1	2	0	6	1	17	1	0	1	2	.333	1	0	4.10
1990	Atl-Phi	NL	15	9	0	1	51.1	227	50	31	29	8	5	0	1	26	1	21	1	0	3	3	.500	0	0	5.08
1991	Philadelphia	NL	36	27	3	3	207.2	857	177	85	78	19	9	11	3	66	4	154	9	1	13	7	.650	2	0	3.38
1992	Philadelphia	NL	13	12	0	0	64.1	298	75	39	38	5	4	2	0	34	2	39	1	0	3	3	.500	0	0	5.32
1993	Philadelphia	NL	31	30	7	0	200	834	175	84	76	12	9	9	3	62	3	167	15	0	16	4	.800	2	0	3.42
1994	Philadelphia	NL	7	7	0	0	35.2	164	37	20	18	5	5	1	0	22	0	28	2	0	2	0	1.000	0	0	4.54
1995	Philadelphia	NL	11	6	0	3	33.2	167	45	32	31	6	2	1	3	20	0	24	3	1	0	5	.000	0	0	8.29
1990	Atlanta	NL	5	2	0	0	12.1	61	14	11	11	3	2	0	1	9	0	4	0	0	1	0	1.000	0	0	8.03
	Philadelphia	NL	10	7	0	1	39	166	36	20	18	5	3	0	0	17	1	17	1	0	2	3	.400	0	0	4.15
	7 ML YEARS		117	95	11	7	619	2650	581	303	282	60	35	26	10	236	11	450	32	2	38	24	.613	5	0	4.10

Willie Greene

Bats: Left **Throws:** Right **Pos:** 3B   **Ht:** 5'11" **Wt:** 185 **Born:** 9/23/71 **Age:** 24

Year	Team	Lg	G	AB	H	2B	3B	HR	(Hm	Rd)	TB	R	RBI	TBB	IBB	SO	HBP	SH	SF	SB	CS	SB%	GDP	Avg	OBP	SLG
1995	Indianapols *	AAA	91	325	79	12	2	19	--	--	152	57	45	38	2	67	3	0	4	3	3	.50	6	.243	.324	.468
1992	Cincinnati	NL	29	93	25	5	2	2	(2	0)	40	10	13	10	0	23	0	0	1	0	2	.00	1	.269	.337	.430
1993	Cincinnati	NL	15	50	8	1	1	2	(2	0)	17	7	5	2	0	19	0	0	1	0	0	.00	1	.160	.189	.340
1994	Cincinnati	NL	16	37	8	2	0	0	(0	0)	10	5	3	6	1	14	0	0	1	0	0	.00	1	.216	.318	.270
1995	Cincinnati	NL	8	19	2	0	0	0	(0	0)	2	1	0	3	0	7	0	0	0	0	0	.00	0	.105	.227	.105
	4 ML YEARS		68	199	43	8	3	4	(4	0)	69	23	21	21	1	63	0	0	3	0	2	.00	4	.216	.287	.347

Mike Greenwell

Bats: Left **Throws:** Right **Pos:** LF   **Ht:** 6' 0" **Wt:** 200 **Born:** 7/18/63 **Age:** 32

Year	Team	Lg	G	AB	H	2B	3B	HR	(Hm	Rd)	TB	R	RBI	TBB	IBB	SO	HBP	SH	SF	SB	CS	SB%	GDP	Avg	OBP	SLG
1995	Pawtucket *	AAA	1	4	2	2	0	0	--	--	4	0	0	1	0	0	0	0	0	1	0	1.00	0	.500	.600	1.000

Year	Team	Lg	G	AB	H	2B	3B	HR	(Hm	Rd)	TB	R	RBI	TBB	IBB	SO	HBP	SH	SF	SB	CS	SB%	GDP	Avg	OBP	SLG
1985	Boston	AL	17	31	10	1	0	4	(1	3)	23	7	8	3	1	4	0	0	0	1	0	1.00	0	.323	.382	.742
1986	Boston	AL	31	35	11	2	0	0	(0	0)	13	4	4	5	0	7	0	0	0	0	0	.00	1	.314	.400	.371
1987	Boston	AL	125	412	135	31	6	19	(8	11)	235	71	89	35	1	40	6	0	3	5	4	.56	7	.328	.386	.570
1988	Boston	AL	158	590	192	39	8	22	(12	10)	313	86	119	87	18	38	9	0	7	16	8	.67	11	.325	.416	.531
1989	Boston	AL	145	578	178	36	0	14	(6	8)	256	87	95	56	15	44	3	0	4	13	5	.72	21	.308	.370	.443
1990	Boston	AL	159	610	181	30	6	14	(6	8)	265	71	73	65	12	43	4	0	3	8	7	.53	19	.297	.367	.434
1991	Boston	AL	147	544	163	26	6	9	(5	4)	228	76	83	43	6	35	3	1	7	15	5	.75	11	.300	.350	.419
1992	Boston	AL	49	180	42	2	0	2	(0	2)	50	16	18	18	1	19	2	0	2	2	3	.40	8	.233	.307	.278
1993	Boston	AL	146	540	170	38	6	13	(6	7)	259	77	72	54	12	46	4	2	3	5	4	.56	17	.315	.379	.480
1994	Boston	AL	95	327	88	25	1	11	(10	1)	148	60	45	38	6	26	4	0	5	2	2	.50	12	.269	.348	.453
1995	Boston	AL	120	481	143	25	4	15	(6	9)	221	67	76	38	4	35	2	0	4	9	5	.64	18	.297	.349	.459
11 ML YEARS			1192	4328	1313	255	37	123	(60	63)	2011	622	682	442	76	337	37	3	38	76	43	.64	125	.303	.370	.465

Kenny Greer

Pitches: Right **Bats:** Right **Pos:** RP **Ht:** 6' 2" **Wt:** 215 **Born:** 5/12/67 **Age:** 29

Year	Team	Lg	G	GS	CG	GF	IP	BFP	H	R	ER	HR	SH	SF	HB	TBB	IBB	SO	WP	Bk	W	L	Pct.	ShO	Sv	ERA
1988	Oneonta	A	15	15	4	0	112.1	470	109	46	30	0	5	4	7	18	2	60	6	6	5	5	.500	0	0	2.40
1989	Pr. William	A	29	13	3	7	111.2	461	101	56	52	3	2	2	7	22	0	44	4	1	7	3	.700	1	2	4.19
1990	Ft. Laud	A	38	5	0	11	89.1	417	115	64	54	5	9	5	7	33	2	55	3	3	4	9	.308	0	1	5.44
	Pr. William	A	1	1	0	0	7.2	32	7	2	2	0	0	1	0	2	0	7	0	0	1	0	1.000	0	0	2.35
1991	Ft. Laud	A	31	1	0	12	57.1	245	49	31	27	3	1	1	7	22	2	46	5	0	4	3	.571	0	0	4.24
1992	Pr. William	A	13	0	0	6	27	112	25	11	11	1	0	0	1	9	0	30	1	0	1	2	.333	0	1	3.67
	Albany-Colo	AA	40	1	0	18	68.2	280	48	19	14	1	2	1	0	30	4	53	6	0	4	1	.800	0	4	1.83
	Columbus	AAA	1	0	0	1	1	7	3	2	1	0	0	0	0	1	0	1	0	0	0	0	.000	0	0	9.00
1993	Columbus	AAA	46	0	0	21	79.1	347	78	41	39	5	4	4	2	36	6	50	2	0	9	4	.692	0	6	4.42
1994	Mets	R	4	2	0	0	6	24	7	2	2	0	0	0	0	0	0	3	1	0	0	0	.000	0	0	3.00
	Norfolk	AAA	25	0	0	12	31	138	35	14	13	2	0	1	3	11	2	18	3	0	1	1	.500	0	1	3.77
1995	Phoenix	AAA	38	0	0	13	63.1	270	65	29	28	1	3	2	2	19	1	41	5	0	5	2	.714	0	1	3.98
1993	New York	NL	1	0	0	1	1	3	0	0	0	0	0	0	0	0	0	2	0	0	1	0	1.000	0	0	0.00
1995	San Francisco	NL	8	0	0	1	12	61	15	12	7	3	2	1	1	5	2	7	0	0	0	2	.000	0	0	5.25
2 ML YEARS			9	0	0	2	13	64	15	12	7	3	2	1	1	5	2	9	0	0	1	2	.333	0	0	4.85

Rusty Greer

Bats: Left **Throws:** Left **Pos:** RF/LF **Ht:** 6' 0" **Wt:** 190 **Born:** 1/21/69 **Age:** 27

Year	Team	Lg	G	AB	H	2B	3B	HR	(Hm	Rd)	TB	R	RBI	TBB	IBB	SO	HBP	SH	SF	SB	CS	SB%	GDP	Avg	OBP	SLG
1990	Butte	R	62	226	78	12	6	10	--	--	132	48	50	41	2	23	1	0	2	9	7	.56	9	.345	.444	.584
1991	Charlotte	A	111	388	114	24	1	5	--	--	155	52	48	66	4	47	2	1	5	12	6	.67	15	.294	.395	.399
	Tulsa	AA	20	64	19	3	2	3	--	--	35	12	12	17	1	6	1	0	0	2	0	1.00	5	.297	.451	.547
1992	Tulsa	AA	106	359	96	22	4	5	--	--	141	47	37	60	6	63	5	0	4	2	2	.50	11	.267	.376	.393
1993	Tulsa	AA	129	474	138	25	6	15	--	--	220	76	59	53	4	79	4	1	3	10	5	.67	11	.291	.365	.464
	Okla. City	AAA	8	27	6	2	0	1	--	--	11	6	4	6	0	7	0	0	0	0	0	.00	0	.222	.364	.407
1994	Okla. City	AAA	31	111	35	12	1	3	--	--	58	18	13	18	1	24	1	0	1	1	1	.50	2	.315	.412	.523
1994	Texas	AL	80	277	87	16	1	10	(3	7)	135	36	46	46	2	46	2	2	4	0	0	.00	3	.314	.410	.487
1995	Texas	AL	131	417	113	21	2	13	(7	6)	177	58	61	55	1	66	1	2	3	3	1	.75	9	.271	.355	.424
2 ML YEARS			211	694	200	37	3	23	(10	13)	312	94	107	101	3	112	3	4	7	3	1	.75	12	.288	.378	.450

Tommy Gregg

Bats: Left **Throws:** Left **Pos:** RF **Ht:** 6' 1" **Wt:** 190 **Born:** 7/29/63 **Age:** 32

Year	Team	Lg	G	AB	H	2B	3B	HR	(Hm	Rd)	TB	R	RBI	TBB	IBB	SO	HBP	SH	SF	SB	CS	SB%	GDP	Avg	OBP	SLG
1995	Charlotte *	AAA	34	124	48	10	1	9	--	--	87	30	32	21	2	13	1	0	1	7	0	1.00	3	.387	.476	.702
1987	Pittsburgh	NL	10	8	2	1	0	0	(0	0)	3	3	0	0	0	2	0	0	0	0	0	.00	2	.250	.250	.375
1988	Atl-Pit	NL	25	44	13	4	0	1	(0	1)	20	5	7	3	1	6	0	0	1	0	1	.00	1	.295	.333	.455
1989	Atlanta	NL	102	276	67	8	0	6	(2	4)	93	24	23	18	2	45	0	3	1	3	4	.43	4	.243	.288	.337
1990	Atlanta	NL	124	239	63	13	1	5	(2	3)	93	18	32	20	4	39	1	0	1	4	3	.57	1	.264	.322	.389
1991	Atlanta	NL	72	107	20	8	1	1	(1	0)	33	13	4	12	2	24	1	0	0	2	2	.50	1	.187	.275	.308
1992	Atlanta	NL	18	19	5	0	0	1	(1	0)	8	1	1	1	0	7	0	0	0	1	0	1.00	1	.263	.300	.421
1993	Cincinnati	NL	10	12	2	0	0	0	(0	0)	2	1	1	0	0	0	0	0	1	0	0	.00	0	.167	.154	.167
1995	Florida	NL	72	156	37	5	0	6	(2	4)	60	20	20	16	1	33	2	0	2	3	1	.75	3	.237	.313	.385
1988	Atlanta	NL	11	29	10	3	0	0	(0	0)	13	1	4	2	1	2	0	0	0	0	0	.00	1	.345	.387	.448
	Pittsburgh	NL	14	15	3	1	0	1	(0	1)	7	4	3	1	0	4	0	0	1	0	0	.00	0	.200	.235	.467
8 ML YEARS			433	861	209	39	2	20	(8	12)	312	85	88	70	10	156	4	3	6	13	11	.54	13	.243	.301	.362

Ken Griffey Jr

Bats: Left **Throws:** Left **Pos:** CF **Ht:** 6' 3" **Wt:** 205 **Born:** 11/21/69 **Age:** 26

Year Team	Lg	G	AB	H	2B	3B	HR	(Hm	Rd)	TB	R	RBI	TBB	IBB	SO	HBP	SH	SF	SB	CS	SB%	GDP	Avg	OBP	SLG
1995 Tacoma *	AAA	1	3	0	0	0	0	--	--	0	0	0	0	0	1	0	0	0	0	0	.00	0	.000	.000	.000
1989 Seattle	AL	127	455	120	23	0	16	(10	6)	191	61	61	44	8	83	2	1	4	16	7	.70	4	.264	.329	.420
1990 Seattle	AL	155	597	179	28	7	22	(8	14)	287	91	80	63	12	81	2	0	4	16	11	.59	12	.300	.366	.481
1991 Seattle	AL	154	548	179	42	1	22	(16	6)	289	76	100	71	21	82	1	4	9	18	6	.75	10	.327	.399	.527
1992 Seattle	AL	142	565	174	39	4	27	(16	11)	302	83	103	44	15	67	5	0	3	10	5	.67	15	.308	.361	.535
1993 Seattle	AL	156	582	180	38	3	45	(21	24)	359	113	109	96	25	91	6	0	7	17	9	.65	14	.309	.408	.617
1994 Seattle	AL	111	433	140	24	4	40	(18	22)	292	94	90	56	19	73	2	0	2	11	3	.79	9	.323	.402	.674
1995 Seattle	AL	72	260	67	7	0	17	(13	4)	125	52	42	52	6	53	0	0	2	4	2	.67	4	.258	.379	.481
7 ML YEARS		917	3440	1039	201	19	189	(102	87)	1845	570	585	426	106	530	18	5	31	92	43	.68	68	.302	.379	.536

Jason Grimsley

Pitches: Right **Bats:** Right **Pos:** RP **Ht:** 6' 3" **Wt:** 180 **Born:** 8/7/67 **Age:** 28

Year Team	Lg	G	GS	CG	GF	IP	BFP	H	R	ER	HR	SH	SF	HB	TBB	IBB	SO	WP	Bk	W	L	Pct.	ShO	Sv	ERA
1995 Buffalo *	AAA	10	10	2	0	68	285	61	26	22	4	2	3	3	19	0	40	4	0	5	3	.625	0	0	2.91
1989 Philadelphia	NL	4	4	0	0	18.1	91	19	13	12	2	1	0	0	19	1	7	2	0	1	3	.250	0	0	5.89
1990 Philadelphia	NL	11	11	0	0	57.1	255	47	21	21	1	2	1	2	43	0	41	6	1	3	2	.600	0	0	3.30
1991 Philadelphia	NL	12	12	0	0	61	272	54	34	33	4	3	2	1	41	3	42	14	0	1	7	.125	0	0	4.87
1993 Cleveland	AL	10	6	0	1	42.1	194	52	26	25	3	1	0	1	20	1	27	2	0	3	4	.429	0	0	5.31
1994 Cleveland	AL	14	13	1	0	82.2	368	91	47	42	7	4	2	6	34	1	59	6	1	5	2	.714	0	0	4.57
1995 Cleveland	AL	15	2	0	2	34	165	37	24	23	4	1	2	2	32	1	25	7	0	0	0	.000	0	1	6.09
6 ML YEARS		66	48	1	3	295.2	1345	300	165	156	21	12	7	14	189	7	201	37	2	13	18	.419	0	1	4.75

Marquis Grissom

Bats: Right **Throws:** Right **Pos:** CF **Ht:** 5'11" **Wt:** 190 **Born:** 4/17/67 **Age:** 29

Year Team	Lg	G	AB	H	2B	3B	HR	(Hm	Rd)	TB	R	RBI	TBB	IBB	SO	HBP	SH	SF	SB	CS	SB%	GDP	Avg	OBP	SLG
1989 Montreal	NL	26	74	19	2	0	1	(0	1)	24	16	2	12	0	21	0	1	0	1	0	1.00	1	.257	.360	.324
1990 Montreal	NL	98	288	74	14	2	3	(2	1)	101	42	29	27	2	40	0	4	1	22	2	.92	3	.257	.320	.351
1991 Montreal	NL	148	558	149	23	9	6	(3	3)	208	73	39	34	0	89	1	4	0	76	17	.82	8	.267	.310	.373
1992 Montreal	NL	159	653	180	39	6	14	(8	6)	273	99	66	42	6	81	5	3	4	78	13	.86	12	.276	.322	.418
1993 Montreal	NL	157	630	188	27	2	19	(9	10)	276	104	95	52	6	76	3	0	8	53	10	.84	9	.298	.351	.438
1994 Montreal	NL	110	475	137	25	4	11	(4	7)	203	96	45	41	4	66	1	0	4	36	6	.86	10	.288	.344	.427
1995 Atlanta	NL	139	551	142	23	3	12	(5	7)	207	80	42	47	4	61	3	1	4	29	9	.76	8	.258	.317	.376
7 ML YEARS		837	3229	889	153	26	66	(31	35)	1292	510	318	255	22	434	13	13	21	295	57	.84	51	.275	.329	.400

Buddy Groom

Pitches: Left **Bats:** Left **Pos:** RP/SP **Ht:** 6' 2" **Wt:** 200 **Born:** 7/10/65 **Age:** 30

Year Team	Lg	G	GS	CG	GF	IP	BFP	H	R	ER	HR	SH	SF	HB	TBB	IBB	SO	WP	Bk	W	L	Pct.	ShO	Sv	ERA
1995 Toledo *	AAA	6	5	1	0	33	132	31	14	7	4	1	0	0	4	0	24	0	0	2	3	.400	0	0	1.91
1992 Detroit	AL	12	7	0	3	38.2	177	48	28	25	4	3	2	0	22	4	15	0	1	0	5	.000	0	0	5.82
1993 Detroit	AL	19	3	0	8	36.2	170	48	25	25	4	2	4	2	13	5	15	2	1	0	0	.000	0	0	6.14
1994 Detroit	AL	40	0	0	10	32	139	31	14	14	4	0	3	2	13	2	27	0	0	0	1	.000	0	1	3.94
1995 Det-Fla		37	4	0	11	55.2	274	81	47	46	8	2	2	2	32	4	35	3	0	2	5	.286	0	1	7.44
1995 Detroit	AL	23	4	0	6	40.2	203	55	35	34	6	2	2	2	26	4	23	3	0	1	3	.250	0	1	7.52
Florida	NL	14	0	0	5	15	71	26	12	12	2	0	0	0	6	0	12	0	0	1	2	.333	0	0	7.20
4 ML YEARS		108	14	0	32	163	760	208	114	110	20	7	11	6	80	15	92	5	2	2	13	.133	0	3	6.07

Kevin Gross

Pitches: Right **Bats:** Right **Pos:** SP **Ht:** 6' 5" **Wt:** 227 **Born:** 6/8/61 **Age:** 35

Year Team	Lg	G	GS	CG	GF	IP	BFP	H	R	ER	HR	SH	SF	HB	TBB	IBB	SO	WP	Bk	W	L	Pct.	ShO	Sv	ERA
1983 Philadelphia	NL	17	17	1	0	96	418	100	46	38	13	2	1	3	35	3	66	4	1	4	6	.400	1	0	3.56
1984 Philadelphia	NL	44	14	1	9	129	566	140	66	59	8	9	3	5	44	4	84	4	4	8	5	.615	0	1	4.12
1985 Philadelphia	NL	38	31	6	0	205.2	873	194	86	78	11	7	5	7	81	6	151	2	0	15	13	.536	2	0	3.41
1986 Philadelphia	NL	37	36	7	0	241.2	1040	240	115	108	28	8	6	5	94	2	154	2	1	12	12	.500	2	0	4.02
1987 Philadelphia	NL	34	33	3	1	200.2	878	205	107	97	26	8	6	10	87	7	110	3	7	9	16	.360	1	0	4.35
1988 Philadelphia	NL	33	33	5	0	231.2	989	209	101	95	18	9	4	11	89	5	162	5	7	12	14	.462	1	0	3.69
1989 Montreal	NL	31	31	4	0	201.1	867	188	105	98	20	10	3	6	88	6	158	5	5	11	12	.478	3	0	4.38
1990 Montreal	NL	31	26	2	3	163.1	712	171	86	83	9	4	9	4	65	7	111	4	1	9	12	.429	1	0	4.57
1991 Los Angeles	NL	46	10	0	16	115.2	509	123	55	46	10	6	4	2	50	6	95	3	0	10	11	.476	0	3	3.58
1992 Los Angeles	NL	34	30	4	0	204.2	856	182	82	72	11	14	6	3	77	10	158	4	2	8	13	.381	3	0	3.17

Year	Team	Lg	G	GS	CG	GF	IP	BFP	H	R	ER	HR	SH	SF	HB	TBB	IBB	SO	WP	Bk	W	L	Pct.	ShO	Sv	ERA
1993	Los Angeles	NL	33	32	3	1	202.1	892	224	110	93	15	11	6	5	74	7	150	2	5	13	13	.500	0	0	4.14
1994	Los Angeles	NL	25	23	1	2	157.1	665	162	64	63	11	4	1	2	43	2	124	4	1	9	7	.563	0	1	3.60
1995	Texas	AL	31	30	4	0	183.2	825	200	124	113	27	5	7	8	89	8	106	5	0	9	15	.375	0	0	5.54
13 ML YEARS			434	346	41	32	2333	10090	2338	1147	1043	207	99	60	74	916	73	1629	47	34	129	149	.464	14	5	4.02

Kip Gross

Pitches: Right **Bats:** Right **Pos:** RP **Ht:** 6' 2" **Wt:** 194 **Born:** 8/24/64 **Age:** 31

			HOW MUCH HE PITCHED						WHAT HE GAVE UP											THE RESULTS					
Year	Team	Lg	G	GS	CG	GF	IP	BFP	H	R	ER	HR	SH	SF	HB	TBB	IBB	SO	WP	Bk	W	L	Pct.	ShO	Sv	ERA
1990	Cincinnati	NL	5	0	0	2	6.1	25	6	3	3	0	0	1	0	2	0	3	0	0	0	0	.000	0	0	4.26
1991	Cincinnati	NL	29	9	1	6	85.2	381	93	43	33	8	6	2	0	40	2	40	5	1	6	4	.600	0	0	3.47
1992	Los Angeles	NL	16	1	0	7	23.2	109	32	14	11	1	0	0	0	10	1	14	1	1	1	1	.500	0	0	4.18
1993	Los Angeles	NL	10	0	0	0	15	59	13	1	1	0	0	0	0	4	0	12	0	0	0	0	.000	0	0	0.60
4 ML YEARS			60	10	1	15	130.2	574	144	61	48	9	6	3	0	56	3	69	6	2	7	5	.583	0	0	3.31

Jeff Grotewold

Bats: Left **Throws:** Right **Pos:** DH **Ht:** 6' 0" **Wt:** 215 **Born:** 12/8/65 **Age:** 30

			BATTING																BASERUNNING				PERCENTAGES		
Year	Team	Lg	G	AB	H	2B	3B	HR	(Hm	Rd)	TB	R	RBI	TBB	IBB	SO	HBP	SH	SF	SB	CS	SB%	GDP	Avg	OBP	SLG
1987	Spartanburg	A	113	381	96	22	2	15	--	--	167	56	70	47	10	114	4	0	3	4	6	.40	5	.252	.338	.438
1988	Clearwater	A	125	442	97	23	2	6	--	--	142	35	39	42	9	103	1	1	1	2	1	.67	16	.219	.288	.321
1989	Clearwater	A	91	301	84	17	2	6	--	--	123	32	55	32	4	43	1	0	4	8	2	.80	12	.279	.346	.409
	Reading	AA	25	80	16	2	0	0	--	--	18	9	11	8	0	14	0	0	2	0	0	.00	2	.200	.267	.225
1990	Reading	AA	127	412	111	33	1	15	--	--	191	56	72	62	5	83	1	2	4	2	2	.50	11	.269	.363	.464
1991	Scranton-Wb	AAA	87	276	71	13	5	5	--	--	109	33	38	25	1	61	1	2	0	0	2	.00	4	.257	.321	.395
1992	Scranton-Wb	AAA	17	51	15	1	1	1	--	--	21	8	8	7	1	10	2	0	0	0	0	.00	1	.294	.400	.412
1993	Portland	AAA	52	151	38	6	3	6	--	--	68	27	30	27	0	41	2	1	1	2	1	.67	7	.252	.370	.450
1994	San Bernrdo	A	32	117	36	10	0	6	--	--	64	19	25	15	0	29	2	0	2	0	3	.00	2	.308	.390	.547
	Duluth-Sup.	IND	35	141	39	7	1	6	--	--	66	15	24	7	1	41	0	0	0	1	1	.50	1	.277	.311	.468
1995	Omaha	AAA	105	350	103	19	0	17	--	--	173	70	60	82	5	88	5	3	1	0	2	.00	14	.294	.434	.494
1992	Philadelphia	NL	72	65	13	2	0	3	(0	3)	24	7	5	9	0	16	1	0	0	0	0	.00	4	.200	.307	.369
1995	Kansas City	AL	15	36	10	1	0	1	(0	1)	14	4	6	9	0	7	0	0	0	0	0	.00	2	.278	.422	.389
2 ML YEARS			87	101	23	3	0	4	(0	4)	38	11	11	18	0	23	1	0	0	0	0	.00	6	.228	.350	.376

Matt Grott

Pitches: Left **Bats:** Left **Pos:** RP **Ht:** 6' 1" **Wt:** 205 **Born:** 12/5/67 **Age:** 28

			HOW MUCH HE PITCHED						WHAT HE GAVE UP											THE RESULTS					
Year	Team	Lg	G	GS	CG	GF	IP	BFP	H	R	ER	HR	SH	SF	HB	TBB	IBB	SO	WP	Bk	W	L	Pct.	ShO	Sv	ERA
1989	Athletics	R	9	5	0	0	35	139	29	10	9	0	0	0	2	9	0	44	1	2	3	1	.750	0	0	2.31
1990	Madison	A	22	0	0	19	25	102	15	5	1	0	0	0	0	14	1	36	1	1	2	0	1.000	0	12	0.36
	Modesto	A	12	0	0	8	17.2	78	10	7	4	0	1	0	0	14	1	28	4	0	2	0	1.000	0	4	2.04
	Huntsville	AA	10	0	0	6	15.2	62	8	5	5	1	1	3	0	10	0	12	0	0	0	0	.000	0	1	2.87
1991	Huntsville	AA	42	0	0	23	57.2	276	65	40	33	6	8	3	0	37	7	65	6	0	2	9	.182	0	3	5.15
	Harrisburg	AA	10	1	0	2	15.1	69	14	8	8	4	0	0	0	8	0	16	0	0	2	1	.667	0	1	4.70
1992	Chattanooga	AA	32	0	0	20	40.1	180	39	16	12	4	4	1	0	25	4	44	5	2	1	2	.333	0	6	2.68
1993	Indianapols	AAA	33	9	0	10	100.1	423	88	45	40	8	3	4	1	40	2	73	7	1	7	5	.583	0	1	3.59
1994	Indianapols	AAA	26	16	2	2	116.1	468	106	44	33	10	5	1	0	32	0	64	7	1	10	3	.769	1	1	2.55
1995	Indianapols	AAA	25	18	2	2	114.2	468	99	61	54	10	2	5	3	24	2	74	11	0	7	3	.700	1	2	4.24
1995	Cincinnati	NL	2	0	0	0	1.2	11	6	4	4	1	0	0	0	0	0	2	0	0	0	0	.000	0	0	21.60

Mark Grudzielanek

Bats: Right **Throws:** Right **Pos:** SS/2B/3B **Ht:** 6' 1" **Wt:** 180 **Born:** 6/30/70 **Age:** 26

			BATTING																BASERUNNING				PERCENTAGES		
Year	Team	Lg	G	AB	H	2B	3B	HR	(Hm	Rd)	TB	R	RBI	TBB	IBB	SO	HBP	SH	SF	SB	CS	SB%	GDP	Avg	OBP	SLG
1991	Jamestown	A	72	275	72	9	3	2	--	--	93	44	32	18	0	42	3	3	3	14	4	.78	6	.262	.311	.338
1992	Rockford	A	128	496	122	12	5	5	--	--	159	64	54	22	1	59	5	0	0	25	4	.86	10	.246	.285	.321
1993	W. Palm Bch	A	86	300	80	11	6	1	--	--	106	41	34	14	0	42	7	0	0	17	10	.63	6	.267	.315	.353
1994	Harrisburg	AA	122	488	157	37	3	11	--	--	233	92	66	43	2	66	8	5	5	32	10	.76	15	.322	.382	.477
1995	Ottawa	AAA	49	181	54	9	1	1	--	--	68	26	22	10	0	17	4	2	4	12	1	.92	6	.298	.342	.376
1995	Montreal	NL	78	269	66	12	2	1	(1	0)	85	27	20	14	4	47	7	3	0	8	3	.73	7	.245	.300	.316

Eddie Guardado

Pitches: Left **Bats:** Right **Pos:** RP/SP **Ht:** 6' 0" **Wt:** 193 **Born:** 10/2/70 **Age:** 25

			HOW MUCH HE PITCHED						WHAT HE GAVE UP											THE RESULTS					
Year	Team	Lg	G	GS	CG	GF	IP	BFP	H	R	ER	HR	SH	SF	HB	TBB	IBB	SO	WP	Bk	W	L	Pct.	ShO	Sv	ERA
1993	Minnesota	AL	19	16	0	2	94.2	426	123	68	65	13	1	3	1	36	2	46	0	0	3	8	.273	0	0	6.18

Year Team	Lg	G	GS	CG	GF	IP	BFP	H	R	ER	HR	SH	SF	HB	TBB	IBB	SO	WP	Bk	W	L	Pct.	ShO	Sv	ERA
1994 Minnesota	AL	4	4	0	0	17	81	26	16	16	3	1	2	0	4	0	8	0	0	0	2	.000	0	0	8.47
1995 Minnesota	AL	51	5	0	10	91.1	410	99	54	52	13	6	5	0	45	2	71	5	1	4	9	.308	0	2	5.12
3 ML YEARS		74	25	0	12	203	917	248	138	133	29	8	10	1	85	4	125	5	1	7	19	.269	0	2	5.90

Mark Gubicza

Pitches: Right **Bats:** Right **Pos:** SP   **Ht:** 6' 5" **Wt:** 230 **Born:** 8/14/62 **Age:** 33

		HOW MUCH HE PITCHED						WHAT HE GAVE UP												THE RESULTS					
Year Team	Lg	G	GS	CG	GF	IP	BFP	H	R	ER	HR	SH	SF	HB	TBB	IBB	SO	WP	Bk	W	L	Pct.	ShO	Sv	ERA
1984 Kansas City	AL	29	29	4	0	189	800	172	90	85	13	4	9	5	75	0	111	3	1	10	14	.417	2	0	4.05
1985 Kansas City	AL	29	28	0	0	177.1	760	160	88	80	14	1	6	5	77	0	99	12	0	14	10	.583	2	0	4.06
1986 Kansas City	AL	35	24	3	2	180.2	765	155	77	73	8	4	8	5	84	2	118	15	0	12	6	.667	2	0	3.64
1987 Kansas City	AL	35	35	10	0	241.2	1036	231	114	107	18	6	11	6	120	3	166	14	1	13	18	.419	2	0	3.98
1988 Kansas City	AL	35	35	8	0	269.2	1111	237	94	81	11	3	6	6	83	3	183	12	4	20	8	.714	4	0	2.70
1989 Kansas City	AL	36	36	8	0	255	1060	252	100	86	10	11	8	5	63	8	173	9	0	15	11	.577	2	0	3.04
1990 Kansas City	AL	16	16	2	0	94	409	101	48	47	5	6	4	4	38	4	71	2	1	4	7	.364	0	0	4.50
1991 Kansas City	AL	26	26	0	0	133	601	168	90	84	10	3	5	6	42	1	89	5	0	9	12	.429	0	0	5.68
1992 Kansas City	AL	18	18	2	0	111.1	470	110	47	46	8	5	3	1	36	3	81	5	1	7	6	.538	1	0	3.72
1993 Kansas City	AL	49	6	0	12	104.1	474	128	61	54	2	6	6	2	43	8	80	12	0	5	8	.385	0	2	4.66
1994 Kansas City	AL	22	22	0	0	130	561	158	74	65	11	5	5	0	26	5	59	9	2	7	9	.438	0	0	4.50
1995 Kansas City	AL	33	33	3	0	213.1	898	222	97	89	21	9	6	6	62	2	81	4	1	12	14	.462	2	0	3.75
12 ML YEARS		363	308	40	14	2099.1	8945	2094	980	897	131	63	77	51	749	39	1311	102	11	128	123	.510	15	2	3.85

Lee Guetterman

Pitches: Left **Bats:** Left **Pos:** RP   **Ht:** 6' 8" **Wt:** 230 **Born:** 11/22/58 **Age:** 37

		HOW MUCH HE PITCHED						WHAT HE GAVE UP												THE RESULTS					
Year Team	Lg	G	GS	CG	GF	IP	BFP	H	R	ER	HR	SH	SF	HB	TBB	IBB	SO	WP	Bk	W	L	Pct.	ShO	Sv	ERA
1995 Tacoma *	AAA	33	1	0	9	36.2	147	33	12	12	2	0	1	0	9	2	21	1	0	1	2	.333	0	4	2.95
1984 Seattle	AL	3	0	0	1	4.1	22	9	2	2	0	0	0	0	2	0	1	1	0	0	0	.000	0	0	4.15
1986 Seattle	AL	41	4	1	8	76	353	108	67	62	7	3	5	4	30	3	38	2	0	0	4	.000	0	0	7.34
1987 Seattle	AL	25	17	2	3	113.1	483	117	60	48	13	2	5	2	35	2	42	3	0	11	4	.733	1	0	3.81
1988 New York	AL	20	2	0	7	40.2	177	49	21	21	2	1	1	1	14	0	15	2	0	1	2	.333	0	0	4.65
1989 New York	AL	70	0	0	38	103	412	98	31	28	6	4	2	0	26	9	51	4	0	5	5	.500	0	13	2.45
1990 New York	AL	64	0	0	21	93	376	80	37	35	6	8	3	0	26	7	48	1	1	11	7	.611	0	2	3.39
1991 New York	AL	64	0	0	37	88	376	91	42	36	6	4	4	3	25	5	35	4	0	3	4	.429	0	6	3.68
1992 NYA-NYN		58	0	0	22	66	310	92	52	52	10	2	5	1	27	8	20	4	0	4	5	.444	0	2	7.09
1993 St. Louis	NL	40	0	0	14	46	192	41	18	15	1	1	2	2	16	5	19	1	0	3	3	.500	0	1	2.93
1995 Seattle	AL	23	0	0	3	17	85	21	13	13	1	1	0	3	11	0	11	0	0	0	0	.000	0	0	6.88
1992 New York	AL	15	0	0	7	22.2	114	35	24	24	5	0	2	0	13	3	5	1	0	1	1	.500	0	0	9.53
New York	NL	43	0	0	15	43.1	196	57	28	28	5	2	3	1	14	5	15	3	0	3	4	.429	0	2	5.82
10 ML YEARS		408	23	3	154	647.1	2786	706	343	312	52	26	27	16	212	39	281	22	1	38	34	.528	1	25	4.34

Ozzie Guillen

Bats: Left **Throws:** Right **Pos:** SS   **Ht:** 5'11" **Wt:** 164 **Born:** 1/20/64 **Age:** 32

		BATTING																	BASERUNNING				PERCENTAGES		
Year Team	Lg	G	AB	H	2B	3B	HR	(Hm	Rd)	TB	R	RBI	TBB	IBB	SO	HBP	SH	SF	SB	CS	SB%	GDP	Avg	OBP	SLG
1985 Chicago	AL	150	491	134	21	9	1	(1	0)	176	71	33	12	1	36	1	8	1	7	4	.64	5	.273	.291	.358
1986 Chicago	AL	159	547	137	19	4	2	(1	1)	170	58	47	12	1	52	1	12	5	8	4	.67	14	.250	.265	.311
1987 Chicago	AL	149	560	156	22	7	2	(2	0)	198	64	51	22	2	52	1	13	8	25	8	.76	10	.279	.303	.354
1988 Chicago	AL	156	566	148	16	7	0	(0	0)	178	58	39	25	3	40	2	10	3	25	13	.66	14	.261	.294	.314
1989 Chicago	AL	155	597	151	20	8	1	(0	1)	190	63	54	15	3	48	0	11	3	36	17	.68	8	.253	.270	.318
1990 Chicago	AL	160	516	144	21	4	1	(1	0)	176	61	58	26	8	37	1	15	5	13	17	.43	6	.279	.312	.341
1991 Chicago	AL	154	524	143	20	3	3	(1	2)	178	52	49	11	1	38	0	13	7	21	15	.58	7	.273	.284	.340
1992 Chicago	AL	12	40	8	4	0	0	(0	0)	12	5	7	1	0	5	0	1	1	1	0	1.00	1	.200	.214	.300
1993 Chicago	AL	134	457	128	23	4	4	(3	1)	171	44	50	10	0	41	0	13	6	5	4	.56	6	.280	.292	.374
1994 Chicago	AL	100	365	105	9	5	1	(0	1)	127	46	39	14	2	35	0	7	4	5	4	.56	7	.288	.311	.348
1995 Chicago	AL	122	415	103	20	3	1	(1	0)	132	50	41	13	1	25	0	4	1	6	7	.46	11	.248	.270	.318
11 ML YEARS		1451	5078	1357	195	54	16	(10	6)	1708	572	468	161	22	409	6	107	44	152	93	.62	87	.267	.288	.336

Eric Gunderson

Pitches: Left **Bats:** Right **Pos:** RP   **Ht:** 6' 0" **Wt:** 195 **Born:** 3/29/66 **Age:** 30

		HOW MUCH HE PITCHED						WHAT HE GAVE UP												THE RESULTS					
Year Team	Lg	G	GS	CG	GF	IP	BFP	H	R	ER	HR	SH	SF	HB	TBB	IBB	SO	WP	Bk	W	L	Pct.	ShO	Sv	ERA
1990 San Francisco	NL	7	4	0	1	19.2	94	24	14	12	2	1	0	0	11	1	14	0	0	1	2	.333	0	0	5.49
1991 San Francisco	NL	2	0	0	1	3.1	18	6	4	2	0	0	0	0	1	0	2	0	0	0	0	.000	0	0	5.40
1992 Seattle	AL	9	0	0	4	9.1	45	12	12	9	1	0	2	1	5	3	2	0	0	2	1	.667	0	0	8.68
1994 New York	NL	14	0	0	3	9	31	5	0	0	0	0	0	0	4	0	4	0	0	0	0	.000	0	0	0.00
1995 NYN-Bos		49	0	0	8	36.2	161	38	17	17	2	2	2	3	17	4	28	1	0	3	2	.600	0	0	4.17

Year Team	Lg	G	GS	CG	GF	IP	BFP	H	R	ER	HR	SH	SF	HB	TBB	IBB	SO	WP	Bk	W	L	Pct.	ShO	Sv	ERA
1995 New York	NL	30	0	0	7	24.1	103	25	10	10	2	0	1	1	8	3	19	1	0	1	1	.500	0	0	3.70
Boston	AL	19	0	0	1	12.1	58	13	7	7	0	2	1	2	9	1	9	0	0	2	1	.667	0	0	5.11
5 ML YEARS		81	4	0	17	78	349	85	47	40	5	3	4	4	38	8	50	1	2	6	5	.545	0	1	4.62

Mark Guthrie

Pitches: Left   **Bats:** Right   **Pos:** RP   **Ht:** 6' 4"   **Wt:** 207   **Born:** 9/22/65   **Age:** 30

		HOW MUCH HE PITCHED						WHAT HE GAVE UP												THE RESULTS					
Year Team	Lg	G	GS	CG	GF	IP	BFP	H	R	ER	HR	SH	SF	HB	TBB	IBB	SO	WP	Bk	W	L	Pct.	ShO	Sv	ERA
1989 Minnesota	AL	13	8	0	2	57.1	254	66	32	29	7	1	5	1	21	1	38	1	0	2	4	.333	0	0	4.55
1990 Minnesota	AL	24	21	3	0	144.2	603	154	65	61	8	6	0	1	39	3	101	9	0	7	9	.438	1	0	3.79
1991 Minnesota	AL	41	12	0	13	98	432	116	52	47	11	4	3	1	41	2	72	7	0	7	5	.583	0	2	4.32
1992 Minnesota	AL	54	0	0	15	75	303	59	27	24	7	4	2	0	23	7	76	2	0	2	3	.400	0	5	2.88
1993 Minnesota	AL	22	0	0	2	21	94	20	11	11	2	1	2	0	16	2	15	1	3	2	1	.667	0	0	4.71
1994 Minnesota	AL	50	2	0	13	51.1	234	65	43	35	8	2	6	2	18	2	38	7	0	4	2	.667	0	1	6.14
1995 Min-LA		60	0	0	14	62	272	66	33	29	6	4	0	2	25	5	67	5	1	5	5	.500	0	0	4.21
1995 Minnesota	AL	36	0	0	7	42.1	181	47	22	21	5	2	0	1	16	3	48	3	1	5	3	.625	0	0	4.46
Los Angeles	NL	24	0	0	7	19.2	91	19	11	8	1	2	0	1	9	2	19	2	0	0	2	.000	0	0	3.66
7 ML YEARS		264	43	3	59	509.1	2192	546	263	236	49	22	18	7	183	22	407	32	4	29	29	.500	1	8	4.17

Ricky Gutierrez

Bats: Right   **Throws:** Right   **Pos:** SS   **Ht:** 6' 1"   **Wt:** 175   **Born:** 5/23/70   **Age:** 26

		BATTING																BASERUNNING				PERCENTAGES		
Year Team	Lg	G	AB	H	2B	3B	HR	(Hm | Rd)	TB	R	RBI	TBB	IBB	SO	HBP	SH	SF	SB	CS	SB%	GDP	Avg	OBP	SLG
1995 Tucson *	AAA	64	236	71	12	4	1	--	--	94	46	26	28	4	28	3	1	2	9	7	.56	6	.301	.379	.398
1993 San Diego	NL	133	438	110	10	5	5	(5 | 0)	145	76	26	50	2	97	5	1	1	4	3	.57	7	.251	.334	.331
1994 San Diego	NL	90	275	66	11	2	1	(1 | 0)	84	27	28	32	1	54	2	2	3	2	6	.25	8	.240	.321	.305
1995 Houston	NL	52	156	43	6	0	0	(0 | 0)	49	22	12	10	3	33	1	1	1	5	0	1.00	4	.276	.321	.314
3 ML YEARS		275	869	219	27	7	6	(6 | 0)	278	125	66	92	6	184	8	4	5	11	9	.55	19	.252	.328	.320

Juan Guzman

Pitches: Right   **Bats:** Right   **Pos:** SP   **Ht:** 5'11"   **Wt:** 195   **Born:** 10/28/66   **Age:** 29

		HOW MUCH HE PITCHED						WHAT HE GAVE UP												THE RESULTS					
Year Team	Lg	G	GS	CG	GF	IP	BFP	H	R	ER	HR	SH	SF	HB	TBB	IBB	SO	WP	Bk	W	L	Pct.	ShO	Sv	ERA
1995 Syracuse *	AAA	1	1	0	0	5	18	1	0	0	0	0	0	0	3	0	5	1	0	0	0	.000	0	0	0.00
1991 Toronto	AL	23	23	1	0	138.2	574	98	53	46	6	2	5	4	66	0	123	10	0	10	3	.769	0	0	2.99
1992 Toronto	AL	28	28	1	0	180.2	733	135	56	53	6	5	3	1	72	2	165	14	2	16	5	.762	0	0	2.64
1993 Toronto	AL	33	33	2	0	221	963	211	107	98	17	5	9	3	110	2	194	26	1	14	3	.824	1	0	3.99
1994 Toronto	AL	25	25	2	0	147.1	671	165	102	93	20	1	6	3	76	1	124	13	1	12	11	.522	0	0	5.68
1995 Toronto	AL	24	24	3	0	135.1	619	151	101	95	13	3	2	3	73	6	94	8	0	4	14	.222	0	0	6.32
5 ML YEARS		133	133	9	0	823	3560	760	419	385	62	16	25	14	397	11	700	71	4	56	36	.609	1	0	4.21

Chris Gwynn

Bats: Left   **Throws:** Left   **Pos:** LF   **Ht:** 6' 0"   **Wt:** 220   **Born:** 10/13/64   **Age:** 31

		BATTING																BASERUNNING				PERCENTAGES		
Year Team	Lg	G	AB	H	2B	3B	HR	(Hm | Rd)	TB	R	RBI	TBB	IBB	SO	HBP	SH	SF	SB	CS	SB%	GDP	Avg	OBP	SLG
1987 Los Angeles	NL	17	32	7	1	0	0	(0 | 0)	8	2	2	1	0	7	0	1	0	0	0	.00	0	.219	.242	.250
1988 Los Angeles	NL	12	11	2	0	0	0	(0 | 0)	2	1	0	1	0	2	0	0	0	0	0	.00	0	.182	.250	.182
1989 Los Angeles	NL	32	68	16	4	1	0	(0 | 0)	22	8	7	2	0	9	0	2	1	1	0	1.00	1	.235	.254	.324
1990 Los Angeles	NL	101	141	40	2	1	5	(0 | 5)	59	19	22	7	2	28	0	0	3	0	1	.00	2	.284	.311	.418
1991 Los Angeles	NL	94	139	35	5	1	5	(3 | 2)	57	18	22	10	1	23	1	1	3	1	0	1.00	5	.252	.301	.410
1992 Kansas City	AL	34	84	24	3	2	1	(0 | 1)	34	10	7	3	0	10	0	1	2	0	0	.00	1	.286	.303	.405
1993 Kansas City	AL	103	287	86	14	4	1	(0 | 1)	111	36	25	24	5	34	1	2	2	0	1	.00	7	.300	.354	.387
1994 Los Angeles	NL	58	71	19	0	0	3	(0 | 3)	28	9	13	7	0	7	0	0	0	0	2	.00	1	.268	.333	.394
1995 Los Angeles	NL	67	84	18	3	2	1	(1 | 0)	28	8	10	6	1	23	1	0	1	0	0	.00	5	.214	.272	.333
9 ML YEARS		518	917	247	32	11	16	(4 | 12)	349	111	108	61	9	143	3	7	12	2	4	.33	22	.269	.313	.381

Tony Gwynn

Bats: Left   **Throws:** Left   **Pos:** RF   **Ht:** 5'11"   **Wt:** 215   **Born:** 5/9/60   **Age:** 36

		BATTING																BASERUNNING				PERCENTAGES		
Year Team	Lg	G	AB	H	2B	3B	HR	(Hm | Rd)	TB	R	RBI	TBB	IBB	SO	HBP	SH	SF	SB	CS	SB%	GDP	Avg	OBP	SLG
1982 San Diego	NL	54	190	55	12	2	1	(0 | 1)	74	33	17	14	0	16	0	4	1	8	3	.73	5	.289	.337	.389
1983 San Diego	NL	86	304	94	12	2	1	(0 | 1)	113	34	37	23	5	21	0	4	3	7	4	.64	9	.309	.355	.372
1984 San Diego	NL	158	606	213	21	10	5	(3 | 2)	269	88	71	59	13	23	2	6	2	33	18	.65	15	.351	.410	.444
1985 San Diego	NL	154	622	197	29	5	6	(3 | 3)	254	90	46	45	4	33	2	1	1	14	11	.56	17	.317	.364	.408
1986 San Diego	NL	160	642	211	33	7	14	(8 | 6)	300	107	59	52	11	35	3	2	2	37	9	.80	20	.329	.381	.467
1987 San Diego	NL	157	589	218	36	13	7	(5 | 2)	301	119	54	82	26	35	3	2	4	56	12	.82	13	.370	.447	.511
1988 San Diego	NL	133	521	163	22	5	7	(3 | 4)	216	64	70	51	13	40	0	4	2	26	11	.70	11	.313	.373	.415

Year	Team	Lg	G	AB	H	2B	3B	HR	(Hm	Rd)	TB	R	RBI	TBB	IBB	SO	HBP	SH	SF	SB	CS	SB%	GDP	Avg	OBP	SLG
1989	San Diego	NL	158	604	**203**	27	7	4	(3	1)	256	82	62	56	16	30	1	11	7	40	16	.71	12	**.336**	.389	.424
1990	San Diego	NL	141	573	177	29	10	4	(2	2)	238	79	72	44	20	23	1	7	4	17	8	.68	13	.309	.357	.415
1991	San Diego	NL	134	530	168	27	11	4	(1	3)	229	69	62	34	8	19	0	0	5	8	8	.50	11	.317	.355	.432
1992	San Diego	NL	128	520	165	27	3	6	(4	2)	216	77	41	46	12	16	0	0	3	3	6	.33	13	.317	.371	.415
1993	San Diego	NL	122	489	175	41	3	7	(4	3)	243	70	59	36	11	19	1	1	7	14	1	.93	18	.358	.398	.497
1994	San Diego	NL	110	419	**165**	35	1	12	(4	8)	238	79	64	48	16	19	2	1	5	5	0	1.00	20	**.394**	**.454**	.568
1995	San Diego	NL	135	535	**197**	33	1	9	(5	4)	259	82	90	35	10	15	1	0	6	17	5	.77	20	**.368**	.404	.484
	14 ML YEARS		1830	7144	2401	384	80	87	(45	42)	3206	1073	804	625	165	344	16	43	52	285	112	.72	197	.336	.388	.449

John Habyan

Pitches: Right **Bats:** Right **Pos:** RP **Ht:** 6' 2" **Wt:** 195 **Born:** 1/29/64 **Age:** 32

			HOW MUCH HE PITCHED						WHAT HE GAVE UP										THE RESULTS				
Year	Team	Lg	G	GS	CG	GF	IP	BFP	H	R	ER	HR	SH	SF	HB	TBB	IBB	SO	WP	Bk	W	L	Pct.	ShO	Sv	ERA
1985	Baltimore	AL	2	0	0	1	2.2	12	3	1	0	0	0	0	0	0	0	2	0	0	1	0	1.000	0	0	0.00
1986	Baltimore	AL	6	5	0	1	26.1	117	24	17	13	3	2	1	0	18	2	14	1	0	1	3	.250	0	0	4.44
1987	Baltimore	AL	27	13	0	4	116.1	493	110	67	62	20	4	4	2	40	1	64	3	0	6	7	.462	0	1	4.80
1988	Baltimore	AL	7	0	0	1	14.2	68	22	10	7	2	0	2	0	4	0	4	1	1	1	0	1.000	0	0	4.30
1990	New York	AL	6	0	0	1	8.2	37	10	2	2	0	0	0	1	2	0	4	1	0	0	0	.000	0	0	2.08
1991	New York	AL	66	0	0	16	90	349	73	28	23	2	2	1	2	20	2	70	1	2	4	2	.667	0	2	2.30
1992	New York	AL	56	0	0	20	72.2	316	84	32	31	6	5	3	2	21	5	44	2	1	5	6	.455	0	7	3.84
1993	KC-NYA	AL	48	0	0	23	56.1	239	59	27	26	6	0	2	0	20	4	39	0	2	2	1	.667	0	1	4.15
1994	St. Louis	NL	52	0	0	10	47.1	204	50	17	17	2	2	0	0	20	8	46	4	0	1	0	1.000	0	1	3.23
1995	Stl-Cal		59	0	0	16	73.1	311	68	34	28	2	6	3	2	27	4	60	4	3	4	4	.500	0	3	3.44
1993	Kansas City	AL	12	0	0	2	14	58	14	7	7	1	0	0	0	4	2	10	0	0	0	0	.000	0	0	4.50
	New York	AL	36	0	0	21	42.1	181	45	20	19	5	0	2	0	16	2	29	0	2	2	1	.667	0	1	4.04
1995	St. Louis	NL	31	0	0	9	40.2	165	32	18	13	0	4	1	1	15	4	35	2	3	3	2	.600	0	2	2.88
	California	AL	28	0	0	7	32.2	146	36	16	15	2	2	2	1	12	0	25	2	0	1	2	.333	0	1	4.13
	10 ML YEARS		329	18	0	93	508.1	2146	503	235	209	43	21	16	9	172	26	347	17	9	25	23	.521	0	12	3.70

Dave Hajek

Bats: Right **Throws:** Right **Pos:** PH **Ht:** 5'10" **Wt:** 165 **Born:** 10/14/67 **Age:** 28

			BATTING																	BASERUNNING				PERCENTAGES		
Year	Team	Lg	G	AB	H	2B	3B	HR	(Hm	Rd)	TB	R	RBI	TBB	IBB	SO	HBP	SH	SF	SB	CS	SB%	GDP	Avg	OBP	SLG
1990	Asheville	A	135	498	155	28	0	6	--	--	201	86	60	61	1	50	2	6	10	43	24	.64	16	.311	.382	.404
1991	Osceola	A	63	232	61	9	4	0	--	--	78	35	20	23	0	30	1	4	1	8	5	.62	5	.263	.331	.336
	Jackson	AA	37	94	18	6	0	0	--	--	24	10	9	7	2	12	0	0	1	2	0	1.00	1	.191	.245	.255
1992	Osceola	A	5	18	2	1	0	0	--	--	3	3	1	1	0	1	0	0	0	1	0	1.00	0	.111	.158	.167
	Jackson	AA	103	326	88	12	3	1	--	--	109	36	18	31	2	25	0	10	3	8	3	.73	5	.270	.331	.334
1993	Jackson	AA	110	332	97	20	2	5	--	--	136	50	27	17	2	14	2	1	3	6	5	.55	10	.292	.328	.410
1994	Tucson	AAA	129	484	157	29	5	7	--	--	217	71	70	29	5	23	2	5	5	12	7	.63	10	.324	.362	.448
1995	Tucson	AAA	131	502	164	37	4	4	--	--	221	99	79	39	7	27	2	5	6	12	7	.63	11	.327	.373	.440
1995	Houston	NL	5	2	0	0	0	0	(0	0)	0	0	0	0	0	1	0	2	0	1	0	1.00	0	.000	.333	.000

Chip Hale

Bats: Left **Throws:** Right **Pos:** DH **Ht:** 5'11" **Wt:** 186 **Born:** 12/2/64 **Age:** 31

			BATTING																	BASERUNNING				PERCENTAGES		
Year	Team	Lg	G	AB	H	2B	3B	HR	(Hm	Rd)	TB	R	RBI	TBB	IBB	SO	HBP	SH	SF	SB	CS	SB%	GDP	Avg	OBP	SLG
1995	Salt Lake *	AAA	16	49	14	4	0	0	--	--	18	5	2	7	1	5	0	0	2	0	1	.00	2	.286	.375	.367
1989	Minnesota	AL	28	67	14	3	0	0	(0	0)	17	6	4	1	0	6	0	1	2	0	0	.00	1	.209	.214	.254
1990	Minnesota	AL	1	2	0	0	0	0	(0	0)	0	0	2	0	0	1	0	0	2	0	0	.00	0	.000	.000	.000
1993	Minnesota	AL	69	186	62	6	1	3	(1	2)	79	25	27	18	0	17	6	2	1	2	1	.67	3	.333	.408	.425
1994	Minnesota	AL	67	118	31	9	0	1	(0	1)	43	13	11	16	1	14	1	1	2	0	2	.00	4	.263	.350	.364
1995	Minnesota	AL	69	103	27	4	0	2	(0	2)	37	10	18	11	1	20	0	0	0	0	0	.00	6	.262	.333	.359
	5 ML YEARS		234	476	134	22	1	6	(1	5)	176	54	62	46	2	58	7	4	7	2	3	.40	11	.282	.349	.370

Darren Hall

Pitches: Right **Bats:** Right **Pos:** RP **Ht:** 6' 3" **Wt:** 205 **Born:** 7/14/64 **Age:** 31

			HOW MUCH HE PITCHED						WHAT HE GAVE UP										THE RESULTS				
Year	Team	Lg	G	GS	CG	GF	IP	BFP	H	R	ER	HR	SH	SF	HB	TBB	IBB	SO	WP	Bk	W	L	Pct.	ShO	Sv	ERA
1986	Medicne Hat	R	17	16	1	0	89.1		91	64	38	3	0	0	3	47	0	60	12	0	5	7	.417	1	0	3.83
1987	Myrtle Bch	A	41	0	0	28	66.2	288	57	31	26	7	2	2	0	28	5	68	1	0	5	5	.500	0	6	3.51
1988	Dunedin	A	4	0	0	2	9.1	39	6	2	2	0	0	0	1	5	3	15	2	0	1	1	.500	0	1	1.93
	Knoxville	AA	37	0	0	35	40.1	172	28	11	10	3	2	2	2	17	1	33	4	1	3	2	.600	0	17	2.23
1989	Dunedin	A	16	14	0	0	51	222	46	25	20	2	1	1	3	21	0	42	3	1	1	4	.200	0	0	3.53
	Knoxville	AA	13	0	0	8	19.2	92	21	12	8	2	1	0	1	10	0	10	3	0	0	2	.000	0	1	3.66
1990	Knoxville	AA	28	0	0	13	33.1	161	29	23	18	6	4	1	4	33	6	28	7	1	3	5	.375	0	1	4.86
1991	Knoxville	AA	42	0	0	24	69.1	287	56	23	20	4	6	3	2	27	2	78	9	0	5	3	.625	0	2	2.60
1992	Syracuse	AAA	55	0	0	26	69	301	62	36	33	5	3	1	2	35	2	49	11	0	4	6	.400	0	5	4.30

91

Year	Team	Lg	G	GS	CG	GF	IP	BFP	H	R	ER	HR	SH	SF	HB	TBB	IBB	SO	WP	Bk	W	L	Pct.	ShO	Sv	ERA
1993	Syracuse	AAA	60	0	0	41	79.1	347	75	51	47	10	7	4	4	31	4	68	5	1	6	7	.462	0	13	5.33
1994	Syracuse	AAA	6	0	0	6	5.2	25	5	2	1	0	0	0	1	2	0	7	0	0	1	0	1.000	0	3	1.59
1994	Toronto	AL	30	0	0	28	31.2	131	26	12	12	3	1	0	1	14	1	28	1	0	2	3	.400	0	17	3.41
1995	Toronto	AL	17	0	0	11	16.1	77	21	9	8	2	0	0	0	9	0	11	0	0	0	2	.000	0	3	4.41
	2 ML YEARS		47	0	0	39	48	208	47	21	20	5	1	0	1	23	1	39	1	0	2	5	.286	0	20	3.75

Joe Hall

Bats: Right **Throws:** Right **Pos:** LF   **Ht:** 6' 0" **Wt:** 180 **Born:** 3/6/66 **Age:** 30

						BATTING													BASERUNNING				PERCENTAGES		
Year	Team	Lg	G	AB	H	2B	3B	HR	(Hm	Rd)	TB	R	RBI	TBB	IBB	SO	HBP	SH	SF	SB	CS	SB%	GDP	Avg	OBP	SLG
1988	Hamilton	A	70	274	78	9	1	2	--	--	95	46	37	30	1	37	5	1	2	30	8	.79	6	.285	.363	.347
	Springfield	A	1	1	0	0	0	0	--	--	0	0	0	0	0	1	0	0	0	0	0	.00	0	.000	.000	.000
1989	St. Pete	A	134	504	147	9	3	0	--	--	162	72	54	60	2	57	8	3	9	45	28	.62	11	.292	.370	.321
1990	Arkansas	AA	115	399	108	14	4	4	--	--	142	44	44	35	4	41	3	2	6	21	14	.60	7	.271	.330	.356
1991	Vancouver	AAA	118	427	106	16	1	4	--	--	136	41	39	23	2	45	4	3	4	11	11	.50	18	.248	.290	.319
1992	Vancouver	AAA	112	367	104	19	7	6	--	--	155	46	56	60	1	44	4	10	3	11	5	.69	15	.283	.387	.422
1993	Nashville	AAA	116	424	123	33	5	10	--	--	196	66	58	52	3	56	4	1	2	10	9	.53	14	.290	.371	.462
1994	Birmingham	AA	19	67	14	6	0	0	--	--	20	9	6	15	0	11	1	0	1	0	0	.00	4	.209	.357	.299
	Nashville	AAA	22	72	21	7	0	4	--	--	40	14	21	16	1	10	2	0	2	0	0	.00	1	.292	.424	.556
1995	Toledo	AAA	91	319	102	19	2	11	--	--	158	52	47	36	1	50	2	1	2	4	1	.80	7	.320	.390	.495
1994	Chicago	AL	17	28	11	3	0	1	(1	0)	17	6	5	2	0	4	1	0	0	0	0	.00	2	.393	.452	.607
1995	Detroit	AL	7	15	2	0	0	0	(0	0)	2	2	0	2	0	3	0	0	0	0	0	.00	1	.133	.235	.133
	2 ML YEARS		24	43	13	3	0	1	(1	0)	19	8	5	4	0	7	1	0	0	0	0	.00	3	.302	.375	.442

Bob Hamelin

Bats: Left **Throws:** Left **Pos:** DH   **Ht:** 6' 0" **Wt:** 235 **Born:** 11/29/67 **Age:** 28

						BATTING													BASERUNNING				PERCENTAGES		
Year	Team	Lg	G	AB	H	2B	3B	HR	(Hm	Rd)	TB	R	RBI	TBB	IBB	SO	HBP	SH	SF	SB	CS	SB%	GDP	Avg	OBP	SLG
1995	Omaha *	AAA	36	119	35	12	0	10	--	--	77	25	32	31	5	34	0	0	2	2	3	.40	2	.294	.434	.647
1993	Kansas City	AL	16	49	11	3	0	2	(1	1)	20	2	5	6	0	15	0	0	0	0	0	.00	2	.224	.309	.408
1994	Kansas City	AL	101	312	88	25	1	24	(13	11)	187	64	65	56	3	62	1	0	5	4	3	.57	6	.282	.388	.599
1995	Kansas City	AL	72	208	35	7	1	7	(3	4)	65	20	25	26	1	56	6	0	1	0	1	.00	6	.168	.278	.313
	3 ML YEARS		189	569	134	35	2	33	(17	16)	272	86	95	88	4	133	7	0	6	4	4	.50	12	.236	.342	.478

Darryl Hamilton

Bats: Left **Throws:** Right **Pos:** CF   **Ht:** 6' 1" **Wt:** 188 **Born:** 12/3/64 **Age:** 31

						BATTING													BASERUNNING				PERCENTAGES		
Year	Team	Lg	G	AB	H	2B	3B	HR	(Hm	Rd)	TB	R	RBI	TBB	IBB	SO	HBP	SH	SF	SB	CS	SB%	GDP	Avg	OBP	SLG
1988	Milwaukee	AL	44	103	19	4	0	1	(1	0)	26	14	11	12	0	9	1	0	1	7	3	.70	2	.184	.274	.252
1990	Milwaukee	AL	89	156	46	5	0	1	(1	0)	54	27	18	9	0	12	0	3	0	10	3	.77	2	.295	.333	.346
1991	Milwaukee	AL	122	405	126	15	6	1	(0	1)	156	64	57	33	2	38	0	7	3	16	6	.73	10	.311	.361	.385
1992	Milwaukee	AL	128	470	140	19	7	5	(1	4)	188	67	62	45	0	42	1	4	7	41	14	.75	10	.298	.356	.400
1993	Milwaukee	AL	135	520	161	21	1	9	(5	4)	211	74	48	45	5	62	3	4	1	21	13	.62	9	.310	.367	.406
1994	Milwaukee	AL	36	141	37	10	1	1	(0	1)	52	23	13	15	1	17	0	2	1	3	0	1.00	2	.262	.331	.369
1995	Milwaukee	AL	112	398	108	20	6	5	(3	2)	155	54	44	47	3	35	3	8	3	11	1	.92	9	.271	.350	.389
	7 ML YEARS		666	2193	637	94	21	23	(11	12)	842	323	253	206	11	215	8	28	16	109	40	.73	44	.290	.351	.384

Joey Hamilton

Pitches: Right **Bats:** Right **Pos:** SP   **Ht:** 6' 4" **Wt:** 230 **Born:** 9/9/70 **Age:** 25

						HOW MUCH HE PITCHED			WHAT HE GAVE UP											THE RESULTS					
Year	Team	Lg	G	GS	CG	GF	IP	BFP	H	R	ER	HR	SH	SF	HB	TBB	IBB	SO	WP	Bk	W	L	Pct.	ShO	Sv	ERA
1992	Charlstn-Sc	A	7	7	0	0	34.2	146	37	24	13	2	0	0	0	14	0	35	6	4	2	2	.500	0	0	3.38
	High Desert	A	9	8	0	0	49.1	211	46	20	15	0	1	0	4	18	0	43	2	2	4	3	.571	0	0	2.74
	Wichita	AA	6	6	0	0	34.2	141	33	12	11	2	0	1	1	11	1	26	1	0	3	0	1.000	0	0	2.86
1993	Rancho Cuca	A	2	2	0	0	11	49	11	5	5	0	0	1	1	2	0	6	0	0	1	0	1.000	0	0	4.09
	Wichita	AA	15	15	0	0	90.2	408	101	55	40	3	1	1	5	36	2	50	2	1	4	9	.308	0	0	3.97
	Las Vegas	AAA	8	8	0	0	47	213	49	25	23	0	2	1	4	22	1	33	6	0	3	2	.600	0	0	4.40
1994	Las Vegas	AAA	9	9	1	0	59.1	256	69	25	18	2	1	0	1	22	0	32	3	0	3	5	.375	1	0	2.73
1994	San Diego	NL	16	16	1	0	108.2	447	98	40	36	7	4	2	6	29	3	61	6	0	9	6	.600	1	0	2.98
1995	San Diego	NL	31	30	2	1	204.1	850	189	89	70	17	12	4	11	56	5	123	2	0	6	9	.400	2	0	3.08
	2 ML YEARS		47	46	3	1	313	1297	287	129	106	24	16	6	17	85	8	184	8	0	15	15	.500	3	0	3.05

Atlee Hammaker

Pitches: Left **Bats:** Both **Pos:** RP **Ht:** 6' 2" **Wt:** 204 **Born:** 1/24/58 **Age:** 38

Year Team	Lg	G	GS	CG	GF	IP	BFP	H	R	ER	HR	SH	SF	HB	TBB	IBB	SO	WP	Bk	W	L	Pct.	ShO	Sv	ERA
1995 Nashville *	AAA	15	0	0	5	28.1	115	27	4	4	1	1	0	0	7	2	20	0	0	1	2	.333	0	1	1.27
1981 Kansas City	AL	10	6	0	2	39	169	44	24	24	2	2	1	0	12	1	11	0	1	1	3	.250	0	0	5.54
1982 San Francisco	NL	29	27	4	0	175	725	189	86	80	16	12	4	2	28	8	102	2	4	12	8	.600	1	0	4.11
1983 San Francisco	NL	23	23	8	0	172.1	695	147	57	43	9	10	4	3	32	12	127	6	2	10	9	.526	3	0	**2.25**
1984 San Francisco	NL	6	6	0	0	33	139	32	10	8	2	3	2	0	9	1	24	0	2	2	0	1.000	0	0	2.18
1985 San Francisco	NL	29	29	1	0	170.2	713	161	81	71	17	8	6	0	47	5	100	4	4	5	12	.294	1	0	3.74
1987 San Francisco	NL	31	27	2	1	168.1	706	159	73	67	22	3	3	3	57	10	107	8	7	10	10	.500	0	0	3.58
1988 San Francisco	NL	43	17	3	11	144.2	607	136	68	60	11	10	4	3	41	9	65	1	2	9	9	.500	1	5	3.73
1989 San Francisco	NL	28	9	0	5	76.2	322	78	34	32	5	6	4	1	23	2	30	1	2	6	6	.500	0	0	3.76
1990 SD-SF	NL	34	7	0	8	86.2	363	85	44	42	8	4	4	0	27	5	44	4	2	4	9	.308	0	0	4.36
1991 San Diego	NL	1	1	0	0	4.2	27	8	7	3	0	2	0	0	3	0	1	1	0	0	1	.000	0	0	5.79
1994 Chicago	AL	2	0	0	0	1.1	5	1	0	0	0	0	0	0	0	0	1	1	0	0	0	.000	0	0	0.00
1995 Chicago	AL	13	0	0	2	6.1	38	11	9	9	2	1	0	1	8	1	3	0	0	0	0	.000	0	0	12.79
1990 San Diego	NL	9	1	0	3	19.1	81	16	11	10	1	0	0	0	6	1	16	1	1	0	4	.000	0	0	4.66
San Francisco		25	6	0	5	67.1	282	69	33	32	7	4	4	0	21	4	28	3	1	4	5	.444	0	0	4.28
12 ML YEARS		249	152	18	29	1078.2	4509	1051	493	439	94	61	32	13	287	54	615	28	26	59	67	.468	6	5	3.66

Chris Hammond

Pitches: Left **Bats:** Left **Pos:** SP **Ht:** 6' 1" **Wt:** 195 **Born:** 1/21/66 **Age:** 30

Year Team	Lg	G	GS	CG	GF	IP	BFP	H	R	ER	HR	SH	SF	HB	TBB	IBB	SO	WP	Bk	W	L	Pct.	ShO	Sv	ERA
1995 Brevard Cty *	A	1	1	0	0	4	16	3	1	0	0	1	0	0	0	0	4	0	0	0	0	.000	0	0	0.00
Charlotte *	AAA	1	1	0	0	4	19	3	1	0	0	0	0	0	2	0	3	1	0	0	0	.000	0	0	0.00
1990 Cincinnati	NL	3	3	0	0	11.1	56	13	9	8	2	1	0	0	12	1	4	1	3	0	2	.000	0	0	6.35
1991 Cincinnati	NL	20	18	0	0	99.2	425	92	51	45	4	6	1	2	48	3	50	3	0	7	7	.500	0	0	4.06
1992 Cincinnati	NL	28	26	0	1	147.1	627	149	75	69	13	5	3	3	55	6	79	6	0	7	10	.412	0	0	4.21
1993 Florida	NL	32	32	1	0	191	826	207	106	99	18	10	2	1	66	2	108	10	5	11	12	.478	0	0	4.66
1994 Florida	NL	13	13	1	0	73.1	312	79	30	25	5	5	2	1	23	1	40	3	0	4	4	.500	1	0	3.07
1995 Florida	NL	25	24	3	0	161	683	157	73	68	17	7	7	9	47	2	126	3	1	9	6	.600	2	0	3.80
6 ML YEARS		121	116	5	1	683.2	2929	697	344	314	59	34	15	16	251	15	407	26	9	38	41	.481	3	0	4.13

Jeffrey Hammonds

Bats: Right **Throws:** Right **Pos:** RF **Ht:** 6' 0" **Wt:** 195 **Born:** 3/5/71 **Age:** 25

Year Team	Lg	G	AB	H	2B	3B	HR	(Hm	Rd)	TB	R	RBI	TBB	IBB	SO	HBP	SH	SF	SB	CS	SB%	GDP	Avg	OBP	SLG
1995 Bowie *	AA	9	31	12	3	1	1	--	--	20	7	11	10	0	7	0	0	1	3	0	1.00	0	.387	.524	.645
1993 Baltimore	AL	33	105	32	8	0	3	(2	1)	49	10	19	2	1	16	0	1	2	4	0	1.00	3	.305	.312	.467
1994 Baltimore	AL	68	250	74	18	2	8	(6	2)	120	45	31	17	1	39	2	0	5	5	0	1.00	3	.296	.339	.480
1995 Baltimore	AL	57	178	43	9	1	4	(2	2)	66	18	23	9	0	30	1	1	2	4	2	.67	3	.242	.279	.371
3 ML YEARS		158	533	149	35	3	15	(10	5)	235	73	73	28	2	85	3	2	9	13	2	.87	9	.280	.314	.441

Mike Hampton

Pitches: Left **Bats:** Right **Pos:** SP **Ht:** 5'10" **Wt:** 180 **Born:** 9/9/72 **Age:** 23

Year Team	Lg	G	GS	CG	GF	IP	BFP	H	R	ER	HR	SH	SF	HB	TBB	IBB	SO	WP	Bk	W	L	Pct.	ShO	Sv	ERA
1993 Seattle	AL	13	3	0	2	17	95	28	20	18	3	1	1	0	17	3	8	1	1	1	3	.250	0	1	9.53
1994 Houston	NL	44	0	0	7	41.1	181	46	19	17	4	0	0	2	16	1	24	5	1	2	1	.667	0	0	3.70
1995 Houston	NL	24	24	0	0	150.2	641	141	73	56	13	11	5	4	49	3	115	3	1	9	8	.529	0	0	3.35
3 ML YEARS		81	27	0	9	209	917	215	112	91	20	12	6	6	82	7	147	9	3	12	12	.500	0	1	3.92

Lee Hancock

Pitches: Left **Bats:** Left **Pos:** RP **Ht:** 6' 4" **Wt:** 215 **Born:** 6/27/67 **Age:** 29

Year Team	Lg	G	GS	CG	GF	IP	BFP	H	R	ER	HR	SH	SF	HB	TBB	IBB	SO	WP	Bk	W	L	Pct.	ShO	Sv	ERA
1988 Bellingham	A	16	16	2	0	100.1	411	83	37	29	3	2	3	2	31	0	102	5	2	6	5	.545	0	0	2.60
1989 San Bernrdo	A	26	26	5	0	173	720	131	69	50	5	5	3	5	82	2	119	11	2	12	7	.632	0	0	2.60
1990 Williamsprt	AA	7	7	0	0	47	193	39	20	14	2	0	1	0	20	1	27	1	0	3	2	.600	0	0	2.68
Harrisburg	AA	20	19	3	0	117.2	513	106	51	45	4	5	0	1	57	1	65	8	4	6	7	.462	1	0	3.44
Buffalo	AAA	1	0	0	0	0	1	0	0	0	0	0	0	0	1	0	0	0	0	0	0	.000	0	0	0.00
1991 Carolina	AA	37	11	0	10	98	420	93	48	41	3	5	3	2	42	4	66	8	0	4	7	.364	0	4	3.77
1992 Buffalo	AAA	10	0	0	7	9	38	9	2	2	0	1	0	0	3	1	5	2	1	0	2	.000	0	2	2.00
Carolina	AA	23	1	0	6	40.1	166	32	13	10	2	0	0	0	12	4	40	6	0	1	1	.500	0	0	2.23
1993 Carolina	AA	25	11	0	3	99.2	409	87	42	28	3	2	1	4	32	2	85	5	0	7	3	.700	0	0	2.53

Year Team	Lg	G	GS	CG	GF	IP	BFP	H	R	ER	HR	SH	SF	HB	TBB	IBB	SO	WP	Bk	W	L	Pct.	ShO	Sv	ERA
Buffalo	AAA	11	11	0	0	66	278	73	38	36	4	4	3	0	14	0	30	2	0	2	6	.250	0	0	4.91
1994 Buffalo	AAA	37	7	0	8	86.2	371	103	35	33	8	0	3	1	22	3	39	1	0	4	5	.444	0	1	3.43
1995 Calgary	AAA	34	17	1	5	113.2	510	146	78	64	9	5	0	4	27	2	49	4	1	6	10	.375	0	0	5.07
1995 Pittsburgh	NL	11	0	0	3	14	54	10	3	3	0	0	0	0	2	0	6	2	0	0	0	.000	0	0	1.93

Chris Haney

Pitches: Left **Bats:** Left **Pos:** SP **Ht:** 6' 3" **Wt:** 195 **Born:** 11/16/68 **Age:** 27

Year Team	Lg	G	GS	CG	GF	IP	BFP	H	R	ER	HR	SH	SF	HB	TBB	IBB	SO	WP	Bk	W	L	Pct.	ShO	Sv	ERA
1991 Montreal	NL	16	16	0	0	84.2	387	94	49	38	6	6	1	1	43	1	51	9	0	3	7	.300	0	0	4.04
1992 KC-Mon		16	13	2	2	80	339	75	43	41	11	0	6	4	26	2	54	5	1	4	6	.400	2	0	4.61
1993 Kansas City	AL	23	23	1	0	124	556	141	87	83	13	3	4	3	53	2	65	6	1	9	9	.500	1	0	6.02
1994 Kansas City	AL	6	6	0	0	28.1	127	36	25	23	2	3	4	1	11	1	18	2	0	2	2	.500	0	0	7.31
1995 Kansas City	AL	16	13	1	0	81.1	338	78	35	33	7	1	4	2	33	0	31	0	0	3	4	.429	1	0	3.65
1992 Kansas City	AL	7	7	1	0	42	174	35	18	18	5	0	3	0	16	2	27	0	0	2	3	.400	1	0	3.86
Montreal	NL	9	6	1	2	38	165	40	25	23	6	0	3	4	10	0	27	5	1	2	3	.400	1	0	5.45
5 ML YEARS		77	71	4	2	398.1	1747	424	239	218	39	13	19	11	166	6	219	24	2	21	28	.429	4	0	4.93

Todd Haney

Bats: Right **Throws:** Right **Pos:** 2B **Ht:** 5' 9" **Wt:** 165 **Born:** 7/30/65 **Age:** 30

Year Team	Lg	G	AB	H	2B	3B	HR	(Hm	Rd)	TB	R	RBI	TBB	IBB	SO	HBP	SH	SF	SB	CS	SB%	GDP	Avg	OBP	SLG
1987 Bellingham	A	66	252	64	11	2	5	--	--	94	57	27	44	0	33	2	1	2	18	10	.64	1	.254	.367	.373
1988 Wausau	A	132	452	127	23	2	7	--	--	175	66	52	56	0	54	7	8	2	35	10	.78	7	.281	.368	.387
1989 San Bernrdo	A	25	107	27	5	0	0	--	--	32	10	7	7	0	14	0	0	1	2	3	.40	2	.252	.296	.299
Williamsprt	AA	115	401	108	20	4	2	--	--	142	59	31	49	2	43	5	7	3	13	8	.62	7	.269	.354	.354
1990 Williamsprt	AA	1	2	1	1	0	0	--	--	2	0	0	1	0	0	0	0	0	0	0	.00	1	.500	.667	1.000
Calgary	AAA	108	419	142	15	6	1	--	--	172	81	36	37	1	38	4	6	0	16	11	.59	11	.339	.398	.411
1991 Indianapols	AAA	132	510	159	32	3	2	--	--	203	68	39	47	3	49	9	7	4	11	10	.52	7	.312	.377	.398
1992 Indianapols	AAA	57	200	53	14	0	6	--	--	85	30	33	37	0	34	1	3	2	1	0	1.00	7	.265	.379	.425
1993 Ottawa	AAA	136	506	147	30	4	3	--	--	194	69	46	36	1	56	3	5	2	11	8	.58	15	.291	.340	.383
1994 Iowa	AAA	83	305	89	22	1	3	--	--	122	48	35	28	0	29	8	3	2	9	6	.60	8	.292	.364	.400
1995 Iowa	AAA	90	326	102	20	2	4	--	--	138	38	30	28	0	21	6	4	2	2	2	.50	17	.313	.376	.423
1992 Montreal	NL	7	10	3	1	0	0	(0	0)	4	0	1	0	0	0	1	0	0	0	0	.00	1	.300	.300	.400
1994 Chicago	NL	17	37	6	0	0	1	(0	1)	9	6	2	3	0	3	1	1	1	2	1	.67	0	.162	.238	.243
1995 Chicago	NL	25	73	30	8	0	2	(1	1)	44	11	6	7	0	11	0	1	0	0	0	.00	0	.411	.463	.603
3 ML YEARS		49	120	39	9	0	3	(1	2)	57	17	9	10	0	14	1	3	1	2	1	.67	1	.325	.379	.475

Greg Hansell

Pitches: Right **Bats:** Right **Pos:** RP **Ht:** 6' 5" **Wt:** 218 **Born:** 3/12/71 **Age:** 25

Year Team	Lg	G	GS	CG	GF	IP	BFP	H	R	ER	HR	SH	SF	HB	TBB	IBB	SO	WP	Bk	W	L	Pct.	ShO	Sv	ERA
1989 Red Sox	R	10	8	0	2	57	246	51	23	16	1	3	1	4	23	0	44	3	3	3	2	.600	0	2	2.53
1990 Winter Havn	A	21	21	2	0	115.1	502	95	63	46	8	4	4	9	64	0	79	4	4	7	10	.412	1	0	3.59
St. Lucie	A	6	6	0	0	38	168	34	22	11	0	1	1	3	15	0	16	3	0	2	4	.333	0	0	2.61
1991 Bakersfield	A	25	25	0	0	150.2	625	142	56	48	5	10	2	5	42	1	132	3	0	14	5	.737	0	0	2.87
1992 Albuquerque	AAA	13	13	0	0	68.2	321	84	46	40	9	1	1	2	35	3	38	4	0	1	5	.167	0	0	5.24
San Antonio	AA	14	14	0	0	92.1	380	80	40	29	6	2	1	3	33	2	64	1	2	6	4	.600	0	0	2.83
1993 Albuquerque	AAA	26	20	0	3	101.1	478	131	86	78	9	1	4	3	60	1	60	10	0	5	10	.333	0	0	6.93
1994 Albuquerque	AAA	47	6	0	19	123.1	498	109	44	41	7	3	4	6	31	3	101	8	0	10	2	.833	0	8	2.99
1995 Albuquerque	AAA	8	1	0	3	16	77	25	15	15	2	1	0	1	6	1	15	0	0	1	1	.500	0	1	8.44
Salt Lake	AAA	7	5	0	0	32.1	141	39	20	18	3	1	1	1	4	1	17	3	1	3	1	.750	0	0	5.01
1995 Los Angeles	NL	20	0	0	7	19.1	93	29	17	16	5	1	1	2	6	1	13	0	0	0	0	.000	0	0	7.45

Dave Hansen

Bats: Left **Throws:** Right **Pos:** 3B **Ht:** 6' 0" **Wt:** 195 **Born:** 11/24/68 **Age:** 27

Year Team	Lg	G	AB	H	2B	3B	HR	(Hm	Rd)	TB	R	RBI	TBB	IBB	SO	HBP	SH	SF	SB	CS	SB%	GDP	Avg	OBP	SLG
1990 Los Angeles	NL	5	7	1	0	0	0	(0	0)	1	0	1	0	0	3	0	0	0	0	0	.00	0	.143	.143	.143
1991 Los Angeles	NL	53	56	15	4	0	1	(0	1)	22	3	5	2	0	12	0	0	0	1	0	1.00	2	.268	.293	.393
1992 Los Angeles	NL	132	341	73	11	0	6	(1	5)	102	30	22	34	3	49	1	0	2	0	2	.00	9	.214	.286	.299
1993 Los Angeles	NL	84	105	38	3	0	4	(2	2)	53	13	30	21	3	13	0	0	1	0	1	.00	0	.362	.465	.505
1994 Los Angeles	NL	40	44	15	3	0	0	(0	0)	18	3	5	5	0	5	0	0	0	0	0	.00	0	.341	.408	.409
1995 Los Angeles	NL	100	181	52	10	0	1	(0	1)	65	19	14	28	4	28	1	0	1	0	0	.00	4	.287	.384	.359
6 ML YEARS		414	734	194	31	0	12	(3	9)	261	68	77	90	10	110	2	0	4	1	3	.25	15	.264	.345	.356

Erik Hanson

Pitches: Right **Bats:** Right **Pos:** SP   **Ht:** 6' 6" **Wt:** 210 **Born:** 5/18/65 **Age:** 31

		HOW MUCH HE PITCHED						WHAT HE GAVE UP												THE RESULTS					
Year Team	Lg	G	GS	CG	GF	IP	BFP	H	R	ER	HR	SH	SF	HB	TBB	IBB	SO	WP	Bk	W	L	Pct.	ShO	Sv	ERA
1988 Seattle	AL	6	6	0	0	41.2	168	35	17	15	4	3	0	1	12	1	36	2	2	2	3	.400	0	0	3.24
1989 Seattle	AL	17	17	1	0	113.1	465	103	44	40	7	4	1	5	32	1	75	3	0	9	5	.643	0	0	3.18
1990 Seattle	AL	33	33	5	0	236	964	205	88	85	15	5	6	2	68	6	211	10	1	18	9	.667	1	0	3.24
1991 Seattle	AL	27	27	2	0	174.2	744	182	82	74	16	2	8	2	56	2	143	14	1	8	8	.500	1	0	3.81
1992 Seattle	AL	31	30	6	0	186.2	809	209	110	100	14	8	9	7	57	1	112	6	0	8	17	.320	1	0	4.82
1993 Seattle	AL	31	30	7	0	215	898	215	91	83	17	10	4	5	60	6	163	8	0	11	12	.478	0	0	3.47
1994 Cincinnati	NL	22	21	0	1	122.2	519	137	60	56	10	5	4	3	23	3	101	8	1	5	5	.500	0	0	4.11
1995 Boston	AL	29	29	1	0	186.2	800	187	94	88	17	6	8	1	59	0	139	5	0	15	5	.750	1	0	4.24
8 ML YEARS		196	193	22	1	1276.2	5367	1273	586	541	100	43	40	26	367	20	980	56	5	76	64	.543	4	0	3.81

Shawn Hare

Bats: Left **Throws:** Left **Pos:** RF   **Ht:** 6' 2" **Wt:** 200 **Born:** 3/26/67 **Age:** 29

		BATTING																	BASERUNNING				PERCENTAGES		
Year Team	Lg	G	AB	H	2B	3B	HR	(Hm	Rd)	TB	R	RBI	TBB	IBB	SO	HBP	SH	SF	SB	CS	SB%	GDP	Avg	OBP	SLG
1995 Okla. City *	AAA	68	238	63	13	3	4	--	--	94	27	30	23	2	47	4	1	1	3	1	.75	9	.265	.338	.395
1991 Detroit	AL	9	19	1	1	0	0	(0	0)	2	0	0	2	0	1	0	0	0	0	0	.00	3	.053	.143	.105
1992 Detroit	AL	15	26	3	1	0	0	(0	0)	4	0	5	2	0	4	0	0	0	0	0	.00	1	.115	.172	.154
1994 New York	NL	22	40	9	1	1	0	(0	0)	12	7	2	4	0	11	0	0	0	0	0	.00	4	.225	.295	.300
1995 Texas	AL	18	24	6	1	0	0	(0	0)	7	2	2	4	0	6	0	0	0	0	0	.00	1	.250	.357	.292
4 ML YEARS		64	109	19	4	1	0	(0	0)	25	9	9	12	0	22	0	0	0	0	0	.00	8	.174	.254	.229

Tim Harikkala

Pitches: Right **Bats:** Right **Pos:** RP   **Ht:** 6' 2" **Wt:** 185 **Born:** 7/15/71 **Age:** 24

		HOW MUCH HE PITCHED						WHAT HE GAVE UP												THE RESULTS					
Year Team	Lg	G	GS	CG	GF	IP	BFP	H	R	ER	HR	SH	SF	HB	TBB	IBB	SO	WP	Bk	W	L	Pct.	ShO	Sv	ERA
1992 Bellingham	A	15	2	0	2	33.1	145	37	15	10	2	3	2	0	16	0	18	1	2	2	0	1.000	0	1	2.70
1993 Bellingham	A	4	0	0	0	8	30	3	1	1	0	0	0	1	2	0	12	0	0	1	0	1.000	0	0	1.13
Appleton	A	15	4	0	5	38.2	175	50	30	28	3	2	1	2	12	2	33	4	3	3	3	.500	0	0	6.52
1994 Appleton	A	13	13	3	0	93.2	373	69	31	20	6	2	3	5	24	0	63	5	0	8	3	.727	0	0	1.92
Riverside	A	4	4	0	0	29	108	16	6	2	1	0	1	0	10	0	30	1	0	4	0	1.000	0	0	0.62
Jacksonvlle	AA	9	9	0	0	54.1	245	70	30	24	4	1	3	1	19	0	22	4	0	4	1	.800	0	0	3.98
1995 Tacoma	AAA	25	24	4	0	146.1	638	151	78	69	13	3	4	2	55	3	73	7	0	5	12	.294	1	0	4.24
1995 Seattle	AL	1	0	0	1	3.1	18	7	6	6	1	0	0	0	1	0	1	0	0	0	0	.000	0	0	16.20

Mike Harkey

Pitches: Right **Bats:** Right **Pos:** SP/RP   **Ht:** 6' 5" **Wt:** 235 **Born:** 10/25/66 **Age:** 29

		HOW MUCH HE PITCHED						WHAT HE GAVE UP												THE RESULTS					
Year Team	Lg	G	GS	CG	GF	IP	BFP	H	R	ER	HR	SH	SF	HB	TBB	IBB	SO	WP	Bk	W	L	Pct.	ShO	Sv	ERA
1988 Chicago	NL	5	5	0	0	34.2	155	33	14	10	0	5	0	2	15	3	18	2	1	0	3	.000	0	0	2.60
1990 Chicago	NL	27	27	2	0	173.2	728	153	71	63	14	5	4	7	59	8	94	8	1	12	6	.667	1	0	3.26
1991 Chicago	NL	4	4	0	0	18.2	84	21	11	11	3	0	1	0	6	1	15	1	0	0	2	.000	0	0	5.30
1992 Chicago	NL	7	7	0	0	38	159	34	13	8	4	1	2	1	15	0	21	3	1	4	0	1.000	0	0	1.89
1993 Chicago	NL	28	28	1	0	157.1	676	187	100	92	17	8	8	3	43	4	67	1	3	10	10	.500	0	0	5.26
1994 Colorado	NL	24	13	0	3	91.2	415	125	61	59	10	5	2	1	35	4	39	0	2	1	6	.143	0	0	5.79
1995 Oak-Cal	AL	26	20	1	1	127.1	573	155	78	77	24	4	4	4	47	2	56	2	0	8	9	.471	0	0	5.44
1995 Oakland	AL	14	12	0	1	66	296	75	46	46	12	3	2	3	31	0	28	2	0	4	6	.400	0	0	6.27
California	AL	12	8	1	0	61.1	277	80	32	31	12	1	2	1	16	2	28	0	0	4	3	.571	0	0	4.55
7 ML YEARS		121	104	4	4	641.1	2790	708	348	320	72	28	21	18	220	22	310	17	8	35	36	.493	1	0	4.49

Pete Harnisch

Pitches: Right **Bats:** Right **Pos:** SP   **Ht:** 6' 0" **Wt:** 207 **Born:** 9/23/66 **Age:** 29

		HOW MUCH HE PITCHED						WHAT HE GAVE UP												THE RESULTS					
Year Team	Lg	G	GS	CG	GF	IP	BFP	H	R	ER	HR	SH	SF	HB	TBB	IBB	SO	WP	Bk	W	L	Pct.	ShO	Sv	ERA
1988 Baltimore	AL	2	2	0	0	13	61	13	8	8	1	2	0	0	9	1	10	1	0	0	2	.000	0	0	5.54
1989 Baltimore	AL	18	17	2	1	103.1	468	97	55	53	10	4	5	5	64	3	70	5	1	5	9	.357	0	0	4.62
1990 Baltimore	AL	31	31	3	0	188.2	821	189	96	91	17	6	5	1	86	5	122	2	2	11	11	.500	0	0	4.34
1991 Houston	NL	33	33	4	0	216.2	900	169	71	65	14	9	7	5	83	3	172	5	2	12	9	.571	2	0	2.70
1992 Houston	NL	34	34	0	0	206.2	859	182	92	85	18	5	5	5	64	3	164	4	1	9	10	.474	0	0	3.70
1993 Houston	NL	33	33	5	0	217.2	896	171	84	72	20	9	4	6	79	5	185	3	1	16	9	.640	4	0	2.98
1994 Houston	NL	17	17	1	0	95	419	100	59	57	13	3	2	3	39	1	62	2	0	8	5	.615	0	0	5.40
1995 New York	NL	18	18	0	0	110	462	111	55	45	13	4	6	3	24	4	82	0	1	2	8	.200	0	0	3.68
8 ML YEARS		186	185	15	1	1151	4886	1032	520	476	106	42	34	28	448	25	867	22	8	63	63	.500	6	0	3.72

95

Brian Harper

Bats: Right **Throws:** Right **Pos:** C **Ht:** 6' 2" **Wt:** 206 **Born:** 10/16/59 **Age:** 36

								BATTING											BASERUNNING				PERCENTAGES		
Year Team	Lg	G	AB	H	2B	3B	HR	(Hm Rd)	TB	R	RBI	TBB	IBB	SO	HBP	SH	SF	SB	CS	SB%	GDP	Avg	OBP	SLG
1979 California	AL	1	2	0	0	0	0	(0 0)	0	0	0	0	0	1	0	0	0	0	0	.00	0	.000	.000	.000
1981 California	AL	4	11	3	0	0	0	(0 0)	3	1	1	0	0	0	0	0	1	1	0	1.00	0	.273	.250	.273
1982 Pittsburgh	NL	20	29	8	1	0	2	(0 2)	15	4	4	1	1	4	0	1	0	0	0	.00	1	.276	.300	.517
1983 Pittsburgh	NL	61	131	29	4	1	7	(5 2)	56	16	20	2	0	15	1	2	4	0	0	.00	3	.221	.232	.427
1984 Pittsburgh	NL	46	112	29	4	0	2	(1 1)	39	4	11	5	0	11	2	1	1	0	0	.00	4	.259	.300	.348
1985 St. Louis	NL	43	52	13	4	0	0	(0 0)	17	5	8	2	0	3	0	0	1	0	0	.00	2	.250	.273	.327
1986 Detroit	AL	19	36	5	1	0	0	(0 0)	6	2	3	3	0	3	0	1	1	0	0	.00	1	.139	.200	.167
1987 Oakland	AL	11	17	4	1	0	0	(0 0)	5	1	3	0	0	4	0	1	1	0	0	.00	1	.235	.222	.294
1988 Minnesota	AL	60	166	49	11	1	3	(0 3)	71	15	20	10	1	12	3	2	1	0	3	.00	12	.295	.344	.428
1989 Minnesota	AL	126	385	125	24	0	8	(4 4)	173	43	57	13	3	16	6	4	4	2	4	.33	11	.325	.353	.449
1990 Minnesota	AL	134	479	141	42	3	6	(1 5)	207	61	54	19	2	27	7	0	4	3	2	.60	20	.294	.328	.432
1991 Minnesota	AL	123	441	137	28	1	10	(4 6)	197	54	69	14	3	22	6	2	6	1	2	.33	14	.311	.336	.447
1992 Minnesota	AL	140	502	154	25	0	9	(3 6)	206	58	73	26	7	22	7	1	10	0	1	.00	15	.307	.343	.410
1993 Minnesota	AL	147	530	161	26	1	12	(6 6)	225	52	73	29	9	29	9	0	5	1	3	.25	15	.304	.347	.425
1994 Milwaukee	AL	64	251	73	15	0	4	(2 2)	100	23	32	9	1	18	3	0	1	0	2	.00	8	.291	.318	.398
1995 Oakland	AL	2	7	0	0	0	0	(0 0)	0	0	0	0	0	1	0	0	0	0	0	.00	0	.000	.000	.000
16 ML YEARS		1001	3151	931	186	7	63	(26 37)	1320	339	428	133	27	188	44	15	43	8	17	.32	107	.295	.329	.419

Gene Harris

Pitches: Right **Bats:** Right **Pos:** RP **Ht:** 5'11" **Wt:** 195 **Born:** 12/5/64 **Age:** 31

		HOW MUCH HE PITCHED						WHAT HE GAVE UP												THE RESULTS					
Year Team	Lg	G	GS	CG	GF	IP	BFP	H	R	ER	HR	SH	SF	HB	TBB	IBB	SO	WP	Bk	W	L	Pct.	ShO	Sv	ERA
1989 Sea-Mon		21	6	0	9	53.1	236	63	38	35	4	7	4	1	25	1	25	3	0	2	5	.286	0	1	5.91
1990 Seattle	AL	25	0	0	12	38	176	31	25	20	5	0	2	1	30	5	43	2	0	1	2	.333	0	0	4.74
1991 Seattle	AL	8	0	0	3	13.1	66	15	8	6	1	1	0	0	10	3	6	1	0	0	0	.000	0	1	4.05
1992 Sea-SD		22	1	0	4	30.1	130	23	15	14	3	3	0	1	15	0	25	1	2	0	2	.000	0	0	4.15
1993 San Diego	NL	59	0	0	48	59.1	269	57	27	20	3	5	2	1	37	8	39	7	0	6	6	.500	0	23	3.03
1994 Det-SD		24	0	0	6	23.2	117	34	21	20	3	2	0	1	12	3	19	4	0	1	1	.500	0	1	7.61
1995 Phi-Bal		24	0	0	5	23	99	23	11	11	2	2	0	0	9	0	13	2	0	2	2	.500	0	0	4.30
1989 Seattle	AL	10	6	0	2	33.1	152	47	27	24	3	0	3	1	15	1	14	0	0	1	4	.200	0	1	6.48
Montreal	NL	11	0	0	7	20	84	16	11	11	1	7	1	0	10	0	11	3	0	1	1	.500	0	0	4.95
1992 Seattle	AL	8	0	0	2	9	40	8	7	7	3	0	0	0	6	0	6	0	1	0	0	.000	0	0	7.00
San Diego	NL	14	1	0	2	21.1	90	15	8	7	0	3	0	1	9	0	19	1	1	0	2	.000	0	0	2.95
1994 Detroit	AL	11	0	0	3	11.1	53	13	10	9	1	0	0	1	4	1	10	1	0	0	0	.000	0	1	7.15
San Diego	NL	13	0	0	3	12.1	64	21	11	11	2	2	0	0	8	2	9	3	0	1	1	.500	0	0	8.03
1995 Philadelphia	NL	21	0	0	5	19	82	19	9	9	2	1	0	0	8	0	9	0	0	2	2	.500	0	0	4.26
Baltimore	AL	3	0	0	0	4	17	4	2	2	0	1	0	0	1	0	4	2	0	0	0	.000	0	0	4.50
7 ML YEARS		183	7	0	87	241	1093	246	145	126	21	20	8	5	138	20	170	20	2	12	18	.400	0	26	4.71

Greg Harris

Pitches: Right **Bats:** Both **Pos:** RP **Ht:** 6' 0" **Wt:** 175 **Born:** 11/2/55 **Age:** 40

		HOW MUCH HE PITCHED						WHAT HE GAVE UP												THE RESULTS					
Year Team	Lg	G	GS	CG	GF	IP	BFP	H	R	ER	HR	SH	SF	HB	TBB	IBB	SO	WP	Bk	W	L	Pct.	ShO	Sv	ERA
1995 Ottawa *	AAA	11	0	0	8	17	60	7	3	2	1	1	1	0	3	0	17	0	0	3	0	1.000	0	1	1.06
1981 New York	NL	16	14	0	2	69	300	65	36	34	8	4	1	2	28	2	54	3	2	3	5	.375	0	1	4.43
1982 Cincinnati	NL	34	10	1	9	91.1	398	96	56	49	12	5	3	2	37	1	67	2	2	2	6	.250	0	1	4.83
1983 Cincinnati	NL	1	0	0	0	1	9	2	3	3	0	1	0	1	3	2	1	0	0	0	0	.000	0	0	27.00
1984 Mon-SD	NL	34	1	0	14	54.1	226	38	18	15	3	2	3	4	25	1	45	3	0	2	2	.500	0	3	2.48
1985 Texas	AL	58	0	0	35	113	450	74	35	31	7	3	2	5	43	3	111	2	1	5	4	.556	0	11	2.47
1986 Texas	AL	73	0	0	63	111.1	462	103	40	35	12	3	6	1	42	6	95	2	1	10	8	.556	0	20	2.83
1987 Texas	AL	42	19	0	14	140.2	629	157	92	76	18	7	3	4	56	3	106	4	2	5	10	.333	0	0	4.86
1988 Philadelphia	NL	66	1	0	19	107	446	80	34	28	7	6	2	4	52	14	71	8	2	4	6	.400	0	1	2.36
1989 Bos-Phi		59	0	0	24	103.1	442	85	46	38	8	4	3	2	58	9	76	12	0	4	4	.500	0	1	3.31
1990 Boston	AL	34	30	1	3	184.1	803	186	90	82	13	8	9	6	77	7	117	8	1	13	9	.591	0	0	4.00
1991 Boston	AL	53	21	1	15	173	731	157	79	74	13	4	8	5	69	5	127	6	1	11	12	.478	0	2	3.85
1992 Boston	AL	70	2	1	22	107.2	459	82	38	30	6	8	5	4	60	11	73	5	0	4	9	.308	0	4	2.51
1993 Boston	AL	80	0	0	24	112.1	494	95	55	47	7	10	4	10	60	14	103	8	1	6	7	.462	0	8	3.77
1994 Bos-NYA		38	0	0	10	50.2	240	64	49	45	9	4	2	3	26	7	48	6	0	3	5	.375	0	2	7.99
1995 Montreal	NL	45	0	0	12	48.1	204	45	18	14	6	3	0	1	16	1	47	3	0	2	3	.400	0	0	2.61
1984 Montreal	NL	15	0	0	4	17.2	68	10	4	4	0	1	0	2	7	1	15	0	0	0	1	.000	0	1	2.04
San Diego	NL	19	1	0	10	36.2	158	28	14	11	3	1	3	2	18	0	30	3	0	2	1	.667	0	1	2.70
1989 Boston	AL	15	0	0	7	28	118	21	12	8	1	1	1	0	15	2	25	2	0	2	2	.500	0	0	2.57
Philadelphia	NL	44	0	0	17	75.1	324	64	34	30	7	3	2	2	43	7	51	10	0	2	2	.500	0	0	3.58

Year	Team	Lg	G	GS	CG	GF	IP	BFP	H	R	ER	HR	SH	SF	HB	TBB	IBB	SO	WP	Bk	W	L	Pct.	ShO	Sv	ERA
1994	Boston	AL	35	0	0	9	45.2	215	60	44	42	8	3	1	1	23	6	44	6	0	3	4	.429	0	2	8.28
	New York	AL	3	0	0	1	5	25	4	5	3	1	1	1	2	3	1	4	0	0	0	1	.000	0	0	5.40
	15 ML YEARS		703	98	4	266	1467.1	6293	1329	689	601	129	72	51	54	652	86	1141	72	13	74	90	.451	0	54	3.69

Greg W. Harris

Pitches: Right **Bats:** Right **Pos:** SP **Ht:** 6' 2" **Wt:** 191 **Born:** 12/1/63 **Age:** 32

			HOW MUCH HE PITCHED						WHAT HE GAVE UP											THE RESULTS					
Year	Team	Lg	G	GS	CG	GF	IP	BFP	H	R	ER	HR	SH	SF	HB	TBB	IBB	SO	WP	Bk	W	L	Pct.	ShO	Sv	ERA
1995	Fort Myers *	A	3	3	1	0	19	69	12	3	2	1	1	0	0	4	0	11	1	0	1	1	.500	0	0	0.95
1988	San Diego	NL	3	1	1	2	18	68	13	3	3	0	0	0	0	3	0	15	0	0	2	0	1.000	0	0	1.50
1989	San Diego	NL	56	8	0	25	135	554	106	43	39	8	5	2	2	52	9	106	3	3	8	9	.471	0	6	2.60
1990	San Diego	NL	73	0	0	33	117.1	488	92	35	30	6	9	7	4	49	13	97	2	3	8	8	.500	0	9	2.30
1991	San Diego	NL	20	20	3	0	133	537	116	42	33	16	9	2	1	27	6	95	2	0	9	5	.643	2	0	2.23
1992	San Diego	NL	20	20	1	0	118	496	113	62	54	13	8	3	2	35	2	66	2	1	4	8	.333	0	0	4.12
1993	SD-Col	NL	35	35	4	0	225.1	975	239	127	115	33	14	4	7	69	9	123	6	6	11	17	.393	0	0	4.59
1994	Colorado	NL	29	19	1	2	130	588	154	99	96	22	12	6	5	52	4	82	5	1	3	12	.200	0	1	6.65
1995	Minnesota	AL	7	6	0	0	32.2	160	50	35	32	5	1	2	0	16	0	21	3	0	0	5	.000	0	0	8.82
1993	San Diego	NL	22	22	4	0	152	639	151	65	62	18	8	2	3	39	6	83	2	3	10	9	.526	0	0	3.67
	Colorado	NL	13	13	0	0	73.1	336	88	62	53	15	6	2	4	30	3	40	4	3	1	8	.111	0	0	6.50
	8 ML YEARS		243	109	10	62	909.1	3866	883	446	402	103	58	26	21	303	43	605	23	14	45	64	.413	2	16	3.98

Lenny Harris

Bats: Left **Throws:** Right **Pos:** 3B/1B **Ht:** 5'10" **Wt:** 210 **Born:** 10/28/64 **Age:** 31

			BATTING															BASERUNNING				PERCENTAGES		
Year	Team	Lg	G	AB	H	2B	3B	HR	(Hm | Rd)	TB	R	RBI	TBB	IBB	SO	HBP	SH	SF	SB	CS	SB%	GDP	Avg	OBP	SLG
1988	Cincinnati	NL	16	43	16	1	0	0	(0 | 0)	17	7	8	5	0	4	0	1	2	4	1	.80	1	.372	.420	.395
1989	Cin-LA	NL	115	335	79	10	1	3	(1 | 2)	100	36	26	20	0	33	2	1	0	14	9	.61	14	.236	.283	.299
1990	Los Angeles	NL	137	431	131	16	4	2	(0 | 2)	161	61	29	29	2	31	1	3	1	15	10	.60	8	.304	.348	.374
1991	Los Angeles	NL	145	429	123	16	1	3	(1 | 2)	150	59	38	37	5	32	5	12	2	12	3	.80	16	.287	.349	.350
1992	Los Angeles	NL	135	347	94	11	0	0	(0 | 0)	105	28	30	24	3	24	1	6	2	19	7	.73	10	.271	.318	.303
1993	Los Angeles	NL	107	160	38	6	1	2	(0 | 2)	52	20	11	15	4	15	0	1	0	3	1	.75	4	.238	.303	.325
1994	Cincinnati	NL	66	100	31	3	1	0	(0 | 0)	36	13	14	5	0	13	0	0	1	7	2	.78	5	.310	.340	.360
1995	Cincinnati	NL	101	197	41	8	3	2	(0 | 2)	61	32	16	14	0	20	0	3	1	10	1	.91	6	.208	.259	.310
1989	Cincinnati	NL	61	188	42	4	0	2	(0 | 2)	52	17	11	9	0	20	1	1	0	10	6	.63	5	.223	.263	.277
	Los Angeles	NL	54	147	37	6	1	1	(1 | 0)	48	19	15	11	0	13	1	0	0	4	3	.57	9	.252	.308	.327
	8 ML YEARS		822	2042	553	71	11	12	(2 | 10)	682	256	172	149	14	172	9	27	9	84	34	.71	58	.271	.322	.334

Dean Hartgraves

Pitches: Left **Bats:** Right **Pos:** RP **Ht:** 6' 0" **Wt:** 185 **Born:** 8/12/66 **Age:** 29

			HOW MUCH HE PITCHED						WHAT HE GAVE UP											THE RESULTS					
Year	Team	Lg	G	GS	CG	GF	IP	BFP	H	R	ER	HR	SH	SF	HB	TBB	IBB	SO	WP	Bk	W	L	Pct.	ShO	Sv	ERA
1987	Auburn	A	23	0	0	12	31.2	157	31	24	14	1	3	0	1	27	4	42	1	0	0	5	.000	0	2	3.98
1988	Asheville	A	34	13	2	7	118.1	523	131	70	59	9	2	8	5	47	2	83	8	5	5	9	.357	1	0	4.49
1989	Asheville	A	19	19	4	0	120.1	542	140	66	55	6	5	3	4	49	2	87	5	3	5	8	.385	0	0	4.11
	Osceola	A	7	6	1	0	39.2	165	36	20	13	0	2	2	2	12	0	21	4	0	3	3	.500	1	0	2.95
1990	Columbus	AA	33	14	0	6	99.2	454	108	66	52	8	7	4	3	48	1	64	6	0	8	8	.500	0	0	4.70
1991	Jackson	AA	19	9	3	5	74	302	60	25	22	3	6	4	2	25	3	44	4	0	6	5	.545	0	0	2.68
	Tucson	AAA	16	3	1	4	43.2	189	47	17	15	2	2	3	0	20	1	18	2	0	3	0	1.000	1	0	3.09
1992	Tucson	AAA	5	1	0	0	8	61	26	24	22	1	0	0	0	9	0	6	4	0	0	1	.000	0	0	24.75
	Jackson	AA	22	22	3	0	146.2	585	127	54	45	7	4	1	3	40	1	92	9	1	9	6	.600	2	0	2.76
1993	Tucson	AAA	23	10	0	2	77.2	369	90	65	55	7	2	6	4	40	0	42	5	0	1	6	.143	0	0	6.37
1994	Tucson	AAA	47	4	0	16	97.2	429	106	64	55	11	3	4	1	36	2	54	4	0	7	2	.778	0	3	5.07
1995	Tucson	AAA	14	0	0	9	21.1	91	21	6	5	0	0	1	1	5	2	15	0	0	3	2	.600	0	2	2.11
1995	Houston	NL	40	0	0	11	36.1	150	30	14	13	2	1	1	0	16	2	24	1	0	2	0	1.000	0	0	3.22

Mike Hartley

Pitches: Right **Bats:** Right **Pos:** RP **Ht:** 6' 1" **Wt:** 195 **Born:** 8/31/61 **Age:** 34

			HOW MUCH HE PITCHED						WHAT HE GAVE UP											THE RESULTS					
Year	Team	Lg	G	GS	CG	GF	IP	BFP	H	R	ER	HR	SH	SF	HB	TBB	IBB	SO	WP	Bk	W	L	Pct.	ShO	Sv	ERA
1995	Pawtucket *	AAA	26	1	0	10	46.2	196	47	21	21	7	1	2	3	12	0	39	2	2	1	1	.500	0	1	4.05
	Rochester *	AAA	8	0	0	6	11	39	4	1	1	0	0	0	0	2	1	12	0	0	0	1	.000	0	0	0.82
1989	Los Angeles	NL	5	0	0	3	6	20	2	1	1	0	0	0	0	0	0	4	0	0	0	1	.000	0	0	1.50
1990	Los Angeles	NL	32	6	1	8	79.1	325	58	32	26	7	2	1	2	30	2	76	3	0	6	3	.667	1	1	2.95
1991	LA-Phi	NL	58	0	0	16	83.1	368	74	40	39	11	2	1	6	47	8	63	10	2	4	1	.800	0	2	4.21
1992	Philadelphia	NL	46	0	0	15	55	243	54	23	21	5	5	1	2	23	6	53	4	0	7	6	.538	0	0	3.44
1993	Minnesota	AL	53	0	0	21	81	359	86	38	36	4	4	6	7	36	3	57	8	0	1	2	.333	0	1	4.00
1995	Bos-Bal	AL	8	0	0	2	14	58	13	8	8	1	2	2	2	3	0	7	0	0	1	0	1.000	0	0	5.14

Year	Team	Lg	G	GS	CG	GF	IP	BFP	H	R	ER	HR	SH	SF	HB	TBB	IBB	SO	WP	Bk	W	L	Pct.	ShO	Sv	ERA
1991	Los Angeles	NL	40	0	0	11	57	258	53	29	28	7	1	1	3	37	7	44	8	1	2	0	1.000	0	1	4.42
	Philadelphia	NL	18	0	0	5	26.1	110	21	11	11	4	1	0	3	10	1	19	2	1	2	1	.667	0	1	3.76
1995	Boston	AL	5	0	0	2	7	33	8	7	7	1	1	2	2	2	0	2	0	0	0	0	.000	0	0	9.00
	Baltimore	AL	3	0	0	0	7	25	5	1	1	0	1	0	0	1	0	4	0	0	1	0	1.000	0	0	1.29
	6 ML YEARS		202	6	1	65	318.2	1373	287	142	131	28	15	11	19	139	19	259	25	2	19	13	.594	1	4	3.70

Bryan Harvey

Pitches: Right **Bats:** Right **Pos:** RP **Ht:** 6' 2" **Wt:** 212 **Born:** 6/2/63 **Age:** 33

			HOW MUCH HE PITCHED						WHAT HE GAVE UP										THE RESULTS					
Year	Team	Lg	G	GS	CG	GF	IP	BFP	H	R	ER	HR	SH	SF	HB	TBB	IBB	SO	WP	Bk	W	L	Pct.	ShO	Sv	ERA
1987	California	AL	3	0	0	2	5	22	6	0	0	0	0	0	0	2	0	3	3	0	0	0	.000	0	0	0.00
1988	California	AL	50	0	0	38	76	303	59	22	18	4	3	3	1	20	6	67	4	1	7	5	.583	0	17	2.13
1989	California	AL	51	0	0	42	55	245	36	21	21	6	5	2	0	41	1	78	5	0	3	3	.500	0	25	3.44
1990	California	AL	54	0	0	47	64.1	267	45	24	23	4	4	4	0	35	6	82	7	1	4	4	.500	0	25	3.22
1991	California	AL	67	0	0	63	78.2	309	51	20	14	6	3	2	1	17	3	101	2	2	2	4	.333	0	46	1.60
1992	California	AL	25	0	0	22	28.2	122	22	12	9	4	2	3	0	11	1	34	4	0	0	4	.000	0	13	2.83
1993	Florida	NL	59	0	0	54	69	264	45	14	13	4	3	6	0	13	2	73	0	1	1	5	.167	0	45	1.70
1994	Florida	NL	12	0	0	10	10.1	47	12	6	6	1	0	0	0	4	0	10	0	0	0	0	.000	0	6	5.23
1995	Florida	NL	1	0	0	0	0	3	2	3	3	1	0	0	0	1	0	0	0	0	0	0	.000	0	0	----
	9 ML YEARS		322	0	0	278	387	1582	278	122	107	30	20	20	2	144	19	448	25	5	17	25	.405	0	177	2.49

Bill Haselman

Bats: Right **Throws:** Right **Pos:** C **Ht:** 6' 3" **Wt:** 215 **Born:** 5/25/66 **Age:** 30

					BATTING														BASERUNNING				PERCENTAGES		
Year	Team	Lg	G	AB	H	2B	3B	HR	(Hm	Rd)	TB	R	RBI	TBB	IBB	SO	HBP	SH	SF	SB	CS	SB%	GDP	Avg	OBP	SLG
1990	Texas	AL	7	13	2	0	0	0	(0	0)	2	0	3	1	0	5	0	0	0	0	0	.00	0	.154	.214	.154
1992	Seattle	AL	8	19	5	0	0	0	(0	0)	5	1	0	0	0	7	0	0	0	0	0	.00	1	.263	.263	.263
1993	Seattle	AL	58	137	35	8	0	5	(3	2)	58	21	16	12	0	19	1	2	2	2	1	.67	5	.255	.316	.423
1994	Seattle	AL	38	83	16	7	1	1	(1	0)	28	11	8	3	0	11	1	1	0	1	0	1.00	3	.193	.230	.337
1995	Boston	AL	64	152	37	6	1	5	(3	2)	60	22	23	17	0	30	2	0	3	0	2	.00	4	.243	.322	.395
	5 ML YEARS		175	404	95	21	2	11	(7	4)	153	55	50	33	0	72	4	3	5	3	3	.50	12	.235	.296	.379

Billy Hatcher

Bats: Right **Throws:** Right **Pos:** RF **Ht:** 5'10" **Wt:** 190 **Born:** 10/4/60 **Age:** 35

					BATTING														BASERUNNING				PERCENTAGES		
Year	Team	Lg	G	AB	H	2B	3B	HR	(Hm	Rd)	TB	R	RBI	TBB	IBB	SO	HBP	SH	SF	SB	CS	SB%	GDP	Avg	OBP	SLG
1995	Omaha *	AAA	26	105	29	5	1	1	(0	0)	39	14	12	9	2	6	2	0	1	4	2	.67	5	.276	.342	.371
1984	Chicago	NL	8	9	1	0	0	0	(0	0)	1	1	0	1	1	0	0	0	0	2	0	1.00	6	.111	.200	.111
1985	Chicago	NL	53	163	40	12	1	2	(2	0)	60	24	10	8	0	12	3	2	2	2	4	.33	9	.245	.290	.368
1986	Houston	NL	127	419	108	15	4	6	(2	4)	149	55	36	22	1	52	5	6	1	38	14	.73	3	.258	.302	.356
1987	Houston	NL	141	564	167	28	3	11	(3	8)	234	96	63	42	1	70	9	7	5	53	9	.85	11	.296	.352	.415
1988	Houston	NL	145	530	142	25	4	7	(3	4)	196	79	52	37	4	56	8	8	8	32	13	.71	6	.268	.321	.370
1989	Hou-Pit	NL	135	481	111	19	3	4	(0	4)	148	59	51	30	2	62	2	3	4	24	7	.77	4	.231	.277	.308
1990	Cincinnati	NL	139	504	139	28	5	5	(2	3)	192	68	25	33	5	42	6	1	1	30	10	.75	4	.276	.327	.381
1991	Cincinnati	NL	138	442	116	25	3	4	(2	2)	159	45	41	26	4	55	7	4	3	11	9	.55	9	.262	.312	.360
1992	Bos-Cin		118	409	102	19	2	3	(1	2)	134	47	33	22	1	52	3	6	4	4	8	.33	11	.249	.290	.328
1993	Boston	AL	136	508	146	24	3	9	(5	4)	203	71	57	28	4	46	11	11	4	14	7	.67	14	.287	.336	.400
1994	Bos-Phi		87	298	73	14	2	3	(0	3)	100	39	31	17	0	28	1	5	6	8	6	.57	5	.245	.283	.336
1995	Texas	AL	6	12	1	1	0	0	(0	0)	2	2	0	1	0	1	0	0	0	0	0	.00	0	.083	.154	.167
1989	Houston	NL	108	395	90	15	3	3	(0	3)	120	49	44	30	2	53	1	3	4	22	6	.79	3	.228	.281	.304
	Pittsburgh	NL	27	86	21	4	0	1	(0	1)	28	10	7	0	0	9	1	0	0	2	1	.67	1	.244	.253	.326
1992	Boston	AL	75	315	75	16	2	1	(1	0)	98	37	23	17	1	41	3	6	1	4	6	.40	9	.238	.283	.311
	Cincinnati	NL	43	94	27	3	0	2	(0	2)	36	10	10	5	0	11	0	0	3	0	2	.00	2	.287	.314	.383
1994	Boston	AL	44	164	40	9	1	1	(0	1)	54	24	18	11	0	14	1	3	2	4	5	.44	3	.244	.292	.329
	Philadelphia	NL	43	134	33	5	1	2	(0	2)	46	15	13	6	0	14	0	2	4	4	1	.80	2	.246	.271	.343
	12 ML YEARS		1233	4339	1146	210	30	54	(20	34)	1578	586	399	267	23	476	55	56	53	218	87	.71	76	.264	.312	.364

Scott Hatteberg

Bats: Left **Throws:** Right **Pos:** C **Ht:** 6' 1" **Wt:** 195 **Born:** 12/14/69 **Age:** 26

					BATTING														BASERUNNING				PERCENTAGES		
Year	Team	Lg	G	AB	H	2B	3B	HR	(Hm	Rd)	TB	R	RBI	TBB	IBB	SO	HBP	SH	SF	SB	CS	SB%	GDP	Avg	OBP	SLG
1991	Winter Havn	A	56	191	53	7	3	1	--	--	69	21	24	22	4	22	0	2	2	1	2	.33	6	.277	.349	.361
	Lynchburg	A	8	25	5	1	0	0	--	--	6	4	3	7	0	6	0	0	0	0	0	.00	0	.200	.375	.240
1992	New Britain	AA	103	297	69	13	2	1	--	--	89	28	30	41	2	49	2	1	3	1	3	.25	6	.232	.327	.300
1993	New Britain	AA	68	227	63	10	2	7	--	--	98	35	28	42	3	38	1	1	0	1	3	.25	6	.278	.393	.432
	Pawtucket	AAA	18	53	10	0	0	1	--	--	13	6	6	6	0	12	1	2	0	0	0	.00	5	.189	.283	.245
1994	New Britain	AA	20	68	18	4	1	1	--	--	27	6	9	7	1	9	0	0	1	0	2	.00	2	.265	.329	.397
	Pawtucket	AAA	78	238	56	14	0	7	--	--	91	26	19	32	1	49	3	2	1	2	1	.67	14	.235	.332	.382

		G	AB	H	2B	3B	HR	(Hm	Rd)	TB	R	RBI	TBB	IBB	SO	HBP	SH	SF	SB	CS	SB%	GDP	Avg	OBP	SLG
1995 Pawtucket	AAA	85	251	68	15	1	7	--	--	106	36	27	40	2	39	4	1	3	2	0	1.00	8	.271	.376	.422
1995 Boston	AL	2	2	1	0	0	0	(0	0)	1	1	0	0	0	0	0	0	0	0	0	.00	1	.500	.500	.500

LaTroy Hawkins

Pitches: Right **Bats:** Right **Pos:** SP   **Ht:** 6' 5" **Wt:** 193 **Born:** 12/21/72 **Age:** 23

			HOW MUCH HE PITCHED					WHAT HE GAVE UP									THE RESULTS				
Year Team	Lg	G	GS	CG	GF	IP	BFP	H	R	ER	HR	SH	SF	HB	TBB	IBB	SO	WP	Bk	W	L	Pct.	ShO	Sv	ERA
1991 Twins	R	11	11	0	0	55	251	62	34	29	2	0	1	3	26	0	47	6	3	4	3	.571	0	0	4.75
1992 Twins	R	6	6	1	0	36.1	161	36	19	13	1	0	0	3	10	0	35	3	2	3	2	.600	0	0	3.22
Elizabethtn	R	5	5	1	0	26.2	115	21	12	10	2	0	0	0	11	0	36	0	1	0	1	.000	0	0	3.38
1993 Fort Wayne	A	26	23	4	1	157.1	619	110	53	36	5	4	4	4	41	0	179	8	2	15	5	.750	3	0	2.06
1994 Fort Myers	A	6	6	1	0	38.2	153	32	10	10	1	2	0	2	6	0	36	0	0	4	0	1.000	0	0	2.33
Nashville	AA	11	11	1	0	73.1	297	50	23	19	2	3	1	3	28	0	53	2	1	9	2	.818	0	0	2.33
Salt Lake	AAA	12	12	1	0	81.2	353	92	42	37	8	2	2	5	33	0	37	4	2	5	4	.556	0	0	4.08
1995 Salt Lake	AAA	22	22	4	0	144.1	601	150	63	57	7	5	2	1	40	1	74	6	1	9	7	.563	1	0	3.55
1995 Minnesota	AL	6	6	1	0	27	131	39	29	26	3	0	3	1	12	0	9	1	1	2	3	.400	0	0	8.67

Charlie Hayes

Bats: Right **Throws:** Right **Pos:** 3B   **Ht:** 6' 0" **Wt:** 224 **Born:** 5/29/65 **Age:** 31

								BATTING											BASERUNNING				PERCENTAGES		
Year Team	Lg	G	AB	H	2B	3B	HR	(Hm	Rd)	TB	R	RBI	TBB	IBB	SO	HBP	SH	SF	SB	CS	SB%	GDP	Avg	OBP	SLG
1988 San Francisco	NL	7	11	1	0	0	0	(0	0)	1	0	0	0	0	3	0	0	0	0	0	.00	0	.091	.091	.091
1989 Phi-SF	NL	87	304	78	15	1	8	(3	5)	119	26	43	11	1	50	0	2	3	3	1	.75	6	.257	.280	.391
1990 Philadelphia	NL	152	561	145	20	0	10	(3	7)	195	56	57	28	3	91	2	0	6	4	4	.50	12	.258	.293	.348
1991 Philadelphia	NL	142	460	106	23	1	12	(6	6)	167	34	53	16	3	75	1	2	1	3	3	.50	13	.230	.257	.363
1992 New York	AL	142	509	131	19	2	18	(7	11)	208	52	66	28	0	100	3	3	6	3	5	.38	12	.257	.297	.409
1993 Colorado	NL	157	573	175	45	2	25	(17	8)	299	89	98	43	6	82	5	1	8	11	6	.65	25	.305	.355	.522
1994 Colorado	NL	113	423	122	23	4	10	(4	6)	183	46	50	36	4	71	3	0	1	3	6	.33	11	.288	.348	.433
1995 Philadelphia	NL	141	529	146	30	3	11	(6	5)	215	58	85	50	2	88	4	0	6	5	1	.83	22	.276	.340	.406
1989 Philadelphia	NL	84	299	77	15	1	8	(3	5)	118	26	43	11	1	49	0	2	3	3	1	.75	6	.258	.281	.395
San Francisco	NL	3	5	1	0	0	0	(0	0)	1	0	0	0	0	1	0	0	0	0	0	.00	0	.200	.200	.200
8 ML YEARS		941	3370	904	175	13	94	(46	48)	1387	361	452	212	19	560	18	8	31	32	26	.55	101	.268	.312	.412

Jimmy Haynes

Pitches: Right **Bats:** Right **Pos:** SP   **Ht:** 6' 4" **Wt:** 175 **Born:** 9/5/72 **Age:** 23

			HOW MUCH HE PITCHED					WHAT HE GAVE UP									THE RESULTS				
Year Team	Lg	G	GS	CG	GF	IP	BFP	H	R	ER	HR	SH	SF	HB	TBB	IBB	SO	WP	Bk	W	L	Pct.	ShO	Sv	ERA
1991 Orioles	R	14	8	1	4	62	256	44	27	11	0	1	3	0	21	0	67	6	1	3	2	.600	0	2	1.60
1992 Kane County	A	24	24	4	0	144	616	131	66	41	2	4	9	4	45	0	141	12	7	7	11	.389	0	0	2.56
1993 Frederick	A	27	27	2	0	172.1	707	139	73	58	13	2	3	1	61	1	174	20	4	12	8	.600	1	0	3.03
1994 Rochester	AAA	3	3	0	0	13.1	68	20	12	10	3	0	1	1	6	0	14	0	0	1	0	1.000	0	0	6.75
Bowie	AA	25	25	5	0	173.2	705	154	67	56	16	6	4	3	46	1	177	8	3	13	8	.619	1	0	2.90
1995 Rochester	AAA	26	25	3	0	167	691	162	77	61	16	4	7	0	49	0	140	6	1	12	8	.600	1	0	3.29
1995 Baltimore	AL	4	3	0	0	24	94	11	6	6	2	1	0	0	12	1	22	0	0	2	1	.667	0	0	2.25

Eric Helfand

Bats: Left **Throws:** Right **Pos:** C   **Ht:** 6' 0" **Wt:** 195 **Born:** 3/25/69 **Age:** 27

								BATTING											BASERUNNING				PERCENTAGES		
Year Team	Lg	G	AB	H	2B	3B	HR	(Hm	Rd)	TB	R	RBI	TBB	IBB	SO	HBP	SH	SF	SB	CS	SB%	GDP	Avg	OBP	SLG
1995 Edmonton *	AAA	19	56	12	4	2	1	--	--	23	5	12	9	1	10	0	5	1	0	1	.00	3	.214	.318	.411
1993 Oakland	AL	8	13	3	0	0	0	(0	0)	3	1	1	0	0	1	0	0	0	0	0	.00	0	.231	.231	.231
1994 Oakland	AL	7	6	1	0	0	0	(0	0)	1	1	1	0	0	1	0	0	0	0	0	.00	0	.167	.167	.167
1995 Oakland	AL	38	86	14	2	1	0	(0	0)	18	9	7	11	0	25	1	3	0	0	0	.00	2	.163	.265	.209
3 ML YEARS		53	105	18	2	1	0	(0	0)	22	11	9	11	0	27	1	3	0	0	0	.00	2	.171	.256	.210

Rick Helling

Pitches: Right **Bats:** Right **Pos:** SP   **Ht:** 6' 3" **Wt:** 215 **Born:** 12/15/70 **Age:** 25

			HOW MUCH HE PITCHED					WHAT HE GAVE UP									THE RESULTS				
Year Team	Lg	G	GS	CG	GF	IP	BFP	H	R	ER	HR	SH	SF	HB	TBB	IBB	SO	WP	Bk	W	L	Pct.	ShO	Sv	ERA
1992 Charlotte	A	3	3	0	0	19.2	79	13	5	5	1	0	1	2	4	0	20	1	1	1	1	.500	0	0	2.29
1993 Tulsa	AA	26	26	2	0	177.1	725	150	76	71	14	4	3	10	46	1	188	3	3	12	8	.600	2	0	3.60
Okla. City	AAA	2	2	1	0	11	41	5	3	2	0	0	1	0	3	0	17	0	0	1	1	.500	0	0	1.64
1994 Okla. City	AAA	20	20	2	0	132.1	585	133	93	85	17	7	9	6	43	2	85	8	2	4	12	.250	0	0	5.78
1995 Okla. City	AAA	20	20	3	0	109.2	493	132	73	65	13	2	6	10	41	1	80	3	1	4	8	.333	1	0	5.33
1994 Texas	AL	9	9	1	0	52	228	62	34	34	14	0	0	0	18	0	25	4	1	3	2	.600	1	0	5.88
1995 Texas	AL	3	3	0	0	12.1	62	17	11	9	2	0	2	2	8	0	5	0	0	0	2	.000	0	0	6.57
2 ML YEARS		12	12	1	0	64.1	290	79	45	43	16	0	2	2	26	0	30	4	1	3	4	.429	1	0	6.02

Scott Hemond

Bats: Right **Throws:** Right **Pos:** C **Ht:** 6' 0" **Wt:** 215 **Born:** 11/18/65 **Age:** 30

					BATTING														BASERUNNING				PERCENTAGES		
Year Team	Lg	G	AB	H	2B	3B	HR	(Hm	Rd)	TB	R	RBI	TBB	IBB	SO	HBP	SH	SF	SB	CS	SB%	GDP	Avg	OBP	SLG
1995 Louisville *	AAA	1	3	0	0	0	0	--	--	0	1	0	0	0	0	0	0	0	0	0	.00	0	.000	.000	.000
1989 Oakland	AL	4	0	0	0	0	0	(0	0)	0	2	0	0	0	0	0	0	0	0	0	.00	0	.000	.000	.000
1990 Oakland	AL	7	13	2	0	0	0	(0	0)	2	0	1	0	0	5	0	0	0	0	0	.00	0	.154	.154	.154
1991 Oakland	AL	23	23	5	0	0	0	(0	0)	5	4	0	1	0	7	0	0	0	1	2	.33	0	.217	.250	.217
1992 ChA-Oak	AL	25	40	9	2	0	0	(0	0)	11	8	2	4	0	13	0	0	1	1	0	1.00	2	.225	.289	.275
1993 Oakland	AL	91	215	55	16	0	6	(3	3)	89	31	26	32	0	55	1	6	1	14	5	.74	2	.256	.353	.414
1994 Oakland	AL	91	198	44	11	0	3	(2	1)	64	23	24	16	0	51	0	2	0	7	6	.54	5	.222	.280	.323
1995 St. Louis	NL	57	118	17	1	0	3	(3	0)	27	11	9	12	0	31	2	1	1	0	0	.00	8	.144	.233	.229
1992 Chicago	AL	8	13	3	1	0	0	(0	0)	4	1	1	1	0	6	0	0	1	0	0	.00	0	.231	.267	.308
Oakland	AL	17	27	6	1	0	0	(0	0)	7	7	1	3	0	7	0	0	0	1	0	1.00	2	.222	.300	.259
7 ML YEARS		298	607	132	30	0	12	(8	4)	198	79	58	65	0	162	3	9	3	23	13	.64	17	.217	.295	.326

Rickey Henderson

Bats: Right **Throws:** Left **Pos:** LF/DH **Ht:** 5'10" **Wt:** 190 **Born:** 12/25/58 **Age:** 37

					BATTING														BASERUNNING				PERCENTAGES		
Year Team	Lg	G	AB	H	2B	3B	HR	(Hm	Rd)	TB	R	RBI	TBB	IBB	SO	HBP	SH	SF	SB	CS	SB%	GDP	Avg	OBP	SLG
1979 Oakland	AL	89	351	96	13	3	1	(1	0)	118	49	26	34	0	39	2	8	3	33	11	.75	4	.274	.338	.336
1980 Oakland	AL	158	591	179	22	4	9	(3	6)	236	111	53	117	7	54	5	6	3	100	26	.79	6	.303	.420	.399
1981 Oakland	AL	108	423	135	18	7	6	(5	1)	185	89	35	64	4	68	2	0	4	56	22	.72	7	.319	.408	.437
1982 Oakland	AL	149	536	143	24	4	10	(5	5)	205	119	51	116	1	94	2	0	4	130	42	.76	5	.267	.398	.382
1983 Oakland	AL	145	513	150	25	7	9	(5	4)	216	105	48	103	8	80	4	1	1	108	19	.85	11	.292	.414	.421
1984 Oakland	AL	142	502	147	27	4	16	(7	9)	230	113	58	86	1	81	5	1	3	66	18	.79	7	.293	.399	.458
1985 New York	AL	143	547	172	28	5	24	(8	16)	282	146	72	99	1	65	3	0	5	80	10	.89	8	.314	.419	.516
1986 New York	AL	153	608	160	31	5	28	(13	15)	285	130	74	89	2	81	2	0	2	87	18	.83	12	.263	.358	.469
1987 New York	AL	95	358	104	17	3	17	(10	7)	178	78	37	80	1	52	2	0	0	41	8	.84	10	.291	.423	.497
1988 New York	AL	140	554	169	30	2	6	(2	4)	221	118	50	82	1	54	3	2	6	93	13	.88	6	.305	.394	.399
1989 NYA-Oak	AL	150	541	148	26	3	12	(7	5)	216	113	57	126	5	68	3	0	4	77	14	.85	8	.274	.411	.399
1990 Oakland	AL	136	489	159	33	3	28	(8	20)	282	119	61	97	2	60	4	2	2	65	10	.87	13	.325	.439	.577
1991 Oakland	AL	134	470	126	17	1	18	(8	10)	199	105	57	98	7	73	7	0	3	58	18	.76	7	.268	.400	.423
1992 Oakland	AL	117	396	112	18	3	15	(10	5)	181	77	46	95	5	56	6	0	3	48	11	.81	5	.283	.426	.457
1993 Oak-Tor	AL	134	481	139	22	2	21	(10	11)	228	114	59	120	7	65	4	1	4	53	8	.87	9	.289	.432	.474
1994 Oakland	AL	87	296	77	13	0	6	(4	2)	108	66	20	72	1	45	5	1	2	22	7	.76	0	.260	.411	.365
1995 Oakland	AL	112	407	122	31	1	9	(3	6)	182	67	54	72	2	66	4	1	3	32	10	.76	8	.300	.407	.447
1989 New York	AL	65	235	58	13	1	3	(1	2)	82	41	22	56	0	29	1	0	1	25	8	.76	0	.247	.392	.349
Oakland	AL	85	306	90	13	2	9	(6	3)	134	72	35	70	5	39	2	0	3	52	6	.90	8	.294	.425	.438
1993 Oakland	AL	90	318	104	19	1	17	(8	9)	176	77	47	85	6	46	2	0	2	31	6	.84	8	.327	.469	.553
Toronto	AL	44	163	35	3	1	4	(2	2)	52	37	12	35	1	19	2	1	2	22	2	.92	1	.215	.356	.319
17 ML YEARS		2192	8063	2338	395	57	235	(109	126)	3552	1719	858	1550	55	1101	63	23	50	1149	265	.81	126	.290	.406	.441

Tom Henke

Pitches: Right **Bats:** Right **Pos:** RP **Ht:** 6' 5" **Wt:** 228 **Born:** 12/21/57 **Age:** 38

			HOW MUCH HE PITCHED					WHAT HE GAVE UP										THE RESULTS					
Year Team	Lg	G	GS	CG	GF	IP	BFP	H	R	ER	HR	SH	SF	HB	TBB	IBB	SO	WP	Bk	W	L	Pct.	ShO	Sv	ERA
1982 Texas	AL	8	0	0	6	15.2	67	14	2	2	0	1	0	1	8	2	9	0	0	1	0	1.000	0	0	1.15
1983 Texas	AL	8	0	0	5	16	65	16	6	6	1	0	0	0	4	0	17	0	0	1	0	1.000	0	1	3.38
1984 Texas	AL	25	0	0	13	28.1	141	36	21	20	0	1	4	1	20	2	25	2	2	1	1	.500	0	2	6.35
1985 Toronto	AL	28	0	0	22	40	153	29	12	9	4	2	2	0	8	2	42	0	0	3	3	.500	0	13	2.03
1986 Toronto	AL	63	0	0	51	91.1	370	63	39	34	6	2	6	1	32	4	118	3	1	9	5	.643	0	27	3.35
1987 Toronto	AL	72	0	0	62	94	363	62	27	26	10	3	5	0	25	3	128	5	0	0	6	.000	0	34	2.49
1988 Toronto	AL	52	0	0	44	68	285	60	23	22	6	4	2	2	24	3	66	0	0	4	4	.500	0	25	2.91
1989 Toronto	AL	64	0	0	56	89	356	66	20	19	5	4	3	2	25	4	116	2	0	8	3	.727	0	20	1.92
1990 Toronto	AL	61	0	0	58	74.2	297	58	18	18	8	4	1	1	19	2	75	6	0	2	4	.333	0	32	2.17
1991 Toronto	AL	49	0	0	31	50.1	190	33	13	13	4	0	0	0	11	2	53	1	0	0	2	.000	0	32	2.32
1992 Toronto	AL	57	0	0	50	55.2	228	40	19	14	5	0	3	0	22	2	46	4	0	3	2	.600	0	34	2.26
1993 Texas	AL	66	0	0	60	74.1	302	55	25	24	7	3	3	1	27	3	79	3	0	5	5	.500	0	40	2.91
1994 Texas	AL	37	0	0	31	38	156	33	16	16	6	1	1	0	12	0	39	3	0	3	6	.333	0	15	3.79
1995 St. Louis	NL	52	0	0	47	54.1	221	42	11	11	2	2	0	0	18	0	48	1	0	1	1	.500	0	36	1.82
14 ML YEARS		642	0	0	548	789.2	3194	607	252	234	64	27	30	9	255	29	861	30	3	41	42	.494	0	311	2.67

Mike Henneman

Pitches: Right **Bats:** Right **Pos:** RP **Ht:** 6' 3" **Wt:** 212 **Born:** 12/11/61 **Age:** 34

Year Team	Lg	G	GS	CG	GF	IP	BFP	H	R	ER	HR	SH	SF	HB	TBB	IBB	SO	WP	Bk	W	L	Pct.	ShO	Sv	ERA
1987 Detroit	AL	55	0	0	28	96.2	399	86	36	32	8	2	2	3	30	5	75	7	0	11	3	.786	0	7	2.98
1988 Detroit	AL	65	0	0	51	91.1	364	72	23	19	7	5	2	2	24	10	58	8	1	9	6	.600	0	22	1.87
1989 Detroit	AL	60	0	0	35	90	401	84	46	37	4	7	3	5	51	15	69	0	1	11	4	.733	0	8	3.70
1990 Detroit	AL	69	0	0	53	94.1	399	90	36	32	4	5	2	3	33	12	50	3	0	8	6	.571	0	22	3.05
1991 Detroit	AL	60	0	0	50	84.1	358	81	29	27	2	5	5	0	34	8	61	5	0	10	2	.833	0	21	2.88
1992 Detroit	AL	60	0	0	53	77.1	321	75	36	34	6	3	5	0	20	10	58	7	0	2	6	.250	0	24	3.96
1993 Detroit	AL	63	0	0	50	71.2	316	69	28	21	4	5	2	2	32	8	58	4	0	5	3	.625	0	24	2.64
1994 Detroit	AL	30	0	0	23	34.2	167	43	27	20	5	2	1	2	17	7	27	5	0	1	3	.250	0	8	5.19
1995 Det-Hou		50	0	0	44	50.1	205	45	12	12	1	1	2	2	13	2	43	5	0	0	2	.000	0	26	2.15
1995 Detroit	AL	29	0	0	26	29.1	118	24	5	5	0	1	0	0	9	1	24	2	0	0	1	.000	0	18	1.53
Houston	NL	21	0	0	18	21	87	21	7	7	1	0	2	2	4	1	19	3	0	0	1	.000	0	8	3.00
9 ML YEARS		512	0	0	387	690.2	2930	645	273	234	41	35	24	19	254	77	499	44	2	57	35	.620	0	162	3.05

Butch Henry

Pitches: Left **Bats:** Left **Pos:** SP **Ht:** 6' 1" **Wt:** 205 **Born:** 10/7/68 **Age:** 27

Year Team	Lg	G	GS	CG	GF	IP	BFP	H	R	ER	HR	SH	SF	HB	TBB	IBB	SO	WP	Bk	W	L	Pct.	ShO	Sv	ERA
1992 Houston	NL	28	28	2	0	165.2	710	185	81	74	16	12	7	1	41	7	96	2	2	6	9	.400	1	0	4.02
1993 Mon-Col	NL	30	16	1	4	103	467	135	76	70	15	6	6	1	28	2	47	1	0	3	9	.250	0	0	6.12
1994 Montreal	NL	24	15	0	1	107.1	433	97	30	29	10	5	3	2	20	1	70	1	0	8	3	.727	0	1	2.43
1995 Montreal	NL	21	21	1	0	126.2	524	133	47	40	11	7	3	2	28	3	60	0	1	7	9	.438	1	0	2.84
1993 Montreal	NL	10	1	0	3	18.1	77	18	10	8	1	0	1	0	4	0	8	0	0	1	1	.500	0	0	3.93
Colorado	NL	20	15	1	1	84.2	390	117	66	62	14	6	5	1	24	2	39	1	0	2	8	.200	0	0	6.59
4 ML YEARS		103	80	4	5	502.2	2134	550	234	213	52	30	19	6	117	13	273	4	3	24	30	.444	2	1	3.81

Doug Henry

Pitches: Right **Bats:** Right **Pos:** RP **Ht:** 6' 4" **Wt:** 205 **Born:** 12/10/63 **Age:** 32

Year Team	Lg	G	GS	CG	GF	IP	BFP	H	R	ER	HR	SH	SF	HB	TBB	IBB	SO	WP	Bk	W	L	Pct.	ShO	Sv	ERA
1991 Milwaukee	AL	32	0	0	25	36	137	16	4	4	1	1	2	0	14	1	28	0	0	2	1	.667	0	15	1.00
1992 Milwaukee	AL	68	0	0	56	65	277	64	34	29	6	1	2	0	24	4	52	4	0	1	4	.200	0	29	4.02
1993 Milwaukee	AL	54	0	0	41	55	260	67	37	34	7	5	4	3	25	8	38	4	0	4	4	.500	0	17	5.56
1994 Milwaukee	AL	25	0	0	7	31.1	143	32	17	16	7	1	0	1	23	1	20	3	0	2	3	.400	0	0	4.60
1995 New York	NL	51	0	0	20	67	273	48	23	22	7	3	2	1	25	6	62	6	1	3	6	.333	0	4	2.96
5 ML YEARS		230	0	0	149	254.1	1090	227	115	105	28	11	10	5	111	20	200	17	1	12	18	.400	0	65	3.72

Dwayne Henry

Pitches: Right **Bats:** Right **Pos:** RP **Ht:** 6' 3" **Wt:** 230 **Born:** 2/16/62 **Age:** 34

Year Team	Lg	G	GS	CG	GF	IP	BFP	H	R	ER	HR	SH	SF	HB	TBB	IBB	SO	WP	Bk	W	L	Pct.	ShO	Sv	ERA
1995 Toledo *	AAA	41	0	0	28	48.1	212	43	21	18	3	1	3	3	24	0	52	5	0	1	1	.500	0	11	3.35
1984 Texas	AL	3	0	0	1	4.1	25	5	4	4	0	1	0	0	7	0	2	0	0	0	1	.000	0	0	8.31
1985 Texas	AL	16	0	0	10	21	86	16	7	6	0	2	1	0	7	0	20	1	0	2	2	.500	0	3	2.57
1986 Texas	AL	19	0	0	4	19.1	93	14	11	10	1	1	2	1	22	0	17	7	1	1	0	1.000	0	0	4.66
1987 Texas	AL	5	0	0	1	10	50	12	10	10	2	0	0	0	9	0	7	1	0	0	0	.000	0	0	9.00
1988 Texas	AL	11	0	0	5	10.1	59	15	10	10	1	0	1	3	9	1	10	3	1	0	1	.000	0	1	8.71
1989 Atlanta	NL	12	0	0	6	12.2	55	12	6	6	2	2	0	0	5	1	16	1	0	0	2	.000	0	1	4.26
1990 Atlanta	NL	34	0	0	14	38.1	176	41	26	24	3	0	1	0	25	0	34	2	1	2	2	.500	0	0	5.63
1991 Houston	NL	52	0	0	25	67.2	282	51	25	24	7	6	2	2	39	7	51	5	0	3	2	.600	0	2	3.19
1992 Cincinnati	NL	60	0	0	11	83.2	352	59	31	31	4	7	3	1	44	6	72	12	0	3	3	.500	0	3	3.33
1993 Sea-Cin		34	1	0	16	58.2	275	62	48	42	6	3	4	2	39	5	37	8	0	2	2	.500	0	2	6.44
1995 Detroit	AL	10	0	0	6	8.2	47	11	6	6	0	1	0	0	10	2	9	1	0	1	0	1.000	0	5	6.23
1993 Seattle	AL	31	1	0	15	54	249	56	40	40	6	3	4	2	35	4	35	7	0	2	1	.667	0	2	6.67
Cincinnati	NL	3	0	0	1	4.2	26	6	8	2	0	0	0	0	4	1	2	1	0	0	1	.000	0	0	3.86
11 ML YEARS		256	1	0	99	334.2	1500	298	184	173	26	23	14	9	216	22	275	41	3	14	15	.483	0	14	4.65

Pat Hentgen

Pitches: Right **Bats:** Right **Pos:** SP **Ht:** 6' 2" **Wt:** 200 **Born:** 11/13/68 **Age:** 27

Year Team	Lg	G	GS	CG	GF	IP	BFP	H	R	ER	HR	SH	SF	HB	TBB	IBB	SO	WP	Bk	W	L	Pct.	ShO	Sv	ERA
1991 Toronto	AL	3	1	0	1	7.1	30	5	2	2	1	1	0	2	3	0	3	1	0	0	0	.000	0	0	2.45
1992 Toronto	AL	28	2	0	10	50.1	229	49	30	30	7	2	2	0	32	5	39	2	1	5	2	.714	0	0	5.36
1993 Toronto	AL	34	32	3	0	216.1	926	215	103	93	27	6	5	7	74	0	122	11	1	19	9	.679	3	0	3.87
1994 Toronto	AL	24	24	6	0	174.2	728	158	74	66	21	6	3	3	59	1	147	5	1	13	8	.619	3	0	3.40

Year Team	Lg	G	GS	CG	GF	IP	BFP	H	R	ER	HR	SH	SF	HB	TBB	IBB	SO	WP	Bk	W	L	Pct.	ShO	Sv	ERA
1995 Toronto	AL	30	30	2	0	200.2	913	**236**	**129**	**114**	24	2	1	5	90	6	135	7	2	10	14	.417	0	0	5.11
5 ML YEARS		119	89	11	11	649.1	2826	663	338	305	80	17	11	17	258	12	446	26	5	47	33	.588	3	0	4.23

Gil Heredia

Pitches: Right **Bats:** Right **Pos:** RP/SP   **Ht:** 6' 1" **Wt:** 205 **Born:** 10/26/65 **Age:** 30

		HOW MUCH HE PITCHED						WHAT HE GAVE UP												THE RESULTS					
Year Team	Lg	G	GS	CG	GF	IP	BFP	H	R	ER	HR	SH	SF	HB	TBB	IBB	SO	WP	Bk	W	L	Pct.	ShO	Sv	ERA
1991 San Francisco	NL	7	4	0	1	33	126	27	14	14	4	2	1	0	7	2	13	1	0	0	2	.000	0	0	3.82
1992 Mon-SF	NL	20	5	0	4	44.2	187	44	23	21	4	2	1	1	20	1	22	1	0	2	3	.400	0	0	4.23
1993 Montreal	NL	20	9	1	2	57.1	246	66	28	25	4	4	1	2	14	2	40	0	0	4	2	.667	0	2	3.92
1994 Montreal	NL	39	3	0	8	75.1	325	85	34	29	7	3	4	2	13	3	62	4	1	6	3	.667	0	0	3.46
1995 Montreal	NL	40	18	0	5	119	509	137	60	57	7	9	4	5	21	1	74	1	0	5	6	.455	0	1	4.31
1992 Montreal	NL	7	1	0	1	14.2	55	12	3	3	1	2	1	0	4	0	7	0	0	0	0	.000	0	0	1.84
San Francisco	NL	13	4	0	3	30	132	32	20	18	3	0	0	1	16	1	15	1	0	2	3	.400	0	0	5.40
5 ML YEARS		126	39	1	20	329.1	1393	359	159	146	26	20	11	10	75	9	211	7	1	17	16	.515	0	3	3.99

Wilson Heredia

Pitches: Right **Bats:** Right **Pos:** RP   **Ht:** 6' 0" **Wt:** 165 **Born:** 3/30/72 **Age:** 24

		HOW MUCH HE PITCHED						WHAT HE GAVE UP												THE RESULTS					
Year Team	Lg	G	GS	CG	GF	IP	BFP	H	R	ER	HR	SH	SF	HB	TBB	IBB	SO	WP	Bk	W	L	Pct.	ShO	Sv	ERA
1991 Rangers	R	17	0	0	8	33.2	153	25	18	8	1	0	2	4	20	0	22	1	1	2	4	.333	0	4	2.14
1992 Gastonia	A	39	1	0	22	63.1	301	71	45	36	4	8	2	5	30	2	64	11	7	1	2	.333	0	5	5.12
1993 Charlotte	A	34	0	0	29	38.2	165	30	17	16	0	2	4	1	20	1	26	4	0	1	5	.167	0	15	3.72
1994 Tulsa	AA	18	1	0	5	43	171	35	23	18	6	4	1	0	8	0	53	5	2	3	2	.600	0	0	3.77
1995 Okla. City	AAA	8	7	0	0	31.2	158	40	26	24	3	1	1	5	25	1	21	1	0	1	4	.200	0	0	6.82
Tulsa	AA	8	7	1	1	45.1	194	42	19	16	4	3	1	2	21	3	34	1	3	4	2	.667	1	1	3.18
Portland	AA	4	4	0	0	27	115	22	7	6	2	1	1	1	14	0	19	0	0	4	0	1.000	0	0	2.00
1995 Texas	AL	6	0	0	0	12	58	9	5	5	2	2	1	0	15	2	6	0	0	0	1	.000	0	0	3.75

Dustin Hermanson

Pitches: Right **Bats:** Right **Pos:** RP   **Ht:** 6' 2" **Wt:** 195 **Born:** 12/21/72 **Age:** 23

		HOW MUCH HE PITCHED						WHAT HE GAVE UP												THE RESULTS					
Year Team	Lg	G	GS	CG	GF	IP	BFP	H	R	ER	HR	SH	SF	HB	TBB	IBB	SO	WP	Bk	W	L	Pct.	ShO	Sv	ERA
1994 Wichita	AA	16	0	0	14	21	82	13	1	1	0	1	0	1	6	2	30	2	1	1	0	1.000	0	8	0.43
Las Vegas	AAA	7	0	0	7	7.1	33	6	5	5	1	0	1	0	5	0	6	0	0	0	0	.000	0	3	6.14
1995 Las Vegas	AAA	31	0	0	22	36	174	35	23	14	5	0	0	2	29	0	42	1	1	0	1	.000	0	11	3.50
1995 San Diego	NL	26	0	0	6	31.2	151	35	26	24	3	0		1	22	1	19	3	0	3	1	.750	0	0	6.82

Carlos Hernandez

Bats: Right **Throws:** Right **Pos:** C   **Ht:** 5'11" **Wt:** 215 **Born:** 5/24/67 **Age:** 29

		BATTING																			BASERUNNING				PERCENTAGES		
Year Team	Lg	G	AB	H	2B	3B	HR	(Hm	Rd)	TB	R	RBI	TBB	IBB	SO	HBP	SH	SF	SB	CS	SB%	GDP	Avg	OBP	SLG
1990 Los Angeles	NL	10	20	4	1	0	0	(0	0)	5	2	1	0	0	2	0	0	0	0	0	.00	0	.200	.200	.250
1991 Los Angeles	NL	15	14	3	1	0	0	(0	0)	4	1	1	0	0	5	1	0	1	1	0	1.00	2	.214	.250	.286
1992 Los Angeles	NL	69	173	45	4	0	3	(1	2)	58	11	17	11	1	21	4	0	2	0	1	.00	8	.260	.316	.335
1993 Los Angeles	NL	50	99	25	5	0	2	(1	1)	36	6	7	2	0	11	0	1	0	0	0	.00	0	.253	.267	.364
1994 Los Angeles	NL	32	64	14	2	0	2	(0	2)	22	6	6	1	0	14	0	0	0	0	0	.00	0	.219	.231	.344
1995 Los Angeles	NL	45	94	14	1	0	2	(1	1)	21	3	8	7	0	25	1	1	0	0	0	.00	5	.149	.216	.223
6 ML YEARS		221	464	105	14	0	9	(3	6)	146	29	40	21	1	78	6	2	3	1	1	.50	15	.226	.267	.315

Jeremy Hernandez

Pitches: Right **Bats:** Right **Pos:** RP   **Ht:** 6' 7" **Wt:** 210 **Born:** 7/6/66 **Age:** 29

		HOW MUCH HE PITCHED						WHAT HE GAVE UP												THE RESULTS					
Year Team	Lg	G	GS	CG	GF	IP	BFP	H	R	ER	HR	SH	SF	HB	TBB	IBB	SO	WP	Bk	W	L	Pct.	ShO	Sv	ERA
1995 Brevard Cty *	A	4	2	0	0	7.2	29	5	2	2	0	0	0	0	2	0	5	2	0	0	0	.000	0	0	2.35
Charlotte *	AAA	15	3	0	6	30.2	142	37	20	19	6	1	1	0	15	0	24	5	0	0	2	.000	0	0	5.58
1991 San Diego	NL	9	0	0	7	14.1	56	8	1	0	0	0	0	0	5	0	9	0	0	0	0	.000	0	2	0.00
1992 San Diego	NL	26	0	0	11	36.2	157	39	17	17	4	6	5	1	11	5	25	0	0	1	4	.200	0	1	4.17
1993 Cle-SD		70	0	0	31	111.2	467	116	52	45	14	4	6	0	34	7	70	2	2	6	7	.462	0	8	3.63
1994 Florida	NL	21	0	0	17	23.1	97	16	9	7	0	2	1	2	14	3	13	1	0	3	3	.500	0	9	2.70
1995 Florida	NL	7	0	0	3	7	36	12	9	9	2	1	1	1	3	1	5	0	0	0	0	.000	0	0	11.57
1993 Cleveland	AL	49	0	0	22	77.1	321	75	33	27	12	2	5	0	27	6	44	2	0	6	5	.545	0	8	3.14
San Diego	NL	21	0	0	9	34.1	146	41	19	18	2	2	1	0	7	1	26	0	0	2	0	.000	0	0	4.72
5 ML YEARS		133	0	0	69	193	813	191	88	78	20	13	13	4	67	16	122	5	2	10	14	.417	0	20	3.64

Jose Hernandez

Bats: Right **Throws:** Right **Pos:** SS/2B/3B | **Ht:** 6' 1" **Wt:** 180 **Born:** 7/14/69 **Age:** 26

							BATTING											BASERUNNING				PERCENTAGES		
Year Team	Lg	G	AB	H	2B	3B	HR	(Hm | Rd)	TB	R	RBI	TBB	IBB	SO	HBP	SH	SF	SB	CS	SB%	GDP	Avg	OBP	SLG
1991 Texas	AL	45	98	18	2	1	0	(0 | 0)	22	8	4	3	0	31	0	6	0	0	1	.00	2	.184	.208	.224
1992 Cleveland	AL	3	4	0	0	0	0	(0 | 0)	0	0	0	0	0	2	0	0	0	0	0	.00	0	.000	.000	.000
1994 Chicago	NL	56	132	32	2	3	1	(0 | 1)	43	18	9	8	0	29	1	5	0	2	2	.50	4	.242	.291	.326
1995 Chicago	NL	93	245	60	11	4	13	(6 | 7)	118	37	40	13	3	69	0	8	2	1	0	1.00	8	.245	.281	.482
4 ML YEARS		197	479	110	15	8	14	(6 | 8)	183	63	53	24	3	131	1	19	2	3	3	.50	14	.230	.267	.382

Roberto Hernandez

Pitches: Right **Bats:** Right **Pos:** RP | **Ht:** 6' 4" **Wt:** 235 **Born:** 11/11/64 **Age:** 31

		HOW MUCH HE PITCHED						WHAT HE GAVE UP									THE RESULTS					
Year Team	Lg	G	GS	CG	GF	IP	BFP	H	R	ER	HR	SH	SF	HB	TBB	IBB	SO	WP	Bk	W	L	Pct.	ShO	Sv	ERA
1991 Chicago	AL	9	3	0	1	15	69	18	15	13	1	0	0	0	7	0	6	1	0	1	0	1.000	0	0	7.80
1992 Chicago	AL	43	0	0	27	71	277	45	15	13	4	0	3	4	20	1	68	2	0	7	3	.700	0	12	1.65
1993 Chicago	AL	70	0	0	67	78.2	314	66	21	20	6	2	2	0	20	1	71	2	0	3	4	.429	0	38	2.29
1994 Chicago	AL	45	0	0	43	47.2	206	44	29	26	5	0	1	1	19	1	50	1	0	4	4	.500	0	14	4.91
1995 Chicago	AL	60	0	0	57	59.2	272	63	30	26	9	4	0	3	28	4	84	1	0	3	7	.300	0	32	3.92
5 ML YEARS		227	3	0	195	272	1138	236	110	98	25	6	6	8	94	7	279	7	0	18	18	.500	0	96	3.24

Xavier Hernandez

Pitches: Right **Bats:** Left **Pos:** RP | **Ht:** 6' 2" **Wt:** 195 **Born:** 8/16/65 **Age:** 30

		HOW MUCH HE PITCHED						WHAT HE GAVE UP									THE RESULTS					
Year Team	Lg	G	GS	CG	GF	IP	BFP	H	R	ER	HR	SH	SF	HB	TBB	IBB	SO	WP	Bk	W	L	Pct.	ShO	Sv	ERA
1989 Toronto	AL	7	0	0	2	22.2	101	25	15	12	2	0	2	1	8	0	7	1	0	1	0	1.000	0	0	4.76
1990 Houston	NL	34	1	0	10	62.1	268	60	34	32	8	2	4	4	24	5	24	6	0	2	1	.667	0	0	4.62
1991 Houston	NL	32	6	0	8	63	285	66	34	33	6	1	1	0	32	7	55	0	0	2	7	.222	0	3	4.71
1992 Houston	NL	77	0	0	25	111	454	81	31	26	5	3	2	3	42	7	96	5	0	9	1	.900	0	7	2.11
1993 Houston	NL	72	0	0	29	96.2	389	75	37	28	6	3	3	1	28	3	101	6	0	4	5	.444	0	9	2.61
1994 New York	AL	31	0	0	14	40	187	48	27	26	7	2	2	2	21	3	37	3	0	4	4	.500	0	6	5.85
1995 Cincinnati	NL	59	0	0	19	90	391	95	47	46	8	6	2	4	31	1	84	7	0	7	2	.778	0	3	4.60
7 ML YEARS		312	7	0	107	485.2	2075	450	225	203	42	17	16	15	186	26	404	28	0	29	20	.592	0	28	3.76

Jose Herrera

Bats: Left **Throws:** Left **Pos:** CF | **Ht:** 6' 0" **Wt:** 165 **Born:** 8/30/72 **Age:** 23

							BATTING											BASERUNNING				PERCENTAGES		
Year Team	Lg	G	AB	H	2B	3B	HR	(Hm	Rd)	TB	R	RBI	TBB	IBB	SO	HBP	SH	SF	SB	CS	SB%	GDP	Avg	OBP	SLG
1991 Medicne Hat	R	40	143	35	5	1	1	--	--	45	21	11	6	1	38	3	1	0	6	7	.46	0	.245	.289	.315
St. Cathrns	A	3	9	3	1	0	0	--	--	4	3	2	1	0	2	1	0	0	0	1	.00	0	.333	.455	.444
1992 Medicne Hat	R	72	265	72	9	2	0	--	--	85	45	21	32	1	62	6	7	0	32	8	.80	4	.272	.363	.321
1993 Hagerstown	A	95	388	123	22	5	5	--	--	170	60	42	26	1	63	7	5	4	36	20	.64	3	.317	.367	.438
Madison	A	4	14	3	0	0	0	--	--	3	1	0	0	0	6	0	1	0	1	1	.50	0	.214	.214	.214
1994 Modesto	A	103	370	106	20	3	11	--	--	165	59	56	38	3	76	10	5	6	21	12	.64	5	.286	.363	.446
1995 Huntsville	AA	92	358	101	11	4	6	--	--	138	37	45	27	2	58	2	0	2	9	8	.53	8	.282	.334	.385
1995 Oakland	AL	33	70	17	1	2	0	(0	0)	22	9	2	6	0	11	0	0	1	1	3	.25	1	.243	.299	.314

Orel Hershiser

Pitches: Right **Bats:** Right **Pos:** SP | **Ht:** 6' 3" **Wt:** 195 **Born:** 9/16/58 **Age:** 37

		HOW MUCH HE PITCHED						WHAT HE GAVE UP									THE RESULTS					
Year Team	Lg	G	GS	CG	GF	IP	BFP	H	R	ER	HR	SH	SF	HB	TBB	IBB	SO	WP	Bk	W	L	Pct.	ShO	Sv	ERA
1983 Los Angeles	NL	8	0	0	4	8	37	7	6	3	1	1	0	0	6	0	5	1	0	0	0	.000	0	1	3.38
1984 Los Angeles	NL	45	20	8	10	189.2	771	160	65	56	9	2	3	4	50	8	150	8	1	11	8	.579	4	2	2.66
1985 Los Angeles	NL	36	34	9	1	239.2	953	179	72	54	8	5	4	6	68	5	157	5	0	19	3	.864	5	0	2.03
1986 Los Angeles	NL	35	35	8	0	231.1	988	213	112	99	13	14	6	5	86	11	153	12	3	14	14	.500	1	0	3.85
1987 Los Angeles	NL	37	35	10	2	264.2	1093	247	105	90	17	8	2	9	74	5	190	11	2	16	16	.500	1	1	3.06
1988 Los Angeles	NL	35	34	15	1	267	1068	208	73	67	18	9	6	4	73	10	178	6	5	23	8	.742	8	1	2.26
1989 Los Angeles	NL	35	33	8	0	256.2	1047	226	75	66	9	19	6	3	77	14	178	8	4	15	15	.500	4	0	2.31
1990 Los Angeles	NL	4	4	0	0	25.1	106	26	12	12	1	1	0	1	4	0	16	0	1	1	1	.500	0	0	4.26
1991 Los Angeles	NL	21	21	0	0	112	473	112	43	43	3	2	1	5	32	6	73	2	4	7	2	.778	0	0	3.46
1992 Los Angeles	NL	33	33	1	0	210.2	910	209	101	86	15	15	6	8	69	13	130	10	0	10	15	.400	0	0	3.67
1993 Los Angeles	NL	33	33	5	0	215.2	913	201	106	86	17	12	4	7	72	13	141	7	0	12	14	.462	1	0	3.59
1994 Los Angeles	NL	21	21	1	0	135.1	575	146	67	57	15	4	3	2	42	6	72	6	2	6	6	.500	0	0	3.79
1995 Cleveland	AL	26	26	1	0	167.1	683	151	76	72	21	3	4	5	51	1	111	3	0	16	6	.727	1	0	3.87
13 ML YEARS		369	329	66	18	2323.1	9617	2085	913	791	147	95	45	59	704	92	1554	79	22	150	108	.581	25	5	3.06

Phil Hiatt

Bats: Right **Throws:** Right **Pos:** RF **Ht:** 6' 3" **Wt:** 200 **Born:** 5/1/69 **Age:** 27

Year	Team	Lg	G	AB	H	2B	3B	HR	(Hm	Rd)	TB	R	RBI	TBB	IBB	SO	HBP	SH	SF	SB	CS	SB%	GDP	Avg	OBP	SLG
1990	Eugene	A	73	289	85	18	5	2	--	--	119	33	44	17	1	69	1	1	4	15	4	.79	1	.294	.331	.412
1991	Baseball Cy	A	81	315	94	21	6	5	--	--	142	41	33	22	4	70	3	1	2	28	14	.67	8	.298	.348	.451
	Memphis	AA	56	206	47	7	1	6	--	--	74	29	33	9	1	63	3	0	6	6	1	.86	3	.228	.263	.359
1992	Memphis	AA	129	487	119	20	5	27	--	--	230	71	83	25	1	157	1	1	3	5	10	.33	11	.244	.287	.472
	Omaha	AAA	5	14	3	0	0	2	--	--	9	3	4	2	0	3	0	0	0	1	0	1.00	0	.214	.313	.643
1993	Omaha	AAA	12	51	12	2	0	3	--	--	23	8	10	4	0	20	1	0	0	0	0	.00	0	.235	.304	.451
1994	Omaha	AAA	6	22	4	1	0	1	--	--	8	2	2	0	0	4	1	1	0	1	0	1.00	2	.182	.217	.364
	Memphis	AA	108	400	120	26	4	17	--	--	205	57	66	40	4	116	13	2	2	12	8	.60	4	.300	.380	.513
1995	Omaha	AAA	20	76	12	5	0	2	--	--	23	7	8	2	0	25	0	0	1	0	0	.00	0	.158	.177	.303
1993	Kansas City	AL	81	238	52	12	1	7	(4	3)	87	30	36	16	0	82	7	0	2	6	3	.67	8	.218	.285	.366
1995	Kansas City	AL	52	113	23	6	0	4	(1	3)	41	11	12	9	0	37	0	2	0	1	0	1.00	3	.204	.262	.363
	2 ML YEARS		133	351	75	18	1	11	(5	6)	128	41	48	25	0	119	7	2	2	7	3	.70	11	.214	.278	.365

Greg Hibbard

Pitches: Left **Bats:** Left **Pos:** SP **Ht:** 6' 0" **Wt:** 185 **Born:** 9/13/64 **Age:** 31

Year	Team	Lg	G	GS	CG	GF	IP	BFP	H	R	ER	HR	SH	SF	HB	TBB	IBB	SO	WP	Bk	W	L	Pct.	ShO	Sv	ERA
1989	Chicago	AL	23	23	2	0	137.1	581	142	58	49	5	5	4	2	41	0	55	4	0	6	7	.462	0	0	3.21
1990	Chicago	AL	33	33	3	0	211	871	202	80	74	11	8	10	6	55	2	92	2	1	14	9	.609	1	0	3.16
1991	Chicago	AL	32	29	5	1	194	806	196	107	93	23	8	2	2	57	1	71	1	0	11	11	.500	0	0	4.31
1992	Chicago	AL	31	28	0	2	176	755	187	92	86	17	10	6	7	57	2	69	1	1	10	7	.588	0	0	4.40
1993	Chicago	NL	31	31	1	0	191	800	209	96	84	19	9	10	3	47	9	82	1	2	15	11	.577	0	0	3.96
1994	Seattle	AL	15	14	0	0	80.2	392	115	78	60	11	6	2	2	31	1	39	5	0	1	5	.167	0	0	6.69
	6 ML YEARS		165	158	11	3	990	4205	1051	511	446	86	46	34	22	288	15	408	14	4	57	50	.533	1	1	4.05

Bryan Hickerson

Pitches: Left **Bats:** Left **Pos:** RP **Ht:** 6' 2" **Wt:** 190 **Born:** 10/13/63 **Age:** 32

Year	Team	Lg	G	GS	CG	GF	IP	BFP	H	R	ER	HR	SH	SF	HB	TBB	IBB	SO	WP	Bk	W	L	Pct.	ShO	Sv	ERA
1991	San Francisco	NL	17	6	0	4	50	212	53	20	20	3	2	0	0	17	3	43	2	0	2	2	.500	0	0	3.60
1992	San Francisco	NL	61	1	0	8	87.1	345	74	31	30	7	4	5	1	21	2	68	4	1	5	3	.625	0	0	3.09
1993	San Francisco	NL	47	15	0	5	120.1	525	137	58	57	14	11	4	1	39	3	69	4	0	7	5	.583	0	1	4.26
1994	San Francisco	NL	28	14	0	1	98.1	436	118	60	59	20	4	1	1	38	6	59	2	1	4	8	.333	0	0	5.40
1995	ChN-Col	NL	56	0	0	13	48.1	239	69	52	46	8	2	0	1	28	5	40	5	1	3	3	.500	0	1	8.57
1995	Chicago	NL	38	0	0	8	31.2	144	36	28	24	3	2	0	0	15	4	28	3	0	2	3	.400	0	1	6.82
	Colorado	NL	18	0	0	5	16.2	95	33	24	22	5	0	0	1	13	1	12	2	1	1	0	1.000	0	0	11.88
	5 ML YEARS		209	36	0	31	404.1	1757	451	221	212	52	23	10	4	143	19	279	17	3	21	21	.500	0	2	4.72

Bob Higginson

Bats: Left **Throws:** Right **Pos:** RF/LF **Ht:** 5'11" **Wt:** 180 **Born:** 8/18/70 **Age:** 25

Year	Team	Lg	G	AB	H	2B	3B	HR	(Hm	Rd)	TB	R	RBI	TBB	IBB	SO	HBP	SH	SF	SB	CS	SB%	GDP	Avg	OBP	SLG
1992	Niagara Fal	A	70	232	68	17	4	2	--	--	99	35	37	33	0	47	1	2	0	12	8	.60	4	.293	.383	.427
1993	Lakeland	A	61	223	67	11	7	3	--	--	101	42	25	40	1	31	1	2	2	8	3	.73	6	.300	.406	.453
	London	AA	63	224	69	15	4	4	--	--	104	25	35	19	1	37	0	0	3	3	4	.43	6	.308	.358	.464
1994	Toledo	AAA	137	476	131	28	3	23	--	--	234	81	67	46	3	99	5	0	3	16	8	.67	9	.275	.343	.492
1995	Detroit	AL	131	410	92	17	5	14	(10	4)	161	61	43	62	3	107	5	2	7	6	4	.60	5	.224	.329	.393

Glenallen Hill

Bats: Right **Throws:** Right **Pos:** RF **Ht:** 6' 2" **Wt:** 220 **Born:** 3/22/65 **Age:** 31

Year	Team	Lg	G	AB	H	2B	3B	HR	(Hm	Rd)	TB	R	RBI	TBB	IBB	SO	HBP	SH	SF	SB	CS	SB%	GDP	Avg	OBP	SLG
1989	Toronto	AL	19	52	15	0	0	1	(1	0)	18	4	7	3	0	12	0	0	0	2	1	.67	0	.288	.327	.346
1990	Toronto	AL	84	260	60	11	3	12	(7	5)	113	47	32	18	0	62	0	0	0	8	3	.73	5	.231	.281	.435
1991	Cle-Tor	AL	72	221	57	8	2	8	(3	5)	93	29	25	23	0	54	0	1	3	6	4	.60	7	.258	.324	.421
1992	Cleveland	AL	102	369	89	16	1	18	(7	11)	161	38	49	20	0	73	4	0	1	9	6	.60	11	.241	.287	.436
1993	Cle-ChN	AL	97	261	69	14	2	15	(5	10)	132	33	47	17	1	71	1	0	4	8	3	.73	4	.264	.307	.506
1994	Chicago	NL	89	269	80	12	1	10	(3	7)	124	48	38	29	0	57	0	0	1	19	6	.76	5	.297	.365	.461
1995	San Francisco	NL	132	497	131	29	4	24	(13	11)	240	71	86	39	4	98	1	0	2	25	5	.83	11	.264	.317	.483
1991	Cleveland	AL	37	122	32	3	0	5	(1	4)	50	15	14	16	0	30	0	1	1	4	2	.67	5	.262	.345	.410
	Toronto	AL	35	99	25	5	2	3	(2	1)	43	14	11	7	0	24	0	0	2	2	2	.50	2	.253	.296	.434
1993	Cleveland	AL	66	174	39	7	2	6	(0	5)	65	19	25	11	1	50	1	0	1	7	3	.70	3	.224	.268	.374
	Chicago	NL	31	87	30	7	0	10	(5	5)	67	14	22	6	0	21	0	0	0	1	0	1.00	1	.345	.387	.770
	7 ML YEARS		595	1929	501	90	13	88	(39	49)	881	270	284	149	5	427	6	2	11	77	28	.73	43	.260	.313	.457

Ken Hill

Pitches: Right **Bats:** Right **Pos:** SP **Ht:** 6' 2" **Wt:** 205 **Born:** 12/14/65 **Age:** 30

		HOW	MUCH	HE	PITCHED				WHAT	HE	GAVE	UP						THE	RESULTS			
Year Team	Lg	G	GS	CG	GF	IP	BFP	H	R	ER	HR	SH	SF	HB	TBB	IBB	SO	WP	Bk	W	L	Pct.	ShO	Sv	ERA
1988 St. Louis	NL	4	1	0	0	14	62	16	9	8	0	0	0	0	6	0	6	1	0	0	1	.000	0	0	5.14
1989 St. Louis	NL	33	33	2	0	196.2	862	186	92	83	9	14	5	5	99	6	112	11	2	7	15	.318	1	0	3.80
1990 St. Louis	NL	17	14	1	1	78.2	343	79	49	48	7	5	5	1	33	1	58	5	0	5	6	.455	0	0	5.49
1991 St. Louis	NL	30	30	0	0	181.1	743	147	76	72	15	7	7	6	67	4	121	7	1	11	10	.524	0	0	3.57
1992 Montreal	NL	33	33	3	0	218	908	187	76	65	13	15	3	3	75	4	150	11	4	16	9	.640	3	0	2.68
1993 Montreal	NL	28	28	2	0	183.2	780	163	84	66	7	9	7	6	74	7	90	6	2	9	7	.563	0	0	3.23
1994 Montreal	NL	23	23	2	0	154.2	647	145	61	57	12	6	6	6	44	7	85	3	0	16	5	.762	1	0	3.32
1995 StL-Cle		30	29	1	0	185	817	202	107	95	21	12	3	1	77	4	98	6	0	10	8	.556	0	0	4.62
1995 St. Louis	NL	18	18	0	0	110.1	493	125	71	62	16	9	2	0	45	4	50	3	0	6	7	.462	0	0	5.06
Cleveland	AL	12	11	1	0	74.2	324	77	36	33	5	3	1	1	32	0	48	3	0	4	1	.800	0	0	3.98
8 ML YEARS		198	191	11	1	1212	5162	1125	554	494	84	68	36	28	475	33	720	50	9	74	61	.548	5	0	3.67

Eric Hillman

Pitches: Left **Bats:** Left **Pos:** SP/RP **Ht:** 6'10" **Wt:** 225 **Born:** 4/27/66 **Age:** 30

		HOW	MUCH	HE	PITCHED				WHAT	HE	GAVE	UP						THE	RESULTS			
Year Team	Lg	G	GS	CG	GF	IP	BFP	H	R	ER	HR	SH	SF	HB	TBB	IBB	SO	WP	Bk	W	L	Pct.	ShO	Sv	ERA
1992 New York	NL	11	8	0	2	52.1	227	67	31	31	9	3	1	2	10	2	16	1	0	2	2	.500	1	0	5.33
1993 New York	NL	27	22	3	1	145	627	173	83	64	12	10	10	4	24	2	60	0	1	2	9	.182	1	0	3.97
1994 New York	NL	11	6	0	0	34.2	156	45	30	30	9	2	1	2	11	3	20	1	1	0	3	.000	0	0	7.79
3 ML YEARS		49	36	3	3	232	1010	285	144	125	30	15	12	8	45	7	96	2	2	4	14	.222	1	0	4.85

Sterling Hitchcock

Pitches: Left **Bats:** Left **Pos:** SP **Ht:** 6' 1" **Wt:** 192 **Born:** 4/29/71 **Age:** 25

		HOW	MUCH	HE	PITCHED				WHAT	HE	GAVE	UP						THE	RESULTS			
Year Team	Lg	G	GS	CG	GF	IP	BFP	H	R	ER	HR	SH	SF	HB	TBB	IBB	SO	WP	Bk	W	L	Pct.	ShO	Sv	ERA
1992 New York	AL	3	3	0	0	13	68	23	12	12	2	0	0	1	6	0	6	0	0	0	2	.000	0	0	8.31
1993 New York	AL	6	6	0	0	31	135	32	18	16	4	0	2	1	14	1	26	3	2	1	2	.333	0	0	4.65
1994 New York	AL	23	5	1	4	49.1	218	48	24	23	3	1	7	0	29	1	37	5	0	4	1	.800	0	2	4.20
1995 New York	AL	27	27	4	0	168.1	719	155	91	88	22	5	9	5	68	1	121	5	2	11	10	.524	1	0	4.70
4 ML YEARS		59	41	5	4	261.2	1140	258	145	139	31	6	18	7	117	3	190	13	4	16	15	.516	1	2	4.78

Denny Hocking

Bats: Both **Throws:** Right **Pos:** SS **Ht:** 5'10" **Wt:** 174 **Born:** 4/2/70 **Age:** 26

				BATTING														BASERUNNING				PERCENTAGES		
Year Team	Lg	G	AB	H	2B	3B	HR	(Hm	Rd)	TB	R	RBI	TBB	IBB	SO	HBP	SH	SF	SB	CS	SB%	GDP	Avg	OBP	SLG
1990 Elizabethtn	R	54	201	59	6	2	6	--	--	87	45	30	40	1	25	6	1	2	13	4	.76	6	.294	.422	.433
1991 Kenosha	A	125	432	110	17	8	2	--	--	149	72	36	77	4	69	6	3	4	22	10	.69	6	.255	.372	.345
1992 Visalia	A	135	550	182	34	9	7	--	--	255	117	81	72	1	77	8	2	2	38	18	.68	7	.331	.415	.464
1993 Nashville	AA	107	409	109	9	4	8	--	--	150	54	50	34	0	66	4	3	2	15	5	.75	12	.267	.327	.367
1994 Salt Lake	AAA	112	394	110	14	6	5	--	--	151	61	57	28	1	57	2	5	4	13	7	.65	6	.279	.327	.383
1995 Salt Lake	AAA	117	397	112	24	2	8	--	--	164	51	75	25	1	41	2	8	5	12	8	.60	10	.282	.324	.413
1993 Minnesota	AL	15	36	5	1	0	0	(0	0)	6	7	0	6	0	8	0	0	0	1	0	1.00	1	.139	.262	.167
1994 Minnesota	AL	11	31	10	3	0	0	(0	0)	13	3	2	0	0	4	0	0	0	2	0	1.00	1	.323	.323	.419
1995 Minnesota	AL	9	25	5	0	2	0	(0	0)	9	4	3	2	1	2	0	1	0	1	0	1.00	1	.200	.259	.360
3 ML YEARS		35	92	20	4	2	0			28	14	5	8	1	14	0	1	0	4	0	1.00	3	.217	.280	.304

Trevor Hoffman

Pitches: Right **Bats:** Right **Pos:** RP **Ht:** 6' 0" **Wt:** 205 **Born:** 10/13/67 **Age:** 28

		HOW	MUCH	HE	PITCHED				WHAT	HE	GAVE	UP						THE	RESULTS			
Year Team	Lg	G	GS	CG	GF	IP	BFP	H	R	ER	HR	SH	SF	HB	TBB	IBB	SO	WP	Bk	W	L	Pct.	ShO	Sv	ERA
1993 SD-Fla	NL	67	0	0	26	90	391	80	43	39	10	4	5	1	39	13	79	5	0	4	6	.400	0	5	3.90
1994 San Diego	NL	47	0	0	41	56	225	39	16	16	4	1	2	0	20	6	68	3	0	4	4	.500	0	20	2.57
1995 San Diego	NL	55	0	0	51	53.1	218	48	25	23	10	0	0	0	14	3	52	1	0	7	4	.636	0	31	3.88
1993 San Diego	NL	39	0	0	13	54.1	239	56	30	26	5	2	4	1	20	6	53	2	0	2	4	.333	0	3	4.31
Florida	NL	28	0	0	13	35.2	152	24	13	13	5	2	1	0	19	7	26	3	0	2	2	.500	0	2	3.28
3 ML YEARS		169	0	0	118	199.1	834	167	84	78	24	5	7	1	73	22	199	9	0	15	14	.517	0	56	3.52

Chris Hoiles

Bats: Right **Throws:** Right **Pos:** C **Ht:** 6' 0" **Wt:** 213 **Born:** 3/20/65 **Age:** 31

				BATTING														BASERUNNING				PERCENTAGES		
Year Team	Lg	G	AB	H	2B	3B	HR	(Hm	Rd)	TB	R	RBI	TBB	IBB	SO	HBP	SH	SF	SB	CS	SB%	GDP	Avg	OBP	SLG
1989 Baltimore	AL	6	9	1	1	0	0	(0	0)	2	0	1	1	0	3	0	0	0	0	0	.00	0	.111	.200	.222

Year	Team	Lg	G	AB	H	2B	3B	HR	(Hm	Rd)	TB	R	RBI	TBB	IBB	SO	HBP	SH	SF	SB	CS	SB%	GDP	Avg	OBP	SLG
1990	Baltimore	AL	23	63	12	3	0	1	(1	0)	18	7	6	5	1	12	0	0	0	0	0	.00	0	.190	.250	.286
1991	Baltimore	AL	107	341	83	15	0	11	(5	6)	131	36	31	29	1	61	1	0	1	0	2	.00	11	.243	.304	.384
1992	Baltimore	AL	96	310	85	10	1	20	(8	12)	157	49	40	55	2	60	2	1	3	0	2	.00	8	.274	.384	.506
1993	Baltimore	AL	126	419	130	28	0	29	(16	13)	245	80	82	69	4	94	9	3	3	1	1	.50	10	.310	.416	.585
1994	Baltimore	AL	99	332	82	10	0	19	(11	8)	149	45	53	63	2	73	5	1	4	2	0	1.00	6	.247	.371	.449
1995	Baltimore	AL	114	352	88	15	1	19	(9	10)	162	53	58	67	3	80	4	0	3	1	0	1.00	11	.250	.373	.460
7 ML YEARS			571	1826	481	82	2	99	(50	49)	864	270	271	289	13	383	21	5	14	4	5	.44	46	.263	.368	.473

Ray Holbert

Bats: Right **Throws:** Right **Pos:** SS   **Ht:** 6' 0" **Wt:** 175 **Born:** 9/25/70 **Age:** 25

						BATTING													BASERUNNING				PERCENTAGES		
Year	Team	Lg	G	AB	H	2B	3B	HR	(Hm	Rd)	TB	R	RBI	TBB	IBB	SO	HBP	SH	SF	SB	CS	SB%	GDP	Avg	OBP	SLG
1988	Padres	R	49	170	44	1	0	3	--	--	54	38	19	37	0	32	2	1	0	20	7	.74	4	.259	.397	.318
1989	Waterloo	A	117	354	55	7	1	0	--	--	64	37	20	41	0	99	2	7	1	13	13	.50	9	.155	.246	.181
1990	Waterloo	A	133	411	84	10	1	3	--	--	105	51	37	51	0	117	4	9	1	16	16	.50	10	.204	.298	.255
1991	High Desert	A	122	386	102	14	2	4	--	--	132	76	51	56	1	83	6	9	3	19	6	.76	10	.264	.364	.342
1992	Wichita	AA	95	304	86	7	3	2	--	--	105	46	23	42	2	68	1	3	1	26	8	.76	7	.283	.371	.345
1993	Wichita	AA	112	388	101	13	5	5	--	--	139	56	48	54	0	87	2	3	9	30	17	.64	6	.260	.347	.358
1994	Las Vegas	AAA	118	426	128	21	5	8	--	--	183	68	52	50	2	99	2	10	4	27	11	.71	8	.300	.373	.430
1995	Las Vegas	AAA	9	26	3	1	0	0	--	--	4	3	3	5	0	10	0	0	0	1	1	.50	1	.115	.258	.154
1994	San Diego	NL	5	5	1	0	0	0	(0	0)	1	1	0	0	0	4	0	0	0	0	0	.00	0	.200	.200	.200
1995	San Diego	NL	63	73	13	2	1	2	(1	1)	23	11	5	8	1	20	2	3	0	4	0	1.00	3	.178	.277	.315
2 ML YEARS			68	78	14	2	1	2	(1	1)	24	12	5	8	1	24	2	3	0	4	0	1.00	3	.179	.273	.308

Todd Hollandsworth

Bats: Left **Throws:** Left **Pos:** CF   **Ht:** 6' 2" **Wt:** 193 **Born:** 4/20/73 **Age:** 23

						BATTING													BASERUNNING				PERCENTAGES		
Year	Team	Lg	G	AB	H	2B	3B	HR	(Hm	Rd)	TB	R	RBI	TBB	IBB	SO	HBP	SH	SF	SB	CS	SB%	GDP	Avg	OBP	SLG
1991	Dodgers	R	6	16	5	0	0	0	--	--	5	1	0	6	0	6	0	0	0	0	0	.00	1	.313	.313	.313
	Yakima	A	56	203	48	5	1	8	--	--	79	34	33	27	3	57	4	0	0	11	1	.92	2	.236	.338	.389
1992	Bakersfield	A	119	430	111	23	5	13	--	--	183	70	58	50	5	113	3	0	2	27	13	.68	6	.258	.338	.426
1993	San Antonio	AA	126	474	119	24	9	17	--	--	212	57	63	29	2	101	5	2	5	23	12	.66	7	.251	.298	.447
1994	Albuquerque	AAA	132	505	144	31	5	19	--	--	242	80	91	46	5	96	0	1	3	15	9	.63	15	.285	.343	.479
1995	San Bernrdo	A	1	2	1	0	0	0	--	--	1	0	0	0	0	1	0	0	0	0	1	.00	0	.500	.500	.500
	Albuquerque	AAA	10	38	9	2	0	2	--	--	17	9	4	6	2	8	1	0	0	1	0	1.00	1	.237	.356	.447
1995	Los Angeles	NL	41	103	24	2	0	5	(3	2)	41	16	13	10	2	29	1	0	1	2	1	.67	1	.233	.304	.398

Dave Hollins

Bats: Both **Throws:** Right **Pos:** 1B   **Ht:** 6' 1" **Wt:** 207 **Born:** 5/25/66 **Age:** 30

						BATTING													BASERUNNING				PERCENTAGES		
Year	Team	Lg	G	AB	H	2B	3B	HR	(Hm	Rd)	TB	R	RBI	TBB	IBB	SO	HBP	SH	SF	SB	CS	SB%	GDP	Avg	OBP	SLG
1990	Philadelphia	NL	72	114	21	0	0	5	(2	3)	36	14	15	10	3	28	1	0	2	0	0	.00	1	.184	.252	.316
1991	Philadelphia	NL	56	151	45	10	2	6	(3	3)	77	18	21	17	1	26	3	0	1	1	1	.50	2	.298	.378	.510
1992	Philadelphia	NL	156	586	158	28	4	27	(14	13)	275	104	93	76	4	110	19	0	4	9	6	.60	8	.270	.369	.469
1993	Philadelphia	NL	143	543	148	30	4	18	(9	9)	240	104	93	85	5	109	5	0	7	2	3	.40	15	.273	.372	.442
1994	Philadelphia	NL	44	162	36	7	1	4	(1	3)	57	28	26	23	0	32	4	0	3	1	0	1.00	6	.222	.328	.352
1995	Phi-Bos		70	218	49	12	2	7	(5	2)	86	48	26	57	4	45	5	0	4	1	1	.50	4	.225	.391	.394
1995	Philadelphia	NL	65	205	47	12	2	7	(5	2)	84	46	25	53	4	38	5	0	4	1	1	.50	4	.229	.393	.410
	Boston	AL	5	13	2	0	0	0	(0	0)	2	2	1	4	0	7	0	0	0	0	0	.00	0	.154	.353	.154
6 ML YEARS			541	1774	457	87	13	67	(34	33)	771	316	274	268	17	350	37	0	21	14	11	.56	36	.258	.363	.435

Darren Holmes

Pitches: Right **Bats:** Right **Pos:** RP   **Ht:** 6' 0" **Wt:** 200 **Born:** 4/25/66 **Age:** 30

			HOW MUCH HE PITCHED					WHAT HE GAVE UP												THE RESULTS					
Year	Team	Lg	G	GS	CG	GF	IP	BFP	H	R	ER	HR	SH	SF	HB	TBB	IBB	SO	WP	Bk	W	L	Pct.	ShO	Sv	ERA
1990	Los Angeles	NL	14	0	0	1	17.1	77	15	10	10	1	1	2	0	11	3	19	1	0	0	1	.000	0	0	5.19
1991	Milwaukee	AL	40	0	0	9	76.1	344	90	43	40	6	8	3	1	27	1	59	6	0	1	4	.200	0	3	4.72
1992	Milwaukee	AL	41	0	0	25	42.1	173	35	12	12	1	4	0	2	11	4	31	0	0	4	4	.500	0	6	2.55
1993	Colorado	NL	62	0	0	51	66.2	274	56	31	30	6	0	0	2	20	1	60	2	1	3	3	.500	0	25	4.05
1994	Colorado	NL	29	0	0	14	28.1	142	35	25	20	5	4	1	1	24	4	33	2	0	0	3	.000	0	3	6.35
1995	Colorado	NL	68	0	0	33	66.2	286	59	26	24	3	5	3	1	28	3	61	7	1	6	1	.857	0	14	3.24
6 ML YEARS			254	0	0	133	297.2	1296	290	147	136	22	22	9	7	121	16	263	18	2	14	16	.467	0	51	4.11

Mark Holzemer

Pitches: Left **Bats:** Left **Pos:** RP **Ht:** 6' 0" **Wt:** 165 **Born:** 8/20/69 **Age:** 26

Year Team	Lg	G	GS	CG	GF	IP	BFP	H	R	ER	HR	SH	SF	HB	TBB	IBB	SO	WP	Bk	W	L	Pct.	ShO	Sv	ERA
1988 Bend	A	13	13	1	0	68.2	311	59	51	40	3	0	1	6	47	1	72	8	6	4	6	.400	1	0	5.24
1989 Quad City	A	25	25	3	0	139.1	603	122	68	52	4	3	5	5	64	1	131	12	4	12	7	.632	1	0	3.36
1990 Midland	AA	15	15	1	0	77	363	92	55	45	10	2	1	6	41	0	54	6	0	1	7	.125	0	0	5.26
1991 Midland	AA	2	2	0	0	6.1	28	3	2	1	0	1	0	1	5	0	7	2	0	0	0	.000	0	0	1.42
1992 Palm Spring	A	5	5	2	0	30	124	23	10	10	2	1	0	3	13	0	32	0	0	3	2	.600	0	0	3.00
Midland	AA	7	7	2	0	44.2	188	45	22	19	4	0	1	1	13	0	36	3	1	2	5	.286	0	0	3.83
Edmonton	AAA	17	16	4	1	89	416	114	69	66	12	2	6	7	55	1	49	6	1	5	7	.417	0	0	6.67
1993 Vancouver	AAA	24	23	2	0	145.2	642	158	94	78	9	6	4	4	70	2	80	5	5	9	6	.600	0	0	4.82
1994 Vancouver	AAA	29	17	0	5	117.1	540	144	93	86	19	4	5	6	58	1	77	15	0	5	10	.333	0	0	6.60
1995 Vancouver	AAA	28	4	0	11	54.2	228	45	18	15	2	5	0	3	24	4	35	2	0	3	2	.600	0	0	2.47
1993 California	AL	5	4	0	1	23.1	117	34	24	23	2	1	0	3	13	0	10	1	0	0	3	.000	0	0	8.87
1995 California	AL	12	0	0	5	8.1	45	11	6	5	1	1	0	1	7	1	5	0	0	0	1	.000	0	0	5.40
2 ML YEARS		17	4	0	6	31.2	162	45	30	28	3	2	0	4	20	1	15	1	0	0	4	.000	0	0	7.96

Rick Honeycutt

Pitches: Left **Bats:** Left **Pos:** RP **Ht:** 6' 1" **Wt:** 195 **Born:** 6/29/54 **Age:** 42

Year Team	Lg	G	GS	CG	GF	IP	BFP	H	R	ER	HR	SH	SF	HB	TBB	IBB	SO	WP	Bk	W	L	Pct.	ShO	Sv	ERA
1977 Seattle	AL	10	3	0	3	29	125	26	16	14	7	0	2	3	11	2	17	2	1	0	1	.000	0	0	4.34
1978 Seattle	AL	26	24	4	0	134	594	150	81	73	12	9	7	3	49	5	50	3	0	5	11	.313	1	0	4.90
1979 Seattle	AL	33	28	8	2	194	839	201	103	87	22	11	6	6	67	7	83	5	1	11	12	.478	1	0	4.04
1980 Seattle	AL	30	30	9	0	203	871	221	99	89	22	11	7	3	60	7	79	4	0	10	17	.370	1	0	3.95
1981 Texas	AL	20	20	8	0	128	509	120	49	47	12	5	0	0	17	1	40	1	0	11	6	.647	2	0	3.30
1982 Texas	AL	30	26	4	3	164	728	201	103	96	20	4	8	3	54	4	64	3	1	5	17	.227	1	0	5.27
1983 Tex-LA		34	32	6	0	213.2	865	214	85	72	15	5	6	8	50	6	74	1	3	16	11	.593	2	0	3.03
1984 Los Angeles	NL	29	28	6	0	183.2	762	180	72	58	11	6	5	2	51	11	75	1	2	10	9	.526	2	0	2.84
1985 Los Angeles	NL	31	25	1	2	142	600	141	71	54	9	5	4	1	49	7	67	2	0	8	12	.400	0	1	3.42
1986 Los Angeles	NL	32	28	0	2	171	713	164	71	63	9	6	1	3	45	4	100	4	1	11	9	.550	0	0	3.32
1987 Oak-LA		34	24	1	1	139.1	631	158	91	73	13	1	3	4	54	4	102	5	1	3	16	.158	1	0	4.72
1988 Oakland	AL	55	0	0	17	79.2	330	74	36	31	6	3	6	3	25	2	47	3	8	3	2	.600	0	7	3.50
1989 Oakland	AL	64	0	0	24	76.2	305	56	26	20	5	5	2	1	26	3	52	6	1	2	2	.500	0	12	2.35
1990 Oakland	AL	63	0	0	13	63.1	256	46	23	19	2	2	6	1	22	2	38	1	1	2	2	.500	0	7	2.70
1991 Oakland	AL	43	0	0	7	37.2	167	37	16	15	3	2	1	2	20	3	26	0	0	2	4	.333	0	0	3.58
1992 Oakland	AL	54	0	0	7	39	169	41	19	16	2	4	1	3	10	3	32	2	0	1	4	.200	0	3	3.69
1993 Oakland	AL	52	0	0	7	41.2	174	30	18	13	2	7	4	1	20	6	21	0	0	1	4	.200	0	1	2.81
1994 Texas	AL	42	0	0	9	25	122	37	21	20	4	5	0	2	9	1	18	0	0	1	2	.333	0	1	7.20
1995 Oak-NYA	AL	52	0	0	6	45.2	180	39	16	15	6	3	1	1	10	0	21	0	0	5	1	.833	0	2	2.96
1983 Texas	AL	25	25	5	0	174.2	693	168	59	47	9	3	6	6	37	2	56	1	2	14	8	.636	2	0	2.42
Los Angeles	NL	9	7	1	0	39	172	46	26	25	6	2	0	2	13	4	18	0	1	2	3	.400	0	0	5.77
1987 Oakland	AL	7	4	0	1	23.2	106	25	17	14	3	1	3	2	9	0	10	1	1	1	4	.200	0	0	5.32
Los Angeles	NL	27	20	1	0	115.2	525	133	74	59	10	0	0	2	45	4	92	4	0	2	12	.143	1	0	4.59
1995 Oakland	AL	49	0	0	6	44.2	174	37	13	12	5	3	1	1	9	0	21	0	0	5	1	.833	0	2	2.42
New York	AL	3	0	0	0	1	6	2	3	3	1	0	0	0	1	0	0	0	0	0	0	.000	0	0	27.00
19 ML YEARS		734	268	47	103	2110.1	8940	2136	1016	875	182	94	70	50	649	78	1006	43	20	107	142	.430	11	34	3.73

Chris Hook

Pitches: Right **Bats:** Right **Pos:** RP **Ht:** 6' 5" **Wt:** 230 **Born:** 8/4/68 **Age:** 27

Year Team	Lg	G	GS	CG	GF	IP	BFP	H	R	ER	HR	SH	SF	HB	TBB	IBB	SO	WP	Bk	W	L	Pct.	ShO	Sv	ERA
1989 Reds	R	14	9	0	1	51	209	43	19	18	1	1	4	4	17	0	39	4	2	4	1	.800	0	0	3.18
1990 Charlstn-Wv	A	30	16	0	3	119.1	537	117	65	54	3	4	3	8	62	4	87	19	1	6	5	.545	0	0	4.07
1991 Charlstn-Wv	A	45	0	0	19	71	306	52	26	19	1	4	1	11	40	1	79	8	0	8	2	.800	0	2	2.41
1992 Cedar Rapds	A	26	25	1	1	159	664	138	59	48	2	7	5	10	53	0	144	5	6	14	8	.636	0	0	2.72
1993 Chattanooga	AA	28	28	1	0	166.2	723	163	85	67	7	11	7	12	66	2	122	9	1	12	8	.600	0	0	3.62
1994 Phoenix	AAA	27	11	0	8	90	401	109	48	46	6	3	4	5	29	0	57	4	1	7	2	.778	0	2	4.60
1995 Phoenix	AAA	4	0	0	0	6	22	2	1	1	0	0	0	0	3	0	5	0	0	0	0	.000	0	0	1.50
1995 San Francisco	NL	45	0	0	14	52.1	239	55	33	32	7	3	3	3	29	3	40	2	0	5	1	.833	0	0	5.50

John Hope

Pitches: Right **Bats:** Right **Pos:** RP **Ht:** 6' 3" **Wt:** 206 **Born:** 12/21/70 **Age:** 25

Year Team	Lg	G	GS	CG	GF	IP	BFP	H	R	ER	HR	SH	SF	HB	TBB	IBB	SO	WP	Bk	W	L	Pct.	ShO	Sv	ERA
1995 Calgary *	AAA	13	13	3	0	80.2	322	76	29	25	3	3	1	3	11	0	41	1	0	7	1	.875	1	0	2.79

Year	Team	Lg	G	GS	CG	GF	IP	BFP	H	R	ER	HR	SH	SF	HB	TBB	IBB	SO	WP	Bk	W	L	Pct.	ShO	Sv	ERA
1993	Pittsburgh	NL	7	7	0	0	38	166	47	19	17	2	5	1	2	8	3	8	1	0	0	2	.000	0	0	4.03
1994	Pittsburgh	NL	9	0	0	1	14	64	18	12	9	1	0	0	2	4	0	6	1	0	0	0	.000	0	0	5.79
1995	Pittsburgh	NL	3	0	0	0	2.1	21	8	8	8	0	0	1	3	4	0	7	0	0	0	0	.000	0	0	30.86
	3 ML YEARS		19	7	0	1	54.1	251	73	39	34	3	5	2	7	16	3	16	2	0	0	2	.000	0	0	5.63

Sam Horn

Bats: Left   **Throws:** Left   **Pos:** DH   **Ht:** 6' 5"   **Wt:** 247   **Born:** 11/2/63   **Age:** 32

Year	Team	Lg	G	AB	H	2B	3B	HR	(Hm	Rd)	TB	R	RBI	TBB	IBB	SO	HBP	SH	SF	SB	CS	SB%	GDP	Avg	OBP	SLG
1995	Calgary *	AAA	36	99	33	8	2	8	--	--	69	21	22	14	0	21	0	0	1	0	0	.00	5	.333	.412	.697
	Okla. City *	AAA	46	156	48	9	0	12	--	--	93	26	42	25	3	49	0	0	1	0	2	.00	4	.308	.401	.596
1987	Boston	AL	46	158	44	7	0	14	(6	8)	93	31	34	17	0	55	2	0	0	0	1	.00	5	.278	.356	.589
1988	Boston	AL	24	61	9	0	0	2	(2	0)	15	4	8	11	3	20	0	0	1	0	0	.00	4	.148	.274	.246
1989	Boston	AL	33	54	8	2	0	0	(0	0)	10	1	4	8	1	16	0	0	0	0	0	.00	4	.148	.258	.185
1990	Baltimore	AL	79	246	61	13	0	14	(8	6)	116	30	45	32	1	62	0	0	2	0	0	.00	8	.248	.332	.472
1991	Baltimore	AL	121	317	74	16	0	23	(12	11)	159	45	61	41	4	99	3	0	1	0	0	.00	10	.233	.326	.502
1992	Baltimore	AL	63	162	38	10	1	5	(2	3)	65	13	19	21	2	60	1	0	1	0	0	.00	8	.235	.324	.401
1993	Cleveland	AL	12	33	15	1	0	4	(2	2)	28	8	8	1	0	5	1	0	1	0	0	.00	1	.455	.472	.848
1995	Texas	AL	11	9	1	0	0	0	(0	0)	1	0	1	0	0	6	0	0	0	0	0	.00	0	.111	.200	.111
	8 ML YEARS		389	1040	250	49	1	62	(32	30)	487	132	179	132	11	323	7	0	6	0	1	.00	37	.240	.328	.468

Vince Horsman

Pitches: Left   **Bats:** Right   **Pos:** RP   **Ht:** 6' 2"   **Wt:** 180   **Born:** 3/9/67   **Age:** 29

Year	Team	Lg	G	GS	CG	GF	IP	BFP	H	R	ER	HR	SH	SF	HB	TBB	IBB	SO	WP	Bk	W	L	Pct.	ShO	Sv	ERA
1995	Salt Lake *	AAA	16	0	0	7	13	64	23	15	15	3	0	0	0	4	2	10	1	0	1	0	1.000	0	0	10.38
1991	Toronto	AL	4	0	0	2	4	16	2	0	0	0	1	0	0	3	1	2	0	0	0	0	.000	0	0	0.00
1992	Oakland	AL	58	0	0	9	43.1	180	39	13	12	3	3	1	0	21	4	18	1	0	2	1	.667	0	1	2.49
1993	Oakland	AL	40	0	0	5	25	116	25	15	15	2	0	0	3	15	1	17	1	0	2	0	1.000	0	1	5.40
1994	Oakland	AL	33	0	0	6	29.1	127	29	17	16	2	3	3	1	11	2	20	1	1	0	1	.000	0	0	4.91
1995	Minnesota	AL	6	0	0	3	9	43	12	8	7	2	2	1	0	4	1	4	0	0	0	0	.000	0	0	7.00
	5 ML YEARS		141	0	0	25	110.2	482	107	53	50	9	9	5	4	54	9	61	3	1	4	2	.667	0	1	4.07

Dwayne Hosey

Bats: Both   **Throws:** Right   **Pos:** CF   **Ht:** 5'10"   **Wt:** 175   **Born:** 3/11/67   **Age:** 29

Year	Team	Lg	G	AB	H	2B	3B	HR	(Hm	Rd)	TB	R	RBI	TBB	IBB	SO	HBP	SH	SF	SB	CS	SB%	GDP	Avg	OBP	SLG
1987	White Sox	R	41	129	36	2	1	1	--	--	43	26	10	18	1	22	3	0	2	19	4	.83	1	.279	.375	.333
1988	South Bend	A	95	311	71	11	0	2	--	--	88	53	24	28	2	55	5	4	2	36	15	.71	5	.228	.301	.283
	Utica	A	3	7	1	0	0	0	--	--	1	0	0	2	0	1	0	0	0	1	0	1.00	0	.143	.333	.143
1989	Madison	A	123	470	115	16	6	11	--	--	176	72	51	44	3	82	8	2	2	33	18	.65	9	.245	.319	.374
1990	Modesto	A	113	453	133	21	5	16	--	--	212	77	61	50	5	70	8	8	2	30	23	.57	2	.294	.372	.468
1991	Huntsville	AA	28	102	25	6	0	1	--	--	34	16	7	9	1	15	1	1	1	5	4	.56	1	.245	.310	.333
	Stockton	A	85	356	97	12	7	15	--	--	168	55	62	31	1	58	3	1	9	22	8	.73	4	.272	.328	.472
1992	Wichita	AA	125	427	108	23	5	9	--	--	168	56	68	40	3	70	10	1	7	16	11	.59	3	.253	.326	.393
1993	Wichita	AA	86	326	95	19	2	18	--	--	172	52	61	25	4	44	2	0	4	13	4	.76	2	.291	.342	.528
	Las Vegas	AAA	32	110	29	4	4	3	--	--	50	21	12	11	1	17	4	0	0	7	4	.64	0	.264	.352	.455
1994	Omaha	AAA	112	406	135	23	8	27	--	--	255	95	80	61	10	85	8	0	6	27	12	.69	3	.333	.424	.628
1995	Omaha	AAA	75	271	80	21	4	12	--	--	145	59	50	29	2	45	1	1	2	15	6	.71	1	.295	.363	.535
1995	Boston	AL	24	68	23	8	1	3	(1	2)	42	20	7	8	0	16	0	1	0	6	0	1.00	0	.338	.408	.618

Chris Howard

Pitches: Left   **Bats:** Right   **Pos:** RP   **Ht:** 6' 0"   **Wt:** 185   **Born:** 11/18/65   **Age:** 30

Year	Team	Lg	G	GS	CG	GF	IP	BFP	H	R	ER	HR	SH	SF	HB	TBB	IBB	SO	WP	Bk	W	L	Pct.	ShO	Sv	ERA
1995	Sarasota *	A	6	5	0	0	10.1	45	10	6	6	1	1	2	0	4	0	7	1	3	0	2	.000	0	0	5.23
	Pawtucket *	AAA	17	0	0	2	20.2	91	25	11	9	6	0	2	0	4	1	19	0	0	3	1	.750	0	0	3.92
1993	Chicago	AL	3	0	0	0	2.1	10	2	0	0	0	0	0	0	3	1	1	0	0	0	0	.000	0	0	0.00
1994	Boston	AL	37	0	0	5	39.2	166	35	17	16	5	2	2	0	12	4	22	1	0	1	0	1.000	0	1	3.63
1995	Texas	AL	4	0	0	1	4	15	3	0	0	0	0	1	0	1	0	2	1	0	0	0	.000	0	0	0.00
	3 ML YEARS		44	0	0	6	46	191	40	17	16	5	2	3	0	16	5	25	2	0	2	0	1.000	0	1	3.13

Dave Howard

Bats: Both   **Throws:** Right   **Pos:** 2B/SS/LF/CF   **Ht:** 6' 0"   **Wt:** 175   **Born:** 2/26/67   **Age:** 29

Year	Team	Lg	G	AB	H	2B	3B	HR	(Hm	Rd)	TB	R	RBI	TBB	IBB	SO	HBP	SH	SF	SB	CS	SB%	GDP	Avg	OBP	SLG
1991	Kansas City	AL	94	236	51	7	0	1	(0	1)	61	20	17	16	0	45	1	9	2	3	2	.60	1	.216	.267	.258

Year Team	Lg	G	AB	H	2B	3B	HR	(Hm	Rd)	TB	R	RBI	TBB	IBB	SO	HBP	SH	SF	SB	CS	SB%	GDP	Avg	OBP	SLG
1992 Kansas City	AL	74	219	49	6	2	1	(1	0)	62	19	18	15	0	43	0	8	2	3	4	.43	3	.224	.271	.283
1993 Kansas City	AL	15	24	8	0	1	0	(0	0)	10	5	2	2	0	5	0	2	1	1	0	1.00	0	.333	.370	.417
1994 Kansas City	AL	46	83	19	4	0	1	(0	1)	26	9	13	11	0	23	0	3	3	3	2	.60	1	.229	.309	.313
1995 Kansas City	AL	95	255	62	13	4	0	(0	0)	83	23	19	24	1	41	1	6	1	6	1	.86	7	.243	.310	.325
5 ML YEARS		324	817	189	30	7	3	(1	2)	242	76	69	68	1	157	2	28	9	16	9	.64	12	.231	.289	.296

Thomas Howard

Bats: Both **Throws:** Right **Pos:** CF/LF/RF **Ht:** 6' 2" **Wt:** 205 **Born:** 12/11/64 **Age:** 31

Year Team	Lg	G	AB	H	2B	3B	HR	(Hm	Rd)	TB	R	RBI	TBB	IBB	SO	HBP	SH	SF	SB	CS	SB%	GDP	Avg	OBP	SLG
1990 San Diego	NL	20	44	12	2	0	0	(0	0)	14	4	0	0	0	11	0	1	0	0	1	.00	1	.273	.273	.318
1991 San Diego	NL	106	281	70	12	3	4	(4	0)	100	30	22	24	4	57	1	2	1	10	7	.59	4	.249	.309	.356
1992 Cle-SD		122	361	100	15	2	2	(1	1)	125	37	32	17	1	60	0	11	2	15	8	.65	4	.277	.308	.346
1993 Cle-Cin		112	319	81	15	3	7	(5	2)	123	48	36	24	0	63	0	0	5	10	7	.59	9	.254	.302	.386
1994 Cincinnati	NL	83	178	47	11	0	5	(4	1)	73	24	24	10	1	30	0	3	1	4	2	.67	2	.264	.302	.410
1995 Cincinnati	NL	113	281	85	15	2	3	(1	2)	113	42	26	20	0	37	1	1	1	17	8	.68	3	.302	.350	.402
1992 Cleveland	AL	117	358	99	15	2	2	(1	1)	124	36	32	17	1	60	0	10	2	15	8	.65	4	.277	.308	.346
San Diego	NL	5	3	1	0	0	0	(0	0)	1	1	0	0	0	0	0	1	0	0	0	.00	0	.333	.333	.333
1993 Cleveland	AL	74	178	42	7	0	3	(3	0)	58	26	23	12	0	42	0	0	4	5	1	.83	5	.236	.278	.326
Cincinnati	NL	38	141	39	8	3	4	(2	2)	65	22	13	12	0	21	0	0	1	5	6	.45	4	.277	.331	.461
6 ML YEARS		556	1464	395	70	10	21	(15	6)	548	185	140	95	6	258	2	18	10	56	33	.63	23	.270	.313	.374

Steve Howe

Pitches: Left **Bats:** Left **Pos:** RP **Ht:** 6' 2" **Wt:** 198 **Born:** 3/10/58 **Age:** 38

Year Team	Lg	G	GS	CG	GF	IP	BFP	H	R	ER	HR	SH	SF	HB	TBB	IBB	SO	WP	Bk	W	L	Pct.	ShO	Sv	ERA
1980 Los Angeles	NL	59	0	0	36	85	359	83	33	25	1	8	3	2	22	10	39	1	0	7	9	.438	0	17	2.65
1981 Los Angeles	NL	41	0	0	25	54	227	51	17	15	2	4	4	0	18	7	32	0	0	5	3	.625	0	8	2.50
1982 Los Angeles	NL	66	0	0	41	99.1	393	87	27	23	3	10	3	0	17	11	49	1	0	7	5	.583	0	13	2.08
1983 Los Angeles	NL	46	0	0	33	68.2	274	55	15	11	2	5	3	1	12	7	52	3	0	4	7	.364	0	18	1.44
1985 Min-LA		32	0	0	19	41	198	58	33	25	3	2	5	1	12	4	21	3	0	3	4	.429	0	3	5.49
1987 Texas	AL	24	0	0	15	31.1	131	33	15	15	2	2	0	3	8	1	19	2	1	3	3	.500	0	1	4.31
1991 New York	AL	37	0	0	10	48.1	189	39	12	9	1	2	1	3	7	2	34	2	0	3	1	.750	0	3	1.68
1992 New York	AL	20	0	0	10	22	79	9	7	6	1	1	1	0	3	1	12	1	0	3	0	1.000	0	6	2.45
1993 New York	AL	51	0	0	19	50.2	215	58	31	28	7	5	2	3	10	4	19	0	0	3	5	.375	0	4	4.97
1994 New York	AL	40	0	0	25	40	152	28	8	8	2	1	0	0	7	1	18	1	0	3	0	1.000	0	15	1.80
1995 New York	AL	56	0	0	20	49	230	66	29	27	7	3	2	4	17	3	28	1	0	6	3	.667	0	2	4.96
1985 Minnesota	AL	13	0	0	5	19	94	28	16	13	1	0	3	0	7	2	10	1	0	2	3	.400	0	0	6.16
Los Angeles	NL	19	0	0	14	22	104	30	17	12	2	2	2	1	5	2	11	2	0	1	1	.500	0	3	4.91
11 ML YEARS		472	0	0	253	589.1	2447	567	227	192	31	43	24	17	133	51	323	15	1	47	40	.540	0	90	2.93

Mike Hubbard

Bats: Right **Throws:** Right **Pos:** C **Ht:** 6' 1" **Wt:** 195 **Born:** 2/16/71 **Age:** 25

Year Team	Lg	G	AB	H	2B	3B	HR	(Hm	Rd)	TB	R	RBI	TBB	IBB	SO	HBP	SH	SF	SB	CS	SB%	GDP	Avg	OBP	SLG
1992 Geneva	A	50	183	44	4	4	3	--	--	65	25	25	7	0	29	3	4	4	6	4	.60	2	.240	.274	.355
1993 Daytona	A	68	245	72	10	3	1	--	--	91	25	20	18	0	41	5	2	5	10	6	.63	4	.294	.348	.371
1994 Orlando	AA	104	357	102	13	3	11	--	--	154	52	39	29	4	58	8	2	2	7	7	.50	5	.286	.351	.431
1995 Iowa	AAA	75	254	66	6	3	5	--	--	93	28	23	26	1	60	0	6	3	6	1	.86	5	.260	.325	.366
1995 Chicago	NL	15	23	4	0	0	0	(0	0)	4	2	1	2	0	7	0	0	0	0	0	.00	1	.174	.240	.174

Trent Hubbard

Bats: Right **Throws:** Right **Pos:** CF **Ht:** 5' 8" **Wt:** 180 **Born:** 5/11/66 **Age:** 30

Year Team	Lg	G	AB	H	2B	3B	HR	(Hm	Rd)	TB	R	RBI	TBB	IBB	SO	HBP	SH	SF	SB	CS	SB%	GDP	Avg	OBP	SLG
1986 Auburn	A	70	242	75	12	1	1	--	--	92	42	32	28	0	42	1	2	2	35	5	.88	2	.310	.381	.380
1987 Asheville	A	101	284	67	8	1	1	--	--	80	39	35	28	1	42	0	0	7	28	13	.68	4	.236	.298	.282
1988 Osceola	A	130	446	116	15	11	3	--	--	162	68	65	61	0	72	3	1	3	44	18	.71	10	.260	.351	.363
1989 Tucson	AAA	21	50	11	2	0	0	--	--	13	3	2	1	0	10	1	0	0	3	3	.50	2	.220	.250	.260
Columbus	AA	104	348	92	7	8	3	--	--	124	55	37	43	3	53	2	4	2	28	6	.82	8	.264	.347	.356
1990 Tucson	AAA	12	27	6	2	2	0	--	--	12	5	2	3	0	6	0	0	0	1	1	.50	1	.222	.300	.444
Columbus	AA	95	335	84	14	4	4	--	--	118	39	35	37	0	51	3	8	2	17	8	.68	7	.251	.329	.352
1991 Jackson	AA	126	455	135	21	3	2	--	--	168	78	41	65	2	81	9	3	2	39	17	.70	3	.297	.384	.369
Tucson	AAA	2	4	0	0	0	0	--	--	0	0	0	0	0	0	0	0	0	0	0	.00	0	.000	.000	.000
1992 Tucson	AAA	115	420	130	16	4	2	--	--	160	69	33	45	1	68	4	9	2	34	10	.77	7	.310	.380	.381
1993 Colo. Sprng	AAA	117	439	138	24	8	7	--	--	199	83	56	47	3	57	6	5	1	33	18	.65	4	.314	.387	.453
1994 Colo. Sprng	AAA	79	320	116	22	5	8	--	--	172	78	38	44	1	40	2	2	1	28	10	.74	7	.363	.441	.538

Year	Team	Lg	G	AB	H	2B	3B	HR	(Hm	Rd)	TB	R	RBI	TBB	IBB	SO	HBP	SH	SF	SB	CS	SB%	GDP	Avg	OBP	SLG
1995	Colo. Sprng	AAA	123	480	163	29	7	12	--	--	242	102	66	61	5	59	5	2	5	37	14	.73	2	.340	.416	.504
1994	Colorado	NL	18	25	7	1	1	1	(1	0)	13	3	3	3	0	4	0	0	0	0	0	.00	1	.280	.357	.520
1995	Colorado	NL	24	58	18	4	0	3	(2	1)	31	13	9	8	0	6	0	1	0	2	1	.67	2	.310	.394	.534
	2 ML YEARS		42	83	25	5	1	4	(3	1)	44	16	12	11	0	10	0	1	0	2	1	.67	3	.301	.383	.530

John Hudek

Pitches: Right **Bats:** Both **Pos:** RP **Ht:** 6' 1" **Wt:** 200 **Born:** 8/8/66 **Age:** 29

			HOW MUCH HE PITCHED					WHAT HE GAVE UP									THE RESULTS					
Year	Team	Lg	G	GS	CG	GF	IP	BFP	H	R	ER	HR	SH	SF	HB	TBB	IBB	SO	WP	Bk	W	L	Pct.	ShO	Sv	ERA
1988	South Bend	A	26	0	0	18	54.2	234	45	19	12	4	3	1	3	21	3	35	3	0	7	2	.778	0	8	1.98
1989	Sarasota	A	27	0	0	25	43	165	22	10	8	1	2	4	2	13	2	39	1	1	1	3	.250	0	15	1.67
	Birmingham	AA	18	0	0	16	17	72	14	8	8	2	1	0	0	9	0	10	0	0	1	1	.500	0	11	4.24
1990	Birmingham	AA	42	10	0	23	92.1	418	84	59	47	9	2	8	6	52	3	67	5	0	6	6	.500	0	4	4.58
1991	Birmingham	AA	51	0	0	42	65.2	292	58	39	28	4	7	5	6	28	7	49	5	0	5	10	.333	0	13	3.84
1992	Birmingham	AA	5	0	0	4	11.2	55	9	4	3	0	2	0	0	11	2	9	0	0	0	1	.000	0	1	2.31
	Vancouver	AAA	39	3	1	19	85.1	367	69	36	30	4	6	5	4	45	9	61	6	0	8	1	.889	1	2	3.16
1993	Toledo	AAA	16	5	0	2	38.2	180	44	26	25	2	2	3	1	22	0	32	2	0	1	3	.250	0	0	5.82
	Tucson	AAA	13	1	0	3	19	83	17	11	8	1	0	1	2	11	1	18	1	0	3	1	.750	0	0	3.79
1994	Tucson	AAA	6	0	0	4	7.1	28	3	4	4	0	0	0	0	3	0	14	1	0	0	0	.000	0	2	4.91
1994	Houston	NL	42	0	0	33	39.1	159	24	14	13	5	0	2	1	18	2	39	0	0	0	2	.000	0	16	2.97
1995	Houston	NL	19	0	0	16	20	83	19	12	12	3	1	0	0	5	0	29	2	0	2	2	.500	0	7	5.40
	2 ML YEARS		61	0	0	49	59.1	242	43	26	25	8	1	2	1	23	2	68	2	0	2	4	.333	0	23	3.79

Rex Hudler

Bats: Right **Throws:** Right **Pos:** 2B/LF **Ht:** 6' 0" **Wt:** 195 **Born:** 9/2/60 **Age:** 35

			BATTING																BASERUNNING				PERCENTAGES		
Year	Team	Lg	G	AB	H	2B	3B	HR	(Hm	Rd)	TB	R	RBI	TBB	IBB	SO	HBP	SH	SF	SB	CS	SB%	GDP	Avg	OBP	SLG
1984	New York	AL	9	7	1	1	0	0	(0	0)	2	2	0	1	0	5	1	0	0	0	0	.00	0	.143	.333	.286
1985	New York	AL	20	51	8	0	1	0	(0	0)	10	4	1	1	0	9	0	5	0	0	1	.00	0	.157	.173	.196
1986	Baltimore	AL	14	1	0	0	0	0	(0	0)	0	1	0	0	0	0	0	0	0	1	0	1.00	0	.000	.000	.000
1988	Montreal	NL	77	216	59	14	2	4	(1	3)	89	38	14	10	6	34	0	1	2	29	7	.81	2	.273	.303	.412
1989	Montreal	NL	92	155	38	7	0	6	(3	3)	63	21	13	6	2	23	1	0	0	15	4	.79	2	.245	.278	.406
1990	Mon-StL	NL	93	220	62	11	2	7	(2	5)	98	31	22	12	1	32	2	2	1	18	10	.64	3	.282	.323	.445
1991	St. Louis	NL	101	207	47	10	2	1	(1	0)	64	21	15	10	1	29	0	2	2	12	8	.60	1	.227	.260	.309
1992	St. Louis	NL	61	98	24	4	0	3	(2	1)	37	17	5	2	0	23	1	1	1	2	6	.25	0	.245	.265	.378
1994	California	AL	56	124	37	8	0	8	(4	4)	69	17	20	6	0	28	0	4	2	2	2	.50	7	.298	.326	.556
1995	California	AL	84	223	59	16	0	6	(4	2)	93	30	27	10	1	48	5	2	1	13	0	1.00	2	.265	.310	.417
1990	Montreal	NL	4	3	1	0	0	0	(0	0)	1	1	0	0	0	1	0	0	0	0	0	.000	.333	.333	.333
	St. Louis	NL	89	217	61	11	2	7	(2	5)	97	30	22	12	1	31	2	2	1	18	10	.64	3	.281	.323	.447
	10 ML YEARS		607	1302	335	71	7	35	(17	18)	525	182	117	58	11	231	10	17	9	92	38	.71	17	.257	.292	.403

Joe Hudson

Pitches: Right **Bats:** Right **Pos:** RP **Ht:** 6' 1" **Wt:** 175 **Born:** 9/29/70 **Age:** 25

			HOW MUCH HE PITCHED					WHAT HE GAVE UP									THE RESULTS					
Year	Team	Lg	G	GS	CG	GF	IP	BFP	H	R	ER	HR	SH	SF	HB	TBB	IBB	SO	WP	Bk	W	L	Pct.	ShO	Sv	ERA
1992	Elmira	A	19	7	0	6	72	320	76	46	35	2	3	0	2	33	0	38	4	2	3	3	.500	0	0	4.38
1993	Lynchburg	A	49	1	0	30	84.1	372	97	46	38	1	2	2	2	38	2	62	10	2	8	6	.571	0	6	4.06
1994	Sarasota	A	30	0	0	21	48.1	215	42	20	12	0	1	1	2	27	0	33	6	0	3	1	.750	0	7	2.23
	New Britain	AA	23	0	0	11	39	183	49	18	17	0	3	1	2	18	1	24	1	1	5	3	.625	0	0	3.92
1995	Trenton	AA	22	0	0	17	31.2	133	20	6	6	0	1	0	1	17	3	24	2	1	0	1	.000	0	8	1.71
1995	Boston	AL	39	0	0	11	46	205	53	21	21	2	3	1	2	23	1	29	6	0	0	1	.000	0	1	4.11

Michael Huff

Bats: Right **Throws:** Right **Pos:** CF/RF **Ht:** 6' 1" **Wt:** 190 **Born:** 8/11/63 **Age:** 32

			BATTING																BASERUNNING				PERCENTAGES		
Year	Team	Lg	G	AB	H	2B	3B	HR	(Hm	Rd)	TB	R	RBI	TBB	IBB	SO	HBP	SH	SF	SB	CS	SB%	GDP	Avg	OBP	SLG
1989	Los Angeles	NL	12	25	5	1	0	1	(0	1)	9	4	2	3	0	6	1	1	0	0	1	.00	0	.200	.310	.360
1991	ChA-Cle	AL	102	243	61	10	2	3	(1	2)	84	42	25	37	2	48	6	6	2	14	4	.78	7	.251	.361	.346
1992	Chicago	AL	60	115	24	5	0	0	(0	0)	29	13	8	10	1	24	1	2	2	1	2	.33	2	.209	.273	.252
1993	Chicago	AL	43	44	8	2	0	1	(0	1)	13	4	6	9	0	15	1	1	2	1	0	1.00	0	.182	.321	.295
1994	Toronto	AL	80	207	63	15	3	3	(1	2)	93	31	25	27	2	27	3	0	0	2	1	.67	6	.304	.392	.449
1995	Toronto	AL	61	138	32	9	1	1	(0	1)	46	14	9	22	0	21	1	5	2	1	1	.50	4	.232	.337	.333
1991	Chicago	AL	51	97	26	4	1	1	(0	1)	35	14	15	12	2	18	2	3	1	3	2	.60	5	.268	.357	.361
	Cleveland	AL	51	146	35	6	1	2	(1	1)	49	28	10	25	0	30	4	3	1	11	2	.85	2	.240	.364	.336
	6 ML YEARS		358	772	193	42	6	9	(2	7)	274	108	75	108	5	141	13	15	8	19	9	.68	19	.250	.349	.355

Rick Huisman

Pitches: Right **Bats:** Right **Pos:** RP   **Ht:** 6' 3" **Wt:** 200 **Born:** 5/17/69 **Age:** 27

| | | | | | | | HOW MUCH HE PITCHED | | | WHAT HE GAVE UP | | | | | | | | | | | | THE RESULTS | | | | | |
Year	Team	Lg	G	GS	CG	GF	IP	BFP	H	R	ER	HR	SH	SF	HB	TBB	IBB	SO	WP	Bk	W	L	Pct.	ShO	Sv	ERA
1990	Everett	A	1	0	0	0	2	10	3	1	1	0	0	0	0	2	0	2	1	0	0	0	.000	0	0	4.50
	Clinton	A	14	13	0	0	79	315	57	19	18	2	1	2	0	33	0	103	5	4	6	5	.545	0	0	2.05
1991	San Jose	A	26	26	7	0	182.1	720	126	45	37	5	11	3	3	73	1	216	13	3	16	4	.800	4	0	1.83
1992	Shreveport	AA	17	16	1	0	103.1	403	79	33	27	3	2	0	5	31	1	100	3	1	7	4	.636	1	0	2.35
	Phoenix	AAA	9	8	0	0	56	230	45	16	15	3	1	1	1	24	0	44	1	0	3	2	.600	0	0	2.41
1993	San Jose	A	4	4	1	0	23.1	97	19	6	6	0	2	1	2	12	0	15	1	0	2	1	.667	0	0	2.31
	Phoenix	AAA	14	14	0	0	72.1	333	78	54	48	5	1	1	1	45	0	59	8	4	3	4	.429	0	0	5.97
	Tucson	AAA	2	0	0	0	3.2	18	6	5	3	0	0	0	0	1	0	4	5	0	1	0	1.000	0	0	7.36
1994	Jackson	AA	49	0	0	46	50.1	204	32	10	9	1	1	1	2	24	2	63	1	0	3	0	1.000	0	31	1.61
1995	Tucson	AAA	42	0	0	28	54.2	246	58	33	27	1	0	3	1	28	3	47	3	1	6	1	.857	0	6	4.45
	Omaha	AAA	5	0	0	3	5	19	3	1	1	1	0	0	0	1	0	13	0	0	0	0	.000	0	1	1.80
1995	Kansas City	AL	7	0	0	2	9.2	44	14	8	8	2	1	0	1	1	0	12	0	0	0	0	.000	0	0	7.45

Tim Hulett

Bats: Right **Throws:** Right **Pos:** 2B   **Ht:** 6' 0" **Wt:** 199 **Born:** 1/12/60 **Age:** 36

| | | | | | | | | | BATTING | | | | | | | | | | | BASERUNNING | | | | PERCENTAGES | | |
Year	Team	Lg	G	AB	H	2B	3B	HR	(Hm	Rd)	TB	R	RBI	TBB	IBB	SO	HBP	SH	SF	SB	CS	SB%	GDP	Avg	OBP	SLG
1995	Louisville *	AAA	3	10	3	1	0	0	--	--	4	1	3	2	1	0	0	0	0	0	1	.00	0	.300	.417	.400
	Okla. City *	AAA	39	141	30	6	1	1	--	--	41	14	7	7	0	33	0	0	0	0	0	.00	1	.213	.250	.291
1983	Chicago	AL	6	5	1	0	0	0	(0	0)	1	0	0	0	0	0	0	0	0	1	0	1.00	0	.200	.200	.200
1984	Chicago	AL	8	7	0	0	0	0	(0	0)	0	1	0	1	0	4	0	0	0	1	0	1.00	0	.000	.125	.000
1985	Chicago	AL	141	395	106	19	4	5	(2	3)	148	52	37	30	1	81	4	4	3	6	4	.60	8	.268	.324	.375
1986	Chicago	AL	150	520	120	16	5	17	(7	10)	197	53	44	21	0	91	1	6	4	4	1	.80	11	.231	.260	.379
1987	Chicago	AL	68	240	52	10	0	7	(3	4)	83	20	28	10	1	41	0	5	2	0	2	.00	6	.217	.246	.346
1989	Baltimore	AL	33	97	27	5	0	3	(2	1)	41	12	18	10	0	17	0	1	1	0	0	.00	3	.278	.343	.423
1990	Baltimore	AL	53	153	39	7	1	3	(2	1)	57	16	16	15	0	41	0	1	0	1	0	1.00	2	.255	.321	.373
1991	Baltimore	AL	79	206	42	9	0	7	(1	6)	72	29	18	13	0	49	1	1	0	0	1	.00	3	.204	.255	.350
1992	Baltimore	AL	57	142	41	7	2	2	(1	1)	58	11	21	10	1	31	1	0	0	0	1	.00	7	.289	.340	.408
1993	Baltimore	AL	85	260	78	15	0	2	(2	0)	99	40	23	23	1	56	3	1	2	1	2	.33	5	.300	.361	.381
1994	Baltimore	AL	36	92	21	2	1	2	(2	0)	31	11	15	12	0	24	0	1	1	0	0	.00	2	.228	.314	.337
1995	St. Louis	NL	4	11	2	0	0	0	(0	0)	2	0	0	0	0	3	0	0	0	0	0	.00	0	.182	.182	.182
	12 ML YEARS		720	2128	529	90	13	48	(22	26)	789	245	220	145	4	438	10	20	13	14	11	.56	47	.249	.298	.371

David Hulse

Bats: Left **Throws:** Left **Pos:** LF/CF/RF   **Ht:** 5'11" **Wt:** 175 **Born:** 2/25/68 **Age:** 28

| | | | | | | | | | BATTING | | | | | | | | | | | BASERUNNING | | | | PERCENTAGES | | |
Year	Team	Lg	G	AB	H	2B	3B	HR	(Hm	Rd)	TB	R	RBI	TBB	IBB	SO	HBP	SH	SF	SB	CS	SB%	GDP	Avg	OBP	SLG
1992	Texas	AL	32	92	28	4	0	0	(0	0)	32	14	2	3	0	18	0	2	0	3	1	.75	0	.304	.326	.348
1993	Texas	AL	114	407	118	9	10	1	(0	1)	150	71	29	26	1	57	1	5	2	29	9	.76	9	.290	.333	.369
1994	Texas	AL	77	310	79	8	4	1	(1	0)	98	58	19	21	0	53	2	7	1	18	2	.90	1	.255	.305	.316
1995	Milwaukee	AL	119	339	85	11	6	3	(1	2)	117	46	47	18	2	60	0	2	5	15	3	.83	3	.251	.285	.345
	4 ML YEARS		342	1148	310	32	20	5	(2	3)	397	189	97	68	3	188	3	16	8	65	15	.81	13	.270	.311	.346

Todd Hundley

Bats: Both **Throws:** Right **Pos:** C   **Ht:** 5'11" **Wt:** 185 **Born:** 5/27/69 **Age:** 27

| | | | | | | | | | BATTING | | | | | | | | | | | BASERUNNING | | | | PERCENTAGES | | |
Year	Team	Lg	G	AB	H	2B	3B	HR	(Hm	Rd)	TB	R	RBI	TBB	IBB	SO	HBP	SH	SF	SB	CS	SB%	GDP	Avg	OBP	SLG
1990	New York	NL	36	67	14	6	0	0	(0	0)	20	8	2	6	0	18	0	1	0	0	0	.00	1	.209	.274	.299
1991	New York	NL	21	60	8	0	1	1	(1	0)	13	5	7	6	0	14	1	1	1	0	0	.00	3	.133	.221	.217
1992	New York	NL	123	358	75	17	0	7	(2	5)	113	32	32	19	4	76	4	7	2	3	0	1.00	3	.209	.256	.316
1993	New York	NL	130	417	95	17	2	11	(5	6)	149	40	53	23	7	62	2	2	4	1	1	.50	10	.228	.269	.357
1994	New York	NL	91	291	69	10	1	16	(8	8)	129	45	42	25	4	73	3	3	1	2	1	.67	3	.237	.303	.443
1995	New York	NL	90	275	77	11	0	15	(6	9)	133	39	51	42	5	64	5	1	3	1	0	1.00	4	.280	.382	.484
	6 ML YEARS		491	1468	338	61	4	50	(22	28)	557	169	187	121	20	307	15	15	11	7	2	.78	29	.230	.293	.379

Brian Hunter

Bats: Right **Throws:** Left **Pos:** 1B   **Ht:** 6' 0" **Wt:** 195 **Born:** 3/4/68 **Age:** 28

| | | | | | | | | | BATTING | | | | | | | | | | | BASERUNNING | | | | PERCENTAGES | | |
Year	Team	Lg	G	AB	H	2B	3B	HR	(Hm	Rd)	TB	R	RBI	TBB	IBB	SO	HBP	SH	SF	SB	CS	SB%	GDP	Avg	OBP	SLG
1995	Indianapols *	AAA	9	36	13	5	0	4	--	--	30	7	11	6	1	11	0	0	0	0	1	.00	0	.361	.452	.833
1991	Atlanta	NL	97	271	68	16	1	12	(7	5)	122	32	50	17	0	48	1	0	2	0	2	.00	0	.251	.296	.450
1992	Atlanta	NL	102	238	57	13	2	14	(9	5)	116	34	41	21	3	50	0	1	8	1	2	.33	2	.239	.292	.487

Year	Team	Lg	G	AB	H	2B	3B	HR	(Hm	Rd)	TB	R	RBI	TBB	IBB	SO	HBP	SH	SF	SB	CS	SB%	GDP	Avg	OBP	SLG
1993	Atlanta	NL	37	80	11	3	1	0	(0	0)	16	4	8	2	1	15	0	0	3	0	0	.00	1	.138	.153	.200
1994	Cin-Pit	NL	85	256	60	16	1	15	(4	11)	123	34	57	17	2	56	0	0	5	0	0	.00	3	.234	.277	.480
1995	Cincinnati	NL	40	79	17	6	0	1	(0	1)	26	9	9	11	1	21	1	0	2	2	1	.67	2	.215	.312	.329
1994	Cincinnati	NL	9	23	7	1	0	4	(0	4)	20	6	10	2	0	1	0	0	1	0	0	.00	0	.304	.346	.870
	Pittsburgh	NL	76	233	53	15	1	11	(4	7)	103	28	47	15	2	55	0	0	4	0	0	.00	3	.227	.270	.442
	5 ML YEARS		361	924	213	54	5	42	(20	22)	403	113	165	68	7	190	2	1	20	3	5	.38	14	.231	.279	.436

Brian L. Hunter

Bats: Right **Throws:** Right **Pos:** CF — **Ht:** 6' 4" **Wt:** 180 **Born:** 3/5/71 **Age:** 25

Year	Team	Lg	G	AB	H	2B	3B	HR	(Hm	Rd)	TB	R	RBI	TBB	IBB	SO	HBP	SH	SF	SB	CS	SB%	GDP	Avg	OBP	SLG
1989	Astros	R	51	206	35	2	0	0	--	--	37	15	13	7	0	42	1	0	0	12	6	.67	1	.170	.201	.180
1990	Asheville	A	127	445	111	14	6	0	--	--	137	84	16	60	1	72	8	1	1	45	13	.78	3	.249	.348	.308
1991	Osceola	A	118	392	94	15	3	1	--	--	118	51	30	45	2	75	1	5	5	32	9	.78	6	.240	.316	.301
1992	Osceola	A	131	489	146	18	9	1	--	--	185	62	62	31	0	76	5	6	4	39	19	.67	7	.299	.344	.378
1993	Jackson	AA	133	523	154	22	5	10	--	--	216	84	52	34	4	85	1	5	2	35	18	.66	11	.294	.338	.413
1994	Tucson	AAA	128	513	191	28	9	10	--	--	267	113	51	52	5	52	5	3	4	49	14	.78	11	.372	.432	.520
1995	Tucson	AAA	38	155	51	5	1	1	--	--	61	28	16	17	0	13	0	0	0	11	3	.79	1	.329	.395	.394
	Jackson	AA	2	6	3	0	0	0	--	--	3	1	0	1	0	0	0	0	0	0	0	.00	1	.500	.571	.500
1994	Houston	NL	6	24	6	1	0	0	(0	0)	7	2	0	1	0	6	0	1	0	2	1	.67	0	.250	.280	.292
1995	Houston	NL	78	321	97	14	5	2	(0	2)	127	52	28	21	0	52	2	2	3	24	7	.77	2	.302	.346	.396
	2 ML YEARS		84	345	103	15	5	2	(0	2)	134	54	28	22	0	58	2	3	3	26	8	.76	2	.299	.341	.388

Edwin Hurtado

Pitches: Right **Bats:** Right **Pos:** SP — **Ht:** 6' 3" **Wt:** 208 **Born:** 2/1/70 **Age:** 26

Year	Team	Lg	G	GS	CG	GF	IP	BFP	H	R	ER	HR	SH	SF	HB	TBB	IBB	SO	WP	Bk	W	L	Pct.	ShO	Sv	ERA
1993	St. Cathrns	A	15	15	3	0	101	402	69	34	28	6	1	3	4	34	0	87	3	3	10	2	.833	1	0	2.50
1994	Hagerstown	A	33	16	1	9	134.1	553	118	53	44	8	0	4	1	46	0	121	5	2	11	2	.846	0	2	2.95
1995	Knoxville	AA	11	11	0	0	54.2	240	54	34	27	7	1	4	0	25	0	38	4	0	2	4	.333	0	0	4.45
1995	Toronto	AL	14	10	1	0	77.2	345	81	50	47	11	2	3	5	40	3	33	11	0	5	2	.714	0	0	5.45

Butch Huskey

Bats: Right **Throws:** Right **Pos:** 3B — **Ht:** 6' 3" **Wt:** 244 **Born:** 11/10/71 **Age:** 24

Year	Team	Lg	G	AB	H	2B	3B	HR	(Hm	Rd)	TB	R	RBI	TBB	IBB	SO	HBP	SH	SF	SB	CS	SB%	GDP	Avg	OBP	SLG
1989	Mets	R	54	190	50	14	2	6	--	--	86	27	34	14	0	36	1	0	0	4	1	.80	2	.263	.317	.453
1990	Kingsport	R	72	279	75	12	0	14	--	--	129	39	53	24	1	74	2	0	5	4	3	.57	2	.269	.326	.462
1991	Columbia	A	134	492	141	27	5	26	--	--	256	88	99	54	6	90	4	1	7	22	10	.69	11	.287	.357	.520
1992	St. Lucie	A	134	493	125	17	1	18	--	--	198	65	75	33	6	74	1	0	5	7	3	.70	5	.254	.299	.402
1993	Binghamton	AA	139	526	132	23	1	25	--	--	232	72	98	48	3	102	2	0	8	11	2	.85	14	.251	.312	.441
1994	Norfolk	AAA	127	474	108	23	3	10	--	--	167	59	57	37	2	88	3	4	5	16	7	.70	9	.228	.285	.352
1995	Norfolk	AAA	109	394	112	18	1	28	--	--	216	66	87	39	4	88	6	0	3	8	6	.57	9	.284	.355	.548
1993	New York	NL	13	41	6	1	0	0	(0	0)	7	2	3	1	1	13	0	0	2	0	0	.00	0	.146	.159	.171
1995	New York	NL	28	90	17	1	0	3	(2	1)	27	8	11	10	0	16	0	1	1	1	0	1.00	3	.189	.267	.300
	2 ML YEARS		41	131	23	2	0	3	(2	1)	34	10	14	11	1	29	0	1	3	1	0	1.00	3	.176	.234	.260

Jeff Huson

Bats: Left **Throws:** Right **Pos:** 3B/2B — **Ht:** 6' 3" **Wt:** 180 **Born:** 8/15/64 **Age:** 31

Year	Team	Lg	G	AB	H	2B	3B	HR	(Hm	Rd)	TB	R	RBI	TBB	IBB	SO	HBP	SH	SF	SB	CS	SB%	GDP	Avg	OBP	SLG
1995	Rochester *	AAA	60	223	56	9	0	3	--	--	74	28	21	26	2	29	0	2	1	16	5	.76	7	.251	.328	.332
1988	Montreal	NL	20	42	13	2	0	0	(0	0)	15	7	3	4	2	3	0	0	0	2	1	.67	2	.310	.370	.357
1989	Montreal	NL	32	74	12	5	0	0	(0	0)	17	1	2	6	3	6	0	3	0	3	0	1.00	6	.162	.225	.230
1990	Texas	AL	145	396	95	12	2	0	(0	0)	111	57	28	46	0	54	2	7	3	12	4	.75	4	.240	.320	.280
1991	Texas	AL	119	268	57	8	3	2	(1	1)	77	36	26	39	0	32	0	9	1	8	3	.73	6	.213	.312	.287
1992	Texas	AL	123	318	83	14	3	4	(0	4)	115	49	24	41	2	43	1	8	6	18	6	.75	7	.261	.342	.362
1993	Texas	AL	23	45	6	1	1	0	(0	0)	9	3	2	0	0	10	0	1	0	0	0	.00	0	.133	.133	.200
1995	Baltimore	AL	66	161	40	4	2	1	(0	1)	51	24	19	15	1	20	1	2	1	5	4	.56	4	.248	.315	.317
	7 ML YEARS		528	1304	306	46	11	7	(1	6)	395	177	104	151	8	168	4	30	11	48	18	.73	33	.235	.314	.303

Tim Hyers

Bats: Left **Throws:** Left **Pos:** 1B — **Ht:** 6' 1" **Wt:** 195 **Born:** 10/3/71 **Age:** 24

Year	Team	Lg	G	AB	H	2B	3B	HR	(Hm	Rd)	TB	R	RBI	TBB	IBB	SO	HBP	SH	SF	SB	CS	SB%	GDP	Avg	OBP	SLG
1990	Medcne Hat	R	61	224	49	7	2	2	--	--	66	29	19	29	1	22	1	0	2	4	1	.80	5	.219	.309	.295
1991	Myrtle Bch	A	132	398	80	8	0	3	--	--	97	31	37	27	0	52	2	4	3	4	4	.50	10	.201	.253	.244

Year	Team	Lg	G	AB	H	2B	3B	HR	(Hm	Rd)	TB	R	RBI	TBB	IBB	SO	HBP	SH	SF	SB	CS	SB%	GDP	Avg	OBP	SLG
1992	Dunedin	A	124	464	114	24	3	8	--	--	168	54	59	41	4	54	3	2	5	2	1	.67	9	.246	.308	.362
1993	Knoxville	AA	140	487	149	26	3	3	--	--	190	72	61	53	5	51	2	5	2	12	3	.80	7	.306	.375	.390
1994	Las Vegas	AAA	14	47	12	1	0	1	--	--	16	4	5	4	0	4	0	0	0	0	0	.00	2	.255	.314	.340
1995	Las Vegas	AAA	82	259	75	12	1	1	--	--	92	46	23	24	3	33	1	2	1	0	3	.00	7	.290	.351	.355
1994	San Diego	NL	52	118	30	3	0	0	(0	0)	33	13	7	9	0	15	0	2	0	3	0	1.00	1	.254	.307	.280
1995	San Diego	NL	6	5	0	0	0	0	(0	0)	0	0	0	0	0	1	0	0	0	0	0	.00	1	.000	.000	.000
	2 ML YEARS		58	123	30	3	0	0	(0	0)	33	13	7	9	0	16	0	2	0	3	0	1.00	2	.244	.295	.268

Mike Ignasiak

Pitches: Right **Bats:** Both **Pos:** RP **Ht:** 5'11" **Wt:** 189 **Born:** 3/12/66 **Age:** 30

	HOW MUCH HE PITCHED						WHAT HE GAVE UP											THE RESULTS					
Year	Team	Lg	G	GS	CG	GF	IP	BFP	H	R	ER	HR	SH	SF	HB	TBB	IBB	SO	WP	Bk	W	L	Pct.	ShO	Sv	ERA
1995	Beloit *	A	1	1	0	0	3	11	0	0	0	0	0	0	0	2	0	4	0	0	0	0	.000	0	0	0.00
	New Orleans *	AAA	4	2	0	1	18	71	9	5	5	2	0	0	0	8	0	19	1	0	1	1	.500	0	0	2.50
1991	Milwaukee	AL	4	1	0	0	12.2	51	7	8	8	2	0	0	0	8	0	10	0	0	2	1	.667	0	0	5.68
1993	Milwaukee	AL	27	0	0	4	37	158	32	17	15	2	1	1	2	21	4	28	0	0	1	1	.500	0	0	3.65
1994	Milwaukee	AL	23	5	0	5	47.2	201	51	25	24	5	1	1	1	13	2	24	1	1	3	1	.750	0	0	4.53
1995	Milwaukee	AL	25	0	0	2	39.2	186	51	27	26	5	1	3	2	23	3	26	1	0	4	1	.800	0	0	5.90
	4 ML YEARS		79	6	0	11	137	596	141	77	73	14	3	5	5	65	9	88	2	1	10	4	.714	0	0	4.80

Pete Incaviglia

Bats: Right **Throws:** Right **Pos:** LF **Ht:** 6' 1" **Wt:** 225 **Born:** 4/2/64 **Age:** 32

	BATTING																			BASERUNNING				PERCENTAGES		
Year	Team	Lg	G	AB	H	2B	3B	HR	(Hm	Rd)	TB	R	RBI	TBB	IBB	SO	HBP	SH	SF	SB	CS	SB%	GDP	Avg	OBP	SLG
1986	Texas	AL	153	540	135	21	2	30	(17	13)	250	82	88	55	2	185	4	0	7	3	2	.60	9	.250	.320	.463
1987	Texas	AL	139	509	138	26	4	27	(11	16)	253	85	80	48	1	168	1	0	5	9	3	.75	8	.271	.332	.497
1988	Texas	AL	116	418	104	19	3	22	(12	10)	195	59	54	39	3	153	7	0	3	6	4	.60	6	.249	.321	.467
1989	Texas	AL	133	453	107	27	4	21	(13	8)	205	48	81	32	0	136	6	0	4	5	7	.42	12	.236	.293	.453
1990	Texas	AL	153	529	123	27	0	24	(15	9)	222	59	85	45	5	146	9	0	4	3	4	.43	18	.233	.302	.420
1991	Detroit	AL	97	337	72	12	1	11	(6	5)	119	38	38	36	0	92	1	1	2	1	3	.25	6	.214	.290	.353
1992	Houston	NL	113	349	93	22	1	11	(6	5)	150	31	44	25	2	99	3	0	2	2	2	.50	6	.266	.319	.430
1993	Philadelphia	NL	116	368	101	16	3	24	(15	9)	195	60	89	21	1	82	6	0	7	1	1	.50	9	.274	.318	.530
1994	Philadelphia	NL	80	244	56	10	1	13	(6	7)	107	28	32	16	3	71	0	0	2	1	0	1.00	3	.230	.278	.439
	9 ML YEARS		1100	3747	929	180	19	183	(101	82)	1696	490	591	317	17	1132	38	1	36	31	26	.54	77	.248	.310	.453

Garey Ingram

Bats: Right **Throws:** Right **Pos:** 3B **Ht:** 5'11" **Wt:** 185 **Born:** 7/25/70 **Age:** 25

	BATTING																			BASERUNNING				PERCENTAGES		
Year	Team	Lg	G	AB	H	2B	3B	HR	(Hm	Rd)	TB	R	RBI	TBB	IBB	SO	HBP	SH	SF	SB	CS	SB%	GDP	Avg	OBP	SLG
1990	Great Falls	R	56	198	68	12	8	2	--	--	102	43	21	22	0	37	3	0	1	10	6	.63	3	.343	.415	.515
1991	Bakersfield	A	118	445	132	16	4	9	--	--	183	75	64	52	4	70	14	5	6	30	13	.70	5	.297	.383	.411
	San Antonio	AA	1	1	0	0	0	0	--	--	0	0	1	0	0	1	0	0	0	0	0	.00	0	.000	.000	.000
1992	San Antonio	AA	65	198	57	9	5	2	--	--	82	34	17	28	2	43	12	2	1	11	6	.65	4	.288	.406	.414
1993	San Antonio	AA	84	305	82	14	5	6	--	--	124	43	33	31	0	50	5	2	2	19	6	.76	3	.269	.344	.407
1994	San Antonio	AA	99	345	89	24	3	8	--	--	143	68	28	43	3	61	9	2	0	19	5	.79	5	.258	.355	.414
	Albuquerque	AAA	2	8	2	0	0	0	--	--	2	2	0	0	0	1	0	0	0	1	0	1.00	1	.250	.250	.250
1995	Albuquerque	AAA	63	232	57	11	4	1	--	--	79	28	30	21	1	40	3	0	3	10	4	.71	4	.246	.313	.341
1994	Los Angeles	NL	26	78	22	1	0	3	(1	2)	32	10	8	7	3	22	0	1	0	0	0	.00	3	.282	.341	.410
1995	Los Angeles	NL	44	55	11	2	0	0	(0	0)	13	5	3	9	0	8	0	2	0	3	0	1.00	0	.200	.313	.236
	2 ML YEARS		70	133	33	3	0	3	(1	2)	45	15	11	16	3	30	0	3	0	3	0	1.00	3	.248	.329	.338

Riccardo Ingram

Bats: Right **Throws:** Right **Pos:** DH **Ht:** 6' 0" **Wt:** 205 **Born:** 9/10/66 **Age:** 29

	BATTING																			BASERUNNING				PERCENTAGES		
Year	Team	Lg	G	AB	H	2B	3B	HR	(Hm	Rd)	TB	R	RBI	TBB	IBB	SO	HBP	SH	SF	SB	CS	SB%	GDP	Avg	OBP	SLG
1988	Lakeland	A	37	117	24	3	1	0	--	--	29	10	10	10	0	30	0	1	0	2	0	1.00	1	.205	.268	.248
1989	Lakeland	A	109	365	88	13	3	6	--	--	125	40	30	29	1	56	1	0	3	5	2	.71	13	.241	.296	.342
1990	London	AA	92	271	69	10	2	0	--	--	83	27	26	27	1	49	4	1	0	3	1	.75	8	.255	.331	.306
1991	London	AA	118	421	114	14	1	18	--	--	184	57	64	40	4	77	4	5	3	6	5	.55	15	.271	.338	.437
1992	Toledo	AAA	121	410	103	15	6	8	--	--	154	45	41	31	4	52	5	4	5	8	6	.57	11	.251	.308	.376
1993	Toledo	AAA	123	415	112	20	4	13	--	--	179	41	62	32	5	66	5	0	5	9	7	.56	6	.270	.326	.431
1994	Toledo	AAA	90	314	90	16	4	9	--	--	141	39	56	24	3	45	5	0	3	11	6	.65	9	.287	.344	.449
1995	Salt Lake	AAA	122	477	166	43	2	12	--	--	249	80	85	41	3	60	3	0	6	4	5	.44	22	.348	.399	.522
1994	Detroit	AL	12	23	5	0	0	0	(0	0)	5	3	2	1	0	2	0	0	1	0	1	.00	0	.217	.240	.217
1995	Minnesota	AL	4	8	1	0	0	0	(0	0)	1	0	1	2	0	1	0	0	0	0	0	.00	1	.125	.300	.125
	2 ML YEARS		16	31	6	0	0	0	(0	0)	6	3	3	3	0	3	0	0	1	0	1	.00	1	.194	.257	.194

Jason Isringhausen

Pitches: Right **Bats:** Right **Pos:** SP **Ht:** 6' 3" **Wt:** 196 **Born:** 9/7/72 **Age:** 23

Year Team	Lg	G	GS	CG	GF	IP	BFP	H	R	ER	HR	SH	SF	HB	TBB	IBB	SO	WP	Bk	W	L	Pct.	ShO	Sv	ERA
1992 Mets	R	6	6	0	0	29	133	26	19	14	0	0	0	3	17	1	25	2	0	2	4	.333	0	0	4.34
Kingsport	R	7	6	1	0	36	160	32	22	13	2	0	3	1	12	1	24	2	1	4	1	.800	1	0	3.25
1993 Pittsfield	A	15	15	2	0	90.1	375	68	45	33	7	4	6	3	28	0	104	8	0	7	4	.636	0	0	3.29
1994 St. Lucie	A	14	14	6	0	101	391	76	31	25	2	1	1	2	27	2	59	4	0	6	4	.600	3	0	2.23
Binghamton	AA	14	14	2	0	92.1	368	78	35	31	6	4	5	2	23	0	69	5	1	5	4	.556	0	0	3.02
1995 Binghamton	AA	6	6	1	0	41	164	26	15	13	1	0	0	3	12	0	59	6	0	2	1	.667	0	0	2.85
Norfolk	AAA	12	12	3	0	87	343	64	17	15	2	2	0	2	24	0	75	4	1	9	1	.900	3	0	1.55
1995 New York	NL	14	14	1	0	93	385	88	29	29	6	3	3	2	31	2	55	4	1	9	2	.818	0	0	2.81

Danny Jackson

Pitches: Left **Bats:** Right **Pos:** SP **Ht:** 6' 0" **Wt:** 220 **Born:** 1/5/62 **Age:** 34

Year Team	Lg	G	GS	CG	GF	IP	BFP	H	R	ER	HR	SH	SF	HB	TBB	IBB	SO	WP	Bk	W	L	Pct.	ShO	Sv	ERA
1995 Louisville *	AAA	1	1	0	0	7	30	8	1	1	0	0	0	1	2	0	2	0	0	1	0	1.000	0	0	1.29
1983 Kansas City	AL	4	3	0	0	19	87	26	12	11	1	1	0	0	6	0	9	0	0	1	1	.500	0	0	5.21
1984 Kansas City	AL	15	11	1	3	76	338	84	41	36	4	3	0	5	35	0	40	3	2	2	6	.250	0	0	4.26
1985 Kansas City	AL	32	32	4	0	208	893	209	94	79	7	5	4	6	76	2	114	4	2	14	12	.538	3	0	3.42
1986 Kansas City	AL	32	27	4	3	185.2	789	177	83	66	13	10	4	4	79	1	115	7	0	11	12	.478	1	1	3.20
1987 Kansas City	AL	36	34	11	1	224	981	219	115	100	11	8	7	7	109	1	152	5	0	9	18	.333	2	0	4.02
1988 Cincinnati	NL	35	35	15	0	260.2	1034	206	86	79	13	13	5	2	71	6	161	5	2	23	8	.742	6	0	2.73
1989 Cincinnati	NL	20	20	1	0	115.2	519	122	78	72	10	6	4	1	57	7	70	3	2	6	11	.353	0	0	5.60
1990 Cincinnati	NL	22	21	0	1	117.1	499	119	54	47	11	4	5	2	40	4	76	3	1	6	6	.500	0	0	3.61
1991 Chicago	NL	17	14	0	0	70.2	347	89	59	53	8	8	2	1	48	4	31	1	1	1	5	.167	0	0	6.75
1992 ChN-Pit	NL	34	34	0	0	201.1	883	211	99	86	6	17	10	4	77	6	97	2	2	8	13	.381	0	0	3.84
1993 Philadelphia	NL	32	32	2	0	210.1	919	214	105	88	12	14	8	4	80	2	120	4	0	12	11	.522	1	0	3.77
1994 Philadelphia	NL	25	25	4	0	179.1	755	183	71	65	13	14	6	2	46	1	129	2	0	14	6	.700	1	0	3.26
1995 St. Louis	NL	19	19	2	0	100.2	467	120	82	66	10	10	7	6	48	1	52	6	0	2	12	.143	1	0	5.90
1992 Chicago	NL	19	19	0	0	113	501	117	59	53	5	11	5	3	48	3	51	1	2	4	9	.308	0	0	4.22
Pittsburgh	NL	15	15	0	0	88.1	382	94	40	33	1	6	5	1	29	3	46	1	0	4	4	.500	0	0	3.36
13 ML YEARS		323	307	44	8	1968.2	8511	1979	979	848	119	113	62	44	772	35	1166	45	12	109	121	.474	15	1	3.88

Darrin Jackson

Bats: Right **Throws:** Right **Pos:** RF/CF **Ht:** 6' 0" **Wt:** 185 **Born:** 8/22/63 **Age:** 32

Year Team	Lg	G	AB	H	2B	3B	HR	(Hm	Rd)	TB	R	RBI	TBB	IBB	SO	HBP	SH	SF	SB	CS	SB%	GDP	Avg	OBP	SLG
1985 Chicago	NL	5	11	1	0	0	0	(0	0)	1	0	0	0	0	3	0	0	0	0	0	.00	0	.091	.091	.091
1987 Chicago	NL	7	5	4	1	0	0	(0	0)	5	2	0	0	0	0	0	0	0	0	0	.00	0	.800	.800	1.000
1988 Chicago	NL	100	188	50	11	3	6	(3	3)	85	29	20	1	1	28	1	2	1	4	1	.80	3	.266	.287	.452
1989 ChN-SD	NL	70	170	37	7	0	4	(1	3)	56	17	20	13	5	34	0	0	2	1	4	.20	2	.218	.270	.329
1990 San Diego	NL	58	113	29	3	0	3	(1	2)	41	10	9	5	1	24	0	1	1	3	0	1.00	1	.257	.286	.363
1991 San Diego	NL	122	359	94	12	1	21	(12	9)	171	51	49	27	2	66	2	3	3	5	3	.63	5	.262	.315	.476
1992 San Diego	NL	155	587	146	23	5	17	(11	6)	230	72	70	26	4	106	4	6	5	14	3	.82	21	.249	.283	.392
1993 Tor-NYN	NL	77	263	55	9	0	6	(4	2)	82	19	26	10	0	75	0	6	1	0	2	.00	9	.209	.237	.312
1994 Chicago	AL	104	369	115	17	3	10	(4	6)	168	43	51	27	3	56	3	2	2	7	1	.88	5	.312	.362	.455
1989 Chicago	NL	45	83	19	4	0	1	(0	1)	26	7	8	6	1	17	0	0	0	1	2	.33	0	.229	.281	.313
San Diego	NL	25	87	18	3	0	3	(1	2)	30	10	12	7	4	17	0	0	2	0	2	.00	1	.207	.260	.345
1993 Toronto	AL	46	176	38	8	0	5	(4	1)	61	15	19	8	0	53	0	5	0	0	2	.00	0	.216	.250	.347
New York	NL	31	87	17	1	0	1	(0	1)	21	4	7	2	0	22	0	1	1	0	0	.00	0	.195	.211	.241
9 ML YEARS		698	2065	531	83	12	67	(36	31)	839	243	245	113	16	392	10	20	15	34	14	.71	46	.257	.297	.406

Mike Jackson

Pitches: Right **Bats:** Right **Pos:** RP **Ht:** 6' 2" **Wt:** 225 **Born:** 12/22/64 **Age:** 31

Year Team	Lg	G	GS	CG	GF	IP	BFP	H	R	ER	HR	SH	SF	HB	TBB	IBB	SO	WP	Bk	W	L	Pct.	ShO	Sv	ERA
1995 Chattanooga *	AA	3	2	0	0	3	11	2	0	0	0	0	0	0	0	0	2	0	0	0	0	.000	0	0	0.00
Indianapolis *	AAA	2	1	0	1	2	6	0	0	0	0	0	0	0	0	0	1	0	0	0	0	.000	0	0	0.00
1986 Philadelphia	NL	9	0	0	4	13.1	54	12	5	5	2	0	0	2	4	1	3	0	0	0	0	.000	0	0	3.38
1987 Philadelphia	NL	55	7	0	8	109.1	468	88	55	51	16	3	4	3	56	6	93	6	8	3	10	.231	0	1	4.20
1988 Seattle	AL	62	0	0	29	99.1	412	74	37	29	10	3	10	2	43	10	76	6	6	6	5	.545	0	4	2.63
1989 Seattle	AL	65	0	0	27	99.1	431	81	43	35	8	6	2	6	54	6	94	1	2	4	6	.400	0	7	3.17
1990 Seattle	AL	63	0	0	28	77.1	338	64	42	39	8	8	5	2	44	12	69	9	2	5	7	.417	0	3	4.54
1991 Seattle	AL	72	0	0	35	88.2	363	64	35	32	5	4	0	6	34	11	74	3	0	7	7	.500	0	14	3.25
1992 San Francisco	NL	67	0	0	24	82	346	76	35	34	7	5	2	4	33	10	80	1	0	6	6	.500	0	2	3.73

Year	Team	Lg	G	GS	CG	GF	IP	BFP	H	R	ER	HR	SH	SF	HB	TBB	IBB	SO	WP	Bk	W	L	Pct.	ShO	Sv	ERA
1993	San Francisco	NL	81	0	0	17	77.1	317	58	28	26	7	4	2	3	24	6	70	2	2	6	6	.500	0	1	3.03
1994	San Francisco	NL	36	0	0	12	42.1	158	23	8	7	4	4	1	2	11	0	51	0	0	3	2	.600	0	4	1.49
1995	Cincinnati	NL	40	0	0	10	49	200	38	13	13	5	1	1	1	19	1	41	1	1	6	1	.857	0	2	2.39
	10 ML YEARS		550	7	0	194	738	3087	578	301	271	72	38	27	31	322	63	651	29	21	46	50	.479	0	38	3.30

Jason Jacome

Pitches: Left **Bats:** Left **Pos:** SP **Ht:** 6' 0" **Wt:** 180 **Born:** 11/24/70 **Age:** 25

			HOW MUCH HE PITCHED						WHAT HE GAVE UP												THE RESULTS					
Year	Team	Lg	G	GS	CG	GF	IP	BFP	H	R	ER	HR	SH	SF	HB	TBB	IBB	SO	WP	Bk	W	L	Pct.	ShO	Sv	ERA
1991	Kingsport	R	12	7	3	5	55.1	210	35	18	10	1	3	2	0	13	2	48	6	1	5	4	.556	1	2	1.63
1992	Columbia	A	8	8	1	0	52.2	209	40	7	6	2	0	0	0	15	0	49	4	1	4	1	.800	0	0	1.03
	St. Lucie	A	17	17	5	0	114.1	454	98	45	36	7	4	3	3	30	0	66	6	0	6	7	.462	1	0	2.83
1993	St. Lucie	A	14	14	2	0	99.1	409	106	37	34	2	1	1	0	23	1	66	2	4	6	3	.667	2	0	3.08
	Binghamton	AA	14	14	0	0	87	374	85	36	31	6	5	2	4	38	1	56	3	0	8	4	.667	0	0	3.21
1994	Norfolk	AAA	19	19	4	0	126.2	540	138	57	40	8	3	5	3	42	1	80	3	0	8	6	.571	1	0	2.84
1995	Norfolk	AAA	8	8	0	0	43.2	181	40	21	19	5	4	1	1	13	0	31	1	0	2	4	.333	0	0	3.92
1994	New York	NL	8	8	1	0	54	222	54	17	16	3	3	1	0	17	2	30	2	0	4	3	.571	1	0	2.67
1995	NYN-KC		20	19	1	0	105	474	134	76	74	18	3	4	2	36	2	50	1	1	4	10	.286	0	0	6.34
1995	New York	NL	5	5	0	0	21	110	33	24	24	3	1	1	1	15	0	11	1	0	0	4	.000	0	0	10.29
	Kansas City	AL	15	14	1	0	84	364	101	52	50	15	2	3	1	21	2	39	0	1	4	6	.400	0	0	5.36
	2 ML YEARS		28	27	2	0	159	696	188	93	90	21	6	5	2	53	4	80	3	1	8	13	.381	1	0	5.09

John Jaha

Bats: Right **Throws:** Right **Pos:** 1B **Ht:** 6' 1" **Wt:** 222 **Born:** 5/27/66 **Age:** 30

			BATTING														BASERUNNING				PERCENTAGES		
Year	Team	Lg	G	AB	H	2B	3B	HR	(Hm	Rd)	TB	R	RBI	TBB	IBB	SO	HBP	SH	SF	SB	CS	SB%	GDP	Avg	OBP	SLG
1995	Beloit *	A	1	4	0	0	0	0	--	--	0	1	0	0	0	1	0	0	0	0	0	.00	0	.000	.000	.000
	New Orleans *	AAA	3	10	4	1	0	1	--	--	8	2	3	2	1	1	0	0	0	0	0	.00	1	.400	.500	.800
1992	Milwaukee	AL	47	133	30	3	1	2	(1	1)	41	17	10	12	1	30	2	1	4	10	0	1.00	1	.226	.291	.308
1993	Milwaukee	AL	153	515	136	21	0	19	(5	14)	214	78	70	51	4	109	8	4	4	13	9	.59	6	.264	.337	.416
1994	Milwaukee	AL	84	291	70	14	0	12	(5	7)	120	45	39	32	3	75	10	1	4	3	3	.50	6	.241	.332	.412
1995	Milwaukee	AL	88	316	99	20	2	20	(8	12)	183	59	65	36	0	66	4	0	1	2	1	.67	8	.313	.389	.579
	4 ML YEARS		372	1255	335	58	3	53	(19	34)	558	199	184	131	8	280	24	6	13	28	13	.68	23	.267	.344	.445

Chris James

Bats: Right **Throws:** Right **Pos:** DH **Ht:** 6' 1" **Wt:** 202 **Born:** 10/4/62 **Age:** 33

			BATTING														BASERUNNING				PERCENTAGES		
Year	Team	Lg	G	AB	H	2B	3B	HR	(Hm	Rd)	TB	R	RBI	TBB	IBB	SO	HBP	SH	SF	SB	CS	SB%	GDP	Avg	OBP	SLG
1995	Omaha *	AAA	3	12	2	1	0	1	--	--	6	3	3	1	0	2	0	0	0	0	0	.00	0	.167	.231	.500
1986	Philadelphia	NL	16	46	13	3	0	1	(0	1)	19	5	5	1	0	13	0	1	0	0	0	.00	1	.283	.298	.413
1987	Philadelphia	NL	115	358	105	20	6	17	(9	8)	188	48	54	27	0	67	2	1	3	3	1	.75	4	.293	.344	.525
1988	Philadelphia	NL	150	566	137	24	1	19	(10	9)	220	57	66	31	2	73	3	0	5	7	4	.64	15	.242	.283	.389
1989	Phi-SD	NL	132	482	117	17	2	13	(7	6)	177	55	65	26	2	68	1	4	3	5	2	.71	20	.243	.281	.367
1990	Cleveland	AL	140	528	158	32	4	12	(6	6)	234	62	70	31	4	71	4	3	3	4	3	.57	11	.299	.341	.443
1991	Cleveland	AL	115	437	104	16	2	5	(1	4)	139	31	41	18	2	61	4	2	2	3	4	.43	9	.238	.273	.318
1992	San Francisco	NL	111	248	60	10	4	5	(3	2)	93	25	32	14	2	45	2	0	3	2	3	.40	4	.242	.285	.375
1993	Tex-Hou		73	160	44	11	1	9	(6	3)	84	24	26	18	2	40	1	1	2	2	0	1.00	3	.275	.348	.525
1994	Texas	AL	52	133	34	8	4	7	(4	3)	71	28	19	20	0	38	3	1	2	0	0	.00	3	.256	.361	.534
1995	KC-Bos	AL	42	82	22	4	0	2	(0	2)	32	8	8	7	0	14	1	1	2	1	0	1.00	2	.268	.326	.390
1989	Philadelphia	NL	45	179	37	4	0	2	(1	1)	47	14	19	4	0	23	0	1	1	3	1	.75	9	.207	.223	.263
	San Diego	NL	87	303	80	13	2	11	(6	5)	130	41	46	22	2	45	1	3	2	2	1	.67	11	.264	.314	.429
1993	Texas	AL	8	31	11	1	0	3	(0	3)	21	5	7	3	0	6	0	0	0	0	0	.00	0	.355	.412	.677
	Houston	NL	65	129	33	10	1	6	(6	0)	63	19	19	15	2	34	1	1	2	2	0	1.00	3	.256	.333	.488
1995	Kansas City	AL	26	58	18	3	0	2	(0	2)	27	6	7	6	0	10	1	0	2	1	0	1.00	1	.310	.373	.466
	Boston	AL	16	24	4	1	0	0	(0	0)	5	2	1	1	0	4	0	2	0	0	0	.00	1	.167	.200	.208
	10 ML YEARS		946	3040	794	145	24	90	(46	44)	1257	343	386	193	14	490	21	15	25	27	17	.61	69	.261	.307	.413

Dion James

Bats: Left **Throws:** Left **Pos:** DH/LF **Ht:** 6' 1" **Wt:** 185 **Born:** 11/9/62 **Age:** 33

			BATTING														BASERUNNING				PERCENTAGES		
Year	Team	Lg	G	AB	H	2B	3B	HR	(Hm | Rd)	TB	R	RBI	TBB	IBB	SO	HBP	SH	SF	SB	CS	SB%	GDP	Avg	OBP	SLG
1983	Milwaukee	AL	11	20	2	0	0	0	(0 | 0)	2	1	1	2	0	2	0	0	0	1	0	1.00	0	.100	.182	.100
1984	Milwaukee	AL	128	387	114	19	5	1	(1 | 0)	146	52	30	32	1	41	3	6	3	10	10	.50	7	.295	.351	.377
1985	Milwaukee	AL	18	49	11	1	0	0	(0 | 0)	12	5	3	6	0	6	0	0	0	0	0	.00	0	.224	.309	.245
1987	Atlanta	NL	134	494	154	37	6	10	(5 | 5)	233	80	61	70	2	63	2	5	3	10	8	.56	5	.312	.397	.472
1988	Atlanta	NL	132	386	99	17	5	3	(1 | 2)	135	46	30	58	5	59	1	2	2	9	9	.50	12	.256	.353	.350
1989	Cle-Atl		134	415	119	18	0	5	(1 | 4)	152	41	40	49	6	49	1	5	0	2	7	.22	9	.287	.363	.366
1990	Cleveland	AL	87	248	68	15	2	1	(0 | 1)	90	28	22	27	3	23	1	3	1	5	3	.63	6	.274	.347	.363
1992	New York	AL	67	145	38	8	0	3	(2 | 1)	55	24	17	22	0	15	1	0	2	1	0	1.00	3	.262	.359	.379

115

Year	Team	Lg	G	AB	H	2B	3B	HR	(Hm	Rd)	TB	R	RBI	TBB	IBB	SO	HBP	SH	SF	SB	CS	SB%	GDP	Avg	OBP	SLG
1993	New York	AL	115	343	114	21	2	7	(5	2)	160	62	36	31	1	31	2	1	1	0	0	.00	5	.332	.390	.466
1995	New York	AL	85	209	60	6	1	2	(1	1)	74	22	26	20	2	16	0	0	2	4	1	.80	5	.287	.346	.354
1989	Cleveland	AL	71	245	75	11	0	4	(1	3)	98	26	29	24	4	26	0	2	0	1	4	.20	5	.306	.368	.400
	Atlanta	NL	63	170	44	7	0	1	(0	1)	54	15	11	25	2	23	1	3	1	1	3	.25	4	.259	.355	.318
10 ML YEARS			911	2696	779	142	21	32	(16	16)	1059	361	266	317	20	305	11	22	15	42	38	.53	55	.289	.364	.393

Mike James

Pitches: Right **Bats:** Right **Pos:** RP **Ht:** 6' 3" **Wt:** 180 **Born:** 8/15/67 **Age:** 28

			HOW MUCH HE PITCHED					WHAT HE GAVE UP									THE RESULTS					
Year	Team	Lg	G	GS	CG	GF	IP	BFP	H	R	ER	HR	SH	SF	HB	TBB	IBB	SO	WP	Bk	W	L	Pct.	ShO	Sv	ERA
1988	Great Falls	R	14	12	0	0	67	299	61	36	28	7	2	3	2	41	0	59	2	5	7	1	.875	0	0	3.76
1989	Bakersfield	A	27	27	1	0	159.2	706	144	82	67	11	3	3	12	78	1	127	13	0	11	8	.579	1	0	3.78
1990	San Antonio	AA	26	26	3	0	157	681	144	73	58	14	4	7	9	78	1	97	10	0	11	4	.733	1	0	3.32
1991	San Antonio	AA	15	15	2	0	89.1	402	88	54	45	10	2	1	4	51	1	74	5	0	9	5	.643	1	0	4.53
	Albuquerque	AAA	13	8	0	3	45	208	51	36	33	7	0	3	2	30	0	39	5	1	1	3	.250	0	0	6.60
1992	San Antonio	AA	8	8	0	0	54	214	39	16	16	3	2	0	1	20	0	52	1	1	2	1	.667	0	0	2.67
	Albuquerque	AAA	18	6	0	3	46.2	211	55	35	29	4	3	2	2	22	0	33	4	0	2	1	.667	0	1	5.59
1993	Albuquerque	AAA	16	0	0	5	31.1	154	38	28	26	5	1	2	4	19	3	32	2	0	1	0	1.000	0	2	7.47
	Vero Beach	A	30	1	0	15	60.1	271	54	37	33	2	2	2	5	33	5	60	5	1	2	3	.400	0	5	4.92
1994	Vancouver	AAA	37	10	0	18	91.1	402	101	56	53	15	1	3	6	34	1	66	3	0	5	3	.625	0	8	5.22
1995	Lk Elsinore	A	5	1	0	1	5.2	29	9	6	6	1	0	0	0	3	0	8	0	0	0	0	.000	0	0	9.53
1995	California	AL	46	0	0	11	55.2	237	49	27	24	6	2	0	3	26	2	36	1	0	3	0	1.000	0	1	3.88

Kevin Jarvis

Pitches: Right **Bats:** Left **Pos:** SP/RP **Ht:** 6' 2" **Wt:** 200 **Born:** 8/1/69 **Age:** 26

			HOW MUCH HE PITCHED					WHAT HE GAVE UP									THE RESULTS					
Year	Team	Lg	G	GS	CG	GF	IP	BFP	H	R	ER	HR	SH	SF	HB	TBB	IBB	SO	WP	Bk	W	L	Pct.	ShO	Sv	ERA
1991	Princeton	R	13	13	4	0	85.2	365	73	34	23	6	1	0	3	29	3	79	6	4	5	6	.455	1	0	2.42
1992	Cedar Rapids	A	1	0	0	0	1	3	1	0	0	0	0	0	0	0	0	0	0	0	0	0	.000	0	0	0.00
	Charlstn-Wv	A	28	18	2	3	133	550	123	59	46	3	3	3	1	37	1	131	9	2	6	8	.429	1	0	3.11
1993	Winston-Sal	A	21	20	2	0	145	609	133	68	55	13	6	4	0	48	2	101	6	2	7	5	.533	1	0	3.41
	Chattanooga	AA	7	3	2	0	37.1	141	26	7	7	0	1	0	1	11	0	18	1	0	3	1	.750	0	0	1.69
1994	Indianapols	AAA	21	20	2	0	132.1	562	136	55	52	13	4	1	1	34	2	90	9	1	10	2	.833	0	0	3.54
1995	Indianapols	AAA	10	10	2	0	60.2	262	62	33	30	2	0	2	0	18	1	37	5	0	4	2	.667	1	0	4.45
1994	Cincinnati	NL	6	3	0	0	17.2	79	22	14	14	4	1	0	0	5	0	10	1	0	1	1	.500	0	0	7.13
1995	Cincinnati	NL	19	11	0	2	79	354	91	56	50	13	2	5	3	32	2	33	2	0	3	4	.429	1	0	5.70
2 ML YEARS			25	14	1	2	96.2	433	113	70	64	17	3	5	3	37	2	43	3	0	4	5	.444	1	0	5.96

Stan Javier

Bats: Both **Throws:** Right **Pos:** CF/LF **Ht:** 6' 0" **Wt:** 185 **Born:** 1/9/64 **Age:** 32

			BATTING																	BASERUNNING				PERCENTAGES		
Year	Team	Lg	G	AB	H	2B	3B	HR	(Hm	Rd)	TB	R	RBI	TBB	IBB	SO	HBP	SH	SF	SB	CS	SB%	GDP	Avg	OBP	SLG
1984	New York	AL	7	7	1	0	0	0	(0	0)	1	1	0	0	0	1	0	0	0	0	0	.00	0	.143	.143	.143
1986	Oakland	AL	59	114	23	8	0	0	(0	0)	31	13	8	16	0	27	1	0	0	8	0	1.00	2	.202	.305	.272
1987	Oakland	AL	81	151	28	3	1	2	(1	1)	39	22	9	19	3	33	0	6	0	3	2	.60	2	.185	.276	.258
1988	Oakland	AL	125	397	102	13	3	2	(0	2)	127	49	35	32	1	63	2	6	3	20	1	.95	13	.257	.313	.320
1989	Oakland	AL	112	310	77	12	3	1	(1	0)	98	42	28	31	1	45	1	4	2	12	2	.86	6	.248	.317	.316
1990	Oak-LA	AL	123	309	92	9	6	3	(1	2)	122	60	27	40	2	50	0	6	2	15	7	.68	6	.298	.376	.395
1991	Los Angeles	NL	121	176	36	5	3	1	(1	0)	50	21	11	16	0	36	0	3	2	7	1	.88	4	.205	.268	.284
1992	LA-Phi	NL	130	334	83	17	1	1	(1	0)	105	42	29	37	2	54	3	3	2	18	3	.86	4	.249	.327	.314
1993	California	AL	92	237	69	10	4	3	(0	3)	96	33	28	27	1	33	1	1	3	12	2	.86	7	.291	.362	.405
1994	Oakland	AL	109	419	114	23	0	10	(1	9)	167	75	44	49	1	76	2	7	3	24	7	.77	7	.272	.349	.399
1995	Oakland	AL	130	442	123	20	2	8	(3	5)	171	81	56	49	3	63	4	5	4	36	5	.88	8	.278	.353	.387
1990	Oakland	AL	19	33	8	0	2	0	(0	0)	12	4	3	3	0	6	0	0	0	0	0	.00	0	.242	.306	.364
	Los Angeles	NL	104	276	84	9	4	3	(1	2)	110	56	24	37	2	44	0	6	2	15	7	.68	6	.304	.384	.399
1992	Los Angeles	NL	56	58	11	3	0	1	(1	0)	17	6	5	6	2	11	1	1	0	2	1	.33	0	.190	.277	.293
	Philadelphia	NL	74	276	72	14	1	0	(0	0)	88	36	24	31	0	43	2	2	2	17	1	.94	4	.261	.338	.319
11 ML YEARS			1089	2896	748	120	23	31	(8	23)	1007	439	275	316	14	481	14	41	21	155	30	.84	59	.258	.332	.348

Gregg Jefferies

Bats: Both **Throws:** Right **Pos:** 1B/LF **Ht:** 5'10" **Wt:** 185 **Born:** 8/1/67 **Age:** 28

			BATTING																	BASERUNNING				PERCENTAGES		
Year	Team	Lg	G	AB	H	2B	3B	HR	(Hm	Rd)	TB	R	RBI	TBB	IBB	SO	HBP	SH	SF	SB	CS	SB%	GDP	Avg	OBP	SLG
1987	New York	NL	6	6	3	1	0	0	(0	0)	4	0	2	0	0	0	0	0	0	0	0	.00	0	.500	.500	.667
1988	New York	NL	29	109	35	8	2	6	(3	3)	65	19	17	8	0	10	0	0	1	5	2	.71	3	.321	.364	.596
1989	New York	NL	141	508	131	28	2	12	(7	5)	199	72	56	39	8	46	1	5	2	21	6	.78	16	.258	.314	.392
1990	New York	NL	153	604	171	40	3	15	(9	6)	262	96	68	46	2	40	5	0	4	11	2	.85	12	.283	.337	.434

Year Team	Lg	G	AB	H	2B	3B	HR	(Hm	Rd)	TB	R	RBI	TBB	IBB	SO	HBP	SH	SF	SB	CS	SB%	GDP	Avg	OBP	SLG
1991 New York	NL	136	486	132	19	2	9	(5	4)	182	59	62	47	2	38	2	1	3	26	5	.84	12	.272	.336	.374
1992 Kansas City	AL	152	604	172	36	3	10	(3	7)	244	66	75	43	4	29	1	0	9	19	9	.68	24	.285	.329	.404
1993 St. Louis	NL	142	544	186	24	3	16	(10	6)	264	89	83	62	7	32	2	0	4	46	9	.84	15	.342	.408	.485
1994 St. Louis	NL	103	397	129	27	1	12	(7	5)	194	52	55	45	12	26	1	0	4	12	5	.71	9	.325	.391	.489
1995 Philadelphia	NL	114	480	147	31	2	11	(4	7)	215	69	56	35	5	26	0	0	6	9	5	.64	15	.306	.349	.448
9 ML YEARS		976	3738	1106	214	18	91	(48	43)	1629	522	474	325	40	247	16	3	36	149	42	.78	104	.296	.352	.436

Reggie Jefferson

Bats: Left **Throws:** Left **Pos:** DH **Ht:** 6' 4" **Wt:** 210 **Born:** 9/25/68 **Age:** 27

			BATTING																BASERUNNING				PERCENTAGES		
Year Team	Lg	G	AB	H	2B	3B	HR	(Hm	Rd)	TB	R	RBI	TBB	IBB	SO	HBP	SH	SF	SB	CS	SB%	GDP	Avg	OBP	SLG
1991 Cle-Cin		31	108	21	3	0	3	(2	1)	33	11	13	4	0	24	0	0	1	0	0	.00	1	.194	.221	.306
1992 Cleveland	AL	24	89	30	6	2	1	(1	0)	43	8	6	1	0	17	1	0	0	0	0	.00	2	.337	.352	.483
1993 Cleveland	AL	113	366	91	11	2	10	(4	6)	136	35	34	28	7	78	5	3	1	1	3	.25	7	.249	.310	.372
1994 Seattle	AL	63	162	53	11	0	8	(4	4)	88	24	32	17	5	32	1	0	1	0	0	.00	6	.327	.392	.543
1995 Boston	AL	46	121	35	8	0	5	(1	4)	58	21	26	9	1	24	0	0	2	0	0	.00	3	.289	.333	.479
1991 Cleveland	AL	26	101	20	3	0	2	(1	1)	29	10	12	3	0	22	0	0	1	0	0	.00	1	.198	.219	.287
Cincinnati	NL	5	7	1	0	0	1	(1	0)	4	1	1	1	0	2	0	0	0	0	0	.00	0	.143	.250	.571
5 ML YEARS		277	846	230	39	4	27	(12	15)	358	99	111	59	13	175	7	3	5	1	3	.25	19	.272	.323	.423

Derek Jeter

Bats: Right **Throws:** Right **Pos:** SS **Ht:** 6' 3" **Wt:** 185 **Born:** 6/26/74 **Age:** 22

			BATTING																BASERUNNING				PERCENTAGES		
Year Team	Lg	G	AB	H	2B	3B	HR	(Hm	Rd)	TB	R	RBI	TBB	IBB	SO	HBP	SH	SF	SB	CS	SB%	GDP	Avg	OBP	SLG
1992 Yankees	R	47	173	35	10	0	3	--	--	54	19	25	19	0	36	5	0	2	2	2	.50	4	.202	.296	.312
Greensboro	A	11	37	9	0	0	1	--	--	12	4	4	7	0	16	1	0	0	0	1	.00	0	.243	.378	.324
1993 Greensboro	A	128	515	152	14	11	5	--	--	203	85	71	58	1	95	11	2	4	18	9	.67	9	.295	.376	.394
1994 Tampa	A	69	292	96	13	8	0	--	--	125	61	39	23	2	30	3	3	3	28	2	.93	4	.329	.380	.428
Albany-Colo	AA	34	122	46	7	2	2	--	--	63	17	13	15	0	16	1	3	1	12	2	.86	3	.377	.446	.516
Columbus	AAA	35	126	44	7	1	3	--	--	62	25	16	20	1	15	1	3	1	10	4	.71	6	.349	.439	.492
1995 Columbus	AAA	123	486	154	27	9	2	--	--	205	96	45	61	1	56	4	2	5	20	12	.63	9	.317	.394	.422
1995 New York	AL	15	48	12	4	1	0	(0	0)	18	5	7	3	0	11	0	0	0	0	0	.00	0	.250	.294	.375

Doug Johns

Pitches: Left **Bats:** Right **Pos:** SP **Ht:** 6' 2" **Wt:** 185 **Born:** 12/19/67 **Age:** 28

		HOW MUCH HE PITCHED						WHAT HE GAVE UP									THE RESULTS					
Year Team	Lg	G	GS	CG	GF	IP	BFP	H	R	ER	HR	SH	SF	HB	TBB	IBB	SO	WP	Bk	W	L	Pct.	ShO	Sv	ERA
1990 Sou. Oregon	A	6	2	0	4	11	57	13	9	7	0	0	0	0	11	1	9	2	2	0	1	.000	0	1	5.73
Athletics	R	8	7	1	1	44	172	36	17	9	1	0	0	0	9	1	37	2	0	3	1	.750	0	0	1.84
1991 Madison	A	38	14	1	9	128.1	549	108	59	46	5	6	2	8	54	1	104	13	0	12	6	.667	0	2	3.23
1992 Reno	A	27	26	4	1	179.1	776	194	98	65	11	7	4	1	64	3	101	5	2	13	10	.565	1	0	3.26
Huntsville	AA	3	1	0	1	16	74	21	11	7	0	1	0	0	5	0	4	1	0	0	0	.000	0	0	3.94
1993 Huntsville	AA	40	6	0	11	91	379	82	41	30	3	7	2	2	31	4	56	2	1	7	5	.583	0	1	2.97
1994 Huntsville	AA	9	0	0	2	15	70	16	2	2	1	2	0	1	12	5	9	1	3	3	0	1.000	0	0	1.20
Tacoma	AAA	22	19	2	2	134	549	114	55	43	10	4	3	7	48	0	65	2	2	9	8	.529	1	0	2.89
1995 Edmonton	AAA	23	21	0	1	132	567	148	55	50	8	3	1	3	43	3	70	6	3	9	5	.643	0	0	3.41
1995 Oakland	AL	11	9	1	1	54.2	229	44	32	28	5	2	1	5	26	1	25	5	1	5	3	.625	1	0	4.61

Brian Johnson

Bats: Right **Throws:** Right **Pos:** C **Ht:** 6' 2" **Wt:** 210 **Born:** 1/8/68 **Age:** 28

			BATTING																BASERUNNING				PERCENTAGES		
Year Team	Lg	G	AB	H	2B	3B	HR	(Hm	Rd)	TB	R	RBI	TBB	IBB	SO	HBP	SH	SF	SB	CS	SB%	GDP	Avg	OBP	SLG
1989 Yankees	R	17	61	22	1	1	0	--	--	25	7	8	4	0	5	1	0	0	0	1	.00	1	.361	.409	.410
1990 Greensboro	A	137	496	118	15	0	7	--	--	154	58	51	57	4	65	4	2	4	4	6	.40	18	.238	.319	.310
1991 Ft. Laud	A	113	394	94	19	0	1	--	--	116	35	44	34	2	67	6	2	3	4	6	.40	14	.239	.307	.294
Albany-Colo	AA	2	8	0	0	0	0	--	--	0	0	0	0	0	2	0	0	0	0	0	.00	0	.000	.000	.000
1992 Wichita	AA	75	245	71	20	0	3	--	--	100	30	26	22	1	32	3	1	1	3	0	1.00	8	.290	.354	.408
1993 Las Vegas	AAA	115	416	141	35	6	10	--	--	218	58	71	41	2	53	5	0	5	0	0	.00	18	.339	.400	.524
1994 Las Vegas	AAA	15	51	11	1	0	2	--	--	18	6	9	8	1	6	1	0	0	0	1	.00	2	.216	.333	.353
1994 San Diego	NL	36	93	23	4	1	3	(3	0)	38	7	16	5	0	21	0	2	1	0	0	.00	4	.247	.283	.409
1995 San Diego	NL	68	207	52	9	0	3	(1	2)	70	20	29	11	2	39	1	1	4	0	0	.00	2	.251	.287	.338
2 ML YEARS		104	300	75	13	1	6	(4	2)	108	27	45	16	2	60	1	3	5	0	0	.00	6	.250	.286	.360

Charles Johnson

Bats: Right **Throws:** Right **Pos:** C **Ht:** 6' 2" **Wt:** 215 **Born:** 7/20/71 **Age:** 24

Year	Team	Lg	G	AB	H	2B	3B	HR	(Hm	Rd)	TB	R	RBI	TBB	IBB	SO	HBP	SH	SF	SB	CS	SB%	GDP	Avg	OBP	SLG
1993	Kane County	A	135	488	134	29	5	19	--	--	230	74	94	62	9	111	2	0	4	9	1	.90	12	.275	.356	.471
1994	Portland	AA	132	443	117	29	1	28	--	--	232	64	80	74	2	97	3	0	3	4	5	.44	14	.264	.371	.524
1995	Portland	AA	2	7	0	0	0	0	--	--	0	0	0	1	0	3	0	0	0	0	0	.00	0	.000	.125	.000
1994	Florida	NL	4	11	5	1	0	1	(1	0)	9	5	4	1	0	4	0	0	1	0	0	.00	1	.455	.462	.818
1995	Florida	NL	97	315	79	15	1	11	(3	8)	129	40	39	46	2	71	4	4	2	0	2	.00	11	.251	.351	.410
	2 ML YEARS		101	326	84	16	1	12	(4	8)	138	45	43	47	2	75	4	4	3	0	2	.00	12	.258	.355	.423

Howard Johnson

Bats: Both **Throws:** Right **Pos:** 3B/LF **Ht:** 5'10" **Wt:** 195 **Born:** 11/29/60 **Age:** 35

Year	Team	Lg	G	AB	H	2B	3B	HR	(Hm	Rd)	TB	R	RBI	TBB	IBB	SO	HBP	SH	SF	SB	CS	SB%	GDP	Avg	OBP	SLG
1982	Detroit	AL	54	155	49	5	0	4	(1	3)	66	23	14	16	1	30	1	1	0	7	4	.64	3	.316	.384	.426
1983	Detroit	AL	27	66	14	0	0	3	(2	1)	23	11	5	7	0	10	1	0	0	0	0	.00	1	.212	.297	.348
1984	Detroit	AL	116	355	88	14	1	12	(4	8)	140	43	50	40	1	67	1	4	2	10	6	.63	6	.248	.324	.394
1985	New York	NL	126	389	94	18	4	11	(6	5)	153	38	46	34	10	78	0	1	4	6	4	.60	6	.242	.300	.393
1986	New York	NL	88	220	54	14	0	10	(5	5)	98	30	39	31	8	64	1	1	0	8	1	.89	2	.245	.341	.445
1987	New York	NL	157	554	147	22	1	36	(13	23)	279	93	99	83	18	113	5	0	3	32	10	.76	8	.265	.364	.504
1988	New York	NL	148	495	114	21	1	24	(9	15)	209	85	68	86	25	104	3	2	8	23	7	.77	6	.230	.343	.422
1989	New York	NL	153	571	164	41	3	36	(19	17)	319	104	101	77	8	126	1	0	6	41	8	.84	4	.287	.369	.559
1990	New York	NL	154	590	144	37	3	23	(13	10)	256	89	90	69	12	100	0	0	9	34	8	.81	7	.244	.319	.434
1991	New York	NL	156	564	146	34	4	38	(21	17)	302	108	117	78	12	120	1	0	15	30	16	.65	4	.259	.342	.535
1992	New York	NL	100	350	78	19	0	7	(2	5)	118	48	43	55	5	79	2	0	3	22	5	.81	7	.223	.329	.337
1993	New York	NL	72	235	56	8	2	7	(3	4)	89	32	26	43	3	43	0	0	2	6	4	.60	3	.238	.354	.379
1994	Colorado	NL	93	227	48	10	2	10	(3	7)	92	30	40	39	2	73	0	0	3	11	3	.79	2	.211	.323	.405
1995	Chicago	NL	87	169	33	4	1	7	(6	1)	60	26	22	34	0	46	1	0	2	1	1	.50	2	.195	.330	.355
	14 ML YEARS		1531	4940	1229	247	22	228	(106	122)	2204	760	760	692	105	1053	17	9	57	231	77	.75	61	.249	.340	.446

Lance Johnson

Bats: Left **Throws:** Left **Pos:** CF **Ht:** 5'11" **Wt:** 160 **Born:** 7/6/63 **Age:** 32

Year	Team	Lg	G	AB	H	2B	3B	HR	(Hm	Rd)	TB	R	RBI	TBB	IBB	SO	HBP	SH	SF	SB	CS	SB%	GDP	Avg	OBP	SLG
1987	St. Louis	NL	33	59	13	2	1	0	(0	0)	17	4	7	4	1	6	0	0	0	6	1	.86	2	.220	.270	.288
1988	Chicago	AL	33	124	23	4	1	0	(0	0)	29	11	6	6	0	11	0	2	0	6	2	.75	1	.185	.223	.234
1989	Chicago	AL	50	180	54	8	2	0	(0	0)	66	28	16	17	0	24	0	2	0	16	3	.84	1	.300	.360	.367
1990	Chicago	AL	151	541	154	18	9	1	(0	1)	193	76	51	33	2	45	1	8	4	36	22	.62	12	.285	.325	.357
1991	Chicago	AL	160	588	161	14	13	0	(0	0)	201	72	49	26	2	58	1	6	3	26	11	.70	14	.274	.304	.342
1992	Chicago	AL	157	567	158	15	12	3	(2	1)	206	67	47	34	4	33	1	4	5	41	14	.75	20	.279	.318	.363
1993	Chicago	AL	147	540	168	18	14	0	(0	0)	214	75	47	36	1	33	0	3	0	35	7	.83	10	.311	.354	.396
1994	Chicago	AL	106	412	114	11	14	3	(1	2)	162	56	54	26	5	23	2	0	3	26	6	.81	8	.277	.321	.393
1995	Chicago	AL	142	607	186	18	12	10	(2	8)	258	98	57	32	2	31	1	2	3	40	6	.87	7	.306	.341	.425
	9 ML YEARS		979	3618	1031	108	78	17	(5	12)	1346	487	334	214	17	264	6	27	18	232	72	.76	75	.285	.324	.372

Mark Johnson

Bats: Left **Throws:** Left **Pos:** 1B **Ht:** 6' 4" **Wt:** 230 **Born:** 10/17/67 **Age:** 28

Year	Team	Lg	G	AB	H	2B	3B	HR	(Hm	Rd)	TB	R	RBI	TBB	IBB	SO	HBP	SH	SF	SB	CS	SB%	GDP	Avg	OBP	SLG
1990	Welland	A	5	8	3	1	0	0	--	--	4	2	2	2	0	0	0	0	0	0	0	.00	0	.375	.500	.500
	Augusta	A	43	144	36	7	0	0	--	--	43	12	19	24	2	18	0	0	2	4	2	.67	3	.250	.353	.299
1991	Augusta	A	49	139	36	7	4	2	--	--	57	23	25	29	1	14	0	1	2	4	2	.67	2	.259	.382	.410
	Salem	A	37	103	26	2	0	2	--	--	34	12	13	18	0	25	1	0	0	0	0	.00	2	.252	.369	.330
1992	Carolina	AA	122	383	89	16	1	7	--	--	128	40	45	55	4	94	3	1	0	16	11	.59	8	.232	.333	.334
1993	Carolina	AA	125	399	93	18	4	14	--	--	161	48	52	66	7	93	3	2	3	6	2	.75	8	.233	.344	.404
1994	Carolina	AA	111	388	107	20	2	23	--	--	200	69	85	67	11	89	4	0	4	6	6	.50	7	.276	.384	.515
1995	Calgary	AAA	9	23	7	4	0	2	--	--	17	7	8	6	1	4	1	0	0	1	0	1.00	0	.304	.467	.739
1995	Pittsburgh	NL	79	221	46	6	1	13	(7	6)	93	32	28	37	2	66	2	0	1	5	2	.71	2	.208	.326	.421

Randy Johnson

Pitches: Left **Bats:** Right **Pos:** SP **Ht:** 6'10" **Wt:** 225 **Born:** 9/10/63 **Age:** 32

			HOW MUCH HE PITCHED						WHAT HE GAVE UP										THE RESULTS				
Year	Team	Lg	G	GS	CG	GF	IP	BFP	H	R	ER	HR	SH	SF	HB	TBB	IBB	SO	WP	Bk	W	L	Pct.	ShO	Sv	ERA
1988	Montreal	NL	4	4	1	0	26	109	23	8	7	3	0	0	0	7	0	25	3	0	3	0	1.000	0	0	2.42
1989	Sea-Mon		29	28	2	1	160.2	715	147	100	86	13	10	13	3	96	2	130	7	7	7	13	.350	0	0	4.82
1990	Seattle	AL	33	33	5	0	219.2	944	174	103	89	26	7	6	5	120	2	194	4	2	14	11	.560	2	0	3.65

Year	Team	Lg	G	GS	CG	GF	IP	BFP	H	R	ER	HR	SH	SF	HB	TBB	IBB	SO	WP	Bk	W	L	Pct.	ShO	Sv	ERA
1991	Seattle	AL	33	33	2	0	201.1	889	151	96	89	15	9	8	12	152	0	228	12	2	13	10	.565	1	0	3.98
1992	Seattle	AL	31	31	6	0	210.1	922	154	104	88	13	3	8	18	144	1	241	13	1	12	14	.462	2	0	3.77
1993	Seattle	AL	35	34	10	1	255.1	1043	185	97	92	22	8	7	16	99	1	308	8	2	19	8	.704	3	1	3.24
1994	Seattle	AL	23	23	9	0	172	694	132	65	61	14	3	1	6	72	2	204	5	0	13	6	.684	4	0	3.19
1995	Seattle	AL	30	30	6	0	214.1	866	159	65	59	12	2	1	6	65	1	294	5	2	18	2	.900	3	0	2.48
1989	Seattle	AL	22	22	2	0	131	572	118	75	64	11	7	9	3	70	1	104	5	5	7	9	.438	0	0	4.40
	Montreal	NL	7	6	0	0	29.2	143	29	25	22	2	3	4	0	26	1	26	2	2	0	4	.000	0	0	6.67
8 ML YEARS			218	216	41	2	1459.2	6182	1125	638	571	118	42	44	66	755	9	1624	57	16	99	64	.607	15	0	3.52

Joel Johnston

Pitches: Right **Bats:** Right **Pos:** RP　　　　**Ht:** 6' 4" **Wt:** 234 **Born:** 3/8/67 **Age:** 29

			HOW MUCH HE PITCHED						WHAT HE GAVE UP												THE RESULTS				
Year	Team	Lg	G	GS	CG	GF	IP	BFP	H	R	ER	HR	SH	SF	HB	TBB	IBB	SO	WP	Bk	W	L	Pct.	ShO	Sv	ERA
1995	Pawtucket *	AAA	30	0	0	13	41.1	194	54	31	31	4	1	2	2	19	1	39	3	1	1	2	.333	0	6	6.75
	Colo. Sprng *	AAA	18	0	0	6	22.2	106	26	16	15	1	3	2	2	12	0	14	0	0	2	2	.500	0	0	5.96
1991	Kansas City	AL	13	0	0	1	22.1	85	9	1	1	0	1	0	0	9	3	21	0	0	1	0	1.000	0	0	0.40
1992	Kansas City	AL	5	0	0	1	2.2	13	3	4	4	2	0	0	0	2	0	1	1	0	0	0	.000	0	0	13.50
1993	Pittsburgh	NL	33	0	0	16	53.1	210	38	20	20	7	4	0	0	19	5	31	1	0	2	4	.333	0	2	3.38
1994	Pittsburgh	NL	4	0	0	1	3.1	30	14	12	11	0	0	0	2	4	0	5	1	0	0	0	.000	0	0	29.70
1995	Boston	AL	4	0	0	0	4	18	2	5	5	1	0	0	1	3	0	4	0	0	0	1	.000	0	0	11.25
5 ML YEARS			59	0	0	18	85.2	356	66	42	41	10	5	0	3	37	8	61	3	0	3	5	.375	0	2	4.31

John Johnstone

Pitches: Right **Bats:** Right **Pos:** RP　　　　**Ht:** 6' 3" **Wt:** 195 **Born:** 11/25/68 **Age:** 27

			HOW MUCH HE PITCHED						WHAT HE GAVE UP												THE RESULTS				
Year	Team	Lg	G	GS	CG	GF	IP	BFP	H	R	ER	HR	SH	SF	HB	TBB	IBB	SO	WP	Bk	W	L	Pct.	ShO	Sv	ERA
1993	Florida	NL	7	0	0	3	10.2	54	16	8	7	1	0	0	0	7	0	5	1	0	0	2	.000	0	0	5.91
1994	Florida	NL	17	0	0	7	21.1	105	23	20	14	4	1	0	1	16	5	23	0	0	1	2	.333	0	0	5.91
1995	Florida	NL	4	0	0	0	4.2	23	7	2	2	1	0	0	0	2	1	3	0	0	0	0	.000	0	0	3.86
3 ML YEARS			28	0	0	10	36.2	182	46	30	23	6	1	0	1	25	6	31	1	0	1	4	.200	0	0	5.65

Bobby Jones

Pitches: Right **Bats:** Right **Pos:** SP　　　　**Ht:** 6' 4" **Wt:** 225 **Born:** 2/10/70 **Age:** 26

			HOW MUCH HE PITCHED						WHAT HE GAVE UP												THE RESULTS				
Year	Team	Lg	G	GS	CG	GF	IP	BFP	H	R	ER	HR	SH	SF	HB	TBB	IBB	SO	WP	Bk	W	L	Pct.	ShO	Sv	ERA
1993	New York	NL	9	9	0	0	61.2	265	61	35	25	6	5	3	2	22	1	35	1	0	2	4	.333	0	0	3.65
1994	New York	NL	24	24	1	0	160	685	157	75	56	10	11	4	4	56	9	80	1	3	12	7	.632	1	0	3.15
1995	New York	NL	30	30	3	0	195.2	839	209	107	91	20	11	6	7	53	6	127	2	1	10	10	.500	1	0	4.19
3 ML YEARS			63	63	4	0	417.1	1789	427	217	172	36	27	13	13	131	18	242	4	4	24	21	.533	2	0	3.71

Chipper Jones

Bats: Both **Throws:** Right **Pos:** 3B/LF　　　　**Ht:** 6' 3" **Wt:** 195 **Born:** 4/24/72 **Age:** 24

			BATTING																	BASERUNNING				PERCENTAGES		
Year	Team	Lg	G	AB	H	2B	3B	HR	(Hm	Rd)	TB	R	RBI	TBB	IBB	SO	HBP	SH	SF	SB	CS	SB%	GDP	Avg	OBP	SLG
1990	Braves	R	44	140	32	1	1	1	--	--	38	20	18	14	1	25	6	2	2	5	3	.63	3	.229	.321	.271
1991	Macon	A	136	473	153	24	11	15	--	--	244	104	98	69	4	70	3	1	10	39	11	.78	6	.323	.405	.516
1992	Durham	A	70	264	73	22	1	4	--	--	109	43	39	31	1	34	2	1	3	10	8	.56	5	.277	.353	.413
	Greenville	AA	67	266	92	17	11	9	--	--	158	43	42	11	1	32	0	4	4	14	1	.93	5	.346	.367	.594
1993	Richmond	AAA	139	536	174	31	12	13	--	--	268	97	89	57	5	70	1	3	6	23	7	.77	8	.325	.387	.500
1993	Atlanta	NL	8	3	2	1	0	0	(0	0)	3	2	0	1	0	1	0	0	0	0	0	.00	0	.667	.750	1.000
1995	Atlanta	NL	140	524	139	22	3	23	(15	8)	236	87	86	73	1	99	0	1	4	8	4	.67	10	.265	.353	.450
2 ML YEARS			148	527	141	23	3	23	(15	8)	239	89	86	74	1	100	0	1	4	8	4	.67	10	.268	.355	.454

Chris Jones

Bats: Right **Throws:** Right **Pos:** RF/LF　　　　**Ht:** 6' 2" **Wt:** 205 **Born:** 12/16/65 **Age:** 30

			BATTING																	BASERUNNING				PERCENTAGES		
Year	Team	Lg	G	AB	H	2B	3B	HR	(Hm	Rd)	TB	R	RBI	TBB	IBB	SO	HBP	SH	SF	SB	CS	SB%	GDP	Avg	OBP	SLG
1995	Norfolk *	AAA	33	114	38	12	1	3	--	--	61	20	19	11	1	20	1	0	3	5	2	.71	2	.333	.388	.535
1991	Cincinnati	NL	52	89	26	1	2	2	(0	2)	37	14	6	2	0	31	0	0	1	2	1	.67	2	.292	.304	.416
1992	Houston	NL	54	63	12	2	1	1	(1	0)	19	7	4	7	0	21	0	3	0	3	0	1.00	1	.190	.271	.302
1993	Colorado	NL	86	209	57	11	4	6	(2	4)	94	29	31	10	1	48	0	5	1	9	4	.69	6	.273	.305	.450
1994	Colorado	NL	21	40	12	2	1	0	(0	0)	16	6	2	2	1	14	0	0	0	0	1	.00	1	.300	.333	.400
1995	New York	NL	79	182	51	6	2	8	(4	4)	85	33	31	13	1	45	1	2	3	2	1	.67	2	.280	.327	.467
5 ML YEARS			292	583	158	22	10	17	(7	10)	251	89	74	34	3	159	1	10	5	16	7	.70	12	.271	.310	.431

Doug Jones

Pitches: Right **Bats:** Right **Pos:** RP   **Ht:** 6' 2" **Wt:** 195 **Born:** 6/24/57 **Age:** 39

Year Team	Lg	G	GS	CG	GF	IP	BFP	H	R	ER	HR	SH	SF	HB	TBB	IBB	SO	WP	Bk	W	L	Pct.	ShO	Sv	ERA
1982 Milwaukee	AL	4	0	0	2	2.2	14	5	3	3	1	0	0	0	1	0	1	0	0	0	0	.000	0	0	10.13
1986 Cleveland	AL	11	0	0	5	18	79	18	5	5	0	1	1	1	6	1	12	0	0	1	0	1.000	0	1	2.50
1987 Cleveland	AL	49	0	0	29	91.1	400	101	45	32	4	5	5	6	24	5	87	0	0	6	5	.545	0	8	3.15
1988 Cleveland	AL	51	0	0	46	83.1	338	69	26	21	1	3	0	2	16	3	72	2	3	3	4	.429	0	37	2.27
1989 Cleveland	AL	59	0	0	53	80.2	331	76	25	21	4	8	6	1	13	4	65	1	1	7	10	.412	0	32	2.34
1990 Cleveland	AL	66	0	0	64	84.1	331	66	26	24	5	2	2	2	22	4	55	2	0	5	5	.500	0	43	2.56
1991 Cleveland	AL	36	4	0	29	63.1	293	87	42	39	7	2	2	0	17	5	48	1	0	4	8	.333	0	7	5.54
1992 Houston	NL	80	0	0	70	111.2	440	96	29	23	5	9	0	5	17	5	93	2	1	11	8	.579	0	36	1.85
1993 Houston	NL	71	0	0	60	85.1	381	102	46	43	7	9	4	5	21	6	66	3	0	4	10	.286	0	26	4.54
1994 Philadelphia	NL	47	0	0	42	54	226	55	14	13	2	4	0	0	6	0	38	1	0	2	4	.333	0	27	2.17
1995 Baltimore	AL	52	0	0	47	46.2	211	55	30	26	6	1	0	2	16	2	42	0	0	0	4	.000	0	22	5.01
11 ML YEARS		526	4	0	447	721.1	3044	730	291	250	42	44	20	24	159	35	579	12	5	43	58	.426	0	239	3.12

Todd Jones

Pitches: Right **Bats:** Left **Pos:** RP   **Ht:** 6' 3" **Wt:** 200 **Born:** 4/24/68 **Age:** 28

Year Team	Lg	G	GS	CG	GF	IP	BFP	H	R	ER	HR	SH	SF	HB	TBB	IBB	SO	WP	Bk	W	L	Pct.	ShO	Sv	ERA
1993 Houston	NL	27	0	0	8	37.1	150	28	14	13	4	2	1	1	15	2	25	1	1	1	2	.333	0	2	3.13
1994 Houston	NL	48	0	0	20	72.2	288	52	23	22	3	3	1	1	26	4	63	1	0	5	2	.714	0	5	2.72
1995 Houston	NL	68	0	0	40	99.2	442	89	38	34	8	5	4	6	52	17	96	5	0	6	5	.545	0	15	3.07
3 ML YEARS		143	0	0	68	209.2	880	169	75	69	15	10	6	8	93	23	184	7	1	12	9	.571	0	22	2.96

Brian Jordan

Bats: Right **Throws:** Right **Pos:** RF/CF   **Ht:** 6' 1" **Wt:** 215 **Born:** 3/29/67 **Age:** 29

Year Team	Lg	G	AB	H	2B	3B	HR	(Hm	Rd)	TB	R	RBI	TBB	IBB	SO	HBP	SH	SF	SB	CS	SB%	GDP	Avg	OBP	SLG
1992 St. Louis	NL	55	193	40	9	4	5	(3	2)	72	17	22	10	1	48	1	0	0	7	2	.78	6	.207	.250	.373
1993 St. Louis	NL	67	223	69	10	6	10	(4	6)	121	33	44	12	0	35	4	0	3	6	6	.50	6	.309	.351	.543
1994 St. Louis	NL	53	178	46	8	2	5	(4	1)	73	14	15	16	0	40	1	0	2	4	3	.57	6	.258	.320	.410
1995 St. Louis	NL	131	490	145	20	4	22	(14	8)	239	83	81	22	4	79	11	0	2	24	9	.73	5	.296	.339	.488
4 ML YEARS		306	1084	300	47	16	42	(25	17)	505	147	162	60	5	202	17	0	7	41	20	.67	23	.277	.323	.466

Kevin Jordan

Bats: Right **Throws:** Right **Pos:** 2B   **Ht:** 6' 1" **Wt:** 194 **Born:** 10/9/69 **Age:** 26

Year Team	Lg	G	AB	H	2B	3B	HR	(Hm	Rd)	TB	R	RBI	TBB	IBB	SO	HBP	SH	SF	SB	CS	SB%	GDP	Avg	OBP	SLG
1990 Oneonta	A	73	276	92	13	7	4	--	--	131	47	54	23	0	31	5	0	1	19	6	.76	3	.333	.393	.475
1991 Ft. Laud	A	121	448	122	25	5	4	--	--	169	61	53	37	4	66	11	0	6	15	3	.83	13	.272	.339	.377
1992 Pr. William	A	112	438	136	29	8	8	--	--	205	67	63	27	3	54	3	1	5	6	4	.60	9	.311	.351	.468
1993 Albany-Colo	AA	135	513	145	33	4	16	--	--	234	87	87	41	2	53	9	0	4	8	4	.67	8	.283	.344	.456
1994 Scranton-Wb	AAA	81	314	91	22	1	12	--	--	151	44	57	29	2	28	3	0	7	0	2	.00	9	.290	.348	.481
1995 Scranton-Wb	AAA	106	410	127	29	4	5	--	--	179	61	60	28	0	36	8	1	6	3	0	1.00	14	.310	.361	.437
1995 Philadelphia	NL	24	54	10	1	0	2	(1	1)	17	6	6	2	1	9	1	0	0	0	0	.00	0	.185	.228	.315

Ricardo Jordan

Pitches: Left **Bats:** Left **Pos:** RP   **Ht:** 6' 0" **Wt:** 180 **Born:** 6/27/70 **Age:** 26

Year Team	Lg	G	GS	CG	GF	IP	BFP	H	R	ER	HR	SH	SF	HB	TBB	IBB	SO	WP	Bk	W	L	Pct.	ShO	Sv	ERA
1990 Dunedin	A	13	2	0	4	22.2	103	15	9	6	0	1	1	1	19	3	16	1	5	0	2	.000	0	0	2.38
1991 Myrtle Bch	A	29	23	3	3	144.2	606	100	58	44	3	4	4	6	79	0	152	3	5	9	8	.529	1	1	2.74
1992 Dunedin	A	45	0	0	32	47	208	44	26	20	3	3	0	2	28	3	49	7	2	0	5	.000	0	15	3.83
1993 Dunedin	A	15	0	0	3	24.2	104	20	13	12	0	1	0	1	15	1	24	3	0	2	0	1.000	0	1	4.38
Knoxville	AA	25	0	0	8	36.2	158	33	17	10	2	5	1	0	18	1	35	0	0	1	4	.200	0	2	2.45
1994 Knoxville	AA	53	0	0	40	64.1	273	54	25	19	2	4	2	4	23	2	70	4	0	4	3	.571	0	17	2.66
1995 Syracuse	AAA	13	0	0	5	12.1	59	15	9	9	1	0	0	1	7	1	17	2	0	0	0	.000	0	0	6.57
1995 Toronto	AL	15	0	0	3	15	76	18	11	11	3	0	2	2	13	1	10	1	0	1	0	1.000	0	1	6.60

Felix Jose

Bats: Both **Throws:** Right **Pos:** RF **Ht:** 6' 1" **Wt:** 220 **Born:** 5/8/65 **Age:** 31

Year Team	Lg	G	AB	H	2B	3B	HR	(Hm	Rd)	TB	R	RBI	TBB	IBB	SO	HBP	SH	SF	SB	CS	SB%	GDP	Avg	OBP	SLG
1995 Iowa *	AAA	10	37	5	3	0	0	--	--	8	2	1	1	0	6	1	0	0	0	0	.00	1	.135	.179	.216
1988 Oakland	AL	8	6	2	1	0	0	(0	0)	3	2	1	0	0	1	0	0	0	1	0	1.00	0	.333	.333	.500
1989 Oakland	AL	20	57	11	2	0	0	(0	0)	13	3	5	4	0	13	0	0	0	0	1	.00	2	.193	.246	.228
1990 Oak-StL		126	426	113	16	1	11	(5	6)	164	54	52	24	0	81	5	2	1	12	6	.67	9	.265	.311	.385
1991 St. Louis	NL	154	568	173	40	6	8	(3	5)	249	69	77	50	8	113	2	0	5	20	12	.63	12	.305	.360	.438
1992 St. Louis	NL	131	509	150	22	3	14	(12	2)	220	62	75	40	8	100	1	0	1	28	12	.70	9	.295	.347	.432
1993 Kansas City	AL	149	499	126	24	3	6	(2	4)	174	64	43	36	5	95	1	1	2	31	13	.70	5	.253	.303	.349
1994 Kansas City	AL	99	366	111	28	1	11	(1	10)	174	56	55	35	6	75	0	0	2	10	12	.45	9	.303	.362	.475
1995 Kansas City	AL	9	30	4	1	0	0	(0	0)	5	2	1	2	0	9	0	0	0	0	0	.00	0	.133	.188	.167
1990 Oakland	AL	101	341	90	12	0	8	(3	5)	126	42	39	16	0	65	5	2	1	8	2	.80	8	.264	.306	.370
St. Louis	NL	25	85	23	4	1	3	(2	1)	38	12	13	8	0	16	0	0	0	4	4	.50	1	.271	.333	.447
8 ML YEARS		696	2461	690	134	14	50	(23	27)	1002	312	309	191	27	487	9	3	11	102	56	.65	47	.280	.333	.407

Wally Joyner

Bats: Left **Throws:** Left **Pos:** 1B **Ht:** 6' 2" **Wt:** 200 **Born:** 6/16/62 **Age:** 34

Year Team	Lg	G	AB	H	2B	3B	HR	(Hm	Rd)	TB	R	RBI	TBB	IBB	SO	HBP	SH	SF	SB	CS	SB%	GDP	Avg	OBP	SLG
1986 California	AL	154	593	172	27	3	22	(11	11)	271	82	100	57	8	58	2	10	12	5	2	.71	11	.290	.348	.457
1987 California	AL	149	564	161	33	1	34	(19	15)	298	100	117	72	12	64	5	2	10	8	2	.80	14	.285	.366	.528
1988 California	AL	158	597	176	31	2	13	(6	7)	250	81	85	55	14	51	5	0	6	8	2	.80	16	.295	.356	.419
1989 California	AL	159	593	167	30	2	16	(8	8)	249	78	79	46	7	58	6	1	8	3	2	.60	15	.282	.335	.420
1990 California	AL	83	310	83	15	0	8	(5	3)	122	35	41	41	4	34	1	1	5	2	1	.67	10	.268	.350	.394
1991 California	AL	143	551	166	34	3	21	(10	11)	269	79	96	52	4	66	1	2	5	2	0	1.00	11	.301	.360	.488
1992 Kansas City	AL	149	572	154	36	2	9	(1	8)	221	66	66	55	4	50	4	0	2	11	5	.69	19	.269	.336	.386
1993 Kansas City	AL	141	497	145	36	3	15	(4	11)	232	83	65	66	13	67	3	2	5	5	9	.36	6	.292	.375	.467
1994 Kansas City	AL	97	363	113	20	3	8	(2	6)	163	52	57	47	3	43	0	2	5	3	2	.60	12	.311	.386	.449
1995 Kansas City	AL	131	465	144	28	0	12	(6	6)	208	69	83	69	10	65	2	5	9	3	2	.60	10	.310	.394	.447
10 ML YEARS		1364	5105	1481	290	19	158	(72	86)	2283	725	789	560	79	556	29	25	67	50	27	.65	124	.290	.359	.447

Jeff Juden

Pitches: Right **Bats:** Right **Pos:** SP **Ht:** 6' 8" **Wt:** 265 **Born:** 1/19/71 **Age:** 25

Year Team	Lg	G	GS	CG	GF	IP	BFP	H	R	ER	HR	SH	SF	HB	TBB	IBB	SO	WP	Bk	W	L	Pct.	ShO	Sv	ERA
1995 Scranton-Wb*	AAA	14	13	0	0	83.1	354	73	43	38	4	4	3	9	33	1	65	4	1	6	4	.600	0	0	4.10
1991 Houston	NL	4	3	0	0	18	81	19	14	12	3	2	3	0	7	1	11	0	1	0	2	.000	0	0	6.00
1993 Houston	NL	2	0	0	1	5	23	4	3	3	1	0	1	0	4	1	7	0	0	0	1	.000	0	0	5.40
1994 Philadelphia	NL	6	5	0	0	27.2	121	29	25	19	4	1	2	1	12	0	22	0	2	1	4	.200	0	0	6.18
1995 Philadelphia	NL	13	10	1	0	62.2	271	53	31	28	6	5	4	5	31	0	47	4	1	2	4	.333	0	0	4.02
4 ML YEARS		25	18	1	1	113.1	496	105	73	62	14	8	10	6	54	2	87	4	4	3	11	.214	0	0	4.92

Dave Justice

Bats: Left **Throws:** Left **Pos:** RF **Ht:** 6' 3" **Wt:** 200 **Born:** 4/14/66 **Age:** 30

Year Team	Lg	G	AB	H	2B	3B	HR	(Hm	Rd)	TB	R	RBI	TBB	IBB	SO	HBP	SH	SF	SB	CS	SB%	GDP	Avg	OBP	SLG
1989 Atlanta	NL	16	51	12	3	0	1	(1	0)	18	7	3	3	1	9	1	1	0	2	1	.67	1	.235	.291	.353
1990 Atlanta	NL	127	439	124	23	2	28	(19	9)	235	76	78	64	4	92	0	0	1	11	6	.65	2	.282	.373	.535
1991 Atlanta	NL	109	396	109	25	1	21	(11	10)	199	67	87	65	9	81	3	0	5	8	8	.50	4	.275	.377	.503
1992 Atlanta	NL	144	484	124	19	5	21	(10	11)	216	78	72	79	8	85	2	0	6	2	4	.33	1	.256	.359	.446
1993 Atlanta	NL	157	585	158	15	4	40	(18	22)	301	90	120	78	12	90	3	0	4	3	5	.38	9	.270	.357	.515
1994 Atlanta	NL	104	352	110	16	2	19	(9	10)	187	61	59	69	5	45	2	0	1	2	4	.33	8	.313	.427	.531
1995 Atlanta	NL	120	411	104	17	2	24	(15	9)	197	73	78	73	5	68	2	0	5	4	2	.67	5	.253	.365	.479
7 ML YEARS		777	2718	741	118	16	154	(83	71)	1353	452	497	431	44	470	13	1	22	32	30	.52	30	.273	.372	.498

Scott Kamieniecki

Pitches: Right **Bats:** Right **Pos:** SP **Ht:** 6' 0" **Wt:** 195 **Born:** 4/19/64 **Age:** 32

Year Team	Lg	G	GS	CG	GF	IP	BFP	H	R	ER	HR	SH	SF	HB	TBB	IBB	SO	WP	Bk	W	L	Pct.	ShO	Sv	ERA
1995 Tampa *	A	1	1	0	0	5	22	6	2	1	0	0	0	1	1	0	2	1	0	1	0	1.000	0	0	1.80
Columbus *	AAA	1	1	0	0	6.2	23	2	0	0	0	0	1	0	1	0	10	0	0	1	0	1.000	0	0	0.00
1991 New York	AL	9	9	0	0	55.1	239	54	24	24	8	2	1	3	22	1	34	1	0	4	4	.500	0	0	3.90
1992 New York	AL	28	28	4	0	188	804	193	100	91	13	3	5	5	74	9	88	9	1	6	14	.300	0	0	4.36
1993 New York	AL	30	20	2	4	154.1	659	163	73	70	17	3	5	3	59	7	72	2	0	10	7	.588	0	1	4.08

1994 New York	AL	22	16	1	2	117.1	509	115	53	49	13	4	3	3	59	5	71	4	0	8	6	.571	0	0	3.76
1995 New York	AL	17	16	1	1	89.2	391	83	43	40	8	1	0	3	49	1	43	4	0	7	6	.538	0	0	4.01
5 ML YEARS		106	89	8	7	604.2	2602	608	293	274	59	13	14	17	263	23	308	20	1	35	37	.486	0	1	4.08

Matt Karchner

Pitches: Right **Bats:** Right **Pos:** RP   **Ht:** 6' 4" **Wt:** 210 **Born:** 6/28/67 **Age:** 29

		HOW MUCH HE PITCHED						WHAT HE GAVE UP												THE RESULTS					
Year Team	Lg	G	GS	CG	GF	IP	BFP	H	R	ER	HR	SH	SF	HB	TBB	IBB	SO	WP	Bk	W	L	Pct.	ShO	Sv	ERA
1989 Eugene	A	8	5	0	0	30	131	30	19	13	1	0	1	5	8	0	25	7	0	1	1	.500	0	0	3.90
1990 Appleton	A	27	11	1	5	71	308	70	42	38	3	2	1	6	31	2	58	4	1	2	7	.222	0	0	4.82
1991 Baseball Cy	A	38	0	0	16	73	295	49	28	16	1	5	0	5	25	3	65	7	1	6	3	.667	0	5	1.97
1992 Memphis	AA	33	18	2	2	141	606	161	83	70	5	6	2	11	35	4	88	8	1	8	8	.500	0	1	4.47
1993 Memphis	AA	6	5	0	1	30	126	34	16	14	2	2	0	4	4	0	14	1	0	3	2	.600	0	0	4.20
1994 Birmingham	AA	39	0	0	33	43	177	36	10	6	0	3	2	2	14	1	29	5	0	5	2	.714	0	6	1.26
Nashville	AAA	17	0	0	11	26.1	101	18	5	4	0	4	1	1	7	2	19	1	0	4	2	.667	0	2	1.37
1995 Nashville	AAA	28	0	0	21	37.1	156	39	7	6	3	5	0	0	10	5	29	2	0	3	3	.500	0	9	1.45
1995 Chicago	AL	31	0	0	10	32	137	33	8	6	2	0	4	1	12	2	24	1	0	4	2	.667	0	0	1.69

Ron Karkovice

Bats: Right **Throws:** Right **Pos:** C   **Ht:** 6' 1" **Wt:** 219 **Born:** 8/8/63 **Age:** 32

		BATTING																BASERUNNING				PERCENTAGES		
Year Team	Lg	G	AB	H	2B	3B	HR	(Hm | Rd)	TB	R	RBI	TBB	IBB	SO	HBP	SH	SF	SB	CS	SB%	GDP	Avg	OBP	SLG
1986 Chicago	AL	37	97	24	7	0	4	(1 | 3)	43	13	13	9	0	37	1	1	1	1	0	1.00	3	.247	.315	.443
1987 Chicago	AL	39	85	6	0	0	2	(1 | 1)	12	7	7	7	0	40	2	1	0	3	0	1.00	2	.071	.160	.141
1988 Chicago	AL	46	115	20	4	0	3	(1 | 2)	33	10	9	7	0	30	1	3	0	4	2	.67	1	.174	.228	.287
1989 Chicago	AL	71	182	48	9	2	3	(0 | 3)	70	21	24	10	0	56	2	7	2	0	0	.00	0	.264	.306	.385
1990 Chicago	AL	68	183	45	10	0	6	(0 | 6)	73	30	20	16	1	52	1	7	1	2	0	1.00	1	.246	.308	.399
1991 Chicago	AL	75	167	41	13	0	5	(0 | 5)	69	25	22	15	1	42	1	9	1	0	0	.00	4	.246	.310	.413
1992 Chicago	AL	123	342	81	12	1	13	(5 | 8)	134	39	50	30	1	89	3	4	2	10	4	.71	3	.237	.302	.392
1993 Chicago	AL	128	403	92	17	1	20	(6 | 14)	171	60	54	29	1	126	6	11	4	2	2	.50	12	.228	.287	.424
1994 Chicago	AL	77	207	44	9	1	11	(6 | 5)	88	33	29	36	2	68	0	2	3	0	3	.00	0	.213	.325	.425
1995 Chicago	AL	113	323	70	14	1	13	(5 | 8)	125	44	51	39	0	84	5	9	6	2	3	.40	5	.217	.306	.387
10 ML YEARS		777	2104	471	95	6	80	(25 | 55)	818	282	279	198	6	624	22	54	20	24	14	.63	29	.224	.295	.389

Scott Karl

Pitches: Left **Bats:** Left **Pos:** SP/RP   **Ht:** 6' 2" **Wt:** 195 **Born:** 8/9/71 **Age:** 24

		HOW MUCH HE PITCHED						WHAT HE GAVE UP												THE RESULTS					
Year Team	Lg	G	GS	CG	GF	IP	BFP	H	R	ER	HR	SH	SF	HB	TBB	IBB	SO	WP	Bk	W	L	Pct.	ShO	Sv	ERA
1992 Helena	R	9	9	1	0	61.2	245	54	13	10	2	1	1	2	16	0	57	5	1	7	0	1.000	1	0	1.46
1993 El Paso	AA	27	27	4	0	180	732	172	67	49	9	6	3	6	35	0	95	6	7	13	8	.619	2	0	2.45
1994 El Paso	AA	8	8	3	0	54.2	219	44	21	18	2	2	1	1	15	1	51	3	0	5	1	.833	1	0	2.96
New Orleans	AAA	15	13	2	0	89	375	92	38	38	10	3	2	4	33	1	54	2	0	5	5	.500	0	0	3.84
1995 New Orleans	AAA	8	6	1	1	46.1	191	47	18	17	3	0	1	2	12	2	29	1	0	3	4	.429	1	0	3.30
1995 Milwaukee	AL	25	18	1	3	124	548	141	65	57	10	3	3	3	50	6	59	0	0	6	7	.462	0	0	4.14

Ryan Karp

Pitches: Left **Bats:** Left **Pos:** RP   **Ht:** 6' 4" **Wt:** 217 **Born:** 4/5/70 **Age:** 26

		HOW MUCH HE PITCHED						WHAT HE GAVE UP												THE RESULTS					
Year Team	Lg	G	GS	CG	GF	IP	BFP	H	R	ER	HR	SH	SF	HB	TBB	IBB	SO	WP	Bk	W	L	Pct.	ShO	Sv	ERA
1992 Oneonta	A	14	13	1	0	70.1	300	66	38	32	2	1	1	3	30	0	58	2	0	6	4	.600	1	0	4.09
1993 Greensboro	A	17	17	0	0	109.1	436	73	26	22	2	0	2	2	40	0	132	6	1	13	1	.929	0	0	1.81
Pr. William	A	8	8	1	0	49	189	35	17	12	4	2	2	2	12	0	34	5	1	3	2	.600	1	0	2.20
Albany-Colo	AA	3	3	0	0	13	60	13	7	6	1	0	1	0	9	0	10	1	0	0	0	.000	0	0	4.15
1994 Reading	AA	21	21	0	0	121.1	528	123	67	60	12	0	4	3	54	3	96	4	0	4	11	.267	0	0	4.45
1995 Reading	AA	7	7	0	0	47	190	44	18	16	4	3	0	0	15	0	37	1	2	1	2	.333	0	0	3.06
Scranton-Wb	AAA	13	13	0	0	81.1	357	81	43	38	6	2	2	4	31	0	73	2	0	7	1	.875	0	0	4.20
1995 Philadelphia	NL	1	0	0	0	2	10	1	1	1	0	0	0	0	3	0	2	1	0	0	0	.000	0	0	4.50

Eric Karros

Bats: Right **Throws:** Right **Pos:** 1B   **Ht:** 6' 4" **Wt:** 222 **Born:** 11/4/67 **Age:** 28

		BATTING																BASERUNNING				PERCENTAGES		
Year Team	Lg	G	AB	H	2B	3B	HR	(Hm | Rd)	TB	R	RBI	TBB	IBB	SO	HBP	SH	SF	SB	CS	SB%	GDP	Avg	OBP	SLG
1991 Los Angeles	NL	14	14	1	1	0	0	(0 | 0)	2	0	1	1	0	6	0	0	0	0	0	.00	0	.071	.133	.143
1992 Los Angeles	NL	149	545	140	30	1	20	(6 | 14)	232	63	88	37	3	103	2	0	5	2	4	.33	15	.257	.304	.426
1993 Los Angeles	NL	158	619	153	27	2	23	(13 | 10)	253	74	80	34	1	82	2	0	3	0	1	.00	17	.247	.287	.409

							(Hm	Rd)																
1994 Los Angeles	NL	111	406	108	21	1	14	(5 | 9)	173	51	46	29	1	53	2	0	11	2	0	1.00	13	.266	.310	.426
1995 Los Angeles	NL	143	551	164	29	3	32	(19 | 13)	295	83	105	61	4	115	4	0	4	4	4	.50	14	.298	.369	.535
5 ML YEARS		575	2135	566	108	7	89	(43 | 46)	955	271	320	162	9	359	10	0	23	8	9	.47	59	.265	.317	.447

Steve Karsay

Pitches: Right **Bats:** Right **Pos:** SP — **Ht:** 6' 3" **Wt:** 205 **Born:** 3/24/72 **Age:** 24

		HOW MUCH HE PITCHED						WHAT HE GAVE UP										THE RESULTS					
Year Team	Lg	G	GS	CG	GF	IP	BFP	H	R	ER	HR	SH	SF	HB	TBB	IBB	SO	WP	Bk	W	L	Pct.	ShO	Sv	ERA
1993 Oakland	AL	8	8	0	0	49	210	49	23	22	4	0	2	2	16	1	33	1	0	3	3	.500	0	0	4.04
1994 Oakland	AL	4	4	1	0	28	115	26	8	8	1	2	1	1	8	0	15	0	0	1	1	.500	0	0	2.57
2 ML YEARS		12	12	1	0	77	325	75	31	30	5	2	3	3	24	1	48	1	0	4	4	.500	0	0	3.51

Mike Kelly

Bats: Right **Throws:** Right **Pos:** LF/RF — **Ht:** 6' 4" **Wt:** 195 **Born:** 6/2/70 **Age:** 26

		BATTING																BASERUNNING				PERCENTAGES		
Year Team	Lg	G	AB	H	2B	3B	HR	(Hm | Rd)	TB	R	RBI	TBB	IBB	SO	HBP	SH	SF	SB	CS	SB%	GDP	Avg	OBP	SLG
1991 Durham	A	35	124	31	6	1	6	--	--	57	29	17	19	0	47	2	0	1	6	2	.75	0	.250	.356	.460
1992 Greenville	AA	133	471	108	18	4	25	--	--	209	83	71	65	2	162	6	0	3	22	11	.67	7	.229	.328	.444
1993 Richmond	AAA	123	424	103	13	1	19	--	--	175	63	58	36	1	109	14	0	1	11	7	.61	3	.243	.322	.413
1994 Richmond	AAA	82	313	82	14	4	15	--	--	149	46	45	32	1	96	3	0	2	9	6	.60	5	.262	.334	.476
1995 Richmond	AAA	15	45	13	1	0	2	--	--	20	5	8	5	0	17	2	0	0	1	0	1.00	0	.289	.385	.444
1994 Atlanta	NL	30	77	21	10	1	2	(0 | 2)	39	14	9	2	0	17	1	0	0	0	1	.00	0	.273	.300	.506
1995 Atlanta	NL	97	137	26	6	1	3	(0 | 3)	43	26	17	11	0	49	2	2	1	7	3	.70	2	.190	.258	.314
2 ML YEARS		127	214	47	16	2	5	(0 | 5)	82	40	26	13	0	66	3	2	1	7	4	.64	2	.220	.273	.383

Pat Kelly

Bats: Right **Throws:** Right **Pos:** 2B — **Ht:** 6' 0" **Wt:** 182 **Born:** 10/14/67 **Age:** 28

		BATTING																BASERUNNING				PERCENTAGES		
Year Team	Lg	G	AB	H	2B	3B	HR	(Hm | Rd)	TB	R	RBI	TBB	IBB	SO	HBP	SH	SF	SB	CS	SB%	GDP	Avg	OBP	SLG
1995 Yankees *	R	1	2	0	0	0	0	--	--	0	2	1	1	0	0	2	0	0	0	0	.00	0	.000	.600	.000
Tampa *	A	3	17	4	1	0	0	--	--	5	0	2	0	0	1	0	0	0	0	0	.00	0	.235	.235	.294
1991 New York	AL	96	298	72	12	4	3	(3 | 0)	101	35	23	15	0	52	5	2	2	12	1	.92	5	.242	.288	.339
1992 New York	AL	106	318	72	22	2	7	(3 | 4)	119	38	27	25	1	72	10	6	3	8	5	.62	6	.226	.301	.374
1993 New York	AL	127	406	111	24	1	7	(4 | 3)	158	49	51	24	0	68	5	10	6	14	11	.56	9	.273	.317	.389
1994 New York	AL	93	286	80	21	2	3	(1 | 2)	114	35	41	19	1	51	6	5	5	6	5	.55	10	.280	.330	.399
1995 New York	AL	89	270	64	12	1	4	(1 | 3)	90	32	29	23	0	65	5	10	2	8	3	.73	5	.237	.307	.333
5 ML YEARS		511	1578	399	91	10	24	(12 | 12)	582	189	171	106	2	308	30	42	18	48	25	.66	35	.253	.309	.369

Roberto Kelly

Bats: Right **Throws:** Right **Pos:** CF/LF — **Ht:** 6' 2" **Wt:** 202 **Born:** 10/1/64 **Age:** 31

		BATTING																BASERUNNING				PERCENTAGES		
Year Team	Lg	G	AB	H	2B	3B	HR	(Hm | Rd)	TB	R	RBI	TBB	IBB	SO	HBP	SH	SF	SB	CS	SB%	GDP	Avg	OBP	SLG
1987 New York	AL	23	52	14	3	0	1	(0 | 1)	20	12	7	5	0	15	0	1	1	9	3	.75	0	.269	.328	.364
1988 New York	AL	38	77	19	4	1	1	(1 | 0)	28	9	7	3	0	15	0	3	1	5	2	.71	0	.247	.272	.364
1989 New York	AL	137	441	133	18	3	9	(2 | 7)	184	65	48	41	3	89	6	8	0	35	12	.74	9	.302	.369	.417
1990 New York	AL	162	641	183	32	4	15	(5 | 10)	268	85	61	33	0	148	4	4	4	42	17	.71	7	.285	.323	.418
1991 New York	AL	126	486	130	22	2	20	(11 | 9)	216	68	69	45	2	77	5	2	5	32	9	.78	14	.267	.333	.444
1992 New York	AL	152	580	158	31	2	10	(6 | 4)	223	81	66	41	4	96	4	1	6	28	5	.85	19	.272	.322	.384
1993 Cincinnati	NL	78	320	102	17	3	9	(4 | 5)	152	44	35	17	0	43	2	0	3	21	5	.81	10	.319	.354	.475
1994 Atl-Cin	NL	110	434	127	23	3	9	(4 | 5)	183	73	45	31	1	71	3	0	8	19	11	.63	8	.293	.347	.422
1995 Mon-LA	NL	136	504	140	23	2	7	(2 | 5)	188	58	57	22	6	79	6	0	7	19	10	.66	14	.278	.312	.373
1994 Atlanta	NL	63	255	73	15	3	6	(3 | 3)	112	44	24	24	0	36	0	0	2	10	3	.77	5	.286	.345	.439
Cincinnati	NL	47	179	54	8	0	3	(1 | 2)	71	29	21	11	1	35	3	0	1	9	8	.53	3	.302	.351	.397
1995 Montreal	NL	24	95	26	4	0	1	(0 | 1)	33	11	9	7	1	14	2	0	0	4	3	.57	4	.274	.337	.347
Los Angeles	NL	112	409	114	19	2	6	(2 | 4)	155	47	48	15	5	65	4	0	7	15	7	.68	10	.279	.306	.379
9 ML YEARS		962	3535	1006	173	20	81	(35 | 46)	1462	495	395	242	16	633	30	19	30	210	74	.74	81	.285	.333	.414

Jeff Kent

Bats: Right **Throws:** Right **Pos:** 2B — **Ht:** 6' 1" **Wt:** 185 **Born:** 3/7/68 **Age:** 28

		BATTING																BASERUNNING				PERCENTAGES		
Year Team	Lg	G	AB	H	2B	3B	HR	(Hm | Rd)	TB	R	RBI	TBB	IBB	SO	HBP	SH	SF	SB	CS	SB%	GDP	Avg	OBP	SLG
1992 Tor-NYN		102	305	73	21	2	11	(4 | 7)	131	52	50	27	0	76	7	0	4	2	3	.40	5	.239	.312	.430
1993 New York	NL	140	496	134	24	0	21	(9 | 12)	221	65	80	30	2	88	8	6	4	4	4	.50	11	.270	.320	.446
1994 New York	NL	107	415	121	24	5	14	(10 | 4)	197	53	68	23	3	84	10	1	3	1	4	.20	7	.292	.341	.475
1995 New York	NL	125	472	131	22	3	20	(11 | 9)	219	65	65	29	3	89	8	1	4	3	3	.50	9	.278	.327	.464
1992 Toronto	AL	65	192	46	13	1	8	(2 | 6)	85	36	35	20	0	47	6	0	4	2	1	.67	3	.240	.324	.443
New York	NL	37	113	27	8	1	3	(2 | 1)	46	16	15	7	0	29	1	0	0	0	2	.00	2	.239	.289	.407
4 ML YEARS		474	1688	459	91	10	66	(34 | 32)	768	235	263	109	8	337	33	8	15	10	14	.42	32	.272	.326	.455

Jimmy Key

Pitches: Left **Bats:** Right **Pos:** SP · **Ht:** 6' 1" **Wt:** 185 **Born:** 4/22/61 **Age:** 35

Year	Team	Lg	G	GS	CG	GF	IP	BFP	H	R	ER	HR	SH	SF	HB	TBB	IBB	SO	WP	Bk	W	L	Pct.	ShO	Sv	ERA
1984	Toronto	AL	63	0	0	24	62	285	70	37	32	8	6	1	1	32	8	44	3	1	4	5	.444	0	10	4.65
1985	Toronto	AL	35	32	3	0	212.2	856	188	77	71	22	5	5	2	50	1	85	6	1	14	6	.700	0	0	3.00
1986	Toronto	AL	36	35	4	0	232	959	222	98	92	24	10	6	3	74	1	141	3	0	14	11	.560	2	0	3.57
1987	Toronto	AL	36	36	8	0	261	1033	210	93	80	24	11	3	2	66	6	161	8	5	17	8	.680	1	0	**2.76**
1988	Toronto	AL	21	21	2	0	131.1	551	127	55	48	13	4	3	5	30	2	65	1	0	12	5	.706	2	0	3.29
1989	Toronto	AL	33	33	5	0	216	886	226	99	93	18	9	9	3	27	2	118	4	1	13	14	.481	1	0	3.88
1990	Toronto	AL	27	27	0	0	154.2	636	169	79	73	20	5	6	1	22	2	88	0	1	13	7	.650	0	0	4.25
1991	Toronto	AL	33	33	2	0	209.1	877	207	84	71	12	10	5	3	44	3	125	1	0	16	12	.571	2	0	3.05
1992	Toronto	AL	33	33	4	0	216.2	900	205	88	85	24	2	7	4	59	0	117	5	0	13	13	.500	2	0	3.53
1993	New York	AL	34	34	4	0	236.2	948	219	84	79	26	6	9	1	43	1	173	3	0	18	6	.750	2	0	3.00
1994	New York	AL	25	**25**	1	0	168	710	177	68	61	10	4	2	3	52	0	97	8	1	**17**	4	.810	0	0	3.27
1995	New York	AL	5	5	0	0	30.1	134	40	20	19	3	3	1	0	6	1	14	1	0	1	2	.333	0	0	5.64
	12 ML YEARS		381	314	33	24	2130.2	8775	2060	882	804	204	75	57	28	505	27	1228	43	10	152	93	.620	12	10	3.40

Brian Keyser

Pitches: Right **Bats:** Right **Pos:** RP/SP · **Ht:** 6' 1" **Wt:** 180 **Born:** 10/31/66 **Age:** 29

Year	Team	Lg	G	GS	CG	GF	IP	BFP	H	R	ER	HR	SH	SF	HB	TBB	IBB	SO	WP	Bk	W	L	Pct.	ShO	Sv	ERA
1989	Utica	A	14	13	2	0	93.2	374	79	37	31	6	2	2	4	22	0	70	5	3	4	4	.500	0	0	2.98
1990	Sarasota	A	38	10	2	13	115.2	475	107	54	47	5	3	6	1	40	1	83	6	3	6	7	.462	1	2	3.66
1991	Sarasota	A	27	14	2	9	129	527	110	40	33	5	8	3	6	45	8	94	3	3	6	7	.462	1	2	2.30
	Birmingham	AA	3	3	0	0	18	78	19	10	10	2	0	1	0	9	0	9	0	1	0	1	.000	0	0	5.00
1992	Birmingham	AA	28	27	7	1	183.1	754	173	86	76	12	1	7	4	60	1	99	9	0	9	10	.474	3	0	3.73
1993	Birmingham	AA	2	2	1	0	11	50	15	9	7	0	1	1	0	5	0	8	0	0	0	2	.000	0	0	5.73
	Nashville	AAA	30	18	2	4	121.2	511	142	70	63	8	2	4	1	27	4	44	4	1	9	5	.643	0	1	4.66
1994	Birmingham	AA	1	1	0	0	6	23	4	1	1	1	0	0	1	1	0	5	0	0	0	0	.000	0	0	1.50
	Nashville	AAA	37	10	2	15	135.2	556	123	49	42	9	7	5	3	36	4	76	9	0	9	5	.643	1	2	2.79
1995	Nashville	AAA	10	10	2	0	72.1	273	49	23	19	4	3	3	1	9	0	40	1	0	2	4	.333	1	0	2.36
1995	Chicago	AL	23	10	0	0	92.1	404	114	53	51	10	0	2	2	27	1	48	1	1	5	6	.455	0	0	4.97

Mark Kiefer

Pitches: Right **Bats:** Right **Pos:** RP · **Ht:** 6' 4" **Wt:** 194 **Born:** 11/13/68 **Age:** 27

Year	Team	Lg	G	GS	CG	GF	IP	BFP	H	R	ER	HR	SH	SF	HB	TBB	IBB	SO	WP	Bk	W	L	Pct.	ShO	Sv	ERA
1988	Helena	R	15	9	2	4	68	296	76	30	20	3	3	0	6	17	0	51	4	3	4	4	.500	0	0	2.65
1989	Beloit	A	30	15	7	5	131.2	533	106	44	34	4	1	4	8	32	2	100	6	0	9	6	.600	2	1	2.32
1990	Brewers	R	1	1	0	0	2.1	10	3	1	1	0	0	0	0	1	0	2	0	0	0	0	.000	0	0	3.86
	Stockton	A	11	10	0	1	60	261	65	23	22	5	0	1	8	17	0	37	3	1	5	2	.714	0	0	3.30
1991	El Paso	AA	12	12	0	0	75.2	325	62	33	28	4	2	2	1	43	2	72	6	0	7	1	.875	0	0	3.33
	Denver	AAA	17	17	3	0	101.1	449	104	55	52	7	4	1	9	41	0	68	6	0	9	5	.643	2	0	4.62
1992	Denver	AAA	27	26	1	0	162.2	706	168	95	83	25	3	4	9	65	1	145	8	3	7	13	.350	0	0	4.59
1993	El Paso	AA	11	11	0	0	51.2	221	48	29	23	5	1	0	2	19	0	44	6	3	3	4	.429	0	0	4.01
	New Orleans	AAA	5	5	0	0	28.1	126	28	20	16	4	1	1	0	17	0	23	4	0	3	2	.600	0	0	5.08
1994	New Orleans	AAA	21	21	0	0	124.2	531	111	61	54	17	2	3	15	48	0	116	13	0	9	7	.563	0	0	3.90
1995	New Orleans	AAA	12	12	1	0	70.1	290	60	22	22	5	1	0	5	19	0	52	6	0	8	2	.800	0	0	2.82
1993	Milwaukee	AL	6	0	0	4	9.1	37	3	0	0	0	0	0	1	5	0	7	0	0	0	0	.000	0	1	0.00
1994	Milwaukee	AL	7	0	0	1	10.2	52	15	12	10	4	0	2	0	8	0	8	0	0	1	0	1.000	0	0	8.44
1995	Milwaukee	AL	24	0	0	7	49.2	209	37	20	19	6	0	0	0	27	2	41	4	0	4	1	.800	0	0	3.44
	3 ML YEARS		37	0	0	12	69.2	298	55	32	29	10	0	2	1	40	2	56	4	0	5	1	.833	0	1	3.75

Darryl Kile

Pitches: Right **Bats:** Right **Pos:** SP · **Ht:** 6' 5" **Wt:** 185 **Born:** 12/2/68 **Age:** 27

Year	Team	Lg	G	GS	CG	GF	IP	BFP	H	R	ER	HR	SH	SF	HB	TBB	IBB	SO	WP	Bk	W	L	Pct.	ShO	Sv	ERA
1995	Tucson *	AAA	4	4	0	0	24.1	113	29	23	23	0	1	0	4	12	0	15	5	0	2	1	.667	0	0	8.51
1991	Houston	NL	37	22	0	5	153.2	689	144	81	63	16	9	5	6	84	4	100	5	4	7	11	.389	0	0	3.69
1992	Houston	NL	22	22	2	0	125.1	524	124	61	55	8	5	6	4	63	4	90	3	4	5	10	.333	0	0	3.95
1993	Houston	NL	32	26	4	0	171.2	733	152	73	67	12	5	7	15	69	1	141	9	3	15	8	.652	2	0	3.51
1994	Houston	NL	24	24	0	0	147.2	664	153	84	75	13	14	2	9	**82**	6	105	**10**	0	9	6	.600	0	0	4.57
1995	Houston	NL	25	21	0	0	127	570	114	81	70	5	7	3	12	73	2	113	11	1	4	12	.250	0	0	4.96
	5 ML YEARS		140	115	6	6	725.1	3210	687	380	330	54	40	23	46	371	17	549	38	12	40	47	.460	2	0	4.09

Jeff King

Bats: Right **Throws:** Right **Pos:** 3B/1B   **Ht:** 6' 1" **Wt:** 185 **Born:** 12/26/64 **Age:** 31

				BATTING															BASERUNNING				PERCENTAGES		
Year Team	Lg	G	AB	H	2B	3B	HR	(Hm	Rd)	TB	R	RBI	TBB	IBB	SO	HBP	SH	SF	SB	CS	SB%	GDP	Avg	OBP	SLG
1989 Pittsburgh	NL	75	215	42	13	3	5	(3	2)	76	31	19	20	1	34	2	2	4	4	2	.67	3	.195	.266	.353
1990 Pittsburgh	NL	127	371	91	17	1	14	(9	5)	152	46	53	21	1	50	1	2	7	3	3	.50	12	.245	.283	.410
1991 Pittsburgh	NL	33	109	26	1	1	4	(3	1)	41	16	18	14	3	15	1	0	1	3	1	.75	3	.239	.328	.376
1992 Pittsburgh	NL	130	480	111	21	2	14	(6	8)	178	56	65	27	3	56	2	8	5	4	6	.40	8	.231	.272	.371
1993 Pittsburgh	NL	158	611	180	35	3	9	(4	5)	248	82	98	59	4	54	4	1	8	8	6	.57	17	.295	.356	.406
1994 Pittsburgh	NL	94	339	89	23	0	5	(2	3)	127	36	42	30	1	38	0	2	7	3	2	.60	7	.263	.316	.375
1995 Pittsburgh	NL	122	445	118	27	2	18	(7	11)	203	61	87	55	5	63	1	0	8	7	4	.64	10	.265	.342	.456
7 ML YEARS		739	2570	657	137	12	69	(34	35)	1025	328	382	226	18	310	11	15	40	32	24	.57	60	.256	.314	.399

Kevin King

Pitches: Left **Bats:** Left **Pos:** RP   **Ht:** 6' 4" **Wt:** 200 **Born:** 2/11/69 **Age:** 27

		HOW MUCH HE PITCHED						WHAT HE GAVE UP										THE RESULTS					
Year Team	Lg	G	GS	CG	GF	IP	BFP	H	R	ER	HR	SH	SF	HB	TBB	IBB	SO	WP	Bk	W	L	Pct.	ShO	Sv	ERA
1995 Tacoma *	AAA	16	0	0	6	16.2	85	33	14	14	2	1	0	0	7	1	10	2	1	0	0	.000	0	0	7.56
Port City *	AA	20	0	0	6	31	136	35	15	13	2	1	1	3	11	1	19	4	1	1	2	.333	0	0	3.77
1993 Seattle	AL	13	0	0	3	11.2	49	9	8	8	3	3	2	1	4	1	8	0	0	0	1	.000	0	0	6.17
1994 Seattle	AL	19	0	0	1	15.1	81	21	13	12	0	0	0	1	17	3	6	0	0	0	2	.000	0	0	7.04
1995 Seattle	AL	2	0	0	0	3.2	20	7	5	5	0	0	1	1	1	0	3	1	0	0	0	.000	0	0	12.27
3 ML YEARS		34	0	0	4	30.2	150	37	26	25	3	3	3	3	22	4	17	1	0	0	3	.000	0	0	7.34

Mike Kingery

Bats: Left **Throws:** Left **Pos:** CF   **Ht:** 6' 0" **Wt:** 185 **Born:** 3/29/61 **Age:** 35

				BATTING															BASERUNNING				PERCENTAGES		
Year Team	Lg	G	AB	H	2B	3B	HR	(Hm	Rd)	TB	R	RBI	TBB	IBB	SO	HBP	SH	SF	SB	CS	SB%	GDP	Avg	OBP	SLG
1986 Kansas City	AL	62	209	54	8	5	3	(1	2)	81	25	14	12	2	30	0	0	2	7	3	.70	4	.258	.296	.388
1987 Seattle	AL	120	354	99	25	4	9	(5	4)	159	38	52	27	0	43	2	1	6	7	9	.44	4	.280	.329	.449
1988 Seattle	AL	57	123	25	6	0	1	(1	0)	34	21	9	19	1	23	1	1	1	3	1	.75	1	.203	.313	.276
1989 Seattle	AL	31	76	17	3	0	2	(2	0)	26	14	6	7	0	14	0	0	1	1	1	.50	2	.224	.286	.342
1990 San Francisco	NL	105	207	61	7	1	0	(0	0)	70	24	24	12	0	19	1	5	1	6	1	.86	1	.295	.335	.338
1991 San Francisco	NL	91	110	20	2	2	0	(0	0)	26	13	8	15	1	21	0	0	0	1	0	1.00	3	.182	.280	.236
1992 Oakland	AL	12	28	3	0	0	0	(0	0)	3	3	1	1	0	3	0	0	0	0	0	.00	1	.107	.138	.107
1994 Colorado	NL	105	301	105	27	8	4	(0	4)	160	56	41	30	2	26	2	5	8	5	7	.42	5	.349	.402	.532
1995 Colorado	NL	119	350	94	18	4	8	(4	4)	144	66	37	45	1	40	0	6	1	13	5	.72	7	.269	.351	.411
9 ML YEARS		702	1758	478	96	24	27	(13	14)	703	260	192	168	7	219	6	18	20	43	27	.61	31	.272	.334	.400

Wayne Kirby

Bats: Left **Throws:** Right **Pos:** RF/CF   **Ht:** 5'10" **Wt:** 190 **Born:** 1/22/64 **Age:** 32

				BATTING															BASERUNNING				PERCENTAGES		
Year Team	Lg	G	AB	H	2B	3B	HR	(Hm	Rd)	TB	R	RBI	TBB	IBB	SO	HBP	SH	SF	SB	CS	SB%	GDP	Avg	OBP	SLG
1991 Cleveland	AL	21	14	3	2	0	0	(0	0)	11	4	5	2	0	6	0	1	1	1	2	.33	2	.209	.239	.256
1992 Cleveland	AL	21	18	3	1	0	1	(0	1)	7	9	1	3	0	2	0	0	0	0	3	.00	1	.167	.286	.389
1993 Cleveland	AL	131	458	123	19	5	6	(4	2)	170	71	60	37	2	58	3	7	6	17	5	.77	8	.269	.323	.371
1994 Cleveland	AL	78	191	56	6	0	5	(3	2)	77	33	23	13	0	30	1	2	0	11	4	.73	1	.293	.341	.403
1995 Cleveland	AL	101	188	39	10	2	1	(0	1)	56	29	14	13	0	32	1	1	2	10	3	.77	4	.207	.260	.298
5 ML YEARS		352	898	230	38	7	13	(7	6)	321	146	103	68	2	128	5	11	9	39	17	.70	16	.256	.309	.357

Ryan Klesko

Bats: Left **Throws:** Left **Pos:** LF   **Ht:** 6' 3" **Wt:** 220 **Born:** 6/12/71 **Age:** 25

				BATTING															BASERUNNING				PERCENTAGES		
Year Team	Lg	G	AB	H	2B	3B	HR	(Hm	Rd)	TB	R	RBI	TBB	IBB	SO	HBP	SH	SF	SB	CS	SB%	GDP	Avg	OBP	SLG
1995 Greenville *	AA	4	13	3	0	0	1	--	--	6	1	4	2	0	1	0	0	0	0	0	.00	1	.231	.333	.462
1992 Atlanta	NL	13	14	0	0	0	0	(0	0)	0	0	1	0	0	5	1	0	0	0	0	.00	0	.000	.067	.000
1993 Atlanta	NL	22	17	6	1	0	2	(2	0)	13	3	5	3	1	4	0	0	0	0	0	.00	0	.353	.450	.765
1994 Atlanta	NL	92	245	68	13	3	17	(7	10)	138	42	47	26	3	48	1	0	4	1	0	1.00	8	.278	.344	.563
1995 Atlanta	NL	107	329	102	25	2	23	(15	8)	200	48	70	47	10	72	2	0	3	5	4	.56	8	.310	.396	.608
4 ML YEARS		234	605	176	39	5	42	(24	18)	351	93	123	76	14	129	4	0	7	6	4	.60	16	.291	.370	.580

Scott Klingenbeck

Pitches: Right **Bats:** Right **Pos:** RP/SP   **Ht:** 6' 2" **Wt:** 205 **Born:** 2/3/71 **Age:** 25

		HOW MUCH HE PITCHED						WHAT HE GAVE UP										THE RESULTS					
Year Team	Lg	G	GS	CG	GF	IP	BFP	H	R	ER	HR	SH	SF	HB	TBB	IBB	SO	WP	Bk	W	L	Pct.	ShO	Sv	ERA
1992 Kane County	A	11	11	0	0	68.1	283	50	31	20	3	2	0	1	28	1	64	4	8	3	4	.429	0	0	2.63
1993 Frederick	A	23	23	0	0	139	593	151	62	46	7	2	2	2	35	1	146	5	2	13	4	.765	0	0	2.98

125

Year Team	Lg	G	GS	CG	GF	IP	BFP	H	R	ER	HR	SH	SF	HB	TBB	IBB	SO	WP	Bk	W	L	Pct.	ShO	Sv	ERA
1994 Bowie	AA	25	25	3	0	143.2	613	151	76	58	15	2	4	5	37	2	120	6	3	7	5	.583	0	0	3.63
1995 Rochester	AAA	8	7	0	0	43	177	46	14	13	2	3	2	1	10	0	29	2	0	3	1	.750	0	0	2.72
1994 Baltimore	AL	1	1	0	0	7	31	6	4	3	1	0	1	1	4	1	5	0	0	1	0	1.000	0	0	3.86
1995 Bal-Min	AL	24	9	0	4	79.2	373	101	65	63	22	3	1	4	42	0	42	7	0	2	4	.333	0	0	7.12
1995 Baltimore	AL	6	5	0	0	31.1	137	32	17	17	6	0	0	0	18	0	15	2	0	2	2	.500	0	0	4.88
Minnesota	AL	18	4	0	4	48.1	236	69	48	46	16	3	1	4	24	0	27	5	0	0	2	.000	0	0	8.57
2 ML YEARS		25	10	0	4	86.2	404	107	69	66	23	3	2	5	46	1	47	7	0	3	4	.429	0	0	6.85

Joe Kmak

Bats: Right **Throws:** Right **Pos:** C **Ht:** 6' 0" **Wt:** 185 **Born:** 5/3/63 **Age:** 33

								BATTING											BASERUNNING				PERCENTAGES		
Year Team	Lg	G	AB	H	2B	3B	HR	(Hm Rd)	TB	R	RBI	TBB	IBB	SO	HBP	SH	SF	SB	CS	SB%	GDP	Avg	OBP	SLG
1985 Everett	A	40	129	40	10	1	1	-- --	55	21	14	20	0	23	3	0	2	0	1	.00	3	.310	.409	.426
1986 Fresno	A	60	163	44	5	0	1	-- --	52	23	9	15	0	38	3	0	1	3	2	.60	6	.270	.341	.319
1987 Fresno	A	48	154	34	8	0	0	-- --	42	18	12	15	0	32	3	3	0	1	2	.33	3	.221	.302	.273
Shreveport	AA	15	41	8	0	1	0	-- --	10	5	3	3	0	4	1	0	0	0	0	.00	1	.195	.267	.244
1988 Shreveport	AA	71	178	40	5	2	1	-- --	52	16	14	11	2	19	4	1	1	0	0	.00	3	.225	.284	.292
1989 Reno	A	78	248	68	10	5	4	-- --	100	39	34	40	1	41	5	0	1	8	4	.67	9	.274	.384	.403
1990 El Paso	AA	35	109	31	3	2	2	-- --	44	8	11	7	0	22	2	3	2	0	0	.00	2	.284	.333	.404
Denver	AAA	28	95	22	3	0	1	-- --	28	12	10	4	0	16	3	5	0	1	1	.50	3	.232	.284	.295
1991 Denver	AAA	100	294	70	17	2	1	-- --	94	34	33	28	0	44	5	8	1	7	3	.70	5	.238	.314	.320
1992 Denver	AAA	67	225	70	11	4	3	-- --	98	27	31	19	0	39	3	5	2	6	3	.67	5	.311	.369	.436
1993 New Orleans	AAA	24	76	23	3	2	1	-- --	33	9	13	8	0	14	0	0	0	1	0	1.00	1	.303	.369	.434
1994 Norfolk	AAA	86	264	66	5	0	5	-- --	86	28	31	31	1	51	5	1	1	2	3	.40	6	.250	.339	.326
1995 Iowa	AAA	34	98	17	3	0	2	-- --	26	6	7	6	0	24	0	3	2	0	0	.00	4	.173	.217	.265
1993 Milwaukee	AL	51	110	24	5	0	0	(0 0)	29	9	7	14	0	13	2	1	0	6	2	.75	2	.218	.317	.264
1995 Chicago	NL	19	53	13	3	0	1	(1 0)	19	7	6	6	0	12	1	0	1	0	0	.00	2	.245	.328	.358
2 ML YEARS		70	163	37	8	0	1	(1 0)	48	16	13	20	0	25	3	1	1	6	2	.75	4	.227	.321	.294

Chuck Knoblauch

Bats: Right **Throws:** Right **Pos:** 2B **Ht:** 5' 9" **Wt:** 181 **Born:** 7/7/68 **Age:** 27

								BATTING											BASERUNNING				PERCENTAGES		
Year Team	Lg	G	AB	H	2B	3B	HR	(Hm Rd)	TB	R	RBI	TBB	IBB	SO	HBP	SH	SF	SB	CS	SB%	GDP	Avg	OBP	SLG
1991 Minnesota	AL	151	565	159	24	6	1	(1 0)	198	78	50	59	0	40	4	1	5	25	5	**.83**	8	.281	.351	.350
1992 Minnesota	AL	155	600	178	19	6	2	(0 2)	215	104	56	88	1	60	5	2	12	34	13	.72	8	.297	.384	.358
1993 Minnesota	AL	153	602	167	27	4	2	(2 0)	208	82	41	65	1	44	9	4	5	29	11	.73	11	.277	.354	.346
1994 Minnesota	AL	109	445	139	**45**	3	5	(1 4)	205	85	51	41	2	56	10	0	3	35	6	.85	13	.312	.381	.461
1995 Minnesota	AL	136	538	179	34	8	11	(4 7)	262	107	63	78	3	95	10	0	3	46	18	.72	15	.333	.424	.487
5 ML YEARS		704	2750	822	149	27	21	(8 13)	1088	456	261	331	7	295	38	7	28	169	53	.76	55	.299	.378	.396

Randy Knorr

Bats: Right **Throws:** Right **Pos:** C **Ht:** 6' 2" **Wt:** 215 **Born:** 11/12/68 **Age:** 27

								BATTING											BASERUNNING				PERCENTAGES		
Year Team	Lg	G	AB	H	2B	3B	HR	(Hm Rd)	TB	R	RBI	TBB	IBB	SO	HBP	SH	SF	SB	CS	SB%	GDP	Avg	OBP	SLG
1995 Syracuse *	AAA	18	67	18	5	1	1	-- --	28	6	6	5	0	14	0	0	1	0	0	.00	1	.269	.315	.418
1991 Toronto	AL	3	1	0	0	0	0	(0 0)	0	0	0	1	0	1	0	0	0	0	0	.00	0	.000	.500	.000
1992 Toronto	AL	8	19	5	0	0	1	(0 1)	8	1	2	1	1	5	0	0	0	0	0	.00	0	.263	.300	.421
1993 Toronto	AL	39	101	25	3	2	4	(2 2)	44	11	20	9	0	29	0	2	0	0	0	.00	7	.248	.309	.436
1994 Toronto	AL	40	124	30	2	0	7	(4 3)	53	20	19	10	0	35	1	0	1	0	0	.00	7	.242	.301	.427
1995 Toronto	AL	45	132	28	8	0	3	(2 1)	45	18	16	11	0	28	0	1	0	0	0	.00	5	.212	.273	.341
5 ML YEARS		135	377	88	13	2	15	(8 7)	150	50	57	32	1	98	1	3	1	0	0	.00	14	.233	.294	.398

Dennis Konuszewski

Pitches: Right **Bats:** Right **Pos:** RP **Ht:** 6' 3" **Wt:** 210 **Born:** 2/4/71 **Age:** 25

				HOW MUCH HE PITCHED					WHAT HE GAVE UP										THE RESULTS					
Year Team	Lg	G	GS	CG	GF	IP	BFP	H	R	ER	HR	SH	SF	HB	TBB	IBB	SO	WP	Bk	W	L	Pct.	ShO	Sv	ERA
1992 Welland	A	2	2	0	0	7	30	6	1	1	0	0	0	0	4	0	4	1	1	0	0	.000	0	1	1.29
Augusta	A	17	8	0	4	62.1	258	50	19	16	1	4	0	5	19	0	45	2	7	3	3	.500	0	1	2.31
1993 Salem	A	39	13	0	7	103	463	121	66	53	14	3	7	5	43	3	81	6	4	4	10	.286	0	1	4.63
1994 Carolina	AA	51	0	0	19	77.2	346	81	39	31	5	2	2	2	31	5	53	6	1	6	5	.545	0	1	3.59
1995 Carolina	AA	48	0	0	18	61.2	278	63	33	25	3	3	1	1	26	5	48	5	1	7	7	.500	0	2	3.65
1995 Pittsburgh	NL	1	0	0	0	0.1	5	3	2	2	0	0	0	0	1	0	0	0	0	0	0	.000	0	0	54.00

Brian Kowitz

Bats: Left **Throws:** Left **Pos:** RF **Ht:** 5'10" **Wt:** 182 **Born:** 8/7/69 **Age:** 26

								BATTING											BASERUNNING				PERCENTAGES		
Year Team	Lg	G	AB	H	2B	3B	HR	(Hm Rd)	TB	R	RBI	TBB	IBB	SO	HBP	SH	SF	SB	CS	SB%	GDP	Avg	OBP	SLG
1990 Pulaski	R	43	182	59	13	1	8	-- --	98	40	19	16	2	16	1	2	2	12	6	.67	4	.324	.378	.538

	Lg	G	AB	H	2B	3B	HR	(Hm	Rd)	TB	R	RBI	TBB	IBB	SO	HBP	SH	SF	SB	CS	SB%	GDP	Avg	OBP	SLG
Greenville	AA	20	68	9	0	0	0	--	--	9	4	4	8	1	10	0	1	0	1	0	1.00	2	.132	.224	.132
1991 Durham	A	86	323	82	13	5	3	--	--	114	41	21	23	0	56	3	4	1	18	8	.69	3	.254	.309	.353
Greenville	AA	35	112	26	5	0	3	--	--	40	15	17	10	0	7	2	2	2	1	4	.20	3	.232	.302	.357
1992 Durham	A	105	382	115	14	7	7	--	--	164	53	64	44	4	53	2	6	7	22	11	.67	3	.301	.370	.429
Greenville	AA	21	56	16	4	0	0	--	--	20	9	6	6	0	10	0	0	0	1	4	.20	0	.286	.355	.357
1993 Greenville	AA	122	450	125	20	5	5	--	--	170	63	48	60	0	56	2	1	1	13	10	.57	7	.278	.365	.378
Richmond	AAA	12	45	12	1	3	0	--	--	19	10	8	5	0	8	1	2	1	1	0	1.00	0	.267	.346	.422
1994 Richmond	AAA	124	466	140	29	7	8	--	--	207	68	57	43	2	53	2	1	7	22	8	.73	8	.300	.357	.444
1995 Richmond	AAA	100	353	99	14	5	2	--	--	129	53	34	41	1	43	3	3	0	11	8	.58	4	.280	.360	.365
1995 Atlanta	NL	10	24	4	1	0	0	(0	0)	5	3	3	2	0	5	1	1	0	0	1	.00	0	.167	.259	.208

Chad Kreuter

Bats: Both **Throws:** Right **Pos:** C **Ht:** 6' 2" **Wt:** 200 **Born:** 8/26/64 **Age:** 31

		BATTING																	BASERUNNING				PERCENTAGES		
Year Team	Lg	G	AB	H	2B	3B	HR	(Hm	Rd)	TB	R	RBI	TBB	IBB	SO	HBP	SH	SF	SB	CS	SB%	GDP	Avg	OBP	SLG
1995 Tacoma *	AAA	15	48	14	5	0	1	--	--	22	6	11	8	0	11	0	0	0	0	0	.00	3	.292	.393	.458
1988 Texas	AL	16	51	14	2	1	1	(0	1)	21	3	5	7	0	13	0	0	0	0	0	.00	1	.275	.362	.412
1989 Texas	AL	87	158	24	3	0	5	(2	3)	42	16	9	27	0	40	0	6	1	0	1	.00	4	.152	.274	.266
1990 Texas	AL	22	22	1	1	0	0	(0	0)	2	2	2	8	0	9	0	1	1	0	0	.00	0	.045	.290	.091
1991 Texas	AL	3	4	0	0	0	0	(0	0)	0	0	0	0	0	1	0	0	0	0	0	.00	0	.000	.000	.000
1992 Detroit	AL	67	190	48	9	0	2	(2	0)	63	22	16	20	1	38	0	3	2	0	1	.00	8	.253	.321	.332
1993 Detroit	AL	119	374	107	23	3	15	(9	6)	181	59	51	49	4	92	3	2	3	2	1	.67	5	.286	.371	.484
1994 Detroit	AL	65	170	38	8	0	1	(1	0)	49	17	19	28	0	36	0	2	4	0	1	.00	3	.224	.327	.288
1995 Seattle	AL	26	75	17	5	0	1	(0	1)	25	12	8	5	0	22	2	1	0	0	0	.00	0	.227	.293	.333
8 ML YEARS		405	1044	249	51	4	25	(14	11)	383	131	110	144	5	251	5	15	11	2	4	.33	21	.239	.331	.367

Rick Krivda

Pitches: Left **Bats:** Right **Pos:** SP **Ht:** 6' 1" **Wt:** 180 **Born:** 1/19/70 **Age:** 26

		HOW MUCH HE PITCHED						WHAT HE GAVE UP										THE RESULTS					
Year Team	Lg	G	GS	CG	GF	IP	BFP	H	R	ER	HR	SH	SF	HB	TBB	IBB	SO	WP	Bk	W	L	Pct.	ShO	Sv	ERA
1991 Bluefield	R	15	8	0	2	67	265	48	20	14	0	2	1	0	24	0	79	1	4	7	1	.875	0	1	1.88
1992 Kane County	A	18	18	2	0	121.2	502	108	53	41	6	0	3	1	41	0	124	5	1	12	5	.706	0	0	3.03
Frederick	A	9	9	1	0	57.1	236	51	23	19	7	0	0	1	15	0	64	1	1	5	1	.833	1	0	2.98
1993 Bowie	AA	22	22	0	0	125.2	522	114	46	43	10	2	1	2	50	0	108	1	2	7	5	.583	0	0	3.08
Rochester	AAA	5	5	0	0	33.1	133	20	7	7	2	1	0	1	16	0	23	1	0	3	0	1.000	0	0	1.89
1994 Rochester	AAA	28	26	3	2	163	688	149	75	64	12	1	6	4	73	4	122	9	1	9	10	.474	2	0	3.53
1995 Rochester	AAA	16	16	1	0	101.2	429	96	44	36	11	6	4	2	32	0	74	3	3	6	5	.545	0	0	3.19
1995 Baltimore	AL	13	13	1	0	75.1	319	76	40	38	9	0	4	4	25	1	53	2	2	2	7	.222	0	0	4.54

Marc Kroon

Pitches: Right **Bats:** Right **Pos:** RP **Ht:** 6' 2" **Wt:** 195 **Born:** 4/2/73 **Age:** 23

		HOW MUCH HE PITCHED						WHAT HE GAVE UP										THE RESULTS					
Year Team	Lg	G	GS	CG	GF	IP	BFP	H	R	ER	HR	SH	SF	HB	TBB	IBB	SO	WP	Bk	W	L	Pct.	ShO	Sv	ERA
1991 Mets	R	12	10	1	2	47.2	208	39	33	24	1	0	1	4	22	0	39	10	5	2	3	.400	0	0	4.53
1992 Kingsport	R	12	12	0	0	68	307	52	41	31	3	0	3	1	57	0	60	13	2	3	5	.375	0	0	4.10
1993 Capital Cty	A	29	19	0	8	124.1	542	123	65	48	6	1	8	5	70	0	122	10	2	2	11	.154	0	2	3.47
1994 Rancho Cuca	A	26	26	0	0	143.1	655	143	86	77	14	4	9	11	81	1	153	9	3	11	6	.647	0	0	4.83
1995 Memphis	AA	22	19	0	2	115.1	497	90	49	45	12	2	2	6	61	1	123	16	1	7	5	.583	0	2	3.51
1995 San Diego	NL	2	0	0	1	1.2	7	1	2	2	0	0	0	0	2	0	2	0	0	0	1	.000	0	0	10.80

Bill Krueger

Pitches: Left **Bats:** Left **Pos:** RP/SP **Ht:** 6' 5" **Wt:** 215 **Born:** 4/24/58 **Age:** 38

		HOW MUCH HE PITCHED						WHAT HE GAVE UP										THE RESULTS					
Year Team	Lg	G	GS	CG	GF	IP	BFP	H	R	ER	HR	SH	SF	HB	TBB	IBB	SO	WP	Bk	W	L	Pct.	ShO	Sv	ERA
1995 Tacoma *	AAA	10	8	0	0	50.2	213	52	30	24	4	1	1	2	9	0	39	2	0	5	3	.625	0	0	4.26
1983 Oakland	AL	17	16	2	0	109.2	473	104	54	44	7	0	5	2	53	1	58	1	1	7	6	.538	0	0	3.61
1984 Oakland	AL	26	24	1	0	142	647	156	95	75	9	4	8	2	85	2	61	5	1	10	10	.500	0	0	4.75
1985 Oakland	AL	32	23	2	4	151.1	674	165	95	76	13	1	5	2	69	1	56	6	3	9	10	.474	0	0	4.52
1986 Oakland	AL	11	3	0	4	34.1	149	40	25	23	4	1	2	0	13	0	10	3	1	1	2	.333	0	1	6.03
1987 Oak-LA		11	0	0	1	8	46	12	9	6	0	0	0	0	9	3	4	0	1	0	3	.000	0	0	6.75
1988 Los Angeles	NL	1	1	0	0	2.1	14	4	3	3	0	0	0	1	2	1	1	0	0	0	0	.000	0	0	11.57
1989 Milwaukee	AL	34	5	0	8	93.2	403	96	49	40	9	5	1	0	33	3	72	10	1	3	2	.600	0	3	3.84
1990 Milwaukee	AL	30	17	0	4	129	566	137	70	57	10	3	10	3	54	6	64	8	0	6	8	.429	0	0	3.98
1991 Seattle	AL	35	25	1	2	175	751	194	82	70	15	6	9	4	60	4	91	10	1	11	8	.579	0	0	3.60
1992 Min-Mon		36	29	2	3	178.2	765	189	95	90	18	4	1	4	53	2	99	12	0	10	8	.556	2	0	4.53
1993 Detroit	AL	32	7	0	7	82	356	90	43	31	6	3	3	4	30	5	60	8	0	6	4	.600	0	0	3.40
1994 Det-SD		24	9	1	0	60.2	276	68	48	43	8	3	4	2	24	2	47	4	1	3	4	.429	0	0	6.38

Year	Team	Lg	G	GS	CG	GF	IP	BFP	H	R	ER	HR	SH	SF	HB	TBB	IBB	SO	WP	Bk	W	L	Pct.	ShO	Sv	ERA
1995	SD-Sea		12	5	0	1	27.2	137	50	23	19	5	3	0	0	8	2	16	3	0	2	1	.667	0	0	6.18
1987	Oakland	AL	9	0	0	1	5.2	33	9	7	6	0	0	0	0	8	3	2	0	1	0	3	.000	0	0	9.53
	Los Angeles	NL	2	0	0	0	2.1	13	3	2	0	0	0	0	0	1	0	2	0	0	0	0	.000	0	0	0.00
1992	Minnesota	AL	27	27	2	0	161.1	684	166	82	77	18	4	1	3	46	2	86	11	0	10	6	.625	2	0	4.30
	Montreal	NL	9	2	0	3	17.1	81	23	13	13	0	0	0	1	7	0	13	1	0	0	2	.000	0	0	6.75
1994	Detroit	AL	16	2	0	0	19.2	104	26	24	21	3	2	3	1	17	1	17	2	0	0	2	.000	0	0	9.61
	San Diego	NL	8	7	1	0	41	172	42	24	22	5	1	1	1	7	1	30	2	1	3	2	.600	0	0	4.83
1995	San Diego	NL	6	0	0	0	7.2	41	13	6	6	1	2	0	0	4	1	6	2	0	0	0	.000	0	0	7.04
	Seattle	AL	6	5	0	1	20	96	37	17	13	4	1	0	0	4	1	10	1	0	2	1	.667	0	0	5.85
13	ML YEARS		301	164	9	34	1194.1	5257	1305	685	577	104	33	48	24	493	32	639	70	10	68	66	.507	2	4	4.35

John Kruk

Bats: Left   **Throws:** Left   **Pos:** DH   **Ht:** 5'10" **Wt:** 214 **Born:** 2/9/61 **Age:** 35

						BATTING														BASERUNNING				PERCENTAGES		
Year	Team	Lg	G	AB	H	2B	3B	HR	(Hm	Rd)	TB	R	RBI	TBB	IBB	SO	HBP	SH	SF	SB	CS	SB%	GDP	Avg	OBP	SLG
1986	San Diego	NL	122	278	86	16	2	4	(1	3)	118	33	38	45	0	58	0	2	2	2	4	.33	11	.309	.403	.424
1987	San Diego	NL	138	447	140	14	2	20	(8	12)	218	72	91	73	15	93	0	3	4	18	10	.64	6	.313	.406	.488
1988	San Diego	NL	120	378	91	17	1	9	(8	1)	137	54	44	80	12	68	0	3	5	5	3	.63	7	.241	.369	.362
1989	Phi-SD	NL	112	357	107	13	6	8	(6	2)	156	53	44	44	2	53	0	2	3	3	0	1.00	11	.300	.374	.437
1990	Philadelphia	NL	142	443	129	25	8	7	(2	5)	191	52	67	69	16	70	0	2	1	10	5	.67	11	.291	.386	.431
1991	Philadelphia	NL	152	538	158	27	6	21	(8	13)	260	84	92	67	16	100	1	0	9	7	0	1.00	11	.294	.367	.483
1992	Philadelphia	NL	144	507	164	30	4	10	(7	3)	232	86	70	92	8	88	1	0	7	3	5	.38	11	.323	.423	.458
1993	Philadelphia	NL	150	535	169	33	5	14	(8	6)	254	100	85	111	10	87	0	0	5	6	2	.75	11	.316	.430	.475
1994	Philadelphia	NL	75	255	77	17	0	5	(3	2)	109	35	38	42	4	51	0	0	4	4	1	.80	9	.302	.395	.427
1995	Chicago	AL	45	159	49	7	0	2	(2	0)	62	13	23	26	0	33	0	0	3	0	1	.00	5	.308	.399	.390
1989	Philadelphia	NL	81	281	93	13	6	5	(4	1)	133	46	38	27	2	39	0	1	3	3	0	1.00	5	.331	.386	.473
	San Diego	NL	31	76	14	0	0	3	(2	1)	23	7	6	17	0	14	0	1	0	0	0	.00	5	.184	.333	.303
10	ML YEARS		1200	3897	1170	199	34	100	(53	47)	1737	582	592	649	83	701	2	12	43	58	31	.65	92	.300	.397	.446

Tim Laker

Bats: Right **Throws:** Right **Pos:** C   **Ht:** 6' 3" **Wt:** 200 **Born:** 11/27/69 **Age:** 26

						BATTING														BASERUNNING				PERCENTAGES		
Year	Team	Lg	G	AB	H	2B	3B	HR	(Hm	Rd)	TB	R	RBI	TBB	IBB	SO	HBP	SH	SF	SB	CS	SB%	GDP	Avg	OBP	SLG
1992	Montreal	NL	28	46	10	3	0	0	(0	0)	13	8	4	2	0	14	0	0	1	1	1	.50	1	.217	.250	.283
1993	Montreal	NL	43	86	17	2	1	0	(0	0)	21	3	7	2	0	16	1	3	1	2	0	1.00	2	.198	.222	.244
1995	Montreal	NL	64	141	33	8	1	3	(1	2)	52	17	20	14	4	38	1	1	1	0	1	.00	5	.234	.306	.369
3	ML YEARS		135	273	60	13	2	3	(1	2)	86	28	31	18	4	68	2	4	2	3	2	.60	8	.220	.271	.315

Tom Lampkin

Bats: Left   **Throws:** Right **Pos:** C   **Ht:** 5'11" **Wt:** 185 **Born:** 3/4/64 **Age:** 32

						BATTING														BASERUNNING				PERCENTAGES		
Year	Team	Lg	G	AB	H	2B	3B	HR	(Hm	Rd)	TB	R	RBI	TBB	IBB	SO	HBP	SH	SF	SB	CS	SB%	GDP	Avg	OBP	SLG
1988	Cleveland	AL	4	4	0	0	0	0	(0	0)	0	0	0	1	0	0	0	0	0	0	0	.00	1	.000	.200	.000
1990	San Diego	NL	26	63	14	0	1	1	(1	0)	19	4	4	4	1	9	0	0	0	0	1	.00	2	.222	.269	.302
1991	San Diego	NL	38	58	11	3	1	0	(0	0)	16	4	3	3	0	9	0	0	0	0	0	.00	2	.190	.230	.276
1992	San Diego	NL	9	17	4	0	0	0	(0	0)	4	3	0	6	0	1	1	0	0	2	1	.00	0	.235	.458	.235
1993	Milwaukee	AL	73	162	32	8	0	4	(1	3)	52	22	25	20	3	26	0	2	4	7	3	.70	2	.198	.280	.321
1995	San Francisco	NL	65	76	21	2	0	1	(1	0)	26	8	9	9	1	8	1	0	0	2	0	1.00	1	.276	.360	.342
6	ML YEARS		215	380	82	13	2	6	(3	3)	117	41	41	43	5	53	2	2	4	11	4	.73	6	.216	.296	.308

Mark Langston

Pitches: Left **Bats:** Right **Pos:** SP   **Ht:** 6' 2" **Wt:** 184 **Born:** 8/20/60 **Age:** 35

			HOW MUCH HE PITCHED						WHAT HE GAVE UP												THE RESULTS					
Year	Team	Lg	G	GS	CG	GF	IP	BFP	H	R	ER	HR	SH	SF	HB	TBB	IBB	SO	WP	Bk	W	L	Pct.	ShO	Sv	ERA
1984	Seattle	AL	35	33	5	0	225	965	188	99	85	16	13	7	8	118	5	204	4	2	17	10	.630	2	0	3.40
1985	Seattle	AL	24	24	2	0	126.2	577	122	85	77	22	3	2	2	91	2	72	3	3	7	14	.333	0	0	5.47
1986	Seattle	AL	37	36	9	1	239.1	1057	234	142	129	30	5	8	4	123	1	245	10	3	12	14	.462	0	0	4.85
1987	Seattle	AL	35	35	14	0	272	1152	242	132	116	30	12	6	5	114	2	262	9	2	19	13	.594	3	0	3.84
1988	Seattle	AL	35	35	9	0	261.1	1078	222	108	97	32	6	5	3	110	2	235	7	4	15	11	.577	3	0	3.34
1989	Sea-Mon		34	34	8	0	250	1037	198	87	76	16	9	7	4	112	6	235	6	4	16	14	.533	5	0	2.74
1990	California	AL	33	33	5	0	223	950	215	120	109	13	6	6	5	104	1	195	8	0	10	17	.370	1	0	4.40
1991	California	AL	34	34	7	0	246.1	992	190	89	82	30	4	6	2	96	3	183	6	0	19	8	.704	0	0	3.00
1992	California	AL	32	32	9	0	229	941	206	103	93	14	4	5	6	74	2	174	5	0	13	14	.481	2	0	3.66
1993	California	AL	35	35	7	0	256.1	1039	220	100	91	22	3	8	1	85	2	196	10	2	16	11	.593	0	0	3.20
1994	California	AL	18	18	2	0	119.1	517	121	67	62	19	3	8	0	54	1	109	6	0	7	8	.467	1	0	4.68
1995	California	AL	31	31	2	0	200.1	859	212	109	103	21	11	3	3	64	1	142	5	1	15	7	.682	1	0	4.63

Year Team	Lg	G	GS	CG	SHO	IP	BFP	H	R	ER	HR	HB	BB	IBB	SO	WP	Bk	W	L	Pct	ShO	Sv	ERA
1989 Seattle	AL	10	10	2	0	73.1	297	60	30	29	3	0	3	4	19	0	60	1	2	4	5	.444	1	0	3.56
Montreal	NL	24	24	6	0	176.2	740	138	57	47	13	9	4	0	93	6	175	5	2	12	9	.571	4	0	2.39
12 ML YEARS		383	380	79	1	2648.2	11164	2370	1241	1120	265	79	71	43	1145	26	2252	79	21	166	141	.541	18	0	3.81

Ray Lankford

Bats: Left   **Throws:** Left   **Pos:** CF   **Ht:** 5'11"   **Wt:** 200   **Born:** 6/5/67   **Age:** 29

							BATTING												BASERUNNING				PERCENTAGES		
Year Team	Lg	G	AB	H	2B	3B	HR	(Hm	Rd)	TB	R	RBI	TBB	IBB	SO	HBP	SH	SF	SB	CS	SB%	GDP	Avg	OBP	SLG
1990 St. Louis	NL	39	126	36	10	1	3	(2	1)	57	12	12	13	0	27	0	0	0	8	2	.80	1	.286	.353	.452
1991 St. Louis	NL	151	566	142	23	15	9	(4	5)	222	83	69	41	1	114	1	4	3	44	20	.69	4	.251	.301	.392
1992 St. Louis	NL	153	598	175	40	6	20	(13	7)	287	87	86	72	6	147	5	2	5	42	24	.64	5	.293	.371	.480
1993 St. Louis	NL	127	407	97	17	3	7	(6	1)	141	64	45	81	7	111	3	1	3	14	14	.50	5	.238	.366	.346
1994 St. Louis	NL	109	416	111	25	5	19	(8	11)	203	89	57	58	3	113	4	0	4	11	10	.52	0	.267	.359	.488
1995 St. Louis	NL	132	483	134	35	2	25	(16	9)	248	81	82	63	6	110	2	0	5	24	8	.75	10	.277	.360	.513
6 ML YEARS		711	2596	695	150	32	83	(49	34)	1158	416	351	328	23	622	15	7	20	143	78	.65	25	.268	.351	.446

Mike Lansing

Bats: Right   **Throws:** Right   **Pos:** 2B   **Ht:** 6'0"   **Wt:** 180   **Born:** 4/3/68   **Age:** 28

							BATTING												BASERUNNING				PERCENTAGES		
Year Team	Lg	G	AB	H	2B	3B	HR	(Hm	Rd)	TB	R	RBI	TBB	IBB	SO	HBP	SH	SF	SB	CS	SB%	GDP	Avg	OBP	SLG
1993 Montreal	NL	141	491	141	29	1	3	(1	2)	181	64	45	46	2	56	5	10	3	23	5	.82	16	.287	.352	.369
1994 Montreal	NL	106	394	105	21	2	5	(3	2)	145	44	35	30	3	37	7	2	2	12	8	.60	10	.266	.328	.368
1995 Montreal	NL	127	467	119	30	2	10	(4	6)	183	47	62	28	2	65	3	1	3	27	4	.87	14	.255	.299	.392
3 ML YEARS		374	1352	365	80	5	18	(8	10)	509	155	142	104	7	158	15	13	8	62	17	.78	40	.270	.327	.376

Barry Larkin

Bats: Right   **Throws:** Right   **Pos:** SS   **Ht:** 6'0"   **Wt:** 195   **Born:** 4/28/64   **Age:** 32

							BATTING												BASERUNNING				PERCENTAGES		
Year Team	Lg	G	AB	H	2B	3B	HR	(Hm	Rd)	TB	R	RBI	TBB	IBB	SO	HBP	SH	SF	SB	CS	SB%	GDP	Avg	OBP	SLG
1986 Cincinnati	NL	41	159	45	4	3	3	(3	0)	64	27	19	9	1	21	0	0	1	8	0	1.00	2	.283	.320	.403
1987 Cincinnati	NL	125	439	107	16	2	12	(6	6)	163	64	43	36	3	52	5	5	3	21	6	.78	8	.244	.306	.371
1988 Cincinnati	NL	151	588	174	32	5	12	(9	3)	252	91	56	41	3	24	8	10	5	40	7	.85	7	.296	.347	.429
1989 Cincinnati	NL	97	325	111	14	4	4	(1	3)	145	47	36	20	5	23	2	2	8	10	5	.67	7	.342	.375	.446
1990 Cincinnati	NL	158	614	185	25	6	7	(4	3)	243	85	67	49	3	49	7	7	4	30	5	.86	14	.301	.358	.396
1991 Cincinnati	NL	123	464	140	27	4	20	(16	4)	235	88	69	55	1	64	3	3	2	24	6	.80	7	.302	.378	.506
1992 Cincinnati	NL	140	533	162	32	6	12	(8	4)	242	76	78	63	8	58	4	2	7	15	4	.79	13	.304	.377	.454
1993 Cincinnati	NL	100	384	121	20	3	8	(4	4)	171	57	51	51	6	33	1	1	3	14	1	.93	13	.315	.394	.445
1994 Cincinnati	NL	110	427	119	23	5	9	(3	6)	179	78	52	64	3	58	0	5	5	26	2	.93	6	.279	.369	.419
1995 Cincinnati	NL	131	496	158	29	6	15	(8	7)	244	98	66	61	2	49	3	3	4	51	5	.91	6	.319	.394	.492
10 ML YEARS		1176	4429	1322	222	44	102	(62	40)	1938	711	537	449	35	431	33	38	42	239	41	.85	83	.298	.364	.438

Mike LaValliere

Bats: Left   **Throws:** Right   **Pos:** C   **Ht:** 5'9"   **Wt:** 205   **Born:** 8/18/60   **Age:** 35

							BATTING												BASERUNNING				PERCENTAGES		
Year Team	Lg	G	AB	H	2B	3B	HR	(Hm	Rd)	TB	R	RBI	TBB	IBB	SO	HBP	SH	SF	SB	CS	SB%	GDP	Avg	OBP	SLG
1995 South Bend *	A	2	5	3	1	0	0	--	--	4	1	1	1	0	0	0	0	0	0	0	.00	0	.600	.667	.800
1984 Philadelphia	NL	6	7	0	0	0	0	(0	0)	0	0	0	2	0	2	0	0	0	0	0	.00	0	.000	.222	.000
1985 St. Louis	NL	12	34	5	1	0	0	(0	0)	6	2	6	7	0	3	0	0	3	0	0	.00	0	.147	.273	.176
1986 St. Louis	NL	110	303	71	10	2	3	(1	2)	94	18	30	36	5	37	1	10	0	0	1	.00	7	.234	.318	.310
1987 Pittsburgh	NL	121	340	102	19	0	1	(1	0)	124	33	36	43	9	32	1	3	3	0	0	.00	4	.300	.377	.365
1988 Pittsburgh	NL	120	352	92	18	0	2	(0	2)	116	24	47	50	10	34	2	1	4	3	2	.60	8	.261	.353	.330
1989 Pittsburgh	NL	68	190	60	10	0	2	(2	0)	76	15	23	29	7	24	0	4	0	0	2	.00	4	.316	.406	.400
1990 Pittsburgh	NL	96	279	72	15	0	3	(2	1)	96	27	31	44	8	20	2	4	1	0	3	.00	6	.258	.362	.344
1991 Pittsburgh	NL	108	336	97	11	2	3	(1	2)	121	25	41	33	4	27	2	1	5	2	1	.67	10	.289	.351	.360
1992 Pittsburgh	NL	95	293	75	13	1	2	(1	1)	96	22	29	44	14	21	1	0	5	0	3	.00	8	.256	.350	.328
1993 ChA-Pit		38	102	26	2	0	0	(0	0)	28	6	8	4	0	14	0	7	2	0	1	.00	1	.255	.278	.275
1994 Chicago	AL	59	139	39	4	0	1	(0	1)	46	6	24	20	0	15	1	9	3	0	2	.00	4	.281	.368	.331
1995 Chicago	AL	46	98	24	6	0	1	(0	1)	33	7	19	9	0	15	0	0	2	0	0	.00	3	.245	.303	.337
1993 Chicago	AL	37	97	25	2	0	0	(0	0)	27	6	8	4	0	14	0	7	2	0	1	.00	1	.258	.282	.278
Pittsburgh	NL	1	5	1	0	0	0	(0	0)	1	0	0	0	0	0	0	0	0	0	0	.00	0	.200	.200	.200
12 ML YEARS		879	2473	663	109	5	18	(8	10)	836	185	294	321	57	244	10	39	28	5	15	.25	57	.268	.351	.338

Matt Lawton

Bats: Left **Throws:** Right **Pos:** CF   **Ht:** 5'10" **Wt:** 196 **Born:** 11/3/71 **Age:** 24

Year Team	Lg	G	AB	H	2B	3B	HR	(Hm	Rd)	TB	R	RBI	TBB	IBB	SO	HBP	SH	SF	SB	CS	SB%	GDP	Avg	OBP	SLG
1992 Twins	R	53	173	45	8	3	2	--	--	65	39	26	27	0	27	9	1	7	20	1	.95	2	.260	.375	.376
1993 Fort Wayne	A	111	340	97	21	3	9	--	--	151	50	38	65	3	43	8	0	2	23	15	.61	8	.285	.410	.444
1994 Fort Myers	A	122	446	134	30	1	7	--	--	187	79	51	80	3	64	2	2	3	42	19	.69	7	.300	.407	.419
1995 New Britain	AA	114	412	111	19	5	13	--	--	179	75	54	56	1	70	12	2	3	26	9	.74	8	.269	.371	.434
1995 Minnesota	AL	21	60	19	4	1	1	(1	0)	28	11	12	7	0	11	3	0	0	1	1	.50	1	.317	.414	.467

Aaron Ledesma

Bats: Right **Throws:** Right **Pos:** 3B   **Ht:** 6'2" **Wt:** 200 **Born:** 6/3/71 **Age:** 25

Year Team	Lg	G	AB	H	2B	3B	HR	(Hm	Rd)	TB	R	RBI	TBB	IBB	SO	HBP	SH	SF	SB	CS	SB%	GDP	Avg	OBP	SLG
1990 Kingsport	R	66	243	81	11	1	5	--	--	109	50	38	30	2	28	8	0	4	23	6	.79	4	.333	.418	.449
1991 Columbia	A	33	115	39	8	0	1	--	--	50	19	14	8	0	16	4	3	3	3	2	.60	1	.339	.392	.435
1992 St. Lucie	A	134	456	120	17	2	2	--	--	147	51	50	46	1	66	11	2	7	20	12	.63	13	.263	.340	.322
1993 Binghamton	AA	66	206	55	12	0	5	--	--	82	23	22	14	0	43	2	4	1	2	1	.67	6	.267	.318	.398
1994 Norfolk	AAA	119	431	118	20	1	3	--	--	149	49	56	28	0	41	6	9	6	18	8	.69	16	.274	.323	.346
1995 Norfolk	AAA	56	201	60	12	1	0	--	--	74	26	28	10	1	22	1	1	0	6	3	.67	5	.299	.335	.368
1995 New York	NL	21	33	8	0	0	0	(0	0)	8	4	3	6	1	7	0	0	0	0	0	.00	2	.242	.359	.242

Manuel Lee

Bats: Both **Throws:** Right **Pos:** 2B   **Ht:** 5'9" **Wt:** 161 **Born:** 6/17/65 **Age:** 31

Year Team	Lg	G	AB	H	2B	3B	HR	(Hm	Rd)	TB	R	RBI	TBB	IBB	SO	HBP	SH	SF	SB	CS	SB%	GDP	Avg	OBP	SLG
1995 St. Pete *	A	6	17	6	1	0	0	--	--	7	2	3	2	0	3	0	0	0	0	0	.00	1	.353	.421	.412
Louisville *	AAA	6	22	6	0	0	0	--	--	6	2	0	0	0	2	0	0	0	0	0	1.00	1	.273	.273	.273
1985 Toronto	AL	64	40	8	0	0	0	(0	0)	8	9	0	2	0	9	0	1	0	1	4	.20	2	.200	.238	.200
1986 Toronto	AL	35	78	16	0	1	1	(1	0)	21	8	7	4	0	10	0	2	1	0	1	.00	5	.205	.241	.269
1987 Toronto	AL	56	121	31	2	3	1	(0	1)	42	14	11	6	0	13	0	1	1	2	0	1.00	1	.256	.289	.347
1988 Toronto	AL	116	381	111	16	3	2	(2	0)	139	38	38	26	1	64	0	4	4	3	3	.50	13	.291	.333	.365
1989 Toronto	AL	99	300	78	9	2	3	(1	2)	100	27	34	20	1	60	0	1	1	4	2	.67	8	.260	.305	.333
1990 Toronto	AL	117	391	95	12	4	6	(2	4)	133	45	41	26	0	90	0	1	3	3	1	.75	9	.243	.288	.340
1991 Toronto	AL	138	445	104	18	3	0	(0	0)	128	41	29	24	0	107	2	10	4	7	2	.78	11	.234	.274	.288
1992 Toronto	AL	128	396	104	10	1	3	(1	2)	125	49	39	50	0	73	0	8	3	6	2	.75	8	.263	.343	.316
1993 Texas	AL	73	205	45	3	1	1	(0	1)	53	31	12	22	3	39	2	9	1	2	4	.33	2	.220	.300	.259
1994 Texas	AL	95	335	93	18	2	2	(1	1)	121	41	38	21	0	66	0	6	1	3	1	.75	8	.278	.319	.361
1995 St. Louis	NL	1	1	1	0	0	0	(0	0)	1	1	0	0	0	0	0	0	0	0	0	.00	0	1.000	1.000	1.000
11 ML YEARS		922	2693	686	88	20	19	(8	11)	871	304	249	201	5	531	4	43	19	31	20	.61	67	.255	.305	.323

Mark Lee

Pitches: Left **Bats:** Left **Pos:** RP   **Ht:** 6'3" **Wt:** 200 **Born:** 7/20/64 **Age:** 31

Year Team	Lg	G	GS	CG	GF	IP	BFP	H	R	ER	HR	SH	SF	HB	TBB	IBB	SO	WP	Bk	W	L	Pct.	ShO	Sv	ERA
1995 Rochester *	AAA	25	0	0	8	28.2	108	18	6	5	0	1	2	0	5	0	35	1	0	4	2	.667	0	3	1.57
1988 Kansas City	AL	4	0	0	4	5	21	6	2	2	0	0	0	0	1	0	2	0	0	0	0	.000	0	0	3.60
1990 Milwaukee	AL	11	0	0	1	21.1	85	20	5	5	1	1	2	0	4	0	14	0	0	1	0	1.000	0	0	2.11
1991 Milwaukee	AL	62	0	0	9	67.2	291	72	33	29	10	4	1	1	31	7	43	0	0	2	5	.286	0	1	3.86
1995 Baltimore	AL	39	0	0	7	33.1	148	31	18	18	5	1	2	1	18	3	27	0	0	2	0	1.000	0	0	4.86
4 ML YEARS		116	0	0	21	127.1	545	129	58	54	16	6	5	2	54	10	84	0	0	5	5	.500	0	2	3.82

Dave Leiper

Pitches: Left **Bats:** Left **Pos:** RP   **Ht:** 6'1" **Wt:** 172 **Born:** 6/18/62 **Age:** 34

Year Team	Lg	G	GS	CG	GF	IP	BFP	H	R	ER	HR	SH	SF	HB	TBB	IBB	SO	WP	Bk	W	L	Pct.	ShO	Sv	ERA
1995 Edmonton *	AAA	2	0	0	1	1.1	10	4	2	2	0	0	0	1	2	1	1	0	0	1	0	1.000	0	0	13.50
Ottawa *	AAA	2	0	0	0	3	11	1	0	0	0	0	0	0	1	0	2	0	0	0	0	.000	0	0	0.00
1984 Oakland	AL	8	0	0	2	7	39	12	7	7	2	0	0	0	5	0	3	1	0	1	0	1.000	0	0	9.00
1986 Oakland	AL	33	0	0	9	31.2	136	28	17	17	3	2	3	2	18	4	15	2	0	2	2	.500	0	1	4.83
1987 Oak-SD		57	0	0	7	68.1	291	65	36	30	8	4	4	1	23	0	43	3	1	3	1	.750	0	2	3.95
1988 San Diego	NL	35	0	0	10	54	217	45	19	13	1	3	5	0	14	5	33	2	0	3	0	1.000	0	1	2.17
1989 San Diego	NL	22	0	0	11	28.2	143	40	19	16	2	1	0	2	20	4	7	2	1	0	1	.000	0	0	5.02
1994 Oakland	AL	26	0	0	8	18.2	75	13	4	4	0	3	2	1	6	1	14	0	0	0	0	.000	0	1	1.93
1995 Oak-Mon	AL	50	0	0	10	44.2	191	39	18	16	5	2	0	1	19	1	22	0	1	1	3	.250	0	2	3.22
1987 Oakland	AL	45	0	0	6	52.1	224	49	28	22	6	2	4	1	18	0	33	3	0	2	1	.667	0	1	3.78
San Diego	NL	12	0	0	1	16	67	16	8	8	1	2	0	0	5	0	10	0	1	1	0	1.000	0	1	4.50

Year Team	Lg	G	GS	CG	GF	IP	BFP	H	R	ER	HR	SH	SF	HB	TBB	IBB	SO	WP	Bk	W	L	Pct.	ShO	Sv	ERA
1995 Oakland	AL	24	0	0	3	22.2	103	23	10	9	3	0	0	1	13	1	10	0	0	1	1	.500	0	0	3.57
Montreal	NL	26	0	0	7	22	88	16	8	7	2	2	0	0	6	0	12	0	1	0	2	.000	0	2	2.86
7 ML YEARS		231	0	0	57	253	1092	242	120	103	21	15	14	7	105	15	137	10	3	10	7	.588	0	7	3.66

Al Leiter

Pitches: Left **Bats:** Left **Pos:** SP   **Ht:** 6' 3" **Wt:** 215 **Born:** 10/23/65 **Age:** 30

		HOW MUCH HE PITCHED						WHAT HE GAVE UP												THE RESULTS					
Year Team	Lg	G	GS	CG	GF	IP	BFP	H	R	ER	HR	SH	SF	HB	TBB	IBB	SO	WP	Bk	W	L	Pct.	ShO	Sv	ERA
1987 New York	AL	4	4	0	0	22.2	104	24	16	16	2	1	0	0	15	0	28	4	0	2	2	.500	0	0	6.35
1988 New York	AL	14	14	0	0	57.1	251	49	27	25	7	1	0	5	33	0	60	1	4	4	4	.500	0	0	3.92
1989 NYA-Tor	AL	5	5	0	0	33.1	154	32	23	21	2	1	1	2	23	0	26	2	1	1	2	.333	0	0	5.67
1990 Toronto	AL	4	0	0	2	6.1	22	1	0	0	0	0	0	0	2	0	5	0	0	0	0	.000	0	0	0.00
1991 Toronto	AL	3	0	0	1	1.2	13	3	5	5	0	1	0	0	5	0	1	0	0	0	0	.000	0	0	27.00
1992 Toronto	AL	1	0	0	0	1	7	1	1	1	0	0	0	0	2	0	0	0	0	0	0	.000	0	0	9.00
1993 Toronto	AL	34	12	1	4	105	454	93	52	48	8	3	3	4	56	2	66	2	2	9	6	.600	1	2	4.11
1994 Toronto	AL	20	20	1	0	111.2	516	125	68	63	6	3	8	2	65	3	100	7	5	6	7	.462	0	0	5.08
1995 Toronto	AL	28	28	2	0	183	805	162	80	74	15	6	4	6	108	1	153	14	0	11	11	.500	1	0	3.64
1989 New York	AL	4	4	0	0	26.2	123	23	20	18	1	1	1	2	21	0	22	1	1	1	2	.333	0	0	6.08
Toronto	AL	1	1	0	0	6.2	31	9	3	3	1	0	0	0	2	0	4	1	0	0	0	.000	0	0	4.05
9 ML YEARS		113	83	4	7	522	2326	490	272	253	40	16	16	19	309	6	439	30	12	33	32	.508	2	2	4.36

Mark Leiter

Pitches: Right **Bats:** Right **Pos:** SP   **Ht:** 6' 3" **Wt:** 210 **Born:** 4/13/63 **Age:** 33

		HOW MUCH HE PITCHED						WHAT HE GAVE UP												THE RESULTS					
Year Team	Lg	G	GS	CG	GF	IP	BFP	H	R	ER	HR	SH	SF	HB	TBB	IBB	SO	WP	Bk	W	L	Pct.	ShO	Sv	ERA
1990 New York	AL	8	3	0	2	26.1	119	33	20	20	5	2	1	2	9	0	21	0	0	1	1	.500	0	0	6.84
1991 Detroit	AL	38	15	1	7	134.2	578	125	66	63	16	5	6	6	50	4	103	2	0	9	7	.563	0	1	4.21
1992 Detroit	AL	35	14	1	7	112	475	116	57	52	9	2	8	3	43	5	75	3	0	8	5	.615	0	0	4.18
1993 Detroit	AL	27	13	1	4	106.2	471	111	61	56	17	3	5	3	44	5	70	5	0	6	6	.500	0	0	4.73
1994 California	AL	40	7	0	15	95.1	425	99	56	50	13	4	4	9	35	6	71	2	0	4	7	.364	0	2	4.72
1995 San Francisco	NL	30	29	7	0	195.2	817	185	91	83	19	10	6	17	55	4	129	9	3	10	12	.455	1	0	3.82
6 ML YEARS		178	81	10	35	670.2	2885	669	351	324	79	26	30	40	236	24	469	21	3	38	38	.500	1	3	4.35

Scott Leius

Bats: Right **Throws:** Right **Pos:** 3B   **Ht:** 6' 3" **Wt:** 200 **Born:** 9/24/65 **Age:** 30

		BATTING																BASERUNNING				PERCENTAGES		
Year Team	Lg	G	AB	H	2B	3B	HR	(Hm	Rd)	TB	R	RBI	TBB	IBB	SO	HBP	SH	SF	SB	CS	SB%	GDP	Avg	OBP	SLG
1990 Minnesota	AL	14	25	6	1	0	1	(0	1)	10	4	4	2	0	2	0	1	0	0	0	.00	2	.240	.296	.400
1991 Minnesota	AL	109	199	57	7	2	5	(2	3)	83	35	20	30	1	35	0	5	1	5	5	.50	4	.286	.378	.417
1992 Minnesota	AL	129	409	102	18	2	2	(2	0)	130	50	35	34	0	61	1	5	0	6	5	.55	10	.249	.309	.318
1993 Minnesota	AL	10	18	3	0	0	0	(0	0)	3	4	2	2	0	4	0	0	2	0	0	.00	1	.167	.227	.167
1994 Minnesota	AL	97	350	86	16	1	14	(7	7)	146	57	49	37	0	58	1	1	2	2	4	.33	9	.246	.318	.417
1995 Minnesota	AL	117	372	92	16	5	4	(2	2)	130	51	45	49	3	54	2	0	4	2	1	.67	14	.247	.335	.349
6 ML YEARS		476	1373	346	58	10	26	(13	13)	502	201	155	154	4	214	4	12	9	15	15	.50	40	.252	.327	.366

Mark Lemke

Bats: Both **Throws:** Right **Pos:** 2B   **Ht:** 5' 9" **Wt:** 167 **Born:** 8/13/65 **Age:** 30

		BATTING																BASERUNNING				PERCENTAGES		
Year Team	Lg	G	AB	H	2B	3B	HR	(Hm	Rd)	TB	R	RBI	TBB	IBB	SO	HBP	SH	SF	SB	CS	SB%	GDP	Avg	OBP	SLG
1988 Atlanta	NL	16	58	13	4	0	0	(0	0)	17	8	2	4	0	5	0	2	0	0	2	.00	1	.224	.274	.293
1989 Atlanta	NL	14	55	10	2	1	2	(1	1)	20	4	10	5	0	7	0	0	0	0	1	.00	6	.182	.250	.364
1990 Atlanta	NL	102	239	54	13	0	0	(0	0)	67	22	21	3	22	0	4	2	0	1	2	.33	9	.226	.286	.280
1991 Atlanta	NL	136	269	63	11	2	2	(2	0)	84	36	23	29	2	27	0	6	4	1	2	.33	9	.234	.305	.312
1992 Atlanta	NL	155	427	97	7	4	6	(4	2)	130	38	26	50	11	39	0	12	2	0	3	.00	9	.227	.307	.304
1993 Atlanta	NL	151	493	124	19	2	7	(3	4)	168	52	49	65	13	50	0	5	6	1	2	.33	21	.252	.335	.341
1994 Atlanta	NL	104	350	103	15	0	3	(2	1)	127	40	31	38	12	37	0	6	0	0	3	.00	11	.294	.363	.363
1995 Atlanta	NL	116	399	101	16	5	5	(3	2)	142	42	38	44	4	40	0	7	3	2	2	.50	12	.253	.325	.356
8 ML YEARS		794	2290	565	87	14	25	(15	10)	755	242	200	256	45	227	0	42	17	4	16	.20	75	.247	.320	.330

Mark Leonard

Bats: Left **Throws:** Right **Pos:** RF   **Ht:** 6' 1" **Wt:** 195 **Born:** 8/14/64 **Age:** 31

		BATTING																BASERUNNING				PERCENTAGES		
Year Team	Lg	G	AB	H	2B	3B	HR	(Hm	Rd)	TB	R	RBI	TBB	IBB	SO	HBP	SH	SF	SB	CS	SB%	GDP	Avg	OBP	SLG
1995 Phoenix *	AAA	112	392	116	25	3	14	--	--	189	73	79	81	8	63	0	1	10	3	2	.60	19	.296	.408	.482
1990 San Francisco	NL	11	17	3	1	0	1	(0	1)	7	3	2	3	0	8	0	0	0	0	0	.00	0	.176	.300	.412
1991 San Francisco	NL	64	129	31	7	1	2	(0	2)	46	14	14	12	1	25	1	1	2	0	1	.00	3	.240	.306	.357

Year Team	Lg	G	AB	H	2B	3B	HR	(Hm	Rd)	TB	R	RBI	TBB	IBB	SO	HBP	SH	SF	SB	CS	SB%	GDP	Avg	OBP	SLG
1992 San Francisco	NL	55	128	30	7	0	4	(3	1)	49	13	16	16	0	31	3	0	1	0	1	.00	3	.234	.331	.383
1993 Baltimore	AL	10	15	1	1	0	0	(0	0)	2	1	3	3	0	7	0	0	3	0	0	.00	0	.067	.190	.133
1994 San Francisco	NL	14	11	4	1	1	0	(0	0)	7	2	2	3	0	2	0	0	0	0	0	.00	0	.364	.500	.636
1995 San Francisco	NL	14	21	4	1	0	1	(1	0)	8	4	4	5	1	2	0	0	0	0	0	.00	0	.190	.346	.381
6 ML YEARS		168	321	73	18	2	8	(4	4)	119	37	41	42	2	75	4	1	6	0	2	.00	6	.227	.319	.371

Curt Leskanic

Pitches: Right **Bats:** Right **Pos:** RP **Ht:** 6' 0" **Wt:** 180 **Born:** 4/2/68 **Age:** 28

| | | HOW MUCH HE PITCHED | | | | | | WHAT HE GAVE UP | | | | | | | | | | | | THE RESULTS | | | | |
Year Team	Lg	G	GS	CG	GF	IP	BFP	H	R	ER	HR	SH	SF	HB	TBB	IBB	SO	WP	Bk	W	L	Pct.	ShO	Sv	ERA
1993 Colorado	NL	18	8	0	1	57	260	59	40	34	7	5	4	2	27	1	30	8	2	1	5	.167	0	0	5.37
1994 Colorado	NL	8	3	0	2	22.1	98	27	14	14	2	2	0	0	10	0	17	2	0	1	1	.500	0	0	5.64
1995 Colorado	NL	76	0	0	27	98	406	83	38	37	7	3	2	0	33	1	107	6	1	6	3	.667	0	10	3.40
3 ML YEARS		102	11	0	30	177.1	764	169	92	85	16	10	6	2	70	2	154	16	3	8	9	.471	0	10	4.31

Jesse Levis

Bats: Left **Throws:** Right **Pos:** C **Ht:** 5' 9" **Wt:** 180 **Born:** 4/14/68 **Age:** 28

| | | BATTING | | | | | | | | | | | | | | | | | BASERUNNING | | | | PERCENTAGES | | |
Year Team	Lg	G	AB	H	2B	3B	HR	(Hm	Rd)	TB	R	RBI	TBB	IBB	SO	HBP	SH	SF	SB	CS	SB%	GDP	Avg	OBP	SLG
1995 Buffalo *	AAA	66	196	61	16	0	4	--	--	89	26	20	32	0	11	2	1	0	0	3	.00	7	.311	.413	.454
1992 Cleveland	AL	28	43	12	4	0	1	(0	1)	19	2	3	0	5	0	0	0		0	0	.00	0	.279	.279	.442
1993 Cleveland	AL	31	63	11	2	0	0	(0	0)	13	7	4	2	0	10	0	1	1	0	0	.00	0	.175	.197	.206
1994 Cleveland	AL	1	1	1	0	0	0	(0	0)	1	0	0	0	0	0	0	0	0	0	0	.00	0	1.000	1.000	1.000
1995 Cleveland	AL	12	18	6	2	0	0	(0	0)	8	1	3	1	0	0	0	1	2	0	0	.00	1	.333	.333	.444
4 ML YEARS		72	125	30	8	0	1	(0	1)	41	10	10	3	0	15	0	2	3	0	0	.00	2	.240	.252	.328

Darren Lewis

Bats: Right **Throws:** Right **Pos:** CF **Ht:** 6' 0" **Wt:** 189 **Born:** 8/28/67 **Age:** 28

| | | BATTING | | | | | | | | | | | | | | | | | BASERUNNING | | | | PERCENTAGES | | |
Year Team	Lg	G	AB	H	2B	3B	HR	(Hm	Rd)	TB	R	RBI	TBB	IBB	SO	HBP	SH	SF	SB	CS	SB%	GDP	Avg	OBP	SLG
1990 Oakland	AL	25	35	8	0	0	0	(0	0)	8	4	1	7	0	4	1	3	0	2	0	1.00	2	.229	.372	.229
1991 San Francisco	NL	72	222	55	5	3	1	(0	1)	69	41	15	36	0	30	1	2	7	13	7	.65	1	.248	.358	.311
1992 San Francisco	NL	100	320	74	8	1	1	(1	0)	87	38	18	29	0	46	1	10	2	28	8	.78	3	.231	.295	.272
1993 San Francisco	NL	136	522	132	17	7	2	(2	0)	169	84	48	30	0	40	7	12	1	46	15	.75	4	.253	.302	.324
1994 San Francisco	NL	114	451	116	15	9	4	(4	0)	161	70	29	53	0	50	4	4	1	30	13	.70	6	.257	.340	.357
1995 SF-Cin	NL	132	472	118	13	3	1	(1	0)	140	66	24	34	0	57	8	12	1	32	18	.64	9	.250	.311	.297
1995 San Francisco	NL	74	309	78	10	3	1	(1	0)	97	47	16	17	0	37	6	7	1	21	7	.75	6	.252	.303	.314
Cincinnati	NL	58	163	40	3	0	0	(0	0)	43	19	8	17	0	20	2	5	0	11	11	.50	3	.245	.324	.264
6 ML YEARS		579	2022	503	58	23	9	(8	1)	634	303	135	189	0	227	23	48	5	151	61	.71	25	.249	.319	.314

Mark Lewis

Bats: Right **Throws:** Right **Pos:** 3B **Ht:** 6' 1" **Wt:** 190 **Born:** 11/30/69 **Age:** 26

| | | BATTING | | | | | | | | | | | | | | | | | BASERUNNING | | | | PERCENTAGES | | |
Year Team	Lg	G	AB	H	2B	3B	HR	(Hm	Rd)	TB	R	RBI	TBB	IBB	SO	HBP	SH	SF	SB	CS	SB%	GDP	Avg	OBP	SLG
1991 Cleveland	AL	84	314	83	15	1	0	(0	0)	100	29	30	15	0	45	0	2	5	2	2	.50	12	.264	.293	.318
1992 Cleveland	AL	122	413	109	21	0	5	(2	3)	145	44	30	25	1	69	3	1	4	4	5	.44	12	.264	.308	.351
1993 Cleveland	AL	14	52	13	2	0	1	(1	0)	18	6	5	0	0	7	0	1	0	3	0	1.00	1	.250	.250	.346
1994 Cleveland	AL	20	73	15	5	0	1	(1	0)	23	6	8	2	0	13	0	1	0	1	0	1.00	2	.205	.227	.315
1995 Cincinnati	NL	81	171	58	13	1	3	(1	2)	82	25	30	21	2	33	0	0	2	0	3	.00	1	.339	.407	.480
5 ML YEARS		321	1023	278	56	2	10	(5	5)	368	110	103	63	3	167	3	5	11	10	10	.50	28	.272	.313	.360

Richie Lewis

Pitches: Right **Bats:** Right **Pos:** RP **Ht:** 5'10" **Wt:** 175 **Born:** 1/25/66 **Age:** 30

| | | HOW MUCH HE PITCHED | | | | | | WHAT HE GAVE UP | | | | | | | | | | | | THE RESULTS | | | | |
Year Team	Lg	G	GS	CG	GF	IP	BFP	H	R	ER	HR	SH	SF	HB	TBB	IBB	SO	WP	Bk	W	L	Pct.	ShO	Sv	ERA
1995 Charlotte *	AAA	17	8	1	4	59	243	50	22	21	5	2	4	0	20	0	45	4	2	5	2	.714	0	0	3.20
1992 Baltimore	AL	2	2	0	0	6.2	40	13	8	8	1	0	1	0	7	0	4	0	0	1	1	.500	0	0	10.80
1993 Florida	NL	57	0	0	14	77.1	341	68	37	28	7	8	4	1	43	6	65	9	1	6	3	.667	0	0	3.26
1994 Florida	NL	45	0	0	9	54	261	62	44	34	7	3	1	1	38	9	45	10	1	1	4	.200	0	0	5.67
1995 Florida	NL	21	1	0	6	36	152	30	15	15	9	2	0	1	15	1	32	1	2	0	1	.000	0	0	3.75
4 ML YEARS		125	3	0	29	174	794	173	104	85	24	13	6	3	103	20	146	20	4	8	9	.471	0	0	4.40

Jim Leyritz

Bats: Right **Throws:** Right **Pos:** C/1B/DH **Ht:** 6' 0" **Wt:** 195 **Born:** 12/27/63 **Age:** 32

					BATTING												BASERUNNING				PERCENTAGES		
Year Team	Lg	G	AB	H	2B	3B	HR	(Hm Rd)	TB	R	RBI	TBB	IBB	SO	HBP	SH	SF	SB	CS	SB%	GDP	Avg	OBP	SLG
1990 New York	AL	92	303	78	13	1	5	(1 4)	108	28	25	27	1	51	7	1	1	2	3	.40	11	.257	.331	.356
1991 New York	AL	32	77	14	3	0	0	(0 0)	17	8	4	13	0	15	0	1	0	0	1	.00	2	.182	.300	.221
1992 New York	AL	63	144	37	6	0	7	(3 4)	64	17	26	14	1	22	6	0	3	0	0	.00	12	.257	.341	.444
1993 New York	AL	95	259	80	14	0	14	(6 8)	136	43	53	37	3	59	8	0	1	0	0	.00	12	.309	.410	.525
1994 New York	AL	75	249	66	12	0	7	(4 13)	129	47	58	35	1	61	6	0	0	0	0	.00	9	.265	.365	.518
1995 New York	AL	77	264	71	12	0	7	(3 4)	104	37	37	37	2	73	8	0	1	1	1	.50	4	.269	.374	.394
6 ML YEARS		434	1296	346	60	1	50	(17 33)	558	180	203	163	8	281	35	2	9	3	6	.33	38	.267	.362	.431

Jon Lieber

Pitches: Right **Bats:** Left **Pos:** SP/RP **Ht:** 6' 3" **Wt:** 220 **Born:** 4/2/70 **Age:** 26

		HOW MUCH HE PITCHED						WHAT HE GAVE UP										THE RESULTS					
Year Team	Lg	G	GS	CG	GF	IP	BFP	H	R	ER	HR	SH	SF	HB	TBB	IBB	SO	WP	Bk	W	L	Pct.	ShO	Sv	ERA
1992 Eugene	A	5	5	0	0	31	117	26	6	4	1	0	0	0	2	0	23	0	1	3	0	1.000	0	0	1.16
Baseball Cy	A	7	6	0	1	31	142	45	20	16	2	1	1	1	8	0	19	0	0	3	3	.500	0	0	4.65
1993 Wilmington	A	17	16	2	0	114.2	476	125	47	34	4	4	1	2	9	1	89	3	1	9	3	.750	0	0	2.67
Memphis	AA	4	4	0	0	21	100	32	16	16	4	0	0	0	6	0	17	0	0	2	1	.667	0	0	6.86
Carolina	AA	6	6	0	0	34	146	39	15	15	3	3	1	1	10	0	28	3	1	4	2	.667	0	0	3.97
1994 Carolina	AA	3	3	1	0	21	78	13	4	3	0	0	0	0	2	0	21	0	0	2	0	1.000	1	0	1.29
Buffalo	AAA	3	3	0	0	21.1	79	16	4	4	1	0	1	0	1	0	21	0	0	1	1	.500	0	0	1.69
1995 Calgary	AAA	14	14	0	0	77	365	122	69	60	6	1	0	0	19	0	34	0	0	1	5	.167	0	0	7.01
1994 Pittsburgh	NL	17	17	1	0	108.2	460	116	62	45	12	3	3	1	25	3	71	2	3	6	7	.462	0	0	3.73
1995 Pittsburgh	NL	21	12	0	3	72.2	327	103	56	51	7	5	6	4	14	0	45	3	0	4	7	.364	0	0	6.32
2 ML YEARS		38	29	1	3	181.1	787	219	118	96	19	8	9	5	39	3	116	5	3	10	14	.417	0	0	4.76

Mike Lieberthal

Bats: Right **Throws:** Right **Pos:** C **Ht:** 6' 0" **Wt:** 180 **Born:** 1/18/72 **Age:** 24

					BATTING												BASERUNNING				PERCENTAGES		
Year Team	Lg	G	AB	H	2B	3B	HR	(Hm Rd)	TB	R	RBI	TBB	IBB	SO	HBP	SH	SF	SB	CS	SB%	GDP	Avg	OBP	SLG
1990 Martinsville	R	49	184	42	9	0	4	-- --	63	26	22	11	0	40	2	0	0	2	0	1.00	3	.228	.279	.342
1991 Spartanburg	A	72	243	74	17	0	0	-- --	91	34	31	23	0	25	5	0	3	1	2	.33	4	.305	.372	.374
Clearwater	A	16	52	15	2	0	0	-- --	17	7	7	3	0	12	1	1	1	0	0	.00	2	.288	.333	.327
1992 Reading	AA	86	309	88	16	1	2	-- --	112	30	37	19	0	26	10	1	4	4	1	.80	15	.285	.342	.362
Scranton-Wb	AAA	16	45	9	1	0	0	-- --	10	4	4	2	0	5	1	1	1	0	0	.00	2	.200	.245	.222
1993 Scranton-Wb	AAA	112	382	100	17	0	7	-- --	138	35	40	24	3	32	6	1	4	2	0	1.00	15	.262	.313	.361
1994 Scranton-Wb	AAA	84	296	69	16	0	1	-- --	88	23	32	21	2	29	2	0	3	1	1	.50	7	.233	.286	.297
1995 Scranton-Wb	AAA	85	278	78	20	2	6	-- --	120	44	42	44	2	26	9	2	7	1	4	.20	14	.281	.388	.432
1994 Philadelphia	NL	24	79	21	3	1	1	(1 0)	29	6	5	3	0	5	1	1	1	0	0	.00	4	.266	.301	.367
1995 Philadelphia	NL	16	47	12	2	0	0	(0 0)	14	1	4	5	0	5	0	2	0	0	0	.00	1	.255	.327	.298
2 ML YEARS		40	126	33	5	1	1	(1 0)	43	7	9	8	0	10	1	3	1	0	0	.00	5	.262	.311	.341

Derek Lilliquist

Pitches: Left **Bats:** Left **Pos:** RP **Ht:** 5'10" **Wt:** 195 **Born:** 2/20/66 **Age:** 30

		HOW MUCH HE PITCHED						WHAT HE GAVE UP										THE RESULTS					
Year Team	Lg	G	GS	CG	GF	IP	BFP	H	R	ER	HR	SH	SF	HB	TBB	IBB	SO	WP	Bk	W	L	Pct.	ShO	Sv	ERA
1995 Albuquerque *	AAA	13	0	0	12	13.1	55	18	4	4	1	0	0	0	3	2	9	0	0	0	0	.000	0	5	2.70
1989 Atlanta	NL	32	30	0	0	165.2	718	202	87	73	16	8	3	2	34	5	79	4	3	8	10	.444	0	0	3.97
1990 Atl-SD	NL	28	18	1	3	122	537	136	74	72	16	9	5	3	42	5	63	2	3	5	11	.313	1	0	5.31
1991 San Diego	NL	6	2	0	0	14.1	70	25	14	14	3	0	0	0	4	1	7	0	0	0	2	.000	0	0	8.79
1992 Cleveland	AL	71	0	0	22	61.2	239	39	13	12	5	5	4	2	18	6	47	2	0	5	3	.625	0	6	1.75
1993 Cleveland	AL	56	2	0	28	64	271	64	20	16	5	6	2	1	19	5	40	1	0	4	4	.500	0	10	2.25
1994 Cleveland	AL	36	0	0	12	29.1	127	34	17	16	6	3	3	1	8	1	15	0	0	1	3	.250	0	1	4.91
1995 Boston	AL	28	0	0	6	23	103	27	17	16	7	2	3	0	7	2	9	1	0	2	1	.667	0	0	6.26
1990 Atlanta	NL	12	11	0	0	61.2	279	75	45	43	10	6	4	1	19	4	34	0	0	2	8	.200	0	0	6.28
San Diego	NL	16	7	1	2	60.1	258	61	29	29	6	3	1	2	23	1	29	2	1	3	3	.500	1	0	4.33
7 ML YEARS		257	52	1	72	480	2065	527	242	219	58	33	20	9	134	25	260	10	6	25	34	.424	1	17	4.11

Jose Lima

Pitches: Right **Bats:** Right **Pos:** SP **Ht:** 6' 2" **Wt:** 170 **Born:** 9/30/72 **Age:** 23

		HOW MUCH HE PITCHED						WHAT HE GAVE UP										THE RESULTS					
Year Team	Lg	G	GS	CG	GF	IP	BFP	H	R	ER	HR	SH	SF	HB	TBB	IBB	SO	WP	Bk	W	L	Pct.	ShO	Sv	ERA
1990 Bristol	R	14	12	1	2	75.1	328	89	49	42	9	5	0	3	22	3	64	4	1	3	8	.273	0	1	5.02
1991 Lakeland	A	4	1	0	2	8.2	43	16	10	10	1	2	1	0	2	0	5	1	2	0	1	.000	0	0	10.38
Fayetteville	A	18	7	0	4	58	249	53	38	32	4	0	3	1	25	0	60	2	4	1	3	.250	0	0	4.97

Year	Team	Lg	G	GS	CG	GF	IP	BFP	H	R	ER	HR	SH	SF	HB	TBB	IBB	SO	WP	Bk	W	L	Pct.	ShO	Sv	ERA
1992	Lakeland	A	25	25	5	0	151	587	132	57	53	14	3	2	5	21	2	137	3	4	5	11	.313	2	0	3.16
1993	London	AA	27	27	2	0	177	744	160	96	80	19	2	6	5	59	4	138	7	13	8	13	.381	0	0	4.07
1994	Toledo	AAA	23	22	3	0	142.1	582	124	70	57	16	3	2	2	48	1	117	4	2	7	9	.438	2	0	3.60
1995	Lakeland	A	4	4	0	0	21	86	23	11	6	2	0	0	0	0	0	20	1	0	3	1	.750	0	0	2.57
	Toledo	AAA	11	11	1	0	74.2	301	69	26	25	9	3	4	1	14	2	40	2	0	5	3	.625	0	0	3.01
1994	Detroit	AL	3	1	0	1	6.2	34	11	10	10	2	0	0	0	3	1	7	1	0	0	1	.000	0	0	13.50
1995	Detroit	AL	15	15	0	0	73.2	320	85	52	50	10	2	1	4	18	4	37	5	0	3	9	.250	0	0	6.11
	2 ML YEARS		18	16	0	1	80.1	354	96	62	60	12	2	1	4	21	5	44	6	0	3	10	.231	0	0	6.72

Jose Lind

Bats: Right **Throws:** Right **Pos:** 2B **Ht:** 5'11" **Wt:** 180 **Born:** 5/1/64 **Age:** 32

					BATTING															BASERUNNING				PERCENTAGES		
Year	Team	Lg	G	AB	H	2B	3B	HR	(Hm	Rd)	TB	R	RBI	TBB	IBB	SO	HBP	SH	SF	SB	CS	SB%	GDP	Avg	OBP	SLG
1995	Vancouver *	AAA	10	36	8	2	0	0	(--	--)	10	2	5	1	0	4	0	0	0	0	1	1.00	0	.222	.243	.278
1987	Pittsburgh	NL	35	143	46	8	4	0	(0	0)	62	21	11	8	1	12	0	6	0	2	1	.67	5	.322	.358	.434
1988	Pittsburgh	NL	154	611	160	24	4	2	(1	1)	198	82	49	42	0	75	0	12	3	15	4	.79	11	.262	.308	.324
1989	Pittsburgh	NL	153	578	134	21	3	2	(2	0)	167	52	48	39	7	64	2	13	5	15	1	.94	13	.232	.280	.289
1990	Pittsburgh	NL	152	514	134	28	5	1	(1	0)	175	46	48	35	19	52	1	4	7	8	0	1.00	20	.261	.305	.340
1991	Pittsburgh	NL	150	502	133	16	6	3	(2	1)	170	53	54	30	10	56	2	5	6	7	4	.64	20	.265	.306	.339
1992	Pittsburgh	NL	135	468	110	14	1	0	(0	0)	126	38	39	26	12	29	1	7	4	3	1	.75	14	.235	.275	.269
1993	Kansas City	AL	136	431	107	13	2	0	(0	0)	124	33	37	13	0	36	2	13	5	3	2	.60	7	.248	.271	.288
1994	Kansas City	AL	85	290	78	16	2	1	(0	1)	101	34	31	16	1	34	0	8	1	9	5	.64	7	.269	.306	.348
1995	KC-Cal	AL	44	140	33	5	0	0	(0	0)	38	9	7	6	0	12	0	1	0	0	1	.00	5	.236	.267	.271
1995	Kansas City	AL	29	97	26	3	0	0	(0	0)	29	4	6	3	0	8	0	1	0	0	1	.00	2	.268	.290	.299
	California	AL	15	43	7	2	0	0	(0	0)	9	5	1	3	0	4	0	0	0	0	0	.00	3	.163	.217	.209
	9 ML YEARS		1044	3677	935	145	27	9	(6	3)	1161	368	324	215	50	370	8	69	31	62	19	.77	102	.254	.295	.316

Doug Linton

Pitches: Right **Bats:** Right **Pos:** RP **Ht:** 6' 1" **Wt:** 190 **Born:** 9/2/65 **Age:** 30

			HOW MUCH HE PITCHED						WHAT HE GAVE UP											THE RESULTS					
Year	Team	Lg	G	GS	CG	GF	IP	BFP	H	R	ER	HR	SH	SF	HB	TBB	IBB	SO	WP	Bk	W	L	Pct.	ShO	Sv	ERA
1995	Omaha *	AAA	18	18	2	0	108.1	472	129	60	53	9	5	3	7	24	2	85	3	1	7	7	.500	1	0	4.40
1992	Toronto	AL	8	3	0	2	24	116	31	23	23	5	1	2	0	17	0	16	2	0	1	3	.250	0	0	8.63
1993	Cal-Tor	AL	23	1	0	6	36.2	178	46	30	30	8	0	3	1	23	1	23	2	0	2	1	.667	0	0	7.36
1994	New York	NL	32	3	0	8	50.1	241	74	27	25	4	3	1	0	20	3	29	2	0	6	2	.750	0	0	4.47
1995	Kansas City	AL	7	2	0	0	22.1	98	22	21	18	4	0	0	2	10	1	13	0	0	0	1	.000	0	0	7.25
1993	California	AL	19	0	0	6	25.2	123	35	22	22	8	0	1	0	14	1	19	2	0	2	1	1.000	0	0	7.71
	Toronto	AL	4	1	0	0	11	55	11	8	8	0	0	2	1	9	0	4	0	0	0	0	.000	0	0	6.55
	4 ML YEARS		70	9	0	16	133.1	633	173	101	96	21	4	6	3	70	5	81	6	0	9	7	.563	0	0	6.48

Felipe Lira

Pitches: Right **Bats:** Right **Pos:** SP/RP **Ht:** 6' 0" **Wt:** 170 **Born:** 4/26/72 **Age:** 24

			HOW MUCH HE PITCHED						WHAT HE GAVE UP											THE RESULTS					
Year	Team	Lg	G	GS	CG	GF	IP	BFP	H	R	ER	HR	SH	SF	HB	TBB	IBB	SO	WP	Bk	W	L	Pct.	ShO	Sv	ERA
1990	Bristol	R	13	10	2	2	78.1	318	70	26	21	4	0	1	3	16	1	71	4	2	5	5	.500	1	1	2.41
	Lakeland	A	1	0	0	0	1.2	11	3	1	1	0	0	1	0	3	0	4	0	0	0	0	.000	0	0	5.40
1991	Fayetteville	A	15	13	0	2	73.1	315	79	43	38	8	4	2	1	19	0	56	6	4	5	5	.500	0	1	4.66
1992	Lakeland	A	32	8	2	2	109	441	95	36	29	6	3	1	7	16	1	84	4	0	11	5	.688	1	1	2.39
1993	London	AA	22	22	2	0	152	641	157	63	57	16	5	3	6	39	2	122	8	1	10	4	.714	0	0	3.38
	Toledo	AAA	5	5	0	0	31.1	135	32	18	16	5	0	3	1	11	1	23	0	1	1	2	.333	0	0	4.60
1994	Toledo	AAA	26	26	1	0	151.1	669	171	91	79	19	4	9	6	45	4	110	16	0	7	12	.368	1	0	4.70
1995	Detroit	AL	37	22	0	7	146.1	635	151	74	70	17	4	9	8	56	7	89	5	1	9	13	.409	0	1	4.31

Nelson Liriano

Bats: Both **Throws:** Right **Pos:** 2B **Ht:** 5'10" **Wt:** 178 **Born:** 6/3/64 **Age:** 32

					BATTING															BASERUNNING				PERCENTAGES		
Year	Team	Lg	G	AB	H	2B	3B	HR	(Hm	Rd)	TB	R	RBI	TBB	IBB	SO	HBP	SH	SF	SB	CS	SB%	GDP	Avg	OBP	SLG
1987	Toronto	AL	37	158	38	6	2	2	(1	1)	54	29	10	16	2	22	0	2	0	13	2	.87	3	.241	.310	.342
1988	Toronto	AL	99	276	73	6	2	3	(0	3)	92	36	23	11	0	40	2	5	1	12	5	.71	4	.264	.297	.333
1989	Toronto	AL	132	418	110	26	3	5	(3	2)	157	51	53	49	0	51	2	10	5	16	7	.70	10	.263	.331	.376
1990	Min-Tor	AL	103	355	83	12	9	1	(1	0)	116	46	28	38	0	44	1	4	2	8	7	.53	8	.234	.308	.327
1991	Kansas City	AL	10	22	9	0	0	0	(0	0)	9	5	1	0	0	2	0	1	0	0	1	.00	0	.409	.409	.409
1993	Colorado	NL	48	151	46	6	3	2	(0	2)	64	28	15	18	2	22	0	5	1	6	4	.60	6	.305	.376	.424
1994	Colorado	NL	87	255	65	17	5	3	(2	1)	101	39	31	42	5	44	0	3	3	0	2	.00	4	.255	.357	.396
1995	Pittsburgh	NL	107	259	74	12	1	5	(2	3)	103	29	38	24	3	34	2	1	3	2	2	.50	2	.286	.347	.398
1990	Minnesota	AL	53	185	47	5	7	0	(0	0)	66	30	13	22	0	24	0	3	1	5	2	.71	3	.254	.332	.357
	Toronto	AL	50	170	36	7	2	1	(1	0)	50	16	15	16	0	20	1	1	1	3	5	.38	5	.212	.282	.294
	8 ML YEARS		623	1894	498	85	25	21	(9	12)	696	263	199	192	12	259	7	31	15	57	30	.66	37	.263	.331	.367

Pat Listach

Bats: Both   **Throws:** Right   **Pos:** 2B/SS   **Ht:** 5' 9"   **Wt:** 180   **Born:** 9/12/67   **Age:** 28

Year Team	Lg	G	AB	H	2B	3B	HR	(Hm	Rd)	TB	R	RBI	TBB	IBB	SO	HBP	SH	SF	SB	CS	SB%	GDP	Avg	OBP	SLG
1992 Milwaukee	AL	149	579	168	19	6	1	(0	1)	202	93	47	55	0	124	1	12	2	54	18	.75	3	.290	.352	.349
1993 Milwaukee	AL	98	356	87	15	1	3	(0	3)	113	50	30	37	0	70	3	5	2	18	9	.67	7	.244	.319	.317
1994 Milwaukee	AL	16	54	16	3	0	0	(0	0)	19	8	2	3	0	8	0	0	0	2	1	.67	1	.296	.333	.352
1995 Milwaukee	AL	101	334	73	8	2	0	(0	0)	85	35	25	25	0	61	2	7	1	13	3	.81	6	.219	.276	.254
4 ML YEARS		364	1323	344	45	9	4	(0	4)	419	186	104	120	0	263	6	24	5	87	31	.74	17	.260	.323	.317

Scott Livingstone

Bats: Left   **Throws:** Right   **Pos:** 1B/3B   **Ht:** 6' 0"   **Wt:** 190   **Born:** 7/15/65   **Age:** 30

Year Team	Lg	G	AB	H	2B	3B	HR	(Hm	Rd)	TB	R	RBI	TBB	IBB	SO	HBP	SH	SF	SB	CS	SB%	GDP	Avg	OBP	SLG
1991 Detroit	AL	44	127	37	5	0	2	(1	1)	48	19	11	10	0	25	0	1	1	2	1	.67	0	.291	.341	.378
1992 Detroit	AL	117	354	100	21	0	4	(2	2)	133	43	46	21	1	36	0	3	4	1	3	.25	8	.282	.319	.376
1993 Detroit	AL	98	304	89	10	2	2	(1	1)	109	39	39	19	1	32	0	1	6	1	3	.25	4	.293	.328	.359
1994 Det-SD		72	203	54	13	1	2	(1	1)	75	11	11	7	0	26	0	0	1	2	2	.50	5	.266	.289	.369
1995 San Diego	NL	99	196	66	15	0	5	(1	4)	96	26	32	15	1	22	0	0	2	2	1	.67	3	.337	.380	.490
1994 Detroit	AL	15	23	5	1	0	0	(0	0)	6	0	1	1	0	4	0	0	0	0	0	.00	0	.217	.250	.261
San Diego	NL	57	180	49	12	1	2	(1	1)	69	11	10	6	0	22	0	0	1	2	2	.50	5	.272	.294	.383
5 ML YEARS		430	1184	346	64	3	15	(6	9)	461	138	139	72	3	141	0	5	14	8	10	.44	20	.292	.329	.389

Graeme Lloyd

Pitches: Left   **Bats:** Left   **Pos:** RP   **Ht:** 6' 7"   **Wt:** 234   **Born:** 4/9/67   **Age:** 29

Year Team	Lg	G	GS	CG	GF	IP	BFP	H	R	ER	HR	SH	SF	HB	TBB	IBB	SO	WP	Bk	W	L	Pct.	ShO	Sv	ERA
1993 Milwaukee	AL	55	0	0	12	63.2	269	64	24	20	5	1	2	3	13	3	31	4	0	3	4	.429	0	0	2.83
1994 Milwaukee	AL	43	0	0	21	47	203	49	28	27	4	1	2	3	15	6	31	2	0	2	3	.400	0	3	5.17
1995 Milwaukee	AL	33	0	0	14	32	127	28	16	16	4	1	4	0	8	2	13	3	0	0	5	.000	0	4	4.50
3 ML YEARS		131	0	0	47	142.2	599	141	68	63	13	3	8	6	36	11	75	9	0	5	12	.294	0	7	3.97

Esteban Loaiza

Pitches: Right   **Bats:** Right   **Pos:** SP   **Ht:** 6' 4"   **Wt:** 190   **Born:** 12/31/71   **Age:** 24

Year Team	Lg	G	GS	CG	GF	IP	BFP	H	R	ER	HR	SH	SF	HB	TBB	IBB	SO	WP	Bk	W	L	Pct.	ShO	Sv	ERA
1991 Pirates	R	11	11	0	0	51.2	220	48	17	13	0	0	2	5	14	0	41	1	0	5	1	.833	1	0	2.26
1992 Augusta	A	26	25	3	1	143.1	613	134	72	62	7	2	3	10	60	0	123	7	4	10	8	.556	0	0	3.89
1993 Salem	A	17	17	3	0	109	462	113	53	41	7	2	4	4	30	0	115	8	0	6	7	.462	0	0	3.39
Carolina	AA	7	7	1	0	43	176	39	18	18	5	0	2	0	12	1	40	3	0	2	1	.667	0	0	3.77
1994 Carolina	AA	24	24	3	0	154.1	647	169	69	65	15	5	3	5	30	0	115	1	1	10	5	.667	0	0	3.79
1995 Pittsburgh	NL	32	31	1	0	172.2	762	205	115	99	21	10	9	5	55	3	85	6	1	8	9	.471	0	0	5.16

Keith Lockhart

Bats: Left   **Throws:** Right   **Pos:** 2B/3B   **Ht:** 5'10"   **Wt:** 170   **Born:** 11/10/64   **Age:** 31

Year Team	Lg	G	AB	H	2B	3B	HR	(Hm	Rd)	TB	R	RBI	TBB	IBB	SO	HBP	SH	SF	SB	CS	SB%	GDP	Avg	OBP	SLG
1986 Billings	R	53	202	70	11	3	7	--	--	108	51	31	35	0	22	4	0	3	4	2	.67	0	.347	.447	.535
Cedar Rapids	A	13	42	8	2	0	0	--	--	10	4	1	6	0	6	1	0	0	1	1	.50	0	.190	.306	.238
1987 Cedar Rapids	A	140	511	160	37	5	23	--	--	276	101	84	86	7	70	13	1	6	20	8	.71	6	.313	.420	.540
1988 Chattanooga	AA	139	515	137	27	3	12	--	--	206	74	67	61	4	59	5	3	11	7	5	.58	9	.266	.343	.400
1989 Nashville	AAA	131	479	128	21	6	14	--	--	203	77	58	61	4	41	6	2	4	4	3	.57	6	.267	.355	.424
1990 Nashville	AAA	126	431	112	25	4	9	--	--	172	48	63	51	3	74	5	1	4	8	7	.53	4	.260	.342	.399
1991 Nashville	AAA	116	411	107	25	3	8	--	--	162	53	36	24	2	64	2	2	1	3	7	.30	5	.260	.334	.394
1992 Tacoma	AAA	107	363	101	25	3	5	--	--	147	44	37	29	1	21	3	2	3	5	3	.63	3	.278	.334	.405
1993 Louisville	AAA	132	467	140	24	3	13	--	--	209	66	68	60	4	43	7	2	6	3	3	.50	6	.300	.383	.448
1994 Las Vegas	AAA	89	331	106	15	5	7	--	--	152	61	43	26	3	37	2	1	4	3	4	.43	6	.320	.369	.459
1995 Omaha	AAA	44	148	56	7	1	5	--	--	80	24	19	16	3	10	1	1	0	1	3	.25	0	.378	.442	.541
1994 San Diego	NL	27	43	9	0	0	2	(2	0)	15	4	6	4	0	10	1	1	1	0	1	1.00	0	.209	.262	.349
1995 Kansas City	AL	94	274	88	19	3	6	(3	3)	131	41	33	14	2	21	4	1	7	8	1	.89	4	.321	.355	.478
2 ML YEARS		121	317	97	19	3	8	(5	3)	146	45	39	18	2	31	5	2	8	9	1	.90	4	.306	.345	.461

Kenny Lofton

Bats: Left **Throws:** Left **Pos:** CF **Ht:** 6' 0" **Wt:** 180 **Born:** 5/31/67 **Age:** 29

Year	Team	Lg	G	AB	H	2B	3B	HR	(Hm	Rd)	TB	R	RBI	TBB	IBB	SO	HBP	SH	SF	SB	CS	SB%	GDP	Avg	OBP	SLG
1991	Houston	NL	20	74	15	1	0	0	(0	0)	16	9	0	5	0	19	0	0	0	2	1	.67	0	.203	.253	.216
1992	Cleveland	AL	148	576	164	15	8	5	(3	2)	210	96	42	68	3	54	2	4	1	66	12	.85	7	.285	.362	.365
1993	Cleveland	AL	148	569	185	28	8	1	(1	0)	232	116	42	81	6	83	1	2	4	70	14	.83	8	.325	.408	.408
1994	Cleveland	AL	112	459	160	32	9	12	(10	2)	246	105	57	52	5	56	2	4	6	60	12	.83	5	.349	.412	.536
1995	Cleveland	AL	118	481	149	22	13	7	(5	2)	218	93	53	40	6	49	1	4	3	54	15	.78	6	.310	.362	.453
	5 ML YEARS		546	2159	673	98	38	25	(19	6)	922	419	194	246	20	261	6	14	14	252	54	.82	26	.312	.381	.427

Kevin Lomon

Pitches: Right **Bats:** Right **Pos:** RP **Ht:** 6' 1" **Wt:** 195 **Born:** 11/20/71 **Age:** 24

Year	Team	Lg	G	GS	CG	GF	IP	BFP	H	R	ER	HR	SH	SF	HB	TBB	IBB	SO	WP	Bk	W	L	Pct.	ShO	Sv	ERA
1991	Pulaski	R	10	5	1	1	44	168	17	9	3	0	0	1	4	13	0	70	4	6	6	0	1.000	1	1	0.61
	Macon	A	1	0	0	1	5	17	2	1	1	0	0	0	0	1	0	2	0	0	1	0	1.000	0	0	1.80
1992	Durham	A	27	27	0	0	135	609	147	83	74	13	5	3	11	63	1	113	16	3	8	9	.471	0	0	4.93
1993	Durham	A	14	14	1	0	85	358	80	36	35	6	0	1	2	30	1	68	5	3	4	2	.667	0	0	3.71
	Greenville	AA	13	13	1	0	79.1	338	76	41	34	4	3	3	4	31	2	68	4	0	3	4	.429	1	0	3.86
1994	Richmond	AAA	28	26	0	0	147	628	159	69	63	12	1	2	3	53	2	97	9	0	10	8	.556	0	0	3.86
1995	Richmond	AAA	32	3	0	8	60	261	62	23	20	2	4	4	0	32	4	52	4	0	1	2	.333	0	1	3.00
1995	New York	NL	6	0	0	1	9.1	47	17	8	7	0	0	0	0	5	1	6	0	0	0	1	.000	0	0	6.75

Tony Longmire

Bats: Left **Throws:** Right **Pos:** LF **Ht:** 6' 1" **Wt:** 202 **Born:** 8/12/68 **Age:** 27

Year	Team	Lg	G	AB	H	2B	3B	HR	(Hm	Rd)	TB	R	RBI	TBB	IBB	SO	HBP	SH	SF	SB	CS	SB%	GDP	Avg	OBP	SLG
1993	Philadelphia	NL	11	13	3	0	0	0	(0	0)	3	1	1	0	0	1	0	0	0	0	0	.00	0	.231	.231	.231
1994	Philadelphia	NL	69	139	33	11	0	0	(0	0)	44	10	17	10	1	27	1	1	2	2	1	.67	5	.237	.289	.317
1995	Philadelphia	NL	59	104	37	7	0	3	(2	1)	53	21	19	11	1	19	1	0	1	1	1	.50	1	.356	.419	.510
	3 ML YEARS		139	256	73	18	0	3	(2	1)	100	32	37	21	2	47	2	1	3	3	2	.60	6	.285	.340	.391

Brian Looney

Pitches: Left **Bats:** Left **Pos:** RP **Ht:** 5'10" **Wt:** 185 **Born:** 9/26/69 **Age:** 26

Year	Team	Lg	G	GS	CG	GF	IP	BFP	H	R	ER	HR	SH	SF	HB	TBB	IBB	SO	WP	Bk	W	L	Pct.	ShO	Sv	ERA
1991	Jamestown	A	11	11	2	0	62.1	246	42	12	8	0	2	2	0	28	0	64	6	0	7	1	.875	1	0	1.16
1992	Rockford	A	17	0	0	5	31.1	141	28	13	11	0	2	0	1	23	0	34	1	0	3	1	.750	0	0	3.16
	Albany	A	11	11	1	0	67.1	265	51	22	16	1	1	3	0	30	0	56	4	0	3	2	.600	1	0	2.14
1993	W. Palm Bch	A	18	16	0	1	106	451	108	48	37	2	7	3	5	29	0	109	2	1	4	6	.400	0	0	3.14
	Harrisburg	AA	8	8	1	0	56.2	221	36	15	15	2	1	1	1	17	1	76	0	0	3	2	.600	1	0	2.38
1994	Ottawa	AAA	27	16	0	2	124.2	565	134	71	60	10	3	6	3	67	4	90	2	0	7	7	.500	0	0	4.33
1995	Pawtucket	AAA	18	18	1	0	100.2	438	106	44	39	9	2	0	3	33	0	78	7	2	4	7	.364	0	0	3.49
1993	Montreal	NL	3	1	0	1	6	28	8	2	2	0	0	0	0	2	0	7	0	1	0	0	.000	0	0	3.00
1994	Montreal	NL	1	0	0	0	2	11	4	5	5	1	0	0	1	0	0	2	0	0	0	0	.000	0	0	22.50
1995	Boston	AL	3	1	0	0	4.2	29	12	9	9	1	1	2	0	4	1	2	0	0	0	1	.000	0	0	17.36
	3 ML YEARS		7	2	0	1	12.2	68	24	16	16	2	1	2	1	6	1	11	0	1	0	1	.000	0	0	11.37

Albie Lopez

Pitches: Right **Bats:** Right **Pos:** RP **Ht:** 6' 2" **Wt:** 205 **Born:** 8/18/71 **Age:** 24

Year	Team	Lg	G	GS	CG	GF	IP	BFP	H	R	ER	HR	SH	SF	HB	TBB	IBB	SO	WP	Bk	W	L	Pct.	ShO	Sv	ERA
1995	Buffalo *	AAA	18	18	1	0	101.1	448	101	57	50	10	0	5	2	51	0	82	8	0	5	10	.333	1	0	4.44
1993	Cleveland	AL	9	9	0	0	49.2	222	49	34	33	7	1	1	1	32	1	25	0	0	3	1	.750	0	0	5.98
1994	Cleveland	AL	4	4	1	0	17	76	20	11	8	3	0	0	1	6	0	18	3	0	1	2	.333	1	0	4.24
1995	Cleveland	AL	6	2	0	0	23	92	17	8	8	4	0	1	1	7	1	22	2	0	0	0	.000	0	0	3.13
	3 ML YEARS		19	15	1	0	89.2	390	86	53	49	14	1	2	3	45	2	65	5	0	4	3	.571	1	0	4.92

Javy Lopez

Bats: Right **Throws:** Right **Pos:** C   **Ht:** 6' 3" **Wt:** 200 **Born:** 11/5/70 **Age:** 25

Year Team	Lg	G	AB	H	2B	3B	HR	(Hm	Rd)	TB	R	RBI	TBB	IBB	SO	HBP	SH	SF	SB	CS	SB%	GDP	Avg	OBP	SLG
1992 Atlanta	NL	9	16	6	2	0	0	(0	0)	8	3	2	0	0	1	0	0	0	0	0	.00	0	.375	.375	.500
1993 Atlanta	NL	8	16	6	1	1	1	(0	1)	12	1	2	0	0	2	1	0	0	0	0	.00	0	.375	.412	.750
1994 Atlanta	NL	80	277	68	9	0	13	(4	9)	116	27	35	17	0	61	5	2	2	0	2	.00	12	.245	.299	.419
1995 Atlanta	NL	100	333	105	11	4	14	(8	6)	166	37	51	14	0	57	2	0	3	0	1	.00	13	.315	.344	.498
4 ML YEARS		197	642	185	23	5	28	(12	16)	302	68	90	31	0	121	8	2	5	0	3	.00	25	.288	.327	.470

Luis Lopez

Bats: Both **Throws:** Right **Pos:** SS/2B   **Ht:** 5'11" **Wt:** 175 **Born:** 9/4/70 **Age:** 25

Year Team	Lg	G	AB	H	2B	3B	HR	(Hm	Rd)	TB	R	RBI	TBB	IBB	SO	HBP	SH	SF	SB	CS	SB%	GDP	Avg	OBP	SLG
1993 San Diego	NL	17	43	5	1	0	0	(0	0)	6	1	1	0	0	8	0	0	1	0	0	.00	0	.116	.114	.140
1994 San Diego	NL	77	235	65	16	1	2	(2	0)	89	29	20	15	2	39	3	2	2	3	2	.60	7	.277	.325	.379
2 ML YEARS		94	278	70	17	1	2	(2	0)	95	30	21	15	2	47	3	2	3	3	2	.60	7	.252	.294	.342

Mark Loretta

Bats: Right **Throws:** Right **Pos:** SS   **Ht:** 6' 0" **Wt:** 175 **Born:** 8/14/71 **Age:** 24

Year Team	Lg	G	AB	H	2B	3B	HR	(Hm	Rd)	TB	R	RBI	TBB	IBB	SO	HBP	SH	SF	SB	CS	SB%	GDP	Avg	OBP	SLG
1993 Helena	R	6	28	9	1	0	1	--	--	13	5	8	1	0	4	1	0	0	0	0	.00	1	.321	.367	.464
Stockton	A	53	201	73	4	1	4	--	--	91	36	31	22	0	17	2	2	2	8	2	.80	6	.363	.427	.453
1994 El Paso	AA	77	302	95	13	6	0	--	--	120	50	38	27	0	33	2	9	5	8	5	.62	12	.315	.369	.397
New Orleans	AAA	43	138	29	7	0	1	--	--	39	16	14	12	0	13	3	3	3	2	1	.67	2	.210	.282	.283
1995 New Orleans	AAA	127	479	137	22	5	7	--	--	190	48	79	34	1	47	9	5	7	8	9	.47	12	.286	.340	.397
1995 Milwaukee	AL	19	50	13	3	0	1	(0	1)	19	13	3	4	0	7	1	1	0	1	1	.50	1	.260	.327	.380

Andrew Lorraine

Pitches: Left **Bats:** Left **Pos:** RP   **Ht:** 6' 3" **Wt:** 195 **Born:** 8/11/72 **Age:** 23

			HOW MUCH HE PITCHED						WHAT HE GAVE UP									THE RESULTS					
Year Team	Lg	G	GS	CG	GF	IP	BFP	H	R	ER	HR	SH	SF	HB	TBB	IBB	SO	WP	Bk	W	L	Pct.	ShO	Sv	ERA
1993 Boise	A	6	6	3	0	42	159	33	6	6	3	0	0	2	6	0	39	0	0	4	1	.800	1	0	1.29
1994 Vancouver	AAA	22	22	4	0	142	599	156	63	54	13	2	4	11	34	1	90	1	1	12	4	.750	2	0	3.42
1995 Vancouver	AAA	18	18	4	0	97.2	420	105	49	43	7	4	3	3	30	0	51	4	0	6	6	.500	1	0	3.96
Nashville	AAA	7	7	0	0	39	184	51	29	26	4	1	3	1	12	0	26	2	0	4	1	.800	0	0	6.00
1994 California	AL	4	3	0	0	18.2	96	30	23	22	7	2	1	0	11	0	10	0	0	0	2	.000	0	0	10.61
1995 Chicago	AL	5	0	0	2	8	30	3	3	3	0	0	0	1	2	0	5	0	0	0	0	.000	0	0	3.38
2 ML YEARS		9	3	0	2	26.2	126	33	26	25	7	2	1	1	13	0	15	0	0	0	2	.000	0	0	8.44

Barry Lyons

Bats: Right **Throws:** Right **Pos:** C   **Ht:** 6' 1" **Wt:** 200 **Born:** 6/3/60 **Age:** 36

Year Team	Lg	G	AB	H	2B	3B	HR	(Hm	Rd)	TB	R	RBI	TBB	IBB	SO	HBP	SH	SF	SB	CS	SB%	GDP	Avg	OBP	SLG
1995 Nashville *	AAA	71	265	68	16	1	8	--	--	110	37	38	20	4	56	4	1	4	0	0	.00	0	.257	.314	.415
1986 New York	NL	6	9	0	0	0	0	(0	0)	0	1	2	1	1	2	0	0	0	0	0	.00	0	.000	.100	.000
1987 New York	NL	53	130	33	4	1	4	(4	0)	51	15	24	8	1	24	2	0	3	0	0	.00	4	.254	.301	.392
1988 New York	NL	50	91	21	7	1	0	(0	0)	30	5	11	3	0	12	0	3	1	0	0	.00	3	.231	.253	.330
1989 New York	NL	79	235	58	13	0	3	(1	2)	80	15	27	11	1	28	2	1	3	0	1	.00	7	.247	.283	.340
1990 LA-NYN	NL	27	85	20	0	0	3	(1	2)	29	9	9	2	0	10	1	0	0	0	0	.00	2	.235	.261	.341
1991 Cal-LA		11	14	1	0	0	0	(0	0)	1	0	0	0	0	2	0	0	0	0	0	.00	0	.071	.071	.071
1995 Chicago	AL	27	64	17	2	0	5	(3	2)	34	8	16	4	0	14	0	1	1	0	0	.00	0	.266	.304	.531
1990 Los Angeles	NL	3	5	1	0	0	1	(0	1)	4	1	2	0	0	1	0	0	0	0	0	.00	0	.200	.200	.800
New York	NL	24	80	19	0	0	2	(1	1)	25	8	7	2	0	9	1	0	0	0	0	.00	2	.238	.265	.313
1991 California	AL	2	5	1	0	0	0	(0	0)	1	0	0	0	0	0	0	0	0	0	0	.00	0	.200	.200	.200
Los Angeles	NL	9	9	0	0	0	0	(0	0)	0	0	0	0	0	2	0	0	0	0	0	.00	0	.000	.000	.000
7 ML YEARS		253	628	150	26	2	15	(9	6)	225	53	89	29	3	92	5	5	8	0	1	.00	13	.239	.275	.358

Kevin Maas

Bats: Left **Throws:** Left **Pos:** DH   **Ht:** 6' 3" **Wt:** 209 **Born:** 1/20/65 **Age:** 31

Year Team	Lg	G	AB	H	2B	3B	HR	(Hm	Rd)	TB	R	RBI	TBB	IBB	SO	HBP	SH	SF	SB	CS	SB%	GDP	Avg	OBP	SLG
1995 Yankees *	R	2	9	4	0	0	1	--	--	7	1	3	0	0	0	0	0	0	0	0	.00	0	.444	.444	.778
Columbus *	AAA	44	161	45	7	2	9	--	--	83	28	33	23	0	40	2	0	2	0	0	.00	1	.280	.372	.516
1990 New York	AL	79	254	64	9	0	21	(12	9)	136	42	41	43	10	76	3	0	0	1	2	.33	2	.252	.367	.535
1991 New York	AL	148	500	110	14	1	23	(8	15)	195	69	63	83	3	128	4	0	5	5	1	.83	4	.220	.333	.390
1992 New York	AL	98	286	71	12	0	11	(7	4)	116	35	35	25	4	63	0	0	4	3	1	.75	1	.248	.305	.406
1993 New York	AL	59	151	31	4	0	9	(7	2)	62	20	25	24	2	32	1	0	1	1	1	.50	2	.205	.316	.411
1995 Minnesota	AL	22	57	11	4	0	1	(1	0)	18	5	5	7	2	11	0	0	0	0	0	.00	4	.193	.281	.316
5 ML YEARS		406	1248	287	43	1	65	(35	30)	527	171	169	182	21	310	8	0	10	10	5	.67	13	.230	.329	.422

John Mabry

Bats: Left **Throws:** Right **Pos:** 1B/LF/RF   **Ht:** 6' 4" **Wt:** 195 **Born:** 10/17/70 **Age:** 25

Year Team	Lg	G	AB	H	2B	3B	HR	(Hm	Rd)	TB	R	RBI	TBB	IBB	SO	HBP	SH	SF	SB	CS	SB%	GDP	Avg	OBP	SLG
1991 Hamilton	A	49	187	58	12	0	1	--	--	73	25	31	17	2	18	2	0	2	9	3	.75	6	.310	.370	.390
Savannah	A	22	86	20	6	1	0	--	--	28	10	8	7	2	12	0	0	2	1	0	1.00	2	.233	.284	.326
1992 Springfield	A	115	438	115	13	6	11	--	--	173	63	57	24	2	39	0	1	1	2	8	.20	12	.263	.300	.395
1993 Arkansas	AA	136	528	153	32	2	16	--	--	237	68	72	27	2	68	4	3	5	7	15	.32	17	.290	.326	.449
Louisville	AAA	4	7	1	0	0	0	--	--	1	0	1	0	0	1	0	0	0	0	0	.00	1	.143	.143	.143
1994 Louisville	AAA	122	477	125	30	1	15	--	--	202	76	68	32	1	67	3	1	2	2	6	.25	14	.262	.311	.423
1995 Louisville	AAA	4	12	1	0	0	0	--	--	1	0	0	0	0	0	0	0	0	0	0	.00	0	.083	.083	.083
1994 St. Louis	NL	6	23	7	3	0	0	(0	0)	10	2	3	2	0	4	0	0	0	0	0	.00	0	.304	.360	.435
1995 St. Louis	NL	129	388	119	21	1	5	(2	3)	157	35	41	24	5	45	2	0	4	0	3	.00	6	.307	.347	.405
2 ML YEARS		135	411	126	24	1	5	(2	3)	167	37	44	26	5	49	2	0	4	0	3	.00	6	.307	.348	.406

Bob MacDonald

Pitches: Left **Bats:** Left **Pos:** RP   **Ht:** 6' 3" **Wt:** 208 **Born:** 4/27/65 **Age:** 31

Year Team	Lg	G	GS	CG	GF	IP	BFP	H	R	ER	HR	SH	SF	HB	TBB	IBB	SO	WP	Bk	W	L	Pct.	ShO	Sv	ERA
1995 Columbus *	AAA	13	0	0	2	19.1	84	22	7	5	1	1	1	0	5	0	13	0	0	2	1	.667	0	0	2.33
1990 Toronto	AL	4	0	0	1	2.1	8	0	0	0	0	0	0	0	2	0	0	0	0	0	0	.000	0	0	0.00
1991 Toronto	AL	45	0	0	10	53.2	231	51	19	17	5	2	2	0	25	4	24	1	1	3	3	.500	0	0	2.85
1992 Toronto	AL	27	0	0	9	47.1	204	50	24	23	4	1	1	1	16	3	26	0	0	1	0	1.000	0	0	4.37
1993 Detroit	AL	68	0	0	24	65.2	293	67	42	39	8	4	5	1	33	5	39	3	1	3	3	.500	0	3	5.35
1995 New York	AL	33	0	0	5	46.1	202	50	25	25	7	2	0	1	22	0	41	1	0	1	1	.500	0	0	4.86
5 ML YEARS		177	0	0	49	215.1	938	218	110	104	24	9	8	3	98	12	130	5	2	8	7	.533	0	3	4.35

Mike Macfarlane

Bats: Right **Throws:** Right **Pos:** C   **Ht:** 6' 1" **Wt:** 205 **Born:** 4/12/64 **Age:** 32

Year Team	Lg	G	AB	H	2B	3B	HR	(Hm	Rd)	TB	R	RBI	TBB	IBB	SO	HBP	SH	SF	SB	CS	SB%	GDP	Avg	OBP	SLG
1987 Kansas City	AL	8	19	4	1	0	0	(0	0)	5	0	3	2	0	2	0	0	0	0	0	.00	1	.211	.286	.263
1988 Kansas City	AL	70	211	56	15	0	4	(2	2)	83	25	26	21	2	37	1	1	2	0	0	.00	5	.265	.332	.393
1989 Kansas City	AL	69	157	35	6	0	2	(0	2)	47	13	19	7	0	27	2	0	1	0	0	.00	8	.223	.263	.299
1990 Kansas City	AL	124	400	102	24	4	6	(1	5)	152	37	58	25	2	69	7	1	6	1	0	1.00	9	.255	.306	.380
1991 Kansas City	AL	84	267	74	18	2	13	(6	7)	135	34	41	17	0	52	6	1	4	1	0	1.00	9	.277	.330	.506
1992 Kansas City	AL	129	402	94	28	3	17	(7	10)	179	51	48	30	2	89	15	1	2	1	5	.17	8	.234	.310	.445
1993 Kansas City	AL	117	388	106	27	0	20	(7	13)	193	55	67	40	2	83	16	1	6	2	5	.29	8	.273	.360	.497
1994 Kansas City	AL	92	314	80	17	3	14	(9	5)	145	53	47	35	1	71	18	0	3	1	0	1.00	8	.255	.359	.462
1995 Boston	AL	115	364	82	18	1	15	(7	8)	147	45	51	38	0	78	14	0	4	2	1	.67	9	.225	.319	.404
9 ML YEARS		808	2522	633	154	13	91	(39	52)	1086	313	360	215	9	508	79	5	28	8	11	.42	61	.251	.326	.431

Shane Mack

Bats: Right **Throws:** Right **Pos:** LF/CF   **Ht:** 6' 0" **Wt:** 190 **Born:** 12/7/63 **Age:** 32

Year Team	Lg	G	AB	H	2B	3B	HR	(Hm	Rd)	TB	R	RBI	TBB	IBB	SO	HBP	SH	SF	SB	CS	SB%	GDP	Avg	OBP	SLG
1987 San Diego	NL	105	238	57	11	3	4	(2	2)	86	28	25	18	0	47	3	6	2	4	6	.40	11	.239	.299	.361
1988 San Diego	NL	56	119	29	3	0	0	(0	0)	32	13	12	14	0	21	3	3	1	5	1	.83	2	.244	.336	.269
1990 Minnesota	AL	125	313	102	10	4	8	(5	3)	144	50	44	29	1	69	5	6	0	13	4	.76	7	.326	.392	.460
1991 Minnesota	AL	143	442	137	27	8	18	(4	14)	234	79	74	34	1	79	6	2	5	13	9	.59	11	.310	.363	.529
1992 Minnesota	AL	156	600	189	31	6	16	(10	6)	280	101	75	64	1	106	15	11	2	26	14	.65	8	.315	.394	.467
1993 Minnesota	AL	128	503	139	30	4	10	(3	7)	207	66	61	41	1	76	4	3	2	15	5	.75	13	.276	.335	.412
1994 Minnesota	AL	81	303	101	21	2	15	(7	8)	171	55	61	32	1	51	6	1	5	4	1	.80	11	.333	.402	.564
7 ML YEARS		794	2518	754	133	27	71	(32	39)	1154	392	352	232	5	449	42	32	17	80	40	.67	63	.299	.366	.458

138

Greg Maddux

Pitches: Right **Bats:** Right **Pos:** SP

Ht: 6' 0" **Wt:** 175 **Born:** 4/14/66 **Age:** 30

		HOW MUCH HE PITCHED						WHAT HE GAVE UP										THE RESULTS				
Year Team	Lg	G	GS	CG	GF	IP	BFP	H	R	ER	HR	SH	SF	HB	TBB	IBB	SO	WP	Bk	W	L	Pct.	ShO	Sv	ERA
1986 Chicago	NL	6	5	1	1	31	144	44	20	19	3	1	0	1	11	2	20	2	0	2	4	.333	0	0	5.52
1987 Chicago	NL	30	27	1	2	155.2	701	181	111	97	17	7	1	4	74	13	101	4	7	6	14	.300	1	0	5.61
1988 Chicago	NL	34	34	9	0	249	1047	230	97	88	13	11	2	9	81	16	140	3	6	18	8	.692	3	0	3.18
1989 Chicago	NL	35	35	7	0	238.1	1002	222	90	78	13	18	6	6	82	13	135	5	3	19	12	.613	1	0	2.95
1990 Chicago	NL	35	35	8	0	237	1011	242	116	91	11	18	5	4	71	10	144	3	3	15	15	.500	2	0	3.46
1991 Chicago	NL	37	37	7	0	263	1070	232	113	98	18	16	3	6	66	9	198	6	3	15	11	.577	2	0	3.35
1992 Chicago	NL	35	35	9	0	268	1061	201	68	65	7	15	3	14	70	7	199	5	0	20	11	.645	4	0	2.18
1993 Atlanta	NL	36	36	8	0	267	1064	228	85	70	14	15	7	6	52	7	197	5	1	20	10	.667	1	0	2.36
1994 Atlanta	NL	25	25	10	0	202	774	150	44	35	4	6	5	6	31	3	156	3	1	16	6	.727	3	0	1.56
1995 Atlanta	NL	28	28	10	0	209.2	785	147	39	38	8	9	1	4	23	3	181	1	0	19	2	.905	3	0	1.63
10 ML YEARS		301	297	70	3	2120.2	8659	1877	783	679	108	116	33	60	561	83	1471	37	24	150	93	.617	20	0	2.88

Mike Maddux

Pitches: Right **Bats:** Left **Pos:** RP/SP

Ht: 6' 2" **Wt:** 190 **Born:** 8/27/61 **Age:** 34

		HOW MUCH HE PITCHED						WHAT HE GAVE UP										THE RESULTS				
Year Team	Lg	G	GS	CG	GF	IP	BFP	H	R	ER	HR	SH	SF	HB	TBB	IBB	SO	WP	Bk	W	L	Pct.	ShO	Sv	ERA
1986 Philadelphia	NL	16	16	0	0	78	351	88	56	47	6	3	3	3	34	4	44	4	2	3	7	.300	0	0	5.42
1987 Philadelphia	NL	7	2	0	0	17	72	17	5	5	0	0	0	0	5	0	15	1	0	2	0	1.000	0	0	2.65
1988 Philadelphia	NL	25	11	0	4	88.2	380	91	41	37	6	7	3	5	34	4	59	4	2	4	3	.571	0	0	3.76
1989 Philadelphia	NL	16	4	2	1	43.2	191	52	29	25	3	3	1	2	14	3	26	3	1	1	3	.250	1	1	5.15
1990 Los Angeles	NL	11	2	0	3	20.2	88	24	15	15	3	0	1	1	4	0	11	2	0	0	1	.000	0	0	6.53
1991 San Diego	NL	64	1	0	27	98.2	388	78	30	27	4	5	2	1	27	3	57	5	0	7	2	.778	0	5	2.46
1992 San Diego	NL	50	1	0	14	79.2	330	71	25	21	2	2	3	0	24	4	60	4	1	2	2	.500	0	5	2.37
1993 New York	NL	58	0	0	31	75	320	67	34	30	3	7	6	4	27	7	57	4	1	3	8	.273	0	5	3.60
1994 New York	NL	27	0	0	12	44	186	45	25	25	7	0	2	0	13	4	32	2	0	2	1	.667	0	2	5.11
1995 Pit-Bos		44	4	0	7	98.2	409	100	49	45	5	1	1	2	18	4	69	6	0	5	1	.833	0	1	4.10
1995 Pittsburgh	NL	8	0	1	1	9	42	14	9	9	0	0	0	0	3	1	4	1	0	1	0	1.000	0	0	9.00
Boston	AL	36	4	0	6	89.2	367	86	40	36	5	1	1	2	15	3	65	5	0	4	1	.800	0	1	3.61
10 ML YEARS		318	41	2	99	644	2715	633	309	277	39	28	22	18	200	33	430	35	7	29	28	.509	1	19	3.87

Dave Magadan

Bats: Left **Throws:** Right **Pos:** 3B/1B

Ht: 6' 3" **Wt:** 205 **Born:** 9/30/62 **Age:** 33

		BATTING																BASERUNNING				PERCENTAGES		
Year Team	Lg	G	AB	H	2B	3B	HR	(Hm	Rd)	TB	R	RBI	TBB	IBB	SO	HBP	SH	SF	SB	CS	SB%	GDP	Avg	OBP	SLG
1986 New York	NL	10	18	8	0	0	0	(0	0)	8	3	3	3	0	1	0	0	0	0	0	.00	1	.444	.524	.444
1987 New York	NL	85	192	61	13	1	3	(2	1)	85	21	24	22	2	22	0	1	1	0	0	.00	5	.318	.386	.443
1988 New York	NL	112	314	87	15	0	1	(1	0)	105	39	35	60	4	39	2	1	3	0	1	.00	9	.277	.393	.334
1989 New York	NL	127	374	107	22	3	4	(3	1)	147	47	41	49	6	37	1	1	4	1	0	1.00	2	.286	.367	.393
1990 New York	NL	144	451	148	28	6	6	(2	4)	206	74	72	74	4	55	2	4	10	2	1	.67	11	.328	.417	.457
1991 New York	NL	124	418	108	23	0	4	(2	2)	143	58	51	83	3	50	2	7	7	1	1	.50	5	.258	.378	.342
1992 New York	NL	99	321	91	9	1	3	(2	1)	111	33	28	56	3	44	0	2	0	1	0	1.00	6	.283	.390	.346
1993 Sea-Fla		137	455	124	23	0	5	(3	2)	162	49	50	80	7	63	1	2	6	2	1	.67	12	.273	.378	.356
1994 Florida	NL	74	211	58	7	0	1	(1	0)	68	30	17	39	0	25	1	0	3	0	0	.00	8	.275	.386	.322
1995 Houston	NL	127	348	109	24	0	2	(0	2)	139	44	51	71	9	56	0	1	2	2	1	.67	9	.313	.428	.399
1993 Seattle	AL	71	228	59	11	0	1	(0	1)	73	27	21	36	3	33	0	2	3	2	0	1.00	9	.259	.356	.320
Florida	NL	66	227	65	12	0	4	(3	1)	89	22	29	44	4	30	1	0	3	0	1	.00	3	.286	.400	.392
10 ML YEARS		1039	3102	901	164	11	29	(16	13)	1174	398	372	537	38	392	9	19	36	9	5	.64	68	.290	.393	.378

Mike Magnante

Pitches: Left **Bats:** Left **Pos:** RP

Ht: 6' 1" **Wt:** 190 **Born:** 6/17/65 **Age:** 31

		HOW MUCH HE PITCHED						WHAT HE GAVE UP										THE RESULTS				
Year Team	Lg	G	GS	CG	GF	IP	BFP	H	R	ER	HR	SH	SF	HB	TBB	IBB	SO	WP	Bk	W	L	Pct.	ShO	Sv	ERA
1995 Omaha *	AAA	15	8	0	3	57	235	55	23	18	3	1	3	1	13	0	38	5	0	5	1	.833	0	0	2.84
1991 Kansas City	AL	38	0	0	10	55	236	55	19	15	3	2	1	0	23	3	42	1	0	0	1	.000	0	0	2.45
1992 Kansas City	AL	44	12	0	11	89.1	403	115	53	49	5	5	7	2	35	5	31	2	0	4	9	.308	0	0	4.94
1993 Kansas City	AL	7	6	0	0	35.1	145	37	16	16	3	1	1	1	11	1	16	1	0	1	2	.333	0	0	4.08
1994 Kansas City	AL	36	1	0	10	47	211	55	27	24	5	2	3	0	16	1	21	3	0	2	3	.400	0	0	4.60
1995 Kansas City	AL	28	0	0	7	44.2	190	45	23	21	6	2	2	2	16	1	28	2	0	1	1	.500	0	0	4.23
5 ML YEARS		153	19	0	38	271.1	1185	307	138	125	22	12	14	5	101	11	138	9	0	8	16	.333	0	0	4.15

Ron Mahay

Bats: Left **Throws:** Left **Pos:** CF **Ht:** 6' 2" **Wt:** 175 **Born:** 6/28/71 **Age:** 25

Year	Team	Lg	G	AB	H	2B	3B	HR	(Hm	Rd)	TB	R	RBI	TBB	IBB	SO	HBP	SH	SF	SB	CS	SB%	GDP	Avg	OBP	SLG
1991	Red Sox	R	54	187	51	6	5	1	--	--	70	30	29	33	0	40	4	2	2	2	0	1.00	4	.273	.389	.374
1992	Winter Havn	A	19	63	16	2	1	0	--	--	20	6	4	2	0	19	0	1	0	0	1	.00	4	.254	.277	.317
1993	New Britain	AA	8	25	3	0	0	1	--	--	6	2	2	1	0	6	0	0	0	1	0	1.00	1	.120	.154	.240
	Lynchburg	A	73	254	54	8	1	5	--	--	79	28	23	11	1	63	5	4	1	2	2	.50	6	.213	.258	.311
1994	Sarasota	A	105	367	102	18	0	4	--	--	132	43	46	39	3	67	2	7	4	3	5	.38	9	.278	.347	.360
1995	Pawtucket	AAA	11	44	14	4	0	0	--	--	18	5	3	4	1	9	0	0	0	1	0	1.00	2	.318	.375	.409
	Trenton	AA	93	310	73	12	3	5	--	--	106	37	28	44	3	90	3	2	4	5	6	.45	5	.235	.332	.342
1995	Boston	AL	5	20	4	2	0	1	(0	1)	9	3	3	1	0	6	1	0	0	0	0	.00	0	.200	.273	.450

Pat Mahomes

Pitches: Right **Bats:** Right **Pos:** RP/SP **Ht:** 6' 4" **Wt:** 212 **Born:** 8/9/70 **Age:** 25

Year	Team	Lg	G	GS	CG	GF	IP	BFP	H	R	ER	HR	SH	SF	HB	TBB	IBB	SO	WP	Bk	W	L	Pct.	ShO	Sv	ERA
1992	Minnesota	AL	14	13	0	1	69.2	302	73	41	39	5	0	3	0	37	0	44	2	1	3	4	.429	0	0	5.04
1993	Minnesota	AL	12	5	0	4	37.1	173	47	34	32	8	1	3	1	16	0	23	3	0	1	5	.167	0	0	7.71
1994	Minnesota	AL	21	21	0	0	120	517	121	68	63	22	1	4	1	62	1	53	3	0	9	5	.643	0	0	4.73
1995	Minnesota	AL	47	7	0	16	94.2	423	100	74	67	22	3	2	2	47	1	67	6	0	4	10	.286	0	3	6.37
	4 ML YEARS		94	46	0	21	321.2	1415	341	217	201	57	5	12	4	162	2	187	14	1	17	24	.415	0	3	5.62

Candy Maldonado

Bats: Right **Throws:** Right **Pos:** RF/LF **Ht:** 6' 0" **Wt:** 220 **Born:** 9/5/60 **Age:** 35

Year	Team	Lg	G	AB	H	2B	3B	HR	(Hm	Rd)	TB	R	RBI	TBB	IBB	SO	HBP	SH	SF	SB	CS	SB%	GDP	Avg	OBP	SLG
1981	Los Angeles	NL	11	12	1	0	0	0	(0	0)	1	0	0	0	0	5	0	0	0	0	0	.00	0	.083	.083	.083
1982	Los Angeles	NL	6	4	0	0	0	0	(0	0)	0	0	0	1	1	2	0	0	0	0	0	.00	0	.000	.200	.000
1983	Los Angeles	NL	42	62	12	1	1	1	(1	0)	18	5	6	5	0	14	0	1	0	0	0	.00	1	.194	.254	.290
1984	Los Angeles	NL	116	254	68	14	0	5	(1	4)	97	25	28	19	0	29	1	1	3	0	3	.00	6	.268	.318	.382
1985	Los Angeles	NL	121	213	48	7	1	5	(2	3)	72	20	19	19	4	40	0	2	1	1	1	.50	3	.225	.288	.338
1986	San Francisco	NL	133	405	102	31	3	18	(6	12)	193	49	85	20	4	77	3	0	4	4	4	.50	12	.252	.289	.477
1987	San Francisco	NL	118	442	129	28	4	20	(14	6)	225	69	85	34	4	78	6	0	7	8	8	.50	9	.292	.346	.509
1988	San Francisco	NL	142	499	127	23	1	12	(5	7)	188	53	68	37	1	89	7	3	6	6	5	.55	13	.255	.311	.377
1989	San Francisco	NL	129	345	75	23	0	9	(1	8)	125	39	41	37	4	69	3	1	3	4	1	.80	8	.217	.296	.362
1990	Cleveland	AL	155	590	161	32	2	22	(12	10)	263	76	95	49	4	134	5	0	7	3	5	.38	13	.273	.330	.446
1991	Mil-Tor	AL	86	288	72	15	0	12	(7	5)	123	37	48	36	4	76	6	0	3	4	0	1.00	8	.250	.342	.427
1992	Toronto	AL	137	489	133	25	4	20	(8	12)	226	64	66	59	3	112	7	2	3	2	2	.50	13	.272	.357	.462
1993	Cle-ChN		98	221	46	7	0	8	(5	3)	77	19	35	24	2	58	1	1	1	0	1	.00	5	.208	.287	.348
1994	Cleveland	AL	42	92	18	5	1	5	(4	1)	40	14	12	19	1	31	0	0	0	1	1	.50	4	.196	.333	.435
1995	Tor-Tex	AL	74	190	50	16	0	9	(7	2)	93	28	30	32	0	50	2	0	3	1	2	.33	6	.263	.370	.489
1991	Milwaukee	AL	34	111	23	6	0	5	(3	2)	44	11	20	13	0	23	0	0	1	0	0	1.00	4	.207	.288	.396
	Toronto	AL	52	177	49	9	0	7	(4	3)	79	26	28	23	4	53	6	0	2	3	0	1.00	4	.277	.375	.446
1993	Cleveland	AL	28	81	20	2	0	5	(4	1)	37	11	20	11	2	18	0	1	1	0	1	.00	2	.247	.333	.457
	Chicago	NL	70	140	26	5	0	3	(1	2)	40	8	15	13	0	40	1	0	0	0	0	.00	3	.186	.260	.286
1995	Toronto	AL	61	160	43	13	0	7	(5	2)	77	22	25	25	0	45	2	0	3	1	1	.50	5	.269	.368	.481
	Texas	AL	13	30	7	3	0	2	(2	0)	16	6	5	7	0	5	0	0	0	0	1	.00	1	.233	.378	.533
	15 ML YEARS		1410	4106	1042	227	17	146	(73	73)	1741	498	618	391	32	864	41	11	41	34	33	.51	98	.254	.322	.424

Matt Mantei

Pitches: Right **Bats:** Right **Pos:** RP **Ht:** 6' 1" **Wt:** 181 **Born:** 7/7/73 **Age:** 22

Year	Team	Lg	G	GS	CG	GF	IP	BFP	H	R	ER	HR	SH	SF	HB	TBB	IBB	SO	WP	Bk	W	L	Pct.	ShO	Sv	ERA
1991	Mariners	R	17	5	0	4	40.1	202	54	40	30	0	2	3	1	28	2	28	7	8	1	5	.167	0	0	6.69
1992	Mariners	R	3	3	0	0	16	68	18	10	10	1	0	0	0	5	0	19	0	0	1	1	.500	0	0	5.63
1993	Bellingham	A	26	0	0	21	25.2	120	26	19	17	2	4	0	1	15	0	34	4	0	1	1	.500	0	12	5.96
1994	Appleton	A	48	0	0	43	48	201	42	14	11	2	2	2	1	21	3	70	6	0	5	1	.833	0	26	2.06
1995	Portland	AA	8	0	0	4	11.1	48	10	3	3	0	1	0	1	5	0	15	0	0	1	0	1.000	0	1	2.38
	Charlotte	AAA	6	0	0	1	7	27	1	3	2	1	0	1	1	5	0	10	0	0	0	1	.000	0	0	2.57
1995	Florida	NL	12	0	0	3	13.1	64	12	8	7	1	1	1	0	13	0	15	1	0	0	1	.000	0	0	4.73

Jeff Manto

Bats: Right **Throws:** Right **Pos:** 3B/DH **Ht:** 6' 3" **Wt:** 210 **Born:** 8/23/64 **Age:** 31

Year	Team	Lg	G	AB	H	2B	3B	HR	(Hm	Rd)	TB	R	RBI	TBB	IBB	SO	HBP	SH	SF	SB	CS	SB%	GDP	Avg	OBP	SLG
1995	Bowie *	AA	1	4	1	0	0	0	--	--	1	1	0	0	0	2	0	0	0	0	0	.00	0	.250	.250	.250

Year Team	Lg	G	AB	H	2B	3B	HR	(Hm	Rd)	TB	R	RBI	TBB	IBB	SO	HBP	SH	SF	SB	CS	SB%	GDP	Avg	OBP	SLG
Frederick *	A	2	8	3	0	0	1	--	--	6	1	3	0	0	1	0	0	0	0	1	.00	0	.375	.375	.750
1990 Cleveland	AL	30	76	17	5	1	2	(1	1)	30	12	14	21	1	18	0	0	0	0	1	.00	0	.224	.392	.395
1991 Cleveland	AL	47	128	27	7	0	2	(0	2)	40	15	13	14	0	22	4	1	1	2	0	1.00	3	.211	.306	.313
1993 Philadelphia	NL	8	18	1	0	0	0	(0	0)	1	0	0	0	0	3	1	0	0	0	0	.00	0	.056	.105	.056
1995 Baltimore	AL	89	254	65	9	0	17	(12	5)	125	31	38	24	0	69	2	0	0	0	3	.00	6	.256	.325	.492
4 ML YEARS		174	476	110	21	1	21	(13	8)	196	58	65	59	1	112	7	1	1	2	4	.33	9	.231	.324	.412

Kirt Manwaring

Bats: Right **Throws:** Right **Pos:** C   **Ht:** 5'11" **Wt:** 203 **Born:** 7/15/65 **Age:** 30

						BATTING														BASERUNNING				PERCENTAGES		
Year Team	Lg	G	AB	H	2B	3B	HR	(Hm	Rd)	TB	R	RBI	TBB	IBB	SO	HBP	SH	SF	SB	CS	SB%	GDP	Avg	OBP	SLG
1987 San Francisco	NL	6	7	1	0	0	0	(0	0)	1	0	0	0	0	1	1	0	0	0	0	.00	1	.143	.250	.143
1988 San Francisco	NL	40	116	29	7	0	1	(0	1)	39	12	15	2	0	21	3	1	1	0	1	.00	2	.250	.279	.336
1989 San Francisco	NL	85	200	42	4	2	0	(0	0)	50	14	18	11	1	28	4	7	1	2	1	.67	5	.210	.264	.250
1990 San Francisco	NL	8	13	2	0	1	0	(0	0)	4	0	1	0	0	3	0	0	0	0	0	.00	0	.154	.154	.308
1991 San Francisco	NL	67	178	40	9	0	0	(0	0)	49	16	19	9	0	22	3	7	2	1	1	.50	2	.225	.271	.275
1992 San Francisco	NL	109	349	85	10	5	4	(1	3)	117	24	26	29	0	42	5	6	0	2	1	.67	12	.244	.311	.335
1993 San Francisco	NL	130	432	119	15	1	5	(3	2)	151	48	49	41	13	76	6	5	2	1	3	.25	14	.275	.345	.350
1994 San Francisco	NL	97	316	79	17	1	1	(0	1)	101	30	29	25	3	50	3	4	3	1	1	.50	10	.250	.308	.320
1995 San Francisco	NL	118	379	95	15	2	4	(4	0)	126	21	36	27	6	72	10	4	4	0	1	1.00	8	.251	.314	.332
9 ML YEARS		660	1990	492	77	12	15	(8	7)	638	165	193	144	23	315	35	34	13	8	8	.50	53	.247	.308	.321

Josias Manzanillo

Pitches: Right **Bats:** Right **Pos:** RP   **Ht:** 6'0" **Wt:** 190 **Born:** 10/16/67 **Age:** 28

		HOW MUCH HE PITCHED						WHAT HE GAVE UP												THE RESULTS					
Year Team	Lg	G	GS	CG	GF	IP	BFP	H	R	ER	HR	SH	SF	HB	TBB	IBB	SO	WP	Bk	W	L	Pct.	ShO	Sv	ERA
1991 Boston	AL	1	0	0	1	1	8	2	2	2	0	0	0	0	3	0	1	0	0	0	0	.000	0	0	18.00
1993 Mil-NYN		16	1	0	6	29	140	30	27	22	2	3	3	2	19	3	21	1	0	1	1	.500	0	1	6.83
1994 New York	NL	37	0	0	14	47.1	186	34	15	14	4	0	0	3	13	2	48	2	0	3	2	.600	0	2	2.66
1995 NYN-NYA		23	0	0	8	33.1	154	37	19	18	4	2	1	2	15	4	25	6	0	1	2	.333	0	0	4.86
1993 Milwaukee	AL	10	1	0	4	17	86	22	20	18	1	2	2	2	10	3	10	1	0	1	1	.500	0	1	9.53
New York	NL	6	0	0	2	12	54	8	7	4	1	1	1	0	9	0	11	0	0	0	2	.000	0	0	3.00
1995 New York	NL	12	0	0	4	16	73	18	15	14	3	0	1	0	6	2	14	5	0	1	2	.333	0	0	7.88
New York	AL	11	0	0	4	17.1	81	19	4	4	1	2	0	2	9	2	11	1	0	0	0	.000	0	0	2.08
4 ML YEARS		77	1	0	29	110.2	488	103	63	56	10	5	4	7	50	9	95	9	0	5	5	.500	0	3	4.55

Ravelo Manzanillo

Pitches: Left **Bats:** Left **Pos:** RP   **Ht:** 5'10" **Wt:** 195 **Born:** 10/17/63 **Age:** 32

		HOW MUCH HE PITCHED						WHAT HE GAVE UP												THE RESULTS					
Year Team	Lg	G	GS	CG	GF	IP	BFP	H	R	ER	HR	SH	SF	HB	TBB	IBB	SO	WP	Bk	W	L	Pct.	ShO	Sv	ERA
1995 Calgary *	AAA	8	1	0	0	12	65	23	18	17	4	0	1	1	10	0	2	1	3	0	2	.000	0	0	12.75
1988 Chicago	AL	2	2	0	0	9.1	46	7	6	6	1	0	0	1	12	0	10	1	0	0	1	.000	0	0	5.79
1994 Pittsburgh	NL	46	0	0	11	50	236	45	30	23	4	2	5	3	42	5	39	2	5	4	2	.667	0	1	4.14
1995 Pittsburgh	NL	5	0	0	0	3.2	16	3	3	2	0	0	0	1	2	0	1	0	0	0	0	.000	0	0	4.91
3 ML YEARS		53	2	0	11	63	298	55	39	31	5	2	5	5	56	5	50	3	5	4	3	.571	0	1	4.43

Isidro Marquez

Pitches: Right **Bats:** Right **Pos:** RP   **Ht:** 6'3" **Wt:** 190 **Born:** 5/15/65 **Age:** 31

		HOW MUCH HE PITCHED						WHAT HE GAVE UP												THE RESULTS					
Year Team	Lg	G	GS	CG	GF	IP	BFP	H	R	ER	HR	SH	SF	HB	TBB	IBB	SO	WP	Bk	W	L	Pct.	ShO	Sv	ERA
1988 Bakersfield	A	20	20	1	0	125.1	546	114	54	43	7	7	2	9	77	1	106	5	1	8	3	.727	0	0	3.09
1989 San Antonio	AA	39	0	0	21	62.1	273	61	33	30	2	4	3	2	34	6	52	6	1	1	4	.200	0	4	4.33
Bakersfield	A	17	0	0	16	36	140	21	5	3	0	0	2	2	11	0	44	2	0	6	0	1.000	0	8	0.75
1990 San Antonio	AA	13	0	0	7	16.2	75	20	10	9	0	1	0	0	8	0	15	1	0	3	1	.750	0	4	4.86
1991 San Antonio	AA	34	0	0	22	47.1	199	42	16	11	1	1	0	1	19	8	36	1	0	4	1	.800	0	3	2.09
Albuquerque	AAA	1	0	0	1	1	5	1	0	0	0	0	0	0	1	0	1	0	0	0	0	.000	0	0	0.00
1993 San Antonio	AA	30	0	0	29	31.2	136	34	13	10	1	2	0	1	8	3	25	1	0	1	4	.200	0	12	2.84
Albuquerque	AAA	9	0	0	3	12	42	7	2	2	0	2	1	0	3	0	10	2	0	1	0	1.000	0	2	1.50
1994 Nashville	AAA	39	0	0	24	63.2	268	48	32	20	4	4	0	3	27	6	63	1	0	3	3	.500	0	11	2.83
1995 Nashville	AAA	46	0	0	17	72	315	80	41	38	8	6	3	2	27	5	57	0	0	7	4	.636	0	4	4.75
1995 Chicago	AL	7	0	0	2	6.2	31	9	5	5	3	1	0	0	2	0	8	0	0	0	0	.000	0	0	6.75

Tom Marsh

Bats: Right **Throws:** Right **Pos:** LF   **Ht:** 6'2" **Wt:** 190 **Born:** 12/27/65 **Age:** 30

						BATTING														BASERUNNING				PERCENTAGES		
Year Team	Lg	G	AB	H	2B	3B	HR	(Hm	Rd)	TB	R	RBI	TBB	IBB	SO	HBP	SH	SF	SB	CS	SB%	GDP	Avg	OBP	SLG
1995 Scranton-Wb *	AAA	78	296	91	22	5	10	--	--	153	46	47	13	1	39	4	0	2	9	3	.75	10	.307	.343	.517
1992 Philadelphia	NL	42	125	25	3	2	2	(1	1)	38	7	16	2	0	23	1	2	2	0	1	.00	2	.200	.215	.304

Year	Team	Lg	G	AB	H	2B	3B	HR	(Hm	Rd)	TB	R	RBI	TBB	IBB	SO	HBP	SH	SF	SB	CS	SB%	GDP	Avg	OBP	SLG
1994	Philadelphia	NL	8	18	5	1	1	0	(0	0)	8	3	3	1	0	1	0	1	0	0	0	.00	0	.278	.316	.444
1995	Philadelphia	NL	43	109	32	3	1	3	(1	2)	46	13	15	4	0	25	0	0	1	0	1	.00	1	.294	.316	.422
	3 ML YEARS		93	252	62	7	4	5	(2	3)	92	23	34	7	0	49	1	3	3	0	2	.00	3	.246	.266	.365

Al Martin

Bats: Left **Throws:** Left **Pos:** LF/CF **Ht:** 6' 2" **Wt:** 210 **Born:** 11/24/67 **Age:** 28

			BATTING																BASERUNNING				PERCENTAGES		
Year	Team	Lg	G	AB	H	2B	3B	HR	(Hm | Rd)	TB	R	RBI	TBB	IBB	SO	HBP	SH	SF	SB	CS	SB%	GDP	Avg	OBP	SLG
1992	Pittsburgh	NL	12	12	2	0	1	0	(0 | 0)	4	1	2	0	0	5	0	0	1	0	0	.00	0	.167	.154	.333
1993	Pittsburgh	NL	143	480	135	26	8	18	(15 | 3)	231	85	64	42	5	122	1	2	3	16	9	.64	5	.281	.338	.481
1994	Pittsburgh	NL	82	276	79	12	4	9	(6 | 3)	126	48	33	34	3	56	2	0	1	15	6	.71	3	.286	.367	.457
1995	Pittsburgh	NL	124	439	124	25	3	13	(8 | 5)	194	70	41	44	6	92	2	1	0	20	11	.65	5	.282	.351	.442
	4 ML YEARS		361	1207	340	63	16	40	(29 | 11)	555	204	140	120	14	275	5	3	5	51	26	.66	13	.282	.348	.460

Norberto Martin

Bats: Right **Throws:** Right **Pos:** 2B **Ht:** 5'10" **Wt:** 164 **Born:** 12/10/66 **Age:** 29

			BATTING																BASERUNNING				PERCENTAGES		
Year	Team	Lg	G	AB	H	2B	3B	HR	(Hm	Rd)	TB	R	RBI	TBB	IBB	SO	HBP	SH	SF	SB	CS	SB%	GDP	Avg	OBP	SLG
1993	Chicago	AL	8	14	5	0	0	0	(0	0)	5	3	2	1	0	1	0	0	0	0	0	.00	0	.357	.400	.357
1994	Chicago	AL	45	131	36	7	1	1	(0	1)	48	19	16	9	0	16	0	3	2	4	2	.67	2	.275	.317	.366
1995	Chicago	AL	72	160	43	7	4	2	(1	1)	64	17	17	3	0	25	1	2	3	5	0	1.00	5	.269	.281	.400
	3 ML YEARS		125	305	84	14	5	3	(1	2)	117	39	35	13	0	42	1	5	5	9	2	.82	7	.275	.302	.384

Carlos Martinez

Bats: Right **Throws:** Right **Pos:** 3B **Ht:** 6' 6" **Wt:** 205 **Born:** 8/11/65 **Age:** 30

			BATTING																BASERUNNING				PERCENTAGES		
Year	Team	Lg	G	AB	H	2B	3B	HR	(Hm	Rd)	TB	R	RBI	TBB	IBB	SO	HBP	SH	SF	SB	CS	SB%	GDP	Avg	OBP	SLG
1995	Vancouver *	AAA	25	97	24	3	0	1	--	--	30	17	6	7	2	17	2	0	0	1	2	.33	4	.247	.311	.309
1988	Chicago	AL	17	55	9	1	0	0	(0	0)	10	5	0	0	0	12	0	0	0	1	0	1.00	1	.164	.164	.182
1989	Chicago	AL	109	350	105	22	0	5	(2	3)	142	44	32	21	2	57	1	6	1	4	1	.80	14	.300	.340	.406
1990	Chicago	AL	92	272	61	6	5	4	(2	2)	89	18	24	10	2	40	0	1	0	0	4	.00	8	.224	.252	.327
1991	Cleveland	AL	72	257	73	14	0	5	(3	2)	102	22	30	10	2	43	2	1	5	3	2	.60	10	.284	.310	.397
1992	Cleveland	AL	69	228	60	9	1	5	(2	3)	86	23	35	7	0	21	1	1	4	2	2	.33	5	.263	.283	.377
1993	Cleveland	AL	80	262	64	10	0	5	(2	3)	89	26	31	20	3	29	0	0	3	1	1	.50	5	.244	.295	.340
1995	California	AL	26	61	11	1	0	1	(0	1)	15	7	9	6	2	7	1	0	0	0	0	.00	2	.180	.265	.246
	7 ML YEARS		465	1485	383	63	6	25	(11	14)	533	145	161	74	11	209	5	9	13	10	10	.50	45	.258	.293	.359

Dave Martinez

Bats: Left **Throws:** Left **Pos:** 1B/LF/RF **Ht:** 5'10" **Wt:** 175 **Born:** 9/26/64 **Age:** 31

			BATTING																BASERUNNING				PERCENTAGES		
Year	Team	Lg	G	AB	H	2B	3B	HR	(Hm	Rd)	TB	R	RBI	TBB	IBB	SO	HBP	SH	SF	SB	CS	SB%	GDP	Avg	OBP	SLG
1986	Chicago	NL	53	108	15	1	1	1	(1	0)	21	13	7	6	0	22	1	0	1	4	2	.67	1	.139	.190	.194
1987	Chicago	NL	142	459	134	18	8	8	(5	3)	192	70	36	57	4	96	2	1	1	16	8	.67	4	.292	.372	.418
1988	ChN-Mon	NL	138	447	114	13	6	6	(2	4)	157	51	46	38	8	94	2	2	5	23	9	.72	3	.255	.313	.351
1989	Montreal	NL	126	361	99	16	7	3	(1	2)	138	41	27	27	2	57	0	7	1	23	4	.85	1	.274	.324	.382
1990	Montreal	NL	118	391	109	13	5	11	(5	6)	165	60	39	24	2	48	1	3	2	13	11	.54	8	.279	.321	.422
1991	Montreal	NL	124	396	117	18	5	7	(3	4)	166	47	42	20	3	54	3	5	3	16	7	.70	3	.295	.332	.419
1992	Cincinnati	NL	135	393	100	20	5	3	(3	0)	139	47	31	42	4	54	0	6	4	12	8	.60	6	.254	.323	.354
1993	San Francisco	NL	91	241	58	12	1	5	(1	4)	87	28	27	27	3	39	0	0	0	6	3	.67	5	.241	.317	.361
1994	San Francisco	NL	97	235	58	9	3	4	(1	3)	85	23	27	21	1	22	2	2	0	3	4	.43	6	.247	.314	.362
1995	Chicago	AL	118	303	93	16	4	5	(2	3)	132	49	37	32	2	41	1	9	4	8	2	.80	6	.307	.371	.436
1988	Chicago	NL	75	256	65	10	1	4	(2	2)	89	27	34	21	5	46	2	0	4	7	3	.70	2	.254	.311	.348
	Montreal	NL	63	191	49	3	5	2	(0	2)	68	24	12	17	3	48	0	2	1	16	6	.73	1	.257	.316	.356
	10 ML YEARS		1142	3334	897	136	45	53	(24	29)	1282	429	319	294	29	527	12	35	21	124	58	.68	43	.269	.329	.385

Dennis Martinez

Pitches: Right **Bats:** Right **Pos:** SP **Ht:** 6' 1" **Wt:** 180 **Born:** 5/14/55 **Age:** 41

			HOW MUCH HE PITCHED						WHAT HE GAVE UP										THE RESULTS						
Year	Team	Lg	G	GS	CG	GF	IP	BFP	H	R	ER	HR	SH	SF	HB	TBB	IBB	SO	WP	Bk	W	L	Pct.	ShO	Sv	ERA
1976	Baltimore	AL	4	2	1	1	28	106	23	8	8	1	1	0	0	8	0	18	1	0	1	2	.333	0	0	2.57
1977	Baltimore	AL	42	13	5	19	167	709	157	86	76	10	8	8	8	64	5	107	5	0	14	7	.667	0	4	4.10
1978	Baltimore	AL	40	38	15	0	276	1140	257	121	108	20	8	7	3	93	4	142	8	0	16	11	.593	2	0	3.52
1979	Baltimore	AL	40	39	18	0	292	1206	279	129	119	28	12	12	1	78	1	132	9	2	15	16	.484	3	0	3.67
1980	Baltimore	AL	25	12	2	8	100	428	103	44	44	12	1	3	2	44	6	42	0	1	6	4	.600	0	1	3.96
1981	Baltimore	AL	25	24	9	0	179	753	173	84	66	10	2	5	2	62	1	88	6	1	14	5	.737	2	0	3.32
1982	Baltimore	AL	40	39	10	0	252	1093	262	123	118	30	11	7	7	87	2	111	7	1	16	12	.571	2	0	4.21
1983	Baltimore	AL	32	25	4	3	153	688	209	108	94	21	3	5	2	45	0	71	2	0	7	16	.304	0	0	5.53

Year Team	Lg	G	GS	CG	GF	IP	BFP	H	R	ER	HR	SH	SF	HB	TBB	IBB	SO	WP	Bk	W	L	Pct	ShO	Sv	ERA
1984 Baltimore	AL	34	20	2	4	141.2	599	145	81	79	26	0	5	5	37	2	77	13	0	6	9	.400	0	0	5.02
1985 Baltimore	AL	33	31	3	1	180	789	203	110	103	29	0	11	9	63	3	68	4	1	13	11	.542	1	0	5.15
1986 Bal-Mon		23	15	1	2	104.2	449	114	57	55	11	8	2	3	30	4	65	3	2	3	6	.333	1	0	4.73
1987 Montreal	NL	22	22	2	0	144.2	599	133	59	53	9	4	3	6	40	2	84	4	2	11	4	.733	1	0	3.30
1988 Montreal	NL	34	34	9	0	235.1	968	215	94	71	21	2	6	6	55	3	120	5	10	15	13	.536	2	0	2.72
1989 Montreal	NL	34	33	5	1	232	950	227	88	82	21	8	2	7	49	4	142	5	2	16	7	.696	2	0	3.18
1990 Montreal	NL	32	32	7	0	226	908	191	80	74	16	11	3	6	49	9	156	1	1	10	11	.476	2	0	2.95
1991 Montreal	NL	31	31	9	0	222	905	187	70	59	9	7	3	4	62	3	123	3	0	14	11	.560	5	0	2.39
1992 Montreal	NL	32	32	6	0	226.1	900	172	75	62	12	12	5	9	60	3	147	2	0	16	11	.593	0	0	2.47
1993 Montreal	NL	35	34	2	1	224.2	945	211	110	96	27	10	4	11	64	7	138	2	4	15	9	.625	0	1	3.85
1994 Cleveland	AL	24	24	7	0	176.2	730	166	75	69	14	3	5	7	44	2	92	4	3	11	6	.647	3	0	3.52
1995 Cleveland	AL	28	28	3	0	187	771	174	71	64	17	4	4	12	46	2	99	3	0	12	5	.706	2	0	3.08
1986 Baltimore	AL	4	0	0	1	6.2	33	11	5	5	0	0	1	0	2	0	2	1	0	0	0	.000	0	0	6.75
Montreal	NL	19	15	1	1	98	416	103	52	50	11	8	1	3	28	4	63	2	2	3	6	.333	1	0	4.59
20 ML YEARS		610	528	120	40	3748	15636	3601	1673	1500	344	115	100	110	1080	63	2022	87	30	231	176	.568	28	6	3.60

Edgar Martinez

Bats: Right **Throws:** Right **Pos:** DH **Ht:** 5'11" **Wt:** 190 **Born:** 1/2/63 **Age:** 33

Year Team	Lg	G	AB	H	2B	3B	HR	(Hm	Rd)	TB	R	RBI	TBB	IBB	SO	HBP	SH	SF	SB	CS	SB%	GDP	Avg	OBP	SLG
1987 Seattle	AL	13	43	13	2	0	0	(0	0)	25	6	5	2	0	5	1	0	0	0	0	.00	0	.372	.413	.581
1988 Seattle	AL	14	32	9	4	0	0	(0	0)	13	0	5	4	0	7	0	1	1	0	0	.00	0	.281	.351	.406
1989 Seattle	AL	65	171	41	5	0	2	(0	2)	52	20	20	17	1	26	3	2	3	2	1	.67	3	.240	.314	.304
1990 Seattle	AL	144	487	147	27	2	11	(3	8)	211	71	49	74	3	62	5	1	3	1	4	.20	13	.302	.397	.433
1991 Seattle	AL	150	544	167	35	1	14	(8	6)	246	98	52	84	9	72	8	2	4	0	3	.00	19	.307	.405	.452
1992 Seattle	AL	135	528	181	46	3	18	(11	7)	287	100	73	54	2	61	4	1	5	14	4	.78	15	.343	.404	.544
1993 Seattle	AL	42	135	32	7	0	4	(1	3)	51	20	13	28	1	19	0	1	1	0	0	.00	4	.237	.366	.378
1994 Seattle	AL	89	326	93	23	1	13	(4	9)	157	47	51	53	3	42	3	2	3	6	2	.75	2	.285	.387	.482
1995 Seattle	AL	145	511	182	52	0	29	(16	13)	321	121	113	116	19	87	8	0	4	4	3	.57	11	.356	.479	.628
9 ML YEARS		797	2777	868	204	9	91	(43	48)	1363	483	381	432	38	381	32	10	24	27	17	.61	67	.313	.408	.491

Pedro Martinez

Pitches: Right **Bats:** Right **Pos:** SP **Ht:** 5'11" **Wt:** 170 **Born:** 10/25/71 **Age:** 24

Year Team	Lg	G	GS	CG	GF	IP	BFP	H	R	ER	HR	SH	SF	HB	TBB	IBB	SO	WP	Bk	W	L	Pct	ShO	Sv	ERA
1992 Los Angeles	NL	2	1	0	1	8	31	6	2	2	0	0	0	0	1	0	8	0	0	0	1	.000	0	0	2.25
1993 Los Angeles	NL	65	2	0	21	107	444	76	34	31	5	0	5	4	57	4	119	3	1	10	5	.667	0	2	2.61
1994 Montreal	NL	24	23	1	1	144.2	584	115	58	55	11	2	3	11	45	3	142	6	0	11	5	.688	1	1	3.42
1995 Montreal	NL	30	30	2	0	194.2	784	158	79	76	21	7	3	11	66	1	174	5	2	14	10	.583	2	0	3.51
4 ML YEARS		121	56	3	22	454.1	1843	355	173	164	37	9	11	26	169	8	443	14	3	35	21	.625	3	3	3.25

Pedro A. Martinez

Pitches: Left **Bats:** Right **Pos:** RP **Ht:** 6' 2" **Wt:** 185 **Born:** 9/29/68 **Age:** 27

Year Team	Lg	G	GS	CG	GF	IP	BFP	H	R	ER	HR	SH	SF	HB	TBB	IBB	SO	WP	Bk	W	L	Pct	ShO	Sv	ERA
1995 Tucson *	AAA	20	3	0	6	34	158	44	28	25	2	2	4	2	13	1	21	0	0	1	1	.500	0	2	6.62
1993 San Diego	NL	32	0	0	9	37	148	23	11	10	4	0	0	1	13	1	32	0	0	3	1	.750	0	3	2.43
1994 San Diego	NL	48	1	0	18	68.1	308	52	31	22	4	9	1	1	49	9	52	2	1	3	2	.600	0	3	2.90
1995 Houston	NL	25	0	0	3	20.2	109	29	18	17	3	2	1	2	16	1	17	0	0	0	0	.000	0	0	7.40
3 ML YEARS		105	1	0	30	126	565	104	60	49	11	11	2	4	78	11	101	2	2	6	3	.667	0	3	3.50

Ramon Martinez

Pitches: Right **Bats:** Left **Pos:** SP **Ht:** 6' 4" **Wt:** 186 **Born:** 3/22/68 **Age:** 28

Year Team	Lg	G	GS	CG	GF	IP	BFP	H	R	ER	HR	SH	SF	HB	TBB	IBB	SO	WP	Bk	W	L	Pct	ShO	Sv	ERA
1988 Los Angeles	NL	9	6	0	0	35.2	151	27	17	15	0	4	0	0	22	1	23	1	0	1	3	.250	0	0	3.79
1989 Los Angeles	NL	15	15	2	0	98.2	410	79	39	35	11	4	0	5	41	1	89	1	0	6	4	.600	2	0	3.19
1990 Los Angeles	NL	33	33	12	0	234.1	950	191	89	76	22	7	5	4	67	5	223	3	3	20	6	.769	3	0	2.92
1991 Los Angeles	NL	33	33	6	0	220.1	916	190	89	80	18	8	4	7	69	4	150	6	0	17	13	.567	4	0	3.27
1992 Los Angeles	NL	25	25	1	0	150.2	662	141	82	67	11	12	1	5	69	4	101	9	0	8	11	.421	1	0	4.00
1993 Los Angeles	NL	32	32	4	0	211.2	918	202	88	81	15	12	5	4	104	9	127	2	2	10	12	.455	3	0	3.44
1994 Los Angeles	NL	24	24	4	0	170	718	160	83	75	18	6	8	6	56	2	119	2	0	12	7	.632	3	0	3.97
1995 Los Angeles	NL	30	30	4	0	206.1	859	176	95	84	19	7	5	5	81	5	138	3	0	17	7	.708	2	0	3.66
8 ML YEARS		201	198	33	0	1327.2	5584	1166	582	513	114	60	28	36	509	31	970	27	5	91	63	.591	18	0	3.48

Sandy Martinez

Bats: Left **Throws:** Right **Pos:** C   **Ht:** 6' 4" **Wt:** 200 **Born:** 10/3/72 **Age:** 23

								BATTING												BASERUNNING				PERCENTAGES		
Year Team	Lg	G	AB	H	2B	3B	HR	(Hm	Rd)	TB	R	RBI	TBB	IBB	SO	HBP	SH	SF	SB	CS	SB%	GDP	Avg	OBP	SLG
1991 Dunedin	A	12	38	7	1	0	0	--	--	8	3	3	7	0	7	1	2	0	0	0	.00	0	.184	.326	.211
Medcine Hat	R	34	98	17	1	0	2	--	--	24	8	16	12	1	29	2	2	2	0	1	.00	2	.173	.272	.245
1992 Dunedin	A	4	15	3	1	0	2	--	--	10	4	4	0	0	3	1	0	0	0	0	.00	1	.200	.250	.667
Medcine Hat	R	57	206	52	15	0	4	--	--	79	27	39	14	0	62	1	0	2	0	0	.00	6	.252	.300	.383
1993 Hagerstown	A	94	338	89	16	1	9	--	--	134	41	46	19	0	71	6	0	1	1	1	.50	8	.263	.313	.396
1994 Dunedin	A	122	450	117	14	6	7	--	--	164	50	52	22	1	79	11	3	1	1	3	.25	15	.260	.310	.364
1995 Knoxville	AA	41	144	33	8	1	2	--	--	49	14	22	6	0	34	0	0	2	0	1	.00	1	.229	.257	.340
1995 Toronto	AL	62	191	46	12	0	2	(1	1)	64	12	25	7	0	45	1	0	1	0	0	.00	1	.241	.270	.335

Tino Martinez

Bats: Left **Throws:** Right **Pos:** 1B   **Ht:** 6' 2" **Wt:** 210 **Born:** 12/7/67 **Age:** 28

								BATTING												BASERUNNING				PERCENTAGES		
Year Team	Lg	G	AB	H	2B	3B	HR	(Hm	Rd)	TB	R	RBI	TBB	IBB	SO	HBP	SH	SF	SB	CS	SB%	GDP	Avg	OBP	SLG
1990 Seattle	AL	24	68	15	4	0	0	(0	0)	19	4	5	9	0	9	0	0	1	0	0	.00	0	.221	.308	.279
1991 Seattle	AL	36	112	23	2	0	4	(3	1)	37	11	9	11	0	24	0	0	2	0	0	.00	2	.205	.272	.330
1992 Seattle	AL	136	460	118	19	2	16	(10	6)	189	53	66	42	9	77	2	1	8	2	1	.67	24	.257	.316	.411
1993 Seattle	AL	109	408	108	25	1	17	(9	8)	186	48	60	45	9	56	5	3	3	0	3	.00	7	.265	.343	.456
1994 Seattle	AL	97	329	86	21	0	20	(8	12)	167	42	61	29	2	52	1	4	3	1	2	.33	9	.261	.320	.508
1995 Seattle	AL	141	519	152	35	3	31	(14	17)	286	92	111	62	15	91	4	2	6	0	0	.00	10	.293	.369	.551
6 ML YEARS		543	1896	502	106	6	88	(44	44)	884	250	312	198	35	309	12	10	23	3	6	.33	52	.265	.334	.466

John Marzano

Bats: Right **Throws:** Right **Pos:** C   **Ht:** 5'11" **Wt:** 195 **Born:** 2/14/63 **Age:** 33

								BATTING												BASERUNNING				PERCENTAGES		
Year Team	Lg	G	AB	H	2B	3B	HR	(Hm	Rd)	TB	R	RBI	TBB	IBB	SO	HBP	SH	SF	SB	CS	SB%	GDP	Avg	OBP	SLG
1995 Okla. City *	AAA	120	427	132	41	3	9	--	--	206	55	56	33	2	54	8	0	6	3	4	.43	17	.309	.365	.482
1987 Boston	AL	52	168	41	11	0	5	(4	1)	67	20	24	7	0	41	3	2	2	0	1	.00	3	.244	.283	.399
1988 Boston	AL	10	29	4	1	0	0	(0	0)	5	3	1	1	0	3	0	0	0	0	0	.00	1	.138	.167	.172
1989 Boston	AL	7	18	8	3	0	1	(1	0)	14	5	3	0	0	2	0	1	1	0	0	.00	0	.444	.421	.778
1990 Boston	AL	32	83	20	4	0	0	(0	0)	24	8	6	5	0	10	0	2	1	0	1	.00	0	.241	.281	.289
1991 Boston	AL	49	114	30	8	0	0	(0	0)	38	10	9	1	0	16	1	1	2	0	0	.00	5	.263	.271	.333
1992 Boston	AL	19	50	4	2	1	0	(0	0)	8	4	1	2	0	12	1	1	0	0	0	.00	0	.080	.132	.160
1995 Texas	AL	2	6	2	0	0	0	(0	0)	2	1	0	0	0	0	0	0	0	0	0	.00	0	.333	.333	.333
7 ML YEARS		171	468	109	29	1	6	(5	1)	158	51	44	16	0	84	5	7	6	0	2	.00	10	.233	.263	.338

Dan Masteller

Bats: Left **Throws:** Left **Pos:** 1B/RF   **Ht:** 6' 0" **Wt:** 190 **Born:** 3/17/68 **Age:** 28

								BATTING												BASERUNNING				PERCENTAGES		
Year Team	Lg	G	AB	H	2B	3B	HR	(Hm	Rd)	TB	R	RBI	TBB	IBB	SO	HBP	SH	SF	SB	CS	SB%	GDP	Avg	OBP	SLG
1989 Elizabethtn	R	9	38	13	0	0	2	--	--	19	8	9	6	0	2	0	0	0	0	2	.50	0	.342	.432	.500
Visalia	A	53	181	46	5	1	3	--	--	62	24	16	18	2	36	1	0	1	0	0	.00	2	.254	.323	.343
1990 Visalia	A	135	473	133	20	5	4	--	--	175	71	73	81	0	76	9	4	3	2	5	.29	15	.281	.394	.370
1991 Orlando	AA	124	370	91	14	5	5	--	--	130	44	35	43	6	43	3	3	2	6	4	.60	5	.246	.328	.351
1992 Orlando	AA	116	365	96	24	4	8	--	--	152	42	42	23	1	36	4	3	1	2	4	.33	7	.263	.313	.416
1993 Nashville	AA	36	121	33	3	0	3	--	--	45	19	16	11	0	19	1	2	0	2	1	.67	0	.273	.338	.372
Portland	AAA	61	211	68	13	4	7	--	--	110	35	47	24	3	25	1	1	7	3	4	.43	2	.322	.383	.521
1994 Salt Lake	AAA	98	338	102	26	3	8	--	--	158	53	58	21	1	27	1	2	4	4	1	.80	9	.302	.341	.467
1995 Salt Lake	AAA	48	152	46	10	7	4	--	--	82	25	18	15	3	17	3	1	3	4	1	.80	3	.303	.370	.539
1995 Minnesota	AL	71	198	47	12	0	3	(1	2)	68	21	21	18	0	19	1	1	1	1	2	.33	7	.237	.303	.343

Mike Matheny

Bats: Right **Throws:** Right **Pos:** C   **Ht:** 6' 3" **Wt:** 205 **Born:** 9/22/70 **Age:** 25

								BATTING												BASERUNNING				PERCENTAGES		
Year Team	Lg	G	AB	H	2B	3B	HR	(Hm	Rd)	TB	R	RBI	TBB	IBB	SO	HBP	SH	SF	SB	CS	SB%	GDP	Avg	OBP	SLG
1991 Helena	R	64	255	72	14	0	2	--	--	92	35	34	19	0	51	6	3	1	2	4	.33	10	.282	.345	.361
1992 Stockton	A	106	333	73	13	2	6	--	--	108	42	46	35	1	81	3	5	3	2	2	.50	11	.219	.297	.324
1993 El Paso	AA	107	339	86	21	2	2	--	--	117	39	28	17	2	73	2	13	1	1	4	.20	6	.254	.292	.345
1994 New Orleans	AAA	57	177	39	10	1	4	--	--	63	20	21	16	1	39	4	6	0	1	1	.50	5	.220	.299	.356
1995 New Orleans	AAA	6	17	6	2	0	3	--	--	17	3	4	0	0	5	3	0	0	0	0	.00	0	.353	.450	1.000
1994 Milwaukee	AL	28	53	12	3	0	1	(1	0)	18	3	2	3	0	13	2	1	0	0	1	.00	1	.226	.293	.340
1995 Milwaukee	AL	80	166	41	9	1	0	(0	0)	52	13	21	12	0	28	2	1	0	2	1	.67	3	.247	.306	.313
2 ML YEARS		108	219	53	12	1	1	(1	0)	70	16	23	15	0	41	4	2	0	2	2	.50	4	.242	.303	.320

T.J. Mathews

Pitches: Right **Bats:** Right **Pos:** RP **Ht:** 6' 2" **Wt:** 200 **Born:** 1/19/70 **Age:** 26

			HOW MUCH HE PITCHED						WHAT HE GAVE UP									THE RESULTS				
Year Team	Lg	G	GS	CG	GF	IP	BFP	H	R	ER	HR	SH	SF	HB	TBB	IBB	SO	WP	Bk	W	L	Pct.	ShO	Sv	ERA
1992 Hamilton	A	14	14	1	0	86.2	351	70	25	21	4	3	0	2	30	0	89	4	2	10	1	.909	0	0	2.18
1993 Springfield	A	25	25	5	0	159.1	634	121	59	48	7	7	4	6	29	0	144	1	3	12	9	.571	2	0	2.71
1994 St. Pete	A	11	11	1	0	66.1	270	52	22	18	1	1	0	2	23	0	62	1	1	5	5	.500	0	0	2.44
Arkansas	AA	16	16	1	0	97	395	83	37	34	8	6	2	6	24	1	93	1	0	5	5	.500	0	0	3.15
1995 Louisville	AAA	32	7	0	10	66.2	298	60	35	20	2	0	3	3	27	2	50	1	0	9	4	.692	0	1	2.70
1995 St. Louis	NL	23	0	0	12	29.2	120	21	7	5	1	4	0	0	11	1	28	2	0	1	1	.500	0	2	1.52

Terry Mathews

Pitches: Right **Bats:** Left **Pos:** RP **Ht:** 6' 2" **Wt:** 225 **Born:** 10/5/64 **Age:** 31

			HOW MUCH HE PITCHED						WHAT HE GAVE UP									THE RESULTS				
Year Team	Lg	G	GS	CG	GF	IP	BFP	H	R	ER	HR	SH	SF	HB	TBB	IBB	SO	WP	Bk	W	L	Pct.	ShO	Sv	ERA
1995 Charlotte *	AAA	2	0	0	0	3.2	15	5	2	2	0	0	0	0	0	0	5	0	0	0	0	.000	0	0	4.91
1991 Texas	AL	34	2	0	8	57.1	236	54	24	23	5	2	0	1	18	3	51	5	0	4	0	1.000	0	1	3.61
1992 Texas	AL	40	0	0	11	42.1	199	48	29	28	4	1	3	1	31	3	26	2	1	2	4	.333	0	0	5.95
1994 Florida	NL	24	2	0	5	43	179	45	16	16	4	1	0	1	9	1	21	1	0	2	1	.667	0	0	3.35
1995 Florida	NL	57	0	0	14	82.2	332	70	32	31	9	5	1	1	27	4	72	3	0	4	4	.500	0	3	3.38
4 ML YEARS		155	4	0	38	225.1	946	217	101	98	22	9	4	4	85	11	170	11	1	12	9	.571	0	4	3.91

Don Mattingly

Bats: Left **Throws:** Left **Pos:** 1B **Ht:** 6' 0" **Wt:** 200 **Born:** 4/20/61 **Age:** 35

			BATTING														BASERUNNING				PERCENTAGES		
Year Team	Lg	G	AB	H	2B	3B	HR	(Hm | Rd)	TB	R	RBI	TBB	IBB	SO	HBP	SH	SF	SB	CS	SB%	GDP	Avg	OBP	SLG
1982 New York	AL	7	12	2	0	0	0	(0 | 0)	2	0	1	0	0	1	0	0	1	0	0	.00	2	.167	.154	.167
1983 New York	AL	91	279	79	15	4	4	(0 | 4)	114	34	32	21	5	31	1	2	2	0	0	.00	8	.283	.333	.409
1984 New York	AL	153	603	207	44	2	23	(12 | 11)	324	91	110	41	8	33	1	8	9	1	1	.50	15	.343	.381	.537
1985 New York	AL	159	652	211	48	3	35	(22 | 13)	370	107	145	56	13	41	2	2	15	2	2	.50	15	.324	.371	.567
1986 New York	AL	162	677	238	53	2	31	(17 | 14)	388	117	113	53	11	35	1	1	10	0	0	.00	17	.352	.394	.573
1987 New York	AL	141	569	186	38	2	30	(17 | 13)	318	93	115	51	13	38	1	0	8	1	4	.20	16	.327	.378	.559
1988 New York	AL	144	599	186	37	0	18	(11 | 7)	277	94	88	41	14	29	3	0	8	1	0	1.00	13	.311	.353	.462
1989 New York	AL	158	631	191	37	2	23	(19 | 4)	301	79	113	51	18	30	1	0	10	3	0	1.00	13	.303	.351	.477
1990 New York	AL	102	394	101	16	0	5	(4 | 1)	132	40	42	28	13	20	3	0	3	1	0	1.00	13	.256	.308	.335
1991 New York	AL	152	587	169	35	0	9	(7 | 2)	231	64	68	46	11	42	4	0	9	2	0	1.00	21	.288	.339	.394
1992 New York	AL	157	640	184	40	0	14	(6 | 8)	266	89	86	39	7	43	1	0	6	3	0	1.00	11	.288	.327	.416
1993 New York	AL	134	530	154	27	2	17	(8 | 9)	236	78	86	61	9	42	2	0	3	0	0	.00	20	.291	.364	.445
1994 New York	AL	97	372	113	20	1	6	(3 | 3)	153	62	51	60	7	24	0	0	4	0	0	.00	8	.304	.397	.411
1995 New York	AL	128	458	132	32	2	7	(5 | 2)	189	59	49	40	7	35	1	0	8	0	2	.00	17	.288	.341	.413
14 ML YEARS		1785	7003	2153	442	20	222	(131 | 91)	3301	1007	1099	588	136	444	21	13	96	14	9	.61	191	.307	.358	.471

Tim Mauser

Pitches: Right **Bats:** Right **Pos:** RP **Ht:** 6' 0" **Wt:** 195 **Born:** 10/4/66 **Age:** 29

			HOW MUCH HE PITCHED						WHAT HE GAVE UP									THE RESULTS				
Year Team	Lg	G	GS	CG	GF	IP	BFP	H	R	ER	HR	SH	SF	HB	TBB	IBB	SO	WP	Bk	W	L	Pct.	ShO	Sv	ERA
1995 Las Vegas *	AAA	35	0	0	15	50.2	233	63	39	27	6	4	13	1	20	2	32	1	0	3	4	.429	0	0	4.80
1991 Philadelphia	NL	3	0	0	1	10.2	53	18	10	9	3	1	0	0	3	0	6	0	0	0	0	.000	0	0	7.59
1993 Phi-SD	NL	36	0	0	16	54	235	51	28	24	6	1	1	1	24	5	46	2	0	0	1	.000	0	0	4.00
1994 San Diego	NL	35	0	0	12	49	211	50	21	19	3	2	3	1	19	3	32	5	1	2	4	.333	0	2	3.49
1995 San Diego	NL	5	0	0	1	5.2	30	4	6	6	0	0	0	0	9	0	9	0	0	0	1	.000	0	0	9.53
1993 Philadelphia	NL	8	0	0	1	16.1	71	15	9	9	1	0	1	0	7	0	14	1	0	0	0	.000	0	0	4.96
San Diego	NL	28	0	0	15	37.2	164	36	19	15	5	1	1	0	17	5	32	1	0	0	1	.000	0	0	3.58
4 ML YEARS		79	0	0	30	119.1	529	123	65	58	12	4	4	2	55	8	93	7	1	2	6	.250	0	2	4.37

Brian Maxcy

Pitches: Right **Bats:** Right **Pos:** RP **Ht:** 6' 1" **Wt:** 170 **Born:** 5/4/71 **Age:** 25

			HOW MUCH HE PITCHED						WHAT HE GAVE UP									THE RESULTS				
Year Team	Lg	G	GS	CG	GF	IP	BFP	H	R	ER	HR	SH	SF	HB	TBB	IBB	SO	WP	Bk	W	L	Pct.	ShO	Sv	ERA
1992 Bristol	R	14	7	2	7	49.1	204	41	24	19	4	0	2	0	17	1	43	3	1	4	2	.667	2	3	3.47
1993 Fayetteville	A	39	12	1	20	113.2	501	111	51	37	2	5	3	13	42	3	101	5	0	12	4	.750	1	9	2.93
1994 Trenton	AA	5	0	0	2	10.2	45	6	1	0	0	0	0	1	4	0	5	0	0	0	0	.000	0	1	0.00
Toledo	AAA	24	1	0	6	44.1	182	31	12	8	1	2	1	0	18	1	43	1	0	2	3	.400	0	3	1.62
1995 Toledo	AAA	20	0	0	9	25.2	120	32	20	15	3	4	0	1	11	1	11	3	0	1	3	.250	0	2	5.26
1995 Detroit	AL	41	0	0	14	52.1	247	61	48	40	6	3	3	2	31	7	20	6	2	4	5	.444	0	0	6.88

Darrell May

Pitches: Left **Bats:** Left **Pos:** RP **Ht:** 6' 2" **Wt:** 170 **Born:** 6/13/72 **Age:** 24

		HOW MUCH HE PITCHED						WHAT HE GAVE UP												THE RESULTS					
Year Team	Lg	G	GS	CG	GF	IP	BFP	H	R	ER	HR	SH	SF	HB	TBB	IBB	SO	WP	Bk	W	L	Pct.	ShO	Sv	ERA
1992 Braves	R	12	7	0	4	53	204	34	13	8	0	2	0	2	13	0	61	2	1	4	3	.571	0	1	1.36
1993 Macon	A	17	17	0	0	104.1	404	81	29	26	6	0	0	1	22	1	111	3	0	10	4	.714	0	0	2.24
Durham	A	9	9	0	0	51.2	213	44	18	12	4	4	2	1	16	0	47	2	1	5	2	.714	0	0	2.09
1994 Durham	A	12	12	1	0	74.2	307	74	29	25	6	0	1	3	17	1	73	3	0	8	2	.800	0	0	3.01
Greenville	AA	11	11	1	0	63.2	265	61	25	22	4	1	2	2	17	0	42	6	0	5	3	.625	0	0	3.11
1995 Greenville	AA	15	15	0	0	91.1	377	81	44	36	18	2	5	3	20	0	79	4	0	2	8	.200	0	0	3.55
Richmond	AAA	9	9	0	0	51	216	53	21	21	1	1	3	0	16	1	42	2	0	4	2	.667	0	0	3.71
1995 Atlanta	NL	2	0	0	1	4	21	10	5	5	0	0	1	0	0	0	1	0	0	0	0	.000	0	0	11.25

Derrick May

Bats: Left **Throws:** Right **Pos:** LF/RF **Ht:** 6' 4" **Wt:** 225 **Born:** 7/14/68 **Age:** 27

		BATTING																BASERUNNING				PERCENTAGES		
Year Team	Lg	G	AB	H	2B	3B	HR	(Hm	Rd)	TB	R	RBI	TBB	IBB	SO	HBP	SH	SF	SB	CS	SB%	GDP	Avg	OBP	SLG
1990 Chicago	NL	17	61	15	3	0	1	(1	0)	21	8	11	2	0	7	0	0	0	1	0	1.00	1	.246	.270	.344
1991 Chicago	NL	15	22	5	2	0	1	(1	0)	10	4	3	2	0	1	0	0	1	0	0	.00	1	.227	.280	.455
1992 Chicago	NL	124	351	96	11	0	8	(3	5)	131	33	45	14	4	40	3	2	1	5	3	.63	10	.274	.306	.373
1993 Chicago	NL	128	465	137	25	2	10	(3	7)	196	62	77	31	6	41	1	0	6	10	3	.77	15	.295	.336	.422
1994 Chicago	NL	100	345	98	19	2	8	(5	3)	145	43	51	30	4	34	0	1	2	3	2	.60	11	.284	.340	.420
1995 Mil-Hou		110	319	90	18	2	9	(4	5)	139	44	50	24	0	42	2	0	3	5	1	.83	5	.282	.333	.436
1995 Milwaukee	AL	32	113	28	3	1	1	(1	0)	36	15	9	5	0	18	1	0	0	0	1	.00	1	.248	.286	.319
Houston	NL	78	206	62	15	1	8	(3	5)	103	29	41	19	0	24	1	0	3	5	0	1.00	4	.301	.358	.500
6 ML YEARS		494	1563	441	78	6	37	(17	20)	642	194	237	103	14	165	6	3	13	24	9	.73	43	.282	.326	.411

Brent Mayne

Bats: Left **Throws:** Right **Pos:** C **Ht:** 6' 1" **Wt:** 190 **Born:** 4/19/68 **Age:** 28

		BATTING																BASERUNNING				PERCENTAGES		
Year Team	Lg	G	AB	H	2B	3B	HR	(Hm	Rd)	TB	R	RBI	TBB	IBB	SO	HBP	SH	SF	SB	CS	SB%	GDP	Avg	OBP	SLG
1990 Kansas City	AL	5	13	3	0	0	0	(0	0)	3	2	1	3	0	3	0	0	0	0	1	.00	0	.231	.375	.231
1991 Kansas City	AL	85	231	58	8	0	3	(2	1)	75	22	31	23	4	42	0	2	3	2	4	.33	6	.251	.315	.325
1992 Kansas City	AL	82	213	48	10	0	0	(0	0)	58	16	18	11	0	26	0	2	3	0	4	.00	5	.225	.260	.272
1993 Kansas City	AL	71	205	52	9	1	2	(0	2)	69	22	22	18	7	31	1	3	0	3	2	.60	6	.254	.317	.337
1994 Kansas City	AL	46	144	37	5	1	2	(1	1)	50	19	20	14	1	27	0	0	0	1	0	1.00	3	.257	.323	.347
1995 Kansas City	AL	110	307	77	18	1	1	(1	0)	100	23	27	25	1	41	3	11	1	0	1	.00	16	.251	.313	.326
6 ML YEARS		399	1113	275	50	3	8	(4	4)	355	104	119	94	13	170	4	18	7	6	12	.33	36	.247	.306	.319

Jamie McAndrew

Pitches: Right **Bats:** Right **Pos:** RP/SP **Ht:** 6' 2" **Wt:** 190 **Born:** 9/2/67 **Age:** 28

		HOW MUCH HE PITCHED						WHAT HE GAVE UP												THE RESULTS					
Year Team	Lg	G	GS	CG	GF	IP	BFP	H	R	ER	HR	SH	SF	HB	TBB	IBB	SO	WP	Bk	W	L	Pct.	ShO	Sv	ERA
1989 Great Falls	R	13	13	1	0	76.1	296	49	16	14	5	2	0	4	27	0	72	2	0	11	0	1.000	0	0	1.65
1990 Bakersfield	A	14	14	1	0	95	388	88	31	24	2	1	0	5	29	1	82	6	4	10	3	.769	1	0	2.27
San Antonio	AA	12	12	0	0	79.1	327	69	28	18	2	3	1	4	32	2	50	1	0	7	3	.700	0	0	2.04
1991 Albuquerque	AAA	28	26	0	2	155.1	691	167	105	87	11	5	2	3	76	1	91	7	5	12	10	.545	0	1	5.04
1992 Albuquerque	AAA	5	5	0	0	29.1	137	41	20	19	1	3	1	0	14	0	9	0	1	1	3	.250	0	0	5.83
San Antonio	AA	11	8	0	1	50.1	215	50	26	20	2	1	1	1	19	2	35	0	0	3	4	.429	0	0	3.58
1993 New Orleans	AAA	27	25	5	0	166.2	693	172	78	73	19	1	6	2	45	3	97	5	2	11	6	.647	1	0	3.94
1995 New Orleans	AAA	17	17	3	0	104.1	443	102	48	46	8	1	3	2	44	1	62	1	1	7	5	.583	1	0	3.97
1995 Milwaukee	AL	10	4	0	2	36.1	153	37	21	19	2	1	0	1	12	2	19	0	0	2	3	.400	0	0	4.71

Dave McCarty

Bats: Right **Throws:** Left **Pos:** 1B **Ht:** 6' 5" **Wt:** 213 **Born:** 11/23/69 **Age:** 26

		BATTING																BASERUNNING				PERCENTAGES		
Year Team	Lg	G	AB	H	2B	3B	HR	(Hm	Rd)	TB	R	RBI	TBB	IBB	SO	HBP	SH	SF	SB	CS	SB%	GDP	Avg	OBP	SLG
1995 Indianapolis *	AAA	37	140	47	10	1	8	(--	--)	83	31	32	15	0	30	1	1	1	0	0	.00	5	.336	.401	.593
Phoenix *	AAA	37	151	53	19	2	4	(--	--)	88	31	19	17	1	27	6	0	1	1	1	.50	6	.351	.434	.583
1993 Minnesota	AL	98	350	75	15	2	2	(2	0)	100	36	21	19	0	80	1	1	0	2	6	.25	13	.214	.257	.286
1994 Minnesota	AL	44	131	34	8	2	1	(1	0)	49	21	12	7	1	32	5	0	0	1	1	.67	3	.260	.322	.374
1995 Min-SF		37	75	17	4	1	0	(0	0)	23	11	6	6	0	22	1	0	1	1	1	.50	1	.227	.289	.307
1995 Minnesota	AL	25	55	12	3	1	0	(0	0)	17	10	4	4	0	18	1	0	1	0	1	.00	1	.218	.279	.309
San Francisco	NL	12	20	5	1	0	0	(0	0)	6	1	2	2	0	4	0	0	0	1	0	1.00	0	.250	.318	.300
3 ML YEARS		179	556	126	27	5	3	(3	0)	172	68	39	32	1	134	7	1	1	5	8	.38	17	.227	.277	.309

Kirk McCaskill

Pitches: Right **Bats:** Right **Pos:** RP   **Ht:** 6' 1" **Wt:** 205 **Born:** 4/9/61 **Age:** 35

		HOW MUCH HE PITCHED					WHAT HE GAVE UP										THE RESULTS					
Year Team	Lg	G	GS	CG	GF	IP	BFP	H	R	ER	HR	SH	SF	HB	TBB	IBB	SO	WP	Bk	W	L	Pct.	ShO	Sv	ERA
1985 California	AL	30	29	6	0	189.2	807	189	105	99	23	2	5	4	64	1	102	5	0	12	12	.500	1	0	4.70
1986 California	AL	34	33	10	1	246.1	1013	207	98	92	19	6	5	5	92	1	202	10	2	17	10	.630	2	0	3.36
1987 California	AL	14	13	1	0	74.2	334	84	52	47	14	3	1	2	34	0	56	1	0	4	6	.400	1	0	5.67
1988 California	AL	23	23	4	0	146.1	635	155	78	70	9	1	6	1	61	3	98	13	2	8	6	.571	2	0	4.31
1989 California	AL	32	32	6	0	212	864	202	73	69	16	3	4	3	59	1	107	7	2	15	10	.600	4	0	2.93
1990 California	AL	29	29	2	0	174.1	738	161	77	63	9	3	1	2	72	1	78	6	1	12	11	.522	1	0	3.25
1991 California	AL	30	30	1	0	177.2	762	193	93	84	19	6	6	3	66	1	71	6	0	10	19	.345	0	0	4.26
1992 Chicago	AL	34	34	0	0	209	911	193	116	97	11	7	7	6	95	5	109	6	2	12	13	.480	0	0	4.18
1993 Chicago	AL	30	14	0	6	113.2	502	144	71	66	12	2	3	1	36	6	65	6	0	4	8	.333	0	2	5.23
1994 Chicago	AL	40	0	0	18	52.2	228	51	22	20	6	1	3	0	22	4	37	1	0	1	4	.200	0	3	3.42
1995 Chicago	AL	55	1	0	17	81	365	97	50	44	10	3	3	5	33	4	50	10	0	6	4	.600	0	2	4.89
11 ML YEARS		351	238	30	42	1677.1	7159	1676	835	751	148	37	44	32	634	27	975	71	9	101	103	.495	11	7	4.03

Quinton McCracken

Bats: Both **Throws:** Right **Pos:** CF   **Ht:** 5' 7" **Wt:** 170 **Born:** 3/16/70 **Age:** 26

		BATTING																BASERUNNING				PERCENTAGES		
Year Team	Lg	G	AB	H	2B	3B	HR	(Hm	Rd)	TB	R	RBI	TBB	IBB	SO	HBP	SH	SF	SB	CS	SB%	GDP	Avg	OBP	SLG
1992 Bend	A	67	232	65	13	2	0	--	--	82	37	27	25	0	39	0	7	2	18	6	.75	6	.280	.347	.353
1993 Central Val	A	127	483	141	17	7	2	--	--	178	94	58	78	4	90	2	12	4	60	19	.76	15	.292	.390	.369
1994 New Haven	AA	136	544	151	27	4	5	--	--	201	94	39	48	4	72	4	10	4	36	19	.65	6	.278	.338	.369
1995 New Haven	AA	55	221	79	11	4	1	--	--	101	33	26	21	3	32	3	1	1	26	8	.76	2	.357	.419	.457
Colo. Sprng	AAA	61	244	88	14	6	3	--	--	123	55	28	23	3	30	1	2	0	17	6	.74	1	.361	.418	.504
1995 Colorado	NL	3	1	0	0	0	0	(0	0)	0	0	0	0	0	1	0	0	0	0	0	.00	0	.000	.000	.000

Jeff McCurry

Pitches: Right **Bats:** Right **Pos:** RP   **Ht:** 6' 7" **Wt:** 210 **Born:** 1/21/70 **Age:** 26

		HOW MUCH HE PITCHED					WHAT HE GAVE UP										THE RESULTS					
Year Team	Lg	G	GS	CG	GF	IP	BFP	H	R	ER	HR	SH	SF	HB	TBB	IBB	SO	WP	Bk	W	L	Pct.	ShO	Sv	ERA
1991 Pirates	R	6	1	0	0	14	68	19	10	4	0	0	1	2	4	0	8	2	1	1	0	1.000	0	0	2.57
Welland	A	9	0	0	5	15.2	70	11	4	1	0	3	0	0	10	3	18	5	1	2	1	.667	0	0	0.57
1992 Augusta	A	19	0	0	13	30	142	36	14	11	1	6	1	3	15	1	34	4	1	2	1	.667	0	7	3.30
Salem	A	30	0	0	15	62.2	255	49	22	20	3	4	2	3	24	3	52	7	0	6	2	.750	0	3	2.87
1993 Salem	A	41	0	0	36	44	184	41	21	19	3	3	3	0	15	3	32	5	0	1	4	.200	0	22	3.89
Carolina	AA	23	0	0	5	29	121	24	11	9	1	2	1	0	14	2	14	2	0	2	1	.667	0	0	2.79
1994 Carolina	AA	48	2	0	32	81.1	350	74	35	29	7	5	1	6	30	3	60	9	1	6	5	.545	0	11	3.21
1995 Calgary	AAA	3	0	0	0	5	22	3	1	1	0	0	0	2	2	0	2	0	0	0	0	.000	0	0	1.80
1995 Pittsburgh	NL	55	0	0	10	61	282	82	38	34	9	4	0	5	30	4	27	2	0	1	4	.200	0	1	5.02

Ray McDavid

Bats: Left **Throws:** Right **Pos:** CF   **Ht:** 6' 2" **Wt:** 200 **Born:** 7/20/71 **Age:** 24

		BATTING																BASERUNNING				PERCENTAGES		
Year Team	Lg	G	AB	H	2B	3B	HR	(Hm	Rd)	TB	R	RBI	TBB	IBB	SO	HBP	SH	SF	SB	CS	SB%	GDP	Avg	OBP	SLG
1990 Padres	R	13	41	6	0	2	0	--	--	10	4	1	6	1	5	0	1	0	3	2	.60	1	.146	.255	.244
1991 Charlstn-Sc	A	127	425	105	16	9	10	--	--	169	93	45	106	1	119	8	0	0	60	14	.81	3	.247	.406	.398
1992 High Desert	A	123	428	118	22	5	24	--	--	222	94	94	94	1	126	7	3	6	43	9	.83	3	.276	.409	.519
1993 Wichita	AA	126	441	119	18	5	11	--	--	180	65	55	70	6	104	6	0	8	33	17	.66	6	.270	.371	.408
1994 Las Vegas	AAA	128	476	129	24	6	13	--	--	204	85	62	67	4	110	8	1	1	24	15	.62	9	.271	.370	.429
1995	R	9	28	13	2	1	1	--	--	20	13	6	8	0	7	0	0	0	3	1	.75	0	.464	.583	.714
Las Vegas	AAA	52	166	45	8	1	5	--	--	70	28	27	30	0	35	4	0	1	7	1	.88	2	.271	.393	.422
1994 San Diego	NL	9	28	7	1	0	0	(0	0)	8	2	2	1	0	8	0	0	0	0	0	1.00	1	.250	.276	.286
1995 San Diego	NL	11	17	3	0	0	0	(0	0)	3	2	0	2	0	6	0	0	0	1	1	.50	1	.176	.263	.176
2 ML YEARS		20	45	10	1	0	0	(0	0)	11	4	2	3	0	14	0	0	0	2	1	.67	1	.222	.271	.244

Ben McDonald

Pitches: Right **Bats:** Right **Pos:** SP   **Ht:** 6' 7" **Wt:** 214 **Born:** 11/24/67 **Age:** 28

		HOW MUCH HE PITCHED					WHAT HE GAVE UP										THE RESULTS					
Year Team	Lg	G	GS	CG	GF	IP	BFP	H	R	ER	HR	SH	SF	HB	TBB	IBB	SO	WP	Bk	W	L	Pct.	ShO	Sv	ERA
1995 Rochester *	AAA	1	1	0	0	3.2	17	1	2	1	0	0	0	0	4	0	1	1	0	0	0	.000	0	0	2.45
1989 Baltimore	AL	6	0	0	2	7.1	33	8	7	7	2	0	1	0	4	0	3	1	1	1	0	1.000	0	0	8.59
1990 Baltimore	AL	21	15	3	2	118.2	472	88	36	32	9	3	5	0	35	0	65	5	0	8	5	.615	2	0	2.43
1991 Baltimore	AL	21	21	1	0	126.1	532	126	71	68	16	2	3	1	43	2	85	3	0	6	8	.429	0	0	4.84
1992 Baltimore	AL	35	35	4	0	227	958	213	113	107	32	6	6	9	74	5	158	3	2	13	13	.500	2	0	4.24
1993 Baltimore	AL	34	34	7	0	220.1	914	185	92	83	17	7	4	5	86	4	171	7	1	13	14	.481	1	0	3.39

147

1994 Baltimore	AL	24	24	5	0	157.1	655	151	75	71	14	6	1	2	54	2	94	3	1	14	7	.667	1	0	4.06
1995 Baltimore	AL	14	13	1	1	80	342	67	40	37	10	0	2	3	38	3	62	4	2	3	6	.333	0	0	4.16
7 ML YEARS		155	142	21	5	937	3906	838	434	405	100	24	22	20	334	16	638	26	7	58	53	.523	6	0	3.89

Jack McDowell

Pitches: Right **Bats:** Right **Pos:** SP **Ht:** 6' 5" **Wt:** 188 **Born:** 1/16/66 **Age:** 30

		HOW MUCH HE PITCHED						WHAT HE GAVE UP												THE RESULTS					
Year Team	Lg	G	GS	CG	GF	IP	BFP	H	R	ER	HR	SH	SF	HB	TBB	IBB	SO	WP	Bk	W	L	Pct.	ShO	Sv	ERA
1987 Chicago	AL	4	4	0	0	28	103	16	6	6	1	0	2	0	6	0	15	0	0	3	0	1.000	0	0	1.93
1988 Chicago	AL	26	26	1	0	158.2	687	147	85	70	12	6	7	7	68	5	84	11	1	5	10	.333	0	0	3.97
1990 Chicago	AL	33	33	4	0	205	866	189	93	87	20	1	5	7	77	0	165	7	1	14	9	.609	0	0	3.82
1991 Chicago	AL	35	35	15	0	253.2	1028	212	97	96	19	8	4	4	82	2	191	10	1	17	10	.630	3	0	3.41
1992 Chicago	AL	34	34	13	0	260.2	1079	247	95	92	21	8	6	7	75	9	178	6	0	20	10	.667	1	0	3.18
1993 Chicago	AL	34	34	10	0	256.2	1067	261	104	96	20	8	6	3	69	6	158	8	1	22	10	.688	4	0	3.37
1994 Chicago	AL	25	25	6	0	181	755	186	82	75	12	4	4	5	42	2	127	4	0	10	9	.526	2	0	3.73
1995 New York	AL	30	30	8	0	217.2	927	211	106	95	25	8	6	5	78	1	157	9	1	15	10	.600	2	0	3.93
8 ML YEARS		221	221	57	0	1561.1	6512	1469	668	617	130	43	38	40	497	25	1075	55	5	106	68	.609	12	0	3.56

Roger McDowell

Pitches: Right **Bats:** Right **Pos:** RP **Ht:** 6' 1" **Wt:** 195 **Born:** 12/21/60 **Age:** 35

		HOW MUCH HE PITCHED						WHAT HE GAVE UP												THE RESULTS					
Year Team	Lg	G	GS	CG	GF	IP	BFP	H	R	ER	HR	SH	SF	HB	TBB	IBB	SO	WP	Bk	W	L	Pct.	ShO	Sv	ERA
1985 New York	NL	62	2	0	36	127.1	516	108	43	40	9	6	2	1	37	8	70	6	2	6	5	.545	0	17	2.83
1986 New York	NL	75	0	0	52	128	524	107	48	43	4	7	3	3	42	5	65	3	3	14	9	.609	0	22	3.02
1987 New York	NL	56	0	0	45	88.2	384	95	41	41	7	5	5	2	28	4	32	3	1	7	5	.583	0	25	4.16
1988 New York	NL	62	0	0	41	89	378	80	31	26	1	3	5	3	31	7	46	6	1	5	5	.500	0	16	2.63
1989 NYN-Phi	NL	69	0	0	56	92	387	79	36	20	3	6	1	3	38	8	47	3	1	4	8	.333	0	23	1.96
1990 Philadelphia	NL	72	0	0	60	86.1	373	92	41	37	2	10	4	2	35	9	39	1	1	6	8	.429	0	22	3.86
1991 LA-Phi	NL	71	0	0	34	101.1	445	100	40	33	4	11	3	2	48	20	50	2	0	9	9	.500	0	10	2.93
1992 Los Angeles	NL	65	0	0	39	83.2	393	103	46	38	3	10	3	1	42	13	50	4	1	6	10	.375	0	14	4.09
1993 Los Angeles	NL	54	0	0	19	68	300	76	32	17	2	3	1	2	30	10	27	5	0	5	3	.625	0	2	2.25
1994 Los Angeles	NL	32	0	0	11	41.1	193	50	25	24	3	5	0	1	22	6	29	3	0	0	3	.000	0	0	5.23
1995 Texas	AL	64	0	0	26	85	362	86	39	38	5	6	5	6	34	7	49	1	1	7	4	.636	0	4	4.02
1989 New York	NL	25	0	0	15	35.1	156	34	21	13	1	3	1	2	16	3	15	3	1	1	5	.167	0	4	3.31
Philadelphia	NL	44	0	0	41	56.2	231	45	15	7	2	3	0	1	22	5	32	0	0	3	3	.500	0	19	1.11
1991 Los Angeles	NL	33	0	0	18	42.1	174	39	12	12	3	4	2	0	16	8	22	1	0	6	3	.667	0	7	2.55
Philadelphia	NL	38	0	0	16	59	271	61	28	21	1	7	1	2	32	12	28	1	0	3	6	.333	0	3	3.20
11 ML YEARS		682	2	0	419	990.2	4255	976	422	357	43	72	32	26	387	97	504	37	11	69	69	.500	0	155	3.24

Chuck McElroy

Pitches: Left **Bats:** Left **Pos:** RP **Ht:** 6' 0" **Wt:** 195 **Born:** 10/1/67 **Age:** 28

		HOW MUCH HE PITCHED						WHAT HE GAVE UP												THE RESULTS					
Year Team	Lg	G	GS	CG	GF	IP	BFP	H	R	ER	HR	SH	SF	HB	TBB	IBB	SO	WP	Bk	W	L	Pct.	ShO	Sv	ERA
1989 Philadelphia	NL	11	0	0	4	10.1	46	12	2	2	1	0	0	0	4	1	8	0	0	0	0	.000	0	0	1.74
1990 Philadelphia	NL	16	0	0	8	14	76	24	13	12	0	0	1	0	10	2	16	0	0	0	1	.000	0	0	7.71
1991 Chicago	NL	71	0	0	12	101.1	419	73	33	22	7	9	6	0	57	7	92	1	0	6	2	.750	0	3	1.95
1992 Chicago	NL	72	0	0	30	83.2	369	73	40	33	5	5	5	0	51	10	83	3	0	4	7	.364	0	6	3.55
1993 Chicago	NL	49	0	0	11	47.1	214	51	30	24	4	5	1	1	25	5	31	3	0	2	2	.500	0	0	4.56
1994 Cincinnati	NL	52	0	0	13	57.2	230	52	15	15	3	2	0	0	15	2	38	4	0	1	2	.333	0	5	2.34
1995 Cincinnati	NL	44	0	0	11	40.1	178	46	29	27	5	1	3	1	15	3	27	1	0	3	4	.429	0	0	6.02
7 ML YEARS		315	0	0	89	354.2	1532	331	162	135	25	22	16	2	177	30	295	12	0	16	18	.471	0	14	3.43

Willie McGee

Bats: Both **Throws:** Right **Pos:** RF/CF **Ht:** 6' 1" **Wt:** 185 **Born:** 11/2/58 **Age:** 37

		BATTING																		BASERUNNING				PERCENTAGES		
Year Team	Lg	G	AB	H	2B	3B	HR	(Hm	Rd)	TB	R	RBI	TBB	IBB	SO	HBP	SH	SF	SB	CS	SB%	GDP	Avg	OBP	SLG
1995 Pawtucket *	AAA	5	21	10	0	0	0	--	--	10	9	2	0	0	4	0	0	0	2	0	1.00	0	.476	.476	.476
1982 St. Louis	NL	123	422	125	12	8	4	(2	2)	165	43	56	12	2	58	2	2	1	24	12	.67	9	.296	.318	.391
1983 St. Louis	NL	147	601	172	22	8	5	(4	1)	225	75	75	26	2	98	0	1	3	39	8	.83	8	.286	.314	.374
1984 St. Louis	NL	145	571	166	19	11	6	(2	4)	225	82	50	29	2	80	1	0	3	43	10	.81	12	.291	.325	.394
1985 St. Louis	NL	152	612	216	26	18	10	(3	7)	308	114	82	34	2	86	0	1	5	56	16	.78	3	.353	.384	.503
1986 St. Louis	NL	124	497	127	22	7	7	(7	0)	184	65	48	37	7	82	1	0	4	19	16	.54	8	.256	.306	.370
1987 St. Louis	NL	153	620	177	37	11	11	(6	5)	269	76	105	24	5	90	2	1	5	16	4	.80	24	.285	.312	.434
1988 St. Louis	NL	137	562	164	24	6	3	(1	2)	209	73	50	32	5	84	1	2	3	41	6	.87	10	.292	.329	.372
1989 St. Louis	NL	58	199	47	10	2	3	(1	2)	70	23	17	10	0	34	1	0	1	8	6	.57	2	.236	.275	.352
1990 Oak-StL		154	614	199	35	7	3	(1	2)	257	99	77	48	6	104	1	0	2	31	9	.78	13	.324	.373	.419

148

Year Team	Lg	G	AB	H	2B	3B	HR	(Hm	Rd)	TB	R	RBI	TBB	IBB	SO	HBP	SH	SF	SB	CS	SB%	GDP	Avg	OBP	SLG
1991 San Francisco	NL	131	497	155	30	3	4	(2	2)	203	67	43	34	3	74	2	8	2	17	9	.65	11	.312	.357	.408
1992 San Francisco	NL	138	474	141	20	2	1	(0	1)	168	56	36	29	3	88	1	5	1	13	4	.76	7	.297	.339	.354
1993 San Francisco	NL	130	475	143	28	1	4	(0	4)	185	53	46	38	7	67	1	3	2	10	9	.53	12	.301	.353	.389
1994 San Francisco	NL	45	156	44	3	0	5	(2	3)	62	19	23	15	2	24	0	1	4	3	0	1.00	8	.282	.337	.397
1995 Boston	AL	67	200	57	11	3	2	(1	1)	80	32	15	9	0	41	0	5	3	5	2	.71	5	.285	.311	.400
1990 Oakland	AL	29	113	31	3	2	0	(0	0)	38	23	15	10	0	18	0	0	0	3	0	1.00	4	.274	.333	.336
St. Louis	NL	125	501	168	32	5	3	(1	2)	219	76	62	38	6	86	1	0	2	28	9	.76	9	.335	.382	.437
14 ML YEARS		1704	6500	1933	299	87	68	(32	36)	2610	877	723	377	46	1010	13	29	39	325	111	.75	132	.297	.335	.402

Russ McGinnis

Bats: Right **Throws:** Right **Pos:** 1B **Ht:** 6' 3" **Wt:** 225 **Born:** 6/18/63 **Age:** 33

Year Team	Lg	G	AB	H	2B	3B	HR	(Hm	Rd)	TB	R	RBI	TBB	IBB	SO	HBP	SH	SF	SB	CS	SB%	GDP	Avg	OBP	SLG
1985 Helena	R	48	150	46	7	0	5	--	--	68	33	38	31	1	19	4	0	2	2	2	.50	5	.307	.433	.453
1986 Beloit	A	124	413	102	24	2	16	--	--	178	62	59	52	2	79	12	3	4	5	2	.71	13	.247	.345	.431
1987 Beloit	A	51	189	58	10	0	13	--	--	107	34	35	19	2	36	2	1	0	1	2	.33	4	.307	.376	.566
Modesto	A	47	165	42	9	0	8	--	--	75	24	31	23	1	33	2	3	3	1	1	.50	4	.255	.347	.455
1988 Huntsville	AA	23	77	20	9	0	2	--	--	35	9	15	7	0	13	0	0	0	1	0	1.00	1	.260	.321	.455
Tacoma	AAA	63	186	47	13	1	2	--	--	68	25	22	21	0	38	1	3	1	1	0	1.00	7	.253	.330	.366
1989 Tacoma	AAA	110	380	105	25	0	7	--	--	151	42	60	45	0	78	6	2	5	0	1	.00	6	.276	.358	.397
1990 Tacoma	AAA	110	359	89	19	1	13	--	--	149	57	77	75	2	70	6	1	7	2	1	.67	15	.248	.380	.415
1991 Iowa	AAA	111	374	105	18	2	15	--	--	172	70	70	63	6	68	6	1	4	3	1	.75	12	.281	.389	.460
1992 Okla. City	AAA	99	330	87	19	1	18	--	--	162	63	51	79	1	52	7	2	2	0	6	.00	15	.264	.414	.491
1993 Omaha	AAA	78	275	80	20	2	16	--	--	152	53	54	42	1	44	7	0	5	1	0	1.00	11	.291	.392	.553
1994 Omaha	AAA	98	344	97	21	1	24	--	--	192	73	70	64	1	64	14	0	5	1	3	.25	11	.282	.410	.558
1995 Rochester	AAA	20	55	10	2	0	3	--	--	21	8	11	17	0	19	2	0	3	0	0	.00	4	.182	.377	.382
1992 Texas	AL	14	33	8	4	0	0	(0	0)	12	2	4	3	0	7	0	0	0	0	0	.00	1	.242	.306	.364
1995 Kansas City	AL	3	5	0	0	0	0	(0	0)	0	1	0	1	0	1	0	0	0	0	0	.00	0	.000	.167	.000
2 ML YEARS		17	38	8	4	0	0	(0	0)	12	3	4	4	0	8	0	0	0	0	0	.00	1	.211	.286	.316

Fred McGriff

Bats: Left **Throws:** Left **Pos:** 1B **Ht:** 6' 3" **Wt:** 215 **Born:** 10/31/63 **Age:** 32

Year Team	Lg	G	AB	H	2B	3B	HR	(Hm	Rd)	TB	R	RBI	TBB	IBB	SO	HBP	SH	SF	SB	CS	SB%	GDP	Avg	OBP	SLG
1986 Toronto	AL	3	5	1	0	0	0	(0	0)	1	1	0	0	0	2	0	0	0	0	0	.00	0	.200	.200	.200
1987 Toronto	AL	107	295	73	16	0	20	(7	13)	149	58	43	60	4	104	1	0	0	3	2	.60	3	.247	.376	.505
1988 Toronto	AL	154	536	151	35	4	34	(18	16)	296	100	82	79	3	149	4	0	4	6	1	.86	15	.282	.376	.552
1989 Toronto	AL	161	551	148	27	3	36	(18	18)	289	98	92	119	12	132	4	1	5	7	4	.64	14	.269	.399	.525
1990 Toronto	AL	153	557	167	21	1	35	(14	21)	295	91	88	94	12	108	2	1	4	5	3	.63	7	.300	.400	.530
1991 San Diego	NL	153	528	147	19	1	31	(18	13)	261	84	106	105	26	135	2	0	7	4	1	.80	14	.278	.396	.494
1992 San Diego	NL	152	531	152	30	4	35	(21	14)	295	79	104	96	23	108	1	0	4	8	6	.57	14	.286	.394	.556
1993 Atl-SD	NL	151	557	162	29	2	37	(15	22)	306	111	101	76	6	106	2	0	5	5	3	.63	14	.291	.375	.549
1994 Atlanta	NL	113	424	135	25	1	34	(13	21)	264	81	94	50	8	76	1	0	3	7	3	.70	8	.318	.389	.623
1995 Atlanta	NL	144	528	148	27	1	27	(15	12)	258	85	93	65	6	99	5	0	6	3	6	.33	19	.280	.361	.489
1993 Atlanta	NL	68	255	79	18	1	19	(8	11)	156	59	55	34	2	51	1	0	1	1	0	1.00	5	.310	.392	.612
San Diego	NL	83	302	83	11	1	18	(7	11)	150	52	46	42	4	55	1	0	4	4	3	.57	9	.275	.361	.497
10 ML YEARS		1291	4512	1284	229	17	289	(139	150)	2414	788	803	744	100	1019	22	2	38	48	29	.62	108	.285	.386	.535

Mark McGwire

Bats: Right **Throws:** Right **Pos:** 1B **Ht:** 6' 5" **Wt:** 250 **Born:** 10/1/63 **Age:** 32

Year Team	Lg	G	AB	H	2B	3B	HR	(Hm	Rd)	TB	R	RBI	TBB	IBB	SO	HBP	SH	SF	SB	CS	SB%	GDP	Avg	OBP	SLG
1986 Oakland	AL	18	53	10	1	0	3	(1	2)	20	10	9	4	0	18	1	0	0	0	1	.00	0	.189	.259	.377
1987 Oakland	AL	151	557	161	28	4	49	(21	28)	344	97	118	71	8	131	5	0	8	1	1	.50	6	.289	.370	.618
1988 Oakland	AL	155	550	143	22	1	32	(12	20)	263	87	99	76	4	117	4	1	4	0	0	.00	15	.260	.352	.478
1989 Oakland	AL	143	490	113	17	0	33	(12	21)	229	74	95	83	5	94	3	0	11	1	1	.50	23	.231	.339	.467
1990 Oakland	AL	156	523	123	16	0	39	(14	25)	256	87	108	110	9	116	7	1	9	2	1	.67	13	.235	.370	.489
1991 Oakland	AL	154	483	97	22	0	22	(15	7)	185	62	75	93	3	116	3	1	5	2	1	.67	13	.201	.330	.383
1992 Oakland	AL	139	467	125	22	0	42	(24	18)	273	87	104	90	12	105	5	0	9	0	1	.00	10	.268	.385	.585
1993 Oakland	AL	27	84	28	6	0	9	(5	4)	61	16	24	21	5	19	1	0	1	0	1	.00	0	.333	.467	.726
1994 Oakland	AL	47	135	34	3	0	9	(6	3)	64	26	25	37	3	40	0	0	3	0	0	.00	3	.252	.413	.474
1995 Oakland	AL	104	317	87	13	0	39	(15	24)	217	75	90	88	5	77	11	0	6	1	1	.50	9	.274	.441	.685
10 ML YEARS		1094	3659	921	150	5	277	(125	152)	1912	621	747	673	54	833	40	3	53	7	8	.47	92	.252	.369	.523

Mark McLemore

Bats: Both   **Throws:** Right   **Pos:** LF/2B   **Ht:** 5'11"   **Wt:** 207   **Born:** 10/4/64   **Age:** 31

Year	Team	Lg	G	AB	H	2B	3B	HR	(Hm	Rd)	TB	R	RBI	TBB	IBB	SO	HBP	SH	SF	SB	CS	SB%	GDP	Avg	OBP	SLG
1986	California	AL	5	4	0	0	0	0	(0	0)	0	0	0	1	0	2	0	1	0	0	1	.00	0	.000	.200	.000
1987	California	AL	138	433	102	13	3	3	(3	0)	130	61	41	48	0	72	0	15	3	25	8	.76	7	.236	.310	.300
1988	California	AL	77	233	56	11	2	2	(1	1)	77	38	16	25	0	28	0	5	2	13	7	.65	6	.240	.312	.330
1989	California	AL	32	103	25	3	1	0	(0	0)	30	12	14	7	0	19	1	3	1	6	1	.86	2	.243	.295	.291
1990	Cal-Cle	AL	28	60	9	2	0	0	(0	0)	11	6	2	4	0	15	0	1	0	1	0	1.00	1	.150	.203	.183
1991	Houston	NL	21	61	9	1	0	0	(0	0)	10	6	2	6	0	13	0	0	1	0	1	.00	1	.148	.221	.164
1992	Baltimore	AL	101	228	56	7	2	0	(0	0)	67	40	27	21	1	26	0	6	1	11	5	.69	6	.246	.308	.294
1993	Baltimore	AL	148	581	165	27	5	4	(2	2)	214	81	72	64	4	92	1	11	6	21	15	.58	21	.284	.353	.368
1994	Baltimore	AL	104	343	88	11	1	3	(2	1)	110	44	29	51	3	50	1	4	1	20	5	.80	7	.257	.354	.321
1995	Texas	AL	129	467	122	20	5	5	(3	2)	167	73	41	59	6	71	3	10	3	21	11	.66	10	.261	.346	.358
1990	Texas	AL	20	48	7	2	0	0	(0	0)	9	4	2	4	0	9	0	1	0	1	0	1.00	1	.146	.212	.188
	Cleveland	AL	8	12	2	0	0	0	(0	0)	2	2	0	0	0	6	0	0	0	0	0	.00	0	.167	.167	.167
	10 ML YEARS		783	2513	632	95	19	17	(11	6)	816	361	244	286	14	388	6	56	18	118	54	.69	61	.251	.327	.325

Greg McMichael

Pitches: Right   **Bats:** Right   **Pos:** RP   **Ht:** 6'3"   **Wt:** 215   **Born:** 12/1/66   **Age:** 29

			HOW MUCH HE PITCHED						WHAT HE GAVE UP									THE RESULTS					
Year	Team	Lg	G	GS	CG	GF	IP	BFP	H	R	ER	HR	SH	SF	HB	TBB	IBB	SO	WP	Bk	W	L	Pct.	ShO	Sv	ERA
1993	Atlanta	NL	74	0	0	40	91.2	365	68	22	21	3	4	2	0	29	4	89	6	1	2	3	.400	0	19	2.06
1994	Atlanta	NL	51	0	0	41	58.2	259	66	29	25	1	3	1	0	19	6	47	3	1	4	6	.400	0	21	3.84
1995	Atlanta	NL	67	0	0	16	80.2	337	64	27	25	8	5	0	0	32	9	74	3	0	7	2	.778	0	2	2.79
	3 ML YEARS		192	0	0	97	231	961	198	78	71	12	12	3	0	80	19	210	12	2	13	11	.542	0	42	2.77

Craig McMurtry

Pitches: Right   **Bats:** Right   **Pos:** RP   **Ht:** 6'5"   **Wt:** 192   **Born:** 11/5/59   **Age:** 36

			HOW MUCH HE PITCHED						WHAT HE GAVE UP									THE RESULTS					
Year	Team	Lg	G	GS	CG	GF	IP	BFP	H	R	ER	HR	SH	SF	HB	TBB	IBB	SO	WP	Bk	W	L	Pct.	ShO	Sv	ERA
1995	Tucson *	AAA	13	13	1	0	69.2	275	54	11	10	2	3	1	4	19	1	41	5	0	6	1	.857	0	0	1.29
1983	Atlanta	NL	36	35	6	0	224.2	943	204	86	77	13	9	5	1	88	1	105	1	2	15	9	.625	3	0	3.08
1984	Atlanta	NL	37	30	0	1	183.1	811	184	100	88	16	12	9	1	102	4	99	4	3	9	17	.346	0	0	4.32
1985	Atlanta	NL	17	6	0	3	45	220	56	36	33	6	7	2	1	27	1	28	3	0	0	3	.000	0	1	6.60
1986	Atlanta	NL	37	5	0	5	79.2	356	82	46	42	7	0	2	2	43	5	50	2	0	1	6	.143	0	0	4.74
1988	Texas	AL	32	0	0	14	60	236	37	16	15	5	3	3	1	24	4	35	2	2	3	3	.500	0	3	2.25
1989	Texas	AL	19	0	0	4	23	111	29	21	19	3	1	2	1	13	1	14	1	1	0	0	.000	0	0	7.43
1990	Texas	AL	23	3	0	6	41.2	188	43	25	20	4	2	2	1	30	0	14	3	0	0	3	.000	0	0	4.32
1995	Houston	NL	11	0	0	3	10.1	56	15	11	9	2	2	2	1	9	1	4	2	0	0	1	.000	0	0	7.84
	8 ML YEARS		212	79	6	36	667.2	2921	650	341	303	54	36	27	10	336	17	349	18	8	28	42	.400	3	4	4.08

Brian McRae

Bats: Both   **Throws:** Right   **Pos:** CF   **Ht:** 6'0"   **Wt:** 195   **Born:** 8/27/67   **Age:** 28

Year	Team	Lg	G	AB	H	2B	3B	HR	(Hm	Rd)	TB	R	RBI	TBB	IBB	SO	HBP	SH	SF	SB	CS	SB%	GDP	Avg	OBP	SLG
1990	Kansas City	AL	46	168	48	8	3	2	(1	1)	68	21	23	9	0	29	0	3	2	4	3	.57	5	.286	.318	.405
1991	Kansas City	AL	152	629	164	28	9	8	(3	5)	234	86	64	24	1	99	2	3	5	20	11	.65	12	.261	.288	.372
1992	Kansas City	AL	149	533	119	23	5	4	(2	2)	164	63	52	42	1	88	6	7	4	18	5	.78	10	.223	.285	.308
1993	Kansas City	AL	153	627	177	28	9	12	(5	7)	259	78	69	37	1	105	4	14	3	23	14	.62	8	.282	.325	.413
1994	Kansas City	AL	114	436	119	22	6	4	(2	2)	165	71	40	54	3	67	6	6	3	28	8	.78	3	.273	.359	.378
1995	Chicago	NL	137	580	167	38	7	12	(6	6)	255	92	48	47	1	92	7	3	1	27	8	.77	12	.288	.348	.440
	6 ML YEARS		751	2973	794	147	39	42	(19	23)	1145	411	296	213	7	480	25	36	18	120	49	.71	50	.267	.320	.385

Rusty Meacham

Pitches: Right   **Bats:** Right   **Pos:** RP   **Ht:** 6'2"   **Wt:** 175   **Born:** 1/27/68   **Age:** 28

			HOW MUCH HE PITCHED						WHAT HE GAVE UP									THE RESULTS					
Year	Team	Lg	G	GS	CG	GF	IP	BFP	H	R	ER	HR	SH	SF	HB	TBB	IBB	SO	WP	Bk	W	L	Pct.	ShO	Sv	ERA
1991	Detroit	AL	10	4	0	1	27.2	126	35	17	16	4	1	3	0	11	0	14	0	1	2	1	.667	0	0	5.20
1992	Kansas City	AL	64	0	0	20	101.2	412	88	33	31	5	3	9	1	21	5	64	4	0	10	4	.714	0	2	2.74
1993	Kansas City	AL	15	0	0	11	21	104	31	15	13	2	0	1	0	5	1	13	0	0	2	2	.500	0	0	5.57
1994	Kansas City	AL	36	0	0	15	50.2	213	51	23	21	7	1	4	2	12	1	36	4	0	3	3	.500	0	4	3.73
1995	Kansas City	AL	49	0	0	26	59.2	262	72	36	33	6	1	4	1	19	5	30	0	0	4	3	.571	0	2	4.98
	5 ML YEARS		174	4	0	73	260.2	1117	277	130	114	24	6	21	7	68	12	157	8	1	21	13	.618	0	8	3.94

Pat Meares

Bats: Right **Throws:** Right **Pos:** SS   **Ht:** 6' 0" **Wt:** 188 **Born:** 9/6/68 **Age:** 27

Year Team	Lg	G	AB	H	2B	3B	HR	(Hm	Rd)	TB	R	RBI	TBB	IBB	SO	HBP	SH	SF	SB	CS	SB%	GDP	Avg	OBP	SLG
1993 Minnesota	AL	111	346	87	14	3	0	(0	0)	107	33	33	7	0	52	1	4	3	4	5	.44	11	.251	.266	.309
1994 Minnesota	AL	80	229	61	12	1	2	(0	2)	81	29	24	14	0	50	2	6	3	5	1	.83	3	.266	.310	.354
1995 Minnesota	AL	116	390	105	19	4	12	(3	9)	168	57	49	15	0	68	11	4	5	10	4	.71	17	.269	.311	.431
3 ML YEARS		307	965	253	45	8	14	(3	11)	356	119	106	36	0	170	14	14	11	19	10	.66	31	.262	.295	.369

Jim Mecir

Pitches: Right **Bats:** Both **Pos:** RP   **Ht:** 6' 1" **Wt:** 195 **Born:** 5/16/70 **Age:** 26

Year Team	Lg	G	GS	CG	GF	IP	BFP	H	R	ER	HR	SH	SF	HB	TBB	IBB	SO	WP	Bk	W	L	Pct.	ShO	Sv	ERA
1991 San Bernrdo	A	14	12	0	2	70.1	314	72	40	33	3	2	3	3	37	0	48	8	4	3	5	.375	0	1	4.22
1992 San Bernrdo	A	14	11	0	1	61.2	283	72	40	32	8	1	2	5	26	0	53	5	1	4	5	.444	0	0	4.67
1993 Riverside	A	26	26	1	0	145.1	654	160	89	70	3	3	8	15	58	2	85	4	0	9	11	.450	0	0	4.33
1994 Jacksonville	AA	46	0	0	34	80.1	343	73	28	24	5	4	2	4	35	3	53	6	0	6	5	.545	0	13	2.69
1995 Tacoma	AAA	40	0	0	22	69.2	298	63	29	24	3	3	1	1	28	7	46	5	0	1	4	.200	0	8	3.10
1995 Seattle	AL	2	0	0	1	4.2	21	5	1	0	0	0	0	0	2	0	3	0	0	0	0	.000	0	0	0.00

Roberto Mejia

Bats: Right **Throws:** Right **Pos:** 2B   **Ht:** 5'11" **Wt:** 165 **Born:** 4/14/72 **Age:** 24

Year Team	Lg	G	AB	H	2B	3B	HR	(Hm	Rd)	TB	R	RBI	TBB	IBB	SO	HBP	SH	SF	SB	CS	SB%	GDP	Avg	OBP	SLG
1995 Colo. Sprng *	AAA	38	143	42	10	2	2	--	--	62	18	14	7	2	29	1	2	0	0	2	.00	6	.294	.331	.434
1993 Colorado	NL	65	229	53	14	5	5	(3	2)	92	31	20	13	1	63	1	4	1	4	1	.80	2	.231	.275	.402
1994 Colorado	NL	38	116	28	8	1	4	(1	3)	50	11	14	15	2	33	0	0	1	3	1	.75	1	.241	.326	.431
1995 Colorado	NL	23	52	8	1	0	1	(1	0)	12	5	4	0	0	17	1	0	0	0	1	.00	1	.154	.167	.231
3 ML YEARS		126	397	89	23	6	10	(5	5)	154	47	38	28	3	113	2	4	3	7	3	.70	4	.224	.277	.388

Paul Menhart

Pitches: Right **Bats:** Right **Pos:** RP/SP   **Ht:** 6' 2" **Wt:** 190 **Born:** 3/25/69 **Age:** 27

Year Team	Lg	G	GS	CG	GF	IP	BFP	H	R	ER	HR	SH	SF	HB	TBB	IBB	SO	WP	Bk	W	L	Pct.	ShO	Sv	ERA
1990 St. Cathrns	A	8	8	0	0	40	180	34	27	18	2	1	1	5	19	0	38	6	2	0	5	.000	0	0	4.05
Myrtle Bch	A	5	4	1	1	30.2	113	18	5	2	1	1	0	0	5	0	18	1	0	3	0	1.000	0	0	0.59
1991 Dunedin	A	20	20	3	0	128.1	521	114	42	38	3	2	2	3	34	0	114	4	1	10	6	.625	0	0	2.66
1992 Knoxville	AA	28	28	2	0	177.2	735	181	85	76	14	2	6	11	38	0	104	12	1	10	11	.476	1	0	3.85
1993 Syracuse	AAA	25	25	4	0	151	646	143	74	61	16	4	3	7	67	4	108	8	1	9	10	.474	0	0	3.64
1995 Syracuse	AAA	10	10	0	0	51.1	234	62	42	36	5	2	3	0	25	0	30	3	1	2	4	.333	0	0	6.31
1995 Toronto	AL	21	9	1	6	78.2	350	72	49	43	9	3	4	6	47	4	50	6	0	1	4	.200	0	0	4.92

Orlando Merced

Bats: Left **Throws:** Right **Pos:** RF/1B   **Ht:** 5'11" **Wt:** 185 **Born:** 11/2/66 **Age:** 29

Year Team	Lg	G	AB	H	2B	3B	HR	(Hm	Rd)	TB	R	RBI	TBB	IBB	SO	HBP	SH	SF	SB	CS	SB%	GDP	Avg	OBP	SLG
1990 Pittsburgh	NL	25	24	5	1	0	0	(0	0)	6	3	0	1	0	9	0	0	0	0	0	.00	1	.208	.240	.250
1991 Pittsburgh	NL	120	411	113	17	2	10	(5	5)	164	83	50	64	4	81	1	1	1	8	4	.67	6	.275	.373	.399
1992 Pittsburgh	NL	134	405	100	28	5	6	(4	2)	156	50	60	52	8	63	2	1	5	5	4	.56	6	.247	.332	.385
1993 Pittsburgh	NL	137	447	140	26	4	8	(3	5)	198	68	70	77	10	64	1	0	2	3	3	.50	9	.313	.414	.443
1994 Pittsburgh	NL	108	386	105	21	3	9	(4	5)	159	48	51	42	5	58	1	0	2	4	1	.80	17	.272	.343	.412
1995 Pittsburgh	NL	132	487	146	29	4	15	(8	7)	228	75	83	52	9	74	1	0	5	7	2	.78	9	.300	.365	.468
6 ML YEARS		656	2160	609	122	18	48	(24	24)	911	327	314	288	36	349	6	2	15	27	14	.66	48	.282	.366	.422

Henry Mercedes

Bats: Right **Throws:** Right **Pos:** C   **Ht:** 5'11" **Wt:** 185 **Born:** 7/23/69 **Age:** 26

Year Team	Lg	G	AB	H	2B	3B	HR	(Hm	Rd)	TB	R	RBI	TBB	IBB	SO	HBP	SH	SF	SB	CS	SB%	GDP	Avg	OBP	SLG
1988 Athletics	R	2	5	2	0	0	0	--	--	2	1	0	0	0	0	0	0	0	0	0	.00	0	.400	.400	.400
1989 Madison	A	51	152	32	3	0	2	--	--	41	11	13	22	1	46	1	3	0	0	0	.00	1	.211	.314	.270
Modesto	A	16	37	3	0	0	1	--	--	6	6	3	7	0	22	0	0	0	0	0	.00	0	.081	.227	.162
Sou. Oregon	A	22	61	10	0	1	0	--	--	12	6	1	10	0	24	1	0	0	2	0	.00	0	.164	.292	.197
1990 Tacoma	AAA	12	31	6	1	0	0	--	--	7	3	2	3	0	7	0	2	0	0	1	.00	2	.194	.265	.226
Madison	A	90	282	64	13	2	3	--	--	90	29	38	30	0	100	1	6	2	6	0	1.00	5	.227	.302	.319
1991 Modesto	A	116	388	100	17	3	4	--	--	135	55	61	68	1	110	2	3	3	5	8	.38	6	.258	.369	.348
1992 Tacoma	AAA	85	246	57	9	2	0	--	--	70	36	20	26	0	60	0	4	0		3	.25	8	.232	.305	.285

Year Team	Lg	G	AB	H	2B	3B	HR	(Hm	Rd)	TB	R	RBI	TBB	IBB	SO	HBP	SH	SF	SB	CS	SB%	GDP	Avg	OBP	SLG
1993 Tacoma	AAA	85	256	61	13	1	4	--	--	88	37	32	31	2	53	1	3	7	1	2	.33	8	.238	.315	.344
1994 Tacoma	AAA	66	205	39	5	1	1	--	--	49	16	17	13	0	60	0	5	3	1	2	.33	6	.190	.235	.239
1995 Omaha	AAA	86	275	59	12	0	11	--	--	104	37	37	22	0	90	3	6	1	2	0	1.00	7	.215	.279	.378
1992 Oakland	AL	9	5	4	0	1	0	(0	0)	6	1	1	0	0	1	0	0	0	0	0	.00	0	.800	.800	1.200
1993 Oakland	AL	20	47	10	2	0	0	(0	0)	12	5	3	2	0	15	1	0	0	1	1	.50	0	.213	.260	.255
1995 Kansas City	AL	23	43	11	2	0	0	(0	0)	13	7	9	8	0	13	1	1	2	0	0	.00	0	.256	.370	.302
3 ML YEARS		52	95	25	4	1	0	(0	0)	31	13	13	10	0	29	2	1	2	1	1	.50	0	.263	.339	.326

Jose Mercedes

Pitches: Right **Bats:** Right **Pos:** RP **Ht:** 6' 1" **Wt:** 199 **Born:** 3/5/71 **Age:** 25

			HOW MUCH HE PITCHED						WHAT HE GAVE UP											THE RESULTS					
Year Team	Lg	G	GS	CG	GF	IP	BFP	H	R	ER	HR	SH	SF	HB	TBB	IBB	SO	WP	Bk	W	L	Pct.	ShO	Sv	ERA
1992 Orioles	R	8	5	2	1	35.1	143	31	12	7	0	0	1	1	13	0	21	5	1	2	3	.400	0	0	1.78
Kane County	A	8	8	2	0	47.1	199	40	26	14	1	2	0	0	15	0	45	6	2	3	2	.600	2	0	2.66
1993 Bowie	AA	26	23	3	0	147	659	170	86	78	13	6	3	2	65	0	75	9	1	6	8	.429	1	0	4.78
1994 El Paso	AA	3	0	0	0	9.2	44	13	6	5	1	0	1	0	4	0	8	1	0	2	0	1.000	0	0	4.66
New Orleans	AAA	3	3	0	0	18.1	81	19	10	10	1	0	0	2	8	0	7	1	0	0	0	.000	0	0	4.91
1994 Milwaukee	AL	19	0	0	5	31	120	22	9	8	4	0	0	2	16	1	11	0	1	2	0	1.000	0	0	2.32
1995 Milwaukee	AL	5	0	0	0	7.1	42	12	9	8	1	0	2	0	8	0	6	1	0	0	1	.000	0	0	9.82
2 ML YEARS		24	0	0	5	38.1	162	34	18	16	5	0	2	2	24	1	17	1	1	2	1	.667	0	0	3.76

Kent Mercker

Pitches: Left **Bats:** Left **Pos:** SP **Ht:** 6' 2" **Wt:** 195 **Born:** 2/1/68 **Age:** 28

			HOW MUCH HE PITCHED						WHAT HE GAVE UP											THE RESULTS					
Year Team	Lg	G	GS	CG	GF	IP	BFP	H	R	ER	HR	SH	SF	HB	TBB	IBB	SO	WP	Bk	W	L	Pct.	ShO	Sv	ERA
1989 Atlanta	NL	2	1	0	1	4.1	26	8	6	6	0	0	0	0	6	0	4	0	0	0	0	.000	0	0	12.46
1990 Atlanta	NL	36	0	0	28	48.1	211	43	22	17	6	1	2	2	24	3	39	2	0	4	7	.364	0	7	3.17
1991 Atlanta	NL	50	4	0	28	73.1	306	56	23	21	5	2	2	1	35	3	62	4	1	5	3	.625	0	6	2.58
1992 Atlanta	NL	53	0	0	18	68.1	289	51	27	26	4	4	1	3	35	1	49	6	0	3	2	.600	0	6	3.42
1993 Atlanta	NL	43	6	0	9	66	283	52	24	21	2	0	0	2	36	3	59	5	1	3	1	.750	0	0	2.86
1994 Atlanta	NL	20	17	2	0	112.1	461	90	46	43	16	4	3	0	45	3	111	4	1	9	4	.692	1	0	3.45
1995 Atlanta	NL	29	26	0	1	143	622	140	73	66	16	8	7	3	61	2	102	6	2	7	8	.467	0	0	4.15
7 ML YEARS		233	54	2	85	515.2	2198	440	221	200	49	19	15	11	242	15	426	27	5	31	25	.554	1	19	3.49

Matt Merullo

Bats: Left **Throws:** Right **Pos:** C/DH **Ht:** 6' 2" **Wt:** 200 **Born:** 8/4/65 **Age:** 30

			BATTING																BASERUNNING				PERCENTAGES		
Year Team	Lg	G	AB	H	2B	3B	HR	(Hm	Rd)	TB	R	RBI	TBB	IBB	SO	HBP	SH	SF	SB	CS	SB%	GDP	Avg	OBP	SLG
1989 Chicago	AL	9	22	5	1	0	1	(1	0)	22	5	8	6	0	14	0	2	1	0	1	.00	2	.222	.273	.272
1991 Chicago	AL	80	140	32	1	0	5	(1	4)	48	8	21	9	1	18	0	1	4	0	0	.00	1	.229	.268	.343
1992 Chicago	AL	24	50	9	1	1	0	(0	0)	12	3	3	1	0	8	1	0	1	0	0	.00	0	.180	.208	.240
1993 Chicago	AL	8	20	1	0	0	0	(0	0)	1	1	0	0	0	1	0	1	0	0	0	.00	1	.050	.050	.050
1994 Cleveland	AL	4	10	1	0	0	0	(0	0)	1	1	0	2	0	1	0	1	0	0	0	.00	0	.100	.250	.100
1995 Minnesota	AL	76	195	55	14	1	1	(1	0)	74	19	27	14	0	27	3	1	3	0	1	.00	5	.282	.335	.379
6 ML YEARS		223	496	116	17	2	7	(3	4)	158	37	59	32	1	69	4	6	9	0	2	.00	9	.234	.281	.319

Jose Mesa

Pitches: Right **Bats:** Right **Pos:** RP **Ht:** 6' 3" **Wt:** 225 **Born:** 5/22/66 **Age:** 30

			HOW MUCH HE PITCHED						WHAT HE GAVE UP											THE RESULTS					
Year Team	Lg	G	GS	CG	GF	IP	BFP	H	R	ER	HR	SH	SF	HB	TBB	IBB	SO	WP	Bk	W	L	Pct.	ShO	Sv	ERA
1987 Baltimore	AL	6	5	0	0	31.1	143	38	23	21	7	0	0	0	15	0	17	4	0	1	3	.250	0	0	6.03
1990 Baltimore	AL	7	7	0	0	46.2	202	37	20	20	2	2	2	1	27	2	24	1	1	3	2	.600	0	0	3.86
1991 Baltimore	AL	23	23	2	0	123.2	566	151	86	82	11	5	4	3	62	2	64	3	0	6	11	.353	1	0	5.97
1992 Bal-Cle	AL	28	27	1	1	160.2	700	169	86	82	14	2	5	4	70	1	62	2	0	7	12	.368	1	0	4.59
1993 Cleveland	AL	34	33	3	0	208.2	897	232	122	114	21	9	9	7	62	2	118	8	2	10	12	.455	0	0	4.92
1994 Cleveland	AL	51	0	0	22	73	315	71	33	31	3	3	4	3	26	7	63	3	0	7	5	.583	0	2	3.82
1995 Cleveland	AL	62	0	0	57	64	250	49	9	8	3	4	2	0	17	2	58	5	0	3	0	1.000	0	46	1.13
1992 Baltimore	AL	13	12	0	1	67.2	300	77	41	39	9	0	3	2	27	1	22	2	0	3	8	.273	0	0	5.19
Cleveland		15	15	1	0	93	400	92	45	43	5	2	2	2	43	0	40	0	0	4	4	.500	1	0	4.16
7 ML YEARS		211	95	6	80	708	3073	747	379	358	61	25	26	18	279	16	406	26	3	37	45	.451	2	48	4.55

Danny Miceli

Pitches: Right **Bats:** Right **Pos:** RP **Ht:** 6' 0" **Wt:** 207 **Born:** 9/9/70 **Age:** 25

			HOW MUCH HE PITCHED						WHAT HE GAVE UP											THE RESULTS					
Year Team	Lg	G	GS	CG	GF	IP	BFP	H	R	ER	HR	SH	SF	HB	TBB	IBB	SO	WP	Bk	W	L	Pct.	ShO	Sv	ERA
1993 Pittsburgh	NL	9	0	0	1	5.1	25	6	3	3	0	0	0	0	3	0	4	0	1	0	0	.000	0	0	5.06

Year Team	Lg	G	GS	CG	GF	IP	BFP	H	R	ER	HR	SH	SF	HB	TBB	IBB	SO	WP	Bk	W	L	Pct.	ShO	Sv	ERA
1994 Pittsburgh	NL	28	0	0	9	27.1	121	28	19	18	5	1	2	2	11	2	27	2	0	2	1	.667	0	2	5.93
1995 Pittsburgh	NL	58	0	0	51	58	264	61	30	30	7	2	4	4	28	5	56	4	0	4	4	.500	0	21	4.66
3 ML YEARS		95	0	0	61	90.2	410	95	52	51	12	3	6	6	42	7	87	6	1	6	5	.545	0	23	5.06

Matt Mieske

Bats: Right **Throws:** Right **Pos:** RF   **Ht:** 6' 0" **Wt:** 192 **Born:** 2/13/68 **Age:** 28

									BATTING										BASERUNNING				PERCENTAGES		
Year Team	Lg	G	AB	H	2B	3B	HR	(Hm	Rd)	TB	R	RBI	TBB	IBB	SO	HBP	SH	SF	SB	CS	SB%	GDP	Avg	OBP	SLG
1993 Milwaukee	AL	23	58	14	0	0	3	(1	2)	23	9	7	4	0	14	0	1	0	0	2	.00	2	.241	.290	.397
1994 Milwaukee	AL	84	259	67	13	1	10	(7	3)	112	39	38	21	0	62	3	2	1	3	5	.38	6	.259	.320	.432
1995 Milwaukee	AL	117	267	67	13	1	12	(3	9)	118	42	48	27	0	45	4	0	5	2	4	.33	8	.251	.323	.442
3 ML YEARS		224	584	148	26	2	25	(11	14)	253	90	93	52	0	121	7	3	6	5	11	.31	16	.253	.319	.433

Keith Miller

Bats: Right **Throws:** Right **Pos:** LF   **Ht:** 5'11" **Wt:** 185 **Born:** 6/12/63 **Age:** 33

									BATTING										BASERUNNING				PERCENTAGES		
Year Team	Lg	G	AB	H	2B	3B	HR	(Hm	Rd)	TB	R	RBI	TBB	IBB	SO	HBP	SH	SF	SB	CS	SB%	GDP	Avg	OBP	SLG
1995 Omaha *	AAA	7	20	5	2	0	0	--	--	7	3	2	4	0	2	0	0	1	1	0	1.00	1	.250	.360	.350
1987 New York	NL	25	51	19	2	2	0	(0	0)	25	14	1	2	0	6	1	3	0	8	1	.89	1	.373	.407	.490
1988 New York	NL	40	70	15	1	1	1	(1	0)	21	9	5	6	0	10	0	3	0	5	0	1.00	1	.214	.276	.300
1989 New York	NL	57	143	33	7	0	1	(0	1)	43	15	7	5	0	27	1	3	0	6	0	1.00	3	.231	.262	.301
1990 New York	NL	88	233	60	8	0	1	(1	0)	71	42	12	23	1	46	2	2	2	16	3	.84	2	.258	.327	.305
1991 New York	NL	98	275	77	22	1	4	(2	2)	113	41	23	23	0	44	5	0	1	14	4	.78	2	.280	.345	.411
1992 Kansas City	AL	106	416	118	24	4	4	(1	3)	162	57	38	31	0	46	14	1	2	16	6	.73	1	.284	.352	.389
1993 Kansas City	AL	37	108	18	3	0	0	(0	0)	21	9	3	8	0	19	1	0	1	3	1	.75	3	.167	.229	.194
1994 Kansas City	AL	5	15	2	0	0	0	(0	0)	2	1	0	0	0	3	0	0	0	0	0	.00	1	.133	.133	.133
1995 Kansas City	AL	9	15	5	0	0	1	(0	1)	8	2	3	2	0	4	0	0	0	0	0	.00	1	.333	.412	.533
9 ML YEARS		465	1326	347	67	8	12	(5	7)	466	190	92	100	1	205	24	12	6	63	20	.76	14	.262	.323	.351

Orlando Miller

Bats: Right **Throws:** Right **Pos:** SS   **Ht:** 6' 1" **Wt:** 180 **Born:** 1/13/69 **Age:** 27

									BATTING										BASERUNNING				PERCENTAGES		
Year Team	Lg	G	AB	H	2B	3B	HR	(Hm	Rd)	TB	R	RBI	TBB	IBB	SO	HBP	SH	SF	SB	CS	SB%	GDP	Avg	OBP	SLG
1988 Ft. Laud	A	3	11	3	0	0	0	--	--	3	0	1	0	0	1	0	0	0	0	0	.00	1	.273	.273	.273
Yankees	R	14	44	8	1	0	0	--	--	9	5	5	3	0	10	0	0	0	1	0	1.00	0	.182	.234	.205
1989 Oneonta	A	58	213	62	5	2	1	--	--	74	29	25	6	0	38	3	3	1	8	2	.80	3	.291	.318	.347
1990 Asheville	A	121	438	137	29	6	4	--	--	190	60	62	25	2	52	10	2	4	12	5	.71	12	.313	.361	.434
1991 Jackson	AA	23	70	13	6	0	1	--	--	22	5	5	5	1	13	2	2	0	0	0	.00	2	.186	.260	.314
Osceola	A	74	272	81	11	2	0	--	--	96	27	36	13	0	30	8	2	3	1	3	.25	5	.298	.345	.353
1992 Jackson	AA	115	379	100	26	5	5	--	--	151	51	53	16	0	75	4	2	4	7	5	.58	5	.264	.298	.398
Tucson	AAA	10	37	9	0	0	2	--	--	15	4	8	1	0	2	0	0	1	0	0	.00	1	.243	.256	.405
1993 Tucson	AAA	122	471	143	29	16	16	--	--	252	86	89	20	0	95	7	1	4	2	4	.33	12	.304	.339	.535
1994 Tucson	AAA	93	338	87	16	6	10	--	--	145	54	55	16	1	77	6	3	7	3	3	.50	8	.257	.297	.429
1994 Houston	NL	16	40	13	0	1	2	(0	2)	21	3	9	2	2	12	2	0	0	1	0	1.00	0	.325	.386	.525
1995 Houston	NL	92	324	85	20	1	5	(1	4)	122	36	36	22	8	71	5	4	0	3	4	.43	7	.262	.319	.377
2 ML YEARS		108	364	98	20	2	7	(1	6)	143	39	45	24	10	83	7	4	0	4	4	.50	7	.269	.327	.393

Alan Mills

Pitches: Right **Bats:** Both **Pos:** RP   **Ht:** 6' 1" **Wt:** 192 **Born:** 10/18/66 **Age:** 29

				HOW MUCH HE PITCHED				WHAT HE GAVE UP									THE RESULTS						
Year Team	Lg	G	GS	CG	GF	IP	BFP	H	R	ER	HR	SH	SF	HB	TBB	IBB	SO	WP	Bk	W	L	Pct.	ShO	Sv	ERA
1995 Rochester *	AAA	1	1	0	0	2.2	17	2	6	0	0	0	1	0	5	0	2	1	0	0	1	.000	0	0	0.00
Orioles *	R	1	1	0	0	2	11	3	0	0	0	0	0	0	2	0	1	0	1	0	0	.000	0	0	0.00
1990 New York	AL	36	0	0	18	41.2	200	48	21	19	4	4	1	1	33	6	24	3	0	1	5	.167	0	0	4.10
1991 New York	AL	6	2	0	3	16.1	72	16	9	8	1	0	1	0	8	0	11	2	0	1	1	.500	0	0	4.41
1992 Baltimore	AL	35	3	0	12	103.1	428	78	33	30	5	6	5	1	54	10	60	2	0	10	4	.714	0	2	2.61
1993 Baltimore	AL	45	0	0	18	100.1	421	80	39	36	14	4	6	4	51	5	68	3	0	5	4	.556	0	4	3.23
1994 Baltimore	AL	47	0	0	16	45.1	199	43	26	26	7	1	1	2	24	2	44	2	0	3	3	.500	0	2	5.16
1995 Baltimore	AL	21	0	0	1	23	118	30	20	19	0	1	2	1	18	4	16	1	0	3	0	1.000	0	0	7.43
6 ML YEARS		190	5	0	68	330	1438	295	148	138	35	15	15	10	188	27	223	13	0	23	17	.575	0	8	3.76

Michael Mimbs

Pitches: Left **Bats:** Left **Pos:** SP/RP   **Ht:** 6' 2" **Wt:** 180 **Born:** 2/13/69 **Age:** 27

				HOW MUCH HE PITCHED				WHAT HE GAVE UP									THE RESULTS						
Year Team	Lg	G	GS	CG	GF	IP	BFP	H	R	ER	HR	SH	SF	HB	TBB	IBB	SO	WP	Bk	W	L	Pct.	ShO	Sv	ERA
1990 Great Falls	R	3	0	0	0	6.2	32	4	5	3	0	0	0	2	5	0	7	0	1	0	0	.000	0	0	4.05
Yakima	A	12	12	0	0	67.1	295	58	36	29	5	2	2	3	39	0	72	1	2	4	3	.571	0	0	3.88

Year Team	Lg	G	GS	CG	GF	IP	BFP	H	R	ER	HR	SH	SF	HB	TBB	IBB	SO	WP	Bk	W	L	Pct.	ShO	Sv	ERA
1991 Vero Beach	A	24	22	1	0	141.2	601	124	52	42	6	9	1	6	70	2	132	15	3	12	4	.750	1	0	2.67
1992 San Antonio	AA	24	22	2	2	129.2	581	132	65	61	11	10	5	3	73	1	87	7	1	10	8	.556	0	1	4.23
1993 St. Paul	IND	20	16	1	1	98.1	430	94	48	35	4	3	4	5	45	0	97	12	0	8	2	.800	0	0	3.20
1994 Harrisburg	AA	32	21	2	0	153.2	644	130	69	59	11	7	2	3	61	0	145	9	0	11	4	.733	1	0	3.46
1995 Philadelphia	NL	35	19	2	6	136.2	603	127	70	63	10	6	8	6	75	2	93	9	0	9	7	.563	1	1	4.15

Blas Minor

Pitches: Right **Bats:** Right **Pos:** RP   **Ht:** 6' 3" **Wt:** 203 **Born:** 3/20/66 **Age:** 30

		HOW MUCH HE PITCHED						WHAT HE GAVE UP												THE RESULTS					
Year Team	Lg	G	GS	CG	GF	IP	BFP	H	R	ER	HR	SH	SF	HB	TBB	IBB	SO	WP	Bk	W	L	Pct.	ShO	Sv	ERA
1992 Pittsburgh	NL	1	0	0	0	2	9	3	2	1	0	0	0	0	0	0	0	1	0	0	0	.000	0	0	4.50
1993 Pittsburgh	NL	65	0	0	18	94.1	398	94	43	43	8	6	4	4	26	3	84	5	0	8	6	.571	0	2	4.10
1994 Pittsburgh	NL	17	0	0	2	19	90	27	17	17	4	2	1	1	9	2	17	0	0	0	1	.000	0	0	8.05
1995 New York	NL	35	0	0	10	46.2	192	44	21	19	6	4	0	1	13	1	43	3	0	4	2	.667	0	1	3.66
4 ML YEARS		118	0	0	30	162	689	168	83	80	18	12	5	6	48	6	144	9	0	12	9	.571	0	4	4.44

Steve Mintz

Pitches: Right **Bats:** Left **Pos:** RP   **Ht:** 5'11" **Wt:** 195 **Born:** 11/28/68 **Age:** 27

		HOW MUCH HE PITCHED						WHAT HE GAVE UP												THE RESULTS					
Year Team	Lg	G	GS	CG	GF	IP	BFP	H	R	ER	HR	SH	SF	HB	TBB	IBB	SO	WP	Bk	W	L	Pct.	ShO	Sv	ERA
1990 Yakima	A	20	0	0	12	26	113	21	9	7	1	3	1	1	16	1	38	2	1	2	3	.400	0	3	2.42
1991 Bakersfield	A	28	11	0	6	92	419	85	56	44	2	5	4	4	58	1	101	9	1	6	6	.500	0	3	4.30
1992 Vero Beach	A	43	2	0	21	77.2	323	66	29	27	7	5	3	3	30	2	66	7	3	3	6	.333	0	6	3.13
1993 New Britain	AA	43	1	0	20	69.1	287	52	22	16	3	5	1	2	30	5	51	7	0	2	4	.333	0	7	2.08
1994 Phoenix	AAA	24	0	0	13	36	161	40	24	22	8	1	3	1	13	3	27	3	0	0	1	.000	0	3	5.50
Shreveport	AA	30	0	0	12	65.1	261	45	29	16	5	2	1	2	22	1	42	8	0	10	2	.833	0	2	2.20
1995 Phoenix	AAA	31	0	0	19	49	205	42	16	13	4	3	0	2	21	4	36	4	0	5	2	.714	0	7	2.39
1995 San Francisco	NL	14	0	0	3	19.1	96	26	16	16	4	2	1	2	12	3	7	1	0	1	2	.333	0	0	7.45

Angel Miranda

Pitches: Left **Bats:** Left **Pos:** RP/SP   **Ht:** 6' 1" **Wt:** 195 **Born:** 11/9/69 **Age:** 26

		HOW MUCH HE PITCHED						WHAT HE GAVE UP												THE RESULTS					
Year Team	Lg	G	GS	CG	GF	IP	BFP	H	R	ER	HR	SH	SF	HB	TBB	IBB	SO	WP	Bk	W	L	Pct.	ShO	Sv	ERA
1993 Milwaukee	AL	22	17	2	0	120	502	100	53	44	12	3	3	2	52	4	88	4	2	4	5	.444	0	0	3.30
1994 Milwaukee	AL	8	8	1	0	46	196	39	28	27	8	1	1	0	27	0	24	1	1	2	5	.286	0	0	5.28
1995 Milwaukee	AL	30	10	0	5	74	339	83	47	43	8	1	4	0	49	2	45	5	1	4	5	.444	0	1	5.23
3 ML YEARS		60	35	3	5	240	1037	222	128	114	28	5	8	2	128	6	157	10	4	10	15	.400	0	1	4.28

Kevin Mitchell

Bats: Right **Throws:** Right **Pos:** LF   **Ht:** 5'11" **Wt:** 244 **Born:** 1/13/62 **Age:** 34

		BATTING																	BASERUNNING				PERCENTAGES		
Year Team	Lg	G	AB	H	2B	3B	HR	(Hm	Rd)	TB	R	RBI	TBB	IBB	SO	HBP	SH	SF	SB	CS	SB%	GDP	Avg	OBP	SLG
1984 New York	NL	7	14	3	0	0	0	(0	0)	3	0	1	0	0	3	0	0	0	0	1	.00	0	.214	.214	.214
1986 New York	NL	108	328	91	22	2	12	(4	8)	153	51	43	33	0	61	1	1	1	3	3	.50	6	.277	.344	.466
1987 SD-SF	NL	131	464	130	20	2	22	(9	13)	220	68	70	48	4	88	2	0	1	9	6	.60	10	.280	.350	.474
1988 San Francisco	NL	148	505	127	25	7	19	(10	9)	223	60	80	48	7	85	5	1	7	5	5	.50	9	.251	.319	.442
1989 San Francisco	NL	154	543	158	34	6	**47**	(22	25)	345	100	**125**	87	**32**	115	3	0	7	3	4	.43	6	.291	.388	**.635**
1990 San Francisco	NL	140	524	152	24	2	35	(15	20)	285	90	93	58	9	87	2	0	5	4	7	.36	8	.290	.360	.544
1991 San Francisco	NL	113	371	95	13	1	27	(9	18)	191	52	69	43	8	57	5	0	4	2	3	.40	6	.256	.338	.515
1992 Seattle	AL	99	360	103	24	0	9	(5	4)	154	48	67	35	4	46	3	0	4	0	2	.00	4	.286	.351	.428
1993 Cincinnati	NL	93	323	110	21	3	19	(10	9)	194	56	64	25	4	48	1	0	4	1	0	1.00	14	.341	.385	.601
1994 Cincinnati	NL	95	310	101	18	1	30	(18	12)	211	57	77	59	15	62	3	0	8	2	0	1.00	12	.326	.429	.681
1987 San Diego	NL	62	196	48	7	1	7	(2	5)	78	19	26	20	3	38	0	0	1	0	0	.00	5	.245	.313	.398
San Francisco	NL	69	268	82	13	1	15	(7	8)	142	49	44	28	1	50	2	0	0	9	6	.60	5	.306	.376	.530
10 ML YEARS		1088	3742	1070	201	24	220	(102	118)	1979	582	689	436	83	652	25	2	41	29	31	.48	75	.286	.361	.529

Dave Mlicki

Pitches: Right **Bats:** Right **Pos:** SP   **Ht:** 6' 4" **Wt:** 190 **Born:** 6/8/68 **Age:** 28

		HOW MUCH HE PITCHED						WHAT HE GAVE UP												THE RESULTS					
Year Team	Lg	G	GS	CG	GF	IP	BFP	H	R	ER	HR	SH	SF	HB	TBB	IBB	SO	WP	Bk	W	L	Pct.	ShO	Sv	ERA
1992 Cleveland	AL	4	4	0	0	21.2	101	23	14	12	3	2	0	1	16	0	16	1	0	0	0	.000	0	0	4.98
1993 Cleveland	AL	3	3	0	0	13.1	58	11	6	5	2	0	0	2	6	0	7	2	0	0	0	.000	0	0	3.38
1995 New York	NL	29	25	0	1	160.2	696	160	82	76	23	8	5	4	54	2	123	5	1	9	7	.563	0	0	4.26
3 ML YEARS		36	32	0	1	195.2	855	194	102	93	28	10	5	7	76	2	146	8	1	9	9	.500	0	0	4.28

Mike Mohler

Pitches: Left **Bats:** Right **Pos:** RP **Ht:** 6' 2" **Wt:** 195 **Born:** 7/26/68 **Age:** 27

Year Team	Lg	G	GS	CG	GF	IP	BFP	H	R	ER	HR	SH	SF	HB	TBB	IBB	SO	WP	Bk	W	L	Pct.	ShO	Sv	ERA
1995 Edmonton *	AAA	29	0	0	17	45	191	40	16	13	0	3	0	0	20	2	28	4	0	2	1	.667	0	5	2.60
1993 Oakland	AL	42	9	0	4	64.1	290	57	45	40	10	5	2	2	44	4	42	0	1	1	6	.143	0	0	5.60
1994 Oakland	AL	1	1	0	0	2.1	14	2	3	2	1	0	0	0	2	0	4	0	0	0	1	.000	0	0	7.71
1995 Oakland	AL	28	0	0	6	23.2	100	16	8	8	0	1	0	0	18	1	15	1	0	1	1	.500	0	1	3.04
3 ML YEARS		71	10	0	10	90.1	404	75	56	50	11	6	2	2	64	5	61	1	1	2	8	.200	0	1	4.98

Paul Molitor

Bats: Right **Throws:** Right **Pos:** DH **Ht:** 6' 0" **Wt:** 180 **Born:** 8/22/56 **Age:** 39

Year Team	Lg	G	AB	H	2B	3B	HR	(Hm	Rd)	TB	R	RBI	TBB	IBB	SO	HBP	SH	SF	SB	CS	SB%	GDP	Avg	OBP	SLG
1978 Milwaukee	AL	125	521	142	26	4	6	(4	2)	194	73	45	19	2	54	4	7	5	30	12	.71	6	.273	.301	.372
1979 Milwaukee	AL	140	584	188	27	16	9	(3	6)	274	88	62	48	5	48	2	6	5	33	13	.72	9	.322	.372	.469
1980 Milwaukee	AL	111	450	137	29	2	9	(2	7)	197	81	37	48	4	48	3	6	5	34	7	.83	9	.304	.372	.438
1981 Milwaukee	AL	64	251	67	11	0	2	(1	1)	84	45	19	25	1	29	3	5	0	10	6	.63	3	.267	.341	.335
1982 Milwaukee	AL	160	666	201	26	8	19	(9	10)	300	136	71	69	1	93	1	10	5	41	9	.82	9	.302	.366	.450
1983 Milwaukee	AL	152	608	164	28	6	15	(9	6)	249	95	47	59	4	74	2	7	6	41	8	.84	12	.270	.333	.410
1984 Milwaukee	AL	13	46	10	1	0	0	(0	0)	11	3	6	2	0	8	0	0	1	1	0	1.00	6	.217	.245	.239
1985 Milwaukee	AL	140	576	171	28	3	10	(6	4)	235	93	48	54	6	80	1	7	4	21	7	.75	12	.297	.356	.408
1986 Milwaukee	AL	105	437	123	24	6	9	(5	4)	186	62	55	40	0	81	0	2	3	20	5	.80	9	.281	.340	.426
1987 Milwaukee	AL	118	465	164	41	5	16	(7	9)	263	114	75	69	2	67	2	5	1	45	10	.82	4	.353	.438	.566
1988 Milwaukee	AL	154	609	190	34	6	13	(4	9)	275	115	60	71	8	54	2	5	3	41	10	.80	10	.312	.384	.452
1989 Milwaukee	AL	155	615	194	35	4	11	(6	5)	270	84	56	64	4	67	4	4	9	27	11	.71	11	.315	.379	.439
1990 Milwaukee	AL	103	418	119	27	6	12	(6	6)	194	64	45	37	4	51	1	0	2	18	3	.86	7	.285	.343	.464
1991 Milwaukee	AL	158	665	216	32	13	17	(7	10)	325	133	75	77	16	62	6	0	1	19	8	.70	11	.325	.399	.489
1992 Milwaukee	AL	158	609	195	36	7	12	(4	8)	281	89	89	73	12	66	3	4	11	31	6	.84	13	.320	.389	.461
1993 Toronto	AL	160	636	211	37	5	22	(13	9)	324	121	111	77	3	71	3	1	8	22	4	.85	13	.332	.402	.509
1994 Toronto	AL	115	454	155	30	4	14	(8	6)	235	86	75	55	4	48	1	0	5	20	0	1.00	13	.341	.410	.518
1995 Toronto	AL	130	525	142	31	2	15	(6	9)	222	63	60	61	1	57	5	3	4	12	0	1.00	10	.270	.350	.423
18 ML YEARS		2261	9135	2789	503	97	211	(105	106)	4119	1545	1036	948	77	1058	43	72	78	466	119	.80	161	.305	.370	.451

Raul Mondesi

Bats: Right **Throws:** Right **Pos:** RF/CF **Ht:** 5'11" **Wt:** 212 **Born:** 3/12/71 **Age:** 25

Year Team	Lg	G	AB	H	2B	3B	HR	(Hm	Rd)	TB	R	RBI	TBB	IBB	SO	HBP	SH	SF	SB	CS	SB%	GDP	Avg	OBP	SLG
1993 Los Angeles	NL	42	86	25	3	1	4	(2	2)	42	13	10	4	0	16	0	1	0	4	1	.80	1	.291	.322	.488
1994 Los Angeles	NL	112	434	133	27	8	16	(10	6)	224	63	56	16	5	78	2	0	2	11	8	.58	9	.306	.333	.516
1995 Los Angeles	NL	139	536	153	23	6	26	(13	13)	266	91	88	33	4	96	4	0	7	27	4	.87	7	.285	.328	.496
3 ML YEARS		293	1056	311	53	15	46	(25	21)	532	167	154	53	9	190	6	1	9	42	13	.76	17	.295	.329	.504

Rich Monteleone

Pitches: Right **Bats:** Right **Pos:** RP **Ht:** 6' 3" **Wt:** 214 **Born:** 3/22/63 **Age:** 33

Year Team	Lg	G	GS	CG	GF	IP	BFP	H	R	ER	HR	SH	SF	HB	TBB	IBB	SO	WP	Bk	W	L	Pct.	ShO	Sv	ERA
1995 Vancouver *	AAA	7	1	0	1	16.2	73	19	7	6	1	0	1	0	3	0	7	0	0	0	0	1.000	0	0	3.24
1987 Seattle	AL	3	0	0	1	7	34	10	5	5	2	0	0	1	4	0	2	0	0	0	0	.000	0	0	6.43
1988 California	AL	3	0	0	2	4.1	20	4	0	0	0	0	0	1	1	1	3	0	1	0	0	.000	0	0	0.00
1989 California	AL	24	0	0	8	39.2	170	39	15	14	3	1	2	1	13	1	27	2	0	2	2	.500	0	0	3.18
1990 New York	AL	5	0	0	2	7.1	31	8	5	5	0	0	0	0	2	0	8	0	0	0	1	.000	0	0	6.14
1991 New York	AL	26	0	0	10	47	201	42	27	19	5	2	2	0	19	3	34	1	1	3	1	.750	0	0	3.64
1992 New York	AL	47	0	0	15	92.2	380	82	35	34	7	3	1	0	27	3	62	0	3	7	3	.700	0	0	3.30
1993 New York	AL	42	0	0	11	85.2	369	85	52	47	14	4	5	0	35	10	50	1	0	7	4	.636	0	0	4.94
1994 San Francisco	NL	39	0	0	8	45.1	189	43	18	16	6	2	4	0	13	2	16	1	2	4	3	.571	0	0	3.18
1995 California	AL	9	0	0	2	9	36	8	2	2	1	1	2	0	3	0	5	0	0	1	0	1.000	0	0	2.00
9 ML YEARS		198	0	0	59	338	1430	321	159	142	38	13	16	3	117	20	207	5	7	24	14	.632	0	0	3.78

Jeff Montgomery

Pitches: Right **Bats:** Right **Pos:** RP **Ht:** 5'11" **Wt:** 180 **Born:** 1/7/62 **Age:** 34

Year Team	Lg	G	GS	CG	GF	IP	BFP	H	R	ER	HR	SH	SF	HB	TBB	IBB	SO	WP	Bk	W	L	Pct.	ShO	Sv	ERA
1987 Cincinnati	NL	14	1	0	6	19.1	89	25	15	14	2	0	0	0	9	1	13	1	1	2	2	.500	0	0	6.52
1988 Kansas City	AL	45	0	0	13	62.2	271	54	25	24	6	3	2	2	30	1	47	3	6	7	2	.778	0	1	3.45
1989 Kansas City	AL	63	0	0	39	92	363	66	16	14	3	1	1	2	25	4	94	6	1	7	3	.700	0	18	1.37

Year	Team	Lg	G	GS	CG	GF	IP	BFP	H	R	ER	HR	SH	SF	HB	TBB	IBB	SO	WP	Bk	W	L	Pct.	ShO	Sv	ERA
1990	Kansas City	AL	73	0	0	59	94.1	400	81	36	25	6	2	2	5	34	8	94	3	0	6	5	.545	0	24	2.39
1991	Kansas City	AL	67	0	0	55	90	376	83	32	29	6	6	2	2	28	2	77	6	0	4	4	.500	0	33	2.90
1992	Kansas City	AL	65	0	0	62	82.2	333	61	23	20	5	4	2	3	27	2	69	2	0	1	6	.143	0	39	2.18
1993	Kansas City	AL	69	0	0	63	87.1	347	65	22	22	3	5	1	2	23	4	66	3	0	7	5	.583	0	45	2.27
1994	Kansas City	AL	42	0	0	38	44.2	193	48	21	20	5	2	1	1	15	1	50	2	0	2	3	.400	0	27	4.03
1995	Kansas City	AL	54	0	0	46	65.2	275	60	27	25	7	5	5	2	25	4	49	1	1	2	3	.400	0	31	3.43
9 ML YEARS			492	1	0	381	638.2	2647	543	217	193	43	28	16	19	216	27	559	27	9	38	33	.535	0	218	2.72

Mike Moore

Pitches: Right   **Bats:** Right   **Pos:** SP   **Ht:** 6' 4"   **Wt:** 215   **Born:** 11/26/59   **Age:** 36

			HOW MUCH HE PITCHED						WHAT HE GAVE UP											THE RESULTS					
Year	Team	Lg	G	GS	CG	GF	IP	BFP	H	R	ER	HR	SH	SF	HB	TBB	IBB	SO	WP	Bk	W	L	Pct.	ShO	Sv	ERA
1982	Seattle	AL	28	27	1	0	144.1	651	159	91	86	21	8	4	2	79	0	73	6	0	7	14	.333	1	0	5.36
1983	Seattle	AL	22	21	3	1	128	556	130	75	67	10	1	6	3	60	4	108	7	0	6	8	.429	2	0	4.71
1984	Seattle	AL	34	33	6	0	212	937	236	127	117	16	5	6	5	85	10	158	7	2	7	17	.292	0	0	4.97
1985	Seattle	AL	35	34	14	1	247	1016	230	100	95	18	2	7	4	70	2	155	10	3	17	10	.630	2	0	3.46
1986	Seattle	AL	38	37	11	1	266	1145	279	141	127	28	10	6	12	94	6	146	4	1	11	13	.458	1	1	4.30
1987	Seattle	AL	33	33	12	0	231	1020	268	145	121	29	9	8	0	84	3	115	4	2	9	19	.321	0	0	4.71
1988	Seattle	AL	37	32	9	3	228.2	918	196	104	96	24	3	3	3	63	6	182	4	3	9	15	.375	3	1	3.78
1989	Oakland	AL	35	35	6	0	241.2	976	193	82	70	14	5	6	2	83	1	172	17	0	19	11	.633	3	0	2.61
1990	Oakland	AL	33	33	3	0	199.1	862	204	113	103	14	4	7	3	84	2	73	13	0	13	15	.464	0	0	4.65
1991	Oakland	AL	33	33	3	0	210	887	176	75	69	11	5	4	5	105	1	153	14	0	17	8	.680	1	0	2.96
1992	Oakland	AL	36	36	2	0	223	982	229	113	102	20	7	11	8	103	5	117	22	0	17	12	.586	0	0	4.12
1993	Detroit	AL	36	36	4	0	213.2	942	227	135	124	35	4	8	3	89	10	89	9	0	13	9	.591	3	0	5.22
1994	Detroit	AL	25	25	4	0	154.1	679	152	97	93	27	4	4	3	89	8	62	10	0	11	10	.524	0	0	5.42
1995	Detroit	AL	25	25	1	0	132.2	632	179	118	111	24	4	4	2	68	3	64	8	0	5	15	.250	0	0	7.53
14 ML YEARS			450	440	79	6	2831.2	12203	2858	1516	1381	291	71	84	55	1156	61	1667	135	11	161	176	.478	16	2	4.39

Mickey Morandini

Bats: Left   **Throws:** Right   **Pos:** 2B   **Ht:** 5'11"   **Wt:** 176   **Born:** 4/22/66   **Age:** 30

						BATTING													BASERUNNING				PERCENTAGES		
Year	Team	Lg	G	AB	H	2B	3B	HR	(Hm	Rd)	TB	R	RBI	TBB	IBB	SO	HBP	SH	SF	SB	CS	SB%	GDP	Avg	OBP	SLG
1990	Philadelphia	NL	25	79	19	4	0	1	(1	0)	26	9	3	6	0	19	0	2	0	3	0	1.00	1	.241	.294	.329
1991	Philadelphia	NL	98	325	81	11	4	1	(1	0)	103	38	20	29	0	45	2	6	2	13	2	.87	7	.249	.313	.317
1992	Philadelphia	NL	127	422	112	8	8	3	(2	1)	145	47	30	25	2	64	0	6	2	8	3	.73	4	.265	.305	.344
1993	Philadelphia	NL	120	425	105	19	9	3	(2	1)	151	57	33	34	2	73	5	4	2	13	2	.87	7	.247	.309	.355
1994	Philadelphia	NL	87	274	80	16	5	2	(1	1)	112	40	26	34	5	33	4	4	0	10	5	.67	4	.292	.378	.409
1995	Philadelphia	NL	127	494	140	34	7	6	(3	3)	206	65	49	42	3	80	9	4	1	9	6	.60	11	.283	.350	.417
6 ML YEARS			584	2019	537	92	33	16	(10	6)	743	256	161	170	12	314	20	26	7	56	18	.76	34	.266	.328	.368

Mike Mordecai

Bats: Right   **Throws:** Right   **Pos:** 2B   **Ht:** 5'11"   **Wt:** 175   **Born:** 12/13/67   **Age:** 28

						BATTING													BASERUNNING				PERCENTAGES		
Year	Team	Lg	G	AB	H	2B	3B	HR	(Hm	Rd)	TB	R	RBI	TBB	IBB	SO	HBP	SH	SF	SB	CS	SB%	GDP	Avg	OBP	SLG
1989	Burlington	A	65	241	61	11	1	1	--	--	77	39	22	33	0	43	5	4	2	12	5	.71	2	.253	.352	.320
	Greenville	AA	4	8	3	0	0	0	--	--	3	0	1	1	0	1	0	0	0	0	0	.00	0	.375	.444	.375
1990	Durham	A	72	271	76	11	7	3	--	--	110	42	36	42	2	45	2	2	2	10	6	.63	9	.280	.379	.406
1991	Durham	A	109	397	104	15	2	4	--	--	135	52	42	39	0	58	2	6	4	30	16	.65	7	.262	.328	.340
1992	Greenville	AA	65	222	58	13	1	4	--	--	85	31	31	29	2	31	0	1	2	9	6	.60	6	.261	.344	.383
	Richmond	AAA	36	118	29	3	0	1	--	--	35	12	6	5	0	19	0	1	2	0	4	.00	1	.246	.272	.297
1993	Richmond	AAA	72	205	55	8	1	2	--	--	71	29	14	14	0	33	1	1	0	10	2	.83	4	.268	.318	.346
1994	Richmond	AAA	99	382	107	25	1	14	--	--	176	67	57	35	1	50	2	3	5	14	7	.67	5	.280	.340	.461
1994	Atlanta	NL	4	4	1	0	0	1	(1	0)	4	1	3	1	0	0	0	0	0	0	0	.00	0	.250	.400	1.000
1995	Atlanta	NL	69	75	21	6	0	3	(1	2)	36	10	11	9	0	16	0	2	1	0	0	.00	0	.280	.353	.480
2 ML YEARS			73	79	22	6	0	4	(2	2)	40	11	14	10	0	16	0	2	1	0	0	.00	0	.278	.356	.506

Ramon Morel

Pitches: Right   **Bats:** Right   **Pos:** RP   **Ht:** 6' 2"   **Wt:** 175   **Born:** 8/15/74   **Age:** 21

			HOW MUCH HE PITCHED						WHAT HE GAVE UP											THE RESULTS					
Year	Team	Lg	G	GS	CG	GF	IP	BFP	H	R	ER	HR	SH	SF	HB	TBB	IBB	SO	WP	Bk	W	L	Pct.	ShO	Sv	ERA
1992	Pirates	R	14	2	1	7	45.2	193	49	26	22	0	1	0	1	11	0	29	4	2	2	2	.500	1	0	4.34
1993	Welland	A	16	16	0	0	77	344	90	45	36	7	3	0	5	21	0	51	6	0	7	8	.467	0	0	4.21
1994	Augusta	A	28	27	2	0	168.2	689	157	69	53	8	2	4	12	24	0	152	20	0	10	7	.588	1	0	2.83
1995	Lynchburg	A	12	12	1	0	72.2	304	80	35	28	2	2	3	3	13	2	44	2	0	3	7	.300	1	0	3.47
	Carolina	AA	10	10	0	0	69	281	71	31	27	4	1	2	2	10	0	34	2	0	3	3	.500	0	0	3.52
1995	Pittsburgh	NL	5	0	0	0	6.1	23	6	2	2	0	1	0	0	2	1	3	0	0	0	1	.000	0	0	2.84

Mike Morgan

Pitches: Right **Bats:** Right **Pos:** SP   **Ht:** 6' 2" **Wt:** 220 **Born:** 10/8/59 **Age:** 36

		HOW MUCH HE PITCHED						WHAT HE GAVE UP												THE RESULTS					
Year Team	Lg	G	GS	CG	GF	IP	BFP	H	R	ER	HR	SH	SF	HB	TBB	IBB	SO	WP	Bk	W	L	Pct.	ShO	Sv	ERA
1995 Orlando *	AA	2	2	0	0	10.2	48	13	9	9	1	1	0	1	7	0	5	0	0	0	2	.000	0	0	7.59
1978 Oakland	AL	3	3	1	0	12	60	19	12	10	1	1	0	0	8	0	0	0	0	0	3	.000	0	0	7.50
1979 Oakland	AL	13	13	2	0	77	368	102	57	51	7	4	4	3	50	0	17	7	0	2	10	.167	0	0	5.96
1982 New York	AL	30	23	2	2	150.1	661	167	77	73	15	2	4	2	67	5	71	6	0	7	11	.389	0	0	4.37
1983 Toronto	AL	16	4	0	2	45.1	198	48	26	26	6	0	1	0	21	0	22	3	0	0	3	.000	0	0	5.16
1985 Seattle	AL	2	2	0	0	6	33	11	8	8	2	0	0	0	5	0	2	1	0	1	1	.500	0	0	12.00
1986 Seattle	AL	37	33	9	2	216.1	951	243	122	109	24	7	3	4	86	3	116	8	1	11	17	.393	1	1	4.53
1987 Seattle	AL	34	31	8	2	207	898	245	117	107	25	8	5	5	53	3	85	11	0	12	17	.414	2	0	4.65
1988 Baltimore	AL	22	10	2	6	71.1	299	70	45	43	6	1	0	1	23	1	29	5	0	1	6	.143	0	1	5.43
1989 Los Angeles	NL	40	19	0	7	152.2	604	130	51	43	6	8	6	2	33	8	72	6	0	8	11	.421	0	0	2.53
1990 Los Angeles	NL	33	33	6	0	211	891	216	100	88	19	11	4	5	60	5	106	4	0	11	15	.423	4	0	3.75
1991 Los Angeles	NL	34	33	5	1	236.1	949	197	85	73	12	10	4	3	61	10	140	6	0	14	10	.583	1	1	2.78
1992 Chicago	NL	34	34	6	0	240	966	203	80	68	14	10	5	3	79	10	123	11	0	16	8	.667	1	0	2.55
1993 Chicago	NL	32	32	1	0	207.2	883	206	100	93	15	11	5	7	74	8	111	8	2	10	15	.400	1	0	4.03
1994 Chicago	NL	15	15	1	0	80.2	380	111	65	60	12	7	6	4	35	2	57	5	0	2	10	.167	0	0	6.69
1995 ChN-StL	NL	21	21	1	0	131.1	548	133	56	52	12	12	5	6	34	2	61	6	0	7	7	.500	0	0	3.56
1995 Chicago	NL	4	4	0	0	24.2	100	19	8	6	2	2	0	1	9	1	15	0	0	2	1	.667	0	0	2.19
St. Louis	NL	17	17	1	0	106.2	448	114	48	46	10	10	5	5	25	1	46	6	0	5	6	.455	0	0	3.88
15 ML YEARS		366	306	44	22	2045	8689	2101	1001	904	176	92	52	45	689	57	1012	87	4	102	144	.415	10	3	3.98

Russ Morman

Bats: Right **Throws:** Right **Pos:** RF   **Ht:** 6' 4" **Wt:** 220 **Born:** 4/28/62 **Age:** 34

		BATTING															BASERUNNING				PERCENTAGES		
Year Team	Lg	G	AB	H	2B	3B	HR	(Hm | Rd)	TB	R	RBI	TBB	IBB	SO	HBP	SH	SF	SB	CS	SB%	GDP	Avg	OBP	SLG
1995 Charlotte *	AAA	44	169	53	7	1	6	--	--	80	28	36	14	3	22	1	0	3	2	2	.50	4	.314	.364	.473
1986 Chicago	AL	49	159	40	5	0	4	(1 | 3)	57	18	17	16	0	36	2	1	2	1	0	1.00	5	.252	.324	.358
1988 Chicago	AL	40	75	18	2	0	0	(0 | 0)	20	8	3	3	0	17	0	2	0	0	0	.00	5	.240	.269	.267
1989 Chicago	AL	37	58	13	2	0	0	(0 | 0)	15	5	8	6	1	16	0	2	1	1	0	1.00	1	.224	.292	.259
1990 Kansas City	AL	12	37	10	4	2	1	(0 | 1)	21	5	3	3	0	3	0	0	1	0	0	.00	0	.270	.317	.568
1991 Kansas City	AL	12	23	6	0	0	0	(0 | 0)	6	1	1	1	1	5	0	0	0	0	0	.00	0	.261	.292	.261
1994 Florida	NL	13	33	7	0	1	1	(0 | 1)	12	2	2	2	0	9	1	0	0	0	0	.00	1	.212	.278	.364
1995 Florida	NL	34	72	20	2	1	3	(1 | 2)	33	9	7	3	0	12	1	0	0	0	0	.00	5	.278	.316	.458
7 ML YEARS		197	457	114	15	4	9	(2 | 7)	164	48	41	34	2	98	4	5	4	2	0	1.00	17	.249	.305	.359

Hal Morris

Bats: Left **Throws:** Left **Pos:** 1B   **Ht:** 6' 4" **Wt:** 210 **Born:** 4/9/65 **Age:** 31

		BATTING															BASERUNNING				PERCENTAGES		
Year Team	Lg	G	AB	H	2B	3B	HR	(Hm | Rd)	TB	R	RBI	TBB	IBB	SO	HBP	SH	SF	SB	CS	SB%	GDP	Avg	OBP	SLG
1995 Indianapols *	AAA	2	5	2	0	0	0	--	--	2	2	1	1	0	0	0	0	0	0	0	.00	0	.400	.500	.400
1988 New York	AL	15	20	2	0	0	0	(0 | 0)	2	1	0	0	0	9	0	0	0	0	0	.00	0	.100	.100	.100
1989 New York	AL	15	18	5	0	0	0	(0 | 0)	5	2	4	1	0	4	0	0	0	0	0	.00	2	.278	.316	.278
1990 Cincinnati	NL	107	309	105	22	3	7	(3 | 4)	154	50	36	21	4	32	1	3	2	9	3	.75	12	.340	.381	.498
1991 Cincinnati	NL	136	478	152	33	1	14	(9 | 5)	229	72	59	46	7	61	1	5	7	10	4	.71	4	.318	.374	.479
1992 Cincinnati	NL	115	395	107	21	3	6	(3 | 3)	152	41	53	45	8	53	2	2	2	6	6	.50	12	.271	.347	.385
1993 Cincinnati	NL	101	379	120	18	0	7	(2 | 5)	159	48	49	34	4	51	2	0	6	2	2	.50	5	.317	.371	.420
1994 Cincinnati	NL	112	436	146	30	4	10	(5 | 5)	214	60	78	34	8	62	5	2	6	6	2	.75	16	.335	.385	.491
1995 Cincinnati	NL	101	359	100	25	2	11	(6 | 5)	162	53	51	29	7	58	1	1	1	1	1	.50	10	.279	.333	.451
8 ML YEARS		702	2394	737	149	13	55	(28 | 27)	1077	327	330	210	38	330	12	13	24	34	18	.65	61	.308	.363	.450

Jose Mota

Bats: Both **Throws:** Right **Pos:** 2B   **Ht:** 5' 9" **Wt:** 155 **Born:** 3/16/65 **Age:** 31

		BATTING															BASERUNNING				PERCENTAGES		
Year Team	Lg	G	AB	H	2B	3B	HR	(Hm | Rd)	TB	R	RBI	TBB	IBB	SO	HBP	SH	SF	SB	CS	SB%	GDP	Avg	OBP	SLG
1985 Buffalo	AAA	6	18	5	0	0	0	--	--	5	3	1	2	0	0	0	0	0	0	0	.00	1	.278	.350	.278
Niagara Fal	A	65	254	77	9	2	0	--	--	90	35	27	28	3	29	2	5	2	8	5	.62	1	.303	.374	.354
1986 Tulsa	AA	41	158	51	7	3	1	--	--	67	26	11	22	0	13	0	3	1	14	8	.64	0	.323	.403	.424
Okla. City	AAA	71	255	71	9	1	0	--	--	82	38	20	24	1	43	3	5	0	7	5	.58	7	.278	.348	.322
1987 Tulsa	AA	21	71	15	2	0	0	--	--	17	11	4	13	0	12	0	0	1	2	2	.50	0	.211	.329	.239
San Antonio	AA	54	190	50	4	3	0	--	--	60	23	11	21	1	34	2	5	0	3	4	.43	3	.263	.343	.316
1988 Albuquerque	AAA	6	15	5	0	0	0	--	--	5	4	1	3	0	3	0	1	0	1	0	1.00	1	.333	.444	.333
San Antonio	AA	82	214	56	11	1	1	--	--	72	32	18	27	1	35	0	3	1	10	4	.71	7	.262	.343	.336
1989 Huntsville	AA	27	81	11	1	0	0	--	--	12	15	6	30	0	15	1	5	1	3	2	.60	0	.136	.372	.148
Wichita	AA	41	109	35	5	1	1	--	--	45	17	9	17	0	21	0	4	1	3	2	.60	1	.321	.413	.413

157

Year Team	Lg	G	AB	H	2B	3B	HR	(Hm	Rd)	TB	R	RBI	TBB	IBB	SO	HBP	SH	SF	SB	CS	SB%	GDP	Avg	OBP	SLG
1990 Las Vegas	AAA	92	247	74	4	4	4	--	--	98	44	21	42	2	35	3	3	1	2	1	.67	0	.300	.406	.397
1991 Las Vegas	AAA	107	377	109	10	2	1	--	--	126	56	37	54	2	48	2	6	3	15	10	.60	10	.289	.378	.334
1992 Omaha	AAA	131	469	108	11	0	3	--	--	128	45	28	41	1	56	2	7	1	21	8	.72	3	.230	.294	.273
1993 Omaha	AAA	105	330	93	11	2	3	--	--	117	46	35	34	0	34	2	3	5	27	10	.73	4	.282	.348	.355
1994 Omaha	AAA	100	358	92	13	6	0	--	--	117	60	32	47	1	41	1	6	3	25	11	.69	3	.257	.342	.327
1995 Omaha	AAA	27	87	28	4	0	0	--	--	32	6	10	6	0	9	1	4	2	1	2	.33	3	.322	.365	.368
1991 San Diego	NL	17	36	8	0	0	0	(0	0)	8	4	2	2	0	7	1	2	0	0	0	.00	0	.222	.282	.222
1995 Kansas City	AL	2	2	0	0	0	0	(0	0)	0	0	0	0	0	0	0	0	0	0	0	.00	0	.000	.000	.000
2 ML YEARS		19	38	8	0	0	0	(0	0)	8	4	2	2	0	7	1	2	0	0	0	.00	0	.211	.268	.211

James Mouton

Bats: Right **Throws:** Right **Pos:** LF/CF/RF **Ht:** 5' 9" **Wt:** 175 **Born:** 12/29/68 **Age:** 27

		BATTING																	BASERUNNING				PERCENTAGES		
Year Team	Lg	G	AB	H	2B	3B	HR	(Hm	Rd)	TB	R	RBI	TBB	IBB	SO	HBP	SH	SF	SB	CS	SB%	GDP	Avg	OBP	SLG
1991 Auburn	A	76	288	76	15	10	2	--	--	117	71	40	55	1	32	7	2	4	60	18	.77	5	.264	.390	.406
1992 Osceola	A	133	507	143	30	6	11	--	--	218	110	62	71	3	78	8	9	5	51	11	.82	9	.282	.376	.430
1993 Tucson	AAA	134	546	172	42	12	16	--	--	286	126	92	72	0	82	8	7	9	40	18	.69	6	.315	.397	.524
1994 Tucson	AAA	4	17	7	1	0	1	--	--	11	2	1	2	0	3	0	0	0	1	0	1.00	1	.412	.474	.647
1995 Tucson	AAA	3	11	5	0	0	1	--	--	8	1	1	0	0	2	0	0	0	0	1	.00	0	.455	.455	.727
1994 Houston	NL	99	310	76	11	0	2	(1	1)	93	43	16	27	0	69	5	2	1	24	5	.83	6	.245	.315	.300
1995 Houston	NL	104	298	78	18	2	4	(2	2)	112	42	27	25	1	59	4	3	1	25	8	.76	5	.262	.326	.376
2 ML YEARS		203	608	154	29	2	6	(3	3)	205	85	43	52	1	128	9	5	2	49	13	.79	11	.253	.320	.337

Lyle Mouton

Bats: Right **Throws:** Right **Pos:** RF/LF **Ht:** 6' 4" **Wt:** 240 **Born:** 5/13/69 **Age:** 27

		BATTING																	BASERUNNING				PERCENTAGES		
Year Team	Lg	G	AB	H	2B	3B	HR	(Hm	Rd)	TB	R	RBI	TBB	IBB	SO	HBP	SH	SF	SB	CS	SB%	GDP	Avg	OBP	SLG
1991 Oneonta	A	70	272	84	11	2	7	--	--	120	53	41	31	2	39	6	0	3	14	8	.64	1	.309	.388	.441
1992 Pr. William	A	50	189	50	14	1	6	--	--	84	28	34	17	1	42	0	0	4	4	2	.67	3	.265	.319	.444
Albany-Colo	AA	64	214	46	12	2	2	--	--	68	25	27	24	2	55	1	0	1	1	1	.50	9	.215	.296	.318
1993 Albany-Colo	AA	135	491	125	22	3	16	--	--	201	74	76	50	2	125	7	2	1	19	13	.59	13	.255	.332	.409
1994 Albany-Colo	AA	74	274	84	23	1	12	--	--	145	42	42	27	1	62	2	0	4	7	6	.54	8	.307	.368	.529
Columbus	AAA	59	204	64	14	5	4	--	--	100	26	32	14	0	45	1	2	3	5	1	.83	6	.314	.356	.490
1995 Nashville	AAA	71	267	79	17	0	8	--	--	120	40	41	23	2	58	1	0	4	10	4	.71	9	.296	.349	.449
1995 Chicago	AL	58	179	54	16	0	5	(4	1)	85	23	27	19	0	46	2	0	1	1	0	1.00	7	.302	.373	.475

Jamie Moyer

Pitches: Left **Bats:** Left **Pos:** SP/RP **Ht:** 6' 0" **Wt:** 170 **Born:** 11/18/62 **Age:** 33

		HOW MUCH HE PITCHED						WHAT HE GAVE UP										THE RESULTS					
Year Team	Lg	G	GS	CG	GF	IP	BFP	H	R	ER	HR	SH	SF	HB	TBB	IBB	SO	WP	Bk	W	L	Pct.	ShO	Sv	ERA
1986 Chicago	NL	16	16	1	0	87.1	395	107	52	49	10	3	3	3	42	1	45	3	3	7	4	.636	1	0	5.05
1987 Chicago	NL	35	33	1	1	201	899	210	127	114	28	14	7	5	97	9	147	11	2	12	15	.444	0	0	5.10
1988 Chicago	NL	34	30	3	1	202	855	212	84	78	20	14	4	4	55	7	121	4	0	9	15	.375	1	0	3.48
1989 Texas	AL	15	15	1	0	76	337	84	51	41	10	1	4	2	33	0	44	1	0	4	9	.308	0	0	4.86
1990 Texas	AL	33	10	1	6	102.1	447	115	59	53	6	1	7	4	39	4	58	1	0	2	6	.250	0	0	4.66
1991 St. Louis	NL	8	7	0	1	31.1	142	38	21	20	5	4	2	1	16	0	20	2	1	0	5	.000	0	0	5.74
1993 Baltimore	AL	25	25	3	0	152	630	154	63	58	11	3	1	6	38	2	90	1	1	12	9	.571	1	0	3.43
1994 Baltimore	AL	23	23	0	0	149	631	158	81	79	23	5	2	2	38	3	87	1	0	5	7	.417	0	0	4.77
1995 Baltimore	AL	27	18	0	3	115.2	483	117	70	67	18	5	3	3	30	0	65	0	0	8	6	.571	0	0	5.21
9 ML YEARS		216	177	10	12	1116.2	4819	1195	608	559	131	50	33	30	388	26	677	24	7	59	76	.437	3	0	4.51

Terry Mulholland

Pitches: Left **Bats:** Right **Pos:** SP/RP **Ht:** 6' 3" **Wt:** 212 **Born:** 3/9/63 **Age:** 33

		HOW MUCH HE PITCHED						WHAT HE GAVE UP										THE RESULTS					
Year Team	Lg	G	GS	CG	GF	IP	BFP	H	R	ER	HR	SH	SF	HB	TBB	IBB	SO	WP	Bk	W	L	Pct.	ShO	Sv	ERA
1995 Phoenix *	AAA	1	1	0	0	4	18	4	3	1	0	0	0	0	1	0	4	0	0	0	0	.000	0	0	2.25
1986 San Francisco	NL	15	10	0	1	54.2	245	51	33	30	3	5	1	1	35	2	27	6	0	1	7	.125	0	0	4.94
1988 San Francisco	NL	9	6	2	1	46	191	50	20	19	3	5	0	1	7	0	18	1	0	2	1	.667	1	0	3.72
1989 Phi-SF	NL	25	18	2	4	115.1	513	137	66	63	8	7	1	4	36	3	66	3	0	4	7	.364	1	0	4.92
1990 Philadelphia	NL	33	26	6	2	180.2	746	172	78	67	15	7	12	2	42	7	75	7	2	9	10	.474	1	0	3.34
1991 Philadelphia	NL	34	34	8	0	232	956	231	100	93	15	11	6	3	49	2	142	3	0	16	13	.552	3	0	3.61
1992 Philadelphia	NL	32	32	12	0	229	937	227	101	97	14	10	7	3	46	3	125	3	0	13	11	.542	2	0	3.81
1993 Philadelphia	NL	29	28	7	0	191	786	177	80	69	20	5	4	3	40	2	116	5	0	12	9	.571	2	0	3.25
1994 New York	AL	24	19	2	4	120.2	542	150	94	87	24	3	4	3	37	1	72	5	0	6	7	.462	0	0	6.49
1995 San Francisco	NL	29	24	2	2	149	666	190	112	96	25	11	6	4	38	1	65	4	0	5	13	.278	0	0	5.80

Year	Team	Lg	G	GS	CG	GF	IP	BFP	H	R	ER	HR	SH	SF	HB	TBB	IBB	SO	WP	Bk	W	L	Pct.	ShO	Sv	ERA
1989	Philadelphia	NL	20	17	2	2	104.1	462	122	61	58	8	7	1	4	32	3	60	3	0	4	7	.364	1	0	5.00
	San Francisco	NL	5	1	0	2	11	51	15	5	5	0	0	0	0	4	0	6	0	0	0	0	.000	0	0	4.09
	9 ML YEARS		230	197	41	14	1318.1	5582	1385	684	621	127	64	41	24	330	21	706	37	2	68	78	.466	10	0	4.24

Bobby Munoz

Pitches: Right **Bats:** Right **Pos:** SP   **Ht:** 6' 8" **Wt:** 252 **Born:** 3/3/68 **Age:** 28

			HOW MUCH HE PITCHED						WHAT HE GAVE UP											THE RESULTS					
Year	Team	Lg	G	GS	CG	GF	IP	BFP	H	R	ER	HR	SH	SF	HB	TBB	IBB	SO	WP	Bk	W	L	Pct.	ShO	Sv	ERA
1995	Reading *	AA	4	4	0	0	15	74	28	19	18	4	0	0	0	3	0	8	1	0	0	4	.000	0	0	10.80
	Scrantn-WB *	AAA	2	2	1	0	16	57	8	2	1	0	0	0	2	3	1	10	1	0	1	0	1.000	1	0	0.56
1993	New York	AL	38	0	0	12	45.2	208	48	27	27	1	1	3	0	26	5	33	2	0	3	3	.500	0	0	5.32
1994	Philadelphia	NL	21	14	1	1	104.1	447	101	40	31	8	5	5	1	35	0	59	5	1	7	5	.583	0	0	2.67
1995	Philadelphia	NL	3	3	0	0	15.2	70	15	13	10	2	0	2	3	9	0	6	0	0	0	2	.000	0	0	5.74
	3 ML YEARS		62	17	1	13	165.2	725	164	80	68	11	6	10	4	70	5	98	7	1	10	10	.500	0	1	3.69

Mike Munoz

Pitches: Left **Bats:** Left **Pos:** RP   **Ht:** 6' 2" **Wt:** 200 **Born:** 7/12/65 **Age:** 30

			HOW MUCH HE PITCHED						WHAT HE GAVE UP											THE RESULTS					
Year	Team	Lg	G	GS	CG	GF	IP	BFP	H	R	ER	HR	SH	SF	HB	TBB	IBB	SO	WP	Bk	W	L	Pct.	ShO	Sv	ERA
1989	Los Angeles	NL	3	0	0	1	2.2	14	5	5	5	1	0	0	0	2	0	3	0	0	0	0	.000	0	0	16.88
1990	Los Angeles	NL	8	0	0	3	5.2	24	6	2	2	0	1	0	0	3	0	2	0	0	0	1	.000	0	0	3.18
1991	Detroit	AL	6	0	0	4	9.1	46	14	10	10	0	0	1	0	5	0	5	3	1	0	0	.000	0	0	9.64
1992	Detroit	AL	65	0	0	15	48	210	44	16	16	3	4	2	0	25	6	23	2	0	1	2	.333	0	2	3.00
1993	Det-Col		29	0	0	10	21	101	25	14	11	2	3	2	0	15	4	17	2	0	2	2	.500	0	0	4.71
1994	Colorado	NL	57	0	0	8	45.2	200	37	22	19	3	2	1	0	31	5	32	2	0	4	2	.667	0	1	3.74
1995	Colorado	NL	64	0	0	19	43.2	208	54	38	36	9	2	2	1	27	0	37	5	0	2	4	.333	0	2	7.42
1993	Detroit	AL	8	0	0	3	3	19	4	2	2	1	0	0	0	6	1	1	0	0	0	1	.000	0	0	6.00
	Colorado	NL	21	0	0	7	18	82	21	12	9	1	3	2	0	9	3	16	2	0	2	1	.667	0	0	4.50
	7 ML YEARS		232	0	0	60	176	803	185	107	99	18	12	8	1	108	15	117	12	0	9	11	.450	0	5	5.06

Noe Munoz

Bats: Right **Throws:** Right **Pos:** C   **Ht:** 6' 2" **Wt:** 180 **Born:** 12/3/70 **Age:** 25

			BATTING																BASERUNNING				PERCENTAGES		
Year	Team	Lg	G	AB	H	2B	3B	HR	(Hm	Rd)	TB	R	RBI	TBB	IBB	SO	HBP	SH	SF	SB	CS	SB%	GDP	Avg	OBP	SLG
1994	Bakersfield	A	8	26	7	2	0	0	--	--	9	4	3	3	0	5	0	1	0	0	2	.00	0	.269	.345	.346
	San Antonio	AA	51	137	31	4	2	2	--	--	45	12	14	3	1	21	2	3	2	1	1	.50	5	.226	.250	.328
1995	Albuquerque	AAA	23	58	13	1	0	0	--	--	14	1	3	2	0	8	0	0	0	0	0	.00	3	.224	.250	.241
1995	Los Angeles	NL	2	1	0	0	0	0	(0	0)	0	0	0	0	0	0	0	0	0	0	0	.00	0	.000	.000	.000

Oscar Munoz

Pitches: Right **Bats:** Right **Pos:** RP/SP   **Ht:** 6' 3" **Wt:** 222 **Born:** 9/4/69 **Age:** 26

			HOW MUCH HE PITCHED						WHAT HE GAVE UP											THE RESULTS					
Year	Team	Lg	G	GS	CG	GF	IP	BFP	H	R	ER	HR	SH	SF	HB	TBB	IBB	SO	WP	Bk	W	L	Pct.	ShO	Sv	ERA
1990	Watertown	A	2	2	0	0	10.2	43	8	2	2	1	0	0	0	3	0	9	1	1	1	1	.500	0	0	1.69
	Kinston	A	9	9	2	0	64	248	43	18	17	6	1	1	1	18	0	55	3	0	7	0	1.000	1	0	2.39
1991	Kinston	A	14	14	3	0	93.2	375	60	23	15	2	4	0	5	36	0	111	6	0	6	3	.667	1	0	1.44
	Canton-Akrn	AA	15	15	2	0	85	378	88	54	54	5	1	2	0	51	1	71	1	1	3	8	.273	1	0	5.72
1992	Orlando	AA	14	12	1	1	67.2	306	73	44	38	10	1	1	4	32	1	74	6	0	3	5	.375	0	0	5.05
1993	Nashville	AA	20	20	1	0	131.2	567	123	56	45	10	1	4	4	51	0	139	12	0	11	4	.733	0	0	3.08
	Portland	AAA	5	5	0	0	31.1	138	29	18	15	2	2	1	0	17	1	29	6	0	2	2	.500	0	0	4.31
1994	Nashville	AA	3	3	2	0	22	86	16	1	1	0	0	0	1	5	0	21	1	0	3	0	1.000	1	0	0.41
	Salt Lake	AAA	26	26	1	0	139.1	662	180	103	91	20	6	5	3	68	1	100	8	0	9	8	.529	0	0	5.88
1995	Salt Lake	AAA	19	19	1	0	112.2	486	121	67	62	9	0	7	3	35	1	74	7	0	8	6	.571	1	0	4.95
1995	Minnesota	AL	10	3	0	4	35.1	164	40	28	22	6	0	1	1	17	0	25	0	0	2	1	.667	0	0	5.60

Pedro Munoz

Bats: Right **Throws:** Right **Pos:** DH/RF   **Ht:** 5'10" **Wt:** 208 **Born:** 9/19/68 **Age:** 27

			BATTING																BASERUNNING				PERCENTAGES		
Year	Team	Lg	G	AB	H	2B	3B	HR	(Hm	Rd)	TB	R	RBI	TBB	IBB	SO	HBP	SH	SF	SB	CS	SB%	GDP	Avg	OBP	SLG
199u	Minnesota	AL	22	85	23	4	1	0	(0	0)	29	13	5	2	0	16	0	1	2	3	0	1.00	3	.271	.281	.341
1991	Minnesota	AL	51	138	39	7	1	7	(4	3)	69	15	26	9	0	31	1	1	2	3	0	1.00	2	.283	.327	.500
1992	Minnesota	AL	127	418	113	16	3	12	(8	4)	171	44	71	17	1	90	1	0	3	4	5	.44	18	.270	.298	.409
1993	Minnesota	AL	104	326	76	11	1	13	(2	11)	128	34	38	25	2	97	3	0	0	1	2	.33	7	.233	.294	.393
1994	Minnesota	AL	75	244	72	15	2	11	(5	6)	124	35	36	19	0	67	2	0	2	0	0	.00	4	.295	.348	.508
1995	Minnesota	AL	104	376	113	17	0	18	(10	8)	184	45	58	19	0	86	3	0	2	0	3	.00	14	.301	.338	.489
	6 ML YEARS		483	1587	436	70	8	61	(29	32)	705	186	234	91	3	387	10	2	11	11	10	.52	48	.275	.316	.444

159

Rob Murphy

Pitches: Left **Bats:** Left **Pos:** RP   **Ht:** 6' 2" **Wt:** 215 **Born:** 5/26/60 **Age:** 36

			HOW MUCH HE PITCHED					WHAT HE GAVE UP										THE RESULTS					
Year Team	Lg	G	GS	CG	GF	IP	BFP	H	R	ER	HR	SH	SF	HB	TBB	IBB	SO	WP	Bk	W	L	Pct.	ShO	Sv	ERA
1995 Charlotte *	AAA	3	0	0	3	3	11	2	0	0	0	0	0	0	0	0	1	1	0	0	0	.000	0	2	0.00
1985 Cincinnati	NL	2	0	0	2	3	12	2	2	2	1	0	0	0	2	0	1	0	0	0	0	.000	0	0	6.00
1986 Cincinnati	NL	34	0	0	12	50.1	195	26	4	4	0	3	3	0	21	2	36	5	0	6	0	1.000	0	1	0.72
1987 Cincinnati	NL	87	0	0	21	100.2	415	91	37	34	7	1	2	0	32	5	99	1	0	8	5	.615	0	3	3.04
1988 Cincinnati	NL	76	0	0	28	84.2	350	69	31	29	3	9	1	1	38	6	74	5	1	0	6	.000	0	3	3.08
1989 Boston	AL	74	0	0	27	105	438	97	38	32	7	7	3	1	41	8	107	6	0	5	7	.417	0	9	2.74
1990 Boston	AL	68	0	0	20	57	285	85	46	40	10	4	4	1	32	3	54	4	0	0	6	.000	0	7	6.32
1991 Seattle	AL	57	0	0	26	48	211	47	17	16	4	3	0	1	19	4	34	4	0	0	1	.000	0	4	3.00
1992 Houston	NL	59	0	0	6	55.2	242	56	28	25	2	3	3	0	21	4	42	4	0	3	1	.750	0	0	4.04
1993 St. Louis	NL	73	0	0	23	64.2	279	73	37	35	8	4	2	1	20	6	41	5	0	5	7	.417	0	1	4.87
1994 NYA-StL	NL	53	0	0	15	42	174	38	21	20	9	1	0	0	13	2	25	2	0	4	3	.571	0	2	4.29
1995 LA-Fla	NL	14	0	0	1	12.1	58	14	16	15	3	2	0	0	8	1	7	1	0	1	2	.333	0	0	10.95
1994 New York	AL	3	0	0	0	1.2	8	3	3	3	2	0	0	0	0	0	0	0	0	0	0	.000	0	0	16.20
St. Louis	NL	50	0	0	15	40.1	166	35	18	17	7	1	0	0	13	2	25	2	0	4	3	.571	0	2	3.79
1995 Los Angeles	NL	6	0	0	1	5	23	6	7	7	2	0	0	0	3	0	2	1	0	0	1	.000	0	0	12.60
Florida	NL	8	0	0	0	7.1	35	8	9	8	1	2	0	0	5	1	5	0	0	1	1	.500	0	0	9.82
11 ML YEARS		597	0	0	181	623.1	2659	598	277	252	54	37	18	5	247	41	520	37	1	32	38	.457	0	30	3.64

Eddie Murray

Bats: Both **Throws:** Right **Pos:** DH/1B   **Ht:** 6' 2" **Wt:** 220 **Born:** 2/24/56 **Age:** 40

									BATTING										BASERUNNING				PERCENTAGES		
Year Team	Lg	G	AB	H	2B	3B	HR	(Hm	Rd)	TB	R	RBI	TBB	IBB	SO	HBP	SH	SF	SB	CS	SB%	GDP	Avg	OBP	SLG
1977 Baltimore	AL	160	611	173	29	2	27	(14	13)	287	81	88	48	6	104	1	0	6	0	1	.00	22	.283	.333	.470
1978 Baltimore	AL	161	610	174	32	3	27	(10	17)	293	85	95	70	7	97	1	1	8	6	5	.55	15	.285	.356	.480
1979 Baltimore	AL	159	606	179	30	2	25	(10	15)	288	90	99	72	9	78	2	1	6	10	2	.83	16	.295	.369	.475
1980 Baltimore	AL	158	621	186	36	2	32	(10	22)	322	100	116	54	10	71	2	0	6	7	2	.78	18	.300	.354	.519
1981 Baltimore	AL	99	378	111	21	2	22	(12	10)	202	57	78	40	10	43	1	0	3	2	3	.40	10	.294	.360	.534
1982 Baltimore	AL	151	550	174	30	1	32	(18	14)	302	87	110	70	18	82	1	0	7	7	2	.78	17	.316	.391	.549
1983 Baltimore	AL	156	582	178	30	3	33	(16	17)	313	115	111	86	13	90	3	0	9	5	1	.83	13	.306	.393	.538
1984 Baltimore	AL	162	588	180	26	3	29	(18	11)	299	97	110	107	25	87	2	0	8	10	2	.83	9	.306	.410	.509
1985 Baltimore	AL	156	583	173	37	1	31	(15	16)	305	111	124	84	12	68	2	0	8	5	2	.71	8	.297	.383	.523
1986 Baltimore	AL	137	495	151	25	1	17	(9	8)	229	61	84	78	7	49	0	0	5	3	0	1.00	17	.305	.396	.463
1987 Baltimore	AL	160	618	171	28	3	30	(14	16)	295	89	91	73	6	80	0	0	3	1	2	.33	15	.277	.352	.477
1988 Baltimore	AL	161	603	171	27	2	28	(14	14)	286	75	84	75	8	78	0	0	3	5	2	.71	20	.284	.361	.474
1989 Los Angeles	NL	160	594	147	29	1	20	(4	16)	238	66	88	87	24	85	2	0	7	7	2	.78	12	.247	.342	.401
1990 Los Angeles	NL	155	558	184	22	3	26	(12	14)	290	96	95	82	21	64	1	0	4	8	5	.62	19	.330	.414	.520
1991 Los Angeles	NL	153	576	150	23	1	19	(11	8)	232	69	96	55	17	74	0	0	8	10	3	.77	17	.260	.321	.403
1992 New York	NL	156	551	144	37	2	16	(7	9)	233	64	93	66	8	74	0	0	8	4	2	.67	15	.261	.336	.423
1993 New York	NL	154	610	174	28	1	27	(15	12)	285	77	100	40	4	61	0	0	9	2	2	.50	24	.285	.325	.467
1994 Cleveland	AL	108	433	110	21	1	17	(7	10)	184	57	76	31	6	53	0	0	3	8	4	.67	8	.254	.302	.425
1995 Cleveland	AL	113	436	141	21	0	21	(11	10)	225	68	82	39	5	65	0	0	5	5	1	.83	15	.323	.375	.516
19 ML YEARS		2819	10603	3071	532	34	479	(227	252)	5108	1545	1820	1257	216	1403	18	2	115	105	43	.71	287	.290	.362	.482

Matt Murray

Pitches: Right **Bats:** Left **Pos:** RP   **Ht:** 6' 6" **Wt:** 235 **Born:** 9/26/70 **Age:** 25

				HOW MUCH HE PITCHED					WHAT HE GAVE UP										THE RESULTS					
Year Team	Lg	G	GS	CG	GF	IP	BFP	H	R	ER	HR	SH	SF	HB	TBB	IBB	SO	WP	Bk	W	L	Pct.	ShO	Sv	ERA
1988 Pulaski	R	13	8	0	3	54	234	48	32	25	4	4	1	1	26	0	76	5	2	2	4	.333	0	1	4.17
1989 Braves	R	2	2	0	0	7	27	3	0	0	0	0	0	1	0	0	10	0	0	1	0	1.000	0	0	0.00
Sumter	A	12	12	0	0	72.2	295	62	37	35	10	2	2	1	22	0	69	4	1	3	5	.375	0	0	4.33
1990 Burlington	A	26	26	6	0	163	671	139	72	59	9	4	2	3	60	0	134	10	1	11	7	.611	3	0	3.26
1991 Durham	A	2	2	0	0	7	26	5	1	1	0	0	0	0	0	0	7	0	0	1	0	1.000	0	0	1.29
1993 Macon	A	15	15	3	0	83.2	338	70	24	17	3	2	0	3	27	0	77	0	1	7	3	.700	0	0	1.83
1994 Durham	A	15	15	1	0	97.1	398	93	43	41	20	0	1	7	22	3	76	6	0	6	7	.462	0	0	3.79
Greenville	AA	12	12	0	0	67.1	312	89	43	38	7	1	2	2	31	0	48	3	0	3	4	.429	0	0	5.08
1995 Greenville	AA	5	5	0	0	29.1	111	20	5	5	0	1	0	1	8	0	25	2	0	4	0	1.000	0	0	1.53
Richmond	AAA	19	19	0	0	123	501	108	41	38	6	1	4	3	34	1	78	9	1	10	3	.769	0	0	2.78
1995 Atl-Bos		6	2	0	1	14	70	21	18	15	4	1	0	1	8	0	4	0	0	0	3	.000	0	0	9.64
1995 Atlanta	NL	4	1	0	1	10.2	46	10	8	8	3	1	0	1	5	0	3	0	0	0	2	.000	0	0	6.75
Boston	AL	2	1	0	0	3.1	24	11	10	7	1	0	0	0	3	0	1	0	0	0	1	.000	0	0	18.90

Mike Mussina

Pitches: Right **Bats:** Right **Pos:** SP   **Ht:** 6' 2" **Wt:** 185 **Born:** 12/8/68 **Age:** 27

			HOW MUCH HE PITCHED					WHAT HE GAVE UP									THE RESULTS					
Year Team	Lg	G	GS	CG	GF	IP	BFP	H	R	ER	HR	SH	SF	HB	TBB	IBB	SO	WP	Bk	W	L	Pct.	ShO	Sv	ERA
1991 Baltimore	AL	12	12	2	0	87.2	349	77	31	28	7	3	2	1	21	0	52	3	1	4	5	.444	0	0	2.87
1992 Baltimore	AL	32	32	8	0	241	957	212	70	68	16	13	6	2	48	2	130	6	0	18	5	.783	4	0	2.54
1993 Baltimore	AL	25	25	3	0	167.2	693	163	84	83	20	6	4	3	44	2	117	5	0	14	6	.700	2	0	4.46
1994 Baltimore	AL	24	24	3	0	176.1	712	163	63	60	19	3	9	1	42	1	99	0	0	16	5	.762	0	0	3.06
1995 Baltimore	AL	32	32	7	0	221.2	882	187	86	81	24	2	2	1	50	4	158	2	0	19	9	.679	4	0	3.29
5 ML YEARS		125	125	23	0	894.1	3593	802	334	320	86	27	23	8	205	9	556	16	1	71	30	.703	10	0	3.22

Greg Myers

Bats: Left **Throws:** Right **Pos:** C/DH   **Ht:** 6' 2" **Wt:** 215 **Born:** 4/14/66 **Age:** 30

							BATTING												BASERUNNING				PERCENTAGES		
Year Team	Lg	G	AB	H	2B	3B	HR	(Hm	Rd)	TB	R	RBI	TBB	IBB	SO	HBP	SH	SF	SB	CS	SB%	GDP	Avg	OBP	SLG
1987 Toronto	AL	7	9	1	0	0	0	(0	0)	1	1	0	0	0	3	0	0	0	0	0	.00	2	.111	.111	.111
1989 Toronto	AL	17	44	5	2	0	0	(0	0)	7	0	1	2	0	9	0	0	0	0	1	.00	2	.114	.152	.159
1990 Toronto	AL	87	250	59	7	1	5	(3	2)	83	33	22	22	0	33	0	1	4	0	1	.00	12	.236	.293	.332
1991 Toronto	AL	107	309	81	22	0	8	(5	3)	127	25	36	21	4	45	0	0	3	0	0	.00	13	.262	.306	.411
1992 Cal-Tor	AL	30	78	18	7	0	1	(0	1)	28	4	13	5	0	11	0	1	2	0	0	.00	2	.231	.271	.359
1993 California	AL	108	290	74	10	0	7	(4	3)	105	27	40	17	2	47	2	3	3	3	3	.50	8	.255	.298	.362
1994 California	AL	45	126	31	6	0	2	(1	1)	43	10	8	10	3	27	0	5	1	0	2	.00	3	.246	.299	.341
1995 California	AL	85	273	71	12	2	9	(6	3)	114	35	38	17	3	49	1	1	2	0	1	.00	4	.260	.304	.418
1992 California	AL	8	17	4	1	0	0	(0	0)	5	0	0	0	0	6	0	1	0	0	0	.00	0	.235	.235	.294
Toronto	AL	22	61	14	6	0	1	(0	1)	23	4	13	5	0	5	0	0	2	0	0	.00	2	.230	.279	.377
8 ML YEARS		486	1379	340	66	3	32	(19	13)	508	135	158	94	12	224	3	11	15	3	8	.27	46	.247	.293	.368

Mike Myers

Pitches: Left **Bats:** Left **Pos:** RP   **Ht:** 6' 3" **Wt:** 197 **Born:** 6/26/69 **Age:** 27

			HOW MUCH HE PITCHED					WHAT HE GAVE UP									THE RESULTS					
Year Team	Lg	G	GS	CG	GF	IP	BFP	H	R	ER	HR	SH	SF	HB	TBB	IBB	SO	WP	Bk	W	L	Pct.	ShO	Sv	ERA
1990 Everett	A	15	14	1	0	85.1	374	91	43	37	9	0	5	0	30	0	73	7	0	4	5	.444	0	0	3.90
1991 Clinton	A	11	11	1	0	65.1	263	61	23	19	3	2	2	0	18	0	59	4	3	5	3	.625	0	0	2.62
Giants	R	1	0	0	0	3	16	5	5	4	0	0	0	0	2	0	2	0	0	1	0	.000	0	0	12.00
1992 Clinton	A	7	7	0	0	37.2	147	28	11	5	0	1	1	2	8	0	32	4	0	1	2	.333	0	0	1.19
San Jose	A	8	8	0	0	54.2	215	43	20	14	1	1	0	2	17	0	40	3	1	5	1	.833	0	0	2.30
1993 Edmonton	AAA	27	27	3	0	161.2	733	195	109	94	20	5	7	10	52	1	112	7	1	7	14	.333	0	0	5.23
1994 Brevard Cty	A	3	2	0	0	11.1	43	7	1	1	1	1	0	0	4	0	15	0	0	0	0	.000	0	0	0.79
Edmonton	AAA	12	11	0	0	60	282	78	42	37	9	1	3	3	21	0	55	3	0	1	5	.167	0	0	5.55
1995 Charlotte	AAA	37	0	0	12	36.2	162	41	25	23	6	2	0	0	15	1	24	3	0	0	5	.000	0	0	5.65
Toledo	AAA	6	0	0	2	8.1	35	6	4	4	1	0	0	1	3	0	8	2	0	0	0	.000	0	0	4.32
1995 Fla-Det		13	0	0	5	8.1	42	11	7	7	1	0	1	2	7	0	4	0	0	1	0	1.000	0	0	7.56
1995 Florida	NL	2	0	0	2	2	9	1	0	0	0	0	0	0	3	0	0	0	0	0	0	.000	0	0	0.00
Detroit	AL	11	0	0	3	6.1	33	10	7	7	1	0	1	2	4	0	4	0	0	1	0	1.000	0	0	9.95

Randy Myers

Pitches: Left **Bats:** Left **Pos:** RP   **Ht:** 6' 1" **Wt:** 230 **Born:** 9/19/62 **Age:** 33

			HOW MUCH HE PITCHED					WHAT HE GAVE UP									THE RESULTS					
Year Team	Lg	G	GS	CG	GF	IP	BFP	H	R	ER	HR	SH	SF	HB	TBB	IBB	SO	WP	Bk	W	L	Pct.	ShO	Sv	ERA
1985 New York	NL	1	0	0	1	2	7	0	0	0	0	0	0	0	1	0	2	0	0	0	0	.000	0	0	0.00
1986 New York	NL	10	0	0	5	10.2	53	11	5	5	1	0	0	1	9	1	13	0	0	0	0	.000	0	0	4.22
1987 New York	NL	54	0	0	18	75	314	61	36	33	6	7	6	0	30	5	92	3	0	3	6	.333	0	6	3.96
1988 New York	NL	55	0	0	44	68	261	45	15	13	5	3	2	2	17	2	69	2	0	7	3	.700	0	26	1.72
1989 New York	NL	65	0	0	47	84.1	349	62	23	22	4	6	2	0	40	4	88	3	0	7	4	.636	0	24	2.35
1990 Cincinnati	NL	66	0	0	59	86.2	353	59	24	20	6	4	2	3	38	8	98	2	1	4	6	.400	0	31	2.08
1991 Cincinnati	NL	58	12	1	18	132	575	116	61	52	8	8	6	1	80	5	108	2	1	6	13	.316	0	6	3.55
1992 San Diego	NL	66	0	0	57	79.2	348	84	38	38	7	7	5	1	34	3	66	5	0	3	6	.333	0	38	4.29
1993 Chicago	NL	73	0	0	69	75.1	313	65	26	26	7	1	2	1	26	2	86	3	0	2	4	.333	0	53	3.11
1994 Chicago	NL	38	0	0	34	40.1	174	40	18	17	3	3	1	0	16	1	32	2	0	1	5	.167	0	21	3.79
1995 Chicago	NL	57	0	0	47	55.2	240	49	25	24	7	2	3	0	28	1	59	0	0	1	2	.333	0	38	3.88
11 ML YEARS		543	12	1	399	709.2	2987	592	271	250	54	41	29	9	319	32	713	22	2	34	49	.410	0	243	3.17

Chris Nabholz

Pitches: Left **Bats:** Left **Pos:** RP   **Ht:** 6' 5" **Wt:** 215 **Born:** 1/5/67 **Age:** 29

			HOW MUCH HE PITCHED					WHAT HE GAVE UP									THE RESULTS					
Year Team	Lg	G	GS	CG	GF	IP	BFP	H	R	ER	HR	SH	SF	HB	TBB	IBB	SO	WP	Bk	W	L	Pct.	ShO	Sv	ERA
1995 Iowa *	AAA	6	5	0	0	19.2	98	27	17	14	3	0	0	3	12	0	16	3	0	0	2	.000	0	0	6.41

Year	Team	Lg	G	GS	CG	GF	IP	BFP	H	R	ER	HR	SH	SF	HB	TBB	IBB	SO	WP	Bk	W	L	Pct.	ShO	Sv	ERA
1990	Montreal	NL	11	11	1	0	70	282	43	23	22	6	1	2	2	32	1	53	1	1	6	2	.750	1	0	2.83
1991	Montreal	NL	24	24	1	0	153.2	631	134	66	62	5	2	4	2	57	4	99	3	1	8	7	.533	0	0	3.63
1992	Montreal	NL	32	32	1	0	195	812	176	80	72	11	7	4	5	74	2	130	5	1	11	12	.478	1	0	3.32
1993	Montreal	NL	26	21	1	2	116.2	505	100	57	53	9	7	4	8	63	4	74	7	0	9	8	.529	0	0	4.09
1994	Bos-Cle	AL	14	12	0	1	53	254	67	48	45	6	0	2	3	38	1	28	6	0	3	5	.375	0	0	7.64
1995	Chicago	NL	34	0	0	4	23.1	104	22	15	14	4	1	2	0	14	3	21	2	0	0	1	.000	0	0	5.40
1994	Boston	AL	8	8	0	0	42	188	44	32	31	5	0	1	2	29	1	23	5	0	3	4	.429	0	0	6.64
	Cleveland	AL	6	4	0	1	11	66	23	16	14	1	0	1	1	9	0	5	1	0	0	1	.000	0	0	11.45
6 ML YEARS			141	100	4	7	611.2	2588	542	289	268	41	18	18	20	278	15	405	24	3	37	35	.514	2	0	3.94

Tim Naehring

Bats: Right **Throws:** Right **Pos:** 3B **Ht:** 6' 2" **Wt:** 205 **Born:** 2/1/67 **Age:** 29

Year	Team	Lg	G	AB	H	2B	3B	HR	(Hm	Rd)	TB	R	RBI	TBB	IBB	SO	HBP	SH	SF	SB	CS	SB%	GDP	Avg	OBP	SLG
1990	Boston	AL	24	85	23	6	0	2	(2	0)	35	10	12	8	1	15	0	0	0	0	0	.00	2	.271	.333	.412
1991	Boston	AL	20	55	6	1	0	0	(0	0)	7	1	3	6	0	15	0	4	0	0	0	.00	0	.109	.197	.127
1992	Boston	AL	72	186	43	8	0	3	(0	3)	60	12	14	18	0	31	3	6	1	0	0	.00	1	.231	.308	.323
1993	Boston	AL	39	127	42	10	0	1	(0	1)	55	14	17	10	0	26	0	3	1	1	0	1.00	3	.331	.377	.433
1994	Boston	AL	80	297	82	18	1	7	(4	3)	123	41	42	30	1	56	4	7	1	1	3	.25	11	.276	.349	.414
1995	Boston	AL	126	433	133	27	2	10	(5	5)	194	61	57	77	5	66	4	4	2	0	2	.00	16	.307	.415	.448
6 ML YEARS			361	1183	329	70	3	23	(11	12)	474	139	145	149	7	209	11	24	5	2	5	.29	33	.278	.363	.401

Charles Nagy

Pitches: Right **Bats:** Left **Pos:** SP **Ht:** 6' 3" **Wt:** 200 **Born:** 5/5/67 **Age:** 29

Year	Team	Lg	G	GS	CG	GF	IP	BFP	H	R	ER	HR	SH	SF	HB	TBB	IBB	SO	WP	Bk	W	L	Pct.	ShO	Sv	ERA
1990	Cleveland	AL	9	8	0	1	45.2	208	58	31	30	7	1	1	4	21	1	26	1	1	2	4	.333	0	0	5.91
1991	Cleveland	AL	33	33	6	0	211.1	914	228	103	97	15	5	9	6	66	7	109	6	2	10	15	.400	1	0	4.13
1992	Cleveland	AL	33	33	10	0	252	1018	245	91	83	11	6	9	2	57	1	169	7	0	17	10	.630	3	0	2.96
1993	Cleveland	AL	9	9	1	0	48.2	223	66	38	34	6	2	1	2	13	1	30	2	0	2	6	.250	0	0	6.29
1994	Cleveland	AL	23	23	3	0	169.1	717	175	76	65	15	2	2	5	48	1	108	5	1	10	8	.556	0	0	3.45
1995	Cleveland	AL	29	29	2	0	178	771	194	95	90	20	2	5	6	61	0	139	2	0	16	6	.727	1	0	4.55
6 ML YEARS			136	135	22	1	905	3851	966	434	399	74	18	27	22	266	11	581	23	4	57	49	.538	5	0	3.97

Bob Natal

Bats: Right **Throws:** Right **Pos:** C **Ht:** 5'11" **Wt:** 190 **Born:** 11/13/65 **Age:** 30

Year	Team	Lg	G	AB	H	2B	3B	HR	(Hm	Rd)	TB	R	RBI	TBB	IBB	SO	HBP	SH	SF	SB	CS	SB%	GDP	Avg	OBP	SLG
1995	Charlotte *	AAA	53	191	60	14	0	3	--	--	83	23	24	11	1	23	2	0	0	0	0	.00	4	.314	.358	.435
1992	Montreal	NL	5	6	0	0	0	0	(0	0)	0	0	0	1	0	1	0	0	0	0	0	.00	1	.000	.143	.000
1993	Florida	NL	41	117	25	4	1	1	(0	1)	34	3	6	6	0	22	4	3	1	1	0	1.00	6	.214	.273	.291
1994	Florida	NL	10	29	8	2	0	0	(0	0)	10	2	2	5	0	5	0	0	0	1	0	1.00	1	.276	.382	.345
1995	Florida	NL	16	43	10	2	1	2	(2	0)	20	2	6	1	0	9	0	1	1	0	0	.00	0	.233	.244	.465
4 ML YEARS			72	195	43	8	2	3	(2	1)	64	7	14	13	0	37	4	4	2	2	0	1.00	8	.221	.280	.328

Jaime Navarro

Pitches: Right **Bats:** Right **Pos:** SP **Ht:** 6' 4" **Wt:** 225 **Born:** 3/27/68 **Age:** 28

Year	Team	Lg	G	GS	CG	GF	IP	BFP	H	R	ER	HR	SH	SF	HB	TBB	IBB	SO	WP	Bk	W	L	Pct.	ShO	Sv	ERA
1989	Milwaukee	AL	19	17	1	1	109.2	470	119	47	38	6	5	2	1	32	3	56	3	0	7	8	.467	0	0	3.12
1990	Milwaukee	AL	32	22	3	2	149.1	654	176	83	74	11	4	5	4	41	3	75	6	5	8	7	.533	0	1	4.46
1991	Milwaukee	AL	34	34	10	0	234	1002	237	117	102	18	7	8	6	73	3	114	10	0	15	12	.556	2	0	3.92
1992	Milwaukee	AL	34	34	5	0	246	1004	224	98	91	14	9	13	6	64	4	100	6	0	17	11	.607	3	0	3.33
1993	Milwaukee	AL	35	34	5	0	214.1	955	254	135	127	21	6	17	11	73	4	114	11	0	11	12	.478	1	0	5.33
1994	Milwaukee	AL	29	10	0	7	89.2	411	115	71	66	10	2	4	4	35	4	65	3	0	4	9	.308	0	0	6.62
1995	Chicago	NL	29	29	1	0	200.1	837	194	79	73	19	2	3	3	56	7	128	1	0	14	6	.700	1	0	3.28
7 ML YEARS			212	180	25	10	1243.1	5333	1319	630	571	99	35	52	52	374	28	652	40	5	76	65	.539	7	1	4.13

Denny Neagle

Pitches: Left **Bats:** Left **Pos:** SP **Ht:** 6' 2" **Wt:** 216 **Born:** 9/13/68 **Age:** 27

Year	Team	Lg	G	GS	CG	GF	IP	BFP	H	R	ER	HR	SH	SF	HB	TBB	IBB	SO	WP	Bk	W	L	Pct.	ShO	Sv	ERA
1991	Minnesota	AL	7	3	0	2	20	92	28	9	9	3	0	0	0	7	2	14	1	0	0	1	.000	0	0	4.05
1992	Pittsburgh	NL	55	6	0	8	86.1	380	81	46	43	9	4	3	2	43	8	77	3	2	4	6	.400	0	2	4.48
1993	Pittsburgh	NL	50	7	0	13	81.1	360	82	49	48	10	1	1	3	37	3	73	5	0	3	5	.375	0	1	5.31
1994	Pittsburgh	NL	24	24	2	0	137	587	135	80	78	18	7	6	3	49	3	122	2	0	9	10	.474	0	0	5.12

Year Team	Lg	G	GS	CG	GF	IP	BFP	H	R	ER	HR	SH	SF	HB	TBB	IBB	SO	WP	Bk	W	L	Pct.	ShO	Sv	ERA
1995 Pittsburgh	NL	31	31	5	0	209.2	876	221	91	80	20	13	6	3	45	3	150	6	0	13	8	.619	1	0	3.43
5 ML YEARS		167	71	7	23	534.1	2295	547	275	258	60	25	16	11	181	19	436	17	2	29	30	.492	1	3	4.35

Troy Neel

Bats: Left **Throws:** Right **Pos:** 1B/DH **Ht:** 6' 4" **Wt:** 215 **Born:** 9/14/65 **Age:** 30

					BATTING													BASERUNNING				PERCENTAGES		
Year Team	Lg	G	AB	H	2B	3B	HR	(Hm	Rd)	TB	R	RBI	TBB	IBB	SO	HBP	SH	SF	SB	CS	SB%	GDP	Avg	OBP	SLG
1992 Oakland	AL	24	53	14	3	0	3	(2	1)	26	8	9	5	0	15	1	0	0	0	1	.00	1	.264	.339	.491
1993 Oakland	AL	123	427	124	21	0	19	(11	8)	202	59	63	49	5	101	4	0	2	3	5	.38	7	.290	.367	.473
1994 Oakland	AL	83	278	74	13	0	15	(6	9)	132	43	48	38	5	61	2	1	1	2	3	.40	4	.266	.357	.475
3 ML YEARS		230	758	212	37	0	37	(19	18)	360	110	120	92	10	177	7	1	3	5	9	.36	12	.280	.362	.475

Jeff Nelson

Pitches: Right **Bats:** Right **Pos:** RP **Ht:** 6' 8" **Wt:** 235 **Born:** 11/17/66 **Age:** 29

		HOW MUCH HE PITCHED						WHAT HE GAVE UP												THE RESULTS					
Year Team	Lg	G	GS	CG	GF	IP	BFP	H	R	ER	HR	SH	SF	HB	TBB	IBB	SO	WP	Bk	W	L	Pct.	ShO	Sv	ERA
1992 Seattle	AL	66	0	0	27	81	352	71	34	31	7	9	3	6	44	12	46	2	0	1	7	.125	0	6	3.44
1993 Seattle	AL	71	0	0	14	60	269	57	30	29	5	2	4	8	34	10	61	2	0	5	3	.625	0	1	4.35
1994 Seattle	AL	28	0	0	7	42.1	185	35	18	13	3	1	1	8	20	4	44	2	1	0	0	.000	0	0	2.76
1995 Seattle	AL	62	0	0	24	78.2	318	58	21	19	4	5	3	6	27	5	96	1	0	7	3	.700	0	2	2.17
4 ML YEARS		227	0	0	71	262	1124	221	103	92	19	17	11	28	125	31	247	7	0	13	13	.500	0	9	3.16

Robb Nen

Pitches: Right **Bats:** Right **Pos:** RP **Ht:** 6' 4" **Wt:** 190 **Born:** 11/28/69 **Age:** 26

		HOW MUCH HE PITCHED						WHAT HE GAVE UP												THE RESULTS					
Year Team	Lg	G	GS	CG	GF	IP	BFP	H	R	ER	HR	SH	SF	HB	TBB	IBB	SO	WP	Bk	W	L	Pct.	ShO	Sv	ERA
1993 Tex-Fla		24	4	0	5	56	272	63	45	42	6	1	2	0	46	0	39	6	1	2	1	.667	0	0	6.75
1994 Florida	NL	44	0	0	28	58	228	46	20	19	6	3	1	0	17	2	60	3	2	5	5	.500	0	15	2.95
1995 Florida	NL	62	0	0	54	65.2	279	62	26	24	6	0	1	1	23	3	68	2	0	0	7	.000	0	23	3.29
1993 Texas	AL	9	3	0	3	22.2	113	28	17	16	1	0	1	0	26	0	12	2	1	1	1	.500	0	0	6.35
Florida	NL	15	1	0	2	33.1	159	35	28	26	5	1	1	0	20	0	27	4	0	1	0	1.000	0	0	7.02
3 ML YEARS		130	4	0	87	179.2	779	171	91	85	18	4	4	1	86	5	167	11	3	7	13	.350	0	38	4.26

Phil Nevin

Bats: Right **Throws:** Right **Pos:** LF/3B **Ht:** 6' 2" **Wt:** 180 **Born:** 1/19/71 **Age:** 25

					BATTING													BASERUNNING				PERCENTAGES		
Year Team	Lg	G	AB	H	2B	3B	HR	(Hm	Rd)	TB	R	RBI	TBB	IBB	SO	HBP	SH	SF	SB	CS	SB%	GDP	Avg	OBP	SLG
1993 Tucson	AAA	123	448	128	21	3	10	--	--	185	67	93	52	1	99	3	0	7	8	1	.89	12	.286	.359	.413
1994 Tucson	AAA	118	445	117	20	1	12	--	--	175	67	79	55	2	101	1	0	4	3	2	.60	21	.263	.343	.393
1995 Tucson	AAA	62	223	65	16	0	7	--	--	102	31	41	27	1	39	1	1	0	2	3	.40	9	.291	.371	.457
Toledo	AAA	7	23	7	2	0	1	--	--	12	3	3	1	0	5	0	0	0	0	0	.00	0	.304	.333	.522
1995 Hou-Det		47	156	28	4	1	2	(2	0)	40	13	13	18	1	40	4	1	0	1	0	1.00	5	.179	.281	.256
1995 Houston	NL	18	60	7	1	0	0	(0	0)	8	4	1	7	1	13	1	1	0	1	0	1.00	2	.117	.221	.133
Detroit	AL	29	96	21	3	1	2	(2	0)	32	9	12	11	0	27	3	0	0	0	0	.00	3	.219	.318	.333

Marc Newfield

Bats: Right **Throws:** Right **Pos:** LF **Ht:** 6' 4" **Wt:** 205 **Born:** 10/19/72 **Age:** 23

					BATTING													BASERUNNING				PERCENTAGES		
Year Team	Lg	G	AB	H	2B	3B	HR	(Hm	Rd)	TB	R	RBI	TBB	IBB	SO	HBP	SH	SF	SB	CS	SB%	GDP	Avg	OBP	SLG
1995 Tacoma *	AAA	53	198	55	11	0	5	--	--	81	30	30	19	1	30	5	0	0	1	0	1.00	6	.278	.356	.409
Las Vegas *	AAA	20	70	24	5	1	3	--	--	40	10	12	3	0	11	1	1	1	2	0	1.00	1	.343	.373	.571
1993 Seattle	AL	22	66	15	3	0	1	(1	0)	21	5	7	2	0	8	1	0	1	0	1	.00	2	.227	.257	.318
1994 Seattle	AL	12	38	7	1	0	1	(0	1)	11	3	4	2	0	4	0	0	0	0	0	.00	2	.184	.225	.289
1995 Sea-SD		45	140	33	8	1	4	(1	3)	55	13	21	5	1	24	1	0	0	0	0	.00	5	.236	.267	.393
1995 Seattle	AL	24	85	16	3	0	3	(0	3)	28	7	14	3	1	16	1	0	0	0	0	.00	2	.188	.225	.329
San Diego	NL	21	55	17	5	1	1	(1	0)	27	6	7	2	0	8	0	0	0	0	0	.00	3	.309	.333	.491
3 ML YEARS		79	244	55	12	1	6	(2	4)	87	21	32	9	1	36	2	0	1	0	1	.00	9	.225	.258	.357

Warren Newson

Bats: Left **Throws:** Left **Pos:** LF/RF **Ht:** 5' 7" **Wt:** 202 **Born:** 7/3/64 **Age:** 31

					BATTING													BASERUNNING				PERCENTAGES		
Year Team	Lg	G	AB	H	2B	3B	HR	(Hm	Rd)	TB	R	RBI	TBB	IBB	SO	HBP	SH	SF	SB	CS	SB%	GDP	Avg	OBP	SLG
1991 Chicago	AL	71	132	39	5	0	4	(1	3)	56	20	25	28	1	34	0	0	0	2	2	.50	4	.295	.419	.424
1992 Chicago	AL	63	136	30	3	0	1	(1	0)	36	19	11	37	2	38	0	0	0	0	0	1.00	3	.221	.387	.265
1993 Chicago	AL	26	40	12	0	0	2	(2	0)	18	9	6	9	1	12	0	0	0	0	0	.00	2	.300	.429	.450
1994 Chicago	AL	63	102	26	5	0	2	(2	0)	37	16	7	14	1	23	0	2	0	1	0	1.00	3	.255	.345	.363
1995 ChA-Sea	AL	84	157	41	2	2	5	(4	1)	62	34	15	39	0	45	1	0	0	2	1	.67	3	.261	.411	.395
1995 Chicago	AL	51	85	20	0	2	3	(3	0)	33	19	9	23	0	27	1	0	0	1	1	.50	2	.235	.404	.388

		G																							
Seattle	AL	33	72	21	2	0	2	(1	1)	29	15	6	16	0	18	0	0	0	1	0	1.00	1	.292	.420	.403
5 ML YEARS		307	567	148	15	2	14	(10	4)	209	98	64	127	5	152	1	2	0	8	3	.73	16	.261	.397	.369

Rod Nichols

Pitches: Right **Bats:** Right **Pos:** RP **Ht:** 6' 2" **Wt:** 190 **Born:** 12/29/64 **Age:** 31

		HOW MUCH HE PITCHED						WHAT HE GAVE UP											THE RESULTS					
Year Team	Lg	G	GS	CG	GF	IP	BFP	H	R	ER	HR	SH	SF	HB	TBB	IBB	SO	WP	Bk	W	L	Pct.	ShO	Sv	ERA
1995 Richmond *	AAA	41	3	0	37	57	232	54	16	16	5	0	1	2	6	1	57	1	0	1	2	.333	0	25	2.53
1988 Cleveland	AL	11	10	3	1	69.1	297	73	41	39	5	2	2	2	23	1	31	2	3	1	7	.125	0	0	5.06
1989 Cleveland	AL	15	11	0	2	71.2	315	81	42	35	9	3	2	2	24	0	42	0	1	4	6	.400	0	0	4.40
1990 Cleveland	AL	4	2	0	0	16	79	24	14	14	5	1	0	2	6	0	3	0	0	0	3	.000	0	0	7.88
1991 Cleveland	AL	31	16	3	4	137.1	578	145	63	54	6	6	4	6	30	3	76	3	0	2	11	.154	1	1	3.54
1992 Cleveland	AL	30	9	0	5	105.1	456	114	58	53	13	1	5	2	31	1	56	3	0	4	3	.571	0	0	4.53
1993 Los Angeles	NL	4	0	0	2	6.1	28	9	5	4	1	1	0	0	2	2	3	0	0	0	1	.000	0	0	5.68
1995 Atlanta	NL	5	0	0	0	6.2	38	14	11	4	3	0	0	0	5	1	3	0	0	0	0	.000	0	0	5.40
7 ML YEARS		100	48	6	14	412.2	1791	460	234	203	42	14	13	14	121	8	214	8	3	11	31	.262	1	1	4.43

Chris Nichting

Pitches: Right **Bats:** Right **Pos:** RP **Ht:** 6' 1" **Wt:** 205 **Born:** 5/13/66 **Age:** 30

		HOW MUCH HE PITCHED						WHAT HE GAVE UP											THE RESULTS					
Year Team	Lg	G	GS	CG	GF	IP	BFP	H	R	ER	HR	SH	SF	HB	TBB	IBB	SO	WP	Bk	W	L	Pct.	ShO	Sv	ERA
1988 Vero Beach	A	21	19	5	2	138	545	90	40	32	7	0	2	0	51	0	151	7	0	11	4	.733	1	1	2.09
1989 San Antonio	AA	26	26	2	0	154	698	160	96	86	13	9	6	6	101	6	136	14	4	4	14	.222	0	0	5.03
1992 Albuquerque	AAA	10	9	0	0	42	205	64	42	37	2	2	0	0	23	1	25	5	1	1	3	.250	0	0	7.93
San Antonio	AA	13	13	0	0	78.2	309	58	25	22	3	4	0	1	37	0	81	4	0	4	5	.444	0	0	2.52
1993 Vero Beach	A	4	4	0	0	17.1	75	18	9	8	2	0	0	0	6	0	18	1	0	0	1	.000	0	0	4.15
1994 Albuquerque	AAA	10	7	0	1	41.1	209	61	39	34	5	0	0	3	28	1	25	6	0	2	2	.500	0	0	7.40
San Antonio	AA	21	8	0	8	65.2	277	47	21	12	1	4	1	2	34	1	74	7	1	3	4	.429	0	1	1.64
1995 Okla. City	AAA	23	7	3	8	67.2	275	58	19	16	4	4	2	2	19	0	72	2	0	5	5	.500	2	1	2.13
1995 Texas	AL	13	0	0	3	24.1	122	36	19	19	1	1	2	1	13	1	6	3	0	0	0	.000	0	0	7.03

Dave Nied

Pitches: Right **Bats:** Right **Pos:** RP **Ht:** 6' 2" **Wt:** 185 **Born:** 12/22/68 **Age:** 27

		HOW MUCH HE PITCHED						WHAT HE GAVE UP											THE RESULTS					
Year Team	Lg	G	GS	CG	GF	IP	BFP	H	R	ER	HR	SH	SF	HB	TBB	IBB	SO	WP	Bk	W	L	Pct.	ShO	Sv	ERA
1995 Portland *	A	1	1	0	0	3	10	1	0	0	0	0	0	0	1	0	5	0	0	0	0	.000	0	0	0.00
New Haven *	AA	1	1	0	0	3.1	14	4	3	3	2	0	0	0	0	0	0	0	0	0	0	.000	0	0	8.10
Colo. Sprng *	AAA	7	7	0	0	30.2	141	31	18	17	0	4	0	2	25	2	21	2	0	1	1	.500	0	0	4.99
1992 Atlanta	NL	6	2	0	0	23	83	10	3	3	0	1	0	0	5	0	19	0	0	3	0	1.000	0	0	1.17
1993 Colorado	NL	16	16	1	0	87	394	99	53	50	8	9	7	1	42	4	46	1	1	5	9	.357	0	0	5.17
1994 Colorado	NL	22	22	2	0	122	538	137	70	65	15	7	3	4	47	5	74	7	2	9	7	.563	1	0	4.80
1995 Colorado	NL	2	0	0	0	4.1	27	11	10	10	2	0	0	0	3	0	3	0	0	0	0	.000	0	0	20.77
4 ML YEARS		46	40	3	0	236.1	1042	257	136	128	25	17	10	5	97	9	142	8	3	17	16	.515	1	0	4.87

Melvin Nieves

Bats: Both **Throws:** Right **Pos:** LF/RF **Ht:** 6' 2" **Wt:** 210 **Born:** 12/28/71 **Age:** 24

		BATTING																	BASERUNNING				PERCENTAGES		
Year Team	Lg	G	AB	H	2B	3B	HR	(Hm	Rd)	TB	R	RBI	TBB	IBB	SO	HBP	SH	SF	SB	CS	SB%	GDP	Avg	OBP	SLG
1988 Braves	R	56	176	30	6	0	1	--	--	39	16	12	20	0	53	2	1	1	5	4	.56	2	.170	.261	.222
1989 Pulaski	R	64	231	64	16	3	9	--	--	113	43	46	30	4	59	1	3	4	6	4	.60	2	.277	.357	.489
1990 Sumter	A	126	459	130	24	7	9	--	--	195	60	59	53	4	125	9	1	9	10	6	.63	7	.283	.362	.425
1991 Durham	A	64	201	53	11	0	9	--	--	91	31	25	40	2	53	5	0	1	3	8	.27	1	.264	.397	.453
1992 Durham	A	31	106	32	9	1	8	--	--	67	18	32	17	3	33	2	0	4	4	2	.67	1	.302	.395	.632
Greenville	AA	100	350	99	23	5	18	--	--	186	61	76	52	6	98	6	2	4	6	4	.60	4	.283	.381	.531
1993 Richmond	AAA	78	273	76	10	3	10	--	--	122	38	36	25	4	84	2	1	1	4	3	.57	4	.278	.342	.447
Las Vegas	AAA	43	159	49	10	1	7	--	--	82	31	24	18	0	42	2	0	0	2	2	.50	1	.308	.385	.516
1994 Las Vegas	AAA	111	406	125	17	6	25	--	--	229	81	92	58	3	138	8	0	2	1	2	.33	10	.308	.403	.564
1992 Atlanta	NL	12	19	4	1	0	0	(0	0)	5	0	1	2	0	7	0	0	0	0	0	.00	0	.211	.286	.263
1993 San Diego	NL	19	47	9	0	0	2	(2	0)	15	4	3	3	0	21	1	0	0	0	0	.00	0	.191	.255	.319
1994 San Diego	NL	10	19	5	1	0	1	(0	1)	9	2	4	3	0	10	0	0	0	0	0	.00	0	.263	.364	.474
1995 San Diego	NL	98	234	48	6	1	14	(5	9)	98	32	38	19	0	88	5	1	3	2	3	.40	9	.205	.276	.419
4 ML YEARS		139	319	66	8	1	17	(7	10)	127	38	46	27	0	126	6	1	3	2	3	.40	9	.207	.279	.398

Dave Nilsson

Bats: Left **Throws:** Right **Pos:** RF/LF/DH **Ht:** 6' 3" **Wt:** 215 **Born:** 12/14/69 **Age:** 26

Year Team	Lg	G	AB	H	2B	3B	HR	(Hm	Rd)	TB	R	RBI	TBB	IBB	SO	HBP	SH	SF	SB	CS	SB%	GDP	Avg	OBP	SLG
1995 Beloit *	A	3	11	6	3	0	1	--	--	12	2	7	2	0	0	0	0	0	0	0	.00	0	.545	.615	1.091
El Paso *	AA	5	15	7	1	0	1	--	--	11	1	4	0	0	1	0	0	0	1	0	1.00	0	.467	.467	.733
New Orleans *	AAA	3	9	4	0	0	1	--	--	7	1	4	2	0	0	0	0	0	0	0	.00	0	.444	.545	.778
1992 Milwaukee	AL	51	164	38	8	0	4	(1	3)	58	15	25	17	1	18	0	2	0	2	2	.50	1	.232	.304	.354
1993 Milwaukee	AL	100	296	76	10	2	7	(5	2)	111	35	40	37	5	36	0	4	3	3	6	.33	10	.257	.336	.375
1994 Milwaukee	AL	109	397	109	28	3	12	(4	8)	179	51	69	34	9	61	0	1	8	1	0	1.00	7	.275	.326	.451
1995 Milwaukee	AL	81	263	73	12	1	12	(7	5)	123	41	53	24	4	41	2	0	5	2	0	1.00	9	.278	.337	.468
4 ML YEARS		341	1120	296	58	6	35	(17	18)	471	142	187	112	19	156	2	7	16	8	8	.50	27	.264	.328	.421

C.J. Nitkowski

Pitches: Left **Bats:** Left **Pos:** SP **Ht:** 6' 3" **Wt:** 190 **Born:** 3/3/73 **Age:** 23

		HOW MUCH HE PITCHED						WHAT HE GAVE UP												THE RESULTS					
Year Team	Lg	G	GS	CG	GF	IP	BFP	H	R	ER	HR	SH	SF	HB	TBB	IBB	SO	WP	Bk	W	L	Pct.	ShO	Sv	ERA
1994 Chattanooga	AA	14	14	0	0	74.2	318	61	30	29	4	5	0	4	40	0	60	2	5	6	3	.667	0	0	3.50
1995 Chattanooga	AA	8	8	0	0	50.1	204	39	20	14	1	3	0	1	20	0	52	1	1	4	2	.667	0	0	2.50
Indianapols	AAA	6	6	0	0	27.2	120	28	16	16	3	0	2	1	10	0	21	0	1	0	0	.000	0	0	5.20
1995 Cin-Det		20	18	0	0	71.2	338	94	57	53	11	2	4	5	35	3	31	2	2	2	7	.222	0	0	6.66
1995 Cincinnati	NL	9	7	0	0	32.1	154	41	25	22	4	2	1	2	15	1	18	1	2	1	3	.250	0	0	6.12
Detroit	AL	11	11	0	0	39.1	184	53	32	31	7	0	3	3	20	2	13	1	0	1	4	.200	0	0	7.09

Otis Nixon

Bats: Both **Throws:** Right **Pos:** CF **Ht:** 6' 2" **Wt:** 180 **Born:** 1/9/59 **Age:** 37

Year Team	Lg	G	AB	H	2B	3B	HR	(Hm	Rd)	TB	R	RBI	TBB	IBB	SO	HBP	SH	SF	SB	CS	SB%	GDP	Avg	OBP	SLG
1983 New York	AL	13	14	2	0	0	0	(0	0)	2	2	0	1	0	5	0	0	0	2	0	1.00	0	.143	.200	.143
1984 Cleveland	AL	49	91	14	0	0	0	(0	0)	14	16	1	8	0	11	0	3	1	12	6	.67	2	.154	.220	.154
1985 Cleveland	AL	104	162	38	4	0	3	(1	2)	51	34	9	8	0	27	0	4	0	20	11	.65	2	.235	.271	.315
1986 Cleveland	AL	105	95	25	4	1	0	(0	0)	31	33	8	13	0	12	0	2	0	23	6	.79	1	.263	.352	.326
1987 Cleveland	AL	19	17	1	0	0	0	(0	0)	1	2	1	3	0	4	0	0	0	2	3	.40	0	.059	.200	.059
1988 Montreal	NL	90	271	66	8	2	0	(0	0)	78	47	15	28	0	42	0	4	2	46	13	.78	0	.244	.312	.288
1989 Montreal	NL	126	258	56	7	2	0	(0	0)	67	41	21	33	1	36	0	2	0	37	12	.76	4	.217	.306	.260
1990 Montreal	NL	119	231	58	6	2	1	(0	1)	71	46	20	28	0	33	0	3	1	50	13	.79	2	.251	.331	.307
1991 Atlanta	NL	124	401	119	10	1	0	(0	0)	131	81	26	47	3	40	2	7	3	72	21	.77	5	.297	.371	.327
1992 Atlanta	NL	120	456	134	14	2	2	(1	1)	158	79	22	39	0	54	0	5	2	41	18	.69	4	.294	.348	.346
1993 Atlanta	NL	134	461	124	12	3	1	(1	0)	145	77	24	61	2	63	0	5	5	47	13	.78	10	.269	.351	.315
1994 Boston	AL	103	398	109	15	1	0	(0	0)	126	60	25	55	1	65	0	6	2	42	10	.81	6	.274	.360	.317
1995 Texas	AL	139	589	174	21	2	0	(0	0)	199	87	45	58	1	85	0	6	3	50	21	.70	6	.295	.357	.338
13 ML YEARS		1245	3444	920	101	16	7	(3	4)	1074	605	217	382	8	477	2	47	19	444	147	.75	36	.267	.339	.312

Matt Nokes

Bats: Left **Throws:** Right **Pos:** C **Ht:** 6' 1" **Wt:** 210 **Born:** 10/31/63 **Age:** 32

Year Team	Lg	G	AB	H	2B	3B	HR	(Hm	Rd)	TB	R	RBI	TBB	IBB	SO	HBP	SH	SF	SB	CS	SB%	GDP	Avg	OBP	SLG
1995 Colo. Sprng *	AAA	12	37	8	2	0	4	--	--	22	7	10	2	0	4	1	0	3	0	0	.00	1	.216	.256	.595
1985 San Francisco	NL	19	53	11	2	0	2	(1	1)	19	3	5	1	0	9	1	0	0	0	0	.00	2	.208	.236	.358
1986 Detroit	AL	7	24	8	1	0	1	(0	1)	12	2	2	1	1	1	0	0	0	0	0	.00	1	.333	.360	.500
1987 Detroit	AL	135	461	133	14	2	32	(14	18)	247	69	87	35	2	70	6	3	3	2	1	.67	13	.289	.345	.536
1988 Detroit	AL	122	382	96	18	0	16	(9	7)	162	53	53	34	3	58	1	6	2	0	1	.00	11	.251	.313	.424
1989 Detroit	AL	87	268	67	10	0	9	(7	2)	104	15	39	17	1	37	2	1	2	1	0	1.00	7	.250	.298	.388
1990 Det-NYA	AL	136	351	87	9	1	11	(4	7)	131	33	40	24	6	47	6	0	1	2	2	.50	11	.248	.306	.373
1991 New York	AL	135	456	122	20	0	24	(13	11)	214	52	77	25	5	49	5	0	7	3	2	.60	6	.268	.308	.469
1992 New York	AL	121	384	86	9	1	22	(18	4)	163	42	59	37	11	62	3	0	6	0	1	.00	13	.224	.293	.424
1993 New York	AL	76	217	54	8	0	10	(4	6)	92	25	35	16	2	31	2	0	3	0	0	.00	4	.249	.303	.424
1994 New York	AL	28	79	23	3	0	7	(6	1)	47	11	19	5	0	16	0	0	1	0	0	.00	1	.291	.329	.595
1995 Bal-Col		36	60	8	2	0	2	(1	1)	16	5	6	5	1	15	0	0	1	0	0	.00	3	.133	.197	.267
1990 Detroit	AL	44	111	30	5	1	3	(1	2)	46	12	8	4	3	14	2	0	1	0	0	.00	5	.270	.305	.414
New York	AL	92	240	57	4	0	8	(3	5)	85	21	32	20	3	33	4	0	0	2	2	.50	6	.238	.307	.354
1995 Baltimore	AL	26	49	6	1	0	2	(1	1)	13	4	6	4	0	11	0	0	1	0	0	.00	2	.122	.185	.265
Colorado	NL	10	11	2	1	0	0	(0	0)	3	1	0	1	1	4	0	0	0	0	0	.00	1	.182	.250	.273
11 ML YEARS		902	2735	695	96	4	136	(77	59)	1207	310	422	200	32	395	26	10	26	8	7	.53	72	.254	.308	.441

Hideo Nomo

Pitches: Right **Bats:** Right **Pos:** SP **Ht:** 6' 2" **Wt:** 210 **Born:** 8/31/68 **Age:** 27

Year Team	Lg	HOW MUCH HE PITCHED						WHAT HE GAVE UP												THE RESULTS					
		G	GS	CG	GF	IP	BFP	H	R	ER	HR	SH	SF	HB	TBB	IBB	SO	WP	Bk	W	L	Pct.	ShO	Sv	ERA
1995 Bakersfield	A	1	1	0	0	5.1	24	6	2	2	0	0	0	1	1	0	6	1	0	0	1	.000	0	0	3.38
1995 Los Angeles	NL	28	28	4	0	191.1	780	124	63	54	14	11	4	5	78	2	236	19	5	13	6	.684	3	0	2.54

Les Norman

Bats: Right **Throws:** Right **Pos:** RF **Ht:** 6' 1" **Wt:** 185 **Born:** 2/25/69 **Age:** 27

Year Team	Lg	BATTING																	BASERUNNING				PERCENTAGES		
		G	AB	H	2B	3B	HR	(Hm	Rd)	TB	R	RBI	TBB	IBB	SO	HBP	SH	SF	SB	CS	SB%	GDP	Avg	OBP	SLG
1991 Eugene	A	30	102	25	4	1	2	--	--	37	14	18	9	0	18	1	2	1	2	1	.67	4	.245	.310	.363
1992 Appleton	A	59	218	82	17	1	4	--	--	113	38	47	22	0	18	1	2	3	8	6	.57	5	.376	.430	.518
Memphis	AA	72	271	74	14	5	3	--	--	107	32	20	22	0	37	2	1	1	4	4	.50	2	.273	.331	.395
1993 Memphis	AA	133	484	141	32	5	17	--	--	234	78	81	50	3	88	14	7	2	11	9	.55	8	.291	.373	.483
1994 Omaha	AAA	13	38	7	3	0	1	--	--	13	4	4	6	0	11	1	1	0	0	1	.00	2	.184	.311	.342
Memphis	AA	106	383	101	19	4	13	--	--	167	53	55	36	1	44	7	3	2	7	7	.50	0	.264	.336	.436
1995 Omaha	AAA	83	313	89	19	3	9	--	--	141	46	33	18	2	48	4	3	2	5	3	.63	3	.284	.329	.450
1995 Kansas City	AL	24	40	9	0	1	0	(0	0)	11	6	4	6	0	6	0	1	0	0	1	.00	0	.225	.326	.275

Jon Nunnally

Bats: Left **Throws:** Right **Pos:** RF/LF **Ht:** 5'10" **Wt:** 190 **Born:** 11/9/71 **Age:** 24

Year Team	Lg	BATTING																	BASERUNNING				PERCENTAGES		
		G	AB	H	2B	3B	HR	(Hm	Rd)	TB	R	RBI	TBB	IBB	SO	HBP	SH	SF	SB	CS	SB%	GDP	Avg	OBP	SLG
1992 Watertown	A	69	246	59	10	4	5	--	--	92	39	43	32	2	55	1	0	4	12	3	.80	3	.240	.325	.374
1993 Columbus	A	125	438	110	15	2	15	--	--	174	81	56	63	0	108	3	4	6	17	11	.61	5	.251	.345	.397
1994 Kinston	A	132	483	129	29	2	22	--	--	228	70	74	64	3	125	3	1	3	23	11	.68	5	.267	.354	.472
1995 Kansas City	AL	119	303	74	15	6	14	(6	8)	143	51	42	51	5	86	2	4	0	6	4	.60	4	.244	.357	.472

Charlie O'Brien

Bats: Right **Throws:** Right **Pos:** C **Ht:** 6' 2" **Wt:** 205 **Born:** 5/1/61 **Age:** 35

Year Team	Lg	BATTING																	BASERUNNING				PERCENTAGES		
		G	AB	H	2B	3B	HR	(Hm	Rd)	TB	R	RBI	TBB	IBB	SO	HBP	SH	SF	SB	CS	SB%	GDP	Avg	OBP	SLG
1985 Oakland	AL	16	11	3	1	0	0	(0	0)	4	3	1	3	0	3	0	0	0	0	0	.00	0	.273	.429	.364
1987 Milwaukee	AL	10	35	7	3	1	0	(0	0)	12	2	0	4	0	4	0	1	0	0	0	.00	0	.200	.282	.343
1988 Milwaukee	AL	40	118	26	6	0	2	(2	0)	38	12	9	5	0	16	0	4	0	0	1	.00	3	.220	.252	.322
1989 Milwaukee	AL	62	188	44	10	0	6	(4	2)	72	22	35	21	1	11	9	8	0	0	0	.00	11	.234	.339	.383
1990 Mil-NYN		74	213	38	10	2	0	(0	0)	52	17	20	21	3	34	3	10	2	0	0	.00	4	.178	.259	.244
1991 New York	NL	69	168	31	6	0	2	(1	1)	43	16	14	17	1	25	4	0	2	0	2	.00	5	.185	.272	.256
1992 New York	NL	68	156	33	12	0	2	(1	1)	51	15	13	16	1	18	1	4	0	0	1	.00	4	.212	.289	.327
1993 New York	NL	67	188	48	11	0	4	(1	3)	71	15	23	14	1	14	2	3	1	1	1	.50	4	.255	.312	.378
1994 Atlanta	NL	51	152	37	11	0	8	(6	2)	72	24	28	15	2	24	3	1	1	0	0	.00	5	.243	.322	.474
1995 Atlanta	NL	67	198	45	7	0	9	(4	5)	79	18	23	29	2	40	6	0	0	0	0	.00	8	.227	.343	.399
1990 Milwaukee	AL	46	145	27	7	2	0	(0	0)	38	11	11	11	1	26	2	8	0	0	0	.00	3	.186	.259	.262
New York	NL	28	68	11	3	0	0	(0	0)	14	6	9	10	2	8	1	2	2	0	0	.00	1	.162	.272	.206
10 ML YEARS		524	1427	312	77	3	33	(19	14)	494	144	166	145	11	189	28	31	6	1	7	.13	44	.219	.302	.346

Troy O'Leary

Bats: Left **Throws:** Left **Pos:** RF/LF/CF **Ht:** 6' 0" **Wt:** 198 **Born:** 8/4/69 **Age:** 26

Year Team	Lg	BATTING																	BASERUNNING				PERCENTAGES		
		G	AB	H	2B	3B	HR	(Hm	Rd)	TB	R	RBI	TBB	IBB	SO	HBP	SH	SF	SB	CS	SB%	GDP	Avg	OBP	SLG
1993 Milwaukee	AL	19	41	12	3	0	0	(0	0)	15	3	3	5	0	9	0	3	0	0	0	.00	1	.293	.370	.366
1994 Milwaukee	AL	27	66	18	1	1	2	(0	2)	27	9	7	5	0	12	1	0	1	1	1	.50	0	.273	.329	.409
1995 Boston	AL	112	399	123	31	6	10	(5	5)	196	60	49	29	4	64	1	3	2	5	3	.63	8	.308	.355	.491
3 ML YEARS		158	506	153	35	7	12	(5	7)	238	72	59	39	4	85	2	6	3	6	4	.60	9	.302	.353	.470

Paul O'Neill

Bats: Left **Throws:** Left **Pos:** RF/LF **Ht:** 6' 4" **Wt:** 215 **Born:** 2/25/63 **Age:** 33

Year Team	Lg	BATTING																	BASERUNNING				PERCENTAGES		
		G	AB	H	2B	3B	HR	(Hm	Rd)	TB	R	RBI	TBB	IBB	SO	HBP	SH	SF	SB	CS	SB%	GDP	Avg	OBP	SLG
1985 Cincinnati	NL	5	12	4	1	0	0	(0	0)	5	1	1	0	0	2	0	0	0	0	0	.00	0	.333	.333	.417
1986 Cincinnati	NL	3	2	0	0	0	0	(0	0)	0	0	0	0	1	0	0	0	0	0	0	.00	0	.000	.333	.000
1987 Cincinnati	NL	84	160	41	14	1	7	(4	3)	78	24	28	18	1	29	0	0	0	2	1	.67	3	.256	.331	.488
1988 Cincinnati	NL	145	485	122	25	3	16	(12	4)	201	58	73	38	5	65	2	3	5	8	6	.57	7	.252	.306	.414
1989 Cincinnati	NL	117	428	118	24	2	15	(11	4)	191	49	74	46	8	64	2	0	4	20	5	.80	7	.276	.346	.446
1990 Cincinnati	NL	145	503	136	28	0	16	(10	6)	212	59	78	53	13	103	2	1	5	13	11	.54	12	.270	.339	.421

Year Team	Lg	G	AB	H	2B	3B	HR	(Hm	Rd)	TB	R	RBI	TBB	IBB	SO	HBP	SH	SF	SB	CS	SB%	GDP	Avg	OBP	SLG
1991 Cincinnati	NL	152	532	136	36	0	28	(20	8)	256	71	91	73	14	107	1	0	1	12	7	.63	8	.256	.346	.481
1992 Cincinnati	NL	148	496	122	19	1	14	(6	8)	185	59	66	77	15	85	2	3	6	6	3	.67	10	.246	.346	.373
1993 New York	AL	141	498	155	34	1	20	(8	12)	251	71	75	44	5	69	2	0	3	2	4	.33	13	.311	.367	.504
1994 New York	AL	103	368	132	25	1	21	(10	11)	222	68	83	72	13	56	0	0	3	5	4	.56	16	**.359**	.460	.603
1995 New York	AL	127	460	138	30	4	22	(12	10)	242	82	96	71	8	76	1	0	11	1	2	.33	**25**	.300	.387	.526
11 ML YEARS		1170	3944	1104	236	13	159	(93	66)	1843	542	665	493	82	657	12	7	38	69	43	.62	101	.280	.359	.467

Sherman Obando

Bats: Right **Throws:** Right **Pos:** RF   **Ht:** 6' 4" **Wt:** 215 **Born:** 1/23/70 **Age:** 26

			BATTING																BASERUNNING				PERCENTAGES		
Year Team	Lg	G	AB	H	2B	3B	HR	(Hm	Rd)	TB	R	RBI	TBB	IBB	SO	HBP	SH	SF	SB	CS	SB%	GDP	Avg	OBP	SLG
1988 Yankees	R	49	172	44	10	2	4	--	--	70	26	27	16	2	32	3	0	1	8	5	.62	3	.256	.328	.407
1989 Oneonta	A	70	276	86	23	3	6	--	--	133	50	45	16	1	45	6	1	2	8	5	.62	3	.312	.360	.482
1990 Pr. William	A	121	439	117	24	6	10	--	--	183	67	67	42	1	85	11	0	6	5	3	.63	7	.267	.341	.417
1991 Yankees	R	4	17	5	2	0	0	--	--	7	3	1	1	0	2	1	0	0	0	0	.00	0	.294	.368	.412
Pr. William	A	42	140	37	11	1	7	--	--	71	25	31	19	2	28	2	0	2	0	1	.00	1	.264	.356	.507
1992 Albany-Colo	AA	109	381	107	19	3	17	--	--	183	71	56	32	1	67	8	2	4	3	1	.75	12	.281	.346	.480
1993 Bowie	AA	19	58	14	2	0	3	--	--	25	8	12	9	0	11	1	0	3	1	0	1.00	1	.241	.338	.431
1994 Rochester	AAA	109	403	133	36	7	20	--	--	243	67	69	30	4	53	6	0	7	1	1	.50	3	.330	.379	.603
1995 Rochester	AAA	85	324	96	26	6	9	--	--	161	42	53	29	3	57	3	0	4	1	1	.50	11	.296	.356	.497
1993 Baltimore	AL	31	92	25	2	0	3	(2	1)	36	8	15	4	0	26	1	0	0	0	0	.00	1	.272	.309	.391
1995 Baltimore	AL	16	38	10	1	0	0	(0	0)	11	0	3	2	0	12	0	0	1	1	0	1.00	0	.263	.293	.289
2 ML YEARS		47	130	35	3	0	3	(2	1)	47	8	18	6	0	38	1	0	1	1	0	1.00	1	.269	.304	.362

Alex Ochoa

Bats: Right **Throws:** Right **Pos:** RF   **Ht:** 6' 0" **Wt:** 185 **Born:** 3/29/72 **Age:** 24

			BATTING																BASERUNNING				PERCENTAGES		
Year Team	Lg	G	AB	H	2B	3B	HR	(Hm	Rd)	TB	R	RBI	TBB	IBB	SO	HBP	SH	SF	SB	CS	SB%	GDP	Avg	OBP	SLG
1991 Orioles	R	53	179	55	8	3	1	--	--	72	26	30	16	0	14	1	3	1	11	6	.65	2	.307	.365	.402
1992 Kane County	A	133	499	147	22	7	1	--	--	186	65	59	58	5	55	7	5	7	31	17	.65	14	.295	.371	.373
1993 Frederick	A	137	532	147	29	5	13	--	--	225	84	90	46	0	67	9	1	6	34	13	.72	15	.276	.341	.423
1994 Bowie	AA	134	519	156	25	2	14	--	--	227	77	82	49	0	67	1	5	12	28	15	.65	11	.301	.355	.437
1995 Rochester	AAA	91	336	92	18	2	8	--	--	138	41	46	26	1	50	2	1	2	17	7	.71	8	.274	.328	.411
Norfolk	AAA	34	123	38	6	2	2	--	--	54	17	15	14	0	12	0	0	1	7	3	.70	4	.309	.377	.439
1995 New York	NL	11	37	11	1	0	0	(0	0)	12	7	0	2	0	10	0	0	0	1	0	1.00	1	.297	.333	.324

Jose Offerman

Bats: Both **Throws:** Right **Pos:** SS   **Ht:** 6' 0" **Wt:** 188 **Born:** 11/8/68 **Age:** 27

			BATTING																BASERUNNING				PERCENTAGES		
Year Team	Lg	G	AB	H	2B	3B	HR	(Hm	Rd)	TB	R	RBI	TBB	IBB	SO	HBP	SH	SF	SB	CS	SB%	GDP	Avg	OBP	SLG
1990 Los Angeles	NL	29	58	9	0	0	1	(1	0)	12	7	7	4	1	14	0	1	0	1	0	1.00	0	.155	.210	.207
1991 Los Angeles	NL	52	113	22	2	0	0	(0	0)	24	10	3	25	2	32	1	1	0	3	2	.60	5	.195	.345	.212
1992 Los Angeles	NL	149	534	139	20	8	1	(1	0)	178	67	30	57	4	98	0	5	2	23	16	.59	5	.260	.331	.333
1993 Los Angeles	NL	158	590	159	21	6	1	(1	0)	195	77	62	71	7	75	2	**25**	8	30	13	.70	12	.269	.346	.331
1994 Los Angeles	NL	72	243	51	8	4	1	(0	1)	70	27	25	38	4	38	0	6	2	2	1	.67	6	.210	.314	.288
1995 Los Angeles	NL	119	429	123	14	6	4	(2	2)	161	69	33	69	0	67	3	10	0	2	7	.22	5	.287	.389	.375
6 ML YEARS		579	1967	503	65	24	8	(5	3)	640	257	160	264	18	324	6	48	12	61	39	.61	33	.256	.344	.325

Chad Ogea

Pitches: Right **Bats:** Right **Pos:** SP/RP   **Ht:** 6' 2" **Wt:** 200 **Born:** 11/9/70 **Age:** 25

		HOW MUCH HE PITCHED					WHAT HE GAVE UP										THE RESULTS					
Year Team	Lg	G	GS	CG	GF	IP	BFP	H	R	ER	HR	SH	SF	HB	TBB	IBB	SO	WP	Bk	W	L	Pct.	ShO	Sv	ERA
1992 Kinston	A	21	21	5	0	139.1	573	135	61	54	6	6	4	5	29	0	123	7	4	13	3	.813	2	0	3.49
Canton-Akrn	AA	7	7	1	0	49	195	38	12	12	2	1	0	4	12	0	40	3	0	6	1	.857	1	0	2.20
1993 Charlotte	AAA	29	29	2	0	181.2	751	169	91	77	26	4	3	2	54	0	135	6	4	13	8	.619	0	0	3.81
1994 Charlotte	AAA	24	23	6	1	163.2	658	146	80	70	21	4	8	4	34	0	113	3	1	9	10	.474	0	1	3.85
1995 Buffalo	AAA	4	4	0	0	17.2	79	16	12	9	1	0	0	2	8	0	11	0	0	1	0	.000	0	0	4.58
1994 Cleveland	AL	4	1	0	0	16.1	80	21	11	11	2	0	0	1	10	2	11	0	0	0	1	.000	0	0	6.06
1995 Cleveland	AL	20	14	1	3	106.1	442	95	38	36	11	0	5	1	29	0	57	3	1	8	3	.727	0	0	3.05
2 ML YEARS		24	15	1	3	122.2	522	116	49	47	13	0	5	2	39	2	68	3	1	8	4	.667	0	0	3.45

John Olerud

Bats: Left **Throws:** Left **Pos:** 1B   **Ht:** 6' 5" **Wt:** 218 **Born:** 8/5/68 **Age:** 27

			BATTING																BASERUNNING				PERCENTAGES		
Year Team	Lg	G	AB	H	2B	3B	HR	(Hm	Rd)	TB	R	RBI	TBB	IBB	SO	HBP	SH	SF	SB	CS	SB%	GDP	Avg	OBP	SLG
1989 Toronto	AL	6	8	3	0	0	0	(0	0)	3	2	0	1	0	1	0	0	0	0	0	.00	0	.375	.375	.375

Year	Team	Lg	G	AB	H	2B	3B	HR	(Hm	Rd)	TB	R	RBI	TBB	IBB	SO	HBP	SH	SF	SB	CS	SB%	GDP	Avg	OBP	SLG
1990	Toronto	AL	111	358	95	15	1	14	(11	3)	154	43	48	57	6	75	1	1	4	0	2	.00	5	.265	.364	.430
1991	Toronto	AL	139	454	116	30	1	17	(7	10)	199	64	68	68	9	84	6	3	10	0	2	.00	12	.256	.353	.438
1992	Toronto	AL	138	458	130	28	0	16	(4	12)	206	68	66	70	11	61	1	1	7	1	0	1.00	15	.284	.375	.450
1993	Toronto	AL	158	551	200	54	2	24	(9	15)	330	109	107	114	33	65	7	0	7	0	2	.00	12	.363	.473	.599
1994	Toronto	AL	108	384	114	29	2	12	(6	6)	183	47	67	61	12	53	3	0	5	1	2	.33	11	.297	.393	.477
1995	Toronto	AL	135	492	143	32	0	8	(1	7)	199	72	54	84	10	54	4	0	1	0	0	.00	17	.291	.398	.404
	7 ML YEARS		795	2705	801	188	6	91	(38	53)	1274	405	410	454	81	393	22	5	34	2	8	.20	72	.296	.397	.471

Jose Oliva

Bats: Right **Throws:** Right **Pos:** 3B **Ht:** 6' 3" **Wt:** 215 **Born:** 3/3/71 **Age:** 25

			BATTING																	BASERUNNING				PERCENTAGES		
Year	Team	Lg	G	AB	H	2B	3B	HR	(Hm	Rd)	TB	R	RBI	TBB	IBB	SO	HBP	SH	SF	SB	CS	SB%	GDP	Avg	OBP	SLG
1988	Rangers	R	27	70	15	3	0	1	--	--	21	5	11	3	1	14	0	0	1	0	0	.00	1	.214	.243	.300
1989	Butte	R	41	114	24	2	3	4	--	--	44	18	13	14	1	41	1	0	2	4	3	.57	0	.211	.298	.386
1990	Gastonia	A	119	383	80	24	1	10	--	--	136	44	52	26	0	104	4	3	8	9	3	.75	5	.209	.261	.355
1991	Rangers	R	3	11	1	1	0	0	--	--	2	0	1	2	0	3	0	0	1	0	0	.00	0	.091	.214	.182
	Charlotte	A	108	384	92	17	4	14	--	--	159	55	59	44	3	107	5	1	6	9	9	.50	15	.240	.321	.414
1992	Tulsa	AA	124	445	120	28	6	16	--	--	208	57	75	40	3	135	2	2	7	4	0	1.00	7	.270	.328	.467
1993	Richmond	AAA	125	412	97	20	6	21	--	--	192	63	65	35	2	134	4	0	1	1	5	.17	10	.235	.301	.466
1994	Richmond	AAA	99	371	94	17	0	24	--	--	183	52	64	25	3	92	2	0	3	2	2	.50	7	.253	.302	.493
1994	Atlanta	NL	19	59	17	5	0	6	(4	2)	40	9	11	7	0	10	0	0	0	0	1	.00	2	.288	.364	.678
1995	Atl-StL	NL	70	183	26	5	0	7	(2	5)	52	15	20	12	0	46	0	0	1	0	0	.00	7	.142	.202	.284
1995	Atlanta	NL	48	109	17	4	0	5	(1	4)	36	7	12	7	0	22	0	0	0	0	0	.00	2	.156	.207	.330
	St. Louis	NL	22	74	9	1	0	2	(1	1)	16	8	8	5	0	24	2	0	1	0	0	.00	3	.122	.195	.216
	2 ML YEARS		89	242	43	10	0	13	(6	7)	92	24	31	19	0	56	0	0	1	0	1	.00	7	.178	.242	.380

Omar Olivares

Pitches: Right **Bats:** Right **Pos:** RP/SP **Ht:** 6' 1" **Wt:** 193 **Born:** 7/6/67 **Age:** 28

			HOW MUCH HE PITCHED						WHAT HE GAVE UP									THE RESULTS					
Year	Team	Lg	G	GS	CG	GF	IP	BFP	H	R	ER	HR	SH	SF	HB	TBB	IBB	SO	WP	Bk	W	L	Pct.	ShO	Sv	ERA
1995	Colo. Sprng *	AAA	3	2	0	0	11.2	52	14	7	7	1	1	1	1	2	0	6	0	0	0	1	.000	0	0	5.40
	Scrantn-WB *	AAA	7	7	0	0	44.1	197	49	25	24	2	2	0	4	20	2	28	3	0	0	3	.000	0	0	4.87
1990	St. Louis	NL	9	6	0	0	49.1	201	45	17	16	2	1	0	2	17	0	20	1	1	1	1	.500	0	0	2.92
1991	St. Louis	NL	28	24	0	2	167.1	688	148	72	69	13	11	2	5	61	1	91	3	1	11	7	.611	0	1	3.71
1992	St. Louis	NL	32	30	1	1	197	818	189	84	84	20	8	7	4	63	5	124	2	0	9	9	.500	0	0	3.84
1993	St. Louis	NL	58	9	0	11	118.2	537	134	60	55	10	4	4	9	54	7	63	4	3	5	3	.625	0	1	4.17
1994	St. Louis	NL	14	12	1	2	73.2	333	84	53	47	10	3	3	4	37	0	26	5	0	3	4	.429	0	1	5.74
1995	Col-Phi	NL	16	6	0	4	41.2	195	55	34	32	5	2	2	3	23	0	22	4	0	1	4	.200	0	0	6.91
1995	Colorado	NL	11	6	0	1	31.2	151	44	28	26	4	1	1	2	21	0	15	4	0	1	3	.250	0	0	7.39
	Philadelphia	NL	5	0	0	3	10	44	11	6	6	1	1	1	1	2	0	7	0	0	0	1	.000	0	0	5.40
	6 ML YEARS		157	87	2	20	647.2	2772	655	320	303	60	29	18	27	255	13	346	19	5	30	28	.517	0	3	4.21

Darren Oliver

Pitches: Left **Bats:** Right **Pos:** RP/SP **Ht:** 6' 2" **Wt:** 200 **Born:** 10/6/70 **Age:** 25

			HOW MUCH HE PITCHED						WHAT HE GAVE UP									THE RESULTS					
Year	Team	Lg	G	GS	CG	GF	IP	BFP	H	R	ER	HR	SH	SF	HB	TBB	IBB	SO	WP	Bk	W	L	Pct.	ShO	Sv	ERA
1993	Texas	AL	2	0	0	0	3.1	14	2	1	1	0	0	0	0	1	1	4	0	0	0	0	.000	0	0	2.70
1994	Texas	AL	43	0	0	10	50	226	40	24	19	4	6	0	6	35	4	50	2	2	4	0	1.000	0	2	3.42
1995	Texas	AL	17	7	0	2	49	222	47	25	23	3	5	1	1	32	1	39	4	0	4	2	.667	0	0	4.22
	3 ML YEARS		62	7	0	12	102.1	462	89	50	43	8	11	1	7	68	6	93	6	2	8	2	.800	0	2	3.78

Joe Oliver

Bats: Right **Throws:** Right **Pos:** C **Ht:** 6' 3" **Wt:** 220 **Born:** 7/24/65 **Age:** 30

			BATTING																	BASERUNNING				PERCENTAGES		
Year	Team	Lg	G	AB	H	2B	3B	HR	(Hm	Rd)	TB	R	RBI	TBB	IBB	SO	HBP	SH	SF	SB	CS	SB%	GDP	Avg	OBP	SLG
1995	New Orleans *	AAA	4	13	1	1	0	0	--	--	2	0	0	0	0	3	0	0	0	0	0	.00	0	.077	.077	.154
1989	Cincinnati	NL	49	151	41	8	0	3	(1	2)	58	13	23	6	1	28	1	1	2	0	0	.00	3	.272	.300	.384
1990	Cincinnati	NL	121	364	84	23	0	8	(3	5)	131	34	52	37	15	75	2	5	1	1	1	.50	6	.231	.304	.360
1991	Cincinnati	NL	94	269	58	11	0	11	(7	4)	102	21	41	18	5	53	0	4	0	0	0	.00	14	.216	.265	.379
1992	Cincinnati	NL	143	485	131	25	1	10	(7	3)	188	42	57	35	19	75	1	6	7	2	3	.40	12	.270	.316	.388
1993	Cincinnati	NL	139	482	115	28	0	14	(7	7)	185	40	75	27	2	91	1	2	9	0	0	.00	13	.239	.276	.384
1994	Cincinnati	NL	6	19	4	0	0	1	(1	0)	7	1	5	2	1	3	0	0	0	0	0	.00	1	.211	.286	.368
1995	Milwaukee	AL	97	337	92	20	0	12	(4	8)	148	43	51	27	1	66	3	2	0	2	4	.33	11	.273	.332	.439
	7 ML YEARS		649	2107	525	115	1	59	(30	29)	819	194	304	152	44	391	8	20	19	5	8	.38	60	.249	.300	.389

Gregg Olson

Pitches: Right **Bats:** Right **Pos:** RP   **Ht:** 6' 4" **Wt:** 212 **Born:** 10/11/66 **Age:** 29

Year Team	Lg	G	GS	CG	GF	IP	BFP	H	R	ER	HR	SH	SF	HB	TBB	IBB	SO	WP	Bk	W	L	Pct.	ShO	Sv	ERA
1995 Buffalo *	AAA	18	0	0	17	21.2	92	16	6	6	0	1	0	3	9	0	25	0	0	1	0	1.000	0	13	2.49
Omaha *	AAA	1	0	0	1	1	4	0	0	0	0	0	0	0	1	0	1	1	0	0	0	.000	0	0	0.00
1988 Baltimore	AL	10	0	0	4	11	51	10	4	4	1	0	0	0	10	1	9	0	1	1	1	.500	0	0	3.27
1989 Baltimore	AL	64	0	0	52	85	356	57	17	16	1	4	1	1	46	10	90	9	3	5	2	.714	0	27	1.69
1990 Baltimore	AL	64	0	0	58	74.1	305	57	20	20	3	1	2	3	31	3	74	5	0	6	5	.545	0	37	2.42
1991 Baltimore	AL	72	0	0	62	73.2	319	74	28	26	1	5	1	1	29	5	72	8	1	4	6	.400	0	31	3.18
1992 Baltimore	AL	60	0	0	56	61.1	244	46	14	14	3	0	2	0	24	0	58	4	0	1	5	.167	0	36	2.05
1993 Baltimore	AL	50	0	0	45	45	188	37	9	8	1	2	2	0	18	3	44	5	0	0	2	.000	0	29	1.60
1994 Atlanta	NL	16	0	0	6	14.2	77	19	15	15	1	2	1	1	13	3	10	0	2	0	2	.000	0	1	9.20
1995 Cle-KC	AL	23	0	0	12	33	141	28	15	15	4	1	2	0	19	2	21	1	0	3	3	.500	0	3	4.09
1995 Cleveland	AL	3	0	0	2	2.2	14	5	4	4	1	0	0	0	2	0	0	0	0	0	0	.000	0	0	13.50
Kansas City	AL	20	0	0	10	30.1	127	23	11	11	3	1	2	0	17	2	21	1	0	3	3	.500	0	3	3.26
8 ML YEARS		359	0	0	295	398	1681	328	122	118	15	15	11	6	190	27	378	32	7	20	26	.435	0	164	2.67

Steve Ontiveros

Pitches: Right **Bats:** Right **Pos:** SP   **Ht:** 6' 0" **Wt:** 190 **Born:** 3/5/61 **Age:** 35

Year Team	Lg	G	GS	CG	GF	IP	BFP	H	R	ER	HR	SH	SF	HB	TBB	IBB	SO	WP	Bk	W	L	Pct.	ShO	Sv	ERA
1985 Oakland	AL	39	0	0	18	74.2	284	45	17	16	4	2	2	2	19	2	36	1	0	1	3	.250	0	8	1.93
1986 Oakland	AL	46	0	0	27	72.2	305	72	40	38	10	1	6	1	25	3	54	4	0	2	2	.500	0	10	4.71
1987 Oakland	AL	35	22	2	6	150.2	645	141	78	67	19	6	2	4	50	3	97	4	1	10	8	.556	1	1	4.00
1988 Oakland	AL	10	10	0	0	54.2	241	57	32	28	4	5	0	0	21	1	30	5	5	3	4	.429	0	0	4.61
1989 Philadelphia	NL	6	5	0	0	30.2	134	34	15	13	2	1	0	0	15	1	12	2	0	2	1	.667	0	0	3.82
1990 Philadelphia	NL	5	0	0	1	10	43	9	3	3	1	0	0	0	3	0	6	0	0	0	0	.000	0	0	2.70
1993 Seattle	AL	14	0	0	8	18	72	18	3	2	0	1	0	0	6	2	13	1	0	0	2	.000	0	0	1.00
1994 Oakland	AL	27	13	2	5	115.1	463	93	39	34	7	2	1	6	26	1	56	5	0	6	4	.600	0	0	2.65
1995 Oakland	AL	22	22	2	0	129.2	558	144	75	63	12	2	6	4	38	0	77	5	0	9	6	.600	1	0	4.37
9 ML YEARS		204	72	6	65	656.1	2745	613	302	264	59	20	17	17	203	13	381	27	6	33	30	.524	2	19	3.62

Jose Oquendo

Bats: Both **Throws:** Right **Pos:** 2B/SS   **Ht:** 5'10" **Wt:** 171 **Born:** 7/4/63 **Age:** 32

Year Team	Lg	G	AB	H	2B	3B	HR	(Hm	Rd)	TB	R	RBI	TBB	IBB	SO	HBP	SH	SF	SB	CS	SB%	GDP	Avg	OBP	SLG
1983 New York	NL	120	328	70	7	0	1	(0	1)	80	29	17	19	2	60	2	3	1	8	9	.47	10	.213	.260	.244
1984 New York	NL	81	189	42	5	0	0	(0	0)	47	23	10	15	2	26	2	3	2	10	1	.91	2	.222	.284	.249
1986 St. Louis	NL	76	138	41	4	1	0	(0	0)	47	20	13	15	4	20	0	2	3	2	3	.40	3	.297	.359	.341
1987 St. Louis	NL	116	248	71	9	0	1	(0	1)	83	43	24	54	6	29	0	6	4	4	4	.50	6	.286	.408	.335
1988 St. Louis	NL	148	451	125	10	1	7	(4	3)	158	36	46	52	7	40	0	12	3	4	6	.40	8	.277	.350	.350
1989 St. Louis	NL	163	556	162	28	7	1	(0	1)	207	59	48	79	7	59	0	7	8	3	5	.38	12	.291	.375	.372
1990 St. Louis	NL	156	469	118	17	5	1	(1	0)	148	38	37	74	8	46	0	5	5	1	1	.50	7	.252	.350	.316
1991 St. Louis	NL	127	366	88	11	4	1	(0	1)	110	37	26	67	13	48	1	4	3	1	2	.33	5	.240	.357	.301
1992 St. Louis	NL	14	35	9	3	1	0	(0	0)	14	3	3	5	1	3	0	0	0	0	0	.00	0	.257	.350	.400
1993 St. Louis	NL	46	73	15	0	0	0	(0	0)	15	7	4	12	1	8	0	3	0	0	0	.00	5	.205	.314	.205
1994 St. Louis	NL	55	129	34	2	2	0	(0	0)	40	13	9	21	4	16	0	1	1	1	1	.50	6	.264	.364	.310
1995 St. Louis	NL	88	220	46	8	3	2	(0	2)	66	31	17	35	3	21	0	4	1	1	1	.50	1	.209	.316	.300
12 ML YEARS		1190	3202	821	104	24	14	(5	9)	1015	339	254	448	58	376	5	50	32	35	33	.51	65	.256	.346	.317

Mike Oquist

Pitches: Right **Bats:** Right **Pos:** RP   **Ht:** 6' 2" **Wt:** 170 **Born:** 5/30/68 **Age:** 28

Year Team	Lg	G	GS	CG	GF	IP	BFP	H	R	ER	HR	SH	SF	HB	TBB	IBB	SO	WP	Bk	W	L	Pct.	ShO	Sv	ERA
1995 Rochester *	AAA	7	0	0	3	12	56	17	8	7	0	0	0	0	5	1	11	0	0	0	0	.000	0	2	5.25
1993 Baltimore	AL	5	0	0	2	11.2	50	12	5	5	0	0	0	0	4	1	8	0	0	0	0	.000	0	0	3.86
1994 Baltimore	AL	15	9	0	3	58.1	278	75	41	40	7	3	4	6	30	4	39	3	0	3	3	.500	0	0	6.17
1995 Baltimore	AL	27	0	0	2	54	255	51	27	25	6	1	4	2	41	3	27	2	0	2	1	.667	0	0	4.17
3 ML YEARS		47	9	0	7	124	583	138	73	70	13	4	8	8	75	8	74	5	0	5	4	.556	0	0	5.08

Jesse Orosco

Pitches: Left **Bats:** Right **Pos:** RP   **Ht:** 6' 2" **Wt:** 205 **Born:** 4/21/57 **Age:** 39

Year Team	Lg	G	GS	CG	GF	IP	BFP	H	R	ER	HR	SH	SF	HB	TBB	IBB	SO	WP	Bk	W	L	Pct.	ShO	Sv	ERA
1979 New York	NL	18	2	0	6	35	154	33	20	19	4	3	0	2	22	0	22	0	0	1	2	.333	0	0	4.89
1981 New York	NL	8	0	0	4	17	69	13	4	3	2	2	0	0	6	2	18	0	1	0	1	.000	0	1	1.59

Year	Team	Lg	G	GS	CG	GF	IP	BFP	H	R	ER	HR	SH	SF	HB	TBB	IBB	SO	WP	Bk	W	L	Pct.	ShO	Sv	ERA
1982	New York	NL	54	2	0	22	109.1	451	92	37	33	7	5	4	2	40	2	89	3	2	4	10	.286	0	4	2.72
1983	New York	NL	62	0	0	42	110	432	76	27	18	3	4	3	1	38	7	84	1	2	13	7	.650	0	17	1.47
1984	New York	NL	60	0	0	52	87	355	58	29	25	7	3	3	2	34	6	85	1	1	10	6	.625	0	31	2.59
1985	New York	NL	54	0	0	39	79	331	66	26	24	6	1	1	0	34	7	68	4	0	8	6	.571	0	17	2.73
1986	New York	NL	58	0	0	40	81	338	64	23	21	6	2	3	3	35	3	62	2	0	8	6	.571	0	21	2.33
1987	New York	NL	58	0	0	41	77	335	78	41	38	5	5	4	2	31	9	78	2	0	3	9	.250	0	16	4.44
1988	Los Angeles	NL	55	0	0	21	53	229	41	18	16	4	3	3	2	30	3	43	1	0	3	2	.600	0	9	2.72
1989	Cleveland	AL	69	0	0	29	78	312	54	20	18	7	8	3	2	26	4	79	0	0	3	4	.429	0	3	2.08
1990	Cleveland	AL	55	0	0	28	64.2	289	58	35	28	9	5	3	0	38	7	55	1	0	5	4	.556	0	2	3.90
1991	Cleveland	AL	47	0	0	20	45.2	202	52	20	19	4	1	3	1	15	8	36	1	1	2	0	1.000	0	0	3.74
1992	Milwaukee	AL	59	0	0	14	39	158	33	15	14	5	0	2	1	13	1	40	2	0	3	1	.750	0	1	3.23
1993	Milwaukee	AL	57	0	0	27	56.2	233	47	25	20	2	1	2	3	17	3	67	1	0	3	5	.375	0	8	3.18
1994	Milwaukee	AL	40	0	0	5	39	174	32	26	22	4	0	2	2	26	2	36	0	0	3	1	.750	0	0	5.08
1995	Baltimore	AL	65	0	0	23	49.2	200	28	19	18	4	2	4	1	27	7	58	2	1	2	4	.333	0	3	3.26
16 ML YEARS			819	4	0	413	1021	4262	825	385	336	79	45	40	24	432	71	920	23	9	71	68	.511	0	133	2.96

Joe Orsulak

Bats: Left **Throws:** Left **Pos:** LF/RF **Ht:** 6' 1" **Wt:** 205 **Born:** 5/31/62 **Age:** 34

					BATTING														BASERUNNING				PERCENTAGES		
Year	Team	Lg	G	AB	H	2B	3B	HR	(Hm	Rd)	TB	R	RBI	TBB	IBB	SO	HBP	SH	SF	SB	CS	SB%	GDP	Avg	OBP	SLG
1983	Pittsburgh	NL	7	11	2	0	0	0	(0	0)	2	0	1	0	0	2	0	0	1	0	1	.00	0	.182	.167	.182
1984	Pittsburgh	NL	32	67	17	1	2	0	(0	0)	22	12	3	1	0	7	1	3	1	3	1	.75	0	.254	.271	.328
1985	Pittsburgh	NL	121	397	119	14	6	0	(0	0)	145	54	21	26	3	27	1	9	3	24	11	.69	5	.300	.342	.365
1986	Pittsburgh	NL	138	401	100	19	6	2	(0	2)	137	60	19	28	2	38	1	6	1	24	11	.69	4	.249	.299	.342
1988	Baltimore	AL	125	379	109	21	3	8	(3	5)	160	48	27	23	2	30	3	8	3	9	8	.53	7	.288	.331	.422
1989	Baltimore	AL	123	390	111	22	5	7	(0	7)	164	59	55	41	6	35	2	7	6	5	3	.63	8	.285	.351	.421
1990	Baltimore	AL	124	413	111	14	3	11	(9	2)	164	49	57	46	9	48	1	4	1	6	8	.43	7	.269	.343	.397
1991	Baltimore	AL	143	486	135	22	1	5	(3	2)	174	57	43	28	1	45	4	0	3	6	2	.75	9	.278	.321	.358
1992	Baltimore	AL	117	391	113	18	3	4	(2	2)	149	45	39	28	5	34	4	4	1	5	4	.56	3	.289	.342	.381
1993	New York	NL	134	409	116	15	4	8	(5	3)	163	59	35	28	1	25	2	0	2	5	4	.56	6	.284	.331	.399
1994	New York	NL	96	292	76	3	0	8	(4	4)	103	39	42	16	2	21	3	0	7	4	2	.67	11	.260	.299	.353
1995	New York	NL	108	290	82	19	2	1	(1	0)	108	41	37	19	2	35	1	1	6	1	3	.25	3	.283	.323	.372
12 ML YEARS			1268	3926	1091	168	35	54	(27	27)	1491	523	379	284	33	347	23	42	35	92	58	.61	63	.278	.328	.380

Luis Ortiz

Bats: Right **Throws:** Right **Pos:** 3B **Ht:** 6' 0" **Wt:** 195 **Born:** 5/25/70 **Age:** 26

					BATTING														BASERUNNING				PERCENTAGES		
Year	Team	Lg	G	AB	H	2B	3B	HR	(Hm	Rd)	TB	R	RBI	TBB	IBB	SO	HBP	SH	SF	SB	CS	SB%	GDP	Avg	OBP	SLG
1991	Red Sox	R	42	153	51	11	2	4	--	--	78	21	29	7	0	9	2	1	1	2	1	.67	1	.333	.368	.510
1992	Lynchburg	A	94	355	103	28	1	10	--	--	162	43	61	22	3	55	2	0	5	4	2	.67	8	.290	.331	.456
1993	Pawtucket	AAA	102	402	118	28	1	18	--	--	202	45	81	13	3	74	2	0	4	1	1	.50	10	.294	.316	.502
1994	Pawtucket	AAA	81	317	99	15	3	6	--	--	138	47	36	29	5	29	0	0	0	1	4	.20	9	.312	.370	.435
1995	Okla. City	AAA	47	170	52	10	5	2	--	--	78	19	20	8	2	20	0	1	3	1	1	.50	7	.306	.331	.459
1993	Boston	AL	9	12	3	0	0	0	(0	0)	3	0	1	0	0	2	0	0	0	0	0	.00	0	.250	.250	.250
1994	Boston	AL	7	18	3	2	0	0	(0	0)	5	3	6	1	0	5	0	1	3	0	0	.00	0	.167	.182	.278
1995	Texas	AL	41	108	25	5	2	1	(1	0)	37	10	18	6	0	18	0	0	1	0	1	.00	7	.231	.270	.343
3 ML YEARS			57	138	31	7	2	1	(1	0)	45	13	25	7	0	25	0	0	4	0	1	.00	7	.225	.255	.326

Donovan Osborne

Pitches: Left **Bats:** Left **Pos:** SP **Ht:** 6' 2" **Wt:** 195 **Born:** 6/21/69 **Age:** 27

			HOW MUCH HE PITCHED						WHAT HE GAVE UP												THE RESULTS					
Year	Team	Lg	G	GS	CG	GF	IP	BFP	H	R	ER	HR	SH	SF	HB	TBB	IBB	SO	WP	Bk	W	L	Pct.	ShO	Sv	ERA
1995	Arkansas *	AA	2	2	0	0	11	46	12	4	3	0	0	0	1	2	0	6	0	0	0	1	.000	0	0	2.45
	Louisville *	AAA	1	1	0	0	7	30	8	3	3	0	1	0	0	0	3	0	0	0	1	.000	0	0	3.86
1992	St. Louis	NL	34	29	0	2	179	754	193	91	75	14	7	4	2	38	2	104	6	0	11	9	.550	0	0	3.77
1993	St. Louis	NL	26	26	1	0	155.2	657	153	73	65	18	6	2	7	47	4	83	4	0	10	7	.588	0	0	3.76
1995	St. Louis	NL	19	19	0	0	113.1	477	112	58	48	17	8	3	2	34	2	82	0	0	4	6	.400	0	0	3.81
3 ML YEARS			79	74	1	2	448	1888	458	222	188	49	21	9	11	119	8	269	10	0	25	22	.532	0	0	3.78

Antonio Osuna

Pitches: Right **Bats:** Right **Pos:** RP **Ht:** 5'11" **Wt:** 160 **Born:** 4/12/73 **Age:** 23

			HOW MUCH HE PITCHED						WHAT HE GAVE UP												THE RESULTS					
Year	Team	Lg	G	GS	CG	GF	IP	BFP	H	R	ER	HR	SH	SF	HB	TBB	IBB	SO	WP	Bk	W	L	Pct.	ShO	Sv	ERA
1991	Dodgers	R	8	0	0	6	11	44	8	5	1	0	0	0	1	0	0	13	6	1	0	0	.000	0	4	0.82
	Yakima	A	13	0	0	11	25.1	101	18	10	9	1	1	0	4	8	0	38	1	0	0	0	.000	0	5	3.20
1993	Bakersfield	A	14	2	0	11	18.1	76	19	10	10	2	0	0	0	5	0	20	0	1	0	2	.000	0	2	4.91
1994	San Antonio	AA	35	0	0	32	46	172	19	6	5	0	2	0	2	18	1	53	0	3	1	2	.333	0	19	0.98

Team	Lg	G																				Avg		
Albuquerque	AAA	6	0	0	6	6	24	5	1	0	0	0	0	1	1	0	8	1	0	0	0	.000	0	4	0.00
1995 San Bernrdo	A	5	0	0	2	7	31	3	1	1	1	1	0	2	5	0	11	3	1	0	0	.000	0	0	1.29
Albuquerque	AAA	19	0	0	17	18.1	76	15	9	9	2	0	1	0	9	0	19	2	0	0	1	.000	0	11	4.42
1995 Los Angeles	NL	39	0	0	8	44.2	186	39	22	22	5	2	1	1	20	2	46	1	0	2	4	.333	0	4	4.43

Ricky Otero

Bats: Both **Throws:** Right **Pos:** LF   **Ht:** 5' 5" **Wt:** 150 **Born:** 4/15/72 **Age:** 24

Year Team	Lg	G	AB	H	2B	3B	HR	(Hm	Rd)	TB	R	RBI	TBB	IBB	SO	HBP	SH	SF	SB	CS	SB%	GDP	Avg	OBP	SLG
1991 Kingsport	R	66	235	81	16	3	7	--	--	124	47	52	35	5	32	2	1	6	12	4	.75	4	.345	.424	.528
Pittsfield	A	6	24	7	0	0	0	--	--	7	4	2	2	0	1	0	0	0	4	0	1.00	0	.292	.346	.292
1992 Columbia	A	96	353	106	24	4	8	--	--	162	57	60	38	0	53	3	4	6	39	13	.75	4	.300	.368	.459
St. Lucie	A	40	151	48	8	4	0	--	--	64	20	19	9	1	11	2	3	2	10	5	.67	1	.318	.360	.424
1993 Binghamton	AA	124	503	133	21	10	2	--	--	180	63	54	38	2	57	7	7	4	28	15	.65	5	.264	.322	.358
1994 Binghamton	AA	128	531	156	31	9	7	--	--	226	96	57	50	1	49	3	4	4	33	16	.67	7	.294	.355	.426
1995 Norfolk	AAA	72	295	79	8	6	1	--	--	102	37	23	27	0	33	1	2	0	16	13	.55	2	.268	.331	.346
1995 New York	NL	35	51	7	2	0	0	(0	0)	9	5	1	3	0	10	0	1	0	2	1	.67	1	.137	.185	.176

Spike Owen

Bats: Both **Throws:** Right **Pos:** 3B/2B/SS   **Ht:** 5'10" **Wt:** 170 **Born:** 4/19/61 **Age:** 35

Year Team	Lg	G	AB	H	2B	3B	HR	(Hm	Rd)	TB	R	RBI	TBB	IBB	SO	HBP	SH	SF	SB	CS	SB%	GDP	Avg	OBP	SLG
1995 Lk Elsinore *	A	3	10	2	1	0	0	--	--	3	1	0	2	0	2	0	0	0	0	0	.00	0	.200	.333	.300
1983 Seattle	AL	80	306	60	11	3	2	(1	1)	83	36	21	24	0	44	2	5	-3	10	6	.63	2	.196	.257	.271
1984 Seattle	AL	152	530	130	18	8	3	(2	1)	173	67	43	46	0	63	3	9	2	16	8	.67	5	.245	.308	.326
1985 Seattle	AL	118	352	91	10	6	6	(3	3)	131	41	37	34	0	27	0	5	2	11	5	.69	5	.259	.322	.372
1986 Bos-Sea	AL	154	528	122	24	7	1	(0	1)	163	67	45	51	1	51	2	9	3	4	4	.50	13	.231	.300	.309
1987 Boston	AL	132	437	113	17	7	2	(2	0)	150	50	48	53	2	43	1	9	4	11	8	.58	9	.259	.337	.343
1988 Boston	AL	89	257	64	14	1	5	(2	3)	95	40	18	27	0	27	2	7	1	0	1	.00	7	.249	.324	.370
1989 Montreal	NL	142	437	102	17	4	6	(5	1)	145	52	41	76	25	44	3	3	3	3	2	.60	11	.233	.349	.332
1990 Montreal	NL	149	453	106	24	5	5	(2	3)	155	55	35	70	12	60	0	5	5	8	6	.57	6	.234	.333	.342
1991 Montreal	NL	139	424	108	22	8	3	(1	2)	155	39	26	42	11	61	1	4	4	2	6	.25	11	.255	.321	.366
1992 Montreal	NL	122	386	104	16	3	7	(3	4)	147	52	40	50	3	30	0	4	6	9	4	.69	10	.269	.348	.381
1993 New York	AL	103	334	78	16	2	2	(1	1)	104	41	20	29	2	30	0	3	1	3	2	.60	6	.234	.294	.311
1994 California	AL	82	268	83	17	2	3	(2	1)	113	30	37	49	0	17	1	3	0	2	8	.20	4	.310	.418	.422
1995 California	AL	82	218	50	9	3	1	(0	1)	68	17	28	18	1	22	0	1	0	3	2	.60	7	.229	.288	.312
1986 Boston	AL	42	126	23	2	1	1	(1	0)	30	21	10	17	0	9	1	2	1	3	1	.75	2	.183	.283	.238
Seattle	AL	112	402	99	22	6	0	(0	0)	133	46	35	34	1	42	1	7	2	1	3	.25	11	.246	.305	.331
13 ML YEARS		1544	4930	1211	215	59	46	(24	22)	1682	587	439	569	57	519	15	67	34	82	62	.57	96	.246	.324	.341

Eric Owens

Bats: Right **Throws:** Right **Pos:** 3B   **Ht:** 6' 1" **Wt:** 185 **Born:** 2/3/71 **Age:** 25

Year Team	Lg	G	AB	H	2B	3B	HR	(Hm	Rd)	TB	R	RBI	TBB	IBB	SO	HBP	SH	SF	SB	CS	SB%	GDP	Avg	OBP	SLG
1992 Billings	R	67	239	72	10	3	3	--	--	97	41	26	23	0	22	0	3	0	15	4	.79	1	.301	.363	.406
1993 Winston-Sal	A	122	487	132	25	4	10	--	--	195	74	63	53	0	69	4	4	7	20	12	.63	8	.271	.343	.400
1994 Chattanooga	AA	134	523	133	17	3	3	--	--	165	73	36	54	0	86	2	8	2	38	14	.73	10	.254	.325	.315
1995 Indianapols	AAA	108	427	134	24	8	12	--	--	210	86	63	52	2	61	1	3	2	33	12	.73	7	.314	.388	.492
1995 Cincinnati	NL	2	2	2	0	0	0	(0	0)	2	0	1	0	0	0	0	1	0	0	0	.00	0	1.000	1.000	1.000

Jayhawk Owens

Bats: Right **Throws:** Right **Pos:** C   **Ht:** 6' 1" **Wt:** 200 **Born:** 2/10/69 **Age:** 27

Year Team	Lg	G	AB	H	2B	3B	HR	(Hm	Rd)	TB	R	RBI	TBB	IBB	SO	HBP	SH	SF	SB	CS	SB%	GDP	Avg	OBP	SLG
1995 Colo. Sprng *	AAA	70	221	65	13	5	12	--	--	124	47	48	20	2	61	7	1	2	2	1	.67	2	.294	.368	.561
1993 Colorado	NL	33	86	18	5	0	3	(2	1)	32	12	6	6	1	30	2	0	0	1	0	1.00	1	.209	.277	.372
1994 Colorado	NL	6	12	3	0	1	0	(0	0)	5	4	1	3	0	3	0	0	0	0	0	.00	1	.250	.400	.417
1995 Colorado	NL	18	45	11	2	0	4	(3	1)	25	7	12	2	0	15	1	0	1	0	0	.00	0	.244	.286	.556
3 ML YEARS		57	143	32	7	1	7	(5	2)	62	23	19	11	1	48	3	0	1	1	0	1.00	2	.224	.291	.434

Mike Pagliarulo

Bats: Left **Throws:** Right **Pos:** 3B/1B   **Ht:** 6' 2" **Wt:** 201 **Born:** 3/15/60 **Age:** 36

Year Team	Lg	G	AB	H	2B	3B	HR	(Hm	Rd)	TB	R	RBI	TBB	IBB	SO	HBP	SH	SF	SB	CS	SB%	GDP	Avg	OBP	SLG
1984 New York	AL	67	201	48	15	3	7	(4	3)	90	24	34	15	0	46	0	0	3	0	0	.00	5	.239	.288	.448
1985 New York	AL	138	380	91	16	2	19	(8	11)	168	55	62	45	4	86	4	3	3	0	0	.00	6	.239	.324	.442

Year	Team	Lg	G	AB	H	2B	3B	HR	(Hm	Rd)	TB	R	RBI	TBB	IBB	SO	HBP	SH	SF	SB	CS	SB%	GDP	Avg	OBP	SLG
1986	New York	AL	149	504	120	24	3	28	(14	14)	234	71	71	54	10	120	4	1	2	4	1	.80	10	.238	.316	.464
1987	New York	AL	150	522	122	26	3	32	(17	15)	250	76	87	53	9	111	2	2	3	1	3	.25	9	.234	.305	.479
1988	New York	AL	125	444	96	20	1	15	(8	7)	163	46	67	37	9	104	2	1	6	1	0	1.00	5	.216	.276	.367
1989	NYA-SD		124	371	73	17	0	7	(5	2)	111	31	30	37	4	82	3	1	0	3	1	.75	5	.197	.275	.299
1990	San Diego	NL	128	398	101	23	2	7	(1	6)	149	29	38	39	3	66	3	2	4	1	3	.25	12	.254	.322	.374
1991	Minnesota	AL	121	365	102	20	0	6	(4	2)	140	38	36	21	3	55	3	2	2	1	2	.33	9	.279	.322	.384
1992	Minnesota	AL	42	105	21	4	0	0	(0	0)	25	10	9	1	0	17	1	0	1	1	0	1.00	1	.200	.213	.238
1993	Bal-Min	AL	116	370	112	25	4	9	(5	4)	172	55	44	26	2	49	6	2	1	6	6	.50	7	.303	.357	.465
1995	Texas	AL	86	241	56	16	0	4	(1	3)	84	27	27	15	2	49	1	1	3	0	0	.00	10	.232	.277	.349
1989	New York	AL	74	223	44	10	0	4	(3	1)	66	19	16	19	0	43	2	0	0	1	1	.50	2	.197	.266	.296
	San Diego	NL	50	148	29	7	0	3	(2	1)	45	12	14	18	4	39	1	1	0	2	0	1.00	3	.196	.287	.304
1993	Baltimore	AL	33	117	38	9	0	6	(3	3)	65	24	21	8	0	15	1	0	0	0	0	.00	4	.325	.373	.556
	Minnesota	AL	83	253	74	16	4	3	(2	1)	107	31	23	18	2	34	5	2	1	6	6	.50	5	.292	.350	.423
11	ML YEARS		1246	3901	942	206	18	134	(67	67)	1586	462	505	343	46	785	29	16	28	18	16	.53	79	.241	.306	.407

Tom Pagnozzi

Bats: Right **Throws:** Right **Pos:** C   **Ht:** 6' 1" **Wt:** 190 **Born:** 7/30/62 **Age:** 33

			BATTING																	BASERUNNING				PERCENTAGES		
Year	Team	Lg	G	AB	H	2B	3B	HR	(Hm	Rd)	TB	R	RBI	TBB	IBB	SO	HBP	SH	SF	SB	CS	SB%	GDP	Avg	OBP	SLG
1995	Louisville *	AAA	5	16	8	2	0	1	--	--	13	4	3	1	0	0	0	0	0	0	0	.00	1	.500	.529	.813
1987	St. Louis	NL	27	48	9	1	0	2	(2	0)	16	8	9	4	2	13	0	1	0	1	0	1.00	0	.188	.250	.333
1988	St. Louis	NL	81	195	55	9	0	0	(0	0)	64	17	15	11	1	32	0	2	1	0	0	.00	5	.282	.319	.328
1989	St. Louis	NL	52	80	12	2	0	0	(0	0)	14	3	3	6	2	19	1	0	1	0	0	.00	7	.150	.216	.175
1990	St. Louis	NL	69	220	61	15	0	2	(2	0)	82	20	23	14	1	37	1	0	2	1	1	.50	7	.277	.321	.373
1991	St. Louis	NL	140	459	121	24	5	2	(2	0)	161	38	57	36	6	63	4	6	5	9	13	.41	10	.264	.319	.351
1992	St. Louis	NL	139	485	121	26	3	7	(3	4)	174	33	44	28	9	64	1	6	3	2	5	.29	15	.249	.290	.359
1993	St. Louis	NL	92	330	85	15	1	7	(1	6)	123	31	41	19	6	30	1	0	5	1	0	1.00	7	.258	.296	.373
1994	St. Louis	NL	70	243	66	12	1	7	(2	5)	101	21	40	21	5	39	0	0	2	0	0	.00	3	.272	.327	.416
1995	St. Louis	NL	62	219	47	14	1	2	(1	1)	69	17	15	11	0	31	1	0	1	0	1	.00	9	.215	.254	.315
9	ML YEARS		732	2279	577	118	11	29	(13	16)	804	188	247	150	32	328	9	15	20	14	20	.41	56	.253	.299	.353

Lance Painter

Pitches: Left **Bats:** Left **Pos:** RP   **Ht:** 6' 1" **Wt:** 195 **Born:** 7/21/67 **Age:** 28

			HOW MUCH HE PITCHED						WHAT HE GAVE UP												THE RESULTS				
Year	Team	Lg	G	GS	CG	GF	IP	BFP	H	R	ER	HR	SH	SF	HB	TBB	IBB	SO	WP	Bk	W	L	Pct.	ShO	Sv	ERA
1995	Colo. Sprng *	AAA	11	4	0	3	25.2	117	32	20	17	3	0	0	1	11	1	12	0	1	0	3	.000	0	0	5.96
1993	Colorado	NL	10	6	1	2	39	166	52	26	26	5	1	0	0	9	0	16	2	0	2	2	.500	0	0	6.00
1994	Colorado	NL	15	14	0	1	73.2	336	91	51	50	9	3	5	1	26	2	41	3	1	4	6	.400	0	0	6.11
1995	Colorado	NL	33	1	0	7	45.1	198	55	23	22	9	0	0	2	10	0	36	4	1	3	0	1.000	0	1	4.37
3	ML YEARS		58	21	1	10	158	700	198	100	98	23	4	5	3	45	2	93	9	2	9	8	.529	0	1	5.58

Vince Palacios

Pitches: Right **Bats:** Right **Pos:** RP/SP   **Ht:** 6' 3" **Wt:** 175 **Born:** 7/19/63 **Age:** 32

			HOW MUCH HE PITCHED						WHAT HE GAVE UP												THE RESULTS				
Year	Team	Lg	G	GS	CG	GF	IP	BFP	H	R	ER	HR	SH	SF	HB	TBB	IBB	SO	WP	Bk	W	L	Pct.	ShO	Sv	ERA
1987	Pittsburgh	NL	6	4	0	0	29.1	120	27	14	14	1	2	0	1	9	1	13	0	2	2	1	.667	0	0	4.30
1988	Pittsburgh	NL	7	3	0	0	24.1	113	28	18	18	3	2	1	0	15	1	15	2	3	1	2	.333	0	0	6.66
1990	Pittsburgh	NL	7	0	0	4	15	50	4	0	0	0	0	0	0	2	0	8	2	0	0	0	.000	0	3	0.00
1991	Pittsburgh	NL	36	7	1	8	81.2	347	69	34	34	12	4	1	1	38	2	64	6	2	6	3	.667	1	3	3.75
1992	Pittsburgh	NL	20	8	0	4	53	232	56	25	25	1	4	1	0	27	1	33	7	0	3	2	.600	0	0	4.25
1994	St. Louis	NL	31	17	1	5	117.2	484	104	60	58	16	7	7	3	43	2	95	4	0	3	8	.273	1	1	4.44
1995	St. Louis	NL	20	5	0	3	40.1	184	48	29	26	7	2	1	2	19	1	34	1	0	2	3	.400	0	0	5.80
7	ML YEARS		127	44	2	24	361.1	1530	336	180	175	40	21	11	7	153	8	262	22	7	17	19	.472	2	7	4.36

Orlando Palmeiro

Bats: Left **Throws:** Right **Pos:** CF   **Ht:** 5'11" **Wt:** 155 **Born:** 1/19/69 **Age:** 27

			BATTING																	BASERUNNING				PERCENTAGES		
Year	Team	Lg	G	AB	H	2B	3B	HR	(Hm	Rd)	TB	R	RBI	TBB	IBB	SO	HBP	SH	SF	SB	CS	SB%	GDP	Avg	OBP	SLG
1991	Boise	A	70	277	77	11	2	1	--	--	95	56	24	33	0	22	3	6	3	8	8	.50	8	.278	.358	.343
1992	Quad City	A	127	451	143	22	4	0	--	--	173	83	41	56	3	41	5	19	1	31	13	.70	5	.317	.393	.384
1993	Midland	AA	131	535	163	19	5	0	--	--	192	85	64	42	1	35	2	18	3	18	14	.56	13	.305	.356	.359
1994	Vancouver	AAA	117	458	150	28	4	1	--	--	189	79	47	58	4	46	1	4	3	21	16	.57	7	.328	.402	.413
1995	Vancouver	AAA	107	398	122	21	4	0	--	--	151	66	47	41	8	34	3	11	5	16	7	.70	11	.307	.371	.379
1995	California	AL	15	20	7	0	0	0	(0	0)	7	3	1	1	0	1	0	0	0	0	0	.00	0	.350	.381	.350

Rafael Palmeiro

Bats: Left **Throws:** Left **Pos:** 1B   **Ht:** 6' 0" **Wt:** 188 **Born:** 9/24/64 **Age:** 31

Year Team	Lg	G	AB	H	2B	3B	HR	(Hm	Rd)	TB	R	RBI	TBB	IBB	SO	HBP	SH	SF	SB	CS	SB%	GDP	Avg	OBP	SLG
1986 Chicago	NL	22	73	18	4	0	3	(1	2)	31	9	12	4	0	6	1	0	0	1	1	.50	4	.247	.295	.425
1987 Chicago	NL	84	221	61	15	1	14	(5	9)	120	32	30	20	1	26	1	0	2	2	2	.50	4	.276	.336	.543
1988 Chicago	NL	152	580	178	41	5	8	(8	0)	253	75	53	38	6	34	3	2	6	12	2	.86	11	.307	.349	.436
1989 Texas	AL	156	559	154	23	4	8	(4	4)	209	76	64	63	3	48	6	2	2	4	3	.57	18	.275	.354	.374
1990 Texas	AL	154	598	191	35	6	14	(9	5)	280	72	89	40	6	59	3	2	8	3	3	.50	24	.319	.361	.468
1991 Texas	AL	159	631	203	49	3	26	(12	14)	336	115	88	68	10	72	6	2	7	4	3	.57	17	.322	.389	.532
1992 Texas	AL	159	608	163	27	4	22	(8	14)	264	84	85	72	8	83	10	5	6	2	3	.40	10	.268	.352	.434
1993 Texas	AL	160	597	176	40	2	37	(22	15)	331	124	105	73	22	85	5	2	9	22	3	.88	8	.295	.371	.554
1994 Baltimore	AL	111	436	139	32	0	23	(11	12)	240	82	76	54	1	63	2	0	6	7	3	.70	11	.319	.392	.550
1995 Baltimore	AL	143	554	172	30	2	39	(21	18)	323	89	104	62	5	65	3	0	5	3	1	.75	12	.310	.380	.583
10 ML YEARS		1300	4857	1455	296	27	194	(101	93)	2387	758	706	494	62	541	40	15	51	60	24	.71	119	.300	.365	.491

Dean Palmer

Bats: Right **Throws:** Right **Pos:** 3B   **Ht:** 6' 2" **Wt:** 195 **Born:** 12/27/68 **Age:** 27

Year Team	Lg	G	AB	H	2B	3B	HR	(Hm	Rd)	TB	R	RBI	TBB	IBB	SO	HBP	SH	SF	SB	CS	SB%	GDP	Avg	OBP	SLG
1989 Texas	AL	16	19	2	2	0	0	(0	0)	4	0	1	0	0	12	0	0	1	0	0	.00	0	.105	.100	.211
1991 Texas	AL	81	268	50	9	2	15	(6	9)	108	38	37	32	0	98	3	1	0	0	2	.00	4	.187	.281	.403
1992 Texas	AL	152	541	124	25	0	26	(11	15)	227	74	72	62	2	154	4	2	4	10	4	.71	9	.229	.311	.420
1993 Texas	AL	148	519	127	31	2	33	(12	21)	261	88	96	53	4	154	8	0	5	11	10	.52	5	.245	.321	.503
1994 Texas	AL	93	342	84	14	2	19	(11	8)	159	50	59	26	0	89	2	0	1	3	4	.43	7	.246	.302	.465
1995 Texas	AL	36	119	40	6	0	9	(5	4)	73	30	24	21	1	21	4	0	1	1	1	.50	2	.336	.448	.613
6 ML YEARS		526	1808	427	87	6	102	(45	57)	832	280	289	194	7	528	21	3	12	25	21	.54	27	.236	.315	.460

Craig Paquette

Bats: Right **Throws:** Right **Pos:** 3B/LF   **Ht:** 6' 0" **Wt:** 190 **Born:** 3/28/69 **Age:** 27

Year Team	Lg	G	AB	H	2B	3B	HR	(Hm	Rd)	TB	R	RBI	TBB	IBB	SO	HBP	SH	SF	SB	CS	SB%	GDP	Avg	OBP	SLG
1993 Oakland	AL	105	393	86	20	4	12	(8	4)	150	35	46	14	2	108	0	1	1	4	2	.67	7	.219	.245	.382
1994 Oakland	AL	14	49	7	2	0	0	(0	0)	9	0	0	0	0	14	0	1	0	1	0	1.00	0	.143	.143	.184
1995 Oakland	AL	105	283	64	13	1	13	(8	5)	118	42	49	12	0	88	1	3	5	5	2	.71	5	.226	.256	.417
3 ML YEARS		224	725	157	35	5	25	(16	9)	277	77	95	26	2	210	1	5	6	10	4	.71	12	.217	.243	.382

Mark Parent

Bats: Right **Throws:** Right **Pos:** C   **Ht:** 6' 5" **Wt:** 240 **Born:** 9/16/61 **Age:** 34

Year Team	Lg	G	AB	H	2B	3B	HR	(Hm	Rd)	TB	R	RBI	TBB	IBB	SO	HBP	SH	SF	SB	CS	SB%	GDP	Avg	OBP	SLG
1986 San Diego	NL	8	14	2	0	0	0	(0	0)	2	1	0	1	0	3	0	0	0	0	0	.00	1	.143	.200	.143
1987 San Diego	NL	12	25	2	0	0	0	(0	0)	2	0	2	0	0	9	0	0	0	0	0	.00	0	.080	.080	.080
1988 San Diego	NL	41	118	23	3	0	6	(4	2)	44	9	15	6	0	23	0	0	1	0	0	.00	1	.195	.232	.373
1989 San Diego	NL	52	141	27	4	0	7	(6	1)	52	12	21	8	2	34	0	1	4	1	0	1.00	5	.191	.229	.369
1990 San Diego	NL	65	189	42	11	0	3	(1	2)	62	13	16	16	3	29	0	3	0	1	0	1.00	2	.222	.283	.328
1991 Texas	AL	3	1	0	0	0	0	(0	0)	0	0	0	0	0	1	0	0	0	0	0	.00	0	.000	.000	.000
1992 Baltimore	AL	17	34	8	1	0	2	(0	2)	15	4	4	3	0	7	1	2	0	0	0	.00	0	.235	.316	.441
1993 Baltimore	AL	22	54	14	2	0	4	(1	3)	28	7	12	3	0	14	0	3	1	0	0	.00	5	.259	.293	.519
1994 Chicago	NL	44	99	26	4	0	3	(0	3)	39	8	16	13	1	24	1	1	2	0	1	.00	5	.263	.348	.394
1995 Pit-ChN	NL	81	265	62	11	0	18	(7	11)	127	30	38	26	2	69	0	1	0	0	0	.00	6	.234	.302	.479
1995 Pittsburgh	NL	69	233	54	9	0	15	(5	10)	108	25	33	23	2	62	0	1	0	0	0	.00	5	.232	.301	.464
Chicago	NL	12	32	8	2	0	3	(2	1)	19	5	5	3	0	7	0	0	0	0	0	.00	1	.250	.314	.594
10 ML YEARS		345	940	206	36	0	43	(19	24)	371	84	124	79	8	213	2	11	8	2	1	.67	21	.219	.277	.395

Chan Ho Park

Pitches: Right **Bats:** Right **Pos:** SP   **Ht:** 6' 2" **Wt:** 195 **Born:** 6/30/73 **Age:** 23

	HOW MUCH HE PITCHED						WHAT HE GAVE UP											THE RESULTS					
Year Team	Lg	G	GS	CG	GF	IP	BFP	H	R	ER	HR	SH	SF	HB	TBB	IBB	SO	WP	Bk	W	L	Pct.	ShO	Sv	ERA
1994 San Antonio	AA	20	20	0	0	101.1	446	91	52	40	4	5	3	4	57	0	100	7	2	5	7	.417	0	0	3.55
1995 Albuquerque	AAA	23	22	0	0	110	487	93	64	60	10	3	2	6	76	2	101	8	2	6	7	.462	0	0	4.91
1994 Los Angeles	NL	2	0	0	1	4	23	5	5	5	1	0	0	1	5	0	6	0	0	0	0	.000	0	0	11.25
1995 Los Angeles	NL	2	1	0	0	4	16	2	2	2	1	0	0	0	2	0	7	0	1	0	0	.000	0	0	4.50
2 ML YEARS		4	1	0	1	8	39	7	7	7	2	0	0	1	7	0	13	0	1	0	0	.000	0	0	7.88

Rick Parker

Bats: Right **Throws:** Right **Pos:** LF   **Ht:** 6' 0" **Wt:** 185 **Born:** 3/20/63 **Age:** 33

Year Team	Lg	G	AB	H	2B	3B	HR	(Hm	Rd)	TB	R	RBI	TBB	IBB	SO	HBP	SH	SF	SB	CS	SB%	GDP	Avg	OBP	SLG
1995 Albuquerque *	AAA	58	175	49	7	2	1	--	--	63	33	14	27	4	17	3	1	1	1	6	.14	4	.280	.383	.360
1990 San Francisco	NL	54	107	26	5	0	2	(0	2)	37	19	14	10	0	15	1	3	0	6	1	.86	1	.243	.314	.346
1991 San Francisco	NL	13	14	1	0	0	0	(0	0)	1	0	1	1	0	5	0	0	0	0	0	.00	0	.071	.133	.071
1993 Houston	NL	45	45	15	3	0	0	(0	0)	18	11	4	3	0	8	0	1	0	1	2	.33	2	.333	.375	.400
1994 New York	NL	8	16	1	0	0	0	(0	0)	1	1	0	0	0	2	0	0	0	0	0	.00	2	.063	.063	.063
1995 Los Angeles	NL	27	29	8	0	0	0	(0	0)	8	3	4	2	0	4	0	2	0	1	1	.50	1	.276	.323	.276
5 ML YEARS		147	211	51	8	0	2	(0	2)	65	34	23	16	0	34	1	8	0	8	4	.67	4	.242	.298	.308

Jose Parra

Pitches: Right **Bats:** Right **Pos:** SP/RP   **Ht:** 5'11" **Wt:** 165 **Born:** 11/28/72 **Age:** 23

Year Team	Lg	G	GS	CG	GF	IP	BFP	H	R	ER	HR	SH	SF	HB	TBB	IBB	SO	WP	Bk	W	L	Pct.	ShO	Sv	ERA
1990 Dodgers	R	10	10	1	0	57.1	228	50	22	17	1	0	3	1	18	0	50	1	1	5	3	.625	0	0	2.67
1991 Great Falls	R	14	14	1	0	64.1	298	86	58	44	5	2	7	2	18	0	55	0	4	4	6	.400	1	0	6.16
1992 Bakersfield	A	24	23	3	0	143	618	151	73	57	5	4	4	4	47	4	107	5	1	7	8	.467	0	0	3.59
San Antonio	AA	3	3	0	0	14.2	74	22	12	10	0	2	1	1	7	0	7	0	1	2	0	1.000	0	0	6.14
1993 San Antonio	AA	17	17	0	0	111.1	452	103	46	39	10	9	3	6	12	2	87	1	0	1	8	.111	0	0	3.15
1994 Albuquerque	AAA	27	27	1	0	145	636	190	92	77	10	4	4	5	38	2	90	10	0	10	10	.500	0	0	4.78
1995 Albuquerque	AAA	12	10	1	1	52.2	232	62	33	30	7	4	2	1	17	3	33	2	0	3	2	.600	1	1	5.13
1995 LA-Min		20	12	0	0	72	339	93	67	57	13	0	4	3	28	1	36	3	1	1	5	.167	0	0	7.13
1995 Los Angeles	NL	8	0	0	0	10.1	47	10	8	5	2	0	1	1	6	1	7	0	1	0	0	.000	0	0	4.35
Minnesota	AL	12	12	0	0	61.2	292	83	59	52	11	0	3	2	22	0	29	3	0	1	5	.167	0	0	7.59

Jeff Parrett

Pitches: Right **Bats:** Right **Pos:** RP   **Ht:** 6' 3" **Wt:** 195 **Born:** 8/26/61 **Age:** 34

Year Team	Lg	G	GS	CG	GF	IP	BFP	H	R	ER	HR	SH	SF	HB	TBB	IBB	SO	WP	Bk	W	L	Pct.	ShO	Sv	ERA
1986 Montreal	NL	12	0	0	6	20.1	91	19	11	11	3	0	1	0	13	0	21	2	0	0	1	.000	0	0	4.87
1987 Montreal	NL	45	0	0	26	62	267	53	33	29	8	5	1	0	30	4	56	6	1	7	6	.538	0	0	4.21
1988 Montreal	NL	61	0	0	34	91.2	369	66	29	27	8	9	6	1	45	9	62	4	1	12	4	.750	0	6	2.65
1989 Philadelphia	NL	72	0	0	34	105.2	444	90	43	35	6	7	5	0	44	13	98	7	3	12	6	.667	0	6	2.98
1990 Atl-Phi	NL	67	5	0	19	108.2	479	119	62	56	11	7	5	2	55	10	86	5	1	5	10	.333	0	2	4.64
1991 Atlanta	NL	18	0	0	9	21.1	109	31	18	15	2	2	0	0	12	2	14	4	0	1	2	.333	0	1	6.33
1992 Oakland	AL	66	0	0	14	98.1	410	81	35	33	7	4	4	2	42	3	78	13	0	9	1	.900	0	1	3.02
1993 Colorado	NL	40	6	0	13	73.2	341	78	47	44	6	4	5	2	45	9	66	11	1	3	3	.500	0	1	5.38
1995 St. Louis	NL	59	0	0	17	76.2	328	71	33	31	8	5	2	1	28	5	71	7	0	4	7	.364	0	0	3.64
1990 Atlanta	NL	20	0	0	5	27	124	27	11	9	1	4	4	1	19	2	17	2	0	1	1	.500	0	1	3.00
Philadelphia	NL	47	5	0	14	81.2	355	92	51	47	10	3	1	1	36	8	69	3	1	4	9	.308	0	1	5.18
9 ML YEARS		440	11	0	172	658.1	2838	608	311	281	59	43	29	8	314	55	552	59	7	53	40	.570	0	22	3.84

Steve Parris

Pitches: Right **Bats:** Right **Pos:** SP   **Ht:** 6' 0" **Wt:** 190 **Born:** 12/17/67 **Age:** 28

Year Team	Lg	G	GS	CG	GF	IP	BFP	H	R	ER	HR	SH	SF	HB	TBB	IBB	SO	WP	Bk	W	L	Pct.	ShO	Sv	ERA
1989 Batavia	A	13	10	0	0	66.2	291	69	38	29	6	3	2	4	20	1	46	4	0	3	5	.375	0	0	3.92
1990 Batavia	A	14	14	0	0	81.2	333	70	34	24	1	3	4	3	22	2	50	7	3	7	1	.875	0	0	2.64
1991 Clearwater	A	43	6	0	8	93	394	101	43	35	1	4	0	9	25	4	59	3	4	7	5	.583	0	1	3.39
1992 Reading	AA	18	14	0	0	85.1	370	94	55	44	9	3	4	3	21	1	60	2	0	5	7	.417	0	0	4.64
Scranton-Wb	AAA	11	6	0	2	51.1	223	57	25	23	1	1	1	4	17	1	29	6	1	3	3	.500	0	1	4.03
1993 Scranton-Wb	AAA	3	0	0	0	5.2	30	9	9	8	3	0	0	1	3	0	4	1	0	0	0	.000	0	0	12.71
Jacksonvlle	AA	7	1	0	0	13.2	64	15	9	9	3	0	1	2	6	0	5	0	0	0	1	.000	0	0	5.93
1994 Salem	A	17	7	0	1	57	247	58	24	23	7	0	2	6	21	1	48	1	0	3	3	.500	0	0	3.63
1995 Carolina	AA	14	14	2	0	89.2	344	61	25	25	2	3	1	4	16	1	86	3	0	9	1	.900	2	0	2.51
1995 Pittsburgh	NL	15	15	1	0	82	360	89	49	49	12	3	2	7	33	1	61	4	0	6	6	.500	1	0	5.38

Lance Parrish

Bats: Right **Throws:** Right **Pos:** C   **Ht:** 6' 3" **Wt:** 224 **Born:** 6/15/56 **Age:** 40

Year Team	Lg	G	AB	H	2B	3B	HR	(Hm	Rd)	TB	R	RBI	TBB	IBB	SO	HBP	SH	SF	SB	CS	SB%	GDP	Avg	OBP	SLG
1977 Detroit	AL	12	46	9	2	0	3			20	10	7	5	0	12	0	0	0	0	0	.00	2	.196	.275	.435
1978 Detroit	AL	85	288	63	11	3	14	(7	7)	122	37	41	11	0	71	3	1	1	0	0	.00	8	.219	.254	.424
1979 Detroit	AL	143	493	136	26	3	19	(8	11)	225	65	65	49	2	105	2	3	1	6	7	.46	15	.276	.343	.456
1980 Detroit	AL	144	553	158	34	6	24	(7	17)	276	79	82	31	3	109	3	2	3	6	4	.60	24	.286	.325	.499
1981 Detroit	AL	96	348	85	18	2	10	(8	2)	137	39	46	34	6	52	0	1	1	2	3	.40	16	.244	.311	.394

Year	Team	Lg	G	AB	H	2B	3B	HR	(Hm	Rd)	TB	R	RBI	TBB	IBB	SO	HBP	SH	SF	SB	CS	SB%	GDP	Avg	OBP	SLG
1982	Detroit	AL	133	486	138	19	2	32	(22	10)	257	75	87	40	5	99	1	0	2	3	4	.43	5	.284	.338	.529
1983	Detroit	AL	155	605	163	42	3	27	(12	15)	292	80	114	44	7	106	1	0	13	1	3	.25	21	.269	.314	.483
1984	Detroit	AL	147	578	137	16	2	33	(13	20)	256	75	98	41	6	120	2	2	6	2	3	.40	12	.237	.287	.443
1985	Detroit	AL	140	549	150	27	1	28	(11	17)	263	64	98	41	5	90	2	3	5	2	6	.25	10	.273	.323	.479
1986	Detroit	AL	91	327	84	6	1	22	(8	14)	158	53	62	38	3	83	5	1	3	0	0	.00	3	.257	.340	.483
1987	Philadelphia	NL	130	466	114	21	0	17	(5	12)	186	42	67	47	2	104	1	1	3	0	1	.00	23	.245	.313	.399
1988	Philadelphia	NL	123	424	91	17	2	15	(11	4)	157	44	60	47	7	93	2	0	5	0	0	.00	11	.215	.293	.370
1989	California	AL	124	433	103	12	1	17	(8	9)	168	48	50	42	6	104	2	1	4	1	1	.50	10	.238	.306	.388
1990	California	AL	133	470	126	14	0	24	(14	10)	212	54	70	46	4	107	5	0	2	2	2	.50	12	.268	.338	.451
1991	California	AL	119	402	87	12	0	19	(9	10)	156	38	51	35	2	117	5	0	3	0	1	.00	7	.216	.285	.388
1992	Cal-Sea	AL	93	275	64	13	1	12	(7	5)	115	26	32	24	3	70	1	1	3	1	1	.50	7	.233	.294	.418
1993	Cleveland	AL	10	20	4	1	0	1	(1	0)	8	2	2	4	0	5	0	0	0	1	0	1.00	2	.200	.333	.400
1994	Pittsburgh	NL	40	126	34	5	0	3	(3	0)	48	10	16	18	1	28	1	1	1	1	1	.50	5	.270	.363	.381
1995	Toronto	AL	70	178	36	9	0	4	(4	0)	57	15	22	15	0	52	1	6	2	0	0	.00	4	.202	.265	.320
1992	California	AL	24	83	19	2	0	4	(1	3)	33	7	11	5	1	22	0	1	0	0	0	.00	1	.229	.270	.398
	Seattle	AL	69	192	45	11	1	8	(6	2)	82	19	21	19	2	48	1	0	2	1	1	.50	6	.234	.304	.427
19 ML YEARS			1988	7067	1782	305	27	324	(160	164)	3113	856	1070	612	62	1527	37	23	58	28	37	.43	197	.252	.313	.440

Bob Patterson

Pitches: Left **Bats:** Right **Pos:** RP　　　　　**Ht:** 6' 2" **Wt:** 192 **Born:** 5/16/59 **Age:** 37

			HOW MUCH HE PITCHED					WHAT HE GAVE UP												THE RESULTS				
Year	Team	Lg	G	GS	CG	GF	IP	BFP	H	R	ER	HR	SH	SF	HB	TBB	IBB	SO	WP	Bk	W	L	Pct.	ShO	Sv	ERA
1985	San Diego	NL	3	0	0	2	4	26	13	11	11	2	0	0	0	3	0	1	0	1	0	0	.000	0	0	24.75
1986	Pittsburgh	NL	11	5	0	2	36.1	159	49	20	20	0	1	1	0	5	2	20	0	1	2	3	.400	0	0	4.95
1987	Pittsburgh	NL	15	7	0	2	43	201	49	34	32	5	6	3	1	22	4	27	1	0	1	4	.200	0	0	6.70
1989	Pittsburgh	NL	12	3	0	2	26.2	109	23	13	12	3	1	1	0	8	2	20	0	0	4	3	.571	0	1	4.05
1990	Pittsburgh	NL	55	5	0	19	94.2	386	88	33	31	9	5	3	3	21	7	70	1	2	8	5	.615	0	5	2.95
1991	Pittsburgh	NL	54	1	0	19	65.2	270	67	32	30	7	2	2	0	15	1	57	0	0	4	3	.571	0	2	4.11
1992	Pittsburgh	NL	60	0	0	26	64.2	268	59	22	21	7	3	2	0	23	6	43	3	0	6	3	.667	0	9	2.92
1993	Texas	AL	52	0	0	29	52.2	224	59	28	28	8	1	2	1	11	0	46	0	0	2	4	.333	0	1	4.78
1994	California	AL	47	0	0	11	42	170	35	21	19	6	0	0	2	15	2	30	1	0	3	4	.400	0	1	4.07
1995	California	AL	62	0	0	20	53.1	212	48	18	18	6	2	1	1	13	3	41	0	1	5	2	.714	0	0	3.04
10 ML YEARS			371	21	0	132	483	2025	490	232	222	53	21	15	8	136	27	355	6	5	34	30	.531	0	19	4.14

Jeff Patterson

Pitches: Right **Bats:** Right **Pos:** RP　　　　　**Ht:** 6' 2" **Wt:** 200 **Born:** 10/1/68 **Age:** 27

			HOW MUCH HE PITCHED					WHAT HE GAVE UP												THE RESULTS				
Year	Team	Lg	G	GS	CG	GF	IP	BFP	H	R	ER	HR	SH	SF	HB	TBB	IBB	SO	WP	Bk	W	L	Pct.	ShO	Sv	ERA
1989	Martinsvlle	R	7	7	0	0	42.1	171	35	23	17	3	0	0	2	12	0	44	3	4	2	4	.333	0	1	3.61
	Batavia	A	9	7	1	2	53.1	208	44	19	17	4	2	1	1	11	0	41	2	2	2	4	.333	1	1	2.87
1990	Clearwater	A	11	11	0	0	67	283	63	34	22	2	0	2	2	22	0	28	1	2	3	6	.333	0	0	2.96
1991	Spartanburg	A	35	10	2	22	114	480	103	60	56	7	4	7	4	41	0	114	0	2	9	8	.529	1	9	4.42
1992	Clearwater	A	30	0	0	22	36.1	148	29	11	8	0	1	0	2	11	2	33	3	1	2	1	.667	0	14	1.98
	Reading	AA	26	0	0	21	31.1	133	30	16	16	2	1	2	0	14	2	22	2	0	3	1	.750	0	13	4.60
	Scranton-Wb	AAA	11	0	0	10	13.2	58	10	4	4	0	1	1	0	8	3	11	2	1	2	1	.667	0	1	2.63
1993	Scranton-Wb	AAA	62	0	0	31	93.2	390	79	32	28	3	8	3	2	42	11	68	8	1	7	5	.583	0	8	2.69
1994	Scranton-Wb	AAA	52	2	0	32	94	420	102	50	48	8	4	0	5	48	8	64	7	0	6	4	.600	0	5	4.60
1995	Columbus	AAA	33	0	0	8	62.1	268	56	30	25	0	3	3	3	30	2	36	9	0	5	3	.625	0	1	3.61
1995	New York	AL	3	0	0	3	3.1	16	3	1	1	1	0	0	0	3	0	3	0	0	0	0	.000	0	0	2.70

John Patterson

Bats: Both **Throws:** Right **Pos:** 2B　　　　　**Ht:** 5' 9" **Wt:** 168 **Born:** 2/11/67 **Age:** 29

			BATTING																	BASERUNNING			PERCENTAGES		
Year	Team	Lg	G	AB	H	2B	3B	HR	(Hm	Rd)	TB	R	RBI	TBB	IBB	SO	HBP	SH	SF	SB	CS	SB%	GDP	Avg	OBP	SLG
1992	San Francisco	NL	32	103	19	1	1	0	(0	0)	22	10	4	5	0	24	1	0	0	5	1	.83	2	.184	.229	.214
1993	San Francisco	NL	16	16	3	0	1	0	(0	1)	6	1	2	0	0	5	0	0	0	0	0	.00	0	.188	.188	.375
1994	San Francisco	NL	85	240	57	10	1	3	(2	1)	78	36	32	16	0	43	11	7	0	13	3	.81	4	.238	.315	.325
1995	San Francisco	NL	95	205	42	5	3	1	(1	0)	56	27	14	14	1	41	12	6	0	4	2	.67	7	.205	.294	.273
4 ML YEARS			228	564	121	16	5	5	(3	2)	162	74	52	35	1	113	24	13	0	22	7	.76	13	.215	.289	.287

Dave Pavlas

Pitches: Right **Bats:** Right **Pos:** RP　　　　　**Ht:** 6' 7" **Wt:** 205 **Born:** 8/12/62 **Age:** 33

			HOW MUCH HE PITCHED					WHAT HE GAVE UP												THE RESULTS				
Year	Team	Lg	G	GS	CG	GF	IP	BFP	H	R	ER	HR	SH	SF	HB	TBB	IBB	SO	WP	Bk	W	L	Pct.	ShO	Sv	ERA
1995	Columbus *	AAA	48	0	0	32	58.2	233	43	19	17	2	4	1	1	20	2	51	4	0	3	3	.500	0	18	2.61
1990	Chicago	NL	13	0	0	3	21.1	93	23	7	5	2	0	2	0	6	2	12	3	0	2	0	1.000	0	0	2.11
1991	Chicago	NL	1	0	0	1	1	5	3	2	2	1	1	0	0	0	0	0	0	0	0	0	.000	0	0	18.00

Year	Team	Lg	G	GS	CG	GF	IP	BFP	H	R	ER	HR	SH	SF	HB	TBB	IBB	SO	WP	Bk	W	L	Pct.	ShO	Sv	ERA
1995	New York	AL	4	0	0	1	5.2	24	8	2	2	0	0	0	0	0	0	3	0	0	0	0	.000	0	0	3.18
	3 ML YEARS		18	0	0	5	28	122	34	11	9	3	1	2	0	6	2	15	3	0	2	0	1.000	0	0	2.89

Roger Pavlik

Pitches: Right **Bats:** Right **Pos:** SP   **Ht:** 6' 3" **Wt:** 220 **Born:** 10/4/67 **Age:** 28

			HOW MUCH HE PITCHED						WHAT HE GAVE UP										THE RESULTS					
Year	Team	Lg	G	GS	CG	GF	IP	BFP	H	R	ER	HR	SH	SF	HB	TBB	IBB	SO	WP	Bk	W	L	Pct.	ShO	Sv	ERA
1992	Texas	AL	13	12	1	0	62	275	66	32	29	3	0	2	3	34	0	45	9	0	4	4	.500	0	0	4.21
1993	Texas	AL	26	26	2	0	166.1	712	151	69	63	18	6	4	5	80	3	131	6	0	12	6	.667	0	0	3.41
1994	Texas	AL	11	11	0	0	50.1	245	61	45	43	8	4	4	4	30	1	31	5	1	2	5	.286	0	0	7.69
1995	Texas	AL	31	31	2	0	191.2	819	174	96	93	19	4	5	4	90	5	149	10	1	10	10	.500	1	0	4.37
	4 ML YEARS		81	80	5	0	470.1	2051	452	240	228	48	14	15	16	234	9	356	30	2	28	25	.528	1	0	4.36

Steve Pegues

Bats: Right **Throws:** Right **Pos:** LF/RF   **Ht:** 6' 2" **Wt:** 190 **Born:** 5/21/68 **Age:** 28

			BATTING																BASERUNNING				PERCENTAGES		
Year	Team	Lg	G	AB	H	2B	3B	HR	(Hm | Rd)	TB	R	RBI	TBB	IBB	SO	HBP	SH	SF	SB	CS	SB%	GDP	Avg	OBP	SLG
1987	Bristol	R	59	236	67	6	5	2	--	--	89	36	23	16	0	43	0	0	2	22	7	.76	8	.284	.327	.377
1988	Fayetteville	A	118	437	112	17	5	6	--	--	157	50	46	21	3	90	3	2	4	21	11	.66	6	.256	.292	.359
1989	Fayetteville	A	70	269	83	11	6	1	--	--	109	35	38	15	2	52	2	1	3	16	10	.62	5	.309	.346	.405
	Toledo	A	55	193	49	7	2	0	--	--	60	24	15	7	0	19	2	0	1	12	4	.75	5	.254	.286	.311
1990	London	AA	126	483	131	22	5	8	--	--	187	48	63	12	1	58	3	3	4	17	8	.68	17	.271	.291	.387
1991	London	AA	56	216	65	3	2	6	--	--	90	24	26	8	0	24	6	0	2	4	7	.36	6	.301	.341	.417
	Toledo	AAA	68	222	50	13	3	4	--	--	81	21	23	3	0	31	3	1	0	8	5	.62	7	.225	.246	.365
1992	Las Vegas	AAA	123	376	99	21	4	9	--	--	155	51	56	7	1	64	6	3	9	12	3	.80	8	.263	.281	.412
1993	Las Vegas	AAA	68	270	95	20	5	9	--	--	152	52	50	7	0	43	1	0	3	12	6	.67	8	.352	.367	.563
1994	Indianapolis	AAA	63	245	71	16	11	6	--	--	127	36	29	6	0	44	3	1	2	10	3	.77	9	.290	.313	.518
1994	Cin-Pit	NL	18	36	13	2	0	0	(0 | 0)	15	2	2	2	0	5	0	0	2	1	0	1.00	3	.361	.395	.417
1995	Pittsburgh	NL	82	171	42	8	0	6	(5 | 1)	68	17	16	4	0	36	1	0	3	1	2	.33	3	.246	.263	.398
1994	Cincinnati	NL	11	10	3	0	0	0	(0 | 0)	3	1	0	1	0	3	0	0	0	0	0	.00	0	.300	.364	.300
	Pittsburgh	NL	7	26	10	2	0	0	(0 | 0)	12	1	2	1	0	2	0	0	0	1	0	1.00	3	.385	.407	.462
	2 ML YEARS		100	207	55	10	0	6	(5 | 1)	83	19	18	6	0	41	1	0	3	2	2	.50	6	.266	.286	.401

Rudy Pemberton

Bats: Right **Throws:** Right **Pos:** LF   **Ht:** 6' 1" **Wt:** 185 **Born:** 12/17/69 **Age:** 26

			BATTING																BASERUNNING				PERCENTAGES		
Year	Team	Lg	G	AB	H	2B	3B	HR	(Hm | Rd)	TB	R	RBI	TBB	IBB	SO	HBP	SH	SF	SB	CS	SB%	GDP	Avg	OBP	SLG
1988	Bristol	R	6	5	0	0	0	0	--	--	0	2	0	1	0	3	2	0	0	0	0	.00	1	.000	.375	.000
1989	Bristol	R	56	214	58	9	2	6	--	--	89	40	39	14	0	43	4	0	1	19	3	.86	3	.271	.326	.416
1990	Fayetteville	A	127	454	126	14	5	6	--	--	168	60	61	42	1	91	12	1	9	12	9	.57	12	.278	.348	.370
1991	Lakeland	A	111	375	86	15	2	3	--	--	114	40	48	25	2	51	9	6	2	25	15	.63	5	.229	.292	.304
1992	Lakeland	A	104	343	91	16	5	3	--	--	126	41	43	21	2	37	13	2	3	25	10	.71	4	.265	.329	.367
1993	London	AA	124	471	130	22	4	15	--	--	205	70	67	24	1	80	12	0	3	14	12	.54	11	.276	.325	.435
1994	Toledo	AAA	99	360	109	13	3	12	--	--	164	49	58	18	3	62	6	0	6	30	9	.77	8	.303	.341	.456
1995	Toledo	AAA	67	224	77	15	3	7	--	--	119	31	23	15	2	36	5	0	3	8	4	.67	5	.344	.393	.531
1995	Detroit	AL	12	30	9	3	1	0	(0 | 0)	14	3	1	0	0	5	1	0	0	0	0	.00	3	.300	.344	.467

Alejandro Pena

Pitches: Right **Bats:** Right **Pos:** RP   **Ht:** 6' 1" **Wt:** 228 **Born:** 6/25/59 **Age:** 37

			HOW MUCH HE PITCHED						WHAT HE GAVE UP										THE RESULTS					
Year	Team	Lg	G	GS	CG	GF	IP	BFP	H	R	ER	HR	SH	SF	HB	TBB	IBB	SO	WP	Bk	W	L	Pct.	ShO	Sv	ERA
1995	Charlotte *	AAA	9	0	0	8	9.1	31	2	1	1	0	0	0	0	1	0	7	0	0	0	0	.000	0	5	0.96
1981	Los Angeles	NL	14	0	0	7	25	104	18	8	8	2	0	0	0	11	1	14	0	0	1	1	.500	0	2	2.88
1982	Los Angeles	NL	29	0	0	11	35.2	160	37	24	19	2	2	0	1	21	7	20	1	1	0	2	.000	0	0	4.79
1983	Los Angeles	NL	34	26	4	4	177	730	152	67	54	7	8	5	1	51	7	120	2	1	12	9	.571	3	1	2.75
1984	Los Angeles	NL	28	28	8	0	199.1	813	186	67	55	7	6	2	3	46	7	135	5	1	12	6	.667	4	0	2.48
1985	Los Angeles	NL	2	1	0	0	4.1	23	7	5	4	1	0	0	0	3	1	2	0	0	0	1	.000	0	0	8.31
1986	Los Angeles	NL	24	10	0	6	70	309	74	40	38	6	3	1	1	30	5	46	1	1	1	2	.333	0	1	4.89
1987	Los Angeles	NL	37	7	0	17	87.1	377	82	41	34	9	5	6	2	37	5	76	0	1	2	7	.222	0	11	3.50
1988	Los Angeles	NL	60	0	0	31	94.1	378	75	29	20	4	3	3	1	27	6	83	3	2	6	7	.462	0	12	1.91
1989	Los Angeles	NL	53	0	0	28	76	306	62	20	18	6	3	1	2	18	4	75	1	1	4	3	.571	0	5	2.13
1990	New York	NL	52	0	0	32	76	320	71	31	27	4	1	6	1	22	5	76	0	0	3	3	.500	0	5	3.20
1991	Atl-NYN	NL	59	0	0	36	82.1	331	74	23	22	6	3	4	1	22	4	62	1	2	8	1	.889	0	15	2.40
1992	Atlanta	NL	41	0	0	31	42	173	40	19	19	7	2	1	0	13	5	34	0	0	1	6	.143	0	15	4.07
1994	Pittsburgh	NL	22	0	0	15	28.2	118	22	16	16	4	0	0	1	10	2	27	2	0	3	2	.600	0	7	5.02
1995	Bos-Fla-Atl	NL	44	0	0	11	55.1	238	55	32	29	8	0	0	0	19	3	64	0	0	3	1	.750	0	4	4.72
1991	Atlanta	NL	15	0	0	12	19.1	70	11	3	3	1	1	0	0	3	0	13	0	0	2	0	1.000	0	11	1.40
	New York	NL	44	0	0	24	63	261	63	20	19	5	2	4	1	19	4	49	1	2	6	1	.857	0	4	2.71

176

Year Team	Lg	G	GS	CG	GF	IP	BFP	H	R	ER	HR	SH	SF	HB	BB	IBB	SO	WP	Bk	W	L	Pct	ShO	Sv	ERA
1995 Boston	AL	17	0	0	5	24.1	117	33	23	20	5	0	0	0	12	2	25	0	0	1	1	.500	0	0	7.40
Florida	NL	13	0	0	4	18	68	11	3	3	2	0	0	0	3	1	21	0	0	2	0	1.000	0	0	1.50
Atlanta	NL	14	0	0	2	13	53	11	6	6	1	0	0	0	4	0	18	0	0	0	0	.000	0	0	4.15
14 ML YEARS		499	72	12	229	1053.1	4380	955	422	363	73	36	29	13	330	62	834	16	10	56	51	.523	7	74	3.10

Geronimo Pena

Bats: Both **Throws:** Right **Pos:** 2B Ht: 6' 1" Wt: 195 Born: 3/29/67 Age: 29

								BATTING											BASERUNNING				PERCENTAGES		
Year Team	Lg	G	AB	H	2B	3B	HR	(Hm	Rd)	TB	R	RBI	TBB	IBB	SO	HBP	SH	SF	SB	CS	SB%	GDP	Avg	OBP	SLG
1995 Louisville *	AAA	6	21	8	1	0	2	--	--	15	5	6	3	2	1	0	0	0	0	0	.00	0	.381	.458	.714
1990 St. Louis	NL	18	45	11	2	0	0	(0	0)	13	5	2	4	0	14	1	0	1	1	1	.50	0	.244	.314	.289
1991 St. Louis	NL	104	185	45	8	3	5	(1	4)	74	38	17	18	1	45	5	1	3	15	5	.75	3	.243	.322	.400
1992 St. Louis	NL	62	203	62	12	1	7	(4	3)	97	31	31	24	0	37	5	0	4	13	8	.62	1	.305	.386	.478
1993 St. Louis	NL	74	254	65	19	2	5	(2	3)	103	34	30	25	0	71	4	4	2	13	5	.72	3	.256	.330	.406
1994 St. Louis	NL	83	213	54	13	1	11	(7	4)	102	33	34	24	1	54	6	4	1	9	1	.90	3	.254	.344	.479
1995 St. Louis	NL	32	101	27	6	1	1	(1	0)	38	20	8	16	1	30	1	4	2	3	2	.60	2	.267	.367	.376
6 ML YEARS		373	1001	264	60	8	29	(15	14)	427	161	122	111	3	251	22	13	13	54	22	.71	9	.264	.346	.427

Tony Pena

Bats: Right **Throws:** Right **Pos:** C Ht: 6' 0" Wt: 185 Born: 6/4/57 Age: 39

								BATTING											BASERUNNING				PERCENTAGES		
Year Team	Lg	G	AB	H	2B	3B	HR	(Hm	Rd)	TB	R	RBI	TBB	IBB	SO	HBP	SH	SF	SB	CS	SB%	GDP	Avg	OBP	SLG
1980 Pittsburgh	NL	8	21	9	1	1	0	(0	0)	12	1	1	0	0	4	0	0	0	0	1	.00	1	.429	.429	.571
1981 Pittsburgh	NL	66	210	63	9	1	2	(1	1)	80	16	17	8	2	23	1	2	2	1	2	.33	4	.300	.326	.381
1982 Pittsburgh	NL	138	497	147	28	4	11	(5	6)	216	53	63	17	3	57	4	3	2	2	5	.29	17	.296	.323	.435
1983 Pittsburgh	NL	151	542	163	22	3	15	(8	7)	236	51	70	31	8	73	0	6	1	6	7	.46	13	.301	.338	.435
1984 Pittsburgh	NL	147	546	156	27	2	15	(7	8)	232	77	78	36	5	79	4	4	2	12	8	.60	14	.286	.333	.425
1985 Pittsburgh	NL	147	546	136	27	2	10	(2	8)	197	53	59	29	4	67	0	7	5	12	8	.60	19	.249	.284	.361
1986 Pittsburgh	NL	144	510	147	26	2	10	(5	5)	207	56	52	53	6	69	1	0	1	9	10	.47	21	.288	.356	.406
1987 St. Louis	NL	116	384	82	13	4	5	(1	4)	118	40	44	36	9	54	1	2	2	6	1	.86	19	.214	.281	.307
1988 St. Louis	NL	149	505	133	23	1	10	(4	6)	188	55	51	33	11	60	1	3	4	6	2	.75	12	.263	.308	.372
1989 St. Louis	NL	141	424	110	17	2	4	(3	1)	143	36	37	35	19	33	2	2	1	5	3	.63	19	.259	.318	.337
1990 Boston	AL	143	491	129	19	1	7	(3	4)	171	62	56	43	3	71	1	2	3	8	6	.57	23	.263	.322	.348
1991 Boston	AL	141	464	107	23	2	5	(2	3)	149	45	48	37	1	53	4	4	3	8	3	.73	23	.231	.291	.321
1992 Boston	AL	133	410	99	21	1	1	(1	0)	125	39	38	24	0	61	1	13	2	3	2	.60	11	.241	.284	.305
1993 Boston	AL	126	304	55	11	0	4	(2	2)	78	20	19	25	0	46	2	13	3	1	3	.25	12	.181	.246	.257
1994 Cleveland	AL	40	112	33	8	1	2	(1	1)	49	18	10	9	0	11	0	3	2	0	1	.00	6	.295	.341	.438
1995 Cleveland	AL	91	263	69	15	0	5	(1	4)	99	25	28	14	1	44	1	1	0	1	0	1.00	9	.262	.302	.376
16 ML YEARS		1881	6229	1638	290	27	106	(46	60)	2300	647	671	430	72	805	23	65	33	80	62	.56	223	.263	.311	.369

Terry Pendleton

Bats: Both **Throws:** Right **Pos:** 3B Ht: 5' 9" Wt: 195 Born: 7/16/60 Age: 35

								BATTING											BASERUNNING				PERCENTAGES		
Year Team	Lg	G	AB	H	2B	3B	HR	(Hm	Rd)	TB	R	RBI	TBB	IBB	SO	HBP	SH	SF	SB	CS	SB%	GDP	Avg	OBP	SLG
1984 St. Louis	NL	67	262	85	16	3	1	(0	1)	110	37	33	16	3	32	0	0	5	20	5	.80	7	.324	.357	.420
1985 St. Louis	NL	149	559	134	16	3	5	(3	2)	171	56	69	37	4	75	0	3	3	17	12	.59	18	.240	.285	.306
1986 St. Louis	NL	159	578	138	26	5	1	(0	1)	177	56	59	34	10	59	1	6	7	24	6	.80	12	.239	.279	.306
1987 St. Louis	NL	159	583	167	29	4	12	(5	7)	240	82	96	70	6	74	2	3	9	19	12	.61	18	.286	.360	.412
1988 St. Louis	NL	110	391	99	20	2	6	(3	3)	141	44	53	21	4	51	2	4	3	3	3	.50	9	.253	.293	.361
1989 St. Louis	NL	162	613	162	28	5	13	(8	5)	239	83	74	44	3	81	0	2	2	9	5	.64	16	.264	.313	.390
1990 St. Louis	NL	121	447	103	20	2	6	(6	0)	145	46	58	30	8	58	1	0	6	7	5	.58	12	.230	.277	.324
1991 Atlanta	NL	153	586	187	34	8	22	(13	9)	303	94	86	43	8	70	1	7	7	10	2	.83	16	.319	.363	.517
1992 Atlanta	NL	160	640	199	39	1	21	(13	8)	303	98	105	37	8	67	0	5	7	5	2	.71	18	.311	.345	.473
1993 Atlanta	NL	161	633	172	33	1	17	(9	8)	258	81	84	36	5	97	3	3	7	5	1	.83	18	.272	.311	.408
1994 Atlanta	NL	77	309	78	18	3	7	(3	4)	123	25	30	12	3	57	0	3	0	2	0	1.00	8	.252	.280	.398
1995 Florida	NL	133	513	149	32	1	14	(8	6)	225	70	78	38	7	84	2	0	4	1	2	.33	7	.290	.339	.439
12 ML YEARS		1611	6114	1673	311	38	125	(71	54)	2435	772	825	418	69	805	12	36	60	122	55	.69	157	.274	.318	.398

Shannon Penn

Bats: Both **Throws:** Right **Pos:** 2B Ht: 5'10" Wt: 165 Born: 9/11/69 Age: 26

								BATTING											BASERUNNING				PERCENTAGES		
Year Team	Lg	G	AB	H	2B	3B	HR	(Hm	Rd)	TB	R	RBI	TBB	IBB	SO	HBP	SH	SF	SB	CS	SB%	GDP	Avg	OBP	SLG
1989 Rangers	R	47	147	32	2	1	0	--	--	36	19	8	20	0	27	1	0	1	17	7	.71	1	.218	.314	.245
1990 Butte	R	60	197	64	4	2	0	--	--	72	38	18	15	0	35	1	0	2	9	4	.69	0	.325	.372	.365
1992 Niagara Fal	A	70	253	69	9	2	3	--	--	91	47	25	28	2	53	6	3	1	31	10	.76	2	.273	.358	.360
1993 London	AA	128	493	128	12	6	0	--	--	152	78	36	54	1	95	8	7	4	53	16	.77	4	.260	.340	.308

Year Team	Lg	G	AB	H	2B	3B	HR	(Hm	Rd)	TB	R	RBI	TBB	IBB	SO	HBP	SH	SF	SB	CS	SB%	GDP	Avg	OBP	SLG
1994 Toledo	AAA	114	444	126	14	6	2	--	--	158	63	33	30	0	96	5	4	4	45	16	.74	4	.284	.333	.356
1995 Toledo	AAA	63	218	54	4	1	1	--	--	63	41	15	17	0	40	10	2	2	15	9	.63	4	.248	.328	.289
1995 Detroit	AL	3	9	3	0	0	0	(0	0)	3	0	0	1	0	2	0	0	0	0	0	.00	2	.333	.400	.333

Brad Pennington

Pitches: Left **Bats:** Left **Pos:** RP **Ht:** 6' 6" **Wt:** 215 **Born:** 4/14/69 **Age:** 27

		HOW MUCH HE PITCHED					WHAT HE GAVE UP									THE RESULTS				
Year Team	Lg	G	GS	CG	GF	IP	BFP	H	R	ER	HR	SH	SF	HB	TBB	IBB	SO	WP	Bk	W	L	Pct.	ShO	Sv	ERA
1995 Indianapolis *	AAA	11	2	0	1	14	79	17	19	16	3	0	1	0	21	1	11	2	0	0	0	.000	0	0	10.29
1993 Baltimore	AL	34	0	0	16	33	158	34	25	24	7	2	1	2	25	0	39	3	0	3	2	.600	0	4	6.55
1994 Baltimore	AL	8	0	0	3	6	35	9	8	8	2	1	0	0	8	0	7	2	0	0	1	.000	0	0	12.00
1995 Bal-Cin	AL	14	0	0	4	16.1	80	12	15	12	1	0	2	1	22	1	17	4	0	0	1	.000	0	0	6.61
1995 Baltimore	AL	8	0	0	2	6.2	33	3	7	6	1	0	0	0	11	1	10	1	0	0	1	.000	0	0	8.10
Cincinnati	NL	6	0	0	2	9.2	47	9	8	6	0	0	2	1	11	0	7	3	0	0	0	.000	0	0	5.59
3 ML YEARS		56	0	0	23	55.1	273	55	48	44	10	3	3	3	55	1	63	9	0	3	4	.429	0	4	7.16

Troy Percival

Pitches: Right **Bats:** Right **Pos:** RP **Ht:** 6' 3" **Wt:** 200 **Born:** 8/9/69 **Age:** 26

		HOW MUCH HE PITCHED					WHAT HE GAVE UP									THE RESULTS				
Year Team	Lg	G	GS	CG	GF	IP	BFP	H	R	ER	HR	SH	SF	HB	TBB	IBB	SO	WP	Bk	W	L	Pct.	ShO	Sv	ERA
1991 Boise	A	28	0	0	20	38.1	157	23	7	6	0	1	2	2	18	1	63	9	0	2	0	1.000	0	12	1.41
1992 Palm Spring	A	11	0	0	9	10.2	45	6	7	6	0	0	3	2	8	1	16	1	1	1	1	.500	0	2	5.06
Midland	AA	20	0	0	17	19	84	18	5	5	1	0	1	1	11	1	21	1	0	3	0	1.000	0	5	2.37
1993 Vancouver	AAA	18	0	0	11	18.2	94	24	14	13	0	1	3	2	13	1	19	2	0	0	1	.000	0	4	6.27
1994 Vancouver	AAA	49	0	0	32	61	266	63	31	28	4	6	3	7	29	5	73	6	2	1	3	.250	0	15	4.13
1995 California	AL	62	0	0	16	74	284	37	19	16	6	4	1	1	26	2	94	2	2	3	2	.600	0	3	1.95

Carlos Perez

Pitches: Left **Bats:** Left **Pos:** SP/RP **Ht:** 6' 3" **Wt:** 195 **Born:** 1/14/71 **Age:** 25

		HOW MUCH HE PITCHED					WHAT HE GAVE UP									THE RESULTS				
Year Team	Lg	G	GS	CG	GF	IP	BFP	H	R	ER	HR	SH	SF	HB	TBB	IBB	SO	WP	Bk	W	L	Pct.	ShO	Sv	ERA
1990 Expos	R	13	2	0	6	35.2	145	24	14	10	0	1	1	1	15	0	38	1	0	3	1	.750	0	2	2.52
1991 Sumter	A	16	12	0	2	73.2	306	57	29	20	3	0	7	0	32	0	69	3	1	2	2	.500	0	0	2.44
1992 Rockford	A	7	1	0	2	9.1	43	12	7	6	3	1	0	1	5	0	8	1	0	1	0	1.000	0	1	5.79
1993 Burlington	A	12	1	0	5	16.2	69	13	6	6	0	3	0	0	9	0	21	0	1	1	0	1.000	0	1	3.24
San Bernrdo	A	20	18	3	0	131	550	120	57	50	12	3	2	0	44	0	98	9	6	8	7	.533	0	0	3.44
1994 Harrisburg	AA	12	11	2	1	79	307	55	27	17	5	3	0	2	18	0	69	5	0	7	2	.778	2	1	1.94
Ottawa	AAA	17	17	3	0	119	511	130	50	44	8	5	3	3	41	2	82	4	1	7	5	.583	0	0	3.33
1995 Montreal	NL	28	23	2	2	141.1	592	142	61	58	18	6	1	5	28	2	106	8	4	10	8	.556	1	0	3.69

Eddie Perez

Bats: Right **Throws:** Right **Pos:** C **Ht:** 6' 1" **Wt:** 175 **Born:** 5/4/68 **Age:** 28

		BATTING															BASERUNNING				PERCENTAGES		
Year Team	Lg	G	AB	H	2B	3B	HR	(Hm | Rd)	TB	R	RBI	TBB	IBB	SO	HBP	SH	SF	SB	CS	SB%	GDP	Avg	OBP	SLG
1987 Braves	R	31	89	18	1	0	1	--	--	22	8	5	8	0	14	1	1	1	0	0	.00	4	.202	.273	.247
1988 Burlington	A	64	186	43	8	0	4	--	--	63	14	19	10	0	33	0	2	1	1	0	1.00	6	.231	.269	.339
1989 Sumter	A	114	401	93	21	0	5	--	--	129	39	44	44	1	68	5	4	5	2	6	.25	10	.232	.312	.322
1990 Sumter	A	41	123	22	7	1	3	--	--	40	11	17	14	0	18	2	3	1	0	0	.00	7	.179	.271	.325
Durham	A	31	93	22	1	0	3	--	--	32	9	10	1	0	12	1	0	1	0	0	.00	3	.237	.250	.344
1991 Durham	A	91	277	75	10	1	9	--	--	114	38	41	17	2	33	3	2	3	0	3	.00	7	.271	.317	.412
Greenville	AA	1	4	1	0	0	0	--	--	1	0	0	0	0	1	0	0	0	0	0	.00	0	.250	.250	.250
1992 Greenville	AA	91	275	63	16	0	6	--	--	97	28	41	24	0	41	2	1	4	3	3	.50	11	.229	.292	.353
1993 Greenville	AA	28	84	28	6	0	6	--	--	52	15	17	2	0	8	0	0	2	1	0	1.00	4	.333	.341	.619
1994 Richmond	AAA	113	388	101	16	2	9	--	--	148	37	49	18	1	47	3	3	6	1	1	.50	4	.260	.294	.381
1995 Richmond	AAA	92	324	86	19	0	5	--	--	120	31	40	12	0	58	2	1	2	1	2	.33	12	.265	.294	.370
1995 Atlanta	NL	7	13	4	1	0	1	(0 | 1)	8	1	4	0	0	2	0	0	0	0	0	.00	0	.308	.308	.615

Eduardo Perez

Bats: Right **Throws:** Right **Pos:** 3B **Ht:** 6' 4" **Wt:** 215 **Born:** 9/11/69 **Age:** 26

		BATTING															BASERUNNING				PERCENTAGES		
Year Team	Lg	G	AB	H	2B	3B	HR	(Hm | Rd)	TB	R	RBI	TBB	IBB	SO	HBP	SH	SF	SB	CS	SB%	GDP	Avg	OBP	SLG
1995 Vancouver *	AAA	69	246	80	12	7	6	--	--	124	39	39	35	0	34	2	1	4	6	2	.75	5	.325	.386	.504
1993 California	AL	52	180	45	6	2	4	(2 | 2)	67	16	30	9	0	39	2	0	1	5	4	.56	4	.250	.292	.372
1994 California	AL	38	129	27	7	0	5	(3 | 2)	49	10	16	12	1	29	0	1	1	3	0	1.00	5	.209	.275	.380
1995 California	AL	29	71	12	4	1	1	(0 | 1)	21	9	7	12	0	9	2	0	1	0	2	.00	3	.169	.302	.296
3 ML YEARS		119	380	84	17	3	10	(5 | 5)	137	35	53	33	1	77	4	1	3	8	6	.57	12	.221	.288	.361

Melido Perez

Pitches: Right **Bats:** Right **Pos:** SP   **Ht:** 6' 4" **Wt:** 210 **Born:** 2/15/66 **Age:** 30

		HOW MUCH HE PITCHED					WHAT HE GAVE UP										THE RESULTS				
Year Team	Lg	G	GS	CG	GF	IP	BFP	H	R	ER	HR	SH	SF	HB	TBB	IBB	SO	WP	Bk	W	L	Pct.	ShO	Sv	ERA
1995 Norwich *	AA	2	2	0	0	9	35	7	0	0	0	0	0	0	3	0	9	0	1	1	0	1.000	0	0	0.00
1987 Kansas City	AL	3	3	0	0	10.1	53	18	12	9	2	0	0	0	5	0	5	0	0	1	1	.500	0	0	7.84
1988 Chicago	AL	32	32	3	0	197	836	186	105	83	26	5	8	2	72	0	138	13	3	12	10	.545	1	0	3.79
1989 Chicago	AL	31	31	2	0	183.1	810	187	106	102	23	5	4	3	90	3	141	12	5	11	14	.440	2	0	5.01
1990 Chicago	AL	35	35	3	0	197	833	177	111	101	14	4	6	2	86	1	161	8	4	13	14	.481	3	0	4.61
1991 Chicago	AL	49	8	0	16	135.2	553	111	49	47	15	4	1	1	52	0	128	11	1	8	7	.533	0	1	3.12
1992 New York	AL	33	33	10	0	247.2	1013	212	94	79	16	6	8	5	93	5	218	13	0	13	16	.448	1	0	2.87
1993 New York	AL	25	25	0	0	163	718	173	103	94	22	4	2	1	64	5	148	3	1	6	14	.300	0	0	5.19
1994 New York	AL	22	22	1	0	151.1	632	134	74	69	16	5	3	3	58	5	109	7	1	9	4	.692	0	0	4.10
1995 New York	AL	13	12	1	1	69.1	304	70	46	43	10	1	3	1	31	2	44	4	0	5	5	.500	0	0	5.58
9 ML YEARS		243	201	20	17	1354.2	5752	1268	700	627	144	34	35	18	551	21	1092	71	15	78	85	.479	5	1	4.17

Mike Perez

Pitches: Right **Bats:** Right **Pos:** RP   **Ht:** 6' 0" **Wt:** 200 **Born:** 10/19/64 **Age:** 31

		HOW MUCH HE PITCHED					WHAT HE GAVE UP										THE RESULTS				
Year Team	Lg	G	GS	CG	GF	IP	BFP	H	R	ER	HR	SH	SF	HB	TBB	IBB	SO	WP	Bk	W	L	Pct.	ShO	Sv	ERA
1990 St. Louis	NL	13	0	0	7	13.2	55	12	6	6	0	0	2	0	3	0	5	0	1	1	0	1.000	0	1	3.95
1991 St. Louis	NL	14	0	0	2	17	75	19	11	11	1	1	0	1	7	2	7	0	1	0	2	.000	0	0	5.82
1992 St. Louis	NL	77	0	0	22	93	377	70	23	19	4	7	4	1	32	9	46	4	0	9	3	.750	0	0	1.84
1993 St. Louis	NL	65	0	0	25	72.2	298	65	24	20	4	5	5	1	20	1	58	2	0	7	2	.778	0	7	2.48
1994 St. Louis	NL	36	0	0	18	31	155	52	32	30	5	4	5	3	10	1	20	0	0	2	3	.400	0	12	8.71
1995 Chicago	NL	68	0	0	18	71.1	308	72	30	29	8	5	3	4	27	8	49	4	0	2	6	.250	0	2	3.66
6 ML YEARS		273	0	0	92	298.2	1268	290	126	115	22	22	19	10	99	21	185	10	1	21	16	.568	0	22	3.47

Robert Perez

Bats: Right **Throws:** Right **Pos:** RF   **Ht:** 6' 3" **Wt:** 205 **Born:** 6/4/69 **Age:** 27

		BATTING																		BASERUNNING				PERCENTAGES		
Year Team	Lg	G	AB	H	2B	3B	HR	(Hm	Rd)	TB	R	RBI	TBB	IBB	SO	HBP	SH	SF	SB	CS	SB%	GDP	Avg	OBP	SLG
1990 St. Cathrns	A	52	207	54	10	2	5	--	--	83	20	25	8	1	34	2	0	0	7	5	.58	7	.261	.295	.401
Myrtle Bch	A	21	72	21	2	0	1	--	--	26	8	10	3	0	9	2	0	1	2	1	.67	3	.292	.333	.361
1991 Dunedin	A	127	480	145	28	6	4	--	--	197	50	50	22	3	72	5	7	2	8	8	.50	19	.302	.338	.410
Syracuse	AAA	4	20	4	1	0	0	--	--	5	2	1	0	0	2	0	0	0	0	0	.00	0	.200	.200	.250
1992 Knoxville	AA	139	526	137	25	5	9	--	--	199	59	59	13	0	87	2	3	7	11	10	.52	10	.260	.277	.378
1993 Syracuse	AAA	138	524	154	26	10	12	--	--	236	72	64	24	1	65	4	5	1	13	15	.46	19	.294	.329	.450
1994 Syracuse	AAA	128	510	155	28	3	10	--	--	219	63	65	27	7	76	2	4	8	4	7	.36	21	.304	.336	.429
1995 Syracuse	AAA	122	502	172	38	6	9	--	--	249	70	67	13	4	60	2	1	4	7	5	.58	17	.343	.359	.496
1994 Toronto	AL	4	8	1	0	0	0	(0	0)	1	0	0	0	0	1	0	0	0	0	0	.00	1	.125	.125	.125
1995 Toronto	AL	17	48	9	2	0	1	(1	0)	14	2	3	0	0	5	0	0	0	0	0	.00	1	.188	.188	.292
2 ML YEARS		21	56	10	2	0	1	(1	0)	15	2	3	0	0	6	0	0	0	0	0	.00	2	.179	.179	.268

Tomas Perez

Bats: Both **Throws:** Right **Pos:** SS   **Ht:** 5'11" **Wt:** 165 **Born:** 12/29/73 **Age:** 22

		BATTING																		BASERUNNING				PERCENTAGES		
Year Team	Lg	G	AB	H	2B	3B	HR	(Hm	Rd)	TB	R	RBI	TBB	IBB	SO	HBP	SH	SF	SB	CS	SB%	GDP	Avg	OBP	SLG
1993 Expos	R	52	189	46	3	1	2	--	--	57	27	21	23	0	25	0	4	2	7	3	.70	5	.243	.322	.302
1994 Burlington	A	119	465	122	22	1	8	--	--	170	76	47	48	3	78	1	4	5	8	10	.44	2	.262	.329	.366
1995 Toronto	AL	41	98	24	3	1	1	(1	0)	32	12	8	7	0	18	0	0	1	0	1	.00	6	.245	.292	.327

Yorkis Perez

Pitches: Left **Bats:** Left **Pos:** RP   **Ht:** 6' 0" **Wt:** 180 **Born:** 9/30/67 **Age:** 28

		HOW MUCH HE PITCHED					WHAT HE GAVE UP										THE RESULTS				
Year Team	Lg	G	GS	CG	GF	IP	BFP	H	R	ER	HR	SH	SF	HB	TBB	IBB	SO	WP	Bk	W	L	Pct.	ShO	Sv	ERA
1991 Chicago	NL	3	0	0	0	4.1	16	2	1	1	0	0	0	0	2	0	3	2	0	1	0	1.000	0	0	2.08
1994 Florida	NL	44	0	0	11	40.2	167	33	18	16	4	2	0	1	14	3	41	4	1	3	0	1.000	0	0	3.54
1995 Florida	NL	69	0	0	11	46.2	205	35	29	27	6	2	1	2	28	4	47	2	0	2	6	.250	0	1	5.21
3 ML YEARS		116	0	0	22	91.2	388	70	48	44	10	4	3	3	44	7	91	8	1	6	6	.500	0	1	4.32

Gerald Perry

Bats: Left   **Throws:** Right   **Pos:** 1B   **Ht:** 6' 0"   **Wt:** 201   **Born:** 10/30/60   **Age:** 35

Year Team	Lg	G	AB	H	2B	3B	HR	(Hm	Rd)	TB	R	RBI	TBB	IBB	SO	HBP	SH	SF	SB	CS	SB%	GDP	Avg	OBP	SLG
1983 Atlanta	NL	27	39	14	2	0	1	(0	1)	19	5	6	5	0	4	0	0	1	0	1	.00	1	.359	.422	.487
1984 Atlanta	NL	122	347	92	12	2	7	(3	4)	129	52	47	61	5	38	2	2	7	15	12	.56	9	.265	.372	.372
1985 Atlanta	NL	110	238	51	5	0	3	(3	0)	65	22	13	23	1	28	0	0	1	9	5	.64	7	.214	.282	.273
1986 Atlanta	NL	29	70	19	2	0	2	(2	0)	27	6	11	8	1	4	0	1	1	0	1	.00	4	.271	.342	.386
1987 Atlanta	NL	142	533	144	35	2	12	(2	10)	219	77	74	48	1	63	1	3	5	42	16	.72	18	.270	.329	.411
1988 Atlanta	NL	141	547	164	29	1	8	(4	4)	219	61	74	36	9	49	1	1	10	29	14	.67	18	.300	.338	.400
1989 Atlanta	NL	72	266	67	11	0	4	(2	2)	90	24	21	32	5	28	3	0	2	10	6	.63	5	.252	.337	.338
1990 Kansas City	AL	133	465	118	22	2	8	(3	5)	168	57	57	39	4	56	3	0	5	17	4	.81	14	.254	.313	.361
1991 St. Louis	NL	109	242	58	8	4	6	(1	5)	92	29	36	22	1	34	0	0	3	15	8	.65	2	.240	.300	.380
1992 St. Louis	NL	87	143	34	8	0	1	(1	0)	45	13	18	15	4	23	1	0	2	3	6	.33	3	.238	.311	.315
1993 St. Louis	NL	96	98	33	5	0	4	(3	1)	50	21	16	18	2	23	0	0	0	1	1	.50	4	.337	.440	.510
1994 St. Louis	NL	60	77	25	7	0	3	(1	2)	41	12	18	15	1	12	0	0	0	1	1	.50	4	.325	.435	.532
1995 St. Louis	NL	65	79	13	4	0	0	(0	0)	17	4	5	6	0	12	0	0	0	0	0	.00	2	.165	.224	.215
13 ML YEARS		1193	3144	832	150	11	59	(25	34)	1181	383	396	328	34	374	11	7	37	142	75	.65	91	.265	.333	.376

Herbert Perry

Bats: Right   **Throws:** Right   **Pos:** 1B   **Ht:** 6' 2"   **Wt:** 215   **Born:** 9/15/69   **Age:** 26

Year Team	Lg	G	AB	H	2B	3B	HR	(Hm	Rd)	TB	R	RBI	TBB	IBB	SO	HBP	SH	SF	SB	CS	SB%	GDP	Avg	OBP	SLG
1991 Watertown	A	14	53	11	2	0	0	--	--	13	3	5	7	0	7	2	0	0	0	0	.00	3	.208	.323	.245
1992 Kinston	A	121	449	125	16	1	19	--	--	200	74	77	46	1	89	12	4	4	12	0	1.00	9	.278	.358	.445
1993 Canton-Akrn	AA	89	327	88	21	1	9	--	--	138	52	55	37	2	47	15	0	6	7	4	.64	5	.269	.364	.422
1994 Charlotte	AAA	102	376	123	20	4	13	--	--	190	67	70	41	7	55	5	0	4	9	4	.69	10	.327	.397	.505
1995 Buffalo	AAA	49	180	57	14	1	2	--	--	79	27	17	15	2	18	3	3	2	1	0	1.00	4	.317	.375	.439
1994 Cleveland	AL	4	9	1	0	0	0	(0	0)	1	1	1	3	1	1	1	0	1	0	0	.00	0	.111	.357	.111
1995 Cleveland	AL	52	162	51	13	1	3	(3	0)	75	23	23	13	0	28	4	3	2	1	3	.25	5	.315	.376	.463
2 ML YEARS		56	171	52	13	1	3	(3	0)	76	24	24	16	1	29	5	3	3	1	3	.25	5	.304	.374	.444

Robert Person

Pitches: Right   **Bats:** Right   **Pos:** RP   **Ht:** 5'11"   **Wt:** 180   **Born:** 10/6/69   **Age:** 26

Year Team	Lg	G	GS	CG	GF	IP	BFP	H	R	ER	HR	SH	SF	HB	TBB	IBB	SO	WP	Bk	W	L	Pct.	ShO	Sv	ERA
1989 Burlington	R	10	5	0	3	34	145	23	13	12	1	0	1	5	17	0	19	5	0	0	1	.000	0	1	3.18
1990 Kinston	A	4	3	0	1	16.2	74	17	6	5	0	0	1	0	9	0	7	0	0	1	0	1.000	0	0	2.70
Indians	R	8	0	0	7	7.1	34	10	7	6	0	1	0	4	4	1	8	1	0	0	2	.000	0	2	7.36
Watertown	A	5	2	0	2	16.1	62	8	2	2	0	0	0	0	7	0	19	0	0	1	0	1.000	0	0	1.10
1991 Kinston	A	11	11	0	0	52	252	56	37	27	2	3	6	2	42	0	45	2	1	3	5	.375	0	0	4.67
Bend	A	2	2	0	0	10	41	6	6	4	0	0	0	1	5	0	6	1	0	1	1	.500	0	0	3.60
South Bend	A	13	13	0	0	76.1	321	50	35	28	3	3	1	0	56	1	66	4	0	4	3	.571	0	0	3.30
1992 Sarasota	A	19	18	1	0	105.1	458	90	48	42	7	4	0	1	62	1	85	7	0	5	7	.417	0	0	3.59
1993 High Desert	A	28	26	4	1	169	740	184	115	88	13	4	6	4	48	0	107	9	1	12	10	.545	0	0	4.69
1994 Binghamton	AA	31	23	3	4	159	649	124	68	61	18	6	4	3	68	3	130	6	0	9	6	.600	2	0	3.45
1995 Binghamton	AA	26	7	1	13	66.2	263	46	27	23	4	4	1	0	25	0	65	1	0	5	4	.556	0	7	3.11
Norfolk	AAA	5	4	0	0	32	138	30	17	16	2	1	0	0	13	0	33	4	0	2	1	.667	0	0	4.50
1995 New York	NL	3	1	0	0	12	44	5	1	1	1	0	0	0	2	0	10	0	0	1	0	1.000	0	0	0.75

Roberto Petagine

Bats: Left   **Throws:** Left   **Pos:** 1B   **Ht:** 6' 1"   **Wt:** 170   **Born:** 6/2/71   **Age:** 25

Year Team	Lg	G	AB	H	2B	3B	HR	(Hm	Rd)	TB	R	RBI	TBB	IBB	SO	HBP	SH	SF	SB	CS	SB%	GDP	Avg	OBP	SLG
1990 Astros	R	55	187	54	5	4	2	--	--	73	35	24	26	2	23	2	1	2	9	6	.60	4	.289	.378	.390
1991 Burlington	A	124	432	112	24	1	12	--	--	174	72	57	71	3	73	4	1	1	6	5	.55	9	.259	.368	.403
1992 Osceola	A	86	307	90	22	4	7	--	--	141	52	49	47	3	47	5	0	4	3	1	.75	5	.293	.391	.459
Jackson	AA	21	70	21	4	0	4	--	--	37	8	12	6	1	15	2	0	2	1	0	1.00	4	.300	.363	.529
1993 Jackson	AA	128	437	146	36	2	15	--	--	231	73	90	84	14	89	4	0	5	6	5	.55	4	.334	.442	.529
1994 Tucson	AAA	65	247	78	19	0	10	--	--	127	53	44	35	6	54	1	0	3	3	1	.75	7	.316	.399	.514
1995 Las Vegas	AAA	19	56	12	2	1	1	--	--	19	8	5	13	1	17	0	1	0	1	0	1.00	0	.214	.362	.339
1994 Houston	NL	8	7	0	0	0	0	(0	0)	0	0	0	1	0	3	0	0	0	0	0	.00	0	.000	.125	.000
1995 San Diego	NL	89	124	29	8	0	3	(2	1)	46	15	17	26	2	41	0	2	0	0	2	.00	2	.234	.367	.371
2 ML YEARS		97	131	29	8	0	3	(2	1)	46	15	17	27	2	44	0	2	0	0	2	.00	2	.221	.354	.351

Mark Petkovsek

Pitches: Right **Bats:** Right **Pos:** SP/RP　　　　**Ht:** 6' 0" **Wt:** 195 **Born:** 11/18/65 **Age:** 30

		HOW MUCH HE PITCHED						WHAT HE GAVE UP												THE RESULTS					
Year Team	Lg	G	GS	CG	GF	IP	BFP	H	R	ER	HR	SH	SF	HB	TBB	IBB	SO	WP	Bk	W	L	Pct.	ShO	Sv	ERA
1995 Louisville *	AAA	8	8	2	0	54.1	209	38	16	14	3	1	1	1	8	0	30	1	0	4	1	.800	1	0	2.32
1991 Texas	AL	4	1	0	1	9.1	53	21	16	15	4	0	1	0	4	0	6	2	0	0	1	.000	0	0	14.46
1993 Pittsburgh	NL	26	0	0	8	32.1	145	43	25	25	7	4	1	0	9	2	14	4	0	3	0	1.000	0	0	6.96
1995 St. Louis	NL	26	21	1	1	137.1	569	136	71	61	11	4	4	6	35	3	71	1	1	6	6	.500	0	0	4.00
3 ML YEARS		56	22	1	10	179	767	200	112	101	22	8	6	6	48	5	91	7	1	9	7	.563	1	0	5.08

Andy Pettitte

Pitches: Left **Bats:** Left **Pos:** SP/RP　　　　**Ht:** 6' 5" **Wt:** 235 **Born:** 6/15/72 **Age:** 24

		HOW MUCH HE PITCHED						WHAT HE GAVE UP												THE RESULTS					
Year Team	Lg	G	GS	CG	GF	IP	BFP	H	R	ER	HR	SH	SF	HB	TBB	IBB	SO	WP	Bk	W	L	Pct.	ShO	Sv	ERA
1991 Yankees	R	6	6	0	0	36.2	135	16	6	4	0	0	0	1	8	0	51	4	6	4	1	.800	0	0	0.98
Oneonta	A	6	6	1	0	33	150	33	18	8	1	1	2	0	16	0	32	4	0	2	2	.500	0	0	2.18
1992 Greensboro	A	27	27	2	0	168	671	141	53	41	4	3	1	5	55	0	130	11	2	10	4	.714	1	0	2.20
1993 Pr. William	A	26	26	2	0	159.2	651	146	68	54	7	6	4	5	47	0	129	8	1	11	9	.550	1	0	3.04
Albany-Colo	AA	1	1	0	0	5	22	5	4	2	0	0	0	0	2	0	6	0	0	1	0	1.000	0	0	3.60
1994 Albany-Colo	AA	11	11	0	0	73	294	60	32	22	5	1	1	1	18	1	50	5	1	7	2	.778	0	0	2.71
Columbus	AAA	16	16	3	0	96.2	401	101	40	32	3	3	4	2	21	0	61	5	0	7	2	.778	0	0	2.98
1995 Columbus	AAA	2	2	0	0	11.2	38	7	0	0	0	0	0	0	0	0	8	1	0	0	0	.000	0	0	0.00
1995 New York	AL	31	26	3	1	175	745	183	86	81	15	4	5	1	63	3	114	8	1	12	9	.571	0	0	4.17

J.R. Phillips

Bats: Left **Throws:** Left **Pos:** 1B　　　　**Ht:** 6' 1" **Wt:** 185 **Born:** 4/29/70 **Age:** 26

		BATTING																	BASERUNNING				PERCENTAGES		
Year Team	Lg	G	AB	H	2B	3B	HR	(Hm	Rd)	TB	R	RBI	TBB	IBB	SO	HBP	SH	SF	SB	CS	SB%	GDP	Avg	OBP	SLG
1988 Bend	A	56	210	40	8	0	4	--	--	60	24	23	21	1	70	1	1	3	3	1	.75	5	.190	.264	.286
1989 Quad City	A	125	442	85	29	1	8	--	--	140	41	50	49	2	146	4	4	4	3	3	.50	5	.192	.277	.317
1990 Palm Spring	A	46	162	32	4	1	1	--	--	41	14	15	10	1	58	1	1	3	3	1	.75	7	.198	.247	.253
Boise	A	68	238	46	6	0	10	--	--	82	30	34	19	0	78	0	1	2	1	1	.50	4	.193	.251	.345
1991 Palm Spring	A	130	471	117	22	2	20	--	--	203	64	70	57	4	144	3	1	2	15	13	.54	8	.248	.332	.431
1992 Midland	AA	127	497	118	32	4	14	--	--	200	58	77	32	4	165	2	1	4	5	3	.63	9	.237	.284	.402
1993 Phoenix	AAA	134	506	133	35	2	27	--	--	253	80	94	53	9	127	6	0	6	7	5	.58	2	.263	.336	.500
1994 Phoenix	AAA	95	360	108	28	5	27	--	--	227	69	79	45	4	96	4	0	2	4	5	.44	4	.300	.382	.631
1993 San Francisco	NL	11	16	5	1	1	1	(0	1)	11	1	4	0	0	5	0	0	0	0	0	.00	0	.313	.313	.688
1994 San Francisco	NL	15	38	5	0	0	1	(0	1)	8	1	3	1	0	13	0	0	1	1	1	1.00	1	.132	.150	.211
1995 San Francisco	NL	92	231	45	9	0	9	(5	4)	81	27	28	19	2	69	0	2	0	1	1	.50	3	.195	.256	.351
3 ML YEARS		118	285	55	10	1	11	(5	6)	100	29	35	20	2	87	0	2	1	2	1	.67	4	.193	.245	.351

Tony Phillips

Bats: Both **Throws:** Right **Pos:** 3B/LF　　　　**Ht:** 5'10" **Wt:** 175 **Born:** 4/25/59 **Age:** 37

		BATTING																	BASERUNNING				PERCENTAGES		
Year Team	Lg	G	AB	H	2B	3B	HR	(Hm	Rd)	TB	R	RBI	TBB	IBB	SO	HBP	SH	SF	SB	CS	SB%	GDP	Avg	OBP	SLG
1982 Oakland	AL	40	81	17	2	2	0	(0	0)	23	11	8	12	0	26	2	5	0	2	3	.40	0	.210	.326	.284
1983 Oakland	AL	148	412	102	12	3	4	(1	3)	132	54	35	48	1	70	2	11	3	16	5	.76	5	.248	.327	.320
1984 Oakland	AL	154	451	120	24	3	4	(2	2)	162	62	37	42	1	86	0	7	5	10	6	.63	5	.266	.325	.359
1985 Oakland	AL	42	161	45	12	2	4	(2	2)	73	23	17	13	0	34	0	3	1	3	2	.60	1	.280	.331	.453
1986 Oakland	AL	118	441	113	14	5	5	(3	2)	152	76	52	76	0	82	3	9	3	15	10	.60	2	.256	.367	.345
1987 Oakland	AL	111	379	91	20	0	10	(5	5)	141	48	46	57	1	76	0	2	3	7	6	.54	9	.240	.337	.372
1988 Oakland	AL	79	212	43	8	4	2	(2	0)	65	32	17	36	0	50	1	1	1	0	2	.00	6	.203	.320	.307
1989 Oakland	AL	143	451	118	15	6	4	(2	2)	157	48	47	58	2	66	3	5	7	3	8	.27	17	.262	.345	.348
1990 Detroit	AL	152	573	144	23	5	8	(4	4)	201	97	55	99	0	85	4	9	2	19	9	.68	10	.251	.364	.351
1991 Detroit	AL	146	564	160	28	4	17	(9	8)	247	87	72	79	5	95	3	3	6	10	5	.67	8	.284	.371	.438
1992 Detroit	AL	159	606	167	32	3	10	(3	7)	235	114	64	114	2	93	1	5	7	12	10	.55	13	.276	.387	.388
1993 Detroit	AL	151	566	177	27	0	7	(3	4)	225	113	57	132	5	102	4	1	4	16	11	.59	11	.313	.443	.398
1994 Detroit	AL	114	438	123	19	3	19	(12	7)	205	91	61	95	3	105	2	0	3	13	5	.72	8	.274	.409	.468
1995 California *	AL	139	525	137	21	1	27	(13	14)	241	119	61	113	6	135	3	1	1	13	10	.57	5	.261	.394	.459
14 ML YEARS		1696	5860	1557	257	41	121	(61	60)	2259	975	629	974	26	1105	28	62	46	139	92	.60	100	.266	.370	.385

Steve Phoenix

Pitches: Right **Bats:** Right **Pos:** RP　　　　**Ht:** 6' 2" **Wt:** 185 **Born:** 1/31/68 **Age:** 28

		HOW MUCH HE PITCHED						WHAT HE GAVE UP												THE RESULTS					
Year Team	Lg	G	GS	CG	GF	IP	BFP	H	R	ER	HR	SH	SF	HB	TBB	IBB	SO	WP	Bk	W	L	Pct.	ShO	Sv	ERA
1990 Athletics	R	6	6	0	0	31	128	25	14	5	0	1	0	1	4	0	31	0	2	3	1	.750	0	0	1.45
Modesto	A	6	6	0	0	37.1	164	43	21	19	2	0	1	2	10	0	23	3	0	4	1	.800	0	0	4.58

Year	Team	Lg	G	GS	CG	GF	IP	BFP	H	R	ER	HR	SH	SF	HB	TBB	IBB	SO	WP	Bk	W	L	Pct.	ShO	Sv	ERA
1991	Huntsville	AA	2	0	0	1	3	18	7	3	2	1	0	0	0	1	0	3	0	0	0	0	.000	0	0	6.00
	Madison	A	7	2	0	3	21.1	96	26	8	7	0	2	0	0	10	0	19	0	0	3	0	1.000	0	2	2.95
	Modesto	A	27	3	1	10	84.1	372	87	44	35	13	3	1	5	33	4	65	3	0	5	2	.714	1	2	3.74
1992	Huntsville	AA	32	24	0	1	174	722	179	68	54	8	4	5	7	36	1	124	5	1	11	5	.688	0	0	2.79
1993	Tacoma	AAA	11	5	0	1	31	159	42	27	24	4	1	0	0	27	2	21	2	0	2	2	.000	0	0	6.97
	Huntsville	AA	11	0	0	7	19.1	73	13	5	3	0	0	1	0	5	2	15	0	0	2	2	.500	0	1	1.40
1994	Tacoma	AAA	20	0	0	17	22	83	16	5	3	0	2	0	1	4	1	16	2	0	0	0	.000	0	9	1.23
	Huntsville	AA	38	0	0	33	48.2	202	42	9	7	1	3	2	1	16	1	40	0	0	6	2	.750	0	20	1.29
1995	Edmonton	AAA	40	0	0	25	64	280	66	36	32	6	5	3	1	28	4	28	5	0	4	3	.571	0	5	4.50
1994	Oakland	AL	2	0	0	0	4.1	19	4	3	3	0	0	0	0	2	0	3	0	0	0	0	.000	0	0	6.23
1995	Oakland	AL	1	0	0	0	1.2	11	3	6	6	1	1	0	0	3	0	3	0	0	0	0	.000	0	0	32.40
	2 ML YEARS		3	0	0	0	6	30	7	9	9	1	1	0	0	5	0	6	0	0	0	0	.000	0	0	13.50

Mike Piazza

Bats: Right **Throws:** Right **Pos:** C   **Ht:** 6' 3" **Wt:** 215 **Born:** 9/4/68 **Age:** 27

			BATTING														BASERUNNING				PERCENTAGES		
Year	Team	Lg	G	AB	H	2B	3B	HR	(Hm Rd)	TB	R	RBI	TBB	IBB	SO	HBP	SH	SF	SB	CS	SB%	GDP	Avg	OBP	SLG
1992	Los Angeles	NL	21	69	16	3	0	1	(1 0)	22	5	7	4	0	12	1	0	0	0	0	.000	1	.232	.284	.319
1993	Los Angeles	NL	149	547	174	24	2	35	(21 14)	307	81	112	46	6	86	3	0	6	3	4	.43	10	.318	.370	.561
1994	Los Angeles	NL	107	405	129	18	0	24	(13 11)	219	64	92	33	10	65	1	0	2	1	3	.25	11	.319	.370	.541
1995	Los Angeles	NL	112	434	150	17	0	32	(9 23)	263	82	93	39	10	80	1	0	1	0	1	1.00	10	.346	.400	.606
	4 ML YEARS		389	1455	469	62	2	92	(44 48)	811	232	304	122	26	243	6	0	9	5	7	.42	32	.322	.375	.557

Hipolito Pichardo

Pitches: Right **Bats:** Right **Pos:** RP   **Ht:** 6' 1" **Wt:** 185 **Born:** 8/22/69 **Age:** 26

			HOW MUCH HE PITCHED						WHAT HE GAVE UP										THE RESULTS					
Year	Team	Lg	G	GS	CG	GF	IP	BFP	H	R	ER	HR	SH	SF	HB	TBB	IBB	SO	WP	Bk	W	L	Pct.	ShO	Sv	ERA
1992	Kansas City	AL	31	24	1	0	143.2	615	148	71	63	9	4	5	3	49	1	59	3	1	9	6	.600	1	0	3.95
1993	Kansas City	AL	30	25	2	2	165	720	183	85	74	10	3	8	6	53	2	70	5	3	7	8	.467	0	0	4.04
1994	Kansas City	AL	45	0	0	19	67.2	303	82	42	37	4	4	2	7	24	5	36	3	0	5	3	.625	0	3	4.92
1995	Kansas City	AL	44	0	0	16	64	287	66	34	31	4	3	1	4	30	7	43	4	1	8	4	.667	0	1	4.36
	4 ML YEARS		150	49	3	37	440.1	1925	479	232	205	27	14	16	20	156	15	208	15	5	29	21	.580	1	4	4.19

Jeff Pierce

Pitches: Right **Bats:** Right **Pos:** RP   **Ht:** 6' 1" **Wt:** 185 **Born:** 6/7/69 **Age:** 27

			HOW MUCH HE PITCHED						WHAT HE GAVE UP										THE RESULTS					
Year	Team	Lg	G	GS	CG	GF	IP	BFP	H	R	ER	HR	SH	SF	HB	TBB	IBB	SO	WP	Bk	W	L	Pct.	ShO	Sv	ERA
1992	South Bend	A	52	0	0	46	69.2	281	46	22	16	1	5	4	6	18	0	88	8	0	3	5	.375	0	30	2.07
	Sarasota	A	1	0	0	1	0.2	3	0	0	0	0	0	0	0	1	0	1	0	0	0	0	.000	0	0	0.00
1993	Birmingham	AA	33	0	0	26	48.2	188	34	16	14	3	4	2	3	7	0	45	1	1	3	4	.429	0	18	2.59
	Chattanooga	AA	13	0	0	8	20.2	87	17	6	6	1	0	1	0	9	1	22	2	0	0	0	.000	0	4	2.61
1994	New Britain	AA	29	0	0	25	39.1	163	31	13	10	3	1	0	2	12	3	54	4	0	1	2	.333	0	10	2.29
	Pawtucket	AAA	32	0	0	14	60.1	249	53	27	23	4	1	0	0	21	1	57	2	1	6	1	.857	0	2	3.43
1995	Pawtucket	AAA	23	3	0	8	41.1	172	34	21	19	5	2	2	2	16	1	43	2	1	4	2	.667	0	0	4.14
1995	Boston	AL	12	0	0	2	15	72	16	12	11	1	1	1	0	14	4	12	0	0	0	3	.000	0	0	6.60

Greg Pirkl

Bats: Right **Throws:** Right **Pos:** 1B   **Ht:** 6' 5" **Wt:** 240 **Born:** 8/7/70 **Age:** 25

			BATTING														BASERUNNING				PERCENTAGES		
Year	Team	Lg	G	AB	H	2B	3B	HR	(Hm Rd)	TB	R	RBI	TBB	IBB	SO	HBP	SH	SF	SB	CS	SB%	GDP	Avg	OBP	SLG
1995	Tacoma *	AAA	47	174	51	8	2	15	-- --	108	29	44	14	1	28	1	0	1	1	1	.50	3	.293	.347	.621
1993	Seattle	AL	7	23	4	0	0	1	(1 0)	7	1	4	0	0	4	0	0	0	0	0	.00	2	.174	.174	.304
1994	Seattle	AL	19	53	14	3	0	6	(2 4)	35	7	11	1	1	12	1	0	1	0	0	.00	1	.264	.286	.660
1995	Seattle	AL	10	17	4	0	0	0	(0 0)	4	2	0	1	0	7	0	0	0	0	0	.00	0	.235	.278	.235
	3 ML YEARS		36	93	22	3	0	7	(3 4)	46	10	15	2	1	23	1	0	1	0	0	.00	3	.237	.258	.495

Jim Pittsley

Pitches: Right **Bats:** Right **Pos:** SP   **Ht:** 6' 7" **Wt:** 215 **Born:** 4/3/74 **Age:** 22

			HOW MUCH HE PITCHED						WHAT HE GAVE UP										THE RESULTS					
Year	Team	Lg	G	GS	CG	GF	IP	BFP	H	R	ER	HR	SH	SF	HB	TBB	IBB	SO	WP	Bk	W	L	Pct.	ShO	Sv	ERA
1992	Royals	R	9	9	0	0	43.1	175	27	16	16	0	0	2	5	15	0	47	2	2	4	1	.800	0	0	3.32
	Baseball Cy	A	1	1	0	0	3	11	2	0	0	0	0	0	0	1	0	4	0	0	0	0	.000	0	0	0.00
1993	Rockford	A	15	15	2	0	80.1	344	76	43	38	3	2	4	5	32	0	87	5	3	5	5	.500	1	0	4.26
1994	Wilmington	A	27	27	1	0	161.2	673	154	73	57	8	3	9	4	42	0	171	2	1	11	5	.688	1	0	3.17
1995	Omaha	AAA	8	8	0	0	47.2	189	38	20	17	5	0	0	2	16	0	39	1	2	4	1	.800	0	0	3.21
1995	Kansas City	AL	1	1	0	0	3.1	17	7	5	5	3	0	0	0	1	0	3	0	0	0	0	.000	0	0	13.50

Phil Plantier

Bats: Left   **Throws:** Right   **Pos:** LF/RF   **Ht:** 5'11"   **Wt:** 195   **Born:** 1/27/69   **Age:** 27

							BATTING												BASERUNNING				PERCENTAGES		
Year Team	Lg	G	AB	H	2B	3B	HR	(Hm	Rd)	TB	R	RBI	TBB	IBB	SO	HBP	SH	SF	SB	CS	SB%	GDP	Avg	OBP	SLG
1995 Tucson *	AAA	10	24	6	2	0	1	--	--	11	6	4	5	0	4	0	0	0	0	0	.00	1	.250	.379	.458
1990 Boston	AL	14	15	2	1	0	0	(0	0)	3	1	3	4	0	6	1	0	1	0	0	.00	1	.133	.333	.200
1991 Boston	AL	53	148	49	7	1	11	(6	5)	91	27	35	23	2	38	1	0	2	1	0	1.00	2	.331	.420	.615
1992 Boston	AL	108	349	86	19	0	7	(5	2)	126	46	30	44	8	83	2	2	2	2	3	.40	9	.246	.332	.361
1993 San Diego	NL	138	462	111	20	1	34	(16	18)	235	67	100	61	7	124	7	1	5	4	5	.44	4	.240	.335	.509
1994 San Diego	NL	96	341	75	21	0	18	(7	11)	150	44	41	36	6	91	5	1	2	3	1	.75	8	.220	.302	.440
1995 Hou-SD	NL	76	216	55	6	0	9	(1	8)	88	33	34	28	3	48	1	0	3	1	1	.50	3	.255	.339	.407
1995 Houston	NL	22	68	17	2	0	4	(0	4)	31	12	15	11	1	19	1	0	3	0	0	.00	0	.250	.349	.456
San Diego	NL	54	148	38	4	0	5	(1	4)	57	21	19	17	2	29	0	0	0	1	1	.50	3	.257	.333	.385
6 ML YEARS		485	1531	378	74	2	79	(35	44)	693	218	243	196	26	390	17	4	15	11	10	.52	27	.247	.336	.453

Dan Plesac

Pitches: Left   **Bats:** Left   **Pos:** RP   **Ht:** 6'5"   **Wt:** 215   **Born:** 2/4/62   **Age:** 34

			HOW MUCH HE PITCHED					WHAT HE GAVE UP										THE RESULTS					
Year Team	Lg	G	GS	CG	GF	IP	BFP	H	R	ER	HR	SH	SF	HB	TBB	IBB	SO	WP	Bk	W	L	Pct.	ShO	Sv	ERA
1986 Milwaukee	AL	51	0	0	33	91	377	81	34	30	5	6	5	0	29	1	75	4	0	10	7	.588	0	14	2.97
1987 Milwaukee	AL	57	0	0	47	79.1	325	63	30	23	8	1	2	3	23	1	89	6	0	5	6	.455	0	23	2.61
1988 Milwaukee	AL	50	0	0	48	52.1	211	46	14	14	2	2	0	0	12	2	52	4	6	1	2	.333	0	30	2.41
1989 Milwaukee	AL	52	0	0	51	61.1	242	47	16	16	6	0	4	0	17	1	52	0	0	3	4	.429	0	33	2.35
1990 Milwaukee	AL	66	0	0	52	69	299	67	36	34	5	2	2	3	31	6	65	2	0	3	7	.300	0	24	4.43
1991 Milwaukee	AL	45	10	0	25	92.1	402	92	49	44	12	3	7	3	39	1	61	2	1	2	7	.222	0	8	4.29
1992 Milwaukee	AL	44	4	0	13	79	330	64	28	26	5	8	4	3	35	5	54	3	1	5	4	.556	0	1	2.96
1993 Chicago	NL	57	0	0	12	62.2	276	74	37	33	10	4	3	0	21	6	47	5	2	2	1	.667	0	0	4.74
1994 Chicago	NL	54	0	0	14	54.2	235	61	30	28	9	1	1	1	13	0	53	0	0	2	3	.400	0	1	4.61
1995 Pittsburgh	NL	58	0	0	16	60.1	259	53	26	24	3	4	3	1	27	7	57	1	0	4	4	.500	0	3	3.58
10 ML YEARS		534	14	0	311	702	2956	648	300	272	65	31	31	14	247	30	605	27	10	37	45	.451	0	137	3.49

Eric Plunk

Pitches: Right   **Bats:** Right   **Pos:** RP   **Ht:** 6'6"   **Wt:** 220   **Born:** 9/3/63   **Age:** 32

			HOW MUCH HE PITCHED					WHAT HE GAVE UP										THE RESULTS					
Year Team	Lg	G	GS	CG	GF	IP	BFP	H	R	ER	HR	SH	SF	HB	TBB	IBB	SO	WP	Bk	W	L	Pct.	ShO	Sv	ERA
1986 Oakland	AL	26	15	0	2	120.1	537	91	75	71	14	2	3	5	102	2	98	9	6	4	7	.364	0	0	5.31
1987 Oakland	AL	32	11	0	11	95	432	91	53	50	8	3	5	2	62	3	90	5	2	4	6	.400	0	2	4.74
1988 Oakland	AL	49	0	0	22	78	331	62	27	26	6	3	2	1	39	4	79	4	7	7	2	.778	0	5	3.00
1989 NYA-Oak	AL	50	7	0	17	104.1	445	82	43	38	10	3	4	1	64	2	85	10	3	8	6	.571	0	1	3.28
1990 New York	AL	47	0	0	16	72.2	310	58	27	22	6	7	0	2	43	4	67	4	2	6	3	.667	0	0	2.72
1991 New York	AL	43	8	0	6	111.2	521	128	69	59	18	6	4	1	62	1	103	6	2	2	5	.286	0	0	4.76
1992 Cleveland	AL	58	0	0	20	71.2	309	61	31	29	5	3	2	0	38	2	50	5	0	9	6	.600	0	4	3.64
1993 Cleveland	NL	70	0	0	40	71	306	61	29	22	5	4	2	0	30	4	77	6	0	4	5	.444	0	15	2.79
1994 Cleveland	AL	41	0	0	18	71	306	61	25	20	3	2	1	2	37	5	73	7	0	7	2	.778	0	3	2.54
1995 Cleveland	AL	56	0	0	22	64	263	48	19	19	5	2	2	4	27	2	71	3	0	6	2	.750	0	2	2.67
1989 New York	AL	27	7	0	5	75.2	332	65	36	31	9	2	4	0	52	2	61	6	3	7	5	.583	0	0	3.69
Oakland	AL	23	0	0	12	28.2	113	17	7	7	1	1	0	1	12	0	24	4	0	1	1	.500	0	1	2.20
10 ML YEARS		472	41	0	174	859.2	3760	743	398	356	80	35	25	18	504	29	793	59	22	57	44	.564	0	32	3.73

Luis Polonia

Bats: Left   **Throws:** Left   **Pos:** LF   **Ht:** 5'8"   **Wt:** 160   **Born:** 12/10/64   **Age:** 31

							BATTING												BASERUNNING				PERCENTAGES		
Year Team	Lg	G	AB	H	2B	3B	HR	(Hm	Rd)	TB	R	RBI	TBB	IBB	SO	HBP	SH	SF	SB	CS	SB%	GDP	Avg	OBP	SLG
1987 Oakland	AL	125	435	125	16	10	4	(1	3)	173	78	49	32	1	64	0	1	1	29	7	.81	4	.287	.335	.398
1988 Oakland	AL	84	288	84	11	4	2	(1	1)	109	51	27	21	0	40	0	2	1	24	9	.73	3	.292	.338	.378
1989 NYA-Oak	AL	125	433	130	17	6	3	(1	2)	168	70	46	25	1	44	2	2	4	22	8	.73	13	.300	.338	.388
1990 Cal-NYA	AL	120	403	135	7	9	2	(2	0)	166	52	35	25	1	43	1	3	4	21	14	.60	9	.335	.372	.412
1991 California	AL	150	604	179	28	8	2	(1	1)	229	92	50	52	4	74	1	2	3	48	23	.68	11	.296	.352	.379
1992 California	AL	149	577	165	17	4	0	(0	0)	190	83	35	45	6	64	1	8	4	51	21	.71	18	.286	.337	.329
1993 California	AL	152	576	156	17	6	1	(0	1)	188	75	32	48	7	53	2	8	3	55	24	.70	7	.271	.328	.326
1994 New York	AL	95	350	109	21	6	1	(0	1)	145	62	36	37	1	36	4	2	1	20	12	.63	7	.311	.383	.414
1995 NYA-Atl	AL	95	291	76	16	3	2	(2	0)	104	43	17	28	1	38	0	3	4	13	4	.76	3	.261	.322	.357
1989 New York	AL	66	227	71	11	2	2	(1	1)	92	39	29	16	1	29	2	0	3	9	4	.69	8	.313	.359	.405
Oakland	AL	59	206	59	6	4	1	(0	1)	76	31	17	9	0	15	0	2	1	13	4	.76	5	.286	.315	.369
1990 California	AL	109	381	128	7	9	2	(2	0)	159	50	32	25	1	42	1	3	3	20	14	.59	8	.336	.376	.417
New York	AL	11	22	7	0	0	0	(0	0)	7	2	3	0	0	1	0	0	1	1	0	1.00	1	.318	.304	.318
1995 New York	AL	67	238	62	14	3	2	(2	0)	83	37	15	25	1	29	0	0	3	10	4	.71	3	.261	.326	.349

Team	Lg	G	AB	H	2B	3B	HR	(Hm	Rd)	TB	R	RBI	TBB	IBB	SO	HBP	SH	SF	SB	CS	SB%	GDP	Avg	OBP	SLG
Atlanta	NL	28	53	14	7	0	0	(0	0)	21	6	2	3	0	9	0	1	0	3	0	1.00	0	.264	.304	.396
9 ML YEARS		1095	3957	1159	150	56	17	(8	9)	1472	606	327	313	22	456	11	31	26	283	122	.70	75	.293	.344	.372

Jim Poole

Pitches: Left **Bats:** Left **Pos:** RP **Ht:** 6' 2" **Wt:** 203 **Born:** 4/28/66 **Age:** 30

		HOW MUCH HE PITCHED						WHAT HE GAVE UP											THE RESULTS					
Year Team	Lg	G	GS	CG	GF	IP	BFP	H	R	ER	HR	SH	SF	HB	TBB	IBB	SO	WP	Bk	W	L	Pct.	ShO	Sv	ERA
1995 Buffalo *	AAA	1	1	0	0	2.2	17	7	8	8	1	0	0	1	2	0	0	0	0	0	0	.000	0	0	27.00
1990 Los Angeles	NL	16	0	0	4	10.2	46	7	5	5	1	0	0	0	8	4	6	1	0	0	0	.000	0	0	4.22
1991 Bal-Tex	AL	29	0	0	5	42	166	29	14	11	3	3	3	0	12	2	38	2	0	3	2	.600	0	1	2.36
1992 Baltimore	AL	6	0	0	1	3.1	14	3	3	0	0	0	0	0	1	0	3	0	0	0	0	.000	0	0	0.00
1993 Baltimore	AL	55	0	0	11	50.1	197	30	18	12	2	3	2	0	21	5	29	0	0	2	1	.667	0	2	2.15
1994 Baltimore	AL	38	0	0	10	20.1	100	32	15	15	4	0	3	0	11	2	18	1	0	1	0	1.000	0	0	6.64
1995 Cleveland	AL	42	0	0	9	50.1	206	40	22	21	7	1	2	2	17	0	41	2	1	3	3	.500	0	0	3.75
1991 Baltimore	AL	24	0	0	3	36	135	19	10	8	3	3	2	0	9	2	34	2	0	3	2	.600	0	0	2.00
Texas	AL	5	0	0	2	6	31	10	4	3	0	0	1	0	3	0	4	0	0	0	0	.000	0	1	4.50
6 ML YEARS		186	0	0	40	177	729	141	77	64	17	7	10	2	70	13	135	6	1	9	6	.600	0	3	3.25

Mark Portugal

Pitches: Right **Bats:** Right **Pos:** SP **Ht:** 6' 0" **Wt:** 190 **Born:** 10/30/62 **Age:** 33

		HOW MUCH HE PITCHED						WHAT HE GAVE UP											THE RESULTS					
Year Team	Lg	G	GS	CG	GF	IP	BFP	H	R	ER	HR	SH	SF	HB	TBB	IBB	SO	WP	Bk	W	L	Pct.	ShO	Sv	ERA
1985 Minnesota	AL	6	4	0	0	24.1	105	24	16	15	3	0	2	0	14	0	12	1	1	1	3	.250	0	0	5.55
1986 Minnesota	AL	27	15	3	7	112.2	481	112	56	54	10	5	3	1	50	1	67	5	0	6	10	.375	0	1	4.31
1987 Minnesota	AL	13	7	0	3	44	204	58	40	38	13	0	1	1	24	1	28	2	0	1	3	.250	0	0	7.77
1988 Minnesota	AL	26	0	0	9	57.2	242	60	30	29	11	2	3	1	17	1	31	2	2	3	3	.500	0	3	4.53
1989 Houston	NL	20	15	2	1	108	440	91	34	33	7	8	1	2	37	0	86	3	0	7	1	.875	1	0	2.75
1990 Houston	NL	32	32	1	0	196.2	831	187	90	79	21	7	6	4	67	4	136	6	0	11	10	.524	0	0	3.62
1991 Houston	NL	32	27	1	3	168.1	710	163	91	84	19	6	6	2	59	5	120	4	1	10	12	.455	0	1	4.49
1992 Houston	NL	18	16	1	0	101.1	405	76	32	30	7	5	1	1	41	3	62	1	1	6	3	.667	1	0	2.66
1993 Houston	NL	33	33	1	0	208	876	194	75	64	10	11	3	4	77	3	131	9	2	18	4	.818	1	0	2.77
1994 San Francisco	NL	21	21	1	0	137.1	580	135	68	60	17	6	4	6	45	2	87	5	0	10	8	.556	0	0	3.93
1995 SF-Cin	NL	31	31	1	0	181.2	775	185	91	81	17	9	1	4	56	2	96	7	0	11	10	.524	0	0	4.01
1995 San Francisco	NL	17	17	1	0	104	445	106	56	48	10	5	0	2	34	2	63	2	0	5	5	.500	0	0	4.15
Cincinnati	NL	14	14	0	0	77.2	330	79	35	33	7	4	1	2	22	0	33	5	0	6	5	.545	0	0	3.82
11 ML YEARS		259	201	11	23	1340	5649	1285	623	567	135	59	31	26	487	22	856	45	7	84	67	.556	3	5	3.81

Jorge Posada

Bats: Both **Throws:** Right **Pos:** C **Ht:** 6' 2" **Wt:** 205 **Born:** 8/17/71 **Age:** 24

		BATTING																	BASERUNNING				PERCENTAGES		
Year Team	Lg	G	AB	H	2B	3B	HR	(Hm	Rd)	TB	R	RBI	TBB	IBB	SO	HBP	SH	SF	SB	CS	SB%	GDP	Avg	OBP	SLG
1991 Oneonta	A	71	217	51	5	5	4	--	--	78	34	33	51	0	49	4	8	1	6	4	.60	3	.235	.388	.359
1992 Greensboro	A	101	339	94	22	4	12	--	--	160	60	58	58	2	87	6	0	3	11	6	.65	8	.277	.389	.472
1993 Pr. William	A	118	410	106	27	2	17	--	--	188	71	61	67	4	90	6	1	6	17	5	.77	7	.259	.366	.459
Albany-Colo	AA	7	25	7	0	0	0	--	--	7	3	0	2	0	7	0	0	0	0	0	.00	1	.280	.333	.280
1994 Columbus	AAA	92	313	75	13	3	11	--	--	127	46	48	32	1	81	1	4	5	5	5	.50	3	.240	.308	.406
1995 Columbus	AAA	108	368	94	32	5	8	--	--	160	60	51	54	0	101	1	6	3	4	4	.50	14	.255	.350	.435
1995 New York	AL	1	0	0	0	0	0	(0	0)	0	0	0	0	0	0	0	0	0	0	0	.00	0	.000	.000	.000

Jay Powell

Pitches: Right **Bats:** Right **Pos:** RP **Ht:** 6' 4" **Wt:** 225 **Born:** 1/9/72 **Age:** 24

		HOW MUCH HE PITCHED						WHAT HE GAVE UP											THE RESULTS					
Year Team	Lg	G	GS	CG	GF	IP	BFP	H	R	ER	HR	SH	SF	HB	TBB	IBB	SO	WP	Bk	W	L	Pct.	ShO	Sv	ERA
1993 Albany	A	6	6	0	0	27.2	122	29	19	14	0	1	2	0	13	0	29	4	1	0	2	.000	0	0	4.55
1994 Frederick	A	26	20	0	2	123.1	552	132	79	68	13	4	3	1	54	0	87	12	2	7	7	.500	0	1	4.96
1995 Portland	AA	50	0	0	44	53	213	42	12	11	2	3	1	2	15	1	53	2	1	5	4	.556	0	24	1.87
1995 Florida	NL	9	0	0	1	8.1	38	7	2	1	0	2	0	2	6	1	4	0	0	0	0	.000	0	0	1.08

Ross Powell

Pitches: Left **Bats:** Left **Pos:** RP/SP **Ht:** 6' 0" **Wt:** 180 **Born:** 1/24/68 **Age:** 28

		HOW MUCH HE PITCHED						WHAT HE GAVE UP											THE RESULTS					
Year Team	Lg	G	GS	CG	GF	IP	BFP	H	R	ER	HR	SH	SF	HB	TBB	IBB	SO	WP	Bk	W	L	Pct.	ShO	Sv	ERA
1995 Tucson *	AAA	13	4	0	5	38	169	37	16	13	3	5	0	1	15	0	34	1	0	3	3	.500	0	1	3.08
1993 Cincinnati	NL	9	1	0	1	16.1	66	13	8	8	1	2	0	0	6	0	17	0	0	0	3	.000	0	0	4.41
1994 Houston	NL	12	0	0	1	7.1	32	6	1	1	0	1	0	1	5	0	5	0	0	0	0	.000	0	0	1.23
1995 Hou-Pit	NL	27	3	0	6	29.2	148	36	26	23	6	3	1	2	21	4	20	4	0	0	2	.000	0	0	6.98

Year Team	Lg	G	GS	CG	GF	IP	BFP	H	R	ER	HR	SH	SF	HB	TBB	IBB	SO	WP	Bk	W	L	Pct.	ShO	Sv	ERA
1995 Houston	NL	15	0	0	1	9	55	16	12	11	1	1	1	0	11	4	8	1	0	0	0	.000	0	0	11.00
Pittsburgh	NL	12	3	0	5	20.2	93	20	14	12	5	2	0	2	10	0	12	3	0	0	2	.000	0	0	5.23
3 ML YEARS		48	4	0	8	53.1	246	55	35	32	7	6	1	3	32	4	42	4	0	0	5	.000	0	0	5.40

Arquimedez Pozo

Bats: Right **Throws:** Right **Pos:** 2B   **Ht:** 5'10" **Wt:** 160 **Born:** 8/24/73 **Age:** 22

Year Team	Lg	G	AB	H	2B	3B	HR	Hm	Rd	TB	R	RBI	TBB	IBB	SO	HBP	SH	SF	SB	CS	SB%	GDP	Avg	OBP	SLG
1992 San Bernrdo	A	54	199	52	8	4	3	--	--	77	33	19	20	0	41	2	1	0	13	8	.62	2	.261	.335	.387
Bellingham	A	39	149	48	12	0	7	--	--	81	37	21	20	0	24	2	1	1	9	5	.64	1	.322	.407	.544
1993 Riverside	A	127	515	176	44	6	13	--	--	271	98	83	56	4	56	2	1	5	10	10	.50	22	.342	.405	.526
1994 Jacksonvlle	AA	119	447	129	31	1	14	--	--	204	70	54	32	0	43	7	3	6	11	8	.58	8	.289	.341	.456
1995 Tacoma	AAA	122	450	135	19	6	10	--	--	196	57	62	26	1	31	3	1	4	3	3	.50	15	.300	.340	.436
1995 Seattle	AL	1	1	0	0	0	0	(0	0)	0	0	0	0	0	0	0	0	0	0	0	.00	0	.000	.000	.000

Todd Pratt

Bats: Right **Throws:** Right **Pos:** C   **Ht:** 6'3" **Wt:** 220 **Born:** 2/9/67 **Age:** 29

Year Team	Lg	G	AB	H	2B	3B	HR	Hm	Rd	TB	R	RBI	TBB	IBB	SO	HBP	SH	SF	SB	CS	SB%	GDP	Avg	OBP	SLG
1995 Iowa *	AAA	23	58	19	1	0	0	--	--	20	3	5	4	1	17	0	0	0	0	0	.00	0	.328	.371	.345
1992 Philadelphia	NL	16	46	13	1	0	2	(2	0)	20	6	10	4	0	12	0	0	0	0	0	.00	2	.283	.340	.435
1993 Philadelphia	NL	33	87	25	6	0	5	(4	1)	46	8	13	5	0	19	1	1	1	0	0	.00	2	.287	.330	.529
1994 Philadelphia	NL	28	102	20	6	1	2	(1	1)	34	10	9	12	0	29	0	0	0	0	1	.00	3	.196	.281	.333
1995 Chicago	NL	25	60	8	2	0	0	(0	0)	10	3	4	6	1	21	0	1	1	0	0	.00	1	.133	.209	.167
4 ML YEARS		102	295	66	15	1	9	(7	2)	110	27	36	27	1	81	1	1	2	0	1	.00	8	.224	.289	.373

Curtis Pride

Bats: Left **Throws:** Right **Pos:** LF   **Ht:** 6'0" **Wt:** 200 **Born:** 12/17/68 **Age:** 27

Year Team	Lg	G	AB	H	2B	3B	HR	Hm	Rd	TB	R	RBI	TBB	IBB	SO	HBP	SH	SF	SB	CS	SB%	GDP	Avg	OBP	SLG
1986 Kingsport	R	27	46	5	0	0	1	--	--	8	5	4	6	0	24	1	0	0	5	0	1.00	0	.109	.226	.174
1987 Kingsport	R	31	104	25	4	0	1	--	--	32	22	9	16	0	34	1	2	0	14	5	.74	0	.240	.347	.308
1988 Kingsport	R	70	268	76	13	1	8	--	--	115	59	27	50	1	48	1	2	1	23	7	.77	2	.284	.397	.429
1989 Pittsfield	A	55	212	55	7	3	6	--	--	86	35	23	25	1	47	2	2	1	9	2	.82	1	.259	.342	.406
1990 Columbia	A	53	191	52	4	4	6	--	--	82	38	25	21	3	45	0	0	1	11	8	.58	3	.272	.343	.429
1991 St. Lucie	A	116	392	102	21	7	9	--	--	164	57	37	43	4	94	2	3	0	24	5	.83	8	.260	.336	.418
1992 Binghamton	AA	118	388	88	15	3	10	--	--	139	54	42	47	1	110	4	0	1	14	11	.56	5	.227	.316	.358
1993 Harrisburg	AA	50	180	64	6	3	15	--	--	121	51	39	12	0	36	4	2	2	21	6	.78	2	.356	.404	.672
Ottawa	AAA	69	262	79	11	4	6	--	--	116	55	22	34	7	61	3	2	0	29	12	.71	3	.302	.388	.443
1994 W. Palm Bch	A	3	8	6	1	0	1	--	--	10	5	3	4	0	2	0	0	0	2	2	.50	0	.750	.833	1.250
Ottawa	AAA	82	300	77	16	4	9	--	--	128	56	32	39	1	81	2	1	1	22	6	.79	3	.257	.345	.427
1995 Ottawa	AAA	42	154	43	8	3	4	--	--	69	25	24	12	4	35	2	0	0	8	4	.67	2	.279	.339	.448
1993 Montreal	NL	10	9	4	1	1	1	(0	1)	10	3	5	0	0	3	0	0	0	1	0	1.00	0	.444	.444	1.111
1995 Montreal	NL	48	63	11	1	0	0	(0	0)	12	10	2	5	0	16	0	0	1	3	2	.60	2	.175	.235	.190
2 ML YEARS		58	72	15	2	1	1	(0	1)	22	13	7	5	0	19	0	0	1	4	2	.67	2	.208	.260	.306

Ariel Prieto

Pitches: Right **Bats:** Right **Pos:** SP/RP   **Ht:** 6'3" **Wt:** 225 **Born:** 10/22/69 **Age:** 26

Year Team	Lg	G	GS	CG	GF	IP	BFP	H	R	ER	HR	SH	SF	HB	TBB	IBB	SO	WP	Bk	W	L	Pct.	ShO	Sv	ERA
1995 Oakland	AL	14	9	1	1	58	258	57	35	32	4	3	2	5	32	1	37	4	1	2	6	.250	0	0	4.97

Tom Prince

Bats: Right **Throws:** Right **Pos:** C   **Ht:** 5'11" **Wt:** 202 **Born:** 8/13/64 **Age:** 31

Year Team	Lg	G	AB	H	2B	3B	HR	Hm	Rd	TB	R	RBI	TBB	IBB	SO	HBP	SH	SF	SB	CS	SB%	GDP	Avg	OBP	SLG
1995 Albuquerque *	AAA	61	192	61	15	0	7	--	--	97	30	36	27	2	41	2	1	0	0	0	.00	6	.318	.407	.505
1987 Pittsburgh	NL	4	9	2	1	0	1	(0	1)	6	1	2	0	0	2	0	0	0	0	0	.00	0	.222	.222	.667
1988 Pittsburgh	NL	29	74	13	2	0	0	(0	0)	15	3	6	4	0	15	0	2	0	0	0	.00	5	.176	.218	.203
1989 Pittsburgh	NL	21	52	7	4	0	0	(0	0)	11	1	5	6	1	12	0	0	1	1	1	.50	1	.135	.220	.212
1990 Pittsburgh	NL	4	10	1	0	0	0	(0	0)	1	1	0	1	0	2	0	0	0	0	1	.00	0	.100	.182	.100
1991 Pittsburgh	NL	26	34	9	3	0	1	(0	1)	15	4	2	7	0	3	1	0	0	0	0	.00	3	.265	.405	.441
1992 Pittsburgh	NL	27	44	4	2	0	0	(0	0)	6	1	5	6	0	9	0	0	2	1	1	.50	2	.091	.192	.136
1993 Pittsburgh	NL	66	179	35	14	0	2	(2	0)	55	14	24	13	2	38	7	2	3	1	1	.50	5	.196	.272	.307
1994 Los Angeles	NL	3	6	2	0	0	0	(0	0)	2	2	1	1	0	3	0	0	0	0	0	.00	0	.333	.429	.333
1995 Los Angeles	NL	18	40	8	2	1	1	(0	1)	15	3	4	4	0	10	0	0	0	0	0	.00	0	.200	.273	.375
9 ML YEARS		198	448	81	28	1	5	(2	3)	126	30	49	42	3	94	8	4	6	3	4	.43	16	.181	.260	.281

Kirby Puckett

Bats: Right   **Throws:** Right   **Pos:** RF/DH   **Ht:** 5' 9"   **Wt:** 223   **Born:** 3/14/61   **Age:** 35

								BATTING										BASERUNNING				PERCENTAGES		
Year Team	Lg	G	AB	H	2B	3B	HR	(Hm | Rd)	TB	R	RBI	TBB	IBB	SO	HBP	SH	SF	SB	CS	SB%	GDP	Avg	OBP	SLG
1984 Minnesota	AL	128	557	165	12	5	0	(0 | 0)	187	63	31	16	1	69	4	4	2	14	7	.67	11	.296	.320	.336
1985 Minnesota	AL	161	691	199	29	13	4	(2 | 2)	266	80	74	41	0	87	4	5	3	21	12	.64	9	.288	.330	.385
1986 Minnesota	AL	161	680	223	37	6	31	(14 | 17)	365	119	96	34	4	99	7	2	0	20	12	.63	14	.328	.366	.537
1987 Minnesota	AL	157	624	207	32	5	28	(18 | 10)	333	96	99	32	7	91	6	0	6	12	7	.63	16	.332	.367	.534
1988 Minnesota	AL	158	657	234	42	5	24	(13 | 11)	358	109	121	23	4	83	2	0	9	6	7	.46	17	.356	.375	.545
1989 Minnesota	AL	159	635	215	45	4	9	(7 | 2)	295	75	85	41	9	59	3	0	5	11	4	.73	21	.339	.379	.465
1990 Minnesota	AL	146	551	164	40	3	12	(6 | 6)	246	82	80	57	11	73	3	1	3	5	4	.56	15	.298	.365	.446
1991 Minnesota	AL	152	611	195	29	6	15	(7 | 8)	281	92	89	31	4	78	4	8	7	11	5	.69	27	.319	.352	.460
1992 Minnesota	AL	160	639	210	38	4	19	(9 | 10)	313	104	110	44	13	97	6	1	6	17	7	.71	17	.329	.374	.490
1993 Minnesota	AL	156	622	184	39	3	22	(12 | 10)	295	89	89	47	7	93	7	1	5	8	6	.57	15	.296	.349	.474
1994 Minnesota	AL	108	439	139	32	3	20	(12 | 8)	237	79	112	28	7	47	7	1	7	6	3	.67	11	.317	.362	.540
1995 Minnesota	AL	137	538	169	39	0	23	(13 | 10)	277	83	99	56	18	89	3	0	5	3	2	.60	15	.314	.379	.515
12 ML YEARS		1783	7244	2304	414	57	207	(113 | 94)	3453	1071	1085	450	85	965	56	23	58	134	76	.64	188	.318	.360	.477

Tim Pugh

Pitches: Right   **Bats:** Right   **Pos:** RP/SP   **Ht:** 6' 6"   **Wt:** 225   **Born:** 1/26/67   **Age:** 29

		HOW MUCH HE PITCHED						WHAT HE GAVE UP										THE RESULTS					
Year Team	Lg	G	GS	CG	GF	IP	BFP	H	R	ER	HR	SH	SF	HB	TBB	IBB	SO	WP	Bk	W	L	Pct.	ShO	Sv	ERA
1995 Indianapolis *	AAA	6	6	1	0	42.1	184	42	24	22	4	1	4	5	14	1	20	1	0	2	4	.333	1	0	4.68
1992 Cincinnati	NL	7	7	0	0	45.1	187	47	15	13	2	2	1	1	13	3	18	0	0	4	2	.667	0	0	2.58
1993 Cincinnati	NL	31	27	3	3	164.1	738	200	102	96	19	6	5	7	59	1	94	3	2	10	15	.400	1	0	5.26
1994 Cincinnati	NL	10	9	1	0	47.2	227	60	37	32	5	2	5	3	26	0	24	4	0	3	3	.500	0	0	6.04
1995 Cincinnati	NL	28	12	0	4	98.1	413	100	46	42	13	2	2	1	32	2	38	3	1	6	5	.545	0	0	3.84
4 ML YEARS		76	55	4	7	355.2	1565	407	200	183	39	12	13	12	130	6	174	10	3	23	25	.479	1	0	4.63

Harvey Pulliam

Bats: Right   **Throws:** Right   **Pos:** LF   **Ht:** 6' 0"   **Wt:** 205   **Born:** 10/20/67   **Age:** 28

								BATTING										BASERUNNING				PERCENTAGES		
Year Team	Lg	G	AB	H	2B	3B	HR	(Hm	Rd)	TB	R	RBI	TBB	IBB	SO	HBP	SH	SF	SB	CS	SB%	GDP	Avg	OBP	SLG
1995 Colo. Sprng *	AAA	115	407	133	30	6	25	--	--	250	90	91	49	10	59	3	0	6	6	2	.75	11	.327	.398	.614
1991 Kansas City	AL	18	33	9	1	0	3	(2	1)	19	4	4	3	1	9	0	1	0	0	0	.00	1	.273	.333	.576
1992 Kansas City	AL	4	5	1	1	0	0	(0	0)	2	2	0	1	0	3	0	0	0	0	0	.00	0	.200	.333	.400
1993 Kansas City	AL	27	62	16	5	0	1	(0	1)	24	7	6	2	0	14	1	0	0	0	0	.00	3	.258	.292	.387
1995 Colorado	NL	5	5	2	1	0	1	(1	0)	6	1	3	0	0	2	0	0	0	0	0	.00	0	.400	.400	1.200
4 ML YEARS		54	105	28	8	0	5	(3	2)	51	14	13	6	1	28	1	1	0	0	0	.00	4	.267	.313	.486

Bill Pulsipher

Pitches: Left   **Bats:** Left   **Pos:** SP   **Ht:** 6' 3"   **Wt:** 208   **Born:** 10/9/73   **Age:** 22

		HOW MUCH HE PITCHED						WHAT HE GAVE UP										THE RESULTS					
Year Team	Lg	G	GS	CG	GF	IP	BFP	H	R	ER	HR	SH	SF	HB	TBB	IBB	SO	WP	Bk	W	L	Pct.	ShO	Sv	ERA
1992 Pittsfield	A	14	14	0	0	95	413	88	40	30	3	0	1	3	56	0	83	16	1	6	3	.667	0	0	2.84
1993 Capital Cty	A	6	6	1	0	43.1	175	34	17	10	1	2	0	1	12	0	29	1	1	2	3	.400	0	0	2.08
St. Lucie	A	13	13	3	0	96.1	374	63	27	24	2	3	1	0	39	0	102	3	1	7	3	.700	1	0	2.24
1994 Binghamton	AA	28	28	5	0	201	849	179	90	72	18	7	1	3	89	2	171	9	5	14	9	.609	1	0	3.22
1995 Norfolk	AAA	13	13	4	0	91.2	377	84	36	32	3	1	5	1	33	0	63	2	1	6	4	.600	2	0	3.14
1995 New York	NL	17	17	2	0	126.2	530	122	58	56	11	2	1	4	45	0	81	0	1	5	7	.417	0	0	3.98

Eddie Pye

Bats: Right   **Throws:** Right   **Pos:** 3B   **Ht:** 5'10"   **Wt:** 183   **Born:** 2/13/67   **Age:** 29

								BATTING										BASERUNNING				PERCENTAGES		
Year Team	Lg	G	AB	H	2B	3B	HR	(Hm	Rd)	TB	R	RBI	TBB	IBB	SO	HBP	SH	SF	SB	CS	SB%	GDP	Avg	OBP	SLG
1988 Great Falls	R	61	237	71	8	4	2	--	--	93	50	30	29	0	26	4	2	1	19	9	.68	6	.300	.384	.392
1989 Bakersfield	A	129	488	126	21	2	8	--	--	175	59	47	41	1	87	6	3	0	19	9	.68	6	.258	.323	.359
1990 San Antonio	AA	119	455	113	18	7	2	--	--	151	67	44	45	1	68	6	3	5	19	6	.76	7	.248	.321	.332
1991 Albuquerque	AAA	12	30	13	1	0	1	--	--	17	4	8	4	0	4	0	1	0	1	2	.33	0	.433	.500	.567
1992 Albuquerque	AAA	72	222	67	11	2	1	--	--	85	30	25	13	0	41	2	5	2	6	4	.60	4	.302	.343	.383
1993 Albuquerque	AAA	101	365	120	21	7	7	--	--	176	53	66	32	0	43	7	4	3	5	9	.36	13	.329	.391	.482
1994 Albuquerque	AAA	100	361	121	19	6	2	--	--	158	79	42	48	7	43	7	2	4	11	6	.65	5	.335	.419	.438
1995 Albuquerque	AAA	84	302	89	20	1	3	--	--	120	49	32	30	2	36	1	2	2	11	2	.85	7	.295	.358	.397
1994 Los Angeles	NL	7	10	1	0	0	0	(0	0)	1	2	0	1	0	4	0	1	0	0	0	.00	0	.100	.182	.100
1995 Los Angeles	NL	7	8	0	0	0	0	(0	0)	0	0	0	0	0	4	0	0	0	0	0	.00	0	.000	.000	.000
2 ML YEARS		14	18	1	0	0	0	(0	0)	1	2	0	1	0	8	0	1	0	0	0	.00	0	.056	.105	.056

Paul Quantrill

Pitches: Right **Bats:** Left **Pos:** SP   **Ht:** 6' 1" **Wt:** 185 **Born:** 11/3/68 **Age:** 27

			HOW MUCH HE PITCHED						WHAT HE GAVE UP											THE RESULTS					
Year Team	Lg	G	GS	CG	GF	IP	BFP	H	R	ER	HR	SH	SF	HB	TBB	IBB	SO	WP	Bk	W	L	Pct.	ShO	Sv	ERA
1992 Boston	AL	27	0	0	10	49.1	213	55	18	12	1	4	2	1	15	5	24	1	0	2	3	.400	0	1	2.19
1993 Boston	AL	49	14	1	8	138	594	151	73	60	13	4	2	2	44	14	66	0	1	6	12	.333	1	1	3.91
1994 Bos-Phi		35	1	0	9	53	236	64	31	29	7	5	3	5	15	4	28	0	2	3	3	.500	0	1	4.92
1995 Philadelphia	NL	33	29	0	1	179.1	784	212	102	93	20	9	6	6	44	3	103	0	3	11	12	.478	0	0	4.67
1994 Boston	AL	17	0	0	4	23	101	25	10	9	4	2	2	2	5	1	15	0	0	1	1	.500	0	0	3.52
Philadelphia	NL	18	1	0	5	30	135	39	21	20	3	3	1	3	10	3	13	0	2	2	2	.500	0	1	6.00
4 ML YEARS		144	44	1	28	419.2	1827	482	224	194	41	22	13	14	118	26	221	1	6	22	30	.423	1	3	4.16

Brian Raabe

Bats: Right **Throws:** Right **Pos:** 2B   **Ht:** 5' 9" **Wt:** 177 **Born:** 11/5/67 **Age:** 28

					BATTING															BASERUNNING				PERCENTAGES		
Year Team	Lg	G	AB	H	2B	3B	HR	(Hm	Rd)	TB	R	RBI	TBB	IBB	SO	HBP	SH	SF	SB	CS	SB%	GDP	Avg	OBP	SLG
1990 Visalia	A	42	138	34	3	2	0	--	--	41	11	9	10	0	9	1	1	0	5	1	.83	6	.246	.302	.297
1991 Visalia	A	85	311	80	3	1	1	--	--	88	36	22	40	0	14	4	3	2	15	5	.75	8	.257	.347	.283
1992 Miracle	A	102	361	104	16	2	2	--	--	130	52	32	48	1	17	8	1	3	7	6	.54	3	.288	.381	.360
Orlando	AA	32	108	30	6	0	2	--	--	42	12	6	2	0	2	0	3	0	0	4	.00	2	.278	.291	.389
1993 Nashville	AA	134	524	150	23	2	6	--	--	195	80	52	56	1	28	10	10	4	18	8	.69	9	.286	.364	.372
1994 Salt Lake	AAA	123	474	152	26	3	3	--	--	193	78	49	50	1	11	1	0	8	9	8	.53	19	.321	.381	.407
1995 Salt Lake	AAA	112	440	134	32	6	3	--	--	187	88	60	45	2	14	3	2	7	15	0	1.00	12	.305	.368	.425
1995 Minnesota	AL	6	14	3	0	0	0	(0	0)	3	4	1	1	0	0	0	0	0	0	0	.00	0	.214	.267	.214

Scott Radinsky

Pitches: Left **Bats:** Left **Pos:** RP   **Ht:** 6' 3" **Wt:** 204 **Born:** 3/3/68 **Age:** 28

				HOW MUCH HE PITCHED						WHAT HE GAVE UP											THE RESULTS					
Year Team	Lg	G	GS	CG	GF	IP	BFP	H	R	ER	HR	SH	SF	HB	TBB	IBB	SO	WP	Bk	W	L	Pct.	ShO	Sv	ERA
1995 South Bend *	A	6	0	0	5	9.2	33	5	0	0	0	0	0	0	0	0	11	0	0	0	0	.000	0	2	0.00
1990 Chicago	AL	62	0	0	18	52.1	237	47	29	28	1	2	2	2	36	1	46	2	1	6	1	.857	0	4	4.82
1991 Chicago	AL	67	0	0	19	71.1	289	53	18	16	4	4	4	1	23	2	49	0	0	5	5	.500	0	8	2.02
1992 Chicago	AL	68	0	0	33	59.1	261	54	21	18	3	2	1	2	34	5	48	3	0	3	7	.300	0	15	2.73
1993 Chicago	AL	73	0	0	24	54.2	250	61	33	26	3	2	0	1	19	3	44	0	4	8	2	.800	0	4	4.28
1995 Chicago	AL	46	0	0	10	38	171	46	23	23	7	1	4	0	17	4	14	0	0	2	1	.667	0	1	5.45
5 ML YEARS		316	0	0	104	275.2	1208	261	124	111	18	11	11	6	129	15	201	5	5	24	16	.600	0	32	3.62

Brad Radke

Pitches: Right **Bats:** Right **Pos:** SP   **Ht:** 6' 2" **Wt:** 186 **Born:** 10/27/72 **Age:** 23

				HOW MUCH HE PITCHED						WHAT HE GAVE UP											THE RESULTS					
Year Team	Lg	G	GS	CG	GF	IP	BFP	H	R	ER	HR	SH	SF	HB	TBB	IBB	SO	WP	Bk	W	L	Pct.	ShO	Sv	ERA
1991 Twins	R	10	9	0	1	49.2	205	41	21	17	0	1	2	2	14	0	44	0	2	3	4	.429	0	1	3.08
1992 Kenosha	A	26	25	4	1	165.2	680	149	70	54	8	7	6	6	47	1	127	4	0	10	10	.500	1	0	2.93
1993 Fort Myers	A	14	14	0	0	92	376	85	42	39	3	0	1	4	21	1	69	3	0	3	5	.375	0	0	3.82
Nashville	AA	13	13	1	0	76	327	81	42	39	6	1	1	6	16	0	76	5	0	2	6	.250	0	0	4.62
1994 Nashville	AA	29	28	5	0	186.1	741	167	66	55	9	4	2	5	34	0	123	8	1	12	9	.571	1	0	2.66
1995 Minnesota	AL	29	28	2	0	181	772	195	112	107	32	2	9	4	47	0	75	4	0	11	14	.440	1	0	5.32

Tim Raines

Bats: Both **Throws:** Right **Pos:** LF/DH   **Ht:** 5' 8" **Wt:** 186 **Born:** 9/16/59 **Age:** 36

					BATTING															BASERUNNING				PERCENTAGES		
Year Team	Lg	G	AB	H	2B	3B	HR	(Hm	Rd)	TB	R	RBI	TBB	IBB	SO	HBP	SH	SF	SB	CS	SB%	GDP	Avg	OBP	SLG
1979 Montreal	NL	6	0	0	0	0	0	(0	0)	0	3	0	0	0	0	0	0	0	2	1	1.00	0	.000	.000	.000
1980 Montreal	NL	15	20	1	0	0	0	(0	0)	1	5	0	6	0	3	0	1	0	5	0	1.00	0	.050	.269	.050
1981 Montreal	NL	88	313	95	13	7	5	(3	2)	137	61	37	45	5	31	2	0	3	71	11	.87	7	.304	.391	.438
1982 Montreal	NL	156	647	179	32	8	4	(1	3)	239	90	43	75	9	83	2	6	1	78	16	.83	6	.277	.353	.369
1983 Montreal	NL	156	615	183	32	8	11	(5	6)	264	133	71	97	9	70	2	2	4	90	14	.87	12	.298	.393	.429
1984 Montreal	NL	160	622	192	38	9	8	(2	6)	272	106	60	87	7	69	2	3	4	75	10	.88	7	.309	.393	.437
1985 Montreal	NL	150	575	184	30	13	11	(4	7)	273	115	41	81	13	60	3	3	3	70	9	.89	9	.320	.405	.475
1986 Montreal	NL	151	580	194	35	10	9	(4	5)	276	91	62	78	9	60	2	1	3	70	9	.89	6	.334	.413	.476
1987 Montreal	NL	139	530	175	34	8	18	(9	9)	279	123	68	90	26	52	4	0	3	50	5	.91	9	.330	.429	.526
1988 Montreal	NL	109	429	116	19	7	12	(5	7)	185	66	48	53	14	44	2	0	8	33	7	.83	8	.270	.350	.431
1989 Montreal	NL	145	517	148	29	6	9	(6	3)	216	76	60	93	18	48	3	0	5	41	9	.82	8	.286	.395	.418
1990 Montreal	NL	130	457	131	11	5	9	(6	3)	179	65	62	70	8	43	3	0	4	49	16	.75	9	.287	.379	.392
1991 Chicago	AL	155	609	163	20	6	5	(1	4)	210	102	50	83	9	68	5	9	3	51	15	.77	7	.268	.359	.345
1992 Chicago	AL	144	551	162	22	9	7	(4	3)	223	102	54	81	4	48	4	4	8	45	6	.88	5	.294	.380	.405
1993 Chicago	AL	115	415	127	16	4	16	(7	9)	199	75	54	64	4	35	3	2	2	21	7	.75	7	.306	.401	.480

187

Year Team	Lg	G	AB	H	2B	3B	HR	(Hm	Rd)	TB	R	RBI	TBB	IBB	SO	HBP	SH	SF	SB	CS	SB%	GDP	Avg	OBP	SLG
1994 Chicago	AL	101	384	102	15	5	10	(5	5)	157	80	52	61	3	43	1	4	3	13	0	1.00	10	.266	.365	.409
1995 Chicago	AL	133	502	143	25	4	12	(6	6)	212	81	67	70	3	52	3	3	3	13	2	.87	8	.285	.374	.422
17 ML YEARS		2053	7766	2295	371	109	146	(68	78)	3322	1374	829	1134	141	809	37	38	57	777	136	.85	118	.296	.385	.428

Manny Ramirez

Bats: Right **Throws:** Right **Pos:** RF   **Ht:** 6' 0" **Wt:** 190 **Born:** 5/30/72 **Age:** 24

						BATTING													BASERUNNING				PERCENTAGES		
Year Team	Lg	G	AB	H	2B	3B	HR	(Hm	Rd)	TB	R	RBI	TBB	IBB	SO	HBP	SH	SF	SB	CS	SB%	GDP	Avg	OBP	SLG
1993 Cleveland	AL	22	53	9	1	0	2	(0	2)	16	5	5	2	0	8	0	0	0	0	0	.00	3	.170	.200	.302
1994 Cleveland	AL	91	290	78	22	0	17	(9	8)	151	51	60	42	4	72	0	0	4	4	2	.67	6	.269	.357	.521
1995 Cleveland	AL	137	484	149	26	1	31	(12	19)	270	85	107	75	6	112	5	2	5	6	6	.50	13	.308	.402	.558
3 ML YEARS		250	827	236	49	1	50	(21	29)	437	141	172	119	10	192	5	2	9	10	8	.56	22	.285	.375	.528

Joe Randa

Bats: Right **Throws:** Right **Pos:** 3B   **Ht:** 5'11" **Wt:** 190 **Born:** 12/18/69 **Age:** 26

						BATTING													BASERUNNING				PERCENTAGES		
Year Team	Lg	G	AB	H	2B	3B	HR	(Hm	Rd)	TB	R	RBI	TBB	IBB	SO	HBP	SH	SF	SB	CS	SB%	GDP	Avg	OBP	SLG
1991 Eugene	A	72	275	93	20	2	11	--	--	150	53	59	46	4	30	6	0	4	6	1	.86	8	.338	.438	.545
1992 Appleton	A	72	266	80	13	0	5	--	--	108	55	43	34	0	37	6	0	6	6	2	.75	6	.301	.385	.406
Baseball Cy	A	51	189	52	7	0	1	--	--	62	22	12	12	0	21	2	1	1	4	3	.57	4	.275	.324	.328
1993 Memphis	AA	131	505	149	31	5	11	--	--	223	74	72	39	2	64	3	0	10	8	7	.53	10	.295	.343	.442
1994 Omaha	AAA	127	455	125	27	2	10	--	--	186	65	51	30	1	49	8	5	5	5	2	.71	18	.275	.327	.409
1995 Omaha	AAA	64	233	64	10	2	8	--	--	102	33	33	22	0	33	2	1	1	2	2	.50	9	.275	.341	.438
1995 Kansas City	AL	34	70	12	2	0	1	(1	0)	17	6	5	6	0	17	0	0	0	0	1	.00	2	.171	.237	.243

Pat Rapp

Pitches: Right **Bats:** Right **Pos:** SP   **Ht:** 6' 3" **Wt:** 215 **Born:** 7/13/67 **Age:** 28

			HOW MUCH HE PITCHED					WHAT HE GAVE UP									THE RESULTS					
Year Team	Lg	G	GS	CG	GF	IP	BFP	H	R	ER	HR	SH	SF	HB	TBB	IBB	SO	WP	Bk	W	L	Pct.	ShO	Sv	ERA
1995 Charlotte *	AAA	1	1	0	0	6	23	6	4	4	0	0	0	1	0	5	2	0	0	0	1	.000	0	0	6.00
1992 San Francisco	NL	3	2	0	1	10	43	8	8	8	0	2	0	1	6	1	3	0	0	0	2	.000	0	0	7.20
1993 Florida	NL	16	16	1	0	94	412	101	49	42	7	8	4	2	39	1	57	6	0	4	6	.400	0	0	4.02
1994 Florida	NL	24	23	2	1	133.1	582	132	67	57	13	8	4	7	69	3	75	5	1	7	8	.467	1	0	3.85
1995 Florida	NL	28	28	3	0	167.1	716	158	72	64	10	8	0	7	76	2	102	7	0	14	7	.667	2	0	3.44
4 ML YEARS		71	69	6	2	404.2	1755	399	196	171	30	26	8	17	190	7	237	18	1	25	23	.521	3	0	3.80

Dennis Rasmussen

Pitches: Left **Bats:** Left **Pos:** RP   **Ht:** 6' 7" **Wt:** 240 **Born:** 4/18/59 **Age:** 37

			HOW MUCH HE PITCHED					WHAT HE GAVE UP									THE RESULTS					
Year Team	Lg	G	GS	CG	GF	IP	BFP	H	R	ER	HR	SH	SF	HB	TBB	IBB	SO	WP	Bk	W	L	Pct.	ShO	Sv	ERA
1995 Omaha *	AAA	10	10	3	0	65.1	269	63	22	21	7	1	1	2	17	0	51	1	0	6	3	.667	1	0	2.89
1983 San Diego	NL	4	1	0	1	13.2	58	10	5	3	1	0	0	0	8	0	13	1	0	0	0	.000	0	0	1.98
1984 New York	AL	24	24	1	0	147.2	616	127	79	75	16	3	7	4	60	0	110	8	2	9	6	.600	0	0	4.57
1985 New York	AL	22	16	2	1	101.2	429	97	56	45	10	1	5	1	42	1	63	3	1	3	5	.375	0	0	3.98
1986 New York	AL	31	31	3	0	202	819	160	91	87	28	1	5	2	74	0	131	5	0	18	6	.750	1	0	3.88
1987 NYA-Cin		33	32	2	0	191.1	814	184	100	97	36	8	6	5	67	1	128	7	2	13	8	.619	0	0	4.56
1988 Cin-SD	NL	31	31	7	0	204.2	854	199	84	78	17	10	4	4	58	4	112	7	5	16	10	.615	1	0	3.43
1989 San Diego	NL	33	33	1	0	183.2	799	190	100	87	18	9	11	3	72	6	87	4	2	10	10	.500	0	0	4.26
1990 San Diego	NL	32	32	3	0	187.2	825	217	110	94	28	14	4	3	62	4	86	9	1	11	15	.423	1	0	4.51
1991 San Diego	NL	24	24	1	0	146.2	633	155	74	61	12	4	6	2	49	3	75	1	1	6	13	.316	1	0	3.74
1992 KC-ChN		8	6	1	1	42.2	158	32	13	12	2	1	1	1	8	1	12	3	0	4	1	.800	1	0	2.53
1993 Kansas City	AL	9	4	0	3	29	138	40	25	24	4	0	1	1	14	1	12	2	0	1	2	.333	0	0	7.45
1995 Kansas City	AL	5	1	0	1	10	51	13	10	10	3	0	0	0	8	2	6	2	0	0	1	.000	0	0	9.00
1987 New York	AL	26	25	2	0	146	627	145	78	77	31	5	5	4	55	1	89	6	0	9	7	.563	0	0	4.75
Cincinnati	NL	7	7	0	0	45.1	187	39	22	20	5	3	1	1	12	0	39	1	2	4	1	.800	0	0	3.97
1988 Cincinnati	NL	11	11	1	0	56.1	255	68	36	36	8	2	2	2	22	4	27	1	5	2	6	.250	1	0	5.75
San Diego	NL	20	20	6	0	148.1	599	131	48	42	9	8	2	2	36	0	85	6	0	14	4	.778	0	0	2.55
1992 Kansas City	AL	5	5	1	0	37.2	134	25	7	6	0	1	0	0	6	0	12	3	0	4	1	.800	1	0	1.43
Chicago	NL	3	1	0	1	5	24	7	6	6	2	0	1	1	2	1	0	0	0	0	0	.000	0	0	10.80
12 ML YEARS		256	235	21	7	1460.2	6194	1424	747	673	175	51	50	26	522	23	835	52	14	91	77	.542	5	0	4.15

Randy Ready

Bats: Right **Throws:** Right **Pos:** 1B   **Ht:** 5'11" **Wt:** 180 **Born:** 1/8/60 **Age:** 36

						BATTING													BASERUNNING				PERCENTAGES		
Year Team	Lg	G	AB	H	2B	3B	HR	(Hm	Rd)	TB	R	RBI	TBB	IBB	SO	HBP	SH	SF	SB	CS	SB%	GDP	Avg	OBP	SLG
1983 Milwaukee	AL	12	37	15	3	2	1	(0	1)	25	8	6	6	1	3	0	0	0	0	1	.00	0	.405	.488	.676

188

Year	Team	Lg	G	AB	H	2B	3B	HR	(Hm	Rd)	TB	R	RBI	TBB	IBB	SO	HBP	SH	SF	SB	CS	SB%	GDP	Avg	OBP	SLG
1984	Milwaukee	AL	37	123	23	6	1	3	(3	0)	40	13	13	14	0	18	0	3	0	0	0	.00	2	.187	.270	.325
1985	Milwaukee	AL	48	181	48	9	5	1	(0	1)	70	29	21	14	0	23	1	2	2	0	0	.00	6	.265	.318	.387
1986	Mil-SD		24	82	15	4	0	1	(0	1)	22	8	4	9	0	10	0	1	0	2	0	1.00	3	.183	.264	.268
1987	San Diego	NL	124	350	108	26	6	12	(7	5)	182	69	54	67	2	44	3	2	1	7	3	.70	7	.309	.423	.520
1988	San Diego	NL	114	331	88	16	2	7	(3	4)	129	43	39	39	1	38	3	4	3	6	2	.75	3	.266	.346	.390
1989	Phi-SD	NL	100	254	67	13	2	8	(3	5)	108	37	26	42	0	37	2	1	4	4	3	.57	4	.264	.368	.425
1990	Philadelphia	NL	101	217	53	9	1	1	(0	1)	67	26	26	29	0	35	1	3	3	3	2	.60	3	.244	.332	.309
1991	Philadelphia	NL	76	205	51	10	1	1	(1	0)	66	32	20	47	3	25	1	1	4	2	1	.67	5	.249	.385	.322
1992	Oakland	AL	61	125	25	2	0	3	(1	2)	36	17	17	25	1	23	0	2	2	1	0	1.00	1	.200	.329	.288
1993	Montreal	NL	40	134	34	8	1	1	(0	1)	47	22	10	23	0	8	1	1	0	2	1	.67	4	.254	.367	.351
1994	Philadelphia	NL	17	42	16	1	0	1	(0	1)	20	5	3	8	0	6	0	0	0	0	1	.00	1	.381	.480	.476
1995	Philadelphia	NL	23	29	4	0	0	0	(0	0)	4	3	0	3	0	6	0	1	0	1	0	.00	2	.138	.219	.138
1986	Milwaukee	NL	23	79	15	4	0	1	(0	1)	22	8	4	9	0	9	0	1	0	2	0	1.00	3	.190	.273	.278
	San Diego	NL	1	3	0	0	0	0	(0	0)	0	0	0	0	0	1	0	0	0	0	0	.00	0	.000	.000	.000
1989	Philadelphia	NL	72	187	50	11	1	8	(3	5)	87	33	21	31	0	31	2	0	3	4	3	.57	2	.267	.372	.465
	San Diego	NL	28	67	17	2	1	0	(0	0)	21	4	5	11	0	6	0	1	1	0	0	.00	2	.254	.354	.313
13 ML YEARS			777	2110	547	107	21	40	(18	22)	816	312	239	326	8	276	12	21	19	27	15	.64	41	.259	.359	.387

Jeff Reboulet

Bats: Right **Throws:** Right **Pos:** SS/1B/2B/3B **Ht:** 6' 0" **Wt:** 171 **Born:** 4/30/64 **Age:** 32

						BATTING														BASERUNNING				PERCENTAGES		
Year	Team	Lg	G	AB	H	2B	3B	HR	(Hm	Rd)	TB	R	RBI	TBB	IBB	SO	HBP	SH	SF	SB	CS	SB%	GDP	Avg	OBP	SLG
1992	Minnesota	AL	73	137	26	7	1	1	(1	0)	38	15	15	23	0	26	1	7	0	3	2	.60	0	.190	.311	.277
1993	Minnesota	AL	109	240	62	8	0	1	(0	1)	73	33	15	35	0	37	2	5	1	5	5	.50	6	.258	.356	.304
1994	Minnesota	AL	74	189	49	11	1	3	(2	1)	71	28	23	18	0	23	1	2	0	0	0	.00	6	.259	.327	.376
1995	Minnesota	AL	87	216	63	11	0	4	(1	3)	86	39	23	27	0	34	1	2	0	1	2	.33	3	.292	.373	.398
4 ML YEARS			343	782	200	37	2	9	(4	5)	268	115	77	103	0	120	5	16	1	9	9	.50	15	.256	.346	.343

Jeff Reed

Bats: Left **Throws:** Right **Pos:** C **Ht:** 6' 2" **Wt:** 190 **Born:** 11/12/62 **Age:** 33

						BATTING														BASERUNNING				PERCENTAGES		
Year	Team	Lg	G	AB	H	2B	3B	HR	(Hm	Rd)	TB	R	RBI	TBB	IBB	SO	HBP	SH	SF	SB	CS	SB%	GDP	Avg	OBP	SLG
1984	Minnesota	AL	18	21	3	0	0	0	(0	0)	6	3	1	2	0	6	0	1	0	0	0	.00	0	.143	.217	.286
1985	Minnesota	AL	7	10	2	0	0	0	(0	0)	2	2	0	0	0	3	0	0	0	0	0	.00	0	.200	.200	.200
1986	Minnesota	AL	68	165	39	6	1	2	(1	1)	53	13	9	16	0	19	1	3	0	1	0	1.00	4	.236	.308	.321
1987	Montreal	NL	75	207	44	11	0	1	(1	0)	58	15	21	12	1	20	1	4	4	0	1	.00	8	.213	.254	.280
1988	Cin-Mon	NL	92	265	60	9	2	1	(1	0)	76	20	16	28	1	41	0	1	1	1	0	1.00	5	.226	.299	.287
1989	Cincinnati	NL	102	287	64	11	0	3	(1	2)	84	16	23	34	5	46	2	3	4	0	0	.00	6	.223	.306	.293
1990	Cincinnati	NL	72	175	44	8	1	3	(2	1)	63	12	16	24	5	26	0	5	1	0	0	.00	4	.251	.340	.360
1991	Cincinnati	NL	91	270	72	15	2	3	(1	2)	100	20	31	23	3	38	1	1	5	0	1	.00	6	.267	.321	.370
1992	Cincinnati	NL	15	25	4	0	0	0	(0	0)	4	2	2	1	1	4	0	0	0	0	0	.00	1	.160	.192	.160
1993	San Francisco	NL	66	119	31	3	0	6	(5	1)	52	10	12	16	4	22	0	1	0	0	1	.00	2	.261	.346	.437
1994	San Francisco	NL	50	103	18	3	0	1	(0	1)	24	11	7	11	4	21	0	0	0	0	0	.00	3	.175	.254	.233
1995	San Francisco	NL	66	113	30	2	0	0	(0	0)	32	12	9	20	3	17	0	1	0	0	0	.00	3	.265	.376	.283
1988	Cincinnati	NL	49	142	33	6	0	1	(1	0)	42	10	7	15	0	19	0	0	0	0	0	.00	2	.232	.306	.296
	Montreal	NL	43	123	27	3	2	0	(0	0)	34	10	9	13	1	22	0	1	1	1	0	1.00	3	.220	.292	.276
12 ML YEARS			722	1760	411	71	6	20	(12	8)	554	136	147	187	27	263	5	19	16	2	3	.40	40	.234	.306	.315

Jody Reed

Bats: Right **Throws:** Right **Pos:** 2B **Ht:** 5' 9" **Wt:** 165 **Born:** 7/26/62 **Age:** 33

						BATTING														BASERUNNING				PERCENTAGES		
Year	Team	Lg	G	AB	H	2B	3B	HR	(Hm	Rd)	TB	R	RBI	TBB	IBB	SO	HBP	SH	SF	SB	CS	SB%	GDP	Avg	OBP	SLG
1987	Boston	AL	9	30	9	1	1	0	(0	0)	12	4	8	4	0	0	0	1	0	1	1	.50	0	.300	.382	.400
1988	Boston	AL	109	338	99	23	1	1	(1	0)	127	60	28	45	1	21	4	11	2	1	3	.25	5	.293	.380	.376
1989	Boston	AL	146	524	151	42	2	3	(2	1)	206	76	40	73	0	44	4	13	5	4	5	.44	12	.288	.376	.393
1990	Boston	AL	155	598	173	45	0	5	(3	2)	233	70	51	75	4	65	4	11	3	4	4	.50	19	.289	.371	.390
1991	Boston	AL	153	618	175	42	2	5	(3	2)	236	87	60	60	2	53	4	11	3	6	5	.55	15	.283	.349	.382
1992	Boston	AL	143	550	136	27	1	3	(2	1)	174	64	40	62	2	44	0	10	4	7	8	.47	17	.247	.321	.316
1993	Los Angeles	NL	132	445	123	21	2	2	(0	2)	154	48	31	38	10	40	1	17	3	1	3	.25	16	.276	.333	.346
1994	Milwaukee	AL	108	399	108	22	0	2	(1	1)	136	48	37	57	1	34	2	4	3	5	4	.56	8	.271	.362	.341
1995	San Diego	NL	131	445	114	18	1	4	(4	0)	146	58	40	59	1	38	5	3	3	6	4	.60	10	.256	.348	.328
9 ML YEARS			1086	3947	1088	241	10	25	(16	9)	1424	515	335	473	21	339	24	81	26	35	37	.49	101	.276	.355	.361

Rick Reed

Pitches: Right **Bats:** Right **Pos:** SP   **Ht:** 6' 1" **Wt:** 200 **Born:** 8/16/64 **Age:** 31

		HOW MUCH HE PITCHED						WHAT HE GAVE UP												THE RESULTS					
Year Team	Lg	G	GS	CG	GF	IP	BFP	H	R	ER	HR	SH	SF	HB	TBB	IBB	SO	WP	Bk	W	L	Pct.	ShO	Sv	ERA
1995 Indianapols *	AAA	22	21	3	0	135	551	127	60	50	16	4	2	2	26	2	92	0	0	11	4	.733	1	0	3.33
1988 Pittsburgh	NL	2	2	0	0	12	47	10	4	4	1	2	0	0	2	0	6	0	0	1	0	1.000	0	0	3.00
1989 Pittsburgh	NL	15	7	0	2	54.2	232	62	35	34	5	2	3	2	11	3	34	0	3	1	4	.200	0	0	5.60
1990 Pittsburgh	NL	13	8	1	2	53.2	238	62	32	26	6	2	1	1	12	6	27	0	0	2	3	.400	1	1	4.36
1991 Pittsburgh	NL	1	1	0	0	4.1	21	8	6	5	1	0	0	0	1	0	2	0	0	0	0	.000	0	0	10.38
1992 Kansas City	AL	19	18	1	0	100.1	419	105	47	41	10	2	5	5	20	3	49	0	0	3	7	.300	1	0	3.68
1993 KC-Tex	AL	3	0	0	0	7.2	36	12	5	5	1	0	0	2	2	0	5	0	0	1	0	1.000	0	0	5.87
1994 Texas	AL	4	3	0	0	16.2	75	17	13	11	3	0	0	1	7	0	12	0	0	1	1	.500	0	0	5.94
1995 Cincinnati	NL	4	3	0	1	17	70	18	12	11	5	1	0	0	3	0	10	0	0	0	0	.000	0	0	5.82
1993 Kansas City	AL	1	0	0	0	3.2	18	6	4	4	0	0	0	1	1	0	3	0	0	0	0	.000	0	0	9.82
Texas	AL	2	0	0	0	4	18	6	1	1	1	0	0	1	1	0	2	0	0	1	0	1.000	0	0	2.25
8 ML YEARS		61	42	2	5	266.1	1138	294	154	137	32	9	9	11	58	12	145	0	3	9	15	.375	2	1	4.63

Steve Reed

Pitches: Right **Bats:** Right **Pos:** RP   **Ht:** 6' 2" **Wt:** 205 **Born:** 3/11/66 **Age:** 30

		HOW MUCH HE PITCHED						WHAT HE GAVE UP												THE RESULTS					
Year Team	Lg	G	GS	CG	GF	IP	BFP	H	R	ER	HR	SH	SF	HB	TBB	IBB	SO	WP	Bk	W	L	Pct.	ShO	Sv	ERA
1992 San Francisco	NL	18	0	0	2	15.2	63	13	5	4	2	0	0	1	3	0	11	0	0	1	0	1.000	0	0	2.30
1993 Colorado	NL	64	0	0	14	84.1	347	80	47	42	13	2	3	3	30	5	51	1	0	9	5	.643	0	3	4.48
1994 Colorado	NL	61	0	0	11	64	297	79	33	28	9	0	7	6	26	3	51	1	0	3	2	.600	0	3	3.94
1995 Colorado	NL	71	0	0	15	84	327	61	24	20	8	3	1	1	21	3	79	0	2	5	2	.714	0	3	2.14
4 ML YEARS		214	0	0	42	248	1034	233	109	94	32	5	11	11	80	11	192	2	2	18	9	.667	0	9	3.41

Bryan Rekar

Pitches: Right **Bats:** Right **Pos:** SP   **Ht:** 6' 3" **Wt:** 208 **Born:** 6/3/72 **Age:** 24

		HOW MUCH HE PITCHED						WHAT HE GAVE UP												THE RESULTS					
Year Team	Lg	G	GS	CG	GF	IP	BFP	H	R	ER	HR	SH	SF	HB	TBB	IBB	SO	WP	Bk	W	L	Pct.	ShO	Sv	ERA
1993 Bend	A	13	13	1	0	76.1	316	81	36	34	8	0	0	1	18	2	59	8	2	3	5	.375	0	0	4.01
1994 Central Val	A	22	19	0	2	111.1	465	120	54	43	3	4	5	2	31	2	91	12	3	6	6	.500	0	0	3.48
1995 New Haven	AA	12	12	1	0	80.1	325	65	28	19	4	3	0	3	16	1	80	0	0	6	3	.667	1	0	2.13
Colo. Sprng	AAA	7	7	2	0	48.1	182	29	10	8	0	1	0	2	13	0	39	3	0	4	2	.667	1	0	1.49
1995 Colorado	NL	15	14	1	0	85	375	95	51	47	11	7	4	3	24	2	60	3	2	4	6	.400	0	0	4.98

Mike Remlinger

Pitches: Left **Bats:** Left **Pos:** RP   **Ht:** 6' 0" **Wt:** 195 **Born:** 3/23/66 **Age:** 30

		HOW MUCH HE PITCHED						WHAT HE GAVE UP												THE RESULTS					
Year Team	Lg	G	GS	CG	GF	IP	BFP	H	R	ER	HR	SH	SF	HB	TBB	IBB	SO	WP	Bk	W	L	Pct.	ShO	Sv	ERA
1995 Indianapols *	AAA	41	1	0	7	46.2	210	40	24	21	4	2	1	2	32	4	58	8	0	5	3	.625	0	0	4.05
1991 San Francisco	NL	8	6	1	0	35	155	36	17	17	5	1	1	0	20	1	19	2	1	2	1	.667	1	0	4.37
1994 New York	NL	10	9	0	0	54.2	252	55	30	28	9	2	3	1	35	4	33	3	0	1	5	.167	0	0	4.61
1995 NYN-Cin	NL	7	0	0	4	6.2	34	9	6	5	1	1	0	0	5	0	7	0	0	0	1	.000	0	0	6.75
1995 New York	NL	5	0	0	4	5.2	27	7	5	4	1	1	0	0	2	0	6	0	0	0	1	.000	0	0	6.35
Cincinnati	NL	2	0	0	0	1	7	2	1	1	0	0	0	0	3	0	1	0	0	0	0	.000	0	0	9.00
3 ML YEARS		25	15	1	5	96.1	441	100	53	50	15	4	4	1	60	5	59	5	1	3	7	.300	1	0	4.67

Al Reyes

Pitches: Right **Bats:** Right **Pos:** RP   **Ht:** 6' 1" **Wt:** 193 **Born:** 4/10/71 **Age:** 25

		HOW MUCH HE PITCHED						WHAT HE GAVE UP												THE RESULTS					
Year Team	Lg	G	GS	CG	GF	IP	BFP	H	R	ER	HR	SH	SF	HB	TBB	IBB	SO	WP	Bk	W	L	Pct.	ShO	Sv	ERA
1990 W. Palm Bch	A	16	10	0	4	57	253	58	32	30	4	3	3	2	32	2	46	5	0	5	4	.556	0	1	4.74
1991 Rockford	A	3	3	0	0	11.1	50	14	8	7	1	0	0	2	2	0	10	0	0	0	1	.000	0	0	5.56
1992 Albany	A	27	0	0	18	27.1	122	24	14	12	0	0	0	3	13	0	29	4	1	0	2	.000	0	4	3.95
1993 Burlington	A	53	0	0	41	74	308	52	33	22	7	6	2	5	26	3	80	5	0	7	6	.538	0	11	2.68
1994 Harrisburg	AA	60	0	0	53	69.1	284	68	26	25	4	2	2	2	13	0	60	2	0	2	2	.500	0	35	3.25
1995 Milwaukee	AL	27	0	0	13	33.1	138	19	9	9	3	1	2	3	18	2	29	0	0	1	1	.500	0	2	2.43

Carlos Reyes

Pitches: Right **Bats:** Both **Pos:** RP   **Ht:** 6' 1" **Wt:** 190 **Born:** 4/4/69 **Age:** 27

		HOW MUCH HE PITCHED						WHAT HE GAVE UP												THE RESULTS					
Year Team	Lg	G	GS	CG	GF	IP	BFP	H	R	ER	HR	SH	SF	HB	TBB	IBB	SO	WP	Bk	W	L	Pct.	ShO	Sv	ERA
1991 Braves	R	20	0	0	13	45.2	195	44	16	9	1	1	0	0	9	1	37	1	3	3	2	.600	0	5	1.77
1992 Macon	A	23	0	0	7	60	241	57	16	14	2	1	1	5	11	1	57	2	0	2	3	.400	0	2	2.10
Durham	A	21	0	0	12	40.2	158	31	11	11	1	2	1	0	10	0	33	2	0	2	1	.667	0	5	2.43
1993 Greenville	AA	33	2	0	10	70	290	64	22	16	5	2	2	3	24	1	57	2	0	8	1	.889	0	2	2.06

		G	GS	CG	GF	IP	BFP	H	R	ER	HR	SH	SF	HB	TBB	IBB	SO	WP	Bk	W	L	Pct.	ShO	Sv	ERA
Richmond	AAA	18	1	0	11	28.2	130	30	12	12	2	2	0	3	11	3	30	2	1	1	0	1.000	0	1	3.77
1994 Modesto	A	3	3	0	0	5	17	2	0	0	0	0	0	0	0	0	3	1	0	0	0	.000	0	0	0.00
1994 Oakland	AL	27	9	0	8	78	344	71	38	36	10	2	3	2	44	1	57	3	0	0	3	.000	0	1	4.15
1995 Oakland	AL	40	1	0	19	69	306	71	43	39	10	4	0	5	28	4	48	5	0	4	6	.400	0	0	5.09
2 ML YEARS		67	10	0	27	147	650	142	81	75	20	6	3	7	72	5	105	8	0	4	9	.308	0	1	4.59

Shane Reynolds

Pitches: Right **Bats:** Right **Pos:** SP   **Ht:** 6' 3" **Wt:** 210 **Born:** 3/26/68 **Age:** 28

		HOW MUCH HE PITCHED						WHAT HE GAVE UP												THE RESULTS					
Year Team	Lg	G	GS	CG	GF	IP	BFP	H	R	ER	HR	SH	SF	HB	TBB	IBB	SO	WP	Bk	W	L	Pct.	ShO	Sv	ERA
1992 Houston	NL	8	5	0	0	25.1	122	42	22	20	2	6	1	0	6	1	10	1	1	1	3	.250	0	0	7.11
1993 Houston	NL	5	1	0	0	11	49	11	4	1	0	0	0	0	6	1	10	0	0	0	0	.000	0	0	0.82
1994 Houston	NL	33	14	1	5	124	517	128	46	42	10	4	0	6	21	3	110	3	2	8	5	.615	1	0	3.05
1995 Houston	NL	30	30	3	0	189.1	792	196	87	73	15	8	0	2	37	6	175	7	1	10	11	.476	2	0	3.47
4 ML YEARS		76	50	4	5	349.2	1480	377	159	136	27	18	1	8	70	11	305	11	4	19	19	.500	3	0	3.50

Armando Reynoso

Pitches: Right **Bats:** Right **Pos:** SP   **Ht:** 6' 0" **Wt:** 196 **Born:** 5/1/66 **Age:** 30

		HOW MUCH HE PITCHED						WHAT HE GAVE UP												THE RESULTS					
Year Team	Lg	G	GS	CG	GF	IP	BFP	H	R	ER	HR	SH	SF	HB	TBB	IBB	SO	WP	Bk	W	L	Pct.	ShO	Sv	ERA
1995 Colo. Sprng *	AAA	5	5	0	0	23	86	14	4	4	1	0	1	0	6	1	17	0	1	2	1	.667	0	0	1.57
1991 Atlanta	NL	6	5	0	1	23.1	103	26	18	16	4	3	0	3	10	1	10	2	0	2	1	.667	0	0	6.17
1992 Atlanta	NL	3	1	0	1	7.2	32	11	4	4	2	1	0	1	2	1	2	0	0	1	0	1.000	0	1	4.70
1993 Colorado	NL	30	30	4	0	189	830	206	101	84	22	5	8	9	63	7	117	7	6	12	11	.522	0	0	4.00
1994 Colorado	NL	9	9	1	0	52.1	226	54	30	28	5	2	2	6	22	1	25	2	2	3	4	.429	0	0	4.82
1995 Colorado	NL	20	18	0	0	93	418	116	61	55	12	8	2	5	36	3	40	2	0	7	7	.500	0	0	5.32
5 ML YEARS		68	63	5	2	365.1	1609	413	214	187	45	19	12	24	133	13	194	13	8	25	23	.521	0	1	4.61

Arthur Rhodes

Pitches: Left **Bats:** Left **Pos:** RP/SP   **Ht:** 6' 2" **Wt:** 206 **Born:** 10/24/69 **Age:** 26

		HOW MUCH HE PITCHED						WHAT HE GAVE UP												THE RESULTS					
Year Team	Lg	G	GS	CG	GF	IP	BFP	H	R	ER	HR	SH	SF	HB	TBB	IBB	SO	WP	Bk	W	L	Pct.	ShO	Sv	ERA
1995 Rochester *	AAA	4	4	1	0	30	125	27	12	9	2	3	0	1	8	0	33	1	0	2	1	.667	0	0	2.70
1991 Baltimore	AL	8	8	0	0	36	174	47	35	32	4	1	3	0	23	0	23	2	0	0	3	.000	0	0	8.00
1992 Baltimore	AL	15	15	2	0	94.1	394	87	39	38	6	5	1	1	38	2	77	2	1	7	5	.583	1	0	3.63
1993 Baltimore	AL	17	17	0	0	85.2	387	91	62	62	16	2	3	1	49	1	49	2	0	5	6	.455	0	0	6.51
1994 Baltimore	AL	10	10	3	0	52.2	238	51	34	34	8	2	3	2	30	1	47	3	0	3	5	.375	2	0	5.81
1995 Baltimore	AL	19	9	0	3	75.1	336	68	53	52	13	4	0	0	48	1	77	3	1	2	5	.286	0	0	6.21
5 ML YEARS		69	59	5	3	344	1529	344	223	218	47	14	10	4	188	5	273	12	2	17	24	.415	3	0	5.70

Karl Rhodes

Bats: Left **Throws:** Left **Pos:** LF   **Ht:** 6' 0" **Wt:** 195 **Born:** 8/21/68 **Age:** 27

		BATTING																	BASERUNNING				PERCENTAGES		
Year Team	Lg	G	AB	H	2B	3B	HR	(Hm	Rd)	TB	R	RBI	TBB	IBB	SO	HBP	SH	SF	SB	CS	SB%	GDP	Avg	OBP	SLG
1995 Pawtucket *	AAA	69	246	70	13	3	10	--	--	119	40	43	34	3	46	1	1	3	8	6	.57	7	.285	.370	.484
1990 Houston	NL	38	86	21	6	1	1	(0	1)	32	12	8	13	3	12	0	1	1	4	1	.80	1	.244	.340	.372
1991 Houston	NL	44	136	29	3	1	1	(0	1)	37	7	12	14	3	26	1	0	1	2	2	.50	3	.213	.289	.272
1992 Houston	NL	5	4	0	0	0	0	(0	0)	0	0	0	0	0	2	0	0	0	0	0	.00	0	.000	.000	.000
1993 ChN-Hou	NL	20	54	15	2	1	3	(0	3)	28	12	7	11	0	9	0	0	0	2	0	1.00	0	.278	.400	.519
1994 Chicago	NL	95	269	63	17	0	8	(4	4)	104	39	19	33	1	64	1	3	2	6	4	.60	1	.234	.318	.387
1995 ChN-Bos		23	41	4	1	0	0	(0	0)	5	4	3	3	0	8	0	0	1	0	0	.00	2	.098	.156	.122
1993 Chicago	NL	15	52	15	2	1	3	(0	3)	28	12	7	11	0	9	0	0	0	2	0	1.00	0	.288	.413	.538
Houston	NL	5	2	0	0	0	0	(0	0)	0	0	0	0	0	0	0	0	0	0	0	.00	0	.000	.000	.000
1995 Chicago	NL	13	16	2	0	0	0	(0	0)	2	2	2	0	0	4	0	0	1	0	0	.00	1	.125	.118	.125
Boston	AL	10	25	2	1	0	0	(0	0)	3	2	1	3	0	4	0	0	0	0	0	.00	1	.080	.179	.120
6 ML YEARS		225	590	132	29	3	13	(4	9)	206	74	44	74	7	121	2	4	5	14	7	.67	7	.224	.310	.349

Chuck Ricci

Pitches: Right **Bats:** Right **Pos:** RP   **Ht:** 6' 2" **Wt:** 180 **Born:** 11/20/68 **Age:** 27

		HOW MUCH HE PITCHED						WHAT HE GAVE UP												THE RESULTS					
Year Team	Lg	G	GS	CG	GF	IP	BFP	H	R	ER	HR	SH	SF	HB	TBB	IBB	SO	WP	Bk	W	L	Pct.	ShO	Sv	ERA
1987 Bluefield	R	13	12	1	0	62.1	288	74	52	45	11	1	0	2	38	1	40	3	0	5	5	.500	0	0	6.50
1988 Bluefield	R	14	14	1	0	73	355	92	61	54	7	1	3	2	48	0	73	6	0	4	6	.400	0	0	6.66
1989 Waterloo	A	29	25	9	1	181.1	760	160	89	60	11	11	5	12	59	5	89	14	1	10	12	.455	0	0	2.98
1990 Frederick	A	26	18	2	5	122.1	539	126	79	60	8	6	3	6	47	3	94	8	0	7	12	.368	1	0	4.41
1991 Frederick	A	30	29	2	0	173.2	752	147	91	60	12	3	10	3	84	2	144	15	1	12	14	.462	0	0	3.11
1992 Frederick	A	1	0	0	0	2.1	11	2	1	0	0	0	0	0	1	0	2	0	0	0	0	.000	0	0	0.00

			G	GS	CG	GF	IP	BFP	H	R	ER	HR	SH	SF	HB	TBB	IBB	SO	WP	Bk	W	L	Pct.	ShO	Sv	ERA
	Hagerstown	AA	20	6	0	4	57.2	275	58	40	37	4	3	4	3	47	1	58	8	2	1	4	.200	0	0	5.77
1993	Rochester	AAA	4	0	0	3	8	36	11	5	5	1	0	0	0	3	0	6	0	0	0	0	.000	0	0	5.63
	Bowie	AA	34	1	0	16	81.2	334	72	35	29	7	5	2	3	20	0	83	8	0	7	4	.636	0	5	3.20
1994	Reading	AA	14	0	0	2	19	71	10	1	0	0	0	0	2	4	2	23	0	0	1	0	1.000	0	0	0.00
	Scranton-Wb	AAA	44	1	0	17	64.2	274	60	30	29	7	2	3	5	22	5	72	4	0	4	3	.571	0	6	4.04
1995	Scranton-Wb	AAA	68	0	0	48	65	269	48	22	18	6	4	1	4	24	5	66	1	0	4	3	.571	0	25	2.49
1995	Philadelphia	NL	7	0	0	3	10	40	9	2	2	0	1	2	1	3	0	9	0	0	1	0	1.000	0	0	1.80

Dave Righetti

Pitches: Left **Bats:** Left **Pos:** SP **Ht:** 6' 4" **Wt:** 220 **Born:** 11/28/58 **Age:** 37

Year	Team	Lg	G	GS	CG	GF	IP	BFP	H	R	ER	HR	SH	SF	HB	TBB	IBB	SO	WP	Bk	W	L	Pct.	ShO	Sv	ERA
1995	Nashville *	AAA	16	15	1	0	83.2	344	81	40	30	9	3	4	1	20	0	44	2	2	4	5	.444	1	0	3.23
1979	New York	AL	3	3	0	0	17	67	10	7	7	2	1	1	0	10	0	13	0	0	1	0	1.000	0	0	3.71
1981	New York	AL	15	15	2	0	105	422	75	25	24	1	0	2	0	38	0	89	1	1	8	4	.667	0	0	2.06
1982	New York	AL	33	27	4	3	183	804	155	88	77	11	8	5	6	**108**	4	163	9	5	11	10	.524	0	1	3.79
1983	New York	AL	31	31	7	0	217	900	194	96	83	12	10	4	2	67	2	169	10	1	14	8	.636	2	0	3.44
1984	New York	AL	64	0	0	53	96.1	400	79	29	25	5	4	4	0	37	7	90	0	2	5	6	.455	0	31	2.34
1985	New York	AL	74	0	0	60	107	452	96	36	33	5	6	3	0	45	3	92	7	0	12	7	.632	0	29	2.78
1986	New York	AL	74	0	0	**68**	106.2	435	88	31	29	4	5	4	2	35	7	83	1	0	8	8	.500	0	**46**	2.45
1987	New York	AL	60	0	0	54	95	419	95	45	37	9	6	5	2	44	4	77	1	3	8	6	.571	0	31	3.51
1988	New York	AL	60	0	0	41	87	377	86	35	34	5	4	0	1	37	2	70	2	4	5	4	.556	0	25	3.52
1989	New York	AL	55	0	0	53	69	300	73	32	23	3	7	2	1	26	6	51	0	0	2	6	.250	0	25	3.00
1990	New York	AL	53	0	0	47	53	235	48	24	21	8	1	1	2	26	2	43	2	0	1	1	.500	0	36	3.57
1991	San Francisco	NL	61	0	0	49	71.2	304	64	29	27	4	4	2	3	28	6	51	1	1	2	7	.222	0	24	3.39
1992	San Francisco	NL	54	4	0	23	78.1	340	79	47	44	4	6	4	0	36	5	47	5	2	2	7	.222	0	3	5.06
1993	San Francisco	NL	51	0	0	15	47.1	210	58	31	30	11	2	0	1	17	0	31	1	0	1	1	.500	0	1	5.70
1994	Oak-Tor	AL	20	0	0	7	20.1	102	22	23	23	5	1	2	1	19	0	14	0	0	0	1	.000	0	0	10.18
1995	Chicago	AL	10	9	0	1	49.1	221	65	24	23	6	1	2	0	18	0	29	0	0	3	2	.600	0	0	4.20
1994	Oakland	AL	7	0	0	1	7	42	13	13	13	3	0	1	1	9	0	4	0	0	0	0	.000	0	0	16.71
	Toronto	AL	13	0	0	6	13.1	60	9	10	10	2	1	1	0	10	0	10	0	0	0	1	.000	0	0	6.75
	16 ML YEARS		718	89	13	474	1403	5988	1287	602	540	95	66	41	21	591	48	1112	40	19	82	79	.509	2	252	3.46

Ron Rightnowar

Pitches: Right **Bats:** Right **Pos:** RP **Ht:** 6' 3" **Wt:** 190 **Born:** 9/5/64 **Age:** 31

Year	Team	Lg	G	GS	CG	GF	IP	BFP	H	R	ER	HR	SH	SF	HB	TBB	IBB	SO	WP	Bk	W	L	Pct.	ShO	Sv	ERA
1987	Fayetteville	A	39	10	2	19	101.2	450	115	70	56	7	5	6	4	37	1	65	4	1	7	7	.500	0	6	4.96
1988	Lakeland	A	17	2	0	4	49.1	197	41	19	8	1	2	0	4	11	2	32	5	2	2	0	1.000	0	0	1.46
1989	London	AA	36	7	2	14	108	478	132	63	60	10	4	5	4	34	4	46	2	2	2	8	.200	0	5	5.00
1990	Toledo	AAA	28	0	0	16	38	165	46	24	20	5	2	2	0	10	3	28	0	0	4	5	.444	0	6	4.74
	Niagara Fal	A	1	1	1	0	7	26	4	1	0	0	0	0	0	1	0	9	0	0	1	0	1.000	0	0	0.00
	London	AA	23	0	0	18	44.1	182	40	20	16	4	1	2	2	9	0	33	1	0	2	2	.500	0	5	3.25
1991	Toledo	AAA	23	0	0	14	29.2	130	30	15	13	2	1	2	1	15	2	5	0	0	1	1	.500	0	3	3.94
	London	AA	15	0	0	9	25.1	110	28	13	11	0	2	1	0	8	1	18	1	0	2	1	.667	0	3	3.91
1992	Toledo	AAA	34	0	0	20	57	258	68	43	39	10	2	5	5	18	4	33	5	0	3	2	.600	0	3	6.16
1993	Toledo	AAA	22	6	0	4	58.1	255	57	32	23	3	1	2	7	19	0	32	2	0	2	2	.500	0	1	3.55
	New Orleans	AAA	4	0	0	1	8.2	45	19	10	10	1	1	0	1	2	0	8	0	0	0	0	.000	0	0	10.38
1994	New Orleans	AAA	51	2	0	24	88	343	62	25	22	8	3	2	3	21	2	79	3	0	8	2	.800	0	11	2.25
1995	New Orleans	AAA	25	0	0	20	30.1	135	37	16	9	3	2	1	2	9	1	22	3	0	1	1	.500	0	10	2.67
1995	Milwaukee	AL	34	0	0	13	36.2	160	35	23	22	3	5	3	5	18	3	22	1	0	2	1	.667	0	1	5.40

Jose Rijo

Pitches: Right **Bats:** Right **Pos:** SP **Ht:** 6' 3" **Wt:** 215 **Born:** 5/13/65 **Age:** 31

Year	Team	Lg	G	GS	CG	GF	IP	BFP	H	R	ER	HR	SH	SF	HB	TBB	IBB	SO	WP	Bk	W	L	Pct.	ShO	Sv	ERA
1984	New York	AL	24	5	0	8	62.1	289	74	40	33	5	6	1	1	33	1	47	2	1	2	8	.200	0	2	4.76
1985	Oakland	AL	12	9	0	1	63.2	272	57	26	25	6	5	0	1	28	2	65	0	0	6	4	.600	0	0	3.53
1986	Oakland	AL	39	26	4	9	193.2	856	172	116	100	24	10	9	4	108	7	176	6	4	9	11	.450	0	1	4.65
1987	Oakland	AL	21	14	1	3	82.1	394	106	67	54	10	0	3	2	41	1	67	5	2	2	7	.222	0	0	5.90
1988	Cincinnati	NL	49	19	0	12	162	653	120	47	43	7	8	5	3	63	7	160	1	4	13	8	.619	0	0	2.39
1989	Cincinnati	NL	19	19	1	0	111	464	101	39	35	6	3	6	2	48	3	86	4	3	7	6	.538	1	0	2.84
1990	Cincinnati	NL	29	29	7	0	197	801	151	65	59	10	8	1	2	78	1	152	2	5	14	8	.636	1	0	2.70
1991	Cincinnati	NL	30	30	3	0	204.1	825	165	69	57	8	4	8	1	55	4	172	2	4	15	6	.714	1	0	2.51
1992	Cincinnati	NL	33	33	2	0	211	836	185	67	60	15	9	4	3	44	1	171	2	1	15	10	.600	0	0	2.56
1993	Cincinnati	NL	36	**36**	2	0	257.1	1029	218	76	71	19	13	3	2	62	2	**227**	0	1	14	9	.609	1	0	2.48

Year Team	Lg	G	GS	CG	GF	IP	BFP	H	R	ER	HR	SH	SF	HB	TBB	IBB	SO	WP	Bk	W	L	Pct.	ShO	Sv	ERA
1994 Cincinnati	NL	26	**26**	2	0	172.1	733	177	73	59	16	7	2	4	52	1	171	1	2	9	6	.600	0	0	3.08
1995 Cincinnati	NL	14	14	0	0	69	295	76	33	32	6	3	3	0	22	1	62	3	0	5	4	.556	0	0	4.17
12 ML YEARS		332	260	22	33	1786	7447	1602	718	628	132	76	45	27	634	31	1556	28	27	111	87	.561	4	3	3.16

Billy Ripken

Bats: Right **Throws:** Right **Pos:** 2B   **Ht:** 6' 1" **Wt:** 187 **Born:** 12/16/64 **Age:** 31

Year Team	Lg	G	AB	H	2B	3B	HR	(Hm	Rd)	TB	R	RBI	TBB	IBB	SO	HBP	SH	SF	SB	CS	SB%	GDP	Avg	OBP	SLG
1995 Buffalo *	AAA	130	448	131	34	1	4	--	--	179	51	56	28	0	38	2	6	8	6	4	.60	14	.292	.331	.400
1987 Baltimore	AL	58	234	72	9	0	2	(0	2)	87	27	20	21	0	23	0	1	1	4	1	.80	3	.308	.363	.372
1988 Baltimore	AL	150	512	106	18	1	2	(0	2)	132	52	34	33	0	63	5	6	3	8	2	.80	14	.207	.260	.258
1989 Baltimore	AL	115	318	76	11	2	2	(0	2)	97	31	26	22	0	53	0	19	5	1	2	.33	12	.239	.284	.305
1990 Baltimore	AL	129	406	118	28	1	3	(2	1)	157	48	38	28	2	43	4	17	1	5	2	.71	7	.291	.342	.387
1991 Baltimore	AL	104	287	62	11	1	0	(0	0)	75	24	14	15	0	31	0	11	2	0	1	.00	14	.216	.253	.261
1992 Baltimore	AL	111	330	76	15	0	4	(3	1)	103	35	36	18	1	26	3	10	2	2	3	.40	10	.230	.275	.312
1993 Texas	AL	50	132	25	4	0	0	(0	0)	29	12	11	11	0	19	4	5	1	0	2	.00	6	.189	.270	.220
1994 Texas	AL	32	81	25	5	0	0	(0	0)	30	9	6	3	0	11	0	1	0	2	1	1.00	2	.309	.333	.370
1995 Cleveland	AL	8	17	7	0	0	2	(1	1)	13	4	3	0	0	3	0	0	0	0	0	.00	0	.412	.412	.765
9 ML YEARS		757	2317	567	101	5	15	(6	9)	723	242	188	151	3	272	16	70	15	22	13	.63	68	.245	.294	.312

Cal Ripken

Bats: Right **Throws:** Right **Pos:** SS   **Ht:** 6' 4" **Wt:** 220 **Born:** 8/24/60 **Age:** 35

Year Team	Lg	G	AB	H	2B	3B	HR	(Hm	Rd)	TB	R	RBI	TBB	IBB	SO	HBP	SH	SF	SB	CS	SB%	GDP	Avg	OBP	SLG
1981 Baltimore	AL	23	39	5	0	0	0	(0	0)	5	1	0	1	0	8	0	0	0	0	0	.00	4	.128	.150	.128
1982 Baltimore	AL	160	598	158	32	5	28	(11	17)	284	90	93	46	3	95	3	2	6	3	3	.50	16	.264	.317	.475
1983 Baltimore	AL	**162**	**663**	**211**	**47**	2	27	(12	15)	343	**121**	102	58	0	97	0	0	5	0	4	.00	24	.318	.371	.517
1984 Baltimore	AL	**162**	641	195	37	7	27	(16	11)	327	103	86	71	1	89	2	0	2	2	1	.67	16	.304	.374	.510
1985 Baltimore	AL	161	642	181	32	5	26	(15	11)	301	116	110	67	1	68	1	0	8	2	3	.40	32	.282	.347	.469
1986 Baltimore	AL	162	627	177	35	1	25	(10	15)	289	98	81	70	5	60	4	0	6	4	2	.67	19	.282	.355	.461
1987 Baltimore	AL	**162**	624	157	28	3	27	(17	10)	272	97	98	81	0	77	1	0	11	3	5	.38	19	.252	.333	.436
1988 Baltimore	AL	161	575	152	25	1	23	(11	12)	248	87	81	102	7	69	2	0	10	2	2	.50	10	.264	.372	.431
1989 Baltimore	AL	**162**	646	166	30	0	21	(13	8)	259	80	93	57	5	72	3	0	6	3	2	.60	22	.257	.317	.401
1990 Baltimore	AL	161	600	150	28	4	21	(8	13)	249	78	84	82	18	66	5	1	7	3	1	.75	12	.250	.341	.415
1991 Baltimore	AL	**162**	650	210	46	5	34	(16	18)	**368**	99	114	53	15	46	5	0	9	6	1	.86	19	.323	.374	.566
1992 Baltimore	AL	**162**	637	160	29	1	14	(5	9)	233	73	72	64	14	50	7	0	7	4	3	.57	13	.251	.323	.366
1993 Baltimore	AL	**162**	641	165	26	3	24	(14	10)	269	87	90	65	19	58	6	0	6	1	4	.20	17	.257	.329	.420
1994 Baltimore	AL	112	444	140	19	3	13	(5	8)	204	71	75	32	3	41	4	0	4	1	0	1.00	17	.315	.364	.459
1995 Baltimore	AL	144	550	144	33	2	17	(10	7)	232	71	88	52	6	59	2	1	8	0	1	.00	15	.262	.324	.422
15 ML YEARS		2218	8577	2371	447	42	327	(163	164)	3883	1272	1267	901	97	955	45	4	95	34	32	.52	255	.276	.345	.453

Bill Risley

Pitches: Right **Bats:** Right **Pos:** RP   **Ht:** 6' 2" **Wt:** 215 **Born:** 5/29/67 **Age:** 29

Year Team	Lg	G	GS	CG	GF	IP	BFP	H	R	ER	HR	SH	SF	HB	TBB	IBB	SO	WP	Bk	W	L	Pct.	ShO	Sv	ERA
1995 Tacoma *	AAA	1	0	0	0	1	4	0	0	0	0	0	0	0	1	0	2	0	0	0	0	.000	0	0	0.00
1992 Montreal	NL	1	1	0	0	5	19	4	1	1	0	1	0	0	1	0	2	0	0	1	0	1.000	0	0	1.80
1993 Montreal	NL	2	0	0	1	3	14	2	3	2	1	1	0	1	2	0	2	0	0	0	0	.000	0	0	6.00
1994 Seattle	AL	37	0	0	7	52.1	203	31	20	20	7	0	2	0	19	4	61	2	0	9	6	.600	0	0	3.44
1995 Seattle	AL	45	0	0	5	60.1	249	55	21	21	7	2	3	1	18	1	65	2	0	2	1	.667	0	1	3.13
4 ML YEARS		85	1	0	13	120.2	485	92	45	44	15	4	5	2	40	5	130	4	0	12	7	.632	0	1	3.28

Kevin Ritz

Pitches: Right **Bats:** Right **Pos:** SP   **Ht:** 6' 4" **Wt:** 220 **Born:** 6/8/65 **Age:** 31

Year Team	Lg	G	GS	CG	GF	IP	BFP	H	R	ER	HR	SH	SF	HB	TBB	IBB	SO	WP	Bk	W	L	Pct.	ShO	Sv	ERA
1989 Detroit	AL	12	12	1	0	74	334	75	41	36	2	1	5	1	44	5	56	6	0	4	6	.400	0	0	4.38
1990 Detroit	AL	4	4	0	0	7.1	52	14	12	9	0	3	0	0	14	2	3	3	0	0	4	.000	0	0	11.05
1991 Detroit	AL	11	5	0	3	15.1	86	17	22	20	1	1	2	2	22	1	9	0	0	0	3	.000	0	0	11.74
1992 Detroit	AL	23	11	0	4	80.1	368	88	52	50	4	1	4	3	44	4	57	7	1	2	5	.286	0	0	5.60
1994 Colorado	NL	15	15	0	0	73.2	335	88	49	46	5	4	2	4	35	4	53	6	1	5	6	.455	0	0	5.62
1995 Colorado	NL	31	28	0	3	173.1	743	171	91	81	16	8	5	6	65	3	120	6	0	11	11	.500	0	2	4.21
6 ML YEARS		96	75	1	10	424	1918	453	267	242	28	18	18	16	224	19	298	28	2	22	35	.386	0	2	5.14

193

Ben Rivera

Pitches: Right **Bats:** Right **Pos:** SP   **Ht:** 6' 6" **Wt:** 250 **Born:** 1/11/68 **Age:** 28

Year	Team	Lg	G	GS	CG	GF	IP	BFP	H	R	ER	HR	SH	SF	HB	TBB	IBB	SO	WP	Bk	W	L	Pct.	ShO	Sv	ERA
1992	Atl-Phi	NL	28	14	4	7	117.1	487	99	40	40	9	5	2	4	45	4	77	5	0	7	4	.636	1	0	3.07
1993	Philadelphia	NL	30	28	1	1	163	742	175	99	91	16	5	5	6	85	4	123	13	0	13	9	.591	1	0	5.02
1994	Philadelphia	NL	9	7	0	1	38	176	40	29	29	7	6	1	1	22	0	19	3	0	3	4	.429	0	0	6.87
1992	Atlanta	NL	8	0	0	3	15.1	78	21	8	8	1	0	1	2	13	2	11	0	0	0	1	.000	0	0	4.70
	Philadelphia	NL	20	14	4	4	102	409	78	32	32	8	5	1	2	32	2	66	5	0	7	3	.700	1	0	2.82
	3 ML YEARS		67	49	5	9	318.1	1405	314	168	160	32	16	8	11	152	8	219	21	0	23	17	.575	2	0	4.52

Mariano Rivera

Pitches: Right **Bats:** Right **Pos:** SP/RP   **Ht:** 6' 2" **Wt:** 168 **Born:** 11/29/69 **Age:** 26

Year	Team	Lg	G	GS	CG	GF	IP	BFP	H	R	ER	HR	SH	SF	HB	TBB	IBB	SO	WP	Bk	W	L	Pct.	ShO	Sv	ERA
1990	Yankees	R	22	1	1	12	52	180	17	3	1	0	2	2	2	7	0	58	0	0	5	1	.833	1	1	0.17
1991	Greensboro	A	29	15	1	6	114.2	480	102	48	35	2	1	5	3	36	0	123	3	0	4	9	.308	0	0	2.75
1992	Ft. Laud	A	10	10	3	0	59.1	217	40	17	15	5	2	1	0	5	0	42	0	0	5	3	.625	1	0	2.28
1993	Yankees	R	2	2	0	0	4	15	2	1	1	0	0	0	0	1	0	6	1	0	0	1	.000	0	0	2.25
	Greensboro	A	10	10	0	0	39.1	161	31	12	9	0	0	1	0	15	0	32	2	0	1	0	1.000	0	0	2.06
1994	Tampa	A	7	7	0	0	36.2	148	34	12	9	2	1	1	2	12	0	27	0	0	3	0	1.000	0	0	2.21
	Albany-Colo	AA	9	9	0	0	63.1	252	58	20	16	5	3	1	0	8	0	39	1	1	3	0	1.000	0	0	2.27
	Columbus	AAA	6	6	1	0	31	137	34	22	20	5	0	0	0	10	0	23	0	1	4	2	.667	0	0	5.81
1995	Columbus	AAA	7	7	1	0	30	114	25	10	7	2	0	1	0	3	0	30	0	0	2	2	.500	1	0	2.10
1995	New York	AL	19	10	0	2	67	301	71	43	41	11	0	2	2	30	0	51	0	1	5	3	.625	0	0	5.51

Roberto Rivera

Pitches: Left **Bats:** Left **Pos:** RP   **Ht:** 6' 0" **Wt:** 200 **Born:** 1/1/69 **Age:** 27

Year	Team	Lg	G	GS	CG	GF	IP	BFP	H	R	ER	HR	SH	SF	HB	TBB	IBB	SO	WP	Bk	W	L	Pct.	ShO	Sv	ERA
1988	Indians	R	14	12	1	1	69.1	295	64	32	25	2	2	4	3	21	1	38	2	4	6	5	.545	1	0	3.25
1989	Burlington	R	18	2	1	8	51.1	214	44	24	20	4	4	2	1	16	3	42	0	2	3	4	.429	0	2	3.51
1990	Watertown	A	14	13	2	0	85	345	85	43	34	9	2	1	1	10	0	63	2	0	4	4	.500	1	0	3.60
1991	Columbus	A	30	1	0	17	49	207	48	15	9	1	2	0	2	12	3	36	2	2	7	1	.875	0	3	1.65
	Kinston	A	10	0	0	5	10.1	46	10	6	5	1	1	1	0	2	0	9	0	0	1	0	1.000	0	0	4.35
1992	Kinston	A	24	8	4	5	88.2	353	83	35	32	7	3	3	3	11	3	56	4	0	3	5	.375	1	1	3.25
1993	Canton-Akrn	AA	8	0	0	4	14.1	68	22	8	8	0	0	0	2	3	0	6	0	2	0	1	.000	0	0	5.02
	Kinston	A	19	1	0	9	35	150	44	26	24	4	1	2	1	4	0	32	0	0	2	3	.400	0	0	6.17
1994	Peoria	A	14	0	0	6	19.1	90	27	6	5	1	2	0	3	3	1	13	2	0	3	1	.750	0	0	2.33
	Orlando	AA	34	0	0	19	45.2	192	45	14	14	1	2	0	2	11	0	31	2	0	3	2	.600	0	4	2.76
1995	Orlando	AA	49	0	0	14	68	257	50	18	18	4	0	4	0	11	3	34	3	1	6	2	.750	0	6	2.38
1995	Chicago	NL	7	0	0	2	5	23	8	3	3	1	0	0	0	2	0	2	0	0	0	0	.000	0	0	5.40

Ruben Rivera

Bats: Right **Throws:** Right **Pos:** LF   **Ht:** 6' 3" **Wt:** 200 **Born:** 11/14/73 **Age:** 22

Year	Team	Lg	G	AB	H	2B	3B	HR	(Hm	Rd)	TB	R	RBI	TBB	IBB	SO	HBP	SH	SF	SB	CS	SB%	GDP	Avg	OBP	SLG
1992	Yankees	R	53	194	53	10	3	1	--	--	72	37	20	42	0	49	6	2	0	21	6	.78	2	.273	.417	.371
1993	Oneonta	A	55	199	55	7	6	13	--	--	113	45	47	32	1	66	5	1	3	11	5	.69	2	.276	.385	.568
1994	Greensboro	A	105	400	115	24	3	28	--	--	229	83	81	47	1	125	8	0	2	36	5	.88	6	.288	.372	.573
	Tampa	A	34	134	35	4	3	5	--	--	60	18	20	8	0	38	1	0	0	12	5	.71	7	.261	.308	.448
1995	Norwich	AA	71	256	75	16	8	9	--	--	134	49	39	37	2	77	11	0	2	16	8	.67	4	.293	.402	.523
	Columbus	AAA	48	174	47	8	2	15	--	--	104	37	35	26	0	62	3	0	1	8	4	.67	5	.270	.373	.598
1995	New York	AL	5	1	0	0	0	0	(0	0)	0	0	0	0	0	1	0	0	0	0	0	.00	0	.000	.000	.000

Joe Roa

Pitches: Right **Bats:** Right **Pos:** SP   **Ht:** 6' 1" **Wt:** 194 **Born:** 10/11/71 **Age:** 24

Year	Team	Lg	G	GS	CG	GF	IP	BFP	H	R	ER	HR	SH	SF	HB	TBB	IBB	SO	WP	Bk	W	L	Pct.	ShO	Sv	ERA
1989	Braves	R	13	4	0	4	37.1	156	40	18	12	2	0	1	0	10	1	21	3	0	2	2	.500	0	0	2.89
1990	Pulaski	R	14	11	3	1	75.2	313	55	29	25	3	2	1	2	26	0	49	2	2	4	2	.667	1	0	2.97
1991	Macon	A	30	18	4	2	141	556	106	46	33	6	0	3	5	33	4	96	3	0	13	3	.813	2	1	2.11
1992	St. Lucie	A	26	24	2	0	156.1	647	176	80	63	9	6	6	6	15	1	61	0	1	9	7	.563	1	0	3.63
1993	Binghamton	AA	32	23	2	0	167.1	693	190	80	72	9	2	4	10	24	0	73	3	2	12	7	.632	1	0	3.87
1994	Binghamton	AA	3	3	0	0	20	82	18	6	4	0	2	2	1	1	0	11	1	2	2	1	.667	0	0	1.80
	Norfolk	AAA	25	25	5	0	167.2	703	184	82	65	16	3	12	4	34	1	74	4	0	8	8	.500	0	0	3.49

Year Team	Lg	G	GS	CG	GF	IP	BFP	H	R	ER	HR	SH	SF	HB	TBB	IBB	SO	WP	Bk	W	L	Pct.	ShO	Sv	ERA
1995 Buffalo	AAA	25	24	3	1	164.2	678	168	71	64	9	2	5	7	28	1	93	1	2	17	3	.850	0	0	3.50
1995 Cleveland	AL	1	1	0	0	6	28	9	4	4	1	1	0	0	2	0	0	0	0	0	1	.000	0	0	6.00

Kevin Roberson

Bats: Both **Throws:** Right **Pos:** LF   **Ht:** 6' 4" **Wt:** 210 **Born:** 1/29/68 **Age:** 28

						BATTING										BASERUNNING				PERCENTAGES		
Year Team	Lg	G	AB	H	2B	3B	HR	(Hm	Rd)	TB	R	RBI	TBB	IBB	SO	HBP	SH	SF	SB	CS	SB%	GDP	Avg	OBP	SLG
1995 Tacoma *	AAA	42	157	37	6	1	6	--	--	63	17	17	19	1	51	2	0	2	1	1	.50	4	.236	.322	.401
1993 Chicago	NL	62	180	34	4	1	9	(4	5)	67	23	27	12	0	48	3	0	0	0	0	.00	3	.189	.251	.372
1994 Chicago	NL	44	55	12	4	0	4	(2	2)	28	8	9	2	0	14	2	0	0	0	0	.00	1	.218	.271	.509
1995 Chicago	NL	32	38	7	1	0	4	(2	2)	20	5	6	6	0	14	1	0	0	0	1	.00	1	.184	.311	.526
3 ML YEARS		138	273	53	9	1	17	(8	9)	115	36	42	20	0	76	6	0	0	0	2	.00	6	.194	.264	.421

Sid Roberson

Pitches: Left **Bats:** Left **Pos:** SP/RP   **Ht:** 5' 9" **Wt:** 170 **Born:** 9/7/71 **Age:** 24

					HOW MUCH HE PITCHED			WHAT HE GAVE UP										THE RESULTS					
Year Team	Lg	G	GS	CG	GF	IP	BFP	H	R	ER	HR	SH	SF	HB	TBB	IBB	SO	WP	Bk	W	L	Pct.	ShO	Sv	ERA
1992 Helena	R	9	8	1	1	65	276	68	32	25	8	3	1	2	18	0	65	4	1	4	4	.500	1	0	3.46
1993 Stockton	A	24	23	6	0	166	684	157	68	48	8	7	3	12	34	0	87	6	4	12	8	.600	1	0	2.60
1994 El Paso	AA	25	25	8	0	181.1	771	190	70	57	7	5	7	17	48	3	119	4	1	15	8	.652	0	0	2.83
1995 New Orleans	AAA	4	3	0	0	13	69	20	11	11	1	0	2	1	10	0	8	0	0	0	2	.000	0	0	7.62
1995 Milwaukee	AL	26	13	0	8	84.1	379	102	55	54	16	0	2	8	37	3	40	3	0	6	4	.600	0	0	5.76

Bip Roberts

Bats: Both **Throws:** Right **Pos:** LF/2B   **Ht:** 5' 7" **Wt:** 165 **Born:** 10/27/63 **Age:** 32

						BATTING										BASERUNNING				PERCENTAGES		
Year Team	Lg	G	AB	H	2B	3B	HR	(Hm	Rd)	TB	R	RBI	TBB	IBB	SO	HBP	SH	SF	SB	CS	SB%	GDP	Avg	OBP	SLG
1995 Las Vegas *	AAA	3	12	4	0	0	0	--	--	4	1	2	0	0	3	0	0	1	1	0	1.00	0	.333	.308	.333
Rancho Cuc *	A	1	3	0	0	0	0	--	--	0	1	0	1	0	1	0	0	0	1	0	1.00	0	.000	.250	.000
1986 San Diego	NL	101	241	61	5	2	1	(0	1)	73	34	12	14	1	29	0	2	1	14	12	.54	2	.253	.293	.303
1988 San Diego	NL	5	9	3	0	0	0	(0	0)	3	1	0	1	0	2	0	0	0	0	2	.00	0	.333	.400	.333
1989 San Diego	NL	117	329	99	15	8	3	(2	1)	139	81	25	49	0	45	1	6	2	21	11	.66	3	.301	.391	.422
1990 San Diego	NL	149	556	172	36	3	9	(4	5)	241	104	44	55	1	65	6	8	4	46	12	.79	8	.309	.375	.433
1991 San Diego	NL	117	424	119	13	3	3	(3	0)	147	66	32	37	0	71	4	4	3	26	11	.70	6	.281	.342	.347
1992 Cincinnati	NL	147	532	172	34	6	4	(3	1)	230	92	45	62	4	54	2	1	4	44	16	.73	7	.323	.393	.432
1993 Cincinnati	NL	83	292	70	13	0	1	(0	1)	86	46	18	38	1	46	3	0	3	26	6	.81	2	.240	.330	.295
1994 San Diego	NL	105	403	129	15	5	2	(1	1)	160	52	31	39	1	57	3	2	2	21	7	.75	7	.320	.383	.397
1995 San Diego	NL	73	296	90	14	0	2	(2	0)	110	40	25	17	1	36	2	1	0	20	2	.91	2	.304	.346	.372
9 ML YEARS		897	3082	915	145	27	25	(15	10)	1189	516	232	312	9	405	21	24	19	218	79	.73	37	.297	.363	.386

Rich Robertson

Pitches: Left **Bats:** Left **Pos:** RP/SP   **Ht:** 6' 4" **Wt:** 175 **Born:** 9/15/68 **Age:** 27

					HOW MUCH HE PITCHED			WHAT HE GAVE UP										THE RESULTS					
Year Team	Lg	G	GS	CG	GF	IP	BFP	H	R	ER	HR	SH	SF	HB	TBB	IBB	SO	WP	Bk	W	L	Pct.	ShO	Sv	ERA
1995 Salt Lake *	AAA	7	7	1	0	44.1	172	31	13	12	2	2	0	0	12	1	40	1	0	5	0	1.000	0	0	2.44
1993 Pittsburgh	NL	9	0	0	2	9	44	15	6	6	0	1	0	0	4	0	5	0	0	0	1	.000	0	0	6.00
1994 Pittsburgh	NL	8	0	0	1	15.2	76	20	12	12	2	1	1	0	10	4	8	0	0	0	0	.000	0	0	6.89
1995 Minnesota	AL	25	4	1	8	51.2	228	48	28	22	4	5	2	0	31	4	38	0	1	2	0	1.000	0	0	3.83
3 ML YEARS		42	4	1	11	76.1	348	83	46	40	6	7	3	0	45	8	51	0	1	2	1	.667	0	0	4.72

Ken Robinson

Pitches: Right **Bats:** Right **Pos:** RP   **Ht:** 5' 9" **Wt:** 170 **Born:** 11/3/69 **Age:** 26

					HOW MUCH HE PITCHED			WHAT HE GAVE UP										THE RESULTS					
Year Team	Lg	G	GS	CG	GF	IP	BFP	H	R	ER	HR	SH	SF	HB	TBB	IBB	SO	WP	Bk	W	L	Pct.	ShO	Sv	ERA
1991 Medicne Hat	R	6	2	0	3	11.2	51	12	8	5	1	1	0	0	5	0	18	2	4	0	1	.000	0	0	3.86
1992 Myrtle Bch	A	20	0	0	9	38.1	162	25	12	12	2	0	1	3	30	0	45	4	0	1	0	1.000	0	1	2.82
1993 Hagerstown	A	40	0	0	24	71.2	314	74	43	37	6	2	4	6	31	1	65	5	1	4	7	.364	0	7	4.65
1994 Hagerstown	A	10	0	0	6	19.2	78	15	8	7	1	1	2	0	4	0	27	2	0	4	1	.800	0	1	3.20
Dunedin	A	5	0	0	2	10	39	6	2	2	1	0	0	0	4	0	16	0	0	1	1	.500	0	0	1.80
Syracuse	AAA	30	3	0	5	55.1	235	46	27	23	4	0	3	1	25	1	48	1	0	4	2	.667	0	0	3.74
1995 Syracuse	AAA	38	0	0	12	50.1	201	37	18	18	6	2	2	2	12	2	61	2	0	5	3	.625	0	2	3.22
1995 Toronto	AL	21	0	0	9	39	167	25	21	16	7	1	2	2	22	1	31	1	0	1	2	.333	0	0	3.69

Alex Rodriguez

Bats: Right **Throws:** Right **Pos:** SS **Ht:** 6' 3" **Wt:** 190 **Born:** 7/27/75 **Age:** 20

Year Team	Lg	G	AB	H	2B	3B	HR	(Hm	Rd)	TB	R	RBI	TBB	IBB	SO	HBP	SH	SF	SB	CS	SB%	GDP	Avg	OBP	SLG
1994 Appleton	A	65	248	79	17	6	14	--	--	150	49	55	24	4	44	2	1	3	16	5	.76	7	.319	.379	.605
Jacksonville	AA	17	59	17	4	1	1	--	--	26	7	8	10	0	13	1	0	0	2	1	.67	1	.288	.391	.441
Calgary	AAA	32	119	37	7	4	6	--	--	70	22	21	8	0	25	1	0	0	2	4	.33	1	.311	.359	.588
1995 Tacoma	AAA	54	214	77	12	3	15	--	--	140	37	45	18	1	44	2	1	2	2	4	.33	2	.360	.411	.654
1994 Seattle	AL	17	54	11	0	0	0	(0	0)	11	4	2	3	0	20	0	1	1	3	0	1.00	0	.204	.241	.204
1995 Seattle	AL	48	142	33	6	2	5	(1	4)	58	15	19	6	0	42	0	1	0	4	2	.67	0	.232	.264	.408
2 ML YEARS		65	196	44	6	2	5	(1	4)	69	19	21	9	0	62	0	2	1	7	2	.78	0	.224	.257	.352

Carlos Rodriguez

Bats: Both **Throws:** Right **Pos:** 2B **Ht:** 5' 9" **Wt:** 160 **Born:** 11/1/67 **Age:** 28

Year Team	Lg	G	AB	H	2B	3B	HR	(Hm	Rd)	TB	R	RBI	TBB	IBB	SO	HBP	SH	SF	SB	CS	SB%	GDP	Avg	OBP	SLG
1995 Red Sox *	R	13	42	9	3	0	0	--	--	12	12	0	9	0	3	0	1	0	0	1	.00	1	.214	.353	.286
Pawtucket *	AAA	40	133	39	7	0	0	--	--	46	19	13	20	0	8	1	1	2	1	0	1.00	4	.293	.385	.346
1991 New York	AL	15	37	7	0	0	0	(0	0)	7	1	2	1	0	2	0	1	0	0	0	.00	3	.189	.211	.189
1994 Boston	AL	57	174	50	14	1	1	(0	1)	69	15	13	11	0	13	0	7	0	1	0	1.00	3	.287	.330	.397
1995 Boston	AL	13	30	10	2	0	0	(0	0)	12	5	5	2	0	2	1	3	0	0	0	.00	0	.333	.394	.400
3 ML YEARS		85	241	67	16	1	1	(0	1)	88	21	20	14	0	17	1	11	0	1	0	1.00	6	.278	.320	.365

Felix Rodriguez

Pitches: Right **Bats:** Right **Pos:** RP **Ht:** 6' 1" **Wt:** 180 **Born:** 12/5/72 **Age:** 23

Year Team	Lg	G	GS	CG	GF	IP	BFP	H	R	ER	HR	SH	SF	HB	TBB	IBB	SO	WP	Bk	W	L	Pct.	ShO	Sv	ERA
1993 Vero Beach	A	32	20	2	7	132	570	109	71	55	15	6	3	6	71	1	80	9	6	8	8	.500	1	0	3.75
1994 San Antonio	AA	26	26	0	0	136.1	588	106	70	61	8	6	7	4	88	3	126	4	1	6	8	.429	0	0	4.03
1995 Albuquerque	AAA	14	11	0	0	51	224	52	29	24	5	4	1	0	26	0	46	0	1	3	2	.600	0	0	4.24
1995 Los Angeles	NL	11	0	0	5	10.2	45	11	3	3	2	0	0	0	5	0	5	0	0	1	1	.500	0	0	2.53

Frank Rodriguez

Pitches: Right **Bats:** Right **Pos:** SP/RP **Ht:** 6' 0" **Wt:** 195 **Born:** 12/11/72 **Age:** 23

Year Team	Lg	G	GS	CG	GF	IP	BFP	H	R	ER	HR	SH	SF	HB	TBB	IBB	SO	WP	Bk	W	L	Pct.	ShO	Sv	ERA
1992 Lynchburg	A	25	25	1	0	148.2	619	125	56	51	11	5	2	6	65	0	129	6	3	12	7	.632	2	0	3.09
1993 New Britain	AA	28	26	4	1	170.2	722	147	79	71	17	2	2	4	78	4	151	7	3	7	11	.389	1	0	3.74
1994 Pawtucket	AAA	28	28	8	0	186	789	182	95	81	18	3	4	8	60	0	160	5	0	8	13	.381	1	0	3.92
1995 Pawtucket	AAA	13	2	0	8	27	109	19	12	12	2	0	0	3	8	0	18	1	0	1	1	.500	0	2	4.00
1995 Bos-Min	AL	25	18	0	1	105.2	478	114	83	72	11	1	4	5	57	1	59	9	0	5	8	.385	0	0	6.13
1995 Boston	AL	9	2	0	1	15.1	75	21	19	18	3	0	0	0	10	1	14	4	0	0	2	.000	0	0	10.57
Minnesota	AL	16	16	0	0	90.1	403	93	64	54	8	1	4	5	47	0	45	5	0	5	6	.455	0	0	5.38

Henry Rodriguez

Bats: Left **Throws:** Left **Pos:** RF/1B **Ht:** 6' 1" **Wt:** 210 **Born:** 11/8/67 **Age:** 28

Year Team	Lg	G	AB	H	2B	3B	HR	(Hm	Rd)	TB	R	RBI	TBB	IBB	SO	HBP	SH	SF	SB	CS	SB%	GDP	Avg	OBP	SLG
1995 Ottawa *	AAA	4	15	3	1	0	0	--	--	4	0	2	1	0	4	0	0	0	0	0	.00	0	.200	.250	.267
1992 Los Angeles	NL	53	146	32	7	0	3	(2	1)	48	11	14	8	0	30	0	1	1	0	0	.00	2	.219	.258	.329
1993 Los Angeles	NL	76	176	39	10	0	8	(5	3)	73	20	23	11	2	39	0	0	1	1	0	1.00	1	.222	.266	.415
1994 Los Angeles	NL	104	306	82	14	2	8	(5	3)	124	33	49	17	2	58	2	1	4	0	1	.00	9	.268	.307	.405
1995 LA-Mon	NL	45	138	33	4	1	2	(1	1)	45	13	15	11	2	28	0	0	0	0	0	.00	5	.239	.293	.326
1995 Los Angeles	NL	21	80	21	4	1	1	(0	1)	30	6	10	5	2	17	0	0	0	0	1	.00	3	.263	.306	.375
Montreal	NL	24	58	12	0	0	1	(1	0)	15	7	5	6	0	11	0	0	0	0	0	.00	5	.207	.277	.259
4 ML YEARS		278	766	186	35	3	21	(13	8)	290	77	101	47	6	155	2	2	7	1	2	.33	17	.243	.286	.379

Ivan Rodriguez

Bats: Right **Throws:** Right **Pos:** C **Ht:** 5' 9" **Wt:** 205 **Born:** 11/30/71 **Age:** 24

Year Team	Lg	G	AB	H	2B	3B	HR	(Hm	Rd)	TB	R	RBI	TBB	IBB	SO	HBP	SH	SF	SB	CS	SB%	GDP	Avg	OBP	SLG
1991 Texas	AL	88	280	74	16	0	3	(3	0)	99	24	27	5	0	42	0	2	1	0	1	.00	10	.264	.276	.354
1992 Texas	AL	123	420	109	16	1	8	(4	4)	151	39	37	24	2	73	1	7	2	0	0	.00	15	.260	.300	.360
1993 Texas	AL	137	473	129	28	4	10	(7	3)	195	56	66	29	3	70	4	5	8	8	7	.53	16	.273	.315	.412
1994 Texas	AL	99	363	108	19	1	16	(7	9)	177	56	57	31	5	42	7	0	4	6	3	.67	10	.298	.360	.488
1995 Texas	AL	130	492	149	32	2	12	(5	7)	221	56	67	16	2	48	4	0	5	0	2	.00	11	.303	.327	.449
5 ML YEARS		577	2028	569	111	8	49	(26	23)	843	231	254	105	12	275	16	14	20	14	13	.52	62	.281	.318	.416

Rich Rodriguez

Pitches: Left **Bats:** Left **Pos:** RP   **Ht:** 6' 0" **Wt:** 200 **Born:** 3/1/63 **Age:** 33

		HOW MUCH HE PITCHED						WHAT HE GAVE UP										THE RESULTS				
Year Team	Lg	G	GS	CG	GF	IP	BFP	H	R	ER	HR	SH	SF	HB	TBB	IBB	SO	WP	Bk	W	L	Pct.	ShO	Sv	ERA
1990 San Diego	NL	32	0	0	15	47.2	201	52	17	15	2	2	1	0	16	4	22	1	1	1	1	.500	0	1	2.83
1991 San Diego	NL	64	1	0	19	80	335	66	31	29	8	7	2	0	44	8	40	4	1	3	1	.750	0	0	3.26
1992 San Diego	NL	61	1	0	15	91	369	77	28	24	4	2	2	0	29	4	64	1	1	6	3	.667	0	0	2.37
1993 SD-Fla	NL	70	0	0	21	76	331	73	38	32	10	5	0	2	33	8	43	3	0	2	4	.333	0	3	3.79
1994 St. Louis	NL	56	0	0	15	60.1	260	62	30	27	6	2	1	1	26	4	43	4	0	3	5	.375	0	0	4.03
1995 St. Louis	NL	1	0	0	0	1.2	4	0	0	0	0	0	0	0	0	0	0	0	0	0	0	.000	0	0	0.00
1993 San Diego	NL	34	0	0	10	30	133	34	15	11	2	2	0	1	9	3	22	1	0	2	3	.400	0	2	3.30
Florida	NL	36	0	0	11	46	198	39	23	21	8	3	0	1	24	5	21	2	0	0	1	.000	0	1	4.11
6 ML YEARS		284	2	0	85	356.2	1500	330	144	127	30	18	6	4	148	28	212	13	3	15	14	.517	0	4	3.20

Steve Rodriguez

Bats: Right **Throws:** Right **Pos:** 2B   **Ht:** 5' 8" **Wt:** 170 **Born:** 11/29/70 **Age:** 25

		BATTING																BASERUNNING				PERCENTAGES		
Year Team	Lg	G	AB	H	2B	3B	HR	(Hm	Rd)	TB	R	RBI	TBB	IBB	SO	HBP	SH	SF	SB	CS	SB%	GDP	Avg	OBP	SLG
1992 Winter Havn	A	26	87	15	0	0	1	--	--	18	13	5	9	0	17	2	3	0	4	1	.80	3	.172	.265	.207
1993 Lynchburg	A	120	493	135	26	3	3	--	--	176	78	42	31	0	69	4	8	3	20	13	.61	15	.274	.320	.357
1994 New Britain	AA	38	159	45	5	2	0	--	--	54	25	14	9	0	14	1	3	1	8	4	.67	3	.283	.324	.340
Pawtucket	AAA	62	233	70	11	0	1	--	--	84	28	21	14	0	30	1	3	2	11	3	.79	6	.300	.340	.361
1995 Pawtucket	AAA	82	324	78	16	3	1	--	--	103	39	24	25	1	34	4	2	3	12	10	.55	7	.241	.301	.318
1995 Bos-Det	AL	18	39	7	1	0	0	(0	0)	8	5	0	6	0	10	0	1	0	2	2	.50	1	.179	.289	.205
1995 Boston	AL	6	8	1	0	0	0	(0	0)	1	1	0	1	0	1	0	0	0	0	1	1.00	0	.125	.222	.125
Detroit	AL	12	31	6	1	0	0	(0	0)	7	4	0	5	0	9	0	1	0	2	1	.33	1	.194	.306	.226

Jimmy Rogers

Pitches: Right **Bats:** Right **Pos:** RP   **Ht:** 6' 2" **Wt:** 200 **Born:** 1/3/67 **Age:** 29

		HOW MUCH HE PITCHED						WHAT HE GAVE UP										THE RESULTS				
Year Team	Lg	G	GS	CG	GF	IP	BFP	H	R	ER	HR	SH	SF	HB	TBB	IBB	SO	WP	Bk	W	L	Pct.	ShO	Sv	ERA
1987 St. Cathrns	A	13	12	0	0	56.1	241	46	33	21	4	2	0	4	24	0	60	5	0	2	4	.333	0	0	3.36
1988 Myrtle Bch	A	33	32	2	0	188.1	803	145	84	70	10	1	6	5	95	1	198	15	6	18	4	.818	0	0	3.35
1989 Knoxville	AA	32	30	1	0	158	718	136	89	80	12	4	3	5	132	1	120	14	3	12	10	.545	0	0	4.56
1990 Knoxville	AA	31	30	2	0	173.1	789	179	98	86	8	6	12	6	104	1	113	12	4	9	12	.429	1	0	4.47
1991 Knoxville	AA	28	27	4	0	168.1	706	139	70	62	7	4	3	6	90	0	122	11	1	7	11	.389	3	0	3.31
1993 Knoxville	AA	19	19	0	0	100.1	431	107	54	45	9	3	2	2	33	1	80	5	0	7	7	.500	0	0	4.04
1994 Syracuse	AAA	31	10	0	5	94	404	82	51	48	7	0	5	0	49	1	69	4	0	5	4	.556	0	0	4.60
1995 Syracuse	AAA	38	0	0	9	73.2	308	65	26	25	4	3	3	3	31	2	82	6	0	3	4	.429	0	1	3.05
1995 Toronto	AL	19	0	0	9	23.2	110	21	15	15	4	3	1	0	18	4	13	0	0	2	4	.333	0	0	5.70

Kenny Rogers

Pitches: Left **Bats:** Left **Pos:** SP   **Ht:** 6' 1" **Wt:** 205 **Born:** 11/10/64 **Age:** 31

		HOW MUCH HE PITCHED						WHAT HE GAVE UP										THE RESULTS				
Year Team	Lg	G	GS	CG	GF	IP	BFP	H	R	ER	HR	SH	SF	HB	TBB	IBB	SO	WP	Bk	W	L	Pct.	ShO	Sv	ERA
1989 Texas	AL	73	0	0	24	73.2	314	60	28	24	2	6	3	4	42	9	63	6	0	3	4	.429	0	2	2.93
1990 Texas	AL	69	3	0	46	97.2	428	93	40	34	6	7	4	1	42	5	74	5	0	10	6	.625	0	15	3.13
1991 Texas	AL	63	9	0	20	109.2	511	121	80	66	14	9	5	6	61	7	73	3	1	10	10	.500	0	5	5.42
1992 Texas	AL	81	0	0	38	78.2	337	80	32	27	7	4	1	0	26	8	70	4	1	3	6	.333	0	6	3.09
1993 Texas	AL	35	33	5	0	208.1	885	210	108	95	18	7	5	4	71	2	140	6	5	16	10	.615	0	0	4.10
1994 Texas	AL	24	24	6	0	167.1	714	169	93	83	24	3	6	3	52	1	120	3	1	11	8	.579	2	0	4.46
1995 Texas	AL	31	31	3	0	208	877	192	87	78	26	3	5	2	76	1	140	8	1	17	7	.708	1	0	3.38
7 ML YEARS		376	100	14	128	943.1	4066	925	468	407	97	39	29	20	370	33	680	35	9	70	51	.579	3	28	3.88

Kevin Rogers

Pitches: Left **Bats:** Both **Pos:** RP   **Ht:** 6' 2" **Wt:** 198 **Born:** 8/20/68 **Age:** 27

		HOW MUCH HE PITCHED						WHAT HE GAVE UP										THE RESULTS				
Year Team	Lg	G	GS	CG	GF	IP	BFP	H	R	ER	HR	SH	SF	HB	TBB	IBB	SO	WP	Bk	W	L	Pct.	ShO	Sv	ERA
1992 San Francisco	NL	6	6	0	0	34	148	37	17	16	4	2	0	1	13	1	26	2	0	0	2	.000	0	0	4.24
1993 San Francisco	NL	64	0	0	24	80.2	334	71	28	24	3	0	1	4	28	5	62	3	0	2	2	.500	0	0	2.68
1994 San Francisco	NL	9	0	0	2	10.1	46	10	4	4	1	0	0	0	6	0	7	0	0	0	0	.000	0	0	3.48
3 ML YEARS		79	6	0	26	125	528	118	49	44	8	2	1	5	47	6	95	5	0	2	4	.333	0	0	3.17

Mel Rojas

Pitches: Right **Bats:** Right **Pos:** RP   **Ht:** 5'11" **Wt:** 195 **Born:** 12/10/66 **Age:** 29

Year Team	Lg	G	GS	CG	GF	IP	BFP	H	R	ER	HR	SH	SF	HB	TBB	IBB	SO	WP	Bk	W	L	Pct.	ShO	Sv	ERA
1990 Montreal	NL	23	0	0	5	40	173	34	17	16	5	2	0	2	24	4	26	2	0	3	1	.750	0	1	3.60
1991 Montreal	NL	37	0	0	13	48	200	42	21	20	4	0	2	1	13	1	37	3	0	3	3	.500	0	6	3.75
1992 Montreal	NL	68	0	0	26	100.2	399	71	17	16	2	4	2	2	34	8	70	2	0	7	1	.875	0	10	1.43
1993 Montreal	NL	66	0	0	25	88.1	378	80	39	29	6	8	6	4	30	3	48	5	0	5	8	.385	0	10	2.95
1994 Montreal	NL	58	0	0	27	84	341	71	35	31	11	2	1	4	21	0	84	3	0	3	2	.600	0	16	3.32
1995 Montreal	NL	59	0	0	48	67.2	302	69	32	31	2	2	1	7	29	4	61	6	0	1	4	.200	0	30	4.12
6 ML YEARS		311	0	0	144	428.2	1793	367	161	143	30	18	12	20	151	20	326	21	0	22	19	.537	0	73	3.00

John Roper

Pitches: Right **Bats:** Right **Pos:** SP   **Ht:** 6' 0" **Wt:** 175 **Born:** 11/21/71 **Age:** 24

Year Team	Lg	G	GS	CG	GF	IP	BFP	H	R	ER	HR	SH	SF	HB	TBB	IBB	SO	WP	Bk	W	L	Pct.	ShO	Sv	ERA
1995 Chattanooga *	AA	3	3	0	0	9	33	5	1	1	0	0	0	0	1	0	6	0	0	0	0	.000	0	0	1.00
Indianapols *	AAA	8	8	0	0	41.2	186	47	26	23	9	0	0	1	16	1	23	4	0	2	5	.286	0	0	4.97
Phoenix *	AAA	1	1	0	0	3	14	5	3	3	0	0	1	0	0	0	2	0	0	0	1	.000	0	0	9.00
1993 Cincinnati	NL	16	15	0	0	80	360	92	51	50	10	5	3	4	36	3	54	5	1	2	5	.286	0	0	5.63
1994 Cincinnati	NL	16	15	0	0	92	390	90	49	46	16	0	3	4	30	0	51	4	0	6	2	.750	0	0	4.50
1995 Cin-SF	NL	3	2	0	0	8	44	15	12	11	3	1	1	0	6	0	6	0	1	0	0	.000	0	0	12.38
1995 Cincinnati	NL	2	2	0	0	7	37	13	9	8	3	1	0	0	4	0	6	0	1	0	0	.000	0	0	10.29
San Francisco	NL	1	0	0	0	1	7	2	3	3	0	0	1	0	2	0	0	0	0	0	0	.000	0	0	27.00
3 ML YEARS		35	32	0	0	180	794	197	112	107	29	6	7	8	72	3	111	9	3	8	7	.533	0	0	5.35

Joe Rosselli

Pitches: Left **Bats:** Right **Pos:** SP   **Ht:** 6' 1" **Wt:** 170 **Born:** 5/28/72 **Age:** 24

Year Team	Lg	G	GS	CG	GF	IP	BFP	H	R	ER	HR	SH	SF	HB	TBB	IBB	SO	WP	Bk	W	L	Pct.	ShO	Sv	ERA
1990 Everett	A	15	15	0	0	78.1	340	87	47	41	10	0	2	0	29	0	90	4	0	4	4	.500	0	0	4.71
1991 Clinton	A	22	22	2	0	153.2	640	144	70	53	5	4	8	1	49	0	127	11	4	8	7	.533	0	0	3.10
1992 San Jose	A	22	22	4	0	149.2	614	145	50	40	7	2	2	2	46	1	111	2	4	11	4	.733	0	0	2.41
1993 Shreveport	AA	4	4	0	0	23	96	22	9	8	1	0	0	0	7	0	19	1	0	0	1	.000	0	0	3.13
1994 Shreveport	AA	14	14	2	0	90.2	350	67	24	19	2	6	2	0	17	0	54	1	0	7	2	.778	2	0	1.89
Phoenix	AAA	13	13	0	0	74.2	322	96	46	41	10	6	1	1	15	0	35	1	1	1	8	.111	0	0	4.94
1995 Phoenix	AAA	13	13	1	0	79.1	332	94	47	44	8	2	4	0	12	0	34	2	0	4	3	.571	0	0	4.99
1995 San Francisco	NL	9	5	0	0	30	140	39	29	29	5	2	4	0	20	2	7	0	1	2	1	.667	0	0	8.70

Rich Rowland

Bats: Right **Throws:** Right **Pos:** C   **Ht:** 6' 1" **Wt:** 215 **Born:** 2/25/64 **Age:** 32

Year Team	Lg	G	AB	H	2B	3B	HR	(Hm	Rd)	TB	R	RBI	TBB	IBB	SO	HBP	SH	SF	SB	CS	SB%	GDP	Avg	OBP	SLG
1995 Pawtucket *	AAA	34	124	32	7	0	8	--	--	63	20	24	7	1	24	1	0	1	0	1	.00	2	.258	.301	.508
1990 Detroit	AL	7	19	3	1	0	0	(0	0)	4	3	0	2	1	4	0	0	0	0	0	.00	1	.158	.238	.211
1991 Detroit	AL	4	4	1	0	0	0	(0	0)	1	0	1	1	0	2	0	0	1	0	0	.00	0	.250	.333	.250
1992 Detroit	AL	6	14	3	0	0	0	(0	0)	3	2	0	3	0	3	0	0	0	0	0	.00	1	.214	.353	.214
1993 Detroit	AL	21	46	10	3	0	0	(0	0)	13	2	4	5	0	16	0	1	0	0	0	.00	1	.217	.294	.283
1994 Boston	AL	46	118	27	3	0	9	(3	6)	57	14	20	11	0	35	0	0	0	0	0	.00	2	.229	.295	.483
1995 Boston	AL	14	29	5	1	0	0	(0	0)	6	1	1	0	0	11	0	0	0	0	0	.00	0	.172	.172	.207
6 ML YEARS		98	230	49	8	0	9	(3	6)	84	22	26	22	1	71	0	1	1	0	0	.00	5	.213	.281	.365

Kirk Rueter

Pitches: Left **Bats:** Left **Pos:** SP   **Ht:** 6' 3" **Wt:** 195 **Born:** 12/1/70 **Age:** 25

Year Team	Lg	G	GS	CG	GF	IP	BFP	H	R	ER	HR	SH	SF	HB	TBB	IBB	SO	WP	Bk	W	L	Pct.	ShO	Sv	ERA
1995 Ottawa *	AAA	20	20	3	0	120.2	498	120	50	41	7	8	3	1	25	0	67	2	1	9	7	.563	0	0	3.06
1993 Montreal	NL	14	14	1	0	85.2	341	85	33	26	5	1	0	0	18	1	31	0	0	8	0	1.000	0	0	2.73
1994 Montreal	NL	20	20	0	0	92.1	397	106	60	53	11	6	6	2	23	1	50	2	0	7	3	.700	0	0	5.17
1995 Montreal	NL	9	9	1	0	47.1	184	38	17	17	3	4	0	1	9	0	28	0	0	5	3	.625	1	0	3.23
3 ML YEARS		43	43	2	0	225.1	922	229	110	96	19	11	6	3	50	2	109	2	0	20	6	.769	1	0	3.83

Scott Ruffcorn

Pitches: Right **Bats:** Right **Pos:** RP **Ht:** 6' 4" **Wt:** 210 **Born:** 12/29/69 **Age:** 26

Year Team	Lg	G	GS	CG	GF	IP	BFP	H	R	ER	HR	SH	SF	HB	TBB	IBB	SO	WP	Bk	W	L	Pct.	ShO	Sv	ERA
1991 White Sox	R	4	2	0	1	11.1	49	8	7	4	0	0	0	0	5	0	15	1	1	0	0	.000	0	0	3.18
South Bend	A	9	9	0	0	43.2	193	35	26	19	1	2	1	2	25	0	45	1	2	1	3	.250	0	0	3.92
1992 Sarasota	A	25	24	2	0	160.1	642	122	53	39	7	4	5	3	39	0	140	3	1	14	5	.737	0	0	2.19
1993 Birmingham	AA	20	20	3	0	135	563	108	47	41	6	5	0	4	52	0	141	7	0	9	4	.692	3	0	2.73
Nashville	AAA	7	6	1	0	45	172	30	16	14	5	2	1	0	8	1	44	3	0	2	2	.500	0	0	2.80
1994 Nashville	AAA	24	24	3	0	165.2	672	139	57	50	5	3	6	6	40	1	144	6	0	15	3	.833	3	0	2.72
1995 Nashville	AAA	2	2	0	0	0.1	9	3	4	4	0	0	0	2	3	0	1	1	0	0	0	.000	0	0	99.99
White Sox	R	3	3	0	0	10	46	7	4	1	0	0	1	0	5	0	7	1	0	0	0	.000	0	0	0.90
Birmingham	AA	3	3	0	0	16	71	17	11	10	0	0	0	0	10	0	13	2	0	0	0	.000	0	0	5.63
1993 Chicago	AL	3	2	0	1	10	46	11	9	9	2	1	1	0	10	0	2	1	0	0	2	.000	0	0	8.10
1994 Chicago	AL	2	2	0	0	6.1	39	15	11	9	1	0	1	0	5	0	3	0	0	0	2	.000	0	0	12.79
1995 Chicago	AL	4	0	0	0	8	46	10	7	7	0	1	0	2	13	0	5	1	0	0	0	.000	0	0	7.88
3 ML YEARS		9	4	0	1	24.1	131	34	29	25	3	2	2	2	28	0	10	1	0	0	4	.000	0	0	9.25

Bruce Ruffin

Pitches: Left **Bats:** Both **Pos:** RP **Ht:** 6' 2" **Wt:** 213 **Born:** 10/4/63 **Age:** 32

Year Team	Lg	G	GS	CG	GF	IP	BFP	H	R	ER	HR	SH	SF	HB	TBB	IBB	SO	WP	Bk	W	L	Pct.	ShO	Sv	ERA
1995 New Haven *	AA	2	2	0	0	2	7	1	0	0	0	0	0	0	0	0	2	0	0	0	0	.000	0	0	0.00
1986 Philadelphia	NL	21	21	6	0	146.1	600	138	53	40	6	2	4	1	44	6	70	0	1	9	4	.692	0	0	2.46
1987 Philadelphia	NL	35	35	3	0	204.2	884	236	118	99	17	8	10	2	73	4	93	6	0	11	14	.440	1	0	4.35
1988 Philadelphia	NL	55	15	3	14	144.1	646	151	86	71	7	10	3	3	80	6	82	12	0	6	10	.375	0	3	4.43
1989 Philadelphia	NL	24	23	1	0	125.2	576	152	69	62	10	8	1	0	62	6	70	8	0	6	10	.375	0	0	4.44
1990 Philadelphia	NL	32	25	2	1	149	678	178	99	89	14	10	6	1	62	7	79	3	2	6	13	.316	1	0	5.38
1991 Philadelphia	NL	31	15	1	2	119	508	125	52	50	6	6	4	1	38	3	85	4	0	4	7	.364	1	0	3.78
1992 Milwaukee	AL	25	6	1	6	58	272	66	43	43	7	3	3	0	41	3	45	2	0	1	6	.143	0	0	6.67
1993 Colorado	NL	59	12	0	8	139.2	619	145	71	60	10	4	5	1	69	9	126	8	0	6	5	.545	0	2	3.87
1994 Colorado	NL	56	0	0	39	55.2	252	55	28	25	6	1	3	1	30	2	65	5	0	4	5	.444	0	16	4.04
1995 Colorado	NL	37	0	0	19	34	140	26	8	8	1	4	0	0	19	1	23	1	0	0	1	.000	0	11	2.12
10 ML YEARS		375	152	17	89	1176.1	5175	1272	627	547	84	56	39	10	518	47	738	49	3	53	75	.414	3	32	4.19

Johnny Ruffin

Pitches: Right **Bats:** Right **Pos:** RP **Ht:** 6' 3" **Wt:** 170 **Born:** 7/29/71 **Age:** 24

Year Team	Lg	G	GS	CG	GF	IP	BFP	H	R	ER	HR	SH	SF	HB	TBB	IBB	SO	WP	Bk	W	L	Pct.	ShO	Sv	ERA
1995 Indianapols *	AAA	36	1	0	4	49.2	213	27	19	16	3	2	1	0	37	2	58	7	0	3	1	.750	0	2	2.90
1993 Cincinnati	NL	21	0	0	5	37.2	159	36	16	15	4	1	0	1	11	1	30	2	0	2	1	.667	0	2	3.58
1994 Cincinnati	NL	51	0	0	13	70	287	57	26	24	7	2	2	0	27	3	44	5	1	7	2	.778	0	1	3.09
1995 Cincinnati	NL	10	0	0	6	13.1	54	4	3	2	0	0	0	0	11	0	11	3	0	0	0	.000	0	0	1.35
3 ML YEARS		82	0	0	24	121	500	97	45	41	11	3	2	1	49	4	85	10	1	9	3	.750	0	3	3.05

Jeff Russell

Pitches: Right **Bats:** Right **Pos:** RP **Ht:** 6' 3" **Wt:** 205 **Born:** 9/2/61 **Age:** 34

Year Team	Lg	G	GS	CG	GF	IP	BFP	H	R	ER	HR	SH	SF	HB	TBB	IBB	SO	WP	Bk	W	L	Pct.	ShO	Sv	ERA
1983 Cincinnati	NL	10	10	2	0	68.1	282	58	30	23	7	6	5	0	22	3	40	1	1	4	5	.444	0	0	3.03
1984 Cincinnati	NL	33	30	4	1	181.2	787	186	97	86	15	8	3	4	65	8	101	3	3	6	18	.250	2	0	4.26
1985 Texas	AL	13	13	0	0	62	295	85	55	52	10	1	3	2	27	1	44	2	0	3	6	.333	0	0	7.55
1986 Texas	AL	37	0	0	9	82	338	74	40	31	11	1	2	1	31	2	54	5	0	5	2	.714	0	2	3.40
1987 Texas	AL	52	2	0	12	97.1	442	109	56	48	9	0	5	2	52	5	56	6	1	5	4	.556	0	3	4.44
1988 Texas	AL	34	24	5	1	188.2	793	183	86	80	15	4	3	7	66	3	88	5	7	10	9	.526	0	3	3.82
1989 Texas	AL	71	0	0	66	72.2	278	45	21	16	4	1	3	3	24	5	77	6	0	6	4	.600	0	38	1.98
1990 Texas	AL	27	0	0	22	25.1	111	23	15	12	1	3	1	0	16	5	16	2	0	1	5	.167	0	10	4.26
1991 Texas	AL	68	0	0	56	79.1	336	71	36	29	11	3	4	1	26	1	52	6	0	6	4	.600	0	30	3.29
1992 Oak-Tex	AL	59	0	0	46	66.1	276	55	14	12	3	1	2	2	25	3	48	3	0	4	3	.571	0	30	1.63
1993 Boston	AL	51	0	0	48	46.2	189	39	16	14	1	4	1	4	14	1	45	2	0	1	4	.200	0	33	2.70
1994 Bos-Cle	AL	42	0	0	36	40.2	179	43	25	23	5	0	2	1	16	2	28	1	0	1	6	.143	0	17	5.09
1995 Texas	AL	37	0	0	32	32.2	139	36	12	11	3	0	0	0	9	1	21	1	0	1	0	1.000	0	20	3.03
1992 Oakland	AL	8	0	0	4	9.2	35	4	0	0	0	0	0	0	3	0	5	0	0	2	0	1.000	0	2	0.00
Texas	AL	51	0	0	42	56.2	241	51	14	12	3	1	2	2	22	3	43	3	0	2	3	.400	0	28	1.91
1994 Boston	AL	29	0	0	25	28	127	30	17	16	3	0	2	1	13	2	18	1	0	0	5	.000	0	12	5.14
Cleveland	AL	13	0	0	11	12.2	52	13	8	7	2	0	0	0	3	0	10	0	0	1	1	.500	0	5	4.97
13 ML YEARS		534	79	11	329	1043.2	4445	1007	503	437	95	29	37	24	393	40	670	43	12	53	70	.431	2	183	3.77

Ken Ryan

Pitches: Right **Bats:** Right **Pos:** RP **Ht:** 6' 3" **Wt:** 230 **Born:** 10/24/68 **Age:** 27

Year Team	Lg	G	GS	CG	GF	IP	BFP	H	R	ER	HR	SH	SF	HB	TBB	IBB	SO	WP	Bk	W	L	Pct.	ShO	Sv	ERA
1995 Trenton *	AA	11	0	0	7	17	79	23	13	11	1	1	0	0	5	0	16	0	0	0	2	.000	0	2	5.82
Pawtucket *	AAA	9	0	0	5	10	42	12	7	7	1	0	1	0	4	0	6	1	0	0	1	.000	0	0	6.30
1992 Boston	AL	7	0	0	6	7	30	4	5	5	2	1	1	0	5	0	5	0	0	0	0	.000	0	1	6.43
1993 Boston	AL	47	0	0	26	50	223	43	23	20	2	4	4	3	29	5	49	3	0	7	2	.778	0	1	3.60
1994 Boston	AL	42	0	0	26	48	202	46	14	13	1	4	0	1	17	3	32	2	0	2	3	.400	0	13	2.44
1995 Boston	AL	28	0	0	20	32.2	153	34	20	18	4	1	0	1	24	6	34	1	0	0	4	.000	0	7	4.96
4 ML YEARS		124	0	0	78	137.2	608	127	62	56	9	10	5	5	75	14	120	6	0	9	9	.500	0	22	3.66

Bret Saberhagen

Pitches: Right **Bats:** Right **Pos:** SP **Ht:** 6' 1" **Wt:** 200 **Born:** 4/11/64 **Age:** 32

Year Team	Lg	G	GS	CG	GF	IP	BFP	H	R	ER	HR	SH	SF	HB	TBB	IBB	SO	WP	Bk	W	L	Pct.	ShO	Sv	ERA
1984 Kansas City	AL	38	18	2	9	157.2	634	138	71	61	13	8	5	2	36	4	73	7	1	10	11	.476	1	1	3.48
1985 Kansas City	AL	32	32	10	0	235.1	931	211	79	75	19	9	7	1	38	1	158	1	3	20	6	.769	1	0	2.87
1986 Kansas City	AL	30	25	4	4	156	652	165	77	72	15	3	3	2	29	1	112	1	1	7	12	.368	2	0	4.15
1987 Kansas City	AL	33	33	15	0	257	1048	246	99	96	27	8	5	6	53	2	163	6	1	18	10	.643	4	0	3.36
1988 Kansas City	AL	35	35	9	0	260.2	1089	271	122	110	18	8	10	4	59	5	171	9	0	14	16	.467	0	0	3.80
1989 Kansas City	AL	36	35	12	0	262.1	1021	209	74	63	13	9	6	2	43	6	193	8	1	23	6	.793	4	0	2.16
1990 Kansas City	AL	20	20	5	0	135	561	146	52	49	9	4	4	1	28	1	87	1	0	5	9	.357	0	0	3.27
1991 Kansas City	AL	28	28	7	0	196.1	789	165	76	67	12	8	3	9	45	5	136	8	1	13	8	.619	2	0	3.07
1992 New York	NL	17	15	1	0	97.2	397	84	39	38	6	3	3	4	27	1	81	1	2	3	5	.375	1	0	3.50
1993 New York	NL	19	19	4	0	139.1	556	131	55	51	11	6	6	3	17	4	93	2	2	7	7	.500	1	0	3.29
1994 New York	NL	24	24	4	0	177.1	696	169	58	54	13	9	5	4	13	0	143	0	0	14	4	.778	1	0	2.74
1995 NYN-Col	NL	25	25	3	0	153	658	165	71	64	21	7	3	10	33	3	100	3	0	7	6	.538	0	0	4.18
1995 New York	NL	16	16	3	0	110	452	105	45	41	13	5	3	5	20	2	71	2	0	5	5	.500	0	0	3.35
Colorado	NL	9	9	0	0	43	206	60	33	30	8	2	0	5	13	1	29	1	0	2	1	.667	0	0	6.28
12 ML YEARS		337	309	76	13	2227.2	9032	2100	880	807	177	82	60	48	421	33	1510	47	12	141	100	.585	16	1	3.26

Chris Sabo

Bats: Right **Throws:** Right **Pos:** DH **Ht:** 6' 0" **Wt:** 185 **Born:** 1/19/62 **Age:** 34

Year Team	Lg	G	AB	H	2B	3B	HR	(Hm	Rd)	TB	R	RBI	TBB	IBB	SO	HBP	SH	SF	SB	CS	SB%	GDP	Avg	OBP	SLG
1995 Louisville *	AAA	9	28	11	0	0	1	--	--	14	5	4	1	0	4	1	0	0	0	0	.00	0	.393	.433	.500
St. Pete *	A	14	39	9	0	0	2	--	--	15	10	7	10	0	6	1	0	0	1	0	1.00	0	.231	.400	.385
1988 Cincinnati	NL	137	538	146	40	2	11	(8	3)	223	74	44	29	1	52	6	5	4	46	14	.77	12	.271	.314	.414
1989 Cincinnati	NL	82	304	79	21	1	6	(3	3)	120	40	29	25	2	33	1	4	2	14	9	.61	2	.260	.316	.395
1990 Cincinnati	NL	148	567	153	38	2	25	(15	10)	270	95	71	61	7	58	4	1	3	25	10	.71	8	.270	.343	.476
1991 Cincinnati	NL	153	582	175	35	3	26	(15	11)	294	91	88	44	3	79	6	5	3	19	6	.76	13	.301	.354	.505
1992 Cincinnati	NL	96	344	84	19	3	12	(8	4)	145	42	43	30	1	54	1	1	6	4	5	.44	12	.244	.302	.422
1993 Cincinnati	NL	148	552	143	33	2	21	(12	9)	243	86	82	43	5	105	6	2	8	6	4	.60	10	.259	.315	.440
1994 Baltimore	AL	68	258	66	15	3	11	(8	3)	120	41	42	20	2	38	5	4	1	1	1	.50	8	.256	.320	.465
1995 ChA-StL		25	84	20	6	0	1	(1	0)	29	10	11	4	1	14	2	2	2	3	1	1.00	1	.238	.283	.345
1995 Chicago	AL	20	71	18	5	0	1	(1	0)	26	10	8	3	1	12	2	2	2	2	0	1.00	1	.254	.295	.366
St. Louis	NL	5	13	2	1	0	0	(0	0)	3	0	3	1	0	2	0	0	0	1	0	1.00	0	.154	.214	.231
8 ML YEARS		857	3229	866	207	16	113	(65	48)	1444	479	410	256	22	433	31	24	29	118	49	.71	66	.268	.325	.447

A.J. Sager

Pitches: Right **Bats:** Right **Pos:** RP **Ht:** 6' 4" **Wt:** 220 **Born:** 3/3/65 **Age:** 31

Year Team	Lg	G	GS	CG	GF	IP	BFP	H	R	ER	HR	SH	SF	HB	TBB	IBB	SO	WP	Bk	W	L	Pct.	ShO	Sv	ERA
1988 Spokane	A	15	15	2	0	98.2	443	123	67	56	3	2	5	4	27	1	74	3	2	8	3	.727	0	0	5.11
1989 Charlstn-Sc	A	26	25	6	0	167.2	708	166	77	63	4	4	5	7	40	1	105	10	1	14	9	.609	2	0	3.38
1990 Wichita	AA	26	26	2	0	154.1	686	200	105	94	7	8	4	3	29	0	79	3	3	11	12	.478	1	0	5.48
1991 Wichita	AA	10	10	1	0	65.1	275	69	35	30	5	3	2	0	16	0	31	1	0	4	3	.571	0	0	4.13
Las Vegas	AAA	18	18	3	0	109	458	127	63	57	5	1	4	1	20	3	61	4	1	7	5	.583	2	0	4.71
1992 Las Vegas	AAA	30	3	0	7	60	282	89	57	53	8	0	4	1	17	3	40	3	2	1	7	.125	0	1	7.95
1993 Las Vegas	AA	11	11	2	0	73.1	298	69	30	26	5	3	3	1	16	0	49	1	0	5	3	.625	1	0	3.19
Las Vegas	AAA	21	11	2	3	90	379	91	49	37	7	5	2	5	18	1	58	5	2	6	5	.545	1	0	3.70
1994 Las Vegas	AAA	23	2	0	13	40.2	180	57	24	20	3	1	0	1	8	3	23	1	0	1	4	.200	0	5	4.43
1995 Colo. Sprng	AAA	23	22	1	0	133.2	564	153	61	52	14	4	3	2	23	1	80	0	0	8	5	.615	1	0	3.50
1994 San Diego	NL	22	3	0	4	46.2	217	62	34	31	4	6	2	2	16	5	26	0	0	1	4	.200	0	0	5.98
1995 Colorado	NL	10	0	0	2	14.2	70	19	16	12	2	0	0	0	7	1	10	0	0	0	0	.000	0	0	7.36
2 ML YEARS		32	3	0	6	61.1	287	81	50	43	6	6	2	2	23	6	36	0	0	1	4	.200	0	0	6.31

Tim Salmon

Bats: Right **Throws:** Right **Pos:** RF   **Ht:** 6' 3" **Wt:** 220 **Born:** 8/24/68 **Age:** 27

Year	Team	Lg	G	AB	H	2B	3B	HR	(Hm	Rd)	TB	R	RBI	TBB	IBB	SO	HBP	SH	SF	SB	CS	SB%	GDP	Avg	OBP	SLG
1992	California	AL	23	79	14	1	0	2	(1	1)	21	8	6	11	1	23	1	0	1	1	1	.50	1	.177	.283	.266
1993	California	AL	142	515	146	35	1	31	(23	8)	276	93	95	82	5	135	5	0	8	5	6	.45	1	.283	.382	.536
1994	California	AL	100	373	107	18	2	23	(12	11)	198	67	70	54	2	102	5	0	3	1	3	.25	3	.287	.382	.531
1995	California	AL	143	537	177	34	3	34	(15	19)	319	111	105	91	2	111	6	0	4	5	5	.50	9	.330	.429	.594
	4 ML YEARS		408	1504	444	88	6	90	(51	39)	814	279	276	238	10	371	17	0	16	12	15	.44	19	.295	.394	.541

Juan Samuel

Bats: Right **Throws:** Right **Pos:** 1B/LF/DH   **Ht:** 5'11" **Wt:** 180 **Born:** 12/9/60 **Age:** 35

Year	Team	Lg	G	AB	H	2B	3B	HR	(Hm	Rd)	TB	R	RBI	TBB	IBB	SO	HBP	SH	SF	SB	CS	SB%	GDP	Avg	OBP	SLG
1983	Philadelphia	NL	18	65	18	1	2	2	(1	1)	29	14	5	4	1	16	1	0	1	3	2	.60	1	.277	.324	.446
1984	Philadelphia	NL	160	701	191	36	19	15	(8	7)	310	105	69	28	2	168	7	0	1	72	15	.83	6	.272	.307	.442
1985	Philadelphia	NL	161	663	175	31	13	19	(8	11)	289	101	74	33	2	141	6	2	5	53	19	.74	8	.264	.303	.436
1986	Philadelphia	NL	145	591	157	36	12	16	(10	6)	265	90	78	26	3	142	8	1	7	42	14	.75	8	.266	.302	.448
1987	Philadelphia	NL	160	655	178	37	15	28	(15	13)	329	113	100	60	5	162	5	0	6	35	15	.70	12	.272	.335	.502
1988	Philadelphia	NL	157	629	153	32	9	12	(7	5)	239	68	67	39	6	151	12	0	5	33	10	.77	8	.243	.298	.380
1989	NYN-Phi	NL	137	532	125	16	2	11	(5	6)	178	69	48	42	2	120	11	2	2	42	12	.78	7	.235	.303	.335
1990	Los Angeles	NL	143	492	119	24	3	13	(6	7)	188	62	52	51	5	126	5	5	5	38	20	.66	8	.242	.316	.382
1991	Los Angeles	NL	153	594	161	22	6	12	(4	8)	231	74	58	49	4	133	3	10	3	23	8	.74	8	.271	.328	.389
1992	KC-LA		76	224	61	8	4	0	(0	0)	77	22	23	14	4	49	2	4	2	8	3	.73	2	.272	.318	.344
1993	Cincinnati	NL	103	261	60	10	4	4	(1	3)	90	31	26	23	3	53	3	0	2	9	7	.56	2	.230	.298	.345
1994	Detroit	AL	59	136	42	9	5	5	(4	1)	76	32	21	10	0	26	3	0	2	5	2	.71	4	.309	.364	.559
1995	Det-KC	AL	91	205	54	10	1	12	(6	6)	102	31	39	29	1	49	2	1	0	6	4	.60	3	.263	.360	.498
1989	New York	NL	86	333	76	13	1	3	(2	1)	100	37	28	24	1	75	10	2	1	31	9	.78	5	.228	.299	.300
	Philadelphia	NL	51	199	49	3	1	8	(3	5)	78	32	20	18	1	45	1	0	1	11	3	.79	2	.246	.311	.392
1992	Kansas City	AL	29	102	29	5	3	0	(0	0)	40	15	8	7	1	27	1	0	0	6	1	.86	2	.284	.336	.392
	Los Angeles	NL	47	122	32	3	1	0	(0	0)	37	7	15	7	3	22	1	4	2	2	2	.50	0	.262	.303	.303
1995	Detroit	AL	76	171	48	10	1	10	(6	4)	90	28	34	24	0	38	2	1	0	5	4	.56	3	.281	.376	.526
	Kansas City	AL	15	34	6	0	0	2	(0	2)	12	3	5	5	1	11	0	0	0	1	0	1.00	0	.176	.282	.353
	13 ML YEARS		1563	5748	1494	272	95	149	(75	74)	2403	812	660	408	38	1336	68	25	41	369	131	.74	77	.260	.314	.418

Rey Sanchez

Bats: Right **Throws:** Right **Pos:** 2B   **Ht:** 5' 9" **Wt:** 170 **Born:** 10/5/67 **Age:** 28

Year	Team	Lg	G	AB	H	2B	3B	HR	(Hm	Rd)	TB	R	RBI	TBB	IBB	SO	HBP	SH	SF	SB	CS	SB%	GDP	Avg	OBP	SLG
1991	Chicago	NL	13	23	6	0	0	0	(0	0)	6	1	2	4	0	3	0	0	0	0	0	.00	0	.261	.370	.261
1992	Chicago	NL	74	255	64	14	3	1	(1	0)	87	24	19	10	1	17	3	5	2	2	1	.67	7	.251	.285	.341
1993	Chicago	NL	105	344	97	11	2	0	(0	0)	112	35	28	15	7	22	3	9	2	1	1	.50	8	.282	.316	.326
1994	Chicago	NL	96	291	83	13	1	0	(0	0)	98	26	24	20	4	29	7	4	1	2	5	.29	9	.285	.345	.337
1995	Chicago	NL	114	428	119	22	2	3	(0	3)	154	57	27	14	2	48	1	8	2	6	4	.60	9	.278	.301	.360
	5 ML YEARS		402	1341	369	60	8	4	(1	3)	457	143	100	63	14	119	14	26	7	11	11	.50	33	.275	.313	.341

Deion Sanders

Bats: Left **Throws:** Left **Pos:** CF   **Ht:** 6' 1" **Wt:** 195 **Born:** 8/9/67 **Age:** 28

Year	Team	Lg	G	AB	H	2B	3B	HR	(Hm	Rd)	TB	R	RBI	TBB	IBB	SO	HBP	SH	SF	SB	CS	SB%	GDP	Avg	OBP	SLG
1995	Chattanooga *	AA	2	7	4	0	0	1	--	--	7	1	2	0	0	1	0	0	0	1	0	1.00	0	.571	.571	1.000
1989	New York	AL	14	47	11	2	0	2	(0	2)	19	7	7	3	1	8	0	0	0	1	0	1.00	0	.234	.280	.404
1990	New York	AL	57	133	21	2	2	3	(1	2)	36	24	9	13	0	27	1	1	1	8	2	.80	2	.158	.236	.271
1991	Atlanta	NL	54	110	21	1	2	4	(2	2)	38	16	13	12	0	23	0	0	0	11	3	.79	1	.191	.270	.345
1992	Atlanta	NL	97	303	92	6	14	8	(5	3)	150	54	28	18	0	52	2	1	1	26	9	.74	5	.304	.346	.495
1993	Atlanta	NL	95	272	75	18	6	6	(1	5)	123	42	28	16	3	42	3	1	2	19	7	.73	3	.276	.321	.452
1994	Atl-Cin	NL	92	375	106	17	4	4	(2	2)	143	58	28	32	1	63	3	2	2	38	16	.70	5	.283	.342	.381
1995	Cin-SF	NL	85	343	92	11	8	6	(3	3)	137	48	28	27	0	60	4	3	2	24	9	.73	1	.268	.327	.399
1994	Atlanta	NL	46	191	55	10	0	4	(2	2)	77	32	21	16	1	28	1	1	2	19	7	.73	4	.288	.343	.403
	Cincinnati	NL	46	184	51	7	4	0	(0	0)	66	26	7	16	0	35	2	1	0	19	9	.68	1	.277	.342	.359
1995	Cincinnati	NL	33	129	31	2	3	1	(1	0)	42	19	10	9	0	18	2	2	2	16	3	.84	0	.240	.296	.326
	San Francisco	NL	52	214	61	9	5	5	(2	3)	95	29	18	18	0	42	2	1	0	8	6	.57	1	.285	.346	.444
	7 ML YEARS		494	1583	418	57	36	33	(14	19)	646	249	141	121	5	275	13	8	8	127	46	.73	17	.264	.320	.408

Reggie Sanders

Bats: Right **Throws:** Right **Pos:** RF/CF   **Ht:** 6' 1" **Wt:** 185 **Born:** 12/1/67 **Age:** 28

						BATTING													BASERUNNING				PERCENTAGES		
Year Team	Lg	G	AB	H	2B	3B	HR	(Hm	Rd)	TB	R	RBI	TBB	IBB	SO	HBP	SH	SF	SB	CS	SB%	GDP	Avg	OBP	SLG
1991 Cincinnati	NL	9	40	8	0	0	1	(0	1)	11	6	3	0	0	9	0	0	0	1	1	.50	1	.200	.200	.275
1992 Cincinnati	NL	116	385	104	26	6	12	(6	6)	178	62	36	48	2	98	4	0	1	16	7	.70	6	.270	.356	.462
1993 Cincinnati	NL	138	496	136	16	4	20	(8	12)	220	90	83	51	7	118	5	3	8	27	10	.73	10	.274	.343	.444
1994 Cincinnati	NL	107	400	105	20	8	17	(10	7)	192	66	62	41	1	114	2	1	3	21	9	.70	2	.263	.332	.480
1995 Cincinnati	NL	133	484	148	36	6	28	(9	19)	280	91	99	69	4	122	8	0	6	36	12	.75	9	.306	.397	.579
5 ML YEARS		503	1805	501	98	24	78	(33	45)	881	315	283	209	14	461	19	4	18	101	39	.72	28	.278	.355	.488

Scott Sanders

Pitches: Right **Bats:** Right **Pos:** SP   **Ht:** 6' 4" **Wt:** 220 **Born:** 3/25/69 **Age:** 27

		HOW MUCH HE PITCHED						WHAT HE GAVE UP										THE RESULTS					
Year Team	Lg	G	GS	CG	GF	IP	BFP	H	R	ER	HR	SH	SF	HB	TBB	IBB	SO	WP	Bk	W	L	Pct.	ShO	Sv	ERA
1995 Las Vegas *	AAA	1	1	0	0	3	14	3	0	0	0	0	0	0	1	0	2	0	0	0	0	.000	0	0	0.00
1993 San Diego	NL	9	9	0	0	52.1	231	54	32	24	4	1	2	1	23	1	37	0	1	3	3	.500	0	0	4.13
1994 San Diego	NL	23	20	0	2	111	485	103	63	59	10	6	5	5	48	4	109	10	1	4	8	.333	0	1	4.78
1995 San Diego	NL	17	15	1	0	90	383	79	46	43	14	2	2	2	31	4	88	6	1	5	5	.500	0	0	4.30
3 ML YEARS		49	44	1	2	253.1	1099	236	141	126	28	9	9	8	102	9	234	16	3	12	16	.429	0	1	4.48

Scott Sanderson

Pitches: Right **Bats:** Right **Pos:** SP   **Ht:** 6' 5" **Wt:** 192 **Born:** 7/22/56 **Age:** 39

		HOW MUCH HE PITCHED						WHAT HE GAVE UP										THE RESULTS					
Year Team	Lg	G	GS	CG	GF	IP	BFP	H	R	ER	HR	SH	SF	HB	TBB	IBB	SO	WP	Bk	W	L	Pct.	ShO	Sv	ERA
1978 Montreal	NL	10	9	1	1	61	251	52	20	17	3	3	2	1	21	0	50	2	0	4	2	.667	1	0	2.51
1979 Montreal	NL	34	24	5	3	168	696	148	69	64	16	5	7	3	54	4	138	2	3	9	8	.529	3	1	3.43
1980 Montreal	NL	33	33	7	0	211	875	206	76	73	18	11	5	3	56	3	125	6	0	16	11	.593	3	0	3.11
1981 Montreal	NL	22	22	4	0	137	560	122	50	45	10	7	4	1	31	2	77	2	0	9	7	.563	1	0	2.96
1982 Montreal	NL	32	32	7	0	224	922	212	98	86	24	9	6	3	58	5	158	2	1	12	12	.500	0	0	3.46
1983 Montreal	NL	18	16	0	1	81.1	346	98	50	42	12	2	1	0	20	0	55	0	0	6	7	.462	0	1	4.65
1984 Chicago	NL	24	24	3	0	140.2	571	140	54	49	5	6	8	2	24	3	76	3	2	8	5	.615	0	0	3.14
1985 Chicago	NL	19	19	2	0	121	480	100	49	42	13	7	7	0	27	4	80	1	0	5	6	.455	0	0	3.12
1986 Chicago	NL	37	28	1	2	169.2	697	165	85	79	21	6	5	2	37	2	124	3	1	9	11	.450	1	1	4.19
1987 Chicago	NL	32	22	0	5	144.2	631	156	72	69	23	4	5	3	50	1	106	1	0	8	9	.471	0	2	4.29
1988 Chicago	NL	11	0	0	3	15.1	62	13	9	9	1	0	3	0	3	1	6	0	0	1	2	.333	0	0	5.28
1989 Chicago	NL	37	23	2	2	146.1	611	155	69	64	16	8	3	2	31	6	86	1	3	11	9	.550	0	0	3.94
1990 Oakland	AL	34	34	2	0	206.1	885	205	99	89	27	4	8	4	66	2	128	7	1	17	11	.607	1	0	3.88
1991 New York	AL	34	34	2	0	208	837	200	95	88	22	5	5	3	29	0	130	4	1	16	10	.615	2	0	3.81
1992 New York	AL	33	33	2	0	193.1	851	220	116	106	28	3	11	4	64	5	104	4	1	12	11	.522	1	0	4.93
1993 Cal-SF		32	29	4	1	184	777	201	97	86	27	9	10	6	34	7	102	1	5	11	13	.458	1	0	4.21
1994 Chicago	AL	18	14	1	0	92	389	110	57	52	20	3	1	2	12	1	36	0	1	8	4	.667	0	0	5.09
1995 California	AL	7	7	0	0	39.1	170	48	23	18	6	1	2	2	4	1	23	0	1	1	3	.250	0	0	4.12
1993 California	AL	21	21	4	0	135.1	576	153	77	67	15	6	8	5	27	5	66	1	2	7	11	.389	1	0	4.46
San Francisco	NL	11	8	0	1	48.2	201	48	20	19	12	3	2	1	7	2	36	0	3	4	2	.667	0	0	3.51
18 ML YEARS		467	403	43	18	2543	10611	2551	1188	1078	292	93	93	41	621	51	1604	39	20	163	141	.536	14	5	3.82

Mo Sanford

Pitches: Right **Bats:** Right **Pos:** RP   **Ht:** 6' 6" **Wt:** 233 **Born:** 12/24/66 **Age:** 29

		HOW MUCH HE PITCHED						WHAT HE GAVE UP										THE RESULTS					
Year Team	Lg	G	GS	CG	GF	IP	BFP	H	R	ER	HR	SH	SF	HB	TBB	IBB	SO	WP	Bk	W	L	Pct.	ShO	Sv	ERA
1995 Salt Lake *	AAA	4	0	0	0	5.2	27	6	4	4	1	0	0	0	4	0	8	0	0	0	0	.000	0	0	6.35
1991 Cincinnati	NL	5	5	0	0	28	118	19	14	12	3	0	0	1	15	1	31	4	0	1	2	.333	0	0	3.86
1993 Colorado	NL	11	6	0	1	35.2	166	37	25	21	4	4	2	0	27	0	36	2	1	1	2	.333	0	0	5.30
1995 Minnesota	AL	11	0	0	6	18.2	89	16	11	11	7	0	0	2	16	0	17	1	0	0	0	.000	0	0	5.30
3 ML YEARS		27	11	0	7	82.1	373	72	50	44	14	4	2	3	58	1	84	7	1	2	4	.333	0	0	4.81

F.P. Santangelo

Bats: Both **Throws:** Right **Pos:** LF   **Ht:** 5'10" **Wt:** 168 **Born:** 10/24/67 **Age:** 28

						BATTING													BASERUNNING				PERCENTAGES		
Year Team	Lg	G	AB	H	2B	3B	HR	(Hm	Rd)	TB	R	RBI	TBB	IBB	SO	HBP	SH	SF	SB	CS	SB%	GDP	Avg	OBP	SLG
1989 Jamestown	A	2	6	3	1	0	0	--	--	4	0	0	1	0	0	0	0	0	1	0	1.00	0	.500	.571	.667
W. Palm Bch	A	57	173	37	4	0	0	--	--	41	18	14	23	1	12	4	6	0	3	3	.50	5	.214	.320	.237
1990 W. Palm Bch	A	116	394	109	19	2	0	--	--	132	63	38	51	2	49	5	18	2	22	7	.76	5	.277	.365	.335
1991 Harrisburg	AA	132	462	113	12	7	5	--	--	154	78	42	74	0	45	7	13	4	21	7	.75	6	.245	.355	.333
1992 Indianapolis	AAA	137	462	123	25	0	5	--	--	163	83	34	62	4	58	7	13	2	12	11	.52	9	.266	.360	.353
1993 Ottawa	AAA	131	453	124	21	2	4	--	--	161	86	45	59	4	52	14	8	4	18	8	.69	10	.274	.372	.355

Year	Team	Lg	G	AB	H	2B	3B	HR	(Hm	Rd)	TB	R	RBI	TBB	IBB	SO	HBP	SH	SF	SB	CS	SB%	GDP	Avg	OBP	SLG
1994	Ottawa	AAA	119	413	104	28	1	5	--	--	149	62	41	59	0	64	9	10	3	7	9	.44	11	.252	.355	.361
1995	Ottawa	AAA	95	267	68	15	3	2	--	--	95	37	25	32	3	22	6	6	4	7	4	.64	2	.255	.343	.356
1995	Montreal	NL	35	98	29	5	1	1	(1	0)	39	11	9	12	0	9	2	1	0	1	1	.50	0	.296	.384	.398

Benito Santiago

Bats: Right **Throws:** Right **Pos:** C   **Ht:** 6' 1" **Wt:** 185 **Born:** 3/9/65 **Age:** 31

												BATTING									BASERUNNING				PERCENTAGES		
Year	Team	Lg	G	AB	H	2B	3B	HR	(Hm	Rd)	TB	R	RBI	TBB	IBB	SO	HBP	SH	SF	SB	CS	SB%	GDP	Avg	OBP	SLG
1986	San Diego	NL	17	62	18	2	0	3	(2	1)	29	10	6	2	0	12	0	0	1	0	1	.00	0	.290	.308	.468
1987	San Diego	NL	146	546	164	33	2	18	(11	7)	255	64	79	16	2	112	5	1	4	21	12	.64	12	.300	.324	.467
1988	San Diego	NL	139	492	122	22	2	10	(3	7)	178	49	46	24	2	82	1	5	5	15	7	.68	18	.248	.282	.362
1989	San Diego	NL	129	462	109	16	3	16	(8	8)	179	50	62	26	6	89	1	3	2	11	6	.65	9	.236	.277	.387
1990	San Diego	NL	100	344	93	8	5	11	(5	6)	144	42	53	27	2	55	3	1	7	5	5	.50	4	.270	.323	.419
1991	San Diego	NL	152	580	155	22	3	17	(6	11)	234	60	87	23	5	114	4	0	7	8	10	.44	21	.267	.296	.403
1992	San Diego	NL	106	386	97	21	0	10	(8	2)	148	37	42	21	1	52	0	0	4	2	5	.29	14	.251	.287	.383
1993	Florida	NL	139	469	108	19	6	13	(6	7)	178	49	50	37	2	88	5	0	4	10	7	.59	9	.230	.291	.380
1994	Florida	NL	101	337	92	14	2	11	(4	7)	143	35	41	25	1	57	1	2	4	1	2	.33	11	.273	.322	.424
1995	Cincinnati	NL	81	266	76	20	0	11	(7	4)	129	40	44	24	1	48	4	0	2	2	2	.50	7	.286	.351	.485
	10 ML YEARS		1110	3944	1034	177	23	120	(60	60)	1617	436	510	225	22	709	24	12	40	75	57	.57	105	.262	.303	.410

Mackey Sasser

Bats: Left **Throws:** Right **Pos:** C   **Ht:** 6' 1" **Wt:** 210 **Born:** 8/3/62 **Age:** 33

												BATTING									BASERUNNING				PERCENTAGES		
Year	Team	Lg	G	AB	H	2B	3B	HR	(Hm	Rd)	TB	R	RBI	TBB	IBB	SO	HBP	SH	SF	SB	CS	SB%	GDP	Avg	OBP	SLG
1987	Pit-SF	NL	14	27	5	0	0	0	(0	0)	5	2	2	0	0	2	0	0	0	0	0	.00	1	.185	.185	.185
1988	New York	NL	60	123	35	10	1	1	(0	1)	50	9	17	6	4	9	0	0	2	0	0	.00	4	.285	.313	.407
1989	New York	NL	72	182	53	14	2	1	(1	0)	74	17	22	7	4	15	0	1	1	0	1	.00	3	.291	.316	.407
1990	New York	NL	100	270	83	14	0	6	(3	3)	115	31	41	15	9	19	1	0	2	0	0	.00	7	.307	.344	.426
1991	New York	NL	96	228	62	14	2	5	(3	2)	95	18	35	9	2	19	1	1	4	0	2	.00	6	.272	.298	.417
1992	New York	NL	92	141	34	6	0	2	(1	1)	46	7	18	3	0	10	0	0	5	0	0	.00	4	.241	.248	.326
1993	Seattle	AL	83	188	41	10	2	1	(0	1)	58	18	21	15	6	30	1	0	4	1	0	1.00	7	.218	.274	.309
1994	Seattle	AL	3	4	0	0	0	0	(0	0)	0	0	0	0	0	0	0	0	0	0	0	.00	0	.000	.000	.000
1995	Pittsburgh	NL	14	26	4	1	0	0	(0	0)	5	1	0	0	0	0	0	0	0	0	0	.00	0	.154	.154	.192
1987	Pittsburgh	NL	12	23	5	0	0	0	(0	0)	5	2	2	0	0	2	0	0	0	0	0	.00	1	.217	.217	.217
	San Francisco	NL	2	4	0	0	0	0	(0	0)	0	0	0	0	0	0	0	0	0	0	0	.00	0	.000	.000	.000
	9 ML YEARS		534	1189	317	69	7	16	(8	8)	448	103	156	55	25	104	3	2	18	1	3	.25	32	.267	.296	.377

Bob Scanlan

Pitches: Right **Bats:** Right **Pos:** SP   **Ht:** 6' 8" **Wt:** 215 **Born:** 8/9/66 **Age:** 29

			HOW MUCH HE PITCHED					WHAT HE GAVE UP										THE RESULTS					
Year	Team	Lg	G	GS	CG	GF	IP	BFP	H	R	ER	HR	SH	SF	HB	TBB	IBB	SO	WP	Bk	W	L	Pct.	ShO	Sv	ERA
1995	New Orleans *	AAA	3	3	0	0	11.2	51	17	7	7	0	0	0	1	3	0	5	1	0	0	1	.000	0	0	5.40
1991	Chicago	NL	40	13	0	16	111	482	114	60	48	5	8	6	3	40	3	44	5	1	7	8	.467	0	1	3.89
1992	Chicago	NL	69	0	0	41	87.1	360	76	32	28	4	4	2	1	30	6	42	6	4	3	6	.333	0	14	2.89
1993	Chicago	NL	70	0	0	13	75.1	323	79	41	38	6	2	6	3	28	7	44	0	2	4	5	.444	0	0	4.54
1994	Milwaukee	AL	30	12	0	9	103	441	117	53	47	11	1	2	4	28	2	65	3	1	2	6	.250	0	2	4.11
1995	Milwaukee	AL	17	14	0	1	83.1	389	101	66	61	9	0	6	7	44	3	29	3	0	4	7	.364	0	0	6.59
	5 ML YEARS		226	39	0	80	460	1995	487	252	222	35	15	22	18	170	21	224	17	8	20	32	.385	0	17	4.34

Steve Scarsone

Bats: Right **Throws:** Right **Pos:** 3B/1B/2B   **Ht:** 6' 2" **Wt:** 195 **Born:** 4/11/66 **Age:** 30

												BATTING									BASERUNNING				PERCENTAGES		
Year	Team	Lg	G	AB	H	2B	3B	HR	(Hm	Rd)	TB	R	RBI	TBB	IBB	SO	HBP	SH	SF	SB	CS	SB%	GDP	Avg	OBP	SLG
1992	Bal-Phi		18	30	5	0	0	0	(0	0)	5	3	0	2	0	12	0	1	0	0	0	.00	0	.167	.219	.167
1993	San Francisco	NL	44	103	26	9	0	2	(1	1)	41	16	15	4	0	32	0	4	1	0	1	.00	0	.252	.278	.398
1994	San Francisco	NL	52	103	28	8	0	2	(0	2)	42	21	13	10	1	20	0	3	2	0	2	.00	1	.272	.330	.408
1995	San Francisco	NL	80	233	62	10	3	11	(7	4)	111	33	29	18	0	82	6	3	1	3	2	.60	2	.266	.333	.476
1992	Baltimore	AL	11	17	3	0	0	0	(0	0)	3	2	0	1	0	6	0	1	0	0	0	.00	0	.176	.222	.176
	Philadelphia	NL	7	13	2	0	0	0	(0	0)	2	1	0	1	0	6	0	0	0	0	0	.00	0	.154	.214	.154
	4 ML YEARS		194	469	121	27	3	15	(8	7)	199	73	57	34	1	146	6	11	4	3	5	.38	3	.258	.314	.424

Gene Schall

Bats: Right **Throws:** Right **Pos:** 1B   **Ht:** 6' 3" **Wt:** 201 **Born:** 6/5/70 **Age:** 26

												BATTING									BASERUNNING				PERCENTAGES		
Year	Team	Lg	G	AB	H	2B	3B	HR	(Hm	Rd)	TB	R	RBI	TBB	IBB	SO	HBP	SH	SF	SB	CS	SB%	GDP	Avg	OBP	SLG
1991	Batavia	A	13	44	15	1	0	2	--	--	22	5	8	3	2	16	0	0	0	0	1	.00	1	.341	.383	.500
1992	Spartanburg	A	77	276	74	13	1	8	--	--	113	44	41	29	0	52	3	2	2	3	2	.60	8	.268	.342	.409
	Clearwater	A	40	133	33	4	2	4	--	--	53	16	19	14	0	29	4	1	3	1	2	.33	2	.248	.331	.398

Year	Team	Lg																										
1993	Reading	AA	82	285	93	12	4	15	--	--	158	51	60	24	0	56	10	0	3	2	1	.67	15	.326	.394	.554
	Scranton-Wb	AAA	40	139	33	6	1	4	--	--	53	16	16	19	1	38	7	1	1	4	2	.67	2	.237	.355	.381
1994	Scranton-Wb	AAA	127	463	132	35	4	15	--	--	223	54	89	50	5	86	6	0	6	9	1	.90	11	.285	.358	.482
1995	Scranton-Wb	AAA	92	320	100	25	4	12	--	--	169	52	63	49	2	54	10	0	4	3	3	.50	14	.313	.415	.528
1995	Philadelphia	NL	24	65	15	2	0	0	(0	0)	17	2	5	6	1	16	1	0	0	0	0	.00	1	.231	.306	.262

Rich Scheid

Pitches: Left **Bats:** Left **Pos:** RP **Ht:** 6' 3" **Wt:** 200 **Born:** 2/3/65 **Age:** 31

			HOW MUCH HE PITCHED						WHAT HE GAVE UP											THE RESULTS					
Year	Team	Lg	G	GS	CG	GF	IP	BFP	H	R	ER	HR	SH	SF	HB	TBB	IBB	SO	WP	Bk	W	L	Pct.	ShO	Sv	ERA
1986	Oneonta	A	15	15	3	0	93	368	62	30	23	2	1	0	3	32	1	100	6	2	9	3	.750	1	0	2.23
1987	Ft. Laud	A	9	8	1	1	55	236	43	25	18	1	1	3	0	29	0	49	3	0	7	0	1.000	0	0	2.95
	Albany-Colo	AA	9	9	1	0	48	221	44	33	29	2	1	4	5	33	1	33	5	3	2	3	.400	1	0	5.44
	Pittsfield	AA	11	6	0	2	28	145	44	27	23	1	0	2	1	19	0	13	2	0	2	0	1.000	0	0	7.39
1988	Pittsfield	AA	24	20	1	1	118.1	522	119	58	49	6	9	6	1	62	3	75	10	10	6	6	.500	0	1	3.73
1989	Iowa	AAA	7	0	0	2	7.1	42	8	6	4	0	0	0	0	10	1	7	0	1	0	0	.000	0	0	4.91
	Charlotte	AA	17	6	1	2	46.1	209	43	30	21	8	1	1	2	27	2	37	7	7	4	1	.800	0	0	4.08
1990	Birmingham	AA	25	0	0	13	44.2	192	37	17	11	0	0	5	1	21	4	37	4	3	2	1	.667	0	4	2.22
	Vancouver	AAA	20	2	0	10	39.1	173	37	19	14	2	1	0	0	24	1	38	2	3	2	2	.500	0	0	3.20
1991	Vancouver	AAA	47	0	0	20	66.2	293	65	46	45	7	4	1	2	33	4	57	6	0	6	7	.462	0	3	6.08
1992	Vancouver	AAA	29	0	0	6	35.1	160	29	13	11	0	2	1	0	28	4	24	3	0	1	2	.333	0	0	2.80
	Tucson	AAA	12	8	0	1	57	236	49	23	16	4	2	2	1	23	2	34	4	3	2	3	.400	0	1	2.53
1993	Edmonton	AAA	38	12	0	15	110	490	130	68	62	9	10	4	4	38	1	84	4	2	5	7	.417	0	1	5.07
1994	Edmonton	AAA	17	17	2	0	102.1	441	110	50	46	7	3	4	0	41	0	86	2	3	9	4	.692	2	0	4.05
1995	Charlotte	AAA	19	8	0	1	54.2	246	74	40	36	10	1	4	2	15	0	37	1	0	1	4	.200	0	0	5.93
1992	Houston	NL	7	1	0	3	12	56	14	8	8	2	0	0	0	6	1	8	1	1	0	1	.000	0	0	6.00
1994	Florida	NL	8	5	0	1	32.1	142	35	18	12	6	2	0	2	8	0	17	2	1	1	3	.250	0	0	3.34
1995	Florida	NL	6	0	0	1	10.1	50	14	7	7	1	1	1	0	7	0	10	1	0	0	0	.000	0	0	6.10
	3 ML YEARS		21	6	0	5	54.2	248	63	33	27	9	3	1	2	21	1	35	4	2	1	4	.200	0	0	4.45

Curt Schilling

Pitches: Right **Bats:** Right **Pos:** SP **Ht:** 6' 4" **Wt:** 225 **Born:** 11/14/66 **Age:** 29

			HOW MUCH HE PITCHED						WHAT HE GAVE UP											THE RESULTS					
Year	Team	Lg	G	GS	CG	GF	IP	BFP	H	R	ER	HR	SH	SF	HB	TBB	IBB	SO	WP	Bk	W	L	Pct.	ShO	Sv	ERA
1988	Baltimore	AL	4	4	0	0	14.2	76	22	19	16	3	0	3	1	10	1	4	2	0	0	3	.000	0	0	9.82
1989	Baltimore	AL	5	1	0	0	8.2	38	10	6	6	2	0	0	0	3	0	6	1	0	0	1	.000	0	0	6.23
1990	Baltimore	AL	35	0	0	16	46	191	38	13	13	1	2	4	0	19	0	32	0	0	1	2	.333	0	3	2.54
1991	Houston	NL	56	0	0	34	75.2	336	79	35	32	2	5	1	0	39	7	71	4	1	3	5	.375	0	8	3.81
1992	Philadelphia	NL	42	26	10	10	226.1	895	165	67	59	11	7	8	1	59	4	147	4	0	14	11	.560	4	2	2.35
1993	Philadelphia	NL	34	34	7	0	235.1	982	234	114	105	23	9	7	4	57	6	186	9	3	16	7	.696	2	0	4.02
1994	Philadelphia	NL	13	13	1	0	82.1	360	87	42	41	10	6	1	3	28	3	58	3	1	2	8	.200	0	0	4.48
1995	Philadelphia	NL	17	17	1	0	116	473	96	52	46	12	5	2	3	26	2	114	0	1	7	5	.583	0	0	3.57
	8 ML YEARS		206	95	19	60	805	3351	731	348	318	64	34	26	12	241	23	618	23	6	43	42	.506	6	13	3.56

Curt Schmidt

Pitches: Right **Bats:** Right **Pos:** RP **Ht:** 6' 5" **Wt:** 200 **Born:** 3/16/70 **Age:** 26

			HOW MUCH HE PITCHED						WHAT HE GAVE UP											THE RESULTS					
Year	Team	Lg	G	GS	CG	GF	IP	BFP	H	R	ER	HR	SH	SF	HB	TBB	IBB	SO	WP	Bk	W	L	Pct.	ShO	Sv	ERA
1992	Jamestown	A	29	1	1	19	63.1	261	42	21	19	1	3	0	5	29	2	61	6	1	3	4	.429	1	2	2.70
	W. Palm Bch	A	3	0	0	2	5	18	3	0	0	0	0	0	0	1	0	3	0	0	0	0	.000	0	0	0.00
1993	Expos	R	1	1	0	0	5	16	1	0	0	0	0	0	0	0	0	7	0	0	1	0	1.000	0	0	0.00
	W. Palm Bch	A	44	2	0	22	65.1	285	63	32	23	3	5	1	0	25	3	51	1	1	4	6	.400	0	5	3.17
1994	Harrisburg	AA	53	0	0	26	71.2	291	51	19	15	4	6	4	0	29	1	75	4	0	6	2	.750	0	5	1.88
1995	Ottawa	AAA	43	0	0	38	52.2	206	40	14	13	1	0	1	4	18	0	38	2	0	5	0	1.000	0	15	2.22
1995	Montreal	NL	11	0	0	0	10.1	54	15	8	8	1	1	0	2	9	0	7	0	0	0	0	.000	0	0	6.97

Jason Schmidt

Pitches: Right **Bats:** Right **Pos:** RP **Ht:** 6' 5" **Wt:** 185 **Born:** 1/29/73 **Age:** 23

			HOW MUCH HE PITCHED						WHAT HE GAVE UP											THE RESULTS					
Year	Team	Lg	G	GS	CG	GF	IP	BFP	H	R	ER	HR	SH	SF	HB	TBB	IBB	SO	WP	Bk	W	L	Pct.	ShO	Sv	ERA
1991	Braves	R	11	11	0	0	45.1	193	32	21	12	0	0	1	0	23	0	44	8	0	3	4	.429	0	0	2.38
1992	Macon	A	7	7	0	0	24.2	119	31	18	11	2	0	1	1	19	0	33	2	2	0	3	.000	0	0	4.01
	Pulaski	R	11	11	0	0	58.1	258	55	38	26	4	0	1	3	31	0	56	3	0	3	4	.429	0	0	4.01
1993	Durham	A	22	22	0	0	116.2	508	128	69	64	12	4	2	8	47	3	110	4	1	7	11	.389	0	0	4.94
1994	Greenville	AA	24	24	1	0	140.2	599	135	64	57	9	6	2	8	54	1	131	9	0	8	7	.533	0	0	3.65

Year Team	Lg	G	GS	CG	GF	IP	BFP	H	R	ER	HR	SH	SF	HB	TBB	IBB	SO	WP	Bk	W	L	Pct.	ShO	Sv	ERA
1995 Richmond	AAA	19	19	0	0	116	484	97	40	29	2	15	1	3	48	3	95	4	1	8	6	.571	0	0	2.25
1995 Atlanta	NL	9	2	0	1	25	119	27	17	16	2	2	4	1	18	3	19	1	0	2	2	.500	0	0	5.76

Dick Schofield

Bats: Right **Throws:** Right **Pos:** SS **Ht:** 5'10" **Wt:** 179 **Born:** 11/21/62 **Age:** 33

Year Team	Lg	G	AB	H	2B	3B	HR	(Hm	Rd)	TB	R	RBI	TBB	IBB	SO	HBP	SH	SF	SB	CS	SB%	GDP	Avg	OBP	SLG
1995 Vancouver *	AAA	16	53	10	4	0	0	--	--	14	5	9	3	0	3	1	1	2	0	0	.00	1	.189	.237	.264
1983 California	AL	21	54	11	2	0	3	(2	1)	22	4	4	6	0	8	1	1	0	0	0	.00	2	.204	.295	.407
1984 California	AL	140	400	77	10	3	4	(0	4)	105	39	21	33	0	79	6	13	0	5	2	.71	7	.193	.264	.263
1985 California	AL	147	438	96	19	3	8	(5	3)	145	50	41	35	0	70	8	12	3	11	4	.73	8	.219	.287	.331
1986 California	AL	139	458	114	17	6	13	(7	6)	182	67	57	48	2	55	5	9	9	23	5	.82	8	.249	.321	.397
1987 California	AL	134	479	120	17	3	9	(4	5)	170	52	46	37	0	63	2	10	3	19	3	.86	4	.251	.305	.355
1988 California	AL	155	527	126	11	6	6	(3	3)	167	61	34	40	0	57	9	11	2	20	5	.80	5	.239	.303	.317
1989 California	AL	91	302	69	11	2	4	(1	3)	96	42	26	28	0	47	3	11	4	9	3	.75	4	.228	.299	.318
1990 California	AL	99	310	79	8	1	1	(1	0)	92	41	18	52	3	61	2	13	2	3	4	.43	3	.255	.363	.297
1991 California	AL	134	427	96	19	3	0	(0	0)	111	44	31	50	2	69	3	7	0	8	4	.67	3	.225	.310	.260
1992 Cal-NYN		143	423	87	18	2	4	(3	1)	121	52	36	61	4	82	5	10	3	11	4	.73	11	.206	.311	.286
1993 Toronto	AL	36	110	21	1	2	0	(0	0)	26	11	5	16	0	25	0	2	0	3	0	1.00	1	.191	.294	.236
1994 Toronto	AL	95	325	83	14	1	4	(2	2)	111	38	32	34	0	62	4	8	2	7	7	.50	2	.255	.332	.342
1995 LA-Cal		21	30	6	0	0	0	(0	0)	6	1	2	5	0	5	0	2	0	0	0	.00	1	.200	.314	.200
1992 California	AL	1	3	1	0	0	0	(0	0)	1	0	0	1	0	0	0	0	0	0	0	.00	0	.333	.500	.333
New York	NL	142	420	86	18	2	4	(3	1)	120	52	36	60	4	82	5	10	3	11	4	.73	11	.205	.309	.286
1995 Los Angeles	NL	9	10	1	0	0	0	(0	0)	1	0	0	1	0	3	0	0	0	0	0	.00	0	.100	.182	.100
California	AL	12	20	5	0	0	0	(0	0)	5	1	2	4	0	2	0	2	0	0	0	.00	1	.250	.375	.250
13 ML YEARS		1355	4283	985	137	32	56	(28	28)	1354	502	353	445	11	683	48	109	26	119	41	.74	59	.230	.308	.316

Pete Schourek

Pitches: Left **Bats:** Left **Pos:** SP **Ht:** 6'5" **Wt:** 205 **Born:** 5/10/69 **Age:** 27

Year Team	Lg	G	GS	CG	GF	IP	BFP	H	R	ER	HR	SH	SF	HB	TBB	IBB	SO	WP	Bk	W	L	Pct.	ShO	Sv	ERA
1991 New York	NL	35	8	1	7	86.1	385	82	49	41	7	5	4	2	43	4	67	1	0	5	4	.556	1	2	4.27
1992 New York	NL	22	21	0	0	136	578	137	60	55	9	4	4	2	44	6	60	4	2	6	8	.429	0	0	3.64
1993 New York	NL	41	18	0	6	128.1	586	168	90	85	13	3	8	3	45	7	72	1	2	5	12	.294	0	0	5.96
1994 Cincinnati	NL	22	10	0	3	81.1	354	90	39	37	11	6	2	3	29	4	69	0	0	7	2	.778	0	0	4.09
1995 Cincinnati	NL	29	29	2	0	190.1	754	158	72	68	17	4	4	8	45	3	160	1	1	18	7	.720	0	0	3.22
5 ML YEARS		149	86	3	16	622.1	2657	635	310	286	57	22	22	18	206	24	428	7	5	41	33	.554	1	2	4.14

Erik Schullstrom

Pitches: Right **Bats:** Right **Pos:** RP **Ht:** 6'5" **Wt:** 235 **Born:** 3/25/69 **Age:** 27

Year Team	Lg	G	GS	CG	GF	IP	BFP	H	R	ER	HR	SH	SF	HB	TBB	IBB	SO	WP	Bk	W	L	Pct.	ShO	Sv	ERA
1990 Wausau	A	5	5	0	0	19.1	82	20	12	10	0	1	0	1	7	0	21	0	2	0	2	.000	0	0	4.66
Frederick	A	2	2	0	0	13	54	9	5	5	0	1	2	1	6	0	8	0	0	2	0	1.000	0	0	3.46
1991 Frederick	A	19	17	1	0	86	361	70	32	29	5	4	1	1	45	1	73	4	2	5	6	.455	1	0	3.03
Hagerstown	AA	2	2	0	0	13	54	11	5	4	0	1	0	1	3	0	9	1	0	1	0	1.000	0	0	2.77
1992 Hagerstown	AA	23	22	2	0	127	556	120	66	51	7	6	2	3	63	0	128	7	3	5	9	.357	0	0	3.61
Las Vegas	AAA	1	1	0	0	5	20	3	0	0	0	0	0	0	3	0	4	0	0	1	0	1.000	0	0	0.00
1993 Bowie	AA	24	14	2	4	109.2	480	119	63	52	6	6	3	3	45	0	97	7	0	5	10	.333	0	1	4.27
Nashville	AA	4	3	0	0	13	61	16	7	7	1	0	1	0	6	0	11	1	0	1	0	1.000	0	0	4.85
1994 Nashville	AA	26	0	0	17	41	164	36	14	12	2	4	1	1	6	0	43	2	0	1	2	.333	0	8	2.63
Salt Lake	AAA	8	0	0	7	11.1	47	12	5	5	0	0	0	0	3	2	8	0	0	0	1	.000	0	2	3.97
1995 Salt Lake	AAA	10	0	0	7	9.2	43	12	5	5	1	0	0	0	4	0	8	0	0	2	0	1.000	0	2	4.66
1994 Minnesota	AL	9	0	0	5	13	57	13	7	4	0	1	0	1	5	0	13	0	0	0	0	.000	0	1	2.77
1995 Minnesota	AL	37	0	0	16	47	225	66	36	36	8	2	1	1	22	1	21	5	0	0	0	.000	0	0	6.89
2 ML YEARS		46	0	0	21	60	282	79	43	40	8	3	1	2	27	1	34	5	0	0	0	.000	0	1	6.00

Tim Scott

Pitches: Right **Bats:** Right **Pos:** RP **Ht:** 6'2" **Wt:** 205 **Born:** 11/16/66 **Age:** 29

Year Team	Lg	G	GS	CG	GF	IP	BFP	H	R	ER	HR	SH	SF	HB	TBB	IBB	SO	WP	Bk	W	L	Pct.	ShO	Sv	ERA
1991 San Diego	NL	2	0	0	0	1	5	2	2	1	0	0	0	0	0	0	1	0	0	0	0	.000	0	0	9.00
1992 San Diego	NL	34	0	0	16	37.2	173	39	24	22	4	4	1	1	21	6	30	0	1	4	1	.800	0	0	5.26
1993 Mon-SD	NL	56	0	0	18	71.2	317	69	28	24	4	3	2	4	34	2	65	2	1	7	2	.778	0	1	3.01
1994 Montreal	NL	40	0	0	8	53.1	223	51	17	16	0	0	2	1	18	3	37	1	1	5	2	.714	0	1	2.70
1995 Montreal	NL	62	0	0	15	63.1	268	52	30	28	6	4	1	6	23	2	57	4	0	2	0	1.000	0	2	3.98
1993 Montreal	NL	32	0	0	16	34	148	31	15	14	3	1	0	0	19	2	35	1	0	5	2	.714	0	1	3.71

	Lg	G	GS	CG	GF	IP	BFP	H	R	ER	HR	SH	SF	HB	TBB	IBB	SO	WP	Bk	W	L	Pct.	ShO	Sv	ERA
San Diego	NL	24	0	0	2	37.2	169	38	13	10	1	2	2	4	15	0	30	1	1	2	0	1.000	0	0	2.39
5 ML YEARS		194	0	0	57	227	986	213	101	91	14	11	4	13	96	13	190	7	3	18	5	.783	0	4	3.61

Rudy Seanez

Pitches: Right **Bats:** Right **Pos:** RP **Ht:** 5'10" **Wt:** 190 **Born:** 10/20/68 **Age:** 27

		HOW MUCH HE PITCHED						WHAT HE GAVE UP												THE RESULTS					
Year Team	Lg	G	GS	CG	GF	IP	BFP	H	R	ER	HR	SH	SF	HB	TBB	IBB	SO	WP	Bk	W	L	Pct.	ShO	Sv	ERA
1995 San Bernrdo *	A	4	0	0	2	6	23	2	0	0	0	0	0	0	3	0	5	0	0	2	0	1.000	0	1	0.00
1989 Cleveland	AL	5	0	0	2	5	20	1	2	2	0	0	2	0	4	1	7	1	1	0	0	.000	0	0	3.60
1990 Cleveland	AL	24	0	0	12	27.1	127	22	17	17	2	0	1	1	25	1	24	5	0	2	1	.667	0	0	5.60
1991 Cleveland	AL	5	0	0	0	5	33	10	12	9	2	0	0	0	7	0	7	2	0	0	0	.000	0	0	16.20
1993 San Diego	NL	3	0	0	3	3.1	20	8	6	5	1	1	0	0	2	0	1	0	0	0	0	.000	0	0	13.50
1994 Los Angeles	NL	17	0	0	6	23.2	104	24	7	7	2	4	2	1	9	1	18	3	0	1	1	.500	0	0	2.66
1995 Los Angeles	NL	37	0	0	12	34.2	159	39	27	26	5	3	0	1	18	3	29	0	0	1	3	.250	0	3	6.75
6 ML YEARS		91	0	0	35	99	463	104	71	66	12	8	5	3	65	6	86	11	1	4	5	.444	0	3	6.00

Kevin Sefcik

Bats: Right **Throws:** Right **Pos:** 3B **Ht:** 5'10" **Wt:** 175 **Born:** 2/10/71 **Age:** 25

		BATTING																BASERUNNING				PERCENTAGES		
Year Team	Lg	G	AB	H	2B	3B	HR	(Hm | Rd)	TB	R	RBI	TBB	IBB	SO	HBP	SH	SF	SB	CS	SB%	GDP	Avg	OBP	SLG
1993 Batavia	A	74	281	84	24	4	2	--	--	122	49	28	27	2	22	3	7	5	20	7	.74	5	.299	.361	.434
1994 Clearwater	A	130	516	147	29	8	2	--	--	198	83	46	49	2	43	7	4	6	30	13	.70	7	.285	.351	.384
1995 Scranton-Wb	AAA	7	26	9	6	1	0	--	--	17	5	6	3	0	1	0	0	1	0	0	.00	1	.346	.400	.654
Reading	AA	128	508	138	18	4	4	--	--	176	68	46	38	0	48	12	3	3	14	11	.56	5	.272	.335	.346
1995 Philadelphia	NL	5	4	0	0	0	0	(0 | 0)	0	1	0	0	0	2	0	0	0	0	0	.00	0	.000	.000	.000

David Segui

Bats: Both **Throws:** Left **Pos:** 1B/LF **Ht:** 6'1" **Wt:** 202 **Born:** 7/19/66 **Age:** 29

		BATTING																BASERUNNING				PERCENTAGES		
Year Team	Lg	G	AB	H	2B	3B	HR	(Hm | Rd)	TB	R	RBI	TBB	IBB	SO	HBP	SH	SF	SB	CS	SB%	GDP	Avg	OBP	SLG
1990 Baltimore	AL	40	123	30	7	0	2	(1 | 1)	43	14	15	11	2	15	1	1	0	0	0	.00	12	.244	.311	.350
1991 Baltimore	AL	86	212	59	7	0	2	(1 | 1)	72	15	22	12	2	19	0	3	1	1	1	.50	7	.278	.316	.340
1992 Baltimore	AL	115	189	44	9	0	1	(1 | 0)	56	21	17	20	3	23	0	2	0	1	0	1.00	4	.233	.306	.296
1993 Baltimore	AL	146	450	123	27	0	10	(6 | 4)	180	54	60	58	4	53	0	3	8	2	1	.67	18	.273	.351	.400
1994 New York	NL	92	336	81	17	1	10	(5 | 5)	130	46	43	33	6	43	1	1	3	0	0	.00	6	.241	.308	.387
1995 NYN-Mon	NL	130	456	141	25	4	12	(6 | 6)	210	68	68	40	5	47	3	8	3	2	7	.22	10	.309	.367	.461
1995 New York	NL	33	73	24	3	1	2	(2 | 0)	35	9	11	12	1	9	1	4	2	1	3	.25	2	.329	.420	.479
Montreal	NL	97	383	117	22	3	10	(4 | 6)	175	59	57	28	4	38	2	4	1	1	4	.20	8	.305	.355	.457
6 ML YEARS		609	1766	478	92	5	37	(20 | 17)	691	218	225	174	22	200	5	18	15	6	9	.40	57	.271	.335	.391

Kevin Seitzer

Bats: Right **Throws:** Right **Pos:** 3B/1B/DH **Ht:** 5'11" **Wt:** 193 **Born:** 3/26/62 **Age:** 34

		BATTING																BASERUNNING				PERCENTAGES		
Year Team	Lg	G	AB	H	2B	3B	HR	(Hm | Rd)	TB	R	RBI	TBB	IBB	SO	HBP	SH	SF	SB	CS	SB%	GDP	Avg	OBP	SLG
1986 Kansas City	AL	28	96	31	4	1	2	(1 | 1)	43	16	11	19	0	14	1	0	0	0	0	.00	0	.323	.440	.448
1987 Kansas City	AL	161	641	207	33	8	15	(7 | 8)	301	105	83	80	0	85	2	1	1	12	7	.63	18	.323	.399	.470
1988 Kansas City	AL	149	559	170	32	5	5	(4 | 1)	227	90	60	72	4	64	6	3	3	10	8	.56	15	.304	.388	.406
1989 Kansas City	AL	160	597	168	17	2	4	(2 | 2)	201	78	48	102	7	76	5	4	7	17	8	.68	16	.281	.387	.337
1990 Kansas City	AL	158	622	171	31	5	6	(5 | 1)	230	91	38	67	2	66	2	4	2	7	5	.58	11	.275	.346	.370
1991 Kansas City	AL	85	234	62	11	3	1	(0 | 1)	82	28	25	29	3	21	2	1	1	4	1	.80	4	.265	.350	.350
1992 Milwaukee	AL	148	540	146	35	1	5	(2 | 3)	198	74	71	57	4	44	2	7	9	13	11	.54	16	.270	.337	.367
1993 Mil-Oak	AL	120	417	112	16	2	11	(6 | 5)	165	45	57	44	1	48	2	3	5	7	7	.50	14	.269	.338	.396
1994 Milwaukee	AL	80	309	97	24	2	5	(4 | 1)	140	44	49	30	1	38	2	4	3	2	1	.67	7	.314	.375	.453
1995 Milwaukee	AL	132	492	153	33	3	5	(2 | 3)	207	56	69	64	2	57	6	5	3	2	0	1.00	13	.311	.395	.421
1993 Milwaukee	AL	47	162	47	6	0	7	(4 | 3)	74	21	30	17	0	15	1	1	1	3	0	1.00	7	.290	.359	.457
Oakland	AL	73	255	65	10	2	4	(2 | 2)	91	24	27	27	1	33	1	2	4	4	7	.36	7	.255	.324	.357
10 ML YEARS		1221	4507	1317	236	32	59	(32 | 27)	1794	627	511	564	24	513	30	32	34	74	48	.61	114	.292	.372	.398

Aaron Sele

Pitches: Right **Bats:** Right **Pos:** SP **Ht:** 6'5" **Wt:** 215 **Born:** 6/25/70 **Age:** 26

		HOW MUCH HE PITCHED						WHAT HE GAVE UP												THE RESULTS					
Year Team	Lg	G	GS	CG	GF	IP	BFP	H	R	ER	HR	SH	SF	HB	TBB	IBB	SO	WP	Bk	W	L	Pct.	ShO	Sv	ERA
1995 Sarasota *	A	2	2	0	0	7	27	6	0	0	0	0	0	0	1	0	8	0	0	0	0	.000	0	0	0.00
Trenton *	AA	2	2	0	0	8	33	8	3	3	0	0	1	2	2	0	9	0	0	0	1	.000	0	0	3.38
Pawtucket *	AAA	2	2	0	0	5	25	9	5	5	3	0	0	1	2	0	1	0	0	0	0	.000	0	0	9.00
1993 Boston	AL	18	18	0	0	111.2	484	100	42	34	5	2	5	7	48	2	93	5	0	7	2	.778	0	0	2.74
1994 Boston	AL	22	22	2	0	143.1	615	140	68	61	13	4	5	9	60	2	105	4	0	8	7	.533	0	0	3.83

Year Team	Lg	G	GS	CG	GF	IP	BFP	H	R	ER	HR	SH	SF	HB	TBB	IBB	SO	WP	Bk	W	L	Pct.	ShO	Sv	ERA
1995 Boston	AL	6	6	0	0	32.1	146	32	14	11	3	1	1	3	14	0	21	3	0	3	1	.750	0	0	3.06
3 ML YEARS		46	46	2	0	287.1	1245	272	124	106	21	7	11	19	122	4	219	12	0	18	10	.643	0	0	3.32

Scott Servais

Bats: Right **Throws:** Right **Pos:** C   **Ht:** 6' 2" **Wt:** 195 **Born:** 6/4/67 **Age:** 29

								BATTING										BASERUNNING				PERCENTAGES		
Year Team	Lg	G	AB	H	2B	3B	HR	(Hm	Rd)	TB	R	RBI	TBB	IBB	SO	HBP	SH	SF	SB	CS	SB%	GDP	Avg	OBP	SLG
1991 Houston	NL	16	37	6	3	0	0	(0	0)	9	0	6	4	0	8	0	1	0	0	0	.00	0	.162	.244	.243
1992 Houston	NL	77	205	49	9	0	0	(0	0)	58	12	15	11	2	25	5	6	0	0	0	.00	7	.239	.294	.283
1993 Houston	NL	85	258	63	11	0	11	(5	6)	107	24	32	22	2	45	5	3	3	0	0	.00	6	.244	.313	.415
1994 Houston	NL	78	251	49	15	1	9	(3	6)	93	27	41	10	0	44	4	7	3	0	0	.00	6	.195	.235	.371
1995 Hou-ChN	NL	80	264	70	22	0	13	(8	5)	131	38	47	32	8	52	3	2	3	2	2	.50	9	.265	.348	.496
1995 Houston	NL	28	89	20	10	0	1	(1	0)	33	7	12	9	2	15	1	1	1	0	1	.00	4	.225	.300	.371
Chicago	NL	52	175	50	12	0	12	(7	5)	98	31	35	23	6	37	2	1	2	2	1	.67	5	.286	.371	.560
5 ML YEARS		336	1015	237	60	1	33	(16	17)	398	101	141	79	12	174	17	19	9	2	2	.50	28	.233	.297	.392

Scott Service

Pitches: Right **Bats:** Right **Pos:** RP   **Ht:** 6' 6" **Wt:** 226 **Born:** 2/26/67 **Age:** 29

			HOW MUCH HE PITCHED					WHAT HE GAVE UP												THE RESULTS					
Year Team	Lg	G	GS	CG	GF	IP	BFP	H	R	ER	HR	SH	SF	HB	TBB	IBB	SO	WP	Bk	W	L	Pct.	ShO	Sv	ERA
1995 Indianapols *	AAA	36	0	0	32	41.1	175	33	13	10	4	2	1	3	15	2	48	1	0	4	1	.800	0	18	2.18
1988 Philadelphia	NL	5	0	0	1	5.1	23	7	1	1	0	0	0	1	1	0	6	0	0	0	0	.000	0	0	1.69
1992 Montreal	NL	5	0	0	1	7	41	15	11	11	1	0	0	0	5	0	11	0	0	0	0	.000	0	0	14.14
1993 Cin-Col	NL	29	0	0	7	46	197	44	24	22	6	2	4	2	16	4	43	0	0	2	2	.500	0	2	4.30
1994 Cincinnati	NL	6	0	0	2	7.1	35	8	9	6	2	2	0	0	3	0	5	0	0	1	2	.333	0	0	7.36
1995 San Francisco	NL	28	0	0	6	31	129	18	11	11	4	3	2	2	20	4	30	3	0	3	1	.750	0	0	3.19
1993 Cincinnati	NL	26	0	0	7	41.1	173	36	19	17	5	2	2	1	15	4	40	0	0	2	2	.500	0	2	3.70
Colorado	NL	3	0	0	0	4.2	24	8	5	5	1	0	2	1	1	0	3	0	0	0	0	.000	0	0	9.64
5 ML YEARS		73	0	0	16	96.2	425	92	56	51	13	7	6	5	45	8	95	3	0	6	5	.545	0	2	4.75

Mike Sharperson

Bats: Right **Throws:** Right **Pos:** 3B   **Ht:** 6' 3" **Wt:** 205 **Born:** 10/4/61 **Age:** 34

								BATTING										BASERUNNING				PERCENTAGES		
Year Team	Lg	G	AB	H	2B	3B	HR	(Hm	Rd)	TB	R	RBI	TBB	IBB	SO	HBP	SH	SF	SB	CS	SB%	GDP	Avg	OBP	SLG
1995 Richmond *	AAA	87	298	95	16	1	3	--	--	122	42	47	35	3	34	2	1	7	7	2	.78	6	.319	.386	.409
1987 Tor-LA		42	129	29	6	1	0	(0	0)	37	11	10	11	1	20	1	1	0	2	1	.67	3	.225	.291	.287
1988 Los Angeles	NL	46	59	16	1	0	0	(0	0)	17	8	4	1	0	12	1	2	1	0	1	.00	1	.271	.290	.288
1989 Los Angeles	NL	27	28	7	3	0	0	(0	0)	10	2	5	4	1	7	0	1	1	0	1	.00	1	.250	.333	.357
1990 Los Angeles	NL	129	357	106	14	2	3	(1	2)	133	42	36	46	6	39	1	8	3	15	6	.71	5	.297	.376	.373
1991 Los Angeles	NL	105	216	60	11	2	2	(1	1)	81	24	20	25	0	24	1	10	0	1	3	.25	2	.278	.355	.375
1992 Los Angeles	NL	128	317	95	21	0	3	(2	1)	125	48	36	47	1	33	0	5	3	2	2	.50	9	.300	.387	.394
1993 Los Angeles	NL	73	90	23	4	0	2	(1	1)	33	13	10	5	0	17	1	0	1	2	0	1.00	2	.256	.299	.367
1995 Atlanta	NL	7	7	1	1	0	0	(0	0)	2	1	2	0	0	2	0	0	0	0	0	.00	0	.143	.143	.286
1987 Toronto	AL	32	96	20	4	1	0	(0	0)	26	4	9	7	0	15	1	1	0	2	1	.67	2	.208	.269	.271
Los Angeles	NL	10	33	9	2	0	0	(0	0)	11	7	1	4	1	5	0	0	0	0	0	.00	1	.273	.351	.333
8 ML YEARS		557	1203	337	61	5	10	(5	5)	438	149	123	139	9	154	5	27	9	22	14	.61	23	.280	.355	.364

Jeff Shaw

Pitches: Right **Bats:** Right **Pos:** RP   **Ht:** 6' 2" **Wt:** 200 **Born:** 7/7/66 **Age:** 29

			HOW MUCH HE PITCHED					WHAT HE GAVE UP												THE RESULTS					
Year Team	Lg	G	GS	CG	GF	IP	BFP	H	R	ER	HR	SH	SF	HB	TBB	IBB	SO	WP	Bk	W	L	Pct.	ShO	Sv	ERA
1990 Cleveland	AL	12	9	0	0	48.2	229	73	38	36	11	1	3	0	20	0	25	3	0	3	4	.429	0	0	6.66
1991 Cleveland	AL	29	1	0	9	72.1	311	72	34	27	6	1	4	4	27	5	31	6	0	0	5	.000	0	1	3.36
1992 Cleveland	AL	2	1	0	1	7.2	33	7	7	7	2	2	0	0	4	0	3	0	0	0	1	.000	0	0	8.22
1993 Montreal	NL	55	8	0	13	95.2	404	91	47	44	12	5	2	7	32	2	50	2	0	2	7	.222	0	0	4.14
1994 Montreal	NL	46	0	0	15	67.1	287	67	32	29	8	2	4	2	15	2	47	5	0	5	2	.714	0	1	3.88
1995 Mon-ChA		59	0	0	18	72	309	70	42	39	6	7	1	4	27	4	51	0	0	1	6	.143	0	3	4.88
1995 Montreal	NL	50	0	0	17	62.1	268	58	35	32	4	6	1	3	26	4	45	0	0	1	6	.143	0	3	4.62
Chicago	AL	9	0	0	1	9.2	41	12	7	7	2	1	0	1	1	0	6	0	0	0	0	.000	0	0	6.52
6 ML YEARS		203	19	0	56	363.2	1573	380	200	182	45	18	14	17	125	13	207	16	0	11	25	.306	0	5	4.50

Danny Sheaffer

Bats: Right **Throws:** Right **Pos:** C   **Ht:** 6' 0" **Wt:** 195 **Born:** 8/2/61 **Age:** 34

								BATTING										BASERUNNING				PERCENTAGES		
Year Team	Lg	G	AB	H	2B	3B	HR	(Hm	Rd)	TB	R	RBI	TBB	IBB	SO	HBP	SH	SF	SB	CS	SB%	GDP	Avg	OBP	SLG
1987 Boston	AL	25	66	8	1	0	1	(0	1)	12	5	5	0	0	14	0	1	1	0	0	.00	2	.121	.119	.182
1989 Cleveland	AL	7	16	1	0	0	0	(0	0)	1	1	0	2	0	2	0	1	0	0	0	.00	0	.063	.167	.063
1993 Colorado	NL	82	216	60	9	1	4	(2	2)	83	26	32	8	0	15	1	2	6	2	3	.40	9	.278	.299	.384

Year	Team	Lg	G	AB	H	2B	3B	HR	(Hm	Rd)	TB	R	RBI	TBB	IBB	SO	HBP	SH	SF	SB	CS	SB%	GDP	Avg	OBP	SLG
1994	Colorado	NL	44	110	24	4	0	1	(0	1)	31	11	12	10	0	11	0	0	0	0	2	.00	2	.218	.283	.282
1995	St. Louis	NL	76	208	48	10	1	5	(2	3)	75	24	30	23	2	38	0	0	1	0	0	.00	8	.231	.306	.361
	5 ML YEARS		234	616	141	24	2	11	(4	7)	202	67	79	43	2	80	1	4	8	2	5	.29	21	.229	.277	.328

Gary Sheffield

Bats: Right **Throws:** Right **Pos:** RF   **Ht:** 5'11" **Wt:** 190 **Born:** 11/18/68 **Age:** 27

						BATTING														BASERUNNING				PERCENTAGES		
Year	Team	Lg	G	AB	H	2B	3B	HR	(Hm	Rd)	TB	R	RBI	TBB	IBB	SO	HBP	SH	SF	SB	CS	SB%	GDP	Avg	OBP	SLG
1988	Milwaukee	AL	24	80	19	1	0	4	(1	3)	32	12	12	7	0	7	0	1	1	3	1	.75	5	.238	.295	.400
1989	Milwaukee	AL	95	368	91	18	0	5	(2	3)	124	34	32	27	0	33	4	3	3	10	6	.63	4	.247	.303	.337
1990	Milwaukee	AL	125	487	143	30	1	10	(3	7)	205	67	67	44	1	41	3	4	9	25	10	.71	11	.294	.350	.421
1991	Milwaukee	AL	50	175	34	12	2	2	(2	0)	56	25	22	19	1	15	3	1	5	5	5	.50	3	.194	.277	.320
1992	San Diego	NL	146	557	184	34	3	33	(23	10)	323	87	100	48	5	40	6	0	7	5	6	.45	19	**.330**	.385	.580
1993	SD-Fla	NL	140	494	145	20	5	20	(10	10)	235	67	73	47	6	64	9	0	7	17	5	.77	11	.294	.361	.476
1994	Florida	NL	87	322	89	16	1	27	(15	12)	188	61	78	51	11	50	6	0	5	12	6	.67	10	.276	.380	.584
1995	Florida	NL	63	213	69	8	0	16	(4	12)	125	46	46	55	8	45	4	0	2	19	4	.83	3	.324	.467	.587
1993	San Diego	NL	68	258	76	12	2	10	(6	4)	122	34	36	18	0	30	3	0	3	5	1	.83	9	.295	.344	.473
	Florida	NL	72	236	69	8	3	10	(4	6)	113	33	37	29	6	34	6	0	4	12	4	.75	2	.292	.378	.479
	8 ML YEARS		730	2696	774	139	12	117	(60	57)	1288	399	430	298	32	295	35	9	39	96	43	.69	66	.287	.361	.478

Keith Shepherd

Pitches: Right **Bats:** Right **Pos:** RP   **Ht:** 6'2" **Wt:** 215 **Born:** 1/21/68 **Age:** 28

			HOW MUCH HE PITCHED						WHAT HE GAVE UP									THE RESULTS					
Year	Team	Lg	G	GS	CG	GF	IP	BFP	H	R	ER	HR	SH	SF	HB	TBB	IBB	SO	WP	Bk	W	L	Pct.	ShO	Sv	ERA
1995	Charlotte *	AAA	4	0	0	1	4.2	29	11	11	11	1	0	1	1	3	0	2	0	0	1	1	.500	0	0	21.21
1992	Philadelphia	NL	12	0	0	6	22	91	19	10	8	0	4	3	0	6	1	10	1	0	1	1	.500	0	3	3.27
1993	Colorado	NL	14	1	0	3	19.1	85	26	16	15	4	1	1	1	4	0	7	1	0	1	3	.250	0	1	6.98
1995	Boston	AL	2	0	0	0	1	9	4	4	4	0	0	0	0	2	0	0	0	0	0	0	.000	0	0	36.00
	3 ML YEARS		28	1	0	9	42.1	185	49	30	27	4	5	4	1	12	1	17	2	0	2	4	.333	0	3	5.74

Craig Shipley

Bats: Right **Throws:** Right **Pos:** 3B/SS   **Ht:** 6'1" **Wt:** 190 **Born:** 1/7/63 **Age:** 33

						BATTING														BASERUNNING				PERCENTAGES		
Year	Team	Lg	G	AB	H	2B	3B	HR	(Hm	Rd)	TB	R	RBI	TBB	IBB	SO	HBP	SH	SF	SB	CS	SB%	GDP	Avg	OBP	SLG
1986	Los Angeles	NL	12	27	3	1	0	0	(0	0)	4	3	4	2	1	5	1	1	0	0	0	.00	1	.111	.200	.148
1987	Los Angeles	NL	26	35	9	1	0	0	(0	0)	10	3	2	0	0	6	0	0	0	0	0	.00	2	.257	.257	.286
1989	New York	NL	4	7	1	0	0	0	(0	0)	1	3	0	0	0	1	0	0	0	0	0	.00	0	.143	.143	.143
1991	San Diego	NL	37	91	25	3	0	1	(0	1)	31	6	6	2	0	14	1	1	0	0	1	.00	1	.275	.298	.341
1992	San Diego	NL	52	105	26	6	0	0	(0	0)	32	7	7	2	1	21	0	1	0	1	1	.50	2	.248	.262	.305
1993	San Diego	NL	105	230	54	9	0	4	(2	2)	75	25	22	10	0	31	3	1	1	12	3	.80	3	.235	.275	.326
1994	San Diego	NL	81	240	80	14	4	4	(2	2)	114	32	30	9	1	28	3	4	2	6	6	.50	3	.333	.362	.475
1995	Houston	NL	92	232	61	8	1	3	(1	2)	80	23	24	8	3	28	2	1	2	6	1	.86	13	.263	.291	.345
	8 ML YEARS		409	967	259	42	5	12	(5	7)	347	102	95	33	6	134	10	9	5	25	12	.68	25	.268	.298	.359

Paul Shuey

Pitches: Right **Bats:** Right **Pos:** RP   **Ht:** 6'3" **Wt:** 215 **Born:** 9/16/70 **Age:** 25

			HOW MUCH HE PITCHED						WHAT HE GAVE UP									THE RESULTS					
Year	Team	Lg	G	GS	CG	GF	IP	BFP	H	R	ER	HR	SH	SF	HB	TBB	IBB	SO	WP	Bk	W	L	Pct.	ShO	Sv	ERA
1992	Columbus	A	14	14	0	0	78	335	62	35	29	2	2	2	3	47	2	73	5	5	5	5	.500	0	0	3.35
1993	Canton-Akrn	AA	27	7	0	10	61.2	291	76	50	50	13	1	4	3	36	3	41	5	0	4	8	.333	0	0	7.30
	Kinston	A	15	0	0	7	22.1	99	29	12	12	1	0	1	1	8	0	27	4	1	1	0	1.000	0	4	4.84
1994	Kinston	A	13	0	0	12	12	49	10	5	5	1	1	1	0	3	0	16	1	0	1	0	1.000	0	8	3.75
	Charlotte	AAA	20	0	0	18	23.1	95	15	9	5	1	1	0	1	10	0	25	3	0	2	1	.667	0	10	1.93
1995	Buffalo	AAA	25	0	0	19	27.1	108	21	9	8	2	3	0	0	7	0	27	2	0	1	2	.333	0	11	2.63
1994	Cleveland	AL	14	0	0	11	11.2	62	14	11	11	1	0	0	0	12	1	16	4	0	0	1	.000	0	5	8.49
1995	Cleveland	AL	7	0	0	3	6.1	28	5	4	3	0	2	0	0	5	0	5	1	0	0	2	.000	0	0	4.26
	2 ML YEARS		21	0	0	14	18	90	19	15	14	1	2	0	0	17	1	21	5	0	0	3	.000	0	5	7.00

Terry Shumpert

Bats: Right **Throws:** Right **Pos:** 2B   **Ht:** 5'11" **Wt:** 185 **Born:** 8/16/66 **Age:** 29

						BATTING														BASERUNNING				PERCENTAGES		
Year	Team	Lg	G	AB	H	2B	3B	HR	(Hm	Rd)	TB	R	RBI	TBB	IBB	SO	HBP	SH	SF	SB	CS	SB%	GDP	Avg	OBP	SLG
1995	Pawtucket *	AAA	37	133	36	7	0	2	--	--	49	17	11	14	0	27	1	2	0	10	4	.71	3	.271	.345	.368
1990	Kansas City	AL	32	91	25	6	1	0	(0	0)	33	7	8	2	0	17	1	0	2	3	3	.50	4	.275	.292	.363
1991	Kansas City	AL	144	369	80	16	4	5	(1	4)	119	45	34	30	0	75	5	10	3	17	11	.61	10	.217	.283	.322
1992	Kansas City	AL	36	94	14	5	1	1	(0	1)	24	6	11	3	0	17	0	2	0	2	2	.50	2	.149	.175	.255
1993	Kansas City	AL	8	10	1	0	0	0	(0	0)	1	0	0	2	0	2	0	0	0	1	0	1.00	0	.100	.250	.100

1994 Kansas City	AL	64	183	44	6	2	8	(2	6)	78	28	24	13	0	39	0	5	1	18	3	.86	0	.240	.289	.426
1995 Boston	AL	21	47	11	3	0	0	(0	0)	14	6	3	4	0	13	0	0	0	3	1	.75	0	.234	.294	.298
6 ML YEARS		305	794	175	36	8	14	(3	11)	269	92	80	54	0	163	6	17	6	44	20	.69	16	.220	.273	.339

Joe Siddall

Bats: Left **Throws:** Right **Pos:** C **Ht:** 6' 1" **Wt:** 197 **Born:** 10/25/67 **Age:** 28

							BATTING												BASERUNNING				PERCENTAGES		
Year Team	Lg	G	AB	H	2B	3B	HR	(Hm	Rd)	TB	R	RBI	TBB	IBB	SO	HBP	SH	SF	SB	CS	SB%	GDP	Avg	OBP	SLG
1988 Jamestown	A	53	178	38	5	3	1	--	--	52	18	16	14	1	29	1	4	2	5	4	.56	3	.213	.272	.292
1989 Rockford	A	98	313	74	15	2	4	--	--	105	36	38	26	2	56	6	5	4	8	5	.62	3	.236	.304	.335
1990 W. Palm Bch	A	106	348	78	12	1	0	--	--	92	29	32	20	0	55	1	10	2	6	7	.46	7	.224	.267	.264
1991 Harrisburg	AA	76	235	54	6	1	1	--	--	65	28	23	23	2	53	1	2	3	8	3	.73	7	.230	.298	.277
1992 Harrisburg	AA	95	288	68	12	0	2	--	--	86	26	27	29	1	55	3	1	3	4	4	.50	7	.236	.310	.299
1993 Ottawa	AAA	48	136	29	6	0	1	--	--	38	14	16	19	5	33	0	3	2	2	2	.50	6	.213	.306	.279
1994 Ottawa	AAA	38	110	19	2	1	3	--	--	32	9	13	10	2	21	2	7	2	1	1	.50	3	.173	.250	.291
1995 Ottawa	AAA	83	248	53	14	2	1	--	--	74	26	23	23	0	42	4	2	0	3	3	.50	6	.214	.291	.298
1993 Montreal	NL	19	20	2	1	0	0	(0	0)	3	0	1	1	1	5	0	0	0	0	0	.00	0	.100	.143	.150
1995 Montreal	NL	7	10	3	0	0	0	(0	0)	3	4	1	3	0	3	1	0	0	0	0	.00	0	.300	.500	.300
2 ML YEARS		26	30	5	1	0	0	(0	0)	6	4	2	4	1	8	1	0	0	0	0	.00	0	.167	.286	.200

Ruben Sierra

Bats: Both **Throws:** Right **Pos:** RF/DH **Ht:** 6' 1" **Wt:** 200 **Born:** 10/6/65 **Age:** 30

							BATTING												BASERUNNING				PERCENTAGES		
Year Team	Lg	G	AB	H	2B	3B	HR	(Hm	Rd)	TB	R	RBI	TBB	IBB	SO	HBP	SH	SF	SB	CS	SB%	GDP	Avg	OBP	SLG
1986 Texas	AL	113	382	101	13	10	16	(8	8)	182	50	55	22	3	65	1	1	5	7	8	.47	8	.264	.302	.476
1987 Texas	AL	158	643	169	35	4	30	(15	15)	302	97	109	39	4	114	2	0	12	16	11	.59	18	.263	.302	.470
1988 Texas	AL	156	615	156	32	2	23	(15	8)	261	77	91	44	10	91	1	0	8	18	4	.82	15	.254	.301	.424
1989 Texas	AL	162	634	194	35	14	29	(21	8)	344	101	119	43	2	82	2	0	10	8	2	.80	7	.306	.347	.543
1990 Texas	AL	159	608	170	37	2	16	(10	6)	259	70	96	49	13	86	1	0	8	9	0	1.00	15	.280	.330	.426
1991 Texas	AL	161	661	203	44	5	25	(12	13)	332	110	116	56	7	91	0	0	9	16	4	.80	17	.307	.357	.502
1992 Oak-Tex	AL	151	601	167	34	7	17	(10	7)	266	83	87	45	12	68	0	0	10	14	4	.78	11	.278	.323	.443
1993 Oakland	AL	158	630	147	23	5	22	(9	13)	246	77	101	52	16	97	0	0	10	25	5	.83	17	.233	.288	.390
1994 Oakland	AL	110	426	114	21	1	23	(11	12)	206	71	92	23	4	64	0	0	11	8	5	.62	15	.268	.298	.484
1995 Oak-NYA	AL	126	479	126	32	0	19	(8	11)	215	73	86	46	4	76	0	0	8	5	4	.56	8	.263	.323	.449
1992 Oakland	AL	27	101	28	4	1	3	(2	1)	43	17	17	14	6	9	0	0	2	2	0	1.00	2	.277	.359	.426
Texas		124	500	139	30	6	14	(8	6)	223	66	70	31	6	59	0	0	8	12	4	.75	9	.278	.315	.446
1995 Oakland	AL	70	264	70	17	0	12	(3	9)	123	40	42	24	2	42	0	0	3	4	4	.50	2	.265	.323	.466
New York	AL	56	215	56	15	0	7	(5	2)	92	33	44	22	2	34	0	0	5	1	0	1.00	6	.260	.322	.428
10 ML YEARS		1454	5679	1547	306	50	220	(119	101)	2613	809	952	419	75	834	7	1	91	126	47	.73	131	.272	.318	.460

Dave Silvestri

Bats: Right **Throws:** Right **Pos:** 2B **Ht:** 6' 0" **Wt:** 180 **Born:** 9/29/67 **Age:** 28

							BATTING												BASERUNNING				PERCENTAGES		
Year Team	Lg	G	AB	H	2B	3B	HR	(Hm	Rd)	TB	R	RBI	TBB	IBB	SO	HBP	SH	SF	SB	CS	SB%	GDP	Avg	OBP	SLG
1992 New York	AL	7	13	4	0	2	0	(0	0)	8	3	1	0	0	3	0	0	0	0	0	.00	1	.308	.308	.615
1993 New York	AL	7	21	6	1	0	1	(0	1)	10	4	4	5	0	3	0	0	0	0	0	.00	1	.286	.423	.476
1994 New York	AL	12	18	2	0	1	1	(1	0)	7	3	2	4	0	9	0	0	1	0	1	.00	0	.111	.261	.389
1995 NYA-Mon		56	93	21	6	0	3	(0	3)	36	16	11	13	0	36	1	1	2	2	0	1.00	3	.226	.321	.387
1995 New York	AL	17	21	2	0	0	1	(0	1)	5	4	4	4	0	9	1	0	1	0	0	.00	1	.095	.259	.238
Montreal	NL	39	72	19	6	0	2	(0	2)	31	12	7	9	0	27	0	1	1	2	0	1.00	2	.264	.341	.431
4 ML YEARS		82	145	33	7	3	5	(1	4)	61	26	18	22	0	51	1	1	3	2	1	.67	5	.228	.327	.421

Bill Simas

Pitches: Right **Bats:** Right **Pos:** RP **Ht:** 6' 3" **Wt:** 225 **Born:** 11/28/71 **Age:** 24

			HOW MUCH HE PITCHED				WHAT HE GAVE UP										THE RESULTS					
Year Team	Lg	G	GS	CG	GF	IP	BFP	H	R	ER	HR	SH	SF	HB	TBB	IBB	SO	WP	Bk	W	L	Pct.	ShO	Sv	ERA
1992 Boise	A	14	12	0	1	70.2	320	82	44	31	0	2	4	3	29	2	39	4	1	6	5	.545	0	1	3.95
1993 Cedar Rapds	A	7	6	0	0	80	376	93	60	44	8	5	4	3	36	1	62	4	1	5	8	.385	0	0	4.95
1994 Midland	AA	13	0	0	11	15.1	52	5	1	1	0	0	0	0	2	0	12	0	0	2	0	1.000	0	6	0.59
Lk Elsinore	A	37	0	0	27	47	194	44	17	11	2	3	2	3	10	1	34	3	2	5	2	.714	0	13	2.11
1995 Vancouver	AAA	30	0	0	24	38	175	44	19	15	1	1	1	4	14	2	44	1	0	6	3	.667	0	6	3.55
Nashville	AAA	7	0	0	3	11.2	50	12	5	5	0	1	0	0	3	1	12	0	0	1	1	.500	0	0	3.86
1995 Chicago	AL	14	0	0	4	14	66	15	5	4	1	0	0	1	10	2	16	1	0	1	1	.500	0	0	2.57

Mike Simms

Bats: Right **Throws:** Right **Pos:** 1B/RF   **Ht:** 6' 4" **Wt:** 185 **Born:** 1/12/67 **Age:** 29

Year Team	Lg	G	AB	H	2B	3B	HR	(Hm	Rd)	TB	R	RBI	TBB	IBB	SO	HBP	SH	SF	SB	CS	SB%	GDP	Avg	OBP	SLG
1995 Tucson *	AAA	85	319	94	26	8	13	--	--	175	56	66	35	0	65	3	0	4	10	2	.83	6	.295	.366	.549
1990 Houston	NL	12	13	4	1	0	1	(0	1)	8	3	2	0	0	4	0	0	0	0	0	.00	1	.308	.308	.615
1991 Houston	NL	49	123	25	5	0	3	(1	2)	39	18	16	18	0	38	0	0	2	1	0	1.00	2	.203	.301	.317
1992 Houston	NL	15	24	6	1	0	1	(0	1)	10	1	3	2	0	9	1	0	0	0	0	.00	1	.250	.333	.417
1994 Houston	NL	6	12	1	1	0	0	(0	0)	2	1	0	0	0	5	0	0	0	0	1	1.00	0	.083	.083	.167
1995 Houston	NL	50	121	31	4	0	9	(5	4)	62	14	24	13	0	28	3	0	1	1	2	.33	3	.256	.341	.512
5 ML YEARS		132	293	67	12	0	14	(6	8)	121	37	45	33	0	84	4	0	3	3	2	.60	7	.229	.312	.413

Duane Singleton

Bats: Left **Throws:** Right **Pos:** CF   **Ht:** 6' 1" **Wt:** 177 **Born:** 8/6/72 **Age:** 23

Year Team	Lg	G	AB	H	2B	3B	HR	(Hm	Rd)	TB	R	RBI	TBB	IBB	SO	HBP	SH	SF	SB	CS	SB%	GDP	Avg	OBP	SLG
1990 Brewers	R	46	134	31	6	1	1	--	--	42	30	13	41	0	39	1	1	1	5	9	.36	1	.231	.412	.313
1991 Beloit	A	101	388	112	13	7	3	--	--	148	57	44	40	7	57	3	5	2	42	17	.71	7	.289	.358	.381
1992 Salinas	A	19	72	22	5	2	1	--	--	34	6	8	6	0	11	0	0	0	4	1	.80	0	.306	.359	.472
Stockton	A	97	389	112	15	10	5	--	--	162	73	51	39	0	66	3	3	6	34	15	.69	7	.288	.352	.416
1993 El Paso	AA	125	456	105	21	6	2	--	--	144	52	61	34	0	90	3	2	5	23	19	.55	4	.230	.285	.316
1994 Stockton	A	38	134	39	6	0	4	--	--	57	31	13	18	0	23	0	0	0	15	6	.71	1	.291	.375	.425
El Paso	AA	39	139	40	11	3	2	--	--	63	25	24	19	0	33	2	1	0	10	5	.67	6	.288	.381	.453
New Orleans	AAA	41	133	37	4	5	0	--	--	51	26	14	18	0	26	0	5	1	6	4	.60	1	.278	.362	.383
1995 New Orleans	AAA	106	355	95	10	4	4	--	--	125	48	29	39	2	63	3	3	1	31	15	.67	7	.268	.344	.352
1994 Milwaukee	AL	2	0	0	0	0	0	(0	0)	0	0	0	0	0	0	0	0	0	0	0	.00	0	.000	.000	.000
1995 Milwaukee	AL	13	31	2	0	0	0	(0	0)	2	0	0	1	0	10	0	0	0	1	0	1.00	0	.065	.094	.065
2 ML YEARS		15	31	2	0	0	0	(0	0)	2	0	0	1	0	10	0	0	0	1	0	1.00	0	.065	.094	.065

Mike Sirotka

Pitches: Left **Bats:** Left **Pos:** SP   **Ht:** 6' 1" **Wt:** 200 **Born:** 5/13/71 **Age:** 25

Year Team	Lg	G	GS	CG	GF	IP	BFP	H	R	ER	HR	SH	SF	HB	TBB	IBB	SO	WP	Bk	W	L	Pct.	ShO	Sv	ERA
1993 White Sox	R	3	0	0	1	5	21	4	1	0	0	0	0	0	2	0	8	0	0	0	0	.000	0	0	0.00
South Bend	A	7	1	0	3	10.1	50	12	8	7	3	0	0	0	6	0	12	0	1	0	1	.000	0	0	6.10
1994 South Bend	A	27	27	8	0	196.2	824	183	99	67	11	9	6	3	58	1	173	7	2	12	9	.571	2	0	3.07
1995 Birmingham	AA	16	16	1	0	101.1	412	95	42	36	11	3	3	2	22	0	79	4	1	7	6	.538	0	0	3.20
Nashville	AAA	8	8	0	0	54	217	51	21	17	4	2	3	1	13	1	34	1	0	1	5	.167	0	0	2.83
1995 Chicago	AL	6	6	0	0	34.1	152	39	16	16	2	1	3	0	17	0	19	2	0	1	2	.333	0	0	4.19

Don Slaught

Bats: Right **Throws:** Right **Pos:** C   **Ht:** 6' 1" **Wt:** 185 **Born:** 9/11/58 **Age:** 37

Year Team	Lg	G	AB	H	2B	3B	HR	(Hm	Rd)	TB	R	RBI	TBB	IBB	SO	HBP	SH	SF	SB	CS	SB%	GDP	Avg	OBP	SLG
1995 Carolina *	AA	3	12	3	1	0	0	--	--	4	1	1	0	0	3	0	0	0	0	0	.00	0	.250	.250	.333
1982 Kansas City	AL	43	115	32	6	0	3	(0	3)	47	14	8	9	0	12	0	2	0	0	0	.00	3	.278	.331	.409
1983 Kansas City	AL	83	276	86	13	4	0	(0	0)	107	21	28	11	0	27	0	1	2	3	1	.75	8	.312	.336	.388
1984 Kansas City	AL	124	409	108	27	4	4	(1	3)	155	48	42	20	4	55	2	8	7	0	0	.00	8	.264	.297	.379
1985 Texas	AL	102	343	96	17	4	8	(4	4)	145	34	35	20	1	41	6	1	0	5	4	.56	5	.280	.331	.423
1986 Texas	AL	95	314	83	17	1	13	(5	8)	141	39	46	16	0	59	5	3	3	3	2	.60	8	.264	.308	.449
1987 Texas	AL	95	237	53	15	2	8	(5	3)	96	25	16	24	3	51	1	4	0	0	3	.00	7	.224	.298	.405
1988 New York	AL	97	322	91	25	1	9	(7	2)	145	33	43	24	3	54	3	5	4	1	0	1.00	10	.283	.334	.450
1989 New York	AL	117	350	88	21	3	5	(3	2)	130	34	38	30	3	57	5	2	5	1	1	.50	9	.251	.315	.371
1990 Pittsburgh	NL	84	230	69	18	3	4	(1	3)	105	27	29	27	2	27	3	3	4	0	1	.00	2	.300	.375	.457
1991 Pittsburgh	NL	77	220	65	17	1	1	(0	1)	87	19	29	21	1	32	3	5	1	1	0	1.00	6	.295	.363	.395
1992 Pittsburgh	NL	87	255	88	17	3	4	(2	2)	123	26	37	17	5	23	2	6	5	2	2	.50	6	.345	.384	.482
1993 Pittsburgh	NL	116	377	113	19	2	10	(1	9)	166	34	55	29	2	56	6	4	4	2	1	.67	13	.300	.356	.440
1994 Pittsburgh	NL	76	240	69	7	0	2	(1	1)	82	21	21	34	2	31	3	1	1	0	0	.00	5	.288	.381	.342
1995 Pittsburgh	NL	35	112	34	6	0	0	(0	0)	40	13	13	9	2	8	1	1	0	0	0	.00	5	.304	.361	.357
14 ML YEARS		1231	3800	1075	225	28	71	(30	41)	1569	388	440	291	28	533	40	46	36	18	15	.55	98	.283	.337	.413

Heathcliff Slocumb

Pitches: Right **Bats:** Right **Pos:** RP   **Ht:** 6' 3" **Wt:** 215 **Born:** 6/7/66 **Age:** 30

Year Team	Lg	G	GS	CG	GF	IP	BFP	H	R	ER	HR	SH	SF	HB	TBB	IBB	SO	WP	Bk	W	L	Pct.	ShO	Sv	ERA
1991 Chicago	NL	52	0	0	21	62.2	274	53	29	24	3	6	3	6	30	6	34	9	0	2	1	.667	0	1	3.45
1992 Chicago	NL	30	0	0	11	36	174	52	27	26	3	2	2	1	21	3	27	1	0	0	3	.000	0	1	6.50
1993 Cle-ChN		30	0	0	9	38	164	35	19	17	3	1	3	0	20	2	22	0	0	4	1	.800	0	0	4.03

1994 Philadelphia	NL	52	0	0	16	72.1	322	75	32	23	0	2	4	2	28	4	58	9	0	5	1	.833	0	0	2.86
1995 Philadelphia	NL	61	0	0	54	65.1	289	64	26	21	2	4	0	1	35	3	63	3	0	5	6	.455	0	32	2.89
1993 Cleveland	AL	20	0	0	5	27.1	122	28	14	13	3	1	2	0	16	2	18	0	0	3	1	.750	0	0	4.28
Chicago	NL	10	0	0	4	10.2	42	7	5	4	0	0	1	0	4	0	4	0	0	1	0	1.000	0	0	3.38
5 ML YEARS		225	0	0	111	274.1	1223	279	133	111	11	15	15	7	134	18	204	22	0	16	12	.571	0	34	3.64

Joe Slusarski

Pitches: Right **Bats:** Right **Pos:** RP **Ht:** 6' 4" **Wt:** 195 **Born:** 12/19/66 **Age:** 29

Year Team	Lg	HOW MUCH HE PITCHED						WHAT HE GAVE UP												THE RESULTS					
		G	GS	CG	GF	IP	BFP	H	R	ER	HR	SH	SF	HB	TBB	IBB	SO	WP	Bk	W	L	Pct.	ShO	Sv	ERA
1995 Buffalo *	AAA	4	2	0	0	15.2	67	18	12	11	2	0	1	1	4	0	9	0	0	1	1	.500	0	0	6.32
New Orleans *	AAA	33	0	0	23	48.1	188	37	10	6	4	1	1	0	11	2	30	0	0	1	1	.500	0	11	1.12
1991 Oakland	AL	20	19	1	0	109.1	486	121	69	64	14	0	3	4	52	1	60	4	0	5	7	.417	0	0	5.27
1992 Oakland	AL	15	14	0	1	76	338	85	52	46	15	1	5	6	27	0	38	0	1	5	5	.500	0	0	5.45
1993 Oakland	AL	2	1	0	0	8.2	43	9	5	5	1	2	0	0	11	3	1	0	0	0	0	.000	0	0	5.19
1995 Milwaukee	AL	12	0	0	6	15	73	21	16	9	3	1	1	2	6	1	6	0	0	1	1	.500	0	0	5.40
4 ML YEARS		49	34	1	7	209	940	236	137	124	33	4	9	12	96	5	105	4	1	11	13	.458	0	0	5.34

Aaron Small

Pitches: Right **Bats:** Right **Pos:** RP **Ht:** 6' 5" **Wt:** 208 **Born:** 11/23/71 **Age:** 24

Year Team	Lg	HOW MUCH HE PITCHED						WHAT HE GAVE UP												THE RESULTS					
		G	GS	CG	GF	IP	BFP	H	R	ER	HR	SH	SF	HB	TBB	IBB	SO	WP	Bk	W	L	Pct.	ShO	Sv	ERA
1989 Medicne Hat	R	15	14	0	0	70.2	326	80	55	46	2	3	2	3	31	1	40	9	5	1	7	.125	0	0	5.86
1990 Myrtle Bch	A	27	27	1	0	147.2	643	150	72	46	6	2	7	4	56	2	96	16	5	9	9	.500	0	0	2.80
1991 Dunedin	A	24	23	1	0	148.1	595	129	51	45	5	5	5	5	42	1	92	7	0	8	7	.533	0	0	2.73
1992 Knoxville	AA	27	24	2	0	135	610	152	94	79	13	2	4	6	61	0	79	14	0	5	12	.294	1	0	5.27
1993 Knoxville	AA	48	9	0	32	93	408	99	44	35	5	3	0	2	40	4	44	8	0	4	4	.500	0	16	3.39
1994 Syracuse	AAA	13	0	0	6	24.1	99	19	8	6	2	2	0	1	9	2	15	2	0	3	2	.600	0	0	2.22
Knoxville	AA	29	11	1	13	96.1	405	92	37	32	4	3	5	3	38	0	75	5	1	5	5	.500	1	5	2.99
1995 Syracuse	AAA	1	0	0	0	1.2	9	3	1	1	1	0	0	0	1	0	2	0	0	0	0	.000	0	0	5.40
Charlotte	AAA	33	0	0	17	40.2	170	36	15	13	2	0	1	2	10	1	31	3	0	2	1	.667	0	10	2.88
1994 Toronto	AL	1	0	0	1	2	13	5	2	2	1	0	1	0	2	0	5	0	0	0	0	.000	0	0	9.00
1995 Florida	NL	7	0	0	1	6.1	32	7	2	1	1	0	0	0	6	0	5	0	0	1	0	1.000	0	0	1.42
2 ML YEARS		8	0	0	2	8.1	45	12	4	3	2	0	1	0	8	0	5	0	0	1	0	1.000	0	0	3.24

John Smiley

Pitches: Left **Bats:** Left **Pos:** SP **Ht:** 6' 4" **Wt:** 210 **Born:** 3/17/65 **Age:** 31

Year Team	Lg	HOW MUCH HE PITCHED						WHAT HE GAVE UP												THE RESULTS					
		G	GS	CG	GF	IP	BFP	H	R	ER	HR	SH	SF	HB	TBB	IBB	SO	WP	Bk	W	L	Pct.	ShO	Sv	ERA
1986 Pittsburgh	NL	12	0	0	2	11.2	42	4	6	5	2	0	0	0	4	0	9	0	0	1	0	1.000	0	0	3.86
1987 Pittsburgh	NL	63	0	0	19	75	336	69	49	48	7	0	3	0	50	8	58	5	1	5	5	.500	0	4	5.76
1988 Pittsburgh	NL	34	32	5	0	205	835	185	81	74	15	11	8	3	46	4	129	6	6	13	11	.542	1	0	3.25
1989 Pittsburgh	NL	28	28	8	0	205.1	835	174	78	64	22	5	7	4	49	5	123	5	2	12	8	.600	1	0	2.81
1990 Pittsburgh	NL	26	25	2	0	149.1	632	161	83	77	15	5	4	2	36	1	86	2	2	9	10	.474	0	0	4.64
1991 Pittsburgh	NL	33	32	2	0	207.2	836	194	78	71	17	11	4	3	44	0	129	3	1	**20**	8	**.714**	1	0	3.08
1992 Minnesota	AL	34	34	5	0	241	972	205	93	86	17	4	9	6	65	0	163	4	0	16	9	.640	2	0	3.21
1993 Cincinnati	NL	18	18	2	0	105.2	455	117	69	66	15	10	3	2	31	0	60	2	1	3	9	.250	0	0	5.62
1994 Cincinnati	NL	24	24	1	0	158.2	672	169	80	68	18	**16**	0	4	37	3	112	4	2	11	10	.524	1	0	3.86
1995 Cincinnati	NL	28	27	1	0	176.2	724	173	72	68	11	17	5	4	39	3	124	5	1	12	5	.706	0	0	3.46
10 ML YEARS		300	220	26	21	1536	6337	1451	689	627	139	79	43	28	401	24	993	36	16	102	75	.576	6	4	3.67

Dwight Smith

Bats: Left **Throws:** Right **Pos:** RF/LF **Ht:** 5'11" **Wt:** 195 **Born:** 11/8/63 **Age:** 32

Year Team	Lg	BATTING																		BASERUNNING				PERCENTAGES		
		G	AB	H	2B	3B	HR	(Hm	Rd)	TB	R	RBI	TBB	IBB	SO	HBP	SH	SF	SB	CS	SB%	GDP	Avg	OBP	SLG
1989 Chicago	NL	109	343	111	19	6	9	(5	4)	169	52	52	31	0	51	2	4	1	9	4	.69	4	.324	.382	.493
1990 Chicago	NL	117	290	76	15	0	6	(3	3)	109	34	27	28	2	46	2	0	2	11	6	.65	7	.262	.329	.376
1991 Chicago	NL	90	167	38	7	2	3	(2	1)	58	16	21	11	2	32	1	1	0	2	3	.40	2	.228	.279	.347
1992 Chicago	NL	109	217	60	10	3	3	(3	0)	85	28	24	13	0	40	1	0	2	9	8	.53	1	.276	.318	.392
1993 Chicago	NL	111	310	93	17	5	11	(6	5)	153	51	35	25	1	51	3	1	3	8	6	.57	3	.300	.355	.494
1994 Bal-Cal	AL	73	196	55	7	2	8	(2	6)	90	31	30	12	1	37	1	0	1	2	4	.33	3	.281	.324	.459
1995 Atlanta	NL	103	131	33	8	2	3	(1	2)	54	16	21	13	1	35	2	0	1	0	3	.00	2	.252	.327	.412
1994 Baltimore	AL	28	74	23	2	1	3	(0	3)	36	12	12	5	1	17	1	0	0	0	1	.00	2	.311	.363	.486
California	AL	45	122	32	5	1	5	(2	3)	54	19	18	7	0	20	0	0	1	2	3	.40	1	.262	.300	.443
7 ML YEARS		712	1654	466	83	20	43	(22	21)	718	228	210	133	7	292	12	6	10	41	34	.55	22	.282	.338	.434

211

Lee Smith

Pitches: Right **Bats:** Right **Pos:** RP **Ht:** 6' 6" **Wt:** 269 **Born:** 12/4/57 **Age:** 38

Year	Team	Lg	G	GS	CG	GF	IP	BFP	H	R	ER	HR	SH	SF	HB	TBB	IBB	SO	WP	Bk	W	L	Pct.	ShO	Sv	ERA
1980	Chicago	NL	18	0	0	6	22	97	21	9	7	0	1	1	0	14	5	17	0	0	2	0	1.000	0	0	2.86
1981	Chicago	NL	40	1	0	12	67	280	57	31	26	2	8	2	1	31	8	50	7	1	3	6	.333	0	1	3.49
1982	Chicago	NL	72	5	0	38	117	480	105	38	35	5	6	5	3	37	5	99	6	1	2	5	.286	0	17	2.69
1983	Chicago	NL	66	0	0	56	103.1	413	70	23	19	5	9	2	1	41	14	91	5	2	4	10	.286	0	29	1.65
1984	Chicago	NL	69	0	0	59	101	428	98	42	41	6	4	5	0	35	7	86	6	0	9	7	.563	0	33	3.65
1985	Chicago	NL	65	0	0	57	97.2	397	87	35	33	9	3	1	1	32	6	112	4	0	7	4	.636	0	33	3.04
1986	Chicago	NL	66	0	0	59	90.1	372	69	32	31	7	6	3	0	42	11	93	2	0	9	9	.500	0	31	3.09
1987	Chicago	NL	62	0	0	55	83.2	280	84	30	29	4	4	0	0	32	5	96	4	0	4	10	.286	0	36	3.12
1988	Boston	AL	64	0	0	57	83.2	363	72	34	26	7	3	2	1	37	6	96	2	0	4	5	.444	0	29	2.80
1989	Boston	AL	64	0	0	50	70.2	290	53	30	28	6	2	2	0	33	6	96	1	0	6	1	.857	0	25	3.57
1990	Bos-StL		64	0	0	53	83	344	71	24	19	3	2	3	0	29	7	87	2	0	5	5	.500	0	31	2.06
1991	St. Louis	NL	67	0	0	61	73	300	70	19	19	5	5	1	0	13	5	67	1	0	6	3	.667	0	47	2.34
1992	St. Louis	NL	70	0	0	55	75	310	62	28	26	4	2	1	0	26	4	60	2	0	4	9	.308	0	43	3.12
1993	NYA-StL		63	0	0	56	58	239	53	25	25	11	0	3	0	14	2	60	1	0	2	4	.333	0	46	3.88
1994	Baltimore	AL	41	0	0	39	38.1	160	34	16	14	6	5	2	0	11	1	42	0	0	1	4	.200	0	33	3.29
1995	California	AL	52	0	0	51	49.1	209	42	19	19	3	3	3	1	25	4	43	1	0	0	5	.000	0	37	3.47
1990	Boston	AL	11	0	0	8	14.1	64	13	4	3	0	0	0	0	9	2	17	1	0	2	1	.667	0	4	1.88
	St. Louis	NL	53	0	0	45	68.2	280	58	20	16	3	2	3	0	20	5	70	1	0	3	4	.429	0	27	2.10
1993	New York	AL	8	0	0	8	8	33	4	0	0	0	0	1	0	5	1	11	0	0	0	0	.000	0	3	0.00
	St. Louis	NL	55	0	0	48	50	206	49	25	25	11	0	2	0	9	1	49	1	0	2	4	.333	0	43	4.50
16 ML YEARS			943	6	0	764	1213	5042	1048	435	397	83	63	36	8	452	96	1195	44	4	68	87	.439	0	471	2.95

Mark Smith

Bats: Right **Throws:** Right **Pos:** RF/LF **Ht:** 6' 3" **Wt:** 205 **Born:** 5/7/70 **Age:** 26

Year	Team	Lg	G	AB	H	2B	3B	HR	(Hm	Rd)	TB	R	RBI	TBB	IBB	SO	HBP	SH	SF	SB	CS	SB%	GDP	Avg	OBP	SLG
1991	Frederick	A	38	148	37	5	1	4	--	--	56	20	29	9	0	24	2	0	3	1	3	.25	4	.250	.296	.378
1992	Hagerstown	AA	128	472	136	32	6	4	--	--	192	51	62	45	9	55	4	0	6	15	5	.75	17	.288	.351	.407
1993	Rochester	AAA	129	485	136	27	1	12	--	--	201	69	68	37	3	90	9	0	2	4	6	.40	9	.280	.341	.414
1994	Rochester	AAA	114	437	108	27	1	19	--	--	194	69	66	35	1	88	7	1	3	4	3	.57	13	.247	.311	.444
1995	Rochester	AAA	96	364	101	25	3	12	--	--	168	55	66	24	1	69	7	1	7	7	3	.70	8	.277	.328	.462
1994	Baltimore	AL	3	7	1	0	0	0	(0	0)	1	0	2	0	0	2	0	0	0	0	0	.00	0	.143	.143	.143
1995	Baltimore	AL	37	104	24	5	0	3	(1	2)	38	11	15	12	2	22	1	2	1	3	0	1.00	4	.231	.314	.365
2 ML YEARS			40	111	25	5	0	3	(1	2)	39	11	17	12	2	24	1	2	1	3	0	1.00	4	.225	.304	.351

Ozzie Smith

Bats: Both **Throws:** Right **Pos:** SS **Ht:** 5'10" **Wt:** 170 **Born:** 12/26/54 **Age:** 41

Year	Team	Lg	G	AB	H	2B	3B	HR	(Hm	Rd)	TB	R	RBI	TBB	IBB	SO	HBP	SH	SF	SB	CS	SB%	GDP	Avg	OBP	SLG
1978	San Diego	NL	159	590	152	17	6	1	(0	1)	184	69	46	47	0	43	0	28	3	40	12	.77	11	.258	.311	.312
1979	San Diego	NL	156	587	124	18	6	0	(0	0)	154	77	27	37	5	37	2	22	1	28	7	.80	11	.211	.260	.262
1980	San Diego	NL	158	609	140	18	5	0	(0	0)	168	67	35	71	1	49	5	23	4	57	15	.79	9	.230	.313	.276
1981	San Diego	NL	110	450	100	11	2	0	(0	0)	115	53	21	41	1	37	5	10	1	22	12	.65	8	.222	.294	.256
1982	St. Louis	NL	140	488	121	24	1	2	(0	2)	153	58	43	68	12	32	2	4	5	25	5	.83	10	.248	.339	.314
1983	St. Louis	NL	159	552	134	30	6	3	(1	2)	185	69	50	64	9	36	1	7	2	34	7	.83	10	.243	.321	.335
1984	St. Louis	NL	124	412	106	20	5	1	(1	0)	139	53	44	56	5	17	2	11	3	35	7	.83	8	.257	.347	.337
1985	St. Louis	NL	158	537	148	22	3	6	(2	4)	194	70	54	65	11	27	2	9	2	31	8	.79	13	.276	.355	.361
1986	St. Louis	NL	153	514	144	19	4	0	(0	0)	171	67	54	79	13	27	2	11	3	31	7	.82	9	.280	.376	.333
1987	St. Louis	NL	158	600	182	40	4	0	(0	0)	230	104	75	89	3	36	1	12	4	43	9	.83	9	.303	.392	.383
1988	St. Louis	NL	153	575	155	27	1	3	(2	1)	193	80	51	74	2	43	1	12	7	57	9	.86	7	.270	.350	.336
1989	St. Louis	NL	155	593	162	30	8	2	(1	1)	214	82	50	55	3	37	2	11	3	29	7	.81	10	.273	.335	.361
1990	St. Louis	NL	143	512	130	21	1	1	(0	1)	156	61	50	61	4	33	2	7	10	32	6	.84	8	.254	.330	.305
1991	St. Louis	NL	150	550	157	30	3	3	(2	1)	202	96	50	83	2	36	1	6	1	35	9	.80	8	.285	.380	.367
1992	St. Louis	NL	132	518	153	20	2	0	(0	0)	177	73	31	59	4	34	0	12	1	43	9	.83	11	.295	.367	.342
1993	St. Louis	NL	141	545	157	22	6	1	(1	0)	194	75	53	43	1	18	1	7	7	21	8	.72	11	.288	.337	.356
1994	St. Louis	NL	98	381	100	18	3	3	(1	2)	133	51	30	38	3	26	0	10	4	6	3	.67	3	.262	.326	.349
1995	St. Louis	NL	44	156	31	5	1	0	(0	0)	38	16	11	17	0	12	2	5	2	4	3	.57	6	.199	.282	.244
18 ML YEARS			2491	9169	2396	392	67	26	(11	15)	3000	1221	775	1047	79	580	31	207	63	573	143	.80	162	.261	.337	.327

Pete Smith

Pitches: Right **Bats:** Right **Pos:** RP   **Ht:** 6' 2" **Wt:** 200 **Born:** 2/27/66 **Age:** 30

		HOW MUCH HE PITCHED						WHAT HE GAVE UP									THE RESULTS					
Year Team	Lg	G	GS	CG	GF	IP	BFP	H	R	ER	HR	SH	SF	HB	TBB	IBB	SO	WP	Bk	W	L	Pct.	ShO	Sv	ERA
1995 Charlotte *	AAA	10	8	0	1	49	206	51	21	21	5	1	2	1	17	0	20	2	2	2	1	.667	0	0	3.86
1987 Atlanta	NL	6	6	0	0	31.2	143	39	21	17	3	0	2	0	14	0	11	3	1	1	2	.333	0	0	4.83
1988 Atlanta	NL	32	32	5	0	195.1	837	183	89	80	15	12	4	1	88	3	124	5	7	7	15	.318	3	0	3.69
1989 Atlanta	NL	28	27	1	0	142	613	144	83	75	13	4	5	0	57	2	115	3	7	5	14	.263	0	0	4.75
1990 Atlanta	NL	13	13	3	0	77	327	77	45	41	11	4	3	0	24	2	56	2	1	5	6	.455	0	0	4.79
1991 Atlanta	NL	14	10	0	2	48	211	48	33	27	5	2	4	0	22	3	29	1	4	1	3	.250	0	0	5.06
1992 Atlanta	NL	12	11	2	0	79	323	63	19	18	3	4	1	0	28	2	43	2	1	7	0	1.000	1	0	2.05
1993 Atlanta	NL	20	14	0	2	90.2	390	92	45	44	15	6	5	2	36	3	53	1	1	4	8	.333	0	0	4.37
1994 New York	NL	21	21	1	0	131.1	565	145	83	81	25	5	7	2	42	4	62	3	1	4	10	.286	0	0	5.55
1995 Cincinnati	NL	11	2	0	3	24.1	106	30	19	18	8	1	3	1	7	1	14	1	0	1	2	.333	0	0	6.66
9 ML YEARS		157	136	12	7	819.1	3515	821	437	401	98	38	34	6	318	20	507	21	23	35	60	.368	4	0	4.40

Zane Smith

Pitches: Left **Bats:** Left **Pos:** SP   **Ht:** 6' 1" **Wt:** 207 **Born:** 12/28/60 **Age:** 35

		HOW MUCH HE PITCHED						WHAT HE GAVE UP									THE RESULTS					
Year Team	Lg	G	GS	CG	GF	IP	BFP	H	R	ER	HR	SH	SF	HB	TBB	IBB	SO	WP	Bk	W	L	Pct.	ShO	Sv	ERA
1995 Pawtucket *	AAA	1	1	0	0	7	23	5	0	0	0	0	0	0	0	0	5	0	0	0	0	.000	0	0	0.00
1984 Atlanta	NL	3	3	0	0	20	87	16	7	5	1	1	0	0	13	2	16	0	0	1	0	1.000	0	0	2.25
1985 Atlanta	NL	42	18	2	3	147	631	135	70	62	4	16	1	3	80	5	85	2	0	9	10	.474	2	0	3.80
1986 Atlanta	NL	38	32	3	2	204.2	889	209	109	92	8	13	6	5	105	6	139	8	0	8	16	.333	1	1	4.05
1987 Atlanta	NL	36	36	9	0	242	1035	245	130	110	19	12	5	5	91	6	130	5	1	15	10	.600	3	0	4.09
1988 Atlanta	NL	23	22	3	0	140.1	609	159	72	67	8	15	2	3	44	4	59	2	2	5	10	.333	0	0	4.30
1989 Atl-Mon	NL	48	17	0	10	147	634	141	76	57	7	15	5	3	52	7	93	4	0	1	13	.071	0	2	3.49
1990 Mon-Pit	NL	33	31	4	1	215.1	860	196	77	61	15	3	3	3	50	4	130	2	0	12	9	.571	2	0	2.55
1991 Pittsburgh	NL	35	35	6	0	228	916	234	95	81	15	7	5	2	29	3	120	1	0	16	10	.615	3	0	3.20
1992 Pittsburgh	NL	23	22	4	0	141	566	138	56	48	8	12	4	2	19	3	56	0	0	8	8	.500	3	0	3.06
1993 Pittsburgh	NL	14	14	1	0	83	353	97	43	42	5	6	0	0	22	3	32	2	0	3	7	.300	0	0	4.55
1994 Pittsburgh	NL	25	24	2	0	157	645	162	67	57	18	7	3	0	34	7	57	2	0	10	8	.556	1	0	3.27
1995 Boston	AL	24	21	0	0	110.2	484	144	78	69	7	0	5	1	23	1	47	0	1	8	8	.500	0	0	5.61
1989 Atlanta	NL	17	17	0	0	99	432	102	65	49	5	10	5	2	33	3	58	3	0	1	12	.077	0	0	4.45
Montreal	NL	31	0	0	10	48	202	39	11	8	2	5	0	1	19	4	35	1	0	0	1	.000	0	2	1.50
1990 Montreal	NL	22	21	1	0	139.1	578	141	57	50	11	2	2	3	41	3	80	1	0	6	7	.462	0	0	3.23
Pittsburgh	NL	11	10	3	1	76	282	55	20	11	4	1	1	0	9	1	50	1	0	6	2	.750	2	0	1.30
12 ML YEARS		344	275	34	16	1836	7709	1876	880	751	115	107	39	27	562	51	964	28	4	96	109	.468	15	3	3.68

John Smoltz

Pitches: Right **Bats:** Right **Pos:** SP   **Ht:** 6' 3" **Wt:** 185 **Born:** 5/15/67 **Age:** 29

		HOW MUCH HE PITCHED						WHAT HE GAVE UP									THE RESULTS					
Year Team	Lg	G	GS	CG	GF	IP	BFP	H	R	ER	HR	SH	SF	HB	TBB	IBB	SO	WP	Bk	W	L	Pct.	ShO	Sv	ERA
1988 Atlanta	NL	12	12	0	0	64	297	74	40	39	10	2	0	2	33	4	37	2	1	2	7	.222	0	0	5.48
1989 Atlanta	NL	29	29	5	0	208	847	160	79	68	15	10	7	2	72	2	168	8	3	12	11	.522	0	0	2.94
1990 Atlanta	NL	34	34	6	0	231.1	966	206	109	99	20	9	8	1	90	3	170	14	3	14	11	.560	2	0	3.85
1991 Atlanta	NL	36	36	5	0	229.2	947	206	101	97	16	9	9	3	77	1	148	20	2	14	13	.519	0	0	3.80
1992 Atlanta	NL	35	35	9	0	246.2	1021	206	90	78	17	7	8	5	80	5	215	17	1	15	12	.556	3	0	2.85
1993 Atlanta	NL	35	35	3	0	243.2	1028	208	104	98	23	13	4	6	100	12	208	13	1	15	11	.577	1	0	3.62
1994 Atlanta	NL	21	21	1	0	134.2	568	120	69	62	15	7	6	4	48	4	113	7	0	6	10	.375	0	0	4.14
1995 Atlanta	NL	29	29	2	0	192.2	808	166	76	68	15	13	5	4	72	8	193	13	0	12	7	.632	1	0	3.18
8 ML YEARS		231	231	31	0	1550.2	6482	1346	668	609	131	70	47	27	572	39	1252	94	11	90	82	.523	7	0	3.53

Chris Snopek

Bats: Right **Throws:** Right **Pos:** 3B   **Ht:** 6' 1" **Wt:** 185 **Born:** 9/20/70 **Age:** 25

		BATTING																	BASERUNNING			PERCENTAGES		
Year Team	Lg	G	AB	H	2B	3B	HR	(Hm	Rd)	TB	R	RBI	TBB	IBB	SO	HBP	SH	SF	SB	CS	SB%	GDP	Avg	OBP	SLG
1992 Utica	A	73	245	69	15	1	2	--	--	92	49	29	52	4	44	2	1	4	14	4	.78	4	.282	.406	.376
1993 South Bend	A	22	72	28	8	1	5	--	--	53	20	18	15	0	13	3	0	2	1	1	.50	1	.389	.500	.736
Sarasota	A	107	371	91	21	4	10	--	--	150	61	50	65	2	67	1	3	6	3	2	.60	2	.245	.354	.404
1994 Birmingham	AA	106	365	96	25	3	6	--	--	145	58	54	58	3	49	5	3	5	9	4	.69	7	.263	.367	.397
1995 Nashville	AAA	113	393	127	23	4	12	--	--	194	56	55	50	1	72	4	6	3	2	5	.29	5	.323	.402	.494
1995 Chicago	AL	22	68	22	4	0	1	(1	0)	29	12	7	9	0	12	0	0	0	1	0	1.00	2	.324	.403	.426

J.T. Snow

Bats: Both **Throws:** Left **Pos:** 1B **Ht:** 6' 2" **Wt:** 202 **Born:** 2/26/68 **Age:** 28

Year Team	Lg	G	AB	H	2B	3B	HR	(Hm	Rd)	TB	R	RBI	TBB	IBB	SO	HBP	SH	SF	SB	CS	SB%	GDP	Avg	OBP	SLG
1992 New York	AL	7	14	2	1	0	0	(0	0)	3	1	2	5	1	5	0	0	0	0	0	.00	0	.143	.368	.214
1993 California	AL	129	419	101	18	2	16	(10	6)	171	60	57	55	4	88	2	7	6	3	0	1.00	10	.241	.328	.408
1994 California	AL	61	223	49	4	0	8	(7	1)	77	22	30	19	1	48	3	2	1	0	1	.00	2	.220	.289	.345
1995 California	AL	143	544	157	22	1	24	(14	10)	253	80	102	52	4	91	3	5	2	2	1	.67	16	.289	.353	.465
4 ML YEARS		340	1200	309	45	3	48	(31	17)	504	163	191	131	10	232	8	14	9	5	2	.71	28	.258	.332	.420

Clint Sodowsky

Pitches: Right **Bats:** Left **Pos:** SP **Ht:** 6' 3" **Wt:** 180 **Born:** 7/13/72 **Age:** 23

| | HOW MUCH HE PITCHED | | | | | | WHAT HE GAVE UP | | | | | | | | | | | | THE RESULTS | | | | | |
Year Team	Lg	G	GS	CG	GF	IP	BFP	H	R	ER	HR	SH	SF	HB	TBB	IBB	SO	WP	Bk	W	L	Pct.	ShO	Sv	ERA
1991 Bristol	R	14	8	0	3	55	253	49	34	23	3	2	1	2	34	0	44	8	4	0	5	.000	0	0	3.76
1992 Bristol	R	15	6	0	2	56	243	46	35	22	3	1	2	4	29	0	48	6	1	2	2	.500	0	0	3.54
1993 Fayettevlle	A	27	27	1	0	155.2	676	177	101	88	11	2	6	6	51	0	80	4	5	14	10	.583	0	0	5.09
1994 Lakeland	A	19	18	1	1	110.1	466	111	58	47	5	2	2	6	34	0	73	12	0	6	3	.667	1	0	3.83
1995 Jacksonvlle	AA	19	19	5	0	123.2	497	102	46	35	4	2	2	5	50	1	77	3	0	5	5	.500	3	0	2.55
Toledo	AAA	9	9	1	0	60	247	47	21	19	5	2	0	3	30	1	32	1	0	5	1	.833	0	0	2.85
1995 Detroit	AL	6	6	0	0	23.1	112	24	15	13	4	1	0	0	18	0	14	1	1	2	2	.500	0	0	5.01

Luis Sojo

Bats: Right **Throws:** Right **Pos:** SS/2B **Ht:** 5'11" **Wt:** 175 **Born:** 1/3/66 **Age:** 30

Year Team	Lg	G	AB	H	2B	3B	HR	(Hm	Rd)	TB	R	RBI	TBB	IBB	SO	HBP	SH	SF	SB	CS	SB%	GDP	Avg	OBP	SLG
1995 Tacoma *	AAA	4	17	3	0	0	1	--	--	6	1	1	0	0	2	0	0	0	0	0	.00	0	.176	.176	.353
1990 Toronto	AL	33	80	18	3	0	1	(0	1)	24	14	9	5	0	5	0	0	0	1	1	.50	1	.225	.271	.300
1991 California	AL	113	364	94	14	1	3	(1	2)	119	38	20	14	0	26	5	19	0	4	2	.67	12	.258	.295	.327
1992 California	AL	106	368	100	12	3	7	(2	5)	139	37	43	14	0	24	1	7	1	7	11	.39	14	.272	.299	.378
1993 Toronto	AL	19	47	8	2	0	0	(0	0)	10	5	6	4	0	2	0	2	1	0	0	.00	3	.170	.231	.213
1994 Seattle	AL	63	213	59	9	2	6	(4	2)	90	32	22	8	0	25	2	3	1	2	1	.67	2	.277	.308	.423
1995 Seattle	AL	102	339	98	18	2	7	(4	3)	141	50	39	23	0	19	1	6	1	4	2	.67	9	.289	.335	.416
6 ML YEARS		436	1411	377	58	8	24	(11	13)	523	176	139	68	0	101	9	37	4	18	17	.51	41	.267	.304	.371

Paul Sorrento

Bats: Left **Throws:** Right **Pos:** 1B **Ht:** 6' 2" **Wt:** 220 **Born:** 11/17/65 **Age:** 30

Year Team	Lg	G	AB	H	2B	3B	HR	(Hm	Rd)	TB	R	RBI	TBB	IBB	SO	HBP	SH	SF	SB	CS	SB%	GDP	Avg	OBP	SLG
1989 Minnesota	AL	14	21	5	0	0	0	(0	0)	5	2	1	5	1	4	0	0	1	0	0	.00	0	.238	.370	.238
1990 Minnesota	AL	41	121	25	4	1	5	(2	3)	46	11	13	12	0	31	1	0	1	1	1	.50	3	.207	.281	.380
1991 Minnesota	AL	26	47	12	2	0	4	(2	2)	26	6	13	4	2	11	0	0	0	0	0	.00	3	.255	.314	.553
1992 Cleveland	AL	140	458	123	24	1	18	(11	7)	203	52	60	51	7	89	1	1	3	0	3	.00	13	.269	.341	.443
1993 Cleveland	AL	148	463	119	26	1	18	(8	10)	201	75	65	58	11	121	2	0	4	3	1	.75	10	.257	.340	.434
1994 Cleveland	AL	95	322	90	14	0	14	(8	6)	146	43	62	34	6	68	0	1	3	0	1	.00	7	.280	.345	.453
1995 Cleveland	AL	104	323	76	14	0	25	(12	13)	165	50	79	51	6	71	0	0	4	1	1	.50	10	.235	.336	.511
7 ML YEARS		568	1755	450	84	3	84	(43	41)	792	239	293	215	33	395	4	2	16	5	7	.42	46	.256	.336	.451

Sammy Sosa

Bats: Right **Throws:** Right **Pos:** RF **Ht:** 6' 0" **Wt:** 185 **Born:** 11/12/68 **Age:** 27

Year Team	Lg	G	AB	H	2B	3B	HR	(Hm	Rd)	TB	R	RBI	TBB	IBB	SO	HBP	SH	SF	SB	CS	SB%	GDP	Avg	OBP	SLG
1989 ChA-Tex	AL	58	183	47	8	0	4	(1	3)	67	27	13	11	2	47	2	5	2	7	5	.58	6	.257	.303	.366
1990 Chicago	AL	153	532	124	26	10	15	(10	5)	215	72	70	33	4	150	6	2	6	32	16	.67	10	.233	.282	.404
1991 Chicago	AL	116	316	64	10	1	10	(3	7)	106	39	33	14	2	98	2	5	1	13	6	.68	5	.203	.240	.335
1992 Chicago	NL	67	262	68	7	2	8	(4	4)	103	41	25	19	1	63	4	4	2	15	7	.68	4	.260	.317	.393
1993 Chicago	NL	159	598	156	25	5	33	(23	10)	290	92	93	38	6	135	4	0	1	36	11	.77	14	.261	.309	.485
1994 Chicago	NL	105	426	128	17	6	25	(11	14)	232	59	70	25	1	92	2	1	4	22	13	.63	7	.300	.339	.545
1995 Chicago	NL	144	564	151	17	3	36	(19	17)	282	89	119	58	11	134	5	0	2	34	7	.83	8	.268	.340	.500
1989 Chicago	AL	33	99	27	5	0	3	(1	2)	41	19	10	11	2	27	2	1	2	7	3	.70	3	.273	.351	.414
Texas	AL	25	84	20	3	0	1	(0	1)	26	8	3	0	0	20	0	4	0	0	2	.00	3	.238	.238	.310
7 ML YEARS		802	2881	738	110	27	131	(71	60)	1295	419	423	198	27	719	25	17	18	159	65	.71	54	.256	.308	.449

Steve Sparks

Pitches: Right **Bats:** Right **Pos:** SP/RP   **Ht:** 6' 0" **Wt:** 180 **Born:** 7/2/65 **Age:** 30

| | | | HOW MUCH HE PITCHED | | | | | WHAT HE GAVE UP | | | | | | | | | | THE RESULTS | | | | |
Year	Team	Lg	G	GS	CG	GF	IP	BFP	H	R	ER	HR	SH	SF	HB	TBB	IBB	SO	WP	Bk	W	L	Pct.	ShO	Sv	ERA
1987	Helena	R	10	9	2	0	57.2	256	68	44	30	8	3	1	4	20	1	47	5	0	6	3	.667	0	0	4.68
1988	Beloit	A	25	24	5	0	164	688	162	80	69	8	4	2	7	51	2	96	5	5	9	13	.409	1	0	3.79
1989	Stockton	A	23	22	3	0	164	660	125	55	44	6	0	1	10	53	0	126	6	0	13	5	.722	2	0	2.41
1990	El Paso	AA	7	6	0	1	30.1	143	43	24	22	4	0	1	1	15	0	17	2	0	1	2	.333	0	0	6.53
	Stockton	A	19	19	5	0	129.1	549	136	63	53	4	4	3	8	31	0	77	7	1	10	7	.588	1	0	3.69
1991	El Paso	AA	4	4	0	0	17	90	30	22	18	1	0	0	0	9	0	10	2	1	1	2	.333	0	0	9.53
	Stockton	A	24	24	8	0	179.2	762	160	70	61	4	3	4	7	98	2	139	13	0	9	10	.474	2	0	3.06
1992	El Paso	AA	28	22	3	3	140.2	613	159	99	84	11	6	10	8	50	1	79	6	3	9	8	.529	0	1	5.37
1993	New Orleans	AAA	29	28	7	0	180.1	767	174	89	77	17	4	9	5	80	1	104	7	2	9	13	.409	1	0	3.84
1994	New Orleans	AAA	28	27	5	0	183.2	787	183	101	91	23	2	4	11	68	0	105	14	3	10	12	.455	1	0	4.46
1995	Milwaukee	AL	33	27	3	2	202	875	210	111	104	17	5	12	5	86	1	96	5	1	9	11	.450	0	0	4.63

Tim Spehr

Bats: Right **Throws:** Right **Pos:** C   **Ht:** 6' 2" **Wt:** 200 **Born:** 7/2/66 **Age:** 29

| | | | BATTING | | | | | | | | | | | | | | BASERUNNING | | | | PERCENTAGES | | |
Year	Team	Lg	G	AB	H	2B	3B	HR	(Hm	Rd)	TB	R	RBI	TBB	IBB	SO	HBP	SH	SF	SB	CS	SB%	GDP	Avg	OBP	SLG
1991	Kansas City	AL	37	74	14	5	0	3	(1	2)	28	7	14	9	0	18	1	3	1	1	0	1.00	2	.189	.282	.378
1993	Montreal	NL	53	87	20	6	0	2	(0	2)	32	14	10	6	1	20	1	3	2	2	0	1.00	0	.230	.281	.368
1994	Montreal	NL	52	36	9	3	1	0	(0	0)	14	8	5	4	0	11	0	1	0	2	0	1.00	0	.250	.325	.389
1995	Montreal	NL	41	35	9	5	0	1	(0	1)	17	4	3	6	0	7	0	3	0	0	0	.00	0	.257	.366	.486
	4 ML YEARS		183	232	52	19	1	6	(1	5)	91	33	32	25	1	56	2	10	3	5	0	1.00	2	.224	.302	.392

Bill Spiers

Bats: Left **Throws:** Right **Pos:** 3B   **Ht:** 6' 2" **Wt:** 190 **Born:** 6/5/66 **Age:** 30

| | | | BATTING | | | | | | | | | | | | | | BASERUNNING | | | | PERCENTAGES | | |
Year	Team	Lg	G	AB	H	2B	3B	HR	(Hm	Rd)	TB	R	RBI	TBB	IBB	SO	HBP	SH	SF	SB	CS	SB%	GDP	Avg	OBP	SLG
1995	Norfolk *	AAA	12	41	9	2	0	0	--	--	11	4	4	8	0	6	0	1	1	0	1	.00	4	.220	.340	.268
1989	Milwaukee	AL	114	345	88	9	3	4	(1	3)	115	44	33	21	1	63	1	4	2	10	2	.83	2	.255	.298	.333
1990	Milwaukee	AL	112	363	88	15	3	2	(2	0)	115	44	36	16	0	45	1	6	3	11	6	.65	12	.242	.274	.317
1991	Milwaukee	AL	133	414	117	13	6	8	(1	7)	166	71	54	34	0	55	2	10	4	14	8	.64	9	.283	.337	.401
1992	Milwaukee	AL	12	16	5	2	0	0	(0	0)	7	2	2	1	0	4	0	1	0	1	1	.50	0	.313	.353	.438
1993	Milwaukee	AL	113	340	81	8	4	2	(2	0)	103	43	36	29	2	51	4	9	4	9	8	.53	11	.238	.302	.303
1994	Milwaukee	AL	73	214	54	10	1	0	(0	0)	66	27	17	19	1	42	1	3	0	7	1	.88	5	.252	.316	.308
1995	New York	NL	63	72	15	2	1	0	(0	0)	19	5	11	12	1	15	0	1	2	0	1	.00	0	.208	.314	.264
	7 ML YEARS		620	1764	448	59	18	16	(6	10)	591	236	189	132	5	275	9	34	15	52	27	.66	39	.254	.307	.335

Ed Sprague

Bats: Right **Throws:** Right **Pos:** 3B   **Ht:** 6' 2" **Wt:** 210 **Born:** 7/25/67 **Age:** 28

| | | | BATTING | | | | | | | | | | | | | | BASERUNNING | | | | PERCENTAGES | | |
Year	Team	Lg	G	AB	H	2B	3B	HR	(Hm	Rd)	TB	R	RBI	TBB	IBB	SO	HBP	SH	SF	SB	CS	SB%	GDP	Avg	OBP	SLG
1991	Toronto	AL	61	160	44	7	0	4	(3	1)	63	17	20	19	2	43	3	0	1	0	3	.00	2	.275	.361	.394
1992	Toronto	AL	22	47	11	2	0	1	(1	0)	16	6	7	3	0	7	0	0	0	0	0	.00	0	.234	.280	.340
1993	Toronto	AL	150	546	142	31	1	12	(8	4)	211	50	73	32	1	85	10	2	6	1	0	1.00	23	.260	.310	.386
1994	Toronto	AL	109	405	97	19	1	11	(6	5)	151	38	44	23	1	95	11	2	4	1	0	1.00	11	.240	.296	.373
1995	Toronto	AL	144	521	127	27	2	18	(12	6)	212	77	74	58	3	96	15	1	7	0	0	.00	19	.244	.333	.407
	5 ML YEARS		486	1679	421	86	4	46	(30	16)	653	188	218	135	7	326	39	6	18	2	3	.40	55	.251	.318	.389

Dennis Springer

Pitches: Right **Bats:** Right **Pos:** SP   **Ht:** 5'10" **Wt:** 185 **Born:** 2/12/65 **Age:** 31

| | | | HOW MUCH HE PITCHED | | | | | WHAT HE GAVE UP | | | | | | | | | | THE RESULTS | | | | |
Year	Team	Lg	G	GS	CG	GF	IP	BFP	H	R	ER	HR	SH	SF	HB	TBB	IBB	SO	WP	Bk	W	L	Pct.	ShO	Sv	ERA
1987	Great Falls	R	23	5	1	13	65.2	290	70	38	21	3	4	2	2	16	2	54	4	0	4	3	.571	0	6	2.88
1988	Bakersfield	A	32	20	6	7	154	657	135	75	56	13	8	7	5	62	4	108	12	1	13	7	.650	4	2	3.27
	Vero Beach	A	1	1	0	0	5.2	25	6	3	3	0	0	0	0	2	0	4	0	0	0	0	.000	0	0	4.76
1989	San Antonio	AA	19	19	4	0	140	583	128	58	49	13	10	2	4	46	2	89	3	0	6	8	.429	1	0	3.15
	Albuquerque	AAA	8	7	0	0	41	193	58	28	22	5	1	0	0	14	0	18	1	0	4	1	.800	0	0	4.83
1990	Albuquerque	AAA	2	2	0	0	6.1	37	10	4	4	1	0	0	2	7	0	2	0	0	0	0	.000	0	0	5.68
	San Antonio	AA	24	24	3	0	163.1	691	147	76	60	8	5	6	4	73	0	77	7	1	8	6	.571	0	0	3.31
1991	San Antonio	AA	30	24	2	0	164.2	725	153	96	81	18	6	11	5	91	2	138	7	0	10	10	.500	1	0	4.43
1992	San Antonio	AA	18	18	4	0	122	525	114	61	59	6	3	2	4	49	3	73	4	0	6	7	.462	2	0	4.35
	Albuquerque	AAA	11	11	1	0	62	269	70	45	39	7	4	1	4	22	0	36	3	0	2	7	.222	0	0	5.66
1993	Albuquerque	AAA	35	18	0	5	130.2	591	173	104	87	18	5	6	2	39	1	69	7	1	3	8	.273	0	0	5.99
1994	Reading	AA	24	19	2	3	135	567	125	74	51	11	4	4	1	44	1	118	14	0	5	8	.385	2	0	3.40

1995 Scranton-Wb	AAA	30	23	4	3	171	715	163	101	89	19	0	10	7	47	1	115	8	0	10	11	.476	0	0	4.68
1995 Philadelphia	NL	4	4	0	0	22.1	94	21	15	12	3	2	0	1	9	1	15	1	0	0	3	.000	0	0	4.84

Russ Springer

Pitches: Right **Bats:** Right **Pos:** RP/SP **Ht:** 6' 4" **Wt:** 195 **Born:** 11/7/68 **Age:** 27

		HOW MUCH HE PITCHED						WHAT HE GAVE UP												THE RESULTS					
Year Team	Lg	G	GS	CG	GF	IP	BFP	H	R	ER	HR	SH	SF	HB	TBB	IBB	SO	WP	Bk	W	L	Pct.	ShO	Sv	ERA
1995 Vancouver *	AAA	6	6	0	0	34	146	24	16	13	3	0	0	3	23	0	23	3	0	2	0	1.000	0	0	3.44
1992 New York	AL	14	0	0	5	16	75	18	11	11	0	0	0	1	10	0	12	0	0	0	0	.000	0	0	6.19
1993 California	AL	14	9	1	3	60	278	73	48	48	11	1	1	3	32	1	31	6	0	1	6	.143	0	0	7.20
1994 California	AL	18	5	0	6	45.2	198	53	28	28	9	1	1	0	14	0	28	2	0	2	2	.500	0	2	5.52
1995 Cal-Phi		33	6	0	6	78.1	350	82	48	46	16	2	2	7	35	4	70	2	0	1	2	.333	0	1	5.29
1995 California	AL	19	6	0	3	51.2	238	60	37	35	11	1	0	5	25	1	38	1	0	1	2	.333	0	1	6.10
Philadelphia	NL	14	0	0	3	26.2	112	22	11	11	5	1	2	2	10	3	32	1	0	0	0	.000	0	0	3.71
4 ML YEARS		79	20	1	20	200	901	226	135	133	36	4	4	11	91	5	141	10	0	4	10	.286	0	3	5.99

Scott Stahoviak

Bats: Left **Throws:** Right **Pos:** 1B/3B **Ht:** 6' 5" **Wt:** 222 **Born:** 3/6/70 **Age:** 26

		BATTING																BASERUNNING				PERCENTAGES		
Year Team	Lg	G	AB	H	2B	3B	HR	(Hm	Rd)	TB	R	RBI	TBB	IBB	SO	HBP	SH	SF	SB	CS	SB%	GDP	Avg	OBP	SLG
1991 Visalia	A	43	158	44	9	1	1	--	--	58	29	25	22	2	28	3	2	0	9	3	.75	3	.278	.377	.367
1992 Visalia	A	110	409	126	26	3	5	--	--	173	62	68	82	2	66	3	0	2	17	6	.74	6	.308	.425	.423
1993 Nashville	AA	93	331	90	25	1	12	--	--	153	40	56	56	2	95	1	1	4	10	2	.83	5	.272	.375	.462
1994 Salt Lake	AAA	123	437	139	41	6	13	--	--	231	96	94	70	5	90	5	0	6	6	8	.43	12	.318	.413	.529
1995 Salt Lake	AAA	9	33	10	1	0	0	--	--	11	6	5	6	0	3	0	0	0	2	0	1.00	0	.303	.410	.333
1993 Minnesota	AL	20	57	11	4	0	0	(0	0)	15	1	1	3	0	22	0	0	0	2	0	.00	2	.193	.233	.263
1995 Minnesota	AL	94	263	70	19	0	3	(1	2)	98	28	23	30	1	61	1	0	2	5	1	.83	5	.266	.341	.373
2 ML YEARS		114	320	81	23	0	3	(1	2)	113	29	24	33	1	83	1	0	2	5	3	.63	5	.253	.323	.353

Matt Stairs

Bats: Left **Throws:** Right **Pos:** LF **Ht:** 5' 9" **Wt:** 180 **Born:** 2/27/69 **Age:** 27

		BATTING																BASERUNNING				PERCENTAGES		
Year Team	Lg	G	AB	H	2B	3B	HR	(Hm	Rd)	TB	R	RBI	TBB	IBB	SO	HBP	SH	SF	SB	CS	SB%	GDP	Avg	OBP	SLG
1995 Pawtucket *	AAA	75	271	77	17	0	13	--	--	133	40	56	29	3	41	1	1	3	3	3	.50	10	.284	.352	.491
1992 Montreal	NL	13	30	5	2	0	0	(0	0)	7	2	5	7	0	7	0	0	1	0	0	.00	0	.167	.316	.233
1993 Montreal	NL	6	8	3	1	0	0	(0	0)	4	1	2	0	0	1	0	0	0	0	0	.00	1	.375	.375	.500
1995 Boston	AL	39	88	23	7	1	1	(0	1)	35	8	17	4	0	14	1	1	1	0	1	.00	4	.261	.298	.398
3 ML YEARS		58	126	31	10	1	1	(0	1)	46	11	24	11	0	22	1	1	2	0	1	.00	5	.246	.307	.365

Andy Stankiewicz

Bats: Right **Throws:** Right **Pos:** SS **Ht:** 5' 9" **Wt:** 165 **Born:** 8/10/64 **Age:** 31

		BATTING																BASERUNNING				PERCENTAGES		
Year Team	Lg	G	AB	H	2B	3B	HR	(Hm	Rd)	TB	R	RBI	TBB	IBB	SO	HBP	SH	SF	SB	CS	SB%	GDP	Avg	OBP	SLG
1995 Tucson *	AAA	25	87	24	4	0	1	--	--	31	16	15	14	0	8	0	2	1	3	1	.75	3	.276	.373	.356
1992 New York	AL	116	400	107	22	2	2	(2	0)	139	52	25	38	0	42	5	7	1	9	5	.64	13	.268	.338	.348
1993 New York	AL	16	9	0	0	0	0	(0	0)	0	5	0	1	0	1	0	0	0	0	0	.00	0	.000	.100	.000
1994 Houston	NL	37	54	14	3	0	0	(0	0)	20	10	5	12	0	12	1	2	0	1	1	.50	2	.259	.403	.370
1995 Houston	NL	43	52	6	1	0	0	(0	0)	7	6	7	12	2	19	0	1	0	4	2	.67	1	.115	.281	.135
4 ML YEARS		212	515	127	26	2	3	(3	0)	166	73	37	63	2	74	6	10	1	14	8	.64	16	.247	.335	.322

Mike Stanley

Bats: Right **Throws:** Right **Pos:** C **Ht:** 6' 0" **Wt:** 190 **Born:** 6/25/63 **Age:** 33

		BATTING																BASERUNNING				PERCENTAGES		
Year Team	Lg	G	AB	H	2B	3B	HR	(Hm	Rd)	TB	R	RBI	TBB	IBB	SO	HBP	SH	SF	SB	CS	SB%	GDP	Avg	OBP	SLG
1986 Texas	AL	15	30	10	3	0	1	(0	1)	16	4	1	3	0	7	0	0	0	1	0	1.00	0	.333	.394	.533
1987 Texas	AL	78	216	59	8	1	6	(3	3)	87	34	37	31	0	48	1	1	4	3	0	1.00	6	.273	.361	.403
1988 Texas	AL	94	249	57	8	0	3	(1	2)	74	21	27	37	0	62	0	1	5	0	0	.00	6	.229	.323	.297
1989 Texas	AL	67	122	30	3	1	1	(1	0)	38	9	11	12	1	29	2	1	0	1	0	1.00	5	.246	.324	.311
1990 Texas	AL	103	189	47	8	1	2	(1	1)	63	21	19	30	2	25	0	6	1	1	0	1.00	4	.249	.350	.333
1991 Texas	AL	95	181	45	13	1	3	(1	2)	69	25	25	34	0	44	2	5	1	0	0	.00	2	.249	.372	.381
1992 New York	AL	68	173	43	7	0	8	(5	3)	74	24	27	33	0	45	1	0	0	0	0	.00	6	.249	.372	.428
1993 New York	AL	130	423	129	17	1	26	(17	9)	226	70	84	57	4	85	5	0	6	1	1	.50	10	.305	.389	.534
1994 New York	AL	82	290	87	20	0	17	(8	9)	158	54	57	39	2	56	2	0	2	0	0	.00	10	.300	.384	.545
1995 New York	AL	118	399	107	29	1	18	(13	5)	192	63	63	57	1	106	5	0	9	1	1	.50	14	.268	.360	.481
10 ML YEARS		850	2272	614	116	6	85	(50	35)	997	325	371	333	10	507	18	14	28	8	2	.80	63	.270	.364	.439

Mike Stanton

Pitches: Left **Bats:** Left **Pos:** RP **Ht:** 6' 1" **Wt:** 190 **Born:** 6/2/67 **Age:** 29

Year	Team	Lg	G	GS	CG	GF	IP	BFP	H	R	ER	HR	SH	SF	HB	TBB	IBB	SO	WP	Bk	W	L	Pct.	ShO	Sv	ERA
1989	Atlanta	NL	20	0	0	10	24	94	17	4	4	0	4	0	0	8	1	27	1	0	0	1	.000	0	7	1.50
1990	Atlanta	NL	7	0	0	4	7	42	16	16	14	1	1	0	1	4	2	7	1	0	0	3	.000	0	2	18.00
1991	Atlanta	NL	74	0	0	20	78	314	62	27	25	6	6	0	1	21	6	54	0	0	5	5	.500	0	7	2.88
1992	Atlanta	NL	65	0	0	23	63.2	264	59	32	29	6	1	2	2	20	2	44	3	0	5	4	.556	0	8	4.10
1993	Atlanta	NL	63	0	0	41	52	236	51	35	27	4	5	2	0	29	7	43	1	0	4	6	.400	0	27	4.67
1994	Atlanta	NL	49	0	0	15	45.2	197	41	18	18	2	2	1	3	26	3	35	1	0	3	1	.750	0	3	3.55
1995	Atl-Bos		48	0	0	22	40.1	178	48	23	19	6	2	1	1	14	2	23	2	1	2	1	.667	0	1	4.24
1995	Atlanta	NL	26	0	0	10	19.1	94	31	14	12	3	2	1	1	6	2	13	1	1	1	1	.500	0	1	5.59
	Boston	AL	22	0	0	12	21	84	17	9	7	3	0	0	0	8	0	10	1	0	1	0	1.000	0	0	3.00
7 ML YEARS			326	0	0	135	310.2	1325	294	155	136	25	21	6	8	122	23	233	9	1	19	21	.475	0	55	3.94

Terry Steinbach

Bats: Right **Throws:** Right **Pos:** C **Ht:** 6' 1" **Wt:** 195 **Born:** 3/2/62 **Age:** 34

Year	Team	Lg	G	AB	H	2B	3B	HR	(Hm	Rd)	TB	R	RBI	TBB	IBB	SO	HBP	SH	SF	SB	CS	SB%	GDP	Avg	OBP	SLG
1986	Oakland	AL	6	15	5	0	0	2	(0	2)	11	3	4	1	0	0	0	0	0	0	0	.00	0	.333	.375	.733
1987	Oakland	AL	122	391	111	16	3	16	(6	10)	181	66	56	32	2	66	9	3	3	1	2	.33	10	.284	.349	.463
1988	Oakland	AL	104	351	93	19	1	9	(6	3)	141	42	51	33	2	47	6	3	5	3	0	1.00	13	.265	.334	.402
1989	Oakland	AL	130	454	124	13	1	7	(5	2)	160	37	42	30	2	66	2	2	3	1	2	.33	14	.273	.319	.352
1990	Oakland	AL	114	379	95	15	2	9	(3	6)	141	32	57	19	1	66	4	5	3	0	1	.00	11	.251	.291	.372
1991	Oakland	AL	129	456	125	31	1	6	(1	5)	176	50	67	22	4	70	7	0	9	2	2	.50	15	.274	.312	.386
1992	Oakland	AL	128	438	122	20	1	12	(3	9)	180	48	53	45	3	58	1	0	3	2	3	.40	20	.279	.345	.411
1993	Oakland	AL	104	389	111	19	1	10	(5	5)	162	47	43	25	1	65	3	0	1	3	3	.50	13	.285	.333	.416
1994	Oakland	AL	103	369	105	21	2	11	(5	6)	163	51	57	26	4	62	0	1	6	2	1	.67	10	.285	.327	.442
1995	Oakland	AL	114	406	113	26	1	15	(9	6)	186	43	65	25	4	74	3	1	4	1	3	.25	15	.278	.322	.458
10 ML YEARS			1054	3648	1004	180	13	97	(43	54)	1501	419	495	258	23	574	35	15	37	15	17	.47	121	.275	.326	.411

Dave Stevens

Pitches: Right **Bats:** Right **Pos:** RP **Ht:** 6' 3" **Wt:** 205 **Born:** 3/4/70 **Age:** 26

Year	Team	Lg	G	GS	CG	GF	IP	BFP	H	R	ER	HR	SH	SF	HB	TBB	IBB	SO	WP	Bk	W	L	Pct.	ShO	Sv	ERA
1990	Huntington	R	13	11	0	1	56.2	274	47	44	29	3	2	3	7	47	0	55	6	8	2	4	.333	0	0	4.61
1991	Geneva	A	9	9	1	0	47.1	197	49	20	15	3	4	3	2	14	0	44	2	0	2	3	.400	0	0	2.85
1992	Charlotte	AA	26	26	2	0	149.2	642	147	79	65	16	5	6	5	53	1	89	8	1	9	13	.409	0	0	3.91
1993	Orlando	AA	11	11	1	0	70.1	304	69	36	33	7	1	0	2	35	0	49	1	0	6	1	.857	1	0	4.22
	Iowa	AAA	24	0	0	15	34.1	137	24	16	16	3	2	1	1	14	2	29	1	0	4	0	1.000	0	4	4.19
1994	Salt Lake	AAA	23	0	0	20	43	183	41	13	8	2	2	2	1	16	1	30	1	0	6	2	.750	0	3	1.67
1994	Minnesota	AL	24	0	0	6	45	208	55	35	34	6	2	0	1	23	2	24	3	0	5	2	.714	0	0	6.80
1995	Minnesota	AL	56	0	0	34	65.2	302	74	40	37	14	4	5	1	32	1	47	2	0	5	4	.556	0	10	5.07
2 ML YEARS			80	0	0	40	110.2	510	129	75	71	20	6	5	2	55	3	71	5	0	10	6	.625	0	10	5.77

Todd Steverson

Bats: Right **Throws:** Right **Pos:** LF **Ht:** 6' 2" **Wt:** 200 **Born:** 11/15/71 **Age:** 24

Year	Team	Lg	G	AB	H	2B	3B	HR	(Hm	Rd)	TB	R	RBI	TBB	IBB	SO	HBP	SH	SF	SB	CS	SB%	GDP	Avg	OBP	SLG
1992	St. Cathrns	A	65	225	47	9	0	6	--	--	74	26	24	26	0	83	1	0	3	23	7	.77	2	.209	.290	.329
1993	Dunedin	A	106	413	112	32	4	11	--	--	185	68	54	44	2	118	1	3	1	15	12	.56	3	.271	.342	.448
1994	Knoxville	AA	124	415	109	24	5	9	--	--	170	59	38	71	2	112	1	1	1	20	11	.65	3	.263	.371	.410
1995	Toledo	AAA	9	28	3	0	0	1	--	--	6	6	1	5	0	13	0	0	0	2	0	.00	1	.107	.242	.214
1995	Detroit	AL	30	42	11	0	0	2	(0	2)	17	11	6	6	0	10	0	0	2	2	0	1.00	0	.262	.340	.405

Dave Stewart

Pitches: Right **Bats:** Right **Pos:** SP **Ht:** 6' 2" **Wt:** 230 **Born:** 2/19/57 **Age:** 39

Year	Team	Lg	G	GS	CG	GF	IP	BFP	H	R	ER	HR	SH	SF	HB	TBB	IBB	SO	WP	Bk	W	L	Pct.	ShO	Sv	ERA
1978	Los Angeles	NL	1	0	0	1	2	6	1	0	0	0	0	0	0	0	1	0	0	0	0	0	.000	0	0	0.00
1981	Los Angeles	NL	32	0	0	14	43	184	40	13	12	3	7	3	0	14	5	29	4	0	4	3	.571	0	6	2.51
1982	Los Angeles	NL	45	14	0	9	146.1	616	137	72	62	14	10	5	2	49	11	80	3	0	9	8	.529	0	1	3.81
1983	Tex-LA		54	9	2	25	135	565	117	43	39	6	9	4	4	50	7	78	3	0	10	4	.714	0	8	2.60
1984	Texas	AL	32	27	3	2	192.1	847	193	106	101	26	4	5	4	87	3	119	12	0	7	14	.333	0	0	4.73
1985	Tex-Phi		46	5	0	32	85.2	383	91	57	52	13	5	2	2	41	5	66	7	1	0	6	.000	0	4	5.46
1986	Oak-Phi		37	17	4	4	161.2	700	152	76	71	16	4	7	3	69	0	111	10	3	9	5	.643	1	0	3.95
1987	Oakland	AL	37	37	8	0	261.1	1103	224	121	107	24	7	5	6	105	2	205	11	0	20	13	.606	1	0	3.68

Year Team	Lg	G	GS	CG	GF	IP	BFP	H	R	ER	HR	SH	SF	HB	TBB	IBB	SO	WP	Bk	W	L	Pct.	ShO	Sv	ERA
1988 Oakland	AL	37	37	14	0	275.2	1156	240	111	99	14	7	9	3	110	5	192	14	16	21	12	.636	2	0	3.23
1989 Oakland	AL	36	36	8	0	257.2	1081	260	105	95	23	9	10	6	69	0	155	13	0	21	9	.700	0	0	3.32
1990 Oakland	AL	36	36	11	0	267	1088	226	84	76	16	10	10	5	83	1	166	8	0	22	11	.667	4	0	2.56
1991 Oakland	AL	35	35	2	0	226	1014	245	135	130	24	5	15	9	105	1	144	12	0	11	11	.500	1	0	5.18
1992 Oakland	AL	31	31	2	0	199.1	838	175	96	81	25	5	8	8	79	1	130	3	1	12	10	.545	0	0	3.66
1993 Toronto	AL	26	26	0	0	162	687	146	86	80	23	3	4	4	72	0	96	4	1	12	8	.600	0	0	4.44
1994 Toronto	AL	22	22	1	0	133.1	602	151	89	87	26	2	4	4	62	4	111	6	0	7	8	.467	0	0	5.87
1995 Oakland	AL	16	16	0	0	81	381	101	65	62	11	6	3	2	39	1	58	8	1	7	7	.300	0	0	6.89
1983 Texas	AL	8	8	2	0	59	237	50	15	14	2	2	1	2	17	0	24	1	0	5	2	.714	0	0	2.14
Los Angeles	NL	46	1	0	25	76	328	67	28	25	4	7	3	2	33	7	54	2	0	5	2	.714	0	8	2.96
1985 Texas	AL	42	5	0	29	81.1	361	86	53	49	13	5	2	2	37	5	64	5	1	0	6	.000	0	4	5.42
Philadelphia	NL	4	0	0	3	4.1	22	5	4	3	0	0	0	0	4	0	2	2	0	0	0	.000	0	0	6.23
1986 Oakland	AL	29	17	4	2	149.1	644	137	67	62	15	4	4	3	65	0	102	9	0	9	5	.643	1	0	3.74
Philadelphia	NL	8	0	0	2	12.1	56	15	9	9	1	0	3	0	4	0	9	1	3	0	0	.000	0	0	6.57
16 ML YEARS		523	348	55	87	2629.1	11251	2499	1259	1154	264	93	94	62	1034	46	1741	118	23	168	129	.566	9	19	3.95

Shannon Stewart

Bats: Right **Throws:** Right **Pos:** CF   **Ht:** 6' 1" **Wt:** 190 **Born:** 2/25/74 **Age:** 22

Year Team	Lg	G	AB	H	2B	3B	HR	(Hm	Rd)	TB	R	RBI	TBB	IBB	SO	HBP	SH	SF	SB	CS	SB%	GDP	Avg	OBP	SLG
1992 Blue Jays	R	50	172	40	1	0	1	--	--	44	44	11	24	0	27	3	4	2	32	5	.86	3	.233	.333	.256
1993 St. Cathrns	A	75	301	84	15	2	3	--	--	112	53	29	33	1	43	2	3	3	25	10	.71	7	.279	.351	.372
1994 Hagerstown	A	56	225	73	10	5	4	--	--	105	39	25	32	3	43	1	2	2	15	11	.58	3	.324	.386	.467
1995 Knoxville	AA	138	498	143	24	6	5	--	--	194	89	55	89	3	61	6	3	5	42	16	.72	13	.287	.398	.390
1995 Toronto	AL	12	38	8	0	0	0	(0	0)	8	2	1	5	0	5	1	0	0	2	0	1.00	0	.211	.318	.211

Kelly Stinnett

Bats: Right **Throws:** Right **Pos:** C   **Ht:** 5'11" **Wt:** 195 **Born:** 2/14/70 **Age:** 26

Year Team	Lg	G	AB	H	2B	3B	HR	(Hm	Rd)	TB	R	RBI	TBB	IBB	SO	HBP	SH	SF	SB	CS	SB%	GDP	Avg	OBP	SLG
1990 Watertown	A	60	192	46	9	2	2	--	--	65	29	21	40	2	43	4	2	2	3	7	.30	8	.240	.378	.339
1991 Columbus	A	102	384	101	15	1	14	--	--	160	49	74	26	2	70	9	1	5	4	1	.80	17	.263	.321	.417
1992 Canton-Akrn	AA	91	296	84	10	0	6	--	--	112	37	32	16	0	43	4	5	3	7	6	.54	8	.284	.326	.378
1993 Charlotte	AAA	98	288	79	10	3	6	--	--	113	42	33	17	1	52	2	0	1	0	0	.00	4	.274	.318	.392
1994 New York	NL	47	150	38	6	2	2	(0	2)	54	20	14	11	1	28	5	0	1	2	0	1.00	3	.253	.323	.360
1995 New York	NL	77	196	43	8	1	4	(1	3)	65	23	18	29	3	65	6	0	0	2	0	1.00	3	.219	.338	.332
2 ML YEARS		124	346	81	14	3	6	(1	5)	119	43	32	40	4	93	11	0	1	4	0	1.00	6	.234	.332	.344

Kevin Stocker

Bats: Both **Throws:** Right **Pos:** SS   **Ht:** 6' 1" **Wt:** 175 **Born:** 2/13/70 **Age:** 26

Year Team	Lg	G	AB	H	2B	3B	HR	(Hm	Rd)	TB	R	RBI	TBB	IBB	SO	HBP	SH	SF	SB	CS	SB%	GDP	Avg	OBP	SLG
1993 Philadelphia	NL	70	259	84	12	3	2	(1	1)	108	46	31	30	11	43	8	4	1	5	0	1.00	8	.324	.409	.417
1994 Philadelphia	NL	82	271	74	11	2	2	(2	0)	95	38	28	44	8	41	7	4	4	2	2	.50	3	.273	.383	.351
1995 Philadelphia	NL	125	412	90	14	3	1	(1	0)	113	42	32	43	9	75	9	10	3	6	1	.86	7	.218	.304	.274
3 ML YEARS		277	942	248	37	8	5	(4	1)	316	126	91	117	28	159	24	18	8	13	3	.81	18	.263	.357	.335

Todd Stottlemyre

Pitches: Right **Bats:** Left **Pos:** SP   **Ht:** 6' 3" **Wt:** 200 **Born:** 5/20/65 **Age:** 31

Year Team	Lg	G	GS	CG	GF	IP	BFP	H	R	ER	HR	SH	SF	HB	TBB	IBB	SO	WP	Bk	W	L	Pct.	ShO	Sv	ERA
1988 Toronto	AL	28	16	0	2	98	443	109	70	62	15	5	3	4	46	5	67	2	3	4	8	.333	0	0	5.69
1989 Toronto	AL	27	18	0	4	127.2	545	137	56	55	11	3	7	5	44	4	63	4	1	7	7	.500	0	0	3.88
1990 Toronto	AL	33	33	4	0	203	866	214	101	98	18	3	5	8	69	4	115	6	1	13	17	.433	0	0	4.34
1991 Toronto	AL	34	34	1	0	219	921	194	97	92	21	0	8	12	75	3	116	4	0	15	8	.652	0	0	3.78
1992 Toronto	AL	28	27	6	0	174	755	175	99	87	20	2	11	10	63	4	98	7	0	12	11	.522	2	0	4.50
1993 Toronto	AL	30	28	1	0	176.2	786	204	107	95	11	5	11	3	69	5	98	7	1	11	12	.478	1	0	4.84
1994 Toronto	AL	26	19	3	5	140.2	605	149	67	66	19	4	5	7	48	2	105	0	0	7	7	.500	1	1	4.22
1995 Oakland	AL	31	31	2	0	209.2	920	228	117	106	26	4	4	6	80	7	205	11	0	14	7	.667	0	0	4.55
8 ML YEARS		237	206	17	11	1348.2	5841	1410	714	661	141	26	54	55	494	34	867	41	6	83	77	.519	4	1	4.41

Doug Strange

Bats: Both **Throws:** Right **Pos:** 3B   **Ht:** 6' 1" **Wt:** 185 **Born:** 4/13/64 **Age:** 32

Year Team	Lg	G	AB	H	2B	3B	HR	(Hm	Rd)	TB	R	RBI	TBB	IBB	SO	HBP	SH	SF	SB	CS	SB%	GDP	Avg	OBP	SLG
1989 Detroit	AL	64	196	42	4	1	1	(1	0)	51	16	14	17	0	36	1	3	0	3	3	.50	6	.214	.280	.260
1991 Chicago	NL	3	9	4	1	0	0	(0	0)	5	0	1	0	0	1	1	0	1	1	0	1.00	0	.444	.455	.556

Year Team	Lg	G	AB	H	2B	3B	HR	(Hm	Rd)	TB	R	RBI	TBB	IBB	SO	HBP	SH	SF	SB	CS	SB%	GDP	Avg	OBP	SLG
1992 Chicago	NL	52	94	15	1	0	1	(0	1)	19	7	5	10	2	15	0	2	0	1	0	1.00	2	.160	.240	.202
1993 Texas	AL	145	484	124	29	0	7	(4	3)	174	58	60	43	3	69	3	8	4	6	4	.60	12	.256	.318	.360
1994 Texas	AL	73	226	48	12	1	5	(3	2)	77	26	26	15	0	38	3	4	2	1	3	.25	6	.212	.268	.341
1995 Seattle	AL	74	155	42	9	2	2	(1	1)	61	19	21	10	0	25	2	1	0	0	3	.00	3	.271	.323	.394
6 ML YEARS		411	1164	275	56	4	16	(9	7)	387	126	127	95	5	184	10	18	7	12	13	.48	29	.236	.298	.332

Darryl Strawberry

Bats: Left **Throws:** Left **Pos:** DH   **Ht:** 6' 6" **Wt:** 215 **Born:** 3/12/62 **Age:** 34

							BATTING												BASERUNNING				PERCENTAGES		
Year Team	Lg	G	AB	H	2B	3B	HR	(Hm	Rd)	TB	R	RBI	TBB	IBB	SO	HBP	SH	SF	SB	CS	SB%	GDP	Avg	OBP	SLG
1995 Yankees *	R	7	20	5	2	0	0	--	--	7	3	4	9	5	5	0	0	1	2	0	1.00	1	.250	.467	.350
Tampa *	A	2	9	2	1	0	1	--	--	6	1	2	1	0	2	0	0	0	0	0	.00	1	.222	.300	.667
Columbus *	AAA	22	83	25	3	1	7	--	--	51	20	29	15	1	17	1	0	2	1	1	.50	1	.301	.406	.614
1983 New York	NL	122	420	108	15	7	26	(10	16)	215	63	74	47	9	128	4	0	2	19	6	.76	5	.257	.336	.512
1984 New York	NL	147	522	131	27	4	26	(8	18)	244	75	97	75	15	131	0	1	4	27	8	.77	8	.251	.343	.467
1985 New York	NL	111	393	109	15	4	29	(14	15)	219	78	79	73	13	96	1	0	3	26	11	.70	9	.277	.389	.557
1986 New York	NL	136	475	123	27	5	27	(11	16)	241	76	93	72	9	141	6	0	9	28	12	.70	4	.259	.358	.507
1987 New York	NL	154	532	151	32	5	39	(20	19)	310	108	104	97	13	122	7	0	4	36	12	.75	4	.284	.398	.583
1988 New York	NL	153	543	146	27	3	**39**	**(21**	**18)**	296	101	101	85	21	127	3	0	9	29	14	.67	6	.269	.366	**.545**
1989 New York	NL	134	476	107	26	1	29	(15	14)	222	69	77	61	13	105	1	0	3	11	4	.73	4	.225	.312	.466
1990 New York	NL	152	542	150	18	1	37	(24	13)	281	92	108	70	15	110	4	0	5	15	8	.65	5	.277	.361	.518
1991 Los Angeles	NL	139	505	134	22	4	28	(14	14)	248	86	99	75	4	125	3	0	5	10	8	.56	8	.265	.361	.491
1992 Los Angeles	NL	43	156	37	8	0	5	(3	2)	60	20	25	19	4	34	1	0	1	3	1	.75	2	.237	.322	.385
1993 Los Angeles	NL	32	100	14	2	0	5	(3	2)	31	12	12	16	1	19	2	0	2	1	0	1.00	1	.140	.267	.310
1994 San Francisco	NL	29	92	22	3	1	4	(2	2)	39	13	17	19	4	22	0	0	2	0	3	.00	2	.239	.363	.424
1995 New York	AL	32	87	24	4	1	3	(3	0)	39	15	13	10	1	22	2	0	0	0	0	.00	0	.276	.364	.448
13 ML YEARS		1384	4843	1256	226	36	297	(148	149)	2445	808	899	719	122	1182	34	1	49	205	87	.70	58	.259	.356	.505

Franklin Stubbs

Bats: Left **Throws:** Left **Pos:** 1B/LF   **Ht:** 6' 2" **Wt:** 209 **Born:** 10/21/60 **Age:** 35

							BATTING												BASERUNNING				PERCENTAGES		
Year Team	Lg	G	AB	H	2B	3B	HR	(Hm	Rd)	TB	R	RBI	TBB	IBB	SO	HBP	SH	SF	SB	CS	SB%	GDP	Avg	OBP	SLG
1984 Los Angeles	NL	87	217	42	2	3	8	(4	4)	74	22	17	24	3	63	0	3	1	2	2	.50	0	.194	.273	.341
1985 Los Angeles	NL	10	9	2	0	0	0	(0	0)	2	0	2	0	0	3	0	0	0	0	0	.00	0	.222	.222	.222
1986 Los Angeles	NL	132	420	95	11	1	23	(12	11)	177	55	58	37	11	107	2	4	2	7	1	.88	9	.226	.291	.421
1987 Los Angeles	NL	129	386	90	16	3	16	(6	10)	160	48	52	31	9	85	1	3	2	8	1	.89	7	.233	.290	.415
1988 Los Angeles	NL	115	242	54	13	0	8	(3	5)	91	30	34	23	3	61	1	2	5	11	3	.79	4	.223	.288	.376
1989 Los Angeles	NL	69	103	30	6	0	4	(1	3)	48	11	15	16	2	27	0	1	0	3	2	.60	3	.291	.387	.466
1990 Houston	NL	146	448	117	23	2	23	(9	14)	213	59	71	48	3	114	2	1	2	19	6	.76	4	.261	.334	.475
1991 Milwaukee	AL	103	362	77	16	2	11	(8	3)	130	48	38	35	3	71	2	0	5	13	4	.76	4	.213	.282	.359
1992 Milwaukee	AL	92	288	66	11	1	9	(3	6)	106	37	42	27	3	68	1	5	1	11	8	.58	2	.229	.297	.368
1995 Detroit	AL	62	116	29	11	0	2	(1	1)	46	13	19	19	1	27	1	0	1	0	1	.00	3	.250	.358	.397
10 ML YEARS		945	2591	602	109	12	104	(47	57)	1047	323	348	260	38	626	10	19	19	74	28	.73	36	.232	.303	.404

Tanyon Sturtze

Pitches: Right **Bats:** Right **Pos:** RP   **Ht:** 6' 5" **Wt:** 205 **Born:** 10/12/70 **Age:** 25

					HOW MUCH HE PITCHED				WHAT HE GAVE UP									THE RESULTS				
Year Team	Lg	G	GS	CG	GF	IP	BFP	H	R	ER	HR	SH	SF	HB	TBB	IBB	SO	WP	Bk	W	L	Pct.	ShO	Sv	ERA
1990 Athletics	R	12	10	0	1	48	232	55	41	29	0	2	5	26	0	30	5	2	2	5	.286	0	0	5.44
1991 Madison	A	27	27	0	0	163	685	136	77	56	5	6	6	58	5	88	10	5	10	5	.667	0	0	3.09
1992 Modesto	A	25	25	1	0	151	656	143	72	63	6	5	5	78	1	126	5	0	7	11	.389	0	0	3.75
1993 Huntsville	AA	28	28	1	0	165.2	734	169	102	88	16	3	11	85	2	112	11	1	5	12	.294	1	0	4.78
1994 Huntsville	AA	17	17	1	0	103.1	435	100	40	37	5	3	4	39	1	63	1	0	6	3	.667	0	0	3.22
Tacoma	AAA	11	9	0	2	64.2	294	73	36	29	5	0	1	34	2	28	6	0	4	5	.444	0	0	4.04
1995 Iowa	AAA	23	17	1	0	86	398	108	66	65	18	5	2	42	1	48	5	0	4	7	.364	1	0	6.80
1995 Chicago	NL	2	0	0	0	2	9	2	2	1	0	0	0	1	0	0	0	0	0	0	.000	0	0	9.00

Chris Stynes

Bats: Right **Throws:** Right **Pos:** 2B   **Ht:** 5' 9" **Wt:** 175 **Born:** 1/19/73 **Age:** 23

							BATTING												BASERUNNING				PERCENTAGES		
Year Team	Lg	G	AB	H	2B	3B	HR	(Hm	Rd)	TB	R	RBI	TBB	IBB	SO	HBP	SH	SF	SB	CS	SB%	GDP	Avg	OBP	SLG
1991 Blue Jays	R	57	219	67	15	1	4	--	--	96	29	39	9	0	38	1	1	0	10	3	.77	1	.306	.336	.438
1992 Myrtle Bch	A	127	489	139	36	0	7	--	--	196	67	46	16	1	43	8	14	4	28	14	.67	8	.284	.315	.401
1993 Dunedin	A	123	496	151	28	5	7	--	--	210	72	48	25	2	40	3	4	4	19	9	.68	12	.304	.339	.423
1994 Knoxville	AA	136	545	173	32	4	8	--	--	237	79	79	23	4	36	7	5	4	28	12	.70	12	.317	.351	.435
1995 Omaha	AAA	83	306	84	12	5	9	--	--	133	51	42	27	0	24	5	4	5	4	5	.44	7	.275	.338	.435
1995 Kansas City	AL	22	35	6	1	0	0	(0	0)	7	7	2	4	0	3	0	0	0	0	0	.00	3	.171	.256	.200

Scott Sullivan

Pitches: Right **Bats:** Right **Pos:** RP   **Ht:** 6' 4" **Wt:** 210 **Born:** 3/13/71 **Age:** 25

		HOW MUCH HE PITCHED						WHAT HE GAVE UP										THE RESULTS					
Year Team	Lg	G	GS	CG	GF	IP	BFP	H	R	ER	HR	SH	SF	HB	TBB	IBB	SO	WP	Bk	W	L	Pct.	ShO	Sv	ERA
1993 Billings	R	18	7	2	9	54	224	33	13	10	1	3	0	6	25	0	79	2	5	5	0	1.000	2	3	1.67
1994 Chattanooga	AA	34	13	2	16	121.1	508	101	60	46	8	2	1	6	40	1	111	5	4	11	7	.611	0	7	3.41
1995 Indianapols	AAA	44	0	0	21	58.2	253	51	31	23	2	3	4	2	24	4	54	3	0	4	3	.571	0	1	3.53
1995 Cincinnati	NL	3	0	0	1	3.2	17	4	2	2	0	1	0	0	2	0	2	0	0	0	0	.000	0	0	4.91

Jeff Suppan

Pitches: Right **Bats:** Right **Pos:** RP/SP   **Ht:** 6' 2" **Wt:** 210 **Born:** 1/2/75 **Age:** 21

		HOW MUCH HE PITCHED						WHAT HE GAVE UP										THE RESULTS					
Year Team	Lg	G	GS	CG	GF	IP	BFP	H	R	ER	HR	SH	SF	HB	TBB	IBB	SO	WP	Bk	W	L	Pct.	ShO	Sv	ERA
1993 Red Sox	R	10	9	2	1	57.2	239	52	20	14	0	1	0	3	16	0	64	2	0	4	3	.571	1	0	2.18
1994 Sarasota	A	27	27	4	0	174	712	153	74	63	10	6	2	6	50	0	173	9	1	13	7	.650	2	0	3.26
1995 Trenton	AA	15	15	1	0	99	409	86	35	26	5	1	3	8	26	1	88	4	0	6	2	.750	1	0	2.36
Pawtucket	AAA	7	7	0	0	45.2	191	50	29	27	9	0	1	1	9	0	32	2	0	2	3	.400	0	0	5.32
1995 Boston	AL	8	3	0	1	22.2	100	29	15	15	4	1	1	0	5	1	19	0	0	1	2	.333	0	0	5.96

B.J. Surhoff

Bats: Left **Throws:** Right **Pos:** 1B/C/LF   **Ht:** 6' 1" **Wt:** 204 **Born:** 8/4/64 **Age:** 31

		BATTING																BASERUNNING				PERCENTAGES		
Year Team	Lg	G	AB	H	2B	3B	HR	(Hm	Rd)	TB	R	RBI	TBB	IBB	SO	HBP	SH	SF	SB	CS	SB%	GDP	Avg	OBP	SLG
1987 Milwaukee	AL	115	395	118	22	4	7	(5	2)	167	50	68	36	1	30	0	5	9	11	10	.52	13	.299	.350	.423
1988 Milwaukee	AL	139	493	121	21	0	5	(2	3)	157	47	38	31	9	49	3	11	3	21	6	.78	12	.245	.292	.318
1989 Milwaukee	AL	126	436	108	17	4	5	(3	2)	148	42	55	25	1	29	3	3	10	14	12	.54	8	.248	.287	.339
1990 Milwaukee	AL	135	474	131	21	4	6	(4	2)	178	55	59	41	5	37	1	7	7	18	7	.72	8	.276	.331	.376
1991 Milwaukee	AL	143	505	146	19	4	5	(3	2)	188	57	68	26	2	33	0	13	9	5	8	.38	21	.289	.319	.372
1992 Milwaukee	AL	139	480	121	19	1	4	(3	1)	154	63	62	46	8	41	2	5	10	14	8	.64	9	.252	.314	.321
1993 Milwaukee	AL	148	552	151	38	3	7	(4	3)	216	66	79	36	5	47	2	4	5	12	9	.57	9	.274	.318	.391
1994 Milwaukee	AL	40	134	35	11	2	5	(2	3)	65	20	22	16	0	14	0	2	2	0	1	.00	5	.261	.336	.485
1995 Milwaukee	AL	117	415	133	26	3	13	(7	6)	204	72	73	37	4	43	4	2	4	7	3	.70	7	.320	.378	.492
9 ML YEARS		1102	3884	1064	194	24	57	(33	24)	1477	472	524	294	35	323	15	52	59	102	64	.61	92	.274	.323	.380

Dave Swartzbaugh

Pitches: Right **Bats:** Right **Pos:** RP   **Ht:** 6' 2" **Wt:** 195 **Born:** 2/11/68 **Age:** 28

		HOW MUCH HE PITCHED						WHAT HE GAVE UP										THE RESULTS					
Year Team	Lg	G	GS	CG	GF	IP	BFP	H	R	ER	HR	SH	SF	HB	TBB	IBB	SO	WP	Bk	W	L	Pct.	ShO	Sv	ERA
1989 Geneva	A	18	10	0	1	75	338	81	59	41	5	0	3	1	35	1	77	8	1	2	3	.400	0	0	4.92
1990 Peoria	A	29	29	5	0	169.2	736	147	88	72	11	1	3	7	89	1	129	10	4	8	11	.421	2	0	3.82
1991 Peoria	A	5	5	1	0	34.1	145	21	16	7	0	2	1	2	15	1	31	2	2	0	5	.000	0	0	1.83
Winston-Sal	A	15	15	2	0	93.2	379	71	22	19	3	5	1	1	42	1	73	4	0	10	4	.714	1	0	1.83
Charlotte	AA	1	1	0	0	5.1	25	6	7	6	1	0	0	0	3	1	5	1	0	0	1	.000	0	0	10.13
1992 Charlotte	AA	27	27	5	0	165	689	134	78	67	13	5	10	9	62	2	111	5	1	7	10	.412	2	0	3.65
1993 Iowa	AAA	26	9	0	5	86.2	385	90	57	51	16	6	4	5	44	1	69	6	0	4	6	.400	0	1	5.30
Orlando	AA	10	9	1	0	66	268	52	33	31	5	2	1	3	18	0	59	2	0	1	3	.250	0	0	4.23
1994 Iowa	AAA	10	0	0	1	19.1	94	24	18	18	8	1	2	1	15	1	14	2	0	1	0	1.000	0	0	8.38
Orlando	AA	42	1	0	11	79	327	70	36	29	7	5	3	4	19	2	70	0	0	2	4	.333	0	2	3.30
1995 Orlando	AA	16	0	0	3	29	111	18	10	8	1	1	1	2	7	0	37	1	1	4	0	1.000	0	0	2.48
Iowa	AAA	30	0	0	9	47	187	33	10	8	1	2	0	1	18	1	38	1	0	3	0	1.000	0	0	1.53
1995 Chicago	NL	7	0	0	2	7.1	27	5	2	0	0	0	0	0	3	1	5	0	0	0	0	.000	0	0	0.00

Mark Sweeney

Bats: Left **Throws:** Left **Pos:** 1B   **Ht:** 6' 1" **Wt:** 195 **Born:** 10/26/69 **Age:** 26

		BATTING																BASERUNNING				PERCENTAGES		
Year Team	Lg	G	AB	H	2B	3B	HR	(Hm	Rd)	TB	R	RBI	TBB	IBB	SO	HBP	SH	SF	SB	CS	SB%	GDP	Avg	OBP	SLG
1991 Boise	A	70	234	66	10	3	4	(--	--)	94	45	34	51	2	42	5	1	3	9	5	.64	7	.282	.416	.402
1992 Quad City	A	120	424	115	20	5	14	(--	--)	187	65	76	47	3	85	4	6	5	15	11	.58	6	.271	.346	.441
1993 Palm Spring	A	66	245	87	18	3	3	(--	--)	120	41	47	42	6	29	2	0	3	9	6	.60	4	.355	.449	.490
Midland	AA	51	188	67	13	2	9	(--	--)	111	41	32	27	3	22	6	0	4	1	1	.50	5	.356	.444	.590
1994 Midland	AA	14	50	15	3	0	3	(--	--)	27	13	18	10	2	10	0	1	2	1	1	.50	3	.300	.403	.540
Vancouver	AAA	103	344	98	12	3	8	(--	--)	140	59	49	59	3	50	5	1	3	3	3	.50	6	.285	.394	.407
1995 Vancouver	AAA	69	226	78	14	2	7	(--	--)	117	48	59	43	4	33	2	1	1	3	1	.75	6	.345	.452	.518
Louisville	AAA	22	76	28	8	0	2	(--	--)	42	15	22	14	1	8	2	0	2	2	0	1.00	5	.368	.468	.553
1995 St. Louis	NL	37	77	21	2	0	2	(0	2)	29	5	13	10	0	15	0	1	2	1	1	.50	3	.273	.348	.377

Mike Sweeney

Bats: Right **Throws:** Right **Pos:** C   **Ht:** 6' 1" **Wt:** 195 **Born:** 7/22/73 **Age:** 22

				BATTING																BASERUNNING				PERCENTAGES		
Year Team	Lg	G	AB	H	2B	3B	HR	(Hm	Rd)	TB	R	RBI	TBB	IBB	SO	HBP	SH	SF	SB	CS	SB%	GDP	Avg	OBP	SLG
1991 Royals	R	38	102	22	3	0	1	--	--	28	8	11	11	0	9	0	0	2	0	0	.00	2	.216	.287	.275
1992 Eugene	A	59	199	44	12	1	4	--	--	70	17	28	13	0	54	4	1	2	3	3	.50	0	.221	.280	.352
1993 Eugene	A	53	175	42	10	2	6	--	--	74	32	29	30	0	41	3	0	1	1	0	1.00	1	.240	.359	.423
1994 Rockford	A	86	276	83	20	3	10	--	--	139	47	52	55	4	43	9	0	4	0	1	.00	8	.301	.427	.504
1995 Wilmington	A	99	332	103	23	1	18	--	--	182	61	53	60	7	39	9	1	5	6	1	.86	4	.310	.424	.548
1995 Kansas City	AL	4	4	1	0	0	0	(0	0)	1	1	0	0	0	0	0	0	0	0	0	.00	0	.250	.250	.250

Bill Swift

Pitches: Right **Bats:** Right **Pos:** SP   **Ht:** 6' 0" **Wt:** 191 **Born:** 10/27/61 **Age:** 34

		HOW MUCH HE PITCHED						WHAT HE GAVE UP												THE RESULTS					
Year Team	Lg	G	GS	CG	GF	IP	BFP	H	R	ER	HR	SH	SF	HB	TBB	IBB	SO	WP	Bk	W	L	Pct.	ShO	Sv	ERA
1985 Seattle	AL	23	21	0	0	120.2	532	131	71	64	8	6	3	5	48	5	55	5	3	6	10	.375	0	0	4.77
1986 Seattle	AL	29	17	1	3	115.1	534	148	85	70	5	5	3	7	55	2	55	2	1	2	9	.182	0	0	5.46
1988 Seattle	AL	38	24	6	4	174.2	757	199	99	89	10	5	3	8	65	3	47	6	2	8	12	.400	1	0	4.59
1989 Seattle	AL	37	16	0	7	130	551	140	72	64	7	4	3	2	38	4	45	4	1	7	3	.700	0	1	4.43
1990 Seattle	AL	55	8	0	18	128	533	135	46	34	4	5	4	7	21	6	42	8	3	6	4	.600	0	6	2.39
1991 Seattle	AL	71	0	0	30	90.1	359	74	22	20	3	2	0	1	26	4	48	2	1	1	2	.333	0	17	1.99
1992 San Francisco	NL	30	22	3	2	164.2	655	144	41	38	6	5	2	3	43	3	77	0	1	10	4	.714	2	1	**2.08**
1993 San Francisco	NL	34	34	1	0	232.2	928	195	82	73	18	4	2	6	55	5	157	4	1	21	8	.724	1	0	2.82
1994 San Francisco	NL	17	17	0	0	109.1	457	109	49	41	10	7	2	1	31	6	62	2	0	8	7	.533	0	0	3.38
1995 Colorado	NL	19	19	0	0	105.2	463	122	62	58	12	6	1	1	43	2	68	2	0	9	3	.750	0	0	4.94
10 ML YEARS		353	178	11	64	1371.1	5769	1397	629	551	83	49	23	41	425	40	656	35	12	78	62	.557	4	25	3.62

Greg Swindell

Pitches: Left **Bats:** Right **Pos:** SP/RP   **Ht:** 6' 3" **Wt:** 225 **Born:** 1/2/65 **Age:** 31

		HOW MUCH HE PITCHED						WHAT HE GAVE UP												THE RESULTS					
Year Team	Lg	G	GS	CG	GF	IP	BFP	H	R	ER	HR	SH	SF	HB	TBB	IBB	SO	WP	Bk	W	L	Pct.	ShO	Sv	ERA
1986 Cleveland	AL	9	9	1	0	61.2	255	57	35	29	9	3	1	1	15	0	46	3	2	5	2	.714	0	0	4.23
1987 Cleveland	AL	16	15	4	0	102.1	441	112	62	58	18	4	3	1	37	1	97	0	1	3	8	.273	1	0	5.10
1988 Cleveland	AL	33	33	12	0	242	988	234	97	86	18	9	5	1	45	3	180	5	0	18	14	.563	4	0	3.20
1989 Cleveland	AL	28	28	5	0	184.1	749	170	71	69	16	4	4	0	51	1	129	3	1	13	6	.684	2	0	3.37
1990 Cleveland	AL	34	34	3	0	214.2	912	245	110	105	27	8	6	1	47	2	135	3	2	12	9	.571	0	0	4.40
1991 Cleveland	AL	33	33	7	0	238	971	241	112	92	21	**13**	8	3	31	1	169	3	1	9	16	.360	0	0	3.48
1992 Cincinnati	NL	31	30	5	0	213.2	867	210	72	64	14	9	7	2	41	4	138	3	2	12	8	.600	3	0	2.70
1993 Houston	NL	31	30	1	0	190.1	818	215	98	88	24	13	3	1	40	3	124	2	2	12	13	.480	1	0	4.16
1994 Houston	NL	24	24	1	0	148.1	623	175	80	72	20	9	7	1	26	2	74	1	1	8	9	.471	0	0	4.37
1995 Houston	NL	33	26	1	3	153	659	180	86	76	21	4	8	2	39	2	96	3	0	10	9	.526	1	0	4.47
10 ML YEARS		272	262	40	3	1748.1	7283	1839	823	739	188	76	52	13	372	19	1188	26	12	102	94	.520	12	0	3.80

Jeff Tabaka

Pitches: Left **Bats:** Right **Pos:** RP   **Ht:** 6' 2" **Wt:** 195 **Born:** 1/17/64 **Age:** 32

		HOW MUCH HE PITCHED						WHAT HE GAVE UP												THE RESULTS					
Year Team	Lg	G	GS	CG	GF	IP	BFP	H	R	ER	HR	SH	SF	HB	TBB	IBB	SO	WP	Bk	W	L	Pct.	ShO	Sv	ERA
1986 Jamestown	A	13	9	0	3	52.1	238	51	31	25	5	3	1	1	34	1	57	5	0	2	4	.333	0	0	4.30
1987 W. Palm Bch	A	28	15	0	8	95	421	90	46	44	3	2	6	3	58	3	71	6	0	8	6	.571	0	5	4.17
1988 W. Palm Bch	A	16	16	2	0	95	387	71	38	18	0	4	6	1	34	1	52	8	1	7	5	.583	2	0	1.71
Jacksonville	AA	2	2	0	0	11	48	14	8	8	1	0	1	0	5	0	7	0	0	1	0	1.000	0	0	6.55
1989 Scranton-Wb	AAA	6	6	0	0	31.1	148	32	26	22	2	2	3	2	23	0	15	1	1	0	4	.000	0	0	6.32
1989 Reading	AA	21	17	6	1	100.2	461	109	59	52	8	3	3	4	54	3	80	9	0	8	7	.533	1	0	4.65
1990 Clearwater	A	8	5	0	1	35.2	163	38	17	12	1	2	1	0	18	0	22	2	1	5	2	.714	0	0	3.03
1991 Reading	AA	21	20	1	0	108.1	495	117	65	61	8	3	10	4	78	2	68	11	0	4	8	.333	1	0	5.07
Stockton	A	4	4	0	0	17.1	82	19	11	10	1	2	0	0	16	0	19	2	0	0	2	.000	0	0	5.19
1992 El Paso	AA	50	0	0	23	82	332	67	23	23	1	3	7	4	38	1	75	5	0	9	5	.643	0	10	2.52
1993 New Orleans	AAA	53	0	0	22	58.1	254	50	26	21	3	1	4	3	30	2	63	7	1	6	6	.500	0	1	3.24
1994 Buffalo	AAA	9	0	0	5	5.1	23	3	2	2	0	0	0	0	4	0	4	0	0	1	0	1.000	0	1	3.38
1995 Las Vegas	AAA	19	0	0	12	22.2	95	16	6	5	0	2	1	1	14	3	27	2	0	0	1	.000	0	6	1.99
1994 Pit-SD	NL	39	0	0	10	41	181	32	29	24	1	3	1	0	27	3	32	1	0	3	1	.750	0	1	5.27
1995 SD-Hou	NL	34	0	0	6	30.2	128	27	11	11	2	0	0	0	17	1	25	1	0	0	0	1.000	0	0	3.23
1994 Pittsburgh	NL	5	0	0	2	4	24	4	8	8	1	0	0	0	8	0	2	0	0	0	0	.000	0	0	18.00
San Diego	NL	34	0	0	8	37	157	28	21	16	0	3	1	0	19	3	30	1	0	3	1	.750	0	0	3.89
1995 San Diego	NL	10	0	0	3	6.1	32	10	5	5	1	0	0	0	5	1	6	1	0	0	0	.000	0	0	7.11
Houston	NL	24	0	0	3	24.1	96	17	6	6	1	0	1	0	12	0	19	0	0	1	0	1.000	0	0	2.22
2 ML YEARS		73	0	0	16	71.2	309	59	40	35	3	3	1	0	44	4	57	2	0	4	1	.800	0	1	4.40

Kevin Tapani

Pitches: Right **Bats:** Right **Pos:** SP **Ht:** 6' 0" **Wt:** 189 **Born:** 2/18/64 **Age:** 32

		HOW MUCH HE PITCHED					WHAT HE GAVE UP										THE RESULTS				
Year Team	Lg	G	GS	CG	GF	IP	BFP	H	R	ER	HR	SH	SF	HB	TBB	IBB	SO	WP	Bk	W	L	Pct.	ShO	Sv	ERA
1989 Min-NYN		8	5	0	1	40	169	39	18	17	3	1	2	0	12	1	23	0	1	2	2	.500	0	0	3.83
1990 Minnesota	AL	28	28	1	0	159.1	659	164	75	72	12	3	4	2	29	2	101	1	0	12	8	.600	1	0	4.07
1991 Minnesota	AL	34	34	4	0	244	974	225	84	81	23	9	6	2	40	0	135	3	3	16	9	.640	1	0	2.99
1992 Minnesota	AL	34	34	4	0	220	911	226	103	97	17	8	11	5	48	2	138	4	0	16	11	.593	1	0	3.97
1993 Minnesota	AL	36	35	3	0	225.2	964	243	123	111	21	3	5	6	57	1	150	4	0	12	15	.444	1	0	4.43
1994 Minnesota	AL	24	24	4	0	156	672	181	86	80	13	2	5	4	39	0	91	1	0	11	7	.611	1	0	4.62
1995 Min-LA		33	31	3	0	190.2	834	227	116	105	29	6	5	5	48	4	131	4	0	10	13	.435	1	0	4.96
1989 Minnesota	AL	5	5	0	0	32.2	138	34	15	14	2	1	1	0	8	1	21	0	0	2	2	.500	0	0	3.86
New York	NL	3	0	0	1	7.1	31	5	3	3	1	0	1	0	4	0	2	0	1	0	0	.000	0	0	3.68
1995 Minnesota	AL	20	20	3	0	133.2	579	155	79	73	21	3	3	4	34	2	88	3	0	6	11	.353	1	0	4.92
Los Angeles	NL	13	11	0	0	57	255	72	37	32	8	3	2	1	14	2	43	1	0	4	2	.667	0	0	5.05
7 ML YEARS		197	191	19	1	1235.2	5183	1305	605	563	118	32	38	24	273	10	769	17	4	79	65	.549	6	0	4.10

Tony Tarasco

Bats: Left **Throws:** Right **Pos:** RF/LF **Ht:** 6' 1" **Wt:** 205 **Born:** 12/9/70 **Age:** 25

		BATTING														BASERUNNING				PERCENTAGES		
Year Team	Lg	G	AB	H	2B	3B	HR	(Hm | Rd)	TB	R	RBI	TBB	IBB	SO	HBP	SH	SF	SB	CS	SB%	GDP	Avg	OBP	SLG
1993 Atlanta	NL	24	35	8	2	0	0	(0 | 0)	10	6	2	0	0	5	1	0	1	0	1	.00	1	.229	.243	.286
1994 Atlanta	NL	87	132	36	6	0	5	(2 | 3)	57	16	19	9	1	17	0	0	3	5	0	1.00	5	.273	.313	.432
1995 Montreal	NL	126	438	109	18	4	14	(7 | 7)	177	64	40	51	12	78	2	3	1	24	3	.89	2	.249	.329	.404
3 ML YEARS		237	605	153	26	4	19	(9 | 10)	244	86	61	60	13	100	3	3	5	29	4	.88	8	.253	.321	.403

Danny Tartabull

Bats: Right **Throws:** Right **Pos:** DH/RF **Ht:** 6' 1" **Wt:** 204 **Born:** 10/30/62 **Age:** 33

		BATTING														BASERUNNING				PERCENTAGES		
Year Team	Lg	G	AB	H	2B	3B	HR	(Hm | Rd)	TB	R	RBI	TBB	IBB	SO	HBP	SH	SF	SB	CS	SB%	GDP	Avg	OBP	SLG
1984 Seattle	AL	10	20	6	1	0	2	(1 | 1)	13	3	7	2	0	3	1	0	1	0	0	.00	0	.300	.375	.650
1985 Seattle	AL	19	61	20	7	1	1	(0 | 1)	32	8	7	8	0	14	0	0	0	1	0	1.00	1	.328	.406	.525
1986 Seattle	AL	137	511	138	25	6	25	(13 | 12)	250	76	96	61	2	157	1	2	3	4	8	.33	10	.270	.347	.489
1987 Kansas City	AL	158	582	180	27	3	34	(15 | 19)	315	95	101	79	2	136	1	0	5	9	4	.69	14	.309	.390	.541
1988 Kansas City	AL	146	507	139	38	3	26	(15 | 11)	261	80	102	76	4	119	4	0	6	8	5	.62	10	.274	.369	.515
1989 Kansas City	AL	133	441	118	22	0	18	(9 | 9)	194	54	62	69	2	123	3	0	2	4	2	.67	12	.268	.369	.440
1990 Kansas City	AL	88	313	84	19	0	15	(5 | 10)	148	41	60	36	0	93	0	0	3	1	1	.50	9	.268	.341	.473
1991 Kansas City	AL	132	484	153	35	3	31	(13 | 18)	287	78	100	65	6	121	3	0	5	6	3	.67	9	.316	.397	.593
1992 New York	AL	123	421	112	19	0	25	(11 | 14)	206	72	85	103	14	115	0	0	2	2	2	.50	7	.266	.409	.489
1993 New York	AL	138	513	128	33	2	31	(11 | 20)	258	87	102	92	9	156	2	0	4	0	0	.00	4	.250	.363	.503
1994 New York	AL	104	399	102	24	1	19	(10 | 9)	185	68	67	66	3	111	1	0	4	1	1	.50	11	.256	.360	.464
1995 NYA-Oak	AL	83	280	66	16	0	8	(3 | 5)	106	34	35	43	1	82	1	0	4	0	2	.00	9	.236	.335	.379
1995 New York	AL	59	192	43	12	0	6	(2 | 4)	73	25	28	33	1	54	1	0	4	0	0	.00	6	.224	.335	.380
Oakland	AL	24	88	23	4	0	2	(1 | 1)	33	9	7	10	0	28	0	0	0	0	2	.00	3	.261	.337	.375
12 ML YEARS		1271	4532	1246	266	19	235	(106 | 129)	2255	696	824	700	43	1230	17	2	39	36	28	.56	100	.275	.371	.498

Jimmy Tatum

Bats: Right **Throws:** Right **Pos:** LF **Ht:** 6' 2" **Wt:** 200 **Born:** 10/9/67 **Age:** 28

		BATTING														BASERUNNING				PERCENTAGES		
Year Team	Lg	G	AB	H	2B	3B	HR	(Hm	Rd)	TB	R	RBI	TBB	IBB	SO	HBP	SH	SF	SB	CS	SB%	GDP	Avg	OBP	SLG
1995 Colo. Sprng *	AAA	27	93	30	7	0	6	--	--	55	17	18	6	0	21	1	0	2	0	1	.00	2	.323	.363	.591
1992 Milwaukee	AL	5	8	1	0	0	0	(0	0)	1	0	0	1	0	2	0	0	0	0	0	.00	0	.125	.222	.125
1993 Colorado	NL	92	98	20	5	0	1	(0	1)	28	7	12	5	0	27	1	0	2	0	0	.00	0	.204	.245	.286
1995 Colorado	NL	34	34	8	1	1	0	(0	0)	11	4	4	1	0	7	0	0	0	0	0	.00	1	.235	.257	.324
3 ML YEARS		131	140	29	6	1	1	(0	1)	40	11	16	7	0	36	1	0	2	0	0	.00	1	.207	.247	.286

Eddie Taubensee

Bats: Left **Throws:** Right **Pos:** C **Ht:** 6' 4" **Wt:** 205 **Born:** 10/31/68 **Age:** 27

		BATTING														BASERUNNING				PERCENTAGES		
Year Team	Lg	G	AB	H	2B	3B	HR	(Hm | Rd)	TB	R	RBI	TBB	IBB	SO	HBP	SH	SF	SB	CS	SB%	GDP	Avg	OBP	SLG
1991 Cleveland	AL	26	66	16	2	1	0	(0 | 0)	20	5	8	5	1	16	0	0	2	0	0	.00	1	.242	.288	.303
1992 Houston	NL	104	297	66	15	0	5	(3 | 2)	96	23	28	31	3	78	2	0	1	2	1	.67	4	.222	.299	.323
1993 Houston	NL	94	288	72	11	1	9	(4 | 5)	112	26	42	21	5	44	0	1	2	1	0	1.00	8	.250	.299	.389
1994 Cin-Hou	NL	66	187	53	8	2	8	(2 | 6)	89	29	21	15	2	31	0	1	2	2	0	1.00	2	.283	.333	.476
1995 Cincinnati	NL	80	218	62	14	2	9	(4 | 5)	107	32	44	22	2	52	2	1	1	2	2	.50	2	.284	.354	.491

222

1994 Cincinnati	NL	61	177	52	8	2	8	(2	6)	88	29	21	15	2	28	0	1	2	2	0	1.00	1	.294	.345	.497
Houston	NL	5	10	1	0	0	0	(0	0)	1	0	0	0	0	3	0	0	0	0	0	.00	1	.100	.100	.100
5 ML YEARS		370	1056	269	50	6	31	(12	19)	424	115	143	94	13	221	4	3	8	7	3	.70	17	.255	.316	.402

Jesus Tavarez

Bats: Both **Throws:** Right **Pos:** CF/RF **Ht:** 6' 0" **Wt:** 170 **Born:** 3/26/71 **Age:** 25

		BATTING																	BASERUNNING				PERCENTAGES		
Year Team	Lg	G	AB	H	2B	3B	HR	(Hm	Rd)	TB	R	RBI	TBB	IBB	SO	HBP	SH	SF	SB	CS	SB%	GDP	Avg	OBP	SLG
1990 Peninsula	A	108	379	90	10	1	0	--	--	102	39	32	20	0	79	0	2	2	40	12	.77	4	.237	.274	.269
1991 San Bernrdo	A	124	466	132	11	3	5	--	--	164	80	41	39	1	77	4	13	1	69	20	.78	4	.283	.343	.352
1992 Jacksonvlle	AA	105	392	101	9	2	3	--	--	123	38	25	23	0	54	1	4	4	29	14	.67	9	.258	.298	.314
1993 High Desert	A	109	444	130	21	8	7	--	--	188	104	71	57	0	66	4	3	5	47	14	.77	6	.293	.375	.423
1994 Portland	AA	89	353	101	11	8	2	--	--	134	60	32	35	2	63	1	7	1	20	8	.71	1	.286	.351	.380
1995 Charlotte	AAA	39	140	42	6	2	1	--	--	55	15	8	9	0	19	0	0	2	7	7	.50	1	.300	.338	.393
1994 Florida	NL	17	39	7	0	0	0	(0	0)	7	4	4	1	0	5	0	1	0	1	1	.50	0	.179	.200	.179
1995 Florida	NL	63	190	55	6	2	2	(1	1)	71	31	13	16	1	27	1	3	1	7	5	.58	1	.289	.346	.374
2 ML YEARS		80	229	62	6	2	2	(1	1)	78	35	17	17	1	32	1	4	1	8	6	.57	1	.271	.323	.341

Julian Tavarez

Pitches: Right **Bats:** Right **Pos:** RP **Ht:** 6' 2" **Wt:** 165 **Born:** 5/22/73 **Age:** 23

		HOW MUCH HE PITCHED						WHAT HE GAVE UP										THE RESULTS					
Year Team	Lg	G	GS	CG	GF	IP	BFP	H	R	ER	HR	SH	SF	HB	TBB	IBB	SO	WP	Bk	W	L	Pct.	ShO	Sv	ERA
1992 Burlington	R	14	14	2	0	87.1	370	86	41	26	3	2	1	10	12	0	69	5	1	6	3	.667	2	0	2.68
1993 Kinston	A	18	18	2	0	119	489	102	48	32	6	3	4	7	28	0	107	3	1	11	5	.688	0	0	2.42
Canton-Akrn	AA	3	2	1	0	19	69	14	2	2	0	0	0	2	1	0	11	0	1	2	1	.667	1	0	0.95
1994 Charlotte	AAA	26	26	2	0	176	737	167	79	68	15	7	3	8	43	0	102	9	0	15	6	.714	2	0	3.48
1993 Cleveland	AL	8	7	0	0	37	172	53	29	27	7	0	1	2	13	2	19	3	1	2	2	.500	0	0	6.57
1994 Cleveland	AL	1	1	0	0	1.2	14	6	8	4	1	0	1	0	1	1	0	0	0	0	0	.000	0	0	21.60
1995 Cleveland	AL	57	0	0	15	85	350	76	36	23	7	0	2	3	21	0	68	3	2	10	2	.833	0	0	2.44
3 ML YEARS		66	8	0	15	123.2	536	135	73	54	15	0	4	5	35	3	87	6	3	12	5	.706	0	0	3.93

Billy Taylor

Pitches: Right **Bats:** Right **Pos:** RP **Ht:** 6' 8" **Wt:** 200 **Born:** 10/16/61 **Age:** 34

		HOW MUCH HE PITCHED						WHAT HE GAVE UP										THE RESULTS					
Year Team	Lg	G	GS	CG	GF	IP	BFP	H	R	ER	HR	SH	SF	HB	TBB	IBB	SO	WP	Bk	W	L	Pct.	ShO	Sv	ERA
1984 Tulsa	AA	42	2	0	28	80	345	65	38	34	8	3	5	2	51	6	80	7	2	5	3	.625	0	7	3.83
1985 Tulsa	AA	20	17	2	0	103.2	441	84	55	40	7	1	5	2	48	1	87	4	4	3	9	.250	0	0	3.47
1986 Tulsa	AA	11	11	2	0	68.1	307	65	40	30	6	2	2	2	37	3	64	3	0	3	7	.300	1	0	3.95
Okla. City	AAA	16	16	1	0	101.2	447	94	56	52	7	2	2	1	57	0	68	4	6	5	5	.500	0	0	4.60
1987 Okla. City	AAA	28	28	0	0	168.1	769	198	122	105	10	0	4	2	91	0	100	8	2	12	9	.571	0	0	5.61
1988 Okla. City	AAA	20	12	1	4	82	373	98	55	50	4	1	8	2	35	1	42	2	6	4	8	.333	1	1	5.49
1989 Las Vegas	AAA	47	0	0	22	79	352	93	48	45	5	4	1	2	27	5	71	1	3	7	4	.636	0	1	5.13
1990 Durham	A	5	0	0	3	8.1	36	8	3	3	0	1	0	0	1	1	10	0	1	0	0	.000	0	0	3.24
Richmond	AAA	2	0	0	0	2.2	13	4	0	0	0	0	0	0	0	0	0	0	0	0	0	.000	0	0	0.00
1991 Greenville	AA	59	0	0	44	77.2	295	49	16	13	1	5	1	3	15	2	65	3	1	6	2	.750	0	22	1.51
1992 Richmond	AAA	47	0	0	27	79	332	72	27	20	5	4	3	0	27	3	82	0	0	2	3	.400	0	12	2.28
1993 Richmond	AAA	59	0	0	55	68.1	282	56	19	15	3	2	2	2	26	7	81	1	0	2	4	.333	0	26	1.98
1994 Oakland	AL	41	0	0	11	46.1	195	38	24	18	4	1	1	2	18	5	48	0	0	1	3	.250	0	1	3.50

Scott Taylor

Pitches: Right **Bats:** Right **Pos:** SP **Ht:** 6' 3" **Wt:** 200 **Born:** 10/3/66 **Age:** 29

		HOW MUCH HE PITCHED						WHAT HE GAVE UP										THE RESULTS					
Year Team	Lg	G	GS	CG	GF	IP	BFP	H	R	ER	HR	SH	SF	HB	TBB	IBB	SO	WP	Bk	W	L	Pct.	ShO	Sv	ERA
1989 Wausau	A	16	16	6	0	106.1	445	92	49	38	5	3	2	6	37	1	65	8	3	9	7	.563	2	0	3.22
Williamsprt	AA	10	7	1	1	40.2	185	49	26	26	6	1	5	1	20	1	22	2	0	1	4	.200	0	0	5.75
1990 San Bernrdo	A	34	21	1	3	126.1	596	148	100	76	17	0	3	7	69	0	86	10	1	8	8	.500	0	1	5.41
1991 Durham	A	24	16	2	5	111.1	452	94	32	27	3	6	2	2	33	3	78	10	0	10	3	.769	0	3	2.18
Greenville	AA	8	7	1	0	43	191	49	25	20	4	1	1	2	16	2	26	6	0	3	4	.429	1	0	4.19
1992 Greenville	AA	22	4	0	6	39	172	44	31	29	6	0	3	3	18	0	20	3	0	1	1	.500	0	1	6.69
El Paso	AA	11	9	0	0	54.1	224	45	21	21	5	3	1	0	19	1	37	2	1	4	2	.667	0	0	3.48
1993 El Paso	AA	17	16	1	1	104.1	434	105	53	44	4	2	2	11	31	2	76	0	0	6	6	.500	0	0	3.80
New Orleans	AAA	12	8	1	3	62.1	244	48	17	16	3	5	1	2	21	1	47	1	1	5	1	.833	0	0	2.31
1994 New Orleans	AAA	28	27	4	0	165.2	720	177	88	79	12	4	5	12	59	2	106	3	0	14	9	.609	1	0	4.29
1995 New Orleans	AAA	2	2	0	0	11.1	47	10	3	3	0	0	0	0	3	0	9	0	0	1	0	1.000	0	0	2.38
Okla. City	AAA	22	19	1	0	118	510	122	59	48	12	4	2	6	38	0	65	5	0	7	8	.467	1	0	3.66
1995 Texas	AL	3	3	0	0	15.1	71	25	16	16	6	0	0	0	5	0	10	0	0	1	2	.333	0	0	9.39

Dave Telgheder

Pitches: Right **Bats:** Right **Pos:** SP **Ht:** 6' 3" **Wt:** 212 **Born:** 11/11/66 **Age:** 29

Year Team	Lg	G	GS	CG	GF	IP	BFP	H	R	ER	HR	SH	SF	HB	TBB	IBB	SO	WP	Bk	W	L	Pct.	ShO	Sv	ERA
1995 Norfolk *	AAA	29	11	0	8	92.1	356	77	34	23	7	5	2	1	8	0	75	0	2	5	4	.556	0	3	2.24
1993 New York	NL	24	7	0	7	75.2	325	82	40	40	10	2	1	4	21	2	35	1	0	6	2	.750	0	0	4.76
1994 New York	NL	6	0	0	0	10	48	11	8	8	2	1	0	0	8	2	4	0	0	0	1	.000	0	0	7.20
1995 New York	NL	7	4	0	2	25.2	118	34	18	16	4	3	1	0	7	3	16	0	1	1	2	.333	0	0	5.61
3 ML YEARS		37	11	0	9	111.1	491	127	66	64	16	6	2	4	36	7	55	1	1	7	5	.583	0	0	5.17

Mickey Tettleton

Bats: Both **Throws:** Right **Pos:** RF/DH **Ht:** 6' 2" **Wt:** 212 **Born:** 9/16/60 **Age:** 35

Year Team	Lg	G	AB	H	2B	3B	HR	(Hm	Rd)	TB	R	RBI	TBB	IBB	SO	HBP	SH	SF	SB	CS	SB%	GDP	Avg	OBP	SLG
1984 Oakland	AL	33	76	20	2	1	1	(1	0)	27	10	5	11	0	21	0	0	1	0	0	.00	3	.263	.352	.355
1985 Oakland	AL	78	211	53	12	0	3	(1	2)	74	23	15	28	0	59	2	5	0	2	2	.50	6	.251	.344	.351
1986 Oakland	AL	90	211	43	9	0	10	(4	6)	82	26	35	39	0	51	1	7	4	7	1	.88	3	.204	.325	.389
1987 Oakland	AL	82	211	41	3	0	8	(5	3)	68	19	26	30	0	65	0	5	2	1	1	.50	3	.194	.292	.322
1988 Baltimore	AL	86	283	74	11	1	11	(7	4)	120	31	37	28	2	70	2	1	2	0	1	.00	9	.261	.330	.424
1989 Baltimore	AL	117	411	106	21	2	26	(15	11)	209	72	65	73	4	117	1	1	3	3	2	.60	8	.258	.369	.509
1990 Baltimore	AL	135	444	99	21	2	15	(8	7)	169	68	51	106	3	160	5	0	4	2	4	.33	7	.223	.376	.381
1991 Detroit	AL	154	501	132	17	2	31	(15	16)	246	85	89	101	9	131	2	0	4	3	3	.50	12	.263	.387	.491
1992 Detroit	AL	157	525	125	25	0	32	(18	14)	246	82	83	122	18	137	1	0	6	0	0	.00	5	.238	.379	.469
1993 Detroit	AL	152	522	128	25	4	32	(16	16)	257	79	110	109	12	139	0	0	6	3	7	.30	5	.245	.372	.492
1994 Detroit	AL	107	339	84	18	2	17	(9	8)	157	57	51	97	10	98	5	0	3	0	1	.00	4	.248	.419	.463
1995 Texas	AL	134	429	102	19	1	32	(22	10)	219	76	78	107	5	110	7	1	3	0	0	.00	8	.238	.396	.510
12 ML YEARS		1325	4163	1007	183	15	218	(121	97)	1874	628	645	851	63	1158	26	20	38	21	28	.43	73	.242	.371	.450

Bob Tewksbury

Pitches: Right **Bats:** Right **Pos:** SP **Ht:** 6' 4" **Wt:** 208 **Born:** 11/30/60 **Age:** 35

Year Team	Lg	G	GS	CG	GF	IP	BFP	H	R	ER	HR	SH	SF	HB	TBB	IBB	SO	WP	Bk	W	L	Pct.	ShO	Sv	ERA
1995 Charlotte *	A	1	1	0	0	6	22	3	0	0	0	0	0	0	0	0	4	0	0	1	0	1.000	0	0	0.00
1986 New York	AL	23	20	2	0	130.1	558	144	58	48	8	4	7	5	31	0	49	3	2	9	5	.643	0	0	3.31
1987 NYA-ChN		15	9	0	4	51.1	242	79	41	38	6	5	1	1	20	3	22	1	2	1	8	.111	0	0	6.66
1988 Chicago	NL	1	1	0	0	3.1	18	6	5	3	1	0	1	0	2	0	1	0	0	0	0	.000	0	0	8.10
1989 St. Louis	NL	7	4	1	2	30	125	25	12	11	2	1	1	2	10	3	17	0	0	1	0	1.000	1	0	3.30
1990 St. Louis	NL	28	20	3	1	145.1	595	151	67	56	7	5	7	3	15	3	50	2	0	10	9	.526	2	1	3.47
1991 St. Louis	NL	30	30	3	0	191	798	206	86	69	13	12	10	5	38	2	75	0	0	11	12	.478	0	0	3.25
1992 St. Louis	NL	33	32	5	1	233	915	217	63	56	15	9	7	3	20	0	91	2	0	16	5	.762	0	0	2.16
1993 St. Louis	NL	32	32	2	0	213.2	907	258	99	91	15	15	9	6	20	1	97	2	0	17	10	.630	0	0	3.83
1994 St. Louis	NL	24	24	4	0	155.2	667	190	97	92	19	12	4	3	22	1	79	1	0	12	10	.545	1	0	5.32
1995 Texas	AL	21	21	4	0	129.2	561	169	75	66	8	6	3	3	20	4	53	4	0	8	7	.533	1	0	4.58
1987 New York	AL	8	6	0	1	33.1	149	47	26	25	5	2	0	1	7	0	12	0	0	1	4	.200	0	0	6.75
Chicago	NL	7	3	0	3	18	93	32	15	13	1	3	1	0	13	3	10	1	2	0	4	.000	0	0	6.50
10 ML YEARS		214	193	24	8	1283.1	5386	1445	603	530	94	69	50	31	198	17	534	15	4	85	66	.563	5	1	3.72

J.J. Thobe

Pitches: Right **Bats:** Right **Pos:** RP **Ht:** 6' 6" **Wt:** 220 **Born:** 11/19/70 **Age:** 25

Year Team	Lg	G	GS	CG	GF	IP	BFP	H	R	ER	HR	SH	SF	HB	TBB	IBB	SO	WP	Bk	W	L	Pct.	ShO	Sv	ERA
1993 Columbus	A	19	19	2	0	132	523	105	36	28	6	2	4	1	25	0	106	3	1	11	2	.846	0	0	1.91
Kinston	A	4	4	0	0	23	102	26	11	8	1	0	4	1	9	0	11	1	0	1	2	.333	0	0	3.13
1994 W. Palm Bch	A	2	2	0	0	12	50	14	5	5	0	1	1	1	2	0	4	0	0	1	1	.500	0	0	3.75
Harrisburg	AA	21	21	1	0	120.2	513	129	73	58	12	6	5	2	24	0	57	7	0	7	8	.467	0	0	4.33
1995 Ottawa	AAA	55	0	0	25	88	354	79	37	32	8	6	2	1	16	3	36	1	0	5	8	.385	0	5	3.27
1995 Montreal	NL	4	0	0	2	4	21	6	4	4	0	0	0	0	3	0	0	1	0	0	0	.000	0	0	9.00

Tom Thobe

Pitches: Left **Bats:** Left **Pos:** RP **Ht:** 6' 6" **Wt:** 195 **Born:** 9/3/69 **Age:** 26

Year Team	Lg	G	GS	CG	GF	IP	BFP	H	R	ER	HR	SH	SF	HB	TBB	IBB	SO	WP	Bk	W	L	Pct.	ShO	Sv	ERA
1993 Macon	A	43	0	0	22	70.1	299	70	25	21	0	6	1	2	16	1	55	8	0	7	5	.583	0	5	2.69
1994 Greenville	AA	51	0	0	27	63.2	263	56	21	18	3	5	2	0	26	2	52	6	2	7	6	.538	0	9	2.54
1995 Richmond	AAA	48	2	1	15	88	350	65	27	18	2	3	1	1	26	5	57	5	0	7	0	1.000	1	5	1.84
1995 Atlanta	NL	3	0	0	1	3.1	17	7	4	4	0	0	0	0	2	0	0	0	0	0	0	.000	0	0	10.80

Frank Thomas

Bats: Right **Throws:** Right **Pos:** 1B/DH   **Ht:** 6' 5" **Wt:** 257 **Born:** 5/27/68 **Age:** 28

Year Team	Lg	G	AB	H	2B	3B	HR	(Hm	Rd)	TB	R	RBI	TBB	IBB	SO	HBP	SH	SF	SB	CS	SB%	GDP	Avg	OBP	SLG
1990 Chicago	AL	60	191	63	11	3	7	(2	5)	101	39	31	44	0	54	2	0	3	0	1	.00	5	.330	.454	.529
1991 Chicago	AL	158	559	178	31	2	32	(24	8)	309	104	109	138	13	112	1	0	2	1	2	.33	20	.318	.453	.553
1992 Chicago	AL	160	573	185	46	2	24	(10	14)	307	108	115	122	6	88	5	0	11	6	3	.67	19	.323	.439	.536
1993 Chicago	AL	153	549	174	36	0	41	(26	15)	333	106	128	112	23	54	2	0	13	4	2	.67	10	.317	.426	.607
1994 Chicago	AL	113	399	141	34	1	38	(22	16)	291	106	101	109	12	61	2	0	7	2	3	.40	15	.353	.487	.729
1995 Chicago	AL	145	493	152	27	0	40	(15	25)	299	102	111	136	29	74	6	0	12	3	2	.60	14	.308	.454	.606
6 ML YEARS		789	2764	893	185	8	182	(99	83)	1640	565	595	661	83	443	18	0	48	16	13	.55	83	.323	.450	.593

Larry Thomas

Pitches: Left **Bats:** Right **Pos:** RP   **Ht:** 6' 1" **Wt:** 195 **Born:** 10/25/69 **Age:** 26

Year Team	Lg	G	GS	CG	GF	IP	BFP	H	R	ER	HR	SH	SF	HB	TBB	IBB	SO	WP	Bk	W	L	Pct.	ShO	Sv	ERA
1991 Utica	A	11	10	0	0	73.1	288	55	22	12	2	3	2	0	25	1	61	3	0	1	3	.250	0	0	1.47
Birmingham	AA	2	0	0	2	6	28	6	3	2	0	0	0	0	4	1	2	0	0	0	0	.000	0	0	3.00
1992 Sarasota	A	8	8	0	0	55.2	220	44	14	10	1	1	0	0	7	1	50	2	0	5	0	1.000	0	0	1.62
Birmingham	AA	17	17	3	0	120.2	474	102	32	26	4	4	2	1	30	2	72	5	0	8	6	.571	0	0	1.94
1993 Nashville	AAA	18	18	1	0	100.2	441	114	73	67	15	3	6	1	32	4	67	4	1	4	6	.400	0	0	5.99
Sarasota	A	8	8	3	0	61.2	247	52	19	17	3	2	0	0	15	0	27	1	1	4	2	.667	2	0	2.48
Birmingham	AA	1	1	0	0	7	33	9	5	4	1	0	0	1	1	1	5	0	0	0	1	.000	0	0	5.14
1994 Birmingham	AA	24	24	1	0	144	642	159	96	74	17	4	6	5	53	0	77	11	2	5	10	.333	0	0	4.63
1995 Birmingham	AA	35	0	0	9	40.1	156	24	9	6	0	2	2	2	15	1	47	3	0	4	1	.800	0	2	1.34
1995 Chicago	AL	17	0	0	5	13.2	54	8	2	2	1	0	0	0	6	1	12	1	0	0	0	.000	0	0	1.32

Mike Thomas

Pitches: Left **Bats:** Left **Pos:** RP   **Ht:** 6' 2" **Wt:** 205 **Born:** 9/2/69 **Age:** 26

Year Team	Lg	G	GS	CG	GF	IP	BFP	H	R	ER	HR	SH	SF	HB	TBB	IBB	SO	WP	Bk	W	L	Pct.	ShO	Sv	ERA
1989 Mets	R	8	3	0	5	31.1	127	23	5	5	0	0	1	2	14	0	34	2	0	2	0	1.000	0	0	1.44
Kingsport	R	6	3	0	3	19.1	90	13	16	14	1	2	0	1	17	0	17	1	0	1	2	.333	0	0	6.52
1990 Pittsfield	A	28	3	0	13	64	270	51	23	19	3	2	3	3	29	3	80	6	0	3	3	.500	0	3	2.67
1991 Columbia	A	30	0	0	27	41	179	28	15	11	1	3	1	2	30	2	59	3	2	4	2	.667	0	15	2.41
Sumter	A	19	0	0	15	27.1	125	25	13	12	0	1	1	1	18	0	30	5	2	4	1	.800	0	5	3.95
1992 Rockford	A	28	17	1	8	113	473	98	52	45	8	3	7	6	51	0	108	5	4	5	9	.357	0	2	3.58
1993 W. Palm Bch	A	25	0	0	19	27.1	123	19	13	10	0	3	0	2	23	2	28	1	0	1	3	.250	0	9	3.29
Harrisburg	AA	25	0	0	14	32.1	150	34	18	17	3	2	1	1	19	2	40	1	2	2	2	.500	0	6	4.73
1994 El Paso	AA	50	0	0	32	66.1	296	57	36	25	6	7	3	4	42	3	59	6	2	2	3	.400	0	20	3.39
1995 New Orleans	AAA	35	0	0	14	33.1	151	37	18	15	3	0	0	2	18	0	28	3	2	0	1	.000	0	1	4.05
1995 Milwaukee	AL	1	0	0	0	1.1	7	2	0	0	0	0	0	0	1	0	0	0	0	0	0	.000	0	0	0.00

Jim Thome

Bats: Left **Throws:** Right **Pos:** 3B   **Ht:** 6' 4" **Wt:** 220 **Born:** 8/27/70 **Age:** 25

Year Team	Lg	G	AB	H	2B	3B	HR	(Hm	Rd)	TB	R	RBI	TBB	IBB	SO	HBP	SH	SF	SB	CS	SB%	GDP	Avg	OBP	SLG
1991 Cleveland	AL	27	98	25	4	2	1	(0	1)	36	7	9	5	1	16	1	0	1	1	1	.50	4	.255	.298	.367
1992 Cleveland	AL	40	117	24	3	1	2	(1	1)	35	8	12	10	2	34	2	0	2	2	0	1.00	3	.205	.275	.299
1993 Cleveland	AL	47	154	41	11	0	7	(5	2)	73	28	22	29	1	36	4	0	5	2	1	.67	3	.266	.385	.474
1994 Cleveland	AL	98	321	86	20	1	20	(10	10)	168	58	52	46	5	84	0	1	1	3	3	.50	11	.268	.359	.523
1995 Cleveland	AL	137	452	142	29	3	25	(13	12)	252	92	73	97	3	113	5	0	3	4	3	.57	8	.314	.438	.558
5 ML YEARS		349	1142	318	67	7	55	(29	26)	564	193	168	187	12	283	12	1	11	12	8	.60	29	.278	.382	.494

Mark Thompson

Pitches: Right **Bats:** Right **Pos:** RP/SP   **Ht:** 6' 2" **Wt:** 205 **Born:** 4/7/71 **Age:** 25

Year Team	Lg	G	GS	CG	GF	IP	BFP	H	R	ER	HR	SH	SF	HB	TBB	IBB	SO	WP	Bk	W	L	Pct.	ShO	Sv	ERA
1992 Bend	A	16	16	4	0	106.1	421	81	32	23	2	1	2	4	31	1	102	8	4	8	4	.667	0	0	1.95
1993 Central Val	A	11	11	0	0	69.2	279	46	19	17	3	1	4	5	18	0	72	3	2	3	2	.600	0	0	2.20
Colo. Sprng	AAA	4	4	2	0	33.1	137	31	13	10	1	1	0	1	11	0	22	3	0	3	0	1.000	0	0	2.70
1994 Colo. Sprng	AAA	23	23	4	0	140.1	629	169	83	70	11	2	5	8	57	2	82	6	0	8	9	.471	1	0	4.49
1995 Colo. Sprng	AAA	11	10	0	0	62	276	73	43	42	2	2	2	6	25	0	38	0	0	5	3	.625	0	0	6.10
1994 Colorado	NL	2	2	0	0	9	49	16	9	9	2	0	0	1	8	0	5	0	0	1	1	.500	0	0	9.00
1995 Colorado	NL	21	5	0	3	51	240	73	42	37	7	4	4	1	22	2	30	2	0	2	3	.400	0	0	6.53
2 ML YEARS		23	7	0	3	60	289	89	51	46	9	4	4	2	30	2	35	2	0	3	4	.429	0	0	6.90

Milt Thompson

Bats: Left **Throws:** Right **Pos:** RF/LF **Ht:** 5'11" **Wt:** 190 **Born:** 1/5/59 **Age:** 37

Year Team	Lg	G	AB	H	2B	3B	HR	(Hm	Rd)	TB	R	RBI	TBB	IBB	SO	HBP	SH	SF	SB	CS	SB%	GDP	Avg	OBP	SLG
1984 Atlanta	NL	25	99	30	1	0	2	(0	2)	37	16	4	11	1	11	0	1	0	14	2	.88	1	.303	.373	.374
1985 Atlanta	NL	73	182	55	7	2	0	(0	0)	66	17	6	7	0	36	3	1	0	9	4	.69	1	.302	.339	.363
1986 Philadelphia	NL	96	299	75	7	1	6	(4	2)	102	38	23	26	1	62	1	4	2	19	4	.83	4	.251	.311	.341
1987 Philadelphia	NL	150	527	159	26	9	7	(3	4)	224	86	43	42	2	87	0	3	3	46	10	.82	5	.302	.351	.425
1988 Philadelphia	NL	122	378	109	16	2	2	(1	1)	135	53	33	39	6	59	1	2	3	17	9	.65	8	.288	.354	.357
1989 St. Louis	NL	155	545	158	28	8	4	(2	2)	214	60	68	39	5	91	4	0	3	27	8	.77	12	.290	.340	.393
1990 St. Louis	NL	135	418	91	14	7	6	(3	3)	137	42	30	39	5	60	5	1	0	25	5	.83	4	.218	.292	.328
1991 St. Louis	NL	115	326	100	16	5	6	(4	2)	144	55	34	32	7	53	0	2	1	16	9	.64	4	.307	.368	.442
1992 St. Louis	NL	109	208	61	9	1	4	(1	3)	84	31	17	16	3	39	2	0	0	18	6	.75	3	.293	.350	.404
1993 Philadelphia	NL	129	340	89	14	2	4	(2	2)	119	42	44	40	9	57	2	3	2	9	4	.69	8	.262	.341	.350
1994 Hou-Phi	NL	96	241	66	7	0	4	(4	0)	85	34	33	24	4	30	3	1	1	9	2	.82	6	.274	.346	.353
1995 Houston	NL	92	132	29	9	0	2	(0	2)	44	14	19	14	3	37	1	2	1	4	2	.67	3	.220	.297	.333
1994 Houston	NL	9	21	6	0	0	1	(1	0)	9	5	3	1	0	2	0	0	0	2	0	1.00	1	.286	.318	.429
Philadelphia	NL	87	220	60	7	0	3	(3	0)	76	29	30	23	4	28	3	1	1	7	2	.78	5	.273	.348	.345
12 ML YEARS		1297	3695	1022	154	37	47	(24	23)	1391	488	354	329	46	622	22	20	16	213	65	.77	59	.277	.338	.376

Robby Thompson

Bats: Right **Throws:** Right **Pos:** 2B **Ht:** 5'11" **Wt:** 173 **Born:** 5/10/62 **Age:** 34

Year Team	Lg	G	AB	H	2B	3B	HR	(Hm	Rd)	TB	R	RBI	TBB	IBB	SO	HBP	SH	SF	SB	CS	SB%	GDP	Avg	OBP	SLG
1986 San Francisco	NL	149	549	149	27	3	7	(0	7)	203	73	47	42	0	112	5	18	1	12	15	.44	11	.271	.328	.370
1987 San Francisco	NL	132	420	110	26	5	10	(7	3)	176	62	44	40	3	91	8	6	0	16	11	.59	8	.262	.338	.419
1988 San Francisco	NL	138	477	126	24	6	7	(3	4)	183	66	48	40	0	111	4	14	5	14	5	.74	7	.264	.323	.384
1989 San Francisco	NL	148	547	132	26	11	13	(7	6)	219	91	50	51	0	133	13	9	0	12	2	.86	6	.241	.321	.400
1990 San Francisco	NL	144	498	122	22	3	15	(8	7)	195	67	56	34	1	96	6	8	3	14	4	.78	9	.245	.299	.392
1991 San Francisco	NL	144	492	129	24	5	19	(11	8)	220	74	48	63	2	95	6	11	1	14	7	.67	5	.262	.352	.447
1992 San Francisco	NL	128	443	115	25	1	14	(8	6)	184	54	49	43	1	75	8	7	4	5	9	.36	8	.260	.333	.415
1993 San Francisco	NL	128	494	154	30	2	19	(13	6)	245	85	65	45	0	97	7	9	4	10	4	.71	7	.312	.375	.496
1994 San Francisco	NL	35	129	27	8	2	2	(1	1)	45	13	7	15	0	32	0	5	1	3	1	.75	2	.209	.290	.349
1995 San Francisco	NL	95	336	75	15	0	8	(4	4)	114	51	23	42	1	76	4	9	0	1	2	.33	3	.223	.317	.339
10 ML YEARS		1241	4385	1139	227	38	114	(62	52)	1784	636	437	415	8	918	61	96	19	101	60	.63	66	.260	.331	.407

Ryan Thompson

Bats: Right **Throws:** Right **Pos:** CF/LF/RF **Ht:** 6'3" **Wt:** 215 **Born:** 11/4/67 **Age:** 28

Year Team	Lg	G	AB	H	2B	3B	HR	(Hm	Rd)	TB	R	RBI	TBB	IBB	SO	HBP	SH	SF	SB	CS	SB%	GDP	Avg	OBP	SLG
1995 Norfolk *	AAA	15	53	18	3	0	2	--	--	27	7	11	4	0	15	0	0	4	4	1	.80	0	.340	.361	.509
Binghamton *	AA	2	8	4	0	0	1	--	--	7	2	4	1	0	2	0	0	0	0	0	.00	0	.500	.556	.875
1992 New York	NL	30	108	24	7	1	3	(3	0)	42	15	10	8	0	24	0	0	1	2	2	.50	2	.222	.274	.389
1993 New York	NL	80	288	72	19	2	11	(5	6)	128	34	26	19	4	81	3	5	1	2	7	.22	5	.250	.302	.444
1994 New York	NL	98	334	75	14	1	18	(5	13)	145	39	59	28	7	94	10	3	4	1	1	.50	8	.225	.301	.434
1995 New York	NL	75	267	67	13	0	7	(3	4)	101	39	31	19	1	77	4	0	4	3	1	.75	12	.251	.306	.378
4 ML YEARS		283	997	238	53	4	39	(16	23)	416	127	126	74	12	276	17	8	10	8	11	.42	27	.239	.300	.417

Gary Thurman

Bats: Right **Throws:** Right **Pos:** LF **Ht:** 5'10" **Wt:** 175 **Born:** 11/12/64 **Age:** 31

Year Team	Lg	G	AB	H	2B	3B	HR	(Hm	Rd)	TB	R	RBI	TBB	IBB	SO	HBP	SH	SF	SB	CS	SB%	GDP	Avg	OBP	SLG
1995 Tacoma *	AAA	93	363	109	10	12	5	--	--	158	65	46	20	0	62	5	3	1	22	8	.73	2	.300	.344	.435
1987 Kansas City	AL	27	81	24	2	0	0	(0	0)	26	12	5	8	0	20	0	1	0	7	2	.78	1	.296	.360	.321
1988 Kansas City	AL	35	66	11	1	0	0	(0	0)	12	6	2	4	0	20	0	0	0	5	1	.83	0	.167	.214	.182
1989 Kansas City	AL	72	87	17	2	1	0	(0	0)	21	24	5	15	0	26	0	2	1	16	0	1.00	0	.195	.311	.241
1990 Kansas City	AL	23	60	14	3	0	0	(0	0)	17	5	3	2	0	12	0	1	0	1	1	.50	2	.233	.258	.283
1991 Kansas City	AL	80	184	51	9	0	2	(1	1)	66	24	13	11	0	42	1	3	1	15	5	.75	4	.277	.320	.359
1992 Kansas City	AL	88	200	49	6	3	0	(0	0)	61	25	20	9	0	34	1	6	0	9	6	.60	3	.245	.281	.305
1993 Detroit	AL	75	89	19	2	2	0	(0	0)	25	22	13	11	0	30	0	1	1	7	0	1.00	2	.213	.297	.281
1995 Seattle	AL	13	25	8	2	0	0	(0	0)	10	3	3	1	0	3	0	0	1	5	2	.71	0	.320	.333	.400
8 ML YEARS		413	792	193	27	6	2	(1	1)	238	121	64	61	0	187	2	14	4	65	17	.79	12	.244	.298	.301

Mike Timlin

Pitches: Right **Bats:** Right **Pos:** RP **Ht:** 6' 4" **Wt:** 210 **Born:** 3/10/66 **Age:** 30

		HOW MUCH HE PITCHED						WHAT HE GAVE UP										THE RESULTS					
Year Team	Lg	G	GS	CG	GF	IP	BFP	H	R	ER	HR	SH	SF	HB	TBB	IBB	SO	WP	Bk	W	L	Pct.	ShO	Sv	ERA
1995 Syracuse *	AAA	8	0	0	2	17.1	70	13	6	2	2	0	0	0	4	0	13	0	0	1	1	.500	0	0	1.04
1991 Toronto	AL	63	3	0	17	108.1	463	94	43	38	6	6	2	1	50	11	85	5	0	11	6	.647	0	3	3.16
1992 Toronto	AL	26	0	0	14	43.2	190	45	23	20	0	2	1	1	20	5	35	0	0	0	2	.000	0	1	4.12
1993 Toronto	AL	54	0	0	27	55.2	254	63	32	29	7	1	3	1	27	3	49	1	0	4	2	.667	0	1	4.69
1994 Toronto	AL	34	0	0	16	40	179	41	25	23	5	0	0	2	20	0	38	3	0	0	1	.000	0	2	5.18
1995 Toronto	AL	31	0	0	19	42	179	38	13	10	1	3	0	2	17	5	36	3	1	4	3	.571	0	5	2.14
5 ML YEARS		208	3	0	93	289.2	1265	281	136	120	19	12	6	7	134	24	243	12	1	19	14	.576	0	12	3.73

Ozzie Timmons

Bats: Right **Throws:** Right **Pos:** LF **Ht:** 6' 2" **Wt:** 210 **Born:** 9/18/70 **Age:** 25

		BATTING															BASERUNNING				PERCENTAGES		
Year Team	Lg	G	AB	H	2B	3B	HR	(Hm | Rd)	TB	R	RBI	TBB	IBB	SO	HBP	SH	SF	SB	CS	SB%	GDP	Avg	OBP	SLG
1991 Geneva	A	73	294	65	10	1	12	--	--	113	35	47	18	0	39	2	0	4	4	3	.57	1	.221	.267	.384
1992 Charlotte	A	36	122	26	7	0	3	--	--	42	13	13	12	0	26	1	1	0	2	2	.50	2	.213	.289	.344
Winston-Sal	A	86	305	86	18	0	18	--	--	158	64	56	58	3	46	2	4	4	11	0	1.00	5	.282	.396	.518
1993 Orlando	AA	107	359	102	22	2	18	--	--	182	65	58	62	3	80	2	2	1	5	11	.31	6	.284	.392	.507
1994 Iowa	AAA	126	440	116	30	2	22	--	--	216	63	66	36	0	93	1	3	2	0	3	.00	12	.264	.319	.491
1995 Chicago	NL	77	171	45	10	1	8	(5 | 3)	81	30	28	13	2	32	0	0	1	3	0	1.00	8	.263	.314	.474

Ron Tingley

Bats: Right **Throws:** Right **Pos:** C **Ht:** 6' 2" **Wt:** 195 **Born:** 5/27/59 **Age:** 37

		BATTING															BASERUNNING				PERCENTAGES		
Year Team	Lg	G	AB	H	2B	3B	HR	(Hm | Rd)	TB	R	RBI	TBB	IBB	SO	HBP	SH	SF	SB	CS	SB%	GDP	Avg	OBP	SLG
1982 San Diego	NL	8	20	2	0	0	0	(0 | 0)	2	0	0	0	0	7	0	1	0	0	0	.00	0	.100	.100	.100
1988 Cleveland	AL	9	24	4	0	0	1	(0 | 1)	7	1	2	2	0	8	0	0	0	0	0	.00	1	.167	.231	.292
1989 California	AL	4	3	1	0	0	0	(0 | 0)	1	0	0	1	0	0	0	0	0	0	0	.00	0	.333	.500	.333
1990 California	AL	5	3	0	0	0	0	(0 | 0)	0	0	0	1	0	1	0	0	0	0	0	.00	1	.000	.250	.000
1991 California	AL	45	115	23	7	0	1	(1 | 0)	33	11	13	8	0	34	1	4	0	1	1	.50	1	.200	.258	.287
1992 California	AL	71	127	25	2	1	3	(2 | 1)	38	15	8	13	0	35	2	5	0	1	0	.00	4	.197	.282	.299
1993 California	AL	58	90	18	7	0	0	(0 | 0)	25	7	12	9	0	22	1	3	1	1	2	.33	4	.200	.277	.278
1994 ChA-Fla		24	57	9	3	1	1	(0 | 1)	17	4	2	5	0	20	0	0	0	0	2	.00	2	.158	.226	.298
1995 Detroit	AL	54	124	28	8	1	4	(3 | 1)	50	14	18	15	0	38	0	5	1	0	0	.00	1	.226	.307	.403
1994 Chicago	AL	5	5	0	0	0	0	(0 | 0)	0	0	0	0	0	2	0	0	0	0	0	.00	0	.000	.000	.000
Florida	NL	19	52	9	3	1	1	(0 | 1)	17	4	2	5	0	18	0	0	0	0	0	.00	2	.173	.246	.327
9 ML YEARS		278	563	110	27	3	10	(6 | 4)	173	52	55	54	0	165	4	18	2	2	5	.29	14	.195	.270	.307

Lee Tinsley

Bats: Both **Throws:** Right **Pos:** CF **Ht:** 5'10" **Wt:** 195 **Born:** 3/4/69 **Age:** 27

		BATTING															BASERUNNING				PERCENTAGES		
Year Team	Lg	G	AB	H	2B	3B	HR	(Hm | Rd)	TB	R	RBI	TBB	IBB	SO	HBP	SH	SF	SB	CS	SB%	GDP	Avg	OBP	SLG
1995 Trenton *	AA	4	18	7	1	0	0	--	--	8	3	3	1	0	5	0	0	0	0	0	1.00	1	.389	.421	.444
1993 Seattle	AL	11	19	3	1	0	1	(0 | 1)	7	2	2	2	0	9	0	0	0	0	0	.00	1	.158	.238	.368
1994 Boston	AL	78	144	32	4	0	2	(1 | 1)	42	27	14	19	1	36	1	3	1	13	0	1.00	2	.222	.315	.292
1995 Boston	AL	100	341	97	17	1	7	(4 | 3)	137	61	41	39	1	74	1	9	1	18	8	.69	8	.284	.359	.402
3 ML YEARS		189	504	132	22	1	10	(5 | 5)	186	90	57	60	2	119	2	12	2	31	8	.79	11	.262	.342	.369

Andy Tomberlin

Bats: Left **Throws:** Left **Pos:** RF/CF **Ht:** 5'11" **Wt:** 180 **Born:** 11/7/66 **Age:** 29

		BATTING															BASERUNNING				PERCENTAGES		
Year Team	Lg	G	AB	H	2B	3B	HR	(Hm | Rd)	TB	R	RBI	TBB	IBB	SO	HBP	SH	SF	SB	CS	SB%	GDP	Avg	OBP	SLG
1995 Edmonton *	AAA	14	52	13	3	0	2	--	--	22	9	7	5	0	15	1	1	0	0	0	.00	1	.250	.328	.423
1993 Pittsburgh	NL	27	42	12	0	1	1	(0 | 1)	17	4	5	2	0	14	1	0	0	0	0	.00	0	.286	.333	.405
1994 Boston	AL	17	36	7	0	1	1	(0 | 1)	12	1	1	6	0	12	0	0	0	1	0	1.00	0	.194	.310	.333
1995 Oakland	AL	46	85	18	0	0	4	(3 | 1)	30	15	10	5	0	22	0	2	0	4	1	.80	2	.212	.256	.353
3 ML YEARS		90	163	37	0	2	6	(4 | 2)	59	20	16	13	0	48	1	2	0	5	1	.83	2	.227	.288	.362

Dilson Torres

Pitches: Right **Bats:** Right **Pos:** RP **Ht:** 6' 3" **Wt:** 200 **Born:** 5/31/70 **Age:** 26

		HOW MUCH HE PITCHED						WHAT HE GAVE UP										THE RESULTS					
Year Team	Lg	G	GS	CG	GF	IP	BFP	H	R	ER	HR	SH	SF	HB	TBB	IBB	SO	WP	Bk	W	L	Pct.	ShO	Sv	ERA
1993 St. Cathrns	A	17	0	0	12	23	98	21	13	8	3	1	0	0	6	0	23	2	0	1	4	.200	0	3	3.13
1994 Wilmington	A	15	9	0	5	59.1	239	47	15	9	5	3	2	0	15	0	49	2	2	7	2	.778	0	2	1.37

	Lg	G	GS	CG	GF	IP	BFP	H	R	ER	HR	SH	SF	HB	TBB	IBB	SO	WP	Bk	W	L	Pct.	ShO	Sv	ERA
Memphis	AA	10	9	0	0	59	229	47	15	12	3	2	1	5	10	0	47	1	0	6	0	1.000	0	0	1.83
1995 Omaha	AAA	5	5	1	0	27.1	113	28	11	8	2	2	1	1	7	0	12	1	1	3	1	.750	1	0	2.63
1995 Kansas City	AL	24	2	0	7	44.1	198	56	30	30	6	0	0	1	17	2	28	1	0	1	2	.333	0	0	6.09

Salomon Torres

Pitches: Right **Bats:** Right **Pos:** SP/RP   **Ht:** 5'11" **Wt:** 165 **Born:** 3/11/72 **Age:** 24

		HOW MUCH HE PITCHED						WHAT HE GAVE UP										THE RESULTS					
Year Team	Lg	G	GS	CG	GF	IP	BFP	H	R	ER	HR	SH	SF	HB	TBB	IBB	SO	WP	Bk	W	L	Pct.	ShO	Sv	ERA
1995 Phoenix *	AAA	1	0	0	0	2	8	2	0	0	0	1	0	0	0	0	5	0	0	0	0	.000	0	0	0.00
Tacoma *	AAA	5	4	0	1	28	114	20	10	10	2	1	1	2	13	1	19	2	1	1	1	.500	0	0	3.21
1993 San Francisco	NL	8	8	0	0	44.2	196	37	21	20	5	7	1	1	27	3	23	3	1	3	5	.375	0	0	4.03
1994 San Francisco	NL	16	14	1	2	84.1	378	95	55	51	10	4	8	7	34	2	42	4	1	2	8	.200	0	0	5.44
1995 SF-Sea		20	14	1	2	80	384	100	61	56	16	1	0	2	49	3	47	1	2	3	9	.250	0	0	6.30
1995 San Francisco	NL	4	1	0	2	8	40	13	8	8	4	0	0	2	7	0	2	0	0	0	1	.000	0	0	9.00
Seattle	AL	16	13	1	2	72	344	87	53	48	12	1	0	2	42	3	45	1	2	3	8	.273	0	0	6.00
3 ML YEARS		44	36	2	6	209	958	232	137	127	31	12	9	10	110	8	112	8	4	8	22	.267	0	0	5.47

Steve Trachsel

Pitches: Right **Bats:** Right **Pos:** SP   **Ht:** 6'4" **Wt:** 205 **Born:** 10/31/70 **Age:** 25

		HOW MUCH HE PITCHED						WHAT HE GAVE UP										THE RESULTS					
Year Team	Lg	G	GS	CG	GF	IP	BFP	H	R	ER	HR	SH	SF	HB	TBB	IBB	SO	WP	Bk	W	L	Pct.	ShO	Sv	ERA
1993 Chicago	NL	3	3	0	0	19.2	78	16	10	10	4	1	1	0	3	0	14	1	0	0	2	.000	0	0	4.58
1994 Chicago	NL	22	22	1	0	146	612	133	57	52	19	3	3	3	54	4	108	6	0	9	7	.563	0	0	3.21
1995 Chicago	NL	30	29	2	0	160.2	722	174	104	92	25	12	5	0	76	8	117	2	1	7	13	.350	0	0	5.15
3 ML YEARS		55	54	3	0	326.1	1412	323	171	154	48	16	9	3	133	12	239	9	1	16	22	.421	0	0	4.25

Alan Trammell

Bats: Right **Throws:** Right **Pos:** SS   **Ht:** 6'0" **Wt:** 185 **Born:** 2/21/58 **Age:** 38

		BATTING															BASERUNNING				PERCENTAGES		
Year Team	Lg	G	AB	H	2B	3B	HR	(Hm | Rd)	TB	R	RBI	TBB	IBB	SO	HBP	SH	SF	SB	CS	SB%	GDP	Avg	OBP	SLG
1977 Detroit	AL	19	43	8	0	0	0	(0 | 0)	8	6	0	4	0	12	0	1	0	0	0	.00	1	.186	.255	.186
1978 Detroit	AL	139	448	120	14	6	2	(0 | 2)	152	49	34	45	0	56	2	6	3	3	1	.75	12	.268	.335	.339
1979 Detroit	AL	142	460	127	11	4	6	(4 | 2)	164	68	50	43	0	55	0	12	5	17	14	.55	6	.276	.335	.357
1980 Detroit	AL	146	560	168	21	5	9	(5 | 4)	226	107	65	69	2	63	3	13	7	12	12	.50	10	.300	.376	.404
1981 Detroit	AL	105	392	101	15	3	2	(2 | 0)	128	52	31	49	2	31	3	16	3	10	3	.77	10	.258	.342	.327
1982 Detroit	AL	157	489	126	34	3	9	(5 | 4)	193	66	57	52	0	47	0	9	6	19	8	.70	5	.258	.325	.395
1983 Detroit	AL	142	505	161	31	2	14	(8 | 6)	238	83	66	57	2	64	0	15	4	30	10	.75	7	.319	.385	.471
1984 Detroit	AL	139	555	174	34	5	14	(7 | 7)	260	85	69	60	2	63	3	6	2	19	13	.59	8	.314	.382	.468
1985 Detroit	AL	149	605	156	21	7	13	(7 | 6)	230	79	57	50	4	71	2	11	9	14	5	.74	6	.258	.312	.380
1986 Detroit	AL	151	574	159	33	7	21	(8 | 13)	269	107	75	59	4	57	5	11	4	25	12	.68	7	.277	.347	.469
1987 Detroit	AL	151	597	205	34	3	28	(13 | 15)	329	109	105	60	8	47	3	2	6	21	2	.91	11	.343	.402	.551
1988 Detroit	AL	128	466	145	24	1	15	(7 | 8)	216	73	69	46	8	46	4	0	7	7	4	.64	14	.311	.373	.464
1989 Detroit	AL	121	449	109	20	3	5	(2 | 3)	150	54	43	45	1	45	4	3	5	10	2	.83	9	.243	.314	.334
1990 Detroit	AL	146	559	170	37	1	14	(9 | 5)	251	71	89	68	7	55	1	3	6	12	10	.55	11	.304	.377	.449
1991 Detroit	AL	101	375	93	20	0	9	(6 | 3)	140	57	55	37	1	39	3	5	1	11	2	.85	7	.248	.320	.373
1992 Detroit	AL	29	102	28	7	1	1	(0 | 1)	40	11	11	15	0	4	1	1	1	2	2	.50	6	.275	.370	.392
1993 Detroit	AL	112	401	132	25	3	12	(6 | 6)	199	72	60	38	2	38	2	4	2	12	8	.60	7	.329	.388	.496
1994 Detroit	AL	76	292	78	17	1	8	(6 | 2)	121	38	28	16	1	35	1	2	0	3	0	1.00	8	.267	.307	.414
1995 Detroit	AL	74	223	60	12	0	2	(1 | 1)	78	28	23	27	4	19	0	3	2	3	1	.75	8	.269	.345	.350
19 ML YEARS		2227	8095	2320	410	55	184	(96 | 88)	3392	1215	987	840	48	847	37	123	73	230	109	.68	153	.287	.353	.419

Jeff Treadway

Bats: Left **Throws:** Right **Pos:** 2B   **Ht:** 5'11" **Wt:** 170 **Born:** 1/22/63 **Age:** 33

		BATTING															BASERUNNING				PERCENTAGES		
Year Team	Lg	G	AB	H	2B	3B	HR	(Hm | Rd)	TB	R	RBI	TBB	IBB	SO	HBP	SH	SF	SB	CS	SB%	GDP	Avg	OBP	SLG
1987 Cincinnati	NL	23	84	28	4	0	2	(2 | 0)	38	9	4	2	0	6	1	3	0	1	0	1.00	1	.333	.356	.452
1988 Cincinnati	NL	103	301	76	19	4	2	(2 | 0)	109	30	23	27	7	30	3	4	6	2	0	1.00	4	.252	.315	.362
1989 Atlanta	NL	134	473	131	18	3	8	(2 | 6)	179	58	40	30	3	38	0	6	5	3	2	.60	9	.277	.317	.378
1990 Atlanta	NL	128	474	134	20	2	11	(5 | 6)	191	56	59	25	1	42	3	5	4	3	4	.43	10	.283	.320	.403
1991 Atlanta	NL	106	306	98	17	2	3	(1 | 2)	128	41	32	23	1	19	2	2	3	2	2	.50	8	.320	.368	.418
1992 Atlanta	NL	61	126	28	6	1	0	(0 | 0)	36	5	5	9	4	16	0	1	0	1	2	.33	3	.222	.274	.286
1993 Cleveland	AL	97	221	67	14	1	2	(0 | 2)	89	25	27	14	2	21	2	1	2	1	1	.50	6	.303	.347	.403
1994 Los Angeles	NL	52	67	20	3	0	0	(0 | 0)	23	14	5	5	0	8	1	4	1	1	1	.50	1	.299	.343	.343
1995 LA-Mon		58	67	14	2	1	0	(0 | 0)	18	6	13	5	1	4	0	0	0	0	0	.00	0	.209	.264	.269
1995 Los Angeles	NL	17	17	2	0	1	0	(0 | 0)	4	2	3	0	0	2	0	0	0	0	0	.00	0	.118	.118	.235
Montreal	NL	41	50	12	2	0	0	(0 | 0)	14	4	10	5	1	2	0	0	0	0	0	.00	0	.240	.309	.280
9 ML YEARS		762	2119	596	103	14	28	(12 | 16)	811	244	208	140	19	184	12	26	21	14	13	.52	42	.281	.326	.383

Chris Tremie

Bats: Right **Throws:** Right **Pos:** C **Ht:** 6' 0" **Wt:** 200 **Born:** 10/17/69 **Age:** 26

				BATTING															BASERUNNING				PERCENTAGES		
Year Team	Lg	G	AB	H	2B	3B	HR	(Hm Rd)	TB	R	RBI	TBB	IBB	SO	HBP	SH	SF	SB	CS	SB%	GDP	Avg	OBP	SLG
1992 Utica	A	6	16	1	0	0	0	-- --	1	1	0	0	0	5	0	0	0	0	0	.00	0	.063	.063	.063
1993 White Sox	R	2	4	0	0	0	0	-- --	0	0	0	0	0	0	0	0	0	0	0	.00	0	.000	.000	.000
Sarasota	A	14	37	6	1	0	0	-- --	7	2	5	2	0	4	3	0	0	0	0	.00	1	.162	.262	.189
Hickory	A	49	155	29	6	1	1	-- --	40	7	17	9	0	26	4	1	0	0	0	.00	5	.187	.250	.258
1994 Birmingham	AA	92	302	68	13	0	2	-- --	87	32	29	17	0	44	6	3	2	4	1	.80	3	.225	.278	.288
1995 Nashville	AAA	67	190	38	4	0	2	-- --	48	13	16	13	0	37	2	4	0	0	0	.00	6	.200	.259	.253
1995 Chicago	AL	10	24	4	0	0	0	(0 0)	4	0	0	1	0	2	0	1	0	0	0	.00	0	.167	.200	.167

Mike Trombley

Pitches: Right **Bats:** Right **Pos:** SP **Ht:** 6' 2" **Wt:** 206 **Born:** 4/14/67 **Age:** 29

		HOW MUCH HE PITCHED						WHAT HE GAVE UP												THE RESULTS					
Year Team	Lg	G	GS	CG	GF	IP	BFP	H	R	ER	HR	SH	SF	HB	TBB	IBB	SO	WP	Bk	W	L	Pct.	ShO	Sv	ERA
1995 Salt Lake *	AAA	12	12	0	0	69.2	301	71	32	28	3	0	5	2	26	1	59	4	1	5	3	.625	0	0	3.62
1992 Minnesota	AL	10	7	0	0	46.1	194	43	20	17	5	2	0	1	17	0	38	0	0	3	2	.600	0	0	3.30
1993 Minnesota	AL	44	10	0	8	114.1	506	131	72	62	15	3	7	3	41	4	85	5	0	6	6	.500	0	2	4.88
1994 Minnesota	AL	24	0	0	8	48.1	219	56	36	34	10	1	2	3	18	2	32	3	0	2	0	1.000	0	0	6.33
1995 Minnesota	AL	20	18	0	0	97.2	442	107	66	61	18	3	2	3	42	1	68	4	0	4	8	.333	0	0	5.62
4 ML YEARS		98	35	0	16	306.2	1361	337	196	174	48	9	11	10	118	7	223	12	0	15	16	.484	0	2	5.11

Michael Tucker

Bats: Left **Throws:** Right **Pos:** LF/DH **Ht:** 6' 2" **Wt:** 185 **Born:** 6/25/71 **Age:** 25

				BATTING															BASERUNNING				PERCENTAGES		
Year Team	Lg	G	AB	H	2B	3B	HR	(Hm Rd)	TB	R	RBI	TBB	IBB	SO	HBP	SH	SF	SB	CS	SB%	GDP	Avg	OBP	SLG
1993 Wilmington	A	61	239	73	14	2	6	-- --	109	42	44	34	4	49	2	0	4	12	2	.86	0	.305	.391	.456
Memphis	AA	72	244	68	7	4	9	-- --	110	38	35	42	0	51	6	3	4	12	5	.71	1	.279	.392	.451
1994 Omaha	AAA	132	485	134	16	7	21	-- --	227	75	77	69	2	111	3	2	6	11	3	.79	6	.276	.366	.468
1995 Omaha	AAA	71	275	84	18	4	4	-- --	122	37	28	24	5	39	4	2	2	11	4	.73	3	.305	.367	.444
1995 Kansas City	AL	62	177	46	10	0	4	(1 3)	68	23	17	18	2	51	1	2	0	2	3	.40	3	.260	.332	.384

Scooter Tucker

Bats: Right **Throws:** Right **Pos:** C **Ht:** 6' 2" **Wt:** 205 **Born:** 11/18/66 **Age:** 29

				BATTING															BASERUNNING				PERCENTAGES		
Year Team	Lg	G	AB	H	2B	3B	HR	(Hm Rd)	TB	R	RBI	TBB	IBB	SO	HBP	SH	SF	SB	CS	SB%	GDP	Avg	OBP	SLG
1995 Richmond *	AAA	22	66	11	3	1	0	-- --	16	5	6	8	0	16	1	0	1	0	0	.00	2	.167	.263	.242
1992 Houston	NL	20	50	6	1	0	0	(0 0)	7	5	3	3	0	13	2	1	0	1	1	.50	2	.120	.200	.140
1993 Houston	NL	9	26	5	1	0	0	(0 0)	6	1	3	2	0	3	0	0	0	0	0	.00	0	.192	.250	.231
1995 Hou-Cle		22	27	2	0	0	1	(0 1)	5	3	1	5	0	4	1	1	0	0	0	.00	0	.074	.242	.185
1995 Houston	NL	5	7	2	0	0	1	(0 1)	5	1	1	0	0	0	0	0	0	0	0	.00	0	.286	.286	.714
Cleveland	AL	17	20	0	0	0	0	(0 0)	0	2	0	5	0	4	1	1	0	0	0	.00	0	.000	.231	.000
3 ML YEARS		51	103	13	2	0	1	(0 1)	18	9	7	10	0	20	3	2	0	1	1	.50	2	.126	.224	.175

Chris Turner

Bats: Right **Throws:** Right **Pos:** C **Ht:** 6' 1" **Wt:** 190 **Born:** 3/23/69 **Age:** 27

				BATTING															BASERUNNING				PERCENTAGES		
Year Team	Lg	G	AB	H	2B	3B	HR	(Hm Rd)	TB	R	RBI	TBB	IBB	SO	HBP	SH	SF	SB	CS	SB%	GDP	Avg	OBP	SLG
1995 Vancouver *	AAA	80	282	75	20	2	3	-- --	108	44	44	34	2	54	5	1	2	3	0	1.00	5	.266	.353	.383
1993 California	AL	25	75	21	5	0	1	(0 1)	29	9	13	9	0	16	1	0	1	1	1	.50	1	.280	.360	.387
1994 California	AL	58	149	36	7	1	1	(1 0)	48	23	12	10	0	29	1	1	2	3	0	1.00	2	.242	.290	.322
1995 California	AL	5	10	1	0	0	0	(0 0)	1	0	1	0	0	3	0	0	0	0	0	.00	0	.100	.100	.100
3 ML YEARS		88	234	58	12	1	2	(1 1)	78	32	26	19	0	48	2	1	3	4	1	.80	3	.248	.306	.333

Tim Unroe

Bats: Right **Throws:** Right **Pos:** 1B **Ht:** 6' 3" **Wt:** 200 **Born:** 10/7/70 **Age:** 25

				BATTING															BASERUNNING				PERCENTAGES		
Year Team	Lg	G	AB	H	2B	3B	HR	(Hm Rd)	TB	R	RBI	TBB	IBB	SO	HBP	SH	SF	SB	CS	SB%	GDP	Avg	OBP	SLG
1992 Helena	R	74	266	74	13	2	16	-- --	139	61	58	47	1	91	4	1	1	3	4	.43	2	.278	.393	.523
1993 Stockton	A	108	382	96	21	6	12	-- --	165	57	63	36	0	96	7	3	4	9	10	.47	8	.251	.324	.432
1994 El Paso	AA	126	474	147	36	7	15	-- --	242	97	103	42	2	107	5	0	9	14	6	.70	6	.310	.366	.511
1995 New Orleans	AAA	102	371	97	21	2	6	-- --	140	43	45	18	1	94	7	1	5	4	3	.57	9	.261	.304	.377
1995 Milwaukee	AL	2	4	1	0	0	0	(0 0)	1	0	0	0	0	0	0	0	0	0	0	.00	0	.250	.250	.250

Tom Urbani

Pitches: Left **Bats:** Left **Pos:** SP/RP   **Ht:** 6' 1" **Wt:** 210 **Born:** 1/21/68 **Age:** 28

| | | HOW MUCH HE PITCHED | | | | | | WHAT HE GAVE UP | | | | | | | | | | | | THE RESULTS | | | | | |
Year Team	Lg	G	GS	CG	GF	IP	BFP	H	R	ER	HR	SH	SF	HB	TBB	IBB	SO	WP	Bk	W	L	Pct.	ShO	Sv	ERA
1995 Louisville *	AAA	2	2	0	0	15.1	65	16	6	5	0	0	0	0	5	0	11	0	0	1	1	.500	0	0	2.93
1993 St. Louis	NL	18	9	0	2	62	283	73	44	32	4	4	6	0	26	2	33	1	1	1	3	.250	0	0	4.65
1994 St. Louis	NL	20	10	0	2	80.1	354	98	48	46	12	3	2	3	21	0	43	4	1	3	7	.300	0	0	5.15
1995 St. Louis	NL	24	13	0	2	82.2	354	99	40	34	11	6	0	2	21	4	52	5	0	3	5	.375	0	0	3.70
3 ML YEARS		62	32	0	6	225	991	270	132	112	27	13	8	5	68	6	128	10	2	7	15	.318	0	0	4.48

Ugueth Urbina

Pitches: Right **Bats:** Right **Pos:** SP   **Ht:** 6' 2" **Wt:** 185 **Born:** 2/15/74 **Age:** 22

| | | HOW MUCH HE PITCHED | | | | | | WHAT HE GAVE UP | | | | | | | | | | | | THE RESULTS | | | | | |
Year Team	Lg	G	GS	CG	GF	IP	BFP	H	R	ER	HR	SH	SF	HB	TBB	IBB	SO	WP	Bk	W	L	Pct.	ShO	Sv	ERA
1991 Expos	R	10	10	3	0	63	252	58	24	16	2	0	0	4	10	0	51	2	3	3	3	.500	1	0	2.29
1992 Albany	A	24	24	5	0	142.1	582	111	68	51	14	2	5	4	54	0	100	4	4	7	13	.350	2	0	3.22
1993 Burlington	A	16	16	4	0	108.1	436	78	30	24	7	2	1	7	36	1	107	6	5	10	1	.909	1	0	1.99
Harrisburg	AA	11	11	3	0	70	298	66	32	31	5	4	2	5	32	1	45	1	1	4	5	.444	1	0	3.99
1994 Harrisburg	AA	21	21	0	0	120.2	497	96	49	44	11	4	7	3	43	0	86	6	1	9	3	.750	0	0	3.28
1995 W. Palm Bch	A	2	2	0	0	9	30	4	0	0	0	0	0	1	1	0	11	0	0	1	0	1.000	0	0	0.00
Ottawa	AAA	13	11	2	0	68	273	46	26	23	1	3	2	1	26	0	55	1	0	6	2	.750	1	0	3.04
1995 Montreal	NL	7	4	0	0	23.1	109	26	17	16	6	2	0	0	14	1	15	2	0	2	2	.500	0	0	6.17

Ismael Valdes

Pitches: Right **Bats:** Right **Pos:** SP/RP   **Ht:** 6' 3" **Wt:** 207 **Born:** 8/21/73 **Age:** 22

| | | HOW MUCH HE PITCHED | | | | | | WHAT HE GAVE UP | | | | | | | | | | | | THE RESULTS | | | | | |
Year Team	Lg	G	GS	CG	GF	IP	BFP	H	R	ER	HR	SH	SF	HB	TBB	IBB	SO	WP	Bk	W	L	Pct.	ShO	Sv	ERA
1991 Dodgers	R	10	10	0	0	50.1	204	44	15	13	0	2	0	0	13	0	44	0	1	2	2	.500	0	0	2.32
1993 San Antonio	AA	3	2	0	0	13	50	12	2	2	0	0	0	0	0	0	11	0	0	1	0	1.000	0	0	1.38
1994 San Antonio	AA	8	8	0	0	53.1	218	54	22	20	4	2	0	2	9	1	55	3	0	2	3	.400	0	0	3.38
Albuquerque	AAA	8	8	0	0	45	188	44	21	17	2	0	0	3	13	0	39	1	0	4	1	.800	0	0	3.40
1994 Los Angeles	NL	21	1	0	7	28.1	115	21	10	10	2	3	0	0	10	2	28	1	2	3	1	.750	0	0	3.18
1995 Los Angeles	NL	33	27	6	1	197.2	804	168	76	67	17	10	5	1	51	5	150	1	3	13	11	.542	2	1	3.05
2 ML YEARS		54	28	6	8	226	919	189	86	77	19	13	5	1	61	7	178	2	5	16	12	.571	2	1	3.07

Marc Valdes

Pitches: Right **Bats:** Right **Pos:** SP   **Ht:** 6' 0" **Wt:** 187 **Born:** 12/20/71 **Age:** 24

| | | HOW MUCH HE PITCHED | | | | | | WHAT HE GAVE UP | | | | | | | | | | | | THE RESULTS | | | | | |
Year Team	Lg	G	GS	CG	GF	IP	BFP	H	R	ER	HR	SH	SF	HB	TBB	IBB	SO	WP	Bk	W	L	Pct.	ShO	Sv	ERA
1993 Elmira	A	3	3	0	0	9.2	46	8	9	6	0	0	0	3	7	0	15	0	0	0	2	.000	0	0	5.59
1994 Kane County	A	11	11	2	0	76.1	315	62	30	25	3	4	1	8	21	0	68	3	0	7	4	.636	0	0	2.95
Portland	AA	15	15	0	0	99	411	77	31	28	5	3	1	8	39	1	70	4	3	8	4	.667	0	0	2.55
1995 Charlotte	AAA	27	27	3	0	170.1	728	189	98	92	19	3	5	12	59	1	104	2	1	9	13	.409	2	0	4.86
1995 Florida	NL	3	3	0	0	7	49	17	13	11	1	1	1	1	9	0	2	1	0	0	0	.000	0	0	14.14

Carlos Valdez

Pitches: Right **Bats:** Right **Pos:** RP   **Ht:** 5'11" **Wt:** 175 **Born:** 12/26/71 **Age:** 24

| | | HOW MUCH HE PITCHED | | | | | | WHAT HE GAVE UP | | | | | | | | | | | | THE RESULTS | | | | | |
Year Team	Lg	G	GS	CG	GF	IP	BFP	H	R	ER	HR	SH	SF	HB	TBB	IBB	SO	WP	Bk	W	L	Pct.	ShO	Sv	ERA
1991 Giants	R	13	10	0	1	63.1	288	75	48	40	3	1	4	2	32	0	48	6	1	2	3	.400	0	0	5.68
1992 Everett	A	3	0	0	2	6.1	29	4	2	1	0	0	1	2	7	0	6	1	0	0	0	.000	0	0	1.42
Giants	R	6	0	0	3	14.2	56	7	2	0	0	1	0	0	5	0	14	1	0	3	1	.750	0	0	0.00
1993 Clinton	A	35	2	0	14	90.1	389	74	47	40	6	7	3	2	44	1	85	8	0	4	7	.364	0	3	3.99
1994 San Jose	A	36	17	0	10	123.2	536	109	70	62	7	3	6	12	61	0	116	6	0	8	6	.571	0	4	4.51
1995 Shreveport	AA	22	3	0	8	64	240	40	11	9	0	1	0	3	14	2	51	1	0	3	2	.600	0	5	1.27
Phoenix	AAA	18	0	0	12	29.1	131	29	10	9	2	2	0	0	13	2	30	3	0	1	0	1.000	0	2	2.76
1995 San Francisco	NL	11	0	0	3	14.2	69	19	10	10	0	1	1	1	8	1	7	1	1	0	1	.000	0	0	6.14

Sergio Valdez

Pitches: Right **Bats:** Right **Pos:** SP   **Ht:** 6' 1" **Wt:** 190 **Born:** 9/7/65 **Age:** 30

| | | HOW MUCH HE PITCHED | | | | | | WHAT HE GAVE UP | | | | | | | | | | | | THE RESULTS | | | | | |
Year Team	Lg	G	GS	CG	GF	IP	BFP	H	R	ER	HR	SH	SF	HB	TBB	IBB	SO	WP	Bk	W	L	Pct.	ShO	Sv	ERA
1995 Phoenix *	AAA	18	18	2	0	109.1	456	117	58	54	6	3	3	2	25	4	64	14	0	6	7	.462	0	0	4.45
1986 Montreal	NL	5	5	0	0	25	120	39	20	19	2	0	0	1	11	0	20	2	0	0	4	.000	0	0	6.84
1989 Atlanta	NL	19	1	0	8	32.2	145	31	24	22	5	2	0	0	17	3	26	2	0	1	2	.333	0	0	6.06
1990 Cle-Atl		30	13	0	7	107.2	466	115	66	58	17	5	5	1	38	2	66	4	0	6	6	.500	0	0	4.85
1991 Cleveland	AL	6	0	0	1	16.1	70	15	11	10	3	1	1	0	5	1	11	1	0	1	0	1.000	0	0	5.51

230

Year Team	Lg	G	GS	CG	GF	IP	BFP	H	R	ER	HR	SH	SF	HB	TBB	IBB	SO	WP	Bk	W	L	Pct.	ShO	Sv	ERA
1992 Montreal	NL	27	0	0	9	37.1	148	25	12	10	2	1	0	0	12	1	32	4	0	0	2	.000	0	0	2.41
1993 Montreal	NL	4	0	0	1	3	14	4	4	3	1	0	0	0	1	0	2	0	0	0	0	.000	0	0	9.00
1994 Boston	AL	12	1	0	2	14.1	72	25	14	13	4	0	0	0	8	1	4	1	0	0	1	.000	0	0	8.16
1995 San Francisco	NL	13	11	1	0	66.1	290	78	43	35	12	5	3	3	17	3	29	2	1	4	5	.444	0	0	4.75
1990 Cleveland	AL	24	13	0	4	102.1	440	109	62	54	17	4	5	1	35	2	63	3	0	6	6	.500	0	0	4.75
Atlanta	NL	6	0	0	3	5.1	26	6	4	4	0	1	0	0	3	0	3	1	0	0	0	.000	0	0	6.75
8 ML YEARS		116	31	1	28	302.2	1325	332	194	170	46	14	9	5	109	11	190	16	1	12	20	.375	0	0	5.06

John Valentin

Bats: Right **Throws:** Right **Pos:** SS **Ht:** 6' 0" **Wt:** 185 **Born:** 2/18/67 **Age:** 29

				BATTING													BASERUNNING				PERCENTAGES		
Year Team	Lg	G	AB	H	2B	3B	HR	(Hm | Rd)	TB	R	RBI	TBB	IBB	SO	HBP	SH	SF	SB	CS	SB%	GDP	Avg	OBP	SLG
1992 Boston	AL	58	185	51	13	0	5	(1 | 4)	79	21	25	20	0	17	2	4	1	1	0	1.00	5	.276	.351	.427
1993 Boston	AL	144	468	130	40	3	11	(7 | 4)	209	50	66	49	2	77	2	16	4	3	4	.43	9	.278	.346	.447
1994 Boston	AL	84	301	95	26	2	9	(6 | 3)	152	53	49	42	1	38	3	5	4	3	1	.75	3	.316	.400	.505
1995 Boston	AL	135	520	155	37	2	27	(11 | 16)	277	108	102	81	2	67	10	4	6	20	5	.80	7	.298	.399	.533
4 ML YEARS		421	1474	431	116	7	52	(25 | 27)	717	232	242	192	5	199	17	29	15	27	10	.73	24	.292	.377	.486

Jose Valentin

Bats: Both **Throws:** Right **Pos:** SS **Ht:** 5'10" **Wt:** 166 **Born:** 10/12/69 **Age:** 26

				BATTING													BASERUNNING				PERCENTAGES		
Year Team	Lg	G	AB	H	2B	3B	HR	(Hm | Rd)	TB	R	RBI	TBB	IBB	SO	HBP	SH	SF	SB	CS	SB%	GDP	Avg	OBP	SLG
1992 Milwaukee	AL	4	3	0	0	0	0	(0 | 0)	0	1	1	0	0	0	0	0	1	0	0	.00	0	.000	.000	.000
1993 Milwaukee	AL	19	53	13	1	2	1	(1 | 0)	21	10	7	7	1	16	1	2	0	1	0	1.00	1	.245	.344	.396
1994 Milwaukee	AL	97	285	68	19	0	11	(8 | 3)	120	47	46	38	1	75	2	4	2	12	3	.80	1	.239	.330	.421
1995 Milwaukee	AL	112	338	74	23	3	11	(3 | 8)	136	62	49	37	0	83	0	7	4	16	8	.67	0	.219	.293	.402
4 ML YEARS		232	679	155	43	5	23	(12 | 11)	277	120	103	82	2	174	3	13	7	29	11	.73	2	.228	.311	.408

Fernando Valenzuela

Pitches: Left **Bats:** Left **Pos:** SP/RP **Ht:** 5'11" **Wt:** 200 **Born:** 11/1/60 **Age:** 35

		HOW MUCH HE PITCHED						WHAT HE GAVE UP												THE RESULTS					
Year Team	Lg	G	GS	CG	GF	IP	BFP	H	R	ER	HR	SH	SF	HB	TBB	IBB	SO	WP	Bk	W	L	Pct.	ShO	Sv	ERA
1980 Los Angeles	NL	10	0	0	4	18	66	8	2	0	0	1	1	0	5	0	16	0	1	2	0	1.000	0	1	0.00
1981 Los Angeles	NL	25	25	11	0	192	758	140	55	53	11	9	3	1	61	4	180	4	0	13	7	.650	8	0	2.48
1982 Los Angeles	NL	37	37	18	0	285	1156	247	105	91	13	19	6	2	83	12	199	4	0	19	13	.594	4	0	2.87
1983 Los Angeles	NL	35	35	9	0	257	1094	245	122	107	16	27	5	3	99	10	189	12	1	15	10	.600	4	0	3.75
1984 Los Angeles	NL	34	34	12	0	261	1078	218	109	88	14	11	7	2	106	4	240	11	1	12	17	.414	2	0	3.03
1985 Los Angeles	NL	35	35	14	0	272.1	1109	211	92	74	14	13	8	1	101	5	208	10	1	17	10	.630	5	0	2.45
1986 Los Angeles	NL	34	34	20	0	269.1	1102	226	104	94	18	15	3	1	85	5	242	13	0	21	11	.656	3	0	3.14
1987 Los Angeles	NL	34	34	12	0	251	1116	254	120	111	25	18	2	4	124	4	190	14	1	14	14	.500	1	0	3.98
1988 Los Angeles	NL	23	22	3	1	142.1	626	142	71	67	11	15	5	0	76	4	64	7	1	5	8	.385	0	1	4.24
1989 Los Angeles	NL	31	31	3	0	196.2	852	185	89	75	11	7	7	2	98	6	116	6	0	10	13	.435	0	0	3.43
1990 Los Angeles	NL	33	33	5	0	204	900	223	112	104	19	11	4	0	77	4	115	13	1	13	13	.500	2	0	4.59
1991 California	AL	2	2	0	0	6.2	36	14	10	9	3	1	1	0	3	0	5	1	0	0	2	.000	0	0	12.15
1993 Baltimore	AL	32	31	5	0	178.2	768	179	104	98	18	4	7	4	79	2	78	8	0	8	10	.444	2	0	4.94
1994 Philadelphia	NL	8	7	0	0	45	182	42	16	15	8	3	2	0	7	1	19	1	0	1	2	.333	0	0	3.00
1995 San Diego	NL	29	15	0	5	90.1	395	101	53	50	16	10	2	0	34	2	57	4	0	8	3	.727	0	0	4.98
15 ML YEARS		402	375	112	10	2669.1	11238	2435	1164	1036	197	164	63	20	1038	63	1918	108	11	158	133	.543	31	2	3.49

Dave Valle

Bats: Right **Throws:** Right **Pos:** C **Ht:** 6' 2" **Wt:** 200 **Born:** 10/30/60 **Age:** 35

				BATTING													BASERUNNING				PERCENTAGES		
Year Team	Lg	G	AB	H	2B	3B	HR	(Hm | Rd)	TB	R	RBI	TBB	IBB	SO	HBP	SH	SF	SB	CS	SB%	GDP	Avg	OBP	SLG
1984 Seattle	AL	13	27	8	1	0	1	(1 | 0)	12	4	4	1	0	5	0	0	0	0	0	.00	0	.296	.321	.444
1985 Seattle	AL	31	70	11	1	0	0	(0 | 0)	12	2	4	1	0	17	1	1	0	0	0	.00	0	.157	.181	.171
1986 Seattle	AL	22	53	18	3	0	5	(4 | 1)	36	10	15	7	0	7	0	0	0	0	0	.00	2	.340	.417	.679
1987 Seattle	AL	95	324	83	16	3	12	(8 | 4)	141	40	53	15	2	46	3	0	4	0	1	.00	13	.256	.292	.435
1988 Seattle	AL	93	290	67	15	2	10	(5 | 5)	116	29	50	18	0	38	9	3	2	0	1	.00	13	.231	.295	.400
1989 Seattle	AL	94	316	75	10	3	7	(1 | 6)	112	32	34	29	2	32	6	1	3	0	0	.00	13	.237	.311	.354
1990 Seattle	AL	107	308	66	15	0	7	(1 | 6)	102	37	33	45	0	48	7	4	0	1	2	.33	11	.214	.328	.331
1991 Seattle	AL	132	324	63	8	1	8	(0 | 8)	97	38	32	34	0	49	9	6	3	0	2	.00	19	.194	.286	.299
1992 Seattle	AL	124	367	88	16	1	9	(7 | 2)	133	39	30	27	1	58	8	7	1	0	0	.00	7	.240	.305	.362
1993 Seattle	AL	135	423	109	19	0	13	(4 | 9)	167	48	63	48	4	56	17	8	4	1	0	1.00	18	.258	.354	.395
1994 Bos-Mil	AL	46	112	26	8	1	2	(1 | 1)	42	14	10	18	2	22	2	2	0	0	2	.00	3	.232	.348	.375
1995 Texas	AL	36	75	18	3	0	0	(0 | 0)	21	7	5	6	0	18	1	1	0	0	1	1.00	2	.240	.305	.280

Year Team	Lg	G	AB	H	2B	3B	HR	(Hm	Rd)	TB	R	RBI	TBB	IBB	SO	HBP	SH	SF	SB	CS	SB%	GDP	Avg	OBP	SLG
1994 Boston	AL	30	76	12	2	1	1	(0	1)	19	6	5	9	1	18	1	2	0	0	1	.00	2	.158	.256	.250
Milwaukee	AL	16	36	14	6	0	1	(1	0)	23	8	5	9	1	4	1	0	0	0	1	.00	1	.389	.522	.639
12 ML YEARS		928	2689	632	115	11	74	(32	42)	991	300	333	249	11	396	63	33	17	5	7	.42	102	.235	.313	.369

Todd Van Poppel

Pitches: Right **Bats:** Right **Pos:** RP/SP **Ht:** 6' 5" **Wt:** 210 **Born:** 12/9/71 **Age:** 24

		HOW MUCH HE PITCHED						WHAT HE GAVE UP										THE RESULTS					
Year Team	Lg	G	GS	CG	GF	IP	BFP	H	R	ER	HR	SH	SF	HB	TBB	IBB	SO	WP	Bk	W	L	Pct.	ShO	Sv	ERA
1991 Oakland	AL	1	1	0	0	4.2	21	7	5	5	1	0	0	0	2	0	6	0	0	0	0	.000	0	0	9.64
1993 Oakland	AL	16	16	0	0	84	380	76	50	47	10	1	2	2	62	0	47	3	0	6	6	.500	0	0	5.04
1994 Oakland	AL	23	23	0	0	116.2	532	108	80	79	20	4	4	3	89	2	83	3	1	7	10	.412	0	0	6.09
1995 Oakland	AL	36	14	1	10	138.1	582	125	77	75	16	3	6	4	56	1	122	4	0	4	8	.333	0	0	4.88
4 ML YEARS		76	54	1	10	343.2	1515	316	212	206	47	8	12	9	209	3	258	10	1	17	24	.415	0	0	5.39

Andy Van Slyke

Bats: Left **Throws:** Right **Pos:** CF **Ht:** 6' 2" **Wt:** 198 **Born:** 12/21/60 **Age:** 35

		BATTING																	BASERUNNING				PERCENTAGES		
Year Team	Lg	G	AB	H	2B	3B	HR	(Hm	Rd)	TB	R	RBI	TBB	IBB	SO	HBP	SH	SF	SB	CS	SB%	GDP	Avg	OBP	SLG
1995 Bowie *	AA	2	6	3	0	0	0	--	--	3	2	2	3	1	0	0	0	0	0	0	.00	0	.500	.667	.500
Frederick *	A	1	2	0	0	0	0	--	--	0	1	0	2	1	1	0	0	0	1	0	1.00	0	.000	.600	.000
1983 St. Louis	NL	101	309	81	15	5	8	(3	5)	130	51	38	46	5	64	1	2	3	21	7	.75	4	.262	.357	.421
1984 St. Louis	NL	137	361	88	16	4	7	(3	4)	133	45	50	63	9	71	0	0	2	28	5	.85	5	.244	.354	.368
1985 St. Louis	NL	146	424	110	25	6	13	(6	7)	186	61	55	47	6	54	2	1	1	34	6	.85	7	.259	.335	.439
1986 St. Louis	NL	137	418	113	23	7	13	(6	7)	189	48	61	47	5	85	1	1	3	21	8	.72	6	.270	.343	.452
1987 Pittsburgh	NL	157	564	165	36	11	21	(11	10)	286	93	82	56	4	122	4	3	3	34	8	.81	6	.293	.359	.507
1988 Pittsburgh	NL	154	587	169	23	15	25	(16	9)	297	101	100	57	2	126	1	1	13	30	9	.77	8	.288	.345	.506
1989 Pittsburgh	NL	130	476	113	18	9	9	(5	4)	176	64	53	47	3	100	3	1	4	16	4	.80	13	.237	.308	.370
1990 Pittsburgh	NL	136	493	140	26	6	17	(6	11)	229	67	77	66	2	89	1	3	4	14	4	.78	6	.284	.367	.465
1991 Pittsburgh	NL	138	491	130	24	7	17	(9	8)	219	87	83	71	1	85	4	0	11	10	3	.77	5	.265	.355	.446
1992 Pittsburgh	NL	154	614	199	45	12	14	(6	8)	310	103	89	58	4	99	4	0	9	12	3	.80	9	.324	.381	.505
1993 Pittsburgh	NL	83	323	100	13	4	8	(5	3)	145	42	50	24	5	40	2	0	4	11	2	.85	13	.310	.357	.449
1994 Pittsburgh	NL	105	374	92	18	3	6	(4	2)	134	41	30	52	7	72	2	0	2	7	0	1.00	7	.246	.340	.358
1995 Bal-Phi		80	277	62	11	2	6	(1	5)	95	32	24	33	2	56	2	0	2	7	0	1.00	7	.224	.309	.343
1995 Baltimore	AL	17	63	10	1	0	3	(1	2)	20	6	8	5	1	15	0	0	0	0	0	.00	1	.159	.221	.317
Philadelphia	NL	63	214	52	10	2	3	(0	3)	75	26	16	28	1	41	2	0	2	7	0	1.00	6	.243	.333	.350
13 ML YEARS		1658	5711	1562	293	91	164	(79	85)	2529	835	792	667	55	1063	27	12	61	245	59	.81	94	.274	.349	.443

John Vander Wal

Bats: Left **Throws:** Left **Pos:** 1B **Ht:** 6' 2" **Wt:** 190 **Born:** 4/29/66 **Age:** 30

		BATTING																	BASERUNNING				PERCENTAGES		
Year Team	Lg	G	AB	H	2B	3B	HR	(Hm	Rd)	TB	R	RBI	TBB	IBB	SO	HBP	SH	SF	SB	CS	SB%	GDP	Avg	OBP	SLG
1991 Montreal	NL	21	61	13	4	1	1	(0	1)	22	4	8	1	0	18	0	0	0	2	0	.00	2	.213	.222	.361
1992 Montreal	NL	105	213	51	8	2	4	(2	2)	75	21	20	24	2	36	0	0	0	3	0	1.00	2	.239	.316	.352
1993 Montreal	NL	106	215	50	7	4	5	(1	4)	80	34	30	27	2	30	1	0	1	6	3	.67	4	.233	.320	.372
1994 Colorado	NL	91	110	27	3	1	5	(1	4)	47	12	15	16	0	31	0	0	1	2	1	.67	4	.245	.339	.427
1995 Colorado	NL	105	101	35	8	1	5	(2	3)	60	15	21	16	5	23	0	0	1	1	1	.50	2	.347	.432	.594
5 ML YEARS		428	700	176	30	9	20	(6	14)	284	86	94	84	9	138	1	0	4	12	5	.71	14	.251	.331	.406

Tim VanEgmond

Pitches: Right **Bats:** Right **Pos:** RP **Ht:** 6' 2" **Wt:** 180 **Born:** 5/31/69 **Age:** 27

		HOW MUCH HE PITCHED						WHAT HE GAVE UP										THE RESULTS					
Year Team	Lg	G	GS	CG	GF	IP	BFP	H	R	ER	HR	SH	SF	HB	TBB	IBB	SO	WP	Bk	W	L	Pct.	ShO	Sv	ERA
1991 Red Sox	R	3	2	1	0	15	54	6	1	1	0	0	0	1	1	0	20	2	2	2	0	1.000	0	1	0.60
Winter Havn	A	13	10	4	2	68.1	292	69	32	23	2	1	0	2	23	1	47	2	1	4	5	.444	2	2	3.03
1992 Lynchburg	A	28	27	2	0	173.2	727	161	73	66	12	4	1	8	52	0	140	18	1	12	4	.750	1	0	3.42
1993 New Britain	AA	29	29	1	0	190.1	794	182	99	84	18	3	2	14	44	1	163	11	3	6	12	.333	1	0	3.97
1994 Pawtucket	AAA	20	20	1	0	119.1	510	110	58	50	9	0	3	7	42	2	87	5	0	9	5	.643	0	0	3.77
1995 Pawtucket	AAA	12	12	0	0	66.2	279	66	32	29	10	1	2	4	21	1	47	5	0	5	3	.625	0	0	3.92
1994 Boston	AL	7	7	1	0	38.1	173	38	27	27	7	0	3	0	21	3	22	1	0	2	3	.400	0	0	6.34
1995 Boston	AL	4	1	0	1	6.2	35	9	7	7	2	0	0	0	6	0	5	1	0	0	1	.000	0	0	9.45
2 ML YEARS		11	8	1	1	45	208	47	34	34	9	0	3	0	27	3	27	2	0	2	4	.333	0	0	6.80

William VanLandingham

Pitches: Right **Bats:** Right **Pos:** SP **Ht:** 6' 2" **Wt:** 210 **Born:** 7/16/70 **Age:** 25

		HOW MUCH HE PITCHED						WHAT HE GAVE UP										THE RESULTS					
Year Team	Lg	G	GS	CG	GF	IP	BFP	H	R	ER	HR	SH	SF	HB	TBB	IBB	SO	WP	Bk	W	L	Pct.	ShO	Sv	ERA
1991 Everett	A	15	15	0	0	77	353	58	43	35	0	1	1	5	79	0	86	25	2	8	4	.667	0	0	4.09

Year	Team		G	GS	CG	SHO	IP		H	R	ER	HR				BB		SO			W	L	Pct.			ERA
1992	San Jose	A	6	6	0	0	21	96	22	18	13	1	0	0	0	13	0	18	4	1	1	3	.250	0	0	5.57
	Clinton	A	10	10	0	0	54	240	49	40	34	1	0	3	5	29	0	59	6	2	0	4	.000	0	0	5.67
1993	San Jose	A	27	27	1	0	163.1	724	167	103	93	7	5	6	1	87	0	171	15	4	14	8	.636	0	0	5.12
	Phoenix	AAA	1	1	0	0	7	29	8	6	5	0	1	0	0	0	0	2	0	0	1		.000	0	0	6.43
1994	Shreveport	AA	8	8	1	0	51.1	200	41	21	16	4	0	2	0	11	0	45	5	1	4	3	.571	0	0	2.81
	Phoenix	AAA	5	5	0	0	29	126	21	15	8	0	0	1	2	14	0	29	4	0	1	1	.500	0	0	2.48
1995	San Jose	A	1	1	0	0	6.2	26	4	0	0	0	0	0	0	2	0	5	0	0	1	0	1.000	0	0	0.00
1994	San Francisco	NL	16	14	0	1	84	363	70	37	33	4	3	1	2	43	4	56	3	3	8	2	.800	0	0	3.54
1995	San Francisco	NL	18	18	1	0	122.2	523	124	58	50	14	6	5	2	40	2	95	5	4	6	3	.667	0	0	3.67
	2 ML YEARS		34	32	1	1	206.2	886	194	95	83	18	9	6	4	83	6	151	8	7	14	5	.737	0	0	3.61

Gary Varsho

Bats: Left **Throws:** Right **Pos:** RF   **Ht:** 5'11" **Wt:** 185 **Born:** 6/20/61 **Age:** 35

						BATTING														BASERUNNING				PERCENTAGES		
Year	Team	Lg	G	AB	H	2B	3B	HR	(Hm	Rd)	TB	R	RBI	TBB	IBB	SO	HBP	SH	SF	SB	CS	SB%	GDP	Avg	OBP	SLG
1988	Chicago	NL	46	73	20	3	0	0	(0	0)	23	6	5	1	0	6	0	0	1	5	0	1.00	0	.274	.280	.315
1989	Chicago	NL	61	87	16	4	2	0	(0	0)	24	10	6	4	1	13	0	0	0	3	0	1.00	0	.184	.220	.276
1990	Chicago	NL	46	48	12	4	0	0	(0	0)	16	10	1	1	1	6	0	0	0	2	0	1.00	1	.250	.265	.333
1991	Pittsburgh	NL	99	187	51	11	2	4	(1	3)	78	23	23	19	2	34	2	1	1	9	2	.82	2	.273	.344	.417
1992	Pittsburgh	NL	103	162	36	6	3	4	(3	1)	60	22	22	10	1	32	0	0	1	5	2	.71	2	.222	.266	.370
1993	Cincinnati	NL	77	95	22	6	0	2	(1	1)	34	8	11	9	0	19	1	3	1	1	0	1.00	1	.232	.302	.358
1994	Pittsburgh	NL	67	82	21	6	3	0	(0	0)	33	15	5	4	1	19	2	2	0	0	1	.00	1	.256	.307	.402
1995	Philadelphia	NL	72	103	26	1	1	0	(0	0)	29	7	11	7	1	17	2	0	1	2	0	1.00	1	.252	.310	.282
	8 ML YEARS		571	837	204	41	11	10	(5	5)	297	101	84	55	7	146	7	6	5	27	5	.84	8	.244	.294	.355

Greg Vaughn

Bats: Right **Throws:** Right **Pos:** DH   **Ht:** 6' 0" **Wt:** 202 **Born:** 7/3/65 **Age:** 30

						BATTING														BASERUNNING				PERCENTAGES		
Year	Team	Lg	G	AB	H	2B	3B	HR	(Hm	Rd)	TB	R	RBI	TBB	IBB	SO	HBP	SH	SF	SB	CS	SB%	GDP	Avg	OBP	SLG
1989	Milwaukee	AL	38	113	30	3	0	5	(1	4)	48	18	23	13	0	23	0	0	2	4	1	.80	0	.265	.336	.425
1990	Milwaukee	AL	120	382	84	26	2	17	(9	8)	165	51	61	33	1	91	1	7	6	7	4	.64	11	.220	.280	.432
1991	Milwaukee	AL	145	542	132	24	5	27	(16	11)	247	81	98	62	2	125	1	2	7	2	2	.50	5	.244	.319	.456
1992	Milwaukee	AL	141	501	114	18	2	23	(11	12)	205	77	78	60	1	123	5	2	5	15	15	.50	8	.228	.313	.409
1993	Milwaukee	AL	154	569	152	28	2	30	(12	18)	274	97	97	89	14	118	5	0	4	10	7	.59	6	.267	.369	.482
1994	Milwaukee	AL	95	370	94	24	1	19	(9	10)	177	59	55	51	6	93	1	0	1	9	5	.64	6	.254	.345	.478
1995	Milwaukee	AL	108	392	88	19	1	17	(8	9)	160	67	59	55	3	89	0	0	4	10	4	.71	10	.224	.317	.408
	7 ML YEARS		801	2869	694	142	13	138	(66	72)	1276	450	471	363	27	662	13	11	29	57	38	.60	46	.242	.327	.445

Mo Vaughn

Bats: Left **Throws:** Right **Pos:** 1B   **Ht:** 6' 1" **Wt:** 245 **Born:** 12/15/67 **Age:** 28

						BATTING														BASERUNNING				PERCENTAGES		
Year	Team	Lg	G	AB	H	2B	3B	HR	(Hm	Rd)	TB	R	RBI	TBB	IBB	SO	HBP	SH	SF	SB	CS	SB%	GDP	Avg	OBP	SLG
1991	Boston	AL	74	219	57	12	0	4	(1	3)	81	21	32	26	2	43	2	0	4	2	1	.67	7	.260	.339	.370
1992	Boston	AL	113	355	83	16	2	13	(8	5)	142	42	57	47	7	67	3	0	3	3	3	.50	4	.234	.326	.400
1993	Boston	AL	152	539	160	34	1	29	(13	16)	283	86	101	79	23	130	8	0	7	4	3	.57	14	.297	.390	.525
1994	Boston	AL	111	394	122	25	1	26	(15	11)	227	65	82	57	20	112	10	0	2	4	4	.50	7	.310	.408	.576
1995	Boston	AL	140	550	165	28	3	39	(15	24)	316	98	126	68	17	150	14	0	4	11	4	.73	17	.300	.388	.575
	5 ML YEARS		590	2057	587	115	7	111	(52	59)	1049	312	398	277	69	502	37	0	20	24	15	.62	53	.285	.377	.510

Randy Velarde

Bats: Right **Throws:** Right **Pos:** 2B/3B/SS/LF   **Ht:** 6' 0" **Wt:** 192 **Born:** 11/24/62 **Age:** 33

						BATTING														BASERUNNING				PERCENTAGES		
Year	Team	Lg	G	AB	H	2B	3B	HR	(Hm	Rd)	TB	R	RBI	TBB	IBB	SO	HBP	SH	SF	SB	CS	SB%	GDP	Avg	OBP	SLG
1987	New York	AL	8	22	4	0	0	0	(0	0)	4	1	1	0	0	6	0	0	0	0	0	.00	1	.182	.182	.182
1988	New York	AL	48	115	20	6	0	5	(2	3)	41	18	12	8	0	24	2	0	0	1	1	.50	3	.174	.240	.357
1989	New York	AL	33	100	34	4	2	2	(1	1)	48	12	11	7	0	14	1	3	0	0	3	.00	0	.340	.389	.480
1990	New York	AL	95	229	48	6	2	5	(1	4)	73	21	19	20	0	53	1	2	1	0	3	.00	6	.210	.275	.319
1991	New York	AL	80	184	45	11	1	1	(0	1)	61	19	15	18	0	43	3	5	0	3	1	.75	6	.245	.322	.332
1992	New York	AL	121	412	112	24	1	7	(2	5)	159	57	46	38	1	78	2	4	5	7	2	.78	13	.272	.333	.386
1993	New York	AL	85	226	68	13	2	7	(4	3)	106	28	24	18	2	39	4	3	2	2	2	.50	12	.301	.360	.469
1994	New York	AL	77	280	78	16	1	9	(3	6)	123	47	34	22	0	61	4	2	2	4	2	.67	7	.279	.338	.439
1995	New York	AL	111	367	102	19	1	7	(2	5)	144	60	46	55	0	64	4	3	3	5	1	.83	9	.278	.375	.392
	9 ML YEARS		658	1935	511	99	10	43	(15	28)	759	263	208	186	3	382	21	22	13	22	15	.59	57	.264	.333	.392

Robin Ventura

Bats: Left **Throws:** Right **Pos:** 3B/1B   **Ht:** 6' 1" **Wt:** 198 **Born:** 7/14/67 **Age:** 28

Year	Team	Lg	G	AB	H	2B	3B	HR	(Hm	Rd)	TB	R	RBI	TBB	IBB	SO	HBP	SH	SF	SB	CS	SB%	GDP	Avg	OBP	SLG
1989	Chicago	AL	16	45	8	3	0	0	(0	0)	11	5	7	8	0	6	1	1	3	0	0	.00	1	.178	.298	.244
1990	Chicago	AL	150	493	123	17	1	5	(2	3)	157	48	54	55	2	53	1	13	3	1	4	.20	5	.249	.324	.318
1991	Chicago	AL	157	606	172	25	1	23	(16	7)	268	92	100	80	3	67	4	8	7	2	4	.33	22	.284	.367	.442
1992	Chicago	AL	157	592	167	38	1	16	(7	9)	255	85	93	93	9	71	0	1	8	2	4	.33	14	.282	.375	.431
1993	Chicago	AL	157	554	145	27	1	22	(12	10)	240	85	94	105	16	82	3	1	6	1	6	.14	18	.262	.379	.433
1994	Chicago	AL	109	401	113	15	1	18	(8	10)	184	57	78	61	15	69	2	2	8	3	1	.75	8	.282	.373	.459
1995	Chicago	AL	135	492	145	22	0	26	(8	18)	245	79	93	75	11	98	1	1	8	4	3	.57	8	.295	.384	.498
	7 ML YEARS		881	3183	873	147	5	110	(53	57)	1360	451	519	477	56	446	12	27	43	13	22	.37	76	.274	.367	.427

Quilvio Veras

Bats: Both **Throws:** Right **Pos:** 2B   **Ht:** 5' 9" **Wt:** 166 **Born:** 4/3/71 **Age:** 25

Year	Team	Lg	G	AB	H	2B	3B	HR	(Hm	Rd)	TB	R	RBI	TBB	IBB	SO	HBP	SH	SF	SB	CS	SB%	GDP	Avg	OBP	SLG
1990	Mets	R	30	98	29	3	3	1	--	--	41	26	5	19	0	16	3	1	1	16	8	.67	1	.296	.421	.418
	Kingsport	R	24	94	36	5	0	1	--	--	44	21	14	13	1	14	1	1	0	9	5	.64	1	.383	.463	.468
1991	Kingsport	R	64	226	76	11	4	1	--	--	98	54	16	36	0	28	7	5	0	38	11	.78	3	.336	.442	.434
	Pittsfield	A	5	15	4	0	1	0	--	--	6	3	2	5	0	1	0	0	0	2	0	1.00	0	.267	.450	.400
1992	Columbia	A	117	414	132	24	10	2	--	--	182	97	40	84	3	52	9	5	3	66	35	.65	5	.319	.441	.440
1993	Binghamton	AA	128	444	136	19	7	2	--	--	175	87	51	91	0	62	9	4	5	52	23	.69	3	.306	.430	.394
1994	Norfolk	AAA	123	457	114	22	4	0	--	--	144	71	43	59	2	56	4	6	4	40	18	.69	8	.249	.338	.315
1995	Florida	NL	124	440	115	20	7	5	(2	3)	164	86	32	80	0	68	9	7	2	56	21	.73	7	.261	.384	.373

Dave Veres

Pitches: Right **Bats:** Right **Pos:** RP   **Ht:** 6' 2" **Wt:** 195 **Born:** 10/19/66 **Age:** 29

Year	Team	Lg	G	GS	CG	GF	IP	BFP	H	R	ER	HR	SH	SF	HB	TBB	IBB	SO	WP	Bk	W	L	Pct.	ShO	Sv	ERA
1986	Medford	A	15	15	0	0	77.1	0	58	38	28	5	0	0	3	57	0	60	3	1	5	2	.714	0	0	3.26
1987	Modesto	A	26	26	2	0	148.1	667	124	90	79	9	10	6	6	108	3	124	29	0	8	9	.471	0	0	4.79
1988	Modesto	A	19	19	3	0	125	543	100	61	46	7	10	4	4	78	1	91	10	6	4	11	.267	2	0	3.31
	Huntsville	AA	8	8	0	0	39	180	50	20	18	1	1	0	3	15	2	17	3	2	3	4	.429	0	0	4.15
1989	Huntsville	AA	29	28	2	1	159.1	709	160	93	86	15	6	4	4	83	1	105	16	2	8	11	.421	1	0	4.86
1990	Tacoma	AAA	32	23	2	2	151.2	654	136	90	79	13	8	9	3	88	1	88	7	2	11	8	.579	0	1	4.69
1991	Albuquerque	AAA	57	3	0	16	100.2	440	89	52	50	8	6	4	3	52	5	81	9	4	7	6	.538	0	5	4.47
1992	Tucson	AAA	29	1	0	10	52.2	225	60	36	31	1	4	1	0	17	1	46	6	0	2	3	.400	0	5	5.30
1993	Tucson	AAA	43	15	1	18	130.1	578	156	88	71	7	5	4	2	32	1	122	5	3	6	10	.375	0	5	4.90
1994	Tucson	AAA	16	0	0	4	24	101	17	8	5	0	0	1	0	10	2	19	1	0	1	1	.500	0	1	1.88
1994	Houston	NL	32	0	0	7	41	168	39	13	11	4	0	2	1	7	3	28	2	0	3	3	.500	0	1	2.41
1995	Houston	NL	72	0	0	15	103.1	418	89	29	26	5	6	8	4	30	6	94	4	0	5	1	.833	0	1	2.26
	2 ML YEARS		104	0	0	22	144.1	586	128	42	37	9	6	10	5	37	9	122	6	0	8	4	.667	0	2	2.31

Randy Veres

Pitches: Right **Bats:** Right **Pos:** RP   **Ht:** 6' 3" **Wt:** 210 **Born:** 11/25/65 **Age:** 30

Year	Team	Lg	G	GS	CG	GF	IP	BFP	H	R	ER	HR	SH	SF	HB	TBB	IBB	SO	WP	Bk	W	L	Pct.	ShO	Sv	ERA
1995	Charlotte *	AAA	6	0	0	6	6.2	29	3	2	2	1	1	0	0	5	0	5	1	0	1	0	1.000	0	1	2.70
1989	Milwaukee	AL	3	1	0	0	8.1	36	9	5	4	0	0	1	0	4	0	8	0	0	0	1	.000	0	0	4.32
1990	Milwaukee	AL	26	0	0	12	41.2	175	38	17	17	5	2	2	1	16	3	16	3	0	0	3	.000	0	1	3.67
1994	Chicago	NL	10	0	0	9	9.2	43	12	6	6	3	0	1	1	2	0	5	0	0	1	1	.500	0	0	5.59
1995	Florida	NL	47	0	0	15	48.2	215	46	25	21	6	5	4	1	22	7	31	2	0	4	4	.500	0	1	3.88
	4 ML YEARS		86	1	0	29	108.1	469	105	53	48	14	7	8	3	44	10	60	5	0	5	9	.357	0	2	3.99

Ron Villone

Pitches: Left **Bats:** Left **Pos:** RP   **Ht:** 6' 3" **Wt:** 235 **Born:** 1/16/70 **Age:** 26

Year	Team	Lg	G	GS	CG	GF	IP	BFP	H	R	ER	HR	SH	SF	HB	TBB	IBB	SO	WP	Bk	W	L	Pct.	ShO	Sv	ERA
1993	Riverside	A	16	16	0	0	83.1	375	74	47	39	5	1	1	4	62	0	82	7	3	7	4	.636	0	0	4.21
	Jacksonville	AA	11	11	0	0	63.2	269	49	34	30	6	1	2	1	41	3	66	9	0	3	4	.429	0	0	4.24
1994	Jacksonville	AA	41	5	0	19	79.1	360	56	37	34	7	1	4	5	68	3	94	9	0	6	7	.462	0	8	3.86
1995	Tacoma	AAA	22	0	0	16	29.2	117	22	1	2	1	2	0	1	19	0	43	1	0	1	0	1.000	0	13	0.61
1995	Sea-SD		38	0	0	15	45	212	44	31	29	11	3	1	1	34	0	63	3	0	2	3	.400	0	0	5.80
1995	Seattle	AL	19	0	0	7	19.1	101	20	19	17	6	3	0	1	23	0	26	1	0	0	2	.000	0	0	7.91
	San Diego	NL	19	0	0	8	25.2	111	24	12	12	5	0	1	0	11	0	37	2	0	2	1	.667	0	1	4.21

Fernando Vina

Bats: Left   **Throws:** Right   **Pos:** 2B   **Ht:** 5' 9"   **Wt:** 170   **Born:** 4/16/69   **Age:** 27

												BATTING							BASERUNNING				PERCENTAGES		
Year Team	Lg	G	AB	H	2B	3B	HR	(Hm	Rd)	TB	R	RBI	TBB	IBB	SO	HBP	SH	SF	SB	CS	SB%	GDP	Avg	OBP	SLG
1993 Seattle	AL	24	45	10	2	0	0	(0	0)	12	5	2	4	0	3	3	1	0	6	0	1.00	0	.222	.327	.267
1994 New York	NL	79	124	31	6	0	0	(0	0)	37	20	6	12	0	11	12	2	0	3	1	.75	4	.250	.372	.298
1995 Milwaukee	AL	113	288	74	7	7	3	(1	2)	104	46	29	22	0	28	9	4	2	6	3	.67	6	.257	.327	.361
3 ML YEARS		216	457	115	15	7	3	(1	2)	153	71	37	38	0	42	24	7	2	15	4	.79	10	.252	.340	.335

Frank Viola

Pitches: Left   **Bats:** Left   **Pos:** SP   *cancel*   **Ht:** 6' 4"   **Wt:** 210   **Born:** 4/19/60   **Age:** 36

					HOW MUCH HE PITCHED				WHAT HE GAVE UP										THE RESULTS					
Year Team	Lg	G	GS	CG	GF	IP	BFP	H	R	ER	HR	SH	SF	HB	TBB	IBB	SO	WP	Bk	W	L	Pct.	ShO	Sv	ERA
1995 Dunedin *	A	3	3	0	0	11.1	53	12	9	5	2	0	1	1	3	0	8	0	0	0	1	.000	0	0	3.97
Indianapols *	AAA	6	6	0	0	33	138	33	17	15	3	0	2	2	6	0	25	0	0	3	3	.500	0	0	4.09
1982 Minnesota	AL	22	22	3	0	126	543	152	77	73	22	2	0	0	38	2	84	4	1	4	10	.286	1	0	5.21
1983 Minnesota	AL	35	34	4	0	210	949	242	141	128	34	5	2	8	92	7	127	6	2	7	15	.318	0	0	5.49
1984 Minnesota	AL	35	35	10	0	257.2	1047	225	101	92	28	1	5	4	73	1	149	6	1	18	12	.600	4	0	3.21
1985 Minnesota	AL	36	36	9	0	250.2	1059	262	136	114	26	5	5	2	68	3	135	6	2	18	14	.563	0	0	4.09
1986 Minnesota	AL	37	37	7	0	245.2	1053	257	136	123	37	4	5	3	83	0	191	12	0	16	13	.552	1	0	4.51
1987 Minnesota	AL	36	36	7	0	251.2	1037	230	91	81	29	7	3	6	66	1	197	1	1	17	10	.630	1	0	2.90
1988 Minnesota	AL	35	35	7	0	255.1	1031	236	80	75	20	6	6	3	54	2	193	5	1	24	7	.774	2	0	2.64
1989 Min-NYN		36	36	9	0	261	1082	246	115	106	22	12	6	4	74	4	211	8	1	13	17	.433	2	0	3.66
1990 New York	NL	35	35	7	0	249.2	1016	227	83	74	15	13	3	2	60	2	182	11	0	20	12	.625	3	0	2.67
1991 New York	NL	35	35	3	0	231.1	980	259	112	102	25	15	5	1	54	4	132	6	1	13	15	.464	0	0	3.97
1992 Boston	AL	35	35	6	0	238	999	214	99	91	13	7	10	7	89	4	121	12	2	13	12	.520	1	0	3.44
1993 Boston	AL	29	29	2	0	183.2	787	180	76	64	12	8	7	6	72	5	91	5	0	11	8	.579	1	0	3.14
1994 Boston	AL	6	6	0	0	31	136	34	17	16	2	2	2	0	17	0	9	2	0	1	1	.500	0	0	4.65
1995 Cincinnati	NL	3	3	0	0	14.1	64	20	11	10	1	0	1	0	3	1	4	1	0	0	1	.000	0	0	6.28
1989 Minnesota	AL	24	24	7	0	175.2	731	171	80	74	17	9	4	3	47	1	138	5	1	8	12	.400	1	0	3.79
New York	NL	12	12	2	0	85.1	351	75	35	32	5	3	2	1	27	3	73	3	0	5	5	.500	1	0	3.38
14 ML YEARS		415	414	74	0	2806	11783	2784	1275	1149	288	87	60	46	843	36	1826	85	12	175	147	.543	16	0	3.69

Joe Vitiello

Bats: Right   **Throws:** Right   **Pos:** DH   **Ht:** 6' 2"   **Wt:** 215   **Born:** 4/11/70   **Age:** 26

												BATTING							BASERUNNING				PERCENTAGES		
Year Team	Lg	G	AB	H	2B	3B	HR	(Hm	Rd)	TB	R	RBI	TBB	IBB	SO	HBP	SH	SF	SB	CS	SB%	GDP	Avg	OBP	SLG
1991 Eugene	A	19	64	21	2	0	6	--	--	41	16	21	11	1	18	1	0	1	1	1	.50	0	.328	.423	.641
Memphis	AA	36	128	27	4	1	0	--	--	33	15	18	23	0	36	1	0	1	0	0	.00	2	.211	.333	.258
1992 Baseball Cy	A	115	400	113	16	1	8	--	--	155	52	65	46	1	101	7	0	8	5	5	.50	11	.283	.360	.388
1993 Memphis	AA	117	413	119	25	2	15	--	--	193	62	66	57	2	95	5	0	5	2	0	1.00	6	.288	.377	.467
1994 Omaha	AAA	98	352	121	28	3	10	--	--	185	46	61	56	1	63	7	1	3	3	2	.60	15	.344	.440	.526
1995 Omaha	AAA	59	229	64	14	2	12	--	--	118	33	42	12	0	50	6	0	2	0	1	.00	9	.279	.329	.515
1995 Kansas City	AL	53	130	33	4	0	7	(3	4)	58	13	21	8	0	25	4	0	0	0	0	.00	4	.254	.317	.446

Jose Vizcaino

Bats: Both   **Throws:** Right   **Pos:** SS   **Ht:** 6' 1"   **Wt:** 180   **Born:** 3/26/68   **Age:** 28

												BATTING							BASERUNNING				PERCENTAGES		
Year Team	Lg	G	AB	H	2B	3B	HR	(Hm	Rd)	TB	R	RBI	TBB	IBB	SO	HBP	SH	SF	SB	CS	SB%	GDP	Avg	OBP	SLG
1989 Los Angeles	NL	7	10	2	0	0	0	(0	0)	2	2	0	0	0	1	0	1	0	0	0	.00	0	.200	.200	.200
1990 Los Angeles	NL	37	51	14	1	1	0	(0	0)	17	3	2	4	1	8	0	0	0	1	1	.50	1	.275	.327	.333
1991 Chicago	NL	93	145	38	5	0	0	(0	0)	43	7	10	5	0	18	0	2	2	2	1	.67	1	.262	.283	.297
1992 Chicago	NL	86	285	64	10	4	1	(0	1)	85	25	17	14	2	35	0	5	1	3	0	1.00	4	.225	.260	.298
1993 Chicago	NL	151	551	158	19	4	4	(1	3)	197	74	54	46	2	71	3	8	9	12	9	.57	9	.287	.340	.358
1994 New York	NL	103	410	105	13	3	3	(1	2)	133	47	33	33	3	62	2	5	6	1	11	.08	5	.256	.310	.324
1995 New York	NL	135	509	146	21	5	3	(2	1)	186	66	56	35	4	76	1	13	3	8	3	.73	14	.287	.332	.365
7 ML YEARS		612	1961	527	69	17	11	(4	7)	663	224	172	137	12	271	6	34	21	27	25	.52	34	.269	.315	.338

Omar Vizquel

Bats: Both   **Throws:** Right   **Pos:** SS   **Ht:** 5' 9"   **Wt:** 165   **Born:** 4/24/67   **Age:** 29

												BATTING							BASERUNNING				PERCENTAGES		
Year Team	Lg	G	AB	H	2B	3B	HR	(Hm	Rd)	TB	R	RBI	TBB	IBB	SO	HBP	SH	SF	SB	CS	SB%	GDP	Avg	OBP	SLG
1989 Seattle	AL	143	387	85	7	3	1	(1	0)	101	45	20	28	0	40	1	13	2	1	4	.20	6	.220	.273	.261
1990 Seattle	AL	81	255	63	3	2	2	(0	2)	76	19	18	18	0	22	0	10	2	4	1	.80	7	.247	.295	.298
1991 Seattle	AL	142	426	98	16	4	1	(0	1)	125	42	41	45	0	37	0	8	3	7	2	.78	8	.230	.302	.293
1992 Seattle	AL	136	483	142	20	4	0	(0	0)	170	49	21	32	0	38	2	9	1	15	13	.54	14	.294	.340	.352
1993 Seattle	AL	158	560	143	14	2	2	(1	1)	167	68	31	50	2	71	4	13	3	12	14	.46	7	.255	.319	.298

235

1994 Cleveland	AL	69	286	78	10	1	1	(0	1)	93	39	33	23	0	23	0	11	2	13	4	.76	4	.273	.325	.325
1995 Cleveland	AL	136	542	144	28	0	6	(3	3)	190	87	56	59	0	59	1	10	10	29	11	.73	4	.266	.333	.351
7 ML YEARS		865	2939	753	98	16	13	(6	7)	922	349	220	255	2	290	8	74	23	81	49	.62	50	.256	.315	.314

Jack Voigt

Bats: Right **Throws:** Right **Pos:** RF   **Ht:** 6' 1" **Wt:** 175 **Born:** 5/17/66 **Age:** 30

| | | | | | BATTING | | | | | | | | | | | | | | BASERUNNING | | | | PERCENTAGES | | |
Year Team	Lg	G	AB	H	2B	3B	HR	(Hm	Rd)	TB	R	RBI	TBB	IBB	SO	HBP	SH	SF	SB	CS	SB%	GDP	Avg	OBP	SLG
1995 Tulsa *	AA	4	16	3	0	0	1	--	--	6	1	3	2	0	5	0	0	0	1	0	1.00	2	.188	.278	.375
1992 Baltimore	AL	1	0	0	0	0	0	(0	0)	0	0	0	0	0	0	0	0	0	0	0	.00	0	.000	.000	.000
1993 Baltimore	AL	64	152	45	11	1	6	(5	1)	76	32	23	25	0	33	0	0	0	1	0	1.00	3	.296	.395	.500
1994 Baltimore	AL	59	141	34	5	0	3	(1	2)	48	15	20	18	1	25	1	1	2	0	0	.00	2	.241	.327	.340
1995 Bal-Tex	AL	36	63	11	3	0	2	(2	0)	20	9	8	10	0	14	0	0	1	0	0	.00	2	.175	.284	.317
1995 Baltimore	AL	3	1	1	0	0	0	(0	0)	1	1	0	0	0	0	0	0	0	0	0	.00	0	1.000	1.000	1.000
Texas	AL	33	62	10	3	0	2	(2	0)	19	8	8	10	0	14	0	0	1	0	0	.00	2	.161	.274	.306
4 ML YEARS		160	356	90	19	1	11	(8	3)	144	56	51	53	1	72	1	1	3	1	0	1.00	5	.253	.349	.404

Ed Vosberg

Pitches: Left **Bats:** Left **Pos:** RP   **Ht:** 6' 1" **Wt:** 190 **Born:** 9/28/61 **Age:** 34

| | | HOW MUCH HE PITCHED | | | | | | WHAT HE GAVE UP | | | | | | | | | | THE RESULTS | | | | | |
Year Team	Lg	G	GS	CG	GF	IP	BFP	H	R	ER	HR	SH	SF	HB	TBB	IBB	SO	WP	Bk	W	L	Pct.	ShO	Sv	ERA
1995 Okla. City *	AAA	1	0	0	0	1.2	7	1	0	0	0	0	0	0	1	0	2	0	0	1	0	1.000	0	0	0.00
1986 San Diego	NL	5	3	0	0	13.2	65	17	11	10	1	0	0	0	9	1	8	0	1	0	1	.000	0	0	6.59
1990 San Francisco	NL	18	0	0	5	24.1	104	21	16	15	3	2	0	0	12	2	12	0	0	1	1	.500	0	0	5.55
1994 Oakland	AL	16	0	0	2	13.2	56	16	7	6	2	1	0	0	5	0	12	1	1	0	2	.000	0	0	3.95
1995 Texas	AL	44	0	0	20	36	154	32	15	12	3	2	3	0	16	1	36	3	2	5	5	.500	0	4	3.00
4 ML YEARS		83	3	0	27	87.2	379	86	49	43	9	5	3	0	42	4	68	4	4	6	9	.400	0	4	4.41

Terrell Wade

Pitches: Left **Bats:** Left **Pos:** RP   **Ht:** 6' 3" **Wt:** 205 **Born:** 1/25/73 **Age:** 23

| | | HOW MUCH HE PITCHED | | | | | | WHAT HE GAVE UP | | | | | | | | | | THE RESULTS | | | | | |
Year Team	Lg	G	GS	CG	GF	IP	BFP	H	R	ER	HR	SH	SF	HB	TBB	IBB	SO	WP	Bk	W	L	Pct.	ShO	Sv	ERA
1991 Braves	R	10	2	0	0	23	112	29	17	16	0	1	2	0	15	0	22	3	2	2	0	1.000	0	0	6.26
1992 Idaho Falls	R	13	11	0	0	50.1	257	59	46	36	5	4	5	2	42	0	54	5	0	1	4	.200	0	0	6.44
1993 Macon	A	14	14	0	0	83.1	336	57	16	16	1	0	1	1	36	0	121	11	0	8	2	.800	0	0	1.73
Durham	A	5	5	0	0	33	137	26	13	12	3	0	0	1	18	0	47	0	1	2	1	.667	0	0	3.27
Greenville	AA	8	8	1	0	42	179	32	16	15	6	1	0	1	29	0	40	2	0	2	1	.667	1	0	3.21
1994 Greenville	AA	21	21	0	0	105.2	444	87	49	45	7	3	2	0	58	0	105	8	0	9	3	.750	0	0	3.83
Richmond	AAA	4	4	0	0	24	103	23	9	7	1	0	1	0	15	0	26	1	0	2	2	.500	0	0	2.63
1995 Richmond	AAA	24	23	1	0	142	600	137	76	72	10	3	5	1	63	1	124	5	1	10	9	.526	0	0	4.56
1995 Atlanta	NL	3	0	0	0	4	18	3	2	2	1	0	0	0	4	0	3	1	0	0	1	.000	0	0	4.50

Billy Wagner

Pitches: Left **Bats:** Left **Pos:** RP   **Ht:** 5'11" **Wt:** 180 **Born:** 6/25/71 **Age:** 25

| | | HOW MUCH HE PITCHED | | | | | | WHAT HE GAVE UP | | | | | | | | | | THE RESULTS | | | | | |
Year Team	Lg	G	GS	CG	GF	IP	BFP	H	R	ER	HR	SH	SF	HB	TBB	IBB	SO	WP	Bk	W	L	Pct.	ShO	Sv	ERA
1993 Auburn	A	7	7	0	0	28.2	135	25	19	13	2	0	0	1	25	0	31	8	1	1	3	.250	0	0	4.08
1994 Quad City	A	26	26	2	0	153	640	99	71	56	9	7	6	8	91	0	204	12	9	8	9	.471	0	0	3.29
1995 Jackson	AA	12	12	0	0	70	288	49	25	20	7	1	1	4	36	1	77	4	1	2	2	.500	0	0	2.57
Tucson	AAA	13	13	0	0	76.1	325	70	28	27	3	4	2	1	32	0	80	4	0	5	3	.625	0	0	3.18
1995 Houston	NL	1	0	0	0	0.1	1	0	0	0	0	0	0	0	0	0	0	0	0	0	0	.000	0	0	0.00

Paul Wagner

Pitches: Right **Bats:** Right **Pos:** SP/RP   **Ht:** 6' 1" **Wt:** 202 **Born:** 11/14/67 **Age:** 28

| | | HOW MUCH HE PITCHED | | | | | | WHAT HE GAVE UP | | | | | | | | | | THE RESULTS | | | | | |
Year Team	Lg	G	GS	CG	GF	IP	BFP	H	R	ER	HR	SH	SF	HB	TBB	IBB	SO	WP	Bk	W	L	Pct.	ShO	Sv	ERA
1992 Pittsburgh	NL	6	1	0	2	13	52	9	1	1	0	0	0	0	5	0	5	1	0	2	0	1.000	0	0	0.69
1993 Pittsburgh	NL	44	17	1	9	141.1	599	143	72	67	15	6	7	1	42	2	114	12	0	8	8	.500	1	2	4.27
1994 Pittsburgh	NL	29	17	1	4	119.2	534	136	69	61	7	8	4	8	50	4	86	4	0	7	8	.467	0	0	4.59
1995 Pittsburgh	NL	33	25	3	1	165	725	174	96	88	18	7	2	7	72	7	120	8	0	5	16	.238	1	1	4.80
4 ML YEARS		112	60	5	15	439	1910	462	238	217	40	21	13	16	169	13	325	25	0	22	32	.407	2	3	4.45

Tim Wakefield

Pitches: Right **Bats:** Right **Pos:** SP **Ht:** 6' 2" **Wt:** 195 **Born:** 8/2/66 **Age:** 29

Year Team		Lg	G	GS	CG	GF	IP	BFP	H	R	ER	HR	SH	SF	HB	TBB	IBB	SO	WP	Bk	W	L	Pct.	ShO	Sv	ERA
1995 Pawtucket *		AAA	4	4	0	0	25	105	23	10	7	1	0	1	4	9	0	14	0	0	2	1	.667	0	0	2.52
1992 Pittsburgh		NL	13	13	4	0	92	373	76	26	22	3	6	4	1	35	1	51	3	1	8	1	.889	1	0	2.15
1993 Pittsburgh		NL	24	20	3	1	128.1	595	145	83	80	14	7	5	9	75	2	59	6	0	6	11	.353	2	0	5.61
1995 Boston		AL	27	27	6	0	195.1	804	163	76	64	22	3	7	9	68	0	119	11	0	16	8	.667	1	0	2.95
3 ML YEARS			64	60	13	1	415.2	1772	384	185	166	39	16	16	19	178	3	229	20	1	30	20	.600	4	0	3.59

Matt Walbeck

Bats: Both **Throws:** Right **Pos:** C **Ht:** 5'11" **Wt:** 188 **Born:** 10/2/69 **Age:** 26

Year Team		Lg	G	AB	H	2B	3B	HR	(Hm	Rd)	TB	R	RBI	TBB	IBB	SO	HBP	SH	SF	SB	CS	SB%	GDP	Avg	OBP	SLG
1993 Chicago		NL	11	30	6	2	0	1	(1	0)	11	2	6	1	0	6	0	0	0	0	0	.00	0	.200	.226	.367
1994 Minnesota		AL	97	338	69	12	0	5	(0	5)	96	31	35	17	1	37	2	1	1	1	1	.50	7	.204	.246	.284
1995 Minnesota		AL	115	393	101	18	1	1	(1	0)	124	40	44	25	2	71	1	1	2	3	1	.75	11	.257	.302	.316
3 ML YEARS			223	761	176	32	1	7	(2	5)	231	73	85	43	3	114	3	2	3	4	2	.67	18	.231	.274	.304

Larry Walker

Bats: Left **Throws:** Right **Pos:** RF **Ht:** 6' 3" **Wt:** 215 **Born:** 12/1/66 **Age:** 29

Year Team		Lg	G	AB	H	2B	3B	HR	(Hm	Rd)	TB	R	RBI	TBB	IBB	SO	HBP	SH	SF	SB	CS	SB%	GDP	Avg	OBP	SLG
1989 Montreal		NL	20	47	8	0	0	0	(0	0)	8	4	4	5	0	13	1	3	0	1	1	.50	0	.170	.264	.170
1990 Montreal		NL	133	419	101	18	3	19	(9	10)	182	59	51	49	5	112	5	3	2	21	7	.75	8	.241	.326	.434
1991 Montreal		NL	137	487	141	30	2	16	(5	11)	223	59	64	42	2	102	5	1	4	14	9	.61	7	.290	.349	.458
1992 Montreal		NL	143	528	159	31	4	23	(13	10)	267	85	93	41	10	97	6	0	8	18	6	.75	9	.301	.353	.506
1993 Montreal		NL	138	490	130	24	5	22	(13	9)	230	85	86	80	20	76	6	0	6	29	7	.81	8	.265	.371	.469
1994 Montreal		NL	103	395	127	44	2	19	(7	12)	232	76	86	47	5	74	4	0	6	15	5	.75	8	.322	.394	.587
1995 Colorado		NL	131	494	151	31	5	36	(24	12)	300	96	101	49	13	72	14	0	5	16	3	.84	13	.306	.381	.607
7 ML YEARS			805	2860	817	178	21	135	(71	64)	1442	464	485	313	55	546	41	7	31	114	38	.75	53	.286	.361	.504

Mike Walker

Pitches: Right **Bats:** Right **Pos:** RP **Ht:** 6' 1" **Wt:** 205 **Born:** 10/4/66 **Age:** 29

Year Team		Lg	G	GS	CG	GF	IP	BFP	H	R	ER	HR	SH	SF	HB	TBB	IBB	SO	WP	Bk	W	L	Pct.	ShO	Sv	ERA
1995 Iowa *		AAA	16	1	0	3	26.1	122	22	13	12	3	1	1	3	19	4	13	0	0	1	1	.500	0	0	4.10
1988 Cleveland		AL	3	1	0	0	8.2	42	8	7	7	0	1	0	0	10	0	7	0	0	0	0	.000	0	0	7.27
1990 Cleveland		AL	18	11	0	2	75.2	350	82	49	41	6	4	2	6	42	4	34	3	1	2	6	.250	0	0	4.88
1991 Cleveland		AL	5	0	0	3	4.1	22	6	1	1	0	0	0	1	2	1	2	0	0	0	1	.000	0	0	2.08
1995 Chicago		NL	42	0	0	12	44.2	206	45	22	16	2	4	4	0	24	3	20	3	1	1	3	.250	0	1	3.22
4 ML YEARS			68	12	0	17	133.1	620	141	79	65	8	9	6	7	78	8	63	6	2	3	11	.214	0	1	4.39

Pete Walker

Pitches: Right **Bats:** Right **Pos:** RP **Ht:** 6' 2" **Wt:** 195 **Born:** 4/8/69 **Age:** 27

Year Team		Lg	G	GS	CG	GF	IP	BFP	H	R	ER	HR	SH	SF	HB	TBB	IBB	SO	WP	Bk	W	L	Pct.	ShO	Sv	ERA
1990 Pittsfield		A	16	13	1	1	80	346	74	43	37	2	0	4	3	46	0	73	1	0	5	7	.417	0	0	4.16
1991 St. Lucie		A	26	25	1	0	151.1	641	145	77	54	9	9	5	4	52	2	95	7	3	10	12	.455	0	0	3.21
1992 Binghamton		AA	24	23	4	1	139.2	605	159	77	64	9	3	2	3	46	0	72	5	2	7	12	.368	0	0	4.12
1993 Binghamton		AA	45	10	0	33	99.1	423	89	45	38	6	6	1	5	46	1	89	5	0	4	9	.308	0	19	3.44
1994 St. Lucie		A	3	0	0	2	4	16	3	2	1	1	0	0	0	1	0	5	0	0	0	0	.000	0	0	2.25
Norfolk		AAA	37	0	0	19	47.2	207	48	22	21	3	3	2	0	24	2	42	3	0	2	4	.333	0	3	3.97
1995 Norfolk		AAA	34	1	0	25	48.1	207	51	24	21	4	3	1	1	16	1	39	2	1	5	2	.714	0	8	3.91
1995 New York		NL	13	0	0	10	17.2	79	24	9	9	3	2	0	0	5	0	5	0	0	1	0	1.000	0	0	4.58

Donnie Wall

Pitches: Right **Bats:** Right **Pos:** SP **Ht:** 6' 1" **Wt:** 180 **Born:** 7/11/67 **Age:** 28

Year Team		Lg	G	GS	CG	GF	IP	BFP	H	R	ER	HR	SH	SF	HB	TBB	IBB	SO	WP	Bk	W	L	Pct.	ShO	Sv	ERA
1989 Auburn		A	12	8	3	2	65.1	250	45	17	13	2	0	1	3	12	0	69	2	3	7	0	1.000	1	1	1.79
1990 Asheville		A	28	22	1	3	132	586	149	87	76	18	5	6	9	47	1	111	10	0	6	8	.429	0	1	5.18
1991 Burlington		A	16	16	3	0	106.2	421	73	30	24	4	4	2	4	21	1	102	5	0	7	5	.583	1	0	2.03
Osceola		A	12	12	4	0	77.1	295	55	22	18	3	3	2	2	11	1	62	1	0	6	3	.667	2	0	2.09
1992 Osceola		A	7	7	0	0	41	166	37	13	12	1	1	1	2	8	0	30	2	0	3	1	.750	0	0	2.63
Jackson		AA	18	18	2	0	114.1	479	114	51	45	6	2	4	2	26	2	99	4	1	9	6	.600	0	0	3.54

Year Team	Lg	G	GS	CG	GF	IP	BFP	H	R	ER	HR	SH	SF	HB	TBB	IBB	SO	WP	Bk	W	L	Pct.	ShO	Sv	ERA
Tucson	AAA	2	2	0	0	8	35	11	1	1	0	0	0	0	1	0	2	0	0	0	0	.000	0	0	1.13
1993 Tucson	AAA	25	22	0	2	131.2	567	147	73	56	11	7	4	2	35	3	89	4	3	6	4	.600	0	0	3.83
1994 Tucson	AAA	26	24	2	0	148.1	634	171	87	73	9	4	9	3	35	2	84	4	0	11	8	.579	2	0	4.43
1995 Tucson	AAA	28	28	0	0	177.1	732	190	72	65	5	6	4	5	32	1	119	5	1	17	6	.739	0	0	3.30
1995 Houston	NL	6	5	0	0	24.1	110	33	19	15	5	0	2	0	5	0	16	1	0	3	1	.750	0	0	5.55

Tim Wallach

Bats: Right **Throws:** Right **Pos:** 3B

Ht: 6' 3" **Wt:** 207 **Born:** 9/14/57 **Age:** 38

Year Team	Lg	G	AB	H	2B	3B	HR	(Hm	Rd)	TB	R	RBI	TBB	IBB	SO	HBP	SH	SF	SB	CS	SB%	GDP	Avg	OBP	SLG
1995 Albuquerque *	AAA	1	3	1	0	0	0	--	--	1	1	1	0	0	2	0	0	0	0	0	.00	0	.333	.333	.333
San Bernrdo *	A	4	15	7	3	0	0	--	--	10	2	4	0	0	3	0	0	0	0	0	.00	0	.467	.467	.667
1980 Montreal	NL	5	11	2	0	0	1	(0	1)	5	1	2	1	0	5	0	0	0	0	0	.00	0	.182	.250	.455
1981 Montreal	NL	71	212	50	9	1	4	(1	3)	73	19	13	15	2	37	4	0	0	0	1	.00	3	.236	.299	.344
1982 Montreal	NL	158	596	160	31	3	28	(11	17)	281	89	97	36	4	81	4	5	4	6	4	.60	15	.268	.313	.471
1983 Montreal	NL	156	581	156	33	3	19	(9	10)	252	54	70	55	8	97	6	0	5	3	0	.00	9	.269	.335	.434
1984 Montreal	NL	160	582	143	25	4	18	(4	14)	230	55	72	50	6	101	7	0	4	3	7	.30	12	.246	.311	.395
1985 Montreal	NL	155	569	148	36	3	22	(9	13)	256	70	81	38	8	79	5	0	5	9	9	.50	17	.260	.310	.450
1986 Montreal	NL	134	480	112	22	1	18	(6	12)	190	50	71	44	8	72	**10**	0	5	8	4	.67	16	.233	.308	.396
1987 Montreal	NL	153	593	177	**42**	4	26	(13	13)	305	89	123	37	5	98	7	0	7	9	5	.64	6	.298	.343	.514
1988 Montreal	NL	159	592	152	32	5	12	(3	9)	230	52	69	38	7	88	3	0	7	2	6	.25	19	.257	.302	.389
1989 Montreal	NL	154	573	159	**42**	0	13	(6	7)	240	76	77	58	10	81	1	0	7	3	7	.30	**21**	.277	.341	.419
1990 Montreal	NL	161	626	185	37	5	21	(9	12)	295	69	98	42	11	80	3	0	7	6	9	.40	12	.296	.339	.471
1991 Montreal	NL	151	577	130	22	1	13	(5	8)	193	60	73	50	8	100	6	0	4	2	4	.33	12	.225	.292	.334
1992 Montreal	NL	150	537	120	29	1	9	(4	5)	178	53	59	50	2	90	8	0	7	2	2	.50	10	.223	.296	.331
1993 Los Angeles	NL	133	477	106	19	1	12	(4	8)	163	42	62	32	2	70	3	1	9	0	2	.00	10	.222	.271	.342
1994 Los Angeles	NL	113	414	116	21	1	23	(7	16)	208	68	78	46	2	80	4	0	2	0	2	.00	12	.280	.356	.502
1995 Los Angeles	NL	97	327	87	22	2	9	(4	5)	140	24	38	27	4	69	4	0	4	0	0	.00	11	.266	.326	.428
16 ML YEARS		2110	7747	2003	422	35	248	(96	152)	3239	871	1083	619	87	1228	75	6	77	50	65	.43	185	.259	.317	.418

Jerome Walton

Bats: Right **Throws:** Right **Pos:** CF/LF

Ht: 6' 1" **Wt:** 185 **Born:** 7/8/65 **Age:** 30

Year Team	Lg	G	AB	H	2B	3B	HR	(Hm	Rd)	TB	R	RBI	TBB	IBB	SO	HBP	SH	SF	SB	CS	SB%	GDP	Avg	OBP	SLG
1989 Chicago	NL	116	475	139	23	3	5	(3	2)	183	64	46	27	1	77	6	2	5	24	7	.77	6	.293	.335	.385
1990 Chicago	NL	101	392	103	16	2	2	(2	0)	129	63	21	50	1	70	4	1	2	14	7	.67	4	.263	.350	.329
1991 Chicago	NL	123	270	59	13	1	5	(3	2)	89	42	17	19	0	55	3	3	3	7	3	.70	7	.219	.275	.330
1992 Chicago	NL	30	55	7	0	1	0	(0	0)	9	7	1	9	0	13	2	3	0	1	2	.33	1	.127	.273	.164
1993 California	AL	5	2	0	0	0	0	(0	0)	0	2	0	1	0	2	0	0	0	0	1	1.00	0	.000	.333	.000
1994 Cincinnati	NL	46	68	21	4	0	1	(1	0)	28	10	9	4	0	12	0	1	0	1	3	.25	2	.309	.347	.412
1995 Cincinnati	NL	102	162	47	12	1	8	(4	4)	85	32	22	17	0	25	4	3	2	10	7	.59	0	.290	.368	.525
7 ML YEARS		523	1424	376	68	8	21	(13	8)	523	220	116	127	2	254	19	13	12	58	29	.67	20	.264	.330	.367

Duane Ward

Pitches: Right **Bats:** Right **Pos:** RP

Ht: 6' 4" **Wt:** 225 **Born:** 5/28/64 **Age:** 32

Year Team	Lg	G	GS	CG	GF	IP	BFP	H	R	ER	HR	SH	SF	HB	TBB	IBB	SO	WP	Bk	W	L	Pct.	ShO	Sv	ERA
1995 Syracuse *	AAA	6	0	0	1	6	33	14	10	10	0	1	0	0	2	1	4	0	0	1	1	.500	0	0	15.00
Dunedin *	A	3	2	0	0	4.1	19	4	3	3	1	1	0	2	1	0	4	0	1	0	1	.000	0	0	6.23
1986 Tor-Atl		12	1	0	7	18	88	25	17	16	2	2	0	1	12	0	9	1	1	0	2	.000	0	0	8.00
1987 Toronto	AL	12	1	0	4	11.2	57	14	9	9	0	1	1	0	12	2	10	0	0	1	0	1.000	0	0	6.94
1988 Toronto	AL	64	0	0	32	111.2	487	101	46	41	5	4	5	5	60	8	91	10	3	9	3	.750	0	15	3.30
1989 Toronto	AL	66	0	0	39	114.2	494	94	55	48	4	**12**	11	5	58	11	122	13	0	4	10	.286	0	15	3.77
1990 Toronto	AL	73	0	0	39	127.2	508	101	51	49	9	6	2	1	42	10	112	5	0	2	8	.200	0	11	3.45
1991 Toronto	AL	**81**	0	0	46	107.1	428	80	36	33	3	3	4	2	33	3	132	6	0	7	6	.538	0	23	2.77
1992 Toronto	AL	79	0	0	35	101.1	414	76	27	22	5	3	4	1	39	3	103	7	0	7	4	.636	0	12	1.95
1993 Toronto	AL	71	0	0	**70**	71.2	282	49	17	17	4	0	2	1	25	2	97	7	0	2	3	.400	0	**45**	2.13
1995 Toronto	AL	4	0	0	0	2.2	25	11	10	8	0	0	0	0	5	0	3	2	0	0	1	.000	0	0	27.00
1986 Toronto	AL	2	1	0	1	2	15	3	4	3	0	0	0	0	4	0	1	1	0	0	1	.000	0	0	13.50
Atlanta	NL	10	0	0	6	16	73	22	13	13	2	2	0	0	8	0	8	0	1	0	1	.000	0	0	7.31
9 ML YEARS		462	2	0	272	666.2	2783	551	268	243	32	31	29	17	286	39	679	51	4	32	37	.464	0	121	3.28

Turner Ward

Bats: Both **Throws:** Right **Pos:** LF/RF

Ht: 6' 2" **Wt:** 182 **Born:** 4/11/65 **Age:** 31

Year Team	Lg	G	AB	H	2B	3B	HR	(Hm	Rd)	TB	R	RBI	TBB	IBB	SO	HBP	SH	SF	SB	CS	SB%	GDP	Avg	OBP	SLG
1995 Beloit *	A	2	5	0	0	0	0	--	--	0	0	0	3	0	1	0	0	0	0	0	.00	0	.000	.375	.000

New Orleans *	AAA	11	33	8	1	1	1	--	--	14	3	3	4	0	10	0	0	0	0	0	.00	1	.242	.324	.424
1990 Cleveland	AL	14	46	16	2	1	1	(0 | 1)	23	10	10	3	0	8	0	0	0	3	0	1.00	1	.348	.388	.500
1991 Cle-Tor	AL	48	113	27	7	0	0	(0 | 0)	34	12	7	11	0	18	0	4	0	0	0	.00	2	.239	.306	.301
1992 Toronto	AL	18	29	10	3	0	1	(0 | 1)	16	7	3	4	0	4	0	0	0	0	1	.00	1	.345	.424	.552
1993 Toronto	AL	72	167	32	4	2	4	(2 | 2)	52	20	28	23	2	26	1	3	4	3	3	.50	7	.192	.287	.311
1994 Milwaukee	AL	102	367	85	15	2	9	(3 | 6)	131	55	45	52	4	68	3	0	5	6	2	.75	9	.232	.328	.357
1995 Milwaukee	AL	44	129	34	3	1	4	(3 | 1)	51	19	16	14	1	21	1	1	1	6	1	.86	2	.264	.338	.395
1991 Cleveland	AL	40	100	23	7	0	0	(0 | 0)	30	11	5	10	0	16	0	4	0	0	0	.00	1	.230	.300	.300
Toronto		8	13	4	0	0	0	(0 | 0)	4	1	2	1	0	2	0	0	0	0	0	.00	1	.308	.357	.308
6 ML YEARS		298	851	204	34	6	19	(8 | 11)	307	123	109	107	7	145	5	8	10	18	7	.72	22	.240	.325	.361

Jeff Ware

Pitches: Right **Bats:** Right **Pos:** SP **Ht:** 6' 3" **Wt:** 190 **Born:** 11/11/70 **Age:** 25

		HOW MUCH HE PITCHED						WHAT HE GAVE UP												THE RESULTS				
Year Team	Lg	G	GS	CG	GF	IP	BFP	H	R	ER	HR	SH	SF	HB	TBB	IBB	SO	WP	Bk	W	L	Pct.	ShO	Sv	ERA
1992 Dunedin	A	12	12	1	0	75.1	319	64	26	22	1	3	0	3	30	0	49	7	3	5	3	.625	1	0	2.63
1994 Knoxville	AA	10	10	0	0	38	175	50	32	29	5	2	2	2	16	0	31	1	0	0	7	.000	0	0	6.87
1995 Syracuse	AAA	16	16	0	0	75	319	62	29	25	8	0	1	2	46	0	76	3	0	7	0	1.000	0	0	3.00
1995 Toronto	AL	5	5	0	0	26.1	124	28	18	16	2	1	0	1	21	0	18	2	0	2	1	.667	0	0	5.47

John Wasdin

Pitches: Right **Bats:** Right **Pos:** RP **Ht:** 6' 2" **Wt:** 190 **Born:** 8/5/72 **Age:** 23

		HOW MUCH HE PITCHED						WHAT HE GAVE UP												THE RESULTS				
Year Team	Lg	G	GS	CG	GF	IP	BFP	H	R	ER	HR	SH	SF	HB	TBB	IBB	SO	WP	Bk	W	L	Pct.	ShO	Sv	ERA
1993 Athletics	R	1	1	0	0	3	13	3	1	1	0	0	0	1	0	0	1	0	0	0	0	.000	0	0	3.00
Madison	A	9	9	0	0	48.1	185	32	11	10	1	3	0	1	9	1	40	2	3	2	3	.400	0	0	1.86
Modesto	A	3	3	0	0	16.1	68	17	9	7	0	0	0	0	4	0	11	0	0	0	3	.000	0	0	3.86
1994 Modesto	A	6	4	0	2	26.2	102	17	6	5	2	0	0	2	5	0	30	0	0	3	1	.750	0	0	1.69
Huntsville	AA	21	21	0	0	141.2	571	126	61	54	13	3	4	2	29	2	108	7	0	12	3	.800	0	0	3.43
1995 Edmonton	AAA	29	28	2	0	174.1	744	193	117	107	26	3	11	4	38	3	111	10	1	12	8	.600	1	0	5.52
1995 Oakland	AL	5	2	0	3	17.1	69	14	9	9	4	0	0	1	3	0	6	0	0	1	1	.500	0	0	4.67

Scott Watkins

Pitches: Left **Bats:** Left **Pos:** RP **Ht:** 6' 3" **Wt:** 180 **Born:** 5/15/70 **Age:** 26

		HOW MUCH HE PITCHED						WHAT HE GAVE UP												THE RESULTS				
Year Team	Lg	G	GS	CG	GF	IP	BFP	H	R	ER	HR	SH	SF	HB	TBB	IBB	SO	WP	Bk	W	L	Pct.	ShO	Sv	ERA
1992 Kenosha	A	27	0	0	11	46.1	196	43	21	19	4	2	1	3	14	0	58	1	0	2	5	.286	0	1	3.69
1993 Fort Wayne	A	15	0	0	8	24.1	124	26	13	11	0	1	2	1	9	0	31	0	1	2	0	1.000	0	1	3.26
Fort Myers	A	20	0	0	10	27.2	125	27	14	9	0	2	0	0	12	0	41	2	1	2	2	.500	0	3	2.93
Nashville	AA	13	0	0	3	16.2	75	19	15	11	2	0	1	1	7	0	17	2	1	0	1	.000	0	0	5.94
1994 Nashville	AA	11	0	0	8	13.2	60	13	9	7	1	1	2	0	4	0	11	1	0	1	0	1.000	0	3	4.61
Salt Lake	AAA	46	0	0	26	57.1	269	73	46	43	10	4	5	1	28	5	47	1	1	2	6	.250	0	3	6.75
1995 Salt Lake	AAA	45	0	0	33	54.2	217	45	18	17	4	1	3	1	13	1	57	1	0	4	2	.667	0	20	2.80
1995 Minnesota	AL	27	0	0	7	21.2	94	22	14	13	2	1	3	0	11	1	11	0	0	0	0	.000	0	0	5.40

Allen Watson

Pitches: Left **Bats:** Left **Pos:** SP **Ht:** 6' 3" **Wt:** 200 **Born:** 11/18/70 **Age:** 25

		HOW MUCH HE PITCHED						WHAT HE GAVE UP												THE RESULTS				
Year Team	Lg	G	GS	CG	GF	IP	BFP	H	R	ER	HR	SH	SF	HB	TBB	IBB	SO	WP	Bk	W	L	Pct.	ShO	Sv	ERA
1995 Arkansas *	AA	1	1	0	0	5	19	4	1	0	0	0	0	0	0	0	7	0	0	1	0	1.000	0	0	0.00
Louisville *	AAA	4	4	1	0	24	97	20	10	7	1	0	0	0	6	0	19	3	0	2	2	.500	1	0	2.63
1993 St. Louis	NL	16	15	0	1	86	373	90	53	44	11	6	4	3	28	2	49	2	1	6	7	.462	0	0	4.60
1994 St. Louis	NL	22	22	0	0	115.2	523	130	73	71	15	7	0	8	53	0	74	2	2	6	5	.545	0	0	5.52
1995 St. Louis	NL	21	19	0	1	114.1	491	126	68	63	17	2	1	5	41	0	49	2	2	7	9	.438	0	0	4.96
3 ML YEARS		59	56	0	2	316	1387	346	194	178	43	15	5	16	122	2	172	6	5	19	21	.475	0	0	5.07

Dave Weathers

Pitches: Right **Bats:** Right **Pos:** SP/RP **Ht:** 6' 3" **Wt:** 220 **Born:** 9/25/69 **Age:** 26

		HOW MUCH HE PITCHED						WHAT HE GAVE UP												THE RESULTS				
Year Team	Lg	G	GS	CG	GF	IP	BFP	H	R	ER	HR	SH	SF	HB	TBB	IBB	SO	WP	Bk	W	L	Pct.	ShO	Sv	ERA
1995 Brevard Cty *	A	1	1	0	0	4	15	4	0	0	0	0	0	0	1	0	3	0	0	0	0	.000	0	0	0.00
Charlotte *	AAA	1	1	0	0	5	27	10	5	5	0	0	0	0	5	0	1	1	0	0	1	.000	0	0	9.00
1991 Toronto	AL	15	0	0	4	14.2	79	15	9	8	1	2	1	2	17	3	13	0	0	1	0	1.000	0	0	4.91
1992 Toronto	AL	2	0	0	0	3.1	15	5	3	3	1	0	0	0	2	0	3	0	0	0	0	.000	0	0	8.10
1993 Florida	NL	14	6	0	2	45.2	202	57	26	26	3	2	0	1	13	1	34	6	0	2	3	.400	0	0	5.12

Year	Team	Lg	G	GS	CG	GF	IP	BFP	H	R	ER	HR	SH	SF	HB	TBB	IBB	SO	WP	Bk	W	L	Pct.	ShO	Sv	ERA
1994	Florida	NL	24	24	0	0	135	621	166	87	79	13	12	4	4	59	9	72	7	1	8	12	.400	0	0	5.27
1995	Florida	NL	28	15	0	0	90.1	419	104	68	60	8	7	3	5	52	3	60	3	0	4	5	.444	0	0	5.98
	5 ML YEARS		83	45	0	6	289	1336	347	193	176	26	23	8	12	143	16	182	16	1	15	20	.429	0	0	5.48

Lenny Webster

Bats: Right **Throws:** Right **Pos:** C **Ht:** 5' 9" **Wt:** 195 **Born:** 2/10/65 **Age:** 31

			BATTING																	BASERUNNING				PERCENTAGES		
Year	Team	Lg	G	AB	H	2B	3B	HR	(Hm	Rd)	TB	R	RBI	TBB	IBB	SO	HBP	SH	SF	SB	CS	SB%	GDP	Avg	OBP	SLG
1989	Minnesota	AL	14	20	6	2	0	0	(0	0)	8	3	1	3	0	2	0	0	0	0	0	.00	0	.300	.391	.400
1990	Minnesota	AL	2	6	2	1	0	0	(0	0)	3	1	0	1	0	1	0	0	0	0	0	.00	0	.333	.429	.500
1991	Minnesota	AL	18	34	10	1	0	3	(1	2)	20	7	8	6	0	10	0	0	1	0	0	.00	2	.294	.390	.588
1992	Minnesota	AL	53	118	33	10	1	1	(1	0)	48	10	13	9	0	11	0	2	0	0	2	.00	3	.280	.331	.407
1993	Minnesota	AL	49	106	21	2	0	1	(1	0)	26	14	8	11	1	8	0	0	0	1	0	1.00	1	.198	.274	.245
1994	Montreal	NL	57	143	39	10	0	5	(2	3)	64	13	23	16	1	24	6	1	0	0	0	.00	7	.273	.370	.448
1995	Philadelphia	NL	49	150	40	9	0	4	(1	3)	61	18	14	16	0	27	0	1	0	0	0	.00	4	.267	.337	.407
	7 ML YEARS		242	577	151	35	1	14	(6	8)	230	66	67	62	2	83	6	4	1	1	2	.33	17	.262	.339	.399

Mitch Webster

Bats: Both **Throws:** Left **Pos:** LF/RF **Ht:** 6' 1" **Wt:** 191 **Born:** 5/16/59 **Age:** 37

			BATTING																	BASERUNNING				PERCENTAGES		
Year	Team	Lg	G	AB	H	2B	3B	HR	(Hm	Rd)	TB	R	RBI	TBB	IBB	SO	HBP	SH	SF	SB	CS	SB%	GDP	Avg	OBP	SLG
1983	Toronto	AL	11	11	2	0	0	0	(0	0)	2	2	0	1	0	1	0	0	0	0	0	.00	0	.182	.250	.182
1984	Toronto	AL	26	22	5	2	1	0	(0	0)	9	9	4	1	0	7	0	0	0	0	0	.00	1	.227	.261	.409
1985	Tor-Mon		78	213	58	8	2	11	(3	8)	103	32	30	20	3	33	0	1	1	15	10	.60	3	.272	.333	.484
1986	Montreal	NL	151	576	167	31	13	8	(2	6)	248	89	49	57	4	78	4	3	5	36	15	.71	9	.290	.355	.431
1987	Montreal	NL	156	588	165	30	8	15	(9	6)	256	101	63	70	5	95	6	8	4	33	10	.77	6	.281	.361	.435
1988	ChN-Mon	NL	151	523	136	16	8	6	(3	3)	186	69	39	55	2	87	8	5	4	22	14	.61	5	.260	.337	.356
1989	Chicago	NL	98	272	70	12	4	3	(1	2)	99	40	19	30	5	55	1	3	2	14	2	.88	3	.257	.331	.364
1990	Cleveland	AL	128	437	110	20	6	12	(6	6)	178	58	55	20	1	61	3	11	6	22	6	.79	5	.252	.285	.407
1991	Cle-LA-Pit		107	203	42	8	5	2	(2	0)	66	23	19	21	1	61	0	2	0	2	3	.40	3	.207	.281	.325
1992	Los Angeles	NL	135	262	70	12	5	6	(1	5)	110	33	35	27	3	49	2	8	5	11	5	.69	1	.267	.334	.420
1993	Los Angeles	NL	88	172	42	6	2	2	(1	1)	58	26	14	11	2	24	2	4	3	4	6	.40	3	.244	.293	.337
1994	Los Angeles	NL	82	84	23	4	0	4	(1	3)	39	16	12	8	1	13	1	0	1	1	2	.33	2	.274	.344	.464
1995	Los Angeles	NL	54	56	10	1	1	1	(0	1)	16	6	3	4	1	14	1	2	0	0	0	.00	1	.179	.246	.286
1985	Toronto	AL	4	1	0	0	0	0	(0	0)	0	0	0	0	0	0	0	0	0	0	1	.00	0	.000	.000	.000
	Montreal	NL	74	212	58	8	2	11	(3	8)	103	32	30	20	3	33	0	1	1	15	9	.63	3	.274	.335	.486
1988	Chicago	NL	70	264	70	11	6	4	(3	1)	105	36	26	19	0	50	3	1	2	10	4	.71	2	.265	.319	.398
	Montreal	NL	81	259	66	5	2	2	(0	2)	81	33	13	36	2	37	5	4	2	12	10	.55	3	.255	.354	.313
1991	Cleveland	AL	13	32	4	0	0	0	(0	0)	4	2	0	3	0	9	0	1	0	2	2	.50	0	.125	.200	.125
	Los Angeles	NL	58	74	21	5	1	1	(0	1)	31	12	10	9	0	21	0	1	0	0	0	.00	0	.284	.361	.419
	Pittsburgh	NL	36	97	17	3	4	1	(1	0)	31	9	9	9	1	31	0	0	0	0	1	.00	3	.175	.245	.320
	13 ML YEARS		1265	3419	900	150	55	70	(29	41)	1370	504	342	325	28	578	28	47	30	160	73	.69	42	.263	.330	.401

Bill Wegman

Pitches: Right **Bats:** Right **Pos:** RP/SP **Ht:** 6' 5" **Wt:** 220 **Born:** 12/19/62 **Age:** 33

			HOW MUCH HE PITCHED						WHAT HE GAVE UP										THE RESULTS					
Year	Team	Lg	G	GS	CG	GF	IP	BFP	H	R	ER	HR	SH	SF	HB	TBB	IBB	SO	WP	Bk	W	L	Pct.	ShO	Sv	ERA
1985	Milwaukee	AL	3	3	0	0	17.2	73	17	8	7	3	0	1	0	3	0	6	0	1	2	0	1.000	0	0	3.57
1986	Milwaukee	AL	35	32	2	1	198.1	836	217	120	113	32	4	5	7	43	2	82	5	2	5	12	.294	0	0	5.13
1987	Milwaukee	AL	34	33	7	0	225	934	229	113	106	31	4	6	6	53	2	102	0	2	12	11	.522	0	0	4.24
1988	Milwaukee	AL	32	31	4	0	199	847	207	104	91	24	3	10	4	50	5	84	1	1	13	13	.500	1	0	4.12
1989	Milwaukee	AL	11	8	0	1	51	240	69	44	38	6	0	4	0	21	2	27	2	0	2	6	.250	0	0	6.71
1990	Milwaukee	AL	8	5	1	0	29.2	132	37	21	16	6	1	1	0	6	1	20	0	0	2	2	.500	1	0	4.85
1991	Milwaukee	AL	28	28	7	0	193.1	785	176	76	61	16	6	4	7	40	0	89	6	0	15	7	.682	2	0	2.84
1992	Milwaukee	AL	35	35	7	0	261.2	1079	251	104	93	28	7	4	9	55	3	127	1	2	13	14	.481	0	0	3.20
1993	Milwaukee	AL	20	18	5	0	120.2	514	135	70	60	13	3	11	2	34	5	50	0	0	4	14	.222	0	0	4.48
1994	Milwaukee	AL	19	19	0	0	115.2	500	140	64	58	14	4	6	2	26	0	59	3	0	8	4	.667	0	0	4.51
1995	Milwaukee	AL	37	4	0	17	70.2	314	89	45	42	14	3	2	3	21	2	50	1	0	5	7	.417	0	2	5.35
	11 ML YEARS		262	216	33	19	1482.2	6254	1567	769	685	187	35	54	40	352	22	696	19	8	81	90	.474	4	2	4.16

John Wehner

Bats: Right **Throws:** Right **Pos:** 3B/LF **Ht:** 6' 3" **Wt:** 205 **Born:** 6/29/67 **Age:** 29

			BATTING																	BASERUNNING				PERCENTAGES		
Year	Team	Lg	G	AB	H	2B	3B	HR	(Hm	Rd)	TB	R	RBI	TBB	IBB	SO	HBP	SH	SF	SB	CS	SB%	GDP	Avg	OBP	SLG
1995	Calgary *	AAA	40	158	52	12	2	4	--	--	80	30	24	12	1	16	2	1	0	8	4	.67	3	.329	.384	.506
1991	Pittsburgh	NL	37	106	36	7	0	0	(0	0)	43	15	7	7	0	17	0	0	0	3	0	1.00	0	.340	.381	.406
1992	Pittsburgh	NL	55	123	22	6	0	0	(0	0)	28	11	4	12	2	22	0	2	0	3	0	1.00	4	.179	.252	.228

Year Team	Lg	G	AB	H	2B	3B	HR	(Hm	Rd)	TB	R	RBI	TBB	IBB	SO	HBP	SH	SF	SB	CS	SB%	GDP	Avg	OBP	SLG
1993 Pittsburgh	NL	29	35	5	0	0	0	(0	0)	5	3	0	6	1	10	0	2	0	0	0	.00	0	.143	.268	.143
1994 Pittsburgh	NL	2	4	1	1	0	0	(0	0)	2	1	3	0	0	1	0	0	0	0	0	.00	0	.250	.250	.500
1995 Pittsburgh	NL	52	107	33	0	3	0	(0	0)	39	13	5	10	1	17	0	4	2	3	1	.75	2	.308	.361	.364
5 ML YEARS		175	375	97	14	3	0	(0	0)	117	43	19	35	4	67	0	8	2	9	1	.90	6	.259	.320	.312

Walt Weiss

Bats: Both **Throws:** Right **Pos:** SS **Ht:** 6' 0" **Wt:** 175 **Born:** 11/28/63 **Age:** 32

							BATTING													BASERUNNING				PERCENTAGES		
Year Team	Lg	G	AB	H	2B	3B	HR	(Hm	Rd)	TB	R	RBI	TBB	IBB	SO	HBP	SH	SF	SB	CS	SB%	GDP	Avg	OBP	SLG
1987 Oakland	AL	16	26	12	4	0	0	(0	0)	16	3	1	2	0	2	0	1	0	1	2	.33	0	.462	.500	.615
1988 Oakland	AL	147	452	113	17	3	3	(0	3)	145	44	39	35	1	56	9	8	7	4	4	.50	9	.250	.312	.321
1989 Oakland	AL	84	236	55	11	0	3	(2	1)	75	30	21	21	0	39	1	5	0	6	1	.86	5	.233	.298	.318
1990 Oakland	AL	138	445	118	17	1	2	(1	1)	143	50	35	46	5	53	4	6	4	9	3	.75	7	.265	.337	.321
1991 Oakland	AL	40	133	30	6	1	0	(0	0)	38	15	13	12	0	14	0	1	2	6	0	1.00	3	.226	.286	.286
1992 Oakland	AL	103	316	67	5	2	0	(0	0)	76	36	21	43	1	39	1	11	4	6	3	.67	10	.212	.305	.241
1993 Florida	NL	158	500	133	14	2	1	(0	1)	154	50	39	79	13	73	3	5	4	7	3	.70	5	.266	.367	.308
1994 Colorado	NL	110	423	106	11	4	1	(1	0)	128	58	32	56	0	58	0	4	3	12	7	.63	6	.251	.336	.303
1995 Colorado	NL	137	427	111	17	3	1	(0	1)	137	65	25	98	8	57	5	6	1	15	3	.83	7	.260	.403	.321
9 ML YEARS		933	2958	745	102	16	11	(4	7)	912	351	226	392	28	391	23	47	25	66	26	.72	52	.252	.341	.308

Bob Wells

Pitches: Right **Bats:** Right **Pos:** RP/SP **Ht:** 6' 0" **Wt:** 180 **Born:** 11/1/66 **Age:** 29

		HOW MUCH HE PITCHED						WHAT HE GAVE UP										THE RESULTS					
Year Team	Lg	G	GS	CG	GF	IP	BFP	H	R	ER	HR	SH	SF	HB	TBB	IBB	SO	WP	Bk	W	L	Pct.	ShO	Sv	ERA
1989 Martinsville	R	4	0	0	2	6	27	8	5	3	1	0	0	0	2	0	3	1	1	0	0	.000	0	0	4.50
1990 Spartanburg	A	20	19	2	0	113	476	94	47	36	6	2	1	5	40	0	73	4	0	5	8	.385	0	0	2.87
Clearwater	A	6	1	0	2	14.2	64	17	9	8	0	0	0	1	6	1	11	0	0	0	2	.000	0	1	4.91
1991 Clearwater	A	24	9	1	3	75.1	297	63	27	26	5	5	1	4	19	4	66	6	4	7	2	.778	0	0	3.11
Reading	AA	1	1	0	0	5	20	4	2	2	1	0	0	0	1	0	3	0	0	1	0	1.000	0	0	3.60
1992 Clearwater	A	9	0	0	8	9.1	40	10	4	4	0	0	0	0	3	2	9	3	0	1	0	1.000	0	5	3.86
Reading	AA	3	3	0	0	15.1	60	12	2	2	0	1	0	0	5	0	11	0	0	0	1	.000	0	0	1.17
1993 Clearwater	A	12	1	0	7	27.2	109	23	5	3	0	1	0	2	6	1	24	0	0	1	0	1.000	0	2	0.98
Scranton-Wb	AAA	11	0	0	3	19.1	80	19	7	6	1	0	0	1	5	0	8	0	0	1	1	.500	0	2	2.79
1994 Reading	AA	14	0	0	12	19.1	82	18	6	6	3	0	0	4	3	1	19	0	0	1	3	.250	0	4	2.79
Scranton-Wb	AAA	11	0	0	4	14.2	70	18	6	4	1	0	2	2	6	1	13	1	0	0	2	.000	0	0	2.45
Calgary	AAA	6	6	0	0	31.2	149	43	27	23	9	1	3	5	9	0	17	2	0	3	2	.600	0	0	6.54
1994 Sea-Phi		7	0	0	2	9	38	8	2	2	0	0	0	1	4	0	6	0	0	2	0	1.000	0	0	2.00
1995 Seattle	AL	30	4	0	3	76.2	358	88	51	49	11	1	5	3	39	3	38	1	0	4	3	.571	0	0	5.75
1994 Seattle	AL	1	0	0	0	4	17	4	1	1	0	0	0	0	1	0	3	0	0	1	0	1.000	0	0	2.25
Philadelphia	NL	6	0	0	2	5	21	4	1	1	0	0	0	1	3	0	3	0	0	1	0	1.000	0	0	1.80
2 ML YEARS		37	4	0	5	85.2	396	96	53	51	11	1	5	4	43	3	44	1	0	6	3	.667	0	0	5.36

David Wells

Pitches: Left **Bats:** Left **Pos:** SP **Ht:** 6' 4" **Wt:** 225 **Born:** 5/20/63 **Age:** 33

		HOW MUCH HE PITCHED						WHAT HE GAVE UP										THE RESULTS					
Year Team	Lg	G	GS	CG	GF	IP	BFP	H	R	ER	HR	SH	SF	HB	TBB	IBB	SO	WP	Bk	W	L	Pct.	ShO	Sv	ERA
1987 Toronto	AL	18	2	0	6	29.1	132	37	14	13	0	1	0	0	12	0	32	4	0	4	3	.571	0	1	3.99
1988 Toronto	AL	41	0	0	15	64.1	279	65	36	33	12	2	2	2	31	9	56	6	2	3	5	.375	0	4	4.62
1989 Toronto	AL	54	0	0	19	86.1	352	66	25	23	5	3	2	0	28	7	78	6	3	7	4	.636	0	2	2.40
1990 Toronto	AL	43	25	0	8	189	759	165	72	66	14	9	2	2	45	3	115	7	1	11	6	.647	0	3	3.14
1991 Toronto	AL	40	28	2	3	198.1	811	188	88	82	24	6	6	2	49	1	106	10	3	15	10	.600	0	1	3.72
1992 Toronto	AL	41	14	0	14	120	529	138	84	72	16	3	4	8	36	6	62	3	1	7	9	.438	0	2	5.40
1993 Detroit	AL	32	30	0	0	187	776	183	93	87	26	3	3	7	42	6	139	13	0	11	9	.550	0	0	4.19
1994 Detroit	AL	16	16	5	0	111.1	464	113	54	49	13	3	1	2	24	6	71	5	0	5	7	.417	1	0	3.96
1995 Det-Cin		29	29	6	0	203	839	194	88	73	23	7	3	2	53	9	133	7	2	16	8	.667	0	0	3.24
1995 Detroit	AL	18	18	3	0	130.1	539	120	54	44	17	3	2	2	37	5	83	6	1	10	3	.769	0	0	3.04
Cincinnati	NL	11	11	3	0	72.2	300	74	34	29	6	4	1	0	16	4	50	1	1	6	5	.545	0	0	3.59
9 ML YEARS		314	144	13	65	1188.2	4941	1149	554	498	133	37	23	25	320	47	792	61	12	79	61	.564	1	13	3.77

Turk Wendell

Pitches: Right **Bats:** Left **Pos:** RP **Ht:** 6' 2" **Wt:** 190 **Born:** 5/19/67 **Age:** 29

		HOW MUCH HE PITCHED						WHAT HE GAVE UP										THE RESULTS					
Year Team	Lg	G	GS	CG	GF	IP	BFP	H	R	ER	HR	SH	SF	HB	TBB	IBB	SO	WP	Bk	W	L	Pct.	ShO	Sv	ERA
1995 Daytona *	A	4	2	0	0	7.2	30	5	2	1	0	1	0	0	1	0	8	1	0	0	0	.000	0	0	1.17
Orlando *	AA	5	0	0	2	7	30	6	3	3	0	0	0	1	4	0	7	0	0	1	0	1.000	0	1	3.86
1993 Chicago	NL	7	4	0	1	22.2	98	24	13	11	0	2	0	0	8	1	15	1	1	1	2	.333	0	0	4.37

1994 Chicago	NL	6	2	0	1	14.1	76	22	20	19	3	2	1	0	10	1	9	1	0	0	1	.000	0	0	11.93
1995 Chicago	NL	43	0	0	17	60.1	270	71	35	33	11	3	3	2	24	4	50	1	0	3	1	.750	0	0	4.92
3 ML YEARS		56	6	0	19	97.1	444	117	68	63	14	7	4	2	42	6	74	3	1	4	4	.500	0	0	5.83

Don Wengert

Pitches: Right **Bats:** Right **Pos:** RP **Ht:** 6' 2" **Wt:** 205 **Born:** 11/6/69 **Age:** 26

			HOW MUCH HE PITCHED						WHAT HE GAVE UP											THE RESULTS					
Year Team	Lg	G	GS	CG	GF	IP	BFP	H	R	ER	HR	SH	SF	HB	TBB	IBB	SO	WP	Bk	W	L	Pct.	ShO	Sv	ERA
1992 Sou. Oregon	A	6	5	1	0	37	144	32	6	6	1	1	0	1	7	0	29	1	1	2	0	1.000	0	0	1.46
Madison	A	7	7	0	0	40	176	42	20	15	2	2	0	2	17	0	29	1	0	3	4	.429	0	0	3.38
1993 Madison	A	13	13	2	0	78.2	322	79	30	29	5	4	4	1	18	0	46	6	0	6	5	.545	0	0	3.32
Modesto	A	12	12	0	0	70.1	299	75	42	37	8	1	1	3	29	0	43	4	1	3	6	.333	0	0	4.73
1994 Modesto	A	10	7	0	3	42.2	174	40	15	14	1	2	1	1	11	0	52	1	0	4	1	.800	0	2	2.95
Huntsville	AA	17	17	1	0	99.1	411	86	43	36	14	0	0	4	33	1	92	3	1	6	4	.600	0	0	3.26
1995 Edmonton	AAA	16	6	0	4	39	178	55	32	32	5	0	1	1	16	2	20	3	0	1	1	.500	0	1	7.38
1995 Oakland	AL	19	0	0	10	29.2	129	30	14	11	3	1	1	1	12	2	16	1	0	1	1	.500	0	0	3.34

David West

Pitches: Left **Bats:** Left **Pos:** SP **Ht:** 6' 6" **Wt:** 247 **Born:** 9/1/64 **Age:** 31

			HOW MUCH HE PITCHED						WHAT HE GAVE UP											THE RESULTS					
Year Team	Lg	G	GS	CG	GF	IP	BFP	H	R	ER	HR	SH	SF	HB	TBB	IBB	SO	WP	Bk	W	L	Pct.	ShO	Sv	ERA
1995 Scrantn-WB *	AAA	1	1	1	0	7	22	2	0	0	0	0	0	0	0	0	6	0	0	1	0	1.000	1	0	0.00
Reading *	AA	1	1	0	0	6	23	2	1	1	1	0	0	0	3	0	8	0	0	0	0	.000	0	0	1.50
1988 New York	NL	2	1	0	0	6	25	6	2	2	0	0	0	0	3	0	3	0	2	1	0	1.000	0	0	3.00
1989 Min-NYN		21	7	0	4	63.2	294	73	49	48	9	2	3	3	33	3	50	2	0	3	4	.429	0	0	6.79
1990 Minnesota	AL	29	27	2	0	146.1	646	142	88	83	21	6	4	4	78	1	92	4	1	7	9	.438	0	0	5.10
1991 Minnesota	AL	15	12	0	0	71.1	305	66	37	36	13	2	3	1	28	0	52	3	0	4	4	.500	0	0	4.54
1992 Minnesota	AL	9	3	0	1	28.1	139	32	24	22	3	0	2	1	20	0	19	2	0	1	3	.250	0	0	6.99
1993 Philadelphia	NL	76	0	0	27	86.1	375	60	37	28	6	8	2	5	51	4	87	3	0	6	4	.600	0	3	2.92
1994 Philadelphia	NL	31	14	0	7	99	429	74	44	39	7	4	2	1	61	2	83	9	0	4	10	.286	0	0	3.55
1995 Philadelphia	NL	8	8	0	0	38	163	34	17	16	5	2	0	1	19	0	25	1	0	3	2	.600	0	0	3.79
1989 Minnesota	AL	10	5	0	4	39.1	182	48	29	28	5	2	2	2	19	1	31	1	0	3	2	.600	0	0	6.41
New York	NL	11	2	0	0	24.1	112	25	20	20	4	0	1	1	14	2	19	1	0	0	2	.000	0	0	7.40
8 ML YEARS		191	72	2	39	539	2376	487	298	274	64	24	16	16	293	10	411	24	3	29	36	.446	0	3	4.58

John Wetteland

Pitches: Right **Bats:** Right **Pos:** RP **Ht:** 6' 2" **Wt:** 215 **Born:** 8/21/66 **Age:** 29

			HOW MUCH HE PITCHED						WHAT HE GAVE UP											THE RESULTS					
Year Team	Lg	G	GS	CG	GF	IP	BFP	H	R	ER	HR	SH	SF	HB	TBB	IBB	SO	WP	Bk	W	L	Pct.	ShO	Sv	ERA
1989 Los Angeles	NL	31	12	0	7	102.2	411	81	46	43	8	4	2	0	34	4	96	16	1	5	8	.385	0	1	3.77
1990 Los Angeles	NL	22	5	0	7	43	190	44	28	23	6	1	1	4	17	3	36	8	0	2	4	.333	0	0	4.81
1991 Los Angeles	NL	6	0	0	3	9	36	5	2	0	0	0	1	1	3	0	9	1	0	1	0	1.000	0	0	0.00
1992 Montreal	NL	67	0	0	58	83.1	347	64	27	27	6	5	1	4	36	3	99	4	0	4	4	.500	0	37	2.92
1993 Montreal	NL	70	0	0	58	85.1	344	58	17	13	3	5	1	2	28	3	113	7	0	9	3	.750	0	43	1.37
1994 Montreal	NL	52	0	0	43	63.2	261	46	22	20	5	5	4	3	21	4	68	0	0	4	6	.400	0	25	2.83
1995 New York	AL	60	0	0	56	61.1	233	40	22	20	6	1	2	0	14	2	66	1	0	1	5	.167	0	31	2.93
7 ML YEARS		308	17	0	232	448.1	1822	338	164	146	34	21	12	14	153	19	487	37	1	26	30	.464	0	137	2.93

Lou Whitaker

Bats: Left **Throws:** Right **Pos:** 2B **Ht:** 5'11" **Wt:** 185 **Born:** 5/12/57 **Age:** 39

			BATTING																BASERUNNING			PERCENTAGES		
Year Team	Lg	G	AB	H	2B	3B	HR	(Hm	Rd)	TB	R	RBI	TBB	IBB	SO	HBP	SH	SF	SB	CS	SB%	GDP	Avg	OBP	SLG
1977 Detroit	AL	11	32	8	1	0	0	(0	0)	9	5	2	4	0	6	0	1	0	2	2	.50	0	.250	.333	.281
1978 Detroit	AL	139	484	138	12	7	3	(2	1)	173	71	58	61	0	65	1	13	8	7	7	.50	9	.285	.361	.357
1979 Detroit	AL	127	423	121	14	8	3	(3	0)	160	75	42	78	2	66	1	14	4	20	10	.67	10	.286	.395	.378
1980 Detroit	AL	145	477	111	19	1	1	(1	0)	135	68	45	73	0	79	0	12	6	8	4	.67	9	.233	.331	.283
1981 Detroit	AL	109	335	88	14	4	5	(4	1)	125	48	36	40	3	42	1	3	3	5	3	.63	5	.263	.340	.373
1982 Detroit	AL	152	560	160	22	8	15	(9	6)	243	76	65	48	4	58	1	6	4	11	3	.79	8	.286	.341	.434
1983 Detroit	AL	161	643	206	40	6	12	(7	5)	294	94	72	67	8	70	0	2	8	17	10	.63	9	.320	.380	.457
1984 Detroit	AL	143	558	161	25	1	13	(8	5)	227	90	56	62	5	63	0	4	5	6	5	.55	9	.289	.357	.407
1985 Detroit	AL	152	609	170	29	8	21	(11	10)	278	102	73	80	9	56	2	5	5	6	4	.60	3	.279	.362	.456
1986 Detroit	AL	144	584	157	26	6	20	(8	12)	255	95	73	63	5	70	0	0	4	13	8	.62	20	.269	.338	.437
1987 Detroit	AL	149	604	160	38	6	16	(10	6)	258	110	59	71	2	108	1	4	4	13	5	.72	5	.265	.341	.427
1988 Detroit	AL	115	403	111	18	2	12	(8	4)	169	54	55	66	5	61	0	6	2	2	0	1.00	8	.275	.376	.419
1989 Detroit	AL	148	509	128	21	1	28	(17	11)	235	77	85	89	6	59	3	1	9	6	3	.67	7	.251	.361	.462
1990 Detroit	AL	132	472	112	22	2	18	(8	10)	192	75	60	74	7	71	0	1	5	8	2	.80	10	.237	.338	.407

Year Team	Lg	G	AB	H	2B	3B	HR	(Hm	Rd)	TB	R	RBI	TBB	IBB	SO	HBP	SH	SF	SB	CS	SB%	GDP	Avg	OBP	SLG
1991 Detroit	AL	138	470	131	26	2	23	(15	8)	230	94	78	90	6	45	2	2	8	4	2	.67	3	.279	.391	.489
1992 Detroit	AL	130	453	126	26	0	19	(11	8)	209	77	71	81	5	46	1	5	4	6	4	.60	9	.278	.386	.461
1993 Detroit	AL	119	383	111	32	1	9	(5	4)	172	72	67	78	4	46	4	7	4	3	3	.50	5	.290	.412	.449
1994 Detroit	AL	92	322	97	21	2	12	(8	4)	158	67	43	41	4	47	1	3	5	2	0	1.00	8	.301	.377	.491
1995 Detroit	AL	84	249	73	14	0	14	(11	3)	129	36	44	31	4	41	2	0	3	4	0	1.00	6	.293	.372	.518
19 ML YEARS		2390	8570	2369	420	65	244	(146	98)	3651	1386	1084	1197	79	1099	20	89	91	143	75	.66	143	.276	.363	.426

Derrick White

Bats: Right **Throws:** Right **Pos:** 1B **Ht:** 6' 1" **Wt:** 215 **Born:** 10/12/69 **Age:** 26

							BATTING													BASERUNNING				PERCENTAGES		
Year Team	Lg	G	AB	H	2B	3B	HR	(Hm	Rd)	TB	R	RBI	TBB	IBB	SO	HBP	SH	SF	SB	CS	SB%	GDP	Avg	OBP	SLG
1991 Jamestown	A	72	271	89	10	4	6	--	--	125	46	49	40	0	46	7	0	2	8	3	.73	8	.328	.425	.461
1992 Harrisburg	AA	134	495	137	19	2	13	--	--	199	63	81	40	3	73	7	0	2	17	3	.85	16	.277	.338	.402
1993 W. Palm Bch	A	6	25	5	0	0	0	--	--	5	1	1	1	0	2	0	0	0	2	0	1.00	0	.200	.231	.200
Ottawa	AAA	67	249	70	15	1	4	--	--	99	32	29	20	2	52	3	0	1	10	7	.59	10	.281	.341	.398
Harrisburg	AA	21	79	18	1	0	2	--	--	25	14	12	5	0	17	2	0	1	2	0	1.00	2	.228	.287	.316
1994 Ottawa	AAA	47	99	21	4	0	0	--	--	25	13	9	8	1	25	1	1	1	4	1	.80	3	.212	.275	.253
Portland	AA	74	264	71	13	2	4	--	--	100	39	34	28	1	52	3	0	2	14	7	.67	5	.269	.343	.379
1995 Toledo	AAA	87	309	82	15	3	14	--	--	145	50	49	29	3	65	4	0	4	6	6	.50	12	.265	.332	.469
1993 Montreal	NL	17	49	11	3	0	2	(1	1)	20	6	4	2	1	12	1	0	0	2	0	1.00	1	.224	.269	.408
1995 Detroit	AL	39	48	9	2	0	0	(0	0)	11	3	2	0	0	7	0	0	0	1	0	1.00	1	.188	.188	.229
2 ML YEARS		56	97	20	5	0	2	(1	1)	31	9	6	2	1	19	1	0	0	3	0	1.00	2	.206	.230	.320

Devon White

Bats: Both **Throws:** Right **Pos:** CF **Ht:** 6' 2" **Wt:** 190 **Born:** 12/29/62 **Age:** 33

							BATTING													BASERUNNING				PERCENTAGES		
Year Team	Lg	G	AB	H	2B	3B	HR	(Hm	Rd)	TB	R	RBI	TBB	IBB	SO	HBP	SH	SF	SB	CS	SB%	GDP	Avg	OBP	SLG
1985 California	AL	21	7	1	0	0	0	(0	0)	1	7	0	1	0	3	1	0	0	3	1	.75	0	.143	.333	.143
1986 California	AL	29	51	12	1	1	1	(0	1)	18	8	3	6	0	8	0	0	0	6	0	1.00	0	.235	.316	.353
1987 California	AL	159	639	168	33	5	24	(11	13)	283	103	87	39	2	135	2	14	2	32	11	.74	8	.263	.306	.443
1988 California	AL	122	455	118	22	2	11	(3	8)	177	76	51	23	1	84	2	5	1	17	8	.68	5	.259	.297	.389
1989 California	AL	156	636	156	18	13	12	(9	3)	236	86	56	31	3	129	2	7	2	44	16	.73	12	.245	.282	.371
1990 California	AL	125	443	96	17	3	11	(5	6)	152	57	44	44	5	116	3	10	3	21	6	.78	6	.217	.290	.343
1991 Toronto	AL	156	642	181	40	10	17	(9	8)	292	110	60	55	1	135	7	5	6	33	10	.77	7	.282	.342	.455
1992 Toronto	AL	153	641	159	26	7	17	(7	10)	250	98	60	47	0	133	5	0	3	37	4	.90	9	.248	.303	.390
1993 Toronto	AL	146	598	163	42	6	15	(10	5)	262	116	52	57	1	127	7	3	3	34	4	**.89**	3	.273	.341	.438
1994 Toronto	AL	100	403	109	24	6	13	(5	8)	184	67	49	21	3	80	5	4	2	11	3	.79	4	.270	.313	.457
1995 Toronto	AL	101	427	121	23	5	10	(4	6)	184	61	53	29	1	97	5	1	3	11	2	.85	5	.283	.334	.431
11 ML YEARS		1268	4942	1284	246	58	131	(63	68)	2039	789	515	353	17	1047	39	49	25	249	65	.79	59	.260	.313	.413

Gabe White

Pitches: Left **Bats:** Left **Pos:** RP **Ht:** 6' 2" **Wt:** 200 **Born:** 11/20/71 **Age:** 24

						HOW MUCH HE PITCHED				WHAT HE GAVE UP										THE RESULTS				
Year Team	Lg	G	GS	CG	GF	IP	BFP	H	R	ER	HR	SH	SF	HB	TBB	IBB	SO	WP	Bk	W	L	Pct.	ShO	Sv	ERA
1990 Expos	R	11	11	1	0	57.1	233	50	21	20	3	1	1	3	12	0	42	5	1	4	2	.667	0	0	3.14
1991 Sumter	A	24	24	5	0	149	626	129	73	54	7	7	6	5	53	0	138	8	0	6	9	.400	0	0	3.26
1992 Rockford	A	27	27	7	0	187	774	148	73	59	10	9	4	11	61	0	176	9	9	14	8	.636	0	0	2.84
1993 Harrisburg	AA	16	16	2	0	100	394	80	30	24	4	1	1	2	28	0	80	5	2	7	2	.778	1	0	2.16
Ottawa	AAA	6	6	1	0	40.1	165	38	15	14	3	0	1	1	6	0	28	2	0	2	1	.667	1	0	3.12
1994 W. Palm Bch	A	1	1	0	0	6	20	2	2	1	0	0	0	0	1	0	4	1	0	1	0	1.000	0	0	1.50
Ottawa	AAA	14	14	0	0	73	320	77	49	41	11	2	3	2	28	2	63	2	0	8	3	.727	0	0	5.05
1995 Ottawa	AAA	12	12	0	0	62.1	264	58	31	27	10	1	4	4	17	0	37	2	1	2	3	.400	0	0	3.90
1994 Montreal	NL	7	1	0	2	23.2	106	24	16	16	4	1	1	1	11	0	17	0	0	1	1	.500	0	0	6.08
1995 Montreal	NL	19	1	0	8	25.2	115	26	21	20	7	2	3	1	9	0	25	0	0	1	2	.333	0	0	7.01
2 ML YEARS		26	6	0	10	49.1	221	50	37	36	11	3	4	2	20	0	42	0	0	2	3	.400	0	0	6.57

Rick White

Pitches: Right **Bats:** Right **Pos:** SP/RP **Ht:** 6' 4" **Wt:** 215 **Born:** 12/23/68 **Age:** 27

						HOW MUCH HE PITCHED				WHAT HE GAVE UP										THE RESULTS				
Year Team	Lg	G	GS	CG	GF	IP	BFP	H	R	ER	HR	SH	SF	HB	TBB	IBB	SO	WP	Bk	W	L	Pct.	ShO	Sv	ERA
1990 Pirates	R	7	6	0	0	35.2	142	26	11	2	0	1	1	2	4	0	27	2	2	3	1	.750	0	0	0.50
Welland	A	9	5	1	1	38.2	165	38	19	14	2	0	2	2	14	2	43	4	0	1	4	.200	0	0	3.26
1991 Augusta	A	34	0	0	18	63	280	68	26	21	2	0	3	1	18	2	50	4	3	4	4	.500	0	6	3.00
Salem	A	13	5	1	4	46.1	189	41	27	24	2	3	1	0	9	3	36	2	0	2	3	.400	0	1	4.66
1992 Salem	A	18	18	5	0	120.2	490	116	58	51	15	2	4	5	24	1	70	5	0	7	9	.438	0	0	3.80
Carolina	AA	10	10	1	0	57.2	247	59	32	27	8	2	1	3	18	1	45	6	0	1	7	.125	0	0	4.21

Year	Team	Lg	G	GS	CG	GF	IP	BFP	H	R	ER	HR	SH	SF	HB	TBB	IBB	SO	WP	Bk	W	L	Pct.	ShO	Sv	ERA
1993	Carolina	AA	12	12	1	0	69.1	275	59	29	27	5	2	2	4	12	0	52	4	1	4	3	.571	0	0	3.50
	Buffalo	AAA	7	3	0	1	28	117	25	13	11	1	2	0	1	8	0	16	1	0	0	3	.000	0	0	3.54
1995	Calgary	AAA	14	11	1	1	79.1	338	97	40	37	13	0	4	3	10	0	56	2	0	6	4	.600	0	0	4.20
1994	Pittsburgh	NL	43	5	0	23	75.1	317	79	35	32	9	7	5	6	17	3	38	2	2	4	5	.444	0	6	3.82
1995	Pittsburgh	NL	15	9	0	2	55	247	66	33	29	3	3	3	2	18	0	29	2	0	2	3	.400	0	0	4.75
	2 ML YEARS		58	14	0	25	130.1	564	145	68	61	12	10	8	8	35	3	67	4	2	6	8	.429	0	6	4.21

Rondell White

Bats: Right **Throws:** Right **Pos:** CF **Ht:** 6' 1" **Wt:** 205 **Born:** 2/23/72 **Age:** 24

								BATTING											BASERUNNING				PERCENTAGES		
Year	Team	Lg	G	AB	H	2B	3B	HR	(Hm | Rd)	TB	R	RBI	TBB	IBB	SO	HBP	SH	SF	SB	CS	SB%	GDP	Avg	OBP	SLG
1993	Montreal	NL	23	73	19	3	1	2	(1 | 1)	30	9	15	7	0	16	0	2	1	1	2	.33	2	.260	.321	.411
1994	Montreal	NL	40	97	27	10	1	2	(1 | 1)	45	16	13	9	0	18	3	0	0	1	1	.50	1	.278	.358	.464
1995	Montreal	NL	130	474	140	33	4	13	(6 | 7)	220	87	57	41	1	87	6	0	4	25	5	.83	11	.295	.356	.464
	3 ML YEARS		193	644	186	46	6	17	(8 | 9)	295	112	85	57	1	121	9	2	5	27	8	.77	14	.289	.352	.458

Mark Whiten

Bats: Both **Throws:** Right **Pos:** RF **Ht:** 6' 3" **Wt:** 235 **Born:** 11/25/66 **Age:** 29

								BATTING											BASERUNNING				PERCENTAGES		
Year	Team	Lg	G	AB	H	2B	3B	HR	(Hm	Rd)	TB	R	RBI	TBB	IBB	SO	HBP	SH	SF	SB	CS	SB%	GDP	Avg	OBP	SLG
1995	Pawtucket *	AAA	28	102	29	3	1	4	--	--	46	19	13	19	0	30	0	0	0	4	2	.67	3	.284	.397	.451
1990	Toronto	AL	33	88	24	1	1	2	(1	1)	33	12	7	7	0	14	0	1	0	2	0	1.00	2	.273	.323	.375
1991	Cle-Tor	AL	116	407	99	18	7	9	(4	5)	158	46	45	30	2	85	3	0	5	4	3	.57	13	.243	.297	.388
1992	Cleveland	AL	148	508	129	19	4	9	(6	3)	183	73	43	72	10	102	2	3	3	16	12	.57	12	.254	.347	.360
1993	St. Louis	NL	152	562	142	13	4	25	(12	13)	238	81	99	58	9	110	2	0	4	15	8	.65	11	.253	.323	.423
1994	St. Louis	NL	92	334	98	18	2	14	(6	8)	162	57	53	37	9	75	1	0	2	10	5	.67	8	.293	.364	.485
1995	Bos-Phi		92	320	77	13	1	12	(5	7)	128	51	47	39	1	86	1	0	1	8	0	1.00	9	.241	.324	.400
1991	Cleveland	AL	70	258	66	14	4	7	(2	5)	109	34	26	19	1	50	2	0	2	4	2	.67	8	.256	.310	.422
	Toronto	AL	46	149	33	4	3	2	(2	0)	49	12	19	11	1	35	1	0	3	0	1	.00	5	.221	.274	.329
1995	Boston	AL	32	108	20	3	0	1	(0	1)	26	13	10	8	0	23	0	0	1	1	0	1.00	5	.185	.239	.241
	Philadelphia	NL	60	212	57	10	1	11	(5	6)	102	38	37	31	1	63	1	0	0	7	0	1.00	4	.269	.365	.481
	6 ML YEARS		633	2219	569	82	19	71	(34	37)	902	320	294	243	31	472	9	3	16	55	28	.66	55	.256	.330	.406

Matt Whiteside

Pitches: Right **Bats:** Right **Pos:** RP **Ht:** 6' 0" **Wt:** 205 **Born:** 8/8/67 **Age:** 28

			HOW MUCH HE PITCHED						WHAT HE GAVE UP										THE RESULTS					
Year	Team	Lg	G	GS	CG	GF	IP	BFP	H	R	ER	HR	SH	SF	HB	TBB	IBB	SO	WP	Bk	W	L	Pct.	ShO	Sv	ERA
1992	Texas	AL	20	0	0	8	28	118	26	8	6	1	0	1	0	11	2	13	2	0	1	1	.500	0	4	1.93
1993	Texas	AL	60	0	0	10	73	305	78	37	35	7	2	1	1	23	6	39	0	2	2	1	.667	0	1	4.32
1994	Texas	AL	47	0	0	16	61	272	68	40	34	6	3	2	1	28	3	37	1	0	2	2	.500	0	1	5.02
1995	Texas	AL	40	0	0	18	53	223	48	24	24	5	2	3	1	19	2	46	4	0	5	4	.556	0	3	4.08
	4 ML YEARS		167	0	0	52	215	918	220	109	99	19	7	7	3	81	13	135	7	2	10	8	.556	0	9	4.14

Sean Whiteside

Pitches: Left **Bats:** Left **Pos:** RP **Ht:** 6' 4" **Wt:** 190 **Born:** 4/19/71 **Age:** 25

			HOW MUCH HE PITCHED						WHAT HE GAVE UP										THE RESULTS					
Year	Team	Lg	G	GS	CG	GF	IP	BFP	H	R	ER	HR	SH	SF	HB	TBB	IBB	SO	WP	Bk	W	L	Pct.	ShO	Sv	ERA
1992	Niagara Fal	A	15	11	0	0	69.2	289	54	26	19	2	1	2	0	24	0	72	7	5	8	4	.667	0	0	2.45
1993	Fayetteville	A	24	16	0	4	100.2	443	113	68	52	8	0	5	3	41	0	85	18	0	3	5	.375	0	0	4.65
1994	Lakeland	A	13	0	0	6	31.1	126	21	6	4	1	0	0	0	12	0	39	4	0	0	2	.000	0	2	1.15
	Trenton	AA	25	0	0	16	36.2	155	26	13	10	2	2	2	1	15	2	31	4	1	2	2	.500	0	5	2.45
1995	Jacksonville	AA	27	1	0	4	33.1	148	34	17	14	4	2	3	0	20	4	17	4	0	2	0	1.000	0	0	3.78
1995	Detroit	AL	2	0	0	0	3.2	22	7	6	6	1	0	2	0	4	1	2	1	0	0	0	.000	0	0	14.73

Darrell Whitmore

Bats: Left **Throws:** Right **Pos:** CF **Ht:** 6' 1" **Wt:** 210 **Born:** 11/18/68 **Age:** 27

								BATTING											BASERUNNING				PERCENTAGES		
Year	Team	Lg	G	AB	H	2B	3B	HR	(Hm | Rd)	TB	R	RBI	TBB	IBB	SO	HBP	SH	SF	SB	CS	SB%	GDP	Avg	OBP	SLG
1993	Florida	NL	76	250	51	8	2	4	(3 | 1)	75	24	19	10	0	72	5	2	0	4	2	.67	8	.204	.249	.300
1994	Florida	NL	9	22	5	1	0	0	(0 | 0)	6	1	0	3	0	5	0	0	0	0	1	.00	0	.227	.320	.273
1995	Florida	NL	27	58	11	2	0	1	(1 | 0)	16	6	2	5	0	15	0	1	1	0	0	.00	1	.190	.250	.276
	3 ML YEARS		112	330	67	11	2	5	(4 | 1)	97	31	21	18	0	92	5	3	1	4	3	.57	9	.203	.254	.294

Kevin Wickander

Pitches: Left **Bats:** Left **Pos:** RP **Ht:** 6' 3" **Wt:** 200 **Born:** 1/4/65 **Age:** 31

		HOW MUCH HE PITCHED						WHAT HE GAVE UP										THE RESULTS				
Year Team	Lg	G	GS	CG	GF	IP	BFP	H	R	ER	HR	SH	SF	HB	TBB	IBB	SO	WP	Bk	W	L	Pct.	ShO	Sv	ERA
1995 Toledo *	AAA	16	0	0	3	12.2	52	11	3	3	1	0	1	1	5	0	8	0	0	2	1	.667	0	1	2.13
1989 Cleveland	AL	2	0	0	1	2.2	15	6	1	1	0	0	0	0	2	1	0	0	0	0	0	.000	0	0	3.38
1990 Cleveland	AL	10	0	0	3	12.1	53	14	6	5	0	0	2	1	4	0	10	0	0	0	1	.000	0	0	3.65
1992 Cleveland	AL	44	0	0	10	41	187	39	14	14	1	2	2	4	28	3	38	1	1	2	0	1.000	0	0	3.07
1993 Cle-Cin		44	0	0	9	34	170	47	27	23	8	1	0	2	22	1	23	5	1	1	0	1.000	0	0	6.09
1995 Det-Mil	AL	29	0	0	9	23.1	99	19	6	5	1	1	2	1	12	5	11	1	1	0	0	.000	0	1	1.93
1993 Cleveland	AL	11	0	0	1	8.2	44	15	7	4	3	0	0	0	3	0	3	1	0	0	0	.000	0	0	4.15
Cincinnati	NL	33	0	0	8	25.1	126	32	20	19	5	1	0	2	19	1	20	4	1	1	0	1.000	0	0	6.75
1995 Detroit	AL	21	0	0	7	17.1	77	18	6	5	1	0	1	1	9	4	9	1	1	0	0	.000	0	1	2.60
Milwaukee	AL	8	0	0	2	6	22	1	0	0	0	1	1	0	3	1	2	0	0	0	0	.000	0	0	0.00
5 ML YEARS		129	0	0	32	113.1	524	125	54	48	10	4	6	8	68	10	82	7	3	3	1	.750	0	2	3.81

Bob Wickman

Pitches: Right **Bats:** Right **Pos:** RP **Ht:** 6' 1" **Wt:** 212 **Born:** 2/6/69 **Age:** 27

		HOW MUCH HE PITCHED						WHAT HE GAVE UP										THE RESULTS				
Year Team	Lg	G	GS	CG	GF	IP	BFP	H	R	ER	HR	SH	SF	HB	TBB	IBB	SO	WP	Bk	W	L	Pct.	ShO	Sv	ERA
1992 New York	AL	8	8	0	0	50.1	213	51	25	23	2	1	3	2	20	0	21	3	0	6	1	.857	0	0	4.11
1993 New York	AL	41	19	1	9	140	629	156	82	72	13	4	1	5	69	7	70	2	0	14	4	.778	1	4	4.63
1994 New York	AL	53	0	0	19	70	286	54	26	24	3	0	5	1	27	3	56	2	0	5	4	.556	0	6	3.09
1995 New York	AL	63	1	0	14	80	347	77	38	36	6	4	1	5	33	3	51	2	0	2	4	.333	0	1	4.05
4 ML YEARS		165	28	1	42	340.1	1475	338	171	155	24	9	10	13	149	13	198	9	0	27	13	.675	1	11	4.10

Chris Widger

Bats: Right **Throws:** Right **Pos:** C **Ht:** 6' 3" **Wt:** 195 **Born:** 5/21/71 **Age:** 25

		BATTING															BASERUNNING				PERCENTAGES		
Year Team	Lg	G	AB	H	2B	3B	HR	(Hm	Rd)	TB	R	RBI	TBB	IBB	SO	HBP	SH	SF	SB	CS	SB%	GDP	Avg	OBP	SLG
1992 Bellingham	A	51	166	43	7	2	5	--	--	69	28	30	22	0	36	1	0	5	8	1	.89	4	.259	.340	.416
1993 Riverside	A	97	360	95	28	2	9	--	--	154	43	58	19	0	64	3	3	4	5	4	.56	8	.264	.303	.428
1994 Jacksonvlle	AA	116	388	101	15	3	16	--	--	170	58	59	39	4	69	5	0	2	8	7	.53	7	.260	.334	.438
1995 Tacoma	AAA	50	174	48	11	1	9	--	--	88	29	21	9	0	29	0	1	0	0	0	.00	4	.276	.311	.506
1995 Seattle	AL	23	45	9	0	0	1	(1	0)	12	2	2	1	0	11	0	0	1	0	0	.00	0	.200	.245	.267

Rick Wilkins

Bats: Left **Throws:** Right **Pos:** C **Ht:** 6' 2" **Wt:** 215 **Born:** 6/4/67 **Age:** 29

		BATTING															BASERUNNING				PERCENTAGES		
Year Team	Lg	G	AB	H	2B	3B	HR	(Hm	Rd)	TB	R	RBI	TBB	IBB	SO	HBP	SH	SF	SB	CS	SB%	GDP	Avg	OBP	SLG
1995 Jackson *	AA	4	11	0	0	0	0	--	--	0	0	0	3	0	2	0	0	0	0	0	.00	0	.000	.214	.000
Tucson *	AAA	4	12	4	0	0	0	--	--	4	0	4	2	0	0	0	0	1	0	0	.00	0	.333	.400	.333
1991 Chicago	NL	86	203	45	9	0	6	(2	4)	72	21	22	19	2	56	6	7	0	3	3	.50	3	.222	.307	.355
1992 Chicago	NL	83	244	66	9	1	8	(3	5)	101	20	22	28	7	53	0	1	0	0	2	.00	6	.270	.344	.414
1993 Chicago	NL	136	446	135	23	1	30	(10	20)	250	78	73	50	13	99	3	0	1	2	1	.67	6	.303	.376	.561
1994 Chicago	NL	100	313	71	25	2	7	(4	3)	121	44	39	40	5	86	2	1	2	4	3	.57	3	.227	.317	.387
1995 ChN-Hou	NL	65	202	41	3	0	7	(3	4)	65	30	19	46	2	61	1	0	2	0	0	.00	8	.203	.351	.322
1995 Chicago	NL	50	162	31	2	0	6	(3	3)	51	24	14	36	1	51	1	0	1	0	0	.00	8	.191	.340	.315
Houston	NL	15	40	10	1	0	1	(0	1)	14	6	5	10	1	10	0	0	1	0	0	.00	1	.250	.392	.350
5 ML YEARS		470	1408	358	69	4	58	(22	36)	609	193	175	183	29	355	12	9	6	9	9	.50	27	.254	.344	.433

Bernie Williams

Bats: Both **Throws:** Right **Pos:** CF **Ht:** 6' 2" **Wt:** 205 **Born:** 9/13/68 **Age:** 27

		BATTING															BASERUNNING				PERCENTAGES		
Year Team	Lg	G	AB	H	2B	3B	HR	(Hm | Rd)	TB	R	RBI	TBB	IBB	SO	HBP	SH	SF	SB	CS	SB%	GDP	Avg	OBP	SLG
1991 New York	AL	85	320	76	19	4	3	(1 | 2)	112	43	34	48	0	57	1	2	3	10	5	.67	4	.238	.336	.350
1992 New York	AL	62	261	73	14	2	5	(3 | 2)	106	39	26	29	1	36	1	2	0	7	6	.54	5	.280	.354	.406
1993 New York	AL	139	567	152	31	4	12	(5 | 7)	227	67	68	53	4	106	4	1	3	9	9	.50	17	.268	.333	.400
1994 New York	AL	108	408	118	29	1	12	(4 | 8)	185	80	57	61	2	54	3	1	2	16	9	.64	11	.289	.384	.453
1995 New York	AL	144	563	173	29	9	18	(7 | 11)	274	93	82	75	1	98	5	2	3	8	6	.57	12	.307	.392	.487
5 ML YEARS		538	2119	592	122	20	50	(20 | 30)	904	322	267	266	8	351	14	8	11	50	35	.59	49	.279	.362	.427

Brian Williams

Pitches: Right **Bats:** Right **Pos:** RP/SP **Ht:** 6' 2" **Wt:** 225 **Born:** 2/15/69 **Age:** 27

		HOW MUCH HE PITCHED						WHAT HE GAVE UP										THE RESULTS				
Year Team	Lg	G	GS	CG	GF	IP	BFP	H	R	ER	HR	SH	SF	HB	TBB	IBB	SO	WP	Bk	W	L	Pct.	ShO	Sv	ERA
1991 Houston	NL	2	2	0	0	12	49	11	5	5	2	0	0	1	4	0	4	0	0	1	0	1.000	0	0	3.75
1992 Houston	NL	16	16	0	0	96.1	413	92	44	42	10	7	3	0	42	1	54	2	1	7	6	.538	0	0	3.92
1993 Houston	NL	42	5	0	12	82	357	76	48	44	7	5	3	4	38	4	56	9	2	4	4	.500	0	3	4.83

Year	Team	Lg	G	GS	CG	GF	IP	BFP	H	R	ER	HR	SH	SF	HB	TBB	IBB	SO	WP	Bk	W	L	Pct.	ShO	Sv	ERA
1994	Houston	NL	20	13	0	2	78.1	384	112	64	50	9	7	5	4	41	4	49	3	1	6	5	.545	0	0	5.74
1995	San Diego	NL	44	6	0	7	72	337	79	54	48	3	7	1	8	38	4	75	7	1	3	10	.231	0	0	6.00
5	ML YEARS		124	42	0	21	340.2	1540	370	215	189	31	26	12	17	163	13	238	21	5	20	26	.435	0	3	4.99

Eddie Williams

Bats: Right **Throws:** Right **Pos:** 1B **Ht:** 6' 0" **Wt:** 210 **Born:** 11/1/64 **Age:** 31

Year	Team	Lg	G	AB	H	2B	3B	HR	(Hm	Rd)	TB	R	RBI	TBB	IBB	SO	HBP	SH	SF	SB	CS	SB%	GDP	Avg	OBP	SLG
1986	Cleveland	AL	5	7	1	0	0	0	(0	0)	1	2	1	0	0	3	0	0	0	0	0	.00	0	.143	.143	.143
1987	Cleveland	AL	22	64	11	4	0	1	(0	1)	18	9	4	9	0	19	1	0	1	0	0	.00	2	.172	.280	.281
1988	Cleveland	AL	10	21	4	0	0	0	(0	0)	4	3	1	0	0	3	1	1	0	0	0	.00	1	.190	.227	.190
1989	Chicago	AL	66	201	55	8	0	3	(2	1)	72	25	10	18	3	31	4	3	3	1	2	.33	4	.274	.341	.358
1990	San Diego	NL	14	42	12	3	0	3	(1	2)	24	5	4	5	2	6	0	0	0	0	1	.00	1	.286	.362	.571
1994	San Diego	NL	49	175	58	11	1	11	(5	6)	104	32	42	15	1	26	3	2	1	0	1	.00	10	.331	.392	.594
1995	San Diego	NL	97	296	77	11	1	12	(4	8)	126	35	47	23	0	47	4	0	2	0	0	.00	21	.260	.320	.426
7	ML YEARS		263	806	218	37	2	30	(12	18)	349	111	109	70	6	135	13	6	7	1	4	.20	39	.270	.336	.433

George Williams

Bats: Both **Throws:** Right **Pos:** C **Ht:** 5'10" **Wt:** 190 **Born:** 4/22/69 **Age:** 27

Year	Team	Lg	G	AB	H	2B	3B	HR	(Hm	Rd)	TB	R	RBI	TBB	IBB	SO	HBP	SH	SF	SB	CS	SB%	GDP	Avg	OBP	SLG
1991	Sou. Oregon	A	55	174	41	10	0	2	--	--	57	24	24	38	0	36	5	3	1	9	4	.69	1	.236	.385	.328
1992	Madison	A	115	349	106	18	2	5	--	--	143	56	42	76	0	53	8	5	1	9	5	.64	10	.304	.438	.410
1993	Huntsville	AA	124	434	128	26	2	14	--	--	200	80	77	67	0	66	14	1	6	6	3	.67	10	.295	.401	.461
1994	W. Michigan	A	63	221	67	20	1	8	--	--	113	40	48	44	3	47	8	1	0	6	3	.67	3	.303	.436	.511
1995	Edmonton	AAA	81	290	90	20	0	13	--	--	149	53	55	50	6	52	2	3	2	0	4	.00	8	.310	.413	.514
1995	Oakland	AL	29	79	23	5	1	3	(1	2)	39	13	14	11	2	21	2	0	2	0	0	.00	1	.291	.383	.494

Gerald Williams

Bats: Right **Throws:** Right **Pos:** LF/RF **Ht:** 6' 2" **Wt:** 190 **Born:** 8/10/66 **Age:** 29

Year	Team	Lg	G	AB	H	2B	3B	HR	(Hm	Rd)	TB	R	RBI	TBB	IBB	SO	HBP	SH	SF	SB	CS	SB%	GDP	Avg	OBP	SLG
1992	New York	AL	15	27	8	2	0	3	(2	1)	19	7	6	0	0	3	0	0	0	2	0	1.00	0	.296	.296	.704
1993	New York	AL	42	67	10	2	3	0	(0	0)	18	11	6	1	0	14	2	0	1	2	0	1.00	2	.149	.183	.269
1994	New York	AL	57	86	25	8	0	4	(2	2)	45	19	13	4	0	17	0	0	1	1	3	.25	6	.291	.319	.523
1995	New York	AL	100	182	45	18	2	6	(4	2)	85	33	28	22	1	34	1	0	3	4	2	.67	4	.247	.327	.467
4	ML YEARS		214	362	88	30	5	13	(8	5)	167	70	53	27	1	68	3	0	5	9	5	.64	12	.243	.297	.461

Matt Williams

Bats: Right **Throws:** Right **Pos:** 3B **Ht:** 6' 2" **Wt:** 216 **Born:** 11/28/65 **Age:** 30

Year	Team	Lg	G	AB	H	2B	3B	HR	(Hm	Rd)	TB	R	RBI	TBB	IBB	SO	HBP	SH	SF	SB	CS	SB%	GDP	Avg	OBP	SLG
1995	San Jose *	A	4	11	2	0	0	1	--	--	5	2	2	0	0	3	1	0	0	0	0	.00	0	.182	.250	.455
1987	San Francisco	NL	84	245	46	9	2	8	(5	3)	83	28	21	16	4	68	1	3	1	4	3	.57	5	.188	.240	.339
1988	San Francisco	NL	52	156	32	6	1	8	(7	1)	64	17	19	8	0	41	2	3	1	0	1	.00	7	.205	.251	.410
1989	San Francisco	NL	84	292	59	18	1	18	(10	8)	133	31	50	14	1	72	2	1	2	1	2	.33	6	.202	.242	.455
1990	San Francisco	NL	159	617	171	27	2	33	(20	13)	301	87	**122**	33	9	138	7	2	5	7	4	.64	13	.277	.319	.488
1991	San Francisco	NL	157	589	158	24	5	34	(17	17)	294	72	98	33	6	128	6	0	7	5	5	.50	11	.268	.310	.499
1992	San Francisco	NL	146	529	120	13	5	20	(9	11)	203	58	66	39	11	109	6	0	2	7	7	.50	15	.227	.286	.384
1993	San Francisco	NL	145	579	170	33	4	38	(19	19)	325	105	110	27	4	80	4	0	9	1	3	.25	12	.294	.325	.561
1994	San Francisco	NL	112	445	119	16	3	**43**	(20	23)	270	74	96	33	7	87	2	0	3	1	0	1.00	11	.267	.319	.607
1995	San Francisco	NL	76	283	95	17	1	23	(9	14)	183	53	65	30	8	58	2	0	3	2	0	1.00	8	.336	.399	.647
9	ML YEARS		1015	3735	970	163	24	225	(116	109)	1856	525	647	233	50	781	32	9	33	28	25	.53	87	.260	.306	.497

Mike Williams

Pitches: Right **Bats:** Right **Pos:** RP/SP **Ht:** 6' 3" **Wt:** 197 **Born:** 7/29/68 **Age:** 27

Year	Team	Lg	G	GS	CG	GF	IP	BFP	H	R	ER	HR	SH	SF	HB	TBB	IBB	SO	WP	Bk	W	L	Pct.	ShO	Sv	ERA
1995	Scrantn-WB *	AAA	3	3	1	0	9.2	39	8	5	5	0	0	0	0	2	0	8	0	1	0	1	.000	0	0	4.66
1992	Philadelphia	NL	5	5	1	0	28.2	121	29	20	17	3	1	1	0	7	0	5	0	0	1	1	.500	0	0	5.34
1993	Philadelphia	NL	17	4	0	2	51	221	50	32	30	5	1	0	0	22	2	33	2	0	1	3	.250	0	0	5.29
1994	Philadelphia	NL	12	8	0	2	50.1	222	61	31	28	7	2	3	0	20	3	29	0	0	2	4	.333	0	0	5.01
1995	Philadelphia	NL	33	8	0	7	87.2	367	78	37	32	10	5	3	3	29	2	57	7	0	3	3	.500	0	0	3.29
4	ML YEARS		67	25	1	11	217.2	931	218	120	107	25	9	7	3	78	7	124	9	0	7	11	.389	0	0	4.42

Mitch Williams

Pitches: Left **Bats:** Left **Pos:** RP **Ht:** 6' 4" **Wt:** 205 **Born:** 11/17/64 **Age:** 31

Year	Team	Lg	G	GS	CG	GF	IP	BFP	H	R	ER	HR	SH	SF	HB	TBB	IBB	SO	WP	Bk	W	L	Pct.	ShO	Sv	ERA
1986	Texas	AL	80	0	0	38	98	435	69	39	39	8	1	3	11	79	8	90	5	5	8	6	.571	0	8	3.58
1987	Texas	AL	85	1	0	32	108.2	469	63	47	39	9	4	3	7	94	7	129	4	2	8	6	.571	0	6	3.23
1988	Texas	AL	67	0	0	51	68	296	48	38	35	4	3	4	6	47	3	61	5	6	2	7	.222	0	18	4.63
1989	Chicago	NL	76	0	0	61	81.2	365	71	27	24	6	2	5	8	52	4	67	6	4	4	4	.500	0	36	2.64
1990	Chicago	NL	59	2	0	39	66.1	310	60	38	29	4	5	3	1	50	6	55	4	2	1	8	.111	0	16	3.93
1991	Philadelphia	NL	69	0	0	60	88.1	386	56	24	23	4	4	4	8	62	5	84	4	1	12	5	.706	0	30	2.34
1992	Philadelphia	NL	66	0	0	56	81	368	69	39	34	4	8	3	6	64	2	74	5	3	5	8	.385	0	29	3.78
1993	Philadelphia	NL	65	0	0	57	62	281	56	30	23	3	4	2	2	44	1	60	6	0	3	7	.300	0	43	3.34
1994	Houston	NL	25	0	0	18	20	106	21	17	17	4	2	1	1	24	2	21	1	0	1	4	.200	0	6	7.65
1995	California	AL	20	0	0	3	10.2	65	13	10	8	1	0	1	2	21	0	9	2	1	1	2	.333	0	0	6.75
	10 ML YEARS		612	3	0	415	684.2	3081	526	309	271	47	33	29	52	537	38	650	42	24	45	57	.441	0	192	3.56

Reggie Williams

Bats: Both **Throws:** Right **Pos:** LF **Ht:** 6' 1" **Wt:** 189 **Born:** 5/5/66 **Age:** 30

Year	Team	Lg	G	AB	H	2B	3B	HR	(Hm	Rd)	TB	R	RBI	TBB	IBB	SO	HBP	SH	SF	SB	CS	SB%	GDP	Avg	OBP	SLG
1988	Everett	A	60	223	56	8	1	3	--	--	75	52	29	47	0	43	3	0	2	36	10	.78	5	.251	.385	.336
1989	Clinton	A	68	236	46	9	2	3	--	--	68	38	18	29	0	66	3	5	1	14	9	.61	1	.195	.290	.288
	Boise	A	42	153	41	5	1	3	--	--	57	33	14	24	0	29	2	0	1	18	5	.78	2	.268	.372	.373
1990	Quad City	A	58	189	46	11	2	3	--	--	70	50	12	39	0	60	4	2	1	24	6	.80	2	.243	.382	.370
1991	Palm Spring	A	14	44	13	1	0	1	--	--	17	10	2	21	0	15	1	1	0	6	5	.55	0	.295	.530	.386
	Midland	AA	83	319	99	12	3	1	--	--	120	77	30	62	2	67	0	5	3	21	9	.70	3	.310	.419	.376
1992	Edmonton	AAA	139	519	141	26	9	3	--	--	194	96	64	88	1	110	3	7	8	44	14	.76	9	.272	.375	.374
1993	Vancouver	AAA	130	481	132	17	6	2	--	--	167	92	53	88	2	99	5	9	6	50	17	.75	7	.274	.388	.347
1994	Albuquerque	AAA	104	288	90	15	8	4	--	--	133	55	42	33	1	62	0	1	2	21	10	.68	6	.313	.381	.462
1995	Albuquerque	AAA	66	234	73	15	5	6	--	--	116	44	29	30	0	46	1	1	3	6	4	.60	3	.312	.388	.496
1992	California	AL	14	26	6	1	1	0	(0	0)	9	5	2	1	0	10	0	0	0	0	2	.00	0	.231	.259	.346
1995	Los Angeles	NL	15	11	1	0	0	0	(0	0)	1	2	1	2	0	3	0	0	0	0	0	.00	0	.091	.231	.091
	2 ML YEARS		29	37	7	1	1	0	(0	0)	10	7	3	3	0	13	0	0	0	0	2	.00	0	.189	.250	.270

Todd Williams

Pitches: Right **Bats:** Right **Pos:** RP **Ht:** 6' 3" **Wt:** 185 **Born:** 2/13/71 **Age:** 25

Year	Team	Lg	G	GS	CG	GF	IP	BFP	H	R	ER	HR	SH	SF	HB	TBB	IBB	SO	WP	Bk	W	L	Pct.	ShO	Sv	ERA
1991	Great Falls	R	28	0	0	14	53	232	50	26	16	1	0	0	1	24	1	59	4	1	5	2	.714	0	8	2.72
1992	Bakersfield	A	13	0	0	13	15.2	64	11	4	4	1	1	0	0	7	1	11	0	0	0	0	.000	0	9	2.30
	San Antonio	AA	39	0	0	34	44	196	47	17	16	0	4	1	1	23	6	35	3	0	7	4	.636	0	13	3.27
1993	Albuquerque	AAA	65	0	0	50	70.1	321	87	44	39	2	0	1	1	31	6	56	6	0	5	5	.500	0	21	4.99
1994	Albuquerque	AAA	59	0	0	36	72.1	299	78	29	25	5	1	3	6	17	3	30	6	1	4	2	.667	0	13	3.11
1995	Albuquerque	AAA	25	0	0	5	45.1	203	59	21	17	4	1	1	1	15	4	23	1	2	4	1	.800	0	0	3.38
1995	Los Angeles	NL	16	0	0	5	19.1	83	19	11	11	3	3	1	0	7	2	8	0	0	2	2	.500	0	0	5.12

Woody Williams

Pitches: Right **Bats:** Right **Pos:** RP/SP **Ht:** 6' 0" **Wt:** 190 **Born:** 8/19/66 **Age:** 29

Year	Team	Lg	G	GS	CG	GF	IP	BFP	H	R	ER	HR	SH	SF	HB	TBB	IBB	SO	WP	Bk	W	L	Pct.	ShO	Sv	ERA
1995	Syracuse *	AAA	5	1	0	1	7.2	34	5	3	3	0	0	0	0	5	0	13	0	0	0	0	.000	0	1	3.52
1993	Toronto	AL	30	0	0	9	37	172	40	18	18	2	2	1	1	22	3	24	2	1	3	1	.750	0	0	4.38
1994	Toronto	AL	38	0	0	14	59.1	253	44	24	24	5	1	2	2	33	1	56	4	0	1	3	.250	0	0	3.64
1995	Toronto	AL	23	3	0	10	53.2	232	44	23	22	6	2	0	2	28	1	41	0	0	1	2	.333	0	0	3.69
	3 ML YEARS		91	3	0	33	150	657	128	65	64	13	5	3	5	83	5	121	6	1	5	6	.455	0	0	3.84

Carl Willis

Pitches: Right **Bats:** Left **Pos:** RP **Ht:** 6' 4" **Wt:** 213 **Born:** 12/28/60 **Age:** 35

Year	Team	Lg	G	GS	CG	GF	IP	BFP	H	R	ER	HR	SH	SF	HB	TBB	IBB	SO	WP	Bk	W	L	Pct.	ShO	Sv	ERA
1995	Vancouver *	AAA	20	0	0	9	35	154	40	17	16	2	0	2	0	11	2	17	2	0	2	2	.500	0	1	4.11
1984	Det-Cin		17	2	0	5	25.2	113	33	17	17	2	1	0	0	7	2	7	0	0	0	3	.000	0	1	5.96
1985	Cincinnati	NL	11	0	0	6	13.2	69	21	18	14	3	1	2	0	5	0	6	1	0	1	0	1.000	0	1	9.22
1986	Cincinnati	NL	29	0	0	7	52.1	233	54	29	26	4	5	1	1	32	9	24	3	1	1	3	.250	0	4	4.47
1988	Chicago	AL	6	0	0	0	12	55	17	12	11	3	0	1	0	7	1	6	2	0	0	0	.000	0	0	8.25
1991	Minnesota	AL	40	0	0	9	89	355	76	31	26	4	3	4	1	19	2	53	4	1	8	3	.727	0	2	2.63
1992	Minnesota	AL	59	0	0	21	79.1	313	73	25	24	4	2	3	0	11	1	45	2	1	7	3	.700	0	1	2.72

Year	Team	Lg	G	GS	CG	GF	IP	BFP	H	R	ER	HR	SH	SF	HB	TBB	IBB	SO	WP	Bk	W	L	Pct.	ShO	Sv	ERA
1993	Minnesota	AL	53	0	0	21	58	236	56	23	20	2	2	1	0	17	5	44	3	0	3	0	1.000	0	5	3.10
1994	Minnesota	AL	49	0	0	12	59.1	282	89	48	39	6	1	3	0	12	5	37	5	0	2	4	.333	0	3	5.92
1995	Minnesota	AL	3	0	0	0	0.2	12	5	7	7	0	1	0	0	0	0	0	0	0	0	0	.000	0	0	94.50
1984	Detroit	AL	10	2	0	4	16	74	25	13	13	1	0	0	0	5	2	4	0	0	0	2	.000	0	0	7.31
	Cincinnati	NL	7	0	0	1	9.2	39	8	4	4	1	1	0	0	2	0	3	0	0	0	1	.000	0	1	3.72
9 ML YEARS			267	2	0	81	390	1668	424	210	184	28	16	15	2	115	25	222	20	3	22	16	.579	0	13	4.25

Dan Wilson

Bats: Right   **Throws:** Right   **Pos:** C   **Ht:** 6' 3"   **Wt:** 190   **Born:** 3/25/69   **Age:** 27

							BATTING												BASERUNNING				PERCENTAGES		
Year	Team	Lg	G	AB	H	2B	3B	HR	(Hm Rd)	TB	R	RBI	TBB	IBB	SO	HBP	SH	SF	SB	CS	SB%	GDP	Avg	OBP	SLG
1992	Cincinnati	NL	12	25	9	1	0	0	(0 0)	10	2	3	3	0	8	0	0	0	0	0	.00	2	.360	.429	.400
1993	Cincinnati	NL	36	76	17	3	0	0	(0 0)	20	6	8	9	4	16	0	2	1	0	0	.00	2	.224	.302	.263
1994	Seattle	AL	91	282	61	14	2	3	(1 2)	88	24	27	10	0	57	1	8	2	1	2	.33	11	.216	.244	.312
1995	Seattle	AL	119	399	111	22	3	9	(5 4)	166	40	51	33	1	63	2	5	1	2	1	.67	12	.278	.336	.416
4 ML YEARS			258	782	198	40	5	12	(6 6)	284	72	89	55	5	144	3	15	4	3	3	.50	27	.253	.303	.363

Gary Wilson

Pitches: Right   **Bats:** Right   **Pos:** RP   **Ht:** 6' 3"   **Wt:** 190   **Born:** 1/1/70   **Age:** 26

				HOW MUCH HE PITCHED						WHAT HE GAVE UP										THE RESULTS					
Year	Team	Lg	G	GS	CG	GF	IP	BFP	H	R	ER	HR	SH	SF	HB	TBB	IBB	SO	WP	Bk	W	L	Pct.	ShO	Sv	ERA
1992	Welland	A	13	4	0	5	42.1	170	27	9	5	0	0	0	1	13	1	40	1	0	3	2	.600	0	0	1.06
	Augusta	A	7	7	0	0	41.2	177	43	22	17	2	3	3	3	7	0	27	1	1	2	3	.400	0	0	3.67
1993	Salem	A	15	15	0	0	78.1	356	102	58	50	15	1	1	2	25	0	54	3	0	5	5	.500	0	0	5.74
	Augusta	A	20	6	0	4	51	229	66	35	31	4	1	1	3	11	0	42	3	1	3	7	.300	0	0	5.47
1994	Salem	A	6	6	1	0	35	147	41	12	9	2	0	0	0	4	0	26	3	0	3	1	.750	1	0	2.31
	Carolina	AA	22	22	7	0	161.2	654	144	55	46	11	8	5	10	37	0	97	2	0	8	5	.615	2	0	2.56
1995	Calgary	AAA	6	4	0	0	16.1	75	19	16	10	1	1	2	0	9	0	12	2	1	1	2	.333	0	0	5.51
	Carolina	AA	1	1	0	0	4.2	16	0	0	0	0	0	0	0	3	0	5	0	0	0	0	.000	0	0	0.00
1995	Pittsburgh	NL	10	0	0	1	14.1	61	13	8	8	2	0	0	2	5	0	8	1	0	0	1	.000	0	0	5.02

Nigel Wilson

Bats: Left   **Throws:** Left   **Pos:** LF   **Ht:** 6' 1"   **Wt:** 185   **Born:** 1/12/70   **Age:** 26

							BATTING												BASERUNNING				PERCENTAGES		
Year	Team	Lg	G	AB	H	2B	3B	HR	(Hm Rd)	TB	R	RBI	TBB	IBB	SO	HBP	SH	SF	SB	CS	SB%	GDP	Avg	OBP	SLG
1988	St. Cathrns	A	40	103	21	1	2	2	-- --	32	12	11	12	0	32	4	1	1	8	4	.67	0	.204	.308	.311
1989	St. Cathrns	A	42	161	35	5	2	4	-- --	56	17	18	11	0	50	4	1	0	8	2	.80	0	.217	.284	.348
1990	Myrtle Bch	A	110	440	120	23	9	16	-- --	209	77	62	30	3	71	6	2	2	22	12	.65	4	.273	.326	.475
1991	Dunedin	A	119	455	137	18	13	12	-- --	217	64	55	29	4	99	9	4	7	26	11	.70	4	.301	.350	.477
1992	Knoxville	AA	137	521	143	34	7	26	-- --	269	85	69	33	5	137	7	2	2	13	8	.62	2	.274	.325	.516
1993	Edmonton	AAA	96	370	108	26	7	17	-- --	199	66	68	25	7	108	10	1	2	8	3	.73	6	.292	.351	.538
1994	Edmonton	AAA	87	314	97	24	1	12	-- --	159	50	62	22	3	79	10	0	4	2	3	.40	3	.309	.369	.506
1995	Indianapols	AAA	82	304	95	27	3	17	-- --	179	53	51	13	4	95	8	0	1	5	3	.63	2	.313	.356	.589
1993	Florida	NL	7	16	0	0	0	0	(0 0)	0	0	0	0	0	11	0	0	0	0	0	.00	0	.000	.000	.000
1995	Cincinnati	NL	5	7	0	0	0	0	(0 0)	0	0	0	0	0	4	0	0	0	0	0	.00	0	.000	.000	.000
2 ML YEARS			12	23	0	0	0	0	(0 0)	0	0	0	0	0	15	0	0	0	0	0	.00	0	.000	.000	.000

Trevor Wilson

Pitches: Left   **Bats:** Left   **Pos:** SP   **Ht:** 6' 0"   **Wt:** 204   **Born:** 6/7/66   **Age:** 30

				HOW MUCH HE PITCHED						WHAT HE GAVE UP										THE RESULTS					
Year	Team	Lg	G	GS	CG	GF	IP	BFP	H	R	ER	HR	SH	SF	HB	TBB	IBB	SO	WP	Bk	W	L	Pct.	ShO	Sv	ERA
1995	San Jose *	A	2	2	0	0	6.2	29	5	4	1	0	1	0	0	3	0	5	0	0	0	1	.000	0	0	1.35
1988	San Francisco	NL	4	4	0	0	22	96	25	14	10	1	3	1	0	8	0	15	0	1	0	2	.000	0	0	4.09
1989	San Francisco	NL	14	4	0	2	39.1	167	28	20	19	2	3	1	4	24	0	22	0	1	2	3	.400	0	0	4.35
1990	San Francisco	NL	27	17	3	3	110.1	457	87	52	49	11	6	2	1	49	3	66	5	2	8	7	.533	2	0	4.00
1991	San Francisco	NL	44	29	2	6	202	841	173	87	80	13	14	5	5	77	4	139	5	3	13	11	.542	1	0	3.56
1992	San Francisco	NL	26	26	1	0	154	660	152	82	72	18	11	6	6	64	5	88	2	7	8	14	.364	1	0	4.21
1993	San Francisco	NL	22	18	1	1	110	455	110	45	44	8	6	3	6	40	3	57	0	0	7	5	.583	0	0	3.60
1995	San Francisco	NL	17	17	0	0	82.2	354	82	42	36	8	5	2	4	38	1	38	0	1	3	4	.429	0	0	3.92
7 ML YEARS			154	115	7	12	720.1	3031	657	342	310	61	48	20	26	300	16	425	12	15	41	46	.471	4	0	3.87

Dave Winfield

Bats: Right   **Throws:** Right   **Pos:** DH   **Ht:** 6' 6"   **Wt:** 245   **Born:** 10/3/51   **Age:** 44

							BATTING												BASERUNNING				PERCENTAGES		
Year	Team	Lg	G	AB	H	2B	3B	HR	(Hm Rd)	TB	R	RBI	TBB	IBB	SO	HBP	SH	SF	SB	CS	SB%	GDP	Avg	OBP	SLG
1973	San Diego	NL	56	141	39	4	1	3	(2 1)	54	9	12	12	1	19	0	0	1	0	0	.00	5	.277	.331	.383
1974	San Diego	NL	145	498	132	18	4	20	(12 8)	218	57	75	40	2	96	1	0	5	9	7	.56	14	.265	.318	.438

Year	Team	Lg	G	AB	H	2B	3B	HR			TB	R	RBI	BB	IBB	SO	HBP	SH	SF	SB	CS	SB%	GDP	AVG	OBP	SLG
1975	San Diego	NL	143	509	136	20	2	15	(7	8)	205	74	76	69	14	82	3	3	7	23	4	.85	11	.267	.354	.403
1976	San Diego	NL	137	492	139	26	4	13	(4	9)	212	81	69	65	8	78	3	2	5	26	7	.79	14	.283	.366	.431
1977	San Diego	NL	157	615	169	29	7	25	(12	13)	287	104	92	58	10	75	0	0	5	16	7	.70	12	.275	.335	.467
1978	San Diego	NL	158	587	181	30	5	24	(11	13)	293	88	97	55	20	81	2	0	5	21	9	.70	13	.308	.367	.499
1979	San Diego	NL	159	597	184	27	10	34	(16	18)	**333**	97	**118**	85	**24**	71	2	0	2	15	9	.63	9	.308	.395	.558
1980	San Diego	NL	162	558	154	25	6	20	(7	13)	251	89	87	79	14	83	2	0	4	23	7	.77	13	.276	.365	.450
1981	New York	AL	105	388	114	25	1	13	(4	9)	180	52	68	43	3	41	1	1	7	11	1	.92	13	.294	.360	.464
1982	New York	AL	140	539	151	24	8	37	(14	**23**)	302	84	106	45	7	64	0	5	8	5	3	.63	20	.280	.331	.560
1983	New York	AL	152	598	169	26	8	32	(13	19)	307	99	116	58	2	77	2	0	6	15	6	.71	30	.283	.345	.513
1984	New York	AL	141	567	193	34	4	19	(9	10)	292	106	100	53	9	71	0	0	6	6	4	.60	14	.340	.393	.515
1985	New York	AL	155	633	174	34	6	26	(15	11)	298	105	114	52	8	96	0	0	4	19	7	.73	17	.275	.328	.471
1986	New York	AL	154	565	148	31	5	24	(12	12)	261	90	104	77	9	106	2	2	6	5	5	.55	20	.262	.349	.462
1987	New York	AL	156	575	158	22	1	27	(11	16)	263	83	97	76	5	96	0	1	3	5	6	.45	20	.275	.358	.457
1988	New York	AL	149	559	180	37	2	25	(12	13)	296	96	107	69	10	88	2	0	1	9	4	.69	19	.322	.398	.530
1990	New York	AL	132	476	127	21	2	21	(13	8)	215	70	78	52	3	81	2	1	7	0	1	.00	17	.267	.338	.453
1991	California	AL	150	568	149	27	4	28	(13	15)	268	75	86	56	4	109	1	2	6	7	2	.78	21	.262	.326	.472
1992	Toronto	AL	156	583	169	33	3	26	(13	13)	286	92	108	82	10	89	1	1	3	2	3	.40	10	.290	.377	.491
1993	Minnesota	AL	143	547	148	27	2	21	(12	9)	242	72	76	45	2	106	0	0	2	2	3	.40	15	.271	.325	.442
1994	Minnesota	AL	77	294	74	15	3	10	(5	5)	125	35	43	31	5	51	0	1	2	2	1	.67	7	.252	.321	.425
1995	Cleveland	AL	46	115	22	5	0	2	(1	1)	33	11	4	14	2	26	1	0	0	1	0	1.00	5	.191	.285	.287
1990	California	AL	112	414	114	18	2	19	(13	6)	193	63	72	48	3	68	1	1	6	0	1	.00	15	.275	.348	.466
	New York	AL	20	61	13	3	0	2	(0	2)	22	7	6	4	0	13	1	0	1	0	0	.00	2	.213	.269	.361
	22 ML YEARS		2973	11003	3110	540	88	465	(218	247)	5221	1669	1833	1216	172	1686	25	19	95	223	96	.70	319	.283	.353	.475

Bobby Witt

Pitches: Right **Bats:** Right **Pos:** SP   **Ht:** 6' 2" **Wt:** 205 **Born:** 5/11/64 **Age:** 32

			HOW MUCH HE PITCHED						WHAT HE GAVE UP												THE RESULTS					
Year	Team	Lg	G	GS	CG	GF	IP	BFP	H	R	ER	HR	SH	SF	HB	TBB	IBB	SO	WP	Bk	W	L	Pct.	ShO	Sv	ERA
1986	Texas	AL	31	31	0	0	157.2	741	130	104	96	18	3	9	3	**143**	2	174	**22**	3	11	9	.550	0	0	5.48
1987	Texas	AL	26	25	1	0	143	673	114	82	78	10	5	5	3	**140**	1	160	7	2	8	10	.444	0	0	4.91
1988	Texas	AL	22	22	13	0	174.1	736	134	83	76	13	7	6	1	101	2	148	**16**	8	8	10	.444	2	0	3.92
1989	Texas	AL	31	31	5	0	194.1	869	182	123	**111**	14	11	8	2	**114**	3	166	7	4	12	13	.480	1	0	5.14
1990	Texas	AL	33	32	7	1	222	954	197	98	83	12	5	6	4	110	3	221	11	2	17	10	.630	1	0	3.36
1991	Texas	AL	17	16	1	0	88.2	413	84	66	60	4	3	4	1	74	1	82	8	0	3	7	.300	1	0	6.09
1992	Oak-Tex	AL	31	31	0	0	193	848	183	99	92	16	7	10	2	114	2	125	9	1	10	14	.417	0	0	4.29
1993	Oakland	AL	35	33	5	0	220	950	226	112	103	16	9	8	3	91	5	131	8	1	14	13	.519	1	0	4.21
1994	Oakland	AL	24	24	5	0	135.2	618	151	88	76	22	2	7	5	70	4	111	6	1	8	10	.444	3	0	5.04
1995	Fla-Tex		29	29	2	0	172	748	185	87	79	12	7	5	3	68	2	141	7	0	5	11	.313	0	0	4.13
1992	Oakland	AL	6	6	0	0	31.2	140	31	12	12	2	2	2	0	19	1	25	3	0	1	1	.500	0	0	3.41
	Texas	AL	25	25	0	0	161.1	708	152	87	80	14	5	8	2	95	1	100	6	1	9	13	.409	0	0	4.46
1995	Florida	NL	19	19	1	0	110.2	472	104	52	48	8	5	3	2	47	1	95	2	0	2	7	.222	0	0	3.90
	Texas	AL	10	10	1	0	61.1	276	81	35	31	4	2	2	1	21	1	46	5	0	3	4	.429	0	0	4.55
	10 ML YEARS		279	274	39	1	1700.2	7550	1586	942	854	137	59	68	27	1025	25	1459	101	22	96	107	.473	9	0	4.52

Mark Wohlers

Pitches: Right **Bats:** Right **Pos:** RP   **Ht:** 6' 4" **Wt:** 207 **Born:** 1/23/70 **Age:** 26

			HOW MUCH HE PITCHED						WHAT HE GAVE UP												THE RESULTS					
Year	Team	Lg	G	GS	CG	GF	IP	BFP	H	R	ER	HR	SH	SF	HB	TBB	IBB	SO	WP	Bk	W	L	Pct.	ShO	Sv	ERA
1991	Atlanta	NL	17	0	0	4	19.2	89	17	7	7	1	2	1	2	13	3	13	0	0	3	1	.750	0	2	3.20
1992	Atlanta	NL	32	0	0	16	35.1	140	28	11	10	0	5	1	1	14	4	17	1	0	1	2	.333	0	4	2.55
1993	Atlanta	NL	46	0	0	18	48	199	37	25	24	2	5	1	1	22	3	45	0	0	6	2	.750	0	4	4.50
1994	Atlanta	NL	51	0	0	15	51	236	51	35	26	1	4	6	0	33	9	58	2	0	7	2	.778	0	1	4.59
1995	Atlanta	NL	65	0	0	49	64.2	269	51	16	15	2	2	0	1	24	3	90	4	0	7	3	.700	0	25	2.09
	5 ML YEARS		211	0	0	97	218.2	933	184	94	82	6	18	9	5	106	22	223	7	0	24	10	.706	0	32	3.38

Steve Wojciechowski

Pitches: Left **Bats:** Left **Pos:** SP/RP   **Ht:** 6' 2" **Wt:** 195 **Born:** 7/29/70 **Age:** 25

			HOW MUCH HE PITCHED						WHAT HE GAVE UP												THE RESULTS					
Year	Team	Lg	G	GS	CG	GF	IP	BFP	H	R	ER	HR	SH	SF	HB	TBB	IBB	SO	WP	Bk	W	L	Pct.	ShO	Sv	ERA
1991	Sou. Oregon	A	16	11	0	1	67	311	74	45	28	4	4	2	1	29	2	50	6	1	2	5	.286	0	0	3.76
1992	Modesto	A	14	14	0	0	66.1	282	60	32	26	2	2	3	1	27	0	53	5	2	6	3	.667	0	0	3.53
1993	Modesto	A	14	14	1	0	84.2	341	64	29	24	3	3	2	0	36	0	52	1	1	8	2	.800	1	0	2.55
	Huntsville	AA	13	13	1	0	67.2	310	91	50	40	6	1	5	2	30	1	52	5	1	4	6	.400	1	0	5.32
1994	Huntsville	AA	27	26	1	1	177	716	148	72	61	7	7	3	0	62	1	114	10	2	10	5	.667	0	0	3.10
1995	Edmonton	AAA	14	12	2	1	78	320	75	37	32	5	1	4	1	21	0	39	4	2	6	3	.667	1	0	3.69
1995	Oakland	AL	14	7	0	3	48.2	219	51	28	28	7	1	2	1	28	1	13	0	0	2	3	.400	0	0	5.18

Bob Wolcott

Pitches: Right   **Bats:** Right   **Pos:** SP   **Ht:** 6' 0"   **Wt:** 190   **Born:** 9/8/73   **Age:** 22

Year Team	Lg	G	GS	CG	GF	IP	BFP	H	R	ER	HR	SH	SF	HB	TBB	IBB	SO	WP	Bk	W	L	Pct.	ShO	Sv	ERA
1992 Bellingham	A	9	7	0	2	22.1	105	25	18	17	4	0	0	2	19	0	17	3	2	0	1	.000	0	0	6.85
1993 Bellingham	A	15	15	1	0	95.1	386	70	31	28	7	1	2	6	26	1	79	6	1	8	4	.667	0	0	2.64
1994 Calgary	AAA	1	1	0	0	6	25	6	2	2	1	0	0	0	3	0	5	0	0	0	1	.000	0	0	3.00
Riverside	A	26	26	5	0	180.2	761	173	75	57	11	4	4	5	50	4	142	5	0	14	8	.636	1	0	2.84
1995 Port City	AA	12	12	2	0	86	320	60	26	21	6	0	3	3	13	0	53	2	0	7	3	.700	1	0	2.20
Tacoma	AAA	13	13	2	0	79.1	347	94	49	36	10	1	4	5	16	0	43	2	1	6	3	.667	1	0	4.08
1995 Seattle	AL	7	6	0	0	36.2	164	43	18	18	6	0	3	2	14	0	19	0	0	3	2	.600	0	0	4.42

Brad Woodall

Pitches: Left   **Bats:** Both   **Pos:** RP   **Ht:** 6' 0"   **Wt:** 175   **Born:** 6/25/69   **Age:** 27

Year Team	Lg	G	GS	CG	GF	IP	BFP	H	R	ER	HR	SH	SF	HB	TBB	IBB	SO	WP	Bk	W	L	Pct.	ShO	Sv	ERA
1991 Idaho Falls	R	28	0	0	0	39.1	160	29	9	6	1	2	1	0	19	1	57	7	1	4	1	.800	0	11	1.37
Durham	A	4	0	0	2	7.1	29	4	3	2	1	0	0	0	4	0	14	0	0	0	0	.000	0	0	2.45
1992 Durham	A	24	0	0	16	42.1	163	29	11	10	3	3	1	1	11	1	51	1	2	1	2	.333	0	4	2.13
Greenville	AA	21	1	0	10	39.1	155	26	15	14	1	0	2	0	17	2	45	4	0	3	4	.429	0	1	3.20
1993 Durham	A	6	5	1	0	30	120	21	10	10	2	0	1	2	6	1	27	4	0	3	1	.750	1	0	3.00
Greenville	AA	8	7	1	1	53.1	220	43	24	20	1	6	0	2	24	0	38	6	1	2	4	.333	0	0	3.38
Richmond	AAA	10	9	0	0	57.2	246	59	32	27	6	1	2	1	16	0	45	1	0	5	3	.625	0	0	4.21
1994 Richmond	AAA	27	27	4	0	185.2	750	159	62	50	14	7	0	2	49	2	137	7	0	15	6	.714	3	0	2.42
1995 Richmond	AAA	13	11	0	1	65.1	279	70	39	37	5	6	0	3	17	1	44	1	0	4	4	.500	0	0	5.10
1994 Atlanta	NL	1	1	0	0	6	24	5	3	3	2	0	0	0	2	0	2	0	0	0	1	.000	0	0	4.50
1995 Atlanta	NL	9	0	0	3	10.1	52	13	10	7	1	1	1	0	8	1	5	1	0	1	1	.500	0	0	6.10
2 ML YEARS		10	1	0	3	16.1	76	18	13	10	3	1	1	0	10	1	7	1	0	1	2	.333	0	0	5.51

Tim Worrell

Pitches: Right   **Bats:** Right   **Pos:** RP   **Ht:** 6' 4"   **Wt:** 220   **Born:** 7/5/67   **Age:** 28

Year Team	Lg	G	GS	CG	GF	IP	BFP	H	R	ER	HR	SH	SF	HB	TBB	IBB	SO	WP	Bk	W	L	Pct.	ShO	Sv	ERA
1995 Rancho Cuc *	A	9	3	0	2	22.2	103	25	17	13	2	0	1	2	6	1	17	0	0	0	2	.000	0	1	5.16
Las Vegas *	AAA	10	3	0	0	24	121	27	21	16	1	2	0	3	17	0	18	0	0	0	2	.000	0	0	6.00
1993 San Diego	NL	21	16	0	1	100.2	443	104	63	55	11	8	5	0	43	5	52	3	0	2	7	.222	0	0	4.92
1994 San Diego	NL	3	3	0	0	14.2	59	9	7	6	0	0	1	0	5	0	14	0	0	1	0	1.000	0	0	3.68
1995 San Diego	NL	9	0	0	4	13.1	63	16	7	7	2	1	0	1	6	0	13	1	0	1	0	1.000	0	0	4.73
3 ML YEARS		33	19	0	5	128.2	565	129	77	68	13	9	6	1	54	5	79	4	0	3	8	.273	0	0	4.76

Todd Worrell

Pitches: Right   **Bats:** Right   **Pos:** RP   **Ht:** 6' 5"   **Wt:** 227   **Born:** 9/28/59   **Age:** 36

Year Team	Lg	G	GS	CG	GF	IP	BFP	H	R	ER	HR	SH	SF	HB	TBB	IBB	SO	WP	Bk	W	L	Pct.	ShO	Sv	ERA
1985 St. Louis	NL	17	0	0	11	21.2	88	17	7	7	2	0	2	0	7	2	17	2	0	3	0	1.000	0	5	2.91
1986 St. Louis	NL	74	0	0	60	103.2	430	86	29	24	9	7	6	1	41	16	73	1	0	9	10	.474	0	36	2.08
1987 St. Louis	NL	75	0	0	54	94.2	395	86	29	28	8	4	2	0	34	11	92	1	0	8	6	.571	0	33	2.66
1988 St. Louis	NL	68	0	0	54	90	366	69	32	30	7	3	5	1	34	14	78	6	2	5	9	.357	0	32	3.00
1989 St. Louis	NL	47	0	0	39	51.2	219	42	21	17	4	3	1	0	26	13	41	3	3	3	5	.375	0	20	2.96
1992 St. Louis	NL	67	0	0	14	64	256	45	15	15	4	3	0	1	25	5	64	1	1	5	3	.625	0	3	2.11
1993 Los Angeles	NL	35	0	0	22	38.2	167	46	28	26	6	3	6	0	11	1	31	1	0	1	1	.500	0	5	6.05
1994 Los Angeles	NL	38	0	0	27	42	173	37	21	20	4	1	2	1	12	1	44	1	0	6	5	.545	0	11	4.29
1995 Los Angeles	NL	59	0	0	53	62.1	249	50	15	14	4	1	2	1	19	2	61	2	0	4	1	.800	0	32	2.02
9 ML YEARS		480	0	0	334	568.2	2343	478	197	181	48	25	26	5	209	65	501	18	6	44	40	.524	0	177	2.86

Craig Worthington

Bats: Right **Throws:** Right **Pos:** 3B **Ht:** 6' 0" **Wt:** 200 **Born:** 4/17/65 **Age:** 31

								BATTING											BASERUNNING				PERCENTAGES		
Year Team	Lg	G	AB	H	2B	3B	HR	(Hm	Rd)	TB	R	RBI	TBB	IBB	SO	HBP	SH	SF	SB	CS	SB%	GDP	Avg	OBP	SLG
1995 Indianapolis *	AAA	81	277	88	19	0	9	--	--	134	48	41	31	1	51	0	1	4	1	1	.50	5	.318	.381	.484
1988 Baltimore	AL	26	81	15	2	0	2	(0	2)	23	5	4	9	0	24	0	0	0	1	0	1.00	2	.185	.267	.284
1989 Baltimore	AL	145	497	123	23	0	15	(12	3)	191	57	70	61	2	114	4	3	1	1	2	.33	10	.247	.334	.384
1990 Baltimore	AL	133	425	96	17	0	8	(3	5)	137	46	44	63	2	96	3	7	3	1	2	.33	13	.226	.328	.322
1991 Baltimore	AL	31	102	23	3	0	4	(1	3)	38	11	12	12	0	14	1	1	0	0	1	.00	3	.225	.313	.373
1992 Cleveland	AL	9	24	4	0	0	0	(0	0)	4	0	2	2	0	4	0	0	0	0	1	.00	0	.167	.231	.167
1995 Cin-Tex		36	86	20	5	0	3	(1	2)	34	5	8	9	0	9	0	2	0	0	0	.00	6	.233	.305	.395
1995 Cincinnati	NL	10	18	5	1	0	1	(0	1)	9	1	2	2	0	1	0	0	0	0	0	.00	0	.278	.350	.500
Texas	AL	26	68	15	4	0	2	(1	1)	25	4	6	7	0	8	0	2	0	0	0	.00	6	.221	.293	.368
6 ML YEARS		380	1215	281	50	0	32	(17	15)	427	124	140	156	4	261	8	13	4	3	6	.33	34	.231	.322	.351

Anthony Young

Pitches: Right **Bats:** Right **Pos:** RP **Ht:** 6' 2" **Wt:** 215 **Born:** 1/19/66 **Age:** 30

			HOW MUCH HE PITCHED					WHAT HE GAVE UP												THE RESULTS					
Year Team	Lg	G	GS	CG	GF	IP	BFP	H	R	ER	HR	SH	SF	HB	TBB	IBB	SO	WP	Bk	W	L	Pct.	ShO	Sv	ERA
1995 Orlando *	AA	2	2	0	0	5	24	6	1	0	0	0	0	0	3	0	5	0	0	0	0	.000	0	0	0.00
Daytona *	A	6	1	0	3	8	36	5	5	5	0	0	0	0	4	0	3	0	0	0	0	.000	0	0	5.63
Iowa *	AAA	3	1	0	0	4	23	9	5	5	0	0	1	0	4	0	6	0	0	0	1	.000	0	0	11.25
1991 New York	NL	10	8	0	2	49.1	202	48	20	17	4	1	1	1	12	1	20	1	0	2	5	.286	0	0	3.10
1992 New York	NL	52	13	1	26	121	517	134	66	56	8	11	4	1	31	5	64	3	1	2	14	.125	0	15	4.17
1993 New York	NL	39	10	1	19	100.1	445	103	62	42	8	11	3	1	42	9	62	0	2	1	16	.059	0	3	3.77
1994 Chicago	NL	20	19	0	0	114.2	474	103	57	50	12	6	3	0	46	2	65	4	1	4	6	.400	0	0	3.92
1995 Chicago	NL	32	1	0	8	41.1	181	47	20	17	5	1	0	3	14	2	15	6	0	3	4	.429	0	2	3.70
5 ML YEARS		153	51	2	55	426.2	1819	435	225	182	37	30	11	6	145	19	226	14	4	12	45	.211	0	20	3.84

Eric Young

Bats: Right **Throws:** Right **Pos:** 2B/LF **Ht:** 5' 9" **Wt:** 180 **Born:** 5/18/67 **Age:** 29

								BATTING											BASERUNNING				PERCENTAGES		
Year Team	Lg	G	AB	H	2B	3B	HR	(Hm	Rd)	TB	R	RBI	TBB	IBB	SO	HBP	SH	SF	SB	CS	SB%	GDP	Avg	OBP	SLG
1992 Los Angeles	NL	49	132	34	1	0	1	(0	1)	38	9	11	8	0	9	0	4	0	6	1	.86	3	.258	.300	.288
1993 Colorado	NL	144	490	132	16	8	3	(3	0)	173	82	42	63	3	41	4	4	4	42	19	.69	9	.269	.355	.353
1994 Colorado	NL	90	228	62	13	1	7	(6	1)	98	37	30	38	1	17	2	5	2	18	7	.72	5	.272	.378	.430
1995 Colorado	NL	120	366	116	21	9	6	(5	1)	173	68	36	49	3	29	5	3	1	35	12	.74	4	.317	.404	.473
4 ML YEARS		403	1216	344	51	18	17	(14	3)	482	196	119	158	7	96	11	16	7	101	39	.72	19	.283	.369	.396

Ernie Young

Bats: Right **Throws:** Right **Pos:** RF **Ht:** 6' 1" **Wt:** 190 **Born:** 7/8/69 **Age:** 26

								BATTING											BASERUNNING				PERCENTAGES		
Year Team	Lg	G	AB	H	2B	3B	HR	(Hm	Rd)	TB	R	RBI	TBB	IBB	SO	HBP	SH	SF	SB	CS	SB%	GDP	Avg	OBP	SLG
1990 Sou. Oregon	A	50	168	47	6	2	6	--	--	75	34	23	28	2	53	3	0	2	4	4	.50	2	.280	.388	.446
1991 Madison	A	114	362	92	19	2	15	--	--	160	75	71	58	0	115	9	9	6	20	9	.69	4	.254	.366	.442
1992 Modesto	A	74	253	63	12	4	11	--	--	116	55	33	47	1	74	6	2	1	11	3	.79	5	.249	.378	.458
1993 Modesto	A	85	301	92	18	6	23	--	--	191	83	71	72	0	92	4	0	3	23	7	.77	2	.306	.442	.635
Huntsville	AA	45	120	25	5	0	5	--	--	45	26	15	24	0	36	2	2	2	8	5	.62	1	.208	.345	.375
1994 Tacoma	AAA	29	102	29	4	0	6	--	--	51	19	16	13	0	27	2	0	2	0	5	.00	3	.284	.370	.500
Huntsville	AA	72	257	89	19	4	14	--	--	158	45	55	37	2	45	2	2	4	5	6	.45	6	.346	.427	.615
1995 Edmonton	AAA	95	347	96	21	4	15	--	--	170	70	72	49	1	73	3	1	7	2	2	.50	5	.277	.365	.490
1994 Oakland	AL	11	30	2	1	0	0	(0	0)	3	2	3	1	0	8	0	0	0	0	0	.00	1	.067	.097	.100
1995 Oakland	AL	26	50	10	3	0	2	(2	0)	19	9	5	8	0	12	0	0	0	0	0	.00	1	.200	.310	.380
2 ML YEARS		37	80	12	4	0	2	(2	0)	22	11	8	9	0	20	0	0	0	0	0	.00	2	.150	.236	.275

Kevin Young

Bats: Right **Throws:** Right **Pos:** 3B   **Ht:** 6' 2" **Wt:** 219 **Born:** 6/16/69 **Age:** 27

Year Team	Lg	G	AB	H	2B	3B	HR	(Hm	Rd)	TB	R	RBI	TBB	IBB	SO	HBP	SH	SF	SB	CS	SB%	GDP	Avg	OBP	SLG
1995 Calgary *	AAA	45	163	58	23	1	8	--	--	107	24	34	15	0	21	0	0	3	6	3	.67	4	.356	.403	.656
1992 Pittsburgh	NL	10	7	4	0	0	0	(0	0)	4	2	4	2	0	0	0	0	0	1	0	1.00	0	.571	.667	.571
1993 Pittsburgh	NL	141	449	106	24	3	6	(6	0)	154	38	47	36	3	82	9	5	9	2	2	.50	10	.236	.300	.343
1994 Pittsburgh	NL	59	122	25	7	2	1	(1	0)	39	15	11	8	2	34	1	2	1	0	2	.00	3	.205	.258	.320
1995 Pittsburgh	NL	56	181	42	9	0	6	(5	1)	69	13	22	8	0	53	2	1	3	1	3	.25	5	.232	.268	.381
4 ML YEARS		266	759	177	40	5	13	(12	1)	266	68	84	54	5	169	12	8	13	4	7	.36	18	.233	.290	.350

Greg Zaun

Bats: Both **Throws:** Right **Pos:** C   **Ht:** 5'10" **Wt:** 170 **Born:** 4/14/71 **Age:** 25

Year Team	Lg	G	AB	H	2B	3B	HR	(Hm	Rd)	TB	R	RBI	TBB	IBB	SO	HBP	SH	SF	SB	CS	SB%	GDP	Avg	OBP	SLG
1990	A	37	100	13	0	1	1	--	--	18	3	7	7	0	17	1	2	0	0	0	.00	2	.130	.194	.180
Bluefield	R	61	184	57	5	2	2	--	--	72	29	21	23	1	15	1	0	1	5	5	.50	2	.310	.388	.391
1991 Kane County	A	113	409	112	17	5	4	--	--	151	67	51	50	1	41	2	3	4	4	4	.50	10	.274	.353	.369
1992 Frederick	A	108	383	96	18	6	6	--	--	144	54	52	42	0	45	3	1	7	3	5	.38	10	.251	.324	.376
1993 Bowie	AA	79	258	79	10	0	3	--	--	98	25	38	27	4	26	1	0	1	4	7	.36	7	.306	.373	.380
Rochester	AAA	21	78	20	4	2	1	--	--	31	10	11	6	0	11	0	0	2	0	0	.00	1	.256	.302	.397
1994 Rochester	AAA	123	388	92	16	4	7	--	--	137	61	43	56	2	72	4	3	3	4	2	.67	5	.237	.337	.353
1995 Rochester	AAA	42	140	41	13	1	6	--	--	74	26	18	14	2	21	3	0	1	0	3	.00	0	.293	.367	.529
1995 Baltimore	AL	40	104	27	5	0	3	(1	2)	41	18	14	16	0	14	0	2	0	1	1	.50	2	.260	.358	.394

Todd Zeile

Bats: Right **Throws:** Right **Pos:** 3B/1B   **Ht:** 6' 1" **Wt:** 190 **Born:** 9/9/65 **Age:** 30

Year Team	Lg	G	AB	H	2B	3B	HR	(Hm	Rd)	TB	R	RBI	TBB	IBB	SO	HBP	SH	SF	SB	CS	SB%	GDP	Avg	OBP	SLG
1995 Louisville *	AAA	2	8	1	0	0	0	--	--	1	0	0	0	0	2	0	0	0	0	0	.00	0	.125	.125	.125
1989 St. Louis	NL	28	82	21	3	1	1	(0	1)	29	7	8	9	1	14	0	1	1	0	0	.00	0	.256	.326	.354
1990 St. Louis	NL	144	495	121	25	3	15	(8	7)	197	62	57	67	3	77	2	0	6	2	4	.33	11	.244	.333	.398
1991 St. Louis	NL	155	565	158	36	3	11	(7	4)	233	76	81	62	3	94	5	0	6	17	11	.61	15	.280	.353	.412
1992 St. Louis	NL	126	439	113	18	4	7	(4	3)	160	51	48	68	4	70	0	0	7	7	10	.41	11	.257	.352	.364
1993 St. Louis	NL	157	571	158	36	1	17	(8	9)	247	82	103	70	5	76	0	0	6	5	4	.56	15	.277	.352	.433
1994 St. Louis	NL	113	415	111	25	1	19	(9	10)	195	62	75	52	3	56	3	0	7	1	3	.25	13	.267	.348	.470
1995 Stl-ChN	NL	113	426	105	22	0	14	(8	6)	169	50	52	34	1	76	4	4	5	1	0	1.00	13	.246	.305	.397
1995 St. Louis	NL	34	127	37	6	0	5	(2	3)	58	16	22	18	1	23	1	0	2	1	0	1.00	2	.291	.378	.457
Chicago	NL	79	299	68	16	0	9	(6	3)	111	34	30	16	0	53	3	4	3	0	0	.00	11	.227	.271	.371
7 ML YEARS		836	2993	787	165	13	84	(44	40)	1230	390	424	362	20	463	14	5	38	33	32	.51	79	.263	.341	.411

Eddie Zosky

Bats: Right **Throws:** Right **Pos:** SS   **Ht:** 6' 0" **Wt:** 180 **Born:** 2/10/68 **Age:** 28

Year Team	Lg	G	AB	H	2B	3B	HR	(Hm	Rd)	TB	R	RBI	TBB	IBB	SO	HBP	SH	SF	SB	CS	SB%	GDP	Avg	OBP	SLG
1989 Knoxville	AA	56	208	46	5	3	2	--	--	63	21	14	10	0	32	0	2	1	1	1	.50	4	.221	.256	.303
1990 Knoxville	AA	115	450	122	20	7	3	--	--	165	53	45	26	1	73	5	6	3	3	13	.19	7	.271	.316	.367
1991 Syracuse	AAA	119	511	135	18	4	6	--	--	179	69	39	35	1	82	5	7	5	9	4	.69	11	.264	.315	.350
1992 Syracuse	AAA	96	342	79	11	6	4	--	--	114	31	38	19	0	53	1	7	4	3	4	.43	10	.231	.270	.333
1993 Hagerstown	A	5	20	2	0	0	0	--	--	2	2	1	2	0	1	0	0	1	0	0	.00	1	.100	.174	.100
Syracuse	AAA	28	93	20	5	0	0	--	--	25	9	8	1	0	20	4	2	3	0	1	.00	1	.215	.248	.269
1994 Syracuse	AAA	85	284	75	15	3	7	--	--	117	41	37	9	0	46	2	6	5	3	1	.75	8	.264	.287	.412
1995 Charlotte	AAA	92	312	77	15	2	3	--	--	105	27	42	7	0	48	1	5	1	2	3	.40	8	.247	.265	.337
1991 Toronto	AL	18	27	4	1	1	0	(0	0)	7	2	2	0	0	8	0	1	0	0	0	.00	1	.148	.148	.259
1992 Toronto	AL	8	7	2	0	1	0	(0	0)	4	1	1	0	0	2	0	0	1	0	0	.00	0	.286	.250	.571
1995 Florida	NL	6	5	1	0	0	0	(0	0)	1	0	0	0	0	0	0	0	0	0	0	.00	0	.200	.200	.200
3 ML YEARS		32	39	7	1	2	0	(0	0)	12	3	3	0	0	10	0	1	1	0	0	.00	1	.179	.175	.308

1995 Team Statistics

American League Batting

Team	G	AB	H	2B	3B	HR	(Hm	Rd)	TB	R	RBI	TBB	IBB	SO	HBP	SH	SF	SB	CS	SB%	GDP	Avg	OBP	SLG
Cleveland	144	5028	1461	279	23	207	(99	108)	2407	840	803	542	40	766	35	31	48	132	53	.71	128	.291	.361	.479
California	145	5019	1390	252	25	186	(90	96)	2250	801	761	564	40	889	36	33	38	58	39	.60	115	.277	.352	.448
Seattle	145	4996	1377	276	20	182	(101	81)	2239	796	767	549	53	871	39	52	34	110	41	.73	109	.276	.350	.448
Boston	144	4997	1399	286	31	175	(70	105)	2272	791	754	560	38	923	65	45	49	99	44	.69	129	.280	.357	.455
Chicago	145	5060	1417	252	37	146	(59	87)	2181	755	712	576	54	767	32	46	56	110	39	.74	106	.280	.354	.431
New York	145	4947	1365	280	34	122	(69	53)	2079	749	709	625	36	851	39	20	68	50	30	.63	139	.276	.357	.420
Milwaukee	144	5000	1329	249	42	128	(56	72)	2046	740	700	502	20	800	46	41	42	105	40	.72	105	.266	.336	.409
Oakland	144	4916	1296	228	18	169	(80	89)	2067	730	694	565	25	911	45	32	58	112	46	.71	108	.264	.341	.420
Baltimore	144	4837	1267	229	27	173	(90	83)	2069	704	668	574	36	803	39	40	41	92	45	.67	119	.262	.342	.428
Minnesota	144	5005	1398	270	34	120	(59	61)	2096	703	662	471	32	916	58	18	36	105	57	.65	152	.279	.346	.419
Texas	144	4913	1304	247	24	138	(81	57)	2013	691	651	526	28	877	33	49	45	90	47	.66	112	.265	.338	.410
Detroit	144	4865	1204	228	29	159	(92	67)	1967	654	619	551	30	987	41	35	43	73	36	.67	121	.247	.327	.404
Toronto	144	5036	1309	275	27	140	(73	67)	2058	642	613	492	27	906	44	33	45	75	16	.82	119	.260	.328	.409
Kansas City	144	4903	1275	240	35	119	(49	70)	1942	629	578	475	33	849	43	66	39	120	53	.69	105	.260	.328	.396
American	1010	69522	18791	3591	406	2164	(1068	1096)	29686	10225	9691	7572	492	12116	595	541	642	1331	586	.69	1640	.270	.344	.427

American League Pitching

Team	G	GS	CG	GF	IP	BFP	H	R	ER	HR	SH	SF	HB	TBB	IBB	SO	WP	Bk	W	L	Pct.	ShO	Sv	ERA
Cleveland	144	144	10	134	1301	5512	1261	607	554	135	32	44	45	445	16	926	48	5	100	44	.694	10	50	3.83
Baltimore	144	144	19	125	1267	5382	1165	640	607	149	33	34	37	523	40	930	30	9	71	73	.493	10	29	4.31
New York	145	145	18	127	1284.2	5575	1286	688	651	159	35	37	32	535	21	908	50	5	79	65	.549	5	35	4.56
Kansas City	144	144	11	133	1288	5561	1323	691	642	142	39	42	38	503	38	763	45	5	70	74	.486	10	37	4.49
California	145	145	8	137	1284.1	5571	1310	697	645	163	48	45	43	486	23	901	42	10	78	67	.538	9	42	4.52
Boston	144	144	7	137	1292.2	5600	1338	698	631	127	32	47	46	476	28	888	57	1	86	58	.597	9	39	4.39
Seattle	145	145	9	136	1289.1	5743	1343	708	644	149	39	52	47	591	37	1068	50	7	79	66	.545	8	39	4.50
Texas	144	144	14	130	1285	5626	1385	720	665	152	41	48	36	514	38	838	60	6	74	70	.514	4	34	4.66
Milwaukee	144	144	7	137	1286	5707	1391	747	689	146	34	62	47	603	39	699	45	7	65	79	.451	4	31	4.82
Chicago	145	145	12	133	1284.2	5734	1374	758	693	164	37	50	39	617	47	892	45	8	68	76	.472	4	36	4.85
Oakland	144	144	8	136	1273	5606	1320	761	698	153	52	44	53	556	26	890	56	4	67	77	.465	4	34	4.93
Toronto	144	144	16	128	1292.2	5773	1336	777	701	145	36	37	51	654	42	894	73	4	56	88	.389	8	22	4.88
Detroit	144	144	5	139	1275	5774	1509	844	778	170	42	50	45	536	79	729	67	7	60	84	.417	3	38	5.49
Minnesota	144	144	7	137	1272.2	5714	1450	889	815	210	41	50	36	533	18	790	52	4	56	88	.389	2	27	5.76
American	1010	1010	151	859	17976	78878	18791	10225	9413	2164	541	642	595	7572	492	12116	720	82	1009	1009	.500	90	493	4.71

American League Fielding

Team	G	PO	A	E	TC	DP	AVG
Baltimore	144	3801	1441	72	5314	141	.986
New York	145	3854	1416	74	5344	121	.986
Kansas City	144	3864	1660	90	5614	168	.984
Texas	144	3855	1589	98	5542	156	.982
California	145	3853	1416	95	5364	120	.982
Cleveland	144	3903	1598	101	5602	142	.982
Toronto	144	3878	1399	97	5374	131	.982
Minnesota	144	3818	1487	100	5405	141	.981
Milwaukee	144	3858	1669	105	5632	186	.981
Oakland	144	3819	1486	102	5407	151	.981
Detroit	144	3825	1594	106	5525	143	.981
Seattle	145	3868	1357	104	5329	108	.980
Chicago	145	3854	1415	108	5377	131	.980
Boston	144	3878	1581	120	5579	151	.978
American	1010	53928	21108	1372	76408	1990	.982

National League Batting

Team	G	AB	H	2B	3B	HR	(Hm	Rd)	TB	R	RBI	TBB	IBB	SO	HBP	SH	SF	SB	CS	SB%	GDP	Avg	OBP	SLG
Colorado	144	4994	1406	259	43	200	(134	66)	2351	785	749	484	47	943	56	82	31	125	59	.68	118	.282	.350	.471
Cincinnati	144	4903	1326	277	35	161	(76	85)	2156	747	694	519	42	946	40	62	50	190	68	.74	92	.270	.342	.440
Houston	144	5097	1403	260	22	109	(41	68)	2034	747	694	566	58	992	69	78	47	176	60	.75	114	.275	.353	.399
Chicago	144	4963	1315	267	39	158	(83	75)	2134	693	648	440	46	953	34	71	35	105	37	.74	110	.265	.327	.430
Florida	143	4886	1278	214	29	144	(68	76)	1982	673	636	517	36	916	49	69	48	131	53	.71	105	.262	.335	.406
San Diego	144	4950	1345	231	20	116	(55	61)	1964	668	618	447	45	872	35	56	38	124	46	.73	125	.272	.334	.397
New York	144	4958	1323	218	34	125	(63	62)	1984	657	617	446	44	994	42	92	43	58	39	.60	105	.267	.330	.400
San Francisco	144	4971	1256	229	33	152	(76	76)	2007	652	610	472	55	1060	57	79	24	138	46	.75	92	.253	.323	.404
Atlanta	144	4814	1202	210	27	168	(94	74)	1970	645	618	520	37	933	40	56	34	73	43	.63	106	.250	.326	.409
Los Angeles	144	4942	1303	191	31	140	(62	78)	1976	634	593	468	46	1023	30	68	35	127	45	.74	99	.264	.329	.400
Pittsburgh	144	4937	1281	245	27	125	(69	56)	1955	629	587	456	45	972	24	51	33	84	55	.60	88	.259	.323	.396
Montreal	144	4905	1268	265	24	118	(43	75)	1935	621	572	400	43	901	56	58	32	120	49	.71	107	.259	.320	.394
Philadelphia	144	4950	1296	263	30	94	(51	43)	1901	615	576	497	38	884	46	77	41	72	25	.74	107	.262	.332	.384
St. Louis	143	4779	1182	238	24	107	(54	53)	1789	563	533	436	31	920	46	48	40	79	46	.63	110	.247	.314	.374
National	1007	69049	18184	3367	418	1917	(969	948)	28138	9329	8745	6668	613	13309	624	947	531	1602	671	.70	1468	.263	.331	.408

National League Pitching

Team	G	GS	CG	GF	IP	BFP	H	R	ER	HR	SH	SF	HB	TBB	IBB	SO	WP	Bk	W	L	Pct.	ShO	Sv	ERA
Atlanta	144	144	18	126	1291.2	5410	1184	540	494	107	63	34	32	436	46	1087	38	4	90	54	.625	11	34	3.44
Los Angeles	144	144	16	128	1295	5481	1188	609	527	125	59	33	37	462	45	1060	49	12	78	66	.542	11	37	3.66
New York	144	144	9	135	1291	5483	1296	618	556	133	62	40	35	401	48	901	39	12	69	75	.479	9	36	3.88
Cincinnati	144	144	8	136	1289.1	5445	1270	623	578	131	56	43	31	424	32	903	58	10	85	59	.590	10	38	4.03
Montreal	144	144	7	137	1283.2	5491	1286	638	581	128	77	29	59	416	26	950	45	9	66	78	.458	9	42	4.07
Philadelphia	144	144	8	136	1290.1	5575	1241	658	603	134	60	44	55	538	36	980	57	10	69	75	.479	8	41	4.21
St. Louis	143	143	4	139	1265.2	5420	1290	658	575	135	83	35	40	445	37	842	51	6	62	81	.434	6	38	4.09
Chicago	144	144	6	138	1301	5664	1313	671	596	162	63	40	34	518	68	926	38	6	73	71	.507	12	45	4.12
San Diego	144	144	6	138	1284.2	5529	1242	672	589	142	72	28	51	512	37	1047	60	5	70	74	.486	10	35	4.13
Florida	143	143	12	131	1286	5628	1299	673	610	139	73	27	46	562	54	994	36	5	67	76	.469	7	29	4.27
Houston	144	144	6	138	1320.1	5703	1357	674	596	118	56	44	50	460	52	1056	52	6	76	68	.528	8	32	4.06
Pittsburgh	144	144	11	133	1275.1	5618	1407	736	635	130	70	46	57	477	50	871	65	4	58	86	.403	7	29	4.69
San Francisco	144	144	12	132	1293.2	5672	1368	776	699	173	77	53	56	505	51	801	43	15	67	77	.465	5	34	4.86
Colorado	144	144	1	143	1288.1	5706	1443	783	710	160	76	35	41	512	31	891	62	13	77	67	.535	1	43	4.96
National	1007	1007	124	883	18056	77825	18184	9329	8379	1917	947	531	624	6668	613	13309	693	117	1007	1007	.500	114	513	4.18

National League Fielding

Team	G	PO	A	E	TC	DP	AVG
Cincinnati	144	3868	1507	79	5454	140	.986
Philadelphia	144	3871	1520	97	5488	139	.982
Atlanta	144	3875	1569	100	5544	113	.982
Colorado	144	3865	1665	107	5637	146	.981
San Francisco	144	3881	1548	108	5537	142	.980
San Diego	144	3854	1538	108	5500	130	.980
Montreal	144	3851	1557	109	5517	119	.980
St. Louis	143	3797	1622	113	5532	156	.980
New York	144	3873	1602	125	5590	125	.979
Chicago	144	3903	1563	115	5581	115	.979
Florida	143	3858	1467	115	5440	143	.979
Houston	144	3961	1639	121	5721	120	.979
Pittsburgh	144	3826	1589	122	5537	138	.978
Los Angeles	144	3885	1491	130	5506	120	.976
National	1007	54168	21877	1539	77584	1846	.980

1995 Fielding Stats

Eighty years ago, baseballists knew that Rabbit Maranville was a good shortstop, because their eyes told them so. But most fielders weren't/aren't as easy to evaluate as the Rabbit, which is why we like to look at range factor. The original range factor was simply total chances per game played, but the range factor (Rng) you'll find here is a bit more precise: total chances per nine innings. You'll also find all the old standards, like assists, errors, double plays. . . you know the drill. An addition this year are games started by position, here for the first time. Another thing you won't find in other sources are our "special" catcher stats, including stolen-base data and one of our personal favorites, Catcher ERA.

The only important things you need to know before digging in are these: All the fielding stats are unofficial—an assist here or a putout there may change when the official stats arrive in December, but these are very close as they are. The regulars are sorted by range factor, except for the first basemen and the catchers in the first catcher section, who are sorted by fielding percentage. The catchers in the special catcher section are sorted by Catcher ERA (CERA). Remember to consider the pitching staff when looking at those CERAs. (No matter how well you call pitches, it's tough to have a good CERA if you play for the Rockies. Just ask Joe Girardi.) And finally, ties in range or percentage are, in reality, not ties at all, just numbers that don't show enough digits to be unique.

First Basemen - Regulars

Player	Tm	G	GS	Inn	PO	A	E	DP	Pct.	Rng
Joyner,Wally	KC	126	120	1069.2	1111	118	3	119	.998	---
Brogna,Rico	NYN	131	120	1089.2	1113	92	3	93	.998	---
Jaha,John	Mil	81	81	658.0	648	62	2	86	.997	---
Palmeiro,Rafael	Bal	142	142	1238.0	1178	123	4	120	.997	---
Segui,David	TOT	104	98	877.2	883	71	3	71	.997	---
Snow,J.T.	Cal	143	143	1249.0	1161	56	4	106	.997	---
Olerud,John	Tor	133	132	1173.0	1098	90	4	102	.997	---
McGriff,Fred	Atl	144	144	1240.2	1286	93	5	104	.996	---
Colbrunn,Greg	Fla	134	129	1163.2	1070	88	5	107	.996	---
Karros,Eric	LA	143	143	1271.2	1234	109	7	100	.995	---
Grace,Mark	ChN	143	142	1268.0	1211	115	7	91	.995	---
Clark,Will	Tex	122	122	1058.1	1077	87	7	120	.994	---
Morris,Hal	Cin	99	91	790.2	755	72	5	79	.994	---
Bagwell,Jeff	Hou	114	114	1048.1	1004	129	7	78	.994	---
Mabry,John	StL	73	66	566.1	595	51	4	63	.994	---
Mattingly,Don	NYA	125	117	1038.0	994	82	7	90	.994	---
Carreon,Mark	SF	81	80	670.1	703	44	5	65	.993	---
Martinez,Tino	Sea	139	136	1195.2	1043	103	8	86	.993	---
Fielder,Cecil	Det	77	77	635.2	631	73	5	65	.993	---
Sorrento,Paul	Cle	91	85	760.1	816	57	7	87	.992	---
Vaughn,Mo	Bos	138	138	1225.2	1262	94	11	126	.992	---
Thomas,Frank	ChA	91	90	780.1	743	35	7	66	.991	---
Galarraga,Andres	Col	142	139	1229.1	1300	119	13	127	.991	---
Williams,Eddie	SD	81	77	608.2	571	48	7	53	.989	---
Hollins,Dave	Phi	61	60	535.2	533	30	7	53	.988	---
Johnson,Mark	Pit	70	63	533.2	527	34	8	53	.986	---
McGwire,Mark	Oak	91	88	754.2	775	63	12	64	.986	---
Average	---	111	108	952.2	937	79	6	87	.994	---

First Basemen - The Rest

Player	Tm	G	GS	Inn	PO	A	E	DP	Pct.	Rng
Aldrete,Mike	Oak	35	19	187.2	175	10	2	16	.989	---
Aldrete,Mike	Cal	1	0	2.0	1	0	0	0	1.000	---
Andrews,Shane	Mon	29	19	175.0	160	11	4	11	.977	---
Anthony,Eric	Cin	17	12	109.1	102	10	4	11	.966	---
Aude,Rich	Pit	32	26	223.2	223	11	1	27	.996	---
Ausmus,Brad	SD	1	0	2.0	0	0	0	0	.000	---
Benzinger,Todd	SF	5	1	16.0	15	0	0	2	1.000	---
Berry,Sean	Mon	3	3	24.0	22	4	0	0	1.000	---
Berryhill,Damon	Cin	1	0	2.0	1	0	0	0	1.000	---
Blowers,Mike	Sea	7	3	33.2	32	5	1	7	.974	---
Bogar,Tim	NYN	10	6	49.0	47	5	0	6	1.000	---
Boggs,Wade	NYA	9	6	58.2	45	5	0	4	1.000	---
Bonilla,Bobby	NYN	10	9	67.0	85	3	0	5	1.000	---
Branson,Jeff	Cin	1	0	0.2	0	0	0	0	.000	---
Brosius,Scott	Oak	18	14	126.1	110	17	2	26	.984	---
Brumley,Mike	Hou	1	0	2.0	1	1	0	0	1.000	---
Busch,Mike	LA	2	0	7.0	8	1	0	2	1.000	---
Caceres,Edgar	KC	6	0	12.0	11	0	0	2	1.000	---
Carter,Joe	Tor	7	6	56.0	47	3	0	2	1.000	---
Cianfrocco,Archi	SD	30	4	93.0	76	7	0	7	1.000	---
Cirillo,Jeff	Mil	3	0	7.2	16	1	0	1	1.000	---
Clark,Jerald	Min	11	7	52.0	33	3	0	3	1.000	---
Clark,Phil	SD	2	1	9.0	7	0	0	1	1.000	---
Clark,Tony	Det	27	27	231.0	252	18	4	25	.985	---
Coles,Darnell	StL	18	12	116.1	122	7	1	7	.992	---

First Basemen - The Rest

Player	Tm	G	GS	Inn	PO	A	E	DP	Pct.	Rng
Conine,Jeff	Fla	14	11	92.2	97	11	1	10	.991	---
Coomer,Ron	Min	22	18	135.2	131	13	1	13	.993	---
Davis,Russ	NYA	2	0	2.0	1	0	0	0	1.000	---
Decker,Steve	Fla	2	0	2.0	3	0	0	0	1.000	---
Delgado,Carlos	Tor	4	2	21.0	20	1	0	3	1.000	---
Donnels,Chris	Bos	8	3	34.0	36	5	0	7	1.000	---
Duncan,Mariano	Phi	12	9	82.0	90	6	2	10	.980	---
Duncan,Mariano	Cin	6	3	28.0	32	0	0	1	1.000	---
Dunn,Steve	Min	3	0	6.0	5	0	0	2	1.000	---
Elster,Kevin	Phi	4	1	17.1	17	0	0	1	1.000	---
Espinoza,Alvaro	Cle	2	0	7.0	9	0	0	1	1.000	---
Fletcher,Scott	Det	1	0	1.0	2	0	0	0	1.000	---
Floyd,Cliff	Mon	18	15	132.2	143	12	2	13	.987	---
Foley,Tom	Mon	4	3	24.0	21	2	0	1	1.000	---
Franco,Matt	ChN	1	0	2.0	2	0	0	0	1.000	---
Gaetti,Gary	KC	11	10	75.1	92	10	1	10	.990	---
Gates,Brent	Oak	1	1	8.0	8	3	0	1	1.000	---
Giambi,Jason	Oak	26	20	175.1	168	10	1	20	.994	---
Giannelli,Ray	StL	2	0	9.0	8	0	0	1	1.000	---
Gomez,Leo	Bal	3	0	5.0	5	0	0	0	1.000	---
Greer,Rusty	Tex	3	3	30.0	29	0	2	3	.935	---
Gregg,Tommy	Fla	2	2	17.0	17	1	0	2	1.000	---
Grotewold,Jeff	KC	1	0	4.0	3	0	1	1	.750	---
Gwynn,Chris	LA	2	0	5.0	5	1	0	2	1.000	---
Hale,Chip	Min	3	0	9.1	13	0	0	0	1.000	---
Hamelin,Bob	KC	8	7	63.0	66	9	0	11	1.000	---
Hare,Shawn	Tex	1	0	1.0	1	0	0	0	1.000	---
Harris,Lenny	Cin	23	14	141.1	127	13	0	10	1.000	---
Haselman,Bill	Bos	1	0	1.0	2	0	0	0	1.000	---
Howard,Dave	KC	1	0	2.0	3	0	0	0	1.000	---
Hudler,Rex	Cal	2	1	10.0	8	0	0	1	1.000	---
Hunter,Brian	Cin	23	18	147.1	164	11	3	19	.983	---
Hyers,Tim	SD	1	0	1.1	1	1	0	0	1.000	---
James,Dion	NYA	6	3	28.0	31	4	0	1	1.000	---
Jefferies,Gregg	Phi	59	58	518.2	492	33	3	52	.994	---
Jefferson,Reggie	Bos	7	3	32.0	26	4	0	4	1.000	---
Johnson,Brian	SD	2	0	7.0	9	0	1	0	.900	---
Johnson,Howard	ChN	3	1	14.0	15	1	0	3	1.000	---
Jones,Chris	NYN	5	5	34.0	43	3	0	3	1.000	---
King,Jeff	Pit	35	32	289.2	295	26	2	23	.994	---
Kingery,Mike	Col	5	2	22.2	25	1	1	0	.963	---
Klesko,Ryan	Atl	4	0	20.1	20	2	1	0	.957	---
Kruk,John	ChA	1	1	8.0	10	0	1	1	.909	---
Ledesma,Aaron	NYN	2	0	3.1	3	0	0	0	1.000	---
Leyritz,Jim	NYA	18	16	134.0	131	6	1	11	.993	---
Livingstone,Scott	SD	43	39	295.0	298	17	3	25	.991	---
Lyons,Barry	ChA	3	3	27.0	27	3	1	2	.968	---
Maas,Kevin	Min	8	5	47.0	43	1	3	4	.936	---
Magadan,Dave	Hou	11	6	68.1	66	4	0	5	1.000	---
Manto,Jeff	Bal	4	2	21.0	28	2	0	5	1.000	---
Martinez,Carlos	Cal	4	1	23.1	20	0	0	2	1.000	---
Martinez,Dave	ChA	48	40	354.1	311	23	1	37	.997	---
Martinez,Edgar	Sea	3	3	26.0	29	1	1	0	.968	---
Masteller,Dan	Min	48	33	303.0	333	21	2	35	.994	---
May,Derrick	Hou	1	1	2.1	0	0	0	0	.000	---
McCarty,Dave	Min	18	15	125.1	128	10	1	13	.993	---
McCarty,Dave	SF	2	1	11.0	14	0	0	0	1.000	---
McGinnis,Russ	KC	1	1	8.0	8	0	0	0	1.000	---

First Basemen - The Rest

Player	Tm	G	GS	Inn	PO	A	E	DP	Pct.	Rng
Merced,Orlando	Pit	35	19	189.1	175	15	1	22	.995	---
Merullo,Matt	Min	2	0	5.0	5	2	0	0	1.000	---
Mordecai,Mike	Atl	9	0	25.2	24	2	0	3	1.000	---
Morman,Russ	Fla	3	1	10.2	10	1	0	1	1.000	---
Munoz,Pedro	Min	3	1	8.0	7	1	3	1	.727	---
Murray,Eddie	Cle	18	18	156.0	160	22	3	12	.984	---
Nieves,Melvin	SD	2	1	6.1	11	0	1	1	.917	---
Nilsson,Dave	Mil	7	0	14.0	16	2	0	1	1.000	---
Oliva,Jose	Atl	1	0	1.0	0	0	0	0	.000	---
Oliva,Jose	StL	2	2	17.1	16	1	0	2	1.000	---
Oliver,Joe	Mil	2	0	4.0	6	0	1	0	1.000	---
Orsulak,Joe	NYN	1	0	3.1	3	1	0	0	1.000	---
Pagliarulo,Mike	Tex	11	7	71.2	69	8	1	5	.987	---
Paquette,Craig	Oak	3	1	13.0	10	1	0	1	1.000	---
Perez,Eddie	Atl	1	0	4.0	3	0	0	1	1.000	---
Perry,Gerald	StL	11	7	70.0	70	3	0	3	1.000	---
Perry,Herbert	Cle	45	41	377.2	388	30	0	30	1.000	---
Petagine,Roberto	SD	51	22	262.1	263	22	1	21	.997	---
Phillips,J.R.	SF	79	54	527.0	535	36	4	45	.993	---
Pirkl,Greg	Sea	6	3	34.0	32	3	0	1	1.000	---
Ready,Randy	Phi	3	3	23.0	18	1	1	3	.967	---
Reboulet,Jeff	Min	17	9	88.0	80	13	0	7	1.000	---
Rodriguez,Henry	LA	1	0	3.0	1	0	0	0	1.000	---
Rodriguez,Henry	Mon	10	9	78.0	82	7	0	8	1.000	---
Sabo,Chris	ChA	1	1	8.0	10	0	1	1	.909	---
Sabo,Chris	StL	2	2	16.2	11	2	1	1	.929	---
Samuel,Juan	Det	37	27	255.1	271	23	5	26	.983	---
Samuel,Juan	KC	1	1	9.0	8	0	0	0	1.000	---
Santiago,Benito	Cin	8	1	23.0	19	2	0	2	1.000	---
Scarsone,Steve	SF	11	8	69.1	79	6	0	11	1.000	---
Schall,Gene	Phi	14	13	113.2	111	10	2	8	.984	---
Segui,David	NYN	7	4	44.2	41	3	0	4	1.000	---
Segui,David	Mon	97	94	833.0	842	68	3	67	.997	---
Seitzer,Kevin	Mil	36	30	268.0	288	20	3	37	.990	---
Sheaffer,Danny	StL	3	3	25.0	31	5	0	1	1.000	---
Shipley,Craig	Hou	1	0	1.0	1	0	0	0	1.000	---
Silvestri,Dave	NYA	4	3	24.0	25	2	0	2	1.000	---
Silvestri,Dave	Mon	4	1	17.0	22	0	0	4	1.000	---
Simms,Mike	Hou	25	23	198.1	204	18	1	19	.996	---
Sprague,Ed	Tor	7	4	42.2	33	0	1	3	.971	---
Stahoviak,Scott	Min	69	56	493.0	494	61	1	46	.998	---
Steinbach,Terry	Oak	2	1	8.0	5	0	1	3	.833	---
Stubbs,Franklin	Det	20	11	106.2	134	5	4	13	.972	---
Surhoff,B.J.	Mil	55	32	322.1	348	29	3	44	.992	---
Sweeney,Mark	StL	19	18	153.1	153	11	1	20	.994	---
Taubensee,Eddie	Cin	3	2	15.0	12	1	0	2	1.000	---
Tettleton,Mickey	Tex	9	9	83.0	80	6	0	7	1.000	---
Tingley,Ron	Det	1	0	1.0	1	0	0	0	1.000	---
Unroe,Tim	Mil	2	1	12.0	11	0	0	3	1.000	---
Valle,Dave	Tex	7	0	17.0	20	1	0	2	1.000	---
Vander Wal,John	Col	10	3	36.1	42	3	2	3	.957	---
Ventura,Robin	ChA	18	10	107.0	95	10	2	11	.981	---
Vitiello,Joe	KC	8	5	45.0	51	3	1	3	.982	---
Voigt,Jack	Bal	1	0	3.0	1	1	0	0	1.000	---
Voigt,Jack	Tex	5	3	24.0	19	1	1	3	.952	---
Wallach,Tim	LA	1	1	8.1	11	0	0	0	1.000	---
Walton,Jerome	Cin	3	0	4.0	3	0	0	0	1.000	---
White,Derrick	Det	16	2	44.1	47	5	1	4	.981	---

First Basemen - The Rest

Player	Tm	G	GS	Inn	PO	A	E	DP	Pct.	Rng
Wilkins,Rick	ChN	2	0	6.0	6	2	0	1	1.000	---
Worthington,Craig	Cin	4	3	28.0	24	2	0	3	1.000	---
Young,Kevin	Pit	6	4	39.0	30	2	0	2	1.000	---
Zeile,Todd	StL	34	33	291.2	310	29	7	29	.980	---
Zeile,Todd	ChN	1	1	11.0	17	0	0	3	1.000	---

Second Basemen - Regulars

Player	Tm	G	GS	Inn	PO	A	E	DP	Pct.	Rng
Vina,Fernando	Mil	99	62	626.2	183	226	7	69	.983	5.87
Young,Eric	Col	77	74	617.2	164	227	11	54	.973	5.70
Garcia,Carlos	Pit	92	89	767.1	218	264	9	70	.982	5.65
Reed,Jody	SD	130	118	1066.2	304	363	4	77	.994	5.63
Lansing,Mike	Mon	127	127	1105.1	307	372	6	77	.991	5.53
Veras,Quilvio	Fla	122	111	1001.0	298	315	9	85	.986	5.51
Frye,Jeff	Tex	83	76	688.2	172	246	11	51	.974	5.46
Alicea,Luis	Bos	132	130	1150.2	255	429	16	98	.977	5.35
Sanchez,Rey	ChN	111	101	903.2	194	342	7	57	.987	5.34
Morandini,Mickey	Phi	122	112	1027.1	268	336	7	72	.989	5.29
Bates,Jason	Col	81	56	551.0	134	188	3	46	.991	5.26
Gates,Brent	Oak	132	128	1129.0	232	424	12	79	.982	5.23
Baerga,Carlos	Cle	134	133	1165.0	230	444	19	97	.973	5.21
Kent,Jeff	NYN	122	122	1045.2	246	354	10	66	.984	5.16
Kelly,Pat	NYA	87	83	731.2	161	255	7	52	.983	5.12
Alomar,Roberto	Tor	128	128	1126.2	273	365	4	84	.994	5.10
Knoblauch,Chuck	Min	136	136	1159.2	253	400	10	85	.985	5.07
Biggio,Craig	Hou	141	139	1273.1	297	418	10	74	.986	5.05
Boone,Bret	Cin	138	138	1214.1	312	362	4	106	.994	5.00
Barberie,Bret	Bal	74	63	543.0	115	186	7	45	.977	4.99
DeShields,Delino	LA	114	108	968.1	203	330	11	54	.980	4.95
Thompson,Robby	SF	91	90	770.2	181	238	3	49	.993	4.89
Alexander,Manny	Bal	82	64	564.0	137	165	9	44	.971	4.82
Lemke,Mark	Atl	115	115	967.1	205	305	5	61	.990	4.75
Durham,Ray	ChA	122	118	1049.2	245	299	15	66	.973	4.66
Cora,Joey	Sea	112	102	919.2	206	261	22	51	.955	4.57
Easley,Damion	Cal	88	82	701.0	145	209	7	41	.981	4.54
Average	---	110	103	919.2	219	308	9	67	.983	5.17

Second Basemen - The Rest

Player	Tm	G	GS	Inn	PO	A	E	DP	Pct.	Rng
Alfonzo,Edgardo	NYN	29	19	191.0	36	51	1	7	.989	4.10
Arias,Alex	Fla	6	4	37.1	9	19	0	3	1.000	6.75
Bell,David	StL	37	36	317.2	75	103	6	27	.967	5.04
Bell,Juan	Bos	5	3	28.0	9	11	0	4	1.000	6.43
Belliard,Rafael	Atl	32	24	226.1	42	91	0	11	1.000	5.29
Beltre,Esteban	Tex	15	7	77.2	13	28	2	6	.953	4.75
Benjamin,Mike	SF	8	4	43.1	7	14	0	1	1.000	4.36
Bogar,Tim	NYN	7	2	32.0	6	20	2	6	.929	7.31
Brady,Doug	ChA	6	5	45.0	14	21	0	4	1.000	7.00
Branson,Jeff	Cin	6	0	5.1	1	1	0	0	1.000	3.38
Brosius,Scott	Oak	3	2	19.0	3	4	0	1	1.000	3.32
Browne,Jerry	Fla	27	21	189.0	61	66	1	13	.992	6.05
Caceres,Edgar	KC	36	22	201.1	50	71	1	8	.992	5.41
Caraballo,Ramon	StL	24	22	196.2	56	73	6	20	.956	5.90
Cedeno,Domingo	Tor	20	12	124.0	30	42	0	8	1.000	5.23

Second Basemen - The Rest

Player	Tm	G	GS	Inn	PO	A	E	DP	Pct.	Rng
Cianfrocco,Archi	SD	3	2	17.0	7	6	0	1	1.000	6.88
Cirillo,Jeff	Mil	25	24	184.0	51	75	2	16	.984	6.16
Correia,Rod	Cal	3	0	6.0	0	3	0	0	1.000	4.50
Cromer,Tripp	StL	11	9	67.0	15	16	1	3	.969	4.16
Diaz,Mario	Fla	9	7	58.0	16	19	2	8	.946	5.43
Donnels,Chris	Hou	1	1	6.0	0	1	0	0	1.000	1.50
Donnels,Chris	Bos	3	0	5.0	1	1	0	1	1.000	3.60
Duncan,Mariano	Phi	24	22	176.0	50	60	5	17	.957	5.63
Duncan,Mariano	Cin	7	6	54.0	13	13	1	3	.963	4.33
Eenhoorn,Robert	NYA	3	3	22.0	11	6	0	2	1.000	6.95
Elster,Kevin	NYA	1	0	1.0	0	0	0	0	.000	.00
Espinoza,Alvaro	Cle	22	9	102.0	18	39	2	7	.966	5.03
Fermin,Felix	Sea	29	25	207.0	32	75	1	11	.991	4.65
Fernandez,Tony	NYA	4	4	36.0	7	9	0	2	1.000	4.00
Fletcher,Scott	Det	63	49	441.0	109	161	0	48	1.000	5.51
Foley,Tom	Mon	3	1	12.1	2	5	0	2	1.000	5.11
Fonville,Chad	Mon	2	0	2.0	0	0	0	0	.000	.00
Fonville,Chad	LA	36	33	293.2	71	98	6	14	.966	5.18
Franco,Matt	ChN	3	1	9.0	0	2	0	0	1.000	2.00
Frazier,Lou	Mon	1	0	2.0	0	1	0	0	1.000	4.50
Gallego,Mike	Oak	18	14	125.0	25	48	3	9	.961	5.26
Giovanola,Ed	Atl	7	1	26.0	9	5	0	1	1.000	4.85
Gomez,Chris	Det	31	26	232.1	55	82	3	19	.979	5.31
Gonzales,Rene	Cal	6	1	13.1	4	6	0	0	1.000	6.75
Grebeck,Craig	ChA	8	7	59.2	11	14	0	2	1.000	3.77
Grudzielanek,Mark	Mon	13	10	93.2	26	26	2	5	.963	5.00
Hale,Chip	Min	7	0	13.2	2	5	0	1	1.000	4.61
Haney,Todd	ChN	17	14	132.0	31	57	2	12	.978	6.00
Harris,Lenny	Cin	1	0	10.2	2	0	0	0	1.000	1.69
Hemond,Scott	StL	6	3	28.0	4	7	0	0	1.000	3.54
Hernandez,Jose	ChN	29	26	226.0	56	76	4	18	.971	5.26
Holbert,Ray	SD	7	1	15.2	3	3	0	1	1.000	3.45
Howard,Dave	KC	41	28	273.2	68	99	1	20	.994	5.49
Hudler,Rex	Cal	52	37	345.0	93	114	3	32	.986	5.40
Hulett,Tim	StL	2	2	15.0	5	11	1	3	.941	9.60
Huson,Jeff	Bal	21	17	160.0	38	45	0	14	1.000	4.67
Ingram,Garey	LA	7	3	31.0	7	11	0	3	1.000	5.23
Johnson,Howard	ChN	8	2	30.1	7	9	2	2	.889	4.75
Jordan,Kevin	Phi	9	9	78.0	28	33	1	8	.984	7.04
King,Jeff	Pit	8	4	44.2	8	14	0	4	1.000	4.43
Lee,Manuel	StL	1	1	3.0	2	2	1	0	.800	12.00
Lewis,Mark	Cin	2	0	5.0	0	3	0	0	1.000	5.40
Lind,Jose	KC	29	27	238.1	56	75	1	17	.992	4.95
Lind,Jose	Cal	15	14	119.0	24	40	0	10	1.000	4.84
Liriano,Nelson	Pit	67	51	463.1	130	132	5	31	.981	5.09
Listach,Pat	Mil	59	55	450.1	104	169	0	43	1.000	5.46
Livingstone,Scott	SD	4	0	4.1	2	3	0	1	1.000	10.38
Lockhart,Keith	KC	61	52	426.0	107	160	7	43	.974	5.64
Loretta,Mark	Mil	4	3	25.0	5	9	0	2	1.000	5.04
Martin,Norberto	ChA	17	15	130.1	35	41	4	12	.950	5.25
McLemore,Mark	Tex	66	61	518.2	106	184	2	40	.993	5.03
Mejia,Roberto	Col	16	14	119.2	35	30	2	4	.970	4.89
Mordecai,Mike	Atl	21	4	72.0	14	19	0	8	1.000	4.13
Mota,Jose	KC	2	1	5.0	1	3	0	0	1.000	7.20
Oquendo,Jose	StL	62	45	417.0	114	149	5	32	.981	5.68
Owen,Spike	Cal	16	11	100.0	28	21	0	7	1.000	4.41
Patterson,John	SF	53	40	381.0	114	112	4	30	.983	5.34
Pena,Geronimo	StL	25	25	221.1	50	73	3	18	.976	5.00

Second Basemen - The Rest

Player	Tm	G	GS	Inn	PO	A	E	DP	Pct.	Rng
Penn,Shannon	Det	3	2	19.0	10	9	3	4	.864	9.00
Perez,Tomas	Tor	7	4	42.0	10	13	0	3	1.000	4.93
Pozo,Arquimedez	Sea	1	0	2.0	0	1	0	0	1.000	4.50
Puckett,Kirby	Min	1	0	1.0	0	1	0	0	1.000	9.00
Raabe,Brian	Min	4	2	19.2	5	7	0	3	1.000	5.49
Randa,Joe	KC	9	5	53.0	7	15	1	3	.957	3.74
Ready,Randy	Phi	1	1	9.0	1	1	0	0	1.000	2.00
Reboulet,Jeff	Min	15	6	78.1	17	29	1	5	.979	5.29
Ripken,Billy	Cle	7	2	34.0	7	6	0	1	1.000	3.44
Roberts,Bip	SD	25	23	181.0	36	68	2	11	.981	5.17
Rodriguez,Carlos	Bos	7	4	47.0	9	15	1	3	.960	4.60
Rodriguez,Steve	Bos	1	1	8.0	1	2	0	0	1.000	3.38
Rodriguez,Steve	Det	12	11	99.0	21	34	1	6	.982	5.00
Samuel,Juan	Det	6	3	31.0	9	12	1	3	.955	6.10
Santangelo,F.P.	Mon	5	0	10.0	1	0	0	0	1.000	0.90
Scarsone,Steve	SF	13	10	98.2	26	36	3	12	.954	5.66
Shipley,Craig	Hou	5	3	21.0	5	10	0	1	1.000	6.43
Shumpert,Terry	Bos	8	6	54.0	12	15	0	4	1.000	4.50
Silvestri,Dave	NYA	7	2	22.0	2	11	0	1	1.000	5.32
Silvestri,Dave	Mon	3	1	9.0	3	2	0	0	1.000	5.00
Sojo,Luis	Sea	19	17	140.2	23	44	3	5	.957	4.29
Spiers,Bill	NYN	6	1	20.1	4	12	0	1	1.000	7.08
Stankiewicz,Andy	Hou	6	1	20.0	3	7	0	1	1.000	4.50
Strange,Doug	Sea	5	2	20.0	3	5	0	1	1.000	3.60
Stynes,Chris	KC	17	9	90.2	22	35	1	12	.983	5.66
Treadway,Jeff	LA	1	0	2.0	1	1	0	1	1.000	9.00
Treadway,Jeff	Mon	11	5	49.1	12	14	0	2	1.000	4.74
Velarde,Randy	NYA	62	53	472.0	103	140	6	25	.976	4.63
Vizcaino,Jose	NYN	1	0	2.0	0	1	0	0	1.000	4.50
Whitaker,Lou	Det	63	53	452.2	107	162	4	32	.985	5.35
Zosky,Eddie	Fla	1	0	0.2	0	1	0	1	1.000	13.50

Third Basemen - Regulars

Player	Tm	G	GS	Inn	PO	A	E	DP	Pct.	Rng
Williams,Matt	SF	74	74	642.1	49	178	10	10	.958	3.18
Fryman,Travis	Det	144	144	1275.0	106	335	14	38	.969	3.11
Cooper,Scott	StL	110	102	908.0	65	242	18	22	.945	3.04
Branson,Jeff	Cin	98	83	680.2	52	178	7	22	.970	3.04
Cirillo,Jeff	Mil	108	58	614.1	47	153	13	21	.939	2.93
Caminiti,Ken	SD	143	142	1226.0	102	293	27	24	.936	2.90
Berry,Sean	Mon	83	78	674.2	54	163	12	18	.948	2.89
Jones,Chipper	Atl	123	121	1055.0	80	258	25	19	.931	2.88
Seitzer,Kevin	Mil	88	86	660.0	52	159	7	18	.968	2.88
Phillips,Tony	Cal	88	87	734.2	53	178	19	17	.924	2.83
Pendleton,Terry	Fla	130	128	1129.1	104	249	18	21	.951	2.81
Ventura,Robin	ChA	122	118	1016.1	107	206	17	14	.948	2.77
King,Jeff	Pit	84	80	684.0	47	163	13	13	.942	2.76
Naehring,Tim	Bos	124	123	1077.2	86	244	16	22	.954	2.76
Sprague,Ed	Tor	139	138	1215.0	134	234	16	20	.958	2.73
Gaetti,Gary	KC	123	118	1047.2	90	220	15	20	.954	2.66
Magadan,Dave	Hou	100	84	736.2	55	161	18	8	.923	2.64
Hayes,Charlie	Phi	141	141	1255.0	104	262	14	25	.963	2.62
Castilla,Vinny	Col	136	133	1175.2	86	254	15	19	.958	2.60
Boggs,Wade	NYA	117	105	935.0	69	192	5	10	.981	2.51
Bonilla,Bobby	TOT	70	65	569.0	38	119	16	11	.908	2.48
Leius,Scott	Min	112	102	911.2	60	182	14	21	.945	2.39

Third Basemen - Regulars

Player	Tm	G	GS	Inn	PO	A	E	DP	Pct.	Rng
Zeile,Todd	ChN	75	73	641.1	34	134	11	12	.939	2.36
Wallach,Tim	LA	96	92	792.0	50	156	5	9	.976	2.34
Thome,Jim	Cle	134	128	1144.2	75	214	16	19	.948	2.27
Blowers,Mike	Sea	126	113	1008.2	81	167	14	9	.947	2.21
Average	---	111	104	915.2	72	203	14	17	.950	2.71

Third Basemen - The Rest

Player	Tm	G	GS	Inn	PO	A	E	DP	Pct.	Rng
Alexander,Manny	Bal	2	0	6.0	1	0	1	0	.500	1.50
Alfonzo,Edgardo	NYN	58	57	488.0	40	110	6	9	.962	2.77
Andrews,Shane	Mon	51	38	334.2	22	86	3	2	.973	2.90
Arias,Alex	Fla	21	11	116.0	8	23	2	3	.939	2.41
Barberie,Bret	Bal	3	0	3.0	0	1	0	0	1.000	3.00
Bates,Jason	Col	15	11	104.1	10	26	1	1	.973	3.11
Battle,Howard	Tor	6	4	39.0	1	6	0	0	1.000	1.62
Bell,David	Cle	2	0	4.0	0	2	0	0	1.000	4.50
Bell,David	StL	3	2	17.0	2	5	1	0	.875	3.71
Bell,Jay	Pit	3	3	24.2	1	6	0	1	1.000	2.55
Bell,Juan	Bos	1	0	2.0	1	0	0	0	1.000	4.50
Beltre,Esteban	Tex	1	0	1.0	0	0	0	0	.000	.00
Benjamin,Mike	SF	43	30	288.2	29	77	4	3	.964	3.30
Bogar,Tim	NYN	25	9	115.0	9	29	2	4	.950	2.97
Bonilla,Bobby	NYN	46	41	366.0	24	73	13	6	.882	2.39
Bonilla,Bobby	Bal	24	24	203.0	14	46	3	5	.952	2.66
Brosius,Scott	Oak	60	50	445.1	27	96	11	7	.918	2.49
Browne,Jerry	Fla	7	4	35.0	1	10	0	0	1.000	2.83
Brumley,Mike	Hou	1	0	1.1	0	0	0	0	.000	.00
Buechele,Steve	ChN	32	30	268.2	26	55	5	2	.942	2.71
Buechele,Steve	Tex	9	6	62.0	7	11	0	2	1.000	2.61
Busch,Mike	LA	10	2	30.0	2	5	1	0	.875	2.10
Caceres,Edgar	KC	3	0	9.0	2	3	0	1	1.000	5.00
Castellano,Pedro	Col	3	0	8.1	1	0	0	0	1.000	1.08
Castro,Juan	LA	7	0	9.0	2	3	0	1	1.000	5.00
Cedeno,Andujar	SD	1	0	8.0	0	1	1	0	.500	1.13
Cedeno,Domingo	Tor	1	0	2.0	0	0	0	0	.000	.00
Cianfrocco,Archi	SD	3	0	5.0	1	0	0	0	1.000	1.80
Coles,Darnell	StL	22	20	169.1	13	26	2	1	.951	2.07
Coomer,Ron	Min	13	10	81.1	6	20	1	1	.963	2.88
Correia,Rod	Cal	2	1	12.0	0	6	2	1	.750	4.50
Davis,Russ	NYA	34	27	227.2	15	45	2	1	.968	2.37
Diaz,Mario	Fla	3	0	5.2	1	0	0	0	1.000	1.59
Donnels,Chris	Hou	9	4	45.0	3	6	2	2	.818	1.80
Donnels,Chris	Bos	27	18	176.0	17	34	4	2	.927	2.61
Duncan,Mariano	Phi	1	1	9.0	2	2	0	0	1.000	4.00
Elster,Kevin	Phi	2	1	12.1	2	2	0	0	1.000	2.92
Espinoza,Alvaro	Cle	22	16	142.1	10	25	1	1	.972	2.21
Franco,Matt	ChN	1	0	1.1	0	0	0	0	.000	.00
Gallego,Mike	Oak	12	8	71.2	5	10	2	1	.882	1.88
Garcia,Freddy	Pit	8	3	36.0	6	15	1	4	.955	5.25
Giambi,Jason	Oak	30	26	225.0	27	45	3	4	.960	2.88
Giovanola,Ed	Atl	3	0	5.0	0	0	0	0	.000	.00
Gomez,Leo	Bal	44	36	308.0	23	68	2	3	.978	2.66
Gonzales,Rene	Cal	18	2	41.0	2	6	0	0	1.000	1.76
Gonzalez,Alex	Tor	9	2	34.2	6	11	2	1	.895	4.41
Grebeck,Craig	ChA	18	9	104.1	14	18	1	3	.970	2.76
Greene,Willie	Cin	7	6	50.1	1	13	0	1	1.000	2.50

Third Basemen - The Rest

Player	Tm	G	GS	Inn	PO	A	E	DP	Pct.	Rng
Grudzielanek,Mark	Mon	31	25	236.2	18	67	6	2	.934	3.23
Gutierrez,Ricky	Hou	2	0	2.0	0	0	0	0	.000	.00
Hale,Chip	Min	5	0	8.1	1	1	0	1	1.000	2.16
Haney,Todd	ChN	4	2	22.0	3	4	0	0	1.000	2.86
Hansen,Dave	LA	58	43	377.1	27	70	7	6	.933	2.31
Harris,Lenny	Cin	24	15	148.2	9	53	4	3	.939	3.75
Haselman,Bill	Bos	1	0	1.0	0	0	0	0	.000	.00
Hernandez,Jose	ChN	20	10	119.1	12	36	0	1	1.000	3.62
Huskey,Butch	NYN	27	27	213.1	14	59	6	2	.924	3.08
Huson,Jeff	Bal	33	24	220.1	21	44	0	5	1.000	2.66
Ingram,Garey	LA	12	6	69.0	9	15	8	0	.750	3.13
Javier,Stan	Oak	1	0	1.0	0	0	0	0	.000	.00
Johnson,Howard	ChN	34	29	246.1	10	52	5	4	.925	2.27
Jordan,Kevin	Phi	1	1	9.0	1	2	0	0	1.000	3.00
Kmak,Joe	ChN	1	0	2.0	0	1	0	0	1.000	4.50
Ledesma,Aaron	NYN	10	4	47.0	2	12	2	0	.875	2.68
Lewis,Mark	Cin	72	40	400.2	19	104	4	4	.969	2.76
Liriano,Nelson	Pit	5	3	30.0	0	5	0	0	1.000	1.50
Listach,Pat	Mil	2	0	4.0	1	0	0	0	1.000	2.25
Livingstone,Scott	SD	13	2	45.2	1	13	0	0	1.000	2.76
Lockhart,Keith	KC	17	11	93.0	5	18	1	1	.958	2.23
Manto,Jeff	Bal	69	60	526.2	40	100	6	11	.959	2.39
Martin,Norberto	ChA	9	4	36.1	2	7	2	0	.818	2.23
Martinez,Carlos	Cal	16	11	99.0	5	25	1	6	.968	2.73
Martinez,Edgar	Sea	4	4	30.0	1	3	1	0	.800	1.20
McGinnis,Russ	KC	1	0	3.0	1	0	0	0	1.000	3.00
Mordecai,Mike	Atl	6	1	30.1	0	5	0	0	1.000	1.48
Nevin,Phil	Hou	17	17	142.2	10	32	3	3	.933	2.65
Oliva,Jose	Atl	25	22	198.1	14	40	6	3	.900	2.45
Oliva,Jose	StL	18	17	150.1	11	31	1	4	.977	2.51
Oquendo,Jose	StL	2	0	6.0	0	0	0	0	.000	.00
Ortiz,Luis	Tex	35	29	247.0	9	43	8	2	.867	1.89
Owen,Spike	Cal	29	23	211.2	16	36	3	0	.945	2.21
Owens,Eric	Cin	2	0	4.0	0	0	0	0	.000	.00
Pagliarulo,Mike	Tex	68	52	483.0	42	115	6	12	.963	2.93
Palmer,Dean	Tex	35	35	302.2	19	73	5	7	.948	2.74
Paquette,Craig	Oak	75	60	530.0	38	77	8	11	.935	1.95
Parker,Rick	LA	2	0	3.0	0	0	0	0	.000	.00
Perez,Eduardo	Cal	23	21	186.0	16	37	7	3	.883	2.56
Perez,Tomas	Tor	1	0	2.0	0	0	0	0	.000	.00
Perry,Herbert	Cle	1	0	7.0	3	0	0	0	1.000	3.86
Puckett,Kirby	Min	1	0	0.2	0	0	0	0	.000	.00
Pye,Eddie	LA	2	1	10.0	0	0	0	0	.000	.00
Raabe,Brian	Min	2	1	10.0	0	0	0	0	.000	.00
Randa,Joe	KC	22	15	135.1	8	29	2	1	.949	2.46
Reboulet,Jeff	Min	22	13	114.2	14	33	2	2	.959	3.69
Ripken,Billy	Cle	1	0	3.0	0	0	0	0	.000	.00
Rodriguez,Carlos	Bos	1	0	2.0	0	1	0	0	1.000	4.50
Sabo,Chris	ChA	1	1	9.0	0	1	0	0	1.000	1.00
Sabo,Chris	StL	1	1	9.0	0	1	0	0	1.000	1.00
Scarsone,Steve	SF	50	40	362.2	30	70	8	8	.926	2.48
Schofield,Dick	LA	1	0	2.0	0	0	0	0	.000	.00
Sefcik,Kevin	Phi	2	0	5.0	0	1	0	1	1.000	1.80
Sharperson,Mike	Atl	1	0	3.0	0	0	0	0	.000	.00
Sheaffer,Danny	StL	1	1	6.0	0	2	0	0	1.000	3.00
Shipley,Craig	Hou	65	39	387.2	27	80	2	5	.982	2.48
Shumpert,Terry	Bos	5	3	34.0	2	7	0	0	1.000	2.38
Silvestri,Dave	Mon	8	3	36.2	2	13	1	0	.938	3.68

Third Basemen - The Rest

Player	Tm	G	GS	Inn	PO	A	E	DP	Pct.	Rng
Snopek,Chris	ChA	17	13	118.2	11	13	0	0	1.000	1.82
Spiers,Bill	NYN	11	6	61.2	9	18	7	2	.794	3.94
Stahoviak,Scott	Min	22	18	145.2	9	30	4	3	.907	2.41
Stankiewicz,Andy	Hou	3	0	5.0	2	1	0	0	1.000	5.40
Strange,Doug	Sea	41	29	250.2	28	65	5	1	.949	3.34
Treadway,Jeff	LA	2	0	2.2	0	0	0	0	.000	.00
Treadway,Jeff	Mon	1	0	1.0	0	1	0	0	1.000	9.00
Valentin,Jose	Mil	1	0	5.0	0	2	0	1	1.000	3.60
Velarde,Randy	NYA	19	13	122.0	6	30	0	2	1.000	2.66
Vina,Fernando	Mil	2	0	2.2	0	0	0	0	.000	.00
Wehner,John	Pit	19	12	117.1	11	26	0	1	1.000	2.84
Worthington,Craig	Cin	2	0	5.0	2	2	0	0	1.000	7.20
Worthington,Craig	Tex	26	22	189.1	13	35	1	3	.980	2.28
Young,Kevin	Pit	48	43	383.1	28	108	12	7	.919	3.19

Shortstops - Regulars

Player	Tm	G	GS	Inn	PO	A	E	DP	Pct.	Rng
Gil,Benji	Tex	130	126	1100.2	228	409	17	92	.974	5.21
Valentin,Jose	Mil	104	100	884.1	163	333	15	81	.971	5.05
Gagne,Greg	KC	118	112	1008.0	175	387	18	87	.969	5.02
Gomez,Chris	Det	97	90	798.0	155	280	12	59	.973	4.91
Bordick,Mike	Oak	126	124	1073.1	246	338	10	92	.983	4.90
Clayton,Royce	SF	136	133	1169.0	223	412	20	91	.969	4.89
Vizcaino,Jose	NYN	134	128	1119.2	189	411	10	78	.984	4.82
Valentin,John	Bos	135	134	1192.2	225	413	18	94	.973	4.81
Weiss,Walt	Col	136	130	1140.2	202	407	16	97	.974	4.81
Bell,Jay	Pit	136	130	1150.0	205	408	14	89	.978	4.80
Meares,Pat	Min	114	109	953.0	185	317	18	67	.965	4.74
Vizquel,Omar	Cle	136	135	1187.0	211	407	9	85	.986	4.69
Miller,Orlando	Hou	89	85	775.1	133	269	15	49	.964	4.67
Cromer,Tripp	StL	95	86	758.0	111	277	16	58	.960	4.61
Dunston,Shawon	ChN	125	123	1043.2	188	336	17	50	.969	4.52
Guillen,Ozzie	ChA	120	108	967.2	167	318	12	55	.976	4.51
Stocker,Kevin	Phi	125	120	1073.1	148	383	17	71	.969	4.45
Ripken,Cal	Bal	144	144	1250.0	205	409	7	99	.989	4.42
Larkin,Barry	Cin	131	131	1090.2	192	342	11	71	.980	4.41
DiSarcina,Gary	Cal	98	98	864.0	146	275	6	46	.986	4.39
Blauser,Jeff	Atl	115	114	997.0	150	335	15	60	.970	4.38
Offerman,Jose	LA	115	111	988.2	166	312	35	56	.932	4.35
Cedeno,Andujar	SD	116	108	944.1	139	304	16	58	.965	4.22
Fernandez,Tony	NYA	103	101	887.2	140	274	10	61	.976	4.20
Abbott,Kurt	Fla	115	109	975.0	149	290	19	64	.959	4.05
Sojo,Luis	Sea	80	72	653.0	110	175	5	33	.983	4.04
Gonzalez,Alex	Tor	97	96	841.0	158	216	17	44	.957	4.04
Cordero,Wil	Mon	105	105	928.2	123	281	17	44	.960	3.92
Average	---	116	112	992.2	172	332	14	68	.972	4.58

Shortstops - The Rest

Player	Tm	G	GS	Inn	PO	A	E	DP	Pct.	Rng
Alexander,Manny	Bal	7	0	15.0	2	5	0	1	1.000	4.20
Alfonzo,Edgardo	NYN	6	3	27.1	5	9	0	3	1.000	4.61
Arias,Alex	Fla	36	28	258.0	40	85	7	15	.947	4.36
Aurilia,Rich	SF	6	4	35.1	8	16	0	4	1.000	6.11
Bates,Jason	Col	20	10	110.0	24	41	1	5	.985	5.32

Shortstops - The Rest

Player	Tm	G	GS	Inn	PO	A	E	DP	Pct.	Rng
Bell,Juan	Bos	6	5	45.0	6	12	3	1	.857	3.60
Belliard,Rafael	Atl	40	30	280.0	32	87	1	12	.992	3.83
Beltre,Esteban	Tex	36	18	184.1	42	51	3	13	.969	4.54
Benjamin,Mike	SF	16	7	89.1	15	30	0	6	1.000	4.53
Bogar,Tim	NYN	27	13	141.2	20	46	2	5	.971	4.19
Branson,Jeff	Cin	32	11	160.0	31	62	2	15	.979	5.23
Brosius,Scott	Oak	3	0	4.0	2	2	0	1	1.000	9.00
Brumley,Mike	Hou	3	0	7.0	0	1	0	0	1.000	1.29
Caceres,Edgar	KC	8	6	53.0	10	18	0	6	1.000	4.75
Castilla,Vinny	Col	5	4	32.2	3	8	0	1	1.000	3.03
Castro,Juan	LA	4	1	12.0	1	4	0	2	1.000	3.75
Cedeno,Domingo	Tor	30	29	253.2	55	89	3	17	.980	5.11
Cianfrocco,Archi	SD	15	14	116.1	17	35	3	7	.945	4.02
Cirillo,Jeff	Mil	2	0	4.0	0	1	0	0	1.000	2.25
Cora,Joey	Sea	1	0	1.0	0	0	1	0	.000	.00
Correia,Rod	Cal	7	4	39.0	6	12	3	4	.857	4.15
Counsell,Craig	Col	3	0	5.0	1	1	0	1	1.000	3.60
Cruz,Fausto	Oak	8	8	70.0	9	24	1	2	.971	4.24
Diaz,Mario	Fla	5	5	40.0	6	11	0	4	1.000	3.83
Duncan,Mariano	Phi	14	10	99.1	14	51	3	9	.956	5.89
Duncan,Mariano	Cin	6	2	35.2	8	13	0	2	1.000	5.30
Easley,Damion	Cal	25	25	195.0	41	67	3	19	.973	4.98
Eenhoorn,Robert	NYA	2	1	12.0	1	2	1	0	.750	2.25
Elster,Kevin	NYA	10	5	47.0	10	14	0	2	1.000	4.60
Elster,Kevin	Phi	19	14	117.2	18	36	1	11	.982	4.13
Espinoza,Alvaro	Cle	19	9	114.0	13	35	2	8	.960	3.79
Fermin,Felix	Sea	46	35	310.2	75	93	5	30	.971	4.87
Fletcher,Scott	Det	3	0	6.0	0	1	0	0	1.000	1.50
Fonville,Chad	LA	38	31	281.2	38	95	4	13	.971	4.25
Gallego,Mike	Oak	11	11	95.0	16	32	0	5	1.000	4.55
Garcia,Carlos	Pit	15	12	100.1	17	34	6	5	.895	4.57
Giovanola,Ed	Atl	1	0	4.1	0	2	0	0	1.000	4.15
Gonzales,Rene	Cal	1	0	1.0	0	0	0	0	.000	.00
Grebeck,Craig	ChA	31	28	236.0	52	95	6	20	.961	5.61
Grudzielanek,Mark	Mon	34	32	282.2	50	104	2	18	.987	4.90
Gutierrez,Ricky	Hou	44	40	359.2	64	107	8	17	.955	4.65
Hernandez,Jose	ChN	43	19	234.1	44	77	5	16	.960	4.65
Hocking,Denny	Min	6	6	54.2	13	20	1	4	.971	5.43
Holbert,Ray	SD	30	15	160.0	24	55	5	12	.940	4.44
Howard,Dave	KC	33	26	227.0	47	93	2	23	.986	5.55
Hulett,Tim	StL	1	0	3.0	1	2	1	0	.750	9.00
Huson,Jeff	Bal	1	0	2.0	0	1	1	0	.500	4.50
Jeter,Derek	NYA	15	14	120.0	17	34	2	6	.962	3.83
Johnson,Howard	ChN	1	0	3.0	1	2	0	1	1.000	9.00
King,Jeff	Pit	2	0	11.0	0	1	2	0	.333	0.82
Knoblauch,Chuck	Min	2	0	2.2	1	0	0	0	1.000	3.38
Lansing,Mike	Mon	2	0	1.1	0	1	0	0	1.000	6.75
Ledesma,Aaron	NYN	2	0	2.1	0	0	0	0	.000	.00
Leius,Scott	Min	7	0	12.0	0	3	0	0	1.000	2.25
Lewis,Mark	Cin	2	0	3.0	0	1	0	0	1.000	3.00
Liriano,Nelson	Pit	1	1	6.0	0	0	0	0	.000	.00
Listach,Pat	Mil	36	29	260.0	54	103	6	30	.963	5.43
Loretta,Mark	Mil	13	11	97.0	14	33	1	6	.979	4.36
Martin,Norberto	ChA	7	4	35.0	8	17	1	2	.962	6.43
Mordecai,Mike	Atl	6	0	10.1	1	5	0	1	1.000	5.23
Oquendo,Jose	StL	24	16	161.1	20	61	1	14	.988	4.52
Owen,Spike	Cal	25	8	105.1	22	38	3	7	.952	5.13
Paquette,Craig	Oak	8	1	30.2	5	12	0	6	1.000	4.99

Shortstops - The Rest

Player	Tm	G	GS	Inn	PO	A	E	DP	Pct.	Rng
Parker,Rick	LA	2	0	1.0	0	0	0	0	.000	.00
Perez,Tomas	Tor	31	19	198.0	39	65	5	14	.954	4.73
Puckett,Kirby	Min	1	0	0.1	0	0	0	0	.000	.00
Reboulet,Jeff	Min	39	29	249.2	53	84	1	22	.993	4.94
Reed,Jody	SD	5	0	8.0	1	3	0	1	1.000	4.50
Roberts,Bip	SD	7	7	56.0	5	18	1	4	.958	3.70
Rodriguez,Alex	Sea	46	38	342.0	55	106	8	14	.953	4.24
Rodriguez,Carlos	Bos	6	3	30.0	7	11	0	3	1.000	5.40
Rodriguez,Steve	Bos	4	0	7.0	0	2	1	0	.667	2.57
Rodriguez,Steve	Det	1	0	1.0	0	0	0	0	.000	.00
Sanchez,Rey	ChN	4	2	20.0	1	9	0	2	1.000	4.50
Schofield,Dick	LA	3	1	11.2	3	9	0	3	1.000	9.26
Schofield,Dick	Cal	12	10	80.0	8	23	0	2	1.000	3.49
Shipley,Craig	Hou	11	7	69.0	11	24	1	1	.972	4.57
Shumpert,Terry	Bos	3	2	18.0	7	13	2	3	.909	10.00
Silvestri,Dave	NYA	1	0	1.0	0	0	0	0	.000	.00
Silvestri,Dave	Mon	9	7	71.0	8	20	0	1	1.000	3.55
Smith,Ozzie	StL	41	41	343.1	60	128	7	27	.964	4.93
Snopek,Chris	ChA	6	5	46.0	14	18	2	5	.941	6.26
Stankiewicz,Andy	Hou	14	12	109.1	15	51	1	6	.985	5.43
Trammell,Alan	Det	60	54	470.0	86	158	5	34	.980	4.67
Velarde,Randy	NYA	28	24	217.0	38	87	3	21	.977	5.18
Vina,Fernando	Mil	6	4	40.2	11	21	1	4	.970	7.08
Wehner,John	Pit	1	1	8.0	0	2	0	0	1.000	2.25
Zosky,Eddie	Fla	4	1	13.0	1	1	1	0	.667	1.38

Left Fielders - Regulars

Player	Tm	G	GS	Inn	PO	A	E	DP	Pct.	Rng
Cordova,Marty	Min	132	128	1123.1	329	11	4	1	.988	2.72
Anderson,Garret	Cal	99	92	814.2	213	7	5	0	.978	2.43
Polonia,Luis	TOT	75	60	549.1	140	5	0	1	1.000	2.38
Belle,Albert	Cle	142	142	1265.0	304	7	6	1	.981	2.21
Carter,Joe	Tor	116	110	943.0	225	6	7	1	.971	2.20
Gonzalez,Luis	TOT	129	121	1066.0	253	7	6	0	.977	2.20
Bonds,Barry	SF	143	143	1257.0	279	12	6	1	.980	2.08
Raines,Tim	ChA	108	103	878.0	193	7	4	1	.980	2.05
Coleman,Vince	TOT	95	95	816.2	177	9	3	1	.984	2.05
May,Derrick	TOT	74	64	553.1	124	4	4	0	.969	2.03
Henderson,Rickey	Oak	90	89	741.1	161	5	2	1	.988	2.02
Gant,Ron	Cin	117	117	930.1	191	7	3	0	.985	1.92
Gilkey,Bernard	StL	118	117	1021.2	206	10	3	4	.986	1.90
Anderson,Brady	Bal	121	108	939.1	193	0	2	0	.990	1.85
Greenwell,Mike	Bos	118	118	1043.2	202	10	6	1	.972	1.83
Conine,Jeff	Fla	118	112	1010.1	195	7	5	1	.976	1.80
Martin,Al	Pit	95	74	657.1	124	4	4	1	.970	1.75
Bichette,Dante	Col	120	118	1010.2	172	7	3	0	.984	1.59
Klesko,Ryan	Atl	102	100	754.0	111	2	7	0	.942	1.35
Average	---	111	105	914.1	199	6	4	0	.980	2.03

Left Fielders - The Rest

Player	Tm	G	GS	Inn	PO	A	E	DP	Pct.	Rng
Aldrete,Mike	Oak	9	6	46.0	10	0	1	0	.909	1.96
Aldrete,Mike	Cal	2	1	8.0	7	0	0	0	1.000	7.88
Alou,Moises	Mon	62	62	517.0	94	3	2	0	.980	1.69
Amaral,Rich	Sea	53	24	247.0	53	3	1	0	.982	2.04
Amaro,Ruben	Cle	5	1	16.0	5	0	0	0	1.000	2.81
Anthony,Eric	Cin	4	2	17.1	4	1	0	0	1.000	2.60
Ashley,Billy	LA	69	64	490.2	102	2	3	0	.972	1.91
Barry,Jeff	NYN	1	0	5.0	1	0	0	0	1.000	1.80
Bass,Kevin	Bal	32	24	214.1	59	1	1	0	.984	2.52
Battle,Allen	StL	14	11	103.0	31	0	1	0	.969	2.71
Bautista,Danny	Det	2	1	13.0	5	0	0	0	1.000	3.46
Bean,Billy	SD	4	1	21.1	3	0	1	0	.750	1.27
Becker,Rich	Min	2	0	4.0	3	1	0	0	1.000	9.00
Benitez,Yamil	Mon	3	0	8.0	2	0	0	0	1.000	2.25
Berroa,Geronimo	Oak	17	13	114.0	25	1	1	0	.963	2.05
Blowers,Mike	Sea	2	1	8.0	2	0	0	0	1.000	2.25
Bogar,Tim	NYN	1	0	2.0	0	0	0	0	.000	.00
Bonilla,Bobby	NYN	31	29	254.0	55	4	1	0	.983	2.09
Bonilla,Bobby	Bal	1	0	4.1	1	0	0	0	1.000	2.08
Bradshaw,Terry	StL	6	5	44.0	12	1	1	0	.929	2.66
Bragg,Darren	Sea	31	27	232.2	65	5	1	0	.986	2.71
Brosius,Scott	Oak	8	3	37.0	10	0	0	0	1.000	2.43
Browne,Jerry	Fla	11	4	60.1	10	1	1	1	.917	1.64
Brumley,Mike	Hou	3	1	9.2	2	0	0	0	1.000	1.86
Buford,Damon	NYN	25	24	209.1	44	1	2	0	.957	1.93
Bullett,Scott	ChN	54	21	226.2	48	1	1	0	.980	1.95
Burks,Ellis	Col	23	13	125.2	27	1	2	0	.933	2.01
Burnitz,Jeromy	Cle	5	1	18.0	9	0	0	0	1.000	4.50
Cangelosi,John	Hou	26	12	152.2	31	3	2	0	.944	2.00
Carreon,Mark	SF	3	0	6.0	3	0	0	0	1.000	4.50
Cedeno,Roger	LA	19	0	27.2	7	0	1	0	.875	2.28
Cianfrocco,Archi	SD	2	2	15.0	2	2	0	0	1.000	2.40
Clark,Dave	Pit	34	24	224.0	56	0	3	0	.949	2.25
Clark,Jerald	Min	12	11	95.0	25	1	0	0	1.000	2.46
Clark,Phil	SD	14	12	94.0	14	0	0	0	1.000	1.34
Coleman,Vince	KC	57	57	495.0	94	7	2	1	.981	1.84
Coleman,Vince	Sea	38	38	321.2	83	2	1	0	.988	2.38
Coles,Darnell	StL	1	1	8.0	1	0	0	0	1.000	1.13
Cookson,Brent	KC	10	7	56.0	14	0	0	0	1.000	2.25
Cordero,Wil	Mon	26	26	224.2	44	1	5	0	.900	1.80
Cummings,Midre	Pit	8	5	43.2	14	1	0	0	1.000	3.09
Cuyler,Milt	Det	34	22	208.1	47	2	3	0	.942	2.12
Dalesandro,Mark	Cal	1	0	1.0	1	0	0	0	1.000	9.00
Dawson,Andre	Fla	12	11	82.1	11	3	2	2	.875	1.53
Delgado,Carlos	Tor	17	15	125.0	34	1	0	0	1.000	2.52
Devereaux,Mike	Atl	14	2	45.0	13	0	0	0	1.000	2.60
Diaz,Alex	Sea	18	4	69.2	14	0	1	0	.933	1.81
Duncan,Mariano	Cin	3	3	28.0	6	0	0	0	1.000	1.93
Dykstra,Lenny	Phi	9	9	84.0	15	0	0	0	1.000	1.61
Eisenreich,Jim	Phi	39	32	299.2	81	1	0	1	1.000	2.46
Faneyte,Rikkert	SF	3	1	16.0	2	1	1	0	.750	1.69
Flora,Kevin	Phi	5	3	30.0	6	0	0	0	1.000	1.80
Floyd,Cliff	Mon	2	2	12.0	2	0	1	0	.667	1.50
Fonville,Chad	LA	10	9	76.1	13	2	1	1	.938	1.77
Fox,Eric	Tex	3	2	20.0	5	0	0	0	1.000	2.25
Frazier,Lou	Mon	10	4	51.2	10	0	0	0	1.000	1.74
Frazier,Lou	Tex	43	19	215.2	57	2	2	0	.967	2.46
Gallagher,Dave	Phi	8	2	34.2	9	0	0	0	1.000	2.34

Left Fielders - The Rest

Player	Tm	G	GS	Inn	PO	A	E	DP	Pct.	Rng
Gallagher,Dave	Cal	2	1	7.0	3	1	0	0	1.000	5.14
Garcia,Freddy	Pit	10	9	66.0	13	0	0	0	1.000	1.77
Garcia,Karim	LA	2	0	8.1	2	0	0	0	1.000	2.16
Giannelli,Ray	StL	1	0	1.0	0	0	0	0	.000	.00
Gonzalez,Juan	Tex	5	5	36.0	6	1	0	0	1.000	1.75
Gonzalez,Luis	Hou	55	52	464.0	94	2	2	0	.980	1.86
Gonzalez,Luis	ChN	74	69	602.0	159	5	4	0	.976	2.45
Goodwin,Tom	KC	37	35	302.2	76	1	0	0	1.000	2.29
Greer,Rusty	Tex	51	42	328.2	79	6	1	0	.988	2.33
Gregg,Tommy	Fla	6	6	51.0	6	0	0	0	1.000	1.06
Gwynn,Chris	LA	12	8	57.2	15	0	0	0	1.000	2.34
Hall,Joe	Det	5	4	33.0	11	1	0	0	1.000	3.27
Hare,Shawn	Tex	4	1	17.0	4	0	0	0	1.000	2.12
Harris,Lenny	Cin	4	2	12.0	4	0	0	0	1.000	3.00
Hatcher,Billy	Tex	1	1	6.0	1	0	0	0	1.000	1.50
Hiatt,Phil	KC	1	0	2.0	0	1	0	0	1.000	4.50
Higginson,Bob	Det	66	58	517.0	149	7	2	1	.987	2.72
Hollandsworth,Todd	LA	9	0	21.0	4	0	0	0	1.000	1.71
Hosey,Dwayne	Bos	2	0	3.0	0	0	0	0	.000	.00
Howard,Dave	KC	11	3	39.0	10	0	0	0	1.000	2.31
Howard,Thomas	Cin	38	16	183.1	41	0	2	0	.953	2.01
Hubbard,Trent	Col	4	2	18.0	4	0	0	0	1.000	2.00
Hudler,Rex	Cal	18	8	86.2	13	0	1	0	.929	1.35
Huff,Michael	Tor	9	7	57.0	16	1	0	0	1.000	2.68
Hulse,David	Mil	67	39	381.1	84	1	3	1	.966	2.01
Hunter,Brian	Cin	3	1	19.2	5	1	0	0	1.000	2.75
Huskey,Butch	NYN	1	1	8.0	2	0	0	0	1.000	2.25
Ingram,Garey	LA	4	0	8.2	1	0	0	0	1.000	1.04
James,Chris	KC	5	3	28.0	9	0	0	0	1.000	2.89
James,Chris	Bos	4	2	20.0	7	0	0	0	1.000	3.15
James,Dion	NYA	23	20	140.2	26	0	1	0	.963	1.66
Javier,Stan	Oak	32	19	191.2	55	0	0	0	1.000	2.58
Jefferies,Gregg	Phi	55	55	484.1	86	3	0	1	1.000	1.65
Jefferson,Reggie	Bos	2	1	5.0	2	0	0	0	1.000	3.60
Johnson,Howard	ChN	13	7	67.1	12	0	0	0	1.000	1.60
Jones,Chipper	Atl	15	13	122.0	19	0	0	0	1.000	1.40
Jones,Chris	NYN	25	17	151.1	29	0	0	0	1.000	1.72
Kelly,Mike	Atl	58	18	240.0	42	0	4	0	.913	1.58
Kelly,Roberto	LA	61	59	490.0	86	1	3	0	.967	1.60
Kirby,Wayne	Cle	1	0	2.0	0	0	0	0	.000	.00
Kowitz,Brian	Atl	2	0	6.0	1	0	0	0	1.000	1.50
Lampkin,Tom	SF	6	0	11.0	3	0	0	0	1.000	2.45
Lawton,Matt	Min	1	0	2.0	2	1	0	0	1.000	13.50
Leonard,Mark	SF	1	0	2.2	1	0	0	0	1.000	3.38
Listach,Pat	Mil	1	0	1.0	0	0	0	0	.000	.00
Longmire,Tony	Phi	19	16	130.1	28	2	0	0	1.000	2.07
Mabry,John	StL	11	9	85.0	17	1	0	1	1.000	1.91
Maldonado,Candy	Tor	26	10	136.2	22	1	0	0	1.000	1.51
Maldonado,Candy	Tex	9	9	62.0	16	0	0	0	1.000	2.32
Marsh,Tom	Phi	24	21	175.0	35	2	3	0	.925	1.90
Martin,Norberto	ChA	5	2	17.0	4	0	0	0	1.000	2.12
Martinez,Dave	ChA	30	11	126.0	21	0	2	0	.913	1.50
Masteller,Dan	Min	6	4	39.0	11	0	0	0	1.000	2.54
May,Derrick	Mil	32	29	246.2	65	1	2	0	.971	2.41
May,Derrick	Hou	42	35	306.2	59	0	2	0	.967	1.73
McCarty,Dave	Min	2	0	2.0	0	0	0	0	.000	.00
McGee,Willie	Bos	3	1	11.0	2	0	0	0	1.000	1.64
McGinnis,Russ	KC	1	0	2.0	0	0	0	0	.000	.00

Left Fielders - The Rest

Player	Tm	G	GS	Inn	PO	A	E	DP	Pct.	Rng
McLemore,Mark	Tex	69	57	530.2	131	0	1	0	.992	2.22
Merced,Orlando	Pit	4	3	22.0	4	1	0	0	1.000	2.05
Miller,Keith	KC	4	1	12.0	5	1	0	0	1.000	4.50
Morman,Russ	Fla	6	5	41.0	5	0	0	0	1.000	1.10
Mouton,James	Hou	39	34	278.0	63	4	0	0	1.000	2.17
Mouton,Lyle	ChA	29	19	187.0	34	1	1	0	.972	1.68
Munoz,Pedro	Min	1	1	7.0	0	0	0	0	.000	.00
Nevin,Phil	Det	27	27	227.0	50	2	2	0	.963	2.06
Newfield,Marc	Sea	23	23	181.0	44	0	0	0	1.000	2.19
Newfield,Marc	SD	19	13	111.1	24	1	0	0	1.000	2.02
Newson,Warren	ChA	12	10	76.2	19	1	1	0	.952	2.35
Newson,Warren	Sea	18	15	123.0	27	1	1	0	.966	2.05
Nieves,Melvin	SD	62	42	400.0	75	5	1	1	.988	1.80
Nilsson,Dave	Mil	15	11	96.2	19	3	0	0	1.000	2.05
Norman,Les	KC	4	2	22.0	4	0	0	0	1.000	1.64
Nunnally,Jon	KC	16	6	65.0	19	0	0	0	1.000	2.63
O'Leary,Troy	Bos	16	8	81.0	15	0	0	0	1.000	1.67
O'Neill,Paul	NYA	25	21	176.0	28	1	0	0	1.000	1.48
Orsulak,Joe	NYN	56	41	384.0	67	2	4	0	.945	1.62
Otero,Ricky	NYN	15	5	62.1	20	0	0	0	1.000	2.89
Palmeiro,Orlando	Cal	3	0	5.0	1	0	0	0	1.000	1.80
Paquette,Craig	Oak	18	12	105.0	18	1	0	0	1.000	1.63
Parker,Rick	LA	19	4	66.1	16	1	0	1	1.000	2.31
Pegues,Steve	Pit	31	19	171.2	40	2	3	0	.933	2.20
Pemberton,Rudy	Det	6	6	49.0	10	0	0	0	1.000	1.84
Perez,Robert	Tor	5	2	31.0	5	0	0	0	1.000	1.45
Petagine,Roberto	SD	1	1	8.0	0	0	0	0	.000	.00
Phillips,J.R.	SF	1	0	1.0	1	0	0	0	1.000	9.00
Phillips,Tony	Cal	47	43	362.0	100	0	1	0	.990	2.49
Plantier,Phil	Hou	8	7	53.1	11	0	0	0	1.000	1.86
Plantier,Phil	SD	39	38	313.1	64	5	3	1	.958	1.98
Polonia,Luis	NYA	64	56	489.1	134	5	0	1	1.000	2.56
Polonia,Luis	Atl	11	4	60.0	6	0	0	0	1.000	0.90
Pride,Curtis	Mon	24	10	117.0	23	0	2	0	.920	1.77
Pulliam,Harvey	Col	1	0	1.0	0	0	0	0	.000	.00
Rhodes,Karl	ChN	11	0	32.1	8	0	1	0	.889	2.23
Rivera,Ruben	NYA	4	0	5.0	2	0	0	0	1.000	3.60
Roberson,Kevin	ChN	10	4	39.2	6	0	0	0	1.000	1.36
Roberts,Bip	SD	48	35	321.2	82	2	1	0	.988	2.35
Rodriguez,Henry	Mon	4	3	25.0	1	0	0	0	1.000	0.36
Samuel,Juan	Det	9	5	47.1	9	0	3	0	.750	1.71
Samuel,Juan	KC	5	4	31.1	3	0	0	0	1.000	0.86
Santangelo,F.P.	Mon	20	18	152.1	37	0	0	0	1.000	2.19
Schall,Gene	Phi	4	4	28.1	3	0	0	0	1.000	0.95
Segui,David	NYN	18	17	126.0	15	2	0	0	1.000	1.21
Segui,David	Mon	2	0	2.0	0	0	0	0	.000	.00
Sheffield,Gary	Fla	3	3	20.0	1	0	2	0	.333	0.45
Silvestri,Dave	Mon	3	0	9.2	0	0	0	0	.000	.00
Singleton,Duane	Mil	3	0	6.1	2	0	0	0	1.000	2.84
Smith,Dwight	Atl	11	7	64.2	5	0	1	0	.833	0.70
Smith,Mark	Bal	15	12	109.0	33	1	0	0	1.000	2.81
Sojo,Luis	Sea	6	5	36.0	8	1	1	0	.900	2.25
Stairs,Matt	Bos	17	14	129.0	13	1	1	0	.933	0.98
Steverson,Todd	Det	17	6	54.2	11	0	0	0	1.000	1.81
Strange,Doug	Sea	4	3	23.1	8	0	0	0	1.000	3.09
Strawberry,Darryl	NYA	1	1	6.0	1	0	1	0	.500	1.50
Stubbs,Franklin	Det	20	13	102.2	21	0	1	0	.955	1.84
Surhoff,B.J.	Mil	54	50	405.0	105	8	1	1	.991	2.51

Left Fielders - The Rest

Player	Tm	G	GS	Inn	PO	A	E	DP	Pct.	Rng
Sweeney,Mark	StL	1	0	3.0	0	0	1	0	.000	.00
Tarasco,Tony	Mon	11	11	95.1	14	1	2	1	.882	1.42
Tatum,Jimmy	Col	2	0	5.0	1	0	0	0	1.000	1.80
Tavarez,Jesus	Fla	4	2	21.0	4	0	0	0	1.000	1.71
Tettleton,Mickey	Tex	2	2	16.0	3	1	0	0	1.000	2.25
Thompson,Milt	Hou	15	3	56.0	16	1	0	0	1.000	2.73
Thompson,Ryan	NYN	11	10	89.0	23	0	0	0	1.000	2.33
Thurman,Gary	Sea	5	4	38.0	9	0	0	0	1.000	2.13
Timmons,Ozzie	ChN	49	41	319.0	59	1	2	1	.968	1.69
Tomberlin,Andy	Oak	5	0	9.0	0	0	0	0	.000	.00
Tucker,Michael	KC	30	26	233.0	59	2	1	0	.984	2.36
Vander Wal,John	Col	7	2	29.0	9	1	0	0	1.000	3.10
Varsho,Gary	Phi	9	2	24.0	5	0	1	0	.833	1.88
Velarde,Randy	NYA	20	14	108.2	23	1	1	0	.960	1.99
Voigt,Jack	Tex	8	6	53.0	15	0	0	0	1.000	2.55
Walton,Jerome	Cin	36	3	87.1	23	0	0	0	1.000	2.37
Ward,Turner	Mil	26	15	149.0	35	3	0	1	1.000	2.30
Webster,Mitch	LA	11	0	24.2	2	0	0	0	1.000	0.73
Wehner,John	Pit	18	10	90.2	21	1	0	1	1.000	2.18
White,Derrick	Det	4	2	23.0	4	0	0	0	1.000	1.57
White,Rondell	Mon	8	8	69.0	18	1	0	0	1.000	2.48
Widger,Chris	Sea	2	1	9.0	1	0	0	0	1.000	1.00
Williams,Gerald	NYA	70	33	359.0	103	6	0	0	1.000	2.73
Williams,Reggie	LA	10	0	23.2	2	0	0	0	1.000	0.76
Wilson,Nigel	Cin	2	0	11.1	2	0	0	0	1.000	1.59
Young,Eric	Col	19	9	99.0	15	3	0	0	1.000	1.64
Young,Ernie	Oak	7	2	29.0	5	0	0	0	1.000	1.55
Zeile,Todd	ChN	2	2	14.0	0	0	1	0	.000	.00

Center Fielders - Regulars

Player	Tm	G	GS	Inn	PO	A	E	DP	Pct.	Rng
Javier,Stan	Oak	101	92	811.1	277	3	0	1	1.000	3.11
Edmonds,Jim	Cal	139	136	1190.1	402	8	1	2	.998	3.10
Williams,Bernie	NYA	144	143	1274.2	431	1	8	0	.982	3.05
Griffey Jr,Ken	Sea	70	69	596.1	190	5	2	1	.990	2.94
Becker,Rich	Min	99	97	848.0	263	11	4	3	.986	2.91
Lewis,Darren	TOT	130	109	1023.2	321	5	2	0	.994	2.87
Hamilton,Darryl	Mil	109	101	841.0	262	4	3	0	.989	2.85
White,Devon	Tor	100	100	862.1	260	7	3	0	.989	2.79
Tinsley,Lee	Bos	97	83	747.1	227	4	5	1	.979	2.78
Brumfield,Jacob	Pit	104	92	808.0	241	8	8	1	.969	2.77
Carr,Chuck	Fla	103	77	735.1	217	8	3	0	.987	2.75
Sanders,Deion	TOT	85	81	716.1	215	2	5	1	.977	2.73
Goodwin,Curtis	Bal	84	79	684.1	202	1	2	1	.990	2.67
Hunter,Brian L.	Hou	74	71	642.2	182	8	9	1	.955	2.66
Nixon,Otis	Tex	138	138	1221.0	355	4	4	0	.989	2.65
Johnson,Lance	ChA	140	132	1185.2	335	8	3	2	.991	2.60
Curtis,Chad	Det	144	144	1266.0	361	5	3	0	.992	2.60
McRae,Brian	ChN	137	136	1213.0	345	4	3	0	.991	2.59
Lankford,Ray	StL	129	128	1116.0	300	7	3	1	.990	2.48
Grissom,Marquis	Atl	136	135	1158.2	309	9	2	1	.994	2.47
Goodwin,Tom	KC	95	94	800.0	212	5	3	0	.986	2.44
Lofton,Kenny	Cle	114	113	974.0	248	11	8	2	.970	2.39
Van Slyke,Andy	TOT	72	69	617.1	156	7	3	2	.982	2.38
White,Rondell	Mon	111	110	967.0	250	4	4	2	.984	2.36
Butler,Brett	TOT	129	127	1105.2	282	6	2	1	.993	2.34

Center Fielders - Regulars

Player	Tm	G	GS	Inn	PO	A	E	DP	Pct.	Rng
Finley,Steve	SD	138	135	1202.2	289	8	7	0	.977	2.22
Kingery,Mike	Col	108	79	762.0	180	4	4	0	.979	2.17
Kelly,Roberto	TOT	72	72	615.2	138	2	3	0	.979	2.05
Average	---	110	105	928.0	266	5	3	0	.986	2.64

Center Fielders - The Rest

Player	Tm	G	GS	Inn	PO	A	E	DP	Pct.	Rng
Aldrete,Mike	Oak	1	0	1.0	0	0	0	0	.000	.00
Alou,Moises	Mon	4	3	26.2	5	0	0	0	1.000	1.69
Amaral,Rich	Sea	29	26	199.0	60	1	0	0	1.000	2.76
Amaro,Ruben	Cle	14	9	88.0	29	0	0	0	1.000	2.97
Anderson,Brady	Bal	40	32	287.2	75	1	1	0	.987	2.38
Anderson,Garret	Cal	1	0	2.0	0	0	0	0	.000	.00
Anthony,Eric	Cin	1	1	6.1	2	0	0	0	1.000	2.84
Battle,Allen	StL	7	4	38.0	12	0	0	0	1.000	2.84
Bell,Derek	Hou	30	30	260.0	72	0	0	0	1.000	2.49
Benard,Marvin	SF	7	6	53.2	19	0	0	0	1.000	3.19
Benitez,Yamil	Mon	4	0	7.0	2	0	0	0	1.000	2.57
Bradshaw,Terry	StL	3	2	17.0	6	0	0	0	1.000	3.18
Bragg,Darren	Sea	1	0	2.0	0	0	0	0	.000	.00
Brosius,Scott	Oak	22	19	149.1	30	2	1	0	.970	1.93
Brown,Jarvis	Bal	13	6	62.0	13	0	0	0	1.000	1.89
Browne,Jerry	Fla	11	8	63.0	19	0	1	0	.950	2.71
Buford,Damon	Bal	15	11	97.0	31	0	0	0	1.000	2.88
Buford,Damon	NYN	16	11	107.0	23	1	0	0	1.000	2.02
Bullett,Scott	ChN	12	4	54.0	11	0	1	0	.917	1.83
Burks,Ellis	Col	65	54	430.0	131	2	3	0	.978	2.78
Burnitz,Jeromy	Cle	1	0	3.0	1	0	0	0	1.000	3.00
Butler,Brett	NYN	90	88	773.2	207	6	1	1	.995	2.48
Butler,Brett	LA	39	39	332.0	75	0	1	0	.987	2.03
Cameron,Mike	ChA	3	3	20.0	6	0	0	0	1.000	2.70
Cangelosi,John	Hou	32	25	238.2	61	0	3	0	.953	2.30
Carter,Joe	Tor	20	17	148.2	43	3	0	0	1.000	2.78
Cedeno,Roger	LA	13	8	87.2	27	0	0	0	1.000	2.77
Clark,Jerald	Min	10	8	66.1	18	0	0	0	1.000	2.44
Cole,Alex	Min	23	17	158.1	44	1	3	0	.938	2.56
Coleman,Vince	KC	2	0	2.0	1	0	0	0	1.000	4.50
Cordova,Marty	Min	11	8	70.0	16	1	1	0	.944	2.19
Cummings,Midre	Pit	20	19	156.2	47	1	1	0	.980	2.76
Cuyler,Milt	Det	1	0	2.0	1	0	0	0	1.000	4.50
Damon,Johnny	KC	44	40	369.1	103	0	1	0	.990	2.51
Devereaux,Mike	ChA	9	8	56.2	15	1	0	0	1.000	2.54
Devereaux,Mike	Atl	9	4	67.0	24	0	0	0	1.000	3.22
Diaz,Alex	Sea	68	49	483.0	130	4	1	1	.993	2.50
Dykstra,Lenny	Phi	52	52	464.1	137	2	2	1	.986	2.69
Eisenreich,Jim	Phi	6	5	43.0	8	0	0	0	1.000	1.67
Everett,Carl	NYN	10	9	80.0	16	1	0	0	1.000	1.91
Faneyte,Rikkert	SF	22	13	149.2	44	2	0	0	1.000	2.77
Flora,Kevin	Phi	15	14	123.1	27	1	0	0	1.000	2.04
Floyd,Cliff	Mon	1	0	2.0	0	0	0	0	.000	.00
Fonville,Chad	LA	2	1	12.0	3	0	0	0	1.000	2.25
Fox,Eric	Tex	2	0	6.0	3	0	0	0	1.000	4.50
Frazier,Lou	Mon	11	7	66.0	22	0	1	0	.957	3.00
Frazier,Lou	Tex	6	3	29.0	12	0	0	0	1.000	3.72
Gallagher,Dave	Phi	21	15	143.1	35	0	0	0	1.000	2.20
Gallagher,Dave	Cal	3	1	15.0	4	0	0	0	1.000	2.40

Center Fielders - The Rest

Player	Tm	G	GS	Inn	PO	A	E	DP	Pct.	Rng
Gibralter,Steve	Cin	2	0	4.0	1	0	0	0	1.000	2.25
Gonzalez,Luis	ChN	6	4	34.0	13	0	0	0	1.000	3.44
Greer,Rusty	Tex	4	3	29.0	9	0	0	0	1.000	2.79
Gregg,Tommy	Fla	4	3	30.0	11	0	0	0	1.000	3.30
Herrera,Jose	Oak	22	14	131.1	39	2	1	1	.976	2.81
Hiatt,Phil	KC	2	0	3.0	2	0	0	0	1.000	6.00
Hill,Glenallen	SF	1	1	8.0	1	0	0	0	1.000	1.13
Hollandsworth,Todd	LA	25	23	207.0	53	1	3	0	.947	2.35
Hosey,Dwayne	Bos	19	15	141.0	46	1	0	0	1.000	3.00
Howard,Dave	KC	16	7	69.0	31	2	1	0	.971	4.30
Howard,Thomas	Cin	39	35	263.0	71	2	0	0	1.000	2.50
Hubbard,Trent	Col	14	11	89.0	12	1	0	0	1.000	1.31
Hudler,Rex	Cal	4	2	19.0	3	0	0	0	1.000	1.42
Huff,Michael	Tor	33	18	192.2	57	1	2	0	.967	2.71
Hulse,David	Mil	52	30	304.0	80	0	0	0	1.000	2.37
Jordan,Brian	StL	13	9	94.2	24	0	0	0	1.000	2.28
Kelly,Mike	Atl	8	3	39.0	7	0	0	0	1.000	1.62
Kelly,Roberto	Mon	24	24	210.1	42	1	0	0	1.000	1.84
Kelly,Roberto	LA	48	48	405.1	96	1	3	0	.970	2.15
Kirby,Wayne	Cle	34	22	236.0	67	2	1	1	.986	2.63
Kowitz,Brian	Atl	1	0	2.0	0	0	0	0	.000	.00
Lawton,Matt	Min	12	10	90.2	23	0	1	0	.958	2.28
Lewis,Darren	SF	73	72	640.1	200	2	1	0	.995	2.84
Lewis,Darren	Cin	57	37	383.1	121	3	1	0	.992	2.91
Listach,Pat	Mil	10	2	29.0	10	1	0	0	1.000	3.41
Longmire,Tony	Phi	2	2	12.0	0	0	0	0	.000	.00
Mahay,Ron	Bos	5	5	44.0	9	0	0	0	1.000	1.84
Marsh,Tom	Phi	4	3	23.0	6	0	0	0	1.000	2.35
Martin,Al	Pit	42	31	289.2	81	4	1	1	.988	2.64
Martinez,Dave	ChA	5	2	22.1	11	0	0	0	1.000	4.43
McCracken,Quinton	Col	1	0	1.0	0	0	0	0	.000	.00
McDavid,Ray	SD	7	3	27.1	5	0	0	0	1.000	1.65
McGee,Willie	Bos	27	24	200.0	65	5	2	1	.972	3.15
Meares,Pat	Min	2	0	5.0	1	0	0	0	1.000	1.80
Mondesi,Raul	LA	24	24	223.2	55	3	2	0	.967	2.33
Mordecai,Mike	Atl	1	0	0.2	0	0	0	0	.000	.00
Mouton,James	Hou	22	17	166.0	35	0	0	0	1.000	1.90
Newson,Warren	Sea	2	1	8.0	2	0	0	0	1.000	2.25
Nieves,Melvin	SD	6	2	22.0	7	0	0	0	1.000	2.86
Norman,Les	KC	5	2	18.2	6	0	1	0	.857	2.89
Nunnally,Jon	KC	7	0	17.0	5	0	0	0	1.000	2.65
O'Leary,Troy	Bos	13	11	100.1	23	1	1	0	.960	2.15
Otero,Ricky	NYN	9	3	40.0	11	1	0	0	1.000	2.70
Palmeiro,Orlando	Cal	4	2	22.0	6	0	0	0	1.000	2.45
Parker,Rick	LA	1	0	7.0	3	0	0	0	1.000	3.86
Pegues,Steve	Pit	4	2	20.0	5	0	0	0	1.000	2.25
Phillips,Tony	Cal	8	4	36.0	13	1	0	0	1.000	3.50
Polonia,Luis	Atl	4	2	24.1	3	0	0	0	1.000	1.11
Pride,Curtis	Mon	1	0	1.0	0	0	0	0	.000	.00
Puckett,Kirby	Min	5	4	34.0	10	0	0	0	1.000	2.65
Rhodes,Karl	Bos	9	6	60.0	18	0	1	0	.947	2.70
Roberts,Bip	SD	4	4	32.2	10	0	0	0	1.000	2.76
Sanders,Deion	Cin	33	29	274.1	88	2	3	1	.968	2.95
Sanders,Deion	SF	52	52	442.0	127	0	2	0	.984	2.59
Sanders,Reggie	Cin	16	15	110.0	28	0	1	0	.966	2.29
Santangelo,F.P.	Mon	2	0	3.2	3	0	0	0	1.000	7.36
Singleton,Duane	Mil	9	9	77.1	20	1	0	0	1.000	2.44
Steverson,Todd	Det	1	0	7.0	0	1	0	0	1.000	1.29

Center Fielders - The Rest

Center Fielders - The Rest

Player	Tm	G	GS	Inn	PO	A	E	DP	Pct.	Rng
Stewart,Shannon	Tor	12	9	89.0	20	1	1	0	.955	2.12
Surhoff,B.J.	Mil	3	1	11.0	6	0	0	0	1.000	4.91
Tavarez,Jesus	Fla	47	44	359.2	91	1	0	1	1.000	2.30
Thompson,Milt	Hou	1	1	13.0	2	0	0	0	1.000	1.38
Thompson,Ryan	NYN	38	33	290.1	91	0	2	1	.978	2.82
Thurman,Gary	Sea	1	0	1.0	0	0	0	0	.000	.00
Tomberlin,Andy	Oak	18	15	132.0	32	1	1	0	.971	2.25
Tucker,Michael	KC	1	1	9.0	5	0	0	0	1.000	5.00
Van Slyke,Andy	Bal	16	16	136.0	39	2	1	1	.976	2.71
Van Slyke,Andy	Phi	56	53	481.1	117	5	2	1	.984	2.28
Veras,Quilvio	Fla	1	0	1.0	1	0	0	0	1.000	9.00
Walker,Larry	Col	4	0	6.1	1	0	0	0	1.000	1.42
Walton,Jerome	Cin	50	27	248.1	73	1	2	0	.974	2.68
Ward,Turner	Mil	7	1	23.2	3	0	0	0	1.000	1.14
Webster,Mitch	LA	4	1	19.1	5	0	0	0	1.000	2.33
Wehner,John	Pit	2	0	1.0	0	0	0	0	.000	.00
Whitmore,Darrell	Fla	14	11	97.0	23	0	1	0	.958	2.13
Williams,Gerald	NYA	2	2	10.0	3	0	0	0	1.000	2.70
Williams,Reggie	LA	1	0	1.0	0	0	0	0	.000	.00
Young,Ernie	Oak	7	4	48.0	15	0	1	0	.938	2.81

Right Fielders - Regulars

Player	Tm	G	GS	Inn	PO	A	E	DP	Pct.	Rng
Mieske,Matt	Mil	108	67	664.0	177	7	4	0	.979	2.49
Devereaux,Mike	TOT	91	74	682.1	177	3	3	1	.984	2.37
Sosa,Sammy	ChN	143	142	1274.0	320	13	13	2	.962	2.35
Salmon,Tim	Cal	142	142	1257.1	319	7	4	0	.988	2.33
Nunnally,Jon	KC	92	78	696.2	172	5	6	1	.967	2.29
Jordan,Brian	StL	116	113	977.2	244	4	1	2	.996	2.28
Green,Shawn	Tor	109	97	867.1	207	9	6	2	.973	2.24
Bautista,Danny	Det	84	75	657.0	159	3	2	0	.988	2.22
Sanders,Reggie	Cin	125	115	1028.0	240	12	4	2	.984	2.21
Mondesi,Raul	LA	114	113	981.0	226	13	4	2	.984	2.19
Tarasco,Tony	Mon	106	103	910.2	215	6	3	1	.987	2.18
O'Leary,Troy	Bos	91	79	673.0	158	5	4	1	.976	2.18
Everett,Carl	NYN	68	67	586.2	131	9	3	1	.979	2.15
Merced,Orlando	Pit	104	99	855.2	196	7	5	2	.976	2.14
Justice,Dave	Atl	120	120	1035.1	233	4	4	0	.984	2.09
Whiten,Mark	TOT	86	80	730.1	157	8	4	1	.976	2.03
Gwynn,Tony	SD	133	132	1126.2	245	8	2	1	.992	2.02
O'Neill,Paul	NYA	107	96	856.1	190	2	3	0	.985	2.02
Hill,Glenallen	SF	124	123	1085.0	225	10	10	1	.959	1.95
Walker,Larry	Col	129	128	1096.2	224	13	3	0	.988	1.94
Puckett,Kirby	Min	106	104	896.1	184	9	4	0	.980	1.94
Greer,Rusty	Tex	101	59	598.2	124	3	3	0	.977	1.91
Ramirez,Manny	Cle	131	129	1132.0	219	3	5	2	.978	1.77
Bell,Derek	Hou	82	80	725.2	129	10	8	2	.946	1.72
Sierra,Ruben	TOT	72	69	578.0	107	2	5	0	.956	1.70
Buhner,Jay	Sea	120	120	1046.0	177	5	2	0	.989	1.57
Average	---	107	100	885.0	198	7	4	0	.979	2.09

Right Fielders - The Rest

Right Fielders - The Rest

Player	Tm	G	GS	Inn	PO	A	E	DP	Pct.	Rng
Aldrete,Mike	Oak	6	3	23.0	6	0	0	0	1.000	2.35
Alou,Moises	Mon	30	27	230.2	49	2	1	0	.981	1.99
Amaral,Rich	Sea	8	5	45.0	8	2	0	0	1.000	2.00
Amaro,Ruben	Cle	6	0	18.0	1	0	0	0	1.000	0.50
Anderson,Garret	Cal	1	1	9.0	0	0	0	0	.000	.00
Anthony,Eric	Cin	20	19	145.0	33	1	0	0	1.000	2.11
Barry,Jeff	NYN	1	0	2.0	1	0	0	0	1.000	4.50
Bass,Kevin	Bal	53	37	340.1	64	2	1	1	.985	1.75
Battle,Allen	StL	14	9	81.1	17	0	0	0	1.000	1.88
Becker,Rich	Min	5	4	39.2	9	0	0	0	1.000	2.04
Benitez,Yamil	Mon	8	7	63.2	14	1	1	0	.938	2.12
Berroa,Geronimo	Oak	54	51	443.0	105	4	3	1	.973	2.21
Bichette,Dante	Col	35	16	184.2	36	2	0	0	1.000	1.85
Blowers,Mike	Sea	3	2	18.0	2	0	1	0	.667	1.00
Bonilla,Bobby	Bal	38	37	322.0	65	2	2	0	.971	1.87
Bradshaw,Terry	StL	1	1	9.0	1	0	0	0	1.000	1.00
Bragg,Darren	Sea	17	11	108.1	18	2	0	1	1.000	1.66
Brosius,Scott	Oak	22	17	148.1	25	0	1	0	.962	1.52
Brown,Jarvis	Bal	5	2	20.0	3	0	0	0	1.000	1.35
Browne,Jerry	Fla	11	4	57.0	16	1	0	0	1.000	2.68
Buford,Damon	Bal	9	0	19.0	9	0	0	0	1.000	4.26
Burks,Ellis	Col	1	0	3.0	0	0	0	0	.000	.00
Cameron,Mike	ChA	26	7	107.0	27	1	0	0	1.000	2.36
Cangelosi,John	Hou	1	1	8.0	0	0	0	0	.000	.00
Canseco,Jose	Bos	1	1	7.0	1	0	0	0	1.000	1.29
Carreon,Mark	SF	19	15	131.1	26	1	2	0	.931	1.85
Cedeno,Roger	LA	5	1	16.1	9	0	0	0	1.000	4.96
Chamberlain,Wes	Bos	12	9	82.0	20	1	1	0	.955	2.30
Cianfrocco,Archi	SD	5	5	31.2	9	0	0	0	1.000	2.56
Clark,Dave	Pit	29	20	182.2	42	1	1	0	.977	2.12
Clark,Jerald	Min	5	2	20.0	4	0	0	0	1.000	1.80
Clark,Phil	SD	21	2	49.1	11	0	0	0	1.000	2.01
Coleman,Vince	KC	13	12	100.1	12	0	1	0	.923	1.08
Cookson,Brent	KC	2	0	2.0	0	0	0	0	.000	.00
Coomer,Ron	Min	1	0	2.0	1	0	0	0	1.000	4.50
Cummings,Midre	Pit	14	9	88.2	18	0	0	0	1.000	1.83
Cuyler,Milt	Det	1	1	9.0	3	0	1	0	.750	3.00
Damon,Johnny	KC	4	3	27.1	7	0	0	0	1.000	2.30
Dawson,Andre	Fla	47	46	341.0	64	0	6	0	.914	1.69
Devereaux,Mike	ChA	87	73	663.1	173	3	3	1	.983	2.39
Devereaux,Mike	Atl	4	1	19.0	4	0	0	0	1.000	1.89
Diaz,Alex	Sea	4	3	24.2	2	0	0	0	1.000	0.73
Eisenreich,Jim	Phi	68	53	488.2	116	1	0	0	1.000	2.15
Faneyte,Rikkert	SF	11	0	19.1	3	0	0	0	1.000	1.40
Floyd,Cliff	Mon	1	1	9.0	1	0	0	0	1.000	1.00
Fox,Eric	Tex	3	2	20.0	5	0	0	0	1.000	2.25
Frazier,Lou	Mon	5	0	7.0	4	0	0	0	1.000	5.14
Gallagher,Dave	Phi	28	24	190.1	45	1	0	0	1.000	2.18
Gallagher,Dave	Cal	1	1	9.0	2	0	0	0	1.000	2.00
Garcia,Karim	LA	3	3	18.0	3	2	0	1	1.000	2.50
Giannelli,Ray	StL	1	1	9.0	2	0	0	0	1.000	2.00
Gibson,Kirk	Det	1	0	1.2	0	0	0	0	.000	.00
Giles,Brian S.	Cle	3	1	10.0	2	1	0	0	1.000	2.70
Goodwin,Tom	KC	1	0	5.2	2	0	0	0	1.000	3.18
Gregg,Tommy	Fla	30	24	213.0	46	0	1	0	.979	1.94
Gwynn,Chris	LA	5	3	34.0	6	0	0	0	1.000	1.59
Hammonds,Jeffrey	Bal	46	45	373.2	88	1	1	0	.989	2.14
Hare,Shawn	Tex	5	2	28.0	5	1	0	0	1.000	1.93
Harris,Lenny	Cin	4	1	14.0	5	2	0	1	1.000	4.50
Hatcher,Billy	Tex	4	3	27.0	8	1	0	0	1.000	3.00
Herrera,Jose	Oak	5	1	17.0	2	0	1	0	.667	1.06
Hiatt,Phil	KC	45	27	252.0	60	3	3	1	.955	2.25
Higginson,Bob	Det	67	55	494.1	98	6	2	1	.981	1.89
Holbert,Ray	SD	1	0	1.0	0	0	0	0	.000	.00
Hollandsworth,Todd	LA	3	2	22.0	3	0	1	0	.750	1.23
Hollins,Dave	Bos	2	2	12.0	3	0	0	0	1.000	2.25
Hosey,Dwayne	Bos	1	1	9.0	0	0	0	0	.000	.00
Howard,Dave	KC	8	6	49.0	9	1	2	0	.833	1.84
Howard,Thomas	Cin	14	6	64.1	15	0	0	0	1.000	2.10
Hudler,Rex	Cal	1	1	9.0	5	0	0	0	1.000	5.00
Huff,Michael	Tor	15	8	89.2	22	1	0	0	1.000	2.31
Hulse,David	Mil	17	14	106.0	16	1	0	0	1.000	1.44
Hunter,Brian	Cin	1	1	7.0	2	0	0	0	1.000	2.57
James,Chris	Bos	4	3	23.0	7	0	0	0	1.000	2.74
James,Dion	NYA	6	3	29.0	4	0	0	0	1.000	1.24
Javier,Stan	Oak	1	0	1.0	0	0	0	0	.000	.00
Jones,Chipper	Atl	5	4	37.0	3	1	0	0	1.000	0.97
Jones,Chris	NYN	28	18	176.0	50	3	2	1	.964	2.71
Jose,Felix	KC	7	7	60.0	15	2	0	0	1.000	2.55
Kelly,Mike	Atl	17	5	71.0	14	0	0	0	1.000	1.77
Kelly,Roberto	LA	2	0	12.0	1	0	0	0	1.000	0.75
Kirby,Wayne	Cle	35	14	141.0	28	0	0	0	1.000	1.79
Kowitz,Brian	Atl	5	5	45.0	5	0	0	0	1.000	1.00
Lawton,Matt	Min	8	4	44.2	9	0	0	0	1.000	1.81
Leonard,Mark	SF	5	4	36.0	8	0	0	1	1.000	2.00
Listach,Pat	Mil	1	0	1.0	0	0	0	0	.000	.00
Longmire,Tony	Phi	2	2	13.0	5	0	0	0	1.000	3.46
Mabry,John	StL	29	19	186.2	40	4	0	1	1.000	2.12
Maldonado,Candy	Tor	38	30	255.2	56	1	1	0	.983	2.01
Maldonado,Candy	Tex	4	1	13.2	4	1	0	0	1.000	3.29
Marsh,Tom	Phi	1	1	8.2	3	0	0	0	1.000	3.12
Martin,Norberto	ChA	7	6	38.0	3	2	0	0	1.000	1.18
Martinez,Dave	ChA	32	22	196.1	49	2	0	1	1.000	2.34
Masteller,Dan	Min	16	9	86.0	21	0	0	0	1.000	2.20
May,Derrick	Hou	13	11	92.0	17	0	0	0	1.000	1.66
McCarty,Dave	Min	4	1	18.0	2	0	0	0	1.000	1.00
McCarty,Dave	SF	4	2	22.0	5	0	1	0	.833	2.05
McGee,Willie	Bos	47	17	203.0	34	2	1	0	.973	1.60
McLemore,Mark	Tex	5	5	36.0	9	0	1	0	.900	2.25
Meares,Pat	Min	1	0	2.0	0	0	0	0	.000	.00
Miller,Keith	KC	1	0	1.0	0	0	0	0	.000	.00
Morman,Russ	Fla	12	10	78.0	16	0	1	0	.941	1.85
Mouton,James	Hou	37	17	195.2	36	0	0	0	1.000	1.66
Mouton,Lyle	ChA	31	29	204.1	60	4	0	1	1.000	2.82
Munoz,Pedro	Min	24	20	163.2	22	3	2	0	.926	1.37
Newfield,Marc	Sea	1	0	1.0	0	0	0	0	.000	.00
Newson,Warren	ChA	14	8	75.1	25	0	0	0	1.000	2.99
Newson,Warren	Sea	4	1	17.0	4	0	0	0	1.000	2.12
Nieves,Melvin	SD	15	5	69.0	13	0	0	0	1.000	1.70
Nilsson,Dave	Mil	47	41	329.1	80	2	2	0	.976	2.24
Norman,Les	KC	8	7	59.0	13	1	0	0	1.000	2.14
Obando,Sherman	Bal	7	5	39.0	12	0	1	0	.923	2.77
Ochoa,Alex	NYN	10	9	74.0	20	1	0	0	1.000	2.55
Oquendo,Jose	StL	1	0	2.0	0	0	0	0	.000	.00
Orsulak,Joe	NYN	31	19	189.2	41	1	0	0	1.000	1.99
Paquette,Craig	Oak	2	0	6.0	1	0	0	0	1.000	1.50

Right Fielders - The Rest

Player	Tm	G	GS	Inn	PO	A	E	DP	Pct.	Rng
Parker,Rick	LA	1	0	3.0	1	0	0	0	1.000	3.00
Pegues,Steve	Pit	25	15	138.2	36	0	1	0	.973	2.34
Pemberton,Rudy	Det	2	2	16.0	5	0	0	0	1.000	2.81
Perez,Robert	Tor	11	9	80.0	25	0	0	0	1.000	2.81
Petagine,Roberto	SD	1	0	7.0	1	0	0	0	1.000	1.29
Plantier,Phil	Hou	12	12	93.0	14	0	1	0	.933	1.35
Polonia,Luis	Atl	1	0	1.0	0	0	0	0	.000	.00
Raines,Tim	ChA	1	0	0.1	0	0	0	0	.000	.00
Roberson,Kevin	ChN	1	1	8.0	2	0	0	0	1.000	2.25
Rodriguez,Henry	LA	20	19	164.2	37	0	0	0	1.000	2.02
Rodriguez,Henry	Mon	4	2	20.2	5	0	1	0	.833	2.18
Santangelo,F.P.	Mon	7	4	42.0	6	0	1	0	.857	1.29
Sheffield,Gary	Fla	59	58	510.1	107	5	5	1	.957	1.98
Sierra,Ruben	Oak	62	60	500.0	89	1	4	0	.957	1.62
Sierra,Ruben	NYA	10	9	78.0	18	1	1	0	.950	2.19
Simms,Mike	Hou	12	11	86.0	17	0	0	0	1.000	1.78
Smith,Dwight	Atl	14	9	83.1	19	0	1	0	.950	2.05
Smith,Mark	Bal	17	17	145.0	27	1	0	0	1.000	1.74
Stairs,Matt	Bos	6	5	40.0	6	1	1	0	.875	1.58
Steverson,Todd	Det	10	7	63.0	11	0	0	0	1.000	1.57
Strawberry,Darryl	NYA	10	9	68.0	17	2	1	1	.950	2.51
Surhoff,B.J.	Mil	9	6	52.0	13	1	0	0	1.000	2.42
Tartabull,Danny	NYA	18	16	136.0	27	1	0	1	1.000	1.85
Tartabull,Danny	Oak	1	1	4.0	1	0	0	0	1.000	2.25
Tavarez,Jesus	Fla	32	1	70.0	24	0	0	0	1.000	3.09
Tettleton,Mickey	Tex	61	61	462.2	97	2	3	1	.971	1.93
Thompson,Milt	Hou	21	12	120.0	27	1	1	1	.966	2.10
Thompson,Ryan	NYN	31	31	262.2	79	4	1	2	.988	2.84
Thurman,Gary	Sea	4	2	22.1	6	0	0	0	1.000	2.42
Timmons,Ozzie	ChN	6	1	19.0	4	0	0	0	1.000	1.89
Tomberlin,Andy	Oak	20	5	71.0	13	0	0	0	1.000	1.65
Tucker,Michael	KC	5	4	35.0	3	1	0	0	1.000	1.03
Van Slyke,Andy	Bal	1	1	8.0	3	0	0	0	1.000	3.38
Vander Wal,John	Col	3	0	4.0	0	0	0	0	.000	.00
Varsho,Gary	Phi	16	11	103.0	26	0	1	0	.963	2.27
Velarde,Randy	NYA	1	0	1.0	0	0	0	0	.000	.00
Veras,Quilvio	Fla	1	0	5.2	1	0	0	0	1.000	1.59
Voigt,Jack	Tex	17	11	99.0	21	1	0	0	1.000	2.00
Walton,Jerome	Cin	8	2	31.0	11	1	0	0	1.000	3.48
Ward,Turner	Mil	19	16	132.2	43	2	1	0	.978	3.05
Webster,Mitch	LA	11	2	32.0	5	0	0	0	1.000	1.41
Wegman,Bill	Mil	1	0	1.0	0	0	0	0	.000	.00
Wehner,John	Pit	3	1	9.2	1	0	0	0	1.000	0.93
White,Derrick	Det	5	4	34.0	4	0	1	0	.800	1.06
Whiten,Mark	Bos	31	27	243.2	52	4	0	1	1.000	2.07
Whiten,Mark	Phi	55	53	486.2	105	4	4	0	.965	2.02
Whitmore,Darrell	Fla	3	0	11.0	1	0	0	0	1.000	0.82
Widger,Chris	Sea	1	1	7.0	2	0	0	0	1.000	2.57
Williams,Gerald	NYA	26	12	116.1	32	0	1	0	.970	2.48
Williams,Reggie	LA	4	1	12.0	4	0	0	0	1.000	3.00
Young,Ernie	Oak	10	6	59.2	15	0	1	0	.938	2.26

Catchers - Regulars

Player	Tm	G	GS	Inn	PO	A	E	DP	PB	Pct.
Santiago,Benito	Cin	75	71	606.0	462	31	2	4	6	.996
Hoiles,Chris	Bal	107	101	871.2	658	34	3	3	4	.996
Mayne,Brent	KC	103	95	817.1	540	39	3	8	4	.995
Wilson,Dan	Sea	119	117	1017.0	897	51	5	2	8	.995
Daulton,Darren	Phi	95	93	814.2	632	45	4	4	9	.994
Fletcher,Darrin	Mon	98	93	767.0	612	45	4	5	0	.994
Steinbach,Terry	Oak	111	106	916.2	681	57	5	3	3	.993
Eusebio,Tony	Hou	103	87	821.1	644	50	5	6	12	.993
Stanley,Mike	NYA	107	103	893.1	651	35	5	3	15	.993
Macfarlane,Mike	Bos	111	104	899.2	618	49	5	3	26	.993
Ausmus,Brad	SD	100	92	821.0	657	60	6	8	3	.992
Parent,Mark	TOT	77	71	634.0	431	44	4	1	9	.992
Johnson,Charles	Fla	97	95	844.2	641	63	6	3	5	.992
Karkovice,Ron	ChA	113	98	867.0	629	42	6	1	7	.991
Walbeck,Matt	Min	113	107	932.0	604	35	6	3	8	.991
Rodriguez,Ivan	Tex	127	120	1065.0	707	67	8	3	8	.990
Piazza,Mike	LA	112	110	941.0	805	51	9	5	12	.990
Manwaring,Kirt	SF	118	114	971.2	607	55	7	5	5	.990
Lopez,Javy	Atl	93	86	756.2	625	50	8	2	8	.988
Girardi,Joe	Col	122	119	1044.1	729	61	10	2	5	.988
Pena,Tony	Cle	91	78	703.0	508	36	7	2	6	.987
Hundley,Todd	NYN	89	76	680.1	487	28	7	2	6	.987
Fabregas,Jorge	Cal	73	63	558.1	391	36	6	1	8	.986
Oliver,Joe	Mil	91	87	730.1	408	40	8	2	16	.982
Flaherty,John	Det	112	104	916.1	570	33	11	4	0	.982
Servais,Scott	TOT	80	76	672.0	526	48	12	4	9	.980
Average	---	101	94	829.0	604	45	6	3	7	.991

Catchers - The Rest

Player	Tm	G	GS	Inn	PO	A	E	DP	PB	Pct.
Allanson,Andy	Cal	35	25	219.1	164	16	1	1	3	.994
Alomar,Sandy	Cle	61	54	466.2	364	22	2	3	4	.995
Berryhill,Damon	Cin	29	21	208.1	152	12	2	0	1	.988
Borders,Pat	KC	45	35	324.1	182	18	0	2	5	1.000
Borders,Pat	Hou	11	10	83.1	70	5	1	2	2	.987
Brito,Jorge	Col	18	13	127.0	109	6	1	0	4	.991
Castillo,Alberto	NYN	12	9	86.1	66	10	2	0	2	.974
Dalesandro,Mark	Cal	8	1	10.0	10	0	0	0	0	1.000
Decker,Steve	Fla	46	38	346.0	295	25	5	2	3	.985
Devarez,Cesar	Bal	6	0	13.0	14	0	0	0	0	1.000
Encarnacion,A	Pit	55	45	398.2	278	42	7	2	4	.979
Goff,Jerry	Hou	11	7	69.1	80	5	0	1	1	1.000
Harper,Brian	Oak	2	1	13.0	6	0	0	0	0	1.000
Haselman,Bill	Bos	48	36	334.1	257	16	3	0	3	.989
Hatteberg,Scott	Bos	2	0	2.0	4	0	0	0	0	1.000
Helfand,Eric	Oak	36	28	254.0	167	13	1	3	0	.994
Hemond,Scott	StL	38	29	260.1	185	15	3	1	7	.985
Hernandez,Carlos	LA	41	22	241.2	210	24	4	2	5	.983
Hubbard,Mike	ChN	9	6	53.2	33	0	1	0	0	.971
Johnson,Brian	SD	55	52	463.2	394	31	3	2	5	.993
Kmak,Joe	ChN	18	16	144.2	93	8	0	0	1	1.000
Knorr,Randy	Tor	45	41	352.1	243	22	8	1	8	.971
Kreuter,Chad	Sea	23	19	176.1	151	12	4	1	3	.976
Laker,Tim	Mon	61	42	378.2	265	27	7	1	4	.977
Lampkin,Tom	SF	17	6	76.1	59	5	0	0	1	1.000
LaValliere,Mike	ChA	46	30	268.0	202	19	1	1	1	.995

Catchers - The Rest

Player	Tm	G	GS	Inn	PO	A	E	DP	PB	Pct.
Levis,Jesse	Cle	12	5	56.1	33	5	0	0	0	1.000
Leyritz,Jim	NYA	46	42	390.1	287	17	2	1	5	.993
Lieberthal,Mike	Phi	14	13	116.2	95	10	1	1	7	.991
Lyons,Barry	ChA	16	9	84.2	64	10	1	1	4	.987
Martinez,Sandy	Tor	61	54	472.2	329	28	5	5	14	.986
Marzano,John	Tex	2	1	11.0	7	1	0	0	0	1.000
Matheny,Mike	Mil	80	47	460.0	261	18	4	2	10	.986
Mercedes,Henry	KC	22	14	139.1	62	8	1	1	2	.986
Merullo,Matt	Min	46	37	339.1	210	10	3	0	3	.987
Munoz,Noe	LA	2	0	4.0	6	0	0	0	0	1.000
Myers,Greg	Cal	61	53	462.2	340	21	4	5	1	.989
Natal,Bob	Fla	13	10	95.1	80	3	1	1	0	.988
Nilsson,Dave	Mil	2	0	3.0	2	0	0	0	0	1.000
Nokes,Matt	Bal	16	12	99.0	83	5	1	0	1	.989
Nokes,Matt	Col	3	2	10.0	10	0	1	0	0	.909
O'Brien,Charlie	Atl	64	56	510.0	447	23	4	5	0	.992
Owens,Jayhawk	Col	16	10	103.0	79	6	1	2	1	.988
Pagnozzi,Tom	StL	61	61	518.2	336	38	2	1	1	.995
Parent,Mark	Pit	67	63	560.1	365	39	4	1	7	.990
Parent,Mark	ChN	10	8	73.2	66	5	0	0	2	1.000
Parrish,Lance	Tor	67	49	467.2	346	41	0	6	9	1.000
Perez,Eddie	Atl	5	2	25.0	31	2	0	2	0	1.000
Posada,Jorge	NYA	1	0	1.0	1	0	0	0	0	1.000
Pratt,Todd	ChN	25	18	181.0	149	9	3	0	1	.981
Prince,Tom	LA	17	12	108.1	71	8	1	1	2	.988
Reboulet,Jeff	Min	1	0	1.0	0	0	0	0	0	.000
Reed,Jeff	SF	42	24	245.2	175	21	1	2	1	.995
Rowland,Rich	Bos	11	4	56.2	39	3	1	2	0	.977
Sasser,Mackey	Pit	11	6	51.2	35	3	0	0	1	1.000
Servais,Scott	Hou	28	27	231.2	198	17	5	0	0	.977
Servais,Scott	ChN	52	49	440.1	328	31	7	4	9	.981
Sheaffer,Danny	StL	67	53	486.2	360	37	3	6	1	.993
Siddall,Joe	Mon	7	2	28.0	14	1	2	0	2	.882
Slaught,Don	Pit	33	30	263.2	220	9	1	2	1	.996
Spehr,Tim	Mon	38	7	110.0	92	12	1	0	0	.990
Stinnett,Kelly	NYN	67	59	524.1	380	22	7	1	6	.983
Surhoff,B.J.	Mil	18	10	92.2	57	6	1	0	8	.984
Sweeney,Mike	KC	4	0	7.0	7	0	1	0	0	.875
Tatum,Jimmy	Col	1	0	4.0	3	0	0	0	0	1.000
Taubensee,Eddie	Cin	65	52	475.0	326	21	6	0	4	.983
Tettleton,Mickey	Tex	3	1	12.0	5	1	0	0	0	1.000
Tingley,Ron	Det	53	40	358.2	198	19	2	0	3	.991
Tremie,Chris	ChA	9	8	65.0	39	2	1	0	0	.976
Tucker,Scooter	Hou	3	1	10.0	7	1	0	0	0	1.000
Tucker,Scooter	Cle	17	7	75.0	53	3	1	0	1	.982
Turner,Chris	Cal	4	3	25.0	17	2	0	0	1	1.000
Valle,Dave	Tex	29	22	197.0	137	12	1	0	2	.993
Webster,Lenny	Phi	43	39	359.0	275	17	3	1	3	.990
Wehner,John	Pit	1	0	1.0	2	0	0	0	0	1.000
Widger,Chris	Sea	19	9	96.0	61	1	0	0	2	1.000
Wilkins,Rick	ChN	49	47	407.2	288	28	4	1	6	.988
Wilkins,Rick	Hou	13	12	104.2	87	4	0	0	0	1.000
Williams,George	Oak	13	9	89.1	58	7	3	0	1	.956
Zaun,Greg	Bal	39	31	283.1	216	13	3	2	3	.987

Catchers - Regulars - Special

Player	Tm	G	GS	Inn	SBA	CS	PCS	CS%	ER	CERA
Lopez,Javy	Atl	93	86	756.2	78	17	0	.22	273	3.25
Pena,Tony	Cle	91	78	703.0	86	18	3	.21	264	3.38
Piazza,Mike	LA	112	110	941.0	116	29	2	.25	384	3.67
Santiago,Benito	Cin	75	71	606.0	47	13	3	.28	259	3.85
Hundley,Todd	NYN	89	76	680.1	69	18	2	.26	295	3.90
Hoiles,Chris	Bal	107	101	871.2	96	32	10	.33	381	3.93
Eusebio,Tony	Hou	103	87	821.1	95	29	11	.31	368	4.03
Fletcher,Darrin	Mon	98	93	767.0	119	36	11	.30	347	4.07
Servais,Scott	TOT	80	76	672.0	99	26	3	.26	306	4.10
Daulton,Darren	Phi	95	93	814.2	101	27	2	.27	376	4.15
Mayne,Brent	KC	103	95	817.1	70	15	0	.21	382	4.21
Macfarlane,Mike	Bos	111	104	899.2	82	29	7	.35	425	4.25
Wilson,Dan	Sea	119	117	1017.0	106	39	9	.37	493	4.36
Johnson,Charles	Fla	97	95	844.2	89	38	2	.43	418	4.45
Ausmus,Brad	SD	100	92	821.0	93	39	6	.42	415	4.55
Parent,Mark	TOT	77	71	634.0	89	35	6	.39	327	4.64
Stanley,Mike	NYA	107	103	893.1	103	29	12	.28	469	4.72
Girardi,Joe	Col	122	119	1044.1	121	33	7	.27	550	4.74
Rodriguez,Ivan	Tex	127	120	1065.0	77	37	6	.48	563	4.76
Oliver,Joe	Mil	91	87	730.1	99	27	7	.27	389	4.79
Steinbach,Terry	Oak	111	106	916.2	99	39	6	.39	494	4.85
Karkovice,Ron	ChA	113	98	867.0	101	34	4	.34	470	4.88
Manwaring,Kirt	SF	118	114	971.2	98	28	7	.29	530	4.91
Fabregas,Jorge	Cal	73	63	558.1	57	22	2	.39	307	4.95
Flaherty,John	Det	112	104	916.1	102	24	6	.24	551	5.41
Walbeck,Matt	Min	113	107	932.0	84	20	1	.24	583	5.63
Average	---	101	94	829.0	91	28	5	.31	408	4.43

Catchers - The Rest - Special

Player	Tm	G	GS	Inn	SBA	CS	PCS	CS%	ER	CERA
Allanson,Andy	Cal	35	25	219.1	33	10	3	.30	103	4.23
Alomar,Sandy	Cle	61	54	466.2	50	14	1	.28	228	4.40
Berryhill,Damon	Cin	29	21	208.1	22	6	1	.27	90	3.89
Borders,Pat	KC	45	35	324.1	22	10	3	.45	184	5.11
Borders,Pat	Hou	11	10	83.1	12	6	1	.50	50	5.40
Brito,Jorge	Col	18	13	127.0	12	5	1	.42	79	5.60
Castillo,Alberto	NYN	12	9	86.1	9	5	0	.56	27	2.81
Dalesandro,Mark	Cal	8	1	19.0	4	1	1	.25	12	5.68
Decker,Steve	Fla	46	38	346.0	38	12	3	.32	151	3.93
Devarez,Cesar	Bal	6	0	13.0	3	0	0	0	5	3.46
Encarnacion,A	Pit	55	45	398.2	59	21	2	.36	232	5.24
Goff,Jerry	Hou	11	7	69.1	16	4	0	.25	26	3.38
Harper,Brian	Oak	2	1	13.0	0	0	0	0	0	0.00
Haselman,Bill	Bos	48	36	334.1	35	11	4	.31	166	4.47
Hatteberg,Scott	Bos	2	0	2.0	0	0	0	0	0	0.00
Helfand,Eric	Oak	36	28	254.0	29	8	3	.28	140	4.96
Hemond,Scott	StL	38	29	260.1	42	18	8	.43	102	3.53
Hernandez,Carlos	LA	41	22	241.2	24	12	1	.50	102	3.80
Hubbard,Mike	ChN	9	6	53.2	8	2	2	.25	41	6.88
Johnson,Brian	SD	55	52	463.2	52	15	3	.29	174	3.38
Kmak,Joe	ChN	18	16	144.2	16	5	0	.31	50	3.11
Knorr,Randy	Tor	45	41	352.1	50	10	0	.20	193	4.93
Kreuter,Chad	Sea	23	19	176.1	20	7	0	.35	101	5.16
Laker,Tim	Mon	61	42	378.2	55	14	3	.25	158	3.76
Lampkin,Tom	SF	17	6	76.1	6	4	1	.67	47	5.54
LaValliere,Mike	ChA	46	30	268.0	30	16	4	.53	132	4.43

Catchers - The Rest - Special

Player	Tm	G	GS	Inn	SBA	CS	PCS	CS%	ER	CERA
Levis,Jesse	Cle	12	5	56.1	11	3	0	.27	27	4.31
Leyritz,Jim	NYA	46	42	390.1	54	11	6	.20	182	4.20
Lieberthal,Mike	Phi	14	13	116.2	19	4	0	.21	54	4.17
Lyons,Barry	ChA	16	9	84.2	21	6	0	.29	66	7.02
Martinez,Sandy	Tor	61	54	472.2	33	13	0	.39	250	4.76
Marzano,John	Tex	2	1	11.0	4	1	0	.25	4	3.27
Matheny,Mike	Mil	80	47	460.0	36	9	2	.25	253	4.95
Mercedes,Henry	KC	22	14	139.1	15	4	1	.27	73	4.72
Merullo,Matt	Min	46	37	339.1	41	5	1	.12	228	6.05
Munoz,Noe	LA	2	0	4.0	0	0	0	0	1	2.25
Myers,Greg	Cal	61	53	462.2	40	13	5	.33	213	4.14
Natal,Bob	Fla	13	10	95.1	8	3	1	.38	41	3.87
Nilsson,Dave	Mil	2	0	3.0	0	0	0	0	2	6.00
Nokes,Matt	Bal	16	12	99.0	16	3	1	.19	86	7.82
Nokes,Matt	Col	3	2	16.0	0	0	0	0	6	5.40
O'Brien,Charlie	Atl	64	56	510.0	91	20	12	.22	217	3.83
Owens,Jayhawk	Col	16	10	103.0	8	5	0	.63	72	6.29
Pagnozzi,Tom	StL	61	61	518.2	76	28	2	.37	238	4.13
Parent,Mark	Pit	67	63	560.1	81	31	5	.38	278	4.47
Parent,Mark	ChN	10	8	73.2	8	4	1	.50	49	5.99
Parrish,Lance	Tor	67	49	467.2	65	27	2	.42	258	4.97
Perez,Eddie	Atl	5	2	25.0	0	0	0	0	4	1.44
Posada,Jorge	NYA	1	0	1.0	0	0	0	0	0	0.00
Pratt,Todd	ChN	25	18	181.0	25	5	1	.20	55	2.73
Prince,Tom	LA	17	12	108.1	12	4	0	.33	40	3.32
Reboulet,Jeff	Min	1	0	1.0	1	0	0	0	4	36.00
Reed,Jeff	SF	42	24	245.2	29	13	1	.45	122	4.47
Rowland,Rich	Bos	11	4	56.2	4	1	0	.25	40	6.35
Sasser,Mackey	Pit	11	6	51.2	7	3	0	.43	29	5.05
Servais,Scott	Hou	28	27	231.2	33	6	1	.18	102	3.96
Servais,Scott	ChN	52	49	440.1	66	20	2	.30	204	4.17
Sheaffer,Danny	StL	67	53	486.2	78	18	1	.23	235	4.35
Siddall,Joe	Mon	7	2	28.0	7	0	0	0	16	5.14
Slaught,Don	Pit	33	30	263.2	39	6	1	.15	124	4.23
Spehr,Tim	Mon	38	7	110.0	20	6	2	.30	60	4.91
Stinnett,Kelly	NYN	67	59	524.1	89	17	5	.19	234	4.02
Surhoff,B.J.	Mil	18	10	92.2	11	0	0	0	45	4.37
Sweeney,Mike	KC	4	0	7.0	0	0	0	0	3	3.86
Tatum,Jimmy	Col	1	0	4.0	2	0	0	0	3	6.75
Taubensee,Eddie	Cin	65	52	475.0	54	11	4	.20	228	4.32
Tettleton,Mickey	Tex	3	1	12.0	0	0	0	0	9	6.75
Tingley,Ron	Det	53	40	358.2	38	14	1	.37	227	5.70
Tremie,Chris	ChA	9	8	65.0	13	2	1	.15	25	3.46
Tucker,Scooter	Hou	3	1	10.0	2	1	0	.50	7	6.30
Tucker,Scooter	Cle	17	7	75.0	8	3	1	.38	35	4.20
Turner,Chris	Cal	4	3	25.0	0	0	0	0	10	3.60
Valle,Dave	Tex	29	22	197.0	18	6	3	.33	89	4.07
Webster,Lenny	Phi	43	39	359.0	55	7	2	.13	173	4.34
Wehner,John	Pit	1	0	1.0	0	0	0	0	2	18.00
Widger,Chris	Sea	19	9	96.0	8	0	0	0	50	4.69
Wilkins,Rick	ChN	49	47	407.2	56	20	1	.36	197	4.35
Wilkins,Rick	Hou	13	12	104.2	11	3	0	.27	43	3.70
Williams,George	Oak	13	9	89.1	15	4	1	.27	64	6.45
Zaun,Greg	Bal	39	31	283.1	27	9	3	.33	135	4.29

Pitchers Hitting & Fielding, and Hitters Pitching

As in last year's *Major League Handbook*, we've included pitcher pickoffs with the pitcher fielding data—giving you *everything* you'd ever want to know about the subject.

Greg Maddux found himself at the top of nearly every pitching category in 1995—and fielding was no exception. In over 200 innings on the mound, Maddux didn't commit *a single error*. Joey Hamilton on the other hand. . . well, break in a new glove, kid, and try again next season.

The hitting data for pitchers is always fun to look at. Ever since Orel Hershiser's historic "quest for .400" in 1993, we've always enjoyed seeing which pitchers handle the bat better than others. As you know, Hershiser has moved on to the American League, where pitchers don't know a weighted doughnut from a chocolate one. Carrying the torch for Orel in 1995 was Allen Watson, who hit a nifty .417 (15-for-36) with five runs batted in. Enjoy.

Pitchers Hitting, Fielding and Holding Runners

Pitcher	1995 Hitting						Career Hitting										1995 Fielding and Holding Runners											
	Avg	AB	H	HR	RBI	SH	Avg	AB	H	2B	3B	HR	RBI	BB	SO	SH	G	Inn	PO	A	E	DP	Pct.	SBA	CS	PCS	PPO	CS%
Abbott, Jim	.000	0	0	0	0	0	.000	0	0	0	0	0	0	0	0	0	30	197.0	8	30	0	0	1.000	24	5	4	1	.38
Abbott, Kyle	.500	2	1	0	0	0	.097	31	3	1	0	0	2	1	19	6	18	28.1	3	4	1	0	.875	2	0	0	1	.00
Acevedo, Juan	.056	18	1	0	0	0	.056	18	1	0	0	0	0	1	6	0	17	65.2	6	7	1	0	.929	7	2	1	2	.43
Acre, Mark	.000	0	0	0	0	0	.000	0	0	0	0	0	0	0	0	0	43	52.0	3	3	0	0	1.000	3	2	0	0	.67
Adams, Terry	.000	0	0	0	0	0	.000	0	0	0	0	0	0	0	0	0	18	18.0	2	1	0	0	1.000	2	0	0	0	.00
Aguilera, Rick	.000	0	0	0	0	0	.203	138	28	3	0	3	11	6	37	16	52	55.1	2	8	0	0	1.000	16	0	0	0	.00
Aheame, Pat	.000	0	0	0	0	0	.000	0	0	0	0	0	0	0	0	0	4	10.0	3	1	0	0	1.000	1	0	0	0	.00
Alberro, Jose	.000	0	0	0	0	0	.000	0	0	0	0	0	0	0	0	0	12	20.2	2	4	0	0	1.000	1	0	1	0	1.00
Alston, Garvin	.000	0	0	0	0	0	.000	0	0	0	0	0	0	0	0	0	6	6.0	0	0	0	0	.000	0	0	0	0	.00
Alvarez, Tavo	.000	12	0	0	0	2	.000	12	0	0	0	0	0	0	4	2	8	37.1	3	4	1	1	.875	1	0	0	0	.00
Alvarez, Wilson	.000	0	0	0	0	0	.000	0	0	0	0	0	0	0	0	0	29	175.0	7	31	0	1	1.000	17	5	4	1	.53
Anderson, Brian	.000	0	0	0	0	0	.000	0	0	0	0	0	0	0	0	0	18	99.2	4	16	2	1	.909	11	1	2	1	.27
Anderson, Scott	.000	0	0	0	0	0	.000	4	0	0	0	0	0	0	3	1	6	25.1	2	3	0	0	1.000	1	0	0	0	.00
Andujar, Luis	.000	0	0	0	0	0	.000	0	0	0	0	0	0	0	0	0	5	30.1	1	1	0	0	1.000	8	3	0	0	.38
Appier, Kevin	.000	0	0	0	0	0	.000	0	0	0	0	0	0	0	0	0	31	201.1	16	20	0	3	1.000	13	4	0	0	.31
Aquino, Luis	.250	4	1	0	0	0	.114	35	4	0	0	0	0	1	9	5	34	42.1	3	4	0	2	1.000	5	0	0	0	.00
Arocha, Rene	.000	1	0	0	0	0	.103	68	7	2	0	0	3	3	30	10	41	49.2	2	9	0	1	1.000	8	6	0	0	.75
Ashby, Andy	.163	49	8	0	3	17	.146	157	23	3	0	0	5	4	68	31	31	192.2	6	21	1	0	.964	27	9	1	1	.37
Assenmacher, Paul	.000	0	0	0	0	0	.083	36	3	1	0	0	0	5	12	7	46	38.1	0	5	0	1	1.000	5	0	0	0	.00
Astacio, Pedro	.125	24	3	0	0	2	.121	157	19	1	0	0	3	1	71	18	46	104.0	11	11	0	0	1.000	13	6	0	0	.46
Ausanio, Joe	.000	0	0	0	0	0	.000	0	0	0	0	0	0	0	0	0	28	37.2	4	2	0	0	1.000	2	0	0	0	.00
Avery, Steve	.208	53	11	2	4	8	.171	362	62	10	3	2	20	11	112	38	29	173.1	3	37	2	2	.952	41	2	9	4	.27
Ayala, Bobby	.000	0	0	0	0	0	.067	30	2	1	0	0	1	0	13	3	63	71.0	7	6	1	0	.929	4	0	0	0	.00
Bailey, Cory	.000	0	0	0	0	0	.000	0	0	0	0	0	0	0	0	0	3	3.2	0	1	0	0	1.000	0	0	0	0	.00
Bailey, Roger	.125	16	2	0	1	3	.125	16	2	0	0	0	1	1	3	3	39	81.1	3	14	2	2	.895	6	1	0	1	.17
Baker, Scott	.000	0	0	0	0	0	.000	0	0	0	0	0	0	0	0	0	1	3.2	0	0	0	0	.000	0	0	0	0	.00
Baldwin, James	.000	0	0	0	0	0	.000	0	0	0	0	0	0	0	0	0	6	14.2	0	3	1	0	.750	7	2	0	0	.29
Bankhead, Scott	.000	0	0	0	0	0	.222	9	2	0	0	0	0	0	7	2	20	39.0	2	2	0	0	1.000	9	1	0	0	.11
Banks, Willie	.269	26	7	0	1	1	.179	67	12	2	0	0	1	2	22	8	25	90.2	13	10	1	0	.958	11	1	0	0	.09
Barber, Brian	.125	8	1	0	0	0	.125	8	1	0	0	0	0	1	2	0	9	29.1	1	1	0	0	1.000	12	2	0	0	.17
Bark, Brian	.000	0	0	0	0	0	.000	0	0	0	0	0	0	0	0	0	3	2.1	0	0	0	0	.000	0	0	0	0	.00
Barton, Shawn	.000	0	0	0	0	1	.000	0	0	0	0	0	0	0	0	1	52	44.1	4	8	0	2	1.000	6	1	3	1	.67
Bautista, Jose	.000	18	0	0	0	1	.098	41	4	0	0	0	1	1	13	3	52	100.2	5	11	1	0	.941	5	1	0	0	.25
Beck, Rod	.333	3	1	0	0	0	.214	14	3	0	0	0	0	0	7	1	60	58.2	6	7	0	0	1.000	4	1	0	0	.25
Bedrosian, Steve	.000	0	0	0	0	0	.098	153	15	0	0	0	2	3	58	12	29	28.0	0	3	1	0	.750	10	3	0	0	.30
Belcher, Tim	.000	0	0	0	0	0	.124	372	46	8	0	2	25	2	142	41	28	179.1	22	16	1	5	.974	15	11	0	0	.73
Belinda, Stan	.000	0	0	0	0	0	.125	16	2	1	0	0	3	2	9	3	63	69.2	3	5	0	0	1.000	3	1	0	0	.33
Benes, Alan	.000	6	0	0	0	0	.000	6	0	0	0	0	0	0	3	0	3	16.0	1	0	0	0	1.000	2	1	0	0	.50
Benes, Andy	.150	40	6	0	3	3	.126	374	47	8	0	4	24	16	168	48	31	181.2	8	15	1	1	.958	21	10	1	0	.52
Benitez, Armando	.000	0	0	0	0	0	.000	0	0	0	0	0	0	0	0	0	44	47.2	1	0	1	0	.500	7	0	0	0	.00
Bennett, Erik	.000	0	0	0	0	0	.000	0	0	0	0	0	0	0	0	0	1	0.1	0	0	0	0	.000	0	0	0	0	.00
Bere, Jason	.000	0	0	0	0	0	.000	0	0	0	0	0	0	0	0	0	27	137.2	10	19	0	1	1.000	41	5	0	1	.12
Bergman, Sean	.000	0	0	0	0	0	.000	0	0	0	0	0	0	0	0	0	28	135.1	9	15	3	0	.889	28	3	0	0	.11
Bertotti, Mike	.000	0	0	0	0	0	.000	0	0	0	0	0	0	0	0	0	4	14.1	0	0	0	0	.000	0	0	0	0	.00
Berumen, Andres	.000	1	0	0	0	0	.000	1	0	0	0	0	0	0	0	0	37	44.1	4	1	1	0	.833	1	0	1	0	.10
Bielecki, Mike	.000	0	0	0	0	0	.078	270	21	0	0	0	12	11	138	35	22	75.1	6	7	2	0	.867	8	2	0	0	.25
Birkbeck, Mike	.333	6	2	0	0	1	.250	8	2	0	0	0	0	1	1	1	4	27.2	0	5	0	0	1.000	2	0	0	0	.00
Black, Bud	.000	0	0	0	0	0	.145	179	26	4	0	0	12	4	49	27	11	47.1	0	8	0	0	1.000	7	1	1	1	.29
Blair, Willie	.000	24	0	0	1	4	.060	83	5	1	0	0	5	3	55	8	40	114.0	6	13	2	1	.905	14	7	1	1	.57
Blomdahl, Ben	.000	0	0	0	0	0	.000	0	0	0	0	0	0	0	0	0	14	24.1	1	6	0	0	1.000	1	1	0	0	1.00
Bochtler, Doug	.000	2	0	0	0	0	.000	2	0	0	0	0	0	0	0	0	34	45.1	1	7	0	1	1.000	11	2	2	1	.36
Boehringer, Brian	.000	0	0	0	0	0	.000	0	0	0	0	0	0	0	0	0	7	17.2	1	0	0	0	1.000	1	0	0	0	.00
Boever, Joe	.000	0	0	0	0	0	.125	16	2	0	0	0	0	0	3	0	60	98.2	4	10	1	0	.933	11	3	0	0	.27
Bohanon, Brian	.000	0	0	0	0	0	.000	0	0	0	0	0	0	0	0	0	52	105.2	7	13	0	0	1.000	8	2	0	0	.25
Bolton, Rodney	.000	0	0	0	0	0	.000	0	0	0	0	0	0	0	0	0	8	22.0	2	3	0	0	1.000	1	0	0	0	.00
Bones, Ricky	.000	0	0	0	0	0	.077	13	1	0	0	0	1	2	5	4	32	200.1	19	32	0	7	1.000	18	7	0	0	.39
Borbon, Pedro	.000	1	0	0	0	0	.000	1	0	0	0	0	0	0	0	0	41	32.0	1	6	0	1	1.000	8	1	0	0	.13
Borland, Toby	.200	5	1	0	0	1	.125	8	1	0	0	0	2	0	1	1	50	74.0	2	10	2	0	.857	7	0	0	0	.00
Borowski, Joe	.000	0	0	0	0	0	.000	0	0	0	0	0	0	0	0	0	6	7.1	1	2	0	0	1.000	1	0	1	0	1.00
Bosio, Chris	.000	0	0	0	0	0	.000	0	0	0	0	0	0	0	0	0	31	170.0	12	21	3	3	.972	11	5	0	0	.45
Boskie, Shawn	.000	0	0	0	0	0	.184	141	26	5	2	1	8	8	42	9	20	111.2	4	19	0	1	1.000	4	0	1	1	.25
Bottalico, Ricky	.000	5	0	0	0	1	.000	5	0	0	0	0	0	0	4	1	62	87.2	6	7	0	1	1.000	9	3	0	0	.33
Bowen, Ryan	.333	6	2	0	0	0	.176	102	18	4	1	0	3	5	36	5	4	16.2	0	2	0	0	1.000	2	0	0	0	.00
Brandenburg, Mark	.000	0	0	0	0	0	.000	0	0	0	0	0	0	0	0	0	11	27.1	1	2	0	0	1.000	0	0	0	0	.00
Brantley, Jeff	.000	3	0	0	0	0	.119	67	8	1	0	0	5	2	23	9	56	70.1	7	4	0	0	1.000	3	1	0	0	.33
Brewer, Billy	.000	0	0	0	0	0	.000	0	0	0	0	0	0	0	0	0	48	45.1	3	4	1	0	1.000	4	0	0	0	.00
Brewington, Jamie	.217	23	5	0	1	4	.217	23	5	0	0	0	1	0	7	4	13	75.1	3	10	0	1	1.000	8	4	0	0	.50
Briscoe, John	.000	0	0	0	0	0	.000	0	0	0	0	0	0	0	0	0	16	18.1	2	2	0	1	1.000	1	1	0	0	1.00
Brocail, Doug	.250	16	4	0	1	4	.196	56	11	0	1	0	1	0	14	15	36	77.1	11	9	0	0	1.000	9	1	0	0	.11
Bronkey, Jeff	.000	0	0	0	0	0	.000	1	0	0	0	0	0	0	0	0	8	12.1	3	0	0	0	1.000	3	0	0	0	.00
Brown, Kevin	.000	0	0	0	0	0	.000	1	0	0	0	0	0	0	0	0	26	172.1	41	41	2	3	.976	10	2	1	2	.30
Browning, Tom	.000	0	0	0	0	0	.153	621	95	14	1	2	32	25	200	72	2	10.0	0	0	0	0	1.000	1	0	0	0	.00

271

Pitcher	1995 Hitting						Career Hitting										1995 Fielding and Holding Runners											
	Avg	AB	H	HR	RBI	SH	Avg	AB	H	2B	3B	HR	RBI	BB	SO	SH	G	Inn	PO	A	E	DP	Pct.	SBA	CS	PCS	PPO	CS%
Bruske, Jim	.000	0	0	0	0	0	.000	0	0	0	0	0	0	0	0	0	9	10.0	1	0	0	0	1.000	1	0	0	0	.00
Bullinger, Jim	.128	47	6	0	5	8	.156	90	14	5	0	1	11	8	31	14	24	150.0	20	20	0	2	1.000	31	3	1	0	.13
Bunch, Mel	.000	0	0	0	0	0	.000	0	0	0	0	0	0	0	0	0	13	40.0	2	3	1	0	.833	5	2	0	0	.40
Burba, Dave	.067	15	1	0	0	4	.140	50	7	1	0	0	3	5	26	10	52	106.2	10	7	0	0	1.000	11	3	0	0	.27
Burgos, Enrique	.000	0	0	0	0	0	.000	0	0	0	0	0	0	0	0	0	5	8.1	0	0	0	0	.000	6	0	0	0	.00
Burkett, John	.106	66	7	0	3	4	.076	367	28	3	0	0	13	20	161	44	30	188.1	17	26	0	0	1.000	12	3	1	0	.33
Burrows, Terry	.000	0	0	0	0	0	.000	0	0	0	0	0	0	0	0	0	28	44.2	3	4	0	0	1.000	4	2	1	0	.75
Butcher, Mike	.000	0	0	0	0	0	.000	0	0	0	0	0	0	0	0	0	40	51.1	4	3	0	1	1.000	4	3	0	0	.75
Byrd, Paul	1.000	1	1	0	0	0	1.000	1	1	0	0	0	0	0	0	0	17	22.0	1	3	1	0	.800	2	0	0	0	.00
Campbell, Kevin	.000	0	0	0	0	0	.000	0	0	0	0	0	0	0	0	0	6	9.2	2	0	0	0	1.000	2	0	0	0	.00
Candiotti, Tom	.109	55	6	0	2	5	.122	221	27	4	0	0	8	6	47	33	30	190.1	15	24	1	0	.975	23	12	1	1	.57
Carmona, Rafael	.000	0	0	0	0	0	.000	0	0	0	0	0	0	0	0	0	15	47.2	9	5	1	0	.933	3	1	0	0	.33
Carrara, Giovanni	.000	0	0	0	0	0	.000	0	0	0	0	0	0	0	0	0	12	48.2	1	3	0	0	1.000	9	4	0	0	.44
Carrasco, Hector	.000	7	0	0	0	0	.000	13	0	0	0	0	0	0	8	0	64	87.1	4	9	2	1	.867	4	0	0	0	.00
Carter, Andy	1.000	1	1	0	0	0	.143	7	1	0	0	0	0	0	3	0	4	7.1	0	0	0	0	.000	0	0	0	0	.00
Casian, Larry	.000	2	0	0	0	0	.000	2	0	0	0	0	0	0	1	0	42	23.1	2	4	0	0	1.000	1	0	0	1	.00
Castillo, Frank	.102	59	6	0	1	7	.114	211	24	0	0	0	6	10	66	26	29	188.0	11	24	2	0	.946	19	6	1	0	.37
Castillo, Tony	.000	0	0	0	0	0	.083	12	1	0	0	0	0	1	6	4	55	72.2	3	10	0	0	1.000	9	2	1	0	.33
Charlton, Norm	1.000	1	1	0	1	0	.093	86	8	2	0	0	1	3	50	10	55	69.2	2	6	0	0	1.000	9	1	0	0	.11
Christiansen, Jason	.000	1	0	0	0	0	.000	1	0	0	0	0	0	0	1	0	63	56.1	2	8	2	0	.833	7	3	0	0	.43
Christopher, Mike	.000	0	0	0	0	0	.000	0	0	0	0	0	0	0	0	0	36	61.1	4	8	0	0	1.000	6	3	0	0	.50
Clark, Mark	.000	0	0	0	0	0	.116	43	5	0	0	0	1	0	20	5	22	124.2	8	15	0	3	1.000	26	5	2	1	.27
Clark, Terry	.000	0	0	0	0	0	.500	2	1	0	0	0	0	0	0	0	41	42.2	2	3	1	0	.833	5	0	0	0	.00
Clemens, Roger	.000	0	0	0	0	0	.000	0	0	0	0	0	0	0	0	0	23	140.0	13	19	1	1	.970	15	5	2	0	.47
Clontz, Brad	.000	2	0	0	0	0	.000	2	0	0	0	0	0	0	0	0	59	69.0	7	8	0	1	1.000	6	2	0	0	.33
Cone, David	.000	0	0	0	0	0	.154	395	61	8	0	0	20	16	86	36	30	229.1	12	27	3	2	.929	37	9	0	2	.24
Converse, Jim	.000	0	0	0	0	0	.000	0	0	0	0	0	0	0	0	0	15	23.1	1	4	0	0	1.000	1	0	0	0	.00
Cook, Dennis	.000	0	0	0	0	0	.250	96	24	2	1	1	7	3	12	8	46	57.2	0	6	0	0	1.000	6	3	1	0	.67
Cormier, Rheal	.000	0	0	0	0	0	.184	141	26	4	0	0	8	1	31	17	48	115.0	7	21	2	3	.933	5	2	0	2	.40
Cornelius, Reid	.100	20	2	0	0	0	.100	20	2	0	0	0	0	0	7	0	18	66.2	7	12	1	2	.950	17	6	0	0	.35
Cornett, Brad	.000	0	0	0	0	0	.000	0	0	0	0	0	0	0	0	0	5	5.0	0	2	0	0	1.000	1	1	0	0	1.00
Corsi, Jim	.000	0	0	0	0	0	.000	1	0	0	0	0	0	0	1	0	36	45.0	3	9	0	1	1.000	3	1	0	0	.33
Courtright, John	.000	0	0	0	0	0	.000	0	0	0	0	0	0	0	0	0	1	1.0	0	0	0	0	.000	0	0	0	0	.00
Cox, Danny	.000	0	0	0	0	0	.109	359	39	3	1	0	12	13	152	41	24	45.0	2	6	2	1	.800	12	4	0	0	.33
Crabtree, Tim	.000	0	0	0	0	0	.000	0	0	0	0	0	0	0	0	0	31	32.0	2	8	0	1	1.000	2	0	0	0	.00
Creek, Doug	.000	0	0	0	0	0	.000	0	0	0	0	0	0	0	0	0	6	6.2	0	0	0	0	.000	0	0	0	0	.00
Cummings, John	.000	3	0	0	0	0	.000	3	0	0	0	0	0	0	1	0	39	44.1	4	5	0	2	1.000	2	0	0	0	.00
Daal, Omar	.000	0	0	0	0	0	.000	0	0	0	0	0	0	0	0	0	28	20.0	2	0	0	0	1.000	0	0	0	0	.00
Darling, Ron	.000	0	0	0	0	0	.144	526	76	21	2	2	21	15	175	65	21	104.0	10	20	0	2	1.000	7	3	1	0	.57
Darwin, Danny	.000	0	0	0	0	0	.124	193	24	5	2	1	16	5	103	8	20	99.0	3	7	2	1	.833	8	3	0	0	.38
Darwin, Jeff	.000	0	0	0	0	0	.000	0	0	0	0	0	0	0	0	0	0	0.0	0	0	0	0	.000	0	0	0	0	.00
Davis, Tim	.000	0	0	0	0	0	.000	0	0	0	0	0	0	0	0	0	5	24.0	1	7	0	0	1.000	4	2	1	0	.75
Davison, Scott	.000	0	0	0	0	0	.000	0	0	0	0	0	0	0	0	0	3	4.1	0	1	0	0	1.000	0	0	0	0	.00
Dedrick, Jim	.000	0	0	0	0	0	.000	0	0	0	0	0	0	0	0	0	6	7.2	1	1	0	0	1.000	1	0	1	1	1.00
DeLeon, Jose	.000	0	0	0	0	1	.091	419	38	1	1	0	9	16	171	52	45	76.0	0	4	1	0	.800	9	3	0	0	.33
DeLucia, Rich	.200	10	2	0	0	1	.200	10	2	0	0	0	0	1	3	1	56	82.1	3	14	2	1	.895	7	4	0	1	.57
Deshaies, Jim	.000	1	0	0	0	0	.088	373	33	0	0	0	12	23	186	44	2	5.1	0	0	0	0	.000	1	0	0	0	.00
DeSilva, John	.000	0	0	0	0	0	.000	0	0	0	0	0	0	0	0	0	2	8.2	0	2	0	1	1.000	0	0	0	0	.00
Dettmer, John	.000	0	0	0	0	0	.000	0	0	0	0	0	0	0	0	0	1	0.1	0	0	0	0	.000	0	0	0	0	.00
Dewey, Mark	.000	1	0	0	0	0	.250	4	1	0	0	0	0	2	3	0	27	31.2	1	3	1	1	.800	4	2	0	0	.50
Dibble, Rob	.000	0	0	0	0	0	.120	25	3	0	0	0	2	0	5	6	31	26.1	0	3	0	0	1.000	16	2	0	0	.13
DiPoto, Jerry	.000	5	0	0	0	1	.000	5	0	0	0	0	0	0	3	1	58	78.2	4	16	3	1	.870	9	4	0	0	.44
Dishman, Glenn	.200	30	6	0	4	2	.200	30	6	0	0	0	4	0	13	2	19	97.0	4	13	0	1	1.000	8	3	1	0	.50
Doherty, John	.000	0	0	0	0	0	.000	0	0	0	0	0	0	0	0	0	48	113.0	12	17	0	1	1.000	10	1	1	0	.20
Dougherty, Jim	.125	8	1	0	0	0	.125	8	1	0	0	0	0	0	2	1	56	67.2	4	14	0	4	1.000	7	1	0	0	.14
Drabek, Doug	.233	60	14	0	8	8	.166	658	109	16	3	2	43	17	193	58	31	185.0	24	20	2	3	.957	31	10	0	0	.32
Dunbar, Matt	.000	0	0	0	0	0	.000	0	0	0	0	0	0	0	0	0	8	7.0	0	3	0	1	1.000	0	0	0	0	.00
Dyer, Mike	.571	7	4	0	1	1	.500	8	4	0	0	0	1	0	2	1	55	74.2	3	13	0	2	1.000	11	3	0	0	.27
Eckersley, Dennis	.000	0	0	0	0	0	.133	180	24	0	3	3	12	9	84	5	52	50.1	3	5	1	2	.889	10	1	0	0	.10
Eddy, Chris	.000	0	0	0	0	0	.000	0	0	0	0	0	0	0	0	0	6	3.2	1	0	0	0	1.000	0	0	0	0	.00
Edenfield, Ken	.000	0	0	0	0	0	.000	0	0	0	0	0	0	0	0	0	7	12.2	0	2	0	0	1.000	1	0	0	0	.00
Edens, Tom	.000	0	0	0	0	0	.000	6	0	0	0	0	0	0	5	1	5	3.0	1	0	0	0	1.000	0	0	0	0	.00
Eiland, Dave	.000	0	0	0	0	0	.095	21	2	0	0	1	2	0	8	4	4	10.0	3	1	0	0	1.000	0	0	0	0	.00
Eischen, Joey	.000	1	0	0	0	0	.000	1	0	0	0	0	0	0	1	0	17	20.1	3	1	0	0	1.000	3	0	0	0	.00
Eldred, Cal	.000	0	0	0	0	0	.000	0	0	0	0	0	0	0	0	0	4	23.2	2	2	1	0	.800	3	1	0	1	.33
Elliott, Donnie	.000	0	0	0	0	0	.000	1	0	0	0	0	0	0	1	1	1	2.0	0	0	0	0	.000	0	0	0	0	.00
Embree, Alan	.000	0	0	0	0	0	.000	0	0	0	0	0	0	0	0	0	23	24.2	0	3	0	0	1.000	2	0	0	0	.00
Ericks, John	.097	31	3	0	1	6	.097	31	3	1	0	1	1	0	12	6	19	106.0	7	10	3	0	.850	23	8	1	0	.39
Erickson, Scott	.000	0	0	0	0	0	.000	0	0	0	0	0	0	0	0	0	32	196.1	26	40	1	2	.985	15	5	0	1	.33
Eshelman, Vaughn	.000	0	0	0	0	0	.000	0	0	0	0	0	0	0	0	0	23	81.2	6	8	1	1	.933	2	1	1	0	1.00
Estes, Shawn	.000	5	0	0	0	0	.000	5	0	0	0	0	0	0	2	0	3	17.1	0	1	0	0	1.000	5	0	0	0	.00
Eversgerd, Bryan	.000	1	0	0	0	0	.000	7	0	0	0	0	0	0	3	2	25	21.0	2	2	1	0	.800	0	0	0	0	.00
Fajardo, Hector	.000	0	0	0	0	0	.000	3	0	0	0	0	0	0	1	0	4	15.0	0	3	0	0	1.000	1	0	0	0	.00
Farrell, John	.000	0	0	0	0	0	.000	0	0	0	0	0	0	0	0	0	1	4.2	1	0	1	0	.500	0	0	0	0	.00

	1995 Hitting						Career Hitting										1995 Fielding and Holding Runners											
Pitcher	Avg	AB	H	HR	RBI	SH	Avg	AB	H	2B	3B	HR	RBI	BB	SO	SH	G	Inn	PO	A	E	DP	Pct.	SBA	CS	PCS	PPO	CS%
Fassero, Jeff	.070	57	4	0	1	8	.070	143	10	2	1	0	1	9	84	25	30	189.0	7	35	4	1	.913	38	3	9	0	.32
Fermin, Ramon	.000	0	0	0	0	0	.000	0	0	0	0	0	0	0	0	0	1	1.1	0	0	0	0	.000	0	0	0	0	.00
Fernandez, Alex	.000	0	0	0	0	0	.000	0	0	0	0	0	0	0	0	0	30	203.2	11	26	3	5	.925	11	5	0	1	.45
Fernandez, Sid	.043	23	1	0	1	1	.185	519	96	14	2	1	32	13	198	65	19	92.2	0	3	1	0	.750	23	2	1	0	.13
Fetters, Mike	.000	0	0	0	0	0	.000	0	0	0	0	0	0	0	0	0	40	34.2	2	1	1	0	.750	0	0	0	0	.00
Finley, Chuck	.000	0	0	0	0	0	.000	0	0	0	0	0	0	0	0	0	32	203.0	4	18	4	4	.846	26	4	1	1	.19
Fleming, Dave	.000	0	0	0	0	0	.000	0	0	0	0	0	0	0	0	0	25	80.0	5	13	0	1	1.000	14	4	1	0	.36
Fletcher, Paul	.000	0	0	0	0	0	.000	0	0	0	0	0	0	0	0	0	10	13.1	0	1	0	0	1.000	3	0	0	0	.00
Florence, Don	.000	1	0	0	0	0	.000	1	0	0	0	0	0	0	1	0	14	12.0	0	4	0	0	1.000	2	0	1	0	.50
Florie, Bryce	.000	2	0	0	0	0	.000	2	0	0	0	0	0	0	1	2	0	47	68.2	4	10	1	0	.933	12	0	0	0	.00
Fortugno, Tim	.000	0	0	0	0	0	.333	3	1	0	0	0	0	0	2	0	37	38.2	1	7	2	0	.800	2	1	0	1	.50
Fossas, Tony	.000	0	0	0	0	0	.000	0	0	0	0	0	0	0	0	0	56	36.2	1	3	1	0	.800	0	0	0	0	.00
Foster, Kevin	.250	60	15	1	9	5	.191	89	17	1	1	1	9	4	28	8	30	167.2	7	14	0	1	1.000	21	9	1	0	.48
Franco, John	.000	0	0	0	0	0	.100	30	3	0	0	0	1	0	11	3	48	51.2	2	9	0	1	1.000	2	0	1	0	.50
Frascatore, John	.000	7	0	0	0	1	.000	8	0	0	0	0	0	1	7	1	14	32.2	3	2	0	0	1.000	11	3	0	0	.27
Fraser, Willie	.000	2	0	0	0	0	.000	4	0	0	0	0	0	0	2	0	22	25.2	1	4	0	0	1.000	3	0	0	0	.00
Freeman, Marvin	.087	23	2	1	4	6	.111	99	11	1	0	2	7	2	62	15	22	94.2	9	11	3	0	.870	16	2	0	0	.13
Frey, Steve	.000	1	0	0	0	0	.000	4	0	0	0	0	0	1	3	0	31	28.1	1	6	1	0	.875	3	0	0	0	.00
Garces, Rich	.000	0	0	0	0	0	.000	1	0	0	0	0	0	0	0	0	18	24.1	2	1	0	0	1.000	3	2	0	0	.67
Gardiner, Mike	.000	0	0	0	0	0	.000	4	0	0	0	0	0	1	3	0	9	12.1	2	1	0	0	1.000	3	2	0	0	.67
Gardner, Mark	.190	21	4	0	1	4	.114	201	23	1	2	0	8	4	79	29	39	102.1	3	10	2	1	.867	15	5	0	0	.33
Givens, Brian	.000	0	0	0	0	0	.000	0	0	0	0	0	0	0	0	0	19	107.1	4	10	2	2	.875	15	4	1	1	.33
Glavine, Tom	.222	63	14	1	8	8	.187	556	104	8	2	1	41	37	149	71	29	198.2	14	42	1	6	.982	20	5	0	0	.25
Gohr, Greg	.000	0	0	0	0	0	.000	0	0	0	0	0	0	0	0	0	10	10.1	0	1	0	0	1.000	0	0	0	0	.00
Gomez, Pat	.000	1	0	0	0	0	.000	8	0	0	0	0	0	0	2	1	18	14.0	1	1	0	0	1.000	1	0	0	0	.00
Gordon, Tom	.000	0	0	0	0	0	.000	0	0	0	0	0	0	0	0	0	31	189.0	25	26	2	3	.962	17	5	0	0	.29
Gott, Jim	.000	1	0	0	0	0	.178	73	13	2	0	4	5	1	41	5	24	31.1	2	7	1	0	.900	5	1	0	0	.20
Grace, Mike	.000	2	0	0	0	2	.000	2	0	0	0	0	0	0	2	2	2	11.1	1	2	0	0	1.000	3	0	0	0	.00
Grahe, Joe	.417	12	5	0	2	6	.417	12	5	1	0	0	2	0	3	3	17	56.2	5	12	1	0	.944	11	3	0	0	.27
Green, Tyler	.182	44	8	1	5	8	.174	46	8	5	0	1	5	0	18	9	26	140.2	9	17	1	2	.963	17	7	0	2	.41
Greene, Tommy	.000	8	0	0	0	1	.219	210	46	6	0	4	18	12	58	14	11	33.2	3	0	0	0	1.000	8	2	0	0	.25
Greer, Kenny	.000	1	0	0	0	0	.000	1	0	0	0	0	0	0	0	0	8	12.0	0	3	1	0	.750	0	0	0	0	.00
Grimsley, Jason	.000	0	0	0	0	0	.105	38	4	0	0	0	2	3	10	5	15	34.0	0	8	0	1	1.000	7	0	0	0	.00
Groom, Buddy	.000	0	0	0	0	0	.000	0	0	0	0	0	0	0	0	0	37	55.2	2	6	1	0	.889	5	0	2	0	.40
Gross, Kevin	.000	0	0	0	0	0	.161	659	106	19	1	6	36	31	276	66	31	183.2	15	20	2	5	.946	21	7	1	0	.38
Grott, Matt	.000	0	0	0	0	0	.000	0	0	0	0	0	0	0	0	0	2	1.2	0	1	0	0	1.000	0	0	0	0	.00
Guardado, Eddie	.000	0	0	0	0	0	.000	0	0	0	0	0	0	0	0	0	51	91.1	4	8	1	0	.923	11	5	0	0	.45
Gubicza, Mark	.000	0	0	0	0	0	.000	0	0	0	0	0	0	0	0	0	33	213.1	28	36	0	2	1.000	15	4	1	0	.33
Guetterman, Lee	.000	0	0	0	0	0	.250	4	1	1	0	0	1	0	2	0	23	17.0	2	5	0	1	1.000	1	0	0	0	.00
Gunderson, Eric	.000	0	0	0	0	0	.000	6	0	0	0	0	0	0	4	0	49	36.2	3	8	0	0	1.000	2	2	0	0	.50
Guthrie, Mark	.000	1	0	0	0	0	.000	1	0	0	0	0	0	0	0	0	60	62.0	0	5	2	0	.714	7	1	1	0	.29
Guzman, Juan	.000	0	0	0	0	0	.000	0	0	0	0	0	0	0	0	0	24	135.1	7	12	2	0	.905	20	5	0	0	.25
Habyan, John	.000	2	0	0	0	0	.000	2	0	0	0	0	0	1	1	0	59	73.1	4	8	0	0	1.000	9	4	0	0	.44
Hall, Darren	.000	0	0	0	0	0	.000	0	0	0	0	0	0	0	0	0	17	16.1	2	1	0	0	1.000	2	0	0	0	.00
Hamilton, Joey	.108	65	7	0	3	5	.067	105	7	2	0	0	4	4	62	10	31	204.1	12	30	6	1	.875	16	7	1	2	.50
Hammaker, Atlee	.000	0	0	0	0	0	.118	305	36	1	0	0	10	10	99	21	13	6.1	0	2	0	0	1.000	1	0	0	0	.00
Hammond, Chris	.271	48	13	1	4	5	.215	214	46	7	1	4	14	26	85	17	25	161.0	8	21	1	2	.967	7	5	2	2	1.00
Hampton, Mike	.146	48	7	0	0	4	.143	49	7	0	0	0	0	4	15	4	24	150.2	10	24	3	2	.919	24	4	2	1	.25
Hancock, Lee	.000	0	0	0	0	0	.000	0	0	0	0	0	0	0	0	0	11	14.0	1	1	0	1	1.000	1	0	0	0	.00
Haney, Chris	.000	0	0	0	0	0	.114	35	4	0	0	0	4	0	4	4	16	81.1	1	15	0	0	1.000	7	1	2	0	.43
Hansell, Greg	.000	0	0	0	0	0	.000	0	0	0	0	0	0	0	0	0	20	19.1	2	1	0	0	1.000	1	0	0	0	.00
Hanson, Erik	.000	0	0	0	0	0	.154	39	6	1	0	0	3	0	17	2	29	186.2	17	21	2	1	.950	18	6	1	1	.39
Harikkala, Tim	.000	0	0	0	0	0	.000	0	0	0	0	0	0	0	0	0	1	3.1	0	0	0	0	.000	1	0	0	0	.00
Harkey, Mike	.000	0	0	0	0	0	.184	163	30	5	0	0	7	3	50	19	26	127.1	7	17	0	2	1.000	24	4	2	0	.25
Harnisch, Pete	.091	33	3	0	0	3	.125	264	33	11	0	0	14	8	68	27	18	110.0	9	12	2	1	.913	17	5	0	0	.29
Harris, Gene	.000	0	0	0	0	0	.167	6	1	0	0	0	0	0	4	2	24	23.0	0	4	1	0	1.000	4	1	0	0	.25
Harris, Greg	.333	3	1	0	0	0	.221	68	15	3	2	0	4	1	29	2	45	48.1	3	5	2	0	.800	10	2	0	0	.20
Harris, Greg W.	.000	0	0	0	0	0	.119	218	26	6	1	0	9	15	88	26	7	32.2	7	3	0	0	1.000	7	2	1	0	.43
Hartgraves, Dean	.000	2	0	0	0	1	.000	2	0	0	0	0	0	0	1	1	40	36.1	3	5	0	0	1.000	0	0	0	0	.00
Hartley, Mike	.000	0	0	0	0	0	.043	23	1	0	0	0	0	0	10	3	8	14.0	0	3	0	0	1.000	1	1	0	0	1.00
Harvey, Bryan	.000	0	0	0	0	0	.000	0	0	0	0	0	0	0	0	0	1	0.0	0	0	0	0	.000	0	0	0	0	.00
Hawkins, LaTroy	.000	0	0	0	0	0	.000	0	0	0	0	0	0	0	0	0	6	27.0	3	3	0	1	1.000	1	0	0	0	.00
Haynes, Jimmy	.000	0	0	0	0	0	.000	0	0	0	0	0	0	0	0	0	4	24.0	3	3	0	0	1.000	1	1	0	0	1.00
Helling, Rick	.000	0	0	0	0	0	.000	0	0	0	0	0	0	0	0	0	3	12.1	0	1	0	0	1.000	0	0	0	0	.00
Henke, Tom	.000	1	0	0	0	0	.000	1	0	0	0	0	0	0	0	0	52	54.1	4	4	0	1	1.000	15	2	0	0	.13
Henneman, Mike	.000	0	0	0	0	0	.000	1	0	0	0	0	0	0	0	1	50	50.1	3	2	0	0	1.000	2	1	0	0	.50
Henry, Butch	.048	42	2	0	1	5	.139	151	21	1	0	1	12	5	30	18	21	126.2	11	25	0	3	1.000	15	5	3	0	.53
Henry, Doug	1.000	1	1	0	0	1	.500	2	1	0	0	0	0	0	1	1	51	67.0	4	9	1	0	.929	7	2	0	0	.29
Henry, Dwayne	.000	0	0	0	0	0	.167	6	1	0	0	0	0	0	5	0	10	8.2	1	0	0	0	1.000	1	0	0	0	.00
Hentgen, Pat	.000	0	0	0	0	0	.000	0	0	0	0	0	0	0	0	0	30	200.2	12	18	2	2	.938	16	7	0	2	.44
Heredia, Gil	.182	33	6	0	2	5	.218	78	17	1	0	0	3	2	10	10	40	119.0	9	21	0	0	1.000	21	5	0	0	.24
Heredia, Wilson	.000	0	0	0	0	0	.000	0	0	0	0	0	0	0	0	0	6	12.0	1	0	0	0	1.000	1	0	0	0	.00
Hermanson, Dustin	.000	0	0	0	0	0	.000	0	0	0	0	0	0	0	0	0	26	31.2	4	4	0	2	1.000	2	0	0	0	.00
Hernandez, Jeremy	.000	1	0	0	0	0	.000	7	0	0	0	0	0	0	2	0	7	7.0	0	1	0	0	.000	0	0	0	0	.00

273

	1995 Hitting						Career Hitting										1995 Fielding and Holding Runners											
Pitcher	Avg	AB	H	HR	RBI	SH	Avg	AB	H	2B	3B	HR	RBI	BB	SO	SH	G	Inn	PO	A	E	DP	Pct.	SBA	CS	PCS	PPO	CS%
Hernandez, Roberto	.000	0	0	0	0	0	.000	0	0	0	0	0	0	0	0	0	60	59.2	2	5	1	0	.875	6	2	0	0	.33
Hernandez, Xavier	.000	8	0	0	0	0	.029	35	1	0	0	0	0	2	19	3	59	90.0	10	7	0	0	1.000	5	0	0	0	.00
Hershiser, Orel	.000	0	0	0	0	0	.214	672	144	26	2	0	46	23	145	89	26	167.1	16	31	2	1	.959	9	3	1	0	.44
Hickerson, Bryan	.667	3	2	0	3	1	.149	74	11	1	1	0	7	3	31	8	56	48.1	3	0	0	1	1.000	7	3	0	0	.43
Hill, Ken	.194	31	6	0	3	5	.148	324	48	6	1	1	19	24	93	65	30	185.0	23	35	1	2	.983	32	6	0	0	.19
Hitchcock, Sterling	.000	0	0	0	0	0	.000	0	0	0	0	0	0	0	0	0	27	168.1	4	12	0	1	1.000	27	1	3	1	.15
Hoffman, Trevor	.500	2	1	0	2	0	.167	12	2	1	0	0	2	0	2	1	55	53.1	5	1	0	0	1.000	1	0	0	0	.00
Holmes, Darren	.000	1	0	0	0	3	.000	2	0	0	0	0	0	0	1	3	68	66.2	6	13	1	0	.950	10	3	0	0	.30
Holzemer, Mark	.000	0	0	0	0	0	.000	0	0	0	0	0	0	0	0	0	12	8.1	1	3	0	0	1.000	1	0	0	0	.00
Honeycutt, Rick	.000	0	0	0	0	0	.133	181	24	3	0	0	8	16	43	28	52	45.2	3	5	1	0	.889	2	1	0	0	.50
Hook, Chris	.000	3	0	0	0	0	.000	3	0	0	0	0	0	0	2	0	45	52.1	5	4	0	1	1.000	8	1	0	0	.13
Hope, John	.000	0	0	0	0	0	.125	16	2	0	0	0	0	0	8	0	3	2.1	0	0	0	0	.000	0	0	0	0	.00
Horsman, Vince	.000	0	0	0	0	0	.000	0	0	0	0	0	0	0	0	0	6	9.0	1	3	0	0	1.000	2	0	0	0	.00
Howard, Chris	.000	0	0	0	0	0	.000	0	0	0	0	0	0	0	0	0	4	4.0	0	0	0	0	.000	0	0	0	0	.00
Howe, Steve	.000	0	0	0	0	0	.074	27	2	0	0	0	0	2	10	1	56	49.0	3	11	0	1	1.000	1	0	0	0	.00
Hudek, John	1.000	1	1	0	2	0	1.000	1	1	0	0	0	2	0	0	0	19	20.0	1	5	0	0	1.000	1	0	0	0	.00
Hudson, Joe	.000	0	0	0	0	0	.000	0	0	0	0	0	0	0	0	0	39	46.0	1	6	0	1	1.000	3	1	0	0	.33
Huisman, Rick	.000	0	0	0	0	0	.000	0	0	0	0	0	0	0	0	0	7	9.2	0	1	0	0	1.000	1	0	0	0	.00
Hurtado, Edwin	.000	0	0	0	0	0	.000	0	0	0	0	0	0	0	0	0	14	77.2	6	8	0	3	1.000	8	4	0	0	.50
Ignasiak, Mike	.000	0	0	0	0	0	.000	0	0	0	0	0	0	0	0	0	25	39.2	3	2	1	1	1.000	5	0	0	1	.00
Isringhausen, Jason	.148	27	4	0	0	4	.148	27	4	1	0	0	0	2	10	4	14	93.0	8	11	2	1	.905	26	4	0	0	.15
Jackson, Danny	.161	31	5	0	2	4	.123	399	49	10	2	0	24	9	210	52	19	100.2	7	12	3	1	.864	12	1	2	0	.25
Jackson, Mike	.250	4	1	0	0	0	.185	27	5	2	0	0	1	1	4	4	39	49.0	2	3	0	0	1.000	3	1	0	0	.33
Jacome, Jason	.000	7	0	0	0	1	.043	23	1	0	0	0	1	0	15	2	20	105.0	6	24	2	2	.938	11	1	2	0	.27
James, Mike	.000	0	0	0	0	0	.000	0	0	0	0	0	0	0	0	0	46	55.2	2	8	0	0	1.000	1	1	0	0	1.00
Jarvis, Kevin	.143	21	3	0	1	0	.160	25	4	1	0	0	1	0	9	3	19	79.0	8	12	2	1	.909	14	0	0	1	.00
Johns, Doug	.000	0	0	0	0	0	.000	0	0	0	0	0	0	0	0	0	11	54.2	6	10	1	0	.941	6	0	4	0	.67
Johnson, Randy	.000	0	0	0	0	0	.125	16	2	0	0	0	0	0	9	2	30	214.1	7	24	1	0	.969	27	3	5	0	.30
Johnston, Joel	.000	0	0	0	0	0	.333	6	2	1	0	0	0	0	2	1	4	4.0	0	0	0	0	.000	0	0	0	0	.00
Johnstone, John	.000	0	0	0	0	0	.000	0	0	0	0	0	0	0	0	1	4	4.2	1	0	0	0	1.000	0	0	0	0	.00
Jones, Bobby	.161	56	9	0	2	18	.123	122	15	1	0	0	3	1	51	28	30	195.2	11	30	6	1	.872	27	3	0	0	.11
Jones, Doug	.000	0	0	0	0	0	.200	5	1	0	0	0	0	0	2	0	52	46.2	4	6	1	3	.909	0	0	0	0	.00
Jones, Todd	.200	5	1	0	0	0	.300	10	3	1	0	0	0	0	1	0	68	99.2	3	11	1	1	.933	10	1	0	0	.10
Jordan, Ricardo	.000	0	0	0	0	0	.000	0	0	0	0	0	0	0	0	0	15	15.0	1	2	0	0	1.000	1	0	0	0	.00
Juden, Jeff	.056	18	1	1	4	3	.063	32	2	0	0	1	5	0	22	5	13	62.2	3	8	0	1	1.000	16	2	0	0	.13
Kamieniecki, Scott	.000	0	0	0	0	0	.000	0	0	0	0	0	0	0	0	0	17	89.2	3	10	0	2	1.000	13	3	1	1	.31
Karchner, Matt	.000	0	0	0	0	0	.000	0	0	0	0	0	0	0	0	0	31	32.0	6	3	0	2	1.000	4	2	0	0	.50
Karl, Scott	.000	0	0	0	0	0	.000	0	0	0	0	0	0	0	0	0	25	124.0	5	21	3	3	.897	9	0	2	2	.22
Karp, Ryan	.000	0	0	0	0	0	.000	0	0	0	0	0	0	0	0	0	1	2.0	0	0	0	0	.000	0	0	0	0	.00
Key, Jimmy	.000	0	0	0	0	0	.000	0	0	0	0	0	0	0	0	0	5	30.1	4	3	0	2	1.000	1	1	0	0	1.00
Keyser, Brian	.000	0	0	0	0	0	.000	0	0	0	0	0	0	0	0	0	23	92.1	9	17	1	1	.963	6	3	0	2	.50
Kiefer, Mark	.000	0	0	0	0	0	.000	0	0	0	0	0	0	0	0	0	24	49.2	0	3	0	1	1.000	5	2	0	0	.40
Kile, Darryl	.111	36	4	0	6	5	.102	206	21	6	0	1	12	13	106	31	25	127.0	11	25	3	2	.923	15	4	0	1	.27
King, Kevin	.000	0	0	0	0	0	.000	0	0	0	0	0	0	0	0	0	2	3.2	0	1	0	0	.000	1	0	0	0	.00
Klingenbeck, Scott	.000	0	0	0	0	0	.000	0	0	0	0	0	0	0	0	0	24	79.2	8	10	1	0	.947	8	2	1	0	.38
Konuszewski, Dennis	.000	0	0	0	0	0	.000	0	0	0	0	0	0	0	0	0	1	0.1	0	0	0	0	.000	0	0	0	0	.00
Krivda, Rick	.000	0	0	0	0	0	.000	0	0	0	0	0	0	0	0	0	13	75.1	0	7	1	0	.875	10	3	2	0	.50
Kroon, Marc	.000	0	0	0	0	0	.000	0	0	0	0	0	0	0	0	0	2	1.2	0	0	0	0	.000	1	1	0	0	1.00
Krueger, Bill	.000	0	0	0	0	0	.400	15	6	1	0	0	0	0	5	3	12	27.2	0	2	0	1	1.000	7	0	0	0	.00
Langston, Mark	.000	0	0	0	0	0	.167	66	11	2	0	0	3	0	28	1	31	200.1	2	43	3	2	.938	16	9	3	2	.75
Lee, Mark	.000	0	0	0	0	0	.000	0	0	0	0	0	0	0	0	0	39	33.1	2	1	1	0	.750	8	0	0	0	.00
Leiper, Dave	.000	1	0	0	0	0	.250	4	1	0	0	0	1	0	2	0	50	44.2	1	8	0	0	1.000	3	0	0	0	.00
Leiter, Al	.000	0	0	0	0	0	.000	0	0	0	0	0	0	0	0	0	28	183.0	7	15	0	2	1.000	19	8	1	0	.47
Leiter, Mark	.098	61	6	0	5	9	.098	61	6	0	0	0	5	4	33	9	30	195.2	7	19	4	4	.867	16	4	1	3	.31
Leskanic, Curt	.143	7	1	0	0	2	.154	26	4	2	0	0	3	1	9	3	76	98.0	9	17	0	1	1.000	8	2	0	1	.25
Lewis, Richie	.000	1	0	0	0	0	.125	8	1	0	0	0	1	2	3	1	21	36.0	8	2	2	0	.833	3	1	0	0	.33
Lieber, Jon	.048	21	1	0	0	0	.083	60	5	1	0	0	0	1	28	0	21	72.2	2	16	1	0	.947	15	3	1	0	.27
Lilliquist, Derek	.000	0	0	0	0	0	.213	108	23	1	0	2	8	1	20	5	28	23.0	2	2	0	0	1.000	4	0	0	0	.00
Lima, Jose	.000	0	0	0	0	0	.000	0	0	0	0	0	0	0	0	0	15	73.2	5	2	0	0	1.000	4	0	0	0	.00
Linton, Doug	.000	0	0	0	0	0	.000	7	0	0	0	0	0	0	3	2	7	22.1	0	5	0	0	1.000	2	0	0	2	.00
Lira, Felipe	.000	0	0	0	0	0	.000	0	0	0	0	0	0	0	0	0	37	146.1	13	15	0	1	1.000	13	7	0	0	.54
Lloyd, Graeme	.000	0	0	0	0	0	.000	0	0	0	0	0	0	0	0	0	33	32.0	2	7	0	0	1.000	4	0	1	0	.25
Loaiza, Esteban	.192	52	10	0	2	7	.192	52	10	1	1	0	2	1	11	7	32	172.2	13	26	0	3	1.000	27	8	0	0	.30
Lomon, Kevin	.000	0	0	0	0	1	.000	0	0	0	0	0	0	0	0	0	6	9.1	0	1	0	0	.500	2	0	0	0	.00
Looney, Brian	.000	0	0	0	0	0	.000	1	0	0	0	0	0	0	1	0	3	4.2	0	1	0	0	1.000	0	0	0	0	.00
Lopez, Albie	.000	0	0	0	0	0	.000	0	0	0	0	0	0	0	0	0	6	23.0	1	2	0	0	1.000	2	1	0	0	.50
Lorraine, Andrew	.000	0	0	0	0	0	.000	0	0	0	0	0	0	0	0	0	5	8.0	1	0	0	0	1.000	6	3	0	0	.50
MacDonald, Bob	.000	0	0	0	0	0	.000	0	0	0	0	0	0	0	0	0	33	46.1	2	4	0	0	1.000	6	3	0	0	.50
Maddux, Greg	.153	72	11	0	0	6	.182	716	130	15	0	2	35	11	200	70	28	209.2	18	53	0	4	1.000	32	5	1	1	.19
Maddux, Mike	.000	0	0	0	0	0	.068	88	6	1	0	0	4	6	31	14	44	98.2	9	12	1	2	.955	12	3	0	0	.25
Magnante, Mike	.000	0	0	0	0	0	.000	0	0	0	0	0	0	0	0	0	28	44.2	8	9	2	2	.895	4	2	0	0	.50
Mahomes, Pat	.000	0	0	0	0	0	.000	0	0	0	0	0	0	0	0	0	47	94.2	11	9	0	3	1.000	12	1	0	1	.08
Mantei, Matt	.000	0	0	0	0	0	.000	0	0	0	0	0	0	0	0	0	12	13.1	1	2	0	0	1.000	0	0	0	0	.00
Manzanillo, Josias	.000	0	0	0	0	0	.000	5	0	0	0	0	0	0	3	0	23	33.1	2	3	0	1	1.000	3	1	0	0	.33

	1995 Hitting					Career Hitting										1995 Fielding and Holding Runners											
Pitcher	Avg	AB	H	HR	RBI	SH	Avg	AB	H	2B	3B	HR	RBI	BB	SO	SH	G	Inn	PO	A	E	DP	Pct.	SBA	CS	PCS	PPO	CS%
Manzanillo, Ravelo	.000	1	0	0	0	0	.500	4	2	1	0	0	2	0	1	0	5	3.2	0	1	0	0	1.000	1	0	1	0	1.00
Marquez, Isidro	.000	0	0	0	0	0	.000	0	0	0	0	0	0	0	0	0	7	6.2	1	0	0	0	1.000	1	1	0	0	1.00
Martinez, Dennis	.000	0	0	0	0	0	.143	509	73	11	0	0	30	14	161	64	28	187.0	15	46	4	3	.938	20	6	0	3	.30
Martinez, Pedro	.111	63	7	0	2	5	.097	113	11	0	1	0	7	3	54	12	29	194.2	13	23	2	0	.947	22	13	0	5	.59
Martinez, Pedro A.	.000	0	0	0	0	0	.000	9	0	0	0	0	1	1	4	2	25	20.2	3	2	0	0	1.000	5	0	0	0	.00
Martinez, Ramon	.172	64	11	0	4	13	.153	451	69	10	0	1	29	5	148	50	30	206.1	16	27	3	2	.935	21	9	0	0	.43
Mathews, T.J.	.000	2	0	0	0	0	.000	2	0	0	0	0	0	0	1	0	23	29.2	4	5	1	1	.900	7	0	0	0	.00
Mathews, Terry	.462	13	6	0	3	0	.474	19	9	3	0	0	3	0	6	0	57	82.2	6	9	0	0	1.000	12	7	0	1	.58
Mauser, Tim	.000	1	0	0	0	0	.071	14	1	0	0	0	0	2	9	1	5	5.2	0	0	0	0	.000	4	1	0	0	.25
Maxcy, Brian	.000	0	0	0	0	0	.000	0	0	0	0	0	0	0	0	0	41	52.1	6	14	2	1	.909	4	1	0	0	.25
May, Darrell	.000	0	0	0	0	0	.000	0	0	0	0	0	0	0	0	0	2	4.0	1	0	0	0	1.000	2	0	0	0	.00
Mcandrew, Jamie	.000	0	0	0	0	0	.000	0	0	0	0	0	0	0	0	0	10	36.1	3	3	1	0	.857	6	1	0	1	.17
McCaskill, Kirk	.000	0	0	0	0	0	.000	0	0	0	0	0	0	0	0	0	55	81.0	5	13	2	0	.900	6	3	0	3	.50
Mccurry, Jeff	.000	3	0	0	0	0	.000	3	0	0	0	0	0	0	1	0	55	61.0	1	12	0	0	1.000	8	4	0	1	.50
McDonald, Ben	.000	0	0	0	0	0	.000	0	0	0	0	0	0	0	0	0	14	80.0	5	13	1	0	.947	14	4	1	0	.36
McDowell, Jack	.000	0	0	0	0	0	.000	0	0	0	0	0	0	0	0	0	30	217.2	18	23	1	1	.976	35	4	6	2	.29
McDowell, Roger	.000	0	0	0	0	0	.222	72	16	5	0	0	6	5	28	5	64	85.0	8	20	1	3	.966	4	1	1	0	.50
McElroy, Chuck	.000	3	0	0	0	0	.258	31	8	3	1	0	4	0	9	0	44	40.1	2	4	0	1	1.000	4	1	0	0	.25
McMichael, Greg	.000	6	0	0	0	0	.000	11	0	0	0	0	0	1	6	0	67	80.2	4	6	1	0	.909	9	1	1	0	.22
McMurtry, Craig	.000	1	0	0	0	0	.098	153	15	0	1	0	4	6	84	22	11	10.1	1	3	0	0	1.000	1	0	0	0	.00
Meacham, Rusty	.000	0	0	0	0	0	.000	0	0	0	0	0	0	0	0	0	49	59.2	5	9	1	2	.933	2	1	0	0	.50
Mecir, Jim	.000	0	0	0	0	0	.000	0	0	0	0	0	0	0	0	0	2	4.2	0	0	0	0	.000	1	0	0	0	.00
Menhart, Paul	.000	0	0	0	0	0	.000	0	0	0	0	0	0	0	0	0	21	78.2	2	11	1	1	.929	7	2	0	2	.29
Mercedes, Jose	.000	0	0	0	0	0	.000	0	0	0	0	0	0	0	0	0	5	7.1	0	0	0	0	.000	1	0	0	0	.00
Mercker, Kent	.104	48	5	0	5	6	.068	117	8	3	0	0	9	3	56	9	29	143.0	5	23	1	2	.966	10	1	0	0	.10
Mesa, Jose	.000	0	0	0	0	0	.000	0	0	0	0	0	0	0	0	0	62	64.0	6	10	1	0	.941	4	1	0	0	.25
Miceli, Danny	.000	1	0	0	0	0	.000	4	0	0	0	0	0	0	3	0	58	58.0	2	5	0	0	1.000	12	2	0	0	.17
Mills, Alan	.000	0	0	0	0	0	.000	0	0	0	0	0	0	0	0	0	21	23.0	1	0	0	0	1.000	8	0	0	0	.00
Mimbs, Michael	.143	35	5	0	2	8	.143	35	5	1	0	0	2	0	12	8	35	136.2	6	22	1	4	.966	11	6	1	0	.64
Minor, Blas	.000	2	0	0	0	0	.167	12	2	1	0	0	0	0	7	1	35	46.2	3	7	0	0	1.000	6	3	0	0	.50
Mintz, Steve	.000	3	0	0	0	0	.000	3	0	0	0	0	0	0	3	0	14	19.1	1	2	0	0	1.000	1	0	0	0	.00
Miranda, Angel	.000	0	0	0	0	0	.000	0	0	0	0	0	0	0	0	0	30	74.0	5	9	0	1	1.000	7	2	2	0	.57
Mlicki, Dave	.051	39	2	0	2	12	.051	39	2	0	0	0	2	8	12	12	29	160.2	10	15	1	3	.962	20	3	0	0	.15
Mohler, Mike	.000	0	0	0	0	0	.000	0	0	0	0	0	0	0	0	0	28	23.2	2	2	0	0	1.000	0	0	0	0	.00
Monteleone, Rich	.000	0	0	0	0	0	.000	3	0	0	0	0	0	0	0	0	9	9.0	1	0	0	0	1.000	0	0	0	0	.00
Montgomery, Jeff	.000	0	0	0	0	0	.000	2	0	0	0	0	0	0	1	0	54	65.2	13	4	1	1	.944	6	1	0	0	.17
Moore, Mike	.000	0	0	0	0	0	.000	1	0	0	0	0	0	0	0	0	25	132.2	14	20	1	3	.971	21	3	0	0	.14
Morel, Ramon	.000	0	0	0	0	0	.000	0	0	0	0	0	0	0	0	0	5	6.1	1	2	0	0	1.000	0	0	0	0	.00
Morgan, Mike	.053	38	2	0	0	4	.091	385	35	2	0	0	12	12	110	37	20	131.1	13	27	1	2	.976	20	4	0	0	.20
Moyer, Jamie	.000	0	0	0	0	0	.139	151	21	2	0	0	4	14	51	19	27	115.2	8	20	0	4	1.000	14	1	2	0	.21
Mulholland, Terry	.102	49	5	1	3	3	.081	405	33	4	1	1	9	9	180	30	29	149.0	5	23	3	2	.903	7	3	3	2	.86
Munoz, Bobby	.000	5	0	0	0	0	.179	39	7	0	0	1	6	1	13	2	3	15.2	0	3	1	0	.750	5	0	0	1	.00
Munoz, Mike	.500	2	1	0	1	0	.333	3	1	1	0	0	1	2	2	0	64	43.2	5	7	0	0	1.000	3	0	0	0	.00
Munoz, Oscar	.000	2	0	0	0	0	.000	2	0	0	0	0	0	0	0	0	10	35.1	1	4	0	0	1.000	4	0	0	0	.00
Murphy, Rob	1.000	1	1	0	0	0	.250	12	3	0	0	0	4		3	0	14	12.1	0	3	0	0	1.000	1	0	0	0	.00
Murray, Matt	.500	2	1	0	0	0	.500	2	1	0	0	0	1	0			6	14.0	1	5	0	1	1.000	3	0	0	0	.00
Mussina, Mike	.000	0	0	0	0	0	.000	0	0	0	0	0	0	0	0	0	32	221.2	13	26	2	3	.951	10	6	0	1	.60
Myers, Jimmy	.000	0	0	0	0	0	.000	0	0	0	0	0	0	0	0	0	0	0.00	0	0	0	0	.000	0	0	0	0	.00
Myers, Mike	.000	0	0	0	0	0	.000	0	0	0	0	0	0	0	0	0	13	8.1	1	1	0	0	1.000	0	0	0	0	.00
Myers, Randy	.000	0	0	0	1	0	.186	59	11	3	0	0	7	3	32	5	57	55.2	2	9	0	0	1.000	3	1	1	0	.67
Nabholz, Chris	.000	1	0	0	0	0	.107	178	19	3	0	0	4	6	44	15	34	23.1	1	5	0	0	1.000	2	0	0	0	.00
Nagy, Charles	.000	0	0	0	0	0	.000	0	0	0	0	0	0	0	0	0	29	178.0	19	34	1	4	.981	21	3	0	0	.14
Navarro, Jaime	.185	65	12	0	7	8	.185	65	12	5	0	0	7	1	25	8	29	200.1	14	13	1	1	.964	22	6	0	0	.27
Neagle, Denny	.122	74	9	1	8	5	.121	141	17	3	0	2	15	4	45	14	31	209.2	13	32	1	5	.978	24	8	3	0	.46
Nelson, Jeff	.000	0	0	0	0	0	.000	0	0	0	0	0	0	0	0	0	62	78.2	2	10	1	1	.923	14	2	0	0	.14
Nen, Robb	.000	0	0	0	0	0	.000	7	0	0	0	0	0	0	1	0	62	65.2	3	9	0	1	1.000	12	0	0	1	.00
Nichols, Rod	.000	0	0	0	0	0	.000	0	0	0	0	0	0	0	0	0	5	6.2	0	2	1	0	.667	1	0	0	0	.00
Nichting, Chris	.000	0	0	0	0	0	.000	0	0	0	0	0	0	0	0	0	13	24.1	5	7	0	0	1.000	0	0	0	0	.00
Nied, Dave	.000	0	0	0	0	0	.143	70	10	0	0	0	2	4	25	6	2	4.1	0	1	0	0	1.000	0	0	0	0	.00
Nitkowski, C.J.	.200	10	2	0	1	0	.200	10	2	0	0	0	1	0	6	0	20	71.2	5	8	2	0	.867	19	3	3	1	.32
Nomo, Hideo	.091	66	6	0	4	5	.091	66	6	0	0	0	4	0	33	5	28	191.1	6	12	3	0	.857	34	4	1	1	.15
Ogea, Chad	.000	0	0	0	0	0	.000	0	0	0	0	0	0	0	0	0	20	106.1	3	14	0	1	1.000	16	2	0	0	.13
Olivares, Omar	.222	9	2	1	2	1	.229	201	46	7	0	4	21	5	58	13	16	41.2	5	8	0	1	1.000	4	0	0	1	.00
Oliver, Darren	.000	0	0	0	0	0	.000	0	0	0	0	0	0	0	0	0	17	49.0	4	8	0	1	1.000	10	1	2	0	.30
Olson, Gregg	.000	0	0	0	0	0	.000	2	0	0	0	0	0	0	2	0	23	33.0	1	5	0	1	1.000	13	1	0	0	.08
Ontiveros, Steve	.000	0	0	0	0	0	.083	12	1	1	0	0	3	1	2	0	22	129.2	17	26	0	4	1.000	10	5	0	1	.50
Oquist, Mike	.000	0	0	0	0	0	.000	0	0	0	0	0	0	0	0	0	27	54.0	1	8	0	0	1.000	6	2	0	0	.33
Orosco, Jesse	.000	0	0	0	0	0	.169	59	10	0	0	0	4	6	25	7	65	49.2	3	8	0	0	1.000	10	3	0	3	.30
Osborne, Donovan	.161	31	5	0	4	3	.159	138	22	4	1	0	7	6	49	12	19	113.1	3	16	0	0	1.000	18	8	0	1	.44
Osuna, Antonio	.000	2	0	0	0	0	.000	2	0	0	0	0	0	0	0	0	39	44.2	0	7	0	2	1.000	4	1	0	1	.25
Painter, Lance	.111	9	1	0	0	1	.175	40	7	2	1	0	3	2	19	7	33	45.1	3	6	1	0	1.000	2	0	1	0	.50
Palacios, Vince	.167	6	1	0	0	0	.045	88	4	0	0	0		2	43	11	20	40.1	3	4	0	0	1.000	4	4	0	0	1.00
Park, Chan Ho	.000	1	0	0	0	0	.000	1	0	0	0	0	0	0	1	0	2	4.0	0	0	0	0	.000	0	0	0	0	.00
Parra, Jose	.000	0	0	0	0	2	.000	0	0	0	0	0	0	0	0	0	20	72.0	4	9	2	1	.867	7	1	0	0	.14

	1995 Hitting						Career Hitting											1995 Fielding and Holding Runners											
Pitcher	Avg	AB	H	HR	RBI	SH	Avg	AB	H	2B	3B	HR	RBI	BB	SO	SH	G	Inn	PO	A	E	DP	Pct.	SBA	CS	PCS	PPO	CS%
Parrett, Jeff	.500	2	1	0	0	0	.111	36	4	0	0	0	1	2	12	2	59	76.2	7	6	2	0	.867	7	1	0	0	.14
Parris, Steve	.250	28	7	0	4	1	.250	28	7	2	0	0	4	0	10	1	15	82.0	4	10	0	0	1.000	15	8	0	0	.53
Patterson, Bob	.000	0	0	0	0	0	.115	52	6	1	0	0	4	2	22	6	62	53.1	0	5	0	0	1.000	7	3	1	0	.57
Patterson, Jeff	.000	0	0	0	0	0	.000	0	0	0	0	0	0	0	0	0	3	3.1	0	0	0	0	.000	0	0	0	0	.00
Pavlas, Dave	.000	0	0	0	0	0	.000	1	0	0	0	0	0	1	1	0	4	5.2	0	0	0	0	.000	0	0	0	0	.00
Pavlik, Roger	.000	0	0	0	0	0	.000	0	0	0	0	0	0	0	0	0	31	191.2	20	32	1	4	.981	17	8	0	2	.47
Pena, Alejandro	.000	1	0	0	0	0	.110	181	20	3	0	1	7	3	73	9	44	55.1	2	3	0	0	1.000	9	2	0	0	.22
Pennington, Brad	.000	2	0	0	0	0	.000	2	0	0	0	0	0	0	1	0	14	16.1	1	0	1	0	.500	2	0	0	0	.00
Percival, Troy	.000	0	0	0	0	0	.000	0	0	0	0	0	0	0	0	0	62	74.0	2	4	0	0	1.000	9	1	0	0	.11
Perez, Carlos	.133	45	6	1	5	4	.133	45	6	1	1	1	5	4	21	4	28	141.1	6	23	2	1	.935	21	4	3	0	.33
Perez, Melido	.000	0	0	0	0	0	.000	0	0	0	0	0	0	0	0	0	13	69.1	4	4	1	0	.889	5	3	1	0	.80
Perez, Mike	.000	4	0	0	0	1	.000	10	0	0	0	0	0	3	6	3	68	71.1	5	8	1	1	.929	16	4	0	0	.25
Perez, Yorkis	.000	2	0	0	0	0	.000	4	0	0	0	0	0	0	3	0	69	46.2	1	4	0	0	1.000	8	1	0	0	.13
Person, Robert	.667	3	2	0	0	0	.667	3	2	0	0	0	0	0	0	0	3	12.0	0	0	0	0	.000	1	0	0	0	.00
Petkovsek, Mark	.081	37	3	0	2	3	.081	37	3	0	0	0	2	5	11	3	26	137.1	8	17	0	1	1.000	17	7	0	0	.41
Pettitte, Andy	.000	0	0	0	0	0	.000	0	0	0	0	0	0	0	0	0	31	175.0	5	26	1	0	.969	17	1	7	5	.47
Phoenix, Steve	.000	0	0	0	0	0	.000	0	0	0	0	0	0	0	0	0	1	1.2	0	0	0	0	.000	0	0	0	0	.00
Pichardo, Hipolito	.000	2	0	0	0	0	.000	2	0	0	0	0	0	0	0	0	44	64.0	2	12	0	1	1.000	5	1	0	0	.20
Pierce, Jeff	.000	0	0	0	0	0	.000	0	0	0	0	0	0	0	0	0	12	15.0	0	2	0	0	1.000	2	1	0	0	.50
Pittsley, Jim	.000	0	0	0	0	0	.000	0	0	0	0	0	0	0	0	0	1	3.1	0	0	0	0	.000	0	0	0	0	.00
Plesac, Dan	.250	4	1	0	0	0	.111	9	1	0	0	0	0	0	7	0	58	60.1	1	8	0	1	1.000	2	0	0	0	.00
Plunk, Eric	.000	0	0	0	0	0	.000	0	0	0	0	0	0	0	0	0	56	64.0	2	7	0	1	1.000	12	3	0	2	.25
Poole, Jim	.000	0	0	0	0	0	.000	0	0	0	0	0	0	0	0	0	42	50.1	2	9	1	0	.917	6	2	0	1	.33
Portugal, Mark	.138	58	8	0	5	8	.197	345	68	14	1	2	31	15	64	42	31	181.2	9	21	1	2	.968	17	2	0	0	.12
Powell, Jay	.000	0	0	0	0	0	.000	0	0	0	0	0	0	0	0	0	9	8.1	1	3	0	0	1.000	3	0	0	0	.00
Powell, Ross	.000	3	0	0	0	1	.000	4	0	0	0	0	0	0	2	1	27	29.2	1	5	0	0	1.000	5	0	1	0	.20
Prieto, Ariel	.000	0	0	0	0	0	.000	0	0	0	0	0	0	0	0	0	14	58.0	0	8	1	0	.889	6	1	0	0	.17
Pugh, Tim	.143	28	4	0	1	4	.202	109	22	4	0	0	4	4	38	13	28	98.1	10	9	1	0	.950	10	3	0	1	.30
Pulsipher, Bill	.105	38	4	0	4	4	.105	38	4	2	0	0	4	5	19	4	17	126.2	5	18	0	1	1.000	14	3	2	1	.36
Quantrill, Paul	.105	57	6	0	0	7	.100	60	6	0	0	0	0	3	25	7	33	179.1	9	32	1	2	.976	24	3	1	1	.17
Radinsky, Scott	.000	0	0	0	0	0	.000	0	0	0	0	0	0	0	0	0	46	38.0	3	5	0	1	1.000	3	2	0	0	.67
Radke, Brad	.000	0	0	0	0	0	.000	0	0	0	0	0	0	0	0	0	29	181.0	17	20	0	1	1.000	11	4	0	0	.36
Rapp, Pat	.107	56	6	0	5	9	.131	130	17	3	0	0	9	1	51	16	28	167.1	13	20	1	1	.971	20	15	0	1	.75
Rasmussen, Dennis	.000	0	0	0	0	0	.193	259	50	8	0	0	14	13	82	19	5	10.0	0	0	0	0	.000	1	0	0	0	.00
Reed, Rick	.000	3	0	0	0	2	.158	38	6	1	0	0	3	3	12	2	4	17.0	2	1	0	0	1.000	1	1	0	0	1.00
Reed, Steve	.333	3	1	0	0	0	.071	14	1	0	0	0	0	0	5	2	71	84.0	4	16	1	1	.952	7	3	1	0	.57
Rekar, Bryan	.038	26	1	0	0	4	.038	26	1	0	0	0	0	3	15	4	15	85.0	9	16	1	0	.962	4	2	0	0	.50
Remlinger, Mike	.000	1	0	0	0	0	.000	24	0	0	0	0	1	2	8	7	7	6.2	0	0	0	0	.000	1	0	0	0	.00
Reyes, Al	.000	0	0	0	0	0	.000	0	0	0	0	0	0	0	0	0	26	33.1	0	6	0	0	1.000	3	0	0	0	.00
Reyes, Carlos	.000	0	0	0	0	0	.000	0	0	0	0	0	0	0	0	0	40	69.0	3	13	0	0	1.000	12	4	0	0	.33
Reynolds, Shane	.127	63	8	0	1	10	.137	102	14	2	0	0	3	2	45	19	30	189.1	13	38	1	0	.981	22	5	1	0	.27
Reynoso, Armando	.133	30	4	0	0	2	.126	119	15	0	0	2	4	6	41	12	20	93.0	7	29	2	2	.947	14	4	1	6	.36
Rhodes, Arthur	.000	0	0	0	0	0	.000	0	0	0	0	0	0	0	0	0	19	75.1	3	7	2	0	.833	12	3	1	0	.33
Ricci, Chuck	.000	0	0	0	0	0	.000	0	0	0	0	0	0	0	0	0	7	10.0	2	0	0	0	1.000	2	1	0	0	.50
Righetti, Dave	.000	0	0	0	0	0	.182	11	2	0	0	0	1	0	6	5	10	49.1	0	5	1	1	.833	6	3	0	0	.50
Rightnowar, Ron	.000	0	0	0	0	0	.000	0	0	0	0	0	0	0	0	0	34	36.2	0	8	0	1	1.000	1	1	0	0	1.00
Rijo, Jose	.136	22	3	0	3	2	.193	429	83	13	0	2	29	8	94	55	13	69.0	4	9	0	0	1.000	8	0	0	0	.00
Risley, Bill	.000	0	0	0	0	0	.000	2	0	0	0	0	0	0	0	0	45	60.1	2	3	0	0	1.000	5	2	0	0	.40
Ritz, Kevin	.188	48	9	0	2	11	.132	68	9	1	0	0	2	2	33	16	31	173.1	10	39	0	1	1.000	22	3	1	0	.18
Rivera, Mariano	.000	0	0	0	0	0	.000	0	0	0	0	0	0	0	0	0	19	67.0	2	14	0	1	1.000	7	2	0	1	.29
Rivera, Roberto	.000	0	0	0	0	0	.000	0	0	0	0	0	0	0	0	0	7	5.0	0	1	0	0	1.000	1	0	0	0	1.00
Roa, Joe	.000	0	0	0	0	0	.000	0	0	0	0	0	0	0	0	0	1	6.0	2	2	0	0	1.000	0	0	0	0	.00
Roberson, Sid	.000	0	0	0	0	0	.000	0	0	0	0	0	0	0	0	0	26	84.1	2	5	3	0	.700	10	1	1	0	.20
Robertson, Rich	.000	0	0	0	0	0	.250	4	1	0	0	0	0	0	3	0	25	51.2	3	4	1	0	.875	8	4	0	0	.50
Robinson, Ken	.000	0	0	0	0	0	.000	0	0	0	0	0	0	0	0	0	21	39.0	2	1	0	0	1.000	2	0	0	0	.00
Rodriguez, Felix	.000	0	0	0	0	0	.000	0	0	0	0	0	0	0	0	0	10	10.2	0	1	0	1	1.000	0	0	0	0	.00
Rodriguez, Frank	.000	0	0	0	0	0	.000	0	0	0	0	0	0	0	0	0	25	105.2	12	23	0	3	1.000	7	2	1	0	.43
Rodriguez, Rich	.000	0	0	0	0	0	.000	17	0	0	0	0	0	2	3	2	1	1.2	0	0	0	0	.000	0	0	0	0	.00
Rogers, Jimmy	.000	0	0	0	0	0	.000	0	0	0	0	0	0	0	0	0	19	23.2	0	2	0	0	1.000	0	0	0	0	.00
Rogers, Kenny	.000	0	0	0	0	0	.000	0	0	0	0	0	0	0	0	0	31	208.0	10	35	2	2	.957	10	3	2	1	.50
Rojas, Mel	.000	6	0	0	0	2	.080	50	4	0	0	0	0	0	30	6	59	67.2	4	7	0	1	1.000	11	0	0	0	.50
Roper, John	.000	1	0	0	0	0	.177	62	11	1	0	0	4	1	23	4	3	8.0	0	1	0	0	1.000	1	1	0	0	1.00
Rosselli, Joe	.200	10	2	0	1	1	.200	10	2	0	0	0	0	0	3	1	9	30.0	0	5	0	1	1.000	1	1	0	0	1.00
Rueter, Kirk	.000	16	0	0	1	2	.079	76	6	0	0	0	5	5	24	12	9	47.1	8	9	0	1	1.000	3	1	1	0	.67
Ruffcorn, Scott	.000	0	0	0	0	0	.000	0	0	0	0	0	0	0	0	0	4	8.0	1	2	0	0	1.000	2	1	0	0	.50
Ruffin, Bruce	.000	2	0	0	0	0	.082	294	24	4	0	0	7	22	142	23	37	34.0	0	8	0	0	1.000	4	1	1	0	.50
Ruffin, Johnny	.000	2	0	0	0	0	.077	13	1	0	0	0	0	0	4	0	10	13.1	2	1	0	1	1.000	1	0	0	0	.00
Russell, Jeff	.000	0	0	0	0	0	.139	79	11	3	0	1	10	5	33	7	37	32.2	2	2	0	0	1.000	3	2	0	0	.67
Ryan, Ken	.000	0	0	0	0	0	.000	0	0	0	0	0	0	0	0	0	28	32.2	1	1	1	0	.667	4	0	0	0	.00
Saberhagen, Bret	.102	49	5	0	0	5	.128	180	23	4	0	0	1	12	45	24	25	153.0	8	34	1	3	.977	5	1	0	4	.20
Sager, A.J.	.000	3	0	0	0	0	.077	13	1	0	1	0	2	0	6	1	10	14.2	1	5	0	1	1.000	4	1	0	0	.25
Sanders, Scott	.296	27	8	0	4	3	.173	75	13	1	0	0	6	4	25	13	17	90.0	6	3	0	0	1.000	8	3	0	0	.38
Sanderson, Scott	.000	0	0	0	0	0	.097	474	46	13	0	2	26	26	224	66	7	39.1	3	4	0	1	1.000	8	2	0	1	.25
Sanford, Mo	.000	0	0	0	0	0	.000	16	0	0	0	0	0	1	9	3	11	18.2	0	1	0	0	.000	3	1	0	0	.33

	1995 Hitting						Career Hitting										1995 Fielding and Holding Runners											
Pitcher	Avg	AB	H	HR	RBI	SH	Avg	AB	H	2B	3B	HR	RBI	BB	SO	SH	G	Inn	PO	A	E	DP	Pct.	SBA	CS	PCS	PPO	CS%
Scanlan, Bob	.000	0	0	0	0	0	.067	30	2	0	0	0	3	1	12	3	17	83.1	6	14	2	1	.909	25	2	0	0	.08
Scheid, Rich	.000	1	0	0	0	0	.000	9	0	0	0	0	0	0	3	1	6	10.1	1	5	0	0	1.000	3	1	1	0	.67
Schilling, Curt	.175	40	7	0	3	5	.152	210	32	4	0	0	10	4	66	27	17	116.0	2	8	1	1	.909	13	1	1	0	.15
Schmidt, Curt	.000	0	0	0	0	0	.000	0	0	0	0	0	0	0	0	0	11	10.1	0	1	0	0	1.000	4	0	0	0	.00
Schmidt, Jason	.200	5	1	0	0	1	.200	5	1	0	0	0	0	1	2	1	9	25.0	3	3	0	1	1.000	3	0	0	0	.00
Schourek, Pete	.220	59	13	0	4	12	.163	178	29	3	0	1	13	6	48	18	29	190.1	7	29	1	2	.973	19	7	5	0	.63
Schullstrom, Erik	.000	0	0	0	0	0	.000	0	0	0	0	0	0	0	0	0	37	47.0	1	6	0	0	1.000	0	0	0	0	.00
Scott, Tim	.250	4	1	0	0	0	.100	10	1	0	0	0	0	0	7	1	61	63.1	3	4	0	1	1.000	23	1	0	0	.04
Seanez, Rudy	.000	1	0	0	0	0	.000	2	0	0	0	0	0	0	2	0	37	34.2	3	3	1	0	.857	5	1	0	0	.20
Seelbach, Chris	.000	0	0	0	0	0	.000	0	0	0	0	0	0	0	0	0	0	0.00	0	0	0	0	.000	0	0	0	0	.00
Sele, Aaron	.000	0	0	0	0	0	.000	0	0	0	0	0	0	0	0	0	6	32.1	2	5	3	0	.700	1	1	0	0	1.00
Service, Scott	.000	1	0	0	0	0	.100	10	1	0	0	0	1	0	6	0	28	31.0	2	2	0	0	1.000	4	1	1	0	.50
Shaw, Jeff	.000	6	0	0	0	0	.107	28	3	0	0	0	0	3	12	1	59	72.0	7	13	0	1	1.000	8	5	0	1	.63
Shepherd, Keith	.000	0	0	0	0	0	.000	2	0	0	0	0	0	0	0	0	2	1.0	0	1	0	0	1.000	0	0	0	0	.00
Shuey, Paul	.000	0	0	0	0	0	.000	0	0	0	0	0	0	0	0	0	7	6.1	0	2	0	0	1.000	2	1	0	0	.50
Simas, Bill	.000	0	0	0	0	0	.000	0	0	0	0	0	0	0	0	0	14	14.0	0	0	0	0	.000	1	0	0	0	.00
Sirotka, Mike	.000	0	0	0	0	0	.000	0	0	0	0	0	0	0	0	0	6	34.1	1	5	0	0	1.000	2	0	2	0	1.00
Slocumb, Heathcliff	.000	1	0	0	0	0	.091	11	1	0	0	0	2	0	6	1	61	65.1	4	17	1	3	.955	5	1	0	0	.20
Slusarski, Joe	.000	0	0	0	0	0	.000	0	0	0	0	0	0	0	0	0	12	15.0	2	1	0	0	1.000	0	0	0	0	.00
Small, Aaron	.000	0	0	0	0	0	.000	0	0	0	0	0	0	0	0	0	7	6.1	0	1	0	0	1.000	1	0	0	0	.00
Smiley, John	.164	55	9	2	5	6	.141	396	56	11	0	2	27	21	151	39	28	176.2	3	27	0	3	1.000	13	3	1	0	.31
Smith, Lee	.000	0	0	0	0	0	.047	64	3	0	0	1	2	3	42	4	52	49.1	1	4	0	0	1.000	9	5	0	0	.56
Smith, Pete	.000	3	0	0	0	0	.116	233	27	3	1	0	11	16	60	31	11	24.1	1	6	0	0	1.000	0	0	0	0	.00
Smith, Zane	.000	0	0	0	0	0	.158	525	83	12	2	0	29	13	102	70	24	110.2	5	18	1	1	.958	13	1	3	0	.31
Smoltz, John	.107	56	6	0	1	6	.142	457	65	9	1	3	23	44	186	57	29	192.2	12	18	2	0	.938	14	4	0	1	.29
Sodowsky, Clint	.000	0	0	0	0	0	.000	0	0	0	0	0	0	0	0	0	6	23.1	2	1	0	0	1.000	2	1	0	0	.50
Sparks, Steve	.000	0	0	0	0	0	.000	0	0	0	0	0	0	0	0	0	33	202.0	25	43	2	5	.971	23	5	2	2	.30
Springer, Dennis	.125	8	1	0	0	0	.125	8	1	0	0	0	0	0	3	0	4	22.1	2	1	1	0	.750	4	2	0	0	.50
Springer, Russ	.000	1	0	0	0	1	.000	1	0	0	0	0	0	0	1	0	33	78.1	3	10	0	2	1.000	9	1	0	1	.11
Stanton, Mike	.000	0	0	0	0	0	.545	11	6	1	0	0	2	1	1	1	48	40.1	1	9	4	0	.714	2	0	2	2	1.00
Stevens, Dave	.000	0	0	0	0	0	.000	0	0	0	0	0	0	0	0	0	56	65.2	9	7	1	1	.941	7	1	0	0	.14
Stewart, Dave	.000	0	0	0	0	0	.196	51	10	1	1	0	4	3	17	6	16	81.0	5	11	0	0	1.000	12	4	1	1	.42
Stottlemyre, Todd	.000	1	0	0	0	0	.000	1	0	0	0	0	0	0	1	0	31	209.2	16	18	2	1	.944	30	11	1	1	.40
Sturtze, Tanyon	.000	0	0	0	0	0	.000	0	0	0	0	0	0	0	0	0	2	2.0	0	0	0	0	.000	0	0	0	0	.00
Sullivan, Scott	.000	1	0	0	0	0	.000	1	0	0	0	0	0	0	1	0	3	3.2	1	0	0	0	1.000	0	0	0	0	.00
Suppan, Jeff	.000	0	0	0	0	0	.000	0	0	0	0	0	0	0	0	0	8	22.2	2	2	0	0	1.000	3	0	0	0	.00
Suzuki, Makoto	.000	0	0	0	0	0	.000	0	0	0	0	0	0	0	0	0	0	0.00	0	0	0	0	.000	0	0	0	0	.00
Swartzbaugh, Dave	.000	0	0	0	0	0	.000	0	0	0	0	0	0	0	0	0	0	7.1	0	0	0	0	.000	2	0	0	0	1.00
Swift, Bill	.194	36	7	1	4	5	.211	199	42	8	0	1	13	11	47	25	19	105.2	9	27	1	2	.973	9	4	1	0	.56
Swindell, Greg	.240	50	12	0	5	6	.188	234	44	9	0	0	13	4	54	33	33	153.0	9	31	1	3	.976	26	5	7	2	.46
Tabaka, Jeff	.000	1	0	0	0	1	.500	2	1	1	0	0	0	1	0	1	34	30.2	1	3	0	0	1.000	2	0	2	0	1.00
Tapani, Kevin	.176	17	3	0	2	3	.158	19	3	1	0	0	2	0	8	3	33	190.2	20	21	1	1	.976	25	4	0	0	.16
Tavarez, Julian	.000	0	0	0	0	0	.000	0	0	0	0	0	0	0	0	0	57	85.0	7	11	2	1	.900	5	2	1	1	.60
Taylor, Scott M.	.000	0	0	0	0	0	.000	0	0	0	0	0	0	0	0	0	3	15.1	1	3	0	2	1.000	0	0	0	0	.00
Telgheder, Dave	.333	6	2	0	1	1	.143	21	3	1	0	0	1	1	11	5	7	25.2	2	6	0	0	1.000	3	0	0	0	.00
Tewksbury, Bob	.000	1	0	0	0	0	.152	309	47	6	0	0	16	18	119	33	21	129.2	12	24	1	3	.973	6	3	0	0	.50
Thobe, J.J.	.000	0	0	0	0	0	.000	0	0	0	0	0	0	0	0	0	4	4.0	0	0	1	0	.000	1	0	0	0	.00
Thobe, Tom	.000	0	0	0	0	0	.000	0	0	0	0	0	0	0	0	0	3	3.1	0	0	0	0	.000	0	0	0	0	.00
Thomas, Larry	.000	0	0	0	0	0	.000	0	0	0	0	0	0	0	0	0	17	13.2	2	0	0	0	1.000	0	0	0	0	.00
Thomas, Mike	.000	0	0	0	0	0	.000	0	0	0	0	0	0	0	0	0	11	11.1	0	0	0	0	.000	0	0	0	0	.00
Thompson, Mark	.385	13	5	0	0	1	.294	17	5	0	0	0	0	0	11	2	21	51.0	3	10	0	1	1.000	10	2	1	1	.30
Timlin, Mike	.000	0	0	0	0	0	.000	0	0	0	0	0	0	0	0	0	31	42.0	1	9	0	1	1.000	1	1	0	0	1.00
Torres, Dilson	.000	0	0	0	0	0	.000	0	0	0	0	0	0	0	0	0	24	44.1	6	12	0	1	1.000	2	1	1	0	1.00
Torres, Salomon	.000	1	0	0	0	0	.175	40	7	0	0	0	0	0	16	6	20	80.0	9	16	0	2	1.000	11	3	0	0	.27
Trachsel, Steve	.265	49	13	0	4	6	.224	98	22	3	0	0	6	3	28	14	30	160.2	7	13	1	0	.952	26	6	0	1	.23
Trombley, Mike	.000	0	0	0	0	0	.000	0	0	0	0	0	0	0	0	0	20	97.2	9	10	1	2	.950	10	1	0	1	.10
Urbani, Tom	.316	19	6	1	3	2	.254	59	15	1	0	1	4	7	17	7	24	82.2	4	19	0	0	1.000	7	2	1	1	.43
Urbina, Ugueth	.333	6	2	0	0	0	.333	6	2	0	0	0	0	0	4	0	7	23.1	5	4	0	0	1.000	7	1	0	0	.14
Valdes, Ismael	.097	62	6	0	1	7	.094	64	6	0	0	0	1	1	27	7	33	197.2	16	31	1	0	.979	14	3	1	1	.29
Valdes, Marc	.000	2	0	0	0	0	.000	2	0	0	0	0	0	0	0	0	3	7.0	0	0	0	0	.000	0	0	0	0	.00
Valdez, Carlos	.000	1	0	0	0	0	.000	1	0	0	0	0	0	0	1	0	11	14.2	1	2	0	0	1.000	7	2	0	0	.29
Valdez, Sergio	.095	21	2	0	1	3	.121	33	4	0	0	0	1	0	14	3	13	66.1	4	14	2	0	.900	10	4	0	0	.40
Valenzuela, Fernando	.250	32	8	2	8	3	.204	851	174	24	1	10	80	8	127	84	29	90.1	7	27	0	2	1.000	8	2	2	1	.50
Van Poppel, Todd	.000	0	0	0	0	0	.000	0	0	0	0	0	0	0	0	0	36	138.1	4	11	1	0	.938	17	4	1	0	.29
Vanegmond, Tim	.000	0	0	0	0	0	.000	0	0	0	0	0	0	0	0	0	4	6.2	1	1	0	0	1.000	0	0	0	0	.00
VanLandingham, William	.152	46	7	1	3	1	.117	77	9	2	0	1	4	0	41	5	18	122.2	7	19	1	2	.963	17	3	1	0	.24
Veres, Dave	.000	5	0	0	0	1	.143	7	1	0	0	0	0	1	5	2	72	103.1	6	11	1	0	.944	9	3	1	1	.44
Veres, Randy	.000	3	0	0	0	0	.000	4	0	0	0	0	0	0	0	0	47	48.2	2	3	1	0	.833	6	1	0	0	.17
Villone, Ron	.000	1	0	0	0	0	.000	1	0	0	0	0	0	0	0	0	38	45.0	0	4	1	0	.800	4	2	1	0	.75
Viola, Frank	.167	6	1	0	0	0	.141	185	26	3	0	0	6	3	41	22	3	14.1	0	2	0	0	1.000	3	0	1	0	.33
Vosberg, Ed	.000	0	0	0	0	0	.000	2	0	0	0	0	0	0	1	0	44	36.0	0	1	1	0	.500	3	1	0	0	.33
Wade, Terrell	.000	0	0	0	0	0	.000	0	0	0	0	0	0	0	0	0	3	4.0	0	0	0	0	.000	0	0	0	0	.00

	1995 Hitting					Career Hitting										1995 Fielding and Holding Runners											
Pitcher	Avg	AB	H	HR	RBI	SH	Avg	AB	H	2B	3B	HR	RBI	BB	SO	SH	G	Inn	PO	A	E	DP	Pct.	SBA	CS	PCS	PPO	CS%
Wagner, Billy	.000	0	0	0	0	0	.000	0	0	0	0	0	0	0	0	0	1	0.1	0	0	0	0	.000	0	0	0	0	.00
Wagner, Paul	.214	42	9	0	4	6	.194	124	24	2	0	0	7	5	36	12	33	165.0	12	24	0	1	1.000	30	5	0	2	.17
Wakefield, Tim	.000	0	0	0	0	0	.127	71	9	2	0	1	3	1	20	8	27	195.1	15	19	2	4	.944	21	6	2	2	.38
Walker, Mike	.000	3	0	0	0	0	.000	3	0	0	0	0	0	0	1	0	42	44.2	4	7	1	0	.917	6	2	0	0	.33
Walker, Pete	.000	0	0	0	0	0	.000	0	0	0	0	0	0	0	0	0	13	17.2	1	2	0	0	1.000	0	0	0	0	.00
Wall, Donnie	.000	5	0	0	0	3	.000	5	0	0	0	0	0	0	2	3	6	24.1	4	2	1	0	.857	2	1	0	0	.50
Ward, Duane	.000	0	0	0	0	0	.000	1	0	0	0	0	0	0	0	0	4	2.2	0	0	1	0	.000	2	0	0	0	.00
Ware, Jeff	.000	0	0	0	0	0	.000	0	0	0	0	0	0	0	0	5	5	26.1	2	4	0	1	1.000	3	1	0	0	.33
Wasdin, John	.000	0	0	0	0	0	.000	0	0	0	0	0	0	0	0	0	5	17.1	1	0	0	0	1.000	4	0	0	0	.00
Watkins, Scott	.000	0	0	0	0	0	.000	0	0	0	0	0	0	0	0	0	27	21.2	1	4	0	0	1.000	1	0	0	0	.00
Watson, Allen	.417	36	15	0	5	3	.270	100	27	9	1	0	12	4	13	11	21	114.1	7	20	0	0	1.000	20	3	8	0	.55
Weathers, Dave	.154	26	4	0	1	5	.100	80	8	0	0	0	1	3	49	12	28	90.1	3	12	2	0	.882	12	3	0	0	.25
Wegman, Bill	.000	0	0	0	0	0	.000	0	0	0	0	0	0	0	0	0	39	70.2	9	5	1	0	.933	5	1	0	0	.20
Wells, Bob	.000	0	0	0	0	0	.000	0	0	0	0	0	0	0	0	0	30	76.2	7	8	0	0	1.000	6	1	0	0	.17
Wells, David	.143	28	4	0	0	1	.143	28	4	0	0	0	0	0	5	1	29	203.0	15	22	2	2	.949	19	3	3	0	.32
Wendell, Turk	.000	7	0	0	0	0	.063	16	1	0	0	0	0	2	8	0	43	60.1	9	12	1	2	.955	9	3	2	1	.56
Wengert, Don	.000	0	0	0	0	0	.000	0	0	0	0	0	0	0	0	0	19	29.2	3	1	0	0	1.000	0	0	0	0	.00
West, David	.125	8	1	1	3	6	.167	48	8	2	0	1	5	1	20	7	8	38.0	1	3	1	0	.800	7	2	0	0	.29
Wetteland, John	.000	0	0	0	0	0	.146	41	6	1	0	1	7	0	19	9	60	61.1	2	3	1	1	.833	8	1	0	0	.13
White, Gabe	.000	3	0	0	0	0	.000	7	0	0	0	0	0	1	4	2	19	25.2	0	2	0	0	1.000	4	0	0	0	.00
White, Rick	.067	15	1	0	1	2	.071	28	2	1	0	0	1	0	7	2	15	55.0	2	9	1	1	.917	2	0	0	0	.00
Whiteside, Matt	.000	0	0	0	0	0	.000	0	0	0	0	0	0	0	0	0	40	53.0	0	4	0	0	1.000	1	0	0	0	.00
Whiteside, Sean	.000	0	0	0	0	0	.000	0	0	0	0	0	0	0	0	0	2	3.2	0	0	0	0	.000	0	0	0	0	.00
Wickander, Kevin	.000	0	0	0	0	0	.000	2	0	0	0	0	0	0	1	0	29	23.1	1	4	0	0	1.000	0	0	0	0	.00
Wickman, Bob	.000	0	0	0	0	0	.000	0	0	0	0	0	0	0	0	0	63	80.0	4	14	1	1	.947	9	0	0	0	.00
Williams, Brian	.071	14	1	0	0	0	.163	80	13	3	0	0	7	0	25	15	43	72.0	6	9	0	0	1.000	4	2	0	0	.50
Williams, Mike	.125	16	2	0	1	7	.180	50	9	2	0	0	6	1	19	16	33	87.2	4	19	1	0	.958	11	1	1	1	.18
Williams, Mitch	.000	0	0	0	0	0	.188	16	3	0	0	1	4	1	4	0	20	10.2	1	1	0	0	1.000	5	0	1	0	.20
Williams, Todd	.500	2	1	0	0	0	.500	2	1	0	0	0	0	0	0	0	16	19.1	2	5	0	1	1.000	1	1	0	0	1.00
Williams, Woody	.000	0	0	0	0	0	.000	0	0	0	0	0	0	0	0	0	23	53.2	6	6	0	0	1.000	4	0	0	0	.00
Willis, Carl	.000	0	0	0	0	0	.250	4	1	0	0	0	0	1	0	2	3	0.2	0	0	0	0	.000	1	0	0	0	.00
Wilson, Gary	.000	0	0	0	0	1	.000	0	0	0	0	0	0	0	0	1	10	14.1	0	2	0	0	1.000	1	0	1	0	1.00
Wilson, Trevor	.233	30	7	0	3	3	.176	193	34	3	0	2	14	11	67	32	17	82.2	2	18	1	2	.952	6	3	0	0	.50
Witt, Bobby	.063	32	2	0	2	4	.061	33	2	1	0	0	2	1	11	4	29	172.0	8	20	0	0	1.000	22	8	1	0	.41
Wohlers, Mark	.000	3	0	0	0	0	.143	7	1	0	0	0	0	0	6	1	65	64.2	4	3	0	0	1.000	5	0	0	0	.00
Wojciechowski, S	.000	0	0	0	0	0	.000	0	0	0	0	0	0	0	0	0	14	48.2	1	8	0	0	1.000	5	1	1	0	.40
Wolcott, Bob	.000	0	0	0	0	0	.000	0	0	0	0	0	0	0	0	0	7	36.2	4	0	0	0	1.000	2	1	1	0	1.00
Woodall, Brad	1.000	1	1	0	1	0	.667	3	2	0	0	0	1	0	0	0	9	10.1	0	2	0	1	1.000	3	0	0	0	.00
Worrell, Tim	.000	1	0	0	0	0	.059	34	2	1	0	0	1	1	16	3	9	13.1	0	2	0	0	1.000	2	0	0	0	.00
Worrell, Todd	.000	2	0	0	0	0	.074	27	2	0	1	0	0	1	20	2	59	62.1	6	11	0	2	1.000	10	0	0	0	.00
Young, Anthony	.667	3	2	0	0	0	.163	92	15	2	0	0	4	2	31	10	32	41.1	5	3	2	1	.800	5	2	0	0	.40

Hitters Pitching

Player	1995 Pitching											Career Pitching										
	G	W	L	Sv	IP	H	R	ER	BB	SO	ERA	G	W	L	Sv	IP	H	R	ER	BB	SO	ERA
Cangelosi, John	1	0	0	0	1.0	0	0	0	1	0	0.00	2	0	0	0	3.0	1	0	0	1	0	0.00
Canseco, Jose	0	0	0	0	0.0	0	0	0	0	0	0.00	1	0	0	0	1.0	2	3	3	3	0	27.00
Davis, Chili	0	0	0	0	0.0	0	0	0	0	0	0.00	1	0	0	0	2.0	0	0	0	0	0	0.00
Espinoza, Alvaro	0	0	0	0	0.0	0	0	0	0	0	0.00	1	0	0	0	0.2	0	0	0	0	0	0.00
Foley, Tom	0	0	0	0	0.0	0	0	0	0	0	0.00	1	0	0	0	0.1	1	1	1	0	0	27.00
Gonzales, Rene	0	0	0	0	0.0	0	0	0	0	0	0.00	1	0	0	0	1.0	0	0	0	0	0	0.00
Howard, Dave	0	0	0	0	0.0	0	0	0	0	0	0.00	1	0	0	0	2.0	2	1	1	5	0	4.50
Martinez, Dave	1	0	0	0	1.0	0	0	0	2	0	0.00	2	0	0	0	1.1	2	2	2	4	0	13.50
O'Neill, Paul	0	0	0	0	0.0	0	0	0	0	0	0.00	1	0	0	0	2.0	2	3	3	4	2	13.50
Oquendo, Jose	0	0	0	0	0.0	0	0	0	0	0	0.00	3	0	1	0	6.0	10	8	8	9	2	12.00
Seitzer, Kevin	0	0	0	0	0.0	0	0	0	0	0	0.00	1	0	0	0	0.1	0	0	0	0	1	0.00
Tomberlin, Andy	0	0	0	0	0.0	0	0	0	0	0	0.00	1	0	0	0	2.0	1	0	0	1	1	0.00
Wallach, Tim	0	0	0	0	0.0	0	0	0	0	0	0.00	2	0	0	0	2.0	3	1	1	0	0	4.50

Park Data

In the charts that follow, the first block of columns shows how much the featured team totaled at home, how much opponents totaled against the featured team at home and the grand totals of both. The second block of columns shows how much the featured team totaled in away games, how much opponents totaled in away games and the grand totals of both. By combining both the featured team's and opponent totals, most team variance is negated and only the park variance is left.

Now for the Index. In a nutshell, the Index tells you whether the park favors the stat you happen to be looking at. For example, how much of an advantage did Rockies right-handed power hitters have hitting at Coors Field? In 1995, right-handed batters hit 241 home runs in 5194 at-bats at Coors, a frequency of .0464 HR per AB; in Rockies road games, the frequency wass .0246 HR per AB (119/4842). Dividing the Home frequency by the Road Frequency gives us a figure of 1.89. This number is multiplied by 100 to make it more recognizable: 189. What does an Index of 189 mean? It means it was 89% easier for righties to hit home runs at Coors than it was in other National League parks.

The greater the Index is over 100, the more favorable the park is for that statistic. The lower the Index is under 100, the less favorable the park is for that statistic. A park that was neutral in a category will have an Index of 100. *E-Infield* refers to infield *fielding* errors. Obviously, a ballpark itself doesn't have any effect on throwing errors, although there can be some official scoring bias that can affect the number of throwing errors charged.

The indexes for the following categories are determined on a per at-bat basis: 2B, 3B, HR, BB, SO, LHB-HR and RHB-HR. The indexes for AB, R, H, E and E-Infield are determined using per-game ratios. All the other indexes are based on the raw figures shown in the chart.

Finally, for most parks you'll notice that we include 1995 data as well as three-year totals (1993-95). However, for parks where there have been changes over the last three years, we never combine data. For example, for Kauffman Stadium in Kansas City, where they changed the dimensions and playing surface prior to the 1995 season, 1995 data is shown, but is not combined with previous years. Instead, 1993-94 data is shown for comparison purposes.

Atlanta Braves

| | 1995 Season | | | | | | | 1993-1995 | | | | | | |
| | Home Games | | | Away Games | | | | Home Games | | | Away Games | | | |
	Braves	Opp	Total	Braves	Opp	Total	Index	Braves	Opp	Total	Braves	Opp	Total	Index
G	72	72	144	72	72	144	---	208	208	416	212	212	424	---
Avg	.251	.248	.250	.248	.240	.244	102	.259	.247	.253	.259	.238	.249	102
AB	2343	2478	4821	2471	2367	4838	100	6845	7177	14022	7345	6899	14244	100
R	322	295	617	323	245	568	109	918	817	1735	1036	730	1766	100
H	589	615	1204	613	569	1182	102	1775	1771	3546	1902	1639	3541	102
2B	100	115	215	110	109	219	99	303	328	631	344	311	655	98
3B	11	8	19	16	9	25	76	31	27	58	43	28	71	83
HR	94	66	160	74	41	115	140	233	155	388	241	129	370	107
BB	239	230	469	281	206	487	97	688	662	1350	769	632	1401	98
SO	438	569	1007	495	518	1013	100	1165	1507	2672	1382	1481	2863	95
E	50	63	113	69	47	116	97	172	186	358	180	197	377	97
E-Infield	40	41	81	41	33	74	109	116	130	246	110	145	255	98
LHB-Avg	.275	.234	.259	.244	.253	.247	105	.274	.243	.261	.255	.244	.251	104
LHB-HR	67	16	83	37	8	45	174	153	50	203	134	25	159	125
RHB-Avg	.225	.255	.243	.252	.235	.242	100	.243	.249	.246	.263	.234	.247	100
RHB-HR	27	50	77	37	33	70	115	80	105	185	107	104	211	91

ATLANTA

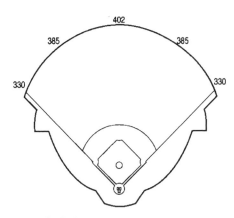

BALTIMORE

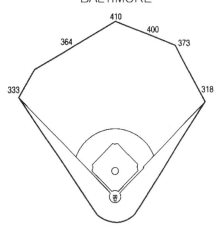

Baltimore Orioles

| | 1995 Season | | | | | | | 1993-1995 | | | | | | |
| | Home Games | | | Away Games | | | | Home Games | | | Away Games | | | |
	Orioles	Opp	Total	Orioles	Opp	Total	Index	Orioles	Opp	Total	Orioles	Opp	Total	Index
G	72	72	144	72	72	144	---	208	208	416	210	210	420	---
Avg	.270	.245	.257	.254	.245	.250	103	.274	.258	.266	.259	.254	.257	103
AB	2357	2423	4780	2480	2332	4812	99	6909	7180	14089	7292	6865	14157	100
R	357	325	682	347	315	662	103	1085	968	2053	994	914	1908	109
H	637	593	1230	630	572	1202	102	1892	1850	3742	1892	1747	3639	104
2B	112	128	240	117	115	232	104	342	360	702	359	366	725	97
3B	9	10	19	18	18	36	53	26	33	59	45	43	88	67
HR	90	84	174	83	65	148	118	252	235	487	217	198	415	118
BB	305	241	546	269	282	551	100	867	704	1571	800	749	1549	102
SO	402	474	876	401	456	857	103	1191	1255	2446	1197	1241	2438	101
E	45	51	96	39	55	94	102	144	146	290	125	150	275	106
E-Infield	33	33	66	27	41	68	97	100	114	214	89	112	201	107
LHB-Avg	.287	.250	.269	.267	.223	.248	108	.295	.263	.279	.270	.242	.258	108
LHB-HR	47	26	73	51	17	68	109	101	70	171	106	52	158	109
RHB-Avg	.252	.240	.246	.238	.262	.251	98	.257	.254	.256	.251	.262	.257	100
RHB-HR	43	58	101	32	48	80	126	151	165	316	111	146	257	123

Boston Red Sox

	1995 Season							1993-1995						
	Home Games			Away Games				Home Games			Away Games			
	Red Sox	Opp	Total	Red Sox	Opp	Total	Index	Red Sox	Opp	Total	Red Sox	Opp	Total	Index
G	72	72	144	72	72	144	---	217	217	434	204	204	408	---
Avg	.294	.271	.283	.266	.264	.265	107	.284	.270	.277	.254	.258	.256	108
AB	2472	2558	5030	2525	2441	4966	101	7379	7688	15067	7054	6787	13841	102
R	387	360	747	404	338	742	101	1100	1076	2176	929	941	1870	109
H	728	694	1422	671	644	1315	108	2098	2073	4171	1790	1748	3538	111
2B	175	134	309	111	130	241	127	501	409	910	326	343	669	125
3B	16	12	28	15	11	26	106	42	41	83	37	38	75	102
HR	70	63	133	105	64	169	78	192	183	375	217	191	408	84
BB	278	231	509	282	245	527	95	792	766	1558	680	712	1392	103
SO	437	451	888	486	437	923	95	1259	1388	2647	1258	1226	2484	98
E	80	68	148	63	51	114	130	223	198	421	148	154	302	131
E-Infield	54	52	106	43	37	80	133	167	146	313	108	114	222	133
LHB-Avg	.291	.257	.276	.275	.260	.268	103	.296	.271	.284	.265	.258	.262	108
LHB-HR	30	18	48	55	28	83	59	92	66	158	107	78	185	81
RHB-Avg	.298	.281	.289	.255	.267	.262	110	.275	.269	.272	.245	.257	.251	108
RHB-HR	40	45	85	50	36	86	94	100	117	217	110	113	223	87

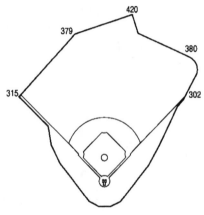

BOSTON

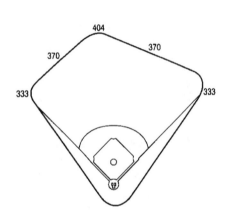

CALIFORNIA

California Angels

	1995 Season							1993-1995						
	Home Games			Away Games				Home Games			Away Games			
	Angels	Opp	Total	Angels	Opp	Total	Index	Angels	Opp	Total	Angels	Opp	Total	Index
G	72	72	144	73	73	146	---	216	216	432	206	206	412	---
Avg	.278	.250	.264	.276	.279	.278	95	.267	.268	.268	.267	.278	.272	98
AB	2437	2491	4928	2582	2458	5040	99	7213	7625	14838	7140	6821	13961	101
R	405	322	727	396	375	771	96	1054	1109	2163	974	1018	1992	104
H	677	623	1300	713	687	1400	94	1926	2044	3970	1905	1897	3802	100
2B	126	114	240	126	146	272	90	337	377	714	352	387	739	91
3B	11	6	17	14	13	27	64	32	17	49	33	36	69	67
HR	90	88	178	96	75	171	106	228	265	493	192	201	393	118
BB	298	247	545	266	239	505	110	793	758	1551	737	714	1451	101
SO	448	469	917	441	432	873	107	1287	1320	2607	1247	1106	2353	104
E	60	53	113	47	54	101	113	204	180	384	146	169	315	116
E-Infield	48	37	85	35	34	69	125	128	126	254	104	119	223	109
LHB-Avg	.293	.263	.281	.271	.272	.271	103	.274	.282	.278	.266	.283	.273	102
LHB-HR	60	32	92	52	25	77	117	107	97	204	90	63	153	124
RHB-Avg	.260	.243	.250	.282	.283	.283	88	.261	.261	.261	.268	.276	.272	96
RHB-HR	30	56	86	44	50	94	97	121	168	289	102	138	240	114

Chicago Cubs

| | 1995 Season | | | | | | | 1993-1995 | | | | | | |
| | Home Games | | | Away Games | | | Index | Home Games | | | Away Games | | | Index |
	Cubs	Opp	Total	Cubs	Opp	Total		Cubs	Opp	Total	Cubs	Opp	Total	
G	72	72	144	72	72	144	---	213	213	426	207	207	414	---
Avg	.270	.266	.268	.260	.258	.259	103	.268	.267	.267	.263	.270	.266	100
AB	2411	2552	4963	2552	2457	5009	99	7176	7511	14687	7332	6971	14303	100
R	339	350	689	354	321	675	102	936	1019	1955	995	940	1935	98
H	652	678	1330	663	635	1298	102	1924	2002	3926	1927	1879	3806	100
2B	121	121	242	146	98	244	100	333	370	703	382	319	701	98
3B	15	13	28	24	10	34	83	43	47	90	54	40	94	93
HR	83	83	166	75	79	154	109	206	248	454	222	187	409	108
BB	218	277	495	222	241	463	108	632	723	1355	618	657	1275	103
SO	447	499	946	506	427	933	102	1272	1353	2625	1354	1195	2549	100
E	76	54	130	65	69	134	97	200	182	382	192	213	405	92
E-Infield	48	38	86	41	51	92	93	122	130	252	108	145	253	97
LHB-Avg	.286	.264	.274	.267	.261	.264	104	.292	.267	.279	.267	.268	.267	104
LHB-HR	27	26	53	25	28	53	99	78	93	171	89	79	168	99
RHB-Avg	.261	.267	.264	.256	.256	.256	103	.252	.266	.259	.260	.271	.265	98
RHB-HR	56	57	113	50	51	101	115	128	155	283	133	108	241	114

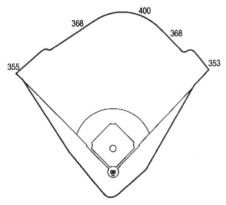

CHICAGO CUBS

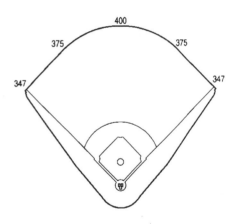

CHICAGO WHITE SOX

Chicago White Sox

| | 1995 Season | | | | | | | 1993-1995 | | | | | | |
| | Home Games | | | Away Games | | | Index | Home Games | | | Away Games | | | Index |
	White Sox	Opp	Total	White Sox	Opp	Total		White Sox	Opp	Total	White Sox	Opp	Total	
G	72	72	144	73	73	146	---	206	206	412	214	214	428	---
Avg	.281	.269	.275	.279	.282	.281	98	.281	.255	.268	.272	.267	.270	99
AB	2448	2528	4976	2612	2463	5075	99	6903	7121	14024	7582	7194	14776	99
R	361	361	722	394	397	791	93	1041	900	1941	1123	1020	2143	94
H	687	680	1367	730	694	1424	97	1938	1815	3753	2066	1921	3987	98
2B	106	119	225	146	104	250	92	297	288	585	358	323	681	91
3B	25	21	46	12	12	24	195	62	37	99	58	31	89	117
HR	59	73	132	87	91	178	76	203	186	389	226	218	444	92
BB	292	293	585	284	324	608	98	815	729	1544	862	831	1693	96
SO	351	432	783	416	460	876	91	977	1285	2262	1192	1335	2527	94
E	53	66	119	69	69	138	87	161	164	325	178	208	386	87
E-Infield	39	50	89	55	49	104	87	121	124	245	138	132	270	94
LHB-Avg	.281	.279	.280	.279	.315	.293	95	.276	.257	.267	.281	.285	.283	95
LHB-HR	24	19	43	37	38	75	58	68	60	128	80	97	177	77
RHB-Avg	.280	.263	.270	.280	.260	.269	100	.286	.254	.268	.264	.255	.259	104
RHB-HR	35	54	89	50	53	103	89	135	126	261	146	121	267	102

Cincinnati Reds

| | 1995 Season | | | | | | | 1993-1995 | | | | | | |
| | Home Games | | | Away Games | | | | Home Games | | | Away Games | | | |
	Reds	Opp	Total	Reds	Opp	Total	Index	Reds	Opp	Total	Reds	Opp	Total	Index
G	72	72	144	72	72	144	---	213	213	426	208	208	416	---
Avg	.271	.260	.266	.270	.259	.265	100	.272	.260	.266	.272	.270	.271	98
AB	2359	2483	4842	2544	2407	4951	98	7055	7377	14432	7364	7026	14390	98
R	358	308	666	389	315	704	95	1027	954	1981	1051	944	1995	97
H	640	646	1286	686	624	1310	98	1922	1918	3840	2003	1899	3902	96
2B	140	128	268	137	118	255	107	383	344	727	366	322	688	105
3B	15	15	30	20	14	34	90	40	48	88	59	57	116	76
HR	76	58	134	85	73	158	87	204	204	408	218	202	420	97
BB	267	214	481	252	210	462	106	734	663	1397	658	608	1266	110
SO	426	455	881	520	448	968	93	1271	1378	2649	1438	1320	2758	96
E	39	70	109	56	78	134	81	159	212	371	177	214	391	93
E-Infield	29	46	75	34	60	94	80	95	134	229	115	152	267	84
LHB-Avg	.262	.267	.264	.250	.261	.255	104	.269	.269	.269	.267	.277	.272	99
LHB-HR	27	25	52	20	27	47	119	54	90	144	51	72	123	114
RHB-Avg	.277	.257	.266	.283	.258	.270	99	.274	.254	.264	.274	.267	.271	98
RHB-HR	49	33	82	65	46	111	73	150	114	264	167	130	297	90

CINCINNATI

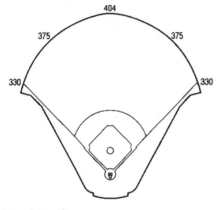

CLEVELAND

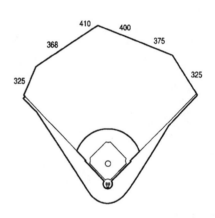

Cleveland Indians

| | 1995 Season | | | | | | | 1994-1995 | | | | | | |
| | Home Games | | | Away Games | | | | Home Games | | | Away Games | | | |
	Indians	Opp	Total	Indians	Opp	Total	Index	Indians	Opp	Total	Indians	Opp	Total	Index
G	72	72	144	72	72	144	---	123	123	246	134	134	268	---
Avg	.293	.242	.267	.288	.268	.278	96	.296	.254	.275	.285	.274	.280	98
AB	2445	2505	4950	2583	2440	5023	99	4250	4380	8630	4800	4547	9347	101
R	400	272	672	440	335	775	87	735	520	1255	784	649	1433	95
H	717	607	1324	744	654	1398	95	1258	1113	2371	1368	1245	2613	99
2B	139	123	262	140	143	283	94	261	221	482	258	239	497	105
3B	14	7	21	9	11	20	107	24	14	38	19	26	45	91
HR	99	60	159	108	75	183	88	186	104	290	188	125	313	100
BB	273	196	469	269	249	518	92	457	369	826	467	480	947	94
SO	369	459	828	397	467	864	97	617	751	1368	778	841	1619	92
E	64	47	111	57	57	114	97	109	100	209	116	108	224	102
E-Infield	40	35	75	41	37	78	96	73	72	145	84	74	158	100
LHB-Avg	.306	.253	.279	.280	.278	.279	100	.308	.260	.284	.288	.283	.285	99
LHB-HR	46	28	74	46	36	82	91	89	45	134	78	59	137	103
RHB-Avg	.280	.231	.255	.296	.257	.278	92	.283	.248	.265	.282	.265	.274	97
RHB-HR	53	32	85	62	39	101	86	97	59	156	110	66	176	99

Colorado Rockies

| | 1995 Season | | | | | | | 1993-1994 | | | | | | |
| | Home Games | | | Away Games | | | | Home Games | | | Away Games | | | |
	Rockies	Opp	Total	Rockies	Opp	Total	Index	Rockies	Opp	Total	Rockies	Opp	Total	Index
G	72	72	144	72	72	144	---	138	138	276	141	141	282	---
Avg	.316	.315	.315	.247	.254	.250	126	.303	.307	.305	.245	.279	.262	117
AB	2515	2679	5194	2479	2363	4842	107	4694	5005	9699	4829	4715	9544	104
R	485	490	975	300	293	593	164	806	907	1713	525	698	1223	143
H	794	843	1637	612	600	1212	135	1422	1535	2957	1183	1314	2497	121
2B	140	165	305	119	112	231	123	263	263	526	221	257	478	108
3B	31	28	59	12	8	20	275	82	68	150	16	31	47	314
HR	134	107	241	66	53	119	189	136	168	304	131	133	264	113
BB	257	252	509	227	260	487	97	408	540	948	358	517	875	107
SO	422	458	880	521	433	954	86	741	834	1575	964	782	1746	89
E	69	65	134	53	60	113	119	186	178	364	108	112	220	169
E-Infield	51	45	96	41	42	83	116	126	128	254	82	76	158	164
LHB-Avg	.322	.315	.318	.252	.278	.266	119	.268	.309	.296	.251	.290	.276	107
LHB-HR	33	36	69	23	21	44	144	9	60	69	30	60	90	79
RHB-Avg	.313	.315	.314	.245	.236	.241	130	.312	.305	.309	.243	.270	.254	121
RHB-HR	101	71	172	43	32	75	215	127	108	235	101	73	174	130

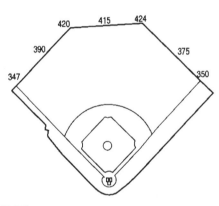

COLORADO

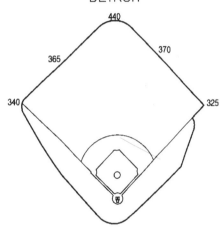

DETROIT

Detroit Tigers

| | 1995 Season | | | | | | | 1993-1995 | | | | | | |
| | Home Games | | | Away Games | | | | Home Games | | | Away Games | | | |
	Tigers	Opp	Total	Tigers	Opp	Total	Index	Tigers	Opp	Total	Tigers	Opp	Total	Index
G	72	72	144	72	72	144	---	211	211	422	210	210	420	---
Avg	.251	.289	.271	.244	.302	.273	99	.266	.278	.272	.260	.291	.276	99
AB	2350	2584	4934	2515	2517	5032	98	7032	7501	14533	7408	7237	14645	99
R	354	426	780	300	418	718	109	1161	1158	2319	1044	1194	2238	103
H	591	748	1339	613	761	1374	97	1870	2087	3957	1928	2108	4036	98
2B	100	147	247	128	153	281	90	340	369	709	386	419	805	89
3B	16	17	33	13	15	28	120	54	42	96	38	50	88	110
HR	92	93	185	67	77	144	131	280	268	548	218	238	456	121
BB	313	252	565	238	284	522	110	974	732	1706	862	795	1657	104
SO	490	383	873	497	346	843	106	1462	1133	2595	1544	984	2528	103
E	68	56	124	58	68	126	98	210	165	375	174	184	358	104
E-Infield	50	42	92	36	34	70	131	134	123	257	122	106	228	112
LHB-Avg	.233	.300	.279	.261	.315	.297	94	.263	.289	.278	.279	.297	.289	96
LHB-HR	29	48	77	12	39	51	148	100	128	228	81	97	178	127
RHB-Avg	.257	.280	.267	.239	.291	.260	103	.268	.269	.268	.250	.287	.267	101
RHB-HR	63	45	108	55	38	93	121	180	140	320	137	141	278	117

285

Florida Marlins

	1995 Season							1994-1995						
	Home Games			Away Games				Home Games			Away Games			
	Marlins	Opp	Total	Marlins	Opp	Total	Index	Marlins	Opp	Total	Marlins	Opp	Total	Index
G	71	71	142	72	72	144	---	130	130	260	128	128	256	---
Avg	.276	.255	.265	.248	.274	.260	102	.273	.271	.272	.254	.265	.259	105
AB	2410	2485	4895	2476	2435	4911	101	4401	4583	8984	4411	4238	8649	102
R	331	321	652	342	352	694	95	576	662	1238	565	587	1152	106
H	665	633	1298	613	666	1279	103	1202	1243	2445	1119	1125	2244	107
2B	95	122	217	119	135	254	86	188	221	409	206	216	422	93
3B	16	24	40	13	14	27	149	33	52	85	20	33	53	154
HR	68	60	128	76	79	155	83	114	130	244	124	129	253	93
BB	233	277	510	284	285	569	90	423	512	935	443	478	921	98
SO	445	514	959	471	480	951	101	816	855	1671	846	788	1634	98
E	75	48	123	68	58	126	99	147	89	236	110	91	201	116
E-Infield	49	38	87	38	40	78	113	93	67	160	70	69	139	113
LHB-Avg	.262	.257	.259	.251	.263	.258	100	.268	.274	.271	.252	.267	.260	104
LHB-HR	11	21	32	13	31	44	70	17	45	62	19	48	67	86
RHB-Avg	.282	.253	.269	.246	.280	.262	103	.276	.269	.273	.254	.265	.259	105
RHB-HR	57	39	96	63	48	111	89	97	85	182	105	81	186	96

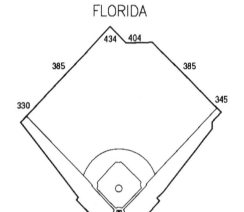

FLORIDA

434 404
385 385
330 345

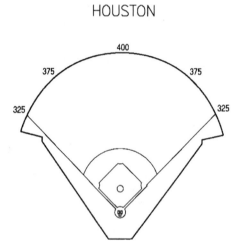

HOUSTON

400
375 375
325 325

Houston Astros

	1995 Season							1994-1995						
	Home Games			Away Games				Home Games			Away Games			
	Astros	Opp	Total	Astros	Opp	Total	Index	Astros	Opp	Total	Astros	Opp	Total	Index
G	72	72	144	72	72	144	---	131	131	262	128	128	256	---
Avg	.262	.250	.256	.287	.283	.285	90	.271	.252	.262	.282	.280	.281	93
AB	2467	2552	5019	2630	2541	5171	97	4450	4572	9022	4602	4451	9053	97
R	321	296	617	426	378	804	77	628	537	1165	721	640	1361	84
H	647	638	1285	756	719	1475	87	1206	1154	2360	1296	1246	2542	91
2B	118	114	232	142	123	265	90	256	199	455	256	229	485	94
3B	9	19	28	13	24	37	78	20	29	49	27	33	60	82
HR	41	48	89	68	70	138	66	98	104	202	131	116	247	82
BB	279	215	494	287	245	532	96	463	401	864	497	426	923	94
SO	491	579	1070	501	477	978	113	868	983	1851	842	812	1654	112
E	58	61	119	91	88	179	66	93	111	204	146	140	286	70
E-Infield	46	47	93	47	64	111	84	71	89	160	84	100	184	85
LHB-Avg	.285	.254	.266	.277	.302	.292	91	.291	.269	.278	.264	.288	.278	100
LHB-HR	5	15	20	20	33	53	40	20	43	63	44	44	88	72
RHB-Avg	.255	.248	.252	.291	.270	.282	89	.262	.241	.253	.289	.274	.282	89
RHB-HR	36	33	69	48	37	85	82	78	61	139	87	72	159	88

Kansas City Royals

| | 1995 Season | | | | | | | 1993-1994 | | | | | | |
| | Home Games | | | Away Games | | | Index | Home Games | | | Away Games | | | Index |
	Royals	Opp	Total	Royals	Opp	Total		Royals	Opp	Total	Royals	Opp	Total	
G	72	72	144	72	72	144	---	140	140	280	137	137	274	---
Avg	.268	.260	.264	.252	.276	.264	100	.289	.256	.272	.242	.256	.249	109
AB	2396	2497	4893	2507	2441	4948	99	4791	4893	9684	4642	4462	9104	104
R	285	346	631	344	345	689	92	695	641	1336	554	585	1139	115
H	643	650	1293	632	673	1305	99	1384	1253	2637	1122	1144	2266	114
2B	118	117	235	122	110	232	102	316	282	598	189	219	408	138
3B	20	15	35	15	14	29	122	50	36	86	23	23	46	176
HR	49	68	117	70	74	144	82	91	97	188	134	103	237	75
BB	224	259	483	251	244	495	99	415	457	872	389	506	895	92
SO	363	359	722	486	404	890	82	728	826	1554	906	876	1782	82
E	53	63	116	58	60	118	98	124	131	255	91	115	206	121
E-Infield	33	47	80	36	36	72	111	82	83	165	57	79	136	119
LHB-Avg	.285	.260	.273	.264	.293	.276	99	.296	.266	.281	.249	.271	.260	108
LHB-HR	24	33	57	29	27	56	106	35	40	75	64	48	112	65
RHB-Avg	.247	.260	.254	.234	.261	.249	102	.283	.248	.265	.235	.244	.239	111
RHB-HR	25	35	60	41	47	88	67	56	57	113	70	55	125	82

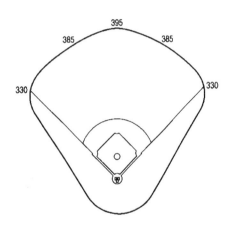

KANSAS CITY

LOS ANGELES

Los Angeles Dodgers

| | 1995 Season | | | | | | | 1993-1995 | | | | | | |
| | Home Games | | | Away Games | | | Index | Home Games | | | Away Games | | | Index |
	Dodgers	Opp	Total	Dodgers	Opp	Total		Dodgers	Opp	Total	Dodgers	Opp	Total	
G	72	72	144	72	72	144	---	208	208	416	212	212	424	---
Avg	.250	.235	.243	.276	.251	.264	92	.264	.242	.253	.265	.265	.265	95
AB	2361	2466	4827	2581	2422	5003	96	6897	7168	14065	7537	7163	14700	98
R	281	276	557	353	333	686	81	841	803	1644	1000	977	1977	85
H	591	580	1171	712	608	1320	89	1820	1737	3557	1996	1898	3894	93
2B	70	89	159	121	124	245	67	235	273	508	350	353	703	76
3B	10	6	16	21	14	35	47	26	24	50	62	60	122	43
HR	62	48	110	78	77	155	74	175	145	320	210	173	383	87
BB	237	209	446	231	253	484	96	670	626	1296	656	757	1413	96
SO	484	528	1012	539	532	1071	98	1236	1431	2667	1411	1404	2815	99
E	74	67	141	78	54	132	107	195	183	378	210	182	392	98
E-Infield	56	49	105	52	36	88	119	149	129	278	148	120	268	106
LHB-Avg	.242	.238	.240	.277	.250	.262	91	.274	.247	.258	.259	.261	.260	99
LHB-HR	8	26	34	11	34	45	78	27	79	106	37	84	121	92
RHB-Avg	.254	.233	.245	.275	.252	.265	92	.259	.238	.249	.268	.269	.268	93
RHB-HR	54	22	76	67	43	110	72	148	66	214	173	89	262	85

Milwaukee Brewers

	1995 Season							1993-1995						
	Home Games			Away Games				Home Games			Away Games			
	Brewers	Opp	Total	Brewers	Opp	Total	Index	Brewers	Opp	Total	Brewers	Opp	Total	Index
G	72	72	144	72	72	144	---	209	209	418	212	212	424	---
Avg	.279	.296	.287	.253	.263	.258	111	.273	.277	.275	.252	.270	.261	106
AB	2483	2604	5087	2517	2357	4874	104	7115	7464	14579	7388	7056	14444	102
R	390	426	816	350	321	671	122	1036	1118	2154	984	1007	1991	110
H	692	770	1462	637	621	1258	116	1939	2071	4010	1861	1902	3763	108
2B	125	155	280	124	108	232	116	356	415	771	371	359	730	105
3B	21	19	40	21	14	35	110	49	52	101	39	54	93	108
HR	56	71	127	72	75	147	83	157	199	356	195	227	422	84
BB	263	301	564	239	302	541	100	771	773	1544	703	773	1476	104
SO	368	344	712	432	355	787	87	1131	1069	2200	1281	1017	2298	95
E	68	53	121	53	54	107	113	204	168	372	165	168	333	113
E-Infield	46	41	87	43	40	83	105	150	112	262	123	114	237	112
LHB-Avg	.284	.306	.295	.249	.248	.249	119	.276	.283	.279	.246	.273	.259	108
LHB-HR	26	29	55	26	25	51	97	70	81	151	67	89	156	94
RHB-Avg	.273	.288	.281	.256	.274	.265	106	.269	.273	.271	.257	.267	.262	104
RHB-HR	30	42	72	46	50	96	76	87	118	205	128	138	266	77

MILWAUKEE

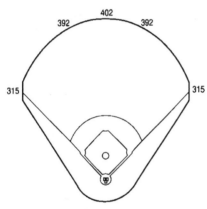

MINNESOTA

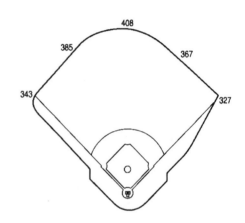

Minnesota Twins

	1995 Season							1994-1995						
	Home Games			Away Games				Home Games			Away Games			
	Twins	Opp	Total	Twins	Opp	Total	Index	Twins	Opp	Total	Twins	Opp	Total	Index
G	72	72	144	72	72	144	---	131	131	262	126	126	252	---
Avg	.285	.279	.282	.274	.296	.285	99	.287	.280	.284	.269	.305	.287	99
AB	2448	2570	5018	2557	2482	5039	100	4471	4687	9158	4486	4374	8860	99
R	368	448	816	335	441	776	105	687	787	1474	610	790	1400	101
H	698	716	1414	700	734	1434	99	1285	1312	2597	1205	1335	2540	98
2B	128	154	282	142	148	290	98	263	286	549	246	291	537	99
3B	23	14	37	11	18	29	128	38	22	60	19	34	53	110
HR	59	120	179	61	90	151	119	107	208	315	116	155	271	112
BB	250	254	504	221	279	500	101	458	453	911	372	468	840	105
SO	465	430	895	451	360	811	111	792	758	1550	759	634	1393	108
E	59	57	116	60	64	124	94	95	92	187	117	114	231	78
E-Infield	37	43	80	44	44	88	91	59	70	129	79	84	163	76
LHB-Avg	.265	.275	.272	.253	.301	.283	96	.268	.274	.272	.249	.301	.280	97
LHB-HR	7	50	57	8	37	45	132	14	77	91	21	60	81	112
RHB-Avg	.294	.282	.289	.284	.290	.286	101	.295	.285	.291	.278	.309	.291	100
RHB-HR	52	70	122	53	53	106	113	93	131	224	95	95	190	112

Montreal Expos

	1995 Season							1993-1995						
	Home Games			Away Games				Home Games			Away Games			
	Expos	Opp	Total	Expos	Opp	Total	Index	Expos	Opp	Total	Expos	Opp	Total	Index
G	72	72	144	72	72	144	---	205	205	410	216	216	432	---
Avg	.263	.256	.259	.255	.268	.261	99	.269	.249	.259	.258	.256	.257	101
AB	2380	2491	4871	2525	2419	4944	99	6793	7112	13905	7605	7222	14827	99
R	303	318	621	318	320	638	97	936	860	1796	1002	914	1916	99
H	625	637	1262	643	649	1292	98	1827	1774	3601	1962	1851	3813	100
2B	137	125	262	128	114	242	110	406	373	779	375	326	701	118
3B	12	22	34	12	16	28	123	37	53	90	53	40	93	103
HR	43	55	98	75	73	148	67	147	152	299	201	195	396	81
BB	206	229	435	194	187	381	116	661	628	1289	660	597	1257	109
SO	438	499	937	463	451	914	104	1146	1312	2458	1284	1377	2661	98
E	82	68	150	51	86	137	109	213	175	388	207	260	467	88
E-Infield	52	36	88	33	60	93	95	151	113	264	153	188	341	82
LHB-Avg	.232	.249	.240	.240	.258	.249	96	.261	.255	.258	.243	.249	.246	105
LHB-HR	17	15	32	21	23	44	76	53	60	113	63	69	132	91
RHB-Avg	.279	.259	.269	.262	.274	.268	100	.273	.246	.260	.266	.261	.264	98
RHB-HR	26	40	66	54	50	104	63	94	92	186	138	126	264	75

MONTREAL

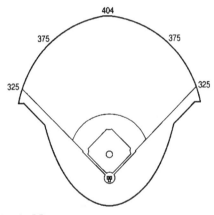

NEW YORK METS

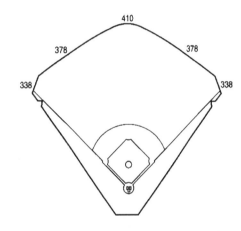

New York Mets

	1995 Season							1993-1995						
	Home Games			Away Games				Home Games			Away Games			
	Mets	Opp	Total	Mets	Opp	Total	Index	Mets	Opp	Total	Mets	Opp	Total	Index
G	72	72	144	72	72	144	---	206	206	412	213	213	426	---
Avg	.268	.258	.263	.266	.267	.266	99	.255	.265	.260	.255	.269	.262	99
AB	2428	2543	4971	2530	2401	4931	101	6869	7279	14148	7406	7133	14539	101
R	308	294	602	349	324	673	89	860	941	1801	975	947	1922	97
H	650	655	1305	673	641	1314	99	1750	1928	3678	1889	1920	3809	100
2B	96	128	224	122	126	248	90	263	355	618	347	385	732	87
3B	18	20	38	16	13	29	130	48	44	92	44	43	87	109
HR	63	68	131	62	65	127	102	191	200	391	209	189	398	101
BB	220	171	391	226	230	456	85	574	559	1133	656	608	1264	92
SO	482	476	958	512	425	937	101	1275	1232	2507	1405	1176	2581	100
E	67	72	139	64	75	139	100	228	183	411	182	191	373	114
E-Infield	51	44	95	48	53	101	94	174	113	287	136	125	261	114
LHB-Avg	.291	.270	.281	.268	.272	.270	104	.269	.263	.266	.255	.282	.267	100
LHB-HR	34	28	62	28	24	52	124	102	76	178	100	65	165	111
RHB-Avg	.247	.249	.248	.264	.263	.264	94	.240	.266	.255	.255	.261	.258	99
RHB-HR	29	40	69	34	41	75	68	89	124	213	109	124	233	94

New York Yankees

| | 1995 Season | | | | | | | 1993-1995 | | | | | | |
| | Home Games | | | Away Games | | | | Home Games | | | Away Games | | | |
	Yankees	Opp	Total	Yankees	Opp	Total	Index	Yankees	Opp	Total	Yankees	Opp	Total	Index
G	73	73	146	72	72	144	---	211	211	422	209	209	418	---
Avg	.297	.255	.275	.255	.267	.261	106	.287	.254	.270	.276	.275	.275	98
AB	2445	2526	4971	2502	2410	4912	100	7039	7257	14296	7509	7121	14630	97
R	411	323	734	338	365	703	103	1091	925	2016	1149	1058	2207	90
H	726	643	1369	639	643	1282	105	2018	1840	3858	2070	1958	4028	95
2B	151	122	273	129	125	254	106	401	314	715	411	411	822	89
3B	16	14	30	18	16	34	87	31	36	67	43	46	89	77
HR	69	76	145	53	83	136	105	220	223	443	219	226	445	102
BB	323	229	552	302	306	608	90	862	663	1525	922	822	1744	89
SO	405	459	864	446	449	895	95	1113	1268	2381	1308	1195	2503	97
E	42	45	87	49	69	118	73	158	147	305	148	187	335	90
E-Infield	26	27	53	31	51	82	64	108	95	203	104	133	237	85
LHB-Avg	.314	.260	.291	.272	.256	.265	110	.306	.260	.287	.281	.264	.274	105
LHB-HR	35	29	64	18	31	49	126	98	75	173	82	73	155	112
RHB-Avg	.275	.251	.261	.238	.275	.258	101	.266	.250	.257	.270	.281	.276	93
RHB-HR	34	47	81	35	52	87	94	122	148	270	137	153	290	97

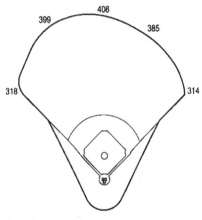

NEW YORK YANKEES

408
399
385
318
314

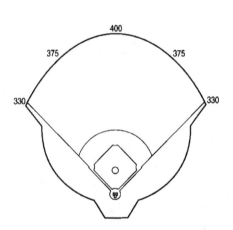

OAKLAND

400
375
375
330
330

Oakland Athletics

| | 1995 Season | | | | | | | 1993-1995 | | | | | | |
| | Home Games | | | Away Games | | | | Home Games | | | Away Games | | | |
	Athletics	Opp	Total	Athletics	Opp	Total	Index	Athletics	Opp	Total	Athletics	Opp	Total	Index
G	72	72	144	72	72	144	---	209	209	418	211	211	422	---
Avg	.262	.248	.255	.266	.291	.278	92	.255	.254	.255	.262	.283	.272	94
AB	2389	2469	4858	2527	2432	4959	98	6910	7211	14121	7434	7119	14553	98
R	330	343	673	400	418	818	82	904	992	1896	1090	1204	2294	83
H	625	613	1238	671	707	1378	90	1764	1834	3598	1949	2016	3965	92
2B	96	98	194	132	138	270	73	279	312	591	387	379	766	80
3B	7	10	17	11	18	29	60	23	33	56	29	54	83	70
HR	80	75	155	89	78	167	95	209	207	416	231	231	462	93
BB	270	269	539	295	287	582	95	805	833	1638	799	913	1712	99
SO	425	476	901	486	414	900	102	1291	1326	2617	1354	1160	2514	107
E	66	67	133	54	64	118	113	191	193	384	168	195	363	107
E-Infield	38	45	83	46	46	92	90	113	133	246	130	141	271	92
LHB-Avg	.224	.258	.246	.275	.290	.284	87	.240	.261	.253	.267	.296	.285	89
LHB-HR	12	33	45	22	35	57	76	53	93	146	73	106	179	85
RHB-Avg	.278	.236	.261	.262	.292	.273	96	.262	.248	.256	.260	.269	.264	97
RHB-HR	68	42	110	67	43	110	107	156	114	270	158	125	283	98

Philadelphia Phillies

	1995 Season							1993-1995						
	Home Games			Away Games				Home Games			Away Games			
	Phillies	Opp	Total	Phillies	Opp	Total	Index	Phillies	Opp	Total	Phillies	Opp	Total	Index
G	72	72	144	72	72	144	---	213	213	426	208	208	416	---
Avg	.264	.253	.258	.260	.256	.258	100	.269	.251	.260	.263	.260	.262	99
AB	2451	2526	4977	2499	2352	4851	103	7241	7538	14779	7321	6917	14238	101
R	336	359	695	279	299	578	120	1045	973	2018	968	922	1890	104
H	646	640	1286	650	601	1251	103	1951	1889	3840	1928	1799	3727	101
2B	143	132	275	120	94	214	125	399	380	779	369	285	654	115
3B	12	14	26	18	11	29	87	51	39	90	58	34	92	94
HR	51	78	129	43	56	99	127	176	175	351	154	186	340	99
BB	250	290	540	247	248	495	106	772	756	1528	786	732	1518	97
SO	428	538	966	456	442	898	105	1258	1547	2805	1386	1249	2635	103
E	55	78	133	55	62	117	114	190	217	407	186	188	374	106
E-Infield	47	50	97	37	34	71	137	158	141	299	130	120	250	117
LHB-Avg	.266	.267	.266	.263	.271	.266	100	.280	.258	.271	.268	.275	.271	100
LHB-HR	29	32	61	22	18	40	148	93	66	159	79	66	145	109
RHB-Avg	.260	.245	.251	.256	.246	.250	100	.254	.247	.250	.256	.251	.253	99
RHB-HR	22	46	68	21	38	59	112	83	109	192	75	120	195	93

PHILADELPHIA

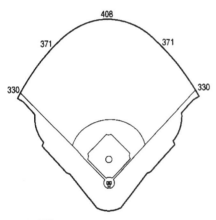

PITTSBURGH

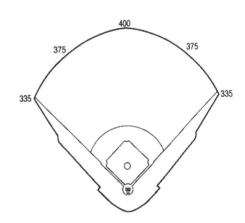

Pittsburgh Pirates

	1995 Season							1993-1995						
	Home Games			Away Games				Home Games			Away Games			
	Pirates	Opp	Total	Pirates	Opp	Total	Index	Pirates	Opp	Total	Pirates	Opp	Total	Index
G	72	72	144	72	72	144	---	214	214	428	206	206	412	---
Avg	.258	.289	.274	.261	.277	.269	102	.263	.279	.271	.261	.284	.272	100
AB	2409	2573	4982	2528	2394	4922	101	7185	7571	14756	7165	6857	14022	101
R	329	396	725	300	340	640	113	972	1075	2047	830	1047	1877	105
H	621	744	1365	660	663	1323	103	1891	2112	4003	1873	1946	3819	101
2B	134	148	282	111	114	225	124	383	431	814	327	379	706	110
3B	6	24	30	21	13	34	87	45	61	106	55	51	106	95
HR	69	67	136	56	63	119	113	178	195	373	137	205	342	104
BB	231	253	484	225	224	449	106	697	667	1364	644	665	1309	99
SO	500	456	956	472	415	887	106	1343	1239	2582	1326	1114	2440	101
E	85	76	161	64	56	120	134	202	220	422	188	153	341	119
E-Infield	51	42	93	44	48	92	101	126	128	254	120	115	235	104
LHB-Avg	.269	.295	.283	.259	.296	.277	102	.268	.279	.273	.265	.297	.280	98
LHB-HR	26	24	50	24	26	50	104	85	67	152	55	69	124	119
RHB-Avg	.252	.286	.269	.262	.265	.264	102	.260	.279	.270	.259	.277	.268	101
RHB-HR	43	43	86	32	37	69	119	93	128	221	82	136	218	95

291

San Diego Padres

	1995 Season							1993-1995						
	Home Games			Away Games				Home Games			Away Games			
	Padres	Opp	Total	Padres	Opp	Total	Index	Padres	Opp	Total	Padres	Opp	Total	Index
G	72	72	144	72	72	144	---	210	210	420	213	213	426	---
Avg	.272	.249	.260	.272	.261	.267	98	.265	.247	.256	.265	.271	.268	96
AB	2359	2454	4813	2591	2411	5002	96	7022	7283	14305	7499	7097	14596	99
R	304	313	617	364	359	723	85	889	940	1829	937	1035	1972	94
H	641	612	1253	704	630	1334	94	1861	1798	3659	1987	1922	3909	95
2B	95	97	192	136	108	244	82	301	291	592	369	330	699	86
3B	8	9	17	12	15	27	65	31	50	81	36	56	92	90
HR	55	72	127	61	70	131	101	193	208	401	168	181	349	117
BB	222	252	474	225	260	485	102	621	697	1318	588	766	1354	99
SO	386	547	933	486	500	986	98	1299	1510	2809	1381	1356	2737	105
E	56	78	134	67	53	120	112	208	196	404	228	193	421	97
E-Infield	42	38	80	51	43	94	85	158	126	284	164	137	301	96
LHB-Avg	.295	.232	.266	.309	.278	.296	90	.277	.245	.261	.293	.285	.289	90
LHB-HR	27	20	47	34	23	57	83	78	81	159	89	66	155	105
RHB-Avg	.250	.261	.256	.238	.251	.245	105	.255	.249	.252	.241	.260	.250	101
RHB-HR	28	52	80	27	47	74	115	115	127	242	79	115	194	127

SAN DIEGO

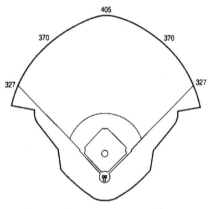

SAN FRANCISCO

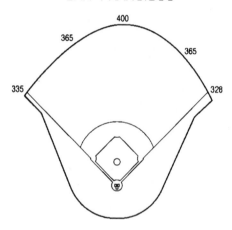

San Francisco Giants

	1995 Season							1993-1995						
	Home Games			Away Games				Home Games			Away Games			
	Giants	Opp	Total	Giants	Opp	Total	Index	Giants	Opp	Total	Giants	Opp	Total	Index
G	72	72	144	72	72	144	---	213	213	426	208	208	416	---
Avg	.240	.256	.248	.265	.294	.279	89	.252	.252	.252	.269	.274	.272	93
AB	2433	2551	4984	2538	2430	4968	100	7064	7380	14444	7333	6942	14275	99
R	305	364	669	347	412	759	88	926	915	1841	1038	997	2035	88
H	583	653	1236	673	715	1388	89	1779	1862	3641	1974	1905	3879	92
2B	100	119	219	129	128	257	85	313	309	622	344	323	667	92
3B	14	11	25	19	17	36	69	41	24	65	57	41	98	66
HR	76	78	154	76	95	171	90	214	233	447	229	230	459	96
BB	247	255	502	225	250	475	105	675	691	1366	677	628	1305	103
SO	523	439	962	537	362	899	107	1342	1349	2691	1367	1089	2456	108
E	71	58	129	60	79	139	93	175	202	377	149	227	376	98
E-Infield	47	50	97	38	57	95	102	121	162	283	109	167	276	100
LHB-Avg	.255	.256	.255	.265	.306	.288	89	.257	.250	.253	.283	.285	.284	89
LHB-HR	25	18	43	25	37	62	66	84	78	162	108	89	197	80
RHB-Avg	.233	.256	.244	.265	.287	.275	89	.249	.254	.251	.262	.267	.265	95
RHB-HR	51	60	111	51	58	109	104	130	155	285	121	141	262	109

Seattle Mariners

	1995 Season							1993-1994						
	Home Games			Away Games				Home Games			Away Games			
	Mariners	Opp	Total	Mariners	Opp	Total	Index	Mariners	Opp	Total	Mariners	Opp	Total	Index
G	73	73	146	72	72	144	---	125	125	250	149	149	298	---
Avg	.285	.258	.271	.266	.279	.272	100	.264	.254	.259	.263	.275	.269	96
AB	2455	2561	5016	2541	2452	4993	99	4192	4378	8570	5185	4941	10126	101
R	424	344	768	372	364	736	103	628	594	1222	675	753	1428	102
H	700	660	1360	677	683	1360	99	1108	1112	2220	1366	1360	2726	97
2B	154	153	307	122	126	248	123	241	245	486	242	242	484	119
3B	8	15	23	12	25	37	62	18	25	43	24	33	57	89
HR	101	73	174	81	76	157	110	137	110	247	177	134	311	94
BB	300	304	604	249	287	536	112	540	483	1023	456	608	1064	114
SO	437	606	1043	434	462	896	116	719	931	1650	834	915	1749	111
E	60	41	101	56	59	115	87	75	97	172	139	128	267	77
E-Infield	44	33	77	48	49	97	78	65	75	140	91	94	185	90
LHB-Avg	.278	.278	.278	.268	.289	.279	100	.271	.260	.266	.264	.287	.274	97
LHB-HR	34	31	65	27	24	51	131	69	35	104	90	39	129	95
RHB-Avg	.290	.241	.267	.265	.270	.267	100	.259	.251	.255	.263	.269	.266	96
RHB-HR	67	42	109	54	52	106	100	68	75	143	87	95	182	93

SEATTLE

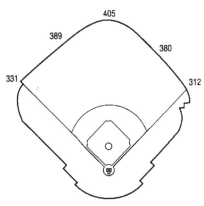

405
389
380
331
312

ST. LOUIS

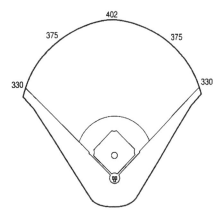

402
375
375
330
330

St. Louis Cardinals

	1995 Season							1993-1995						
	Home Games			Away Games				Home Games			Away Games			
	Cardinals	Opp	Total	Cardinals	Opp	Total	Index	Cardinals	Opp	Total	Cardinals	Opp	Total	Index
G	72	72	144	71	71	142	---	209	209	418	211	211	422	---
Avg	.256	.261	.259	.238	.275	.256	101	.267	.271	.269	.255	.283	.269	100
AB	2383	2507	4890	2396	2310	4706	102	6909	7312	14221	7323	7124	14447	99
R	311	316	627	252	342	594	104	935	952	1887	921	1071	1992	96
H	611	655	1266	571	635	1206	104	1845	1979	3824	1871	2018	3889	99
2B	136	139	275	102	122	224	118	367	417	784	346	383	729	109
3B	15	13	28	9	14	23	117	48	45	93	37	56	93	102
HR	54	60	114	53	75	128	86	163	185	348	170	236	406	87
BB	227	211	438	209	234	443	95	706	567	1273	752	616	1368	95
SO	414	428	842	506	414	920	88	1146	1151	2297	1342	1098	2440	96
E	57	49	106	66	49	115	91	182	153	335	231	186	417	81
E-Infield	49	35	84	54	37	91	91	124	109	233	167	130	297	79
LHB-Avg	.270	.259	.265	.238	.267	.251	105	.276	.272	.274	.257	.276	.265	104
LHB-HR	20	20	40	19	23	42	92	66	64	130	70	71	141	95
RHB-Avg	.247	.263	.255	.238	.279	.259	98	.260	.270	.265	.254	.287	.272	98
RHB-HR	34	40	74	34	52	86	83	97	121	218	100	165	265	83

Texas Rangers

	1995 Season							1994-1995						
	Home Games			Away Games				Home Games			Away Games			
	Rangers	Opp	Total	Rangers	Opp	Total	Index	Rangers	Opp	Total	Rangers	Opp	Total	Index
G	72	72	144	72	72	144	---	135	135	270	123	123	246	---
Avg	.273	.273	.273	.258	.283	.270	101	.277	.278	.277	.267	.287	.277	100
AB	2431	2574	5005	2482	2413	4895	102	4569	4848	9417	4327	4226	8553	100
R	379	368	747	312	352	664	113	713	721	1434	591	696	1287	102
H	663	703	1366	641	682	1323	103	1264	1349	2613	1154	1212	2366	101
2B	124	101	225	123	123	246	89	222	220	442	223	218	441	91
3B	13	15	28	11	13	24	114	28	36	64	23	23	46	126
HR	81	73	154	57	79	136	111	144	140	284	118	169	287	90
BB	281	244	525	245	270	515	100	533	443	976	430	465	895	99
SO	441	407	848	436	431	867	96	820	797	1617	787	724	1511	97
E	63	60	123	50	66	116	106	128	130	258	105	97	202	116
E-Infield	49	40	89	34	48	82	109	100	86	186	75	73	148	115
LHB-Avg	.259	.277	.268	.271	.277	.274	98	.267	.294	.281	.278	.287	.282	99
LHB-HR	39	28	67	22	31	53	124	57	66	123	36	71	107	106
RHB-Avg	.284	.270	.277	.247	.287	.267	104	.284	.267	.275	.258	.286	.272	101
RHB-HR	42	45	87	35	48	83	102	87	74	161	82	98	180	80

TEXAS

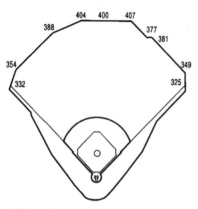

TORONTO

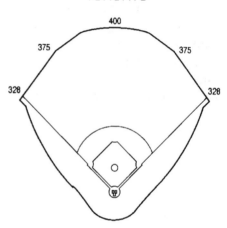

Toronto Blue Jays

	1995 Season							1993-1995						
	Home Games			Away Games				Home Games			Away Games			
	Blue Jays	Opp	Total	Blue Jays	Opp	Total	Index	Blue Jays	Opp	Total	Blue Jays	Opp	Total	Index
G	72	72	144	72	72	144	---	212	212	424	209	209	418	---
Avg	.255	.260	.257	.265	.276	.270	95	.271	.259	.265	.268	.271	.269	98
AB	2492	2584	5076	2544	2410	4954	102	7174	7481	14655	7403	6994	14397	100
R	322	388	710	320	389	709	100	1052	1053	2105	1003	1045	2048	101
H	636	671	1307	673	665	1338	98	1944	1937	3881	1985	1893	3878	99
2B	147	125	272	128	132	260	102	408	353	761	394	333	727	103
3B	15	17	32	12	16	28	112	60	44	104	39	41	80	128
HR	73	79	152	67	66	133	112	226	224	450	188	182	370	119
BB	261	321	582	231	333	564	101	736	885	1621	731	871	1602	99
SO	469	497	966	437	397	834	113	1227	1485	2712	1231	1264	2495	107
E	56	47	103	61	47	108	95	154	151	305	183	178	361	83
E-Infield	38	33	71	39	29	68	104	114	111	225	119	122	241	92
LHB-Avg	.265	.273	.269	.297	.297	.297	91	.283	.273	.277	.296	.286	.291	95
LHB-HR	17	34	51	33	37	70	77	59	103	162	81	79	160	100
RHB-Avg	.249	.247	.248	.241	.252	.246	101	.264	.246	.256	.252	.256	.254	101
RHB-HR	56	45	101	34	29	63	146	167	121	288	107	103	210	134

1995 Lefty-Righty Stats

Platoon stats are probably the forefather of all of today's statistical splits, and their importance can still hardly be overstated. For one reason, lefty/righty match-ups are always changing during a game. A night game starts and finishes in the dark. An Astroturf game starts and finishes on Astroturf. A home game is at home, and a road game on the road. But lefty/righty match-ups fluctuate from the first pitch of a ballgame to the very last. Managers still live by them, and we hope you'll enjoy taking a look as well.

One of the interesting things to do with these splits is find the players that *don't* necessarily follow the traditional platoon trends. One of those players is Seattle's Tino Martinez—a left-handed batter who hit over 40 points higher against lefties in 1995, with some pretty good power. Some pitchers are also able to buck the trend. Remember righthander Joey Hamilton from the fielding section? Well, Hamilton fared better in 1995 against *left-handed* batters than right-handed ones—about 30 points in terms of batting average.

Batters vs. Left-Handed and Right-Handed Pitchers

Batter	vs	Avg	AB	H	2B	3B	HR	BI	BB	SO	OBP	SLG
Abbott,Kurt	L	.244	119	29	5	2	3	13	8	30	.297	.395
Bats Right	R	.259	301	78	13	5	14	47	28	80	.325	.475
Aldrete,Mike	L	.000	6	0	0	0	0	0	2	1	.333	.000
Bats Left	R	.280	143	40	8	0	4	24	17	30	.350	.420
Alexander,M	L	.250	84	21	1	1	2	5	7	11	.308	.357
Bats Right	R	.228	158	36	8	0	1	18	13	19	.295	.297
Alfonzo,E	L	.286	98	28	5	1	2	15	4	12	.314	.418
Bats Right	R	.274	237	65	8	4	2	26	8	25	.296	.367
Alicea,Luis	L	.293	99	29	3	0	2	12	16	11	.388	.384
Bats Both	R	.263	320	84	17	3	4	32	47	50	.361	.372
Allanson,Andy	L	.103	39	4	2	0	0	0	4	4	.186	.154
Bats Right	R	.233	43	10	1	0	3	10	3	8	.298	.465
Alomar,R	L	.231	130	30	2	1	2	9	11	23	.289	.308
Bats Both	R	.323	387	125	22	6	11	57	36	22	.375	.496
Alomar Jr,S	L	.364	44	16	2	0	4	12	1	2	.378	.682
Bats Right	R	.283	159	45	4	0	6	23	6	24	.320	.421
Alou,Moises	L	.341	82	28	8	0	5	19	8	12	.409	.622
Bats Right	R	.252	262	66	14	0	9	39	21	44	.321	.408
Amaral,Rich	L	.273	128	35	8	0	1	8	10	16	.326	.359
Bats Right	R	.291	110	32	6	2	1	11	11	17	.361	.409
Amaro,Ruben	L	.150	40	6	1	0	1	3	1	4	.209	.250
Bats Both	R	.300	20	6	2	0	0	4	3	2	.391	.400
Anderson,B	L	.213	178	38	12	0	3	15	25	51	.320	.331
Bats Left	R	.285	376	107	21	10	13	49	62	60	.394	.497
Anderson,G	L	.252	115	29	4	0	5	23	6	24	.285	.417
Bats Left	R	.351	259	91	15	1	11	46	13	41	.382	.544
Andrews,Shane	L	.203	64	13	2	1	2	12	7	15	.288	.359
Bats Right	R	.218	156	34	8	0	6	19	10	53	.263	.385
Anthony,Eric	L	.294	17	5	0	0	1	5	1	3	.286	.471
Bats Left	R	.265	117	31	6	0	4	18	12	27	.333	.419
Arias,Alex	L	.220	50	11	2	1	0	4	7	2	.310	.300
Bats Right	R	.283	166	47	7	1	3	22	15	18	.346	.392
Ashley,Billy	L	.279	68	19	1	0	2	5	5	31	.329	.382
Bats Right	R	.218	147	32	4	0	6	22	20	57	.316	.367
Aude,Rich	L	.279	61	17	6	0	1	11	3	10	.313	.426
Bats Right	R	.208	48	10	2	0	1	8	3	10	.255	.313
Aurilia,Rich	L	.500	2	1	0	0	1	1	1	0	.667	2.000
Bats Right	R	.471	17	8	3	0	1	3	0	2	.444	.824
Ausmus,Brad	L	.314	70	22	2	1	3	7	12	10	.415	.500
Bats Right	R	.287	258	74	14	3	2	27	19	46	.336	.388
Baerga,Carlos	L	.331	160	53	12	1	4	29	17	10	.389	.494
Bats Both	R	.307	397	122	16	1	11	61	18	21	.340	.436
Bagwell,Jeff	L	.298	84	25	6	0	2	15	20	16	.434	.440
Bats Right	R	.288	364	105	23	0	19	72	59	86	.390	.508
Baines,Harold	L	.290	62	18	1	0	3	5	6	10	.353	.452
Bats Left	R	.300	323	97	18	1	21	58	64	35	.412	.557
Barberie,Bret	L	.152	79	12	6	0	0	8	10	15	.274	.228
Bats Both	R	.285	158	45	8	0	2	17	26	35	.390	.373
Barry,Jeff	L	.143	7	1	1	0	0	0	0	4	.143	.286
Bats Both	R	.125	8	1	0	0	0	1	1	4	.222	.125

Batter	vs	Avg	AB	H	2B	3B	HR	BI	BB	SO	OBP	SLG
Bass,Kevin	L	.252	115	29	4	0	3	13	6	19	.301	.365
Bats Both	R	.239	180	43	8	0	2	19	18	28	.305	.317
Bates,Jason	L	.183	71	13	2	1	2	10	10	22	.284	.324
Bats Both	R	.291	251	73	15	3	6	36	32	48	.375	.446
Battle,Allen	L	.273	44	12	0	0	0	1	6	9	.360	.273
Bats Right	R	.270	74	20	5	0	0	1	9	17	.357	.338
Battle,Howard	L	.667	3	2	0	0	0	0	0	0	.667	.667
Bats Right	R	.083	12	1	0	0	0	0	4	8	.313	.083
Bautista,D	L	.189	95	18	1	0	4	9	1	25	.198	.326
Bats Right	R	.210	176	37	8	0	3	18	11	43	.257	.307
Bean,Billy	L	.000	0	0	0	0	0	0	0	0	.000	.000
Bats Left	R	.000	7	0	0	0	0	0	0	1	.125	.000
Becker,Rich	L	.149	87	13	1	0	0	2	7	33	.237	.161
Bats Left	R	.262	305	80	14	1	2	31	27	62	.322	.334
Bell,David	L	.361	36	13	1	0	0	3	2	5	.395	.389
Bats Right	R	.209	110	23	6	2	2	16	2	20	.235	.355
Bell,Derek	L	.410	100	41	4	0	2	28	7	14	.455	.510
Bats Right	R	.313	352	110	17	2	6	58	26	57	.365	.423
Bell,Jay	L	.306	144	44	10	1	7	17	19	12	.387	.535
Bats Right	R	.246	386	95	18	3	6	38	36	98	.316	.355
Bell,Juan	L	.000	8	0	0	0	0	1	0	4	.000	.000
Bats Both	R	.222	18	4	2	0	1	1	2	6	.300	.500
Belle,Albert	L	.293	133	39	11	1	8	25	24	25	.399	.571
Bats Right	R	.324	413	134	41	4	42	101	49	55	.401	.729
Belliard,R	L	.302	43	13	0	0	0	2	1	8	.318	.302
Bats Right	R	.197	137	27	2	1	0	5	5	20	.236	.226
Beltre,E	L	.222	27	6	3	0	0	3	3	4	.300	.333
Bats Right	R	.215	65	14	5	0	0	4	1	11	.227	.292
Benard,Marvin	L	.167	6	1	0	0	1	2	0	2	.167	.667
Bats Left	R	.429	28	12	2	0	0	2	1	5	.448	.500
Benitez,Yamil	L	.292	24	7	1	1	2	5	1	4	.320	.667
Bats Right	R	.533	15	8	1	0	0	2	0	3	.533	.600
Benjamin,Mike	L	.270	37	10	3	0	1	2	3	5	.325	.432
Bats Right	R	.208	149	31	3	0	2	10	5	46	.239	.268
Bennett,Gary	L	.000	1	0	0	0	0	0	0	1	.000	.000
Bats Right	R	.000	0	0	0	0	0	0	0	0	.000	.000
Benzinger,T	L	.500	4	2	0	0	1	2	0	1	.400	1.250
Bats Both	R	.000	6	0	0	0	0	0	2	2	.250	.000
Berroa,G	L	.237	152	36	7	3	3	17	21	27	.326	.382
Bats Right	R	.294	394	116	15	0	19	71	42	71	.361	.477
Berry,Sean	L	.284	74	21	6	0	1	13	10	12	.372	.405
Bats Right	R	.329	240	79	16	1	13	42	15	41	.365	.567
Berryhill,D	L	.103	39	4	0	0	0	6	6	10	.204	.103
Bats Both	R	.256	43	11	3	0	2	5	4	9	.319	.465
Bichette,D	L	.336	149	50	9	1	14	40	11	23	.377	.691
Bats Right	R	.342	430	147	29	1	26	88	11	73	.360	.595
Biggio,Craig	L	.383	107	41	5	0	7	18	22	5	.493	.626
Bats Right	R	.283	446	126	25	2	15	59	58	80	.384	.448
Blauser,Jeff	L	.226	84	19	2	0	1	5	20	25	.383	.286
Bats Right	R	.207	347	72	14	2	11	26	37	82	.301	.354

Batters vs. Left-Handed and Right-Handed Pitchers

Batter	vs	Avg	AB	H	2B	3B	HR	BI	BB	SO	OBP	SLG	Batter	vs	Avg	AB	H	2B	3B	HR	BI	BB	SO	OBP	SLG
Blowers,Mike	L	.341	129	44	11	0	7	34	15	31	.407	.589	Burnitz,J	L	1.000	1	1	0	0	0	0	0	0	1.000	1.000
Bats Right	R	.223	310	69	13	1	16	62	38	97	.306	.426	Bats Left	R	.500	6	3	1	0	0	0	0	0	.500	.667
Bogar,Tim	L	.377	77	29	6	0	1	16	3	11	.400	.494	Busch,Mike	L	.200	10	2	0	0	1	2	0	5	.200	.500
Bats Right	R	.191	68	13	1	0	0	5	6	14	.253	.206	Bats Right	R	.286	7	2	0	0	2	4	0	2	.286	1.143
Boggs,Wade	L	.311	132	41	2	1	1	15	21	14	.397	.364	Butler,Brett	L	.277	130	36	3	3	1	11	17	15	.358	.369
Bats Left	R	.329	328	108	20	3	4	48	53	36	.418	.445	Bats Left	R	.308	383	118	15	6	0	27	50	36	.384	.379
Bonds,Barry	L	.268	138	37	10	2	5	28	25	23	.388	.478	Caceres,Edgar	L	.160	50	8	2	1	1	8	2	9	.189	.300
Bats Left	R	.304	368	112	20	5	28	76	95	60	.447	.614	Bats Both	R	.299	67	20	4	1	0	9	6	6	.365	.388
Bonilla,Bobby	L	.366	164	60	10	3	8	29	15	20	.420	.610	Cameron,Mike	L	.238	21	5	2	0	1	2	1	7	.273	.476
Bats Both	R	.313	390	122	27	5	20	70	39	59	.374	.562	Bats Right	R	.118	17	2	0	0	0	0	2	8	.211	.118
Boone,Bret	L	.252	123	31	11	0	4	22	8	17	.293	.439	Caminiti,Ken	L	.331	169	56	11	0	10	32	12	19	.374	.574
Bats Right	R	.272	390	106	23	2	11	46	33	67	.336	.426	Bats Both	R	.289	357	103	22	0	16	62	57	75	.383	.485
Borders,Pat	L	.225	89	20	5	0	2	6	5	14	.266	.348	Cangelosi,J	L	.303	33	10	2	0	2	5	6	11	.410	.545
Bats Right	R	.191	89	17	3	1	2	7	4	15	.226	.315	Bats Both	R	.321	168	54	3	2	0	13	42	31	.465	.363
Bordick,Mike	L	.239	109	26	1	0	2	9	10	5	.298	.303	Canseco,Jose	L	.280	93	26	3	0	12	21	19	18	.409	.699
Bats Right	R	.273	319	87	12	0	6	35	25	43	.334	.367	Bats Right	R	.314	303	95	22	1	12	60	23	75	.367	.512
Bradshaw,T	L	.250	4	1	0	0	0	0	1	1	.400	.250	Caraballo,R	L	.261	23	6	0	1	0	0	4	6	.370	.348
Bats Left	R	.225	40	9	1	1	0	2	1	9	.244	.300	Bats Both	R	.184	76	14	4	0	2	3	2	27	.235	.316
Brady,Doug	L	.250	4	1	0	0	0	0	1	0	.400	.250	Carr,Chuck	L	.310	116	36	12	0	2	8	17	19	.403	.466
Bats Both	R	.176	17	3	1	0	0	3	1	4	.222	.235	Bats Left	R	.177	192	34	8	0	0	12	29	30	.286	.219
Bragg,Darren	L	.308	13	4	1	0	0	2	4	3	.474	.385	Carreon,Mark	L	.309	97	30	5	0	3	11	4	4	.330	.454
Bats Left	R	.227	132	30	4	1	3	10	14	34	.313	.341	Bats Right	R	.298	299	89	19	0	14	54	19	33	.347	.502
Branson,Jeff	L	.158	38	6	2	0	0	4	3	11	.238	.211	Carter,Joe	L	.294	136	40	8	0	8	20	8	18	.331	.529
Bats Left	R	.273	293	80	16	2	12	41	41	58	.358	.464	Bats Right	R	.239	422	101	15	0	17	56	29	69	.290	.396
Brito,B	L	.000	1	0	0	0	0	0	0	1	.000	.000	Castellano,P	L	.000	1	0	0	0	0	0	0	1	.000	.000
Bats Right	R	.250	4	1	0	0	1	1	0	2	.400	1.000	Bats Right	R	.000	4	0	0	0	0	0	2	2	.333	.000
Brito,Jorge	L	.071	14	1	0	0	0	0	0	6	.071	.071	Castilla,V	L	.388	134	52	15	0	12	35	8	11	.417	.769
Bats Right	R	.270	37	10	3	0	0	7	2	11	.325	.351	Bats Right	R	.282	393	111	19	2	20	55	22	76	.324	.494
Brogna,Rico	L	.229	118	27	7	0	2	14	6	34	.272	.339	Castillo,A	L	.000	7	0	0	0	0	0	0	1	.000	.000
Bats Left	R	.308	377	116	20	2	20	62	33	77	.363	.531	Bats Right	R	.136	22	3	0	0	0	0	3	8	.269	.136
Brosius,Scott	L	.234	124	29	4	2	3	8	14	29	.324	.371	Castro,Juan	L	.000	0	0	0	0	0	0	0	0	.000	.000
Bats Right	R	.275	265	73	15	0	14	38	27	38	.350	.491	Bats Right	R	.250	4	1	0	0	0	0	1	1	.400	.250
Brown,Jarvis	L	.167	12	2	0	0	0	0	1	4	.231	.167	Cedeno,A	L	.271	96	26	5	0	2	9	6	23	.314	.385
Bats Right	R	.133	15	2	1	0	0	1	6	5	.381	.200	Bats Right	R	.190	294	56	11	2	4	22	22	69	.258	.282
Browne,Jerry	L	.174	46	8	0	0	0	4	7	6	.283	.174	Cedeno,D	L	.256	39	10	1	1	2	7	2	10	.293	.487
Bats Both	R	.283	138	39	4	0	1	13	18	14	.367	.333	Bats Both	R	.230	122	28	5	0	2	7	8	25	.288	.320
Brumfield,J	L	.298	124	37	10	1	1	6	5	15	.326	.419	Cedeno,Roger	L	.267	15	4	1	0	0	0	1	4	.313	.333
Bats Right	R	.259	278	72	13	1	3	20	32	56	.345	.345	Bats Both	R	.222	27	6	1	0	0	3	2	6	.267	.259
Brumley,Mike	L	.000	4	0	0	0	0	0	0	2	.000	.000	Chamberlain,W	L	.200	20	4	1	0	0	0	2	6	.273	.250
Bats Both	R	.071	14	1	0	0	1	2	0	4	.071	.286	Bats Right	R	.045	22	1	0	0	1	1	1	5	.087	.182
Buechele,S	L	.182	33	6	2	0	1	2	6	2	.308	.333	Cianfrocco,A	L	.250	36	9	1	0	0	7	4	8	.325	.278
Bats Right	R	.175	97	17	0	0	0	7	9	20	.245	.175	Bats Right	R	.268	82	22	6	0	5	24	7	20	.337	.524
Buford,Damon	L	.268	56	15	1	0	2	5	10	6	.388	.393	Cirillo,Jeff	L	.294	119	35	6	2	2	15	18	16	.388	.429
Bats Right	R	.170	112	19	4	0	2	9	15	29	.284	.259	Bats Right	R	.268	209	56	13	2	7	24	29	26	.361	.450
Buhner,Jay	L	.254	118	30	5	0	8	30	17	30	.341	.500	Clark,Dave	L	.348	23	8	2	0	1	4	5	6	.464	.565
Bats Right	R	.264	352	93	18	0	32	91	43	90	.343	.588	Bats Left	R	.272	173	47	4	0	3	20	19	32	.344	.347
Bullett,Scott	L	.333	12	4	1	1	0	6	2	5	.429	.583	Clark,Jerald	L	.291	55	16	4	1	2	7	2	6	.310	.509
Bats Left	R	.268	138	37	4	6	3	16	10	25	.322	.449	Bats Right	R	.389	54	21	4	2	1	8	0	5	.400	.593
Burks,Ellis	L	.327	104	34	6	2	5	18	11	23	.397	.567	Clark,Phil	L	.179	67	12	2	0	1	6	5	13	.240	.254
Bats Right	R	.230	174	40	4	4	9	31	28	49	.338	.454	Bats Right	R	.300	30	9	1	0	1	1	3	5	.364	.433

Batters vs. Left-Handed and Right-Handed Pitchers

Batter	vs	Avg	AB	H	2B	3B	HR	BI	BB	SO	OBP	SLG	Batter	vs	Avg	AB	H	2B	3B	HR	BI	BB	SO	OBP	SLG
Clark,Tony	L	.400	20	8	2	0	1	5	0	5	.400	.650	Davis,Russ	L	.311	74	23	4	2	2	10	8	18	.378	.500
Bats Both	R	.198	81	16	3	1	2	6	8	25	.270	.333	Bats Right	R	.167	24	4	1	0	0	2	2	8	.259	.208
Clark,Will	L	.291	148	43	12	0	4	32	22	16	.384	.453	Dawson,Andre	L	.313	80	25	6	1	4	18	2	13	.333	.563
Bats Left	R	.307	306	94	15	3	12	60	46	34	.392	.493	Bats Right	R	.226	146	33	4	2	4	19	7	32	.290	.363
Clayton,Royce	L	.260	104	27	5	0	4	11	7	16	.304	.423	Decker,Steve	L	.241	29	7	1	0	1	3	3	3	.313	.379
Bats Right	R	.240	405	97	24	3	1	47	31	93	.297	.321	Bats Right	R	.221	104	23	1	1	2	10	16	19	.320	.308
Colbrunn,Greg	L	.215	144	31	5	1	3	14	8	26	.257	.326	Delgado,C	L	.273	11	3	2	0	1	2	0	4	.273	.727
Bats Right	R	.299	384	115	17	0	20	75	14	43	.331	.500	Bats Left	R	.150	80	12	1	0	2	9	6	22	.205	.238
Cole,Alex	L	.000	5	0	0	0	0	0	1	1	.286	.000	DeShields,D	L	.207	121	25	5	1	2	11	11	22	.273	.314
Bats Left	R	.365	74	27	3	2	1	14	7	14	.420	.500	Bats Left	R	.276	304	84	13	2	6	26	52	61	.383	.391
Coleman,Vince	L	.254	138	35	5	2	3	10	10	21	.309	.384	Devarez,Cesar	L	.000	0	0	0	0	0	0	0	0	.000	.000
Bats Both	R	.303	317	96	18	4	2	19	27	59	.358	.404	Bats Right	R	.000	4	0	0	0	0	0	0	0	.000	.000
Coles,Darnell	L	.214	70	15	4	0	2	8	5	12	.267	.357	Devereaux,M	L	.308	130	40	7	0	5	26	9	18	.353	.477
Bats Right	R	.235	68	16	3	0	1	8	11	8	.361	.324	Bats Right	R	.295	258	76	17	1	6	37	18	44	.337	.438
Conine,Jeff	L	.317	120	38	6	0	9	24	21	16	.407	.592	Diaz,Alex	L	.304	46	14	5	0	1	8	0	3	.304	.478
Bats Right	R	.298	363	108	20	2	16	81	45	78	.369	.496	Bats Both	R	.237	224	53	9	0	2	19	13	24	.282	.304
Cookson,Brent	L	.125	32	4	0	0	0	3	1	5	.152	.125	Diaz,Mario	L	.206	34	7	1	0	0	1	1	5	.229	.235
Bats Right	R	.333	3	1	1	0	0	2	1	2	.500	.667	Bats Right	R	.245	53	13	2	0	1	5	0	7	.245	.340
Coomer,Ron	L	.319	47	15	2	0	3	12	6	7	.407	.553	DiSarcina,G	L	.289	97	28	10	2	2	14	4	4	.314	.495
Bats Right	R	.204	54	11	1	1	2	7	3	4	.246	.370	Bats Right	R	.313	265	83	18	4	3	27	16	21	.354	.445
Cooper,Scott	L	.206	97	20	4	1	0	18	14	28	.310	.268	Donnels,Chris	L	.111	18	2	0	0	1	1	2	6	.200	.278
Bats Left	R	.238	277	66	14	1	3	22	35	57	.325	.329	Bats Left	R	.291	103	30	2	2	1	12	10	18	.351	.379
Cora,Joey	L	.325	40	13	2	0	0	5	3	3	.391	.375	Duncan,M	L	.298	114	34	7	1	2	17	5	24	.322	.430
Bats Both	R	.295	387	114	17	2	3	34	34	28	.355	.372	Bats Right	R	.278	151	42	7	1	4	19	0	38	.277	.417
Cordero,Wil	L	.306	124	38	12	0	3	19	10	23	.360	.476	Dunn,Steve	L	.000	0	0	0	0	0	0	0	0	.000	.000
Bats Right	R	.279	390	109	23	2	7	30	26	65	.335	.403	Bats Left	R	.000	6	0	0	0	0	0	1	3	.143	.000
Cordova,Marty	L	.323	124	40	10	2	3	20	12	29	.386	.508	Dunston,S	L	.348	138	48	8	2	5	24	4	16	.372	.543
Bats Right	R	.263	388	102	17	2	21	64	40	82	.342	.479	Bats Right	R	.274	339	93	22	4	9	45	6	59	.293	.442
Correia,Rod	L	.000	6	0	0	0	0	0	0	1	.000	.000	Durham,Ray	L	.315	149	47	9	4	3	17	14	29	.373	.490
Bats Right	R	.333	15	5	1	1	0	3	0	4	.333	.533	Bats Both	R	.230	322	74	18	2	4	34	17	54	.277	.335
Counsell,C	L	.000	0	0	0	0	0	0	0	0	.000	.000	Dykstra,Lenny	L	.307	88	27	5	0	1	9	10	13	.380	.398
Bats Left	R	.000	1	0	0	0	0	0	1	0	.500	.000	Bats Left	R	.241	166	40	10	1	1	9	23	15	.339	.331
Cromer,Tripp	L	.190	84	16	7	0	2	6	3	16	.222	.345	Easley,Damion	L	.246	118	29	6	2	2	13	10	13	.302	.381
Bats Right	R	.238	261	62	12	0	3	12	11	50	.273	.318	Bats Right	R	.201	239	48	8	0	2	22	22	34	.281	.259
Cruz,Fausto	L	.286	7	2	0	0	0	3	1	1	.333	.286	Edmonds,Jim	L	.293	164	48	10	0	7	29	15	35	.359	.482
Bats Right	R	.188	16	3	0	0	0	2	2	4	.263	.188	Bats Left	R	.289	394	114	20	4	26	78	36	95	.349	.558
Cummings,M	L	.176	17	3	0	0	1	1	0	4	.176	.353	Eenhoorn,R	L	.143	7	1	1	0	0	1	0	1	.143	.286
Bats Left	R	.252	135	34	7	1	1	14	13	26	.318	.341	Bats Right	R	.143	7	1	0	0	0	1	1	2	.250	.143
Curtis,Chad	L	.348	135	47	9	2	5	16	16	16	.419	.556	Eisenreich,J	L	.213	75	16	3	0	0	9	8	7	.287	.253
Bats Right	R	.244	451	110	20	1	16	51	54	77	.328	.399	Bats Left	R	.341	302	103	19	2	10	46	30	37	.398	.517
Cuyler,Milt	L	.167	30	5	1	0	0	0	1	3	.194	.200	Elster,Kevin	L	.188	32	6	1	1	0	3	3	9	.278	.281
Bats Both	R	.224	58	13	0	4	0	5	7	13	.308	.362	Bats Right	R	.184	38	7	4	0	1	6	5	10	.267	.368
Dalesandro,M	L	.000	4	0	0	0	0	0	0	2	.000	.000	Encarnacion,A	L	.286	42	12	2	1	2	4	1	2	.302	.524
Bats Right	R	.167	6	1	1	0	0	0	0	0	.167	.333	Bats Right	R	.205	117	24	5	1	0	6	12	26	.279	.265
Damon,Johnny	L	.231	39	9	1	1	0	4	2	4	.268	.308	Espinoza,A	L	.218	55	12	1	0	1	6	2	9	.237	.291
Bats Left	R	.295	149	44	10	4	3	19	10	18	.337	.477	Bats Right	R	.273	88	24	3	0	1	11	0	7	.281	.341
Daulton,D	L	.243	111	27	8	1	2	23	17	18	.358	.387	Eusebio,Tony	L	.273	88	24	7	0	1	13	6	16	.323	.386
Bats Left	R	.251	231	58	11	2	7	32	38	34	.359	.407	Bats Right	R	.307	280	86	14	1	5	45	25	43	.363	.418
Davis,Chili	L	.349	129	45	7	0	6	30	22	25	.427	.543	Everett,Carl	L	.210	100	21	5	1	4	14	7	22	.269	.400
Bats Both	R	.305	295	90	16	0	14	56	67	54	.430	.502	Bats Both	R	.286	189	54	8	0	8	40	32	45	.392	.455

Batters vs. Left-Handed and Right-Handed Pitchers

Batter	vs	Avg	AB	H	2B	3B	HR	BI	BB	SO	OBP	SLG	Batter	vs	Avg	AB	H	2B	3B	HR	BI	BB	SO	OBP	SLG
Fabregas,J	L	.179	39	7	1	0	0	6	2	8	.214	.205	Garcia,Carlos	L	.295	105	31	5	0	1	12	8	16	.342	.371
Bats Left	R	.261	188	49	9	0	1	16	15	20	.315	.324	Bats Right	R	.294	262	77	19	2	5	38	17	39	.339	.439
Faneyte,R	L	.182	33	6	1	0	0	3	3	13	.250	.212	Garcia,Freddy	L	.184	38	7	1	1	0	0	7	8	.311	.263
Bats Right	R	.208	53	11	3	1	0	1	8	14	.311	.302	Bats Right	R	.053	19	1	0	0	0	1	1	9	.100	.053
Fermin,Felix	L	.169	89	15	4	0	0	5	2	4	.202	.213	Garcia,Karim	L	.000	1	0	0	0	0	0	0	1	.000	.000
Bats Right	R	.216	111	24	2	0	0	10	4	2	.256	.234	Bats Left	R	.211	19	4	0	0	0	0	0	3	.211	.211
Fernandez,T	L	.195	128	25	3	0	2	13	8	14	.241	.266	Gates,Brent	L	.269	134	36	9	1	2	13	11	28	.322	.396
Bats Both	R	.270	256	69	17	2	3	32	34	26	.359	.387	Bats Both	R	.249	390	97	15	3	3	43	35	56	.303	.326
Fielder,Cecil	L	.265	102	27	1	1	6	18	11	21	.330	.471	Giambi,Jason	L	.222	18	4	0	0	1	2	1	5	.333	.389
Bats Right	R	.237	392	93	17	0	25	64	64	95	.350	.472	Bats Left	R	.259	158	41	7	0	5	23	27	26	.367	.399
Finley,Steve	L	.326	187	61	7	2	3	9	16	28	.388	.433	Giannelli,Ray	L	.000	2	0	0	0	0	0	0	1	.000	.000
Bats Left	R	.283	375	106	16	6	7	35	43	34	.355	.413	Bats Left	R	.111	9	1	0	0	0	0	3	3	.333	.111
Flaherty,John	L	.209	86	18	5	1	0	8	5	8	.261	.291	Gibralter,S	L	.500	2	1	0	0	0	0	0	0	.500	.500
Bats Right	R	.254	268	68	17	0	11	32	13	39	.291	.440	Bats Right	R	.000	1	0	0	0	0	0	0	0	.000	.000
Fletcher,D	L	.227	44	10	2	0	1	8	6	4	.333	.341	Gibson,Kirk	L	.265	34	9	2	0	2	10	2	14	.316	.500
Bats Left	R	.294	306	90	19	1	10	37	26	19	.353	.461	Bats Left	R	.259	193	50	10	2	7	25	31	47	.366	.440
Fletcher,S	L	.161	56	9	3	0	1	5	5	8	.226	.268	Gil,Benji	L	.108	102	11	3	1	0	8	16	43	.225	.157
Bats Right	R	.262	126	33	7	1	0	12	14	19	.350	.333	Bats Right	R	.256	313	80	17	2	9	38	10	104	.281	.409
Flora,Kevin	L	.154	39	6	0	0	0	1	3	13	.214	.154	Giles,B	L	.667	3	2	0	0	0	1	0	0	.667	.667
Bats Right	R	.270	37	10	3	0	2	6	1	10	.289	.514	Bats Left	R	.500	6	3	0	0	1	2	0	1	.500	1.000
Floyd,Cliff	L	.286	7	2	0	0	0	2	0	3	.286	.286	Gilkey,B	L	.311	106	33	9	1	2	15	12	10	.378	.472
Bats Left	R	.113	62	7	1	0	1	6	7	19	.214	.177	Bats Right	R	.294	374	110	24	3	15	54	30	60	.353	.495
Foley,Tom	L	.000	1	0	0	0	0	0	0	1	.000	.000	Giovanola,Ed	L	.000	3	0	0	0	0	0	0	1	.000	.000
Bats Left	R	.217	23	5	2	0	0	2	2	3	.280	.304	Bats Left	R	.091	11	1	0	0	0	0	3	4	.286	.091
Fonville,Chad	L	.241	87	21	3	0	0	4	4	17	.275	.276	Girardi,Joe	L	.250	116	29	3	0	1	10	10	25	.310	.302
Bats Both	R	.292	233	68	3	1	0	12	19	25	.348	.313	Bats Right	R	.266	346	92	14	2	7	45	19	51	.307	.379
Fordyce,Brook	L	.500	2	1	1	0	0	0	1	0	.667	1.000	Goff,Jerry	L	.000	0	0	0	0	0	0	0	0	.000	.000
Bats Right	R	.000	0	0	0	0	0	0	0	0	.000	.000	Bats Left	R	.154	26	4	2	0	1	3	4	13	.267	.346
Fox,Eric	L	.000	5	0	0	0	0	0	1	0	.167	.000	Gomez,Chris	L	.283	113	32	10	0	3	21	16	22	.374	.451
Bats Both	R	.000	10	0	0	0	0	0	2	4	.167	.000	Bats Right	R	.201	318	64	10	2	8	29	25	74	.261	.321
Franco,Matt	L	.000	1	0	0	0	0	0	0	1	.000	.000	Gomez,Leo	L	.273	44	12	1	0	2	6	8	11	.389	.432
Bats Left	R	.313	16	5	1	0	0	1	0	3	.313	.375	Bats Right	R	.217	83	18	4	0	2	6	10	12	.305	.337
Frazier,Lou	L	.216	51	11	1	0	0	7	5	12	.298	.235	Gonzales,Rene	L	.357	14	5	1	0	1	3	0	4	.357	.643
Bats Both	R	.198	111	22	3	0	0	4	10	20	.280	.225	Bats Right	R	.250	4	1	0	0	0	0	0	0	.250	.250
Frye,Jeff	L	.272	92	25	5	0	3	12	8	11	.333	.424	Gonzalez,Alex	L	.273	110	30	6	2	3	10	18	37	.372	.445
Bats Right	R	.281	221	62	10	2	1	17	16	34	.336	.357	Bats Right	R	.230	257	59	13	2	7	32	26	77	.300	.377
Fryman,Travis	L	.211	128	27	2	2	1	16	12	28	.275	.281	Gonzalez,Juan	L	.327	101	33	6	0	9	26	5	20	.352	.653
Bats Right	R	.294	439	129	19	3	14	65	51	72	.367	.446	Bats Right	R	.283	251	71	14	2	18	56	12	46	.312	.570
Gaetti,Gary	L	.212	132	28	2	0	9	23	18	23	.316	.432	Gonzalez,Luis	L	.268	112	30	6	4	4	19	10	14	.346	.500
Bats Right	R	.277	382	106	25	0	26	73	29	68	.333	.547	Bats Left	R	.279	359	100	23	4	9	50	47	49	.361	.440
Gagne,Greg	L	.248	117	29	7	1	1	10	11	21	.308	.350	Goodwin,C	L	.247	77	19	3	0	1	6	3	14	.284	.325
Bats Right	R	.259	313	81	18	3	5	39	27	39	.319	.383	Bats Left	R	.269	212	57	8	3	0	18	12	39	.307	.335
Galarraga,A	L	.270	137	37	8	1	10	33	10	33	.327	.562	Goodwin,Tom	L	.252	115	29	5	0	0	6	9	24	.312	.296
Bats Right	R	.283	417	118	21	2	21	73	22	113	.333	.494	Bats Left	R	.299	365	109	11	3	4	22	29	48	.357	.378
Gallagher,D	L	.301	83	25	8	0	0	6	12	9	.385	.398	Grace,Mark	L	.290	186	54	17	0	3	30	10	22	.330	.430
Bats Right	R	.311	90	28	5	0	1	6	6	12	.354	.400	Bats Left	R	.344	366	126	34	3	13	62	55	24	.425	.560
Gallego,Mike	L	.354	48	17	0	0	0	4	4	9	.404	.354	Grebeck,Craig	L	.241	87	21	7	0	1	4	9	12	.320	.356
Bats Right	R	.153	72	11	0	0	0	4	5	15	.218	.153	Bats Right	R	.284	67	19	5	0	0	14	12	11	.407	.358
Gant,Ron	L	.250	84	21	3	0	7	17	23	21	.413	.536	Green,Shawn	L	.222	45	10	3	1	0	4	1	9	.234	.333
Bats Right	R	.282	326	92	16	4	22	71	51	87	.379	.558	Bats Left	R	.296	334	99	28	3	15	50	19	59	.338	.533

Batters vs. Left-Handed and Right-Handed Pitchers

Batter	vs	Avg	AB	H	2B	3B	HR	BI	BB	SO	OBP	SLG	Batter	vs	Avg	AB	H	2B	3B	HR	BI	BB	SO	OBP	SLG
Greene,Willie	L	.000	1	0	0	0	0	0	0	1	.000	.000	Hatteberg,S	L	.000	1	0	0	0	0	0	0	0	.000	.000
Bats Left	R	.111	18	2	0	0	0	0	3	6	.238	.111	Bats Left	R	1.000	1	1	0	0	0	0	0	0	1.000	1.000
Greenwell,M	L	.268	142	38	5	1	5	22	12	12	.329	.423	Hayes,Charlie	L	.313	147	46	13	1	3	25	17	21	.388	.476
Bats Left	R	.310	339	105	20	3	10	54	26	23	.357	.475	Bats Right	R	.262	382	100	17	2	8	60	33	67	.321	.380
Greer,Rusty	L	.244	78	19	2	0	2	9	7	8	.314	.346	Helfand,Eric	L	.333	12	4	0	0	0	1	1	3	.385	.333
Bats Left	R	.277	339	94	19	2	11	52	48	58	.364	.442	Bats Left	R	.135	74	10	2	1	0	6	10	22	.247	.189
Gregg,Tommy	L	.182	11	2	1	0	0	3	1	1	.231	.273	Hemond,Scott	L	.222	27	6	1	0	1	3	5	6	.364	.370
Bats Left	R	.241	145	35	4	0	6	17	15	32	.319	.393	Bats Right	R	.121	91	11	0	0	2	6	7	25	.190	.187
Griffey Jr,K	L	.279	86	24	3	0	3	10	13	16	.370	.419	Henderson,R	L	.233	120	28	5	0	2	10	27	18	.374	.325
Bats Left	R	.247	174	43	4	0	14	32	39	37	.383	.511	Bats Right	R	.328	287	94	26	1	7	44	45	48	.422	.498
Grissom,M	L	.273	132	36	9	0	4	8	13	17	.338	.432	Hernandez,C	L	.243	37	9	1	0	2	7	2	9	.282	.432
Bats Right	R	.253	419	106	14	3	8	34	34	44	.311	.358	Bats Right	R	.088	57	5	0	0	0	1	5	16	.175	.088
Grotewold,J	L	.000	0	0	0	0	0	0	0	0	.000	.000	Hernandez,J	L	.264	72	19	4	1	4	12	3	16	.293	.514
Bats Left	R	.278	36	10	1	0	1	6	9	7	.422	.389	Bats Right	R	.237	173	41	7	3	9	28	10	53	.276	.468
Grudzielanek,M	L	.343	70	24	4	0	0	9	2	10	.387	.400	Herrera,Jose	L	.214	14	3	0	0	0	1	2	2	.294	.214
Bats Right	R	.211	199	42	8	2	1	11	12	37	.270	.286	Bats Left	R	.250	56	14	1	2	0	1	4	9	.300	.339
Guillen,Ozzie	L	.198	101	20	5	0	0	8	1	10	.204	.248	Hiatt,Phil	L	.235	81	19	6	0	2	8	5	26	.279	.383
Bats Left	R	.264	314	83	15	3	1	33	16	15	.291	.341	Bats Right	R	.125	32	4	0	0	2	4	4	11	.222	.313
Gutierrez,R	L	.250	40	10	1	0	0	2	0	8	.250	.275	Higginson,Bob	L	.212	66	14	2	0	2	5	8	19	.307	.333
Bats Right	R	.284	116	33	5	0	0	10	10	25	.344	.328	Bats Left	R	.227	344	78	15	5	12	38	54	88	.333	.404
Gwynn,Chris	L	.000	2	0	0	0	0	0	0	1	.000	.000	Hill,G	L	.308	91	28	4	0	8	22	7	17	.357	.615
Bats Left	R	.220	82	18	3	2	1	10	6	22	.278	.341	Bats Right	R	.254	406	103	25	4	16	64	32	81	.308	.453
Gwynn,Tony	L	.330	188	62	8	0	2	27	11	4	.365	.404	Hocking,Denny	L	.286	7	2	0	2	0	3	0	0	.286	.857
Bats Left	R	.389	347	135	25	1	7	63	24	11	.424	.527	Bats Both	R	.167	18	3	0	0	0	0	2	2	.250	.167
Hajek,Dave	L	.000	2	0	0	0	0	0	1	1	.333	.000	Hoiles,Chris	L	.300	100	30	4	1	12	27	21	20	.418	.720
Bats Right	R	.000	0	0	0	0	0	0	0	0	.000	.000	Bats Right	R	.230	252	58	11	0	7	31	46	60	.355	.357
Hale,Chip	L	.250	4	1	0	0	0	0	1	1	.400	.250	Holbert,Ray	L	.154	39	6	0	1	2	5	2	8	.214	.359
Bats Left	R	.263	99	26	4	0	2	18	10	19	.330	.364	Bats Right	R	.206	34	7	2	0	0	0	6	12	.341	.265
Hall,Joe	L	.182	11	2	0	0	0	0	2	3	.308	.182	Hollandsworth,T	L	.194	31	6	0	0	1	2	4	12	.286	.290
Bats Right	R	.000	4	0	0	0	0	0	0	0	.000	.000	Bats Left	R	.250	72	18	2	0	4	11	6	17	.313	.444
Hamelin,Bob	L	.233	30	7	1	0	4	10	5	8	.395	.667	Hollins,Dave	L	.254	67	17	4	1	3	4	16	11	.425	.478
Bats Left	R	.157	178	28	6	1	3	15	21	48	.256	.253	Bats Both	R	.212	151	32	8	1	4	22	41	34	.376	.358
Hamilton,D	L	.237	114	27	4	1	0	9	17	13	.346	.289	Horn,Sam	L	.000	0	0	0	0	0	0	0	0	.000	.000
Bats Left	R	.285	284	81	16	5	5	35	30	22	.352	.430	Bats Left	R	.111	9	1	0	0	0	0	1	6	.200	.111
Hammonds,J	L	.208	53	11	2	0	0	7	4	10	.254	.245	Hosey,Dwayne	L	.400	25	10	5	0	1	3	3	4	.464	.720
Bats Right	R	.256	125	32	7	1	4	16	5	20	.290	.424	Bats Both	R	.302	43	13	3	1	2	4	5	12	.375	.558
Haney,Todd	L	.591	22	13	3	0	1	1	3	0	.640	.864	Howard,Dave	L	.243	111	27	4	0	0	5	9	19	.298	.279
Bats Right	R	.333	51	17	5	0	1	5	4	11	.382	.490	Bats Both	R	.243	144	35	9	4	0	14	15	22	.319	.361
Hansen,Dave	L	.154	13	2	1	0	0	1	2	2	.250	.231	Howard,Thomas	L	.158	19	3	2	0	0	0	3	6	.273	.263
Bats Left	R	.298	168	50	9	0	1	13	26	26	.395	.369	Bats Both	R	.313	262	82	13	2	3	26	17	31	.356	.412
Hare,Shawn	L	.000	3	0	0	0	0	0	1	2	.250	.000	Hubbard,Mike	L	.143	14	2	0	0	0	1	1	0	.200	.143
Bats Left	R	.286	21	6	1	0	0	2	3	4	.375	.333	Bats Right	R	.222	9	2	0	0	0	0	1	2	.300	.222
Harper,Brian	L	.000	2	0	0	0	0	0	0	1	.000	.000	Hubbard,Trent	L	.207	29	6	3	0	0	3	4	4	.303	.310
Bats Right	R	.000	5	0	0	0	0	0	0	0	.000	.000	Bats Right	R	.414	29	12	1	0	3	6	4	2	.485	.759
Harris,Lenny	L	.235	17	4	1	0	1	2	1	3	.278	.471	Hudler,Rex	L	.272	92	25	8	0	4	16	8	18	.337	.489
Bats Left	R	.206	180	37	7	3	1	14	13	17	.258	.294	Bats Right	R	.260	131	34	8	0	2	11	2	30	.290	.366
Haselman,Bill	L	.238	42	10	2	0	0	5	8	5	.365	.286	Huff,Michael	L	.200	70	14	5	0	0	4	7	12	.269	.271
Bats Right	R	.245	110	27	4	1	5	18	9	25	.303	.436	Bats Right	R	.265	68	18	4	1	1	5	15	9	.400	.397
Hatcher,Billy	L	.100	10	1	1	0	0	0	1	1	.182	.200	Hulett,Tim	L	.000	2	0	0	0	0	0	0	1	.000	.000
Bats Right	R	.000	2	0	0	0	0	0	0	0	.000	.000	Bats Right	R	.222	9	2	0	0	0	0	0	2	.222	.222

Batters vs. Left-Handed and Right-Handed Pitchers

Batter	vs	Avg	AB	H	2B	3B	HR	BI	BB	SO	OBP	SLG
Hulse,David	L	.263	76	20	3	2	0	11	6	23	.313	.355
Bats Left	R	.247	263	65	8	4	3	36	12	37	.276	.342
Hundley,Todd	L	.300	60	18	5	0	3	12	8	17	.391	.533
Bats Both	R	.274	215	59	6	0	12	39	34	47	.379	.470
Hunter,Brian	L	.308	39	12	4	0	1	7	8	10	.417	.487
Bats Right	R	.125	40	5	2	0	0	2	3	11	.200	.175
Hunter,B	L	.288	80	23	1	3	0	9	8	13	.344	.375
Bats Right	R	.307	241	74	13	2	2	19	13	39	.346	.402
Huskey,Butch	L	.182	22	4	1	0	0	1	3	6	.280	.227
Bats Right	R	.191	68	13	0	0	3	10	7	10	.263	.324
Huson,Jeff	L	.208	24	5	0	0	0	2	0	4	.240	.208
Bats Left	R	.255	137	35	4	2	1	17	15	16	.327	.336
Hyers,Tim	L	.000	1	0	0	0	0	0	0	1	.000	.000
Bats Left	R	.000	4	0	0	0	0	0	0	0	.000	.000
Ingram,Garey	L	.259	27	7	1	0	0	1	5	3	.375	.296
Bats Right	R	.143	28	4	1	0	0	2	4	5	.250	.179
Ingram,R	L	.333	3	1	0	0	0	0	1	1	.500	.333
Bats Right	R	.000	5	0	0	0	0	1	1	0	.167	.000
Jaha,John	L	.324	71	23	5	0	2	13	7	13	.380	.479
Bats Right	R	.310	245	76	15	2	18	52	29	53	.392	.608
James,Chris	L	.290	62	18	4	0	1	7	6	8	.352	.403
Bats Right	R	.200	20	4	0	0	1	1	1	6	.238	.350
James,Dion	L	.188	16	3	0	0	0	0	1	5	.235	.188
Bats Left	R	.295	193	57	6	1	2	26	19	11	.355	.368
Javier,Stan	L	.303	119	36	9	1	3	18	9	11	.359	.471
Bats Both	R	.269	323	87	11	1	5	38	40	52	.351	.356
Jefferies,G	L	.351	151	53	12	0	4	15	11	5	.390	.510
Bats Both	R	.286	329	94	19	2	7	41	24	21	.331	.419
Jefferson,R	L	.286	7	2	0	0	0	0	1	3	.375	.286
Bats Left	R	.289	114	33	8	0	5	26	8	21	.331	.491
Jeter,Derek	L	.357	14	5	3	0	0	4	0	2	.357	.571
Bats Right	R	.206	34	7	1	1	0	3	3	9	.270	.294
Johnson,Brian	L	.270	63	17	3	0	1	11	4	7	.314	.365
Bats Right	R	.243	144	35	6	0	2	18	7	32	.275	.326
Johnson,C	L	.289	83	24	6	0	3	12	19	19	.417	.470
Bats Right	R	.237	232	55	9	1	8	27	27	52	.326	.388
Johnson,H	L	.182	22	4	0	0	0	1	6	6	.357	.182
Bats Both	R	.197	147	29	4	1	7	21	28	40	.326	.381
Johnson,Lance	L	.287	171	49	4	2	1	13	11	17	.328	.351
Bats Left	R	.314	436	137	14	10	9	44	21	14	.346	.454
Johnson,Mark	L	.182	22	4	1	0	1	4	1	5	.217	.364
Bats Left	R	.211	199	42	5	1	12	24	36	61	.336	.427
Jones,Chipper	L	.283	127	36	4	2	3	13	23	22	.393	.417
Bats Both	R	.259	397	103	18	1	20	73	50	77	.339	.461
Jones,Chris	L	.250	84	21	5	0	3	10	5	17	.286	.417
Bats Right	R	.306	98	30	1	2	5	21	8	28	.361	.510
Jordan,Brian	L	.273	121	33	3	2	5	21	9	15	.328	.455
Bats Right	R	.304	369	112	17	2	17	60	13	64	.343	.499
Jordan,Kevin	L	.273	33	9	1	0	2	6	1	5	.314	.485
Bats Right	R	.048	21	1	0	0	0	0	1	4	.091	.048
Jose,Felix	L	.000	8	0	0	0	0	0	2	3	.200	.000
Bats Both	R	.182	22	4	1	0	0	1	0	6	.182	.227
Joyner,Wally	L	.274	146	40	3	0	0	9	12	28	.327	.295
Bats Left	R	.326	319	104	25	0	12	74	57	37	.422	.517
Justice,Dave	L	.241	141	34	2	2	7	23	30	20	.366	.433
Bats Left	R	.259	270	70	15	0	17	55	43	48	.364	.504
Karkovice,Ron	L	.231	104	24	4	1	2	14	12	26	.303	.346
Bats Right	R	.210	219	46	10	0	11	37	27	58	.307	.406
Karros,Eric	L	.315	124	39	5	2	4	17	13	21	.384	.484
Bats Right	R	.293	427	125	24	1	28	88	48	94	.365	.550
Kelly,Mike	L	.217	69	15	4	1	2	13	4	19	.260	.391
Bats Right	R	.162	68	11	2	0	1	4	7	30	.256	.235
Kelly,Pat	L	.272	92	25	6	1	3	13	8	13	.330	.457
Bats Right	R	.219	178	39	6	0	1	16	15	52	.295	.270
Kelly,Roberto	L	.299	117	35	8	1	2	14	5	18	.331	.436
Bats Right	R	.271	387	105	15	1	5	43	17	61	.306	.354
Kent,Jeff	L	.248	133	33	8	0	3	10	11	21	.306	.376
Bats Right	R	.289	339	98	14	3	17	55	18	68	.336	.499
King,Jeff	L	.241	112	27	7	1	7	19	20	11	.348	.509
Bats Right	R	.273	333	91	20	1	11	68	35	52	.340	.438
Kingery,Mike	L	.227	44	10	2	0	0	4	9	11	.358	.273
Bats Left	R	.275	306	84	16	4	8	33	36	29	.350	.431
Kirby,Wayne	L	.267	30	8	2	0	0	3	3	6	.324	.333
Bats Left	R	.196	158	31	8	2	1	11	10	26	.247	.291
Klesko,Ryan	L	.244	78	19	5	1	3	12	11	21	.348	.449
Bats Left	R	.331	251	83	20	1	20	58	36	51	.412	.657
Kmak,Joe	L	.467	15	7	2	0	0	3	2	2	.529	.600
Bats Right	R	.158	38	6	1	0	1	3	4	10	.250	.263
Knoblauch,C	L	.355	141	50	10	3	4	30	12	24	.397	.553
Bats Right	R	.325	397	129	24	5	7	33	66	71	.433	.463
Knorr,Randy	L	.234	47	11	3	0	3	8	4	8	.294	.489
Bats Right	R	.200	85	17	5	0	0	8	7	20	.261	.259
Kowitz,Brian	L	.000	1	0	0	0	0	0	0	1	.000	.000
Bats Left	R	.174	23	4	1	0	0	2	2	5	.269	.217
Kreuter,Chad	L	.333	18	6	2	0	1	5	0	5	.333	.611
Bats Both	R	.193	57	11	3	0	0	3	5	17	.281	.246
Kruk,John	L	.255	51	13	1	0	0	7	13	14	.394	.275
Bats Left	R	.333	108	36	6	0	2	16	13	19	.402	.444
Laker,Tim	L	.209	67	14	4	0	2	10	4	19	.260	.358
Bats Right	R	.257	74	19	4	1	1	10	10	19	.345	.378
Lampkin,Tom	L	.111	9	1	0	0	0	1	1	3	.200	.111
Bats Left	R	.299	67	20	2	0	1	8	8	5	.382	.373
Lankford,Ray	L	.275	142	39	13	1	3	29	17	32	.354	.444
Bats Left	R	.279	341	95	22	1	22	53	46	78	.362	.543
Lansing,Mike	L	.271	107	29	4	0	4	19	9	11	.322	.421
Bats Right	R	.250	360	90	26	2	6	43	19	54	.292	.383
Larkin,Barry	L	.288	111	32	6	1	8	20	15	12	.370	.577
Bats Right	R	.327	385	126	23	5	7	46	46	37	.400	.468
LaValliere,M	L	.200	15	3	0	0	1	4	2	1	.263	.400
Bats Left	R	.253	83	21	6	0	0	15	7	14	.311	.325

Batters vs. Left-Handed and Right-Handed Pitchers

Batter	vs	Avg	AB	H	2B	3B	HR	BI	BB	SO	OBP	SLG
Lawton,Matt	L	.176	17	3	0	0	0	3	0	5	.222	.176
Bats Left	R	.372	43	16	4	1	1	9	7	6	.481	.581
Ledesma,Aaron	L	.385	13	5	0	0	0	2	2	1	.467	.385
Bats Right	R	.150	20	3	0	0	0	1	4	6	.292	.150
Lee,Manuel	L	.000	0	0	0	0	0	0	0	0	.000	.000
Bats Both	R	1.000	1	1	0	0	0	0	0	0	1.000	1.000
Leius,Scott	L	.274	117	32	5	2	1	13	19	13	.372	.376
Bats Right	R	.235	255	60	11	3	3	32	30	41	.317	.337
Lemke,Mark	L	.290	93	27	6	1	2	12	11	15	.362	.441
Bats Both	R	.242	306	74	10	4	3	26	33	25	.314	.330
Leonard,Mark	L	.000	0	0	0	0	0	0	0	0	.000	.000
Bats Left	R	.190	21	4	1	0	1	4	5	2	.346	.381
Levis,Jesse	L	.333	3	1	0	0	0	0	0	0	.333	.333
Bats Left	R	.333	15	5	2	0	0	3	1	0	.333	.467
Lewis,Darren	L	.231	104	24	4	1	0	3	5	6	.270	.288
Bats Right	R	.255	368	94	9	2	1	21	29	51	.322	.299
Lewis,Mark	L	.357	115	41	10	1	2	22	11	20	.409	.513
Bats Right	R	.304	56	17	3	0	1	8	10	13	.403	.411
Leyritz,Jim	L	.322	115	37	5	0	5	18	21	31	.435	.496
Bats Right	R	.228	149	34	7	0	2	19	16	42	.326	.315
Lieberthal,M	L	.300	10	3	0	0	0	0	2	2	.417	.300
Bats Right	R	.243	37	9	2	0	0	4	3	3	.300	.297
Lind,Jose	L	.270	37	10	1	0	0	2	4	6	.341	.297
Bats Right	R	.223	103	23	4	0	0	5	2	6	.238	.262
Liriano,N	L	.283	46	13	1	0	3	11	4	9	.340	.500
Bats Both	R	.286	213	61	11	1	2	27	20	25	.349	.376
Listach,Pat	L	.213	141	30	6	1	0	5	11	32	.273	.270
Bats Both	R	.223	193	43	2	1	0	20	14	29	.279	.244
Livingstone,S	L	.524	21	11	1	0	1	3	0	2	.524	.714
Bats Left	R	.314	175	55	14	0	4	29	15	20	.365	.463
Lockhart,K	L	.188	16	3	1	0	0	0	0	4	.188	.250
Bats Left	R	.329	258	85	18	3	6	33	14	17	.364	.492
Lofton,Kenny	L	.274	146	40	8	1	0	12	15	23	.342	.342
Bats Left	R	.325	335	109	14	12	7	41	25	26	.371	.501
Longmire,Tony	L	.524	21	11	2	0	1	5	5	4	.593	.762
Bats Left	R	.313	83	26	5	0	2	14	6	15	.367	.446
Lopez,Javy	L	.291	86	25	4	0	2	8	6	18	.333	.407
Bats Right	R	.324	247	80	7	4	12	43	8	39	.347	.530
Loretta,Mark	L	.286	14	4	2	0	0	1	2	3	.375	.429
Bats Right	R	.250	36	9	1	0	1	2	4	4	.308	.361
Lyons,Barry	L	.273	22	6	2	0	2	6	3	6	.346	.636
Bats Right	R	.262	42	11	0	0	3	10	1	8	.279	.476
Maas,Kevin	L	.500	2	1	1	0	0	0	0	0	.500	1.000
Bats Left	R	.182	55	10	3	0	1	5	7	11	.294	.291
Mabry,John	L	.330	100	33	3	0	2	14	4	10	.362	.420
Bats Left	R	.299	288	86	18	1	3	27	20	35	.342	.399
Macfarlane,M	L	.300	90	27	5	1	8	15	13	19	.388	.644
Bats Right	R	.201	274	55	13	0	7	36	25	59	.297	.325
Magadan,Dave	L	.171	35	6	1	0	0	4	3	8	.237	.200
Bats Left	R	.329	313	103	23	0	2	47	68	48	.446	.422

Batter	vs	Avg	AB	H	2B	3B	HR	BI	BB	SO	OBP	SLG
Mahay,Ron	L	.250	4	1	1	0	0	2	1	2	.400	.500
Bats Left	R	.188	16	3	1	0	1	1	0	4	.235	.438
Maldonado,C	L	.262	103	27	8	0	5	14	17	24	.367	.485
Bats Right	R	.264	87	23	8	0	4	16	15	26	.374	.494
Manto,Jeff	L	.322	90	29	8	0	7	15	13	28	.413	.644
Bats Both	R	.220	164	36	1	0	10	23	11	41	.273	.409
Manwaring,K	L	.247	85	21	6	1	3	7	8	16	.312	.447
Bats Right	R	.252	294	74	9	1	1	29	19	56	.315	.299
Marsh,Tom	L	.268	56	15	2	0	1	5	3	10	.305	.357
Bats Right	R	.321	53	17	1	1	2	10	1	15	.327	.491
Martin,Al	L	.132	68	9	0	0	1	7	1	22	.145	.176
Bats Left	R	.310	371	115	25	3	12	34	43	70	.385	.491
Martin,N	L	.247	85	21	6	0	1	5	2	15	.273	.353
Bats Right	R	.293	75	22	1	4	1	12	1	10	.291	.453
Martinez,C	L	.233	30	7	0	0	1	4	1	4	.281	.333
Bats Right	R	.129	31	4	1	0	0	5	5	3	.250	.161
Martinez,Dave	L	.212	33	7	0	0	0	1	4	10	.297	.212
Bats Left	R	.319	270	86	16	4	5	36	28	31	.380	.463
Martinez,E	L	.433	127	55	11	0	8	32	39	15	.562	.709
Bats Right	R	.331	384	127	41	0	21	81	77	72	.449	.602
Martinez,S	L	.118	17	2	0	0	0	1	2	8	.211	.118
Bats Left	R	.253	174	44	12	0	2	24	5	37	.276	.356
Martinez,Tino	L	.322	152	49	11	1	10	46	17	33	.389	.605
Bats Left	R	.281	367	103	24	2	21	65	45	58	.361	.529
Marzano,John	L	.000	1	0	0	0	0	0	0	0	.000	.000
Bats Right	R	.400	5	2	0	0	0	0	0	0	.400	.400
Masteller,Dan	L	.143	14	2	0	0	0	2	2	0	.235	.143
Bats Left	R	.245	184	45	12	0	3	19	16	19	.308	.359
Matheny,Mike	L	.246	65	16	3	0	0	6	2	10	.269	.292
Bats Right	R	.248	101	25	6	1	0	15	10	18	.327	.327
Mattingly,Don	L	.265	151	40	10	1	2	15	11	10	.313	.384
Bats Left	R	.300	307	92	22	1	5	34	29	25	.355	.427
May,Derrick	L	.256	39	10	3	0	0	5	1	8	.293	.333
Bats Left	R	.286	280	80	15	2	9	45	23	34	.339	.450
Mayne,Brent	L	.178	45	8	2	0	0	2	2	9	.213	.222
Bats Left	R	.263	262	69	16	1	1	25	23	32	.329	.344
McCarty,Dave	L	.275	40	11	1	1	0	2	6	8	.370	.350
Bats Right	R	.171	35	6	3	0	0	4	0	14	.189	.257
Mccracken,Q	L	.000	0	0	0	0	0	0	0	0	.000	.000
Bats Both	R	.000	1	0	0	0	0	0	0	1	.000	.000
McDavid,Ray	L	.000	4	0	0	0	0	0	0	1	.000	.000
Bats Left	R	.231	13	3	0	0	0	0	2	5	.333	.231
McGee,Willie	L	.341	85	29	6	2	2	9	3	16	.352	.529
Bats Both	R	.243	115	28	5	1	0	6	6	25	.281	.304
McGinnis,Russ	L	.000	3	0	0	0	0	0	1	1	.250	.000
Bats Right	R	.000	2	0	0	0	0	0	0	0	.000	.000
McGriff,Fred	L	.255	188	48	9	1	6	28	19	39	.332	.410
Bats Left	R	.294	340	100	18	0	21	65	46	60	.377	.532
McGwire,Mark	L	.278	79	22	2	0	14	28	30	18	.478	.835
Bats Right	R	.273	238	65	11	0	25	62	58	59	.427	.634

Batters vs. Left-Handed and Right-Handed Pitchers

Batter	vs	Avg	AB	H	2B	3B	HR	BI	BB	SO	OBP	SLG	Batter	vs	Avg	AB	H	2B	3B	HR	BI	BB	SO	OBP	SLG
McLemore,Mark	L	.267	131	35	7	1	1	6	16	21	.358	.359	Nevin,Phil	L	.257	35	9	1	0	0	3	2	10	.297	.286
Bats Both	R	.259	336	87	13	4	4	35	43	50	.341	.357	Bats Right	R	.157	121	19	3	1	2	10	16	30	.277	.248
McRae,Brian	L	.313	163	51	13	0	2	12	5	23	.333	.429	Newfield,Marc	L	.281	57	16	5	0	2	7	4	11	.328	.474
Bats Both	R	.278	417	116	25	7	10	36	42	69	.353	.444	Bats Right	R	.205	83	17	3	1	2	14	1	13	.224	.337
Meares,Pat	L	.231	121	28	7	0	5	11	1	26	.254	.413	Newson,Warren	L	.200	5	1	0	0	0	1	5	3	.636	.200
Bats Right	R	.286	269	77	12	4	7	38	14	42	.336	.439	Bats Left	R	.263	152	40	2	2	5	14	34	42	.398	.401
Mejia,Roberto	L	.182	22	4	0	0	0	1	0	7	.182	.182	Nieves,Melvin	L	.179	56	10	1	0	5	9	4	18	.246	.464
Bats Right	R	.133	30	4	1	0	1	3	0	10	.156	.267	Bats Both	R	.213	178	38	5	1	9	29	15	70	.285	.404
Merced,O	L	.225	120	27	5	1	5	17	14	26	.301	.408	Nilsson,Dave	L	.273	55	15	1	1	2	9	4	11	.328	.435
Bats Left	R	.324	367	119	24	3	10	66	38	48	.386	.488	Bats Right	R	.279	208	58	11	0	10	44	20	30	.339	.476
Mercedes,H	L	.261	23	6	1	0	0	4	3	8	.333	.304	Nixon,Otis	L	.333	177	59	6	1	0	13	12	20	.376	.379
Bats Right	R	.250	20	5	1	0	0	5	5	5	.407	.300	Bats Both	R	.279	412	115	15	1	0	32	46	65	.349	.320
Merullo,Matt	L	.438	32	14	2	0	1	10	3	3	.486	.594	Nokes,Matt	L	.000	7	0	0	0	0	0	1	1	.125	.000
Bats Left	R	.252	163	41	12	1	0	17	11	24	.306	.337	Bats Left	R	.151	53	8	2	0	2	6	4	14	.207	.302
Mieske,Matt	L	.306	121	37	5	1	9	31	12	14	.370	.587	Norman,Les	L	.231	39	9	0	1	0	4	5	6	.318	.282
Bats Right	R	.205	146	30	8	0	3	17	15	31	.285	.322	Bats Right	R	.000	1	0	0	0	0	0	1	0	.500	.000
Miller,Keith	L	.500	8	4	0	0	1	3	2	1	.600	.875	Nunnally,Jon	L	.162	37	6	1	1	1	4	3	13	.225	.324
Bats Right	R	.143	7	1	0	0	0	0	0	3	.143	.143	Bats Left	R	.256	266	68	14	5	13	38	48	73	.373	.492
Miller,O	L	.250	72	18	6	1	0	7	6	14	.316	.361	O'Brien,C	L	.171	35	6	1	0	1	3	8	7	.326	.286
Bats Right	R	.266	252	67	14	0	5	29	16	57	.320	.381	Bats Right	R	.239	163	39	6	0	8	20	21	33	.347	.423
Molitor,Paul	L	.279	111	31	7	1	4	18	18	16	.371	.468	O'Leary,Troy	L	.231	52	12	1	0	0	5	6	11	.310	.250
Bats Right	R	.268	414	111	24	1	11	42	43	41	.343	.411	Bats Left	R	.320	347	111	30	6	10	44	23	53	.362	.527
Mondesi,Raul	L	.250	112	28	6	2	5	16	10	20	.315	.473	O'Neill,Paul	L	.259	170	44	9	2	9	38	18	33	.326	.494
Bats Right	R	.295	424	125	17	4	21	72	23	76	.331	.502	Bats Left	R	.324	290	94	21	2	13	58	53	43	.419	.545
Morandini,M	L	.229	105	24	5	2	1	14	7	23	.287	.343	Obando,S	L	.316	19	6	1	0	0	3	0	4	.300	.368
Bats Left	R	.298	389	116	29	5	5	35	35	57	.367	.437	Bats Right	R	.211	19	4	0	0	0	0	2	8	.286	.211
Mordecai,Mike	L	.385	26	10	4	0	2	4	1	3	.407	.769	Ochoa,Alex	L	.333	18	6	1	0	0	0	2	2	.400	.389
Bats Right	R	.224	49	11	2	0	1	7	8	13	.328	.327	Bats Right	R	.263	19	5	0	0	0	0	0	8	.263	.263
Morman,Russ	L	.233	30	7	1	1	1	3	2	5	.281	.433	Offerman,Jose	L	.301	123	37	8	0	1	7	21	16	.403	.390
Bats Right	R	.310	42	13	1	0	2	4	1	7	.341	.476	Bats Both	R	.281	306	86	6	6	3	26	48	51	.384	.369
Morris,Hal	L	.221	68	15	5	0	0	7	4	19	.274	.294	Olerud,John	L	.259	143	37	10	0	1	17	15	17	.333	.350
Bats Left	R	.292	291	85	20	2	11	44	25	39	.347	.488	Bats Left	R	.304	349	106	22	0	7	37	69	37	.422	.427
Mota,Jose	L	.000	0	0	0	0	0	0	0	0	.000	.000	Oliva,Jose	L	.105	57	6	0	0	2	5	4	17	.164	.211
Bats Both	R	.000	2	0	0	0	0	0	0	0	.000	.000	Bats Right	R	.159	126	20	5	0	5	15	8	29	.219	.317
Mouton,James	L	.328	116	38	7	1	3	10	9	16	.381	.483	Oliver,Joe	L	.260	77	20	8	0	1	8	9	12	.345	.403
Bats Right	R	.220	182	40	11	1	1	17	16	43	.292	.308	Bats Right	R	.277	260	72	12	0	11	43	18	54	.329	.450
Mouton,Lyle	L	.295	78	23	6	0	2	10	11	22	.378	.449	Oquendo,Jose	L	.204	54	11	4	1	2	6	9	7	.317	.426
Bats Right	R	.307	101	31	10	0	3	17	8	24	.369	.495	Bats Both	R	.211	166	35	4	2	0	11	26	14	.316	.259
Munoz,Noe	L	.000	0	0	0	0	0	0	0	0	.000	.000	Orsulak,Joe	L	.160	25	4	1	0	0	6	1	3	.185	.200
Bats Right	R	.000	1	0	0	0	0	0	0	0	.000	.000	Bats Left	R	.294	265	78	18	2	1	31	18	32	.336	.389
Munoz,Pedro	L	.310	126	39	7	0	7	23	11	29	.367	.532	Ortiz,Luis	L	.242	62	15	3	1	1	10	2	10	.262	.371
Bats Right	R	.296	250	74	10	0	11	35	8	57	.322	.468	Bats Right	R	.217	46	10	2	1	0	8	4	8	.280	.304
Murray,Eddie	L	.269	104	28	5	0	3	16	6	17	.304	.404	Otero,Ricky	L	.250	24	6	2	0	0	0	3	3	.333	.333
Bats Both	R	.340	332	113	16	0	18	66	33	48	.397	.551	Bats Both	R	.037	27	1	0	0	0	1	0	7	.037	.037
Myers,Greg	L	.240	75	18	4	1	0	9	4	27	.280	.320	Owen,Spike	L	.205	44	9	3	0	0	8	4	6	.271	.273
Bats Left	R	.268	198	53	8	1	9	29	13	22	.313	.455	Bats Both	R	.236	174	41	6	3	1	20	14	16	.293	.322
Naehring,Tim	L	.275	102	28	4	0	3	11	29	12	.439	.402	Owens,Eric	L	1.000	1	1	0	0	0	0	0	0	1.000	1.000
Bats Right	R	.317	331	105	23	2	7	46	48	54	.406	.462	Bats Right	R	1.000	1	1	0	0	0	1	0	0	1.000	1.000
Natal,Bob	L	.286	14	4	0	1	1	1	1	3	.333	.643	Owens,Jayhawk	L	.500	16	8	2	0	2	9	1	3	.529	1.000
Bats Right	R	.207	29	6	2	0	1	5	0	6	.200	.379	Bats Right	R	.103	29	3	0	0	2	5	1	12	.156	.310

Batters vs. Left-Handed and Right-Handed Pitchers

Batter	vs	Avg	AB	H	2B	3B	HR	BI	BB	SO	OBP	SLG	Batter	vs	Avg	AB	H	2B	3B	HR	BI	BB	SO	OBP	SLG
Pagliarulo,M	L	.222	18	4	2	0	0	5	4	3	.364	.333	Piazza,Mike	L	.326	89	29	1	0	8	15	5	16	.362	.607
Bats Left	R	.233	223	52	14	0	4	22	11	46	.269	.350	Bats Right	R	.351	345	121	16	0	24	78	34	64	.409	.606
Pagnozzi,Tom	L	.242	33	8	5	0	0	1	2	2	.286	.394	Pirkl,Greg	L	.267	15	4	0	0	0	0	0	6	.267	.267
Bats Right	R	.210	186	39	9	1	2	14	9	29	.249	.301	Bats Right	R	.000	2	0	0	0	0	0	1	1	.333	.000
Palmeiro,O	L	.600	5	3	0	0	0	1	0	0	.600	.600	Plantier,Phil	L	.333	45	15	1	0	3	8	6	7	.404	.556
Bats Left	R	.267	15	4	0	0	0	0	1	1	.313	.267	Bats Left	R	.234	171	40	5	0	6	26	22	41	.321	.368
Palmeiro,R	L	.292	202	59	9	0	14	37	17	24	.347	.545	Polonia,Luis	L	.241	29	7	2	0	1	2	3	4	.313	.414
Bats Left	R	.321	352	113	21	2	25	67	45	41	.398	.605	Bats Left	R	.263	262	69	14	3	1	15	25	34	.323	.351
Palmer,Dean	L	.432	37	16	3	0	3	10	5	4	.500	.757	Posada,Jorge	L	.000	0	0	0	0	0	0	0	0	.000	.000
Bats Right	R	.293	82	24	3	0	6	14	16	17	.427	.549	Bats Both	R	.000	0	0	0	0	0	0	0	0	.000	.000
Paquette,C	L	.213	108	23	3	0	6	16	6	36	.254	.407	Pozo,A	L	.000	0	0	0	0	0	0	0	0	.000	.000
Bats Right	R	.234	175	41	10	1	7	33	6	52	.257	.423	Bats Right	R	.000	1	0	0	0	0	0	0	0	.000	.000
Parent,Mark	L	.274	62	17	2	0	9	14	8	9	.357	.742	Pratt,Todd	L	.080	25	2	1	0	0	2	3	9	.172	.120
Bats Right	R	.222	203	45	9	0	9	24	18	60	.285	.399	Bats Right	R	.171	35	6	1	0	0	2	3	12	.237	.200
Parker,Rick	L	.200	10	2	0	0	0	1	0	2	.200	.200	Pride,Curtis	L	.400	5	2	0	0	0	1	0	1	.400	.400
Bats Right	R	.316	19	6	0	0	0	3	2	2	.381	.316	Bats Left	R	.155	58	9	1	0	0	1	5	15	.222	.172
Parrish,Lance	L	.207	58	12	4	0	0	7	6	18	.288	.276	Prince,Tom	L	.083	12	1	0	0	0	0	2	4	.214	.083
Bats Right	R	.200	120	24	5	0	4	15	9	34	.254	.342	Bats Right	R	.250	28	7	2	1	1	4	2	6	.300	.500
Patterson,J	L	.160	25	4	0	0	1	1	3	7	.250	.280	Puckett,Kirby	L	.320	128	41	8	0	6	23	17	24	.404	.523
Bats Both	R	.211	180	38	5	3	0	13	11	34	.300	.272	Bats Right	R	.312	410	128	31	0	17	76	39	65	.371	.512
Pegues,Steve	L	.248	117	29	7	0	3	12	2	21	.254	.385	Pulliam,H	L	.333	3	1	0	0	1	1	0	1	.333	1.333
Bats Right	R	.241	54	13	1	0	3	4	2	15	.281	.426	Bats Right	R	.500	2	1	1	0	0	2	0	1	.500	1.000
Pemberton,R	L	.500	8	4	2	0	0	0	0	2	.556	.750	Pye,Eddie	L	.000	6	0	0	0	0	0	0	3	.000	.000
Bats Right	R	.227	22	5	1	1	0	3	1	3	.261	.364	Bats Right	R	.000	2	0	0	0	0	0	0	1	.000	.000
Pena,Geronimo	L	.379	29	11	5	1	0	1	6	7	.486	.621	Raabe,Brian	L	.200	5	1	0	0	0	1	1	0	.333	.200
Bats Both	R	.222	72	16	1	0	1	7	10	23	.318	.278	Bats Right	R	.222	9	2	0	0	0	0	0	0	.222	.222
Pena,Tony	L	.298	84	25	4	0	1	5	2	11	.322	.381	Raines,Tim	L	.279	140	39	10	0	3	16	26	14	.395	.414
Bats Right	R	.246	179	44	11	0	4	23	12	33	.293	.374	Bats Both	R	.287	362	104	15	4	9	51	44	38	.365	.425
Pendleton,T	L	.336	149	50	9	0	3	23	5	11	.359	.456	Ramirez,Manny	L	.407	123	50	10	0	7	28	24	24	.507	.659
Bats Both	R	.272	364	99	23	1	11	55	33	73	.332	.431	Bats Right	R	.274	361	99	16	1	24	79	51	88	.365	.524
Penn,Shannon	L	1.000	1	1	0	0	0	0	0	0	1.000	1.000	Randa,Joe	L	.190	42	8	2	0	1	3	3	6	.244	.310
Bats Both	R	.250	8	2	0	0	0	0	1	2	.333	.250	Bats Right	R	.143	28	4	0	0	0	2	3	11	.226	.143
Perez,Eddie	L	.000	0	0	0	0	0	0	0	0	.000	.000	Ready,Randy	L	.050	20	1	0	0	0	0	1	6	.095	.050
Bats Right	R	.308	13	4	1	0	1	4	0	2	.308	.615	Bats Right	R	.333	9	3	0	0	0	0	2	0	.455	.333
Perez,Eduardo	L	.154	26	4	2	0	1	5	6	3	.313	.346	Rebboulet,Jeff	L	.281	89	25	5	0	4	12	15	13	.390	.472
Bats Right	R	.178	45	8	2	1	0	2	6	6	.296	.267	Bats Right	R	.299	127	38	6	0	0	11	12	21	.360	.346
Perez,Robert	L	.167	30	5	1	0	1	3	0	5	.167	.300	Reed,Jeff	L	.250	8	2	0	0	0	0	3	2	.455	.250
Bats Right	R	.222	18	4	1	0	0	0	0	0	.222	.278	Bats Left	R	.267	105	28	2	0	0	9	17	15	.369	.286
Perez,Tomas	L	.238	21	5	0	0	1	4	0	7	.238	.381	Reed,Jody	L	.290	131	38	8	1	0	9	22	6	.400	.366
Bats Both	R	.247	77	19	3	1	0	4	7	11	.306	.312	Bats Right	R	.242	314	76	10	0	4	31	37	32	.325	.312
Perry,Gerald	L	.000	5	0	0	0	0	0	0	1	.000	.000	Rhodes,Karl	L	.000	6	0	0	0	0	0	1	0	.143	.000
Bats Left	R	.176	74	13	4	0	0	5	6	11	.238	.230	Bats Left	R	.114	35	4	1	0	0	3	2	8	.158	.143
Perry,Herbert	L	.344	64	22	7	0	3	10	5	9	.403	.594	Ripken,Billy	L	.500	4	2	0	0	1	1	0	1	.500	1.250
Bats Right	R	.296	98	29	6	1	0	13	8	19	.358	.378	Bats Right	R	.385	13	5	0	0	1	2	0	2	.385	.615
Petagine,R	L	.231	13	3	1	0	0	1	4	7	.412	.308	Ripken,Cal	L	.286	154	44	10	0	7	26	18	12	.354	.487
Bats Left	R	.234	111	26	7	0	3	16	22	34	.361	.378	Bats Right	R	.253	396	100	23	2	10	62	34	47	.311	.396
Phillips,J.R.	L	.233	30	7	0	0	1	6	2	8	.281	.333	Rivera,Ruben	L	.000	0	0	0	0	0	0	0	0	.000	.000
Bats Left	R	.189	201	38	9	0	8	22	17	61	.252	.353	Bats Right	R	.000	1	0	0	0	0	0	0	1	.000	.000
Phillips,Tony	L	.280	132	37	6	1	7	13	36	25	.441	.500	Roberson,K	L	.143	7	1	0	0	1	1	2	3	.400	.571
Bats Both	R	.254	393	100	15	0	20	48	77	110	.377	.445	Bats Both	R	.194	31	6	1	0	3	5	4	11	.286	.516

Batters vs. Left-Handed and Right-Handed Pitchers

Batter	vs	Avg	AB	H	2B	3B	HR	BI	BB	SO	OBP	SLG
Roberts,Bip	L	.253	79	20	2	0	0	3	5	9	.306	.278
Bats Both	R	.323	217	70	12	0	2	22	12	27	.361	.406
Rodriguez,A	L	.245	53	13	5	1	2	7	4	15	.298	.491
Bats Right	R	.225	89	20	1	1	3	12	2	27	.242	.360
Rodriguez,C	L	.300	10	3	0	0	0	2	0	1	.300	.300
Bats Both	R	.350	20	7	2	0	0	3	2	1	.435	.450
Rodriguez,H	L	.219	32	7	1	0	0	3	2	8	.257	.250
Bats Left	R	.245	106	26	3	1	2	12	9	20	.304	.349
Rodriguez,I	L	.301	146	44	10	0	4	16	9	16	.340	.452
Bats Right	R	.303	346	105	22	2	8	51	7	32	.321	.448
Rodriguez,S	L	.375	8	3	0	0	0	0	2	1	.500	.375
Bats Right	R	.129	31	4	1	0	0	0	4	9	.229	.161
Rowland,Rich	L	.200	10	2	1	0	0	0	0	4	.200	.300
Bats Right	R	.158	19	3	0	0	0	1	0	7	.158	.158
Sabo,Chris	L	.294	17	5	2	0	1	4	1	3	.368	.588
Bats Right	R	.224	67	15	4	0	0	7	3	11	.260	.284
Salmon,Tim	L	.338	139	47	8	1	11	31	30	23	.456	.647
Bats Right	R	.327	398	130	26	2	23	74	61	88	.420	.575
Samuel,Juan	L	.261	119	31	2	0	8	23	18	33	.362	.479
Bats Right	R	.267	86	23	8	1	4	16	11	16	.357	.523
Sanchez,Rey	L	.263	114	30	6	1	1	7	2	5	.276	.360
Bats Right	R	.283	314	89	16	1	2	20	12	43	.310	.360
Sanders,Deion	L	.213	89	19	3	4	0	7	6	21	.268	.337
Bats Left	R	.287	254	73	8	4	6	21	21	39	.348	.421
Sanders,R	L	.365	104	38	6	2	8	24	17	22	.447	.692
Bats Right	R	.289	380	110	30	4	20	75	52	100	.383	.540
Santangelo,F	L	.281	32	9	2	1	0	3	3	4	.361	.406
Bats Both	R	.303	66	20	3	0	1	6	9	5	.395	.394
Santiago,B	L	.355	62	22	6	0	3	14	10	9	.444	.597
Bats Right	R	.265	204	54	14	0	8	30	14	39	.321	.451
Sasser,Mackey	L	.000	1	0	0	0	0	0	0	0	.000	.000
Bats Left	R	.160	25	4	1	0	0	0	0	0	.160	.200
Scarsone,S	L	.324	71	23	5	1	3	7	4	24	.364	.549
Bats Right	R	.241	162	39	5	2	8	22	14	58	.320	.444
Schall,Gene	L	.269	26	7	2	0	0	2	2	4	.345	.346
Bats Right	R	.205	39	8	0	0	0	3	4	12	.279	.205
Schofield,D	L	.231	13	3	0	0	0	1	4	3	.412	.231
Bats Right	R	.176	17	3	0	0	0	1	1	2	.222	.176
Sefcik,Kevin	L	.000	1	0	0	0	0	0	0	0	.000	.000
Bats Right	R	.000	3	0	0	0	0	0	0	2	.000	.000
Segui,David	L	.330	112	37	7	1	2	17	12	12	.403	.464
Bats Both	R	.302	344	104	18	3	10	51	28	35	.354	.459
Seitzer,Kevin	L	.252	139	35	9	0	0	14	20	19	.342	.317
Bats Right	R	.334	353	118	24	3	5	55	44	38	.416	.462
Servais,Scott	L	.348	69	24	11	0	2	18	13	12	.447	.594
Bats Right	R	.236	195	46	11	0	11	29	19	40	.309	.462
Sharperson,M	L	.333	3	1	1	0	0	2	0	1	.333	.667
Bats Right	R	.000	4	0	0	0	0	0	0	1	.000	.000
Sheaffer,D	L	.205	73	15	4	0	1	13	11	17	.310	.301
Bats Right	R	.244	135	33	6	1	4	17	12	21	.304	.393
Sheffield,G	L	.328	61	20	3	0	3	8	19	8	.488	.525
Bats Right	R	.322	152	49	5	0	13	38	36	37	.459	.612
Shipley,Craig	L	.280	118	33	4	1	1	11	2	8	.293	.356
Bats Right	R	.246	114	28	4	0	2	13	6	20	.289	.333
Shumpert,T	L	.364	11	4	2	0	0	1	2	3	.462	.545
Bats Right	R	.194	36	7	1	0	0	2	2	10	.237	.222
Siddall,Joe	L	.000	1	0	0	0	0	0	0	0	.000	.000
Bats Left	R	.333	9	3	0	0	0	1	3	3	.538	.333
Sierra,Ruben	L	.273	161	44	10	0	5	28	14	20	.326	.429
Bats Both	R	.258	318	82	22	0	14	58	32	56	.321	.459
Silvestri,D	L	.216	37	8	1	0	1	7	5	15	.295	.324
Bats Right	R	.232	56	13	5	0	2	4	8	21	.338	.429
Simms,Mike	L	.291	55	16	3	0	6	14	5	11	.361	.673
Bats Right	R	.227	66	15	1	0	3	10	8	17	.325	.379
Singleton,D	L	.143	7	1	0	0	0	0	0	1	.143	.143
Bats Left	R	.042	24	1	0	0	0	0	1	9	.080	.042
Slaught,Don	L	.280	25	7	3	0	0	4	3	1	.357	.400
Bats Right	R	.310	87	27	3	0	0	9	6	7	.362	.345
Smith,Dwight	L	.125	8	1	0	0	0	0	3	1	.364	.125
Bats Left	R	.260	123	32	8	2	3	21	10	34	.324	.431
Smith,Mark	L	.300	40	12	1	0	1	2	4	11	.364	.400
Bats Right	R	.188	64	12	4	0	2	13	8	11	.284	.344
Smith,Ozzie	L	.143	35	5	2	0	0	2	2	6	.205	.200
Bats Both	R	.215	121	26	3	0	0	9	15	6	.304	.256
Snopek,Chris	L	.407	27	11	1	0	0	2	3	3	.467	.444
Bats Right	R	.268	41	11	3	0	1	5	6	9	.362	.415
Snow,J.T.	L	.267	161	43	5	1	5	28	22	34	.351	.404
Bats Both	R	.298	383	114	17	0	19	74	30	57	.353	.491
Sojo,Luis	L	.360	111	40	9	0	5	19	10	7	.418	.577
Bats Right	R	.254	228	58	9	2	2	20	13	12	.293	.338
Sorrento,Paul	L	.163	43	7	1	0	2	14	7	10	.269	.326
Bats Left	R	.246	280	69	13	0	23	65	44	61	.347	.539
Sosa,Sammy	L	.257	148	38	6	1	9	27	20	37	.345	.493
Bats Right	R	.272	416	113	11	2	27	92	38	97	.338	.502
Spehr,Tim	L	.273	11	3	2	0	1	3	1	1	.333	.727
Bats Right	R	.250	24	6	3	0	0	0	5	6	.379	.375
Spiers,Bill	L	.667	3	2	1	0	0	1	1	0	.750	1.000
Bats Left	R	.188	69	13	1	1	0	10	11	15	.293	.232
Sprague,Ed	L	.222	135	30	1	0	5	14	12	16	.282	.341
Bats Right	R	.251	386	97	26	2	13	60	46	80	.350	.430
Stahoviak,S	L	.077	13	1	0	0	0	0	1	5	.143	.077
Bats Left	R	.276	250	69	19	0	3	23	29	56	.351	.388
Stairs,Matt	L	.333	3	1	0	0	0	0	0	0	.333	.333
Bats Left	R	.259	85	22	7	1	1	17	4	14	.297	.400
Stankiewicz,A	L	.200	20	4	1	0	0	5	4	4	.333	.250
Bats Right	R	.063	32	2	0	0	0	2	8	15	.250	.063
Stanley,Mike	L	.281	139	39	8	0	8	24	23	35	.380	.511
Bats Right	R	.262	260	68	21	1	10	59	34	71	.349	.465
Steinbach,T	L	.301	123	37	7	0	6	25	12	23	.365	.504
Bats Right	R	.269	283	76	19	1	9	40	13	51	.302	.438

Batters vs. Left-Handed and Right-Handed Pitchers

Batter	vs	Avg	AB	H	2B	3B	HR	BI	BB	SO	OBP	SLG	Batter	vs	Avg	AB	H	2B	3B	HR	BI	BB	SO	OBP	SLG
Steverson,T	L	.250	16	4	0	0	1	1	2	5	.333	.438	Tinsley,Lee	L	.250	88	22	3	0	3	9	9	26	.320	.386
Bats Right	R	.269	26	7	0	0	1	5	4	5	.344	.385	Bats Both	R	.296	253	75	14	1	4	32	30	48	.372	.407
Stewart,S	L	.154	13	2	0	0	0	0	2	1	.267	.154	Tomberlin,A	L	.286	7	2	0	0	0	2	0	2	.286	.286
Bats Right	R	.240	25	6	0	0	0	1	3	4	.345	.240	Bats Left	R	.205	78	16	0	0	4	8	5	20	.253	.359
Stinnett,K	L	.224	76	17	2	0	3	10	11	21	.330	.368	Trammell,Alan	L	.311	90	28	8	0	1	11	11	2	.386	.433
Bats Right	R	.217	120	26	6	1	1	8	18	44	.343	.308	Bats Right	R	.241	133	32	4	0	1	12	16	17	.318	.293
Stocker,Kevin	L	.217	115	25	4	0	0	9	7	23	.268	.252	Treadway,Jeff	L	.333	3	1	0	0	0	0	0	1	.333	.333
Bats Both	R	.219	297	65	10	3	1	23	36	52	.317	.283	Bats Left	R	.203	64	13	2	1	0	13	5	3	.261	.266
Strange,Doug	L	.222	9	2	1	0	0	1	0	1	.222	.333	Tremie,Chris	L	.000	8	0	0	0	0	0	0	0	.000	.000
Bats Both	R	.274	146	40	8	2	2	20	10	24	.329	.397	Bats Right	R	.250	16	4	0	0	0	0	1	2	.294	.250
Strawberry,D	L	.167	12	2	0	0	0	0	0	4	.167	.167	Tucker,M	L	.211	19	4	0	0	0	0	0	4	.211	.211
Bats Left	R	.293	75	22	4	1	3	13	10	18	.391	.493	Bats Left	R	.266	158	42	10	0	4	17	18	47	.345	.405
Stubbs,F	L	.250	16	4	1	0	0	2	3	7	.368	.313	Tucker,S	L	.000	11	0	0	0	0	0	1	0	.083	.000
Bats Left	R	.250	100	25	10	0	2	17	16	20	.356	.410	Bats Right	R	.125	16	2	0	0	0	1	4	4	.333	.313
Stynes,Chris	L	.172	29	5	1	0	0	2	2	3	.226	.207	Turner,Chris	L	.111	9	1	0	0	0	1	0	3	.111	.111
Bats Right	R	.167	6	1	0	0	0	0	2	0	.375	.167	Bats Right	R	.000	1	0	0	0	0	0	0	0	.000	.000
Surhoff,B.J.	L	.367	128	47	10	1	3	22	8	8	.409	.531	Unroe,Tim	L	.000	0	0	0	0	0	0	0	0	.000	.000
Bats Left	R	.300	287	86	16	2	10	51	29	35	.365	.474	Bats Right	R	.250	4	1	0	0	0	0	0	0	.250	.250
Sweeney,Mark	L	.308	13	4	2	0	1	4	1	3	.357	.692	Valentin,John	L	.356	132	47	10	0	6	35	26	18	.465	.568
Bats Left	R	.266	64	17	0	0	1	9	9	12	.347	.313	Bats Right	R	.278	388	108	27	2	21	67	55	49	.376	.521
Sweeney,Mike	L	.333	3	1	0	0	0	0	0	0	.333	.333	Valentin,Jose	L	.133	83	11	2	0	0	4	11	24	.232	.157
Bats Right	R	.000	1	0	0	0	0	0	0	0	.000	.000	Bats Both	R	.247	255	63	21	3	11	45	26	59	.313	.482
Tarasco,Tony	L	.247	89	22	3	1	1	7	5	16	.287	.337	Valle,Dave	L	.188	16	3	0	0	0	0	0	7	.188	.188
Bats Left	R	.249	349	87	15	3	13	33	46	62	.339	.421	Bats Right	R	.254	59	15	3	0	0	5	6	11	.333	.305
Tartabull,D	L	.253	99	25	6	0	6	17	23	27	.392	.495	Van Slyke,A	L	.169	59	10	2	2	0	5	9	9	.275	.271
Bats Right	R	.227	181	41	10	0	2	18	20	55	.300	.315	Bats Left	R	.239	218	52	9	0	6	19	24	47	.318	.362
Tatum,Jimmy	L	.235	17	4	1	1	0	4	0	4	.235	.412	Vander Wal,J	L	.400	5	2	1	0	0	2	0	2	.400	.600
Bats Right	R	.235	17	4	0	0	0	0	1	3	.278	.235	Bats Left	R	.344	96	33	7	1	5	19	16	21	.434	.594
Taubensee,E	L	.250	28	7	0	0	2	10	3	8	.344	.464	Varsho,Gary	L	.250	4	1	0	0	0	0	0	2	.250	.250
Bats Left	R	.289	190	55	14	2	7	34	19	44	.355	.495	Bats Left	R	.253	99	25	1	1	0	11	7	15	.312	.283
Tavarez,Jesus	L	.250	24	6	1	0	0	2	2	1	.296	.292	Vaughn,Greg	L	.246	118	29	7	0	5	18	22	23	.362	.432
Bats Both	R	.295	166	49	5	2	2	11	14	26	.354	.386	Bats Right	R	.215	274	59	12	1	12	41	33	66	.297	.398
Tettleton,M	L	.225	142	32	5	1	8	21	29	39	.358	.444	Vaughn,Mo	L	.253	174	44	8	0	6	31	14	52	.330	.402
Bats Both	R	.244	287	70	14	0	24	57	78	71	.413	.544	Bats Left	R	.322	376	121	20	3	33	95	54	98	.414	.654
Thomas,Frank	L	.389	126	49	10	0	16	35	36	13	.524	.849	Velarde,Randy	L	.279	136	38	8	1	1	10	21	18	.377	.375
Bats Right	R	.281	367	103	17	0	24	76	100	61	.430	.523	Bats Right	R	.277	231	64	11	0	6	36	34	46	.374	.403
Thome,Jim	L	.275	109	30	3	2	3	13	18	32	.380	.422	Ventura,Robin	L	.265	132	35	4	0	5	31	17	38	.335	.409
Bats Left	R	.327	343	112	26	1	22	60	79	81	.456	.601	Bats Left	R	.306	360	110	18	0	21	62	58	60	.401	.531
Thompson,Milt	L	.000	5	0	0	0	0	0	0	2	.000	.000	Veras,Quilvio	L	.244	119	29	2	2	3	10	18	17	.362	.370
Bats Left	R	.228	127	29	9	0	2	19	14	35	.308	.346	Bats Both	R	.268	321	86	18	5	2	22	62	51	.392	.374
Thompson,R	L	.247	77	19	4	0	1	5	14	14	.363	.338	Vina,Fernando	L	.278	54	15	1	2	0	6	10	10	.409	.370
Bats Right	R	.216	259	56	11	0	7	18	28	62	.302	.340	Bats Left	R	.252	234	59	6	5	3	23	12	18	.306	.359
Thompson,Ryan	L	.288	73	21	4	0	2	7	5	14	.333	.425	Vitiello,Joe	L	.278	72	20	3	0	6	16	6	11	.358	.569
Bats Right	R	.237	194	46	9	0	5	24	14	63	.296	.361	Bats Right	R	.224	58	13	1	0	1	5	2	14	.262	.293
Thurman,Gary	L	.389	18	7	1	0	0	1	0	0	.389	.444	Vizcaino,Jose	L	.346	130	45	5	0	0	9	9	20	.388	.385
Bats Right	R	.143	7	1	0	0	0	2	1	3	.222	.286	Bats Both	R	.266	379	101	16	5	3	47	26	56	.313	.359
Timmons,Ozzie	L	.315	92	29	5	1	3	14	5	11	.351	.489	Vizquel,Omar	L	.262	168	44	13	0	2	19	18	22	.330	.375
Bats Right	R	.203	79	16	5	0	5	14	8	21	.273	.456	Bats Both	R	.267	374	100	15	0	4	37	41	37	.335	.340
Tingley,Ron	L	.333	33	11	2	0	2	5	5	12	.410	.576	Voigt,Jack	L	.174	46	8	1	0	2	7	7	9	.278	.326
Bats Right	R	.187	91	17	6	1	2	13	10	26	.267	.341	Bats Right	R	.176	17	3	2	0	0	1	3	5	.300	.294

Batters vs. Left-Handed and Right-Handed Pitchers

Batter	vs	Avg	AB	H	2B	3B	HR	BI	BB	SO	OBP	SLG
Walbeck,Matt	L	.308	117	36	5	1	0	15	9	11	.354	.368
Bats Both	R	.236	276	65	13	0	1	29	16	60	.279	.293
Walker,Larry	L	.319	141	45	9	0	7	30	10	22	.389	.532
Bats Left	R	.300	353	106	22	5	29	71	39	50	.378	.637
Wallach,Tim	L	.259	85	22	3	1	4	13	7	16	.315	.459
Bats Right	R	.269	242	65	19	1	5	25	20	53	.330	.417
Walton,Jerome	L	.306	98	30	5	0	6	9	12	15	.391	.541
Bats Right	R	.266	64	17	7	1	2	13	5	10	.329	.500
Ward,Turner	L	.156	45	7	1	0	2	1		8	.170	.200
Bats Both	R	.321	84	27	3	0	4	14	13	13	.418	.500
Webster,Lenny	L	.250	48	12	4	0	1	5	7	9	.345	.396
Bats Right	R	.275	102	28	5	0	3	9	9	18	.333	.412
Webster,Mitch	L	.189	37	7	1	1	1	3	2	9	.231	.351
Bats Both	R	.158	19	3	0	0	0	0	2	5	.273	.158
Wehner,John	L	.289	45	13	0	2	0	3	5	9	.346	.378
Bats Right	R	.323	62	20	0	1	0	2	5	8	.373	.355
Weiss,Walt	L	.263	114	30	2	1	0	2	23	17	.387	.298
Bats Both	R	.259	313	81	15	2	1	23	75	40	.409	.329
Whitaker,Lou	L	.308	26	8	3	0	1	5	1	7	.357	.538
Bats Left	R	.291	223	65	11	0	13	39	30	34	.374	.516
White,Derrick	L	.261	23	6	1	0	0	1	0	2	.261	.304
Bats Right	R	.120	25	3	1	0	0	1	0	5	.120	.160
White,Devon	L	.230	100	23	7	0	1	13	6	23	.287	.330
Bats Both	R	.300	327	98	16	5	9	40	23	74	.348	.462
White,Rondell	L	.377	122	46	15	0	2	18	12	17	.437	.549
Bats Right	R	.267	352	94	18	4	11	39	29	70	.328	.435
Whiten,Mark	L	.209	110	23	1	1	6	15	12	30	.285	.400
Bats Both	R	.257	210	54	12	0	6	32	27	56	.345	.400
Whitmore,D	L	.000	6	0	0	0	0	0	1	3	.143	.000
Bats Left	R	.212	52	11	2	0	1	2	4	12	.263	.308
Widger,Chris	L	.136	22	3	0	0	1	1	0	6	.136	.273
Bats Right	R	.261	23	6	0	0	0	1	3	5	.333	.261
Wilkins,Rick	L	.158	38	6	0	0	1	3	10	13	.327	.237
Bats Left	R	.213	164	35	3	0	6	16	36	48	.356	.341
Williams,B	L	.303	195	59	11	3	13	35	23	29	.378	.590
Bats Both	R	.310	368	114	18	6	5	47	52	69	.399	.432
Williams,E	L	.288	118	34	4	0	7	19	10	16	.341	.500
Bats Right	R	.242	178	43	7	1	5	28	13	31	.306	.376
Williams,G	L	.310	29	9	3	0	1	7	2	6	.344	.517
Bats Both	R	.280	50	14	2	1	2	7	9	15	.403	.480
Williams,G	L	.278	126	35	13	2	4	19	20	24	.378	.508
Bats Right	R	.179	56	10	5	0	2	9	2	10	.200	.375
Williams,Matt	L	.377	53	20	5	0	6	16	9	9	.468	.811
Bats Right	R	.326	230	75	12	1	17	49	21	49	.383	.609
Williams,R	L	.000	2	0	0	0	0	0	1	1	.333	.000
Bats Both	R	.111	9	1	0	0	0	1	1	2	.200	.111
Wilson,Dan	L	.235	102	24	3	0	3	16	10	13	.304	.353
Bats Right	R	.293	297	87	19	3	6	35	23	50	.347	.438
Wilson,Nigel	L	.000	1	0	0	0	0	0	0	0	.000	.000
Bats Left	R	.000	6	0	0	0	0	0	0	4	.000	.000
Winfield,Dave	L	.154	65	10	3	0	1	3	9	13	.257	.246
Bats Right	R	.240	50	12	2	0	1	1	5	13	.321	.340
Worthington,C	L	.300	40	12	3	0	2	6	7	3	.404	.525
Bats Right	R	.174	46	8	2	0	1	2	2	6	.208	.283
Young,Eric	L	.400	125	50	11	4	4	21	11	9	.449	.648
Bats Right	R	.274	241	66	10	5	2	15	38	20	.382	.382
Young,Ernie	L	.250	12	3	1	0	1	1	2	1	.357	.583
Bats Right	R	.184	38	7	2	0	1	4	6	11	.295	.316
Young,Kevin	L	.156	64	10	1	0	3	8	2	19	.191	.313
Bats Right	R	.274	117	32	8	0	3	14	6	34	.310	.419
Zaun,Greg	L	.241	29	7	1	0	1	2	5	4	.353	.379
Bats Both	R	.267	75	20	4	0	2	12	11	10	.360	.400
Zeile,Todd	L	.170	106	18	7	0	3	10	8	12	.226	.321
Bats Right	R	.272	320	87	15	0	11	42	26	64	.331	.422
Zosky,Eddie	L	.333	3	1	0	0	0	0	0	0	.333	.333
Bats Right	R	.000	2	0	0	0	0	0	0	0	.000	.000
AL	L	.268	--	--	--	--	--	--	--	--	.343	.421
	R	.271	--	--	--	--	--	--	--	--	.345	.429
NL	L	.268	--	--	--	--	--	--	--	--	.334	.417
	R	.262	--	--	--	--	--	--	--	--	.331	.404
MLB	L	.268	--	--	--	--	--	--	--	--	.338	.419
	R	.266	--	--	--	--	--	--	--	--	.338	.417

Pitchers vs. Left-Handed and Right-Handed Batters

Pitcher	vs	Avg	AB	H	2B	3B	HR	BI	BB	SO	OBP	SLG
Abbott,Jim	L	.285	144	41	4	1	2	14	11	10	.340	.368
Throws Left	R	.271	620	168	29	0	12	65	53	76	.327	.376
Abbott,Kyle	L	.276	29	8	1	0	1	6	5	5	.371	.414
Throws Left	R	.263	76	20	4	0	2	9	11	16	.356	.395
Acevedo,Juan	L	.385	104	40	10	0	6	23	10	11	.435	.654
Throws Right	R	.271	155	42	6	0	9	26	10	29	.337	.484
Acre,Mark	L	.247	93	23	3	0	2	15	16	28	.369	.344
Throws Right	R	.264	110	29	4	4	5	26	12	19	.331	.509
Adams,Terry	L	.259	27	7	1	1	0	7	7	7	.412	.370
Throws Right	R	.306	49	15	4	2	0	7	3	8	.346	.469
Aguilera,Rick	L	.205	117	24	3	0	2	13	6	32	.244	.282
Throws Right	R	.253	87	22	5	0	4	8	7	20	.305	.448
Ahearne,Pat	L	.375	32	12	1	0	1	6	4	1	.444	.500
Throws Right	R	.444	18	8	2	0	1	5	1	3	.474	.722
Alberro,Jose	L	.295	44	13	0	0	1	9	6	4	.380	.364
Throws Right	R	.302	43	13	2	1	1	12	6	6	.392	.465
Alvarez,Tavo	L	.316	76	24	6	1	1	11	9	7	.395	.461
Throws Right	R	.278	79	22	3	2	1	10	5	10	.337	.405
Alvarez,W	L	.296	108	32	2	3	2	18	14	20	.379	.426
Throws Left	R	.250	555	139	23	5	19	70	79	98	.343	.413
Anderson,B	L	.342	79	27	3	1	6	19	1	11	.354	.633
Throws Left	R	.267	311	83	14	2	18	38	29	34	.329	.498
Anderson,S	L	.408	49	20	6	1	1	7	3	3	.442	.633
Throws Right	R	.176	51	9	3	0	2	5	5	3	.263	.353
Andujar,Luis	L	.246	61	15	4	0	1	4	7	6	.324	.361
Throws Right	R	.212	52	11	4	0	3	8	7	3	.317	.462
Appier,Kevin	L	.253	427	108	21	9	11	53	52	87	.337	.422
Throws Right	R	.177	311	55	13	1	3	26	28	98	.254	.254
Aquino,Luis	L	.313	83	26	7	0	5	23	8	13	.374	.578
Throws Right	R	.316	98	31	8	0	1	19	5	13	.364	.429
Arocha,Rene	L	.278	97	27	5	0	3	14	8	11	.336	.423
Throws Right	R	.318	88	28	5	3	3	13	10	14	.396	.545
Ashby,Andy	L	.273	330	90	19	0	5	29	28	59	.334	.376
Throws Right	R	.236	382	90	11	1	12	40	34	91	.309	.364
Assenmacher,P	L	.177	62	11	0	0	1	4	4	21	.227	.226
Throws Left	R	.263	80	21	5	0	2	7	8	19	.344	.400
Astacio,Pedro	L	.258	194	50	10	2	8	24	16	34	.319	.454
Throws Right	R	.264	201	53	9	0	4	25	13	46	.312	.368
Ausanio,Joe	L	.246	65	16	2	1	3	14	7	22	.315	.446
Throws Right	R	.317	82	26	4	0	6	17	16	14	.424	.585
Avery,Steve	L	.194	93	18	5	0	0	7	11	29	.283	.247
Throws Left	R	.261	563	147	29	5	22	77	41	112	.315	.448
Ayala,Bobby	L	.229	175	40	10	1	5	31	19	49	.307	.383
Throws Right	R	.317	104	33	8	1	4	19	11	28	.403	.529
Bailey,Cory	L	.200	5	1	0	0	0	0	0	2	.200	.200
Throws Right	R	.125	8	1	0	0	0	3	2	3	.300	.125
Bailey,Roger	L	.258	132	34	9	3	1	17	24	19	.372	.394
Throws Right	R	.302	179	54	14	1	8	28	15	14	.355	.525
Baker,Scott	L	.429	7	3	0	0	0	3	3	2	.583	.429
Throws Left	R	.250	8	2	1	0	0	1	2	1	.400	.375

Pitcher	vs	Avg	AB	H	2B	3B	HR	BI	BB	SO	OBP	SLG
Baldwin,James	L	.447	38	17	4	0	2	9	7	4	.533	.711
Throws Right	R	.441	34	15	3	0	4	12	2	6	.472	.882
Bankhead,S	L	.308	65	20	5	0	4	14	5	6	.357	.569
Throws Right	R	.258	93	24	4	0	5	15	11	14	.333	.462
Banks,Willie	L	.289	166	48	3	0	8	33	24	28	.375	.452
Throws Right	R	.297	195	58	11	1	6	28	34	34	.405	.456
Barber,Brian	L	.368	38	14	2	0	1	6	10	8	.500	.500
Throws Right	R	.233	73	17	2	0	3	12	6	19	.280	.384
Bark,Brian	L	.250	4	1	0	0	0	0	0	0	.250	.250
Throws Left	R	.333	3	1	0	0	0	0	1	0	.500	.333
Barton,Shawn	L	.242	62	15	3	0	0	9	7	9	.315	.290
Throws Left	R	.234	94	22	4	0	3	14	12	13	.327	.372
Bautista,Jose	L	.323	161	52	9	1	9	35	16	15	.380	.553
Throws Right	R	.276	246	68	19	2	15	47	10	30	.314	.553
Beck,Rod	L	.275	109	30	3	1	3	22	12	15	.339	.404
Throws Right	R	.259	116	30	2	0	4	13	9	27	.323	.379
Bedrosian,S	L	.333	39	13	0	0	3	14	4	7	.400	.564
Throws Right	R	.365	74	27	6	0	3	18	8	15	.422	.568
Belcher,Tim	L	.268	425	114	19	6	9	45	52	48	.350	.405
Throws Right	R	.269	275	74	19	3	10	39	36	48	.356	.469
Belinda,Stan	L	.209	110	23	5	0	3	12	17	25	.310	.336
Throws Right	R	.201	139	28	7	0	2	21	11	32	.276	.295
Benes,Alan	L	.529	34	18	2	1	0	7	3	6	.579	.647
Throws Right	R	.167	36	6	0	0	2	4	1	14	.189	.333
Benes,Andy	L	.283	381	108	20	4	7	50	52	81	.371	.412
Throws Right	R	.256	332	85	15	3	11	45	26	90	.311	.419
Benitez,A	L	.239	67	16	3	1	2	6	18	21	.420	.403
Throws Right	R	.196	107	21	3	0	6	27	19	35	.321	.393
Bennett,Erik	L	.000	1	0	0	0	0	0	0	0	.000	.000
Throws Right	R	.000	0	0	0	0	0	0	0	0	.000	.000
Bere,Jason	L	.306	284	87	16	1	9	47	70	59	.443	.465
Throws Right	R	.245	261	64	7	1	12	53	36	51	.340	.418
Bergman,Sean	L	.319	335	107	15	3	15	65	41	51	.394	.516
Throws Right	R	.287	216	62	12	0	4	21	26	35	.368	.398
Bertotti,Mike	L	.500	12	6	2	0	2	4	0	2	.500	1.167
Throws Left	R	.333	51	17	4	1	4	15	11	13	.455	.686
Berumen,A	L	.229	70	16	0	1	2	19	18	20	.385	.343
Throws Right	R	.223	94	21	1	1	1	12	18	22	.357	.287
Bielecki,Mike	L	.238	172	41	5	0	9	23	17	30	.307	.424
Throws Right	R	.322	121	39	4	1	6	27	14	15	.393	.521
Birkbeck,Mike	L	.156	45	7	1	0	0	0	0	8	.156	.178
Throws Right	R	.273	55	15	1	1	2	3	2	6	.298	.436
Black,Bud	L	.371	35	13	5	0	3	15	1	2	.368	.771
Throws Left	R	.305	164	50	14	0	5	25	15	32	.361	.482
Blair,Willie	L	.270	163	44	8	2	5	23	27	26	.372	.436
Throws Right	R	.257	265	68	6	4	6	38	18	57	.308	.377
Blomdahl,Ben	L	.351	57	20	2	0	2	12	6	7	.413	.491
Throws Right	R	.364	44	16	3	0	3	9	7	8	.451	.636
Bochtler,Doug	L	.250	56	14	3	1	2	8	10	14	.364	.446
Throws Right	R	.233	103	24	5	0	3	12	9	31	.292	.369

Pitchers vs. Left-Handed and Right-Handed Batters

Pitcher	vs	Avg	AB	H	2B	3B	HR	BI	BB	SO	OBP	SLG
Boehringer,B	L	.333	42	14	3	2	2	12	9	5	.451	.643
Throws Right	R	.303	33	10	2	0	3	7	13	5	.500	.636
Boever,Joe	L	.299	221	66	10	1	10	52	28	40	.370	.489
Throws Right	R	.344	180	62	14	2	7	36	16	31	.401	.561
Bohanon,Brian	L	.250	128	32	5	0	3	16	11	18	.310	.359
Throws Left	R	.301	296	89	28	2	7	51	30	45	.367	.480
Bolton,Rodney	L	.346	52	18	3	0	2	9	11	3	.460	.519
Throws Right	R	.357	42	15	3	1	2	10	3	7	.391	.619
Bones,Ricky	L	.281	449	126	22	2	10	49	42	33	.339	.405
Throws Right	R	.281	327	92	21	3	16	48	41	44	.362	.511
Borbon,Pedro	L	.167	42	7	0	0	1	3	2	13	.205	.238
Throws Left	R	.278	79	22	8	1	1	10	15	20	.396	.443
Borland,Toby	L	.295	122	36	3	0	1	16	12	19	.365	.344
Throws Right	R	.265	170	45	10	1	2	19	25	40	.367	.371
Borowski,Joe	L	.222	9	2	0	0	0	0	1	0	.300	.222
Throws Right	R	.176	17	3	0	0	0	2	3	3	.300	.176
Bosio,Chris	L	.313	377	118	22	6	5	46	40	29	.379	.443
Throws Right	R	.312	298	93	20	1	13	41	29	56	.369	.517
Boskie,Shawn	L	.285	246	70	17	2	8	37	18	32	.339	.467
Throws Right	R	.277	206	57	16	1	8	31	7	19	.306	.481
Bottalico,R	L	.186	113	21	1	1	3	15	25	26	.331	.292
Throws Right	R	.155	187	29	4	1	4	22	17	61	.240	.251
Bowen,Ryan	L	.306	36	11	0	1	1	4	8	7	.432	.444
Throws Right	R	.353	34	12	3	0	2	6	4	8	.400	.618
Brandenburg,M	L	.279	61	17	4	0	1	8	4	11	.328	.393
Throws Right	R	.358	53	19	1	0	4	13	3	10	.393	.604
Brantley,Jeff	L	.227	119	27	5	0	7	15	16	30	.314	.445
Throws Right	R	.188	138	26	3	0	4	12	4	32	.215	.297
Brewer,Billy	L	.299	77	23	1	1	5	18	8	15	.372	.532
Throws Left	R	.284	109	31	3	0	4	22	12	16	.361	.422
Brewington,J	L	.199	136	27	5	1	2	12	28	28	.333	.294
Throws Right	R	.291	141	41	10	0	6	22	17	17	.376	.489
Briscoe,John	L	.286	35	10	1	0	1	11	8	11	.413	.400
Throws Right	R	.405	37	15	4	0	3	12	13	8	.569	.757
Brocail,Doug	L	.313	131	41	4	1	5	19	13	17	.384	.473
Throws Right	R	.256	180	46	10	1	5	23	9	22	.297	.406
Bronkey,Jeff	L	.250	20	5	1	0	0	3	2	1	.318	.300
Throws Right	R	.357	28	10	3	0	0	3	4	4	.438	.464
Brown,Kevin	L	.247	364	90	12	4	5	34	31	49	.311	.343
Throws Right	R	.234	278	65	10	2	5	25	17	68	.291	.338
Browning,Tom	L	.000	3	0	0	0	0	0	0	1	.000	.000
Throws Left	R	.325	40	13	4	0	2	8	5	2	.400	.575
Bruske,Jim	L	.200	15	3	0	0	0	1	2	3	.294	.200
Throws Right	R	.360	25	9	2	1	0	8	2	2	.429	.520
Bullinger,Jim	L	.273	264	72	15	3	5	36	41	32	.377	.409
Throws Right	R	.258	310	80	13	2	9	36	24	61	.318	.400
Bunch,Mel	L	.253	91	23	4	1	6	16	9	10	.320	.516
Throws Right	R	.271	70	19	4	0	5	8	5	9	.320	.543
Burba,Dave	L	.272	158	43	8	1	5	29	23	28	.363	.430
Throws Right	R	.198	237	47	11	0	4	19	28	68	.283	.295
Burgos,E	L	.778	9	7	1	0	1	2	2	1	.818	1.222
Throws Left	R	.250	28	7	1	0	0	3	4	11	.364	.286
Burkett,John	L	.274	361	99	18	8	6	39	33	67	.338	.418
Throws Right	R	.290	376	109	19	4	16	47	24	59	.339	.489
Burrows,Terry	L	.349	63	22	2	0	3	12	4	9	.397	.524
Throws Left	R	.309	123	38	6	0	8	21	15	13	.388	.553
Butcher,Mike	L	.337	83	28	6	0	2	12	16	7	.440	.482
Throws Right	R	.194	108	21	3	2	5	22	15	22	.294	.398
Byrd,Paul	L	.333	33	11	3	0	0	6	2	8	.378	.424
Throws Right	R	.146	48	7	3	0	1	2	5	18	.222	.271
Campbell,K	L	.167	18	3	0	0	0	1	2	1	.250	.167
Throws Right	R	.313	16	5	1	0	0	3	3	4	.421	.375
Candiotti,Tom	L	.267	330	88	16	1	7	27	36	62	.340	.385
Throws Right	R	.246	402	99	20	1	11	56	22	79	.296	.383
Carmona,R	L	.340	106	36	10	2	5	24	18	15	.423	.613
Throws Right	R	.232	82	19	4	0	4	12	16	13	.364	.427
Carrara,G	L	.338	130	44	2	2	5	32	18	17	.420	.500
Throws Right	R	.290	69	20	6	0	5	13	7	10	.351	.594
Carrasco,H	L	.288	146	42	8	2	0	18	22	23	.378	.370
Throws Right	R	.233	189	44	8	0	1	18	24	41	.318	.291
Carter,Andy	L	.200	5	1	0	0	1	2	0	3	.286	.800
Throws Left	R	.158	19	3	0	0	2	2	2	3	.238	.474
Casian,Larry	L	.308	52	16	2	1	0	7	5	7	.362	.385
Throws Left	R	.189	37	7	0	0	1	5	10	4	.354	.270
Castillo,F	L	.256	309	79	13	1	6	23	31	66	.325	.362
Throws Right	R	.242	414	100	10	1	16	46	21	69	.285	.386
Castillo,Tony	L	.263	80	21	3	1	1	21	8	13	.344	.363
Throws Left	R	.235	183	43	6	2	6	29	16	25	.293	.388
Charlton,Norm	L	.195	77	15	1	0	1	7	11	17	.308	.247
Throws Left	R	.187	166	31	3	1	3	18	20	53	.280	.271
Christiansen,J	L	.207	82	17	5	0	2	18	13	22	.327	.341
Throws Left	R	.252	127	32	9	0	3	16	21	31	.358	.394
Christopher,M	L	.331	118	39	10	0	7	20	9	14	.375	.593
Throws Right	R	.256	125	32	5	2	1	9	5	20	.293	.352
Clark,Mark	L	.318	283	90	22	3	10	47	21	39	.364	.523
Throws Right	R	.248	214	53	13	1	3	23	21	29	.320	.360
Clark,Terry	L	.309	68	21	7	0	1	12	9	11	.397	.456
Throws Right	R	.244	90	22	4	1	2	12	11	11	.324	.378
Clemens,Roger	L	.257	303	78	14	1	7	32	33	78	.349	.380
Throws Right	R	.261	241	63	10	1	8	30	27	54	.343	.411
Clontz,Brad	L	.344	93	32	6	1	1	19	12	16	.421	.462
Throws Right	R	.228	171	39	5	0	4	14	10	39	.281	.327
Cone,David	L	.233	497	116	22	2	13	52	55	100	.311	.364
Throws Right	R	.221	358	79	20	2	11	35	33	91	.293	.380
Converse,Jim	L	.368	38	14	3	0	2	8	6	7	.455	.605
Throws Right	R	.264	53	14	2	0	0	4	10	7	.381	.302
Cook,Dennis	L	.284	88	25	3	1	3	21	9	25	.353	.443
Throws Left	R	.292	130	38	7	3	6	23	17	28	.369	.531
Cormier,Rheal	L	.259	108	28	7	0	1	9	9	18	.316	.352
Throws Left	R	.305	338	103	18	1	11	44	22	51	.351	.462

Pitchers vs. Left-Handed and Right-Handed Batters

Pitcher	vs	Avg	AB	H	2B	3B	HR	BI	BB	SO	OBP	SLG	Pitcher	vs	Avg	AB	H	2B	3B	HR	BI	BB	SO	OBP	SLG
Cornelius,R	L	.308	133	41	7	1	7	22	10	19	.359	.534	Drabek,Doug	L	.289	381	110	21	3	10	44	30	75	.343	.438
Throws Right	R	.268	127	34	7	0	4	18	20	20	.371	.417	Throws Right	R	.274	347	95	15	5	8	52	24	68	.330	.415
Cornett,Brad	L	.500	12	6	1	0	0	2	2	3	.571	.583	Dunbar,Matt	L	.267	15	4	0	0	0	4	5	2	.450	.267
Throws Right	R	.333	9	3	1	0	1	1	1	1	.455	.778	Throws Left	R	.500	16	8	2	0	0	3	6	3	.652	.625
Corsi,Jim	L	.213	80	17	2	1	0	7	15	10	.333	.263	Dyer,Mike	L	.358	95	34	7	0	4	19	11	10	.440	.558
Throws Right	R	.192	73	14	3	0	2	6	11	16	.314	.315	Throws Right	R	.244	193	47	8	0	5	21	19	43	.316	.363
Courtright,J	L	.500	2	1	0	0	0	1	0	0	.500	.500	Eckersley,D	L	.347	121	42	10	0	3	21	8	20	.386	.504
Throws Left	R	.500	2	1	0	0	0	0	0	0	.500	.500	Throws Right	R	.145	76	11	2	0	2	7	3	20	.177	.250
Cox,Danny	L	.293	92	27	6	0	3	20	17	22	.400	.457	Eddy,Chris	L	.333	6	2	0	0	0	2	0	0	.429	.333
Throws Right	R	.341	88	30	7	0	1	9	16	16	.439	.455	Throws Left	R	.500	10	5	1	0	0	4	2	2	.615	.600
Crabtree,Tim	L	.296	71	21	5	0	1	9	5	16	.346	.408	Edenfield,Ken	L	.316	19	6	2	0	1	2	2	3	.381	.579
Throws Right	R	.167	54	9	1	0	0	6	8	5	.286	.185	Throws Right	R	.290	31	9	2	0	0	6	3	3	.343	.355
Creek,Doug	L	.000	7	0	0	0	0	0	1	3	.125	.000	Edens,Tom	L	.000	2	0	0	0	0	0	0	0	.000	.000
Throws Left	R	.143	14	2	0	1	0	0	2	7	.250	.286	Throws Right	R	.462	13	6	3	0	0	3	3	2	.563	.692
Cummings,John	L	.306	62	19	2	0	1	7	2	8	.328	.387	Eiland,Dave	L	.333	21	7	2	0	0	3	1	3	.364	.429
Throws Left	R	.245	110	27	9	0	2	12	15	17	.328	.382	Throws Right	R	.360	25	9	3	0	1	7	2	3	.414	.600
Daal,Omar	L	.267	45	12	2	0	0	9	6	6	.346	.311	Eischen,Joey	L	.156	32	5	2	0	1	6	5	7	.270	.313
Throws Left	R	.459	37	17	3	0	1	4	9	5	.574	.622	Throws Left	R	.280	50	14	0	0	0	2	6	8	.379	.280
Darling,Ron	L	.310	245	76	12	2	10	41	20	41	.364	.498	Eldred,Cal	L	.283	46	13	0	1	3	6	5	10	.365	.522
Throws Right	R	.276	174	48	10	1	6	26	26	28	.365	.448	Throws Right	R	.239	46	11	1	0	1	3	5	8	.314	.326
Darwin,Danny	L	.344	253	87	16	3	11	36	22	25	.399	.561	Elliott,D	L	.333	3	1	1	0	0	0	1	1	.500	.667
Throws Right	R	.289	152	44	7	1	14	38	9	33	.329	.625	Throws Right	R	.200	5	1	0	0	0	0	0	2	.200	.200
Davis,Tim	L	.150	20	3	0	0	1	6	2	7	.227	.300	Embree,Alan	L	.217	23	5	2	0	1	4	5	12	.357	.435
Throws Left	R	.346	78	27	7	1	1	11	16	12	.453	.500	Throws Left	R	.265	68	18	2	1	1	11	11	11	.358	.368
Davison,Scott	L	.357	14	5	0	0	1	3	1	2	.400	.571	Ericks,John	L	.285	207	59	7	1	4	23	27	35	.366	.386
Throws Right	R	.333	6	2	0	0	0	0	0	1	.333	.333	Throws Right	R	.241	203	49	10	1	3	29	23	45	.319	.345
Dedrick,Jim	L	.286	7	2	0	1	0	1	3	1	.545	.571	Erickson,S	L	.287	478	137	26	2	10	61	41	55	.344	.412
Throws Right	R	.316	19	6	3	0	1	5	3	2	.375	.632	Throws Right	R	.271	280	76	22	1	8	34	26	51	.339	.443
DeLeon,Jose	L	.276	123	34	5	2	2	19	16	24	.356	.398	Eshelman,V	L	.367	49	18	6	0	0	5	6	8	.436	.490
Throws Right	R	.208	159	33	6	0	10	25	19	41	.308	.434	Throws Left	R	.255	267	68	14	2	3	33	30	33	.329	.356
DeLucia,Rich	L	.237	114	27	7	1	5	15	21	20	.353	.447	Estes,Shawn	L	.250	8	2	0	0	0	2	2	3	.455	.250
Throws Right	R	.198	182	36	3	0	4	21	15	56	.269	.280	Throws Left	R	.226	62	14	2	0	2	8	3	11	.262	.355
Deshaies,Jim	L	.750	4	3	0	0	0	3	0	0	.750	.750	Eversgerd,B	L	.269	26	7	3	0	0	6	0	2	.296	.385
Throws Left	R	.444	27	12	3	0	3	7	1	6	.464	.889	Throws Left	R	.268	56	15	4	0	2	14	9	6	.358	.446
DeSilva,John	L	.143	21	3	0	0	1	3	3	1	.240	.286	Fajardo,H	L	.250	32	8	2	1	2	12	1	4	.294	.563
Throws Right	R	.500	10	5	0	2	2	4	4	0	.667	1.500	Throws Right	R	.379	29	11	1	0	0	3	4	5	.455	.414
Dettmer,John	L	1.000	1	1	0	0	0	1	0	0	.500	1.000	Farrell,John	L	.500	12	6	1	0	0	3	0	2	.462	.583
Throws Right	R	.500	2	1	0	0	0	0	0	0	.500	.500	Throws Right	R	.143	7	1	0	0	0	1	0	2	.143	.143
Dewey,Mark	L	.389	36	14	3	0	2	7	7	6	.488	.639	Fassero,Jeff	L	.175	103	18	3	1	0	10	6	29	.221	.223
Throws Right	R	.195	82	16	5	0	0	8	10	26	.280	.256	Throws Left	R	.301	628	189	36	7	15	79	68	135	.368	.452
Dibble,Rob	L	.150	40	6	0	0	1	10	25	12	.478	.225	Fermin,Ramon	L	.000	3	0	0	0	0	1	1	0	.250	.000
Throws Right	R	.222	45	10	1	1	1	13	21	14	.451	.356	Throws Right	R	.800	5	4	0	0	0	3	0	0	.800	.800
DiPoto,Jerry	L	.268	123	33	5	0	0	14	18	17	.366	.309	Fernandez,A	L	.277	412	114	21	6	11	51	38	91	.336	.437
Throws Right	R	.267	165	44	8	1	2	24	11	32	.319	.344	Throws Right	R	.232	371	86	12	2	8	38	27	68	.282	.340
Dishman,Glenn	L	.167	66	11	4	1	1	7	11	9	.300	.303	Fernandez,Sid	L	.135	52	7	0	0	1	2	4	16	.196	.192
Throws Left	R	.302	308	93	19	0	10	40	23	34	.352	.461	Throws Left	R	.252	306	77	16	1	19	45	34	94	.327	.447
Doherty,John	L	.325	234	76	17	1	7	30	22	29	.390	.496	Fetters,Mike	L	.297	74	22	5	0	2	16	11	16	.388	.446
Throws Right	R	.249	217	54	9	0	3	30	15	17	.304	.332	Throws Right	R	.273	66	18	5	0	1	7	9	17	.355	.394
Dougherty,Jim	L	.420	88	37	5	1	5	23	15	12	.509	.670	Finley,Chuck	L	.248	113	28	2	0	1	15	9	27	.312	.292
Throws Right	R	.227	172	39	6	1	2	19	10	37	.270	.308	Throws Left	R	.249	658	164	38	3	19	82	84	168	.337	.403

Pitchers vs. Left-Handed and Right-Handed Batters

Pitcher	vs	Avg	AB	H	2B	3B	HR	BI	BB	SO	OBP	SLG	Pitcher	vs	Avg	AB	H	2B	3B	HR	BI	BB	SO	OBP	SLG
Fleming,Dave	L	.214	70	15	1	0	3	7	10	14	.313	.357	Greer,Kenny	L	.250	16	4	0	0	0	2	2	1	.316	.250
Throws Left	R	.285	242	69	14	1	16	49	43	26	.392	.550	Throws Right	R	.306	36	11	2	0	3	6	3	6	.375	.611
Fletcher,Paul	L	.333	18	6	1	0	0	1	5	1	.458	.389	Grimsley,J	L	.315	73	23	5	0	3	15	10	12	.398	.507
Throws Right	R	.265	34	9	2	0	2	7	4	9	.359	.500	Throws Right	R	.255	55	14	6	1	1	10	22	13	.469	.455
Florence,Don	L	.364	22	8	0	1	0	3	3	3	.440	.455	Groom,Buddy	L	.348	66	23	4	0	2	18	12	9	.457	.500
Throws Left	R	.321	28	9	0	0	0	3	3	2	.387	.321	Throws Left	R	.341	170	58	8	1	6	31	20	26	.408	.506
Florie,Bryce	L	.202	109	22	0	1	2	10	18	20	.318	.275	Gross,Kevin	L	.280	378	106	17	5	11	52	39	56	.347	.439
Throws Right	R	.203	133	27	2	2	6	24	20	48	.321	.383	Throws Right	R	.278	338	94	15	1	16	49	50	50	.378	.470
Fortugno,Tim	L	.218	55	12	2	1	2	9	7	9	.306	.400	Grott,Matt	L	.500	4	2	1	0	0	2	0	0	.500	.750
Throws Left	R	.209	86	18	1	0	5	13	12	15	.300	.395	Throws Left	R	.571	7	4	1	1	1	4	0	2	.571	1.429
Fossas,Tony	L	.181	72	13	5	0	0	8	2	27	.203	.250	Guardado,E	L	.223	121	27	3	0	2	15	6	34	.254	.298
Throws Left	R	.254	59	15	2	0	1	7	8	13	.348	.339	Throws Left	R	.309	233	72	10	2	11	42	39	37	.405	.511
Foster,Kevin	L	.260	288	75	13	0	12	28	28	65	.323	.431	Gubicza,Mark	L	.270	455	123	20	3	9	49	32	33	.320	.387
Throws Right	R	.222	334	74	15	1	20	51	37	81	.308	.452	Throws Right	R	.275	360	99	23	0	12	38	30	48	.333	.439
Franco,John	L	.281	32	9	2	0	0	3	2	9	.314	.344	Guetterman,L	L	.267	30	8	1	0	0	3	3	6	.333	.300
Throws Left	R	.245	159	39	9	0	4	17	15	32	.310	.377	Throws Left	R	.325	40	13	3	1	1	8	8	5	.471	.525
Frascatore,J	L	.275	51	14	4	0	1	8	10	11	.403	.412	Gunderson,E	L	.250	64	16	5	0	2	13	5	16	.319	.422
Throws Right	R	.313	80	25	6	1	2	10	6	10	.364	.488	Throws Left	R	.301	73	22	9	1	0	7	12	12	.402	.452
Fraser,Willie	L	.277	47	13	2	1	3	6	6	5	.358	.553	Guthrie,Mark	L	.245	94	23	1	0	2	13	7	30	.297	.319
Throws Right	R	.222	54	12	1	0	3	13	3	7	.300	.407	Throws Left	R	.293	147	43	7	2	4	19	18	37	.377	.449
Freeman,M	L	.351	194	68	12	3	8	34	23	21	.419	.567	Guzman,Juan	L	.299	298	89	13	3	5	48	45	41	.390	.413
Throws Right	R	.284	190	54	8	1	7	21	18	40	.347	.447	Throws Right	R	.258	240	62	14	2	8	36	28	53	.342	.433
Frey,Steve	L	.275	51	14	2	0	1	5	5	10	.328	.373	Habyan,John	L	.264	106	28	7	0	1	9	11	14	.333	.358
Throws Left	R	.231	52	12	3	0	1	5	5	4	.310	.346	Throws Right	R	.240	167	40	16	0	1	18	16	46	.308	.353
Garces,Rich	L	.333	39	13	3	0	0	5	3	3	.381	.410	Hall,Darren	L	.257	35	9	0	0	1	4	5	6	.350	.343
Throws Right	R	.211	57	12	1	0	1	6	8	19	.308	.281	Throws Right	R	.364	33	12	1	1	1	5	4	5	.432	.545
Gardiner,Mike	L	.500	32	16	2	1	3	14	1	4	.486	.906	Hamilton,Joey	L	.229	340	78	9	2	9	36	27	49	.290	.347
Throws Right	R	.407	27	11	1	2	2	6	1	3	.429	.815	Throws Right	R	.260	427	111	13	3	8	42	29	74	.318	.361
Gardner,Mark	L	.274	168	46	8	1	6	16	26	25	.378	.440	Hammaker,A	L	.364	11	4	0	0	1	3	3	2	.533	.636
Throws Right	R	.270	233	63	16	2	8	36	17	62	.328	.459	Throws Left	R	.412	17	7	0	0	1	4	5	1	.545	.588
Givens,Brian	L	.212	66	14	4	0	0	4	11	14	.325	.273	Hammond,Chris	L	.217	106	23	3	1	2	12	5	26	.259	.321
Throws Left	R	.287	356	102	23	3	11	58	43	59	.367	.461	Throws Left	R	.264	507	134	36	2	15	53	42	100	.327	.432
Glavine,Tom	L	.313	134	42	7	0	2	17	16	28	.391	.410	Hampton,Mike	L	.272	114	31	5	1	3	14	11	21	.346	.412
Throws Left	R	.231	605	140	27	2	7	51	50	99	.292	.317	Throws Left	R	.240	458	110	17	2	10	46	38	94	.298	.352
Gohr,Greg	L	.350	20	7	3	0	0	0	1	3	.381	.500	Hancock,Lee	L	.118	17	2	0	0	0	2	1	2	.167	.118
Throws Right	R	.118	17	2	0	0	0	1	2	9	.211	.118	Throws Left	R	.235	34	8	1	0	0	2	1	4	.257	.265
Gomez,Pat	L	.381	21	8	1	0	0	7	2	4	.435	.429	Haney,Chris	L	.184	49	9	2	0	0	1	8	4	.298	.224
Throws Left	R	.216	37	8	1	0	2	6	10	11	.383	.405	Throws Left	R	.277	249	69	9	2	7	32	25	27	.343	.414
Gordon,Tom	L	.316	395	125	15	1	5	54	52	61	.392	.397	Hansell,Greg	L	.364	33	12	2	0	3	10	3	7	.447	.697
Throws Right	R	.235	336	79	15	0	7	32	37	58	.312	.342	Throws Right	R	.340	50	17	2	0	2	13	3	6	.370	.500
Gott,Jim	L	.296	54	16	4	2	0	10	8	5	.387	.444	Hanson,Erik	L	.215	409	88	11	2	7	43	29	83	.266	.303
Throws Right	R	.282	78	22	6	0	2	9	4	14	.321	.436	Throws Right	R	.312	317	99	23	2	10	40	30	56	.369	.492
Grace,Mike	L	.348	23	8	1	0	0	1	3	2	.423	.391	Harikkala,Tim	L	.375	8	3	1	0	0	2	0	1	.375	.500
Throws Right	R	.105	19	2	0	0	0	1	1	5	.150	.105	Throws Right	R	.444	9	4	0	0	1	4	1	0	.500	.778
Grahe,Joe	L	.313	112	35	6	0	3	14	12	8	.389	.446	Harkey,Mike	L	.306	281	86	15	0	16	41	34	29	.382	.454
Throws Right	R	.291	117	34	8	0	3	17	15	19	.368	.436	Throws Right	R	.296	233	69	14	2	8	29	13	27	.337	.476
Green,Tyler	L	.304	224	68	11	2	7	40	36	34	.402	.464	Harnisch,Pete	L	.302	199	60	16	2	6	26	14	34	.350	.492
Throws Right	R	.280	318	89	14	2	8	35	30	51	.342	.412	Throws Right	R	.226	226	51	11	1	7	24	10	48	.257	.376
Greene,Tommy	L	.357	70	25	9	0	3	16	11	9	.451	.614	Harris,Gene	L	.182	33	6	0	0	0	1	6	2	.308	.182
Throws Right	R	.282	71	20	6	0	3	15	9	15	.373	.493	Throws Right	R	.309	55	17	0	1	2	9	3	11	.345	.455

Pitchers vs. Left-Handed and Right-Handed Batters

Pitcher	vs	Avg	AB	H	2B	3B	HR	BI	BB	SO	OBP	SLG	Pitcher	vs	Avg	AB	H	2B	3B	HR	BI	BB	SO	OBP	SLG
Harris,Greg	L	.294	85	25	2	0	3	10	7	18	.348	.424	Holmes,Darren	L	.179	106	19	4	2	2	16	13	21	.270	.311
Throws Right	R	.202	99	20	5	2	3	11	9	29	.275	.384	Throws Right	R	.280	143	40	6	1	1	10	15	40	.346	.357
Harris,G	L	.353	85	30	9	1	2	13	8	12	.409	.553	Holzemer,Mark	L	.267	15	4	1	0	0	3	3	3	.389	.333
Throws Right	R	.357	56	20	5	0	3	18	8	9	.424	.607	Throws Left	R	.333	21	7	0	0	1	1	4	2	.462	.476
Hartgraves,D	L	.236	55	13	4	2	0	9	5	9	.300	.382	Honeycutt,R	L	.179	84	15	2	0	0	10	5	10	.222	.202
Throws Left	R	.221	77	17	3	0	2	9	11	15	.315	.338	Throws Left	R	.296	81	24	1	0	6	18	5	11	.345	.531
Hartley,Mike	L	.250	16	4	0	0	0	4	3	1	.350	.250	Hook,Chris	L	.210	62	13	3	0	0	5	17	6	.388	.258
Throws Right	R	.273	33	9	2	0	1	7	0	5	.306	.424	Throws Right	R	.302	139	42	5	2	7	33	12	34	.359	.518
Harvey,Bryan	L	.000	0	0	0	0	0	0	1	0	1.000	.000	Hope,John	L	.400	5	2	0	0	0	1	1	1	.429	.400
Throws Right	R	1.000	2	2	0	0	1	3	0	0	1.000	2.500	Throws Right	R	.750	8	6	1	0	0	7	3	1	.857	.875
Hawkins,L	L	.355	76	27	7	2	1	12	8	4	.414	.539	Horsman,Vince	L	.417	12	5	2	0	1	6	0	1	.417	.833
Throws Right	R	.308	39	12	2	0	2	14	4	5	.364	.513	Throws Left	R	.292	24	7	1	0	1	5	4	3	.379	.458
Haynes,Jimmy	L	.147	34	5	2	0	1	1	5	9	.256	.294	Howard,Chris	L	.125	8	1	0	0	0	0	0	2	.125	.125
Throws Right	R	.128	47	6	0	0	1	4	7	13	.241	.191	Throws Left	R	.400	5	2	1	0	0	1	1	0	.429	.600
Helling,Rick	L	.320	25	8	0	0	1	5	7	2	.457	.440	Howe,Steve	L	.241	79	19	5	0	1	10	1	12	.268	.342
Throws Right	R	.360	25	9	2	0	1	5	1	3	.407	.560	Throws Left	R	.376	125	47	8	0	6	27	16	16	.448	.584
Henke,Tom	L	.192	99	19	5	0	2	5	7	27	.245	.303	Hudek,John	L	.353	34	12	1	2	3	9	2	9	.389	.765
Throws Right	R	.225	102	23	2	0	0	9	11	21	.301	.245	Throws Right	R	.163	43	7	1	0	0	1	3	20	.217	.186
Henneman,Mike	L	.283	99	28	5	1	1	13	6	19	.327	.384	Hudson,Joe	L	.324	71	23	4	0	1	14	12	9	.424	.423
Throws Right	R	.193	88	17	3	0	0	13	7	24	.258	.227	Throws Right	R	.286	105	30	4	0	1	14	11	20	.359	.352
Henry,Butch	L	.273	99	27	6	1	1	6	5	12	.314	.384	Huisman,Rick	L	.412	17	7	1	1	2	4	1	4	.444	.941
Throws Left	R	.275	385	106	20	1	10	37	23	48	.316	.410	Throws Right	R	.280	25	7	1	0	0	1	0	8	.280	.320
Henry,Doug	L	.182	99	18	2	0	2	12	14	21	.287	.263	Hurtado,Edwin	L	.294	170	50	8	0	8	33	23	13	.376	.482
Throws Right	R	.210	143	30	5	2	5	16	11	41	.265	.378	Throws Right	R	.248	125	31	8	0	3	14	17	20	.356	.384
Henry,Dwayne	L	.273	22	6	1	0	0	2	7	6	.448	.318	Ignasiak,Mike	L	.329	73	24	4	0	2	17	11	11	.414	.466
Throws Right	R	.357	14	5	1	0	0	3	3	3	.471	.429	Throws Right	R	.321	84	27	10	1	3	23	12	15	.408	.571
Hentgen,Pat	L	.298	453	135	24	4	11	71	56	69	.379	.442	Isringhausen,J	L	.301	183	55	5	1	3	15	17	22	.363	.388
Throws Right	R	.279	362	101	20	1	13	45	34	66	.343	.448	Throws Right	R	.202	163	33	1	2	3	11	14	33	.264	.288
Heredia,Gil	L	.300	207	62	8	2	4	21	5	29	.316	.415	Jackson,Danny	L	.259	58	15	3	0	1	10	7	10	.348	.362
Throws Right	R	.285	263	75	7	1	3	29	16	45	.333	.354	Throws Left	R	.311	338	105	31	2	9	62	41	42	.386	.494
Heredia,W	L	.250	24	6	2	0	1	4	5	3	.367	.458	Jackson,Mike	L	.197	66	13	1	1	3	3	11	8	.321	.333
Throws Right	R	.188	16	3	0	0	1	2	10	3	.500	.375	Throws Right	R	.223	112	25	8	1	3	15	8	33	.273	.393
Hermanson,D	L	.278	54	15	2	0	3	13	9	5	.381	.481	Jacome,Jason	L	.304	69	21	1	1	2	10	3	11	.333	.435
Throws Right	R	.282	71	20	3	0	5	14	13	14	.400	.535	Throws Left	R	.314	360	113	27	5	16	63	33	39	.371	.550
Hernandez,J	L	.308	13	4	1	0	0	3	1	2	.400	.385	James,Mike	L	.262	84	22	5	1	5	13	12	16	.361	.524
Throws Right	R	.471	17	8	4	0	2	9	2	3	.500	1.059	Throws Right	R	.221	122	27	3	0	1	17	14	20	.312	.270
Hernandez,R	L	.268	127	34	4	1	5	19	21	52	.376	.433	Jarvis,Kevin	L	.269	119	32	3	0	6	18	18	9	.362	.445
Throws Right	R	.264	110	29	5	0	4	21	7	32	.319	.418	Throws Right	R	.306	193	59	14	1	7	30	14	24	.355	.497
Hernandez,X	L	.310	129	40	10	1	5	23	16	28	.388	.519	Johns,Doug	L	.241	54	13	2	0	1	5	4	10	.300	.333
Throws Right	R	.251	219	55	10	2	3	18	15	56	.307	.356	Throws Left	R	.220	141	31	8	0	4	22	22	15	.341	.362
Hershiser,O	L	.281	349	98	21	3	12	46	29	49	.336	.461	Johnson,Randy	L	.129	85	11	3	1	0	5	6	38	.196	.188
Throws Right	R	.196	271	53	13	0	9	27	22	62	.264	.343	Throws Left	R	.209	707	148	34	3	12	54	59	256	.275	.317
Hickerson,B	L	.295	78	23	3	2	1	15	11	22	.389	.423	Johnston,Joel	L	.250	8	2	0	0	1	1	1	0	.333	.625
Throws Left	R	.354	130	46	7	1	7	32	17	18	.429	.569	Throws Right	R	.000	6	0	0	0	0	0	2	4	.333	.000
Hill,Ken	L	.278	371	103	23	3	11	49	44	27	.355	.445	Johnstone,J	L	.143	7	1	0	1	0	0	1	1	.250	.429
Throws Right	R	.280	353	99	21	3	10	47	33	71	.340	.442	Throws Right	R	.429	14	6	4	0	1	4	1	2	.467	.929
Hitchcock,S	L	.304	112	34	10	0	6	23	9	22	.363	.554	Jones,Bobby	L	.248	347	86	22	3	9	34	24	61	.299	.406
Throws Left	R	.233	520	121	17	3	16	51	59	99	.310	.369	Throws Right	R	.296	415	123	24	2	11	60	29	66	.346	.443
Hoffman,T	L	.202	99	20	2	0	3	9	11	33	.282	.313	Jones,Doug	L	.229	105	24	5	0	1	17	11	25	.302	.305
Throws Right	R	.267	105	28	7	0	7	17	3	19	.287	.533	Throws Right	R	.356	87	31	7	0	5	17	5	17	.404	.609

312

Pitchers vs. Left-Handed and Right-Handed Batters

Pitcher	vs	Avg	AB	H	2B	3B	HR	BI	BB	SO	OBP	SLG	Pitcher	vs	Avg	AB	H	2B	3B	HR	BI	BB	SO	OBP	SLG
Jones,Todd	L	.265	166	44	8	2	3	16	31	43	.375	.392	Lilliquist,D	L	.242	33	8	4	1	2	8	4	3	.316	.606
Throws Right	R	.215	209	45	8	1	5	27	21	53	.304	.335	Throws Left	R	.339	56	19	4	0	5	17	5	6	.381	.679
Jordan,R	L	.333	21	7	0	0	2	10	5	5	.500	.619	Lima,Jose	L	.305	177	54	8	0	6	23	11	17	.344	.452
Throws Left	R	.289	38	11	3	1	1	11	8	5	.396	.500	Throws Right	R	.263	118	31	8	2	4	16	7	20	.326	.466
Juden,Jeff	L	.300	90	27	4	0	3	14	14	17	.396	.444	Linton,Doug	L	.286	49	14	3	0	4	12	7	7	.375	.592
Throws Right	R	.191	136	26	8	0	3	13	17	30	.294	.316	Throws Right	R	.216	37	8	2	0	0	6	3	6	.310	.270
Kamieniecki,S	L	.244	176	43	11	1	2	13	30	21	.364	.352	Lira,Felipe	L	.262	332	87	13	4	8	35	35	55	.336	.398
Throws Right	R	.247	162	40	5	2	6	26	19	22	.326	.414	Throws Right	R	.283	226	64	19	1	9	34	21	34	.348	.496
Karchner,Matt	L	.296	54	16	1	0	0	4	3	8	.339	.315	Lloyd,Graeme	L	.239	46	11	0	0	1	2	2	6	.265	.304
Throws Right	R	.258	66	17	4	0	2	12	9	16	.333	.409	Throws Left	R	.250	68	17	2	0	3	14	6	7	.299	.412
Karl,Scott	L	.261	92	24	2	0	4	17	6	7	.317	.413	Loaiza,E	L	.276	304	84	21	0	6	46	37	41	.355	.405
Throws Left	R	.295	397	117	29	5	6	48	44	52	.365	.438	Throws Right	R	.319	379	121	22	3	15	57	18	44	.350	.512
Karp,Ryan	L	.000	2	0	0	0	0	0	1	0	.333	.000	Lomon,Kevin	L	.600	15	9	1	1	0	4	3	2	.667	.800
Throws Left	R	.200	5	1	0	0	0	1	2	2	.429	.200	Throws Right	R	.296	27	8	1	0	0	2	2	4	.345	.333
Key,Jimmy	L	.333	18	6	1	0	0	3	0	1	.333	.389	Looney,Brian	L	.600	5	3	0	0	0	1	0	0	.500	.600
Throws Left	R	.321	106	34	10	1	3	15	6	13	.354	.519	Throws Left	R	.529	17	9	3	0	1	8	4	2	.591	.882
Keyser,Brian	L	.342	202	69	13	5	3	26	12	19	.375	.500	Lopez,Albie	L	.122	41	5	1	0	1	2	3	18	.182	.220
Throws Right	R	.263	171	45	12	0	7	28	15	29	.330	.456	Throws Right	R	.286	42	12	3	0	3	7	4	4	.354	.571
Kiefer,Mark	L	.226	84	19	3	2	4	15	16	16	.350	.452	Lorraine,A	L	.167	6	1	0	0	0	0	1	1	.286	.167
Throws Right	R	.184	98	18	4	1	2	7	11	25	.266	.306	Throws Left	R	.095	21	2	1	0	0	2	1	4	.174	.143
Kile,Darryl	L	.250	216	54	6	0	3	32	47	50	.386	.319	MacDonald,Bob	L	.277	65	18	2	1	3	9	11	20	.382	.477
Throws Right	R	.232	259	60	13	4	2	25	26	63	.324	.336	Throws Left	R	.286	112	32	6	0	4	18	11	21	.355	.446
King,Kevin	L	.250	4	1	0	0	0	1	0	1	.200	.250	Maddux,Greg	L	.194	355	69	8	0	2	14	10	94	.221	.234
Throws Left	R	.462	13	6	3	0	0	4	1	2	.533	.692	Throws Right	R	.198	393	78	14	0	6	21	13	87	.227	.280
Klingenbeck,S	L	.311	183	57	12	2	9	34	20	22	.379	.546	Maddux,Mike	L	.291	182	53	14	2	2	23	11	30	.330	.423
Throws Right	R	.317	139	44	7	1	13	30	22	20	.422	.662	Throws Right	R	.229	205	47	13	1	3	27	7	39	.262	.346
Konuszewski,D	L	1.000	2	2	0	0	0	1	1	0	1.000	1.000	Magnante,Mike	L	.203	69	14	2	0	1	7	7	15	.286	.275
Throws Right	R	1.000	1	1	0	0	0	1	0	0	1.000	1.000	Throws Left	R	.313	99	31	3	0	5	22	9	13	.369	.495
Krivda,Rick	L	.308	52	16	5	1	0	3	2	10	.327	.442	Mahomes,Pat	L	.312	202	63	12	0	12	31	19	32	.372	.550
Throws Left	R	.256	234	60	19	0	9	33	23	43	.330	.453	Throws Right	R	.222	167	37	7	1	10	40	28	35	.335	.455
Kroon,Marc	L	.000	0	0	0	0	0	0	1	0	1.000	.000	Mantei,Matt	L	.267	15	4	1	0	0	7	6	5	.476	.333
Throws Right	R	.200	5	1	0	0	0	0	1	2	.333	.200	Throws Right	R	.235	34	8	2	0	1	6	7	10	.357	.382
Krueger,Bill	L	.379	29	11	0	0	1	6	1	6	.400	.483	Manzanillo,J	L	.309	55	17	3	0	2	8	4	14	.356	.473
Throws Left	R	.402	97	39	9	0	4	16	7	10	.442	.619	Throws Right	R	.253	79	20	5	0	2	9	11	11	.355	.392
Langston,Mark	L	.291	127	37	6	0	3	11	10	16	.343	.409	Manzanillo,R	L	.500	6	3	0	0	0	0	1	1	.625	.500
Throws Left	R	.269	651	175	38	2	18	86	54	126	.326	.416	Throws Left	R	.000	7	0	0	0	0	0	1	0	.125	.000
Lee,Mark	L	.204	49	10	1	0	2	9	10	12	.344	.347	Marquez,I	L	.308	13	4	0	0	3	5	0	4	.308	1.000
Throws Left	R	.273	77	21	7	1	3	8	8	15	.337	.506	Throws Right	R	.333	15	5	0	0	0	3	2	4	.412	.333
Leiper,Dave	L	.197	76	15	2	0	2	8	8	10	.274	.303	Martinez,D	L	.229	424	97	11	1	11	38	27	52	.274	.337
Throws Left	R	.258	93	24	7	0	3	15	11	12	.343	.430	Throws Right	R	.274	281	77	19	1	6	23	19	47	.344	.413
Leiter,Al	L	.254	122	31	9	0	4	16	11	29	.321	.426	Martinez,P	L	.219	366	80	16	6	8	33	41	67	.305	.361
Throws Left	R	.234	559	131	27	2	11	53	97	124	.350	.349	Throws Right	R	.236	331	78	14	3	13	36	25	107	.299	.414
Leiter,Mark	L	.241	315	76	14	2	9	33	36	48	.323	.384	Martinez,P	L	.364	44	16	3	0	1	8	5	7	.442	.500
Throws Right	R	.263	414	109	27	0	10	48	19	81	.315	.401	Throws Left	R	.295	44	13	3	0	2	13	11	10	.436	.500
Leskanic,Curt	L	.242	157	38	8	2	4	19	20	47	.324	.395	Martinez,R	L	.253	320	81	12	2	8	34	55	47	.362	.378
Throws Right	R	.213	211	45	10	1	3	17	9	40	.259	.313	Throws Right	R	.215	441	95	22	1	11	48	26	91	.264	.345
Lewis,Richie	L	.200	55	11	2	1	3	9	9	12	.323	.436	Mathews,T.J.	L	.200	30	6	0	0	0	3	7	6	.351	.200
Throws Right	R	.241	79	19	5	1	6	14	6	20	.294	.557	Throws Right	R	.200	75	15	2	0	1	6	4	22	.241	.267
Lieber,Jon	L	.396	134	53	8	2	6	24	7	14	.420	.619	Mathews,Terry	L	.227	119	27	5	1	4	16	17	19	.328	.387
Throws Right	R	.305	164	50	7	2	1	24	7	31	.341	.390	Throws Right	R	.240	179	43	11	0	5	24	10	53	.279	.385

Pitchers vs. Left-Handed and Right-Handed Batters

Pitcher	vs	Avg	AB	H	2B	3B	HR	BI	BB	SO	OBP	SLG	Pitcher	vs	Avg	AB	H	2B	3B	HR	BI	BB	SO	OBP	SLG
Mauser,Tim	L	.375	8	3	0	0	0	2	2	4	.500	.375	Mohler,Mike	L	.256	39	10	1	0	0	5	5	6	.341	.282
Throws Right	R	.077	13	1	0	0	0	1	7	5	.400	.077	Throws Left	R	.143	42	6	1	0	0	4	13	9	.345	.167
Maxcy,Brian	L	.297	101	30	2	2	4	23	17	9	.398	.475	Monteleone,R	L	.556	9	5	0	0	1	3	1	1	.545	.889
Throws Right	R	.290	107	31	4	1	2	19	14	11	.373	.402	Throws Right	R	.143	21	3	1	0	0	4	2	4	.208	.190
May,Darrell	L	.000	0	0	0	0	0	0	0	0	.000	.000	Montgomery,J	L	.279	136	38	5	1	4	20	15	19	.348	.419
Throws Left	R	.500	20	10	1	0	0	5	0	1	.476	.550	Throws Right	R	.216	102	22	2	0	3	14	10	30	.287	.324
Mcandrew,J	L	.205	88	18	3	0	2	10	4	10	.239	.307	Moore,Mike	L	.332	319	106	15	5	12	63	43	30	.407	.524
Throws Right	R	.373	51	19	4	0	0	4	8	9	.467	.451	Throws Right	R	.311	235	73	20	0	12	42	25	34	.382	.549
McCaskill,K	L	.312	141	44	5	0	5	24	19	21	.402	.454	Morel,Ramon	L	.500	10	5	0	0	0	1	1	2	.545	.500
Throws Right	R	.294	180	53	7	0	5	26	14	29	.348	.417	Throws Right	R	.100	10	1	0	0	0	1	1	1	.182	.100
Mccurry,Jeff	L	.384	86	33	6	2	3	13	13	5	.470	.605	Morgan,Mike	L	.273	227	62	14	0	5	22	24	25	.346	.401
Throws Right	R	.312	157	49	10	1	6	27	17	22	.393	.503	Throws Right	R	.269	264	71	10	1	7	28	10	36	.301	.394
McDonald,Ben	L	.200	150	30	6	0	6	16	16	32	.280	.360	Moyer,Jamie	L	.317	104	33	5	0	2	11	9	11	.379	.423
Throws Right	R	.248	149	37	5	0	4	20	22	30	.351	.362	Throws Left	R	.249	338	84	14	2	16	51	21	54	.293	.444
McDowell,Jack	L	.255	475	121	19	5	15	59	52	71	.326	.411	Mulholland,T	L	.280	107	30	3	1	3	17	8	13	.319	.411
Throws Right	R	.254	355	90	18	2	10	39	26	86	.312	.400	Throws Left	R	.320	500	160	20	5	22	80	30	52	.362	.512
McDowell,R	L	.269	134	36	6	1	2	15	17	17	.367	.373	Munoz,Bobby	L	.296	27	8	1	1	1	5	3	3	.367	.519
Throws Right	R	.282	177	50	5	1	3	26	17	32	.343	.373	Throws Right	R	.241	29	7	3	0	1	7	6	3	.400	.448
McElroy,Chuck	L	.283	60	17	4	1	3	15	6	10	.348	.533	Munoz,Mike	L	.286	84	24	2	1	5	19	8	19	.351	.512
Throws Left	R	.296	98	29	5	1	2	23	9	17	.352	.429	Throws Left	R	.326	92	30	6	1	4	19	19	18	.438	.543
McMichael,G	L	.200	130	26	9	0	3	10	11	28	.262	.338	Munoz,Oscar	L	.324	71	23	9	0	3	13	10	13	.407	.577
Throws Right	R	.224	170	38	6	0	5	10	21	46	.309	.347	Throws Right	R	.230	74	17	5	0	3	15	7	12	.301	.419
McMurtry,C	L	.333	18	6	2	0	0	5	2	3	.400	.444	Murphy,Rob	L	.304	23	7	0	0	1	6	5	2	.429	.435
Throws Right	R	.375	24	9	3	1	0	9	7	1	.500	.583	Throws Left	R	.280	25	7	1	0	2	3	3	5	.357	.560
Meacham,Rusty	L	.287	115	33	7	2	2	25	8	9	.328	.435	Murray,Matt	L	.458	24	11	4	0	1	7	2	1	.500	.750
Throws Right	R	.320	122	39	8	2	4	25	11	21	.375	.516	Throws Right	R	.278	36	10	1	0	3	9	6	3	.395	.556
Mecir,Jim	L	.333	15	5	0	1	0	2	0	3	.333	.467	Mussina,Mike	L	.209	483	101	20	6	9	32	34	98	.261	.331
Throws Right	R	.000	4	0	0	0	0	0	2	0	.333	.000	Throws Right	R	.250	344	86	25	1	15	42	16	60	.285	.459
Menhart,Paul	L	.247	170	42	8	3	5	19	31	26	.365	.418	Myers,Mike	L	.200	15	3	1	0	0	2	4	3	.381	.267
Throws Right	R	.250	120	30	7	1	4	25	16	24	.354	.425	Throws Left	R	.471	17	8	2	0	1	6	3	1	.571	.765
Mercedes,Jose	L	.500	6	3	2	0	0	2	6	0	.643	.833	Myers,Randy	L	.130	46	6	3	0	0	6	4	16	.196	.196
Throws Right	R	.346	26	9	0	0	1	7	2	6	.393	.462	Throws Left	R	.267	161	43	7	1	7	27	24	43	.358	.453
Mercker,Kent	L	.213	75	16	2	0	2	5	8	17	.289	.320	Nabholz,Chris	L	.250	44	11	2	0	1	8	4	12	.306	.364
Throws Left	R	.265	468	124	29	3	14	58	53	85	.339	.429	Throws Left	R	.256	43	11	3	0	3	7	10	9	.389	.535
Mesa,Jose	L	.230	126	29	2	0	0	4	11	29	.290	.246	Nagy,Charles	L	.313	377	118	26	1	6	42	36	52	.375	.435
Throws Right	R	.198	101	20	2	0	3	8	6	29	.241	.307	Throws Right	R	.238	320	76	20	0	14	45	25	87	.296	.431
Miceli,Danny	L	.359	92	33	5	2	5	21	19	18	.452	.620	Navarro,Jaime	L	.250	336	84	11	1	7	29	31	58	.314	.351
Throws Right	R	.209	134	28	7	0	2	18	9	38	.279	.306	Throws Right	R	.252	437	110	16	0	12	40	25	70	.295	.371
Mills,Alan	L	.400	30	12	2	0	1	5	8	3	.525	.567	Neagle,Denny	L	.272	125	34	8	2	5	14	15	26	.350	.488
Throws Right	R	.269	67	18	4	0	3	20	10	13	.372	.463	Throws Left	R	.273	684	187	29	3	15	66	30	124	.304	.390
Mimbs,Michael	L	.214	98	21	6	0	1	11	16	15	.325	.306	Nelson,Jeff	L	.233	120	28	4	0	2	11	15	39	.343	.317
Throws Left	R	.259	410	106	20	2	9	52	59	78	.354	.383	Throws Right	R	.191	157	30	8	0	2	15	12	57	.249	.280
Minor,Blas	L	.292	72	21	7	0	1	9	4	12	.329	.431	Nen,Robb	L	.273	121	33	9	3	3	16	12	27	.336	.471
Throws Right	R	.225	102	23	5	0	5	10	9	31	.295	.422	Throws Right	R	.218	133	29	8	0	3	12	11	41	.283	.346
Mintz,Steve	L	.367	30	11	1	1	2	4	7	1	.500	.667	Nichols,Rod	L	.500	8	4	2	0	1	4	3	1	.636	1.125
Throws Right	R	.306	49	15	0	2	2	5		6	.375	.510	Throws Right	R	.400	25	10	4	0	2	5	2	2	.444	.800
Miranda,Angel	L	.283	53	15	2	0	0	3	11	5	.406	.321	Nichting,C	L	.340	53	18	4	1	1	11	9	3	.438	.509
Throws Left	R	.293	232	68	12	1	8	37	38	40	.387	.457	Throws Right	R	.346	52	18	2	0	0	11	4	3	.386	.385
Mlicki,Dave	L	.309	278	86	15	2	12	34	30	39	.381	.507	Nied,Dave	L	.500	10	5	1	0	1	6	0	0	.500	.900
Throws Right	R	.213	347	74	16	0	11	40	24	84	.263	.354	Throws Right	R	.429	14	6	1	0	1	3	3	3	.529	.714

Pitchers vs. Left-Handed and Right-Handed Batters

Pitcher	vs	Avg	AB	H	2B	3B	HR	BI	BB	SO	OBP	SLG	Pitcher	vs	Avg	AB	H	2B	3B	HR	BI	BB	SO	OBP	SLG
Nitkowski,C	L	.273	55	15	4	0	0	9	1	3	.300	.345	Perez,Melido	L	.260	146	38	11	0	6	23	18	24	.341	.459
Throws Left	R	.333	237	79	23	1	11	47	34	28	.420	.578	Throws Right	R	.262	122	32	8	1	4	18	13	20	.331	.443
Nomo,Hideo	L	.199	317	63	9	3	8	28	34	112	.284	.322	Perez,Mike	L	.290	93	27	1	0	2	9	9	10	.368	.366
Throws Right	R	.168	364	61	14	0	6	25	44	124	.257	.255	Throws Right	R	.256	176	45	8	0	6	28	18	39	.325	.403
Ogea,Chad	L	.226	235	53	10	0	6	22	17	32	.272	.345	Perez,Yorkis	L	.157	83	13	3	1	3	10	14	21	.286	.325
Throws Right	R	.246	171	42	9	0	5	14	12	25	.299	.386	Throws Left	R	.247	89	22	7	1	3	13	14	26	.352	.449
Olivares,Omar	L	.311	61	19	4	0	1	10	13	7	.427	.426	Person,Robert	L	.143	21	3	0	0	1	1	1	4	.182	.286
Throws Right	R	.346	104	36	3	3	4	21	10	15	.415	.548	Throws Right	R	.095	21	2	0	0	0	0	1	6	.136	.095
Oliver,Darren	L	.350	40	14	3	0	1	4	9	11	.469	.500	Petkovsek,M	L	.285	235	67	13	3	4	33	14	17	.324	.417
Throws Left	R	.231	143	33	6	1	2	19	23	28	.339	.329	Throws Right	R	.242	285	69	15	0	7	29	21	54	.304	.368
Olson,Gregg	L	.236	55	13	3	0	2	8	8	7	.328	.400	Pettitte,Andy	L	.256	117	30	5	1	1	10	9	18	.307	.342
Throws Right	R	.234	64	15	2	1	2	12	11	14	.342	.391	Throws Left	R	.276	555	153	29	6	14	64	54	96	.339	.425
Ontiveros,S	L	.262	328	86	15	3	8	33	20	46	.303	.399	Phoenix,Steve	L	.500	4	2	0	0	0	3	1	2	.600	.500
Throws Right	R	.322	180	58	14	0	4	29	18	31	.389	.467	Throws Right	R	.333	3	1	0	0	1	3	2	1	.600	1.333
Oquist,Mike	L	.250	76	19	3	0	3	10	17	5	.389	.408	Pichardo,H	L	.279	129	36	5	0	3	12	14	21	.350	.388
Throws Right	R	.244	131	32	9	2	3	25	24	22	.358	.412	Throws Right	R	.250	120	30	2	0	1	12	16	22	.355	.292
Orosco,Jesse	L	.143	77	11	4	0	1	9	7	28	.212	.234	Pierce,Jeff	L	.320	25	8	2	0	0	3	11	6	.514	.400
Throws Left	R	.191	89	17	6	0	3	16	20	30	.336	.360	Throws Right	R	.258	31	8	4	0	0	7	3	6	.324	.387
Osborne,D	L	.282	71	20	6	2	3	8	11	15	.378	.549	Pittsley,Jim	L	.286	7	2	0	0	1	1	1	0	.375	.714
Throws Left	R	.256	359	92	20	1	14	43	23	67	.302	.435	Throws Right	R	.556	9	5	1	0	2	4	0	0	.556	1.333
Osuna,Antonio	L	.276	58	16	1	1	1	4	14	12	.417	.379	Plesac,Dan	L	.222	81	18	3	2	2	16	9	27	.298	.383
Throws Right	R	.221	104	23	2	1	4	15	6	34	.268	.375	Throws Left	R	.245	143	35	6	1	1	9	18	30	.329	.322
Painter,Lance	L	.292	65	19	4	1	1	7	6	15	.370	.431	Plunk,Eric	L	.222	108	24	6	1	0	13	13	23	.312	.296
Throws Left	R	.298	121	36	8	1	8	20	4	21	.320	.579	Throws Right	R	.200	120	24	3	0	5	9	14	48	.294	.350
Palacios,V	L	.257	70	18	5	1	2	12	7	19	.333	.443	Poole,Jim	L	.213	75	16	4	1	1	5	7	20	.280	.333
Throws Right	R	.333	90	30	4	0	5	17	12	15	.413	.544	Throws Left	R	.220	109	24	3	0	6	16	10	21	.293	.413
Park,Chan Ho	L	.000	5	0	0	0	0	0	2	1	.286	.000	Portugal,Mark	L	.255	345	88	15	2	5	32	33	47	.319	.354
Throws Right	R	.222	9	2	1	0	1	1	0	6	.222	.667	Throws Right	R	.269	360	97	19	2	12	47	23	49	.320	.433
Parra,Jose	L	.285	165	47	4	6	5	28	17	15	.349	.473	Powell,Jay	L	.154	13	2	0	0	0	0	2	1	.313	.154
Throws Right	R	.331	139	46	9	0	8	25	11	21	.386	.568	Throws Right	R	.313	16	5	0	0	0	2	4	3	.476	.313
Parrett,Jeff	L	.214	98	21	6	1	2	7	14	22	.310	.357	Powell,Ross	L	.286	35	10	2	0	2	9	6	8	.409	.514
Throws Right	R	.258	194	50	9	0	6	28	14	49	.310	.397	Throws Left	R	.302	86	26	9	3	4	14	15	12	.406	.616
Parris,Steve	L	.243	140	34	6	0	5	18	18	27	.342	.393	Prieto,Ariel	L	.234	111	26	4	0	1	11	22	22	.363	.297
Throws Right	R	.314	175	55	7	3	7	26	15	34	.378	.509	Throws Right	R	.295	105	31	3	0	3	18	10	15	.375	.410
Patterson,Bob	L	.200	85	17	5	0	2	11	5	19	.250	.329	Pugh,Tim	L	.201	154	31	5	1	3	11	17	17	.279	.305
Throws Left	R	.282	110	31	5	0	4	13	8	22	.331	.436	Throws Right	R	.312	221	69	14	0	10	30	15	21	.357	.511
Patterson,J	L	.200	5	1	0	0	0	0	3	1	.500	.200	Pulsipher,B	L	.254	71	18	3	1	1	6	4	11	.312	.366
Throws Right	R	.250	8	2	0	0	1	4	0	2	.250	.625	Throws Left	R	.256	407	104	17	3	10	45	41	70	.326	.384
Pavlas,Dave	L	.286	7	2	0	0	0	0	0	1	.286	.286	Quantrill,P	L	.351	308	108	26	4	10	44	24	45	.396	.558
Throws Right	R	.353	17	6	1	0	0	4	0	2	.353	.412	Throws Right	R	.253	411	104	18	3	10	49	20	58	.293	.384
Pavlik,Roger	L	.234	410	96	17	4	10	43	48	84	.315	.368	Radinsky,S	L	.339	56	19	6	1	2	10	4	7	.383	.589
Throws Right	R	.255	306	78	18	1	9	37	42	65	.348	.408	Throws Left	R	.290	93	27	3	0	5	14	13	7	.364	.484
Pena,A	L	.205	88	18	2	1	3	12	12	23	.300	.352	Radke,Brad	L	.268	400	107	27	2	14	47	26	40	.313	.450
Throws Right	R	.282	131	37	8	2	5	20	7	41	.319	.489	Throws Right	R	.285	309	88	21	1	18	58	21	35	.329	.534
Pennington,B	L	.167	12	2	2	0	0	6	5	3	.368	.333	Rapp,Pat	L	.242	293	71	17	2	4	25	47	38	.347	.355
Throws Left	R	.233	43	10	5	0	1	3	17	14	.459	.419	Throws Right	R	.262	332	87	10	0	6	35	29	64	.334	.346
Percival,Troy	L	.172	116	20	5	0	2	7	14	40	.262	.267	Rasmussen,D	L	.067	15	1	1	0	0	2	1	3	.125	.133
Throws Right	R	.125	136	17	2	0	4	14	12	54	.200	.228	Throws Left	R	.429	28	12	2	0	3	11	7	3	.543	.821
Perez,Carlos	L	.178	101	18	3	2	1	5	4	21	.224	.277	Reed,Rick	L	.250	28	7	0	0	2	4	2	2	.300	.464
Throws Left	R	.275	451	124	25	1	17	51	24	85	.315	.448	Throws Right	R	.289	38	11	2	0	3	7	1	8	.308	.579

Pitchers vs. Left-Handed and Right-Handed Batters

Pitcher	vs	Avg	AB	H	2B	3B	HR	BI	BB	SO	OBP	SLG
Reed,Steve	L	.216	102	22	3	0	1	8	13	20	.304	.275
Throws Right	R	.196	199	39	4	0	7	23	8	59	.230	.322
Rekar,Bryan	L	.307	166	51	14	1	3	23	14	28	.364	.458
Throws Right	R	.257	171	44	7	2	8	23	10	32	.299	.462
Remlinger,M	L	.400	10	4	1	0	0	2	0	2	.400	.500
Throws Left	R	.278	18	5	3	0	1	5	5	5	.435	.611
Reyes,Al	L	.255	51	13	1	1	2	8	9	11	.365	.431
Throws Right	R	.095	63	6	2	0	1	5	9	18	.230	.175
Reyes,Carlos	L	.283	145	41	5	1	2	14	14	25	.354	.372
Throws Right	R	.242	124	30	3	1	8	25	14	23	.333	.476
Reynolds,S	L	.260	354	92	21	2	6	34	20	90	.299	.381
Throws Right	R	.266	391	104	15	5	9	40	17	85	.300	.399
Reynoso,A	L	.301	163	49	11	1	6	27	16	15	.365	.491
Throws Right	R	.328	204	67	14	3	6	30	20	25	.397	.515
Rhodes,Arthur	L	.149	74	11	2	0	2	7	7	15	.222	.257
Throws Left	R	.271	210	57	10	1	11	42	41	62	.390	.486
Ricci,Chuck	L	.308	13	4	1	0	0	1	2	3	.400	.385
Throws Right	R	.250	20	5	1	0	0	2	1	6	.292	.300
Righetti,Dave	L	.276	29	8	1	0	1	3	3	5	.344	.414
Throws Left	R	.333	171	57	11	0	5	20	15	24	.383	.485
Rightnowar,R	L	.270	63	17	2	0	0	11	5	12	.338	.302
Throws Right	R	.273	66	18	4	0	3	16	13	10	.405	.470
Rijo,Jose	L	.328	128	42	8	1	4	14	13	31	.387	.500
Throws Right	R	.245	139	34	5	2	2	14	9	31	.287	.353
Risley,Bill	L	.234	128	30	4	1	3	18	9	35	.281	.352
Throws Right	R	.258	97	25	4	0	4	17	9	30	.324	.423
Ritz,Kevin	L	.291	299	87	18	0	3	34	42	51	.375	.381
Throws Right	R	.233	360	84	18	1	13	55	23	69	.289	.397
Rivera,M	L	.246	142	35	6	0	6	22	20	26	.337	.415
Throws Right	R	.288	125	36	6	1	5	17	10	25	.348	.472
Rivera,R	L	.250	12	3	1	0	0	1	0	0	.250	.333
Throws Left	R	.556	9	5	0	1	1	4	2	2	.636	1.111
Roa,Joe	L	.176	17	3	1	0	0	2	2	0	.263	.235
Throws Right	R	.750	8	6	1	0	1	2	0	0	.750	1.250
Roberson,Sid	L	.318	66	21	2	0	1	6	7	9	.403	.394
Throws Left	R	.305	266	81	16	1	15	49	30	31	.384	.541
Robertson,R	L	.268	56	15	1	1	0	6	13	13	.406	.321
Throws Left	R	.246	134	33	5	0	4	17	18	25	.331	.373
Robinson,Ken	L	.171	82	14	1	1	2	6	11	18	.263	.280
Throws Right	R	.190	58	11	2	0	5	13	11	13	.338	.483
Rodriguez,F	L	.259	27	7	3	0	0	3	3	3	.333	.370
Throws Right	R	.308	13	4	0	0	2	6	2	2	.400	.769
Rodriguez,F	L	.269	219	59	9	0	3	30	35	24	.364	.352
Throws Right	R	.286	192	55	14	1	8	34	22	35	.374	.495
Rodriguez,R	L	.000	1	0	0	0	0	0	0	0	.000	.000
Throws Left	R	.000	3	0	0	0	0	0	0	0	.000	.000
Rogers,Jimmy	L	.235	51	12	1	1	2	7	11	5	.371	.412
Throws Right	R	.243	37	9	3	0	2	8	7	8	.356	.486
Rogers,Kenny	L	.157	115	18	2	0	2	9	14	30	.248	.226
Throws Left	R	.257	676	174	28	1	24	68	62	110	.319	.408

Pitcher	vs	Avg	AB	H	2B	3B	HR	BI	BB	SO	OBP	SLG
Rojas,Mel	L	.262	130	34	7	1	1	17	19	27	.360	.354
Throws Right	R	.263	133	35	7	0	1	17	10	34	.340	.338
Roper,John	L	.476	21	10	2	0	2	7	4	3	.538	.857
Throws Right	R	.333	15	5	1	0	1	5	2	3	.412	.600
Rosselli,Joe	L	.483	29	14	1	0	2	8	2	2	.516	.724
Throws Left	R	.294	85	25	8	2	3	18	18	5	.402	.541
Rueter,Kirk	L	.143	21	3	0	0	0	0	0	5	.182	.143
Throws Left	R	.235	149	35	2	1	3	15	9	23	.278	.322
Ruffcorn,S	L	.313	16	5	0	0	0	3	8	4	.542	.313
Throws Right	R	.357	14	5	0	0	0	4	5	1	.571	.357
Ruffin,Bruce	L	.242	33	8	1	0	0	2	4	5	.324	.273
Throws Left	R	.214	84	18	1	0	1	8	15	18	.333	.262
Ruffin,Johnny	L	.150	20	3	1	0	0	1	8	3	.393	.200
Throws Right	R	.043	23	1	0	0	0	0	3	8	.154	.043
Russell,Jeff	L	.274	73	20	0	0	2	6	4	12	.312	.356
Throws Right	R	.281	57	16	2	0	1	11	5	9	.339	.368
Ryan,Ken	L	.262	65	17	2	0	1	11	15	19	.400	.338
Throws Right	R	.274	62	17	3	0	3	8	9	15	.375	.468
Saberhagen,B	L	.231	286	66	16	2	8	26	18	52	.275	.385
Throws Right	R	.310	319	99	15	2	13	41	15	48	.359	.492
Sager,A.J.	L	.364	33	12	4	0	0	7	1	5	.382	.485
Throws Right	R	.250	28	7	1	0	1	7	6	5	.382	.393
Sanders,Scott	L	.276	134	37	13	0	5	19	16	23	.355	.485
Throws Right	R	.198	212	42	4	0	9	21	15	65	.253	.344
Sanderson,S	L	.258	89	23	6	1	3	9	2	12	.272	.449
Throws Right	R	.347	72	25	6	0	3	11	2	11	.377	.556
Sanford,Mo	L	.214	28	6	1	0	2	3	7	6	.371	.464
Throws Right	R	.233	43	10	3	0	5	12	9	11	.389	.651
Scanlan,Bob	L	.306	173	53	7	3	5	33	24	21	.392	.468
Throws Right	R	.302	159	48	7	1	4	21	20	8	.389	.434
Scheid,Rich	L	.214	14	3	1	0	0	3	2	5	.313	.286
Throws Left	R	.407	27	11	2	0	1	6	5	5	.485	.593
Schilling,C	L	.233	176	41	6	0	8	23	16	51	.297	.403
Throws Right	R	.211	261	55	12	0	4	20	10	63	.246	.303
Schmidt,Curt	L	.429	14	6	2	0	1	8	3	2	.579	.786
Throws Right	R	.321	28	9	3	0	0	9	6	5	.441	.429
Schmidt,Jason	L	.243	37	9	5	0	0	5	10	8	.388	.378
Throws Right	R	.316	57	18	2	0	2	12	8	11	.397	.456
Schourek,Pete	L	.264	91	24	3	0	4	12	7	18	.320	.429
Throws Left	R	.223	602	134	26	5	13	55	38	142	.275	.347
Schullstrom,E	L	.337	86	29	6	1	4	23	14	7	.431	.570
Throws Right	R	.327	113	37	9	0	4	19	8	14	.372	.513
Scott,Tim	L	.230	113	26	6	1	5	16	13	22	.323	.434
Throws Right	R	.215	121	26	3	2	1	10	10	35	.291	.298
Seanez,Rudy	L	.239	46	11	5	0	2	12	5	7	.327	.478
Throws Right	R	.308	91	28	3	2	3	16	13	22	.394	.484
Sele,Aaron	L	.317	60	19	4	1	2	5	8	6	.408	.517
Throws Right	R	.194	67	13	1	0	1	5	6	15	.270	.254
Service,Scott	L	.171	35	6	2	0	0	5	13	4	.392	.229
Throws Right	R	.179	67	12	2	0	4	10	7	26	.267	.388

Pitchers vs. Left-Handed and Right-Handed Batters

Pitcher	vs	Avg	AB	H	2B	3B	HR	BI	BB	SO	OBP	SLG	Pitcher	vs	Avg	AB	H	2B	3B	HR	BI	BB	SO	OBP	SLG
Shaw,Jeff	L	.295	122	36	6	0	2	14	13	23	.365	.393	Swift,Bill	L	.312	218	68	11	3	6	31	28	26	.393	.472
Throws Right	R	.230	148	34	14	1	4	12	14	28	.309	.419	Throws Right	R	.278	194	54	8	1	6	27	15	42	.329	.423
Shepherd,K	L	.667	3	2	1	0	0	1	0	0	.667	1.000	Swindell,Greg	L	.245	106	26	7	0	1	9	5	27	.277	.340
Throws Right	R	.500	4	2	1	0	0	4	2	0	.667	.750	Throws Left	R	.308	500	154	31	3	20	72	34	69	.350	.502
Shuey,Paul	L	.273	11	3	2	0	0	3	3	4	.429	.455	Tabaka,Jeff	L	.190	42	8	2	0	0	4	9	5	.333	.238
Throws Right	R	.200	10	2	0	0	0	0	2	1	.333	.200	Throws Left	R	.275	69	19	1	1	2	8	8	20	.351	.406
Simas,Bill	L	.133	15	2	2	0	0	0	3	3	.316	.267	Tapani,Kevin	L	.284	419	119	33	2	15	56	26	77	.329	.480
Throws Right	R	.325	40	13	0	0	1	2	7	13	.426	.400	Throws Right	R	.308	351	108	22	1	14	48	22	54	.349	.496
Sirotka,Mike	L	.368	19	7	2	0	0	1	1	3	.400	.474	Tavarez,J	L	.268	153	41	9	0	5	15	12	25	.321	.425
Throws Left	R	.286	112	32	4	1	2	13	16	16	.366	.393	Throws Right	R	.205	171	35	3	0	2	16	9	43	.254	.257
Slocumb,H	L	.224	107	24	2	0	0	5	17	26	.336	.243	Taylor,S	L	.351	37	13	2	1	3	12	2	5	.385	.703
Throws Right	R	.282	142	40	6	0	2	25	18	37	.363	.366	Throws Right	R	.414	29	12	2	0	3	4	3	5	.469	.793
Slusarski,Joe	L	.367	30	11	1	0	1	7	2	4	.424	.500	Telgheder,D	L	.302	53	16	3	1	2	11	2	7	.321	.509
Throws Right	R	.303	33	10	3	0	2	6	4	2	.385	.576	Throws Right	R	.333	54	18	5	0	2	5	5	9	.390	.537
Small,Aaron	L	.333	12	4	0	0	1	3	2	2	.429	.583	Tewksbury,Bob	L	.300	327	98	27	1	5	40	15	37	.331	.434
Throws Right	R	.214	14	3	2	0	0	1	4	3	.389	.357	Throws Right	R	.351	202	71	14	0	3	24	5	16	.370	.465
Smiley,John	L	.225	102	23	5	0	4	14	9	14	.298	.392	Thobe,J.J.	L	.000	4	0	0	0	0	0	1	0	.200	.000
Throws Left	R	.269	557	150	33	3	7	51	30	110	.307	.377	Throws Right	R	.429	14	6	1	0	0	3	2	0	.500	.500
Smith,Lee	L	.235	102	24	5	1	1	10	15	23	.328	.333	Thobe,Tom	L	.333	3	1	0	0	0	0	0	1	.333	.333
Throws Right	R	.240	75	18	5	0	2	12	10	20	.333	.387	Throws Left	R	.429	14	6	1	0	0	2	0	1	.429	.500
Smith,Pete	L	.364	55	20	3	0	5	11	6	7	.426	.691	Thomas,Larry	L	.182	22	4	0	0	0	1	2	7	.250	.182
Throws Right	R	.256	39	10	0	0	3	11	1	7	.273	.487	Throws Left	R	.154	26	4	0	1	1	3	4	5	.267	.346
Smith,Zane	L	.342	73	25	4	2	0	17	1	11	.347	.452	Thomas,Mike	L	.667	3	2	0	0	0	1	1	0	.750	.667
Throws Left	R	.312	382	119	25	0	7	49	22	36	.347	.432	Throws Left	R	.000	3	0	0	0	0	0	0	0	.000	.000
Smoltz,John	L	.261	345	90	16	2	7	35	44	70	.345	.380	Thompson,Mark	L	.378	98	37	11	1	2	17	14	11	.455	.571
Throws Right	R	.206	369	76	16	0	8	33	28	123	.264	.314	Throws Right	R	.324	111	36	6	1	5	28	8	19	.363	.532
Sodowsky,C	L	.318	66	21	2	0	4	12	9	9	.400	.530	Timlin,Mike	L	.298	94	28	4	2	1	12	6	19	.340	.415
Throws Right	R	.111	27	3	0	0	0	1	9	5	.333	.111	Throws Right	R	.159	63	10	1	0	0	6	11	17	.303	.175
Sparks,Steve	L	.277	447	124	25	5	9	50	57	52	.355	.416	Torres,Dilson	L	.304	79	24	3	0	3	10	8	15	.368	.456
Throws Right	R	.269	320	86	17	0	8	35	29	44	.332	.397	Throws Right	R	.317	101	32	7	0	3	20	9	13	.378	.475
Springer,D	L	.212	33	7	2	0	0	0	6	6	.350	.273	Torres,S	L	.345	197	68	14	0	5	26	33	28	.439	.492
Throws Right	R	.286	49	14	2	0	3	11	3	9	.327	.510	Throws Right	R	.237	135	32	5	0	11	32	16	19	.327	.519
Springer,Russ	L	.306	134	41	10	0	5	18	22	21	.415	.493	Trachsel,S	L	.254	295	75	11	3	13	38	41	61	.343	.444
Throws Right	R	.241	170	41	9	1	11	34	13	49	.307	.500	Throws Right	R	.296	334	99	15	2	12	46	35	56	.360	.461
Stanton,Mike	L	.212	52	11	1	0	0	4	3	10	.250	.231	Trombley,Mike	L	.297	219	65	15	4	8	27	28	32	.380	.511
Throws Left	R	.343	108	37	7	0	6	24	11	13	.408	.574	Throws Right	R	.243	173	42	8	1	10	31	14	36	.302	.474
Stevens,Dave	L	.318	129	41	6	2	3	21	14	24	.379	.465	Urbani,Tom	L	.243	74	18	3	2	3	6	5	15	.300	.459
Throws Right	R	.252	131	33	5	1	11	29	18	23	.340	.557	Throws Left	R	.323	251	81	13	0	8	29	16	37	.366	.470
Stewart,Dave	L	.313	198	62	10	1	4	21	26	30	.394	.434	Urbina,Ugueth	L	.279	43	12	2	1	2	7	8	7	.392	.512
Throws Right	R	.293	133	39	7	0	7	33	13	28	.356	.504	Throws Right	R	.280	50	14	3	0	4	10	6	8	.357	.504
Stottlemyre,T	L	.259	483	125	22	3	11	49	52	128	.333	.385	Valdes,Ismael	L	.228	359	82	19	0	13	38	33	59	.294	.390
Throws Right	R	.300	343	103	15	1	15	56	28	77	.356	.481	Throws Right	R	.228	378	86	13	1	4	30	18	91	.261	.299
Sturtze,T	L	.200	5	1	1	0	0	0	1	0	.333	.400	Valdes,Marc	L	.500	18	9	0	0	1	6	4	0	.565	.667
Throws Right	R	.333	3	1	0	0	1	2	0	0	.333	1.333	Throws Right	R	.421	19	8	3	0	0	3	5	2	.560	.579
Sullivan,S	L	.200	5	1	0	0	0	0	2	0	.429	.200	Valdez,Carlos	L	.409	22	9	2	0	1	2	4	1	.500	.636
Throws Right	R	.333	9	3	0	0	0	2	0	2	.333	.333	Throws Right	R	.270	37	10	2	1	0	7	4	6	.349	.378
Suppan,Jeff	L	.300	50	15	6	0	1	8	2	8	.321	.480	Valdez,Sergio	L	.308	130	40	9	1	8	19	9	9	.355	.577
Throws Right	R	.326	43	14	4	0	3	7	3	11	.370	.628	Throws Right	R	.288	132	38	7	1	4	18	8	20	.333	.447
Swartzbaugh,D	L	.167	6	1	0	0	0	0	2	0	.375	.167	Valenzuela,F	L	.317	63	20	6	0	1	4	6	8	.377	.460
Throws Right	R	.222	18	4	1	0	0	2	1	5	.263	.278	Throws Left	R	.283	286	81	21	0	15	44	28	49	.345	.514

Pitchers vs. Left-Handed and Right-Handed Batters

Pitcher	vs	Avg	AB	H	2B	3B	HR	BI	BB	SO	OBP	SLG	Pitcher	vs	Avg	AB	H	2B	3B	HR	BI	BB	SO	OBP	SLG
Van Poppel,T	L	.248	290	72	14	4	10	39	43	63	.345	.428	Wengert,Don	L	.314	51	16	3	2	2	8	9	4	.410	.569
Throws Right	R	.238	223	53	13	0	6	34	13	59	.284	.377	Throws Right	R	.222	63	14	5	0	1	7	3	12	.269	.349
Vanegmond,Tim	L	.350	20	7	0	0	2	5	5	3	.480	.650	West,David	L	.188	16	3	1	0	1	3	3	7	.350	.438
Throws Right	R	.222	9	2	0	0	0	1	1	2	.300	.222	Throws Left	R	.248	125	31	9	0	4	13	16	18	.333	.416
VanLandingham	L	.301	216	65	13	1	4	22	17	31	.350	.426	Wetteland,J	L	.186	113	21	2	1	3	18	10	39	.250	.301
Throws Right	R	.232	254	59	9	1	10	30	23	64	.296	.394	Throws Right	R	.184	103	19	8	0	3	9	4	27	.213	.350
Veres,Dave	L	.243	140	34	7	1	3	6	20	31	.337	.371	White,Gabe	L	.286	21	6	0	0	2	7	1	5	.304	.571
Throws Right	R	.239	230	55	7	1	2	25	10	63	.273	.304	Throws Left	R	.253	79	20	4	0	5	15	8	20	.322	.494
Veres,Randy	L	.262	65	17	1	0	4	13	14	11	.395	.462	White,Rick	L	.308	107	33	7	1	1	17	9	10	.364	.421
Throws Right	R	.246	118	29	2	0	2	19	8	20	.287	.314	Throws Right	R	.289	114	33	5	0	2	13	9	19	.341	.386
Villone,Ron	L	.298	47	14	2	0	2	11	18	20	.492	.468	Whiteside,M	L	.256	78	20	0	1	2	8	10	19	.348	.359
Throws Left	R	.238	126	30	3	1	9	24	16	43	.326	.492	Throws Right	R	.233	120	28	2	0	3	13	9	27	.280	.325
Viola,Frank	L	.250	8	2	0	0	0	1	0	1	.250	.250	Whiteside,S	L	.667	3	2	1	0	0	2	1	0	.500	1.000
Throws Left	R	.346	52	18	0	0	3	8	3	3	.375	.519	Throws Left	R	.385	13	5	2	0	1	5	3	2	.500	.769
Vosberg,Ed	L	.250	52	13	3	0	2	6	8	14	.344	.423	Wickander,K	L	.250	40	10	2	0	0	7	6	3	.347	.300
Throws Left	R	.235	81	19	1	0	1	15	8	22	.297	.284	Throws Left	R	.209	43	9	0	1	1	6	6	8	.306	.326
Wade,Terrell	L	.250	4	1	0	0	0	0	0	1	.250	.250	Wickman,Bob	L	.305	128	39	7	0	3	17	13	15	.369	.430
Throws Left	R	.200	10	2	0	0	1	1	4	2	.429	.500	Throws Right	R	.216	176	38	7	0	3	24	20	36	.312	.307
Wagner,Billy	L	.000	1	0	0	0	0	0	0	0	.000	.000	Williams,B	L	.279	111	31	6	1	0	17	20	29	.403	.351
Throws Left	R	.000	0	0	0	0	0	0	0	0	.000	.000	Throws Right	R	.279	172	48	5	2	3	23	18	46	.362	.384
Wagner,Paul	L	.277	285	79	10	2	5	33	39	34	.365	.379	Williams,Mike	L	.193	145	28	4	2	6	17	18	14	.280	.372
Throws Right	R	.270	352	95	22	5	13	54	33	86	.342	.472	Throws Right	R	.275	182	50	8	3	4	20	11	43	.323	.418
Wakefield,Tim	L	.242	380	92	15	4	13	36	38	58	.308	.405	Williams,M	L	.471	17	8	0	0	1	6	5	1	.625	.647
Throws Right	R	.211	337	71	10	2	9	31	30	61	.290	.332	Throws Left	R	.208	24	5	0	0	0	4	16	8	.512	.208
Walker,Mike	L	.278	54	15	5	1	1	10	7	5	.355	.463	Williams,Todd	L	.214	28	6	2	0	1	4	4	3	.303	.393
Throws Right	R	.250	120	30	5	0	1	17	17	15	.336	.317	Throws Right	R	.295	44	13	1	0	2	7	3	5	.340	.455
Walker,Pete	L	.316	38	12	4	0	1	4	2	2	.350	.500	Williams,W	L	.231	117	27	6	0	4	13	15	31	.323	.385
Throws Right	R	.343	35	12	0	0	2	5	3	3	.385	.514	Throws Right	R	.205	83	17	6	0	2	6	13	10	.320	.349
Wall,Donnie	L	.269	52	14	1	1	3	7	2	9	.291	.500	Willis,Carl	L	1.000	2	2	1	0	0	1	2	0	1.000	1.500
Throws Right	R	.373	51	19	4	0	2	8	3	7	.400	.569	Throws Right	R	.750	4	3	1	0	0	3	3	0	.857	1.000
Ward,Duane	L	.750	12	9	3	0	0	6	2	2	.800	1.000	Wilson,Gary	L	.364	22	8	0	0	1	4	4	3	.462	.500
Throws Right	R	.286	7	2	0	0	0	2	3	1	.500	.286	Throws Right	R	.156	32	5	2	0	1	5	1	5	.229	.313
Ware,Jeff	L	.313	67	21	3	1	2	8	10	10	.403	.478	Wilson,Trevor	L	.255	47	12	3	0	0	3	5	7	.345	.319
Throws Right	R	.206	34	7	2	0	0	5	11	8	.413	.265	Throws Left	R	.271	258	70	11	0	8	24	33	31	.357	.407
Wasdin,John	L	.241	29	7	1	0	2	4	3	4	.313	.483	Witt,Bobby	L	.307	348	107	18	4	8	40	40	66	.382	.451
Throws Right	R	.194	36	7	1	0	2	6	0	2	.216	.389	Throws Right	R	.246	317	78	17	3	4	35	28	75	.305	.356
Watkins,Scott	L	.273	33	9	0	1	0	4	6	3	.385	.333	Wohlers,Mark	L	.234	111	26	2	1	1	9	17	41	.336	.297
Throws Left	R	.283	46	13	2	0	2	12	5	8	.333	.457	Throws Right	R	.191	131	25	4	0	1	10	7	49	.237	.244
Watson,Allen	L	.200	75	15	1	2	3	11	8	6	.286	.387	Wojciechowski	L	.327	55	18	6	2	1	8	4	1	.373	.564
Throws Left	R	.302	367	111	23	3	14	43	33	43	.365	.496	Throws Left	R	.250	132	33	7	1	6	17	24	12	.365	.455
Weathers,Dave	L	.315	143	45	12	0	2	21	28	23	.438	.441	Wolcott,Bob	L	.344	93	32	11	2	3	10	5	9	.376	.602
Throws Right	R	.282	209	59	7	1	6	34	24	37	.356	.411	Throws Right	R	.212	52	11	3	0	3	7	9	10	.333	.442
Wegman,Bill	L	.326	144	47	7	0	8	25	5	21	.349	.542	Woodall,Brad	L	.429	7	3	0	0	0	2	2	1	.500	.429
Throws Right	R	.298	141	42	6	2	6	19	16	29	.377	.496	Throws Left	R	.286	35	10	0	0	1	7	6	4	.390	.371
Wells,Bob	L	.295	139	41	13	2	5	22	18	11	.379	.525	Worrell,Tim	L	.455	22	10	4	0	1	2	3	5	.520	.773
Throws Right	R	.275	171	47	11	1	6	22	21	27	.352	.456	Throws Right	R	.182	33	6	0	0	1	6	3	8	.270	.273
Wells,David	L	.245	147	36	10	2	4	16	7	29	.277	.422	Worrell,Todd	L	.191	115	22	3	0	1	10	10	36	.258	.243
Throws Left	R	.252	627	158	36	3	19	60	46	104	.304	.410	Throws Right	R	.252	111	28	3	0	3	14	9	25	.308	.360
Wendell,Turk	L	.327	98	32	3	0	4	16	11	11	.391	.480	Young,Anthony	L	.271	59	16	4	0	0	2	8	7	.358	.339
Throws Right	R	.279	140	39	7	1	7	26	13	39	.344	.493	Throws Right	R	.298	104	31	9	0	5	18	6	8	.354	.529

Pitchers vs. Left-Handed and Right-Handed Pitchers

Batter	vs	Avg	AB	H	2B	3B	HR	BI	BB	SO	OBP	SLG
AL	L	.276	--	--	--	--	--	--	--	--	.349	.423
	R	.266	--	--	--	--	--	--	--	--	.340	.431
NL	L	.267	--	--	--	--	--	--	--	--	.345	.408
	R	.261	--	--	--	--	--	--	--	--	.322	.407
MLB	L	.272	--	--	--	--	--	--	--	--	.347	.416
	R	.263	--	--	--	--	--	--	--	--	.331	.418

Leader Boards

As in 1994, the 1995 season left us pondering the thought of "what might have been" had a 162-game schedule been in place. Albert Belle put up some unbelievable numbers down the stretch—finishing with 50 home runs despite being shorted 18 games. Might Belle have also finished with 400 total bases? Nobody has done that since Jim Rice in 1978. Might Edgar Martinez have finished first in batting average, on-base percentage *and* slugging percentage? How many more times might Frank Thomas have walked? What might Greg Maddux have done with four extra starts? Would Randy Johnson have managed 300 strikeouts? How many more homers would we have seen in Coors Field?

We'll never, ever know. All of our agonizing (and believe me, we've done *a lot*) won't change anything. Nevertheless, you'll find the names mentioned above throughout the Leader Boards section, along with some new names here and there—names like Reggie Sanders, Hideo Nomo, and Manny Ramirez.

You should also sneak a peek at the career batting and pitching leaders. It's remarkable to see how many current players will make a strong case for the Hall of Fame over the next decade—Wade Boggs, Barry Bonds, Joe Carter, Roger Clemens, Andre Dawson, Tony Gwynn, Rickey Henderson, Greg Maddux, Fred McGriff, Paul Molitor, Eddie Murray, Kirby Pucket, Tim Raines, Cal Ripken, Lee Smith, Ozzie Smith, Dave Winfield—okay, the Hall might be hard pressed to find room for *all* of them, but it's a lot of fun to argue their cases anyway.

1995 American League Batting Leaders

Batting Average

Player, Team	AB	H	AVG
E Martinez, Sea	**511**	**182**	**.356**
C Knoblauch, Min	538	179	.333
T Salmon, Cal	537	177	.330
W Boggs, NYA	460	149	.324
E Murray, Cle	436	141	.323
B Surhoff, Mil	415	133	.320
C Davis, Cal	424	135	.318
A Belle, Cle	546	173	.317
K Puckett, Min	538	169	.314
C Baerga, Cle	557	175	.314

On-Base Percentage

Player, Team	PA	OB	OBP
E Martinez, Sea	**639**	**306**	**.479**
F Thomas, ChA	647	294	.454
J Thome, Cle	557	244	.438
T Salmon, Cal	638	274	.429
C Davis, Cal	522	224	.429
C Knoblauch, Min	629	267	.424
T Naehring, Bos	516	214	.415
W Boggs, NYA	541	223	.412
R Henderson, Oak	486	198	.407
H Baines, Bal	459	185	.403

Slugging Percentage

Player, Team	AB	TB	SLG
A Belle, Cle	**546**	**377**	**.690**
E Martinez, Sea	511	321	.628
F Thomas, ChA	493	299	.606
T Salmon, Cal	537	319	.594
R Palmeiro, Bal	554	323	.583
M Vaughn, Bos	550	316	.575
J Buhner, Sea	470	266	.566
M Ramirez, Cle	484	270	.558
J Thome, Cle	452	252	.558
J Canseco, Bos	396	220	.556

Games

F Thomas, ChA	**145**
E Martinez, Sea	**145**
5 players tied with	144

Plate Appearances

C Curtis, Det	**670**
B Anderson, Bal	657
O Nixon, Tex	656
B Williams, NYA	648
F Thomas, ChA	647

At Bats

L Johnson, ChA	**607**
O Nixon, Tex	589
C Curtis, Det	586
T Fryman, Det	567
B Williams, NYA	563

Hits

L Johnson, ChA	**186**
E Martinez, Sea	182
C Knoblauch, Min	179
T Salmon, Cal	177
C Baerga, Cle	175

Singles

O Nixon, Tex	**151**
L Johnson, ChA	146
C Baerga, Cle	130
C Knoblauch, Min	126
W Boggs, NYA	118

Doubles

E Martinez, Sea	**52**
A Belle, Cle	**52**
K Puckett, Min	39
J Valentin, Bos	37
T Martinez, Sea	35

Triples

K Lofton, Cle	**13**
L Johnson, ChA	12
B Anderson, Bal	10
B Williams, NYA	9
C Knoblauch, Min	8

Home Runs

A Belle, Cle	**50**
J Buhner, Sea	40
F Thomas, ChA	40
3 players tied with	39

Total Bases

A Belle, Cle	**377**
R Palmeiro, Bal	323
E Martinez, Sea	321
T Salmon, Cal	319
M Vaughn, Bos	316

Runs Scored

E Martinez, Sea	**121**
A Belle, Cle	**121**
J Edmonds, Cal	120
T Phillips, Cal	119
T Salmon, Cal	111

Runs Batted In

A Belle, Cle	**126**
M Vaughn, Bos	**126**
J Buhner, Sea	121
E Martinez, Sea	113
2 players tied with	111

Ground Double Play

A Belle, Cle	**24**
P O'Neill, NYA	23
E Sprague, Tor	18
T Fryman, Det	18
M Blowers, Sea	18

Sacrifice Hits

T Goodwin, KC	**14**
L Alicea, Bos	13
J Cora, Sea	13
B Mayne, KC	11
4 players tied with	10

Sacrifice Flies

F Thomas, ChA	**12**
B Gates, Oak	11
P O'Neill, NYA	11
W Clark, Tex	11
O Vizquel, Cle	10

Stolen Bases

K Lofton, Cle	**54**
T Goodwin, KC	50
O Nixon, Tex	50
C Knoblauch, Min	46
V Coleman, Sea	42

Caught Stealing

O Nixon, Tex	**21**
C Knoblauch, Min	18
T Goodwin, KC	18
V Coleman, Sea	16
2 players tied with	15

Walks

F Thomas, ChA	**136**
E Martinez, Sea	116
T Phillips, Cal	113
M Tettleton, Tex	107
J Thome, Cle	97

Intentional Walks

F Thomas, ChA	**29**
E Martinez, Sea	19
K Puckett, Min	18
M Vaughn, Bos	17
T Martinez, Sea	15

Hit by Pitch

E Sprague, Tor	**15**
M Macfarlane, Bos	14
M Vaughn, Bos	14
P Meares, Min	11
M McGwire, Oak	11

Strikeouts

M Vaughn, Bos	**150**
B Gil, Tex	147
T Phillips, Cal	135
J Edmonds, Cal	130
M Blowers, Sea	128

1995 National League Batting Leaders

Batting Average

Player, Team	AB	H	AVG
T Gwynn, SD	**535**	**197**	**.368**
M Piazza, LA	434	150	.346
D Bichette, Col	579	197	.340
D Bell, Hou	452	151	.334
M Grace, ChN	552	180	.326
B Larkin, Cin	496	158	.319
V Castilla, Col	527	163	.309
D Segui, Mon	456	141	.309
G Jefferies, Phi	480	147	.306
R Sanders, Cin	484	148	.306

On-Base Percentage

Player, Team	PA	OB	OBP
B Bonds, SF	**635**	**274**	**.431**
C Biggio, Hou	662	269	.406
T Gwynn, SD	577	233	.404
W Weiss, Col	531	214	.403
M Piazza, LA	475	190	.400
J Bagwell, Hou	539	215	.399
R Sanders, Cin	567	225	.397
M Grace, ChN	626	247	.395
B Larkin, Cin	564	222	.394
J Offerman, LA	501	195	.389

Slugging Percentage

Player, Team	AB	TB	SLG
D Bichette, Col	**579**	**359**	**.620**
L Walker, Col	494	300	.607
M Piazza, LA	434	263	.606
R Sanders, Cin	484	280	.579
B Bonds, SF	506	292	.577
V Castilla, Col	527	297	.564
R Gant, Cin	410	227	.554
E Karros, LA	551	295	.535
J Conine, Fla	483	251	.520
M Grace, ChN	552	285	.516

Games

B Bonds, SF	**144**
F McGriff, Atl	**144**
S Sosa, ChN	**144**
4 players tied with	143

Plate Appearances

C Biggio, Hou	**673**
B McRae, ChN	638
B Bonds, SF	635
S Finley, SD	630
S Sosa, ChN	629

At Bats

B McRae, ChN	**580**
D Bichette, Col	579
S Sosa, ChN	564
S Finley, SD	562
A Galarraga, Col	554

Hits

T Gwynn, SD	**197**
D Bichette, Col	**197**
M Grace, ChN	180
3 players tied with	167

Singles

T Gwynn, SD	**154**
S Finley, SD	126
B Butler, LA	126
D Bell, Hou	120
2 players tied with	117

Doubles

M Grace, ChN	**51**
B McRae, ChN	38
D Bichette, Col	38
R Sanders, Cin	36
2 players tied with	35

Triples

B Butler, LA	**9**
E Young, Col	**9**
S Finley, SD	8
L Gonzalez, ChN	8
D Sanders, SF	8

Home Runs

D Bichette, Col	**40**
L Walker, Col	36
S Sosa, ChN	36
B Bonds, SF	33
3 players tied with	32

Total Bases

D Bichette, Col	**359**
L Walker, Col	300
V Castilla, Col	297
E Karros, LA	295
B Bonds, SF	292

Runs Scored

C Biggio, Hou	**123**
B Bonds, SF	109
S Finley, SD	104
D Bichette, Col	102
B Larkin, Cin	98

Runs Batted In

D Bichette, Col	**128**
S Sosa, ChN	119
A Galarraga, Col	106
J Conine, Fla	105
E Karros, LA	105

Ground Double Play

C Hayes, Phi	**23**
F McGriff, Atl	20
E Williams, SD	20
T Gwynn, SD	19
2 players tied with	17

Sacrifice Hits

B Jones, NYN	**18**
A Ashby, SD	17
R Martinez, LA	13
J Vizcaino, NYN	13
4 players tied with	12

Sacrifice Flies

J Conine, Fla	**12**
J King, Pit	8
5 players tied with	7

Stolen Bases

Q Veras, Fla	**56**
B Larkin, Cin	51
D DeShields, LA	39
R Sanders, Cin	36
S Finley, SD	36

Caught Stealing

Q Veras, Fla	**21**
D Lewis, Cin	18
D DeShields, LA	14
4 players tied with	12

Walks

B Bonds, SF	**120**
W Weiss, Col	98
C Biggio, Hou	80
Q Veras, Fla	80
J Bagwell, Hou	79

Intentional Walks

B Bonds, SF	**22**
J Branson, Cin	14
L Walker, Col	13
J Bagwell, Hou	12
T Tarasco, Mon	12

Hit by Pitch

C Biggio, Hou	**22**
L Walker, Col	14
A Galarraga, Col	13
J Patterson, SF	12
J Blauser, Atl	12

Strikeouts

A Galarraga, Col	**146**
S Sosa, ChN	134
R Sanders, Cin	122
E Karros, LA	115
R Brogna, NYN	111

1995 American League Pitching Leaders

Earned Run Average

Pitcher, Team	IP	ER	ERA
R Johnson, Sea	**214.1**	**59**	**2.48**
T Wakefield, Bos	195.1	64	2.95
D Martinez, Cle	187.0	64	3.08
M Mussina, Bal	221.2	81	3.29
K Rogers, Tex	208.0	78	3.38
D Cone, NYA	229.1	91	3.57
K Brown, Bal	172.1	69	3.60
A Leiter, Tor	183.0	74	3.64
J Abbott, Cal	197.0	81	3.70
M Gubicza, KC	213.1	89	3.75

Won-Lost Percentage

Pitcher, Team	W	L	WL%
R Johnson, Sea	**18**	**2**	**.900**
D Wells, Cin	10	3	.769
E Hanson, Bos	15	5	.750
C Nagy, Cle	16	6	.727
O Hershiser, Cle	16	6	.727
K Rogers, Tex	17	7	.708
D Martinez, Cle	12	5	.706
D Cone, NYA	18	8	.692
M Langston, Cal	15	7	.682
M Mussina, Bal	19	9	.679

Opposition Average

Pitcher, Team	AB	H	AVG
R Johnson, Sea	**792**	**159**	**.201**
K Appier, KC	738	163	.221
M Mussina, Bal	827	187	.226
T Wakefield, Bos	717	163	.227
D Cone, NYA	855	195	.228
A Leiter, Tor	681	162	.238
K Brown, Bal	642	155	.241
K Rogers, Tex	791	192	.243
R Pavlik, Tex	716	174	.243
O Hershiser, Cle	620	151	.244

Games

J Orosco, Bal	**65**
R McDowell, Tex	64
B Wickman, NYA	63
B Ayala, Sea	63
S Belinda, Bos	63

Games Started

M Gubicza, KC	**33**
M Mussina, Bal	32
C Finley, Cal	32
9 pitchers tied with	31

Complete Games

J McDowell, NYA	**8**
M Mussina, Bal	7
S Erickson, Bal	7
3 pitchers tied with	6

Games Finished

R Hernandez, ChA	**57**
J Mesa, Cle	**57**
J Wetteland, NYA	56
R Aguilera, Bos	51
L Smith, Cal	51

Wins

M Mussina, Bal	**19**
D Cone, NYA	18
R Johnson, Sea	18
K Rogers, Tex	17
3 pitchers tied with	16

Losses

J Bere, ChA	**15**
M Moore, Det	**15**
K Gross, Tex	**15**
4 pitchers tied with	14

Saves

J Mesa, Cle	**46**
L Smith, Cal	37
R Aguilera, Bos	32
R Hernandez, ChA	32
2 pitchers tied with	31

Shutouts

M Mussina, Bal	**4**
R Johnson, Sea	3
3 pitchers tied with	2

Hits Allowed

P Hentgen, Tor	**236**
T Stottlemyre, Oak	228
M Gubicza, KC	222
R Bones, Mil	218
S Erickson, Bal	213

Doubles Allowed

B Radke, Min	**48**
S Erickson, Bal	**48**
C Nagy, Cle	46
M Mussina, Bal	45
2 pitchers tied with	44

Triples Allowed

K Appier, KC	**10**
T Belcher, Sea	9
A Fernandez, ChA	8
W Alvarez, ChA	8
4 pitchers tied with	7

Home Runs Allowed

B Radke, Min	**32**
K Gross, Tex	27
T Stottlemyre, Oak	26
R Bones, Mil	26
K Rogers, Tex	26

Batters Faced

D Cone, NYA	**954**
J McDowell, NYA	927
T Stottlemyre, Oak	920
P Hentgen, Tor	913
M Gubicza, KC	898

Innings Pitched

D Cone, NYA	**229.1**
M Mussina, Bal	221.2
J McDowell, NYA	217.2
R Johnson, Sea	214.1
M Gubicza, KC	213.1

Runs Allowed

P Hentgen, Tor	**129**
K Gross, Tex	124
J Bere, ChA	120
M Moore, Det	118
T Stottlemyre, Oak	117

Strikeouts

R Johnson, Sea	**294**
T Stottlemyre, Oak	205
C Finley, Cal	195
D Cone, NYA	191
K Appier, KC	185

Walks Allowed

A Leiter, Tor	**108**
J Bere, ChA	106
W Alvarez, ChA	93
C Finley, Cal	93
P Hentgen, Tor	90
R Pavlik, Tex	90

Hit Batters

R Clemens, Bos	**14**
D Martinez, Cle	12
K Brown, Bal	9
T Wakefield, Bos	9
4 pitchers tied with	8

Wild Pitches

A Leiter, Tor	**14**
S Bergman, Det	13
C Finley, Cal	13
4 pitchers tied with	11

Balks

T Fortugno, Cal	**3**
B Anderson, Cal	**3**
14 pitchers tied with	2

1995 National League Pitching Leaders

Earned Run Average

Pitcher, Team	IP	ER	ERA
G Maddux, Atl	209.2	38	1.63
H Nomo, LA	191.1	54	2.54
A Ashby, SD	192.2	63	2.94
I Valdes, LA	197.2	67	3.05
T Glavine, Atl	198.2	68	3.08
J Hamilton, SD	204.1	70	3.08
J Smoltz, Atl	192.2	68	3.18
F Castillo, ChN	188.0	67	3.21
P Schourek, Cin	190.1	68	3.22
J Navarro, ChN	200.1	73	3.28

Won-Lost Percentage

Pitcher, Team	W	L	WL%
G Maddux, Atl	19	2	.905
P Schourek, Cin	18	7	.720
D Burba, Cin	10	4	.714
R Martinez, LA	17	7	.708
J Navarro, ChN	14	6	.700
J Smiley, Cin	12	5	.706
T Glavine, Atl	16	7	.696
H Nomo, LA	13	6	.684
P Rapp, Fla	14	7	.667
J Smoltz, Atl	12	7	.632

Opposition Average

Pitcher, Team	AB	H	AVG
H Nomo, LA	681	124	.182
G Maddux, Atl	748	147	.197
P Martinez, Mon	697	158	.227
I Valdes, LA	737	168	.228
P Schourek, Cin	693	158	.228
R Martinez, LA	761	176	.231
J Smoltz, Atl	714	166	.232
K Foster, ChN	622	149	.240
T Glavine, Atl	739	182	.246
J Hamilton, SD	767	189	.246

Games

C Leskanic, Col	76
D Veres, Hou	72
S Reed, Col	71
Y Perez, Fla	69
3 pitchers tied with	68

Games Started

D Neagle, Pit	31
M Portugal, Cin	31
A Ashby, SD	31
E Loaiza, Pit	31
D Drabek, Hou	31

Complete Games

G Maddux, Atl	10
M Leiter, SF	7
I Valdes, LA	6
D Neagle, Pit	5
4 pitchers tied with	4

Games Finished

H Slocumb, Phi	54
R Nen, Fla	54
T Worrell, LA	53
R Beck, SF	52
2 pitchers tied with	51

Wins

G Maddux, Atl	19
P Schourek, Cin	18
R Martinez, LA	17
T Glavine, Atl	16
4 pitchers tied with	14

Losses

P Wagner, Pit	16
J Burkett, Fla	14
J Fassero, Mon	14
T Candiotti, LA	14
3 pitchers tied with	13

Saves

R Myers, ChN	38
T Henke, StL	36
R Beck, SF	33
H Slocumb, Phi	32
T Worrell, LA	32

Shutouts

G Maddux, Atl	3
H Nomo, LA	3
10 pitchers tied with	2

Hits Allowed

D Neagle, Pit	221
P Quantrill, Phi	212
B Jones, NYN	209
J Burkett, Fla	208
J Fassero, Mon	207

Doubles Allowed

B Jones, NYN	46
P Quantrill, Phi	44
E Loaiza, Pit	43
M Leiter, SF	41
2 pitchers tied with	39

Triples Allowed

J Burkett, Fla	12
P Martinez, Mon	9
D Drabek, Hou	8
J Fassero, Mon	8
3 pitchers tied with	7

Home Runs Allowed

K Foster, ChN	32
S Trachsel, ChN	25
T Mulholland, SF	25
J Bautista, SF	24
D Mlicki, NYN	23

Batters Faced

D Neagle, Pit	876
R Martinez, LA	859
J Hamilton, SD	850
B Jones, NYN	839
J Navarro, ChN	837

Innings Pitched

D Neagle, Pit	209.2
G Maddux, Atl	209.2
R Martinez, LA	206.1
J Hamilton, SD	204.1
J Navarro, ChN	200.1

Runs Allowed

E Loaiza, Pit	115
T Mulholland, SF	112
B Jones, NYN	107
S Trachsel, ChN	104
D Drabek, Hou	104

Strikeouts

H Nomo, LA	236
J Smoltz, Atl	193
G Maddux, Atl	181
S Reynolds, Hou	175
P Martinez, Mon	174

Walks Allowed

R Martinez, LA	81
H Nomo, LA	78
P Rapp, Fla	76
S Trachsel, ChN	76
M Mimbs, Phi	75

Hit Batters

M Leiter, SF	17
D Kile, Hou	12
J Hamilton, SD	11
A Ashby, SD	11
P Martinez, Mon	11

Wild Pitches

H Nomo, LA	19
H Carrasco, Cin	15
J Smoltz, Atl	13
T Borland, Phi	12
2 pitchers tied with	11

Balks

H Nomo, LA	5
W VanLandingham, SF	4
C Perez, Mon	4
4 pitchers tied with	3

1995 American League Special Batting Leaders

Scoring Position

Player, Team	AB	H	AVG
R Henderson, Oak	**74**	**31**	**.419**
K Lofton, Cle	88	34	.386
E Martinez, Sea	138	53	.384
B Surhoff, Mil	107	41	.383
K Seitzer, Mil	125	47	.376
C Knoblauch, Min	113	41	.363
C Baerga, Cle	144	52	.361
E Murray, Cle	114	40	.351
D White, Tor	82	28	.341
W Clark, Tex	129	44	.341

Leadoff On-Base%

Player, Team	PA	OB	OBP
C Knoblauch, Min	**620**	**262**	**.423**
W Boggs, NYA	238	100	.420
R Henderson, Oak	480	196	.408
T Phillips, Cal	632	250	.396
K Lofton, Cle	524	190	.363
O Nixon, Tex	649	231	.356
B Anderson, Bal	489	174	.356
L Johnson, ChA	553	196	.354
C Curtis, Det	669	234	.350
L Tinsley, Bos	283	98	.346

Cleanup Slugging%

Player, Team	AB	TB	SLG
M McGwire, Oak	**300**	**209**	**.697**
A Belle, Cle	546	377	.690
J Gonzalez, Tex	350	209	.597
T Martinez, Sea	191	109	.571
E Martinez, Sea	152	86	.566
J Canseco, Bos	383	216	.564
B Bonilla, Bal	237	129	.544
D Nilsson, Mil	143	77	.538
J Jaha, Mil	134	71	.530
C Davis, Cal	389	194	.499

Vs LHP

E Martinez, Sea	**.433**
M Ramirez, Cle	.407
F Thomas, ChA	.389
B Surhoff, Mil	.367
L Sojo, Sea	.360

Vs RHP

E Murray, Cle	**.340**
K Seitzer, Mil	.334
E Martinez, Sea	.331
W Boggs, NYA	.329
R Henderson, Oak	.328

Late & Close

J Canseco, Bos	**.404**
E Martinez, Sea	.397
J Cora, Sea	.392
R Alomar, Tor	.389
C Baerga, Cle	.375

Bases Loaded

M Stanley, NYA	**.818**
D White, Tor	.667
M Vaughn, Bos	.600
B Surhoff, Mil	.556
K Seitzer, Mil	.533

OBP vs LHP

E Martinez, Sea	**.562**
F Thomas, ChA	.524
M Ramirez, Cle	.507
M McGwire, Oak	.478
J Valentin, Bos	.465

OBP vs RHP

J Thome, Cle	**.456**
E Martinez, Sea	.449
C Knoblauch, Min	.433
C Davis, Cal	.430
F Thomas, ChA	.430

BA at Home

W Boggs, NYA	**.379**
E Martinez, Sea	.377
C Davis, Cal	.358
T O'Leary, Bos	.349
T Naehring, Bos	.348

BA on the Road

T Salmon, Cal	**.366**
E Martinez, Sea	.336
C Knoblauch, Min	.336
K Puckett, Min	.326
L Johnson, ChA	.324

SLG vs LHP

F Thomas, ChA	**.849**
M McGwire, Oak	.835
C Hoiles, Bal	.720
E Martinez, Sea	.709
J Canseco, Bos	.699

SLG vs RHP

A Belle, Cle	**.729**
M Vaughn, Bos	.654
R Palmeiro, Bal	.605
E Martinez, Sea	.602
J Thome, Cle	.601

SB Success %

R Amaral, Sea	**91.3**
R Alomar, Tor	90.9
S Javier, Oak	87.8
L Johnson, ChA	87.0
C Goodwin, Bal	84.6

Times on Base

E Martinez, Sea	**306**
F Thomas, ChA	294
T Salmon, Cal	274
C Knoblauch, Min	267
2 players tied with	253

AB per HR

A Belle, Cle	**10.9**
J Buhner, Sea	11.8
F Thomas, ChA	12.3
M Tettleton, Tex	13.4
M Vaughn, Bos	14.1

Ground/Fly Ratio

O Nixon, Tex	**3.00**
T Goodwin, KC	2.16
M McLemore, Tex	1.96
B Gates, Oak	1.89
W Boggs, NYA	1.88

GDP/GDP Opp

J Valentin, Mil	**0.0**
B Anderson, Bal	3.2
K Lockhart, KC	4.0
S Stahoviak, Min	4.6
D Hulse, Mil	4.6

% CS by Catchers

I Rodriguez, Tex	**48.1**
L Parrish, Tor	41.5
T Steinbach, Oak	39.4
D Wilson, Sea	36.8
M Macfarlane, Bos	35.4

Pitches Seen

T Phillips, Cal	**2753**
C Curtis, Det	2647
B Anderson, Bal	2642
E Martinez, Sea	2586
J Valentin, Bos	2552

Pitches per PA

R Henderson, Oak	**4.36**
W Boggs, NYA	4.32
M Tettleton, Tex	4.30
T Phillips, Cal	4.28
J Thome, Cle	4.23

% Pitches Taken

M Tettleton, Tex	**66.9**
E Martinez, Sea	66.2
W Boggs, NYA	65.9
T Naehring, Bos	63.7
R Henderson, Oak	63.5

Steals of Third

O Nixon, Tex	**13**
V Coleman, Sea	**13**
K Lofton, Cle	**13**
R Henderson, Oak	11
5 players tied with	9

1995 National League Special Batting Leaders

Scoring Position

Player, Team	AB	H	AVG
T Gwynn, SD	137	54	.394
J Bates, Col	73	27	.370
D Bichette, Col	158	58	.367
D DeShields, LA	75	27	.360
M Piazza, LA	112	40	.357
M Alou, Mon	98	35	.357
B Larkin, Cin	109	38	.349
M Morandini, Phi	107	37	.346
E Karros, LA	145	50	.345
E Taubensee, Cin	79	27	.342

Leadoff On-Base%

Player, Team	PA	OB	OBP
J Cangelosi, Hou	152	69	.454
S Finley, SD	341	138	.405
E Young, Col	388	156	.402
Q Veras, Fla	517	200	.387
B Butler, LA	584	219	.375
R White, Mon	272	102	.375
A Martin, Pit	193	70	.363
T Howard, Cin	152	54	.355
L Dykstra, Phi	291	103	.354
M Morandini, Phi	300	106	.353

Cleanup Slugging%

Player, Team	AB	TB	SLG
R Gant, Cin	127	91	.717
M Grace, ChN	119	79	.664
M Williams, SF	277	178	.643
L Walker, Col	308	192	.623
B Bonilla, Bal	316	190	.601
R Sanders, Cin	357	208	.583
M Piazza, LA	133	76	.571
B Jordan, StL	148	79	.534
K Caminiti, SD	407	210	.516
S Sosa, ChN	427	215	.504

Vs LHP

E Young, Col	.400
V Castilla, Col	.388
C Biggio, Hou	.383
R White, Mon	.377
R Sanders, Cin	.365

Vs RHP

T Gwynn, SD	.389
M Piazza, LA	.351
M Grace, ChN	.344
D Bichette, Col	.342
D Magadan, Hou	.329

Late & Close

R Gant, Cin	.418
E Young, Col	.404
B Larkin, Cin	.397
M Williams, SF	.395
T Gwynn, SD	.387

Bases Loaded

D Sheaffer, StL	.714
T Gwynn, SD	.636
C Everett, NYN	.556
D Magadan, Hou	.500
R Kelly, LA	.500

OBP vs LHP

C Biggio, Hou	.493
E Young, Col	.449
R Sanders, Cin	.447
R White, Mon	.437
V Castilla, Col	.417

OBP vs RHP

B Bonds, SF	.447
D Magadan, Hou	.446
M Grace, ChN	.425
T Gwynn, SD	.424
M Piazza, LA	.409

BA at Home

T Gwynn, SD	.387
V Castilla, Col	.383
D Bichette, Col	.377
M Grace, ChN	.375
J Conine, Fla	.350

BA on the Road

M Piazza, LA	.384
D Bell, Hou	.361
T Gwynn, SD	.349
C Biggio, Hou	.326
D Segui, Mon	.324

SLG vs LHP

V Castilla, Col	.769
R Sanders, Cin	.692
D Bichette, Col	.691
E Young, Col	.648
C Biggio, Hou	.626

SLG vs RHP

L Walker, Col	.637
B Bonds, SF	.614
M Piazza, LA	.606
D Bichette, Col	.595
M Grace, ChN	.560

SB Success %

B Larkin, Cin	91.1
B Roberts, SD	90.9
T Tarasco, Mon	88.9
M Lansing, Mon	87.1
R Mondesi, LA	87.1

Times on Base

B Bonds, SF	274
C Biggio, Hou	269
M Grace, ChN	247
T Gwynn, SD	233
3 players tied with	229

AB per HR

M Piazza, LA	13.6
L Walker, Col	13.7
R Gant, Cin	14.1
D Bichette, Col	14.5
B Bonds, SF	15.3

Ground/Fly Ratio

B Butler, LA	2.58
T Gwynn, SD	2.55
B McRae, ChN	2.16
D Bell, Hou	2.07
W Weiss, Col	2.02

GDP/GDP Opp

T Tarasco, Mon	2.2
C Carr, Fla	3.2
D Daulton, Phi	3.9
C Jones, NYN	4.1
B Jordan, StL	4.3

% CS by Catchers

C Johnson, Fla	42.7
B Ausmus, SD	41.9
M Parent, ChN	39.3
T Pagnozzi, StL	36.8
R Wilkins, Hou	34.3

Pitches Seen

C Biggio, Hou	2488
E Karros, LA	2484
B Bonds, SF	2451
S Sosa, ChN	2441
B McRae, ChN	2439

Pitches per PA

D Justice, Atl	4.21
B Larkin, Cin	4.15
Q Veras, Fla	4.15
R Gant, Cin	4.09
J Bell, Pit	4.09

% Pitches Taken

W Weiss, Col	65.4
D Magadan, Hou	64.7
Q Veras, Fla	64.6
D DeShields, LA	63.9
J Reed, SD	63.9

Steals of Third

B Larkin, Cin	15
Q Veras, Fla	14
E Young, Col	12
C Biggio, Hou	10
S Finley, SD	10

1995 American League Special Pitching Leaders

Baserunners Per 9 IP

Player, Team	IP	BR	BR/9
R Johnson, Sea	214.1	230	9.66
M Mussina, Bal	221.2	238	9.66
T Wakefield, Bos	195.1	240	11.06
K Brown, Bal	172.1	212	11.07
O Hershiser, Cle	167.1	207	11.13
D Martinez, Cle	187.0	232	11.17
K Appier, KC	201.1	251	11.22
D Cone, NYA	229.1	289	11.34
K Rogers, Tex	208.0	270	11.68
A Fernandez, ChA	203.2	265	11.71

Run Support Per 9 IP

Player, Team	IP	R	R/9
C Nagy, Cle	178.0	161	8.14
M Langston, Cal	200.1	160	7.19
S Erickson, Bal	196.1	148	6.78
C Finley, Cal	203.0	150	6.65
E Hanson, Bos	186.2	137	6.61
D Cone, NYA	229.1	166	6.51
T Stottlemyre, Oak	209.2	151	6.48
C Bosio, Sea	170.0	122	6.46
O Hershiser, Cle	167.1	113	6.08
D Martinez, Cle	187.0	122	5.87

Save Percentage

Player, Team	OP	SV	SV%
J Mesa, Cle	48	46	.958
L Smith, Cal	41	37	.902
M Henneman, Hou	20	18	.900
R Aguilera, Bos	36	32	.889
D Jones, Bal	25	22	.880
J Wetteland, NYA	37	31	.838
J Russell, Tex	24	20	.833
J Montgomery, KC	38	31	.816
M Fetters, Mil	27	22	.815
D Eckersley, Oak	38	29	.763

Hits per 9 IP

R Johnson, Sea	6.68
K Appier, KC	7.29
T Wakefield, Bos	7.51
M Mussina, Bal	7.59
D Cone, NYA	7.65

Home Runs per 9 IP

R Johnson, Sea	0.50
K Brown, Bal	0.52
T Gordon, KC	0.57
K Appier, KC	0.63
J Abbott, Cal	0.64

Strikeouts per 9 IP

R Johnson, Sea	12.3
T Stottlemyre, Oak	8.8
C Finley, Cal	8.6
K Appier, KC	8.3
A Leiter, Tor	7.5

GDP per 9 IP

O Hershiser, Cle	1.4
S Sparks, Mil	1.3
S Erickson, Bal	1.2
J Abbott, Cal	1.1
K Brown, Bal	1.1

Vs LHB

M Mussina, Bal	.210
E Hanson, Bos	.215
C Ogea, Cle	.226
B Ayala, Sea	.229
D Martinez, Cle	.229

Vs RHB

K Appier, KC	.177
O Hershiser, Cle	.196
R Johnson, Sea	.209
T Wakefield, Bos	.211
D Cone, NY	.221

OBP Leadoff Inning

D Cone, NYA	.237
D Wells, Cin	.246
K Brown, Bal	.247
M Mussina, Bal	.255
O Hershiser, Cle	.261

BA Allowed ScPos

R Johnson, Sea	.164
D Martinez, Cle	.183
T Wakefield, Bos	.185
M Mussina, Bal	.212
F Lira, Det	.220

SLG Allowed

R Johnson, Sea	.303
K Brown, Bal	.341
K Appier, KC	.351
A Leiter, Tor	.363
D Martinez, Cle	.367

OBP Allowed

R Johnson, Sea	.266
M Mussina, Bal	.270
T Wakefield, Bos	.300
D Martinez, Cle	.302
K Brown, Bal	.302

PkOf Throw/Runner

J McDowell, NYA	1.47
D Cone, NYA	1.44
M Langston, Cal	1.28
K Brown, Bal	1.26
S Hitchcock, NYA	1.24

SB% Allowed

M Langston, Cal	25.0
T Belcher, Sea	26.7
M Mussina, Bal	40.0
F Lira, Det	46.2
W Alvarez, ChA	47.1

Pitches per Batter

J Abbott, Cal	3.48
O Hershiser, Cle	3.54
C Bosio, Sea	3.57
M Gubicza, KC	3.58
S Erickson, Bal	3.58

Grd/Fly Ratio Off

K Brown, Bal	2.68
S Erickson, Bal	2.59
O Hershiser, Cle	2.47
C Nagy, Cle	2.07
M Gubicza, KC	2.01

K/BB Ratio

R Johnson, Sea	4.52
M Mussina, Bal	3.16
T Stottlemyre, Oak	2.56
A Fernandez, ChA	2.45
K Brown, Bal	2.44

Wins in Relief

J Tavarez, Cle	10
S Belinda, Bos	8
H Pichardo, KC	8
J Nelson, Sea	7
R McDowell, Tex	7

Holds

T Percival, Cal	29
B Wickman, NYA	21
J Tavarez, Cle	19
S Belinda, Bos	17
J Orosco, Bal	15

Blown Saves

R Hernandez, ChA	10
D Eckersley, Oak	9
B Wickman, NYA	9
T Castillo, Tor	8
B Ayala, Sea	8

% Inherited Scored

M Christopher, Det	9.1
P Assenmacher, Cle	10.7
J Poole, Cle	14.8
M Lee, Bal	15.4
T Percival, Cal	17.0

1st Batter OBP

J Doherty, Det	.049
J Poole, Cle	.083
J Mesa, Cle	.117
M Lee, Bal	.118
E Plunk, Cle	.163

1995 National League Special Pitching Leaders

Baserunners Per 9 IP

Player, Team	IP	BR	BR/9
G Maddux, Atl	209.2	174	7.47
H Nomo, LA	191.1	207	9.74
P Schourek, Cin	190.1	211	9.98
I Valdes, LA	197.2	220	10.02
P Martinez, Mon	194.2	235	10.86
J Smiley, Cin	176.2	216	11.00
S Reynolds, Hou	189.1	235	11.17
J Hamilton, SD	204.1	256	11.28
J Smoltz, Atl	192.2	242	11.30
F Castillo, ChN	188.0	237	11.35

Run Support Per 9 IP

Player, Team	IP	R	R/9
M Portugal, Cin	181.2	125	6.19
P Rapp, Fla	167.1	115	6.19
J Bullinger, ChN	150.0	99	5.94
K Foster, ChN	167.2	107	5.74
C Hammond, Fla	161.0	102	5.70
D Mlicki, NYN	160.2	100	5.60
M Hampton, Hou	150.2	93	5.56
G Swindell, Hou	153.0	94	5.53
J Fassero, Mon	189.0	116	5.52
P Schourek, Cin	190.1	116	5.49

Save Percentage

Player, Team	OP	SV	SV%
T Henke, StL	38	36	.947
T Worrell, LA	36	32	.889
J Brantley, Cin	32	28	.875
R Myers, ChN	44	38	.864
M Wohlers, Atl	29	25	.862
H Slocumb, Phi	38	32	.842
T Hoffman, SD	38	31	.816
J Franco, NYN	36	29	.806
R Nen, Fla	29	23	.793
D Miceli, Pit	27	21	.778

Hits per 9 IP

H Nomo, LA	5.83
G Maddux, Atl	6.31
P Martinez, Mon	7.30
P Schourek, Cin	7.47
I Valdes, LA	7.65

Home Runs per 9 IP

G Maddux, Atl	0.34
T Glavine, Atl	0.41
P Rapp, Fla	0.54
J Smiley, Cin	0.56
H Nomo, LA	0.66

Strikeouts per 9 IP

H Nomo, LA	11.1
J Smoltz, Atl	9.0
S Reynolds, Hou	8.3
P Martinez, Mon	8.0
K Foster, ChN	7.8

GDP per 9 IP

J Burkett, Fla	1.2
T Glavine, Atl	1.2
A Ashby, SD	1.1
J Smiley, Cin	1.1
P Wagner, Pit	1.0

Vs LHB

G Maddux, Atl	.194
H Nomo, LA	.199
P Martinez, Mon	.219
I Valdes, LA	.228
J Hamilton, SD	.229

Vs RHB

H Nomo, LA	.168
D Burba, Cin	.198
G Maddux, Atl	.198
J Smoltz, Atl	.206
C Shilling, Phi	.211

OBP Leadoff Inning

I Valdes, LA	.240
R Martinez, LA	.250
G Maddux, Atl	.255
M Leiter, SF	.258
S Avery, Atl	.267

BA Allowed ScPos

G Maddux, Atl	.157
C Hammond, Fla	.184
H Nomo, LA	.192
C Perez, Mon	.193
M Morgan, StL	.203

SLG Allowed

G Maddux, Atl	.258
H Nomo, LA	.286
T Glavine, Atl	.334
I Valdes, LA	.343
J Smoltz, Atl	.346

OBP Allowed

G Maddux, Atl	.224
H Nomo, LA	.270
I Valdes, LA	.277
P Schourek, Cin	.281
S Reynolds, Hou	.300

PkOf Throw/Runner

S Trachsel, ChN	1.66
S Avery, Atl	1.63
G Swindell, Hou	1.48
M Leiter, SF	1.45
J Fassero, Mon	1.29

SB% Allowed

C Hammond, Fla	0.0
T Mulholland, SF	14.3
P Rapp, Fla	25.0
P Schourek, Cin	36.8
P Martinez, Mon	40.9

Pitches per Batter

E Loaiza, Pit	3.28
G Maddux, Atl	3.34
T Mulholland, SF	3.36
M Portugal, Cin	3.43
J Smiley, Cin	3.46

Grd/Fly Ratio Off

G Maddux, Atl	3.03
S Reynolds, Hou	2.69
J Hamilton, SD	2.26
A Ashby, SD	2.10
J Fassero, Mon	2.03

K/BB Ratio

G Maddux, Atl	7.87
S Reynolds, Hou	4.73
P Schourek, Cin	3.56
D Neagle, Pit	3.33
J Smiley, Cin	3.18

Wins in Relief

J Dougherty, Hou	8
R DeLucia, StL	8
B Clontz, Atl	8
4 players tied with	7

Holds

R Bottalico, Phi	20
G McMichael, Atl	20
3 players tied with	19

Blown Saves

R Beck, SF	10
M Rojas, Mon	9
T Hoffman, SD	7
J Franco, NYN	7
R Arocha, StL	7

% Inherited Scored

T Scott, Mon	12.5
Y Perez, Fla	14.3
P Borbon, Atl	17.2
C Leskanic, Col	17.4
D Bochtler, SD	21.9

1st Batter OBP

M Wohlers, Atl	.097
Y Perez, Fla	.105
T Worrell, LA	.109
M Jackson, Cin	.135
B Williams, SD	.143

1995 Active Career Batting Leaders

Batting Average

Player, Team	AB	H	AVG
T Gwynn	**7144**	**2401**	**.336**
W Boggs	7599	2541	.334
F Thomas	2764	893	.323
M Piazza	1455	469	.322
K Puckett	7244	2304	.318
E Martinez	2777	868	.313
K Lofton	2159	673	.312
H Morris	2394	737	.308
D Mattingly	7003	2153	.307
M Grace	4356	1333	.306
J Bagwell	2523	771	.306
P Molitor	9135	2789	.305
C Baerga	3185	971	.305
M Greenwell	4328	1313	.303
K Griffey Jr	3440	1039	.302
W Clark	5112	1543	.302
J Kruk	3897	1170	.300
J Conine	1640	492	.300
R Palmeiro	4857	1455	.300
C Knoblauch	2750	822	.299
B Larkin	4429	1322	.298
R Alomar	4460	1329	.298
W McGee	6500	1933	.297
B Roberts	3082	915	.297
J Olerud	2705	801	.296

On-Base Percentage

Player, Team	PA	OB	OBP
F Thomas	**3491**	**1572**	**.450**
W Boggs	8916	3777	.424
E Martinez	3265	1332	.408
R Henderson	9726	3951	.406
B Bonds	6035	2400	.398
J Olerud	3215	1277	.397
J Kruk	4591	1821	.397
J Bagwell	2971	1174	.395
T Salmon	1775	699	.394
D Magadan	3684	1447	.393
T Gwynn	7837	3042	.388
F McGriff	5316	2050	.386
T Raines	8994	3466	.385
J Thome	1352	517	.382
K Lofton	2425	925	.381
W Clark	5871	2227	.379
K Griffey Jr	3915	1483	.379
M Grace	4945	1873	.379
B Butler	8868	3357	.379
C Knoblauch	3147	1191	.378
J Valentin	1698	640	.377
M Vaughn	2391	901	.377
J Cangelosi	1667	628	.377
M Piazza	1592	597	.375
L Dykstra	5094	1906	.374

Slugging Percentage

Player, Team	AB	TB	SLG
F Thomas	**2764**	**1640**	**.593**
A Belle	2839	1620	.571
M Piazza	1455	811	.557
T Salmon	1504	814	.541
B Bonds	5020	2714	.541
K Griffey Jr	3440	1845	.536
F McGriff	4512	2414	.535
J Gonzalez	2589	1379	.533
M McGwire	3659	1912	.523
J Canseco	4711	2428	.515
J Bagwell	2523	1300	.515
M Vaughn	2057	1049	.510
D Strawberry	4843	2445	.505
L Walker	2860	1442	.504
R Mondesi	1056	532	.504
M Alou	1609	802	.498
D Justice	2718	1353	.498
D Tartabull	4532	2255	.498
W Clark	5112	2542	.497
C Fielder	3789	1883	.497
M Williams	3735	1856	.497
V Castilla	1015	504	.497
J Thome	1142	564	.494
R Palmeiro	4857	2387	.491
E Martinez	2777	1363	.491

Games

D Winfield	**2973**
E Murray	2819
A Dawson	2585
O Smith	2491
L Whitaker	2390
P Molitor	2261
A Trammell	2227
C Ripken	2218
R Henderson	2192
H Baines	2183
T Wallach	2110
B Butler	2074
T Raines	2053
W Boggs	1991
L Parrish	1988

Runs Scored

R Henderson	**1719**
D Winfield	1669
P Molitor	1545
E Murray	1545
L Whitaker	1386
T Raines	1374
A Dawson	1367
W Boggs	1287
B Butler	1285
C Ripken	1272
O Smith	1221
A Trammell	1215
T Gwynn	1073
K Puckett	1071
H Baines	1033

Runs Batted In

D Winfield	**1833**
E Murray	1820
A Dawson	1577
C Ripken	1267
H Baines	1261
J Carter	1173
C Davis	1100
D Mattingly	1099
K Puckett	1085
L Whitaker	1084
T Wallach	1083
G Gaetti	1075
L Parrish	1070
P Molitor	1036
A Trammell	987

Stolen Bases

R Henderson	**1149**
T Raines	777
V Coleman	740
O Smith	573
B Butler	535
P Molitor	466
O Nixon	444
J Samuel	369
B Bonds	340
W McGee	325
A Dawson	314
R Alomar	296
M Grissom	295
T Gwynn	285
K Gibson	284

Hits

D Winfield	3110
E Murray	3071
P Molitor	2789
A Dawson	2758
W Boggs	2541
T Gwynn	2401
O Smith	2396
C Ripken	2371
L Whitaker	2369
R Henderson	2338
A Trammell	2320
K Puckett	2304
T Raines	2295
H Baines	2271
B Butler	2243

Home Runs

E Murray	479
D Winfield	465
A Dawson	436
C Ripken	327
J Carter	327
L Parrish	324
H Baines	301
J Canseco	300
D Strawberry	297
G Gaetti	292
B Bonds	292
F McGriff	289
M McGwire	277
C Davis	270
K Gibson	255

Strikeouts

D Winfield	1686
L Parrish	1527
A Dawson	1496
E Murray	1403
C Davis	1385
J Samuel	1336
G Gaetti	1301
K Gibson	1285
J Canseco	1267
D Tartabull	1230
T Wallach	1228
D Strawberry	1182
A Galarraga	1171
H Baines	1163
M Tettleton	1158

AB per HR

M McGwire	13.2
A Belle	14.6
C Fielder	15.2
F Thomas	15.2
J Gonzalez	15.5
F McGriff	15.6
J Canseco	15.7
M Piazza	15.8
D Strawberry	16.3
M Williams	16.6
T Salmon	16.7
S Horn	16.8
B Bonds	17.2
D Justice	17.6
J Buhner	17.7

Doubles

D Winfield	540
E Murray	532
P Molitor	503
A Dawson	501
W Boggs	489
C Ripken	447
D Mattingly	442
T Wallach	422
L Whitaker	420
K Puckett	414
A Trammell	410
R Henderson	395
O Smith	392
H Baines	387
T Gwynn	384

Walks

R Henderson	1550
E Murray	1257
D Winfield	1216
W Boggs	1213
L Whitaker	1197
T Raines	1134
B Butler	1078
O Smith	1047
T Phillips	974
P Molitor	948
C Davis	936
B Bonds	931
C Ripken	901
M Tettleton	851
A Trammell	840

K/BB Ratio

W Boggs	0.49
T Gwynn	0.55
O Smith	0.55
E Young	0.61
M Grace	0.66
F Thomas	0.67
R Henderson	0.71
T Raines	0.71
J Reed	0.72
D Magadan	0.73
D Mattingly	0.76
G Jefferies	0.76
M LaValliere	0.76
M Greenwell	0.76
L Dykstra	0.78

GDP/GDP Opp

D Valle	26.4
M Blowers	27.6
T Pena	28.1
S Horn	28.1
R Gonzales	28.3
B Harper	29.4
G Myers	30.0
T Steinbach	30.1
A Belle	30.2
D Clark	30.5
M Lemke	30.5
B Mayne	30.9
D Segui	31.0
E Sprague	31.1
C Fielder	31.8

Triples

B Butler	127
T Raines	109
A Dawson	98
P Molitor	97
J Samuel	95
A Van Slyke	91
T Fernandez	89
D Winfield	88
V Coleman	88
W McGee	87
T Gwynn	80
L Johnson	78
O Smith	67
L Whitaker	65
S Owen	59

Intentional Walks

E Murray	216
B Bonds	196
D Winfield	172
T Gwynn	165
W Boggs	162
H Baines	155
C Davis	153
A Dawson	143
T Raines	141
D Mattingly	136
W Clark	129
D Strawberry	122
K Griffey Jr	106
H Johnson	105
B Bonilla	103

SB Success %

B Larkin	85.4
T Raines	85.1
M Grissom	83.8
S Javier	83.8
K Lofton	82.4
R Henderson	81.3
V Coleman	80.9
A Van Slyke	80.6
O Smith	80.0
L Dykstra	79.9
P Molitor	79.7
R Alomar	79.6
D White	79.3
J Carter	78.8
K Gibson	78.5

AB per RBI

F Thomas	4.6
A Belle	4.7
M Piazza	4.8
M McGwire	4.9
J Canseco	5.0
C Fielder	5.0
J Gonzalez	5.0
M Vaughn	5.2
J Bagwell	5.4
D Strawberry	5.4
T Salmon	5.4
J Buhner	5.5
D Justice	5.5
D Tartabull	5.5
F McGriff	5.6

1995 Active Career Pitching Leaders

Wins	
D Martinez	231
D Eckersley	192
R Clemens	182
F Viola	175
D Stewart	168
M Langston	166
S Sanderson	163
M Moore	161
F Valenzuela	158
J Key	152
O Hershiser	150
G Maddux	150
D Darwin	148
B Saberhagen	141
R Darling	136

Losses	
D Martinez	176
M Moore	176
D Eckersley	159
D Darwin	150
K Gross	149
F Viola	147
M Morgan	144
R Honeycutt	142
S Sanderson	141
M Langston	141
F Valenzuela	133
D Stewart	129
T Candiotti	124
M Gubicza	123
D Jackson	121

Saves	
L Smith	471
D Eckersley	323
T Henke	311
J Franco	295
D Righetti	252
R Myers	243
D Jones	239
J Montgomery	218
R Aguilera	211
M Williams	192
S Bedrosian	184
J Russell	183
T Worrell	177
B Harvey	177
G Olson	164

Shutouts	
R Clemens	36
F Valenzuela	31
D Martinez	28
O Hershiser	25
D Drabek	21
D Cone	21
D Eckersley	20
G Maddux	20
M Langston	18
R Martinez	18
F Viola	16
M Moore	16
B Saberhagen	16
T Belcher	16
4 players tied with	15

Games	
L Smith	943
D Eckersley	901
J Orosco	819
R Honeycutt	734
S Bedrosian	732
D Righetti	718
G Harris	703
R McDowell	682
J Franco	661
T Henke	642
P Assenmacher	622
D Darwin	618
M Williams	612
D Martinez	610
R Murphy	597

Games Started	
D Martinez	528
M Moore	440
F Viola	414
S Sanderson	403
M Langston	380
F Valenzuela	375
R Darling	364
D Eckersley	361
D Stewart	348
R Clemens	348
K Gross	346
O Hershiser	329
T Candiotti	319
J Key	314
B Saberhagen	309

CG Freq	
F Valenzuela	0.30
D Eckersley	0.28
R Clemens	0.27
J McDowell	0.26
B Saberhagen	0.25
G Maddux	0.24
D Martinez	0.23
T Mulholland	0.21
M Langston	0.21
K Brown	0.20
T Candiotti	0.20
O Hershiser	0.20
D Cone	0.19
C Finley	0.19
R Johnson	0.19

Innings Pitched	
D Martinez	3748.0
D Eckersley	3133.0
M Moore	2831.2
F Viola	2806.0
F Valenzuela	2669.1
M Langston	2648.2
D Stewart	2629.1
D Darwin	2546.2
S Sanderson	2543.0
R Clemens	2533.1
R Darling	2360.1
K Gross	2333.0
O Hershiser	2323.1
B Saberhagen	2227.2
T Candiotti	2165.1

Batters Faced	
D Martinez	15636
D Eckersley	12894
M Moore	12203
F Viola	11783
D Stewart	11251
F Valenzuela	11238
M Langston	11164
D Darwin	10687
S Sanderson	10611
R Clemens	10352
K Gross	10090
R Darling	10032
O Hershiser	9617
T Candiotti	9134
B Saberhagen	9032

Home Runs Allowed	
D Martinez	344
D Eckersley	324
S Sanderson	292
M Moore	291
F Viola	288
M Langston	265
D Stewart	264
D Darwin	256
R Darling	239
T Browning	236
B Black	217
K Gross	207
J Key	204
F Valenzuela	197
G Swindell	188

Walks Allowed	
M Moore	1156
M Langston	1145
D Martinez	1080
F Valenzuela	1038
D Stewart	1034
B Witt	1025
K Gross	916
R Darling	906
F Viola	843
J DeLeon	841
D Jackson	772
C Finley	756
R Johnson	755
D Darwin	753
R Clemens	750

Strikeouts	
R Clemens	2333
D Eckersley	2285
M Langston	2252
D Martinez	2022
F Valenzuela	1918
F Viola	1826
D Stewart	1741
D Cone	1741
D Darwin	1673
M Moore	1667
S Fernandez	1663
K Gross	1629
R Johnson	1624
S Sanderson	1604
J DeLeon	1594

Earned Run Average

Player, Team	IP	ER	ERA
J Franco	**822.0**	**239**	**2.62**
T Henke	789.2	234	2.67
G Maddux	2120.2	679	2.88
L Smith	1213.0	397	2.95
J Orosco	1021.0	336	2.96
R Clemens	2533.1	845	3.00
O Hershiser	2323.1	791	3.06
A Pena	1053.1	363	3.10
J Rijo	1786.0	628	3.16
D Cone	1922.0	678	3.17
M Mussina	894.1	320	3.22
K Appier	1218.1	436	3.22
R McDowell	990.2	357	3.24
R Aguilera	922.0	333	3.25
B Saberhagen	2227.2	807	3.26

Winning Percentage

Player, Team	W	L	W%
M Mussina	**71**	**30**	**.703**
R Clemens	182	98	.650
D Cone	129	78	.623
J Key	152	93	.620
G Maddux	150	93	.617
J McDowell	106	68	.609
R Johnson	99	64	.607
T Glavine	124	82	.602
K Appier	81	54	.600
J Burkett	81	56	.591
R Martinez	91	63	.591
B Saberhagen	141	100	.585
O Hershiser	150	108	.581
K Rogers	70	51	.579
T Browning	123	90	.577

Opposition Batting

Player, Team	AB	H	AVG
S Fernandez	**6541**	**1367**	**.209**
T Henke	2873	607	.211
R Johnson	5275	1125	.213
J Orosco	3721	825	.222
J DeLeon	6942	1556	.224
D Cone	7083	1589	.224
R Clemens	9409	2143	.228
S Bedrosian	4416	1026	.232
J Smoltz	5766	1346	.233
L Smith	4483	1048	.234
E Plunk	3178	743	.234
K Appier	4547	1068	.235
R Martinez	4951	1166	.236
G Maddux	7889	1877	.238
P Harnisch	4334	1032	.238

Hits Per 9 Innings

Player, Team	IP	H	H/9
S Fernandez	**1798.2**	**1367**	**6.84**
T Henke	789.2	607	6.92
R Johnson	1459.2	1125	6.94
J Orosco	1021.0	825	7.27
J DeLeon	1897.1	1556	7.38
D Cone	1922.0	1589	7.44
R Clemens	2533.1	2143	7.61
S Bedrosian	1190.2	1026	7.76
L Smith	1213.0	1048	7.78
E Plunk	859.2	743	7.78
J Smoltz	1550.2	1346	7.81
K Appier	1218.1	1068	7.89
R Martinez	1327.2	1166	7.90
G Maddux	2120.2	1877	7.97
B McDonald	937.0	838	8.05

Homeruns Per 9 Innings

Player, Team	IP	HR	HR/9
R McDowell	**990.2**	**43**	**0.39**
G Maddux	2120.2	108	0.46
J Franco	822.0	46	0.50
K Appier	1218.1	72	0.53
D Jackson	1968.2	119	0.54
B Swift	1371.1	83	0.54
M Gubicza	2099.1	131	0.56
Z Smith	1836.0	115	0.56
O Hershiser	2323.1	147	0.57
K Brown	1451.0	95	0.59
T Glavine	1721.0	113	0.59
D Righetti	1403.0	95	0.61
L Smith	1213.0	83	0.62
R Clemens	2533.1	175	0.62
A Pena	1053.1	73	0.62

Baserunners Per 9 Innings

Player, Team	IP	BR	BR/9
T Henke	**789.2**	**871**	**9.93**
M Mussina	894.1	1015	10.21
B Saberhagen	2227.2	2569	10.38
S Fernandez	1798.2	2094	10.48
R Clemens	2533.1	2975	10.57
G Maddux	2120.2	2498	10.60
D Eckersley	3133.0	3699	10.63
D Drabek	2081.2	2515	10.87
J Key	2130.2	2593	10.95
C Schilling	805.0	984	11.00
J Smiley	1536.0	1880	11.02
O Hershiser	2323.1	2848	11.03
D Cone	1922.0	2360	11.05
A Pena	1053.1	1298	11.09
K Appier	1218.1	1510	11.15

Strikeouts per 9 Innings

Player, Team	IP	K	K/9
R Johnson	**1459.2**	**1624**	**10.01**
T Henke	789.2	861	9.81
L Smith	1213.0	1195	8.87
S Fernandez	1798.2	1663	8.32
E Plunk	859.2	793	8.30
R Clemens	2533.1	2333	8.29
D Cone	1922.0	1741	8.15
J Orosco	1021.0	920	8.11
J Rijo	1786.0	1556	7.84
T Gordon	1149.2	999	7.82
B Witt	1700.2	1459	7.72
J Guzman	823.0	700	7.65
M Langston	2648.2	2252	7.65
J DeLeon	1897.1	1594	7.56
A Benes	1298.0	1081	7.50

Walks per 9 Innings

Player, Team	IP	BB	BB/9
B Tewksbury	**1283.1**	**198**	**1.39**
B Saberhagen	2227.2	421	1.70
G Swindell	1748.1	372	1.91
K Tapani	1235.2	273	1.99
D Eckersley	3133.0	716	2.06
M Mussina	894.1	205	2.06
J Key	2130.2	505	2.13
B Wegman	1482.2	352	2.14
S Sanderson	2543.0	621	2.20
T Mulholland	1318.1	330	2.25
J Burkett	1185.2	302	2.29
J Smiley	1536.0	401	2.35
D Drabek	2081.2	546	2.36
G Maddux	2120.2	561	2.38
T Browning	1921.0	511	2.39

Strikeout to Walk Ratio

Player, Team	K	BB	K/BB
B Saberhagen	**140.1**	**1510**	**3.59**
T Henke	85.0	861	3.38
G Swindell	124.0	1188	3.19
D Eckersley	238.2	2285	3.19
R Clemens	250.0	2333	3.11
R Aguilera	85.2	739	2.88
K Tapani	91.0	769	2.82
M Mussina	68.1	556	2.71
B Tewksbury	66.0	534	2.70
E Hanson	122.1	980	2.67
L Smith	150.2	1195	2.64
G Maddux	187.0	1471	2.62
S Sanderson	207.0	1604	2.58
C Schilling	80.1	618	2.56
A Pena	110.0	834	2.53

1995 American League Bill James Leaders

Top Game Scores of the Year

Pitcher	Date	Opp	IP	H	R	ER	BB	K	SC
C Finley	5/23	NYA	9.0	2	0	0	2	15	96
R Johnson	7/15	Tor	9.0	3	0	0	2	16	95
K Appier	9/15	Cal	9.0	3	0	0	1	13	93

Top Game Scores of the Year

Pitcher	Date	Opp	IP	H	R	ER	BB	K	SC
R Johnson	6/5	Bal	9.0	3	0	0	1	12	92
T Stottlemyre	6/16	KC	10.0	5	1	1	1	15	92
S Ontiveros	5/27	NYA	9.0	1	0	0	2	7	90

Offensive Win Pct

E Martinez, Sea	**.860**
F Thomas, ChA	.813
T Salmon, Cal	.801
J Thome, Cle	.790
A Belle, Cle	.783
C Davis, Cal	.735
R Palmeiro, Bal	.732
J Valentin, Bos	.729
M Ramirez, Cle	.721
M Vaughn, Bos	.713

Runs Created

E Martinez, Sea	**161**
F Thomas, ChA	144
A Belle, Cle	144
T Salmon, Cal	142
R Palmeiro, Bal	124
M Vaughn, Bos	121
J Valentin, Bos	119
J Thome, Cle	118
C Knoblauch, Min	115
B Williams, NYA	109
M Ramirez, Cle	109

Isolated Power (Power Pct)

A Belle, Cle	**.374**
J Buhner, Sea	.304
F Thomas, ChA	.298
M Vaughn, Bos	.275
M Tettleton, Tex	.273
R Palmeiro, Bal	.273
E Martinez, Sea	.272
T Salmon, Cal	.264
T Martinez, Sea	.258
G Gaetti, KC	.257

Power/Speed Number

C Curtis, Det	**23.6**
J Valentin, Bos	23.0
M Cordova, Min	21.8
B Anderson, Bal	19.8
R Alomar, Tor	18.1
C Knoblauch, Min	17.8
T Phillips, Cal	17.5
M Vaughn, Bos	17.2
J Carter, Tor	16.2
L Johnson, ChA	16.0

Secondary Average

F Thomas, ChA	**.576**
M Tettleton, Tex	.522
A Belle, Cle	.513
E Martinez, Sea	.501
J Thome, Cle	.460
T Salmon, Cal	.434
J Buhner, Sea	.430
J Valentin, Bos	.419
T Phillips, Cal	.419
H Baines, Bal	.418

Cheap Wins

C Bosio	**5**
E Hanson	**5**
B Radke	**5**
Z Smith	4
B Tewksbury	4
S Boskie	4
M Clark	4
J Bere	4
15 players tied with	3

Tough Losses

J McDowell	**6**
K Gross	4
C Finley	4
K Brown	4
T Belcher	4
W Alvarez	4
R Pavlik	4
R Krivda	4
8 players tied with	3

Slow Hooks

Blue Jays	27
Brewers	21
Athletics	20
Yankees	19
Rangers	19
White Sox	17
Twins	16
Angels	15
Mariners	15
Red Sox	14
Tigers	14
Royals	14
Indians	7
Orioles	3

Quick Hooks

Tigers	31
White Sox	26
Mariners	25
Royals	22
Brewers	20
Red Sox	18
Athletics	18
Orioles	16
Angels	16
Blue Jays	15
Indians	13
Rangers	13
Yankees	12
Twins	11

1995 National League Bill James Leaders

Pitcher	Date	Opp	IP	H	R	ER	BB	K	SC
F Castillo	9/25	StL	9.0	1	0	0	2	13	96
P Martinez	6/3	SD	9.0	1	0	0	0	9	94
R Martinez	7/14	Fla	9.0	0	0	0	1	8	94

Top Game Scores of the Year

Pitcher	Date	Opp	IP	H	R	ER	BB	K	SC
H Nomo	6/24	SF	9.0	2	0	0	3	13	93
H Nomo	8/5	SF	9.0	1	0	0	3	11	93
P Wagner	8/29	Col	9.0	1	0	0	3	11	93

Offensive Win Pct

B Bonds, SF	**.806**
M Piazza, LA	.806
R Sanders, Cin	.775
L Walker, Col	.770
B Larkin, Cin	.758
M Grace, ChN	.746
D Bichette, Col	.745
C Biggio, Hou	.741
R Gant, Cin	.728
J Bagwell, Hou	.722

Power/Speed Number

S Sosa, ChN	**35.0**
B Bonds, SF	32.0
R Sanders, Cin	31.5
R Mondesi, LA	26.5
C Biggio, Hou	26.4
R Gant, Cin	25.6
G Hill, SF	24.5
R Lankford, StL	24.5
B Larkin, Cin	23.2
B Jordan, StL	23.0

Tough Losses

D Kile	**6**
T Candiotti	5
F Castillo	5
P Martinez	5
S Reynolds	5
I Valdes	5
5 players tied with	4

Slow Hooks

Rockies	15
Giants	14
Dodgers	13
Mets	12
Pirates	12
Cardinals	11
Padres	11
Marlins	9
Cubs	8
Reds	7
Astros	7
Phillies	6
Braves	3
Expos	3

Runs Created

B Bonds, SF	**134**
C Biggio, Hou	121
D Bichette, Col	121
R Sanders, Cin	115
M Grace, ChN	115
L Walker, Col	114
B Larkin, Cin	108
E Karros, LA	107
K Caminiti, SD	105
M Piazza, LA	103

Secondary Average

B Bonds, SF	**.561**
R Gant, Cin	.495
R Sanders, Cin	.465
L Walker, Col	.427
D Justice, Atl	.409
R Lankford, StL	.400
J Bagwell, Hou	.397
B Larkin, Cin	.389
S Sosa, ChN	.383
Q Veras, Fla	.373

Isolated Power (Power Pct)

L Walker, Col	**.302**
B Bonds, SF	.283
D Bichette, Col	.280
R Gant, Cin	.278
R Sanders, Cin	.273
M Piazza, LA	.260
V Castilla, Col	.254
E Karros, LA	.238
R Lankford, StL	.236
S Sosa, ChN	.232

Cheap Wins

P Quantrill	**5**
B Swift	4
K Tapani	4
J Bullinger	4
P Rapp	4
J Burkett	3
K Hill	3
J Navarro	3
K Ritz	3
J Fassero	3
P Martinez	3
K Foster	3
R Bailey	3
18 players tied with	2

Quick Hooks

Rockies	32
Marlins	28
Braves	25
Reds	21
Padres	21
Expos	20
Cubs	15
Astros	15
Phillies	15
Cardinals	15
Giants	15
Dodgers	14
Pirates	13
Mets	9

Player Profiles

As is our custom each year, we include in the *Major League Handbook* statistical profiles for a few of professional baseball's elite. Albert Belle went on a tremendous home-run tear in September (anybody want to check that bat?) while helping the Indians to their first taste of postseason play since Dwight Eisenhower was President. Meanwhile, Greg Maddux continued to just. . . well, we've run out of words to describe Maddux at this point. And Jose Mesa came out of nowhere to have one of the best years a relief pitcher ever had.

If you enjoy these profiles, you might want to check out the *STATS 1996 Player Profiles*, which has breakdowns like these for *every* player who appeared in the majors last season.

	Avg	G	AB	R	H	2B	3B	HR	RBI	BB	SO	HBP	GDP	SB	CS	OBP	SLG	IBB	SH	SF	#Pit	#P/PA	GB	FB	G/F
1995 Season	.317	143	546	121	173	52	1	50	126	73	80	6	24	5	2	.401	.690	5	0	4	2379	3.77	185	186	0.99
Last Five Years	.298	684	2598	445	774	177	9	186	563	284	474	28	89	48	23	.369	.588	34	3	35	10915	3.70	855	827	1.03

1995 Season

	Avg	AB	H	2B	3B	HR	RBI	BB	SO	OBP	SLG		Avg	AB	H	2B	3B	HR	RBI	BB	SO	OBP	SLG
vs. Left	.293	133	39	11	1	8	25	24	25	.399	.571	Scoring Posn	.270	148	40	12	0	13	76	29	26	.388	.615
vs. Right	.324	413	134	41	0	42	101	49	55	.401	.729	Close & Late	.282	85	24	10	0	7	18	10	8	.354	.647
Groundball	.328	119	39	14	0	9	32	21	17	.437	.672	None on/out	.378	143	54	13	1	20	20	22	18	.467	.902
Flyball	.264	121	32	8	0	13	24	12	15	.333	.653	Batting #4	.317	546	173	52	1	50	126	73	80	.401	.690
Home	.328	268	88	28	1	25	53	38	45	.415	.720	Other	.000	0	0	0	0	0	0	0	0	.000	.000
Away	.306	278	85	24	0	25	73	35	35	.387	.662	Total	.317	546	173	52	1	50	126	73	80	.401	.690
Day	.298	168	50	17	1	8	28	24	26	.389	.554	April	.471	17	8	2	0	2	6	2	2	.526	.941
Night	.325	378	123	35	0	42	98	49	54	.406	.751	May	.267	105	28	11	0	4	14	11	14	.336	.486
Grass	.317	482	153	45	1	45	109	65	69	.401	.695	June	.324	105	34	11	1	6	23	14	18	.397	.619
Turf	.313	64	20	7	0	5	17	8	11	.397	.656	July	.265	102	27	5	0	7	21	15	16	.364	.520
First Pitch	.389	95	37	10	0	9	18	3	0	.420	.779	August	.381	118	45	13	0	14	30	16	16	.456	.847
Ahead in Count	.429	154	66	21	0	17	43	38	0	.543	.896	September/October	.313	99	31	10	0	17	32	15	14	.420	.929
Behind in Count	.198	182	36	7	1	14	37	0	60	.200	.478	Pre-All Star	.312	260	81	27	1	14	51	31	40	.384	.585
Two Strikes	.212	217	46	11	0	17	47	31	80	.311	.498	Post-All Star	.322	286	92	25	0	36	75	42	40	.415	.787

1995 By Position

Position	Avg	AB	H	2B	3B	HR	RBI	BB	SO	OBP	SLG	G	GS	Innings	PO	A	E	DP	Fld Pct	Rng Fctr	In Zone	Outs	Zone Rtg	MLB Zone
As lf	.317	542	172	52	1	50	126	73	79	.402	.694	142	142	1265.0	304	7	6	1	.981	2.21	340	290	.853	.811

Last Five Years

	Avg	AB	H	2B	3B	HR	RBI	BB	SO	OBP	SLG		Avg	AB	H	2B	3B	HR	RBI	BB	SO	OBP	SLG
vs. Left	.305	685	209	53	2	45	149	95	126	.385	.585	Scoring Posn	.287	703	202	49	1	53	375	123	149	.384	.586
vs. Right	.295	1913	565	124	7	141	414	189	348	.363	.589	Close & Late	.279	405	113	20	2	27	91	51	80	.356	.538
Groundball	.300	570	171	39	1	30	109	68	115	.379	.530	None on/out	.313	681	213	52	5	43	43	54	115	.368	.593
Flyball	.282	613	173	41	3	55	135	59	111	.346	.628	Batting #4	.298	2516	749	172	9	180	547	281	460	.370	.588
Home	.308	1239	381	87	6	89	276	151	214	.385	.603	Batting #5	.246	61	15	4	0	4	12	2	11	.262	.508
Away	.289	1359	393	90	3	97	287	133	260	.353	.574	Other	.476	21	10	1	0	2	4	1	3	.500	.810
Day	.304	841	256	68	2	53	175	87	150	.372	.579	April	.294	330	97	21	0	24	67	32	67	.366	.576
Night	.295	1757	518	109	7	133	388	197	324	.367	.592	May	.307	488	150	40	3	30	96	62	81	.391	.586
Grass	.299	2233	667	150	8	164	487	250	400	.371	.593	June	.300	430	129	32	3	28	90	50	79	.371	.584
Turf	.293	365	107	27	1	22	76	34	74	.358	.553	July	.295	475	140	21	1	38	110	46	86	.355	.583
First Pitch	.363	476	173	42	1	40	124	25	0	.395	.708	August	.306	454	139	30	0	33	95	50	82	.375	.590
Ahead in Count	.386	611	236	47	2	65	163	114	0	.480	.789	September/October	.283	421	119	33	2	33	105	44	79	.352	.606
Behind in Count	.223	962	215	45	6	42	149	0	355	.229	.414	Pre-All Star	.302	1430	432	105	6	93	292	157	260	.374	.579
Two Strikes	.219	1121	246	55	5	53	191	144	474	.312	.419	Post-All Star	.293	1168	342	72	3	93	271	127	214	.362	.598

Batter vs. Pitcher (career)

Hits Best Against	Avg	AB	H	2B	3B	HR	RBI	BB	SO	OBP	SLG	Hits Worst Against	Avg	AB	H	2B	3B	HR	RBI	BB	SO	OBP	SLG
Jamie Moyer	.727	11	8	4	0	0	4	2	1	.714	1.091	Frank Viola	.059	17	1	1	0	0	3	1	4	.095	.118
Brian Bohanon	.600	15	9	3	0	1	6	3	0	.667	1.000	Dennis Eckersley	.077	13	1	0	1	0	0	0	5	.077	.231
Brad Radke	.545	11	6	2	0	1	4	1	1	.583	1.000	Pat Hentgen	.105	19	2	1	0	0	1	1	3	.150	.158
Mike Trombley	.455	11	5	1	1	2	4	0	2	.455	1.273	Tom Henke	.111	9	1	0	0	0	2	4	.273	.111
Cal Eldred	.438	16	7	0	1	3	7	3	2	.550	1.125	Chris Haney	.182	11	2	0	0	0	1	1	1	.231	.182

Greg Maddux — Braves
Age 30 – Pitches Right (groundball pitcher)

	ERA	W	L	Sv	G	GS	IP	BB	SO	Avg	H	2B	3B	HR	RBI	OBP	SLG	CG	ShO	Sup	QS	#P/S	SB	CS	GB	FB	G/F
1995 Season	1.63	19	2	0	28	28	209.2	23	181	.197	147	22	0	8	35	.224	.258	10	3	4.34	22		26	6	354	117	3.03
Last Five Years	2.28	90	40	0	161	161	1209.2	242	931	.218	958	152	18	51	306	.263	.295	44	13	4.25	128	101	126	38	2024	765	2.65

1995 Season

	ERA	W	L	Sv	G	GS	IP	H	HR	BB	SO		Avg	AB	H	2B	3B	HR	RBI	BB	SO	OBP	SLG
Home	2.23	6	2	0	13	13	97.0	77	5	12	84	vs. Left	.194	355	69	8	0	2	14	10	94	.221	.234
Away	1.12	13	0	0	15	15	112.2	70	3	11	97	vs. Right	.198	393	78	14	0	6	21	13	87	.227	.280
Day	1.44	6	0	0	7	7	50.0	31	3	6	34	Inning 1-6	.190	573	109	12	0	5	24	18	142	.220	.237
Night	1.69	13	2	0	21	21	159.2	116	5	17	147	Inning 7+	.217	175	38	10	0	3	11	5	39	.239	.326
Grass	2.07	10	2	0	18	18	130.2	98	6	19	105	None on	.202	510	103	14	0	5	5	13	124	.225	.259
Turf	0.91	9	0	0	10	10	79.0	49	2	4	76	Runners on	.185	238	44	8	0	3	30	10	57	.223	.256
April	1.80	1	0	0	1	1	5.0	1	1	1	5	Scoring Posn	.157	127	20	3	0	2	26	7	34	.206	.228
May	2.44	3	1	0	6	6	44.1	29	1	5	37	Close & Late	.187	107	20	5	0	2	8	3	27	.209	.290
June	1.18	3	0	0	5	5	38.0	33	2	2	27	None on/out	.241	212	51	8	0	3	3	4	45	.255	.321
July	1.27	4	0	0	6	6	49.2	33	1	5	49	vs. 1st Batr (relief)	.000	0	0	0	0	0	0	0	0	.000	.000
August	2.59	4	1	0	5	5	41.2	30	3	7	34	First Inning Pitched	.224	107	24	3	0	1	10	5	13	.263	.280
September/October	0.29	4	0	0	5	5	31.0	21	0	3	29	First 75 Pitches	.178	572	102	11	0	4	19	16	137	.203	.219
Starter	1.63	19	2	0	28	28	209.2	147	8	23	181	Pitch 76-90	.258	97	25	7	0	2	6	3	18	.294	.392
Reliever	0.00	0	0	0	0	0	0.0	0	0	0	0	Pitch 91-105	.246	57	14	2	0	1	6	2	18	.271	.333
0-3 Days Rest (Start)	0.00	0	0	0	0	0	0.0	0	0	0	0	Pitch 106+	.273	22	6	2	0	1	4	2	8	.333	.500
4 Days Rest	2.08	7	2	0	14	14	99.1	83	2	14	84	First Pitch	.205	112	23	3	0	0	3	2	0	.217	.232
5+ Days Rest	1.22	12	0	0	14	14	110.1	64	6	9	97	Ahead in Count	.136	381	52	10	0	6	16	0	155	.145	.210
Pre-All Star	1.64	8	1	0	14	14	104.1	73	4	8	86	Behind in Count	.349	109	38	4	0	7	9	0	8	.398	.385
Post-All Star	1.62	11	1	0	14	14	105.1	74	4	15	95	Two Strikes	.106	341	36	6	0	5	10	12	181	.141	.167

Last Five Years

	ERA	W	L	Sv	G	GS	IP	H	HR	BB	SO		Avg	AB	H	2B	3B	HR	RBI	BB	SO	OBP	SLG
Home	2.34	39	19	0	76	76	582.0	455	26	120	455	vs. Left	.227	2402	546	77	12	30	179	160	514	.279	.307
Away	2.22	51	21	0	85	85	627.2	503	25	122	476	vs. Right	.207	1994	412	75	6	21	127	82	417	.244	.282
Day	2.37	33	15	0	57	57	417.2	347	19	96	315	Inning 1-6	.212	3416	723	117	14	35	229	182	739	.257	.285
Night	2.23	57	25	0	104	104	792.0	611	32	146	616	Inning 7+	.240	980	235	35	4	16	77	60	192	.286	.333
Grass	2.29	66	28	0	115	115	867.2	676	41	180	668	None on	.214	2790	597	94	8	32	32	132	597	.254	.288
Turf	2.24	24	12	0	46	46	342.0	282	10	62	263	Runners on	.225	1606	361	58	10	19	274	110	334	.279	.309
April	2.48	12	6	0	21	21	152.1	119	7	31	111	Scoring Posn	.205	931	191	27	9	9	236	85	202	.276	.282
May	2.46	14	9	0	29	29	219.1	158	11	49	178	Close & Late	.243	585	142	20	2	10	54	47	129	.303	.335
June	2.61	13	9	0	30	30	220.1	187	11	52	166	None on/out	.244	1183	289	40	3	16	16	60	233	.287	.324
July	2.14	18	5	0	29	29	223.1	187	7	34	176	vs. 1st Batr (relief)	.000	0	0	0	0	0	0	0	0	.000	.000
August	2.20	17	6	0	27	27	212.2	164	10	44	149	First Inning Pitched	.215	590	127	21	2	5	45	43	129	.275	.283
September/October	1.73	16	5	0	25	25	181.2	143	5	32	151	First 75 Pitches	.212	3178	673	100	14	33	201	162	661	.255	.283
Starter	2.28	90	40	0	161	161	1209.2	958	51	242	931	Pitch 76-90	.222	612	136	21	1	6	44	27	136	.259	.301
Reliever	0.00	0	0	0	0	0	0.0	0	0	0	0	Pitch 91-105	.242	393	95	13	1	7	39	32	88	.299	.333
0-3 Days Rest (Start)	2.30	7	1	0	11	11	82.1	65	2	11	63	Pitch 106+	.254	213	54	11	2	5	22	21	46	.325	.394
4 Days Rest	2.43	56	33	0	111	111	818.1	655	35	194	643	First Pitch	.257	712	183	28	3	6	61	21	0	.285	.330
5+ Days Rest	1.86	27	6	0	39	39	309.0	238	14	37	225	Ahead in Count	.153	2062	316	44	6	18	93	0	775	.163	.207
Pre-All Star	2.48	43	28	0	90	90	667.2	527	31	142	523	Behind in Count	.331	835	276	46	6	14	91	120	0	.414	.450
Post-All Star	2.03	47	12	0	71	71	542.0	431	20	100	408	Two Strikes	.131	1909	251	37	6	16	82	101	931	.180	.182

Pitcher vs. Batter (career)

Pitches Best Vs.	Avg	AB	H	2B	3B	HR	RBI	BB	SO	OBP	SLG	Pitches Worst Vs.	Avg	AB	H	2B	3B	HR	RBI	BB	SO	OBP	SLG
Eric Karros	.000	17	0	0	0	0	1	1	3	.056	.000	Franklin Stubbs	.500	24	12	2	1	0	2	2	2	.538	.667
Felix Jose	.000	16	0	0	0	0	0	1	7	.059	.000	Bip Roberts	.471	34	16	4	0	0	3	7	4	.561	.588
Karl Rhodes	.000	10	0	0	0	0	1	1	1	.091	.000	Brad Ausmus	.444	9	4	1	0	0	2	2	2	.545	.556
Phil Plantier	.059	17	1	0	0	0	0	0	5	.059	.059	Andy Van Slyke	.343	67	23	7	0	4	11	11	12	.436	.627
Nelson Liriano	.083	12	1	0	0	0	0	0	4	.083	.083	Dion James	.333	12	4	1	1	1	5	2	2	.429	.833

Jose Mesa — Indians

	ERA	W	L	Sv	G	GS	IP	BB	SO	Avg	H	2B	3B	HR	RBI	OBP	SLG	GF	IR	IRS	Hld	SvOp	SB	CS	GB	FB	G/F
1995 Season	1.13	3	0	46	62	0	64.0	17	58	.216	49	4	0	3	12	.268	.273	57	12	3	0	48	3	1	91	53	1.72
Last Five Years	4.53	33	40	48	198	83	630.0	237	365	.277	672	116	6	52	283	.342	.394	80	64	18	8	54	44	28	855	739	1.16

1995 Season

	ERA	W	L	Sv	G	GS	IP	H	HR	BB	SO		Avg	AB	H	2B	3B	HR	RBI	BB	SO	OBP	SLG
Home	0.28	1	0	21	30	0	31.2	16	1	8	28	vs. Left	.230	126	29	2	0	0	4	11	29	.290	.246
Away	1.95	2	0	25	32	0	32.1	33	2	9	30	vs. Right	.198	101	20	2	0	3	8	6	29	.241	.307
Day	1.35	2	0	17	23	0	26.2	27	2	10	26	Inning 1-6	.000	0	0	0	0	0	0	0	0	.000	.000
Night	0.96	1	0	29	39	0	37.1	22	1	7	32	Inning 7+	.216	227	49	4	0	3	12	17	58	.268	.273
Grass	1.12	3	0	39	54	0	56.1	42	3	14	51	None on	.213	136	29	3	0	2	2	8	37	.257	.279
Turf	1.17	0	0	7	8	0	7.2	7	0	3	7	Runners on	.220	91	20	1	0	1	10	9	21	.284	.264
April	4.50	1	0	0	1	0	2.0	4	1	1	3	Scoring Posn	.122	49	6	1	0	1	10	7	15	.224	.204
May	2.20	0	0	11	15	0	16.1	11	0	4	12	Close & Late	.227	172	39	3	0	3	10	12	45	.274	.297
June	0.90	0	0	9	10	0	10.0	7	0	3	8	None on/out	.175	57	10	2	0	1	1	2	14	.203	.263
July	0.00	0	0	9	10	0	10.0	10	0	2	13	First Inning Pitched	.117	60	7	1	0	1	4	2	16	.145	.183
August	0.60	1	0	9	15	0	15.0	10	1	3	14	First 15 Pitches	.210	214	45	3	0	2	11	15	56	.260	.252
September/October	0.84	1	0	8	11	0	10.2	7	1	4	8	Pitch 16-30	.224	49	11	1	0	1	4	6	15	.309	.306
Starter	0.00	0	0	0	0	0	0.0	0	0	0	0	Pitch 31-45	.182	11	2	0	0	0	0	2	3	.308	.182
Reliever	1.13	3	0	46	62	0	64.0	49	3	17	58	Pitch 46+	.000	0	0	0	0	0	0	0	0	.000	.000
0 Days rest (Relief)	0.51	1	0	16	18	0	17.2	9	0	2	19	First Pitch	.267	30	8	1	0	1	2	1	0	.281	.400
1 or 2 Days rest	1.69	1	0	20	30	0	32.0	23	2	11	27	Ahead in Count	.158	133	21	2	0	2	7	0	53	.158	.218
3+ Days rest	0.63	1	0	10	14	0	14.1	17	1	4	12	Behind in Count	.333	30	10	0	0	0	2	9	0	.475	.333
Pre-All Star	1.84	1	0	21	27	0	29.1	23	1	8	25	Two Strikes	.168	131	22	2	0	1	4	7	58	.210	.206
Post-All Star	0.52	2	0	25	35	0	34.2	26	2	9	33												

Last Five Years

	ERA	W	L	Sv	G	GS	IP	H	HR	BB	SO		Avg	AB	H	2B	3B	HR	RBI	BB	SO	OBP	SLG
Home	4.03	17	21	22	96	41	313.0	314	22	119	176	vs. Left	.292	1209	353	52	0	20	122	121	147	.357	.385
Away	5.03	16	19	26	102	42	317.0	358	30	118	189	vs. Right	.262	1218	319	64	6	32	161	116	218	.328	.403
Day	5.21	7	17	17	69	28	205.2	243	22	86	131	Inning 1-6	.282	1728	488	89	6	41	220	176	225	.350	.412
Night	4.20	26	23	31	129	55	424.1	429	30	151	234	Inning 7+	.263	699	184	27	0	11	63	61	140	.323	.349
Grass	4.45	28	33	41	167	68	527.1	549	43	201	308	None on	.260	1368	355	65	3	27	27	134	198	.328	.371
Turf	4.91	5	7	7	31	15	102.2	123	9	36	57	Runners on	.299	1059	317	51	3	25	256	103	167	.360	.424
April	3.65	7	6	2	24	11	86.1	89	10	24	58	Scoring Posn	.287	606	174	34	2	14	229	74	99	.357	.419
May	3.93	9	9	11	45	18	139.2	136	12	59	78	Close & Late	.247	453	112	16	0	7	40	39	93	.308	.329
June	5.47	6	10	9	39	15	107.0	121	9	40	51	None on/out	.270	625	169	31	0	15	15	44	85	.320	.392
July	3.86	3	4	9	30	9	84.0	90	5	29	57	vs. 1st Batr (relief)	.176	108	19	1	0	1	11	5	26	.211	.213
August	4.33	3	4	9	33	14	114.1	112	8	41	69	First Inning Pitched	.244	694	169	28	1	11	87	75	144	.318	.334
September/October	5.93	5	7	8	27	16	98.2	124	8	44	52	First 15 Pitches	.258	563	145	24	1	10	56	53	97	.322	.357
Starter	5.09	23	35	0	83	83	489.2	550	46	190	244	Pitch 16-30	.276	435	120	14	0	11	56	44	87	.343	.384
Reliever	2.57	10	5	48	115	0	140.1	122	6	47	121	Pitch 31-45	.254	338	86	17	2	6	42	36	54	.325	.370
0 Days rest (Relief)	3.25	4	1	17	33	0	36.0	33	2	9	34	Pitch 46+	.294	1091	321	61	3	25	129	104	127	.358	.424
1 or 2 Days rest	2.11	5	2	21	59	0	76.2	56	3	25	67	First Pitch	.353	337	119	20	3	10	52	13	0	.375	.519
3+ Days rest	2.93	1	2	10	23	0	27.2	33	1	13	20	Ahead in Count	.241	1119	270	42	2	16	111	0	316	.246	.325
Pre-All Star	4.30	23	26	23	115	46	351.1	365	31	135	198	Behind in Count	.297	516	153	36	1	11	63	121	0	.427	.434
Post-All Star	4.81	10	14	25	83	37	278.2	307	21	102	167	Two Strikes	.228	1100	251	34	2	20	99	103	365	.298	.317

Pitcher vs. Batter (career)

Pitches Best Vs.	Avg	AB	H	2B	3B	HR	RBI	BB	SO	OBP	SLG	Pitches Worst Vs.	Avg	AB	H	2B	3B	HR	RBI	BB	SO	OBP	SLG
Matt Nokes	.000	16	0	0	0	0	0	2	3	.111	.000	Gregg Jefferies	.615	13	8	2	0	1	1	0	0	.615	1.000
Jeff Huson	.000	11	0	0	0	0	0	0	1	.000	.000	Chad Kreuter	.600	10	6	2	0	1	4	1	1	.667	1.100
Tim Raines	.077	13	1	0	0	0	0	0	0	.077	.077	Kevin Maas	.571	14	8	1	0	1	2	0	1	.600	.857
Gary Gaetti	.091	11	1	0	0	0	0	0	2	.091	.091	Scott Livingstone	.533	15	8	1	0	0	4	2	0	.556	.600
Felix Jose	.091	11	1	0	0	0	0	0	2	.091	.091	Ken Griffey Jr	.500	20	10	1	0	1	3	0	1	.500	.700

Manager Tendencies

One of the things about baseball which appeal to many of us is the game's endless opportunities for analysis. And few things are analyzed more than managerial decisions. . .

Should Marcel Lachemann have gone to his bullpen earlier in the seventh inning of that regular-season finale?

Speaking of bullpens, did Terry Collins' heavy use of *his* pen contribute to the late-inning collapses against the Cubs on the campaign's final weekend?

How much influence did Gene Mauch have as the Royals' bench coach?

Which managers would have nothing to do with the temporarily-revived four-man rotation?

It's questions like these that get our second-guessing juices going, and it's questions like these that inspired the following pages, which look at managerial tendencies in a number of situations. Once again, the skippers are compared based on offense, defense, lineups, and pitching use. We don't rank the managers; there is plenty of room for argument on whether certain moves are good or bad. We are simply providing fodder for the discussion.

Offensively, managers have control over bunting, stealing and the timing of hit-and-runs. The *Handbook* looks at the quantity, timing and success of these moves.

Defensively, the Handbook looks at the success of pitchouts, the frequency of intentional walks, and the pattern of defensive substitutions.

Most managers spend large amounts of their time devising lineups. The *Handbook* shows the number of lineups used, as well as the platoon percentage. The use of pinch hitters and pinch runners is also explored.

Finally, how does the manager use pitchers? For starters, the *Handbook* shows slow and quick hooks, along with the number of times a starter was allowed to throw more than 120 pitches. For relievers, the number of relief appearances, and how often a pitcher gets a save going more than one inning (a rare occurence these days).

The categories include:

Stolen Base Success Percentage: SB/Attempts

Favorite count: A combination of the most common ball-strike count for the event, as well as how frequently that count is used when seen.

Out Percentage: The proportion of stolen bases on that count.

Sacrifice Bunt Attempts: A bunt is considered a sac attempt if no runner is on third, there are no outs, or the pitcher attempts a bunt.

Sacrifice Bunt Success %: A bunt that results in a sacrifice or a hit, divided by the number of attempts.

Favorite inning: The most common inning in which an event occurred.

Hit and Run Success: The hit and run results in baserunner advancement with no double play.

Intentional Walk Situation: Runners on base, first base open, and anyone but the pitcher up.

Defensive Substitutions: Straight defensive substitutions, with the team leading by four runs or less.

Number of Lineups: Based on batting order, 1-8 for National Leaguers, 1-9 for American Leaguers.

Percent LHB vs. RHSP and RHB vs. LHSP: A measure of platooning. A batter is considered to always have the platoon advantage if he is a switch hitter.

Percent PH platoon: Frequency the manager gets his pinch-hitter the platoon advantage. Switch hitters always have the advantage.

Score Diff: The most common score differential on which an intentional walk is called for.

Slow and Quick hooks: See the glossary for complete information. This measures how often a pitcher is left in longer than is standard practice, or pulled earlier than normal.

3 Pitchers (2 runs or less): The club gives up two runs or less in a game, but uses at least three pitchers.

Offense

	Stolen Bases			Out Percentage			Sacrifice Bunts				Hit and Run		
	Attempts	SB%	Favorite Count	0	1	2	Attempts	Success %	Favorite Inning	Squeezes	Attempts	Success %	Favorite Count
AL Managers													
Anderson, Sparky, Det	109	67.0	0-1	25.7	37.6	36.7	43	83.7	8	0	59	28.8	2-1
Bevington, Terry, ChA	115	71.3	1-0	23.5	40.0	36.5	61	80.3	8	6	83	31.3	2-1
Boone, Bob, KC	173	69.4	0-1	19.7	33.5	46.8	98	76.5	7	4	79	34.2	1-1
Garner, Phil, Mil	145	72.4	3-2	10.3	36.6	53.1	64	76.6	7	8	67	40.3	2-1
Gaston, Cito, Tor	91	82.4	1-2	22.0	33.0	45.1	47	85.1	1	1	20	25.0	2-1
Hargrove, Mike, Cle	185	71.4	2-2	25.4	35.7	38.9	40	90.0	8	2	50	30.0	2-1
Kelly, Tom, Min	162	64.8	3-2	22.2	29.6	48.1	25	76.0	6	2	109	43.1	2-1
Kennedy, Kevin, Bos	143	69.2	2-2	21.0	33.6	45.5	55	83.6	6	1	57	38.6	2-1
La Russa, Tony, Oak	158	70.9	1-1	21.5	32.9	45.6	42	88.1	3	1	105	33.3	1-0
Lachemann, Marcel, Cal	97	59.8	3-2	22.7	37.1	40.2	51	68.6	8	0	77	32.5	1-1
Lamont, Gene, ChA	34	82.4	1-0	23.5	23.5	52.9	12	83.3	4	1	15	26.7	0-1
Oates, Johnny, Tex	137	65.7	0-0	21.2	41.6	37.2	63	87.3	2	5	74	37.8	2-2
Piniella, Lou, Sea	151	72.8	3-1	19.9	43.0	37.1	66	80.3	8	3	77	36.4	2-1
Regan, Phil, Bal	137	67.2	1-2	18.2	34.3	47.4	54	77.8	7	0	70	38.6	2-1
Showalter, Buck, NYA	80	62.5	3-2	11.3	42.5	46.3	27	92.6	9	0	47	46.8	2-2
NL Managers													
Alou, Felipe, Mon	169	71.0	3-1	21.9	36.7	41.4	74	78.4	5	4	104	23.1	2-1
Baker, Dusty, SF	184	75.0	0-0	29.3	38.6	32.1	101	82.2	5	4	128	38.3	1-1
Baylor, Don, Col	184	67.9	0-0	20.1	35.9	44.0	102	85.3	3	6	91	36.3	0-0
Bochy, Bruce, SD	170	72.9	0-0	18.8	36.5	44.7	68	82.4	5	9	108	52.8	2-1
Collins, Terry, Hou	236	74.6	0-0	20.3	38.6	41.1	97	87.6	5	6	130	40.8	2-1
Cox, Bobby, Atl	116	62.9	3-2	17.2	34.5	48.3	77	76.6	2	5	64	50.0	1-1
Fregosi, Jim, Phi	97	74.2	0-0	14.4	33.0	52.6	92	82.6	3	6	49	36.7	2-1
Green, Dallas, NYN	97	59.8	1-0	22.7	27.8	49.5	123	84.6	3	8	83	43.4	2-1
Johnson, Davy, Cin	258	73.6	0-0	27.5	37.2	35.3	87	74.7	2	0	78	29.5	2-1
Jorgensen, Mike, StL	83	60.2	3-2	19.3	30.1	50.6	37	78.4	3	1	47	42.6	2-1
Lachemann, Rene, Fla	184	71.2	0-0	34.8	35.9	29.3	105	75.2	3	11	70	30.0	2-2
Lasorda, Tom, LA	172	73.8	1-1	27.9	34.3	37.8	100	73.0	3	5	77	24.7	1-1
Leyland, Jim, Pit	139	60.4	2-2	24.5	30.2	45.3	69	76.8	2	2	94	33.0	1-0
Riggleman, Jim, ChN	142	73.9	0-0	14.8	34.5	50.7	90	86.7	8	9	104	32.7	1-0
Torre, Joe, StL	42	69.0	2-1	11.9	33.3	54.8	26	73.1	3	0	18	27.8	2-2

Defense

	Pitchout			Non-POut CS%	Intentional BB			Defensive Subs				
	Total	Runners Moving	CS%		IBB	Percent of Situations	Favorite Score Diff.	Total	Favorite Inning	Pos. 1	Pos. 2	Pos. 3
AL Managers												
Anderson, Sparky, Det	77	16	25.0	27.4	63	9.9	-1	11	9	lf-7	1b-2	2b-1
Bevington, Terry, ChA	47	13	53.8	32.1	29	6.2	-2	24	8	rf-8	ss-4	cf-4
Boone, Bob, KC	32	6	83.3	23.8	24	4.7	-1	17	9	rf-6	2b-3	ss-2
Garner, Phil, Mil	52	7	71.4	22.3	23	4.0	0	52	8	2b-13	rf-13	3b-10
Gaston, Cito, Tor	57	12	50.0	32.4	26	4.3	-2	7	4	lf-3	rf-2	2b-1
Hargrove, Mike, Cle	22	7	85.7	21.6	12	1.9	0	21	9	rf-10	c-3	cf-3
Kelly, Tom, Min	26	6	33.3	19.2	11	1.8	-2	4	8	c-1	ss-1	lf-1
Kennedy, Kevin, Bos	17	4	50.0	33.3	20	3.5	-2	21	7	rf-9	cf-5	c-3
La Russa, Tony, Oak	42	12	58.3	33.6	17	3.0	-2	24	9	rf-7	lf-5	2b-3
Lachemann, Marcel, Cal	34	10	60.0	32.3	16	2.9	-2	13	8	3b-7	c-3	cf-2
Lamont, Gene, ChA	20	3	100.0	32.4	11	7.8	1	1	8	rf-1	None	None
Oates, Johnny, Tex	3	1	0.0	44.9	28	5.5	-1	25	8	2b-9	lf-6	3b-4
Piniella, Lou, Sea	40	7	42.9	33.9	32	4.8	-2	22	9	cf-8	lf-5	2b-2
Regan, Phil, Bal	36	7	14.3	31.9	28	5.4	-1	26	8	rf-8	cf-6	2b-4
Showalter, Buck, NYA	29	8	37.5	24.8	15	2.5	0	20	8	lf-10	3b-3	1b-2
NL Managers												
Alou, Felipe, Mon	22	7	14.3	28.4	20	3.2	0	10	8	c-5	3b-3	ss-1
Baker, Dusty, SF	77	14	50.0	31.9	33	5.8	-2	13	9	1b-6	rf-3	cf-2
Baylor, Don, Col	24	3	66.7	29.3	24	3.9	-1	11	9	2b-5	cf-5	ss-1
Bochy, Bruce, SD	38	9	44.4	36.8	26	4.8	-2	23	8	1b-10	2b-4	lf-3
Collins, Terry, Hou	44	13	30.8	28.8	39	5.8	-1	11	7	rf-4	cf-3	c-1
Cox, Bobby, Atl	41	6	33.3	21.5	38	6.2	-2	40	8	lf-18	2b-5	rf-5
Fregosi, Jim, Phi	33	11	18.2	22.0	26	4.2	-2	9	7	lf-4	cf-3	2b-1
Green, Dallas, NYN	30	6	50.0	23.0	38	5.7	-2	10	7	1b-3	3b-2	lf-2
Johnson, Davy, Cin	8	4	50.0	23.5	25	4.7	-2	31	8	cf-10	lf-9	3b-7
Jorgensen, Mike, StL	13	6	66.7	30.4	14	3.5	-1	11	8	c-2	1b-2	2b-2
Lachemann, Rene, Fla	9	1	0.0	39.6	40	6.7	-1	20	7	cf-7	rf-5	1b-3
Lasorda, Tom, LA	18	4	50.0	29.1	29	4.9	0	22	8	lf-15	c-3	3b-3
Leyland, Jim, Pit	51	15	33.3	32.7	36	5.7	0	4	5	ss-2	3b-1	cf-1
Riggleman, Jim, ChN	53	17	47.1	29.6	51	8.8	-1	30	8	lf-10	2b-7	3b-5
Torre, Joe, StL	14	3	33.3	33.9	11	4.3	-1	4	7	2b-2	c-1	rf-1

Lineups

	Starting Lineup			Substitutes					
	Lineups Used	% LHB Vs. RHSP	%RHB vs. LHSP	#PH	#PR	Percent PH Platoon	PH BA	PR SB	PR SB%
AL Managers									
Anderson, Sparky, Det	103	30.3	96.9	151	43	75.5	0.252	1	100.0
Bevington, Terry, ChA	87	67.9	76.8	99	30	75.8	0.291	5	100.0
Boone, Bob, KC	127	74.1	78.9	222	44	83.8	0.218	1	33.3
Garner, Phil, Mil	120	55.8	77.2	83	67	74.7	0.205	7	70.0
Gaston, Cito, Tor	82	53.7	90.9	85	24	84.7	0.192	0	0.0
Hargrove, Mike, Cle	64	63.9	83.5	101	34	69.3	0.163	2	100.0
Kelly, Tom, Min	118	40.5	89.9	190	17	90.0	0.270	0	0.0
Kennedy, Kevin, Bos	107	61.0	75.4	112	29	83.9	0.277	0	0.0
La Russa, Tony, Oak	120	40.5	97.5	113	38	80.5	0.284	1	50.0
Lachemann, Marcel, Cal	93	64.9	77.5	141	16	86.5	0.252	0	0.0
Lamont, Gene, ChA	23	66.7	79.6	39	4	87.2	0.357	0	0.0
Oates, Johnny, Tex	93	59.8	87.9	108	30	75.0	0.244	1	100.0
Piniella, Lou, Sea	98	46.8	84.3	137	41	86.9	0.281	8	100.0
Regan, Phil, Bal	104	63.5	71.2	154	51	83.8	0.308	6	66.7
Showalter, Buck, NYA	107	70.7	80.9	124	30	83.1	0.269	1	50.0
NL Managers									
Alou, Felipe, Mon	116	39.8	84.4	200	36	83.0	0.202	2	66.7
Baker, Dusty, SF	96	29.0	82.6	230	23	79.1	0.210	1	100.0
Baylor, Don, Col	87	36.3	88.9	257	23	70.0	0.299	1	50.0
Bochy, Bruce, SD	96	53.1	76.9	262	30	80.5	0.242	4	80.0
Collins, Terry, Hou	106	28.7	93.8	302	38	78.1	0.297	5	62.5
Cox, Bobby, Atl	59	58.2	67.6	224	48	72.3	0.215	3	60.0
Fregosi, Jim, Phi	96	73.1	74.5	245	6	72.2	0.233	0	0.0
Green, Dallas, NYN	94	57.5	87.7	243	19	79.4	0.274	1	100.0
Johnson, Davy, Cin	106	45.7	86.3	258	18	82.9	0.271	0	0.0
Jorgensen, Mike, StL	84	46.5	71.8	151	8	72.8	0.236	0	0.0
Lachemann, Rene, Fla	104	33.9	97.5	227	24	55.1	0.213	2	66.7
Lasorda, Tom, LA	66	38.0	81.9	270	42	85.9	0.198	2	100.0
Leyland, Jim, Pit	124	44.8	85.6	282	8	68.1	0.257	0	0.0
Riggleman, Jim, ChN	92	39.8	83.1	196	9	75.5	0.242	0	0.0
Torre, Joe, StL	36	43.5	79.6	99	6	69.7	0.239	0	0.0

Pitching

	Starters				Relievers			
	Slow Hooks	Quick Hooks	> 120 Pitches	3 Days Rest	Relief Apperances	Save > 1 IP	1st Batter Platoon Pct	3 Pitchers (2 runs or less)
AL Managers								
Anderson, Sparky, Det	14	31	7	11	366	14	57.1	14
Bevington, Terry, ChA	13	23	22	1	285	5	59.5	9
Boone, Bob, KC	14	22	15	37	308	14	63.6	18
Garner, Phil, Mil	21	20	10	3	321	4	55.8	18
Gaston, Cito, Tor	27	15	40	1	265	10	49.8	8
Hargrove, Mike, Cle	7	13	12	0	335	3	59.0	28
Kelly, Tom, Min	16	11	8	11	336	4	56.5	6
Kennedy, Kevin, Bos	14	18	14	3	370	8	58.1	22
La Russa, Tony, Oak	20	18	19	7	358	7	57.8	20
Lachemann, Marcel, Cal	15	16	20	9	368	5	60.1	22
Lamont, Gene, ChA	4	3	3	0	88	2	63.6	2
Oates, Johnny, Tex	19	13	14	11	310	10	66.8	20
Piniella, Lou, Sea	15	25	30	21	324	20	57.1	15
Regan, Phil, Bal	3	16	27	2	336	5	68.8	24
Showalter, Buck, NYA	19	12	37	5	302	6	66.6	21
NL Managers								
Alou, Felipe, Mon	3	20	7	1	396	18	53.8	25
Baker, Dusty, SF	14	15	8	3	381	8	61.2	14
Baylor, Don, Col	15	32	4	1	456	14	59.4	19
Bochy, Bruce, SD	11	21	17	3	337	3	56.4	22
Collins, Terry, Hou	7	15	8	9	394	8	60.4	26
Cox, Bobby, Atl	3	25	13	0	339	6	56.8	24
Fregosi, Jim, Phi	6	15	11	0	341	11	61.0	24
Green, Dallas, NYN	12	9	14	2	298	10	58.1	12
Johnson, Davy, Cin	7	21	1	4	330	16	55.3	23
Jorgensen, Mike, StL	8	8	1	0	231	6	63.6	13
Lachemann, Rene, Fla	9	28	15	0	400	9	62.5	19
Lasorda, Tom, LA	13	14	24	1	355	5	63.7	21
Leyland, Jim, Pit	12	13	11	33	391	4	64.4	20
Riggleman, Jim, ChN	8	15	13	2	414	12	64.3	18
Torre, Joe, StL	3	7	1	1	146	2	63.0	7

Player Projections

Hi; this is Bill James. This is the part of this book in which we pause a moment to review the projections from last season, point to a few of our successes, acknowledge some of our failures, bow humbly, apologize profusely for failing to give our very best efforts, and promise to do better next year. No, wait a minute; that's the ritual for a Japanese baseball manager. . . we're Americans. We get to brag about the ones we did right.

Whatever. One way we could do this would be to compare lists. We could compare the list of players who we projected to hit 30 home runs, for example, with the list of players who actually did:

Our Projection	Actual Factual
Ken Griffey Jr., 41	Albert Belle, 50
Albert Belle, 40	Dante Bichette, 40
Frank Thomas, 40	Jay Buhner, 40
Barry Bonds, 38	Frank Thomas, 40
Juan Gonzalez, 38	Mark McGwire, 39
Matt Williams, 38	Rafael Palmeiro, 39
Fred McGriff, 36	Mo Vaughn, 39
Manny Ramirez, 36	Sammy Sosa, 36
Cecil Fielder, 34	Larry Walker, 36
Tim Salmon, 34	Gary Gaetti, 35
Jeff Bagwell, 30	Tim Salmon, 34
Jose Canseco, 30	Barry Bonds, 33
Mike Piazza, 30	Jim Edmonds, 33
Sammy Sosa, 30	Vinny Castilla, 32
	Eric Karros, 32
	Mike Piazza, 32
	Mickey Tettleton, 32
	Cecil Fielder, 31
	Andres Galarraga, 31
	Tino Martinez, 31
	Manny Ramirez, 31

As you can see, we projected only 14 players to hit 30 or more home runs. In fact, 21 players hit 30 or more home runs. This is normal. Since we always project players to have typical seasons, rather than good seasons, we will always under-project the players who have career years, and thus under-project the number of 30-home run hitters, 100-RBI men, .300 hitters, or whatever.

Of the 14 players whom we projected to hit 30 homers, eight actually did; that's

Belle, Thomas, Bonds, Ramirez, Fielder, Salmon, Piazza and Sosa. Five of the other six players missed 30 homers simply because they were hurt (Griffey, Canseco, Bagwell, Williams and Gonzalez). As a group, they hit more home runs per at bat (.064) than we had projected for them (.061), but just missed too much playing time, between injuries and the strike, to reach 30. The sixth player we had projected to hit 30 who didn't was the Crime Dog, who had his string of seven straight 30-homer seasons snapped by the shortened schedule. He hit 27 homers; there is very little doubt that, with another 18 games, he would have cleared the barrier.

On the other side, there were 13 players who hit 30 home runs, but whom we had not projected for 30. In the case of Mark McGwire and Mo Vaughn, we had projected 29, so that's not a big problem—in fact, 10 of the 13 were projected in the twenties.

Then there are the ones we just missed—Vinny Castilla, Jim Edmonds, and Gary Gaetti. We had Castilla figured for a seven-homer season. As it turned out, seven homers wouldn't have been a good month for him:

	G	AB	R	H	2B	3B	HR	RBI	BB	SO	SB	CS	Avg	OBA	SPct
Projected	106	332	35	88	19	3	7	34	16	50	2	2	.265	.299	.404
Actual	139	527	82	163	34	2	32	90	30	87	2	8	.309	.347	.564

Jim Edmonds we projected for eight home runs, which was three more than he had ever hit before, but still sold him short by more than two dozen. Then there's Gary Gaetti, for whom we really have no very good excuse:

	G	AB	R	H	2B	3B	HR	RBI	BB	SO	SB	CS	Avg	OBA	SPct
Projected	119	405	41	92	20	1	11	52	24	94	1	1	.227	.289	.363
Actual	137	514	76	134	27	0	35	96	47	91	3	3	.261	.329	.518

Maybe you had figured out John Valentin, but we hadn't; he was way better than we thought he would be, too. We had some good projections, but I'll talk about those in later. The other side of Gary Gaetti would be, I suppose, Carlos Delgado . . .

	G	AB	R	H	2B	3B	HR	RBI	BB	SO	SB	CS	Avg	OBA	SPct
Projected	137	473	75	137	20	0	29	84	73	103	3	2	.290	.385	.516
Actual	37	91	7	15	3	0	3	11	6	26	0	0	.165	.212	.297

. . . or Willie Greene:

	G	AB	R	H	2B	3B	HR	RBI	BB	SO	SB	CS	Avg	OBA	SPct
Projected	148	523	75	139	28	2	26	80	61	120	6	7	.293	.338	.419
Actual	8	19	1	2	0	0	0	0	3	7	0	0	.105	.227	.105

Delgado is having a serious transitional problem in an organization which has become suddenly enamored of Mike Huff and Lance Parrish, but he will eventually have the big seasons we have projected for him. I'm less confident about Willie Greene.

Our greatest over-projections for 1995 were for young players—exactly the opposite of what I would have expected to happen after the strike. There were 17 players that we had projected to hit .300, ten of whom actually did. That list includes:

Player	Projected	Actual
Roberto Alomar	.311	.300
Carlos Baerga	.319	.314
Wade Boggs	.314	.324
Tony Gwynn	.324	.368
Gregg Jefferies	.311	.306
Kenny Lofton	.311	.310
Edgar Martinez	.301	.356
Mike Piazza	.318	.346
Kirby Puckett	.300	.314
Frank Thomas	.333	.308

The highest batting averages we had projected for National Leaguers were for Tony Gwynn and Mike Piazza, in that order. The top two hitters in the National League were Tony Gwynn and Mike Piazza, in that order. The order was scrambled in the American League, but we didn't do too badly there, either. Our highest projected average was for Frank Thomas, who didn't win the batting title, but did hit .308. The actual batting champion was Edgar Martinez, whom we had projected at .301.

While I'm braggin', sort of, we had projected only two major league players, Barry Bonds and Sammy Sosa, to have 30 homers and 30 stolen bases. In fact, only two players did—Barry Bonds and Sammy Sosa.

The seven players we had projected to hit .300 who didn't, in decreasing order of batting average, were:

Player	Projected	Actual
John Olerud	.319	.291
Jeff Bagwell	.310	.290
Hal Morris	.310	.279
Paul Molitor	.301	.275
Chipper Jones	.310	.265
Ken Griffey Jr.	.320	.258
Jeffrey Hammonds	.300	.242

In the case of Hammonds we didn't really have a lot of playing time to go on, majors or minors, but I'm not here to make excuses. There were an astonishing 40 players who hit .300 (in 400 plate appearances), whom we hadn't expected to hit .300. This list includes Mark Grace, whom we had projected at .299, Albert Belle (.298), Will

Clark (.297), Manny Ramirez (.295), and twelve other players we had projected between .280 and .294, but it also includes five players that we had projected to hit less than .260:

Player	Projected	Actual
B.J. Surhoff	.259	.320
Jose Canseco	.259	.306
Bobby Bonilla	.255	.329
Chili Davis	.254	.318
David Segui	.254	.309

David Segui was among our worst projections of the year, but he serves to illustrate the system. Segui had MLEs (major league equivalencies) of several minor league seasons which showed him as a .300 hitter. The first time he appeared in this section, in 1991, we had him projected as a .295 hitter.

Years went by, however, and he didn't do it and he didn't do it. Gradually the minor league records dropped off the screen, and we began to project him completely based on what he had done in the major leagues, which wasn't much. But the minor league records were meaningful; he just had an unusually long and difficult transition.

Chili Davis is a different problem, a player who has a number of atypical years in mid-career. The system, asked to project him from 1994, figures that he's a career .270 hitter, he hit .243 in 1993, he's old, he's probably not going to hit much more than .250. The system was wrong in this case.

But we had some good ones, too. Let's take Jay Bell:

	G	AB	R	H	2B	3B	HR	RBI	BB	SO	SB	CS	Avg	OBA	SPct
Projected	158	622	93	167	33	6	12	57	69	115	10	7	.268	.342	.399
Actual	138	530	79	139	28	4	13	55	55	110	2	5	.262	.336	.404

Give us back the 18 games from the strike, and I think we'd have been pretty much on target there. We can point to a number of those, as you know if you've read this section before. Craig Shipley (projected .264 with 3 homers, 23 RBI; actual .263 with 3 and 24), Andre Dawson, Royce Clayton.

We've always been proud of our ability to project young players, and, despite Carlos Delgado and Willie Greene (and Cliff Floyd and Rich Becker and Roberto Mejia) we still are. Of course, it is nearly impossible to project playing time for a young player, but in this book last year, we projected Rondell White to hit .293 with a .336 on-base percentage and a .451 slugging percentage. He hit .295 with percentages of .356 and .464.

Manny Ramirez before 1995 had played 113 major league games, hitting just

.254—yet we projected him to hit .295 with a .573 slugging percentage. We were damn close:

	G	AB	R	H	2B	3B	HR	RBI	BB	SO	SB	CS	Avg	OBA	SPct
Projected	152	555	100	164	44	1	36	111	69	113	4	3	.295	.373	.573
Actual	137	484	85	149	26	1	31	107	75	112	6	6	.308	.402	.558

We fessed up on Willie Greene, but there's another young Green, Shawn Green. Prior to 1995 he had played 17 major league games, hitting .077—yet we projected him to hit .293 with an occasional homer. He hit .288, with a little more power than we had expected.

We were too high on Chipper Jones' batting average—but he will hit .300. Brian (L.) Hunter didn't play as much as we had guessed he might—but he did play as well:

	G	AB	R	H	2B	3B	HR	RBI	BB	SO	SB	CS	Avg	OBA	SPct
Projected	144	533	77	157	24	4	8	48	31	79	32	13	.295	.333	.400
Actual	78	321	52	97	14	5	2	28	21	52	24	7	.302	.346	.396

We can't control when the manager puts him in the lineup. We missed his batting average by seven points, his slugging percentage by four points, his on base percentage by 13 points. From my standpoint, that's an almost perfect projection.

Of course, we could have projected him to play only 78 games. We have long arguments every year about how much playing time to project for who. What I always argue, and I win as many as I lose, is that if a young player can play, we should project him to play. My thinking is this: if a young player comes along, and you turn to us to see what kind of a hitter he is, and we don't tell you, then we've failed you. We haven't told you what we know.

On the other hand, if we project him to bat 537 times and he doesn't, so what? You didn't really think we knew who was going to play how much, did you? We write this in October. We don't know who is going to play center field for the Twins next year.

What we know is, Matt Lawton can play. So what I say is, let's make a strong statement that Matt Lawton can play. If Tom Kelly doesn't give him a chance to show it, that's on him.

So we project more playing time than actually exists. In part, we do this because we don't know who will get hurt—but we know that somebody will. You can project one extra player per team, and bet that one guy will go out with an injury.

As much as that, though, I hate projecting compromises. Let's take the Twins center field job next year, which is a pretty typical toss-up position. It could go to Rich Becker, it could go to Matt Lawton, it could go to somebody else. We don't know.

We know that there are about 550 at bats there. We could project 275 at bats for each of them, rub our hands contentedly and say we've got the position covered. But have we really minimized our error? The reality is that one of these guys will bat 550 times, and the other guy will be near zero. If we project them both at 550, our gross error will be 550 at bats—about 550 at bats on one guy, but near zero on the other one. If we project them each at 275, our gross error is still 550 at bats—275 on each.

So making the projected at bats match the available playing time doesn't really do anything to minimize the error. It's a compromise; it guarantees that you'll be half wrong. I'd rather be right half the time and wrong half the time than half wrong all the time.

There's a side chart here entitled "These Guys Can Play Too and Might Get a Shot." This includes players that we wouldn't expect to play next year, but who we feel have the ability to play if they get a chance.

Over the years, a surprising number of these players have gotten a shot, and have played well. Jeff Bagwell was in that chart in 1991; we didn't think he would get a chance to play that year. Marty Cordova was in that chart last year (we had him projected to hit .318 with a .494 slugging percentage), along with Edgardo Alfonzo, David Bell, Darren Bragg, Ray Durham and Herb Perry, none of whom we really expected to play. Let's run a couple:

Edgardo Alfonzo

	G	AB	R	H	2B	3B	HR	RBI	BB	SO	SB	CS	Avg	OBA	SPct
Projected	127	477	70	125	29	1	11	59	43	58	9	11	.262	.323	.396
Actual	101	335	26	93	13	5	4	41	12	37	1	1	.278	.301	.382

Herb Perry

	G	AB	R	H	2B	3B	HR	RBI	BB	SO	SB	CS	Avg	OBA	SPct
Projected	102	365	58	112	19	2	11	46	23	47	6	4	.307	.368	.460
Actual	52	162	23	51	13	1	3	23	13	28	1	3	.315	.376	.463

We figured there was no way Perry could get playing time with that lineup, but talent will find a way. The essential point is that minor league hitting statistics will tell you exactly how good a hitter somebody will be in the major leagues—if you know how to read them. Sometimes there's a transitional problem, like Carlos Delgado is having, but minor league batting stats aren't meaningless, as major league executives almost universally believed they were until 1980. There is no such thing as a "minor league hitter."

John Dewan will project the stats for pitchers. That's his baby; I don't really have anything to do with that. I don't want to overstate the accuracy of our projections. Sometimes we're right, sometimes we're wrong; that's what I've tried to say. We're not hiding under the table, and we're not saying "maybe."

—*Bill James*

Pitcher Projections

Well, like last year, our pitcher projections' accuracy was thwarted by two main factors: the season was shorter than we projected due to the strike, and the offensive explosion of the previous few years continued. Over the years we've been doing these pitcher projections, though, we've come to accept that we are attempting the impossible—an accurate prediction of pitching stats. We do get lucky from time to time, though. Here are a couple of the better projections from last year's book:

Mike Mussina

	ERA	W	L	G	IP	H	BB	SO	BR/9
Project	3.05	18	9	34	242	220	49	148	10.0
Actual	3.29	19	9	32	221	187	50	158	9.6

Dennis Eckersley

	ERA	W	Sv	G	IP	H	BB	SO	BR/9
Project	3.98	4	28	59	61	63	14	69	11.4
Actual	4.83	4	29	52	50	53	11	40	11.4

But then there are always the Jimmy Key's of the projection world, too:

Jimmy Key

	ERA	W	L	G	IP	H	BB	SO	BR/9
Project	3.84	15	12	34	232	229	73	154	11.7
Actual	5.64	1	2	5	30	40	6	14	13.7

It's an imperfect science, to say the least, but it's fun.

—*Michael Canter and John Dewan*

Projections for 1996 Batters

Batter	Age	Avg	G	AB	R	H	2B	3B	HR	RBI	BB	SO	SB	CS	OBP	SLG
Abbott,Kurt	27	.260	144	489	63	127	22	5	17	65	30	134	8	5	.303	.429
Aldrete,Mike	35	.250	75	140	18	35	7	0	3	15	18	29	1	1	.335	.364
Alexander,Manny	25	.230	85	274	34	63	12	2	3	25	13	36	12	6	.265	.321
Alfonzo,Edgardo	22	.276	123	424	51	117	23	3	9	54	30	45	6	6	.324	.408
Alicea,Luis	30	.259	147	478	69	124	23	6	7	56	71	73	14	8	.355	.377
Alomar,Roberto	28	.306	151	585	101	179	31	6	14	75	71	60	45	11	.381	.451
Alomar,Sandy	30	.271	107	354	50	96	18	1	11	48	22	44	5	3	.314	.421
Alou,Moises	29	.300	132	487	79	146	32	4	21	83	47	65	12	8	.361	.511
Amaral,Rich	34	.274	104	292	46	80	18	1	2	27	26	42	16	6	.333	.363
Anderson,Brady	32	.244	151	599	95	146	26	5	14	59	87	109	31	9	.340	.374
Anderson,Garret	24	.301	146	522	64	157	33	2	13	85	29	96	4	3	.338	.446
Andrews,Shane	24	.240	74	221	32	53	13	0	7	32	27	60	3	2	.323	.394
Anthony,Eric	28	.248	55	161	21	40	7	0	6	21	17	34	2	1	.320	.404
Arias,Alex	28	.251	114	251	24	63	14	1	2	27	26	26	1	1	.321	.339
Ashley,Billy	25	.260	119	315	41	82	13	0	14	47	26	107	3	2	.317	.435
Aude,Rich	24	.273	79	249	31	68	17	1	8	38	19	43	3	2	.325	.446
Aurilia,Rich	24	.253	63	146	19	37	7	0	3	18	14	20	3	3	.319	.363
Ausmus,Brad	27	.251	128	403	47	101	15	2	6	35	34	72	11	6	.309	.342
Baerga,Carlos	27	.317	154	638	106	202	32	2	23	109	31	55	13	4	.348	.481
Bagwell,Jeff	28	.305	152	564	106	172	35	3	30	109	89	101	16	6	.400	.537
Baines,Harold	37	.270	129	422	57	114	22	2	15	62	57	62	1	1	.357	.438
Barberie,Bret	28	.282	128	412	49	116	20	2	6	41	40	72	3	3	.345	.383
Bass,Kevin	37	.251	80	175	22	44	12	1	3	25	18	28	4	2	.321	.383
Bates,Jason	25	.276	96	297	37	82	14	3	9	38	31	50	3	5	.345	.434
Battle,Allen	27	.279	101	179	29	50	12	2	1	17	19	31	6	3	.348	.385
Bautista,Danny	24	.251	66	199	22	50	8	1	5	24	10	37	6	3	.287	.377
Becker,Rich	24	.282	121	444	74	125	22	3	9	52	62	99	16	8	.370	.405
Bell,David	23	.267	151	574	67	153	23	2	13	73	36	70	4	4	.310	.382
Bell,Derek	27	.297	139	532	70	158	21	3	15	77	34	104	28	9	.339	.432
Bell,Jay	30	.262	157	614	93	161	33	6	12	57	72	123	9	7	.340	.394
Belle,Albert	29	.308	159	603	115	186	42	3	46	131	85	95	15	8	.394	.617
Belliard,Rafael	34	.204	61	93	7	19	2	0	0	5	3	18	1	1	.229	.226
Beltre,Esteban	28	.261	75	161	18	42	6	1	1	15	13	31	4	3	.316	.329
Benard,Marvin	26	.291	86	203	29	59	10	1	2	19	16	31	7	5	.342	.379
Benitez,Yamil	24	.250	82	204	23	51	9	1	6	29	14	55	6	5	.298	.392
Benjamin,Mike	30	.205	61	127	16	26	6	1	2	12	8	27	4	1	.252	.315
Berroa,Geronimo	31	.273	151	579	85	158	30	2	20	91	63	116	8	4	.344	.435
Berry,Sean	30	.272	133	383	50	104	21	2	14	56	41	69	11	5	.342	.446
Bichette,Dante	32	.300	150	611	92	183	34	2	32	108	27	105	19	10	.329	.519
Biggio,Craig	30	.283	160	628	114	178	34	4	16	69	92	93	38	13	.375	.427
Blauser,Jeff	30	.258	139	497	79	128	24	3	11	53	66	99	9	5	.345	.384
Blowers,Mike	31	.259	134	409	54	106	23	1	15	70	47	106	2	2	.336	.430
Bogar,Tim	29	.242	100	194	20	47	13	0	2	23	13	29	1	0	.290	.340
Boggs,Wade	38	.311	135	508	82	158	30	2	7	66	77	48	1	1	.402	.419
Bonds,Barry	31	.288	157	549	118	158	34	4	36	104	123	78	33	12	.418	.561
Bonilla,Bobby	33	.265	147	551	80	146	30	3	24	82	70	110	2	3	.348	.461
Boone,Bret	27	.280	157	567	72	159	30	2	19	84	42	106	5	6	.330	.441
Borders,Pat	33	.241	88	274	22	66	14	1	5	26	13	44	1	1	.275	.354
Bordick,Mike	30	.250	150	512	54	128	17	2	5	46	50	56	10	6	.317	.320
Bragg,Darren	26	.285	70	235	37	67	14	1	6	27	29	43	10	4	.364	.430

Projections for 1996 Batters

Batter	Age	Avg	G	AB	R	H	2B	3B	HR	RBI	BB	SO	SB	CS	OBP	SLG
Branson,Jeff	29	.249	127	333	40	83	15	2	7	34	29	64	2	1	.309	.369
Brogna,Rico	26	.267	152	554	67	148	27	3	21	73	36	118	3	2	.312	.440
Brosius,Scott	29	.244	145	476	64	116	23	1	17	58	40	88	7	5	.302	.403
Browne,Jerry	30	.273	100	264	36	72	11	2	2	23	35	23	3	1	.358	.352
Brumfield,Jacob	31	.272	126	437	70	119	24	2	8	31	39	71	27	13	.332	.391
Buford,Damon	26	.246	44	122	21	30	6	1	2	12	10	21	7	4	.303	.361
Buhner,Jay	31	.264	150	546	92	144	25	2	31	105	89	129	2	2	.367	.487
Bullett,Scott	27	.273	99	161	20	44	6	2	2	16	10	33	8	3	.316	.373
Burks,Ellis	31	.260	120	361	56	94	23	3	14	53	46	83	6	4	.344	.457
Butler,Brett	39	.294	138	534	79	157	17	5	3	32	78	65	34	13	.384	.361
Caminiti,Ken	33	.261	150	559	73	146	29	1	16	78	61	101	9	5	.334	.403
Cangelosi,John	33	.246	93	248	37	61	8	1	2	17	40	44	17	7	.351	.310
Canseco,Jose	31	.267	122	464	75	124	22	1	27	85	56	120	10	6	.346	.494
Caraballo,Ramon	27	.250	60	188	24	47	8	2	3	16	11	34	6	4	.291	.362
Carr,Chuck	27	.252	82	163	23	41	6	1	1	12	15	25	15	6	.315	.319
Carreon,Mark	32	.281	129	481	58	135	22	0	17	77	33	56	1	1	.327	.432
Carter,Joe	36	.247	156	607	81	150	30	2	27	104	46	107	10	3	.300	.437
Castilla,Vinny	28	.287	153	581	77	167	31	4	26	81	31	90	5	7	.324	.489
Cedeno,Andujar	26	.253	132	443	53	112	24	3	10	51	38	94	6	4	.312	.388
Cedeno,Domingo	27	.235	84	251	31	59	8	3	2	21	19	50	5	4	.289	.315
Cianfrocco,Archi	29	.254	74	213	23	54	10	1	6	30	11	48	2	1	.290	.394
Cirillo,Jeff	26	.285	151	519	83	148	33	3	14	71	58	70	5	3	.357	.441
Clark,Dave	33	.268	100	257	40	69	12	1	9	41	31	53	2	1	.347	.428
Clark,Phil	28	.261	60	111	14	29	7	0	3	13	5	14	1	1	.293	.405
Clark,Tony	24	.266	98	316	41	84	15	1	16	56	37	92	1	1	.343	.472
Clark,Will	32	.301	143	525	93	158	31	3	19	95	80	69	2	2	.393	.480
Clayton,Royce	26	.253	157	576	59	146	23	5	6	61	44	106	22	9	.306	.342
Colbrunn,Greg	26	.284	148	549	69	156	29	0	21	91	25	78	9	4	.315	.452
Cole,Alex	30	.276	76	152	24	42	5	2	1	12	18	25	12	6	.353	.355
Coleman,Vince	34	.254	106	417	57	106	13	5	3	25	29	72	42	13	.303	.331
Coles,Darnell	34	.222	47	99	11	22	6	0	2	12	9	17	0	0	.287	.343
Conine,Jeff	30	.293	156	587	75	172	29	4	20	96	60	120	2	1	.359	.458
Coomer,Ron	29	.295	105	390	57	115	23	2	17	73	20	52	2	2	.329	.495
Cooper,Scott	28	.258	118	388	44	100	19	2	7	46	44	71	2	2	.333	.371
Cora,Joey	31	.269	142	509	74	137	15	4	3	41	54	48	17	8	.339	.332
Cordero,Wil	24	.290	154	575	80	167	38	3	16	75	45	83	16	6	.342	.450
Cordova,Marty	26	.292	153	561	94	164	33	4	27	93	61	127	17	9	.362	.510
Cromer,Tripp	28	.230	98	317	34	73	14	2	5	25	16	66	1	1	.267	.334
Cummings,Midre	24	.270	102	318	37	86	18	1	6	35	20	50	3	1	.314	.390
Curtis,Chad	27	.272	159	607	97	165	28	4	15	67	69	93	39	20	.346	.405
Damon,Johnny	22	.301	152	612	100	184	25	13	13	67	57	60	25	6	.360	.448
Daulton,Darren	34	.240	116	400	57	96	19	1	14	66	75	77	3	1	.360	.398
Davis,Chili	36	.271	140	510	79	138	26	1	20	93	85	119	3	2	.375	.443
Davis,Russ	26	.243	111	367	53	89	19	1	15	55	43	96	2	2	.322	.422
Dawson,Andre	41	.250	84	184	18	46	8	1	6	26	7	31	1	1	.277	.402
Decker,Steve	30	.264	70	193	18	51	9	0	4	22	21	23	1	0	.336	.373
Delgado,Carlos	24	.286	121	427	67	122	21	1	25	78	62	97	3	2	.376	.515
DeShields,Delino	27	.280	144	521	86	146	21	5	7	50	83	89	50	15	.379	.380
Devereaux,Mike	33	.263	113	396	52	104	18	2	10	57	29	81	4	3	.313	.394
Diaz,Alex	27	.253	81	190	25	48	9	2	1	17	9	21	10	6	.286	.337

Projections for 1996 Batters

Batter	Age	Avg	G	AB	R	H	2B	3B	HR	RBI	BB	SO	SB	CS	OBP	SLG
DiSarcina,Gary	28	.262	144	503	66	132	24	3	5	47	26	39	7	7	.299	.352
Donnels,Chris	30	.262	91	164	21	43	12	1	2	19	20	29	1	1	.342	.384
Duncan,Mariano	33	.251	103	347	41	87	16	2	7	43	11	73	5	3	.274	.369
Dunston,Shawon	33	.255	140	533	58	136	25	4	14	62	19	87	8	7	.281	.396
Durham,Ray	24	.274	148	559	88	153	30	9	10	59	41	93	29	11	.323	.413
Dykstra,Lenny	33	.273	105	396	74	108	24	2	7	31	75	47	22	8	.389	.396
Easley,Damion	26	.245	113	363	44	89	16	2	5	36	37	50	7	5	.315	.342
Edmonds,Jim	26	.291	153	615	102	179	30	3	24	102	59	142	6	7	.353	.467
Eisenreich,Jim	37	.283	140	385	47	109	22	3	6	51	37	44	6	2	.346	.403
Encarnacion,Angelo	23	.249	77	229	23	57	12	1	3	22	11	32	1	1	.283	.349
Espinoza,Alvaro	34	.245	74	143	16	35	9	0	1	15	4	19	1	1	.265	.329
Eusebio,Tony	29	.289	114	367	42	106	17	1	6	52	26	60	1	1	.336	.390
Everett,Carl	25	.273	134	495	79	135	25	3	17	67	43	112	17	15	.331	.438
Fabregas,Jorge	26	.249	91	285	30	71	12	0	3	31	18	38	1	1	.294	.323
Fermin,Felix	32	.251	86	279	28	70	8	1	1	23	10	13	2	2	.277	.297
Fernandez,Tony	34	.264	134	484	63	128	24	5	6	57	52	50	14	9	.336	.372
Fielder,Cecil	32	.249	152	566	80	141	20	1	32	105	81	136	0	0	.343	.458
Finley,Steve	31	.272	147	580	84	158	21	6	9	47	46	71	27	10	.326	.376
Flaherty,John	28	.235	112	332	32	78	17	0	7	33	19	46	1	1	.276	.349
Fletcher,Darrin	29	.259	133	402	40	104	21	1	11	59	38	33	0	0	.323	.398
Fletcher,Scott	37	.248	75	226	30	56	10	1	2	17	19	22	6	2	.306	.327
Floyd,Cliff	23	.279	126	459	67	128	20	3	15	73	44	90	16	7	.342	.434
Fonville,Chad	25	.283	131	467	65	132	9	1	3	36	35	55	29	13	.333	.325
Frazier,Lou	31	.242	57	91	13	22	3	1	0	8	10	15	8	2	.317	.297
Frye,Jeff	29	.278	116	403	55	112	26	3	3	41	46	52	7	3	.352	.380
Fryman,Travis	27	.281	161	647	97	182	37	4	23	101	76	141	6	4	.357	.457
Gaetti,Gary	37	.243	148	523	68	127	25	1	26	85	40	120	2	2	.297	.444
Gagne,Greg	34	.248	145	505	55	125	25	3	8	55	37	90	8	11	.299	.356
Galarraga,Andres	35	.291	157	592	89	172	32	2	31	108	32	135	8	4	.327	.508
Gallagher,Dave	35	.260	83	150	19	39	7	0	2	14	16	17	1	1	.331	.347
Gallego,Mike	35	.233	46	120	14	28	4	0	2	13	14	21	0	0	.313	.317
Gant,Ron	31	.270	144	525	98	142	28	3	28	99	75	118	27	10	.362	.495
Garcia,Carlos	28	.273	135	524	66	143	25	4	9	51	29	76	16	11	.311	.387
Gates,Brent	26	.282	148	561	69	158	30	3	7	68	56	77	5	3	.347	.383
Giambi,Jason	25	.261	96	280	43	73	19	0	7	44	40	46	1	1	.353	.404
Gil,Benji	23	.244	147	509	58	124	19	3	14	64	37	141	12	8	.295	.375
Gilkey,Bernard	29	.275	144	553	82	152	31	4	15	68	56	79	17	11	.342	.427
Girardi,Joe	31	.269	128	457	56	123	16	2	5	44	31	67	5	4	.316	.346
Gomez,Chris	25	.247	140	453	51	112	23	2	7	52	45	78	6	3	.315	.353
Gomez,Leo	29	.232	101	311	44	72	15	0	13	42	45	65	1	1	.329	.405
Gonzalez,Alex	23	.267	138	501	74	134	27	5	14	58	46	115	20	8	.329	.425
Gonzalez,Juan	26	.297	146	552	94	164	30	3	39	117	37	93	4	2	.341	.574
Gonzalez,Luis	28	.279	146	512	77	143	32	6	15	75	61	74	15	11	.356	.453
Goodwin,Curtis	23	.267	100	352	53	94	10	3	2	25	19	49	27	10	.305	.330
Goodwin,Tom	27	.265	126	415	57	110	12	3	2	29	29	65	37	15	.313	.323
Grace,Mark	32	.301	153	588	84	177	35	3	12	79	69	48	6	4	.374	.432
Grebeck,Craig	31	.255	77	188	26	48	11	1	2	16	26	22	1	0	.346	.356
Green,Shawn	23	.292	141	503	69	147	32	3	15	62	33	83	8	7	.336	.457
Greenwell,Mike	32	.292	130	483	69	141	28	3	13	66	47	38	6	4	.355	.443
Greer,Rusty	27	.279	151	552	81	154	29	3	16	74	73	98	4	2	.363	.429

Projections for 1996 Batters

Batter	Age	Avg	G	AB	R	H	2B	3B	HR	RBI	BB	SO	SB	CS	OBP	SLG
Griffey Jr,Ken	26	.310	152	567	117	176	33	4	40	104	96	92	14	7	.410	.594
Grissom,Marquis	29	.275	136	557	93	153	26	4	12	58	49	67	39	11	.333	.400
Grudzielanek,Mark	26	.279	126	438	58	122	27	2	5	46	26	59	19	7	.319	.384
Guillen,Ozzie	32	.260	128	438	48	114	17	3	2	44	13	34	6	5	.282	.326
Gutierrez,Ricky	26	.256	78	234	33	60	7	2	1	19	24	44	4	3	.326	.316
Gwynn,Tony	36	.336	137	541	71	182	29	4	8	68	46	24	11	3	.388	.449
Hamelin,Bob	28	.229	81	249	36	57	13	1	12	38	38	54	2	2	.331	.434
Hamilton,Darryl	31	.280	109	397	53	111	15	2	5	37	41	42	13	6	.347	.365
Hammonds,Jeffrey	25	.295	110	390	57	115	23	3	11	53	22	61	9	5	.333	.454
Haney,Todd	30	.275	73	171	21	47	10	0	2	15	14	17	3	2	.330	.368
Hansen,Dave	27	.280	112	214	20	60	8	0	3	27	35	30	0	0	.382	.360
Harris,Lenny	31	.252	78	111	16	28	6	1	1	10	8	11	4	2	.303	.351
Haselman,Bill	30	.259	86	212	34	55	13	1	7	30	22	35	1	1	.329	.429
Hayes,Charlie	31	.270	156	578	66	156	29	2	16	77	50	90	7	5	.328	.410
Hemond,Scott	30	.212	48	113	13	24	5	0	2	11	14	27	4	2	.299	.310
Henderson,Rickey	37	.273	127	447	85	122	23	2	11	45	102	75	38	11	.408	.407
Hernandez,Jose	26	.258	115	333	46	86	11	3	8	39	18	76	7	4	.296	.381
Higginson,Bob	25	.263	143	472	73	124	24	4	19	62	56	99	10	7	.341	.451
Hill,Glenallen	31	.258	151	532	72	137	25	3	22	80	43	116	26	8	.313	.440
Hoiles,Chris	31	.268	137	447	69	120	19	0	24	71	82	102	1	1	.382	.472
Hollandsworth,Todd	23	.233	79	227	27	53	9	1	7	28	14	48	7	4	.278	.374
Hollins,Dave	30	.248	91	315	62	78	14	2	10	46	60	64	2	1	.368	.400
Hosey,Dwayne	29	.288	115	372	66	107	26	3	13	54	37	63	15	7	.352	.478
Howard,Dave	29	.226	106	257	22	58	10	2	1	22	22	40	6	3	.287	.292
Howard,Thomas	31	.268	120	284	40	76	14	1	5	30	20	48	12	7	.316	.377
Hubbard,Trent	30	.323	137	511	81	165	26	5	10	51	50	66	27	12	.383	.452
Hudler,Rex	35	.242	100	240	29	58	11	1	6	25	10	53	9	3	.272	.371
Huff,Michael	32	.260	79	150	20	39	7	1	2	13	23	20	3	2	.358	.360
Hulse,David	28	.274	93	310	50	85	10	4	2	29	20	47	18	5	.318	.352
Hundley,Todd	27	.239	123	380	48	91	16	1	14	52	36	78	1	1	.305	.397
Hunter,Brian L.	25	.305	151	574	93	175	25	5	7	55	40	81	38	15	.350	.402
Huskey,Butch	24	.236	72	212	26	50	8	0	8	31	16	42	4	2	.289	.387
Huson,Jeff	31	.233	51	120	14	28	4	0	1	10	11	16	4	3	.298	.292
Jaha,John	30	.273	142	517	83	141	28	1	23	80	58	112	8	5	.346	.464
James,Chris	33	.228	71	149	19	34	7	1	4	16	17	36	1	0	.307	.369
James,Dion	33	.290	86	210	22	61	6	1	2	26	21	16	4	1	.355	.357
Javier,Stan	32	.258	135	453	68	117	15	2	6	46	52	71	29	7	.335	.340
Jefferies,Gregg	28	.308	142	562	81	173	31	2	15	76	58	32	27	10	.373	.450
Jefferson,Reggie	27	.289	82	204	28	59	10	1	7	28	18	37	1	1	.347	.451
Jeter,Derek	22	.313	152	537	94	168	31	6	5	59	62	65	21	8	.384	.421
Johnson,Brian	28	.263	74	213	22	56	12	1	4	28	15	33	0	0	.311	.385
Johnson,Charles	24	.247	132	478	60	118	26	1	20	66	62	106	3	3	.333	.431
Johnson,Howard	35	.217	67	143	21	31	10	1	5	21	27	38	4	2	.341	.406
Johnson,Lance	32	.288	151	593	84	171	17	12	4	53	35	34	39	9	.328	.378
Johnson,Mark	28	.230	82	243	33	56	11	1	10	34	34	58	4	2	.325	.407
Jones,Chipper	24	.292	159	579	99	169	30	6	21	92	71	87	13	7	.369	.473
Jones,Chris	30	.259	96	266	38	69	9	3	8	36	18	64	6	3	.306	.406
Jordan,Brian	29	.289	153	557	77	161	25	6	19	84	36	86	23	13	.332	.458
Joyner,Wally	34	.274	140	503	71	138	29	1	13	71	69	67	4	4	.362	.414
Justice,Dave	30	.279	141	494	85	138	21	2	29	92	85	74	4	4	.385	.506

354

Projections for 1996 Batters

Batter	Age	Avg	G	AB	R	H	2B	3B	HR	RBI	BB	SO	SB	CS	OBP	SLG
Karkovice,Ron	32	.218	124	357	49	78	15	1	13	46	40	105	2	2	.297	.375
Karros,Eric	28	.268	159	612	80	164	30	2	26	88	49	96	3	2	.322	.451
Kelly,Mike	26	.234	66	171	24	40	7	1	6	21	13	49	4	3	.288	.392
Kelly,Pat	28	.264	120	371	47	98	22	2	6	46	26	71	10	7	.312	.383
Kelly,Roberto	31	.287	137	509	68	146	25	2	12	56	28	80	23	10	.324	.415
Kent,Jeff	28	.271	150	558	72	151	30	2	21	80	33	106	3	4	.311	.444
King,Jeff	31	.258	146	550	65	142	28	2	13	82	56	61	7	5	.327	.387
Kingery,Mike	35	.273	112	337	49	92	17	3	6	32	33	29	8	5	.338	.395
Kirby,Wayne	32	.254	75	189	28	48	8	1	3	20	13	27	8	3	.302	.354
Klesko,Ryan	25	.271	142	435	63	118	23	2	23	74	54	87	4	3	.352	.492
Knoblauch,Chuck	27	.296	155	614	102	182	33	5	8	62	73	77	47	15	.371	.406
Knorr,Randy	27	.235	111	323	40	76	15	1	9	41	26	77	0	0	.292	.372
Laker,Tim	26	.251	77	215	25	54	12	1	4	26	19	47	3	2	.312	.372
Lankford,Ray	29	.261	154	548	99	143	33	6	20	77	88	138	20	13	.363	.453
Lansing,Mike	28	.266	150	538	62	143	30	2	7	57	43	59	25	8	.320	.368
Larkin,Barry	32	.305	137	525	95	160	28	4	12	64	71	56	36	5	.388	.442
Lawton,Matt	24	.270	151	564	102	152	27	6	17	78	66	106	27	11	.346	.429
Leius,Scott	30	.244	120	365	54	89	16	3	8	43	44	59	2	2	.325	.370
Lemke,Mark	30	.247	143	473	48	117	15	2	6	44	58	47	2	2	.330	.326
Lewis,Darren	28	.254	114	429	65	109	12	4	2	32	36	43	36	15	.312	.315
Lewis,Mark	26	.267	131	487	71	130	26	1	10	56	37	77	5	4	.319	.386
Leyritz,Jim	32	.262	108	332	50	87	18	0	13	58	49	80	0	0	.357	.434
Lind,Jose	32	.243	63	181	16	44	8	1	1	15	7	17	2	1	.271	.315
Liriano,Nelson	32	.260	84	173	21	45	8	2	2	19	19	24	3	3	.333	.364
Listach,Pat	28	.252	79	262	34	66	9	2	1	23	24	49	12	5	.315	.313
Livingstone,Scott	30	.284	122	320	35	91	17	1	4	35	19	36	2	2	.324	.381
Lockhart,Keith	31	.282	134	472	60	133	25	2	8	51	38	45	5	4	.335	.394
Lofton,Kenny	29	.312	147	587	116	183	26	10	8	59	69	73	74	19	.384	.431
Longmire,Tony	27	.279	99	244	29	68	18	1	3	31	19	40	3	2	.331	.398
Lopez,Javy	25	.285	125	431	52	123	21	2	17	64	18	69	1	2	.314	.462
Mabry,John	25	.276	150	550	65	152	31	1	14	67	30	67	4	7	.314	.413
Macfarlane,Mike	32	.239	131	431	57	103	24	1	16	63	45	91	2	2	.311	.411
Magadan,Dave	33	.272	126	371	43	101	19	1	3	42	71	55	1	1	.389	.353
Maldonado,Candy	35	.219	92	201	25	44	14	1	6	28	31	57	1	1	.323	.388
Manto,Jeff	31	.255	68	196	27	50	12	0	9	32	24	38	1	1	.336	.454
Manwaring,Kirt	30	.234	142	462	38	108	16	2	4	44	39	80	1	1	.293	.303
Marsh,Tom	30	.258	59	198	22	51	10	2	5	24	7	28	3	2	.283	.404
Martin,Al	28	.276	131	445	74	123	22	5	15	51	47	100	20	11	.346	.449
Martin,Norberto	29	.272	111	243	32	66	8	2	2	25	12	27	8	4	.306	.346
Martinez,Dave	31	.274	128	332	42	91	15	4	6	37	33	41	8	4	.340	.398
Martinez,Edgar	33	.319	149	521	96	166	40	1	22	88	99	80	4	3	.427	.526
Martinez,Sandy	23	.227	45	132	10	30	8	0	1	17	4	33	0	0	.250	.311
Martinez,Tino	28	.273	156	567	80	155	34	2	28	97	66	87	1	1	.349	.489
Masteller,Dan	28	.267	61	180	23	48	10	2	4	24	14	20	2	1	.320	.411
Matheny,Mike	25	.232	95	241	22	56	13	1	3	23	14	49	2	2	.275	.332
Mattingly,Don	35	.290	131	487	71	141	32	1	12	67	61	38	0	0	.369	.433
May,Derrick	27	.287	106	321	43	92	16	1	7	47	24	33	5	2	.336	.408
Mayne,Brent	28	.252	116	330	31	83	14	1	3	33	30	46	2	2	.314	.327
McGee,Willie	37	.275	78	247	30	68	13	2	3	24	18	43	5	3	.325	.381
McGriff,Fred	32	.289	154	570	99	165	28	1	35	103	73	104	6	5	.370	.526

Projections for 1996 Batters

Batter	Age	Avg	G	AB	R	H	2B	3B	HR	RBI	BB	SO	SB	CS	OBP	SLG
McGwire,Mark	32	.238	122	378	73	90	15	0	27	76	105	96	1	1	.404	.492
McLemore,Mark	31	.253	148	537	69	136	18	3	4	49	66	83	22	13	.335	.320
McRae,Brian	28	.271	158	642	92	174	32	7	11	60	57	104	29	13	.330	.394
Meares,Pat	27	.270	135	419	52	113	23	3	6	46	18	69	8	6	.300	.382
Merced,Orlando	29	.290	154	549	80	159	30	4	13	81	77	81	5	3	.377	.430
Merullo,Matt	30	.277	79	213	24	59	10	1	5	32	16	25	0	0	.328	.404
Mieske,Matt	28	.249	127	346	54	86	20	2	12	50	35	65	5	5	.318	.422
Miller,Orlando	27	.254	130	406	51	103	22	4	8	52	19	90	3	4	.287	.387
Molitor,Paul	39	.285	139	555	80	158	28	4	13	74	66	69	18	3	.361	.420
Mondesi,Raul	25	.284	156	564	82	160	25	7	20	75	36	104	20	10	.327	.459
Morandini,Mickey	30	.269	144	510	65	137	24	7	5	46	48	77	14	6	.332	.373
Morris,Hal	31	.307	131	476	62	146	27	2	11	73	41	65	3	2	.362	.441
Mouton,James	27	.267	111	348	57	93	20	2	5	36	34	62	27	9	.332	.379
Mouton,Lyle	27	.280	138	514	73	144	31	2	16	76	44	116	12	9	.337	.442
Munoz,Pedro	27	.276	127	421	51	116	21	2	17	56	29	109	1	2	.322	.456
Murray,Eddie	40	.267	127	450	55	120	20	1	16	70	33	60	4	2	.317	.422
Myers,Greg	30	.237	108	317	31	75	15	1	7	37	20	59	2	2	.282	.356
Naehring,Tim	29	.287	143	501	68	144	29	1	11	64	71	75	2	2	.376	.415
Nevin,Phil	25	.250	95	260	32	65	11	1	6	39	28	56	2	1	.323	.369
Newfield,Marc	23	.273	117	319	38	87	19	0	11	42	20	42	1	1	.316	.436
Newson,Warren	31	.287	83	150	30	43	6	0	4	16	31	35	2	1	.409	.407
Nieves,Melvin	24	.262	70	221	32	58	8	1	11	33	21	72	2	2	.326	.457
Nilsson,Dave	26	.291	123	406	56	118	26	3	11	68	39	54	3	3	.353	.451
Nixon,Otis	37	.269	145	587	84	158	17	2	1	33	68	92	49	18	.345	.310
Nunnally,Jon	24	.253	135	356	61	90	18	7	15	50	62	92	8	6	.364	.469
O'Brien,Charlie	35	.217	65	189	18	41	10	0	5	21	20	29	0	0	.292	.349
O'Leary,Troy	26	.299	119	394	60	118	28	5	8	54	39	66	6	3	.363	.457
O'Neill,Paul	33	.287	142	508	78	146	28	1	21	85	71	79	3	4	.375	.470
Ochoa,Alex	24	.270	126	419	50	113	19	1	8	49	29	57	17	9	.317	.377
Offerman,Jose	27	.267	127	393	53	105	12	4	2	39	56	62	11	7	.359	.333
Olerud,John	27	.312	155	557	87	174	37	1	21	88	101	67	1	1	.418	.496
Oliva,Jose	25	.234	58	141	19	33	7	1	6	20	11	36	0	1	.289	.426
Oliver,Joe	30	.242	97	326	31	79	17	0	9	45	23	62	1	1	.292	.377
Oquendo,Jose	32	.245	77	147	19	36	6	1	1	12	24	16	1	1	.351	.320
Orsulak,Joe	34	.266	103	290	39	77	13	2	4	31	18	26	3	2	.308	.366
Ortiz,Luis	26	.278	64	212	24	59	12	2	5	31	12	30	0	0	.317	.425
Owen,Spike	35	.238	59	147	15	35	6	1	1	14	18	13	1	1	.321	.313
Owens,Jayhawk	27	.280	57	132	18	37	7	1	5	19	11	36	1	1	.336	.462
Pagnozzi,Tom	33	.245	103	326	28	80	16	1	5	35	21	43	0	0	.291	.347
Palmeiro,Rafael	31	.285	157	603	99	172	35	2	29	95	73	80	12	4	.362	.494
Palmer,Dean	27	.253	143	517	88	131	25	2	31	89	55	138	8	7	.325	.489
Paquette,Craig	27	.229	82	227	27	52	10	1	8	30	10	64	3	2	.262	.388
Parent,Mark	34	.226	81	226	25	51	10	0	10	32	23	57	0	0	.297	.403
Patterson,John	29	.235	97	234	32	55	13	3	2	28	15	37	7	3	.281	.342
Pegues,Steve	28	.255	60	161	18	41	9	1	3	17	3	29	4	2	.268	.379
Pena,Geronimo	29	.257	79	230	36	59	13	2	6	28	27	55	9	4	.335	.409
Pena,Tony	39	.235	99	251	22	59	13	1	3	21	18	40	1	1	.286	.331
Pendleton,Terry	35	.266	140	546	62	145	27	2	12	65	31	94	3	2	.305	.388
Perry,Herbert	26	.299	119	412	65	123	27	1	10	62	39	55	5	4	.359	.442
Petagine,Roberto	25	.282	145	507	75	143	32	1	16	80	76	119	4	3	.376	.444

356

Projections for 1996 Batters

Batter	Age	Avg	G	AB	R	H	2B	3B	HR	RBI	BB	SO	SB	CS	OBP	SLG
Phillips,J.R.	26	.238	86	164	21	39	9	1	7	24	15	44	2	2	.302	.433
Phillips,Tony	37	.260	144	543	104	141	23	2	13	54	123	130	14	9	.396	.381
Piazza,Mike	27	.324	141	525	85	170	25	1	32	109	49	90	2	2	.382	.558
Plantier,Phil	27	.249	104	321	47	80	15	1	17	52	43	82	3	2	.338	.461
Polonia,Luis	31	.284	107	373	55	106	15	4	2	26	35	39	28	13	.346	.362
Puckett,Kirby	35	.296	148	587	83	174	34	3	19	99	48	87	6	4	.350	.462
Raines,Tim	36	.276	132	486	81	134	23	5	10	59	72	53	16	4	.369	.405
Ramirez,Manny	24	.309	152	554	104	171	38	1	38	120	78	114	5	5	.394	.587
Reboulet,Jeff	32	.251	112	255	38	64	14	1	3	23	32	37	2	2	.334	.349
Reed,Jeff	33	.217	59	83	8	18	5	0	1	7	13	15	0	0	.323	.313
Reed,Jody	33	.263	140	491	61	129	30	1	4	44	60	44	4	4	.343	.352
Ripken,Cal	35	.262	162	645	87	169	33	2	21	99	60	66	1	1	.325	.417
Roberts,Bip	32	.283	114	420	56	119	18	2	3	34	42	57	26	7	.348	.357
Rodriguez,Alex	20	.271	137	521	60	141	23	4	18	69	33	143	11	7	.314	.434
Rodriguez,Henry	28	.234	80	167	17	39	8	1	4	20	11	33	0	0	.281	.365
Rodriguez,Ivan	24	.291	151	529	67	154	29	2	16	76	31	63	6	5	.330	.444
Salmon,Tim	27	.299	158	585	115	175	33	2	38	112	101	146	5	5	.402	.557
Samuel,Juan	35	.248	106	238	37	59	17	4	6	35	25	53	7	5	.319	.429
Sanchez,Rey	28	.270	139	478	53	129	19	3	2	38	22	44	4	4	.302	.335
Sanders,Deion	28	.276	114	417	63	115	14	8	4	39	33	68	35	14	.329	.412
Sanders,Reggie	28	.274	154	562	97	154	29	6	25	94	67	146	33	14	.351	.480
Santangelo,F.P.	28	.241	50	133	17	32	6	0	1	11	16	17	3	2	.322	.308
Santiago,Benito	31	.251	126	414	45	104	20	2	12	49	33	75	5	4	.306	.396
Scarsone,Steve	30	.252	49	103	14	26	5	1	3	12	9	27	1	1	.313	.408
Sequi,David	29	.283	136	467	62	132	24	1	11	64	52	54	2	2	.355	.409
Seitzer,Kevin	34	.281	133	487	57	137	25	2	6	64	57	60	4	3	.357	.378
Servais,Scott	29	.235	111	336	38	79	20	0	11	45	30	56	1	1	.298	.393
Sheaffer,Danny	34	.242	91	223	25	54	11	1	3	29	18	25	1	1	.299	.341
Sheffield,Gary	27	.281	143	501	81	141	26	2	25	86	78	78	22	9	.378	.491
Shipley,Craig	33	.260	100	250	27	65	10	1	3	24	10	32	7	4	.288	.344
Sierra,Ruben	30	.262	150	580	83	152	31	5	23	105	47	88	14	6	.317	.452
Silvestri,Dave	28	.225	78	222	33	50	13	2	7	30	35	76	5	4	.331	.396
Simms,Mike	29	.234	64	167	23	39	9	1	6	25	18	45	2	1	.308	.407
Slaught,Don	37	.297	90	269	27	80	17	1	4	34	30	39	0	0	.368	.413
Smith,Dwight	32	.270	63	115	16	31	7	1	3	15	9	21	2	2	.323	.426
Smith,Mark	26	.242	38	120	15	29	7	0	3	16	8	24	1	1	.289	.375
Smith,Ozzie	41	.244	71	238	27	58	9	1	1	18	21	14	6	3	.305	.303
Snopek,Chris	25	.295	124	403	62	119	24	2	9	56	53	62	5	4	.377	.432
Snow,J.T.	28	.263	149	600	82	158	24	1	22	95	66	111	2	2	.336	.417
Sojo,Luis	30	.256	119	383	49	98	17	2	6	39	23	31	4	2	.298	.358
Sorrento,Paul	30	.249	131	410	61	102	21	1	18	68	57	93	2	1	.340	.437
Sosa,Sammy	27	.274	159	621	92	170	23	5	34	105	49	138	38	14	.327	.491
Sprague,Ed	28	.248	159	573	66	142	29	1	16	75	46	112	1	0	.304	.386
Stahoviak,Scott	26	.280	89	275	39	77	21	1	7	40	38	66	5	3	.367	.440
Stairs,Matt	27	.289	62	142	18	41	9	1	3	24	15	20	2	2	.357	.430
Stanley,Mike	33	.267	127	423	64	113	17	1	17	73	60	97	1	1	.358	.433
Steinbach,Terry	34	.258	128	462	48	119	21	1	12	58	31	81	3	3	.304	.385
Stinnett,Kelly	26	.245	91	229	28	56	7	1	4	22	20	49	1	1	.305	.336
Stocker,Kevin	26	.259	134	455	61	118	19	2	3	41	53	70	8	4	.337	.330
Strange,Doug	32	.247	73	154	17	38	9	0	2	18	12	24	2	1	.301	.344

Projections for 1996 Batters

Batter	Age	Avg	G	AB	R	H	2B	3B	HR	RBI	BB	SO	SB	CS	OBP	SLG
Strawberry,Darryl	34	.246	87	211	35	52	9	1	10	38	36	50	1	2	.356	.441
Surhoff,B.J.	31	.267	142	502	64	134	25	2	9	67	41	48	9	6	.322	.378
Tarasco,Tony	25	.280	140	407	64	114	19	3	13	49	39	64	18	6	.343	.437
Tartabull,Danny	33	.249	97	342	52	85	20	1	15	58	59	102	1	1	.359	.444
Taubensee,Eddie	27	.277	74	206	27	57	11	1	7	30	18	37	1	1	.335	.442
Tavarez,Jesus	25	.268	96	332	44	89	9	3	2	26	23	50	14	9	.315	.331
Tettleton,Mickey	35	.230	145	474	74	109	19	1	24	76	116	135	2	2	.381	.426
Thomas,Frank	28	.325	162	566	126	184	38	2	44	131	149	76	3	3	.466	.633
Thome,Jim	25	.295	154	556	103	164	31	3	25	90	100	138	5	4	.402	.496
Thompson,Milt	37	.255	76	102	12	26	4	1	1	13	11	19	3	1	.327	.343
Thompson,Robby	34	.245	92	322	46	79	16	2	8	28	35	73	4	2	.319	.382
Thompson,Ryan	28	.231	101	350	44	81	15	2	13	44	27	106	4	4	.286	.397
Timmons,Ozzie	25	.267	84	247	38	66	15	1	12	36	25	50	2	3	.335	.482
Tinsley,Lee	27	.262	125	397	64	104	17	5	7	44	42	96	20	8	.333	.383
Trammell,Alan	38	.261	83	207	26	54	9	1	4	22	18	24	4	2	.320	.372
Tucker,Michael	25	.266	104	319	41	85	13	3	8	37	34	64	8	5	.337	.401
Valentin,John	29	.279	151	573	89	160	38	2	20	86	78	81	11	5	.366	.457
Valentin,Jose	26	.243	140	424	66	103	24	4	11	58	52	100	14	9	.326	.396
Van Slyke,Andy	35	.263	77	262	32	69	13	3	6	29	30	47	6	1	.339	.405
Vander Wal,John	30	.272	110	125	18	34	7	1	5	19	17	26	2	1	.359	.464
Vaughn,Greg	30	.238	116	428	69	102	21	2	19	66	64	102	9	5	.337	.430
Vaughn,Mo	28	.279	159	587	93	164	30	1	34	110	83	157	7	4	.369	.508
Velarde,Randy	33	.260	116	366	53	95	17	1	9	40	41	72	4	2	.334	.385
Ventura,Robin	28	.268	155	559	84	150	26	1	23	93	94	95	4	4	.374	.442
Veras,Quilvio	25	.267	152	517	91	138	23	7	4	48	82	69	52	21	.367	.362
Vina,Fernando	27	.241	124	315	41	76	9	4	3	28	20	23	12	7	.287	.324
Vitiello,Joe	26	.280	115	347	41	97	19	1	10	49	33	67	1	1	.342	.427
Vizcaino,Jose	28	.275	154	582	72	160	20	4	4	55	47	83	9	8	.329	.344
Vizquel,Omar	29	.255	148	537	73	137	19	2	3	48	54	56	20	11	.323	.315
Walbeck,Matt	26	.254	140	481	48	122	22	1	7	58	29	65	2	1	.296	.347
Walker,Larry	29	.297	151	556	103	165	35	3	32	110	77	93	24	7	.382	.543
Wallach,Tim	38	.234	101	334	34	78	16	1	9	43	29	66	0	0	.295	.368
Walton,Jerome	30	.266	110	203	35	54	14	1	4	23	19	32	8	6	.329	.404
Ward,Turner	31	.242	64	178	26	43	8	1	4	20	25	30	5	2	.335	.365
Webster,Lenny	31	.255	77	188	22	48	12	0	4	20	18	24	0	0	.320	.383
Wehner,John	29	.256	71	207	29	53	11	1	3	20	20	30	8	3	.322	.362
Weiss,Walt	32	.249	152	515	65	128	17	2	2	37	89	69	11	5	.359	.301
Whitaker,Lou	39	.255	114	357	51	91	18	2	9	45	55	53	3	1	.354	.392
White,Devon	33	.254	132	544	82	138	25	4	13	52	39	118	22	6	.304	.386
White,Rondell	24	.297	152	556	92	165	33	5	16	75	43	92	24	8	.347	.460
Whiten,Mark	29	.255	130	491	74	125	19	3	18	74	57	109	13	6	.332	.415
Wilkins,Rick	29	.243	91	267	39	65	13	1	10	34	39	70	1	1	.340	.412
Williams,Bernie	27	.282	160	632	99	178	36	5	18	83	81	105	13	9	.363	.440
Williams,Eddie	31	.281	98	299	39	84	12	0	13	51	24	43	0	0	.334	.452
Williams,Gerald	29	.251	118	271	45	68	20	3	7	37	18	54	11	5	.298	.424
Williams,Matt	30	.271	143	539	88	146	23	3	36	100	39	95	2	1	.320	.525
Wilson,Dan	27	.249	141	449	41	112	25	2	6	47	33	80	1	1	.301	.354
Young,Eric	29	.286	136	416	71	119	19	5	6	42	58	33	38	16	.373	.399
Young,Kevin	27	.252	90	266	25	67	17	2	5	31	18	58	3	2	.299	.387
Zaun,Greg	25	.253	63	182	23	46	8	1	3	20	19	26	2	2	.323	.357
Zeile,Todd	30	.257	141	522	71	134	27	2	16	77	57	77	3	2	.330	.408

Projections for 1996 Pitchers

Pitcher	Age	ERA	W	L	Sv	G	GS	IP	H	HR	BB	SO	BR/9
Abbott,Jim	28	4.17	13	12	0	33	33	218	226	21	71	105	12.3
Aguilera,Rick	34	3.54	5	3	37	60	0	61	58	8	13	58	10.5
Alvarez,Wilson	26	4.37	13	12	0	33	33	206	189	21	110	137	13.1
Appier,Kevin	28	3.07	16	10	0	34	34	226	184	13	90	207	10.9
Aquino,Luis	31	3.97	3	3	0	42	6	59	63	4	22	32	13.0
Ashby,Andy	28	4.30	12	14	0	35	35	220	230	24	71	165	12.3
Assenmacher,Paul	35	3.27	4	2	0	56	0	44	39	3	15	39	11.0
Astacio,Pedro	26	3.46	6	5	0	47	19	151	141	14	48	106	11.3
Avery,Steve	26	3.41	14	10	0	33	33	203	185	17	61	165	10.9
Ayala,Bobby	26	3.94	5	4	11	70	0	80	77	9	33	80	12.4
Bankhead,Scott	32	3.94	3	2	0	29	1	48	45	6	20	32	12.2
Banks,Willie	27	5.61	5	11	0	29	22	130	141	14	84	85	15.6
Bautista,Jose	31	4.46	4	6	0	64	5	105	112	17	26	59	11.8
Beck,Rod	27	3.43	5	3	34	65	0	63	56	8	18	54	10.6
Belcher,Tim	34	4.70	11	13	0	33	33	203	207	20	99	103	13.6
Belinda,Stan	29	3.24	6	3	2	65	0	75	65	7	27	60	11.0
Benes,Andy	28	4.06	14	12	0	35	35	217	206	20	93	215	12.4
Bere,Jason	25	5.10	10	12	0	31	31	173	151	20	133	149	14.8
Bielecki,Mike	36	5.16	2	3	0	25	10	75	87	11	29	46	13.9
Black,Bud	39	4.74	5	5	0	15	14	76	81	12	26	46	12.7
Blair,Willie	30	4.80	4	6	0	51	10	120	140	13	45	87	13.9
Boever,Joe	35	4.86	5	6	0	68	0	111	120	16	49	73	13.7
Bohanon,Brian	27	5.12	3	5	4	44	10	95	116	10	40	55	14.8
Bones,Ricky	27	4.88	11	16	0	35	34	227	241	30	94	78	13.3
Bosio,Chris	33	4.42	11	11	0	30	30	173	178	17	71	90	13.0
Boskie,Shawn	29	4.26	7	7	0	23	20	114	120	16	25	63	11.4
Brantley,Jeff	32	3.49	5	4	29	65	0	80	67	10	30	65	10.9
Brewer,Billy	28	4.50	3	4	0	58	0	50	47	8	23	34	12.6
Brown,Kevin	31	3.76	13	11	0	31	31	206	215	13	57	142	11.9
Burba,Dave	29	3.87	5	5	0	66	7	114	105	11	55	109	12.6
Burkett,John	31	4.11	12	14	0	34	34	217	227	20	65	130	12.1
Candiotti,Tom	38	3.88	12	12	0	33	32	209	212	18	63	146	11.8
Casian,Larry	30	4.85	2	3	0	50	0	39	46	4	13	17	13.6
Castillo,Frank	27	3.77	10	10	0	27	26	167	162	18	47	119	11.3
Castillo,Tony	33	3.78	5	4	10	60	0	81	78	8	31	46	12.1
Charlton,Norm	33	3.12	6	3	31	62	0	78	61	6	36	88	11.2
Clark,Mark	28	4.57	9	8	0	23	23	136	147	16	46	70	12.8
Clemens,Roger	33	3.64	13	8	0	29	29	188	163	16	81	182	11.7
Cone,David	33	3.19	18	10	0	34	34	254	205	21	97	208	10.7
Cook,Dennis	33	4.57	3	4	0	52	1	61	61	10	23	49	12.4
Cormier,Rheal	29	4.08	5	4	0	41	15	117	126	12	29	68	11.9
Corsi,Jim	34	3.71	3	3	0	43	0	51	47	2	28	26	13.2
Cox,Danny	36	4.02	2	2	0	26	0	47	45	4	22	42	12.8
DeLeon,Jose	35	3.30	5	4	0	55	0	90	68	10	44	79	11.2
DeLucia,Rich	31	4.77	3	4	0	46	1	66	68	10	31	69	13.5
Deshaies,Jim	36	4.91	3	4	0	12	11	55	64	10	9	33	11.9
Dewey,Mark	31	3.53	3	3	0	42	0	51	50	3	19	33	12.2
Dibble,Rob	32	5.10	2	2	0	35	0	30	21	3	39	32	18.0
Doherty,John	29	4.42	5	5	11	42	7	118	139	11	33	41	13.1
Drabek,Doug	33	3.44	14	11	0	34	34	217	205	17	64	164	11.2

Projections for 1996 Pitchers

Pitcher	Age	ERA	W	L	Sv	G	GS	IP	H	HR	BB	SO	BR/9
Eckersley,Dennis	41	4.11	4	4	34	58	0	57	60	7	14	53	11.7
Eldred,Cal	28	3.79	8	7	0	20	20	133	116	14	55	78	11.6
Erickson,Scott	28	4.48	12	13	0	35	34	215	238	20	73	130	13.0
Fassero,Jeff	33	3.71	12	11	0	31	31	194	184	13	76	167	12.1
Fernandez,Alex	26	4.03	15	12	0	34	34	230	223	28	73	171	11.6
Fernandez,Sid	33	3.97	8	8	0	23	23	127	105	20	52	118	11.1
Fetters,Mike	31	3.60	3	3	28	48	0	45	41	2	24	29	13.0
Finley,Chuck	33	4.44	13	14	0	35	35	231	228	23	106	202	13.0
Fleming,Dave	26	4.76	3	5	0	30	20	119	129	14	56	59	14.0
Fossas,Tony	38	3.86	3	3	0	62	0	42	39	4	18	42	12.2
Franco,John	35	3.90	3	4	32	56	0	60	60	6	22	50	12.3
Freeman,Marvin	33	5.02	7	9	0	26	23	129	143	15	56	85	13.9
Frey,Steve	32	4.24	2	3	2	43	0	34	33	4	16	17	13.0
Gardiner,Mike	30	4.76	2	2	0	24	0	34	36	5	14	17	13.2
Gardner,Mark	34	4.54	4	5	5	39	15	119	125	16	47	84	13.0
Glavine,Tom	30	3.42	15	11	0	33	33	224	214	11	74	165	11.6
Gordon,Tom	28	3.98	13	13	0	35	35	217	200	17	102	156	12.5
Gott,Jim	36	4.07	2	3	0	37	0	42	46	3	15	33	13.1
Grahe,Joe	28	4.92	3	4	0	32	7	64	71	5	30	33	14.2
Greene,Tommy	29	4.88	2	4	0	12	9	48	48	4	29	35	14.4
Gross,Kevin	35	4.84	11	14	0	35	33	212	226	20	103	145	14.0
Gubicza,Mark	33	4.17	13	13	0	35	35	220	242	17	64	87	12.5
Guthrie,Mark	30	4.30	4	5	0	70	1	69	70	8	31	57	13.2
Guzman,Juan	29	4.50	10	11	0	29	29	170	165	15	92	134	13.6
Habyan,John	32	3.91	5	4	0	67	0	76	80	5	29	62	12.9
Hammond,Chris	30	3.99	8	9	0	25	23	149	155	14	44	106	12.0
Hanson,Erik	31	4.08	12	9	0	29	29	181	190	15	57	140	12.3
Harkey,Mike	29	5.48	6	10	0	29	21	133	161	19	49	57	14.2
Harnisch,Pete	29	3.29	9	8	0	22	22	134	121	15	29	97	10.1
Harris,Gene	31	4.06	2	2	0	29	0	31	31	2	16	20	13.6
Harris,Greg	40	4.92	2	4	0	47	0	53	58	8	22	51	13.6
Harris,Greg W.	32	5.31	4	6	0	18	14	83	90	11	41	51	14.2
Henke,Tom	38	2.90	4	3	40	57	0	59	46	6	20	56	10.1
Henneman,Mike	34	3.67	3	3	22	53	0	54	53	4	21	45	12.3
Henry,Butch	27	3.88	9	9	0	27	24	153	162	14	34	84	11.5
Henry,Doug	32	4.29	3	4	4	50	0	65	62	8	30	50	12.7
Hentgen,Pat	27	4.73	12	14	0	34	34	232	235	29	104	180	13.2
Hernandez,Roberto	31	3.05	5	3	36	65	0	65	55	6	22	72	10.7
Hernandez,Xavier	30	3.32	5	4	3	57	0	84	75	7	30	81	11.3
Hershiser,Orel	37	4.27	13	10	0	30	30	192	195	25	58	114	11.9
Hickerson,Bryan	32	5.14	3	4	0	54	6	77	88	11	32	49	14.0
Hill,Ken	30	3.87	15	10	0	34	32	214	204	15	90	117	12.4
Hoffman,Trevor	28	3.57	4	4	33	62	0	63	54	8	24	63	11.1
Holmes,Darren	30	3.77	4	3	10	64	0	62	59	5	28	59	12.6
Honeycutt,Rick	42	4.40	3	3	1	54	0	45	48	6	13	27	12.2
Howe,Steve	38	3.50	4	3	1	60	0	54	54	5	13	29	11.2
Jackson,Danny	34	4.50	7	11	0	26	26	158	165	10	75	104	13.7
Jackson,Mike	31	2.59	4	2	6	47	0	59	45	5	17	56	9.5
Johnson,Randy	32	2.56	20	7	0	33	33	239	180	18	72	303	9.5
Jones,Bobby	26	3.79	12	14	0	34	34	223	227	19	61	130	11.6

360

Projections for 1996 Pitchers

Pitcher	Age	ERA	W	L	Sv	G	GS	IP	H	HR	BB	SO	BR/9
Jones,Doug	39	4.03	4	3	14	59	0	58	65	5	13	44	12.1
Jones,Todd	28	2.81	7	4	7	69	0	93	72	6	40	82	10.8
Kamieniecki,Scott	32	4.70	8	8	0	23	21	132	130	12	72	71	13.8
Key,Jimmy	35	3.64	7	5	0	15	15	99	102	10	20	58	11.1
Kile,Darryl	27	4.56	8	11	0	30	27	158	154	12	91	123	14.0
Krueger,Bill	38	6.06	1	2	0	20	8	49	70	7	17	35	16.0
Langston,Mark	35	3.94	13	11	0	32	32	210	204	23	67	166	11.6
Leiper,Dave	34	3.00	4	2	0	51	0	45	37	3	18	23	11.0
Leiter,Al	30	4.64	11	12	0	31	31	190	186	13	113	158	14.2
Leiter,Mark	33	3.94	10	11	0	39	26	192	191	21	54	134	11.5
Lilliquist,Derek	30	3.71	3	2	0	38	0	34	31	4	10	18	10.9
Lloyd,Graeme	29	3.68	3	3	5	45	0	44	45	4	11	24	11.5
MacDonald,Bob	31	4.67	3	3	0	37	0	52	55	6	26	38	14.0
Maddux,Greg	30	1.66	23	4	0	33	33	249	192	9	27	196	7.9
Maddux,Mike	34	3.16	6	3	1	46	3	94	90	6	25	68	11.0
Magnante,Mike	31	4.75	2	3	0	38	0	55	66	5	20	28	14.1
Martinez,Dennis	41	3.35	17	8	0	32	32	215	204	18	53	111	10.8
Martinez,Pedro	24	2.99	16	10	0	34	34	217	174	19	73	210	10.2
Martinez,Ramon	28	3.79	14	13	0	34	34	233	216	20	92	154	11.9
Mathews,Terry	31	3.92	4	4	0	57	1	85	87	8	24	59	11.8
McCaskill,Kirk	35	4.92	4	5	1	62	1	86	100	10	32	53	13.8
McDowell,Jack	30	4.03	15	12	0	34	34	248	248	22	89	176	12.2
McDowell,Roger	35	4.23	5	4	0	63	0	83	91	4	37	45	13.9
McElroy,Chuck	28	3.54	4	3	0	59	0	56	54	4	20	37	11.9
McMichael,Greg	29	3.11	6	4	4	72	0	84	75	5	28	77	11.0
Meacham,Rusty	28	3.76	4	4	1	55	0	67	69	6	19	42	11.8
Mercker,Kent	28	3.55	12	9	0	32	28	170	140	16	73	144	11.3
Mesa,Jose	30	3.78	6	4	48	70	0	81	83	6	24	58	11.9
Mills,Alan	29	3.89	2	2	0	35	0	37	31	5	20	27	12.4
Montgomery,Jeff	34	2.87	5	3	37	60	0	69	58	5	21	56	10.3
Moore,Mike	36	5.92	5	9	0	20	20	108	121	19	56	48	14.8
Morgan,Mike	36	4.03	7	8	0	21	21	125	134	11	32	69	12.0
Moyer,Jamie	33	4.04	10	9	0	31	24	158	160	19	41	83	11.4
Mulholland,Terry	33	4.33	8	11	0	33	25	162	175	20	41	86	12.0
Munoz,Mike	30	4.74	4	4	0	77	0	57	56	6	36	45	14.5
Mussina,Mike	27	3.11	18	10	0	35	35	252	225	24	57	160	10.1
Myers,Randy	33	3.77	4	4	45	61	0	62	59	6	25	63	12.2
Nabholz,Chris	29	4.15	2	3	0	33	7	52	51	4	29	33	13.8
Nagy,Charles	29	4.10	15	10	0	33	33	215	223	18	74	154	12.4
Navarro,Jaime	28	3.93	10	11	0	35	26	190	197	16	53	125	11.8
Neagle,Denny	27	3.91	13	13	0	35	35	221	229	25	48	177	11.3
Nelson,Jeff	29	3.18	6	3	3	62	0	82	68	6	36	90	11.4
Nen,Robb	26	3.41	4	5	27	66	0	74	67	7	36	76	12.5
Olivares,Omar	28	4.70	2	3	0	20	10	67	72	7	33	31	14.1
Olson,Gregg	29	3.86	2	2	2	27	0	35	31	2	20	27	13.1
Ontiveros,Steve	35	3.48	10	8	0	29	24	155	146	12	46	84	11.1
Orosco,Jesse	39	3.33	5	3	4	68	0	54	39	6	31	57	11.7
Parrett,Jeff	34	3.87	4	5	0	66	0	86	80	7	42	79	12.8
Patterson,Bob	37	3.81	4	3	0	67	0	59	55	8	17	41	11.0
Pavlik,Roger	28	4.53	10	11	0	30	29	171	169	18	80	124	13.1

Projections for 1996 Pitchers

Pitcher	Age	ERA	W	L	Sv	G	GS	IP	H	HR	BB	SO	BR/9
Pena,Alejandro	37	3.88	3	3	0	41	0	51	47	7	18	56	11.5
Perez,Melido	30	4.10	8	7	0	20	20	125	115	13	56	91	12.3
Perez,Mike	31	3.52	4	4	2	63	0	64	62	5	21	46	11.7
Pichardo,Hipolito	26	4.09	4	4	0	52	0	77	84	5	27	39	13.0
Plesac,Dan	34	3.86	4	4	3	67	0	70	69	7	22	62	11.7
Plunk,Eric	32	3.15	6	3	2	62	0	80	68	5	36	84	11.7
Poole,Jim	30	3.52	4	2	0	47	0	46	41	5	18	35	11.5
Portugal,Mark	33	3.51	12	10	0	30	30	182	171	15	56	104	11.2
Radinsky,Scott	28	4.19	3	3	1	52	0	43	46	4	17	27	13.2
Reed,Steve	30	3.79	6	5	0	83	0	95	89	11	32	74	11.5
Righetti,Dave	37	5.60	2	3	0	16	7	45	55	7	16	28	14.2
Rijo,Jose	31	3.56	8	7	0	22	22	124	117	10	40	118	11.4
Rogers,Kenny	31	4.07	15	13	0	35	35	239	229	26	88	166	11.9
Rojas,Mel	29	3.03	6	4	42	69	0	86	76	5	29	71	11.0
Ruffin,Bruce	32	4.50	3	3	16	53	0	50	51	5	25	46	13.7
Russell,Jeff	34	3.56	3	2	32	48	0	43	42	3	13	34	11.5
Saberhagen,Bret	32	3.91	14	9	0	30	30	198	192	22	44	144	10.7
Sanderson,Scott	39	5.05	4	5	0	14	12	73	87	15	8	34	11.7
Scanlan,Bob	29	5.23	5	9	0	26	18	117	129	12	62	63	14.7
Schilling,Curt	29	3.09	9	6	0	20	20	134	119	12	30	112	10.0
Schourek,Pete	27	3.97	12	12	0	31	31	197	208	20	47	165	11.6
Scott,Tim	29	3.45	5	4	3	65	0	73	70	5	28	60	12.1
Shaw,Jeff	29	4.00	5	4	1	64	0	81	80	10	25	52	11.7
Slocumb,Heathcliff	30	4.00	4	5	33	68	0	81	88	3	36	65	13.8
Smiley,John	31	3.57	13	11	0	33	31	207	205	20	46	147	10.9
Smith,Lee	38	3.17	4	3	39	57	0	54	45	5	22	51	11.2
Smith,Pete	30	4.39	2	3	0	18	11	80	81	13	25	40	11.9
Smith,Zane	35	4.18	11	9	0	30	27	157	178	15	33	62	12.1
Smoltz,John	29	3.38	14	9	0	31	30	200	170	17	75	185	11.0
Stanton,Mike	29	4.25	4	3	3	60	0	53	53	4	26	37	13.4
Stottlemyre,Todd	31	4.64	12	14	0	35	33	229	245	25	87	203	13.0
Swift,Bill	34	4.66	9	7	0	23	23	139	139	13	59	83	12.8
Swindell,Greg	31	4.32	10	12	0	35	30	179	196	20	46	101	12.2
Tapani,Kevin	32	4.31	12	14	0	37	35	215	239	23	54	137	12.3
Tewksbury,Bob	35	4.37	10	10	0	27	26	167	205	14	26	74	12.4
Timlin,Mike	30	4.14	3	3	20	40	0	50	51	4	23	45	13.3
Valenzuela,Fernando	35	4.45	5	7	0	28	16	99	101	12	37	55	12.5
Wegman,Bill	33	4.25	4	5	0	37	13	110	122	13	28	57	12.3
Wells,David	33	3.95	12	12	0	30	30	212	209	27	56	134	11.3
West,David	31	3.50	5	4	0	22	12	72	58	6	36	58	11.8
Wetteland,John	29	2.22	7	2	35	68	0	73	53	5	21	83	9.1
Whiteside,Matt	28	4.16	4	3	8	51	0	67	70	6	25	43	12.8
Wickman,Bob	27	3.77	6	4	2	72	1	93	91	6	41	58	12.8
Wilson,Trevor	30	4.45	5	7	0	19	19	93	92	9	43	43	13.1
Witt,Bobby	32	4.48	11	12	0	33	33	193	204	18	77	157	13.1
Wohlers,Mark	26	3.09	6	3	32	72	0	70	60	2	33	81	12.0
Worrell,Todd	36	3.18	5	3	35	63	0	68	61	6	19	63	10.6
Young,Anthony	30	4.04	3	3	2	31	7	69	71	6	27	38	12.8

These Guys Can Play Too and Might Get A Shot

The players below saw either little or no major league action last year, but they played well in the minors and might well end up with major league jobs in 1996. We must stress, however, that the numbers below are NOT projections. Rather, they are Major League Equivalencies. For details, we refer you to this book's companion, the Minor League Handbook. But briefly, the MLE's represent the major league equivalent of what the player did in the minors last year. Does that mean he'll do the same thing if given a chance in the majors this season? No, but it does suggest a general level of talent. And we've learned over the years not to ignore the MLE's.

Batter	Age	Avg	G	AB	R	H	2B	3B	HR	RBI	BB	SO	SB	CS	OBP	SLG
Abreu,Bob	22	.263	114	392	53	103	20	10	6	55	49	133	10	14	.345	.411
Arias,George	24	.248	134	499	70	124	15	5	25	81	41	128	1	1	.306	.449
Beamon,Trey	22	.278	118	417	46	116	23	2	3	38	24	57	11	7	.317	.365
Bonnici,James	24	.282	138	507	73	143	39	2	19	89	65	108	1	1	.364	.479
Crespo,Felipe	23	.275	88	338	46	93	18	4	12	34	34	60	9	6	.341	.459
Echevarria,Angel	25	.327	124	471	75	154	32	1	30	97	46	96	6	3	.387	.590
Garciaparra,Nomar	22	.268	125	514	74	138	22	6	7	45	41	44	25	10	.323	.375
Gibralter,Steve	23	.289	79	253	40	73	17	1	14	51	21	71	0	1	.343	.530
Giles,Brian S.	25	.303	123	409	65	124	18	6	14	65	51	41	5	3	.380	.479
Greene,Todd	25	.272	125	467	69	127	17	0	33	74	20	97	2	5	.302	.520
Grijak,Kevin	25	.304	127	372	39	113	18	3	12	55	24	57	0	2	.346	.465
Guerrero,Wilton	21	.314	109	411	51	129	10	3	0	23	18	74	17	9	.343	.353
Jennings,Robin	24	.289	132	485	67	140	26	5	16	75	36	65	5	14	.338	.462
Kendall,Jason	22	.300	117	413	73	124	24	0	6	59	39	23	7	6	.361	.402
Kennedy,Dave	25	.333	128	504	72	168	23	2	32	93	39	136	3	1	.381	.577
Kieschnick,Brooks	24	.276	138	492	52	136	27	0	19	62	50	95	1	3	.343	.447
Malave,Jose	25	.261	91	314	48	82	12	0	19	50	26	70	0	0	.318	.481
McGuire,Ryan	24	.338	109	417	57	141	32	0	6	57	47	54	8	7	.405	.458
McMillon,Billy	24	.285	141	498	73	142	25	2	10	74	65	96	10	9	.368	.404
Owens,Eric	25	.285	108	410	70	117	22	5	9	51	44	62	25	9	.355	.429
Payton,Jay	23	.281	135	533	76	150	26	5	13	69	28	57	19	10	.317	.422
Pough,Chop	26	.267	127	461	75	123	33	4	23	86	47	136	8	4	.335	.505
Ramirez,Roberto	26	.275	129	488	66	134	26	4	16	80	30	109	8	8	.317	.443
Relaford,Desmond	22	.269	120	461	67	124	17	1	8	32	47	92	24	6	.337	.362
Renteria,Edgar	20	.265	135	491	55	130	13	5	5	54	21	91	21	8	.295	.342
Rivera,Ruben	22	.260	119	416	75	108	21	6	20	64	48	145	17	10	.336	.483
Saenz,Olmedo	25	.293	111	409	56	120	24	0	12	70	42	61	0	2	.359	.440
Valdes,Pedro	23	.294	114	422	54	124	27	2	6	64	30	82	2	6	.341	.410
Walker,Todd	23	.283	137	508	82	144	26	2	22	84	54	111	18	7	.352	.472

The Favorite Toy

"The Favorite Toy" is a mathematical formula invented by Bill James to project a player's chances to reach career hit and home run goals like 3,000 hits or 500 home runs. The formula is pretty long and we won't run it here, but what The Favorite Toy does is use a player's age and recent performances to estimate his chances of reaching the goal. Does Frank Thomas have a chance to break Hank Aaron's home run record? The formula says he has a very slight one, well under 10 percent, as does Albert Belle. We'll know a lot more in five years or so, but it's fun to speculate on it *now*.

Bill thought you'd enjoy seeing some Favorite Toy projections . . . they're neat to look at now, and it'll be just as much fun to review them five years from now. Here they are, with the player's age based on how old he'll be on July 1, 1996.

— Don Zminda

Players with at least a 5% Chance for 3000 Hits

Player	Age	Curr. Total	Proj., Total	Chance
Paul Molitor	39.6	2789	3055	76%
Tony Gwynn	35.9	2401	2906	34%
Kirby Puckett	35.1	2304	2841	27%
Roberto Alomar	28.2	1329	2516	21%
Carlos Baerga	27.4	971	2385	20%
Cal Ripken	35.6	2371	2803	19%
Chuck Knoblauch	27.8	822	2175	12%
Travis Fryman	27.0	848	2146	10%
Rafael Palmeiro	31.5	1455	2378	10%
Gregg Jefferies	28.7	1106	2228	9%
Frank Thomas	27.9	893	2137	9%
Ivan Rodriguez	24.4	569	1963	7%
Ruben Sierra	30.5	1547	2350	5%

No players are currently projected to have even a 1 percent chance to reach 4,000 hits or break Pete Rose's career record.

Players with at Least a 10% chance for 500 Home Runs

Player	Age	Curr. Total	Proj., Total	Chance
Eddie Murray	40.1	479	514	96%
Frank Thomas	27.9	182	506	52%
Albert Belle	29.6	194	498	49%
Barry Bonds	31.7	292	496	48%
Ken Griffey Jr	26.4	189	459	37%
Matt Williams	30.4	225	436	27%
Fred McGriff	32.4	289	448	25%
Juan Gonzalez	26.5	167	414	24%
Sammy Sosa	27.4	131	401	23%
Jose Canseco	31.8	300	436	18%
Mo Vaughn	28.3	111	372	17%
Mark McGwire	32.5	277	425	16%
Rafael Palmeiro	31.5	194	383	12%
Mike Piazza	27.6	92	341	11%
Tim Salmon	27.6	90	339	11%
Cecil Fielder	32.5	250	400	10%

Players with at Least a 5% chance for 600 Home Runs

Player	Age	Curr. Total	Proj., Total	Chance
Frank Thomas	27.9	182	506	28%
Albert Belle	29.6	194	498	25%
Barry Bonds	31.7	292	496	16%
Ken Griffey Jr	26.4	189	459	16%
Sammy Sosa	27.4	131	401	8%
Juan Gonzalez	26.5	167	414	7%
Matt Williams	30.4	225	436	6%

Players with at Least a 1% chance for 700 Home Runs

Player	Age	Curr. Total	Proj., Total	Chance
Frank Thomas	27.9	182	506	13%
Albert Belle	29.6	194	498	10%
Ken Griffey	26.4	189	459	3%

Players with at Least a 1% chance for 756 Home Runs

Player	Age	Curr. Total	Proj., Total	Chance
Frank Thomas	27.9	182	506	7%
Albert Belle	29.6	194	498	4%

Players with at Least a 1% chance for 800 Home Runs

Player	Age	Curr. Total	Proj., Total	Chance
Frank Thomas	27.9	182	506	2%

About STATS, Inc.

STATS, Inc. is the nation's leading independent sports information and statistical analysis company, providing detailed sports services for a wide array of clients.

One of the fastest-growing sports companies in the country, STATS provides the most up-to-the-minute sports information to professional teams, print and broadcast media, software developers and interactive srevice providers around the country. Some of our major clients are ESPN, Turner Sports, the Associated Press, *The Sporting News*, Electronic Arts and Motorola. Much of the information we provide is available to the public via STATS On-Line.

STATS Publishing, a division of STATS, Inc., produces 10 annual books, including the *STATS Major League Handbook*, the *Pro Football Handbook*, and the *Pro Basketball Handbook*. These publications deliver STATS expertise to fans, scouts, general managers and media around the country.

In addition, STATS offers the most innovative—and fun—fantasy sports games around, from *Bill James Fantasy Baseball* and *Bill James Classic Baseball* to *STATS Fantasy Football* and *STATS Fantasy Hoops*.

Information technology has grown by leaps and bounds in the last decade, and STATS will continue to be at the forefront as both a vendor and supplier of the most up-to-date, in-depth sports information available. If you haven't already, you will most certainly be seeing us at an infobahn rest stop in the near future.

For more information on our products, or on joining our reporter network, write us at:

STATS, Inc.
8131 Monticello Ave.
Skokie, IL 60076-3300

...or call us at 1-800-63-STATS (1-800-637-8287). Outside the U.S., dial 1-708-676-3383.

Glossary

% Inherited Scored
A Relief Pitching statistic indicating the percentage of runners on base at the time a relief pitcher enters a game that he allows to score.

1st Batter OBP
The On-Base Percentage allowed by a relief pitcher to the first batter he faces in a game.

Active Career Batting Leaders
Minimum of 1,000 At Bats required for Batting Average, On-Base Percentage, Slugging Percentage, At Bats Per HR, At Bats Per GDP, At Bats Per RBI, and K/BB Ratio. One hundred (100) Stolen Base Attempts required for Stolen Base Success %. Any player who appeared in 1995 is eligible for inclusion provided he meets the category's minimum requirements.

Active Career Pitching Leaders
Minimum of 750 Innings Pitched required for Earned Run Average, Opponent Batting Average, all of the "Per 9 Innings" categories, and Strikeout to Walk Ratio. Two hundred fifty (250) Games Started required for Complete Game Frequency. One hundred (100) decisions required for Win-Loss Percentage. Any player who appeared in 1995 is eligible for inclusion provided he meets the category's minimum requirements.

BA ScPos Allowed
Batting Average Allowed with Runners in Scoring Position.

Batting Average
Hits divided by At Bats.

Catcher's ERA
The Earned Run Average of a club's pitchers with a particular catcher behind the plate. To figure this for a catcher, multiply the Earned Runs Allowed by the pitchers while he was catching times nine and divide that by his number of Innings Caught.

Cheap Wins/Tough Losses/Top Game Scores
First determine the starting pitcher's Game Score as follows: (1)Start with 50. (2)Add 1 point for each out recorded by the starting pitcher. (3)Add 2 points for each inning the pitcher completes after the fourth inning. (4)Add 1 point for each strikeout. (5)Subtract 2 points for each hit allowed. (6)Subtract 4 points for each earned run allowed. (7)Subtract 2 points for an unearned run. (8)Subtract 1 point for each walk.

If the starting pitcher scores over 50 and loses, it's a Tough Loss. If he wins with a game score under 50, it's a Cheap Win. The top Game Scores of 1995 are listed.

Cleanup Slugging%
The Slugging Percentage of a player when batting fourth in the batting order.

Complete Game Frequency
Complete Games divided by Games Started.

Earned Run Average
(Earned Runs times 9) divided by Innings Pitched.

Fielding Percentage
(Putouts plus Assists) divided by (Putouts plus Assists plus Errors).

Hold

A Hold is credited any time a relief pitcher enters a game in a Save Situation (see definition below), records at least one out, and leaves the game never having relinquished the lead. Note: a pitcher cannot finish the game and receive credit for a Hold, nor can he earn a hold and a save.

Isolated Power

Slugging Percentage minus Batting Average.

K/BB Ratio

Strikeouts divided by Walks.

Late & Close

A Late & Close situation meets the following requirements: (1)the game is in the seventh inning or later, and (2)the batting team is either leading by one run, tied, or has the potential tying run on base, at bat, or on deck. Note: this situation is very similar to the characteristics of a Save Situation.

Leadoff On Base%

The On-Base Percentage of a player when batting first in the batting order.

Offensive Winning Percentage

The Winning Percentage a team of nine Fred McGriffs (or anybody) would compile against average pitching and defense. The formula: (Runs Created per 27 outs) divided by the League average of runs scored per game. Square the result and divide it by (1+itself).

On Base Percentage

(Hits plus Walks plus Hit by Pitcher) divided by (At Bats plus Walks plus Hit by Pitcher plus Sacrifice Flies).

Opponent Batting Average

Hits Allowed divided by (Batters Faced minus Walks minus Hit Batsmen minus Sacrifice Hits minus Sacrifice Flies minus Catcher's Interference).

PA*

The divisor for On Base Percentage: At Bats plus Walks plus Hit By Pitcher plus Sacrifice Flies; or Plate Appearances minus Sacrifice Hits and Times Reached Base on Defensive Interference.

PCS (Pitchers' Caught Stealing)

The number of runners officially counted as Caught Stealing where the initiator of the fielding play was the pitcher, not the catcher. Note: such plays are often referred to as "pickoffs", but appear in official records as Caught Stealings. The most common "pitcher caught stealing scenario" is a 1-3-6 fielding play, where the runner is officially charged a Caught Stealing because he broke for second base. "Pickoff" (fielding play 1-3 being the most common) is not an official statistic.

PkOf Throw/Runner

The number of pickoff throws made by a pitcher divided by the number of runners on first base.

Plate Appearances

At Bats plus Total Walks plus Hit By Pitcher plus Sacrifice Hits plus Sacrifice Flies plus Times Reached on Defensive Interference.

Power/Speed Number

A way to look at power and speed in one number. A player must score high in both areas to earn a high Power/Speed Number. The formula: (HR x SB x 2) divided by (HR + SB).

Quick Hooks and Slow Hooks

A Quick Hook is the removal of a pitcher who has pitched less than 6 innings and given up 3 runs or less. A Slow Hook occurs when a pitcher pitches more than 9 innings, or allows 7 or more runs, or whose combined innings pitched and runs allowed totals 13 or more.

Range Factor

The number of Chances (Putouts plus Assists) times nine divided by the number of Defensive Innings Played. The average for a Regular Player at each position in 1995:

Second Base: 5.17
Third Base: 2.71
Shortstop: 4.58

Left Field: 2.03
Center Field: 2.64
Right Field: 2.09

Run Support Per 9 IP

The number of runs scored by a pitcher's team while he was still in the game times nine divided by his Innings Pitched.

Runs Created

A way to combine a batter's total offensive contributions into one number. The formula: (H + BB + HBP - CS - GIDP) times (Total Bases + .26(TBB - IBB + HBP) + .52(SH + SF + SB)) divided by (AB + TBB + HBP + SH + SF).

Save Percentage

Saves (SV) divided by Save Opportunities (OP).

Save Situation

A Relief Pitcher is in a Save Situation when:

upon entering the game with his club leading, he has the opportunity to be the finishing pitcher (and is not the winning pitcher of record at the time), and meets any one of the three following conditions:

(1) he has a lead of no more than three runs and has the opportunity to pitch for at least one inning, or

(2) he enters the game, regardless of the count, with the potential tying run either on base, at bat, or on deck; or

(3) he pitches three or more innings regardless of the lead and the official scorer credits him with a save.

SB Success%

Stolen Bases divided by (Stolen Bases plus Caught Stealing).

Secondary Average

A way to look at a player's extra bases gained, independent of Batting Average. The formula: (Total Bases - Hits + TBB + SB) divided by At Bats.

Slugging Percentage

Total Bases divided by At Bats.

Total Bases

Hits plus Doubles plus (2 times Triples) plus (3 times Home runs).

Win-Loss Percentage or Winning Percentage

Wins divided by (Wins plus Losses).

Bill James Classic Baseball

Joe Jackson, Walter Johnson, and Roberto Clemente are back on the field of your dreams!

If you're not ready to give up baseball in the fall, or if you're looking to relive its glorious past, then Bill James Classic Baseball is the game for you!

The Classic Game features players from all eras of Major League Baseball at all performance levels - not just the stars. You could see Honus Wagner, Josh Gibson, Carl Yastrzemski, Bob Uecker, Billy Grabarkewitz, and Dick Fowler...on the SAME team!

As owner, GM and manager all in one, you'll be able to...

- "Buy" your team of up to 25 players from our catalog of over 2,000 historical players (You'll receive $1 million to buy your favorite players)
- Choose the park your team will call home—current or historical, 63 in all!
- Rotate batting lineups for a right- or left-handed starting pitcher
- Change your pitching rotation for each series. Determine your set-up man, closer, and long reliever
- Alter in-game strategies, including stealing frequency, holding runners on base, hit-and-run, and much more!
- Select your best pinch hitter and late-inning defensive replacements (For example, Curt Flood will get to more balls than Hack Wilson!)

How to Play The Classic Game:

1. Sign up to be a team owner TODAY! Leagues forming year-round
2. STATS, Inc. will supply you with a catalog of eligible players and a rule book
3. You'll receive $1 million to buy your favorite major leaguers
4. Take part in a player and ballpark draft with 11 other owners
5. Set your pitching rotation, batting lineup, and managerial strategies
6. STATS runs the game simulation...a 154-game schedule, 14 weeks!
7. You'll receive customized in-depth weekly reports, featuring game summaries, stats, and boxscores

Order from STATS INC. Today!
Use Order Form in This Book, or Call 1-800-63-STATS or 708-676-3383!

Bill James Fantasy Baseball

Bill James Fantasy Baseball enters its eighth season of offering baseball fans the most unique, realistic and exciting game fantasy sports has to offer.

You draft a 25-player roster and can expand to as many as 28. Players aren't ranked like in rotisserie leagues—you'll get credit for everything a player does, like hitting homers, driving in runs, turning double plays, pitching quality outings and more!

Also, the team which scores the most points among all leagues, plus wins the World Series, will receive the John McGraw Award, which includes a one-week trip to the Grapefruit League in spring training, a day at the ballpark with Bill James, and a new fantasy league named in his/her honor!

Unique Features Include:

• **Live fantasy experts** — available seven days a week

• **The best weekly reports in the business** — detailing who is in the lead, win-loss records, MVPs, and team strengths and weaknesses

• **On-Line computer system** — a world of information, including daily updates of fantasy standings and stats

• **Over twice as many statistics as rotisserie**

• **Transactions that are effective the very next day!**

"My goal was to develop a fantasy league based on the simplest yet most realistic principle possible. A league in which the values are as nearly as possible what they ought to be, without being distorted by artificial category values or rankings...."
- Bill James

All this, all summer long...for less than $5 per week!

Order from STATS INC. Today!
Use Order Form in This Book, or Call 1-800-63-STATS or 708-676-3383!

STATS Fantasy Hoops

Soar into the 1995-96 season with STATS Fantasy Hoops! SFH puts YOU in charge. Don't just sit back and watch Grant Hill, Shawn Kemp, and Alonzo Mourning - get in the game and coach your team to the top!

How to Play SFH:
1. Sign up to coach a team.
2. You'll receive a full set of rules and a draft form with SFH point values for all eligible players - anyone who played in the NBA in 1994-95, plus all 1995 NBA draft picks.
3. Complete the draft form and return it to STATS.
4. You will take part in the draft with nine other owners, and we will send you league rosters.
5. You make unlimited weekly transactions including trades, free agent signings, activations, and benchings.
6. Six of the 10 teams in your league advance to postseason play, with two teams ultimately advancing to the Finals.

SFH points values are tested against actual NBA results, mirroring the real thing. Weekly reports will tell you everything you need to know to lead your team to the SFH Championship!

STATS Fantasy Football

STATS Fantasy Football puts YOU in charge! You draft, trade, cut, bench, activate players and even sign free agents each week. SFF pits you head-to-head against 11 other owners.

STATS' scoring system applies realistic values, tested against actual NFL results. Each week, you'll receive a superb in-depth report telling you all about both team and league performances.

How to Play SFF:
1. Sign up today!
2. STATS sends you a draft form listing all eligible NFL players.
3. Fill out the draft form and return it to STATS, and you will take part in the draft along with 11 other team owners.
4. Go head-to-head against the other owners in your league. You'll make week-by-week roster moves and transactions through STATS' Fantasy Football experts, via phone, fax, or on-line!

Order from STATS INC. Today!
Use Order Form in This Book, or Call 1-800-63-STATS or 708-676-3383!

STATS On-Line

Now you can have a direct line to a world of sports information just like the pros use with STATS On-Line. If you love to keep up with your favorite teams and players, STATS On-Line is for you. From Shaquille O'Neal's fast-breaking dunks to Ken Griffey's tape-measure blasts — if you want baseball, basketball, football and hockey stats, we put them at your fingertips!

STATS On-Line

- **Player Profiles and Team Profiles —** The #1 resource for scouting your favorite professional teams and players with information you simply can't find anywhere else! The most detailed info you've ever seen, including real-time stats. Follow baseball pitch-by-pitch, foot ball snap-by-snap, and basketball and hockey shot-by-shot, with scores and player stats updated continually!

- **NO monthly or annual fees**

- **Local access numbers** — avoid costly long-distance charges!

- **Unlimited access** — 24 hours a day, seven days a week

- **Downloadable files** — get year-to-date stats in an ASCII format for baseball, football, basketball, and hockey

- **In-progress box scores** — You'll have access to the most up-to-the-second scoring stats for every team and player. When you log into STATS On-Line, you'll get detailed updates, including player stats and scoring plays while the games are in progress!

- **Other exclusive features** — transactions and injury information, team and player profiles and updates, standings, leader and trailer boards, game-by-game logs, fantasy game features, and much more!

Sign-up fee of $30 (applied towards future use), 24-hour access with usage charges of $.75/min. Mon.-Fri., 8am-6pm CST; $.25/min. all other hours and weekends.

Order from *STATS* INC. Today!
Use Order Form in This Book, or Call 1-800-63-STATS or 708-676-3383!

Exclusive Scouting Reports

STATS Presents... *The Scouting Notebook: 1996*

Building upon seven years of tremendous success, the *Notebook* offers everything to the baseball devotee. STATS and its team of national scouts break new ground by covering every player who appeared in the majors last season, along with all the top prospects.

Unique Features:

☆ Extensive scouting reports on over 700 major league players

☆ Evaluations of nearly 200 minor league prospects

☆ Coverage of every 1995 major leaguer

☆ Written by experts covering every team, including nationally renowned analysts like Peter Gammons and John Benson

☆ Complete coverage of the strengths and weaknesses of each team's top players

*"STATS Scouting Notebook - **the most valuable reference tool a fan can have, short of having lunch with Peter Gammons every week.**"*
— John Hunt, *Baseball Weekly*

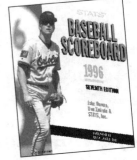
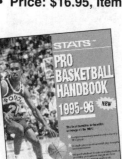

STATS INC Order Form

Name_____ Phone_____

Address_____ Fax_____

City_____ State_____ Zip_____

Method of Payment (U.S. Funds Only):

❏ Check/Money Order   ❏ Visa   ❏ MasterCard

Cardholder Name_____

Credit Card Number_____ Exp. _____

Signature_____

BOOKS

Qty	Product Name	Item #	Price	Total
	STATS 1996 Major League Handbook	HB96	$17.95	
	1996 Major League Hndbk. (Comb-bnd)	HC96	$19.95	
	STATS 1996 Projections Update	PJUP	$9.95	
	The Scouting Notebook: 1996	SN96	$16.95	
	STATS 1996 Player Profiles	PP96	$17.95	
	1996 Player Profiles (Comb-bound)	PC96	$19.95	
	STATS 1996 Minor Lg. Scouting Ntbk.	MN96	$16.95	
	STATS 1996 Minor League Handbook	MH96	$17.95	
	1996 Minor League Hndbk. (Comb-bnd)	MC96	$19.95	
	STATS 1996 BVSP Match-Ups!	BP96	$12.95	
	STATS 1996 Baseball Scoreboard	SB96	$16.95	
	STATS 1995-96 Pro Basketball Hndbk.	BH96	$17.95	
	Pro Football Revealed (1996 Edition)	PF96	$16.95	
	STATS 1996 Pro Football Handbook	FH96	$17.95	

For previous editions, circle appropriate years:

Major League Handbook	91 92 93 94 95	$9.95
Scouting Report/Notebook	92 94 95	$9.95
Player Profiles	93 94 95	$9.95
Minor League Handbook	92 93 94 95	$9.95
Baseball Scoreboard	92 93 94 95	$9.95
Basketball Scoreboard	94 95	$9.95
Pro Football Handbook	95	$9.95
Pro Football Revealed	94 95	$9.95

FANTASY GAMES & STATSfax

Qty	Product Name	Item #	Price	Total
	Bill James Classic Baseball	BJCG	$129.00	
	How to Win The Classic Game (book)	CGBK	$16.95	
	The Classic Game STATSfax	CGX5	$20.00	
	Bill James Fantasy Baseball	BJFB	$89.00	
	BJFB STATSfax/5-day	SFX5	$20.00	
	BJFB STATSfax/7-day	SFX7	$25.00	
	STATS Fantasy Hoops	SFH	$85.00	
	SFH STATSfax/5-day	SFH5	$20.00	
	SFH STATSfax/7-day	SFH7	$25.00	
	STATS Fantasy Football	SFF	$69.00	
	SFF STATSfax/3-day	SFF3	$15.00	

STATS ON-LINE

Qty	Product Name	Item #	Price	Total
	STATS On-Line	ONLE	$30.00	

**For faster service, call
1-800-63-STATS or 708-676-3383,
or fax this form to STATS at
708-676-0821**

1st Fantasy Team Name (ex. Colt 45's):_____ _____

What Fantasy Game is this team for?_____

2nd Fantasy Team Name (ex. Colt 45's):_____ _____

What Fantasy Game is this team for?_____

NOTE: $1.00/player is charged for all roster moves and transactions.

For Bill James Fantasy Baseball

Would you like to play in a league drafted by Bill James?   ❏ Yes   ❏ No

TOTALS

	Price	Total
Product Total (excl. Fantasy Games and On-Line)		
For first class mailing in U.S. add:	+$2.50/book	
Canada—all orders—add:	+$3.50/book	
Order 2 or more books—subtract:	-$1.00/book	
IL residents add 8.5% sales tax		
Subtotal		
Fantasy Games & On-Line Total		
GRAND TOTAL		

FREE Information Kits:

❏ STATS Reporter Networks
❏ Bill James Classic Baseball
❏ Bill James Fantasy Baseball
❏ STATS On-Line
❏ STATS Fantasy Hoops
❏ STATS Fantasy Football
❏ STATS Year-end Reports
❏ STATSfax

Mail to: STATS, Inc., 8131 Monticello Ave., Skokie, IL 60076-3300

BOOK